CRIMINAL JUSTICE SYSTEM

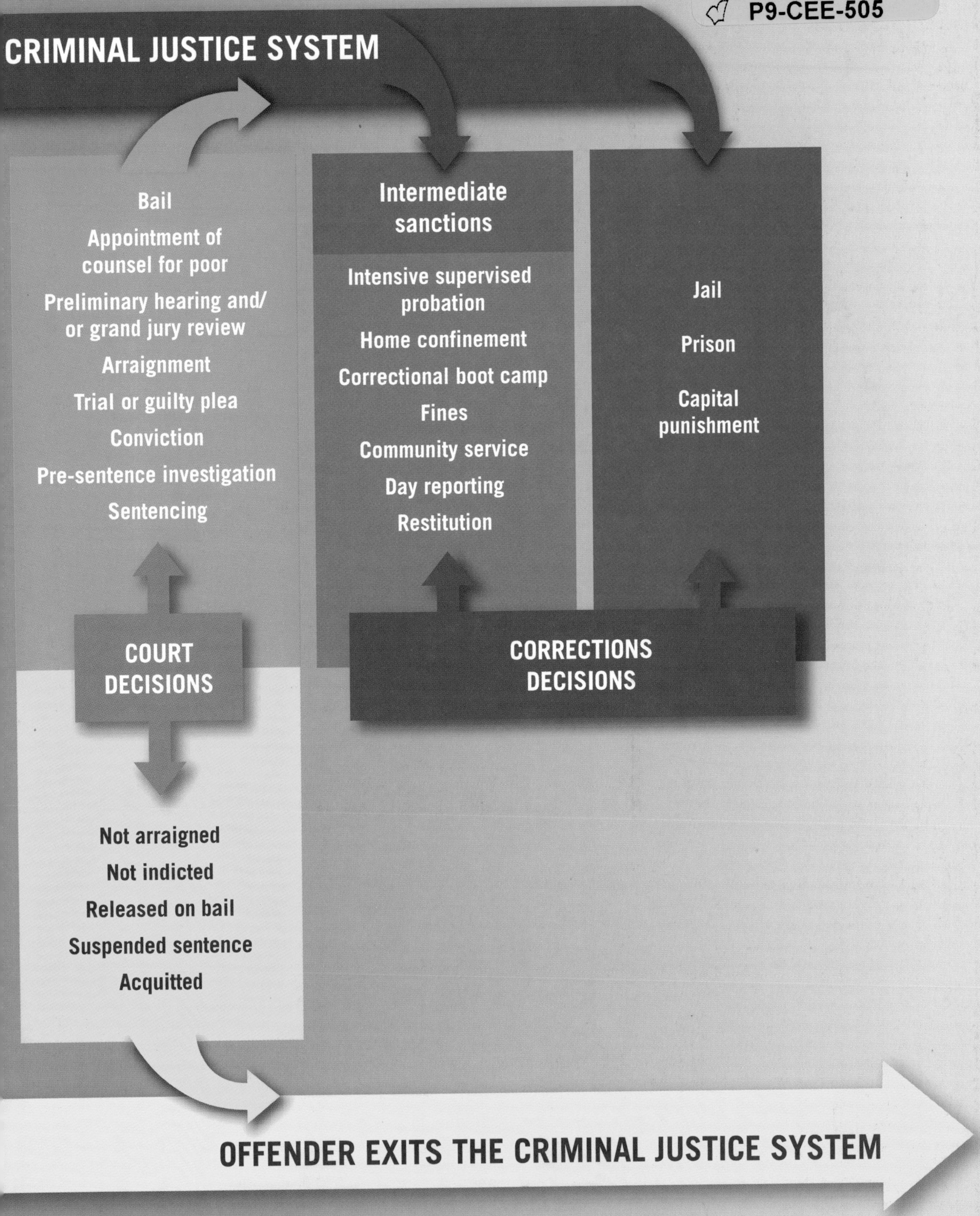

Bail

Appointment of
counsel for poor

Preliminary hearing and/
or grand jury review

Arraignment

Trial or guilty plea

Conviction

Pre-sentence investigation

Sentencing

Intermediate
sanctions

Intensive supervised
probation

Home confinement

Correctional boot camp

Fines

Community service

Day reporting

Restitution

Jail

Prison

Capital
punishment

COURT DECISIONS

CORRECTIONS DECISIONS

Not arraigned

Not indicted

Released on bail

Suspended sentence

Acquitted

OFFENDER EXITS THE CRIMINAL JUSTICE SYSTEM

This book and its **Companion Website** team up—to help you succeed!

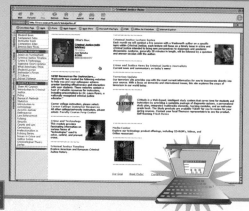

http://cj.wadsworth.com/samaha_cj7e

Thoroughly integrated with the text—chapter by chapter! As you work through this text, you'll find this Companion Website—linked to the book's concepts and topics—to be an invaluable study tool. Success is just a click away!

▶ **Self-Study Assessment:** These Pre-/Post-tests (with rejoinder feedback) provide page numbers for chapter review

▶ **A Final Exam,** with a random selection of tutorial questions

▶ **Direct access** to the Wadsworth Criminal Justice Resource Center and its wide selection of learning tools *(see below)*

▶ **Chapter Outlines, Objectives, Tutorial Quizzes,** and **Summaries** for each chapter

▶ **Access to...**Criminal Justice websites that are organized by chapter, the Constitution (with links to the amendments), Flashcards, and Glossary

---

▶ DECISION ━━ POINT ◀

Does race affect jury deliberations?

Click on this Decision Point at http://cj.wadsworth.com/samaha_cj7e to explore the issue.

★ **Decision Points**—These chapter-related scenarios include critical thinking questions that allow you to explore key issues and gain additional insights into criminal justice concepts

---

CONCEPT | BUILDER

Visit http://cj.wadsworth.com/samaha_cj7e for an interactive exploration of **police effectiveness: myths versus facts.**

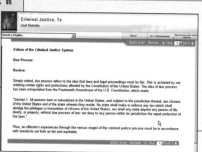

★ **Concept Builders**—Three-step modules that 1) briefly review a key chapter concept, 2) apply the concept to a real-world scenario, and 3) challenge you to apply the concept with a related essay question

---

▶ **InfoTrac® College Edition Keywords** to help guide you to current articles online

▶ **Opposing Viewpoints Resource Center** exercises that help you see all sides of controversial issues

---

The Wadsworth Criminal Justice Resource Center
http://cj.wadsworth.com

Rich with student tools, the site includes hundreds of popular CJ links, many interactive features such as *Crime and Technology* and *What Americans Think,* and a *Student Help Center* with links to career and study tips, and writing and research help. You can also access recent perspectives by clicking on *Terrorism Update.*

Criminal Justice

SEVENTH EDITION

Joel Samaha
University of Minnesota

THOMSON
WADSWORTH

Australia • Brazil • Canada • Mexico • Singapore • Spain
United Kingdom • United States

THOMSON
━━━━━✦━━━━━ ™
WADSWORTH

Criminal Justice, Seventh Edition, Joel Samaha

Senior Acquisitions Editor, Criminal Justice:
  Carolyn Henderson Meier
Senior Development Editor: Sherry Symington
Assistant Editor: Jana Davis
Editorial Assistant: Rebecca Johnson
Technology Project Manager: Susan DeVanna
Marketing Manager: Terra Schultz
Marketing Communications Manager: Stacey Purviance
Project Manager, Editorial Production: Jennie Redwitz
Creative Director: Rob Hugel
Art Director: Vernon Boes
Print Buyer: Barbara Britton
Permissions Editor: Stephanie Lee

Production Service: Ruth Cottrell
Text Designer: Ellen Pettengell
Photo Researcher: Don Murie, Meyers Photo-Art
Copy Editor: Lura Harrison
Illustrator: Judith Ogus
Cover Designer: Bill Stanton
Cover Images: Lady Justice © Benny De Grove/Getty
  Images Inc. Inset images: judge and lawyer: Inmagine/
  BrandXPictures; female prisoner and police officer:
  Inmagine/Thinkstock.
Compositor: R&S Book Composition
Text and Cover Printer: Transcontinental Printing/
  Interglobe

Library of Congress Control Number: 2005925892

Student Edition: ISBN-13: 978-0-534-64557-1
             ISBN-10: 0-534-64557-7

Thomson Higher Education
10 Davis Drive
Belmont, CA 94002-3098
USA

For more information about our products, contact us at:
Thomson Learning Academic Resource Center
1-800-423-0563
For permission to use material from this text or product,
submit a request online at **http://www.thomsonrights.com.**
Any additional questions about permissions can be
submitted by email to **thomsonrights@thomson.com.**

For Steve, Doug, and my students

Brief Contents

Contents

CHAPTER 3

Explanations of Criminal Behavior 68

CHAPTER 4

Criminal Justice and the Law 106

PART 2   *The Police*

CHAPTER 5

*Missions and Roles
of the Police 136*

CHAPTER 6

Policing Strategies 184

PART 3   *The Courts*

PART 4   *Corrections*

Preface

Last September was the 34th Fall term, and the 60th time (give or take a few), I went to Anderson Hall at the University of Minnesota to teach the first day of a criminal justice course. A lot has changed over those years, but one thing has stayed the same: I woke up at about 3 o'clock in the morning, like all the other first days, with butterflies in my stomach. Would it be a good day? Maybe, maybe not. But that's the great thing about teaching criminal justice. When I get up every teaching day, I know it might be a good (maybe even an exciting) day at school. I wrote *Criminal Justice 7* hoping to make the hours you spend studying criminal justice as exciting as my good days teaching it.

But there's more for you in this new edition of *Criminal Justice* than a semester (and maybe the start of a lifetime) of excitement. You're going to be learning about a social issue that deserves a lot of attention. Who can deny the importance of questions like, What's a crime, and who's a criminal? Which illegal drug users go to prison, and which ones get probation? Why do some murderers get executed while others go to prison for 25 years? What happens when prisoners get out of prison? Where do they go? What do they do? Who decides these questions? Are their decisions constitutional? Are they fair? Are they wise? Do police, court, and corrections programs work? And, of course, How much do they cost, and are they worth it?

Three Continuing Themes

Criminal Justice 7 continues, sharpens, expands, and brings up to date three themes that have characterized the previous six editions of the text:

1. *Crime control in a constitutional democracy.* Balancing two conflicting, but absolutely necessary, values in a constitutional democracy: the power of the government to protect public safety and security versus the privacy and liberty of individuals to come and go as they please without government interference.

2. *Decision making in criminal justice.* The formal and informal dimensions of the structure and process of decisions and decision making in the public agencies of crime control (police, courts, and corrections), as well as the legitimate criteria (seriousness of the offense, criminal history of offender, and strength of the case) that underlie legitimate decisions and the discriminatory criteria (race, ethnicity, and class) that infect decisions.

3. *Research and criminal justice policy.* First, basic research that describes and explains crime control policies and how they operate in day-to-day practice. Second, evaluation research that measures the effects of policies and practices: Are they legal? Do they work? Are they fair? Are they smart?

Three Teaching Missions

This edition of *Criminal Justice*, like all its predecessors, is based on three teaching missions:

1. **Description and explanation.** Describe and explain the basic structure, processes, concepts, and decisions needed to understand the criminal justice system.
2. **Critical thinking.** Provide the tools needed to think critically about criminal justice issues.
3. **Readability.** Put these basics and tools into a book written in a direct and relaxed, yet

serious, style that you'll want to read *and* that fits comfortably into one term.

The first mission of *Criminal Justice 7* is huge: describing and explaining the basics. And every year it's a bigger challenge to accomplish, because our knowledge is growing by leaps and bounds. The second mission is just as important: providing you with tools to think critically about the big questions raised by criminal justice. (By the way, don't confuse thinking critically with thinking negatively. By "thinking critically," I mean basing your conclusions on sound information. By "thinking negatively," I mean "dissing" or venting your dislike.) The third mission: writing a book that "works" for a one-term course. The three missions boil down to this: Write a book that covers the basics, challenges you to think critically and gets you ready for advanced criminal justice courses if you're a criminal justice major, and makes all of you better informed about an important social issue. How can I accomplish these three missions? That question has nagged me more every year I teach this huge, exciting, growing, and important subject. Writing *Criminal Justice* gave me the chance to answer this nagging question.

Seven Rules on My Wall

I pasted seven rules on my wall behind my monitor to keep me on track in accomplishing my three missions for the new edition of *Criminal Justice*:

1. Keep it conversational and interesting.
2. Keep it lean.
3. Keep it moving.
4. Keep it current.
5. Keep it serious.
6. Describe and explain the basics with clear examples.
7. Present enough (but not too much) information on all sides of every question to think about it critically (but not negatively).

There's something else pasted on my wall, something Thomas Jefferson wrote in 1820:

> I know no safe depository of the ultimate powers of the society but the people themselves; and if we think them not enlightened enough to exercise their control with a wholesome discretion, the remedy is not to take it from them, but to inform their discretion by education. This is the true corrective of abuses of constitutional power.

Please don't roll your eyes, and forgive me if choosing Jefferson's quote gives away my old-fashioned patriotism about our country and my optimism about your education, but for me, his words boil down why I should be writing and why you should be reading this book: "to inform" our "discretion by education."

Five New Learning Features

1. **Fact or Fiction?** statements at the beginning of each chapter act as a kind of pre-test of students' understandings and misunderstandings about the three themes in *Criminal Justice*. The idea came from something I read once: "People know a lot about criminal justice; unfortunately most of what they know is wrong."
2. **In Focus** boxes throughout the chapters elaborate critical issues related to crime control in a constitutional democracy, decision making in criminal justice, and evaluating the effectiveness, fairness, wisdom, and legality of crime control policies.
3. **CJ & Technology** boxes are included in most chapters. These boxes highlight the powerful effect (and effectiveness of) rapidly advancing information and scientific technology on crime control in our constitutional democracy.
4. **Make Your Decision** sections at the end of every chapter respond to comments by reviewers and my students and my own wish to "dig deeper" and think critically about balancing civil liberties and public safety; about the appropriate criteria (seriousness of the offense, criminal history of the offenders, and strength of the case) supporting good decision making and the inappropriate criteria (race, ethnicity, sexual orientation) infecting criminal justice decision making; and the effectiveness, fairness, wisdom, and legality of crime control policies. These two- to three-page sections include excerpts from enough conflicting empirical and theoretical research, perspectives, and arguments for students to think critically about, and make their own decisions regarding, issues of current importance.
5. **Chapter Summaries** at the end of each chapter consist of a bulleted list that summarizes the main points in the chapter. Each bullet is a capsule of a main chapter topic.

Highlights of New and/or Expanded Sections, Boxes, and Make Your Decision Sections

Chapter 1

New Section: Research and criminal justice

CJ & Technology: Government Thermal Imaging of Your Home: An Invasion of Privacy?

Make Your Decision: Is There a Wartime Exception to the Bill of Rights?

Chapter 2

New Sections:
- Crimes against the state (treason, sedition, terrorism)
- White-collar crime
- National incident-based reporting (NIBRS)

CJ & Technology: Hot Off the Wireless

Make Your Decision: Can We Identify Career Criminals before Their Careers Start?

Chapter 3

New and/or Expanded Sections:
- Biological theories
- Psychological theories
- Developmental criminology
  - Age
  - Life course
- Criminal law and criminal justice explanations

In Focus: Rational Choice Theory: A Sound Basis for Policy?

Make Your Decision: Do Broken Windows Cause Serious Crime?

Chapter 4

Expanded Sections:
- Procedural due process
- Equal protection

In Focus:
- Should Evidence of Rape Victims' Sexual Activities Be Off Limits in Rape Trials?
- Are Some Crimes Inherently Evil?

Make Your Decision: Are Battered Women Justified in Killing Their Batterers?

Chapter 5

New and/or Expanded Sections:
- Federal law enforcement
- Homeland security
- Private police
- Police training and education

CJ & Technology: The DEA "Operation Web Tryp"

In Focus:
- Which Laws Should the Police Enforce?
- Does Field Training Make Better Cops?

Make Your Decision: Are Business Improvement Zones Good Public Policy?

Chapter 6

New and/or Expanded Sections:
- Crime attack: Gun violence
- Law enforcement technology
  - DNA
  - COMPSTAT
- Cost effectiveness of DNA and COMPSTAT

In Focus:
- Is Preventive Patrol a Waste of Police Time and Taxpayers' Money?
- Were the Field Interrogations Appropriate?
- Problem-Oriented Policing in Chicago

CJ & Technology: 3-D Mug Shot

Make Your Decision: Are the Streets "Less Mean" Because of COMPSTAT?

Chapter 7

New and/or Expanded Sections:
- Racial profiling
  - Driving while Black or Brown
  - Constitution and profiling

In Focus:
- Was There Probable Cause to Arrest?
- Do You *Have* to Identify Yourself to Police Officers?
- Do Officers Have to *Mirandize* Suspects When It Would Endanger an Officer or Someone Nearby?
- Interrogating Terrorist Suspects: Does the Constitution Allow It?

CJ & Technology: Are Tasers Safe?

Make Your Decision: Did Ethnicity Infect the Decision to Stop?

CJ & Technology: Is There a Doctor in the House?

Make Your Decision: A Provocative Proposal: Reentry Courts

Chapter 15

New Sections:
- Juvenile delinquency
- Transfer to adult criminal court

In Focus:
- Life Sentence for 12-Year-Old?
- Juvenile Delinquency: Arrest or Detention for Wearing a Low-Cut Midriff Top?
- Arrest a 13-Year-Old for DWI?
- Juvenile Detention of Mentally Ill Juveniles: Substitute for Mental Health Care?

Make Your Decision: Juvenile Corrections: Rehabilitation or Punishment?

Supplements

The new edition is accompanied by a wide array of supplements prepared to create the best learning environment inside as well as outside the classroom for both the instructor and the student. (Available to qualified adopters. Please consult your local sales representative for details.)

For the Instructor

Instructor's Manual with Test Bank Written by George Franks of Stephen F. Austin State University, this *Instructor's Manual* contains resources designed to streamline and maximize the effectiveness of your course preparation: a sample syllabus, chapter objectives, outlines, key terms, and class exercises/discussion questions. The test bank offers approximately 80 test questions per chapter, in multiple-choice, true/false, fill-in-the-blanks, short answer, and essay formats. The *Instructor's Manual* also includes a full answer key and references to main text page numbers for key terms and the answers to test bank questions.

ExamView® Computerized Testing You can create, deliver, and customize tests and study guides (both print and online) in minutes with this easy-to-use assessment and tutorial system.

Resource Integration Guide Included in the Instructor's Edition of *Criminal Justice 7,* this essential guide provides grids that link each chapter's outline—topic by topic—to instructional ideas and corresponding supplement resources. At a glance, you'll see which Microsoft® PowerPoint® slides, videos, test questions, media resources, and lecture suggestions are appropriate for each key chapter topic.

Multimedia Manager Instructor Resource CD: A Microsoft® PowerPoint® Tool With this one-stop digital library and presentation tool, you can assemble, edit, publish, and present custom lectures, bringing together art from this CD-ROM, the web, and your own material. Also includes preloaded Microsoft® PowerPoint® slides for each chapter of the book.

WebTutor ToolBox A free course management option that comes preloaded with content and is available via a free access code when packaged with this text. This tool pairs all the content of this text's rich Book Companion Website with sophisticated course management functionality. You can assign materials (including online quizzes) and have the results flow automatically to your grade book. WebTutor™ ToolBox is ready to use as soon as you log on, or you can customize its preloaded content by uploading images and other resources. Contact your Thomson Wadsworth representative for packaging information.

Wadsworth's Faculty Prep Center This website, at http://cj.wadsworth.com/faculty_course_prep, features Dr. Laura Myers of Prairie View A&M University, who offers many tools to assist in teaching the introductory criminal justice course. Instructors can download Microsoft® PowerPoint® slides that provide tips on teaching and engaging students, join one of Dr. Myers's online workshops using WebEx, or send a syllabus to her for review and advice. This site also gives information on in-service trainings and links to daily crime and justice news that can launch lectures.

Criminal Justice Faculty Development: Teaching Professors to Teach, Second Edition Written by Dr. Laura Myers of Prairie View A&M University, this print guide provides an array of teaching tips to help both new and experienced faculty.

Criminal Justice Video Resource Center At cj.wadsworth.com/videos you can view the complete list of videos that Wadsworth provides to qualified adopters. These include videos from CNN®, CourtTV®, Films for the Humanities and

Social Sciences, the Oral History Project, and the A&E American Justice Series.

CNN Today: Criminal Justice Video Series, Volumes V, VI, and VII Launch lectures with news footage from CNN®. Organized by topics covered in a typical criminal justice course, these videos are divided into exciting clips ranging from two to eight minutes long. Each video includes high-interest news stories that appeal to students, spark classroom discussions, and reinforce the connection of criminal justice to daily life.

America's New War: CNN Looks at Terrorism, Volumes I and II These two videos feature CNN clips with in-depth coverage of recent terrorist attacks and events on the international stage. Volume I covers anthrax and biological warfare, new security measures, al-Qaeda, homeland defense, renewed patriotism, and more. Volume II examines the case of Jose Padilla, Guantanamo Bay detainees, the train bombings in Spain, the capture of Saddam Hussein, the search for weapons of mass destruction, recent incidents of domestic terrorism, and more.

Introduction to Criminal Justice CNN DVD This DVD features selected video clips from the exclusive Wadsworth CNN Today "Introduction to Criminal Justice" video series. It also includes discussion questions that tie the DVD to related chapter topics and spark student participation in class.

Oral History Project Video Series Developed in association with the American Society of Criminology, the Academy of Criminal Justice Society, and the National Institute of Justice, the series includes:

- **Volume 1: Moments in Time** Features such criminal justice experts as Norval Morris, Don Gottfredson, Marvin Wolfgang, Robert Merton, and Joan McCord, who give highlights of the evolution of modern criminal justice.
- **Volume 2: Historical Perspectives** Includes interviews with some of the most influential people in criminal justice, who discuss key moments in the development of the discipline, including Albert Cohen, Travis Hirschi, and Robert Merton.
- **Volume 3: Research Methodology in Criminal Justice** Illustrates groundbreaking research that changed our understanding of the discipline. Researchers include David Farrington, Rolf Loeber, Joan McCord, John Laub, Simon Dinitz, Frank Scarpitti, and Marvin Wolfgang.

For the Student

The following tools are available to aid students in preparing for and passing their course and exploring topics in more depth.

Study Guide Written by George Franks of Stephen F. Austin State University, the Study Guide has been thoroughly updated and includes learning objectives, chapter summaries, key term reviews, and extensive self-tests, including multiple-choice, true/false, fill-in-the-blank, short answer, and essay questions, as well as a full answer key.

Current Perspectives: Readings from InfoTrac College Edition: Cyber Crime Edited and introduced by Roger LeRoy Miller, the 19 articles in this reader cover a wide range of cyber crime topics and provide a good way to introduce students to cyber crime issues. It includes free access to InfoTrac® College Edition and is free when packaged with the text.

Current Perspectives: Readings from InfoTrac College Edition: Terrorism and Homeland Security Edited and introduced by Dipak K. Gupta (San Diego State University), the 16 articles in this reader offer a representative selection that helps you introduce students to terrorism issues. It includes free access to InfoTrac College Edition.

Public Policy and Criminal Justice: The Election of 2004 and the Future This brief booklet gives students an in-depth look at important criminal justice issues that played a part in the 2004 presidential and state elections. It is free when packaged with the book.

Wadsworth's Guide to Careers in Criminal Justice, Second Edition This 60-page booklet provides a brief introduction to careers in criminal justice. Students learn about opportunities in law enforcement, courts, and corrections.

Six Steps to Effective Writing in Criminal Justice Written by Judy Schmidt (Pennsylvania State University) and Mike Hooper (California Department of Justice), this compact resource promotes strong writing skills in students and helps prepare them for their academic and professional writing challenges. It includes sample writing topics, examples, formats, and papers that reflect the criminal justice discipline.

Crime and Evidence in Action CD-ROM With its accompanying Crime and Evidence in Action Website, this CD-ROM places students in the cen-

ter of the action as they make decisions as a patrol officer, detective, prosecutor, defense attorney,
judge, corrections officer, and parole officer.

**Careers in Criminal Justice 3.0 Interactive
CD-ROM** This CD-ROM provides career profiling
information and links to self-assessment testing
and is designed to help students investigate and
focus on criminal justice career choices.

**Crime Scenes 2.0: An Interactive Criminal
Justice CD-ROM** Written by Bruce Berg (California State University, Long Beach), this interactive
CD-ROM features six vignettes that allow students
to play various roles as they explore aspects of the
criminal justice system, such as policing, investigation, courts, sentencing, and corrections.

Web-Based Supplements

Book Companion Website This dynamic site at
http://cj.wadsworth.com/samaha_cj7e includes
many great online resources for instructors and
students, including:

- **Decision Points** Chapter-related scenarios
  with critical thinking questions that allow
  students to explore key issues and gain additional insights.
- **Self-Study Assessment** Pretests and
  posttests with rejoinder feedback that provide students with text page numbers for
  chapter review.
- **Chapter Outlines, Objectives, and Summaries** Overviews of each chapter.
- **Chapter Tutorial Quizzes** Overviews of
  quizzes for each chapter.
- **A Final Exam** With a random selection of
  tutorial questions
- **Direct Access to the Wadsworth Criminal
  Justice Resource Center**
- **Instructor Resources** Password protected,
  including the *Instructor's Manual* and links
  to other resources.
- **Access to . . .** CJ websites organized by
  chapter, the Constitution (with links to the
  amendments), Flash Cards, and Glossary.
- **InfoTrac College Edition Key Words**
  Search words to help guide students to
  current articles online.
- **Opposing Viewpoints Resource Center
  Exercises**
- **Concept Builders** Three-step interactive
  learning modules.

**The Wadsworth Criminal Justice Resource
Center** Rich with student and instructor tools,
the Resource Center, at **http://cj.wadsworth
.com**, includes a direct link to the Terrorism Update Website, hundreds of popular CJ links, many
interactive features such as *Crime and Technology*
and *What Americans Think*, a *Student Help Center*
with links to career and study tips, writing and research help, and much more.

InfoTrac College Edition with InfoMarks
Packaged free with every new student copy of
the text, you and your students will receive four
months of access to reliable resources with Info-
Trac College Edition, the online library. This fully
searchable database offers more than twenty
years' worth of full-text articles (not abstracts)
from almost five thousand diverse sources, such
as top academic journals, newsletters, and peri-
odicals. In addition, students have access to
InfoWrite, which includes guides to writing research papers, grammar, critical thinking guidelines, and much more. InfoTrac College Edition
also includes access to InfoMarks™: stable URLs
that can be linked to articles, journals, and
searches. Ideal for both teaching and research, InfoMarks allow you to use a simple copy-and-paste
technique to create instant and continually updated online readers, content services, bibliogra-
phies, electronic "reserve" readings, and current
topic sites. Contact your Thomson Wadsworth
representative for details.

Opposing Viewpoints Resource Center This
online center, which can be previewed at **http://
www.gale.com/OpposingViewpoints**, helps you
expose students to different sides of compelling
social and scientific issues.

Acknowledgments

This edition of *Criminal Justice* bears the marks
of instructors from all over the country who reviewed previous editions. The list of my creditors
is long and just mentioning their names far from
repays my debt to them. The following instructors reviewed *Criminal Justice 7* and provided
thoughtful and serious evaluations of it:

Leanne Fiftal Alarid, University of Missouri–
Kansas City

Andrea Bannister, Wichita State University

James A. Curry, Baylor University

Stephan D. Kaftan, Hawkeye Community College

Robert NeVille, College of the Siskiyous

Karen F. Parker, University of Florida

Joseph Peterson, University of Illinois–Chicago

Donna M. Sherwood, Macomb Community College

Thomas D. Stucky, Indiana University, Purdue University–Fort Wayne

The instructors who reviewed previous editions include James A. Adamitis, Bonnie Berry, John S. Boyd, Susan Brinkley, Stephen Brown, Orman Buswell, Dave Camp, Paul V. Clark, William J. Cook, Jr., Walt Copley, Jerry Davis, Dana C. DeWitt, Marlon T. Doss, Edna Erez, Walter M. Francis, Peter Grimes, John E. Harlan, Patricia Harris, Vincent Hoffman, Nicholas H. Irons, Michael Israel, Mark Jones, Gary Keveles, Peter B. Kraska, Robert Lockwood, Matthew Lyones, Robert McCormack, Joseph Macy, Stephen Mastrofski, Greg Matoesian, G. Larry Mays, William Michalek, JoAnn Miller, Terry Miller, Robert Murillo, Gordon E. Meisner, Donald R. Morton, Charles E. Myers II, John Northrup, H. Wayne Overson, Mario Peitrucci, Gary Perlstein, Joseph Peterson, Daniel F. Postingle, Harry L. Powell, Joel Powell, Archie Rainey, Christine Rasche, Philip Roades, Ronald Robinson, Glenda Rogers, William Ruefle, Gregory D. Russell, John Scarborough, William Selke, Edward Sieh, Stan Stodkovic, Kenrick Thompson, Myron Utech, Neil R. Vance, Timothy Vieders, Allen Wagner, Mervin White, Thomas Whitt, Warren M. Whitton, Keven Wright, and Stanley Yeldell.

I'm pleased to acknowledge how much two colleagues at the University of Minnesota helped me improve this new edition of *Criminal Justice*. Professor Candace Kruttschnitt provided me with her own invaluable and latest research (and up-to-date references to other scholars' research) on gender and crime and women's prisons and imprisonment. Her research and advice definitely enriched the sections on gender and crime and gender and criminal justice.

Chris Uggen probably doesn't even know how much my informal conversations with him (in the halls, in the elevator, on the phone, in e-mails, on Ph.D. oral exams, and in his office) helped me to formulate my overall plan for focusing and streamlining *Criminal Justice 7*, not to mention his invaluable research on life-course criminology, employment and crime, and felon disenfranchisement.

I'm delighted to acknowledge others whose influence on previous editions still shows. Professor David Ward (retired), Department of Sociology, who was instrumental in bringing me to the University of Minnesota, first as my colleague, and then as my loyal and dear friend for 35 years, knew all the answers to my questions about corrections research. The book is richer because of his knowledge, his experience, and his unlimited generosity in taking the time and energy to share his vast knowledge and experience with me.

Professor Joachim Savelsberg, who carefully reviewed earlier editions, made copious notes and discussed his experiences in using *Criminal Justice* in his sections of our introductory course in criminal justice at the University of Minnesota. Joachim offered not only editorial advice but has also continued to engage me in constructive thinking about the theory and sometimes not too subtle biases that appear in the text. I haven't taken all his suggestions but I've always listened to them.

Norm Carlson, former director of the Federal Bureau of Prisons and until his retirement my colleague at the University of Minnesota, has taken me to correctional facilities, gotten me information and photos I couldn't have gotten on my own, and helpfully criticized the text. But more than that, he set an example that all of us should follow—he remained generous, optimistic, cheerful, and open-minded in the face of what would have soured many others in less challenging positions. His advice, encouragement, and example have all enriched *Criminal Justice*. His advice to me to "show the positive side of criminal justice" I've taken to heart even when it wasn't easy.

It's my pleasure to acknowledge former students who are now experienced and respected criminal justice professionals in their own right, who enriched my classes when they took them, and who now influence my teaching and writing: Deputy Chief Richard Gardell, St. Paul Police Department; Sergeant James De Concini, Minneapolis Police Department (retired); Martin Costello, esq., Hughes and Costello; John Sheehy, esq., Meshbesher and Spence; Jeff Dean, criminal defense sole practitioner; Judge Phil Bush, Hennepin County District Court; David Schwab, U.S. Probation Office; Darin Kearns, U.S. Probation Office; Dennis Benson, Deputy Commissioner, Minnesota Department of Corrections; and David Crist, Warden, Minnesota Department of Corrections. Following their careers, listening to their stories, visiting their facilities, and arguing with their positions has kept me young in mind and in touch (at least secondhand) with the "real world" of criminal justice.

Criminal Justice 7 has profited from the now thousands of my former students not mentioned here. Undergraduates, graduate students, law students, and criminal justice professionals have inspired me (and still do) to give them the most I can and the best I have.

This new edition owes much to the expertise, devotion, and effort of the people at Wadsworth. Thanks first to Criminal Justice Editor Carolyn Henderson Meier. Senior Development Editor Sherry Symington helped me clarify how we'd accomplish the missions of putting the basics of criminal justice and the tools to think critically about criminal justice decision making into a book that would fit realistically into a one-semester course and that students would want to read. Production Editor Ruth Cottrell has never lost her cool with me. She's a glaring exception to the rule that no one's indispensable. She's kind, generous, efficient, smart, and on top of all that, she's really nice. Lura Harrison deserves a lot of credit for careful editing and excellent suggestions, even when—to put it mildly—I didn't want to hear them. Production Project Manager Jennie Redwitz could always tell me who to go to for what I wanted and needed; that's not easy because I'm not what you call organized on these important matters.

My assistant Doug drives me here and there so I can physically do my work. But he does a lot more; he puts up with my mercurial temperament almost every day, often in the early morning (which he hates), and sometimes even at night.

Speaking of putting up with me, my best friend Steve does all the things I can't or won't do because I'm researching, writing, and/or getting ready for class. These necessary jobs started with taking care of my sons when they were young, then expanded to taking care of a kennel of Irish Wolfhounds that sometimes numbered as many as 10 adults and 15 puppies. Now, he still has his hands full with Betty and Allison (the 2 remaining Irish Wolfhounds); Frankie (the Standard Poodle), and Kitty Cat (the Siamese cat).

Give credit to everybody mentioned (and many more who aren't) for making *Criminal Justice 7* a better book. But of course blame me for all its shortcomings.

Joel Samaha
Minneapolis

About the Author

Professor Joel Samaha teaches Introduction to Criminal Justice, Criminal Law, Criminal Procedure, and The Supreme Court and the Bill of Rights at the University of Minnesota. He is both a lawyer and an historian whose primary research interest is constitutional and legal history. He received his B.A., J.D., and Ph.D. from Northwestern University. Professor Samaha also studied under the late Sir Geoffrey Elton at Cambridge University, England.

Professor Samaha was admitted to the Illinois Bar in 1962 and practiced law briefly in Chicago. He taught at UCLA before going to the University of Minnesota in 1971. At the University of Minnesota, he served as Chair of the Department of Criminal Justice Studies from 1974 to 1978. He now teaches and writes full time. He has taught both television and radio courses in criminal justice and has co-taught a National Endowment for the Humanities seminar in legal and constitutional history. He was named Distinguished Teacher at the University of Minnesota in 1974.

In addition to *Law and Order in Historical Perspective* (1974), an analysis of law enforcement in pre-industrial English society, Professor Samaha has transcribed and written a scholarly introduction to a set of criminal justice records in the reign of Elizabeth I. He has also written several articles on the history of criminal justice, published in *Historical Journal, The American Journal of Legal History, Minnesota Law Review, William Mitchell Law Review,* and *Journal of Social History.* In addition to *Criminal Justice,* he has written two other textbooks, *Criminal Law,* Eighth Edition, and *Criminal Procedure,* Sixth Edition.

Criminal Justice

SEVENTH EDITION

Joel Samaha

IN GOD WE TRUST

CHAPTER 1

Criminal Justice in the United States

FACT *or* FICTION?

▶ In a constitutional democracy, the majority determines our rights.

▶ There's a wartime exception to the Bill of Rights.

▶ The police turn suspects into defendants when they arrest them.

▶ Criminal justice is a system because taxes pay for all crime control agencies.

▶ Half of all decision making by the police affecting Blacks is infected.

▶ The history of criminal justice swings like a pendulum between cracking down on crime and protecting individual rights.

DECISION MAKING: LEGITIMATE OR ILLEGITIMATE?

Police officers arrested a Native American found drinking cheap red wine and eating a tuna fish sandwich in a city park. He was later convicted of the offense of "drinking in the park." About the same time, a gourmet club prepared a meal of salmon mousse, bought an expensive imported white wine to go with it, and went to another Minneapolis park to eat in "the right atmosphere." The police saw the event but didn't arrest anyone. On the following Sunday, the society page even wrote a glowing description of the club's event. A local public defender quipped, "What's the problem? The Native American and the club were both eating and drinking in the park, even from the same food groups."

—MY RECOLLECTION FROM THE MID-1970S

As a young law graduate I [the late Professor Frank Remington] found that the real world of the prosecutor's office differed sharply from what one would expect if formal law was applied in practice. Prosecutors used informal, extralegal methods for dealing with minor frauds and other community problems that affected the poor, who were unable to afford legal assistance. In handling a case involving a poor person who had been defrauded by conduct that may or may not have constituted a violation of the criminal law, the prosecutor commonly notified the suspect that a criminal prosecution was being considered. The hope was that the suspect would respond by returning the money obtained from the poor victim. Ultimately the objective was to solve the problem. It was thought less important to decide whether the problem was a criminal fraud.

—REMINGTON 1993, 73–74

You're about to take a journey through U.S. criminal justice. In that journey, you're going to think about questions you already have strong (sometimes *very* strong) feelings about. Here are a few. Why do people commit crimes? (Do they choose to? Or do forces beyond their control decide for them? [Chapter 3]). How *well* (and how *fairly*) do we control crime? (Do police "crackdowns" on disorderly conduct reduce robbery? Or do they just make lower-class people's lives miserable? [Chapter 6]). What's the "just" punishment for a particular crime? (How many years in prison is a robbery worth? [Chapter 11]).

I'm sure some of the answers will frustrate you; some will make you angry; some will confuse you; and sometimes you'll decide there isn't an answer—not yet anyway. But at the end of the journey, you'll have more than *feelings* to base your answers on. You'll have *knowledge* to back up your answers.

Knowledge is worth having for its own sake of course. But there's more to it than that. Crime control is an expensive operation (Figure 1.1), not just because

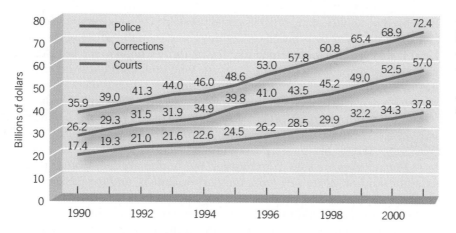

◀ **FIGURE 1.1 Criminal Justice Expenditures, 1990–2001**

Source: Bureau of Justice Statistics, *Justice Expenditures and Employment Extracts, 1992–2001* (Washington, DC: Bureau of Justice Statistics, May 2004), Tables 1 and 3.

of what governments spend on it (although it costs a lot), but because it diverts resources away from other things we want and need (such as roads and schools, just to mention two things close to our everyday lives). Also, crime takes a heavy toll on victims and their families—a toll no amount of money can repay. And families of offenders suffer, too, even when they receive no benefit from the crimes and bear no blame for committing them. Finally, most of the problems linked to crime go a lot deeper than criminal justice can possibly do anything about. For all these reasons (and more you'll discover as you study criminal justice), you need this knowledge.

Criminal justice is a complex subject. There's a lot of detail, and it's easy to get lost in it. So, *Criminal Justice 7* is organized around three themes in U.S. criminal justice. If you make these themes part of your reading, listening, and study habits, they can help you organize, learn, understand, and think about criminal justice so you won't lose your way in your journey through it:

1. *Crime control in a constitutional democracy.* Balancing the power of the government to maintain community safety with the privacy and liberty of individuals to come and go as they please without government interference
2. *Decision making in the criminal justice system.* The formal and informal dimensions to the structure and process of decisions and decision making. Also, the legitimate criteria that produce appropriate decisions and the discriminatory criteria that infect decisions in crime control agencies (police, courts, and corrections)
3. *Research and criminal justice policy.* Research that tells us how crime control policies operate in practice and evaluates the effects of policies and practices (Are they legal? Do they work? Are they fair? Are they smart?)

Let's look at each of these themes, which you'll be learning more about throughout the rest of the book. We'll also take a brief look at the history of crime control.

Crime Control in a Constitutional Democracy

If men were angels, no government would be necessary. If angels were to govern men, neither external nor internal controls on government would be necessary. In framing a government which is to be administered by men over men, the great difficulty lies in this: You must first enable the government to control the governed; and in the next place, oblige it to control itself. (James Madison, 1787, quoted in Cooke, 1961, 349)

If we lived in a police state, officials could break into our houses in the dead of night and shoot us in our beds based on nothing more than the whim of the current dictator. If we lived in a *pure* democracy, the majority who won the last election could pass and enforce a law to lock up everyone who protests the war on terror. But we live in a constitutional democracy where neither a single dictator nor an overwhelming majority of the people has total power over us as individuals.

The heart of our **constitutional democracy** is balance, the balance between two values that make life in a free society worth living—community security and individual liberty and privacy. Community security means we as a community feel safe: our lives are safe from murder; our bodies are safe from rape and other assaults; our homes are safe from burglars, arsonists, and trespassers; our "stuff" is safe from thieves and vandals; and our homeland is safe from foreign and terrorist attacks. The second value is individual autonomy, where I control my life: I can come and go as I please; develop my body and my mind as I wish to do; believe whatever or whomever I want; worship any god I like; "hang" with anybody I pick to hang with; in fact do pretty much anything I want to do (assuming of course I'm a competent adult, I can afford it, and it's not a crime).

Weighed on one side of the balance is the amount of government power needed to control crime for everybody's safety and security. Weighed on the other side of the balance is the amount of control individuals have over their own lives. James Madison (see opening quote in this section, "If men were angels...") and others who wrote and adopted the U.S. Constitution in the 1700s were realists; they accepted human nature for what it is: humans aren't angels. They believed that left to do as they please, ordinary people will break the law. And because they're people, too, government officials left to do as they please will abuse their power. So, the Founders expected excesses from both ordinary people and government officials who live in a real world inhabited by imperfect people.

constitutional democracy balancing community security and individual liberty and privacy

▶ Since community security *and* individual liberty and privacy are equally desired values, striking the balance between them is difficult and where it's struck never satisfies anyone completely. Here a member of the community in Soledad, CA, protests the release of a serial child molester in his town. The security of children from harm seems an obvious value, but what rights does the offender have to liberty and privacy if he has served the full extent of his sentence?

AP/Wide World Photos

Government Thermal Imaging of Your Home: An Invasion of Privacy?

In 1991, Agent William Elliott of the U.S. Department of the Interior came to suspect Danny Kyllo was growing marijuana in his home, part of a triplex on Rhododendron Drive in Florence, Oregon. Indoor marijuana growth typically requires high-intensity lamps. To determine whether an amount of heat was emanating from Kyllo's home consistent with the use of such lamps, at 3:20 A.M. on January 16, 1992, Agent Elliott and Dan Haas used an Agema Thermovision 210 thermal imager to scan the triplex. Thermal imagers detect infrared radiation, which virtually all objects emit but which is not visible to the naked eye. The imager converts radiation into images based on relative warmth—black is cool, white is hot, shades of gray connote relative differences; in that respect, it operates somewhat like a video camera showing heat images.

The scan of Kyllo's home took only a few minutes and was performed from the passenger seat of Agent Elliott's vehicle across the street from the front of the house and also from the street in back of the house. The scan showed that the roof over the garage and a side wall of Kyllo's home were relatively hot compared with the rest of the home and substantially warmer than neighboring homes in the triplex. Agent Elliott concluded that Kyllo was using halide lights to grow marijuana in his house, which indeed he was.

Based partly on the thermal imaging, a judge issued a warrant authorizing a search of Kyllo's home, and the agents found an indoor growing operation involving more than one hundred plants. Kyllo was indicted for manufacturing marijuana. He claimed the thermal imaging invaded his privacy. The U.S. Supreme Court agreed:

> It would be foolish to contend that the degree of privacy secured to citizens by the Fourth Amendment has been entirely unaffected by the advance of technology.... The question we confront today is what limits there are upon this power of technology to shrink the realm of guaranteed privacy. We think that obtaining by sense-enhancing technology any information regarding the interior of the home that could not otherwise have been obtained without physical "intrusion into a constitutionally protected area," constitutes a search—at least where (as here) the technology in question is not in general public use. This assures preservation of that degree of privacy against government.

Not all the justices agreed. According to Justice Stevens:

> The notion that heat emissions from the outside of a dwelling are a private matter...is...quite difficult to take seriously. Heat waves, like aromas that are generated in a kitchen, or in a laboratory or opium den, enter the public domain if and when they leave a building. A subjective expectation that they would remain private is not only implausible but also surely not "one that society is prepared to recognize as 'reasonable.'"...

Source: Kyllo v. U.S., 533 U.S. 27 (2001)

One important point: Because community security *and* individual liberty and privacy are equally desired values, striking the balance between them is difficult, and where it's struck never satisfies everyone completely. U.S. Supreme Court Chief Justice William Rehnquist (1974) put the difficulty and dissatisfaction this way:

> Throughout the long history of...constitutional law in our country, the most difficult cases to decide have been those in which two competing values, each able to marshal respectable claims on its behalf, meet in a contest in which one must prevail over the other. (1)

Another important point: The balance between crime control and individual rights is flexible. Where the balance is struck exactly shifts depending on the circumstances. So, the right balance falls within a zone, not a point on the spectrum between total control and total freedom. The most extreme examples are emergencies, especially a wartime emergency. According to the ancient Latin maxim, "During war the laws are silent." Or as one lawyer prosecuting suspected disloyalists during the Civil War put it, "During wartime the Bill of Rights is put to sleep. We'll wake it up when the emergency passes" (Gayarré 1903, 601).

But it's not just in war emergencies where we'll see the balance struck in various places in the zone. After September 11, Professor William J. Stuntz (2002) summed this point up when he reflected on how the horror of the attacks led to the call for "broader powers for law enforcement and greater restrictions on citizens":

This is not a bad thing. Law enforcement authority naturally varies with the nature and size of the crime problems police must combat.... The Fourth [ban on unreasonable searches and seizures] and Fifth [ban on coerced confessions] Amendment rights have varied with crime before, and they will probably do so in the future. As they must, if the law is to reflect a sensible balance between the social need for order and individuals' desire for privacy and liberty. The terrorist attacks raised the demands on law enforcement. Those increased demands have already led to some increases in law enforcements' legal authority, and that trend will—and probably should—continue, at least for a while. (2138–2139)

Where exactly is the "right" balance between individual rights guaranteed by the U.S. Constitution and government power to protect public safety? (See the CJ & Technology box "Government Thermal Imaging of Your Home: An Invasion of Privacy?") You'll learn more about this balance in chapters on the police, courts, and corrections. In this chapter's Make Your Decision (see later), the U.S. Supreme Court balanced national security against the rights of enemy combatants captured on the battlefields of Afghanistan and Iraq.

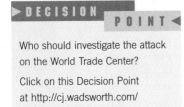

Who should investigate the attack on the World Trade Center?

Click on this Decision Point at http://cj.wadsworth.com/samaha_cj7e to explore the issue.

Criminal Justice Decision Making

Our second theme is decision making in criminal justice. But before we get to the "decision making" part, you need to know something about the structure of the criminal justice system, where the process of decision making takes place. We define the **criminal justice system** as a series of decision points (the criminal justice structure) *and* the decision-making criminal justice process, which takes place in the government crime control agencies (see the endpapers in the front of the book). So, let's look first at the structure and then the process of the criminal justice system. Then, we'll get into the decision-making part, examining formal and informal decision making, the complexity of decision making, and legitimate versus discriminatory decision making.

criminal justice system a series of decision points and decision making

The Criminal Justice Structure

The structure of criminal justice consists of a series of decision points in the three major crime control agencies—police, courts, and corrections. Each criminal justice agency is a point where decisions to keep or release individuals from the criminal justice system are made. The dictionary defines a *system* as a "collection of parts that make up a whole." The parts of the criminal justice system consist of the public agencies of crime control (law enforcement, courts, and corrections) at three levels of government (local, state, and federal). So, there are local, state, and federal law enforcement agencies; local, state, and federal courts; and local, state, and federal corrections agencies. You'll learn more details about these agencies in the appropriate chapters, but in the meantime Table 1.1 should give you the general picture of the structure of the U.S. criminal justice.

Local agencies employ 60 percent of all criminal justice employees; most are law enforcement officers. Criminal justice is (and it's *supposed* to be) mostly a state and a local affair. So, that's what you'll learn most about in this book. But we won't neglect federal criminal justice. Why? First, the role of federal criminal justice has grown steadily since the 1960s; it increased more quickly during the 1980s and 1990s when new federal drug, gun, and violent crime laws were passed.

Second, "9/11" has produced an even greater expansion of federal crime control. The attacks on the World Trade Center and the Pentagon immediately triggered the "largest criminal investigation in the government's history"—7,000 agents and employees were put on the case (Savage and Lichtblau 2001). The USA Patriot Act, signed by President George W. Bush in October 2001, expanded the definitions of federal terrorist crimes and the power of the FBI to investigate and apprehend suspects in these cases. At the signing of the act, the president promised that federal

PATRIOT Act: "PATRIOT" stands for Providing Appropriate Tools Required to Intercept and Obstruct Terrorism. You can review the complete act at this site. To reach this site go to "Web Links" on your Samaha CJ7 website: http://cj.wadsworth.com/samaha_cj7e.

	Local	State	Federal
Law Enforcement	Municipal police departments County sheriff's offices	Highway patrol	U.S. Marshals Federal Bureau of Investigation (FBI) DEA (Drug Enforcement Agency) ATF (Bureau of Alcohol, Firearms, and Tobacco) Secret Service
Courts	Municipal courts District trial courts District appellate courts District (county) attorney's office County public defender's office	Supreme court Attorney general's office Public defender's office	U.S. Magistrates Courts U.S. District Courts U.S. Courts of Appeals U.S. Supreme Court U.S. Attorney's offices U.S. Public Defender's office
Corrections	Municipal holding facilities County jails Probation department	State prisons State parole authority	U.S. jails U.S. prisons U.S. probation and parole departments

law enforcement's highest priority would be to prevent, investigate, and bring violators of antiterrorist laws to justice. As a result, the FBI has expanded its mission (Chapter 5). Also, there's a huge new federal agency, the Department of Homeland Security (Chapter 5), devoted to preventing terrorist attacks.

Third, federal law enforcement, courts, and corrections frequently act as role models for state and local criminal justice agencies. Although federal criminal justice may be a role model, anyone who watches TV cop shows and crime dramas knows that turf wars exist between the "feds" and local criminal justice, especially between law enforcement agencies. Rivalry between federal and local law enforcement is old and natural in our federal system, which divides power among federal, state, and local governments. So, it's not surprising the new emphasis on federal enforcement of laws against terrorism immediately caused a turf war in the investigation of the September 11 attack (Chapter 5).

The Criminal Justice Process

The crime control agencies make up the structure of the criminal justice system, but there's more to the system than its structure. Criminal justice can't decide anything; rather, it's the framework for decision making. Here's where decision making comes in: The criminal justice process is all about decision making in the agencies by criminal justice professionals. Like all processes, criminal justice makes "products." Criminal justice processes people to change their legal status. Also, the decision making among the professionals is interdependent. We'll look at both of these factors, which are central to the criminal justice process.

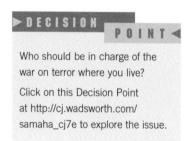

> DECISION POINT ◄

Who should be in charge of the war on terror where you live?

Click on this Decision Point at http://cj.wadsworth.com/ samaha_cj7e to explore the issue.

Producers and Products Who makes the products? What products do they make? Here are the major producers and products you'll learn about in later chapters:

1. *Law enforcement* officers produce suspects when they arrest (or otherwise focus their investigation on) a person.
2. *Prosecutors* produce defendants when they charge suspects with crimes.
3. *Courts* produce offenders when they convict defendants.
4. *Corrections* produce ex-offenders when they release them from custody (Remington, Kimball, Dickey, Goldstein, and Newman 1982, 19–20).

Law enforcement starts the process by deciding whether to investigate crime and apprehend suspects. Prosecutors continue the process by deciding whether to charge suspects and with what crimes to charge them. Next, prosecutors, defense counsel, and judges all participate in deciding bail, disposition (trial or a plea of guilty), and sentencing of offenders. Corrections professionals decide how to supervise offenders in their custody and participate in deciding if, when, and how prisoners return to society. The process boils down to deciding whether to move people further into the system and when and under what conditions to remove them from it. Table 1.2 shows the progression of decision making by producers.

Interdependent Decision Making It's very important for you to understand that decision making among criminal justice agencies is interdependent. Decisions of one agency affect decisions in other agencies. Take, for example, state laws that take away police discretion and command police officers to arrest suspects in all alleged cases of domestic assault. Before these mandatory arrest laws, police officers had discretion to take things like age, mental illness, and the amount of aggressiveness into account when deciding whether to arrest. Since the laws have been passed, do things like age, mental illness, and the amount of aggressiveness matter? Of course they do. But now, prosecutors instead of police officers use their discretionary decision-making power to take them into account when they decide whether to charge arrested men (the assailants are almost always men) with assault. We call the shifting of discretionary decision making from one agency to another the **hydraulic effect.** (When you compress discretion at one decision point in the system it'll pop up at another point.)

hydraulic effect compression of discretion at one point in the system causes discretion to pop up at another point

The criminologist Lloyd E. Ohlin (1993) nicely captures this interdependence in his description of the criminal justice system as:

> a system of complex individualization of justice, adaptively balanced, not easily controlled, and certainly not inevitably improved by attempts to mandate choices, remove discretion, or impose well-meaning but simplistic panaceas on such a highly complex process. (10)

Still, decision making isn't entirely interdependent. First, criminal justice agencies have a lot of independence. They get their authority and their budgets from different sources. Police departments get their power and money from cities and towns. Sheriff's departments, prosecutors, public defenders, jails, and trial courts get their power and money from counties. Appeals courts and prisons get theirs from states.

Second, agencies set their own policies, rarely if ever coordinating them with other agencies. And most professionals within these agencies don't even think about the effects of their decisions on other agencies. For example, when police officers arrest suspected drunk drivers, child molesters, burglars, and thieves, they're not thinking about how their arrests are going to affect the "system" (giving prosecutors more work, courts heavier caseloads, and prisons more prisoners). Why? The consequences of their decisions are too far down the line to worry about them. So, each agency becomes its own little subcriminal justice system. In reality, Professor Ohlin (1993) writes:

> The criminal justice process reduces the cases processed from its broadest net of police intervention to final incarceration in jail or prison. Certainly the cases that go all the way demonstrate the system as a system. But absent rigid legislative mandates or other external controls on discretion, most . . . criminal cases are not subject to maximum processing. So although full enforcement does exist as a total system, other more abbreviated systems exist within it to respond to the different problems and the infinite variety of persons dealt with by enforcement officials. (11)

Formal and Informal Decision Making

formal decision making decision making open to public view, according to written rules

There are two very different kinds of decision making in criminal justice: decision making "by the book" (**formal decision making**) and decision making "in

▼ TABLE 1.2 The Progression of Decision Making by Producers

Producer	Progressive Levels of Decision Making
Police (Chapters 5–7)	Do nothing
	Investigate crime
	Report and record crime
	Arrest criminal suspect
	Search criminal suspect
	Interrogate criminal suspect
	Release criminal suspect
	Warn criminal suspect verbally
	Use force against individuals
	Intervene to maintain the peace (ordering people to "break it up," "move on," or "keep quiet")
	Provide service to people (helping lost persons find their way, helping parents find their children, providing an emergency escort)
Prosecutor (Chapters 8–11)	Take no action
	Divert case or person to another agency
	Charge suspect with a criminal offense
	Recommend bail or detention
	Negotiate a guilty plea
	Recommend harsh or lenient sentence
Judge (Chapters 8–11)	Release on bail
	Detain prior to trial
	Accept negotiated plea
	Reject negotiated plea
	Suspend sentence
	Sentence to probation
	Hand down a minimum sentence
	Hand down a maximum sentence
Probation department (Chapter 12)	Provide little or no supervision
	Provide minimum supervision
	Provide medium supervision
	Provide maximum supervision
	Report probation violations
	Don't revoke probation for violations
	Revoke probation for violations
Prison (Chapters 13–14)	Classify prisoners for type of prison and program
	Place minimum restrictions on prisoners' liberty and privacy
	Place medium restrictions on prisoners' liberty and privacy
	Place maximum restrictions on prisoners' liberty and privacy
	Issue disciplinary reports
	Take disciplinary actions
	Release prisoners
	Supervise prisoners' reentry into the community

▼ **TABLE 1.3 Formal versus Informal Decision Making**

Formal Decision Making	Informal Decision Making
Decisions "by the book" (written rules)	Decisions according to professional judgment (discretionary decision making)
Decisions published or known to the public	Decisions not published and with low visibility
Mission is to provide certainty and predictability in criminal justice	Mission is to provide flexibility to satisfy a need for "play in the joints" of formal criminal justice

▼ **TABLE 1.4 Formal Rules**

Sources	Types of Rules
Constitutional provisions	U.S. Constitution and Bill of Rights
	State constitutions and bills of rights
Statutes	U.S. Code
	State codes
Court decisions	Decisions of federal courts interpreting constitutional provisions and statutes
	Decisions of state courts interpreting constitutional provisions and statutes
Rules of procedure	Federal Rules of Criminal Procedure
	State rules of criminal procedure
	Department and agency rules
	Federal law enforcement agencies' rules and regulations
	U.S. Attorney General's rules
	Federal Bureau of Prisons' rules and regulations
	State and local police departments' rules and regulations
	County and district attorneys' rules and regulations
	State and local prisons' and jails' rules and regulations

informal decision making (discretionary decision making) professional decision making guided by education, training, and experience

action" (**informal decision making**) (Table 1.3). Let's look at formal and informal decision making in criminal justice.

Formal Decision Making Formal decision making is decision making according to written rules (decision making by the book). Formal decision making is open to public view (arrest, court proceedings), and formal decisions are published, or at least known to the public. The rules come from several sources (Table 1.4):

1. U.S. and state constitutions
2. Statutes (written laws) created by the U.S. Congress, state legislatures, and city councils
3. Court decisions of state and federal courts
4. Manuals and written policies of courts and crime control agencies (law enforcement, prosecution, and corrections)

Formal decision making consists of applying (and probably often interpreting) these *written* rules of formal criminal justice. Most formal decision making takes place in courts where judges apply laws. But it also takes place in various kinds of departmental and civilian reviews of police misconduct (Chapter 7) and in disciplinary hearings in prisons (Chapter 14).

The most famous example of formal rules is so embedded in our culture almost everybody can recite it—the *Miranda* warnings—written and published by the U.S. Supreme Court in *Miranda v. Arizona* (1966, Chapter 7). If you watch crime news stories or cop stories on TV, you're almost certain to hear the warnings recited. The rules are the way formal criminal justice carries out one of its most important missions—providing certainty and predictability throughout criminal justice. We should know what to expect and be able to count on it happening (Walker 1993, 18–20).

Informal (Discretionary) Decision Making There's no book of written rules to guide informal decision making (we call it **discretionary decision making**, a term you're going to be seeing and learning a lot about throughout the book). Discretionary decision making operates according to the judgments of criminal justice professionals guided by their education, training, and experience in the field. Their decision making is low visibility (often completely invisible). Their decisions aren't published (and often are not even known to the public).

discretionary decision making decision making according to judgments of criminal justice professionals based on their education, training, and field experience

But don't get the idea that informal criminal justice isn't important. It has missions, too, as important as those of formal criminal justice. One of its most important (you'll learn more of these missions in other chapters): To satisfy the need for flexibility in the vast number of situations that don't fit neatly into the rules in the book of formal criminal justice. We'll call this the need for "play in the joints" of formal criminal justice. Discretionary decision making lies at the heart of the day-to-day reality of criminal justice.

Despite the emphasis on discretionary decision making in this book and its importance in day-to-day criminal justice, remember two important points. First, *both* informal and formal decision making are essential. Criminal justice "rests on, indeed is created and enabled by...law" wrote one of the great authorities on criminal justice decision making and author of his own criminal justice textbook, the late Donald J. Newman (Remington 1993, 279). Second, just because the rules aren't in writing and decision making according to them is invisible doesn't mean discretion is *bad*, as we'll shortly see and be reminded of throughout this book.

The Complexity of Decision Making

Decision making is a complicated business in the real world of criminal justice. The "book" doesn't have a list of simple rules telling police officers, prosecutors, defense lawyers, judges, and corrections officers how to solve most of the problems they run into. Only professional judgment, developed through training and experience (with maybe a little luck thrown in), will do.

Also, the goals of criminal justice are multiple, vague, and often in conflict. Police officers are legally commanded to "enforce all the laws." Informally, they can't (and they *shouldn't*). Prosecutors are told formally to "do justice." Informally, they pursue other goals like winning cases, cracking down on specific crimes, improving efficiency, and saving the people's tax dollars. Judges have to impose sentences that are supposed to punish, incapacitate, and reform individual defendants while protecting the community by sending a message to prevent criminal wannabes from committing crimes. Probation officers are supposed to police and counsel offenders in the community. Corrections officers are supposed to maintain order and prevent escapes from prison, discipline prisoners, and turn them into people who can return to society ready to work and play by the rules.

As if these challenges aren't enough, professionals don't have the luxury of time to consider their decisions. They have to decide *right now* how to accomplish their goals. By now, I think you've got the message you should remember as you begin your journey through criminal justice: There are no simple solutions written in books to solve most of the problems criminal justice professionals have to deal with in their daily work (Walker 1992b, 47).

▼ TABLE 1.5 Legitimate and Discriminatory Decision-Making Criteria

Legitimate Criteria	Discriminatory Criteria
Seriousness of the offense	Race
Dangerousness of offender	Ethnicity
Relationship of offender to victim	Class
Strength of case	Sex
	Sexual orientation

Legitimate versus Discriminatory Decision Making

The last dimension to decision making is the criteria. There are two types of criteria (Table 1.5). We'll call the first **legitimate decision-making criteria,** or criteria that produce legal, fair, and smart (more on smart decisions in the "Research and Criminal Justice" section later in the chapter) decisions. Second, **discriminatory decision-making criteria** infect decision making to produce illegal, discriminatory, and harmful decisions. Criminologists have examined a fairly long list of criteria. (See the In Focus box "Crime and Punishment in New Haven: A Gender Gap.") We'll boil them down to the ones researchers (and the rest of your book) concentrate on. The legitimate criteria include:

1. Seriousness of the offense
2. Dangerousness of the offender
3. Amount and quality of the facts in the case
4. Relationship of the offender to the victim

The discriminatory criteria include:

1. Race (mostly Blacks and Whites)
2. Sex
3. Age
4. Class

I know from experience that lots of you who are reading this are asking: What about other races, like Native Americans and Asians? What about ethnicity (particularly Hispanics, Arabs, and Asians)? What about sexual orientation? What about disability? Of course, we should include all of these, and other noxious criteria that infect decision making I'm sure I've overlooked. Unfortunately, we're badly lacking in enough research to report on. Whenever it's available, it's included in the appropriate places in the book.

There's an enormous amount of research on the criteria for decision making. The "big picture" of all that research (Lauritson and Sampson 1998) shows that

1. Officials rely on legitimate criteria in *most* cases of *serious* crime at *most* decision points in their decision making. (75)
2. "Our review of the literature on minorities and criminal justice suggests that racial discrimination emerges *some* of the time at *some* stages of the system in *some* locations, but there is little evidence that racial disparities reflect systemic, overt bias on the part of criminal justice decision makers." (77–78)

These conclusions leave many gaps in our knowledge, particularly the meaning of the italicized words. Some of the gaps you'll be able to fill in when you read the rest of the chapters. Some you'll have to leave blank because the evidence isn't there, or it conflicts. But the gaps raise a very important question for you to think about when you come to sections focusing on decision-making cri-

legitimate decision-making criteria characteristics for decision making that produce legal, fair, and smart decisions

discriminatory decision-making criteria characteristics that infect decision making to produce illegal, discriminatory, unfair decisions

▶DECISION
POINT◀

How can the police avoid claims of racial profiling?

Click on this Decision Point at http://cj.wadsworth.com/ samaha_cj7e to explore the issue.

Crime and Punishment in New Haven: A Gender Gap?

Case 1. Kate, a White woman in her mid-thirties, waved down a man who was driving along a street frequented by prostitutes. While Kate and the driver exchanged words, a second woman approached the car. Kate moved to the driver's side, opened the car door, and pulled the man out. The other woman put a knife to the man's back. Both women demanded his wallet and car keys. A police officer on patrol saw the three people and, recognizing Kate, stopped. As the officer approached, Kate told the victim she had a gun and showed it to him. Then the two women fled and the officer chased them. He was able to catch only Kate, whom he arrested. Kate was charged with first-degree robbery. Three months later, she pleaded guilty to the charge. At the time, she had more than a dozen previous convictions, and had been in and out of prison since she was 20 years old. She was sentenced to serve two years of incarceration.

Case 2. Casey, a Black man in his mid-twenties, entered an all-night convenience store in a poor neighborhood and asked the clerk (a Black woman in her early twenties) for an item. When she turned around, Casey hit the clerk on the back of the head with a blunt instrument, knocking her to the floor. When she came to, she saw Casey at the cash register and screamed. Casey took about $55. He was charged with and pleaded guilty to first-degree robbery, three months later. Casey had more than a dozen previous convictions and had been in and out of prison since his late teens. He was sentenced to 10 years in prison.

Both Kate and Casey were charged with identical crimes, in the same city, during the same month. Both had similar criminal histories. Yet, despite such strong surface similarities, New Haven's criminal justice system treated them differently. How do you explain these differences under a system that promises "equal justice for all"?

They were both accused and convicted of first-degree robbery; they both had similar criminal records. So, except for race and gender, the two cases appear to be the same. A gender gap, right? Wrong. Although both victimized strangers, Kate's victim wasn't injured; Kate's accomplice, not Kate, pulled the knife; and the victim wasn't *completely* innocent (he was probably cruising for a prostitute). Finally, Kate's admittedly substantial previous crimes were almost all prostitution-related misdemeanors.

By contrast, Casey's female victim was physically and psychologically injured. She was afraid to go back to work and couldn't go anywhere near the store without getting physically ill. Casey had a history of serious offenses, including robbery and assault (Daly 1994, 7).

---

teria: "How much discrimination is too much? Or to put it another way, "How much discrimination is acceptable in a system created and run by *imperfect* people (which of course all of us are)?" We'll close with two answers to these questions: First, here's what Professor Alfred Blumstein (1993), a respected criminologist concluded from his own research:

> Overall, 76 percent of all...[decisions to imprison] were based on...actual offending. That leaves 24 percent that might be based on discrimination. (750–751)

> The principal conclusion of...[our research] was not that racial discrimination does not exist—there are too many anecdotal reports of such discrimination to dismiss that possibility—but, rather, that the *bulk* [my emphasis] of the racial disproportionality in prison is attributable to differential involvement in arrest, and probably in crime, in those most serious offenses that tend to lead to imprisonment. (743, 750)

Professor Katheryn K. Russell (1998) had a very different answer:

> Professor Blumstein surmises that a 20 to 25 percent gap is no great cause for alarm because eliminating this gap would not change the incarceration picture dramatically. By Blumstein's calculation, the 20 to 25 percent gap of unexplained disparity between arrest and incarceration figures represents about 10,000 black prisoners. Although 10,000 prisoners is a statistical drop in the bucket of the overall prison population (less than 1 percent), socially it is no small number. Ten thousand blacks, who may have been more harshly treated by the criminal justice system because of their race, constitutes an enormous social problem. If 10,000 blacks have been subjected to discrimination, this means that some were unjustly convicted and unjustly sentenced to lengthy prison terms.

> ▶ DECISION POINT ◀
>
> How much discrimination is too much?
>
> Click on this Decision Point at http://cj.wadsworth.com/ samaha_cj7e to explore the issue.

► How much discrimination is acceptable in a system created and run by imperfect people? Law enforcement officers have to use their discretionary powers every day and often have to make split-second decisions in tense situations. Many feel that this power often leads to racial discrimination and profiling. Here, Sharif Aleen protests fatal police shootings in Denver, CO, prior to a march in October 2003. The Denver police were under growing scrutiny after a string of fatal shootings, including the death of a developmentally disabled teen and a man officers said was wielding a pickaxe (family members said it was a twig).

AP/Wide World Photos

Criminal Justice Models

Several models of criminal justice should help you understand the themes of crime control in a constitutional democracy and of decision making in criminal justice. Keep in mind that models are simplifications of reality; in highlighting the essentials of reality, they dim its details. Let's look at four of these models:

1. Criminal justice "wedding cake"
2. Criminal justice "funnel"
3. Crime control model
4. Due process model

Before we get to the models, notice (you'll learn more about them in other chapters) four decisions that have to be made *before* the criminal justice process kicks in:

1. Legislatures have to decide to define behavior as criminal. (Chapter 4)
2. Offenders have to decide to commit crimes. (Chapter 3)
3. Victims have to decide to report crimes. (Chapter 2)
4. Law enforcement officers have to decide to arrest people. (Chapter 6)

OK, now let's look at the models.

The Wedding Cake Model

The wedding cake model depicts a process in which criminal justice officials decide how to deal with cases according to their informal discretionary definition of "seriousness." Professionals distinguish between "real crime" and "garbage" (also called "bullsh_t") cases. What determines the difference?

1. Seriousness of the charge (including injury to victims and use of a gun)
2. Past criminal record of the offender
3. Relationship of the victim to the offender
4. Strength of the prosecution's case

Judged by these criteria, it's no surprise that "real crimes" get more attention (as well they should) than "garbage" cases (Gottfredson and Gottfredson 1988;

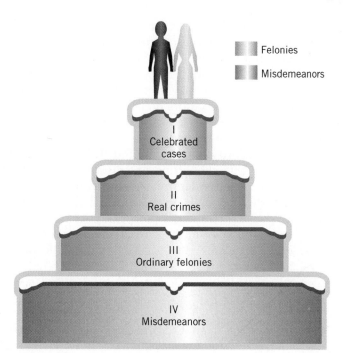

Felonies

Misdemeanors

I
Celebrated cases

II
Real crimes

III
Ordinary felonies

IV
Misdemeanors

Mather 1974, 187–216; Spohn and Cederblom 1991, 306). The tiers of a wedding cake (narrow at the top and increasingly wider toward the bottom (Figure 1.2) represent the decreasing seriousness and increasing numbers of cases.

1. On the small top tier are a tiny number of "celebrated cases."
2. In the second tier are a somewhat larger number of "real crimes."
3. Most "ordinary felonies" are in the third tier.
4. The broad fourth tier represents the vast number of minor crimes.

All three top tiers are **felonies,** crimes that can send convicted offenders to prison for a year or more. First-tier crimes are the "celebrated cases"—the very few felonies that grab public attention because the crime is particularly grisly (Timothy McVeigh who blew up more than a hundred men, women, and children) or a famous person (Martha Stewart) is charged with committing it. In celebrated cases, defendants get all the protections the law allows, including a trial.

felonies crimes punishable by a year or more in prison

Don't get the idea that these full legal protections and a trial are typical; they're the rarest event in real-life criminal justice (Chapter 10). A story will make my point. A former student, now a successful criminal lawyer, defended a man charged with the horrific crime of murdering his girlfriend and her little girl by cutting them up with a hatchet. As you might expect the case got a lot of attention. Because it was a grisly crime and got so much publicity, the case was definitely going to trial. Discouraged at the prospect of having no defense, the attorney complained, "I can't even count on the cops screwing up by violating his rights. They know this case is going to trial and they want a conviction, so they'll handle this sucker with kid gloves so they can put him away."

Second-tier crimes are "real crimes" (felonies like criminal homicide, rape, aggravated assault, and armed robbery). Of course, some celebrated cases (Timothy McVeigh) are "real crimes," too. But the second tier's reserved for what we'll call "pure real crimes" (classified on the seriousness of the offense alone). What makes them serious? They're committed by individuals who have criminal records, are strangers to their victims, use guns, and injure their victims. "Real crimes" are less likely than celebrated cases to go to a full formal trial but more likely than less serious felony and misdemeanor cases.

Third-tier cases are "ordinary felonies," like burglaries, thefts, and unarmed robberies where no one got hurt and the victim knew the offender. "Technically," serious felonies where the event is also a private dispute are classified as "ordinary." Suppose Doug asks his roommate Eli for $25. At the time Eli gives Doug the money, Doug believes the $25 is a gift. A few months later, Eli asks Doug for his $25. When Doug says, "No way, you gave me that $25," Eli grabs Doug's wallet and takes all the money in it, $40. "I'm taking my $25 plus the rest in interest." Police and prosecutors don't call this a "real" robbery no matter what the law says. So, they either divert it out of the system completely or go for a guilty plea to ordinary theft.

The vast majority of cases are fourth-tier crimes, misdemeanors like simple assault, petty theft, shoplifting, and disorderly conduct. Samuel Walker calls this bottom tier the "lower depths." Practically none of these cases go to trial; they're not worth the cost and effort of formal proceedings. So, they're disposed of quickly either in preliminary proceedings or in agreements among prosecutors, defendants, and lawyers. In many, there are no criminal charges at all; they're considered "problems" the parties should settle between themselves (Walker 1994, 29–37).

The Funnel Model

Wide at the top, narrow at the bottom, a funnel is opposite in shape to a wedding cake; but like the wedding cake, it also represents the reality of informal day-to-day discretionary decision making. The wedding cake depicts how a few celebrated cases and serious felonies move through the whole formal criminal justice system and how the many ordinary felonies and the vast majority of misdemeanors are disposed of by informal discretion early in the criminal process. The funnel model of criminal justice shows how decisions made at each stage in the criminal process sort out those people who shouldn't go further from those who should continue. We call this sorting operation **case attrition;** at each stage, the numbers of people in the system shrink as they're sorted out of or into other parts of the formal system.

Some decisions remove people by releasing them outright with no charges. Some decisions remove people by **diversion,** transferring them to other agencies for alcohol and other treatment or family counseling programs. The rest are sent on to the next stage in the formal criminal justice structure and process. Figure 1.3 shows the following about this sorting operation:

1. More people are arrested than charged with crimes.
2. More people are charged with crimes than convicted.
3. More people are convicted than sentenced.
4. More people are sentenced to probation than to prison.

Put another way, there are more suspects than defendants, more defendants than convicted offenders, and more convicted offenders than prisoners.

Don't assume that case attrition is "letting criminals off." In the old days, the view that every arrest would end in conviction and punishment if it weren't for "technicalities," incompetence, softhearted judges, or even corruption was reflected in the phrase **"case mortality."** However, empirical research has repeatedly proven the case mortality view was wrong. Why? Because the decisions to arrest, charge, and convict depend on how much evidence backs them up (the strength of the case criterion). Arrest doesn't mean *guilt* (proof beyond a reasonable doubt); it means *probable cause* (Chapter 7, "Probable Cause" section) to *believe* arrested people are guilty. Prosecutors need more proof to charge defendants, and of course they have to prove guilt beyond a reasonable doubt to convict (Chapter 9, "Decision to Charge," and Chapter 10, "Proving Guilt" sections). Also, judges weigh the three other criteria—the seriousness of the offense, any criminal history of the offender, and the relationship between the offender and the victim—when they decide whether to sentence offenders to prison (Chapter 11, "Sentencing"). So, there will always be more arrests than charges, more

case attrition at each stage, the numbers of people in the system shrink as they're sorted out of or into other parts of the formal system

diversion transferring individuals in the system to other agencies for alcohol and other treatment or family counseling programs

case mortality view that every case would end in conviction and punishment if it weren't for "technicalities," incompetence, softhearted judges, or even corruption

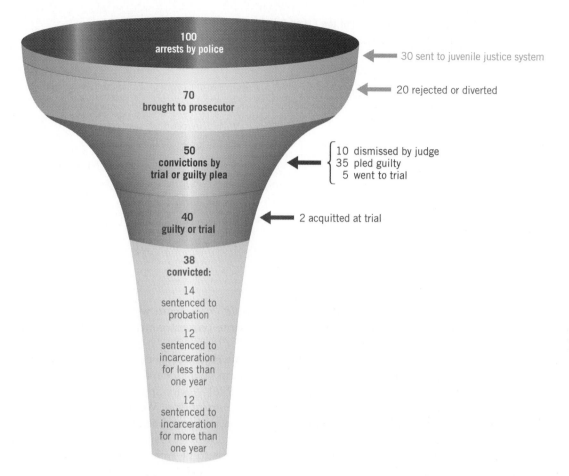

100
arrests by police

→ 30 sent to juvenile justice system

70
brought to prosecutor

← 20 rejected or diverted

50
convictions by
trial or guilty plea

⎧ 10 dismissed by judge
⎨ 35 pled guilty
⎩ 5 went to trial

40
guilty or trial

← 2 acquitted at trial

38
convicted:

14
sentenced to
probation

12
sentenced to
incarceration
for less than
one year

12
sentenced to
incarceration
for more than
one year

▲ **FIGURE 1.3 The Criminal Justice Funnel**
The funnel shows that decisions made at each stage in the criminal process sort out those people who shouldn't go further from those who should continue. *Source:* Brian Forst, "Prosecution," James Q. Wilson and Joan Petersilia, *Crime: Public Policies for Crime Control* (Oakland: Institute for Contemporary Studies, 2004), page 510.

charges than convictions, more convictions than prison sentences, and more short than long prison sentences. (And that's the way it *should* be in a *fair* criminal justice system.)

The Crime Control and Due Process Models

In an influential article written in 1964, Stanford University law professor Herbert Packer (1964) built two models of criminal justice on two values of our constitutional democracy—crime control and due process (113). According to the **value of crime control** model, criminal justice exists to reduce crime for the good of the whole society. According to the **value of due process** model, the mission of criminal justice is to guarantee fair procedures for every individual caught up in the system (Table 1.6). Most people put crime control high on their list of priorities when it comes to criminal justice. But crime control doesn't mean controlling crime at any price. We have to respond to crime within the limits placed on government power by the values of our constitutional democracy. So, officials fighting crime have to respect the life, liberty, privacy, property, and dignity of all people no matter how much we hate them or what they do.

The Crime Control Model The **crime control model** focuses on the need to protect people and their property, partly for the victims' sake but also for the good of the whole society. If people don't feel safe, they lose their capacity to

CONCEPT ‖ BUILDER
Visit http://cj.wadsworth.com/
samaha_cj7e for an interactive
exploration of the **crime control
model.**

value of crime control criminal justice exists to reduce crime for the good of the whole society

value of due process the mission of criminal justice is to guarantee fair procedures for every individual caught up in the system

crime control model focuses on the need to protect people and their property for the good of the whole society

Chapter 1 Criminal Justice in the United States   19

▼ TABLE 1.6 Comparison of the Crime Control and Due Process Models

Crime Control	Due Process
Control crime	Fair procedures
Society's needs	Individual's rights
Confidence in police and prosecutor	Distrust of all government power
Negotiation	Adversary court proceedings
Reliability of informal fact-finding	Reliability of formal fact-finding
Discretion by police and prosecutors	Limited discretion by police and prosecutors
Presumption of guilt	Presumption of innocence
Emphasis on early stages of investigation	Emphasis on trial
Conveyer belt	Obstacle course
Fear of criminals	Fear of government

function and enjoy the rewards that should come from working hard and playing by the rules. At the end of the day, crime control guarantees social freedom by protecting people and their property.

To make good on this guarantee, criminal justice decisions have to sort out the guilty from the innocent; let the innocent go as soon as possible; and convict and punish the guilty (also as soon as possible). Notice *speedy* decisions by themselves aren't good enough; they have to be *correct*, too. We don't want to convict innocent people and let guilty ones go free, not just because it's unfair but because it leads to time-wasting, expensive second-guessing of decisions already made. In other words, we also want decisions to be *right* because we want them to be *final* (Packer 1968, 158).

Informal decision making is the best way to ensure speed and accuracy. In Professor Packer's words, "The process must not be cluttered up with [the] ceremonious rituals" of a formal legal contest. For example, police interrogation gets to the truth faster and better than examination and cross-examination during a trial. Negotiations out of court between prosecutors and defense lawyers are more efficient and fairer than time-consuming, formal court proceedings. According to Packer (1968), the crime control model operates like

> an assembly line conveyer belt [Figure 1.4] down which moves an endless array of cases, never stopping, carrying the cases to workers who stand at fixed stations and who perform on each case as it comes by the same small but essential operation that brings it one step closer to being a finished product, or, to exchange the metaphor, a closed file. (159)

▼ FIGURE 1.4 The Crime Control Conveyer Belt

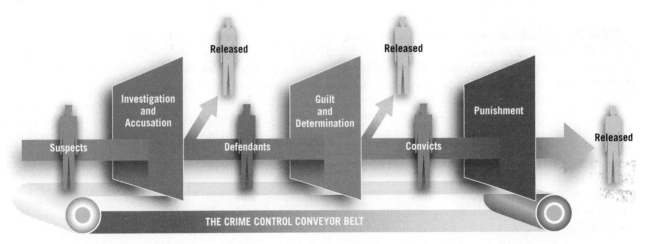

◄ Presumed guilty? 28-year-old Stancy Nesby sued San Francisco officials after she was repeatedly detained, arrested, or jailed based on warrants issued after a woman arrested for cocaine possession used Nesby's name and didn't show up in court.

The **presumption of guilt** (the belief that people caught up in criminal justice are *probably* guilty) fits in with the premium placed on fast and accurate crime control. This is reflected in views such as "the police wouldn't have arrested her and prosecutors wouldn't have charged her unless she'd done something wrong." So, courts shouldn't "handcuff" the police and stymie prosecutors by putting up expensive, time-consuming hurdles to their efforts to find the truth. Give police officers leeway to detain, search, and interrogate suspects so they can sort out the guilty from the innocent. Let prosecutors bargain for guilty pleas to get the guilty to punishment and hopefully redemption as soon as possible. As you can see, the crime control model emphasizes the early stages in criminal justice—police investigation and guilty pleas.

One final point: The crime control model isn't too worried about mistakes and unfairness. Why? First, because it makes three assumptions based on confidence in government power:

1. *Police and prosecutors rarely make mistakes.* They don't base their decisions on personal prejudices even if they *are* prejudiced. And most suspects are guilty of *something.*
2. *The need for crime control outweighs the suffering of the few innocent people who get caught up in the system.* It's better that a few innocent people get convicted than guilty people go free.
3. *Sooner or later innocent people are vindicated* (most of the time sooner). At the end of the day, there's more to fear from criminals going free and innocent people suffering than there is from government power to control crime.

The Due Process Model According to the **due process model,** it's more important to guarantee the rights of individuals to fair procedures than to catch criminals. In fact, the best definition of due process is *fair procedures.* **Fair procedures** means decision making according to formal rules growing out of the Bill of Rights and the due process clauses of the U.S. Constitution and state constitutions (Chapter 4).

The commitment to decision making by formal rules is based on a distrust of government power and the need to control it. In Professor Paul Bator's (1963)

presumption of guilt view that the people caught up in criminal justice are *probably* guilty

due process model it's more important to guarantee the right of individuals to fair practices than to catch criminals

fair procedures decision making according to formal rules growing out of the Bill of Rights and the due process clauses of the U.S. Constitution and state constitutions

► According to the due process model, it's more important to guarantee the rights of individuals to fair procedures than to catch criminals. The media circus around top-tier wedding cake defendants like Scott Peterson, who was convicted of killing his wife and unborn child, can often make it difficult to put together unbiased juries. Is it possible for someone like Peterson to receive a fair trial?

© Frederic Larson/San Francisco/Corbis

harsh words, "The criminal law's notion of just condemnation and punishment is a cruel hypocrisy visited by a smug society on the psychologically and economically crippled." So, we have to throw up barriers to government power at each step in the criminal process to prevent further involvement in this risky business of criminal justice. It shouldn't surprise us that the due process model resembles an obstacle course, not an assembly line (Packer 1968, 170).

Creating due process obstacles (Figure 1.5) is based on the idea that you can't find the truth informally because human failings—like our faulty powers of observation, our motivation of self-interest, our emotions, and our prejudices—stand in the way. The model puts great confidence in the **adversary process**—getting the truth by fighting in court according to the formal rules of criminal procedure (Chapters 8–9). So, in the due process model, the trial is the high point of criminal justice. Why? Formal public proceedings reduce the chances that mistakes, emotions, and prejudices will infect decision making because skilled lawyers argue their side of the story in front of neutral judges acting as umpires, and impartial juries decide who's telling the truth.

Distrust of government power and the need to control it also means operating according to the **presumption of innocence:** The government always has the burden to justify its use of power even against people who turn out to be guilty. When all is said and done, the due process model expresses more fear of government than of criminals.

adversary process getting the truth by fighting in court according to the formal rules of criminal procedure

presumption of innocence the government always has the burden to justify its use of power even against people who turn out to be guilty

The History of Crime Control and Due Process

The tension between the values of due process and crime control is as old as criminal justice. One way (there are others) to interpret the history of criminal justice in Western cultures is as a pendulum swing between a commitment to crime control and a commitment to due process (Figure 1.6).

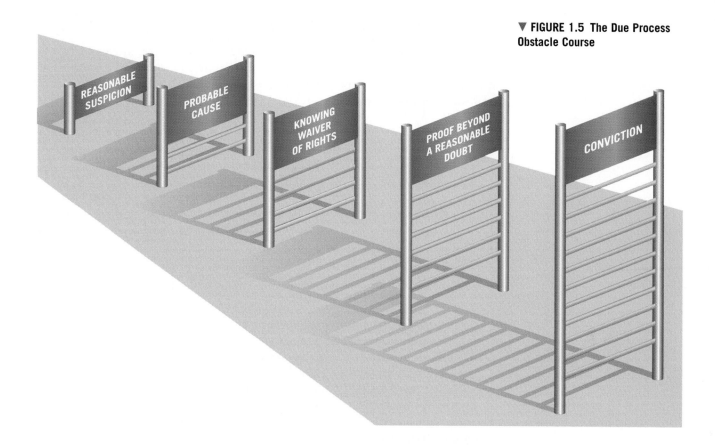

REASONABLE SUSPICION

PROBABLE CAUSE

KNOWING WAIVER OF RIGHTS

PROOF BEYOND A REASONABLE DOUBT

CONVICTION

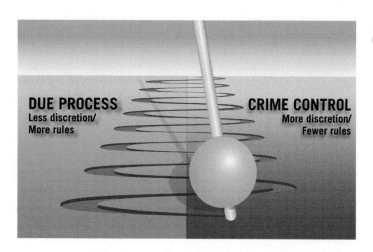

◀ FIGURE 1.6 The Crime Control/Due Process Pendulum

DUE PROCESS
Less discretion/
More rules

CRIME CONTROL
More discretion/
Fewer rules

At one end of the pendulum's swing is the fear of government abuse of power and demands for rules to control it. At the other end is the fear of crime and demands for discretionary power to eliminate it. Fear of government abuse of power has always led to more rules and less discretion. Fear of crime has always produced the opposite, more discretion and fewer rules. No one has stated more eloquently the problem of crime control in a constitutional democracy than James Madison (quoted on p. 5), during the debate over the Bill of Rights in 1787.

In this section, we'll look at the history of the pendulum swing of criminal justice through the early history of criminal justice, colonial America, the revolution and the early republic, the early years of industrialization, the due process revolution, and the return to crime control.

The Early History of Criminal Justice

In the ancient Roman republic, citizens enjoyed strong safeguards against government power. During the later years of the empire, Rome swung to the opposite extreme. The Emperor Hadrian boasted that merely sending a suspect to trial was conclusive proof of guilt (Pound 1921, 1–16; Strachan-Davidson 1912, 114, 168).

English history also experienced this swing of the pendulum between discretionary power and formal checks upon it. After the Norman Conquest in 1066, the Norman kings wielded enormous power; by 1185, the great Angevin King Henry II had consolidated and centralized royal power. By the beginning of the thirteenth century, a reaction occurred, provoked by Henry II's power-hungry son, John. In 1215, King John's barons forced him to accept and sign the Magna Carta, or Great Charter. Among other restrictions, King John agreed to a historic limit on royal power:

> No freeman shall be taken or imprisoned . . . or in any wise destroyed, nor will we go upon him, nor will we send upon him, unless by the lawful judgment of his peers, or by the law of the land. (Plucknett 1956, 24)

These curbs on royal authority emboldened the English nobility into great lawlessness that went on for more than two hundred years. Finally, royal authority reemerged under the Tudor monarchs in the late 1400s and throughout the 1500s, especially during the reigns of Henry VII (1485–1509) and his son, Henry VIII (1509–1547). Complaints that the ordinary courts protected criminals, rioters, and disturbers of the peace led to the creation of special royal courts like the famous Court of the Star Chamber. Unlike the Norman kings, the Tudor monarchs were checked by the rule of law (Elton 1974).

One of these cases (Samaha 1974, 1979) I discovered while searching for the American roots of due process in the Elizabethan borough of Colchester. In 1575, George Dibney, an Elizabethan gentleman, tested the balance between law and royal discretionary power in late Tudor England. Queen Elizabeth suspected Dibney had published seditious libels against Benjamin Clere, one of her supporters. She called on the local constables to go to Dibney's house and search for the libels. When the constables arrived, the following exchanges (somewhat modernized but mostly the actual words) took place:

DIBNEY: By whose authority do you come to search my house?

CONSTABLE: The Queen's authority.

DIBNEY: Not good enough. You need a warrant backed up by probable cause to enter my house and search it.

CONSTABLE: We have probable cause.

DIBNEY: Of what does it consist?

CONSTABLE: We're credibly informed you have libels in this house.

DIBNEY: Who credibly informed you?

DIBNEY (scoffing on hearing the informer's name): You and everybody else knows he's a liar and a knave.

CONSTABLES (impatient, and drawing their daggers): We're coming in whether you like it or not.

DIBNEY: What are your names?

CONSTABLES: Why?

DIBNEY: So that when I sue you in the Queen's Bench, I'll be sure to collect damages for your illegal entry, just as I did with the last lot who illegally searched my house.

Unfortunately, the record ends at that point, so we don't know whether the constables searched his house, or if they did, whether Dibney sued them and collected damages. But one important point we know for sure: "Mere suspicion," even that of the powerful Queen Elizabeth I, wasn't enough to back up entering a private home without probable cause to search (Chapter 7).

The resurgence of royal power under the Tudors emboldened the Stuart monarchs in the 1600s to aggrandize their power. The Stuarts upset the precarious Tudor balance between royal discretionary power and legal limits. By the reign of King Charles I, in the early 1600s, the royal Court of Star Chamber had abandoned procedural safeguards in favor of the royal power to punish troublemakers. Furthermore, royal domination of common-law judges ensured decisions favorable to royal interests and to the members of the aristocracy who supported the Stuart kings.

This aggrandizement, and the abuses accompanying it, eventually led to the English Civil War and later to the Glorious Revolution. Both were fought in part to resolve the struggle between those who favored royal discretionary power (some even claiming the monarch had absolute power above the law) and those who maintained that the law—not kings, queens, and their minions—ruled England (Kenyon 1986).

Colonial America

The first New England colonists came to America not just to establish their own church but also to escape the harsh Stuart criminal law and its arbitrary administration. They established the Massachusetts Body of Liberties, which reduced the number of capital offenses and guaranteed defendants several procedural safeguards. John Winthrop, the leading founder of the Massachusetts Bay Colony, devoted a major part of his life to working out the proper balance between the power of the government to enforce the criminal law and the rights of those charged with committing crimes (Chapter 11, "History of Sentencing" section) (Walker 1980).

Revolution and the Early Republic

The American Revolution, fought in part over the colonists' perception of George III's tyranny, led to the creation of a government of checks and balances, separation of powers, and constitutionally prescribed limits on government's power over individual citizens. All these actions bespoke a hostility to government power, expressed in Victorian historian Lord Acton's famous aphorism, "Power tends to corrupt and absolute power corrupts absolutely."

The authors of the U.S. Constitution believed they could create in a written document a perfect balance between security and liberty, goals expressed in the Preamble as to "insure the domestic tranquillity" *and* "secure the blessings of liberty." But many refused to trust the document unless it included a **bill of rights, a list, among other things, of specific guarantees limiting the power of the government to enforce the criminal law.** These guarantees included the rights against unreasonable searches and seizures, self-incrimination (Chapter 7), and cruel and unusual punishment (Chapter 11) and the guarantees of the rights to a jury trial, to confront witnesses, and to counsel (Chapter 10). These guarantees appeared as amendments and are among those in the Bill of Rights.

The safeguards written into the U.S. Bill of Rights (and similar bills of rights in all the states) established a criminal procedure with strong formal safeguards against government power. This structure existed with minimal complaints as long as a relatively homogeneous, widely scattered, mainly agrarian population dominated American society and its institutions (Pound 1921, 1–16).

In this inspiring story of individual rights and limits on government power in our history, let's remember five groups excluded from the enjoyment of these rights—Blacks (both free and slaves), Native Americans, women, poor people, and immigrants.

bill of rights a list of specific guarantees limiting the power of the government to enforce the criminal law

FindLaw—Bill of Rights and Other Constitutional Amendments: Analysis of each of the amendments, particularly the 4th, 5th, and 6th, which relate to criminal justice and policing. Click on "Annotations" for each of the amendments for further information. To reach this site go to "Web Links" on your Samaha CJ7 website: http://cj.wadsworth.com/samaha_cj7e.

Industrialization, Urbanization, and Immigration

Industrialization, urbanization, and immigration transformed American society and its institutions during the nineteenth century. An agricultural society made up of farmers and small towns was transformed into a manufacturing society made up of wage laborers from widely differing cultural heritages, crowded into cities of teeming millions and causing enormous problems of public order. Although no one at the time was aware of it, the response to the growing disorder was the creation of what would later become the modern criminal justice system. The modern bureaucratic agencies of criminal justice—police, courts, and corrections—originated in the nineteenth century. (We'll discuss the particular histories in the appropriate chapters on police, courts, and corrections.)

We don't have space to develop the point, but you should note that the United States was not unique in these responses to industrialization, immigration, and urbanization; most of the industrial nations of Western Europe and Japan formulated a similar response to similar historic developments (Walker 1998, 49–50).

By the early years of the twentieth century, many influential Americans believed they were in the midst of an epidemic crime wave. The widespread fear of crime led to the questioning of restrictions on the power of government to establish order and to demands that police, prosecutors, and judges crack down on crime and criminals. Some, such as Samuel Untermeyer, a prominent New York attorney, advocated the abolition of the Fourth Amendment's protection against unreasonable searches and seizures and the Fifth Amendment's guarantee against self-incrimination (American Academy of Political and Social Science 1910). Others demanded harsher punishments for even minor offenses, such as life imprisonment and even death for hardened drunkards and prostitutes. This tough stance toward criminals prevailed from the 1920s through the 1950s, when the public feared gangsters, mobsters, and juvenile delinquents more than they feared abuse of government power (Brown and Warner 1992, 296–305; Howe 1910; Walker 1998).

The Due Process Revolution

due process revolution U.S. Supreme Court decisions during the 1960s to expand the rights of criminal defendants, apply the rights to federal and state criminal justice, and include protection for "outsiders"

Then came the **due process revolution** of the 1960s. Before this, the U.S. Supreme Court had interpreted the Bill of Rights to apply only to *federal* criminal proceedings. During the 1960s, the Court adopted an ambitious (some say too ambitious, even unconstitutional) agenda:

1. Expand the rights of criminal defendants.
2. Apply these expanded rights to both federal *and* state criminal proceedings.
3. Include protection for "outsiders"—like poor, minority, and other suspects, defendants, and offenders—within the protection of these expanded rights. (Chapter 2)

The 1960s were turbulent times when "the establishment" was under siege. (I remember, when I was a young lawyer-turned-"do-gooder" high school teacher in Chicago's inner city, an older teacher who began almost every conversation by wringing her hands and saying, "In these times of upheaval and disorder....") Soaring crime rates; an increasingly militant civil rights movement; growing dissension over an unpopular war in Vietnam; a highly publicized youth counterculture; and rioting in the streets and cities left law-abiding citizens reeling (Cronin, Cronin, and Milakovich 1981; Halberstam 1998; Skolnick 1994, 241).

The Return to Crime Control

One popular interpretation of the problems of the 1960s was that a permissive society with too many safeguards for criminal defendants and not enough punishment for offenders emboldened budding criminals to mock the standards of decency, hard work, and "playing by the rules." These "antisocial renegades" lived for sex, drugs, rock and roll, riots, and, eventually, for crime. The popular and political answer was to declare and fight an all-out "war on crime." The elements of this war consisted of more police, more punishment, and fewer rights for criminal defendants.

This resurgence of the value of crime control continued throughout the 1980s and 1990s. And despite reduced crime rates and some public disenchantment with all "domestic wars"—including those on crime and drugs—the belief that law-abiding people are still at war with crime, particularly violent crime and drugs, is very much alive in 2005 (Currie 1998, 3–11; Flanagan and Longmire 1996). There's some speculation (but no hard empirical proof) that the September 11 attack has contributed to a crime control mind-set. But there's also speculation that fighting terror has siphoned off energy from crime control to antiterrorism efforts. (We'll discuss some of these speculations in the appropriate chapters and sections.)

Research and Criminal Justice

As I'm writing this section, a bipartisan unanimous U.S. Senate committee has issued a report concluding that the United States went to war against Iraq based on "bad intelligence." The intelligence agencies told the president there were weapons of mass destruction and where they were in Iraq. According to the report, no weapons were found in those places. The intelligence agencies told the president there was a connection between Saddam Hussein and al-Qaeda terrorists. Again according to the report, there was no connection. I hope I've worded this in a way that makes clear I'm not taking sides in any kind of partisan or ideological debate here. What I *am* doing is pointing out the importance of *knowledge* (which in this book you should take to mean facts, evidence, and good research).

There are two reasons I include research as one of the core themes of the book. First, you can't understand the other themes without knowledge, and knowledge depends on good research. Understanding is your responsibility not just to get a good grade in your class (although of course I hope you do!); not just so you can be a good criminal justice professional (even though that's an important reason, too); but so you can be a good citizen (being informed before you give your opinion or cast your vote or pay your taxes).

Second, the best criminal justice policies and practices depend on research to evaluate these policies and practices. (Of course, sometimes things work even if they're based on hunches or just because of luck, or in spite of bad research. The monster Saddam Hussein is gone even if the reasons we threw him out weren't backed up by good research.) Over the long haul, good research is the best foundation to build a criminal justice system on.

What do we mean by **"good" criminal justice research?** I'm referring to two kinds of research. Basic research describes and explains how practices and policies actually work (not how the officials defining and carrying out the policies say or believe they operate, nor how the public believes or hopes they operate). Evaluation research measures effectiveness, by answering the following questions:

1. *Is it legal?* (Example: Are police crackdowns unreasonable searches and seizures?)
2. *Does it work?* (Example: Do prison treatment programs rehabilitate prisoners?)
3. *Is it fair?* (Example: Do mass public housing searches unnecessarily target minorities?)
4. *Is it smart?* (Example: Does policing crime "hot spots" save money by focusing on the specific corners and buildings where most reports of crime originate?)

▶ DECISION POINT ◀

"Justice for all" or "Just us"?
Click on this Decision Point at http://cj.wadsworth.com/ samaha_cj7e to explore the issue.

"good" criminal justice research research that describes, explains, and evaluates criminal justice practices and policies

National Criminal Justice Reference Service (NCJRS): A databank of statistics, research, and resources on issues related to criminal justice. To reach this site go to "Web Links" on your Samaha CJ7 website: http://cj .wadsworth.com/samaha_cj7e.

MAKE YOUR DECISION *Is There a Wartime Exception to the Bill of Rights?*

FACTS

On September 11, 2001, the al Qaeda terrorist network used hijacked commercial airliners to attack prominent targets in the United States. Approximately 3,000 people were killed in those attacks. One week later, in response to these "acts of treacherous violence," Congress passed a resolution authorizing the President to "use all necessary and appropriate force against those nations, organizations, or persons he determines planned, authorized, committed, or aided the terrorist attacks" or "harbored such organizations or persons, in order to prevent any future acts of international terrorism against the United States by such nations, organizations or persons." Soon thereafter, the President ordered United States Armed Forces to Afghanistan, with a mission to subdue al Qaeda and quell the Taliban regime that was known to support it.

This case arises out of the detention of a man whom the Government alleges took up arms with the Taliban during this conflict. His name is Yaser Esam Hamdi. Born an American citizen in Louisiana in 1980, Hamdi moved with his family to Saudi Arabia as a child. By 2001, he resided in Afghanistan. At some point that year, he was seized by members of the Northern Alliance, a coalition of military groups opposed to the Taliban government, and eventually was turned over to the United States military.

The Government asserts that it initially detained and interrogated Hamdi in Afghanistan before transferring him to the U.S. Naval Base in Guantanamo Bay in January 2002. In April 2002, upon learning that Hamdi is an American citizen, authorities transferred him to a naval brig in Norfolk, Virginia, where he remained until a recent transfer to a brig in Charleston, South Carolina. The Government contends that Hamdi is an "enemy combatant," and that this status justifies holding him in the United States indefinitely—without formal charges or proceedings—unless and until it makes the determination that access to counsel or further process is warranted.

In June 2002, Hamdi's father, Esam Fouad Hamdi, filed a petition for a writ of habeas corpus [a court order challenging the lawfulness of the younger Hamdi's detention] in the Eastern District of Virginia....Hamdi's father claims his son went to Afghanistan to do "relief work," and that he had been in that country less than two months before September 11, 2001, and that he couldn't have received military training. The 20-year-old was traveling on his own for the first time, his father says, and "because of his lack of experience, he was trapped in Afghanistan once that military campaign began." ...

Source: Hamdi v. Rumsfeld (2004)

...The Government filed...a declaration from one Michael Mobbs (hereinafter "Mobbs Declaration"), who identified himself as Special Advisor to the Under Secretary of Defense for Policy. Mobbs set forth what remains the sole evidentiary support that the Government has provided to the courts for Hamdi's detention. The declaration states that Hamdi "traveled to Afghanistan" in July or August 2001, and that he thereafter "affiliated with a Taliban military unit and received weapons training." It asserts that Hamdi "remained with his Taliban unit following the attacks of September 11" and that, during the time when Northern Alliance forces were "engaged in battle with the Taliban," "Hamdi's Taliban unit surrendered" to those forces, after which he "surrender[ed] his Kalishnikov assault rifle" to them.

The Mobbs Declaration also states that, because al Qaeda and the Taliban "were and are hostile forces engaged in armed conflict with the armed forces of the United States, individuals associated with" those groups

AP/Wide World Photos

▲ Yaser E. Hamdi, an American citizen captured in Afghanistan and held incommunicado for more than two years as an enemy combatant, was released and returned to Saudi Arabia after he agreed to renounce his American citizenship and to report possible terrorist activity. Legal analysts said the arrangement would be difficult for the United States to enforce.

"were and continue to be enemy combatants." Mobbs states that Hamdi was labeled an enemy combatant "based upon his interviews and in light of his association with the Taliban." According to the declaration, a series of "U.S. military screening teams" determined that Hamdi met "the criteria for enemy combatants," and "a subsequent interview of Hamdi has confirmed that he surrendered and gave his firearm to Northern Alliance forces, which supports his classification as an enemy combatant." . . .

Majority Opinion

O'CONNOR, J.

I

. . . There is no bar to this Nation's holding one of its own citizens as an enemy combatant. . . . Citizens who associate themselves with the military arm of the enemy government, and with its aid, guidance and direction enter this country bent on hostile acts, are enemy belligerents within the meaning of . . . the law of war. . . .

Hamdi objects, nevertheless, that Congress has not authorized the *indefinite* detention to which he is now subject. . . . We take Hamdi's objection to be . . . the substantial prospect of perpetual detention. We recognize that the national security underpinnings of the "war on terror," although crucially important, are broad and malleable. As the Government concedes, "given its unconventional nature, the current conflict is unlikely to end with a formal cease-fire agreement." [All references to quotations are omitted.] The prospect Hamdi raises is therefore not far-fetched. If the Government does not consider this unconventional war won for two generations, and if it maintains during that time that Hamdi might, if released, rejoin forces fighting against the United States, then the position it has taken throughout the litigation of this case suggests that Hamdi's detention could last for the rest of his life. . . . Active combat operations against Taliban fighters apparently are ongoing in Afghanistan. The United States may detain, for the duration of these hostilities, individuals legitimately determined to be Taliban combatants who "engaged in an armed conflict against the United States."

Even when . . . detention of enemy combatants is legally authorized, there remains the question of what process is constitutionally due to a citizen who disputes his enemy-combatant status. . . . [The government argued that Hamdi is entitled to no (or very little) review of his detention; the decision should be left to the president's and the military's discretion. Hamdi argued that he should get all (or at least most) of the protections defendants get in ordinary criminal trials.] Both of these posi-

tions highlight legitimate concerns. And both emphasize the tension that often exists between the autonomy that the Government asserts is necessary . . . and the process that a citizen contends he is due before he is deprived of a constitutional right. . . .

It is beyond question that substantial interests lie on both sides of the scale in this case. Hamdi's "private interest . . . is the most elemental of liberty interests—the interest in being free from physical detention by one's own government." "Freedom from bodily restraint has always been at the core of the liberty protected by the Due Process Clause from arbitrary governmental action." "In our society liberty is the norm," and detention without trial "is the carefully limited exception." . . .

Nor is the weight on this side of the . . . scale offset by the circumstances of war or the accusation of treasonous behavior, for "it is clear that commitment for *any* purpose constitutes a significant deprivation of liberty . . . of the *erroneously* detained individual. . . .

Moreover, as critical as the Government's interest may be in detaining those who actually pose an immediate threat to the national security of the United States during ongoing international conflict, history and common sense teach us that an unchecked system of detention carries the potential to become a means for oppression and abuse of others who do not present that sort of threat." . . . We live in a society in which "mere public intolerance or animosity cannot constitutionally justify the deprivation of a person's physical liberty." . . .

On the other side of the scale are the . . . governmental interests in ensuring that those who have in fact fought with the enemy during a war do not return to battle against the United States. . . . Without doubt, our Constitution recognizes that core strategic matters of warmaking belong in the hands of those who are best positioned and most politically accountable for making them. [Courts recognize] . . . "broad powers in military commanders engaged in day-to-day fighting in a theater of war." . . .

Striking the proper constitutional balance here is of great importance to the Nation during this period of ongoing combat. But it is equally vital that our calculus not give short shrift to the values that this country holds dear or to the privilege that is American citizenship. . . . "The imperative necessity for safeguarding these rights to procedural due process under the gravest of emergencies has existed throughout our constitutional history, for it is then . . . that there is the greatest temptation to dispense with guarantees which . . . will inhibit government action." . . .

. . . We believe . . . "the risk of erroneous deprivation" of a detainee's liberty interest is unacceptably high under the Government's proposed rule, while some of the "additional or substitute procedural safeguards" suggested by [Hamdi]...are unwarranted in light of...the burdens they may impose on the military in such cases.

We therefore hold that a citizen-detainee seeking to challenge his classification as an enemy combatant must receive notice of the factual basis for his classification, and a fair opportunity to rebut the Government's factual assertions before a neutral decisionmaker....These essential constitutional promises may not be eroded.

At the same time, the...circumstances may demand that...enemy combatant proceedings may be tailored to alleviate their uncommon potential to burden the Executive at a time of ongoing military conflict. Hearsay, for example, may need to be accepted as the most reliable available evidence from the Government in such a proceeding. Likewise, the Constitution would not be offended by a presumption in favor of the Government's evidence, so long as...once the Government puts forth credible evidence...the...petitioner...[can] rebut that evidence....[This] would [insure]...that the errant tourist, embedded journalist, or local aid worker has a chance to prove military error....

We think it unlikely that this basic process will have the dire impact on the central functions of warmaking that the Government forecasts. The parties agree that initial captures on the battlefield need not receive the process we have discussed here; that process is due only when the determination is made to *continue* to hold those who have been seized....This focus meddles little, if at all, in the strategy or conduct of war, inquiring only into the appropriateness of continuing to detain an individual claimed to have taken up arms against the United States.

While we accord the greatest respect and consideration to the judgments of military authorities in matters relating to the actual prosecution of a war, and recognize that the scope of that discretion necessarily is wide... "the military claim must subject itself to the judicial process of having its reasonableness determined and its conflicts with other interests reconciled."

In sum, while the full protections that accompany challenges to detentions in other settings may prove unworkable and inappropriate in the enemy-combatant setting, the threats to military operations posed by a basic system of independent review are not so weighty as to trump a citizen's core rights to challenge meaningfully the Government's case and to be heard by an impartial adjudicator.

...We reject the Government's assertion that separation of powers principles mandate a heavily circumscribed role for the courts in such circumstances....We have long since made clear that a state of war is not a blank check for the President when it comes to the rights of the Nation's citizens....The war power "is a power to wage war successfully, and thus it permits the harnessing of the entire energies of the people in a supreme cooperative effort to preserve the nation. But even the war power does not remove constitutional limitations safeguarding essential liberties."

...The Great Writ of habeas corpus allows the Judicial Branch [to act as an important]...check on the Executive's discretion in the realm of detentions. "At its historical core, the writ of habeas corpus has served as a means of reviewing the legality of Executive detention...." It would turn our system of checks and balances on its head to suggest that a citizen could not make his way to court with a challenge to the factual basis for his detention by his government, simply because the Executive opposes making available such a challenge. Absent suspension of the writ by Congress, a citizen detained as an enemy combatant is entitled to this process....

Dissenting Opinion

SCALIA, J.

...The Founders well understood the difficult tradeoff between safety and freedom. Many think it not only inevitable but entirely proper that liberty give way to security in times of national crisis—that, at the extremes of military exigency, *inter arma silent leges* ["During war the laws are silent."]....

THOMAS, J.

The Executive Branch, acting pursuant to the powers vested in the President by the Constitution and with explicit congressional approval, has determined that Yaser Hamdi is an enemy combatant and should be detained. This detention falls squarely within the Federal Government's war powers, and we lack the expertise and capacity to second-guess that decision. As such, petitioners' habeas challenge should fail...

In a case strikingly similar to this one, the Court addressed a Governor's authority to detain for an extended period a person the executive believed to be responsible, in part, for a local insurrection. Justice Holmes wrote for a unanimous Court:

> When it comes to a decision by the head of the State upon a matter involving its life, the ordinary rights of individuals must yield to what *he deems* the necessities of the moment. Public danger warrants the substitution of executive process for judicial process. This was admitted with regard to killing men in the actual clash of arms, and we think it obvious, although it was disputed, that the same is true of temporary detention to prevent apprehended harm.

The Court answered...the petitioner's claim that he had been denied due process by emphasizing that

> it is familiar that what is due process of law depends on circumstances. It varies with the subject-matter and the necessities of the situation. Thus summary proceedings suffice for taxes, and executive decisions for exclusion from the country....Such arrests are not necessarily for punishment, but are by way of precaution to prevent the exercise of hostile power.

Undeniably, Hamdi has been deprived of a serious interest, one actually protected by the Due Process Clause. Against this, however, is the Government's overriding interest in protecting the Nation....

QUESTIONS

1. Describe the details of both sides of the balance between liberty and security as Justice O'Connor, Justice Scalia, and Justice Thomas see them.
2. Where did Justice O'Connor strike the balance? List and describe her reasons for striking the balance where she did.
3. Where did Justice Scalia strike the balance? List and describe his reasons for striking the balance where he did.
4. Where did Justice Thomas strike the balance? List and describe his reasons for striking the balance where he did.
5. Where would you strike the balance? Defend your answer with details from the case.

The U.S. government released Yaser Hamdi in October 2004 in return for his renouncing his U.S. citizenship and agreeing to severe travel restrictions for the rest of his life. According to Mark Corallo, a U.S. Justice Department spokesman, Hamdi's release would be under conditions that would:

ensure the interests of the United States and our national security. As we have repeatedly stated, the United States has no interest in detaining enemy combatants beyond the point that they pose a threat to the U.S. and our allies. (Savage 2004, 1)

Attorney Kevin J. Barry, a retired military judge who is cofounder of the National Institute of Military Justice, blamed the government for holding Hamdi so long when it apparently did not have evidence to sustain criminal charges. "There seems to be an initial pulling of the trigger in cases like Chaplain Yee and Halabi [two other suspected enemy collaborators who were later released] and Hamdi that, once the dust settles, cannot be borne out," Barry said (Savage 2004, 1).

Among other high-profile legal setbacks in the Bush administration's war on terrorism: None of the hundreds of Muslims detained in federal sweeps after the September 11 attacks ended up facing terrorism charges, though most were deported on minor immigration charges (Savage 2004, 1).

Knowing this, would you change your answer to question 5?

Chapter Summary

▶ Crime control in a constitutional democracy consists of balancing the need for government power to enforce the criminal law against the rights of individuals to come and go as they please and be free from government interference. We need to give the government enough power to make us safe and secure but not so much that it undermines the freedom and privacy that makes society in a constitutional democracy worth living in.

▶ The criminal justice system is both a structure and a process. The structure consists of a series of decision points in the major crime control agencies (police, courts, and corrections). The process consists of decision making about the investigation of suspects, the prosecution and conviction of defendants, the punishment (correction) and supervision of offenders, and the release of ex-offenders from custody.

▶ Criminal justice decision making consists of formal and informal decision making. Formal decision making is decision making according to law and other formal rules. Informal decision making is discretionary decision making according to professional judgment based on education, training, and experience.

▶ Most decision making is based on legitimate criteria (seriousness of offense, dangerousness of offender, strength of the evidence, and relationship of the offender to the victim). But, some decision making is discriminatory, infected by decisions based on race and ethnicity, sex, sexual orientation, and class.

▶ One way to look at the history of criminal justice is as a pendulum swing between due process and crime control. Due process periods emphasize fair procedures for every person caught up in the criminal justice system. Crime control periods stress crime control to make the whole community feel safe.

▶ Basic research in criminal justice is necessary to describe and explain how practices and policies actually work day to day. We also need evaluation research that measures the effectiveness of criminal justice policies and practices. We measure their effectiveness according to whether they're legal; whether they work; whether they're fair; and whether they're smart.

Key Terms

constitutional democracy, p. 6
criminal justice system, p. 8
hydraulic effect, p. 10
formal decision making, p. 10
informal decision making, p. 12
discretionary decision making, p. 13
legitimate decision-making criteria, p. 14
discriminatory decision-making criteria, p. 14

felonies, p. 17
case attrition, p. 18
diversion, p. 18
case mortality, p. 18
value of crime control, p. 19
value of due process, p. 19
crime control model, p. 19
presumption of guilt, p. 21
due process model, p. 21

fair procedures, p. 21
adversary process, p. 22
presumption of innocence, p. 22
bill of rights, p. 25
due process revolution, p. 26
"good" criminal justice research, p. 27

Web Resources

Go to http://cj.wadsworth.com/samaha_cj7e for a wealth of online resources related to your book. Take a "pre-test" and "post-test" for each chapter in order to help master the material. Check out the *Web Links* to access the websites mentioned in the text, as well as many others. Explore the *Decision Points* flagged in the margins of the text for additional insights. You can also access recent perspectives by clicking on *CJ in the News and Terrorism Update* under *Course Resources*.

🖋 Search Online with InfoTrac College Edition

For additional information, explore InfoTrac College Edition, your online library. Go to http://cj.wadsworth.com/samaha_cj7e to access InfoTrac College Edition from your book's website.

Use the passcode that came with your book. You will find InfoTrac College Edition exercises and a list of key words for further research.

CHAPTER 2

Crime, Criminals, and Victims

FACT *or* FICTION?

▶ Most crimes are violent crimes.

▶ Treason is very hard to prove.

▶ White-collar crime doesn't accurately describe
   the type of crime it's intended to define.

▶ There's a dark figure in crime in all the major
   measures of crime.

▶ Violent crime has increased sharply since
   1995.

▶ More people sent to prison translates into
   fewer crimes committed.

▶ Most criminals are White.

▶ Female crime rates have fallen since 1995.

▶ Most criminals know their victims.

"WELCOME TO BLOOMINGTON; YOU'RE UNDER ARREST."

A newspaper headline warns, "Serial Rapist Strikes Again." A judge has ordered a young woman to walk up and down in front of the local Kmart wearing the sign "I stole $5 from Kmart," the local TV news informs us. My student was arrested for "drunk and disorderly" conduct when he got obnoxious in a bar after drinking one beer too many, he tells me. A "deadbeat dad" is barred from having more children until he pays his child support. A local resident is sentenced to thirty days in jail for returning library books late. My neighbor reports me to the local police because I parked my car on my own lawn (a "crime" in the Minnesota town where I live). And the last time I checked, it's still a crime in Minnesota to "fornicate with a bird." Years ago, a Bloomington, Minnesota, police officer told me:

> "We should have a billboard at our city limits reading, 'Welcome to Bloomington, you're under arrest.'"
> "Why?" I asked.
> "Because everything in Bloomington is a crime."

Of course, the police officer was joking but he had a point: The word *crime* covers an enormous range of behavior—technically, whatever the law calls a crime (Chapter 4). In this chapter, we'll look at the types of crime, measures of crimes, trends in crime, criminals, and crime victims.

The Types of Crime

What's the first thing you think of when you hear the word *crime*? I'm sure it won't be parking on your front lawn or returning your library books late. It'll probably be murder, rape, or mugging. After all, they're the crimes that really hurt you and the people you care about. And, of course, they're practically the only crimes you see on TV news. But the truth is violent crimes are only a tiny slice of the total amount of crime, which is generally very few murders, a few more rapes, still a few more robberies and burglaries, lots of thefts, and a deluge of drunk and disorderly conduct charges and "other" crimes like parking on my front lawn (Figure 2.1, Table 2.1).

How can we get a grip on this hodgepodge we call "crime"? One way is to classify crimes into three groups adopted by the official crime statistics you'll learn about in this chapter (another is to apply the legal classifications used in the formal criminal law in Chapter 4):

1. *Violent or personal crime.* Actions that can physically hurt or threaten to hurt people
2. *Property crime.* Actions that take, damage, or destroy or threaten to take, invade, damage, or destroy people's property
3. *Crimes against public order and morals.* Disorderly conduct, public drunkenness, individual drug use, prostitution, and many similar minor offenses (misdemeanors)

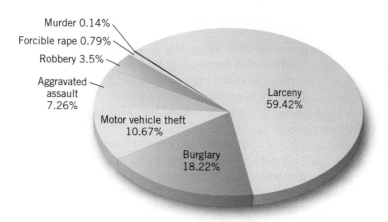

◀ FIGURE 2.1 Crime Index
Offenses, 2003

Source: FBI, *Crime in the United States,
2003* (Washington, DC: FBI, October 27,
2004), calculated from Table 1.

▼ TABLE 2.1 Arrests for Minor Crimes, 2002

Offense	Arrests
All other offenses	3,662,159
Driving under the influence	1,461,746
Disorderly conduct	669,938
Liquor laws	653,819
Drunkenness	572,735
Vandalism	276,697
Curfew and loitering law violations	141,252
Runaways	125,688
Prostitution and commercialized vice	79,733
Vagrancy	27,295
Gambling	10,506
Suspicion	8,899

Source: FBI, *Crime in the United States, 2002* (Washington, DC: FBI, 2003), Section IV, UCR Data, Table 29.

Violent crimes and property crimes have two victims—the individual victims
of crime and the whole community. How can this be? Think about a few examples. The serial rapist doesn't just hurt the individuals he attacks, he undermines the whole community's sense of personal safety. The burglar who breaks
into your house makes all of us feel unsafe in our homes. The corporation that
"cooks" its books and causes you to lose money undermines the public confidence that our market economy depends on.

Most of this book examines decision making about the crimes listed in Figure
2.1 and Table 2.1, as well they should, because over the long haul, they're always
important. But other types of crimes may receive more attention, depending on
the times. Naturally, 9/11 jumps immediately to mind because of its threat to our
personal security. So does white-collar crime because of recent high-profile cases
undermining our confidence in our market economy. And although temporarily
overshadowed by terrorism and corporate crime, crimes motivated by hate for
particular groups haven't gone away. We still need to make decisions about how
best (if at all) criminal justice can play a part in reckoning with discrimination
in our society. In this section, we'll look at crimes against the state, white-collar
crimes, and hate crimes.

Crimes against the State

The revolutionaries who wrote the U.S. Constitution (and the Bill of Rights) knew the constitutional democracy they were creating couldn't survive without the active support (or at least the passive acceptance) of most of the people. They realized it would be some time before the new republican form of government took hold among the people whose loyalty and allegiance they needed for the newborn nation's survival.

They also knew a lot about national security because, just when they needed the people's allegiance and loyalty most, the newborn nation faced enormous threats from enemies inside and outside the country. Benedict Arnold's betrayal of General Washington was fresh in their minds, and English royalists remained deeply committed to King George III. At the same time, powerful unfriendly countries had designs on the fledgling republic's territory. England was hovering just to the north in Canada, smarting from the loss of the American colonies and looking for payback. Spain to the south had just taken back Florida and claimed the whole Mississippi Valley. France had only recently been thrown out of the Ohio Valley. These unfriendly nations formed alliances with Native American nations by taking advantage of deep injustices the Americans continued to inflict on the natives.

Let's first look briefly at the crimes (treason, sedition, sabotage, and espionage) the revolutionaries created (and which are still with us) to protect the nation from its foreign and domestic enemies. Then, we'll look at new criminal laws passed after Timothy McVeigh's domestic terrorist attack on the Oklahoma City federal building in 1993 and al Qaeda's international terrorist attack on the World Trade Center and the Pentagon on September 11, 2001.

Old Crimes against the State: Treason, Sedition, Sabotage, and Espionage

According to Article III, Section 2 of the U.S. Constitution:

treason levying war against the United States, adhering to its enemies, or giving them aid and comfort

> **Treason** against the United States, shall consist only in levying War against them, or in adhering to their Enemies, giving them Aid and Comfort. No Person shall be convicted of Treason unless on the Testimony of two Witnesses to the same overt Act, or on Confession in open Court.

The authors of the Constitution were tough on individuals who broke their allegiance in the face of the dangers just described. But there was a flip side to fighting acts of treason against the new republic. Many of the revolutionaries were traitors themselves under British law. "Treason" consisted of either levying war against the king or giving aid and comfort to the king's enemies. They'd done both. And they knew English prosecutions for treason weren't pretty. Thomas Jefferson referred to the English law of treason as a "deadly weapon" in the hands of "tyrannical kings" and "weak and wicked Ministers which had drawn the blood of the best and honestest men in the kingdom" (Jefferson 1853, 1:215). Treason prosecutions were probably on Benjamin Franklin's mind when he quipped at the signing of the Declaration of Independence, "We must all hang together, or most assuredly we shall all hang separately" (Lederer 1988, 27).

So as much as they recognized the need for allegiance to the new government, their fear of government abuse of treason prosecutions led them to adopt "every limitation that the practice of governments had evolved or that politico-legal philosophy to that time had advanced" (*Cramer v. U.S.* 1945, 23–24). How did they accomplish this? They wrote the definition of treason into the body of the U.S. Constitution (Article III, § 3) (quoted and defined earlier), where it would be very tough to tamper with because of the intentionally cumbersome constitutional amendment process.

This made (and still does make) treason a narrowly defined crime that's very tough to prove. That's just what the authors intended, and they got their wish. There have only been a handful of treason cases in our history.

An artist's sketch of Brian Patrick Regan, a retired Air Force master sergeant sentenced to life in prison without parole for attempting to sell U.S. intelligence secrets to Iraq's Saddam Hussein (for $13 million) and the Chinese government. "We are here today to tell the full story of Brian Patrick Regan's betrayal of his country. We want you to see the magnitude of the damage this man was willing to inflict on his country and fellow citizens" U.S. Attorney Paul McNulty said at a press conference.

But treason isn't the only crime aimed at combating disloyalty and keeping the allegiance of our citizens. Three other, very old crimes—sedition ("stirring up" support for treason), sabotage, and espionage—take aim at upholding these objectives. For centuries, it's been a crime against the state not just to commit treason but to "stir up" others to overthrow the government by violence. Advocating the violent overthrow of the government was called **sedition.** The "stirring up" could be done by speeches (seditious speech); by writings (seditious libel); and by agreement (seditious conspiracy). **Sabotage** is the crime of destroying and damaging property for the purpose of interfering with and hindering preparations for and carrying on war and defense during national emergencies (U.S. Criminal Code 2003, Title 18, Part I, Chapter 105, § 2153). Finally, **espionage (spying)** is the secret observation by special agents of a foreign country on people or their activities or enterprises (such as war production or scientific advancement in military fields) and intelligence (information) gathering about such people, activities, and enterprises for political or military uses (U.S. Criminal Code 2003, Title 18, Chapter 37, § 794).

Antiterrorist Crimes Prosecutors can use treason, sedition, sabotage, and espionage to prosecute suspected terrorists. Murder, attempted murder, and conspiracy to murder also may apply. But there are also specific antiterrorism crimes found in Chapter 113, "Terrorism," of the U.S. Code (Chapter 113B, Title 18):

1. Use of certain weapons of mass destruction (U.S. Code § 2332a)
2. Acts of terrorism transcending national boundaries (U.S. Code § 2332b)
3. Harboring or concealing terrorists (U.S. Code § 2339)
4. Providing material support to terrorists (U.S. Code § 2339A)
5. Providing material support or resources to designated foreign terrorist organizations (U.S. Code § 2339B)

Terrorism (U.S. Code § 2331) means

(A) violent acts or acts dangerous to human life that are a violation of the criminal laws of the United States or of any State, or that would be a criminal violation if committed within the jurisdiction of the United States or of any State;

sedition to "stir up" others to overthrow the government by violence

sabotage the crime of destroying and damaging property for the purpose of interfering with and hindering preparations for and carrying on war and defense during national emergencies

espionage (spying) secret observation by special agents of a foreign country on people or their activities or enterprises (such as war production or scientific advancement in military fields)

terrorism violent acts or acts dangerous to human life that are a violation of the criminal laws of the United States or of any State, or that would be a criminal violation if committed within the jurisdiction of the United States or of any State

Currency or monetary instruments or financial securities	Communications equipment
Financial services	Facilities
Lodging	Weapons, lethal substances, explosives
Training	Personnel
Expert advice or assistance	Transportation
Safehouses	Other physical assets, except medicine or religious materials
False documentation or identification	

Source: U.S. Code, Title 18, § 2339B, § 2339A.

(B) [that] appear to be intended
    (i)   to intimidate or coerce a civilian population;
    (ii) to influence the policy of a government by intimidation or coercion; or
    (iii) to affect the conduct of a government by mass destruction, assassination, or kidnapping;

material support the crime of providing aid to individual terrorists and terrorist organizations, including money, financial services, lodging, training, etc.

Although all these crimes are available to the U.S. government for prosecuting suspected terrorists and convicting guilty ones, so far, the government has used only one. In the more than thirty cases prosecuted since September 11 (Roth 2003), the government's charge of choice has been the crime of providing **"material support"** to terrorists and/or to terrorist organizations (U.S. Code, Title 18, § 2339B) or to individual terrorists (§ 2339A) (Table 2.2). These crimes were created in 1996 after the Oklahoma City bombing in the Antiterrorism and Effective Death Penalty Act (AEDPA).

Slightly amended (the penalties were ratcheted up), the felonies of material support for individual terrorists and terrorist organizations became part of the USA Patriot Act (*U*niting and *S*trengthening *A*merica by *P*roviding *A*ppropriate *T*ools to *I*ntercept and *O*bstruct *T*errorism) (2001). This huge law (300+ pages) passed with lightning speed only six weeks after the September 11 attacks. Most of the act deals with criminal procedure (surveillance and intelligence/law enforcement information sharing, search and seizure, interrogation, and detention), but it's the six-line "material support" for terrorist organizations section that's our main concern. (The criminal procedure provisions are extremely important, too, and you'll learn more about them in other chapters.)

According to § 2339B, it's a crime not just to *provide* material support but to attempt or conspire to provide it. All of these material support provisions are directed at "nipping terrorism in the bud." Hopefully, it helps to prevent what we most want to prevent—killing and destruction by terrorist acts.

White-Collar Crimes

white-collar crime crimes committed by respectable people, or at least respected business and professional people

street crime violent and property crimes reported in the UCR

In 1939, the distinguished president of the American Sociological Association, Edwin Sutherland (1940), introduced the term **white-collar crime** to describe crimes committed by "respectable" people, "or at least respected business and professional men." It's distinguished from **street crime,** violent and property crimes (the crimes now covered by the UCR, NCVS, and NIBRS). Sutherland may have named the concept, but he wasn't the first sociologist to point his finger at the crimes of the "respectable" classes. In 1902, the French sociologist Emile Durkheim (1964) wrote that the most "blameworthy acts are so often absolved by success" that business people could escape liability for the harms they cause (2). A few years later, in 1907, the American sociologist Edward A. Ross (1907) complained that members of a new criminal class, which he called the "criminaloid," used their powerful positions in business to exploit consumers but escaped criminal liability because they didn't fit the accepted definitions of criminals. Since their motive was profit, not injuring others, neither they nor the public considered their actions to be crimes.

Let's look more closely at recent cases and the two ways white-collar crime is defined.

Recent Cases On July 7, 2004, Kenneth Lay, the former CEO of Enron Corporation was indicted for **corporate fraud,** defined by the U.S. Department of Justice as including the following crimes:

1. Falsification of corporate financial information (including, for example, false/fraudulent accounting entries; bogus trades and other transactions designed to artificially inflate revenue; fraudulently overstating assets, earnings, and profits or understating/concealing liabilities and losses; and false transactions designed to evade regulatory oversight)
2. Self-dealing by corporate insiders (for example, insider trading, kickbacks, misuse of corporate property for personal gain and individual tax violations related to any such dealings
3. Obstruction of justice, perjury, witness tampering, or other obstructive behavior relating to either of the categories mentioned above (Corporate Fraud Task Force 2004, 2.2)

The indictment (*U.S. v. Kenneth Lay* 2004) accused Lay and two other Enron executives of

> engaging in a wide-ranging scheme to deceive the investing public, including Enron's shareholders, the SEC [Securities and Exchange Commission], and other…victims… about the performance of Enron's businesses by:
> (a) manipulating Enron's publicly reported financial results; and
> (b) making public statements and representations about Enron's financial performance and results that were false and misleading in that they did not fairly and accurately reflect Enron's actual financial condition and performance, and they omitted to disclose facts necessary to make those statements and representations fair and accurate. (3)

Here's just one of the many examples of how the scheme worked, according to the indictment:

> On September 26, 2001, Lay held an online forum with Enron employees [many of whom had heavily invested in Enron stock as their retirement plan]. Lay stated that "the third quarter is looking great. We will hit our numbers. We are continuing to have strong growth in our businesses, and at this time I think we're positioned for a very strong fourth quarter." He added that "we have record operating and financial results" and that "the balance sheet is strong." In fact, as Lay knew, Enron was preparing to announce an overall quarterly loss for the first time since 1997.…(31)
> Lay announced to the employees, "I have strongly encouraged our 16b [management] officers to buy additional Enron stock. Some, including myself, have done so over the past couple of months and others will probably do so in the future.…My personal belief is that Enron stock is an incredible bargain at current prices." Lay deliberately created the impression with Enron employees that his confidence in Enron's stock was such that he had personally increased his personal ownership in the past two months. In fact, as Lay knew, during the prior "couple of months," Lay had purchased approximately $4 million in Enron stock but sold $24 million in Enron stock in sales that were concealed from Enron employees and the rest of the investing public. (32)

Lay and two other executives also indicted used the scheme to "enrich themselves…through salary, bonuses, grants of stock options, and other profits, and prestige within their professions and communities" (6). Between 1998 and 2001, Lay received $300 million from stock sales and $19 million in salary and bonuses.

If it's proved, the case of Kenneth Lay and other Enron executives is one of corporate crime at its extreme—millions of investors and thousands of employees lost a lot of money and many most of their future retirement security. The Enron case has shaken the public trust and confidence that are at the heart of

▶ Surrounded by reporters, former Enron CEO Kenneth Lay arrives at the FBI in Houston. Lay turned himself in to face criminal charges involving one of the biggest corporate fraud cases in U.S. history.

AP/Wide World Photos

our market economy. Deputy U.S. Attorney General, Larry Thompson, head of the Corporate Fraud Task Force and appointed by the president in July 2002 to conduct a high-profile crackdown on corporate crime, said, "We will go no higher" than Lay, but "we may well go wider."

The Task Force already has, prosecuting Martha Stewart. Stewart is a multimillionaire celebrity with a blue-collar background who worked her way up to become the most powerful woman CEO in the country. However, no hint of scandal has touched Martha Stewart Living Omnimedia, Inc., the highly successful corporation she built from scratch. A jury convicted her of lying to federal officers investigating a $50,000 profit from stock she sold in her personal portfolio (*U.S. v. Martha Stewart and Peter Bacanovic* 2004, 8–9). On July 16, 2004, U.S. District Judge Miriam Goldman Cederbaum sentenced Stewart to five months in prison; then to five months of home detention, wearing an electronic monitor and having her phones tapped; and followed by two years probation. She also fined her $30,000 (Scannell 2004). Outside the courtroom, Stewart talked about her concern for her family and friends and her company. Then, she spoke about her employees:

> More than 200 people have lost their jobs at my company as a result of the situation. I want them to know how very, very sorry I am.... But, I'll be back. I'm not afraid whatsoever. I'm just very, very sorry that it has come to this, that a small personal matter has been able to be blown out of all proportion. (Scannell 2004)

That evening in an interview with Barbara Walters, she spoke of the humiliation she felt at being reduced to a "common criminal" and a "convicted felon" (Walters, July 16, 2004).

Why did the Task Force prosecute Martha Stewart? Prosecutor Karen Patton Seymour put it this way to Judge Cederbaum:

> Citizens like Ms. Stewart who willingly take the steps to lie to officials when they are under investigation about their own conduct, those citizens should not expect the leniency that Ms. Stewart seeks. (McClam 2004)

As of July 2004, the Task Force had prosecuted over seven hundred individuals and gotten over three hundred corporate crime convictions (Anderson 2004). Few doubt the seriousness of these high-profile corporate crime cases (except for Martha Stewart's, which has generated a lot of controversy; many believe she was prosecuted because she's a powerful woman)—nor the value of the public attention they are attracting.

Hot Off the Wireless

In a recent television commercial a stressed-out office worker takes his laptop to a park and uses his wireless access connection to meet his deadline as he basks in the warm sunshine. Other television and radio advertisements promote the same message: wireless connections make life more convenient, faster, easier. But these commercials do not mention the hidden dangers that every consumer—and every law enforcement officer—should watch for.

Statistics released by the Federal Bureau of Investigation in 2003 show that "cybercrime" rates increased for the third straight year. Although most people know about financial fraud, identity theft, and the dangers hackers can pose to conventional systems and networks, most are unaware of the unique risks from the use of wireless access technology.

As information technology companies tout wireless use, consumers buy laptop computers and set up wireless access points in their homes and offices without learning about the need for wireless security, says Robert DeCarlo, Jr., an economic crime specialist with CSL. "The vast majority of crimes involving wireless use go undetected and unreported. The victims don't know they're vulnerable, and law enforcement doesn't know the signs to look for. I think we're on the cusp of an explosion of crime using wireless technology."

Jeffrey Isherwood, a CSL senior engineer, says he can recall officers telling him about only one or two cases in which the suspect had wireless access. Ironically, at least half of the officers he talks with tell him they have wireless access in their homes or precincts. Just like the average consumer, these officers are aware of the benefits of wireless use but not its potential security risks. "Wireless often is the last thing that police think of when someone reports identity theft," Isherwood says. "They ask victims where they've been shopping. If they do check victims' computers, they don't think to ask specifically about wireless."

"It's not that there's a specific crime here; it's a method of perpetrating a crime such as identity theft, and it's a method that's very hard to trace and prove," says Joshua Bartolomie, another CSL electronic crime specialist in wireless issues. "For instance, you might live in an apartment building with 10 apartments and someone might be sitting downstairs collecting all of your information. It's the perfect way to perform identity theft."

Bartolomie also says "WarDrivers" (slang for wireless hackers) drive around and look for wireless networks, hoping to find an open access point in a home or office and break into it or piggyback off it from laptops in their vehicles. They break in, cause problems, and then drive away, leaving no evidence behind.

Isherwood says he and Bartolomie perform test sampling whenever they attend a conference. "We use the same equipment and technology that the hackers use," Isherwood says, "and we get numbers that compare to the nationally reported figures. That is, about 75 percent of all wireless access points are unencrypted and wide open, and anybody who wants to can gain access to them."

Source: TECH Beat, Spring 2004

Definitions There are two definitions of white-collar crime. The *status* definition (high social status, respectable people committed the crime in the course of their occupation) is favored by those who believe differences in power and wealth are the keys to understanding crime and controlling it. So research on crimes of greed and arrogance can be added to crimes of need and desperation to create a fuller picture of crime in general (Shover 1998, 134).

The *abuse-of-trust* definition of white-collar crime focuses on crimes defined as exploitation of a trust relationship by someone who's "responsible for custody, discretion, information, or property rights" (Shover 1998, 135). (See the CJ & Technology box "Hot Off the Wireless.") For example, Enron tells its employees the company's finances are in great shape and employees buy Enron stock for their retirement accounts. But here's another: A gas station attendant steals customers' credit card numbers and sells them. These are both abuses of trust even though one criminal wears a white and the other a blue collar (135). As you can see, the abuse-of-trust definition has nothing to do with status. According to Shover (1998):

> White-collar crime does not occur only where offenders are powerful and victims are ordinary citizens. When citizens do fall prey to white-collar crime, odds are high that they will be victimized by offenders closer to home than international banking conspirators. It is not only managers of Fortune 500 corporations who victimize us but also the local attorney and the neighborhood automotive repair shop. (135)

Hate Crimes

hate crimes crimes motivated by prejudice against groups based on differences in race, ethnicity, religion, physical or mental capacity, or sexual orientation

Hate Crime Statistics: An overview of recent national hate crime statistics. To reach this site go to "Web Links" on your Samaha CJ7 website: http://cj.wadsworth.com/samaha_cj7e.

According to the Hate Crime Statistics Act of 1990, **hate crimes** "are crimes motivated by prejudice against groups based on differences in race, ethnicity, religion, physical or mental capacity, or sexual orientation" (U.S. Code 2004, Title 28, § 234(b)(1)). The FBI is in charge of carrying out the law. With the cooperation of local law enforcement agencies, by 2002, the FBI was collecting data representing 86 percent of the population (FBI, *Hate Crime Statistics* 2003, 1). In 2002, there were over seven thousand hate crime incidents reported to the FBI. Most were motivated by race; two-thirds were against Blacks, and one-fifth were against Whites. Religious bias was the second most frequent motive; two-thirds of these events were against Jews; 11 percent were against Muslims. Sexual orientation came next, followed by ethnicity/national origin, and last was physical or mental disability (Figure 2.2). Two-thirds of the hate crimes reported in 2000 were violent crimes, and most of the rest were property crimes. Sixty-four percent of known hate crime offenders were White; 18 percent were Black (1).

Hate itself isn't a crime; it's the *motive* for committing a crime. That's what these numbers represent. Hate (like any motive) is hard to identify for sure because it's subjective. That's why the FBI standard for reporting it is that there's enough evidence to "lead a reasonable and prudent person to conclude that the offender's *actions* were motivated, in whole or in part, by his or her bias (FBI, *Hate Crime Statistics* 2003, 3).

Why make a crime a special crime when it's motivated by group prejudice? After all, isn't murder still murder, rape still rape, burglary still burglary, and so on, no matter what the motivation for committing them? No, say supporters of singling out hate crimes for special treatment. First, hate crimes are based on the idea that committing crimes because of group characteristics reverberates beyond individual victims to whole groups, communities, and even the entire nation. Second, groups protected by hate laws are especially vulnerable to crime. So we have to compensate these vulnerable victims by harsher punishment.

Opponents don't buy these arguments. First, we don't need special hate crime statutes because all crimes are hate crimes, they argue. Second, current statutes are discriminatory because they leave out many vulnerable groups, like the elderly, children, the diseased, ex-offenders, and so on. Third, where will including vulnerable groups stop? Will it include broad categories like neighborhood, social class, and education? Fourth, hate crime statutes are not constitutional because they violate our right to free speech. Words and thoughts are free; you can't punish people for what they believe or how they feel, only for what they do (Chapter 4). Finally, it's impossible to prove hate because we can't see into the human mind, especially in this age of political correctness when we're so clever at hiding our prejudices.

▶ **FIGURE 2.2** Percentage of Hate Crimes by Motivation, 2002

Source: FBI, *Hate Crime Statistics, 2002* (Washington, DC: FBI, 2003) pp. 9–11.

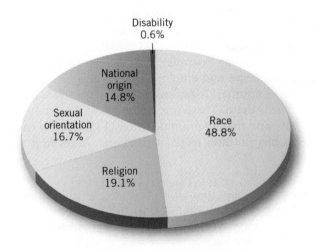

Now that you've got a background in the types of crime, let's turn to the important subject of measuring crime.

Measuring Crime

Societies have kept track of crime for centuries. In 1730, Aarhus Denmark conducted a survey asking people if they'd been crime victims. In the 1800s, an English constable went door to door asking villagers if they'd been victimized. Today, there are two main sources of crime statistics—police reports and victim surveys—and one much less used and less complete statistic, offenders' self-reports of crimes they've committed. Each statistic is based on a different place to look for the best measure of crime: police, victims, and offenders. Let's look at each of these statistics and then consider their strengths and weaknesses (Sparks 1981, 2).

Official Police Reports

Basing crime statistics on police reports stems from the belief that the best way to find out about crime is to ask the police. Certainly, this was the belief of the International Association of Chiefs of Police (IAACP), a police reform organization that planned the first nationwide collection of crime statistics in the United States. In 1930, the FBI collected its first set of data based on official police records, the **Uniform Crime Reports (UCR).** The FBI depended (and still does) on voluntary cooperation from local police departments to collect and report to the FBI summaries of serious (Part I) and minor (Part II) offenses. The FBI publishes these statistics every year in *Crime in the United States*. Let's look at the ways Part I and Part II offenses are measured and reported. Then, we'll contrast the UCR with a new reporting system, the NIBRS.

Crime Index (Part I) Offenses The **Crime Index** (Table 2.3) statistic is a summary of raw numbers of crimes and **crime rates** (the number of crimes reported for every 100,000 people). So, in 2002, there were 11,877,218 Part I offenses known to the police; and the index crime rate was 4118 for every 100,000 people (FBI, *Crime in the United States* 2003). The index consists of eight of the most often reported serious crimes: murder, forcible rape, robbery, aggravated assault, burglary, theft, motor vehicle theft, and arson.

It shouldn't surprise you to learn that these numbers aren't perfect. Why? Because the Crime Index includes only crimes the police know about. So there's always an unknown number of crimes (the **dark figure in crime**). Also, the UCR overrepresents serious crime because it counts attempts as if they were completed crimes. It also overrepresents street crime (crimes committed mostly by poor and minority criminals) because white-collar crimes aren't in the index (Brownstein 1996, 19–25; Schneider and Wiersema 1991, 333–335).

Part II Offenses The less serious offenses in Part II are measured by the raw numbers of arrests for each of the Part II offenses (Table 2.1). In Part II, citations and summonses are counted as arrests. Don't view the number of *arrests* as the number of *persons* arrested. Why? Because a person might be arrested several times in a year.

National Incident-Based Reporting System (NIBRS) To improve its statistics, the UCR is shifting from summaries (lump-sum totals of crimes reported to the police and arrests) to incident-based reporting. (Table 2.5 at the end of this section compares the UCR and the NIBRS.) The new system is called the **National Incident-Based Reporting System (NIBRS).** The NIBRS collects information about two groups of offenses (Table 2.4). Group A includes the 8 UCR

> **DECISION**
> **POINT** ◀

Are crime statistics objective measures or subjective constructions?

Click on this Decision Point at http://cj.wadsworth.com/samaha_cj7e to explore the issue.

Bureau of Justice Statistics: A comprehensive list of statistical data related to criminal justice topics. To reach this site go to "Web Links" on your Samaha CJ7 website: http://cj.wadsworth.com/samaha_cj7e.

Uniform Crime Reports (UCR) official statistics of crimes known to the police, collected by the FBI and published annually as *Crime in the United States*.

Crime Index UCR statistics reporting numbers and rates of eight serious crimes reported to the police

crime rates the number of crimes for every 100,000 individuals in the general population

dark figure in crime the number of crimes committed but not known

Uniform Crime Reports (UCR): The UCR contains the different levels of Index Crimes that local police report to the FBI. This site includes information on how the FBI tabulates crime data on a national basis. To reach this site go to "Web Links" on your Samaha CJ7 website: http://cj.wadsworth.com/samaha_cj7e.

National Incident-Based Reporting System (NIBRS) the official report of crimes known to the police, which collects information about two groups of offenses, with details about each crime

▼ TABLE 2.3 Definitions of Index Crimes

Violent Crimes	
Murder and Nonnegligent Homicide	The willful (nonnegligent) killing of one human being by another. The UCR does not include deaths caused by negligence, suicide, or accident; justifiable homicides; or attempts to murder or assaults to murder, which are classified as aggravated assaults.
Forcible Rape	The carnal knowledge of a female forcibly and against her will. Assaults or attempts to commit rape by force or threat of force are also included; however, statutory rape (without force) and other sex offenses are excluded.
Robbery	The taking or attempting to take anything of value from the care, custody, or control of a person or persons by force or threat of force or violence and/or by putting the victim in fear.
Aggravated Assault	An unlawful attack by one person upon another for the purpose of inflicting severe or aggravated bodily injury. This type of assault is usually accompanied by the use of a weapon or by means likely to produce death or great bodily harm. Attempts involving the display or threat of a gun, knife, or other weapon are included because serious personal injury would likely result if the assault were completed.
Property Crimes	
Burglary	The unlawful entry of a structure to commit a felony or theft. The use of force to gain entry is not required to classify an offense as a burglary. Burglary is categorized into three subclassifications: forcible entry, unlawful entry where no force is used, and attempted forcible entry.
Larceny/Theft	The unlawful taking, carrying, leading, or riding away of property from the possession or constructive possession of another. It includes crimes such as shoplifting, pocket-picking, purse snatching, thefts from motor vehicles, thefts of motor vehicle parts and accessories, bicycle thefts, etc., in which no use of force, violence, or fraud occurs. In the Uniform Crime Reporting Program, this crime category does not include embezzlement, confidence games, forgery, or worthless checks. Motor vehicle theft is also excluded from this category inasmuch as it is a separate Crime Index offense.
Motor Vehicle Theft	The theft or attempted theft of a motor vehicle. This offense includes the stealing of automobiles, trucks, buses, motorcycles, motor scooters, snowmobiles, etc. The taking of a motor vehicle for temporary use by persons having lawful access is excluded from this definition.
Arson	Any willful or malicious burning or attempt to burn, with or without intent to defraud, a dwelling house, public building, motor vehicle or aircraft, personal property of another, etc. Only fires determined through investigation to have been willfully or maliciously set are classified as arsons. Fires of suspicious or unknown origins are excluded.

Source: FBI, *Crime in the United States, 2002* (Washington, DC: FBI, 2003), Appendix II.

incident-based reporting the collecting of detailed information about individual cases for each offense, including offense, victim, property, offender, and witnesses by local law enforcement agencies

🚀 **National Incident-Based Reporting System (NIBRS):** NIBRS is an upgraded reporting system from the UCR. Incident-based data provide an extremely large amount of information about crime. The information is also organized in complex ways, reflecting the many different aspects of a crime incident. To reach this site go to "Web Links" on your Samaha CJ7 website: http://cj.wadsworth.com/samaha_cj7e.

index crimes (with some changes in definition) and adds 14 others. Group B includes some specifically named offenses and then a catchall "all other crimes."

The heart of the NIBRS is incident-based reporting. **Incident-based reporting** means that local law enforcement agencies collect detailed information about individual cases for each offense. The details for Group A incidents include:

1. *The offense.* Attempts are separated from completed crimes.
2. *The victim.* This includes information about age, sex, ethnicity, race, resident or alien status, type of injury, and the relationship of victims to offenders.
3. *The damage to property.* Any property involved.
4. *The offender.* This includes details about age, sex, race, and ethnicity.
5. *The arrestee.* This includes information about the use of alcohol, narcotics, and other drugs.
6. *The witnesses.* Any witnesses.
7. *The incident.* A brief narrative describing the incident.

In Group A incidents, the NIBRS separates attempts from completed crimes (the UCR lumps them together), and it includes information like the age, gender,

Group A (Collects extensive data on the following offenses)		Group B (Collects data only on persons arrested for these offenses)
Arson	Kidnapping/Abduction	Bad checks
Assault offenses • Aggravated assault • Simple assault • Intimidation	Larceny/Theft offenses • Pocket-picking • Purse snatching • Shoplifting • Theft from building • Theft from coin-operated machine or device • Theft from motor vehicle • Theft of motor vehicle parts or accessories • All other larceny	Curfew/Loitering/Vagrancy violations
Bribery		Disorderly conduct
Burglary/Breaking and entering		Driving under the influence
Counterfeiting		Drunkenness
Destruction/Damage/Vandalism of property • Drugs/Narcotic offenses • Drug/Narcotic violations • Drug equipment violations	Motor vehicle theft	Family offenses, nonviolent
	Pornography/Obscene material	Liquor law violations
Embezzlement	Prostitution offenses • Prostitution • Assisting or promoting prostitution	Peeping tom
Extortion/Blackmail		Runaway
Fraud offenses • False pretenses/Swindle/Confidence game • Credit card/Automatic teller machine fraud • Impersonation • Welfare fraud • Wire fraud	Robbery	Trespass of real property
	Sex offenses, forcible • Forcible rape • Forcible sodomy • Sexual assault with an object • Forcible fondling	All other offenses
Gambling offenses • Betting/Wagering • Operating/Promoting/Assisting gambling • Gambling equipment violations • Sports tampering	Sex offenses, nonforcible • Incest • Statutory rape	
	Stolen property offenses (receiving, etc.)	
Homicide offenses • Murder and nonnegligent manslaughter • Negligent manslaughter • Justifiable homicide	Weapons law violations	

Source: FBI, *CJIS Newsletter,* Vol. 4, No. 1 (Washington, DC: U.S. Department of Justice, n.d.), p. 2.

▼ TABLE 2.5 Differences between the UCR and the NIBRS

Uniform Crime Reports (UCR)	National Incident-Based Reporting Systems (NIBRS)
Consists of monthly aggregate crime	Consists of individual incident records for the 8 index crimes and 38 other offenses with details on the • Offense • Offender • Victim • Property
Counts 8 index crimes	
Records one offense per incident as determined by the hierarchy rule, which suppresses counts of lesser offenses in multiple-offense incident	
Does not distinguish between attempted and completed crimes	Records each offense that occurred in the incident
Applies the hotel rule to burglary	Distinguishes between attempted and completed crimes
Records rape of females only	Expands the burglary hotel rule to include rental storage facilities
Collects weapon information for murder, robbery, and aggravated assault	Records rapes of males and females
Provides counts on arrests for the 8 index crimes and 21 other offenses	Restructures the definition of assault
	Collects weapon information for all violent offenses
	Provides details on arrests for the 8 index crimes and 49 other offenses

Source: Ramona R. Rantala, *Effects of NIBRS on Crime Statistics* (Washington, DC: Bureau of Justice Statistics, 2000).

▶ This officer is interviewing a witness to a crime, information that might provide clues to solving the crime but which may also be used to collect information for NIBRS which will turn up more and more in books like this one.

and race of arrested persons, the suspected use of alcohol, narcotics, or other drugs; the use of a weapon in committing the crime; the gender, race, ethnic origin, and resident or nonresident status of victims; the type of injury sustained, and the relationship of the victim to the offender. For Group B incidents, NIBRS collects only information for arrested persons.

States have been slow to adopt the NIBRS. As of February 2004, 24 states have been certified to report to the FBI (accounting for only 15 percent of the nation's reported crime) (IBR 2004). However, that's an improvement over 1997, when the NIBRS covered only 5.7 percent of the population. Why is it taking so long? It's a huge undertaking. According to a report of a joint FBI and Bureau of Justice Statistics IBRS project, "Implementation of a project of this scope is an enormous undertaking, particularly so in that it relies so heavily on the internal informational processing and reporting capabilities of local law enforcement agencies" (BJS, July 1997).

Victim Surveys

Eager to close the gap (which many guessed to be large) between how many crimes the police know about and how much crime there really is, criminologists called for a more complete measure of crime. Believing the best method to find out how much crime there really is was to ask victims, criminologists developed victim surveys. The most extensive (and most expensive) victim survey in history, the **National Crime Victimization Survey (NCVS),** was launched in 1972. The NCVS collects detailed information about violent and property crimes and publishes it in its annual report, *Criminal Victimization in the U.S.* (Figure 2.3). Obviously, it doesn't include homicides because the victims are dead.

How does the NCVS work? Every six months, U.S. Census workers take a telephone poll of a national sample of more than forty thousand households. They ask questions about five topics:

1. *Victimization.* Whether the person was a victim of a crime within the past six months
2. *Victims.* Age, race, sex, educational level, and income of victims
3. *Crime.* Location, amount of personal injury, and economic loss *suffered from the crime*
4. *Perpetrator.* Gender, age, race, and relationship to the victim
5. *Reporting.* Whether victims reported the crimes to the police and the reasons they did or didn't

National Crime Victimization Survey (NCVS) collects detailed information about violent and property crimes and publishes the survey results annually in *Criminal Victimization in the U.S.*

Who uses, is dependent on, and sells drugs?

Click on this Decision Point at http://cj.wadsworth.com/samaha_cj7e to explore the issue.

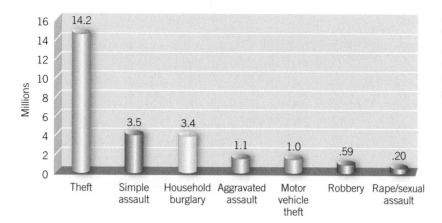

◀ **FIGURE 2.3 Criminal Victimization, 2003**

Source: Bureau of Justice Statistics, *Criminal Victimization in the U.S., 2003* (Washington, DC: Bureau of Justice Statistics, September 2004), Table 1.

In its first annual report, *Criminal Victimization in the U.S., 1972,* the NCVS proved what researchers and policymakers had always said: A lot more crimes are committed than reported to the police. Less than half of the victims of violent crime reported them to the police in 2002 (the latest numbers available); only 40 percent reported property crimes. So, like UCR, there's still a dark figure. Why? For one thing, you *can't* ask dead victims about homicide, the most violent crime. And interviewers *don't* ask whether you're a victim of other crimes, like commercial burglary, commercial theft, and white-collar crime.

Also, victims don't always tell interviewers about the victimizations they *are* asked about. Why don't victims tell interviewers about their victimizations? According to criminologist Wesley Skogan (1990b, 256–272), "Most victimizations are not notable events. The majority are property crimes in which the perpetrator is never detected. The financial stakes are small, and the costs of calling the police greatly outweigh the benefits." Interviewers have uncovered other reasons, including embarrassment, apathy, forgetfulness, and knowing the perpetrator. All these reasons tell us why victims *don't* report minor offenses. But what about serious crimes? Victims *do* report more violent crimes than property crimes, but still less than half were reported in 2002.

Sampling problems are another shortcoming in NCVS. Young Black males and illegal immigrants are consistently underrepresented among those interviewed. So are people with particular lifestyles, like drifters, street hustlers, and homeless people. And NCVS doesn't survey people in prisons, jails, or juvenile corrections facilities. (We know that prisoners have higher victimization rates than the general population.) Wealthy people escape the NCVS by insulating themselves from all kinds of interviews. Another sampling problem is the small number of rapes, robberies, and aggravated assaults reported; for example, the year 2002 sample (Rennison and Rand 2003, 11) turned up only 1.1 rapes and 2.2 robberies for 1,000 households. It's hard to make national generalizations based on so few numbers (which isn't to say even one rape or one robbery isn't serious). Table 2.6 compares the UCR and the NCVS.

Self-Reports

Self-reports are based on the idea that if you want to know about crimes, ask the people who commit them. Self-reports are surveys of special groups in the general population. Self-reports grew out of a distrust of *all* official statistics. During the 1960s crime boom (see the "Trends in Crime" section), some criminologists explained the steep increase in crime figures as not so much a real increase but a reflection of biased, greater enforcement against minorities, poor people, and the youth counterculture.

In a pioneer self-report survey in the late 1950s, James F. Short and F. Ivan Nye asked nondelinquent schoolchildren and children in juvenile institutions

National Crime Victimization Survey (NCVS): An ongoing survey of a nationally representative sample of residential addresses, the NCVS is the primary source of information on the characteristics of criminal victimization and on the number and types of crimes not reported to law enforcement and authorities. To reach this site go to "Web Links" on your Samaha CJ7 website: http://cj .wadsworth.com/samaha_cj7e.

National Archive of Criminal Justice Data (NACJD): To reach this site go to "Web Links" on your Samaha CJ7 website: http://cj.wadsworth.com/ samaha_cj7e.

▶ DECISION POINT ◀

Are surveys of defensive gun users accurate?

Click on this Decision Point at http://cj.wadsworth.com/samaha_ cj7e to explore the issue.

self-reports surveys of special groups in the general population

Self-Report Surveys as Measures of Crime and Criminal Victimization: To reach this pdf file go to "Web Links" on your Samaha CJ7 website: http://cj.wadsworth.com/samaha_cj7e.

▼ TABLE 2.6 Comparison of UCR and NCVS

	Uniform Crime Reports (UCR)	National Crime Victim Survey (NCVS)
Crimes Included	(Index Crimes)	
	Homicide	Rape
	Rape	Robbery
	Robbery	Aggravated assault
	Burglary	Simple assault
	Aggravated assault	Household burglary
	Theft	Personal theft (purse snatching, pick-pocketing)
	Motor vehicle theft	Motor vehicle theft
	Arson	
Persons Arrested	All offenses	
Scope	Crimes reported to the police by victims and witnesses	Nonfatal violent and property crimes against victims 12 years old or older
	Crimes discovered by the police	Victims age, sex, race, ethnicity, marital status, income, and educational level
		Offenders' sex, race, age, and relationship to victim
Excluded	White-collar crime	Homicide
		Commercial crimes (nonresidential burglary)
		White-collar crime
Method	Local law enforcement agencies record crimes reported to or discovered by them and report summary totals to the FBI	U.S. Census Bureau surveys a representative sample of households
		Interviewers ask about crimes committed against household members 12 years or over during the last six months
Source	Federal Bureau of Investigation (FBI), the law enforcement arm of the Department of Justice	Bureau of Justice Statistics (BJS), the research arm of the Department of Justice

about their delinquent acts. Both groups admitted similar behavior—truancy, stealing less than $2, buying and drinking alcohol, driving without a license, and having sex. After that, self-reports grew rapidly until, by the end of the 1960s, they dominated the study of juvenile delinquency (Lafree 1998, 15).

Beginning in the 1980s, a number of self-reports concentrated on adult felons, most of them prisoners. In *The Armed Criminal in America* (1986), James D. Wright surveyed more than eighteen hundred convicted adult male felons incarcerated in 10 states. Prisoners were asked if, how, and why they obtained, carried, and used firearms, especially in committing crimes. The largest group (39 percent), "unarmed criminals," had never committed a crime while armed. About 11 percent ("knife criminals" and "improvisers") had carried a variety of ready-to-hand weapons. The other half were "gun criminals." More than half of the gun criminals (28 percent of all armed criminals) had used a gun only once or sporadically. The rest (about 22 percent)—"handgun predators" and "shotgun predators"—had committed almost half the self-reported crimes.

Gun criminals reported they'd lived around guns all their lives and that it was easier to commit crimes when they had a gun. A majority reported their guns were always loaded and they had shot them a lot—half said they'd shot at other people. Half also said someone had fired at them. Many said a man armed with a gun is "prepared for anything that might happen." When asked how they'd respond to a ban on small, cheap handguns, they said they'd just get bigger, more expensive handguns. Asked about their response to a total ban on handguns, a majority of gun criminals—and more than three-quarters of the "predators"—said they'd carry sawed-off shoulder weapons (Wright 1986).

Still, finding out about crime by asking prisoners creates problems. First, convicted prisoners don't represent all criminals. They overrepresent multiple offenders and "unsuccessful" criminals. Second, even a representative sample doesn't guarantee accuracy. Some prisoners exaggerate their "expertise" and minimize the harm they inflicted on their victims. Many don't trust the researchers or just want to "play games" to liven the monotony of life in prison (Chapter 14). Also, no matter what promises of confidentiality interviewers make, many prisoners still believe what they say will affect their chances for release. So they paint the best possible picture of themselves (Hough 1987, 356; Wright and Decker 1994, 5–6).

The Canadian criminologist Gwynn Nettler had this to say about self-report surveys after he'd reviewed many of them:

> Asking people questions about their behavior is a poor way of observing it. . . . It is particularly ticklish to ask people to recall their "bad" behavior. Confessional data are at least as weak as the official statistics they were supposed to improve upon. (Braithwaite 1979, 21)

Trends in Crime

A crime boom—that's the best way to describe the trend in crime from the 1950s to the early 1990s. Here's the way Professor Gary Lafree (1998) describes the boom:

> Murder rates doubled; rape rates quadrupled; robbery and burglary rates quintupled. By the early 1990s, nearly 25,000 Americans were being murdered each year. In just two years, more Americans were murdered than were killed in the Vietnam War; in twelve years more were murdered than died during World War II. . . . Taken together, there was an eightfold increase in rates of murder, robbery, rape, aggravated assault, burglary, and theft reported to the police between the end of World War II and the early 1990s. (15)

Then came the current crime bust, which began in the early 1990s (Figure 2.4). Violent crime (murder, forcible rape, robbery, and aggravated assault) rates dropped 37 percent, from a high of 758.1 in 1991 to 475 in 2003 (FBI 2003, 9). Still, this is a long way from the low of 38.1 in 1956, clearly demonstrating the current bust can't match the 63 percent increase during the 1960s boom (Lafree 1998, 1).

A hot debate about the causes of the crime boom of the 1960s to the 1990s and of the crime bust that we've enjoyed since the mid-1990s continues to rage. A lot of this debate gets caught up in ideology and politics. In the 1960s, the debate centered on whether the increase in crime was real or whether more and better

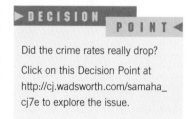

Did the crime rates really drop?

Click on this Decision Point at http://cj.wadsworth.com/samaha_cj7e to explore the issue.

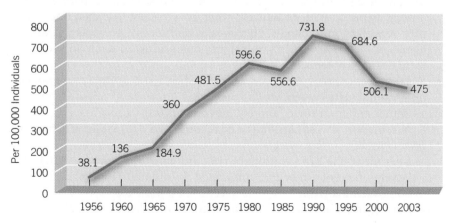

◀ **FIGURE 2.4 Violent Crime Rates, 1956–2003**

Source: FBI, *Crime in the United States* (Washington, DC: FBI), selected years, 1956–2003.

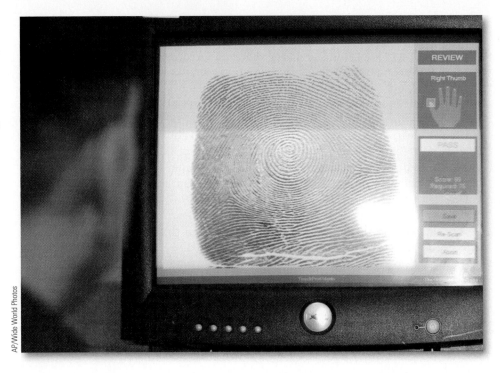

▶ The IAFIS provides automated fingerprint search capabilities, latent searching capability, electronic image storage, and electronic exchange of fingerprints and responses, 24 hours a day, 365 days a year. As a result of submitting fingerprints electronically, agencies receive electronic responses to criminal ten-print fingerprint submissions within two hours and within 24 hours for civil fingerprint submissions.

AP/Wide World Photos

reporting made it *look* real. After the 1960s version of the culture wars subsided, most dispassionate observers concluded that there was a *real* increase in crime, but there was still a lot of disagreement over *why* it occurred. And no one's settled that debate. Turning from the boom to the bust, no one doubts *whether* we're living in a continuing crime bust, but there's controversy over *why*. The U.S. Department of Justice (2004, 1.7–1.10) has suggested a number of changes, mainly taking place since the 1980s, that resulted in the crime bust. You'll learn more about these changes and their effectiveness in later chapters, but here's a brief summary of them:

- *Increased federal assistance.*
  —More federal money to support community policing, domestic violence programs, and victim assistance
  —Increased dissemination of new knowledge about crime, delinquency, and the criminal and juvenile justice systems
  —Increased use of federal laws against criminal organizations and serious offenders
- *More state and local agency collaboration.* Increased use of partnerships among criminal justice agencies, other government agencies, and community organizations (schools, churches, social service providers, health-care agencies, victim advocacy groups, and businesses) to work on specific local crime problems (Chapter 6)
- *Stronger, better prepared local criminal justice agencies.* Increased spending on criminal justice agencies has produced
  —Better staffed, trained, and equipped agencies
  —Automation and enhancement of records and data systems (Chapter 5)
- *Federal agency improvements.*
  —Upgrade of the FBI's National Crime Information Center (NCIC)
  —Development of a new FBI Integrated Automated Fingerprint Identification System (IAFIS)
  —Development of a new FBI Combined DNA Index System (CODIS)

National Crime Information Center (NCIC): To reach this site go to "Web Links" on your Samaha CJ7 website: http://cj.wadsworth.com/samaha_cj7e.

—Deployment of the ATF's (Alcohol, Tobacco, and Firearms Agency) National Integrated Ballistic Identification System (IBIS) equipment for use by local law enforcement

- *Community policing.* Introduction of a new model of policing based on law enforcement's working closely with local community groups, government, and nongovernment agencies to identify and solve specific community problems (Chapter 5)
- *Fighting gun violence.* Tougher gun control measures like background checks, waiting periods, and the establishment of the FBI Instant Background Check to do the checks
- *Sentencing reform.* Shift from indeterminate sentences based on judges' and corrections' professional judgments to tougher fixed sentences with limited discretion to change them (Chapter 12)
- *Imprisonment changes.* More offenders going to prison and being kept there for longer stays (Chapter 13)

Now that you know something about the broad outlines of the kinds of crime and how they've changed and stayed the same over time, how we measure crime and its trends, and possible reasons for these changes, let's turn to the people who commit crimes and the people who suffer as victims of it.

Criminals

We can say seven things with some confidence about the people who commit crimes:

1. Most aren't violent (fewer than 1 out of 100).
2. Eighty-one percent are male.
3. Almost half are under 25.
4. Almost none are over 50.
5. Over two-thirds are White.
6. Over half know their victims.
7. Many are both criminals and crime victims. (Bureau of Justice Statistics 2001c, Table 4)

Let's look more closely at what we know about female criminals, the relationship between race and crime, and the relationships between criminals and their victims.

Female Criminals

We can say at least three things with confidence about women and crime. First, women commit only 10 percent of violent crimes (Figure 2.5). Second, the criminal careers of female criminals begin earlier than those of men, they stop sooner, and they return to committing crimes much less frequently than men. Third, female crime is increasing. Between 1992 and 2002, female arrests for violent crimes grew 15 percent while male arrests declined 3 percent. This sounds dramatic, but before you make too much of what looks like a boom in female violent crime, we should beware of percentages based on small numbers. For example, in 2002, the FBI reported 10,285 murders committed by men and 1108 by women (FBI, *Crime in the United States, 2003*, Table 2.6; Kruttschnitt 2001, 1–37).

What accounts for the enormous differences between female and male criminality and the shorter life of crime for women? Traditional criminologists said it's because women are biologically and psychologically different from men. The great sociologist Emile Durkheim said women faced less strain from bad social and

► **FIGURE 2.5 Female and Male Violent Crime Arrests, 2003**
Source: FBI: *Crime in the U.S., 2003* (Washington, DC: FBI, October 27, 2004), Table 33.

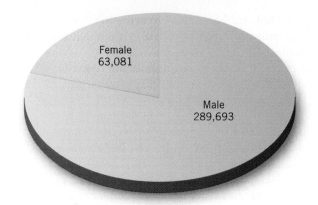

Female
63,081

Male
289,693

economic conditions because "being a more instinctive creature than man, woman has only to follow her instincts." Also, "they are much less involved in collective existence; thus they feel—[the effects of economic and social conditions] good or evil—less strongly." The great psychoanalyst Sigmund Freud said female criminality stemmed from biological problems brought about by the odd functioning of women's genitals, which limited them to family roles. So these distinguished men and a long string of their followers looked to women's biology and psychology to explain their criminality (Steffensmeier and Haynie 2000, 403, 407).

A second (and more congenial to social scientists) school of thought about women criminals says women are affected by social and economic conditions just like men. So poverty, income inequality, race, and other "structural determinants" link women and men to crime. Darrell Steffensmeier and Dana Haynie used arrests in 178 U.S. cities with populations of over 100,000 in 1990 to determine whether things like race, poverty, unemployment, and female-headed households affected arrest rates of men and women. What did they find?

1. Poverty, income inequality, joblessness, and female-headed households affect arrest rates for both Black women and men.
2. But these structural disadvantages affect men more in one crime—homicide of all types except killing spouses or partners. (Steffensmeier and Haynie 2000, 428–429)

spousal and intimate partner homicide exception women commit fewer crimes than men, but women murder their spouses and intimate partners at about the same or higher rates

Let's examine this **spousal and intimate partner homicide exception** closely. This exception is huge because almost all women who kill, kill people they're intimately involved with (unlike men, who kill not only their wives and girlfriends but their "friends" and strangers, too). In fact, it was a dirty little secret until 1992 that wives kill their husbands as often (and in some places more often) than husbands kill their wives, at least in the United States. Margo I. Wilson and Martin Daly examined spousal homicide in the United States and other countries. They found what they call the sex ratio of killing (SROK) (SROK = homicides committed by women for every 100 homicides committed by men) was 75 in the United States, 31 in Canada, and only 6 in parts of Africa. In some cities in the United States, women kill their husbands more often than husbands kill their wives. The Chicago SROK was 102, Detroit's 119 (another study found it was 200!), and Houston's, 137 (Wilson and Daly 1992, 189, Table 1).

How can we explain this major spousal and partner homicide exception in light of the generally low criminality of women? Wilson and Daly say there might be three reasons. First, increased marital conflict takes the form of increased male coercion, which limits women's options which in turn leads women to use drastic forms of escape and self-defense. Second, women kill their husbands when they feel socially empowered to retaliate. For example, in Chicago where the SROK is 102, many Black underclass women maintain strong ties with their relatives and not their husbands' families. This might explain why Latinas have a low SROK; their ties are mainly to their husbands' families.

According to Wilson and Daly (1992), in societies where

women are cut off from their kin and may be treated like household servants by their mothers-in-law, an abused wife may feel she has no recourse other than suicide or flight; violence against the husband is futile and almost unthinkable. Conversely, an abused wife who is surrounded by supportive relatives has more assertive options available for changing her situation, and she may be especially tempted to react violently.... However, the majority presence of the wife's relatives might be expected to deter husbands from seriously assaulting wives, so that the incidence of serious wife battering might be lower in matrilineal kinship systems. (208)

Third, women's deadly actions overtake men's when women are defending their children from prior relationships against their current partners. So Wilson and Daly (1992) say:

Higher SROK values ... may reflect a greater prevalence of stepfathers.... If black children in Chicago, for example, experience higher rates of their fathers' absence and of new men in their mothers' life than white children, and if Latino children experience lower rates of substitute fatherhood than either blacks or whites, this could largely account for the ethnic contrasts in SROK values [blacks, 131; whites 43; and Latinos, 29]. (202, 209)

White and Black Criminals

According to Figure 2.6, almost twice as many Whites are arrested for violent, property, and drug offenses as Blacks. Arrested Whites make up about 15 percent less than their percentage of the general population. On the other hand, arrested Blacks make up about three times more than their percentage of the general population. Why are there so many more Blacks than Whites arrested compared with their percentage of the general population? Does the criminal justice system (in this case the police) discriminate against Blacks? Or do Blacks commit crimes at higher rates than Whites?

We'll talk about discrimination in several other chapters. Here, we have to answer other important questions. First, why are we only talking about Blacks and not other minorities, too? Unfortunately, the arrest statistics lump Whites and Hispanics together, so we can't get those numbers, and the numbers for Asian and Native Americans are so small they're not reliable. Second, why are we looking at arrest rates? Well, to be honest, it's partly because they're easy to get. But there's more to it than that. NCVS data back them up. Remember, NCVS asks victims about the crimes committed against them. One of the questions NCVS asks is the race of victimizers. (Of course, victims have to see their victimizers, which happens only in rape, robbery, and assault.) Victim identifications match

▶ DECISION POINT ◀

Is the number of convenience store robberies high?

Click on this Decision Point at http://cj.wadsworth.com/samaha_cj7e to explore the issue.

▼ FIGURE 2.6 Percentage of Whites and Blacks Arrested Compared to Percent of the General Population, 2003

Source: FBI, *Crime in the U.S., 2003* (Washington, DC: FBI, October 27, 2004). Based on Table 43.

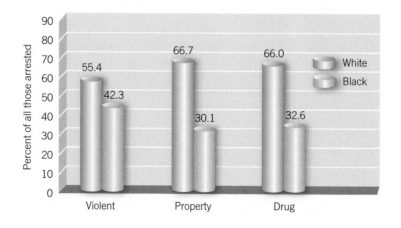

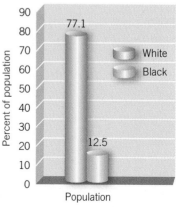

up well with police statistics in cases victims report to the police. This is important because two very different sources—police and victim reports—corroborate each other on race statistics.

Third, do Blacks commit crimes at higher rates than Whites? Or to put it technically, is there more Black criminality than White criminality? A mass of research too powerful to dismiss says yes, Blacks commit more crimes than Whites compared with their numbers in the general population. But let's be clear about two things this *doesn't* tell us. First, it doesn't tell us Blacks are by nature more crime-prone than Whites. According to respected experts on race and crime, Robert J. Sampson and Janet L. Lauritsen (1997):

> The idea that I.Q., temperament, and other individual characteristics explain the race-crime connection is anathema…on political and policy grounds. But there are better reasons to reject the constitutional arguments—empirical validity.…The reason is simple; there are more variations within any race or ethnic group than between them.…"Race" is socially constructed, and the explanation of apparent differences is linked to the fact that race is serving as a proxy for some other set of variables. (331)

Second, it doesn't mean criminal justice doesn't discriminate against Blacks. In fact, two theories (strain and labeling, Chapter 3) look to social structure and the agencies of criminal justice (not race) to explain criminal behavior (Gottfredson and Hirschi 1990, 149–153; Hindelang 1978, 92–109; Tonry 1995, 52–56; Walker, Spohn, and DeLone 2000, 37–48). Traditional explanations of crime focus on the individual level; they try to separate offenders from nonoffenders. Another old idea in criminology focuses on the community level. This isn't done to explain why individuals get involved in crime but to identify characteristics in neighborhoods, cities, states, and countries that lead to high rates of criminality.

The founders of the social ecology theory, Clifford Shaw and Henry McKay, identified three community characteristics of Chicago neighborhoods—low social economic status, racial or ethnic heterogeneity, and high residential mobility—that led first to social disorganization and then to high crime and delinquency rates. Perhaps their most important finding was that high crime rates continued for many years in such neighborhoods no matter how much population turnover there was. Because of this finding, they rejected individual explanations and focused on how community characteristics linked to transmitting criminality from one generation to the next (Sampson and Lauritsen 1997, 351–352).

Later research has backed up Shaw and McKay's social ecology theory to explain higher rates of Black criminality. In an important study, Robert J. Sampson established a link between joblessness among Black males and murder and robbery rates in 150 U.S. cities. He found high numbers of unemployed Black men compared with Black women is directly linked to single-parent families headed by women, and Black family disruption is significantly connected to murder and robbery rates (Sampson 1987, 348–382).

In a later comment on the study and other related research, Sampson and Lauritsen (1997) concluded:

> Despite a large difference in mean levels of family disruption between black and white communities, the percentage of white families headed by a female also had a significant effect on white juvenile and adult violence. The relationships for white robbery were in large part identical in sign and magnitude to those for blacks. As a result, the influence of black family disruption on black crime was independent of alternative explanations (e.g., region, income, density, age composition) and could not be attributed to unique factors within the black community because of the similar effect of white family disruption on white crime. (335)
>
> What does this mean? First, there's no homogeneous Black community. Second, there's no unique "Black subculture of violence." Otherwise, the variations within race don't make sense. For example, if a uniform subculture of violence explains black crime, are we to assume that this subculture is three times as potent in, say, New York as Chicago

(where black homicide differs by a factor of three)? In San Francisco as in Baltimore (3:1 ratio)? These distinct variations exist even at the state level. For example, rates of black homicide in California are triple those for whites in Maryland. Must whites then be part of the black subculture of violence in California, given that white homicide rates are also more than triple those for whites in Maryland? We think not. The sources of violent crime appear to be remarkably invariant across race and rooted instead in the structural differences among communities, cities, and states in economic and family organization. (Sampson 1995, 41)

The debate over the link between race and crime is far from over and is hampered by political correctness and ideological stubbornness, but happily Shaw and McKay's followers have put aside both to advance our knowledge of this important and touchy subject (Sampson and Wilson 1995).

The Relationship between Criminals and Victims

"You always hurt the one you love" goes the old song. It's more true of criminals and their victims than we like to admit. When it comes to criminals, relationships *do* matter, especially four (Table 2.7):

1. *Intimates.* Spouses, ex-spouses, same-sex partners, boyfriends, girlfriends
2. *Relatives.* Parents, children, siblings, grandparents, in-laws, cousins
3. *Acquaintances.* People who know each other, like friends and people from their work, where they shop, where they go for fun
4. *Strangers.* People who don't know each other

Here's some of what we know about crimes involving victims and offenders who have some kind of relationship with each other. Fifty to sixty percent of all husbands assault their wives at least once during marriage (Finkelhor, Gelles, Hotaling, and Straus 1983). Husbands and boyfriends kill 70 percent of women homicide victims! (Bureau of Justice Statistics 1998 (March), 1; Gove, Hughes, and Geerken 1985, 464–465). Parents physically assault 100,000 to 200,000 children every year, sexually abuse 60,000 to 100,000, and kill 5,000! (Straus, Gelles,

▼ **TABLE 2.7 Relationship of Offenders to Victims, 2002**

		Total %	Rape %	Robbery %	Aggravated Assault %	Assault %
Male Victims	Nonstranger	43	52	24	39	47
	Intimate	3	0	4	2	3
	Other relative	4	0	0	5	4
	Friend/Acquaintance	37	52	20	32	41
	Stranger	56	48	74	60	52
	Relationship unknown	1	0	3	1	1
Female Victims	Nonstranger	67	69	55	58	70
	Intimate	20	10	19	19	22
	Other relative	7	2	11	8	7
	Friend/Acquaintance	40	57	25	32	42
	Stranger	31	28	43	37	29
	Relationship unknown	2	3	2	5	1

Note: Percentages may not add up to 100 because of rounding.

Source: BJS, *Criminal Victimization in the U.S., 2002* (Washington, DC: BJS, August 2003), Table 11.

and Steinmetz 1980, 49). The kind of abuse varies by social class. Stephen Brown (1984, 259–278) used an anonymous questionnaire to survey 110 high school freshmen about parental abuse. He found lower-class parents abused their children more often physically and middle-class parents abused their children more often emotionally ("guilt trips" and shaming).

Violence between family members gets most of the attention, but you should also know that property crimes also occur within families. Alan J. Lincoln and Murray A. Straus administered a voluntary anonymous questionnaire to 450 randomly distributed New England college students. The questionnaire asked about property crimes—including forgery, fraud, vandalism, and extortion—committed by one family member against another. Property crimes occurred in 73 percent of the families (Lincoln and Straus 1985, 71–87).

Crime Victims

Crime and Victims: The Bureau of Justice Statistics' site contains information on criminal victimization, crime characteristics, victim characteristics, and incident-based statistics. To reach this site go to "Web Links" on your Samaha CJ7 website: http://cj.wadsworth.com/samaha_cj7e.

Here are the bare facts of criminal victimization reported by the NCVS for the year 2002 (BJS, *Criminal Victimization in the U.S., 2003*):

- There were 23 million victimizations.
- Almost 5.7 million were violent crimes and a little more than 18 million were property crimes.
- Young people were violent crime victims at higher rates (49.7 percent for ages 12–15; 57 percent for ages 16–19) than any other age group (10 percent for ages 50–64).
- There were 26.4 male victims and 21.9 female victims of violent crime for every 1,000 households.
- There were 23.6 White violent crime victims in every 1,000 households, 29.5 Black victims, and 26.5 Hispanic victims.
- The violent crime rate in households with incomes less than $7,500 was 46 for every 1,000 households.
- Most violent crime victims didn't face an armed attacker.

These are the raw numbers. But what about the *experience* of being a crime victim? Numbers can't capture the fear, helplessness, anger, and the desire for revenge like what this husband and wife whose house was burglarized experienced:

WIFE: That made me angry inside, that someone would do that and upset my children....It was somewhat revenge, anger toward that person and feeling like they had no business in my home....The more I thought about it...the more revenge I felt.

HUSBAND: It's unfair that you work for something, like this lawn mower was nothing of value really, but you work hard for it and somebody takes it away from you when you're about to enjoy it or continue to enjoy it. (Greenberg, Ruback, and Westcott 1983, 81)

Another victim went even further:

Six young men rob a teenager of his gold jewelry while he waits for a subway train. The next night the victim chances upon the offenders at the same station. He comes up to them and simply utters, "Remember me?" Although they don't recognize him and look puzzled he takes out a pistol and shoots three of them before fleeing. (Karmen 1990, 2)

Criminals aren't the only source of victim suffering. A bank teller found this out when she handed over money to a robber. The robber had handed her a note that read, "This is a stickup. Put all the money in a bag and no one will get hurt." In her panic she forgot to slip in a specially treated bundle of bills to set off shots of red dye and tear gas at the robber when he tried to leave the bank. The next morning her boss gave her a choice: She could either take a demotion and pay cut or an unpaid indefinite leave of absence. She quit. "I did what any normal person would do—I gave the man the money. For three years I've been a loyal employee and this is what I get" (Karmen 1990, 2).

Let's look at the types of victims and programs for protecting and assisting victims.

The Types of Victim

I've been mugged six (or was it seven?) times in my life. Does this mean I'm victim-prone? Probably not. I haven't been mugged since I've gotten older and stopped going to places and doing things at times I probably shouldn't have. In other words, I was in the right place at the right time ("Routine Activities Theory" in Chapter 3). My own experience illustrates what research clearly demonstrates—victimization isn't a random experience. Take the elderly. The common perception is they're crime-prone. In fact, people 65 or over are five times less often victims of violent crime, four times less often victims of car theft, and half as often victims of home burglaries. Of course, this doesn't mean older people don't suffer from crime. Victimization and the fear of it traumatize older people more than they do younger victims. This fear erodes the quality of their lives, forcing them to stay at home rather than venture outside (Cook 1979, 123; Eve and Eve 1984, 290; Miethe and Meier 1994, 2).

Some empirical research supports the victim proneness theory. Marvin E. Wolfgang, Terence P. Thornberry, and Robert M. Figlio asked birth cohorts (people the same age) about the crimes they committed and the victimizations they suffered between the ages of 12 to 18 and 18 to 26. The responses showed they were both victims and victimizers in violent crimes but not property crimes (Reiss 1980, 47–57; Wolfgang, Thornberry, and Figlio 1987, chap. 13).

Occupation also affects victimization. More than one million people a year are the victims of violent crime on the job. Every year, someone steals personal belongings from more than two million workers while they work, and the cars of another 200,000. These victimizations cost an average of about 3.5 days of work per person every year. Among those victimized while working, men are more likely to be the victims of violent crime, but women are just as likely to be the victims of theft (Bureau of Justice Statistics 1994; *Wall Street Journal* 1994).

Victimization is also related to race. In 2002, the violent crime victimization rate for Whites was 23.6 per 1,000 persons over 12 years of age and for Hispanics higher, 26.5. For Blacks it was higher still, 29.5 (BJS, *Criminal Victimization* 2003). The National Institute for Occupational Health and Safety (OSHA) found the rate of work-related homicides for Blacks was nearly twice that of White workers. Black taxi drivers and gas station attendants experience especially high homicide rates. Finally, most crime is intraracial (within races) not interracial (between races). In other words, most crime is White on White, Black on Black, Hispanic on Hispanic, Asian on Asian, or American Indian on American Indian (Bureau of Justice Statistics 2000c, 3; Walker, Spohn, and DeLone 2000, 24–25).

Victimization strongly correlates with lifestyle. Criminologists have developed theories built around this correlation (Miethe and Meier 1994, 2; Chapter 3). The earliest theorists faced strong opposition on ideological grounds. During the 1970s, feminists and victims' advocates complained such theories blamed the victims. Despite opposition, one of these theories, the lifestyle-exposure theory, has received considerable acceptance among criminologists. Michael S. Hindelang, Michael Gottfredson, and James Garofalo (1978) found different victim lifestyles explain different rates of victimization. Gender, race, and income are linked to different lifestyles and to chances of victimization. According to the theory, crimes take place disproportionately against young, single, low-income Black men because this group spends more time away from home at night, taking part in activities during which crimes often occur (Hindelang, Gottfredson, and Garofalo 1978; Meier and Miethe 1993, 459–465).

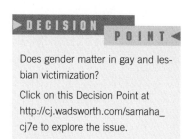

> DECISION POINT ◄

Does gender matter in gay and lesbian victimization?

Click on this Decision Point at http://cj.wadsworth.com/samaha_cj7e to explore the issue.

Where does crime prevention fit today?

Click on this Decision Point at http://cj.wadsworth.com/samaha_ cj7e to explore the issue.

Lawrence W. Sherman, Patrick R. Gartin, and Michael E. Buerger (1989, 27–55) identified "hot spots" (places where most crimes take place, Chapter 6) in Minneapolis. On the basis of more than 300,000 emergency calls for one year, they found most calls reporting robberies, rapes, and thefts came from hot spots. Because older people, married couples, and others with steady employment rarely go to hot spots, particularly at night, they're rarely victims (459–465).

Victim Protection and Assistance

The U.S. Victims of Crime Act created a $100 million crime victims' fund drawn from criminal fines in federal offenses. The money supports state victim-compensation and other programs to assist victims. States have also passed laws to assist crime victims. Most of these statutes compensate violent crime victims who report crimes and cooperate with investigation and prosecution for medical expenses, funeral expenses, lost wages, and the support of deceased victims' dependents. However, the caps on the allowable amounts are too low to make compensation meaningful.

Some states have established victim-witness assistance programs, usually supervised by prosecutors. These programs provide services like

- *Personal advocacy.* Helping victims receive all the services they're entitled to
- *Referral.* Recommending or obtaining other assistance
- *Restitution assistance.* Urging judges to order, or probation authorities to collect, restitution and helping violent crime victims fill out applications to receive compensation
- *Court orientation.* Explaining the criminal justice system and their participation in it
- *Transportation.* Taking victims and witnesses to and from court, to social service agencies, and, if necessary, to shelters
- *Escort services.* Escorting witnesses to court and staying with them during proceedings
- *Emotional support.* Giving victims support during their ordeals with crime and with the criminal justice proceedings following it (National Law Journal 1990, 12)

Thirteen states have even written victim's rights provisions into their constitutions. Typical provisions require the criminal justice system to:

- Treat victims with compassion and respect
- Inform victims of critical stages in the trial process
- Invite victims to attend and comment on trial proceedings

"I feel as if our movement is picking up the steam it needs to carry through all fifty states," said Linda Lowrance, chair of the Victims' Constitutional Amendment Network. But no one has evaluated the *effectiveness* of these provisions, according to John Stein, deputy director of the National Organization for Victim Assistance. However, some evidence shows victim impact statements make people "feel better" about the criminal justice system, even though the statements have little or no effect on sentencing or punishment of convicted offenders. Roberta Roper, whose daughter was raped and murdered, couldn't attend the trial of her daughter's murderers because Maryland has no victims' rights law. Forced to watch the trial by pressing her nose against the small pane of glass in a wooden courtroom door, Roper felt she'd let her daughter down by not being in court. "By being a presence at the trial, we could as a family bear witness to the fact that Stephanie lived, and she mattered. We were denied that" (Bureau of Justice Statistics 1989a; *New York Times* 1992, 156).

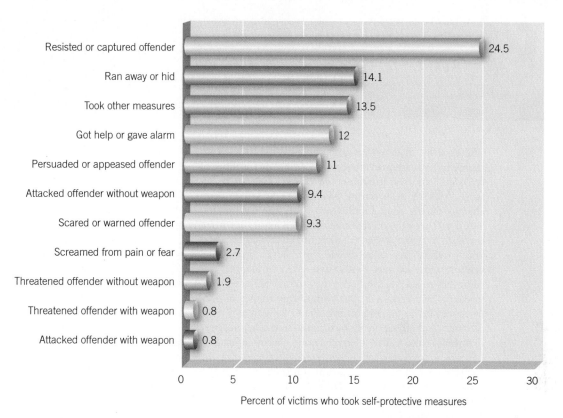

Percent of victims who took self-protective measures

▲ FIGURE 2.7 Self-Protective Measures Taken by Violent Crime Victims, 2002

Source: Bureau of Justice Statistics, *Criminal Victimization, 2002* (Washington, DC: Bureau of justice Statistics, 2003).

At the time of the crime, victims have to depend on self-protection. According to the NCVS, three-quarters of victims reported taking self-protective measures against offenders, including resisting, trying to capture the offender, persuading the offender, and running away. More than half of those who took self-protective measures reported that their actions had a positive effect. About 7 percent reported that the measures made the situation worse, while 6 percent reported that both positive and negative effects resulted (Figure 2.7).

MAKE YOUR DECISION: *Can We Identify Career Criminals before Their Careers Start?*

There's a lot of empirical research proving a sharp increase in both the **prevalence of criminality** (number of *offenders*) and the **incidence of crime** (number of *offenses*), which peak during adolescence and then drop sharply during young adulthood. That's the big picture. But if you zoom in on that picture you'll learn that when it comes to crime and criminality, not all adolescents and young adults are alike. Some have never committed crimes, and they never will. Some don't commit crimes until they're adults. Most don't commit crimes after adolescence. But a *few* will start committing crimes in adolescence and go on committing crimes as long as they're mentally and physically fit to commit them. These **career criminals** (also called *superpredators, chronic offenders, life-course persisters,* and *high-crime offenders*) are the focus of a lot of public and criminal justice research and policy attention (Bennett, DiIulio, and Walters 1996; Laub and Sampson 2003, 18). They're also the subject of this Make Your Decision.

DOES THE EVIDENCE SUPPORT THE NEED FOR A CAREER CRIMINAL POLICY?

Assume you're a policy advisor to an official responsible for career criminal policy. She wants a policy recommendation *tomorrow* on how to identify superpredators, what to do about them, when, and how. So you only have time to read two brief excerpts from two influential but contrasting views on career criminals. Read and summarize what these excerpts say about:

1. The problems in identifying and predicting which adolescents will become career criminals
2. The conflicting theories about the paths to becoming a career criminal
3. The empirical research related to identifying and predicting career criminality and its pathways

After you've completed the summaries, write up the main points in favor of adopting a career criminal policy soon, and summarize the elements of the policy. Then, write up the main points against adopting any career criminal proposal. Finally, write up a recommendation for further study, and list exactly what that further study should be looking for.

Source: Terrie E. Moffitt, *Juvenile Delinquency: Seed of a Career in Violent Crime, Just Sowing Wild Oats—or Both?* Paper presented at the Science and Public Policy Seminars of the Federation of Behavioral, Psychological, and Cognitive Sciences, Washington, DC, September 1991. Reprinted with permission from the author.

ARE SUPER PREDATORS BORN THAT WAY?

Terrie E. Moffitt

There are marked individual differences in the stability of antisocial behavior. Many people behave antisocially, but their antisocial behavior is temporary and situational. In contrast, the antisocial behavior of some people is very stable and persistent. Temporary, situational antisocial behavior is quite common in the population, especially among adolescents. Persistent, stable antisocial behavior is found among a relatively small number of males whose behavior problems are also quite extreme. The central tenet of this article is that temporary versus persistent antisocial persons constitute two qualitatively distinct types of persons. In particular, I suggest that juvenile delinquency conceals two qualitatively distinct categories of individuals, each in need of its own distinct theoretical explanation....

When official rates of crime are plotted against age, the rates for both prevalence and incidence of offending appear highest during adolescence; they peak sharply at about age 17 and drop precipitously in young adulthood. The majority of criminal offenders are teenagers; by the early 20s, the number of active offenders decreases by over 50%, and by age 28, almost 85% of former delinquents desist from offending. With slight variations, this general relationship between age and crime obtains among males and females, for most types of crimes, dur-

▲ Shakespeare said "The child is father to the man." Modern criminologists differ on the point. Some find that adult criminal offending results from an unfolding of what's "already there." Others say development is a "constant interaction between individuals and their environment, coupled with the factor of chance or 'random developmental noise.'"

ing recent historical periods and in numerous Western nations....

But [what explains]...the increase in the prevalence of offenders?...A small group of persons is shown engaging in antisocial behavior of one sort or another at every stage of life. I have labeled these persons life-course-persistent to reflect the continuous course of their antisocial behavior. A larger group of persons fills out the age—crime curve with crime careers of shorter duration. I have labeled these persons adolescence-limited to reflect their more temporary involvement in antisocial behavior....A substantial body of longitudinal research consistently points to a very small group of males who display high rates of antisocial behavior across time and in diverse situations. The professional nomenclature may change, but the faces remain the same as they drift through successive systems aimed at curbing their deviance: schools, juvenile-justice programs, psychiatric treatment centers, and prisons. The topography of their behavior may change with changing opportunities, but the underlying disposition persists throughout the life course.

...Continuity is the hallmark of the small group of life-course-persistent antisocial persons. Across the life course, these individuals exhibit changing manifestations of antisocial behavior: biting and hitting at age 4, shoplifting and truancy at age 10, selling drugs and stealing cars at age 16, robbery and rape at age 22, and fraud and child abuse at age 30; the underlying disposition remains the same, but its expression changes form as new social opportunities arise at different points in development. This pattern of continuity across age is matched also by cross-situational consistency: Life-course-persistent antisocial persons lie at home, steal from shops, cheat at school, fight in bars, and embezzle at work....

Life-course-persistent persons miss out on opportunities to acquire and practice prosocial alternatives at each stage of development. Children with poor self-control and aggressive behavior are often rejected by peers and adults. In turn, children who have learned to expect rejection are likely in later settings to withdraw or strike out preemptively, precluding opportunities to affiliate with prosocial peers. Such children are robbed of chances to practice conventional social skills.

Alternatively, consider this sequence of narrowing options: Behavior problems at school and failure to attain basic math and reading skills place a limit on the variety of job skills that can be acquired and thereby cut off options to pursue legitimate employment as an alternative to the underground economy. Simply put, if social and academic skills are not mastered in childhood, it is very difficult to later recover lost opportunities.

Personal characteristics such as poor self-control, impulsivity, and inability to delay gratification increase the risk that antisocial youngsters will make irrevocable decisions that close the doors of opportunity. Teenaged parenthood, addiction to drugs or alcohol, school dropout, disabling or disfiguring injuries, patchy work histories, and time spent incarcerated are snares that diminish the probabilities of later success by eliminating opportunities for breaking the chain of cumulative continuity.

Similarly, labels accrued early in life can foreclose later opportunities; an early arrest record or a "bad" reputation may rule out lucrative jobs, higher education, or an advantageous marriage. In short, the behavior of life-course-persistent antisocial persons is increasingly maintained and supported by narrowing options for conventional behavior.

Interventions with life-course-persistent persons have met with dismal results. This is not surprising, considering that most interventions are begun relatively late in the chain of cumulative continuity. The forces of continuity are formidable foes. After a protracted deficient learning history, and after options for change have been eliminated, efforts to suppress antisocial behavior will not automatically bring prosocial behavior to the surface in its place.

When in the life course does the potential for change dwindle to nil? How many person-environment interactions must accumulate before the life-course-persistent pattern becomes set?...The well-documented resistance of antisocial personality disorder to treatments of all kinds seems to suggest that the life-course-persistent style is fixed sometime before age 18.

REFERENCES

Elliott, D. S., & Huizinga, D. (1984, April). *The relationship between delinquent behavior and ADM problems.* Paper presented at the ADAMHA/OJJDP State-of-the-Art Research Conference on Juvenile Offenders with Serious Drug, Alcohol, and Mental Health Problems, Rockville, MD.

Farrington, D. P. (1983). Offending from 10 to 25 years of age. In K. Van Dusen & S. A. Mednick (Eds.), *Prospective studies of crime and delinquency* (pp. 17–38). Boston: Kluwer-Nijhoff.

Moffitt, T. E. (1991, September). *Juvenile delinquency: Seed of a career in violent crime, just sowing wild oats—or both?* Paper presented at the Science and Public Policy Seminars of the Federation of Behavioral, Psychological, and Cognitive Sciences, Washington, DC.

DO WE KNOW THE PATH TO BECOMING A SUPER PREDATOR?

...Relying on what Michael Tonry and David Farrington (1995) refer to as the central insight from Shakespeare—that the child is father to the man—researchers have addressed how developmental processes are linked to the onset, continuation, and cessation of criminal and antisocial behavior. Much has been learned and developmental criminology is now ascendant....

Using the analogy of a photographic image, Lewontin (2000) argues that the way the term "development" is used is a process that makes the latent image apparent. This seems to be what developmental criminological theory is all about. For example, in Moffitt's theory of crime, the environment offers a "set of enabling conditions" that allow individual traits to express themselves. Although reciprocal interactions with the environment are allowed, life-course-persistent offenders and adolescence-limited offenders follow a preprogrammed line of development—an unwinding, an unfolding, or an unrolling of what is fundamentally "already there."...

...Some developmentalists recognize social interactions, but in the end they...emphasize the primacy of early childhood attributes that are presumed to be stable. We view the life course as something altogether different....In our theory of crime, development is better conceived as the constant interaction between individuals and their environment, coupled with the factor of chance or "random developmental noise" (Lewontin 2000, 35–36). Recognizing developmental noise implies that "the organism is determined neither by its genes nor by its environment nor even by interaction between them, but bears a significant mark of random processes" (38).

From this view it makes sense that we uncovered enormous heterogeneity in criminal offending over the life course. Some offenders start early and stop; others start early and continue for long periods of time. A sizable portion of the offending population displays a zigzag pattern of offending over long time periods. Most important, long-term patterns of offending cannot be explained by individual differences (for example, low verbal IQ), childhood characteristics (for example, early onset of misbehavior), or adolescent characteristics (for example, chronic juvenile offending). In our conception of development, then, the sum of the parts includes individual differences, environmental differences, social interactions, and random, chance events. All of this leads to considerable "noisy, unpredictable development."... This description captures well the life-course reality of much crime.

On the Dangers of Offender Typologies

...The popularity of typological approaches to crime has...increased in recent years. In our view, the problems with typological approaches are many and far

Source: Reprinted by permission of the publisher from *Shared Beginnings, Divergent Lives: Delinquent Boys to Age 70* by John H. Laub and Robert J. Sampson, pp. 38, 361–362, Cambridge, Mass.: Harvard University Press, Copyright © 2003 by the President and Fellows of Harvard College.

reaching....One fundamental problem is that most typological approaches in criminology are...[after the fact]. After the fact, it appears possible to find groups in any data set, many of which cannot be replicated or validated with independent data. The key finding from our analyses is that the process of desistance [ceasing to commit crimes] follows a remarkably similar path for all offenders, albeit at different rates....

[Another problem is]...linked to interventions. The fundamental idea is that different interventions are needed for different types of offenders (see Gibbons 1985)....An obvious problem is that there is little consistent empirical support in decades of criminological research for the idea of offense specialization and differential causal forces. Moreover..., offender types are at best a loose reflection of reality and do not capture the complexity of offending over the life course....

Finally, the success of specialized, targeted interventions focusing on offender types such as life-course-persistent offenders has not been demonstrated; this approach may lead to grandiose proclamations...that far exceed the state of scientific knowledge in the field of criminology.

...Despite the appeal of groups for simplifying a messy reality, we believe that criminologists may be better served by attending to individual trajectories of crime. Understanding general causal pathways to crime at all points in the life course is the research question that criminology might profitably begin to address.

Reconsidering the Risk-Factor Paradigm

...The conference "Delinquents under 10: Targeting the Young Offender" was held in Minneapolis in 1999. As the name indicates, the risk-factor and prediction paradigm has again taken hold of criminology, especially for those interested in crime prevention and crime control policies. Investigators know what the risk factors are; however, what we don't know very well is which kids will do what and when. In other words..., our ability to predict behavior prospectively over the long term continues to be weak at best.

What is needed...are "observable and identifiable precursors that would allow alarms to be issued with high reliability and accuracy" (Geller et al. 1997, 1616).

> In the field of criminology do such precursors in fact exist? Yes and no. The yes refers once again to the fact that adult criminals seem always to possess early childhood risks (Robins 1966, 1978), a sturdy finding in criminology. The no refers to the prospective reality. There is a lengthy history of prediction research in criminology showing that childhood variables are quite modest prognostic devices, going forward in time. Known as the **false positive problem,** prediction scales often result in the substantial overprediction of future criminality (Loeber and Stouthamer-Loeber 1987; Farrington and Tarling 1985).

Likewise, prediction attempts often fail to identify accurately those who will become criminal even though past behavior suggests otherwise (**false negatives**)....Jennifer White and her colleagues (1990, 521) document that "early antisocial behavior is the best predictor of later antisocial behavior." This study examined behavior from age 3 to age 15. Nevertheless, their data clearly show the limitations of relying only on childhood information to understand behavior over time.

Conclusion

The missing element in traditional social control theory is human agency (1964, 183); motivation has always been its weakest link. And..., traditional social control cannot easily explain...crime that results when individuals are socially bonded and tightly connected to strong subcultures or higher-echelon segments of society. Events such as the Enron and WorldCom scandals, alleged insider trading by Martha Stewart, terrorism here and abroad, and sex abuse by priests in the Catholic Church should cause even the most ardent supporter of traditional social control theory some discomfort and consternation.

Although we do not abandon control theory, we see other concepts as equally relevant for understanding persistent offending and desistance from crime over the life course....These concepts include personal agency and situated choice, routine activities, aging, macro-level historical events, and local culture and community context.

REFERENCES

Farrington, David P., and Roger Tarling, eds. 1985. *Prediction in Criminology.* Albany, NY: State University of New York Press.

Geller, Robert J., David D. Jackson, Yan Y. Kagan, and Francisco Mulargia. 1997. "Earthquakes Cannot Be Predicted." *Science* 275:1616–1617.

Gibbons, Don C. 1985. "The Assumption of the Efficacy of Middle-Range Explanations: Typologies," in *Theoretical Methods in Criminology,* ed. Robert F. Meier. Beverly Hills, CA: Sage Publications.

Lewinton, Richard. 2000. *The Triple Helix: Gene, Organism, and Environment.* Cambridge, MA: Harvard University Press.

Loeber, Rolf, and Magda Stouthamer-Loeber. 1987. "Prediction," in *Handbook of Juvenile Delinquency,* ed. Herbert C. Quay. New York: John Wiley & Sons.

Tonry, Michael, and David P. Farrington. 1995. "Strategic Approaches to Crime Prevention," in *Building a Safer Society: Strategic Approaches to Crime Prevention,* eds. Michael Tonry and David P. Farrington. Chicago: University of Chicago Press.

White, Jennifer L., Terrie E. Moffitt, Felton Earls, Lee Robbins, and Phil A. Silva. 1990. "How Early Can We Tell? Predictors of Childhood Conduct Disorder and Adolescent Delinquency." *Criminology* 28:207–533.

KEY TERMS

prevalence of criminality the number of offenders

incidence of crime the number of offenses

career criminals individuals who start committing crimes very early and continue to commit crimes throughout their lives

false positive problem when prediction scales result in the substantial overprediction of future criminality

false negatives when attempts to predict accurately those who will become criminals based on their past behaviors fail

Is it too early to make policy based on research about crime and drugs?

Click on this Decision Point at http://cj.wadsworth.com/samaha_cj7e to explore the issue.

Can we rely on the evidence of the career patterns of career criminals?

Click on this Decision Point at http://cj.wadsworth.com/samaha_cj7e to explore the issue.

Chapter Summary

▶ One way to help you get a grip on the vast amount of behavior included in the word *crime* is to think about four types: violent crime; property crime; other crimes against society and individuals; and crimes against the state. Violent crimes physically and/or mentally hurt or threaten to hurt individuals. Property crimes take, invade, damage, or destroy other people's property. Violent and property crimes all have two victims, individual victims of crimes and the whole society. Crimes against public order and morals almost never have *complaining* victims; they offend the community generally.

▶ Crimes against the state consist of ancient crimes against disloyalty and the recent crimes against terrorism. The old crime of treason is intentionally very hard to prove because the authors of the U.S. Constitution understood from their own experience it could be misused for punishing more than traitors. They knew King George III also used treason laws to punish his critics. The newer crimes against terrorism are broad in their definition, but in practice, the main crimes prosecuted are providing assistance to individual terrorists and terrorist organizations.

▶ The two definitions of white-collar crimes are related to occupation. The status definition focuses on high-status offenders (usually corporate officers) who use their position to cheat investors, shareholders, employees, and the public. The abuse-of-trust definition focuses on abusing a trust relationship, including anyone (no matter what their status) "responsible for custody, discretion, information, or property rights." This definition would include a corporate CEO who misled employees about the value of their retirement fund as well as a local auto mechanic who replaced your perfectly good brakes.

▶ All crime statistics suffer from a "dark figure" (crimes committed but not known). Official statistics omit crimes not reported to the police and not counted; victim surveys omit crimes interviewers don't ask about and victims don't tell the interviewers about; self-report surveys only select groups and the members of the groups selected don't report all the crimes they've committed.

▶ For the last 10 years, there's been a crime bust. But the volume and rates of crime are still a lot higher than they were before the crime boom that began in the 1960s. Hardly anyone disputes the trends, but there's heated debate about *why* the trends have followed these paths.

▶ Most criminals are nonviolent young White men. Over half know their victims, sometimes intimately. Often criminals are themselves crime victims. The numbers of female criminals are on the rise but they've got a long way to go before they catch up to the numbers of male criminals. One "dirty little secret" about female criminality: women kill their husbands as often (and in some places more often) as husbands kill their wives. The reasons aren't clear, but researchers say it may be that male coercion leaves women with few options; women feel socially empowered to fight back against abuse; and women whose husbands abuse their children take extraordinary measures to protect their children from the abuse.

▶ The ratio of Black criminals to the general population is higher than for Whites. This, however, doesn't prove Blacks are by nature more criminal than Whites. For example, researchers have linked Black murder and robbery rates to high numbers of unemployed Black men compared with Black women. This, in turn, is directly linked to single-parent families headed by women and disruption of Black families.

▶ There's more to victimization than physical injury and property loss—fear, helplessness, anger, pain, and desire for revenge. Victimization is linked to age, race, occupation, and lifestyle. Federal and state governments have adopted a variety of victim protection and assistance programs that by most accounts fall short of the need for them.

Key Terms

Web Resources

Go to http://cj.wadsworth.com/samaha_cj7e for a wealth of online resources related to your book. Take a "pre-test" and "post-test" for each chapter in order to help master the material. Check out the *Web Links* to access the websites mentioned in the text, as well as many others. Explore the *Decision Points* flagged in the margins of the text for additional insights. You can also access recent perspectives by clicking on *CJ in the News* and *Terrorism Update* under *Course Resources*.

Search Online with InfoTrac College Edition

For additional information, explore InfoTrac College Edition, your online library. Go to http://cj.wadsworth.com/samaha_cj7e to access InfoTrac College Edition from your book's website. Use the passcode that came with your book. You will find InfoTrac College Edition exercises and a list of key words for further research.

CHAPTER 3

Explanations of Criminal Behavior

FACT *or* FICTION?

▶ Spiritual explanations of crime can be proven by observation.

▶ According to the evidence, robbers usually take other people's money to pay bills.

▶ The seduction of crime theory focuses on the childhood of offenders to find out what turns them on.

▶ Biological theories are now supported by enough empirical evidence to build policies on them.

▶ Empirical evidence demonstrates a direct causal link between low intelligence and criminal behavior.

▶ Sociological theories assume that social structure and social processes determine criminal behavior.

▶ Empirical evidence demonstrates that the strain theory explains only lower-class male criminal behavior.

▶ According to social control theory, we're all rule breakers by nature.

▶ Most adult criminals were juvenile delinquents.

▶ Criminal law and criminal justice theories shift the emphasis from lawbreakers to law enforcers.

WHAT DOES IT *FEEL* LIKE TO COMMIT A CRIME?

The social science literature contains only scattered evidence of what it means, feels, sounds, tastes, or looks like to commit a particular crime. Readers of research on homicide and assault do not hear the slaps and curses, see the pushes and shoves, or feel the humiliation and rage that may build toward the attack, sometimes persisting after the victim's death. How adolescents manage to make shoplifting or vandalism of cheap and commonplace things a thrilling experience has not been intriguing to many students of delinquency. Researchers of adolescent gangs have never grasped why their subjects so often stubbornly refuse to accept the outsider's insistence that they wear the "gang" label.

—JACK KATZ (1988)

You learned some of the facts about crime, criminals, and victims in Chapter 2. You'll learn about the legal definitions and constitutional limits on the definitions of crime in Chapter 4. In the remaining chapters, you'll learn about how public agencies control crime and criminals. But none of those chapters explains how and why behavior comes to be defined as criminal and why there are crimes and criminals. That's the subject of this chapter. Criminologists develop and test theories to explain crime and criminal behavior. Criminal justice uses (or at least should use) them to create effective responses to crime and criminal behavior. After all, you can't very well solve problems without knowing why they exist.

Over the long sweep of history, two types of theories have been used to explain crime and criminal behavior—spiritual and natural (Vold, Bernard, and Snipes 2002, 2). Spiritual explanations are ancient and at first were the only explanation for crime and punishment. They're based on the belief (faith) that some higher power we can't directly observe controls many aspects of life. Fires, floods, famines, and other natural disasters were explained as punishment for wrongs done by people to the higher powers. In medieval Europe, the beginnings of our criminal justice system were based on a spiritual view of the world that equated crime with sins against God. The early American colonists built their criminal justice system on the union of sin and crime. Many sins (profanity, drunkenness, adultery) were also misdemeanors; felonies (homicide, rape, robbery, burglary, and theft) were also sins. And our modern prison system stems from the Quakers' invention of the penitentiary, where prisoners were locked up in solitary confinement with only a Bible to read and manual labor to perform. That way, they could contemplate their sins, repent, and return to society reformed.

Spiritual explanations are still with us. There are those who believe (some passionately) that crime is the devil's work. Charles Colson (special counsel to President Nixon) is a very influential and passionate proponent of the modern spiritual view of crime. Colson served seven months in prison in 1974 for obstructing justice during the Watergate affair. In 1976, he created Prison Fellowship Ministries, after becoming a born-again Christian. This volunteer organization brings Bible study and a Christian message to prisoners and their families. In 1983, he founded Justice Fellowship to develop "Bible-based criminal justice and prison reform." As I write this, Colson is a syndicated radio host and still contributes the royalties from his many highly successful books to Prison Fellowship (*Washington Post* n.d.).

Spiritual explanations of crime aren't subject to proof by observation (they're faith based) so they can't be discussed as part of the scientific theories of crime discussed in this chapter. But let's be clear. Just because they can't be proven according to the standards set by scientific criminology doesn't mean they're not true. So this book takes no stand on the truth or falsity of spiritual theories.

Natural explanations look to objects and events in this world to explain the meaning of life (and crime). Natural theories are ancient, too. The ancient Greek physician Hippocrates, born in 460 B.C., argued that thinking is physiological; the brain (the organ of the mind) produces it (Vold et al. 2002, 4). By the first century B.C., Roman law fused Hebrew law based on divine sanction with Greek law based on "the nature of things." The great thinkers of the social and political world of the 1500s and 1600s (Hobbes, Locke, Descartes, and others) studied society like "hard" scientists studied the physical world—namely, quantitatively and objectively.

The modern scientific theories of crime you'll read about in this chapter all stem from the natural explanations in the sense that they're based on quantitative, objective observations. The theories focus on relationships between phenomena we can observe (Vold et al. 2002, 4). We'll discuss several of these relationships in other chapters (between race, ethnicity, sex, age, and crime; between crime and punishment; between law enforcement tactics and crime; and others).

The relationship that criminologists seek to prove (or disprove) is the *causal* relationship. Causal relationships consist of several elements, two of which we concentrate on here: correlation and theoretical rationale. **Correlation** means that observable phenomena "*tend* to vary with each other systematically," like height and weight. Positive correlations refer to variations in the same direction (the taller you are the more you weigh). Negative correlations refer to variations in the opposite direction (the more miles on your car the less money it's worth). Notice that the direction doesn't have to be true in all cases—it only has to *tend* to be true (Vold et al. 2002, 6).

Correlations are necessary to causation because if two phenomena don't vary together (like blonde color and being gay), one phenomenon can't cause the other. But correlation isn't enough to prove causation. There has to be a *theoretical rationale*—a sensible explanation for the correlation. Remember this important point: Even if both the elements of correlation and a theoretical rationale are present, cause in theories of crime and criminal behavior is still a statement of *probabilities* not *certainties*. But even probabilities are useful. If we identify a rational theory supporting a correlation, we might be able to influence the direction of the relationship between crime and other phenomena. For example, if, as is widely believed, adult criminal behavior is rooted in early childhood ("Make Your Decision" later), then early childhood intervention can reduce adult crime.

All of the natural scientific theories reflect three very different ways to look at crime. **Classical theories** (also called **utilitarian theories**) are based on the twin pillars of free will (individuals choose to commit crimes) and reason (they choose to do what benefits them). **Positivist theories** are based on **determinism**—the belief that criminal behavior is controlled by factors beyond the control of individuals. These factors might be within an individual (biologically and/or psychologically) or outside (dependent on social structure and social processes). **Criminal law theories** rest on the idea that crime is whatever the law says it is, and so the focus of criminal theories is on lawmakers and law enforcers instead of lawbreakers (Vold et al. 2002, 8–10). We'll look at some of the theories within each of these points of view. Probably because I'm a historian, we'll examine the theories as they were created chronologically, but we'll update each theory before going on to the next one.

Crime Theories: An Educational Resource for the Learning, Researching and Teaching of Theoretical Criminology: A great source for all things related to crime causation theories. Includes a timeline of the theories and their evolution into more current theories. To reach this site go to "Web Links" on your Samaha CJ7 website: http://cj.wadsworth.com/samaha_cj7e.

correlation observable phenomena that "*tend* to vary with each other systematically"

Crime Causation Theories: Synopsis of prevalent crime causation theories by Diane M. DeMelo. To reach this site go to "Web Links" on your Samaha CJ7 website: http://cj.wadsworth.com/samaha_cj7e.

classical (utilitarian) theories theories based on free will and reason

positivist theories theories based on determinism or forces beyond individual control

determinism forces beyond individual control

criminal law theories crime is whatever the law says it is

Classical Theories

During the eighteenth-century Age of Reason (Enlightenment), English philosopher Jeremy Bentham (influenced by the novel ideas of Italian criminologist Cesare Beccaria) developed the utilitarian theory of crime causation. This theory was based on two assumptions: First, it's in human nature to seek pleasure and avoid pain, a view called hedonism—"Nature has placed mankind under two sovereign masters, pain and pleasure," in Bentham's words. Second, individuals are free to choose to commit (or not commit) crimes (free will). So, for example, if the fear of the pain from getting caught and punished for stealing your friend's MP3 player will be more than the pleasure you'll get from stealing it, you won't steal it. In the terms of classical criminology, your decision not to steal is an example of specific deterrence and the resulting decisions by other criminal wannabes not to steal are examples of general deterrence (Chapter 11).

Upon these radical assumptions, the whole structure of our criminal law and criminal justice system was built (Gottfredson and Hirschi 1990, 5). When crime continued to climb in the 1800s, positivist disillusion with the classical theories produced the positivist theories we'll discuss later. And when crime continued its upward climb, even skyrocketed (Chapter 2), policies based on positivist theories were blamed; so during the 1970s, policies based on classical theory assumptions became popular again.

Let's look at two current theories based on classical criminology—rational choice and routine activities theories. Then, we'll examine the theory of the seductions of crime, which seeks to understand what it feels like to commit crimes and how this affects the decision to do so.

Criminology: Dr. Tom O'Connor's website on criminology-related information. A good resource with many useful links for criminal justice students. To reach this site go to "Web Links" on your Samaha CJ7 website: http://cj.wadsworth.com/samaha_cj7e.

The Rational Choice Theory

rational choice theory individuals make decisions according to what they *believe* is in their self-interest

The **rational choice theory** assumes that individuals make decisions according to what they *believe* is (even if it's not) in their self-interest. The explanation allows for *some* irrational and pathological components in criminal behavior. Rational choice theory consists of three elements:

1. A reasoning criminal
2. A crime-specific focus
3. Separate analyses of criminal involvement and criminal events (Cornish and Clarke 1986)

The reasoning criminal element assumes offenders commit crimes to benefit themselves. Getting benefits requires rational decision making, even though the decisions are affected by *some* irrationality and pathology. According to the theory, criminals have specific goals, alternative means of obtaining them, and at least some information for choosing the best alternative to achieve their goals.

The crime-specific element assumes decision making is different for each crime. Burglary, for example, requires decision making different from robbery, and different kinds of burglaries and robberies require different decision making. So deciding to rob a convenience store or a bank or to mug a person on the street each demands a separate analysis. The decision to commit a commercial burglary isn't like the decision to commit a residential burglary. And burglars who target public housing, middle-class neighborhoods, and wealthy enclaves differ as to individual burglars, targets, motivations, and methods.

The third element divides criminal involvement and criminal events. Criminal involvement refers to three critical decisions:

1. Deciding generally to get into crime (Figure 3.1)
2. Deciding to continue committing crimes
3. Deciding to get out of involvement in crime

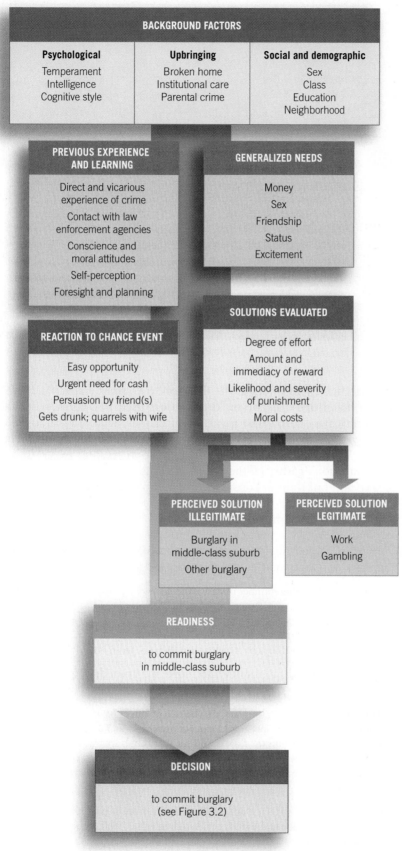

◄ **FIGURE 3.1 Criminal Involvement: The Decision to Get Involved in Crime**

Source: Derek B. Cornish and Ronald V. Clarke, eds., *The Reasoning Criminal: Rational Choice Perspectives on Offending* (New York: Springer-Verlag, 1986), Figure 1.1, 4.

BACKGROUND FACTORS

Psychological	Upbringing	Social and demographic
Temperament	Broken home	Sex
Intelligence	Institutional care	Class
Cognitive style	Parental crime	Education
		Neighborhood

PREVIOUS EXPERIENCE AND LEARNING

Direct and vicarious experience of crime

Contact with law enforcement agencies

Conscience and moral attitudes

Self-perception

Foresight and planning

GENERALIZED NEEDS

Money

Sex

Friendship

Status

Excitement

REACTION TO CHANCE EVENT

Easy opportunity

Urgent need for cash

Persuasion by friend(s)

Gets drunk; quarrels with wife

SOLUTIONS EVALUATED

Degree of effort

Amount and immediacy of reward

Likelihood and severity of punishment

Moral costs

PERCEIVED SOLUTION ILLEGITIMATE

Burglary in middle-class suburb

Other burglary

PERCEIVED SOLUTION LEGITIMATE

Work

Gambling

READINESS

to commit burglary in middle-class suburb

DECISION

to commit burglary (see Figure 3.2)

▶ **FIGURE 3.2 The Criminal Event: The Decision to Commit a Specific Burglary**

Source: Derek B. Cornish and Ronald V. Clarke, eds., *The Reasoning Criminal: Rational Choice Perspectives on Offending* (New York: Springer-Verlag, 1986), Figure 1.2, 5.

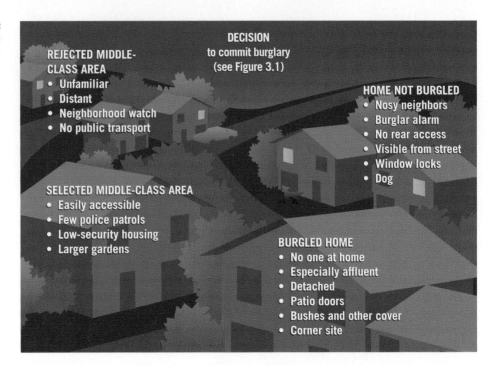

The criminal event refers to the decision to commit a specific crime. Figure 3.2 breaks down one decision-making process used to commit a specific burglary.

Empirical research into a variety of crimes, including shoplifting, burglary, robbery, and illegal drug use, has demonstrated some support for all three elements. It also demonstrates rational decision making exists in a *weak* form. Criminals don't gather *all* they need, and they usually don't use the information they've got; but they *do* consider risks and payoffs. We'll look at what motivates individuals to get into crime, how they view risks versus payoffs, and the policy implications for fighting crime.

Motivation Their analysis of a sample of 105 St. Louis residential burglars led Richard T. Wright and Scott H. Decker (1994) to conclude:

> In the overwhelming number of cases, the decision to commit a residential burglary arises in the face of what offenders perceive to be a pressing need of cash. Previous research consistently has shown this to be so and the results of the present study bear out this point. More than nine out of ten of the offenders in our sample—95 out of 105—reported that they broke into dwellings primarily when they needed money. (36)

Why did they need the money? To "solve an immediate problem." Burglary was a "matter of day-to-day survival." Here's how two burglars put it:

> Usually what I'll do is a burglary, maybe two or three if I have to, and then this will help me get over the rough spot until I can get my shit straightened out. Once I get it straightened out, I just go with the flow until I hit that rough spot where I need money again. And then I hit it.... The only time I would go and commit a burglary is if I needed it in that point in time. That would be strictly to pay light bill, gas bill, rent. (Dan Whiting in Wright and Decker 1994, 37)

> You know how to stretch a dollar? I'll stretch it from here to the parking lot. But I can only stretch it so far and then it breaks. Then I say, "Well, I guess I got to go put on my black clothes. Go on out there like a thief in the night." (Ralph Jones in Wright and Decker 1994, 37)

Another robber told Floyd Feeney (1986), during his interviews with 113 California robbers, why he committed one particular robbery:

There wasn't no food in the house, you know. Scrounging. And I'm forced into having to do something like this. I know I was desperate. Besides, I was going out stealing anything I could get a hold of, get a little money to get some food. (57)

But the motive isn't always to buy food and pay the rent. Sometimes, Wright and Decker's (1994) sample of burglars needed the money to "keep the party going." When the authors asked the burglars in their sample what they spent the money on, almost 75 percent said for "high living." As Janet Wilson, one of the burglars put it, "Long as I got some money, I'm cool. If I ain't got no money and I want to get high, then I go for it." A substantial number of burglars said they "needed" money for "keeping up appearances"—buying brand-name clothes and expensive cars (37–38).

Sometimes, they didn't know what their reason was. One robber told Floyd Feeney:

I have no idea why I did this. Well, guess it was for some money, but I didn't have no problem, really, then. You know, everybody got a little money problem, but not big enough to go and rob somebody. I just can't get off into it. I don't really know why I did it. (Feeney 1986, 57)

Table 3.1 summarizes the reasons robbers give for committing robbery.

Risk Do criminals consider the risks of getting caught? The evidence is mixed. Neal Shover and David Honaker question whether their sample of repeat property offenders in Tennessee state prison were "reasoning criminals." Most of the prisoners (62 percent) said they didn't consider the risk of being arrested; the rest said they thought about it briefly but then quickly got on with their planned burglaries. One burglar put it this way: "You think about going to prison about like you think of dying" (Shover and Honaker 1992, 281).

On the other hand, Julie Horney and Ineke Haen Marshall (1992) found their sample of more than one thousand men in Nebraska prisons for property

▼ **TABLE 3.1 Motivation for Committing Robbery**

Motivation	Percent
Money	(57)
For drugs	17
For food and shelter	8
For other specific items	16
General desire for money	16
Other than Money	(24)
Excitement	6
Anger	6
Impress friends	6
Not sure; drunk or on drugs	6
Not Really a Robber	(19)
Recover money owed	5
Interrupted burglary	4
Fight turned into a robbery	4
Partner started robbery	6

► A New York City drug dealer counts his take. Research shows that even if making huge fortunes from drug dealing is rare, dealing pays a lot more than the legitimate jobs available to most urban men with poor education and job skills. Choosing to make profits in the face of the real risks of getting killed, injured, or going to prison supports rational choice theory, but it presents major problems for law enforcement agencies.

© Alamy Images

offenses thought about getting caught. They also perceived the risk of getting caught and being punished. They'd learned through experience that "what actually happens when rules are violated is often nothing." They take this into account in their decision to commit crimes, which is what we'd expect a reasoning criminal to do according to rational choice theory (572–592).

The responses from a sample of Washington, D.C., drug dealers also support rational choice theory. Rand Corporation researchers selected a sample of persons charged with drug offenses in the District of Columbia between 1985 and 1987. They found drug dealing was profitable. Even if it didn't lead to big fortunes, it paid a lot more than the legitimate jobs available to most urban youths with poor education and job skills. The Rand researchers estimated that drug dealers made an average of $30 an hour (and free drugs if they wanted them). The risks of dealing drugs were high, too. In a year of dealing, dealers faced a 1 percent chance of getting killed, a 7 percent chance of being seriously injured, and a 22 percent chance of going to prison. They took the risks anyway (Reuter, MacCoun, and Murphy 1990, viii–xix).

Choosing to make profits in the face of the real risks of getting killed, being injured, or going to prison supports rational choice theory, but it presents major problems for law enforcement agencies. "Drug selling is an important career choice and a major economic activity for many Black males living in poverty," according to the Rand study. Improving employment prospects would probably do little to reduce drug selling, because many dealers have developed expensive drug habits. Raising legitimate wages by 50 percent, to about $10.50 an hour, is unrealistic in view of the low education and job skill level of most dealers. Besides, even $10.50 an hour falls far short of the $30 an hour they can make dealing drugs. According to researchers, society must teach young people to avoid the lure of short-term gains. The realities of frequent imprisonment and expensive drug dependency are not worth it (Reuter, MacCoun, and Murphy 1990, xiv).

Forty-two out of 60 career robbers and burglars in Kenneth Tunnell's (1990) sample couldn't see any realistic alternative to committing crimes. Approximately equal numbers of the remaining inmates said they'd already tried to live without crime, tried to borrow money, or tried to find a job and failed at all of them (45).

Rational choice doesn't apply to all crimes. By definition, individuals don't choose rationally to commit crimes of passion. Some criminals are psychotic or suffering from biological defects affecting their behavior (see "Biological Theories" later). Furthermore, rational choice plays a larger role in the decision making of experienced criminals than of amateurs.

Policy Implications Rational choice theory can lead to two contrasting policy approaches to reducing crime. One is to raise the cost of illegal behavior through more arrests, convictions, and stiffer punishments. Raising the price of crime enjoys wide public support and is the current policy of choice. So politicians are only too happy (or at least to promise) to "get tough on criminals." The second approach, to increase the gains from lawful behavior, we haven't tried often, and it enjoys little support. Why? For one thing, we'd have to make major changes—some say unwarranted invasions—into areas that aren't the government's business. For example, government could set wage controls, guarantee job security, and order more chances for advancement for car washers. This might well make washing cars attractive enough that former car thieves would rather wash cars than steal them, but that amount of government interference is out of the question in our free market economy. (See the In Focus box "Rational Choice Theory: A Sound Basis for Policy?")

▶ DECISION POINT ◀

Is the economic explanation convincing enough to support public policy?

Click on this Decision Point at http://cj.wadsworth.com/samaha_cj7e to explore the issue.

The Routine Activities Theory

The **routine activities theory,** like classical or rational choice, studies the decision to commit crimes. The focus is the influence of the "location of targets and the movement of offenders and victims in time and space" (Felson 1986) on the decision to commit a crime. Opportunity and temptation are central to routine activities theory. The theory assumes that offenders' decisions are "not calculated to maximize success, but rather to meet their needs with a minimum of effort" (Clarke and Felson 1993, 10–11).

The theory also assumes most criminals (like most people) are "middling in morality, in self-control, in careful effort, in pursuing advantage" (Clarke and Felson 1993, 11). So criminal behavior depends on the situation—specifically, on time, space (perhaps more properly, place), opportunity, and temptation. Situation explanations look at the modus operandi (MO) of offenders "not merely as interesting material for undergraduate classes, but rather as central information for professional criminologists" (11).

According to leading exponents of the theory Lawrence E. Cohen and Marcus Felson (1979):

> No matter at what level data were measured or analyzed, that approach kept returning ... to specific points in time and space ... and to changes from moment to moment and hour to hour in where people are, what they are doing, and what happens to them as a result. (3)

Let's look at the elements of routine activities theory and its policy implications for fighting crime.

Elements The theory includes three elements, all of which include rational choice:

1. A motivated offender
2. A suitable target
3. The absence of a capable guardian

A motivated offender is "anybody who for any reason might commit a crime." The routine activities theory brings time and space into the foreground and pushes into the background both the individual motivation of criminals and the agencies of criminal justice. Whether money, power, status, sex, or thrills motivate offenders to commit crimes is not the significant inquiry; any motivation will do. According to Clarke and Felson (1993), people are

routine activities theory a focus on the influence of the location of targets and movements of offenders and victims in time and space on decision making by criminals

Rational Choice Theory:
A Sound Basis for Policy?

Critics have found much to criticize about the rational choice theory. Some have challenged the free will and rationalist assumptions on which the theory rests. Respected sociologists like Michael Gottfredson and Travis Hirschi say rational choice theory treats criminal behavior like a job. But it's not, they say. The decision to commit crimes, unlike the decision to go to work, doesn't have career characteristics such as specialization; it's not a source of lasting income; its pursuit conflicts with legitimate activities; and criminals don't "respond to fluctuations in risk created by crime-control bureaucrats." Besides, data on property crime simply don't support the "view of crime derived from economic models of work." As an example, Gottfredson and Hirschi (1990) point out that data on burglars refute the rational choice theory:

> The model age for burglars is about seventeen, and the rate of burglary declines rapidly with age. The most likely "pecuniary" outcome for a burglar is no gain, and his next offense is likely to be something else than burglary. Shoplifting of something he does not need and cannot use is high on the list of probabilities, or an offense likely to terminate his legitimate and illegitimate careers—such as rape, assault, or homicide—for (again) no pecuniary gain is also highly probable. In the unlikely event that he is legitimately employed, his most likely victim will be his employer, an act difficult to reconcile with maximization of long-term utility or the equation of legitimate work with risk avoidance. Because research shows that offenders are versatile, our portrait of the burglar applies equally well to the white-collar offender, the organized-crime offender, the dope dealer, and the assaulter; they are, after all, the same people. (74)

According to criminologists Ronald V. Clarke and Marcus Felson (1993), "the economist's image of the self-maximizing decision maker, carefully calculating his or her advantage, did not fit the opportunistic, ill-considered, and even reckless nature of most crime" (5).

Others have criticized the economic model by treating self-interest as the only motive for human behavior. According to Amitai Etzioni, "Individuals are simultaneously under the influence of two major sets of factors—

their pleasure, and their moral duty" (Forst 1995, 5–6). Robert H. Frank, in *Beyond Self-Interest*, argues that we often ignore our self-interest when we

> trudge through snowstorms to cast our ballots, even when we are certain they will make no difference. We leave tips for waitresses in restaurants in distant cities we will never visit again. We make anonymous contributions to private charities. We often refrain from cheating even when we are sure we would not be caught. We sometimes walk away from profitable transactions whose terms we believe to be "unfair." We battle endless red tape to get a $10 refund on a defective product. And so on. (Quoted in Forst 1993, 5–6)

Mitchell B. Chamlin and John K. Cochran (1998) point out:

> The question remains…whether…downturns in the business cycle have much of an effect on the life-style choices of individuals. If…progressive transformations of the social, physical, and economic structure of post-World War II society have produced life-style patterns that embody a greater penchant for the consumption of consumer goods and the enjoyment of leisure activities away from the home…short-term downturns in the economy may have little effect on the day-to-day activities of individuals. Rather than abandoning behavioral patterns that have become ingrained over time, individuals may choose to maintain their life-styles but do so in a more frugal manner (e.g., eat more at fast-food restaurants and less so at more elegant establishments). (426–427)

Others have attacked the highly sophisticated equations that are an essential element in econometric models, claiming they're too mechanistic, too cold, calculated, and unemotional to reflect what most people are really like. Clarke and Felson (1993) maintain that "the formal mathematical modeling of criminal choices by economists often demanded data that was unavailable or could not be pressed into service without making unrealistic assumptions about what they represented" (5).

Still other critics say even if highly refined equations can accurately explain human behavior, they require a lot more sophisticated data than their creators have used up to this point (5).

treated virtually as objects and their motivations scrupulously avoided as a topic of discussion, in stark contrast to the heavy motivational emphasis of virtually all contemporary criminology at that time [1970s].…Thus, at the outset the approach distinguished clearly between criminal inclinations and criminal events and made that distinction a centerpiece rather than a footnote. (1–14)

A suitable target is "any person or object likely to be taken or attacked by the offender" (Clarke and Felson 1993, 2). This includes anyone or any property in the right place at the right time.

The capable guardian can be (but usually isn't) a police officer or a security guard in a position to protect a target. Clarke and Felson (1993) offer this explanation for omitting the police as capable guardians:

> This was the result of a conscious effort to distance routine activity theory from the rest of criminology, which is far too wedded to the criminal justice system as central to crime explanation.... Widespread media linkage of the police and courts to crime [is incorrect].... In fact most crime involves neither agency. Indeed, the most likely persons to prevent a crime are not policemen (who seldom are around to discover crimes in the act) but rather friends, relatives, bystanders, or the owner of the property targeted. (2–3)

Policy Implications What have we learned from routine activities theory? Crime is more likely to occur when targets are more "attractive," aren't as well guarded, and are more exposed to motivated offenders. For example, Americans have increasingly spent more time away from home since World War II. As more people have spent more time away from home (women working and single-parent families), homicide, robbery, rape, assault, and burglary rates have climbed. The number of property crimes has also increased with the number of light portable electronic gadgets (Lafree 1998, 68).

The routine activities theory has stretched criminology beyond motivation and demonstrated the importance of informal social control. But, according to the criminologist Gary Lafree (1998), routine activities theory doesn't

> offer a ready explanation for the observed timing of observed changes in crime rates.... It seems unlikely that the situational variables identified by Cohen and Felson were not also changing when crime rates were...high and constant in the 1980s and 1990s. By concentrating on the supply of suitable crime situations, situational theorists end up treating all motivated offenders as equally motivated and all capable guardians as equally capable. (68)

The Seductions of Crime Theory

In his fascinating book *Seductions of Crime* (1988), Jack Katz explores what he calls the **foreground forces** in crime, "the positive, often wonderful attractions within the lived experience of criminality." Think of these as the immediate causes of committing a particular crime. He goes beyond rational choice theory by exploring the "thrill" of committing crimes. Katz doesn't reject the **background forces,** the underlying causes (which we'll examine in the "Sociological Theories" section later in this chapter). But, Katz argues, traditional criminologists have neglected foreground forces:

foreground forces in crime the immediate causes

background forces the underlying sociological causes

> The description of "cold-blooded senseless murder" has been left to writers outside the social sciences. Neither academic methods nor academic theories seem to be able to grasp why such killers may have been courteous to their victims just moments before the killing, why they often wait until they have dominated victims in sealed-off environments before coldly executing them, or how it makes sense to kill them when only petty cash is at stake. Sociological and psychological studies of robbery rarely focus on the distinctive attractions of robbery, even though research has now clearly documented that alternative forms of criminality are available and familiar to many career robbers. In sum, only rarely have sociologists taken up the challenge of explaining the qualities of deviant experience. (3)

Katz believes studying foreground forces might explain why most people escape the criminogenic forces identified by theories of social structure, process, and control to which they're exposed. And foreground forces might also shed light on why many of those who fit the causal profiles of biological, psychoanalytic, and sociological theories "go for long stretches without committing the crime to which theory directs them." "Why," asks Katz (1988, 4), "are some people who were not determined to commit a crime one moment determined to do so the next?" Katz says it's the "seduction," the "thrill," of crime.

AP/Wide World Photos

► According to Katz's seduction of crime theory, at the moment of the crime there's a transition from the choice to commit crimes rationally to a compulsion to do so, driven by the seductive thrill of crime. The criminal controls the transition from choice to compulsion. The robber in this FBI surveillance image of a Bank of the West branch in Albuquerque, NM, threatened a teller with a needle he said was infected with AIDS, put a device he said was a bomb on the counter, and ordered the teller to put cash in a white envelope. What about this situation might he have found seductive?

The foreground approach looks at what stops people from committing or seduces them into committing crimes that their social, biological, and psychological background can't explain. According to Katz, at the moment of the crime the criminal feels seduced, drawn to, compelled to commit the crime. Seduction isn't special to criminals—everyone gets seduced into something or by someone. What *is* special is the seduction of committing a crime. Compelled doesn't mean there was no choice. At the moment of the crime, says Katz, there's a transition from the choice to commit crimes rationally to a compulsion to do so, driven by the seductive thrill of crime. The criminal controls the transition from choice to compulsion.

It was widely assumed that a criminal law and criminal justice built on hedonism and free will would reduce crime. But that didn't happen. The results of the growing practice of collecting crime statistics (Chapter 2) made clear that crime was steadily rising in countries whose penal systems followed classical theory. Rising crime rates led to the widespread *perception* that deterrence doesn't work. (Whether perception matches reality doesn't matter; as often is the case, perception trumps reality.)

The disillusionment with deterrence and advances in biology and psychology created a climate in the 1800s favorable to criminological theories based on *determinism*—the idea that forces beyond individual control determined behavior. Theories based on determinism are called *positivist theories*. The forces that determine behavior might be inside individuals (biological and psychological) or outside (sociological). Let's look at the positivist theories and their modern descendants.

Biological Theories

"Criminals are born not made," concluded the nineteenth-century Italian psychiatrist turned criminologist Cesare Lombroso. As a young doctor at an asylum in Pavia, Lombroso performed an autopsy on an Italian Jack the Ripper. In the course of his examination, he detected an abnormality in the dead man's skull. Describing his discovery, he wrote:

At the sight of that skull, I seemed to see all at once, standing out clearly illumined as in a vast plain under a flaming sky, the problem of the nature of the criminal, who reproduces in civilised times characteristics, not only of primitive savages, but of still lower types as far back as the carnivora. (Lombroso-Ferrero 1972, 6–7)

So the first positivist theory of criminal behavior was biological. Lombroso is best known for the atavistic theory that criminals are throwbacks to some primitive age of development. (I'm a breeder of Irish Wolfhounds and I see, or think I see, in them from time to time, unwelcome throwbacks, too.) Other early positivists studied faces and body types to find the causes of crime. But Lombroso made a much larger contribution than the atavistic theory suggests; he called for a general theory of crime causation. That general theory became what we know as multiple-factor causation—some factors are determined by biology, others by psychology, and still others by society (Vold et al. 2002, 27).

The early positivists gave biological theories a bad name, especially when their focus on external physical traits was dragooned into the service of racists and extreme nationalists to justify genocide and other horrors. But we've come a long way from that time. Today, much respectable research on the links between biology and crime exists. A panel made up of 19 prominent scholars and scientists of the prestigious National Research Council (the Understanding and Control of Violent Behavior Panel) collected and published an entire volume reporting on the state of our understanding of the links between biology and criminal violence and how to control violent behavior. Much of what's included in this section comes from that work (Reiss and Roth, 1993).

Let's take a brief look at some of these modern reported links between biology and crime, by examining the genetic link, biological markers of violent behavior, and the implications for criminal justice policy.

Genetics

"Like father like son" captures the ancient commonsense observation that kids resemble their parents. Now, we know empirically that genes *do* affect lots of behaviors (reasoning, academic achievement, aggression, and hostility). So it wouldn't be surprising if researchers discovered that criminal behavior had at least *some* genetic component. Identical twin studies make it easier to separate the effects of genes and environment, because twins' genes, which are produced by one egg fertilized by one sperm, are identical. Some twin studies have established that genes contribute substantially to criminal behavior (Miczek, Mirsky, Carey, DeBold, and Raine 1994, 2). But don't make too much of these results.

First, the samples are drawn exclusively from Danish twins, which makes it difficult to apply the results to other cultures. Second, the evidence for the contribution of genes to *violent* criminal behavior is a lot weaker than it is for less serious offenses. Only three samples allowed for measuring the effect of genes on violent criminal behavior, and two of those failed to show a significant effect. The Understanding and Control of Violent Behavior Panel of the prestigious National Research Council reported that "these findings suggest at most a weak role for heredity in violent behavior" (Reiss and Roth 1993). They warned us not to make too much of the connection between genes and violence because

First, evidence for the heritability of individual differences *within* a population cannot be used to explain average differences *between* populations or even within the same populations *over time*. It is unlikely that genetic differences could account for anything but a small fraction of the change in violence over the twentieth century, differences in violent crime among nations, or variance in rates among certain subgroups within a nation.

Second, heritability cannot predict or explain an individual's...[blame for] a particular violent event.

Third, many estimates of heritability are based on Scandinavian countries, where the necessary data are routinely collected in national registries. [Also, the environments in Scandinavian countries and the U.S. differ.] (Miczek, Mirsky, Carey, DeBold, and Raine 1994, 4)

CONCEPT | BUILDER
Visit http://cj.wadsworth.com/ samaha_cj7e for an interactive exploration of the **"nature versus nurture" arguments for criminal behavior.**

Biological Markers of Violent Behavior

Criminal behavior, like all behavior, results from complex processes in the brain. Sometimes, permanent conditions (genetics or brain damage) produce the behavior; sometimes temporary conditions (seizures, use of alcohol or other psychoactive substances) produce it. Let's look briefly at the influence of the conditions most modern research has focused on. As you read the following sections, keep in mind the warning in the Understanding and Control of Violent Behavior Panel (Reiss and Roth 1993) report:

> Interpreting the correlations [between the influences and violent behavior] is difficult. The interactions are complicated, precise measurement of brain activity is difficult, and violent behavior is rare.... Most of the evidence...consists of correlations rather than experimental results. Causal interpretations are therefore tenuous. Not only are hormonal, neurotransmitter, and neurophysiological processes *involved in* violent and nonviolent behavior, these functions can be changed as *consequences of* violent behavior.
>
> Given these difficulties, it should not be surprising that no patterns precise enough to be considered reliable biological markers for violent behavior have yet been identified. Researchers have, however, identified some particularly promising areas for further research that may eventually lead to nonintrusive diagnostic and prognostic indices of individuals' potentials for aggression and perhaps to interventions without unacceptable side effects. (116)

We'll examine the influence of hormones on male violence, hormones on female violence, and neurotransmitters, brain abnormalities and dysfunctions, and diet in violence.

Hormones and Male Violence Testosterone, the chief hormone that produces masculine characteristics, has been frequently studied, especially in sexual violence. High numbers of violent sex offenders have elevated levels of testosterone, but the levels are probably affected by alcohol abuse. Alcohol abuse affects testosterone levels, *and* alcohol itself is associated with violent behavior (Reiss and Roth 1993, 118). Research also points to permanent changes in aggressive behavior in adults exposed to male sex hormones during pregnancy or at birth. For example,

> girls who were accidentally exposed to male sex hormones during fetal development display an unusually high level long-term tendency toward aggression, while boys prenatally exposed to antiandrogens [substances that tend to inhibit the production, activity, or effects of a male sex hormone] show decreased aggressiveness. (118–119)

But (there's almost always an important but) it's not clear whether the hormones cause the elevated aggressiveness or it's the other way around. It may be that peer reaction to the abnormal genital development caused an increase in aggressiveness (Reiss and Roth 1993, 119).

What about using antiandrogens intentionally to reduce violent behavior? Some studies report that antiandrogens reduce the sex drive, but they don't show that it reduces violent behavior (119). Incidentally, no matter what you've heard about athletes, violence, and steroids, in studies of the effects of steroids derived from male sex hormones, "steroids exert at most a weak influence accounting for little variation in violent behavior" (119).

Hormones and Female Violence Sandie Craddock, a 29-year-old London barmaid, had a long criminal record (30 prior sentences for theft, arson, and assault). Her arrest record fit neatly into a 29-day cycle (Henig 1982). Then, she attacked and killed a barmaid she worked with. "PMS turned her into a raging animal each month and forced her to act out of character" (Easteal 1993, 2). Sentencing was delayed for three months to see if she'd respond to progesterone (the hormone that prepares the uterus for pregnancy). Craddock was placed on probation and court-ordered progesterone treatment. Later that year, after no progesterone for four days, she threw a brick through a window and reported herself to the police. She was arrested, received progesterone, and was released. The next year, she began to receive a lower dosage of progesterone. Within a few months she attempted suicide, wrote a threatening poison pen letter to a police sergeant, and waited behind the police station with a knife.

There are plenty of other stories like Sandie Craddock's. Easteal (1993; Chapter 4, "Defenses to Crime" section) reports several. But what's their significance? Is there a link between female sex hormones and violence, as it surely looks like in Sandie Craddock's case? Most of the research on hormones and crime is about men, but there's been a long history of interest in female behavior and menstruation (1). The focus of modern research is on *premenstrual syndrome* (PMS)— the link between heightened levels of female sex hormones just before the onset of menstruation and violent and aggressive behavior.

Diana Fishbein (2001), an expert on biology and crime, reports that research demonstrates that significant numbers of women prisoners committed their crimes just before menstruation (26–38). Let's be clear: Fishbein isn't denying what we all know—the vast number of women don't commit crimes just before their menstrual cycle begins. At this stage of our knowledge it's best to accept the modest conclusion that some women may express more irritability and hostility just before menstruation and that some of those expressions may have a hormonal component. But "it seems unlikely that 'raging hormones' alone account for the violence sometimes associated with the female reproductive cycle" (Brain 1994, 222).

Neurotransmitters There are 50 known *neurotransmitters*, enzymes that translate messages from the brain into action. Researchers have studied a few because they're linked to violent behavior. One of them, dopamine, activates processes for pleasure and reward. Some antipsychotic drugs that affect dopamine levels are used to "quell acute violent outbursts" and as long-term "chemical restraint for violence-prone" inmates of institutions. But these drugs do more than control violence; they also create lots of neurological problems (Reiss and Roth 1993, 119–120).

Serotonin is the most studied neurotransmitter for its effect on violent behavior. Since the late 1970s, researchers have reported negative correlations between serotonin concentrations and aggressive, impulsive, sensation-seeking behavior, alcoholism, suicide, and crime. Again, there's a but:

> More consistent replications and a better understanding of the relationship between measures in blood, spinal fluid, and relevant brain regions are needed before these factors can be accepted as biological markers for violent behavior." (Reiss and Roth 1993, 120–121)

Brain Abnormalities and Dysfunctions Several studies have reported rare violent episodes before or between seizures connected to temporal lobe epilepsy. And here's the but: Researchers haven't demonstrated whether people with seizure disorders have a greater tendency to commit violence than the general population (Reiss and Roth 1993, 122).

There's *indirect* evidence that deficits in memory, attention, and verbal skills due to brain damage are "common in children who exhibit violent or aggressive behavior. . . . This correlation *could* reflect *some* direct relationship between the limbic system [the region of the brain] damage and aggressive behavior" (122). Again, here's the but:

> It is more likely to reflect less direct results of distorted social interactions with peers resulting from impaired communication skills, or to arise from the frustration over the inability to compete successfully with peers in cognitive tasks. (123)

So many "buts" related to connecting violence to brain dysfunctions prompted this statement by the Understanding and Control of Violent Behavior Panel:

From the standpoint of designing violence control interventions, perhaps the most useful information about brain dysfunctions and violent behavior is the extent to which they arise from social-environmental conditions. Some individuals' dysfunctions may well be a result more than a cause: they may originate in head injuries inflicted by others in retaliation. (Reiss and Roth 1993, 123–124)

As for the environmental link between neurology and violence, researchers point to two culprits: (1) childhood exposure to lead (air contaminated by leaded gasoline, paint in older houses, and in old plumbing) and (2) opiate, cocaine, alcohol, and tobacco use during pregnancy (Reiss and Roth 1993). Here, the panel suggests a policy few could disagree with:

In addition to other likely benefits for children's health, interventions to reduce substance abuse by pregnant women and to reduce small children's environmental lead exposure should be considered potential long-range preventive interventions for violence. (124)

Diet "For thousands of years, people have believed that the food they eat can have a powerful effect on their behavior" (Kanarek 1994, 515). We've blamed food for our ills and praised it for its power to cure them. Many primitive peoples believe individuals take on the characteristics of the food they eat (eating a lion makes you aggressive; eating a rabbit makes you timid). Primitive peoples aren't the only ones who believe that foods can cause antisocial and violent behavior; "you are what you eat" was at the heart of the 1800s health reform movement in the United States. "Diet determined not only health and disease, but also spirituality, mental health, intelligence, and temperament...(Kanarek 1994, 516). Sylvester Graham (creator of the graham cracker) and John Harvey Kellogg (creator of dry cereal) lectured widely on their products' health benefits and on the evils of meat, blaming it for everything from headache to aggression. Eating rich, spicy foods, Kellogg warned, was a recipe for moral degeneration and violent behavior (517).

Since the early 1980s, interest in the connection between diet and behavior has exploded. Consumers' obsession with health and fitness has created a huge market for silly, maybe downright harmful but easy and simple, roads to healthy, happy, peaceful lives. Scientific correlations between diet and behavior have been spun to mean cause-and-effect relations. In the specific context of this section (the link between diet and violent behavior), the need for reliable, careful research is especially strong. Why? Because the research results might be the basis for criminal justice policy affecting public resources and individual privacy, liberty, and dignity.

Food may be the most difficult biological factor to separate from nonbiological factors, because it's so intimately connected with our "social functions, religious observations, and cultural rituals" (Kanarek 1994, 517). But that hasn't stopped researchers from trying to establish links between diet and violent behavior.

Of all the things we eat, none has been condemned more than sugar. Sugar is named the culprit in all kinds of negative behavior (hyperactivity, depression, mental confusion, alcohol and other drug addiction, and antisocial behavior). Most notoriously, it was even blamed for a murder. The case became a brief national obsession when in 1978, in San Francisco, City Supervisor Dan White shot and killed the mayor and another supervisor. White's lawyers blamed his irrational actions on the high-sugar content in the junk food their client ate so much of. Although it was never part of the defense in court, it came to be called the "Twinkie defense."

One explanation for the link between sugar and violence is hypoglycemia (low levels of the simple sugar glucose in the blood). A series of studies (Schoenthaler 1982, 1983a–c, 1985) investigated the effects of reducing the sugar intake of inmates in several juvenile detention facilities. The institution modified its food policy to reduce sugar consumption, substituting:

1. Honey for table sugar
2. Molasses for white sugar in cooking
3. Fruit juice for Kool-Aid®
4. Unsweetened for presweetened cereal
5. Fresh fruit, peanuts, coconut, popcorn, or cheese for high-sugar desserts

The dependent variable in the studies was the number of disciplinary actions recorded by the staff before and during the change in policy. Schoenthaler claimed that reducing sugar intake could reduce juvenile offender misbehavior by as much as 54 percent. What's wrong with this claim? Several things according to Kanarek (1994, 525–526):

1. *Independent variable.* Schoenthaler identifies it as sugar intake. Unfortunately, the dietary changes were a doubtful way of reducing sugar intake. Many of the changes just replaced one sugar for another. Also, sugar intake wasn't measured. So, it's impossible to determine whether the change in policy actually reduced sugar intake. Even if sugar intake was reduced, diets during the two periods were different enough to make it difficult to attribute the reduced number of discipline reports to sugar intake.
2. *Behavioral techniques.* None of the studies used *double-blind procedures* (neither the participant nor the administrator know the hypothesis of the study). In Schoenthaler's studies, both the inmates and the institution officials knew about the dietary changes. Knowing the changes and knowing they were participants could have influenced them to change their behavior. As for the officials, knowledge of the changes could have influenced their observations.
3. *Dependent variable.* Official records of disciplinary actions were used to measure changes in violent behavior. In most institutions, the staff has discretion to record (or not to record) incidents. Also, in some of the studies, dietary changes were made during the last stages of inmates' stay.

After pointing out these (and other) problems with the studies, Kanarek (1994) concluded:

Taken together, the studies by Shoenthaler provide little convincing evidence for the claim that sugar intake contributes to antisocial behavior. . . . They leave open the question of whether nonspecific factors were responsible for the changes attributed to diet. (526)

Criminal Justice Policy Implications

It's clear from this section that when it comes to biological theories of crime, we've come a long way from the early positivists. But it's just as clear that we've got a long way to go before we can say the theories are supported by enough (or even any) empirical research to build policies around them. As the reports of the empirical research we've reviewed here advise, the only policy we can advocate is to advance what we know.

Advancing our knowledge is going to be difficult for several reasons (Reiss and Roth 1993, 127–128). One problem in accumulating more understanding is that less-intrusive and broadly accepted research methods produce information that's removed from the cause. For example, analyzing urine and hair samples intrude the least on subjects' privacy and dignity but also their results are the least useful. Why? Because they blend together relevant neurological processes with unrelated events that happened long before or after a violent event. For another example, painful and risky spinal taps can measure ongoing brain activity better, but they're not related to the start or finish of violent acts.

Then, there's the ethical problem. According to Reiss and Roth (1993):

The critical ethical dilemma of experimental research on aggression and violent behavior is the trade-off between experimental preparations with high realism and face validity versus the demand for protection of research subjects against stress and pain. It is unacceptable for experimental biomedical research with humans to achieve high face validity in studies of violent behavior. Therefore, it is necessary to develop and implement animal models, often as a means of building an empirical basis for subsequent research that places acceptable but nonnegligible burdens on human subjects. Each study of animal or human subjects needs to be designed to inflict the least possible stress and harm on the subjects without invalidating the information to be obtained. (128)

Finally, researchers have to contend with suspicion. According to Reiss and Roth:

> For many people, attention to genetic [and other biological]... processes that underlie violent behavior raises concerns about the potential for ethically unacceptable future preventive interventions. The specters of eugenics, preemptive incarceration based on individuals' biomedical profiles, and maintaining classroom discipline with drugs that dull children's creativity are all occasionally raised. Actually..., better biomedical understanding of violence has added violence prevention to the list of justifications for rather benign interventions with families, such as teaching pregnant women to avoid drug use and new mothers to protect their children from head injuries, and interventions in communities, such as reducing children's exposure to lead. (127)

With all the qualifications we've reviewed, the Understanding and Control of Violent Behavior Panel still concluded on an upbeat note. It called for adding biological and genetic factors to social factors in the search for causes of violence. The report fully endorses a multidisciplinary, multicause approach with contributions from sociology, psychology, psychiatry, law, genetics, and biology. In the words of the panel's report:

> Research strongly suggests that violence arises from interactions among individuals' psychosocial development, their neurological and hormonal differences, and social processes. Consequently, we have no basis for considering any of these "levels of explanation" any more fundamental than the others. (Reiss and Roth 1993, 102)

Mark Moore (Butterfield 1992, A12), professor of criminal justice policy at Harvard University, remains pessimistic. Moore offered this bleak assessment of the link between violence and biology: "You come to the important point of view that the causes of violence are complex and therefore elusive. The hope that we might be able to base policy on definite knowledge of the causes of violence is receding."

The report (like all biological theories of crime) also faced criticism that it reflects racism. Just a month before the council announced its report, the federal government, under pressure from protesters, withdrew financial support for a conference on the possible genetic causes of crime (Butterfield 1992).

Psychological Theories

Psychological theories focus on the mental and emotional elements in criminal behavior. There are several kinds of these elements, but most theories and research concentrate on two:

1. Intelligence (measured mostly by low IQ)
2. Personality (antisocial and impulsive behavior)

We'll examine each of these elements.

Low Intelligence

The early positivist criminologists believed that low intelligence was one of the causes of crime. In the early 1900s, they used the then new IQ (intelligence quotient, which was obtained by dividing mental age by chronological age) to identify feebleminded inmates—those with IQs below the mental age of 12. The wave of IQ testing that swept through U.S. prisons seemed to back up their belief. H. H. Goddard (1914) surveyed the results of a large number of studies of feeblemindedness based on prisoners' IQs. He confidently concluded that most prisoners were feebleminded, but that confidence was short lived. During World War I, the U.S. Army tested draftees' intelligence. After the war, when some criminologists compared the results of prisoners' and soldiers' IQs, they found insignificant differences between prisoners and soldiers. Several reported that prisoners scored *higher* (Vold et al. 2002, 61).

After the soldier-prisoner comparison studies, low intelligence disappeared as an explanation for criminal behavior—until 1977. That's when the distinguished scholars Travis Hirschi and Michael Hindelang (1977) reported that their review of research showed the link between IQ and delinquency was at least as strong as race or social class. They conceded, however, the link was *indirect*. Kids with low IQs fail in school, and academic failure is linked to future delinquency and adult criminality. But that didn't make the link any less real.

Hirschi and Hindelang brought back IQ as a psychological explanation of crime. A number of studies in the United States and other countries found similar results. But none was more strong, confident, or controversial than Richard Herrnstein and Charles Murray's *The Bell Curve* (1994). Herrnstein and Murray, after extensively reviewing the IQ-crime research, found that offenders have an average IQ of 92 (8 points below average). Other studies showed that serious offenders' scores are lower than minor offenders, and that low IQ scores in small children are linked to later delinquency and adult offending (Blumstein, Farrington, and Moitra 1985).

Not surprisingly, Hirschi and Hindelang's study, backed up by other research both in the United States and other countries, didn't settle the question. We won't list here the studies supporting and challenging the link between intelligence and crime, but Vold and his colleagues' (2002) conclusion is most likely closest to the mark:

> At present, it seems best to conclude that low intelligence has no direct causal impact on crime and delinquency. The differences in IQ scores between delinquents and nondelinquents probably result from environmental rather than genetic factors. In particular, these differences probably reflect the underachievements of delinquents in schools rather than any genetic inferiority. In addition, if there is any causal link at all between low intelligence and crime, it is probably mediated by some other factor, such as school failure. To the extent that this is the case, then policies to reduce crime and delinquency should deal with the actual cause (e.g., school failure) rather than with the low intelligence. (82)

Personality

What's the first thing that comes to your mind when you think of personality? (Don't include intelligence.) Probably words like *aggressive, argumentative, timid, withdrawn, friendly, likeable,* and others that describe behavioral and emotional traits that hold true most of the time. Sheldon and Eleanor Glueck (1930) compared 500 delinquent and nondelinquent Boston boys during the 1940s and 1950s. They concluded that the "delinquent personality" doesn't depend so much on a list of characteristics as it does on the *relationship* among characteristics:

> Delinquents are more extroverted, vivacious, impulsive and less self-controlled than the non-delinquents. They are more hostile, resentful, defiant, suspicious, and destructive. They are less fearful of failure or defeat than non-delinquents. They are less concerned about meeting conventional expectations, and are more ambivalent toward or far less submissive to authority. They are, as a group, more socially assertive. To a greater extent than the control group, they express feelings of not being recognized or appreciated. (275)

Researchers have built and administered elaborate tools aimed at sorting out the differences in delinquent and criminal personalities from nondelinquent and noncriminal personalities. Although there are many claims that they do a good sorting job, many methodological problems raise questions about their accuracy. Too often, it's not possible to sort out whether the differences are because of environment or personality. So they're not very useful in proving (or disproving) a link between personality and crime.

Sociological Theories

Criminologists are wary of explanations of criminal behavior based on the individual's biology, psychology, and free will. They look for the links between criminal behavior and the structure and processes of society; in social institutions like neighborhoods, family, churches, and schools; in demographics like social status, race, gender, age, and education; and in community values. Let's look at some of these explanations, including social structure theories, social process theories, and developmental, or age and desistance, theories.

Social Structure Theories

social structure theories explain the link between individual criminal behavior, social class, and structural conditions like poverty, unemployment, and poor education

Social structure theories link individual criminal behavior to social class and structural conditions like poverty, unemployment, and poor education. According to social structure theorists, crime is located mainly in lower-income classes because flaws in the social structure increase the odds individuals in that part of society will commit crimes. The nineteenth-century sociologist Emile Durkheim (1951) explained crime as the result of the breakdown of social norms—the **anomie theory.** Durkheim formulated the anomie theory after France had gone through several political revolutions and was in the midst of changing from an agricultural to an industrial society. A society in transition, Durkheim said, weakens the bonds that ordinarily control our natural (but not always desirable) urges; crime follows that weakening. Two forms of the theory, strain and opportunity theories, were developed to describe conditions specific to the United States.

anomie theory crime results from the breakdown of social norms

The Strain Theory In 1938, during the Great Depression, sociologist Robert K. Merton (1968, 185–214) formulated a U.S. version of anomie that came to be called the **strain theory.** According to Merton's theory, society establishes goals we all try to achieve—the goals "worth striving for" (187). In U.S. culture, the most important goal is getting rich; it's not enough just to get rich, the goal is to get as rich as possible. Although society establishes the goals, for some people, social structure blocks achieving them. This blockage creates a strain that leads more people in the lower than in the upper classes to commit crimes.

strain theory American culture defines goals, which the social structure blocks many members of the lower classes from achieving

Second, Merton argued that cultures don't just define the goals; they also define the means to get them. In American culture, the only approved means to get as rich as possible are hard work, honesty, education, and delayed gratification (the work ethic). Criminal means are strictly forbidden, even though they're quicker and more effective. Because not everyone can get as rich as possible (or even rich), the culture tries to keep control by emphasizing, "It's not whether you win, it's how you play the game that counts." But sometimes, the goal becomes more important than the approved means of achieving it: "It's not how you play the game that counts, it's whether you win that counts." And that's what Merton saw in American culture. Getting rich is so important that the means (hard work, honesty, education, and delayed gratification) aren't enough reward. Strain follows.

Strain falls especially hard on the lower classes. Here, it's not just individual worth but the social structure itself that stands in the way of success. In the upper classes, it takes only moderate talent and effort to achieve success by the work ethic. The contradiction between the culture and the social structure is the essence of Merton's strain theory. So the reason for higher crime rates in the lower classes isn't cultural (everyone wants to get rich and everyone has similarly weak ties to the work ethic). The reason lies in the social structure; the lower classes don't have their fair share of opportunities to get rich by hard work.

Several versions of the strain theory exist. We'll look at individual strain, the general strain theory, gender and strain theories, the strain theory and crime in organizations, and the strain theory and crime rates.

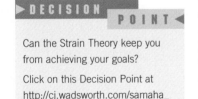

▶DECISION POINT◀

Can the Strain Theory keep you from achieving your goals?

Click on this Decision Point at http://cj.wadsworth.com/samaha_cj7e to explore the issue.

Social and Individual Strain Merton didn't say so, but later theorists have pointed out that *strain* has two completely different meanings. The first is *social strain*, blocks in the social structure to providing legitimate means to achieve culturally promoted goals. The second is *individual strain*, the feelings (stress, frustration, anger, depression) individuals experience because of the blocks in the social structure. The argument goes like this: Individuals who experience a structural strain, blocked from the legitimate opportunity to succeed, may *feel* strained. These feelings prompt them to commit crime at higher rates than those who don't feel strained.

General Strain Theory Robert Agnew (1992), who specializes in juvenile delinquency, has proposed a general strain theory at the individual level. It focuses on negative relationships that cause individuals strain. Negative relationships include those in which someone:

1. Prevents you from achieving a goal you value
2. Takes something you value that you already have
3. Imposes on you something you dislike or don't want

Previous strain theory looked only at relationships that prevented someone from achieving monetary success. The general strain theory broadens the theory to include a "golden rule" to prevent "relationships in which others do not treat an individual as he or she would like to be treated." The strain of these negative relationships can lead to delinquency and crime.

Gender and Strain Theories Agnew and Broidy (1997) found several gender differences in the general strain theory:

1. Females experience as much or more strain than males.
2. Males and females experience different types of strain. (Table 3.2).
3. There are gender differences in the responses to strain. (Table 3.3).

▼ **TABLE 3.2 Gender Differences in the Types of Strain Experienced**

Females	Males
Concerned with creating and maintaining close bonds and relationships with others—thus they commit lower rates of property and violent crimes	Concerned with material success—thus they commit higher rates of property and violent crimes
Face negative treatment, such as discrimination, high demands from family, and restricted behavior	Face more conflict with peers and are likely to be the victims of crime
Failure to achieve goals may lead them to commit self-destructive behavior	Failure to achieve goals may lead them to commit property and violent crimes

Source: Robert Agnew and Lisa Broidy, "Gender and Crime: A General Strain Theory Perspective," *Journal of Research in Crime and Delinquency* 34(3) (1997):275–306.

▼ **TABLE 3.3 Gender Differences in Emotional Response to Strain**

Female	Male
More likely to respond with depression and anger	More likely to respond with anger
Anger is accompanied by fear, guilt, and shame	Anger is followed by moral outrage
More likely to blame themselves and worry about the effects of their anger	Quick to blame others and are less concerned about hurting others
Depression and guilt may lead them to commit self-destructive behaviors (i.e., eating disorders)	Moral outrage may lead them to commit property and violent crimes

Source: Robert Agnew and Lisa Broidy, "Gender and Crime: A General Strain Theory Perspective," *Journal of Research in Crime and Delinquency* 34(3)(1997): 281–283.

Not all research finds gender differences in strain. For example, Hoffmann and Su (1997) found no significant gender differences. Agnew and Broidy admit "there are many gaps in the data that must be filled."

Strain Theory and Crime in Organizations Some theorists have extended the strain theory to help explain crime in organizations. Feeling deprived when others around them are doing better causes strain for less successful members of the organization. They may be doing exceptionally well by the standards of people below them, but they don't look down; instead, they yearn for the salary, power, and prestige of those above them. This anomie of affluence leads some people to put rules aside to reduce their deprivation (lack of success) (Lafree 1998, 57; Simon and Gagnon 1976, 356–378; Thio 1975, 135–158).

Strain Theory and Crime Rates Does strain affect crime rates? The strain theory doesn't fit the crime trends of the last 50 years. The theory treats strain caused by trying to get ahead and roadblocks to it like a permanent characteristic, but crime trends have been anything but constant. Our biggest crime boom (the 1960s) took place when there were both more opportunities to get ahead and fewer roadblocks to getting there (Lafree 1998, 64–65).

Strain and Illegitimate Opportunity Theory Merton emphasized the lack of opportunity by the lower class to pursue legitimate means to success; Cloward and Ohlin (1960) pointed out the abundance of illegitimate opportunities open to them. According to Cloward and Ohlin's illegitimate opportunity theory, when you can't get money, power, and prestige legally, you break the law to get them. In Clifford Shaw's (1966) classic book, *The Jack-Roller,* the delinquent youth Stanley describes a community with criminal opportunities:

> Stealing in the neighborhood was a common practice among the children and approved by the parents. Whenever the boys got together they talked about robbing and made more plans for stealing. I hardly knew any boys who did not go robbing. The little fellows went in for petty stealing, breaking into freight cars, and stealing junk. The older guys did big jobs like stick-up, burglary, and stealing autos. The little fellows admired the "big shots" and longed for the day when they could get into the big racket. (54)

Social Process Theories

Social structure theory doesn't pretend to explain all criminal behavior. After all, crime occurs in all social classes, and most people in the lower classes don't commit crimes. **Social process theories** look for explanations of crime in social processes (interactions among members) of families, peer groups, schools, churches, neighborhoods, and other social institutions. There's a lot of empirical research linking experiences with these institutions to criminal behavior. For example, most prison inmates come from single-parent homes, have relatives and friends who have served time in prison, are school dropouts or underachievers, and have poor work skills and employment records (Chapter 12).

Social process theorists agree that criminogenic forces in society affect behavior, but they disagree over *how.* **Social learning theories** assume individuals are born like blank slates and can learn any values and behavior. **Social control theory** assumes everybody is born with the desire to break the rules. **Labeling theory** assumes the criminal justice system creates criminals. Whether individuals have actually broken the law doesn't matter. Society's actions shape the self-image and behavior of people who have been labeled criminals.

Social Learning Theories When I was a boy, a neighbor told her son to stay away from that Joel Samaha because I'd "put bad bugs in his head." The commonsense notion that people learn criminal behavior from others underlies so-

social process theories explanations of crime based on the interactions among members of families, peer groups, schools, churches, neighborhoods, and other social institutions

social learning theory individuals learn behavior from others

social control theory individuals are rule breakers by nature

labeling theory criminal behavior is learned by being labeled a criminal by the criminal justice system

cial learning theory. This notion depends on the assumption that we're blank slates at birth and our parents, friends, teachers, religious leaders, and government write the attitudes, beliefs, and values on our behavioral slates.

The criminologist Edwin Sutherland formulated the most prominent social learning theory: differential association theory. According to Sutherland, criminal behavior, just like any other behavior, depends on our associations with other people. If we associate more with lawbreakers than law-abiders, chances are we'll commit crimes. Some associations are stronger than others. The more intense the relationships, the more we learn from them and the longer we retain what we've learned. So our families and our friendships teach us the most enduring lessons about how to behave. People in low-income neighborhoods who associate with "street criminals" learn to act like street criminals, not because people who live in poor neighborhoods are "bad" but because that's the way social beings behave. By the same reasoning, corporate criminals learn criminal behavior, too (Sutherland and Cressey 1978, 83–87).

▶ D E C I S I O N
P O I N T ◀

Do abused children become adult violent criminals?

Click on this Decision Point at http://cj.wadsworth.com/samaha_cj7e to explore the issue.

The Social Control Theory Social control theory assumes that people are rule breakers by nature. As Travis Hirschi (1969), the leading proponent of social control theory, put it: "The question 'Why did they do it?' is simply not the question the theory is designed to answer. The question is, 'Why don't we do it?' There is much evidence that we would, if we dared" (34). Why do we obey rules when we're rule breakers by nature? Because our ties to established institutions of social control (families, peer groups, churches, and schools) check our natural desire to break rules and satisfy our selfish interests. When ties to these institutions weaken, criminal behavior is likely to follow. Social bonds don't reduce our desire to get what we want; they reduce the chance we'll give in to our desire (Cullen 1983, 134–142).

Hirschi identified four elements in the social bond that curb the natural desire to break rules (Table 3.4). First, attachment to others makes us sensitive to their opinions. Attachment to those whose opinions we care about (parents, teachers, coaches, neighbors, and friends) predicts best whether we'll follow rules. Second, commitment to the conventional order keeps us in line. The stronger our desire to get a job, get an education, and protect our reputation, the greater the chances we'll follow the rules. Third, involvement in legal activities leaves us less time to get into trouble; "idle hands are the devil's workshop." Fourth, the stronger we believe in the conventional order, the less likely we are to break its rules. Hirschi reports the results of testing his theory in *Causes of Delinquency* (1969). Police reports, self-reports, and schools for more than three thousand boys in a California youth project backed up Hirschi's theory. Further empirical studies have yielded similar results.

Control theory is an appealing explanation for crime trends since 1950, a period that saw ties to traditional institutions weakened. Empirical evidence strongly supports the argument that juveniles and young adults with strong ties to their families and schools are less likely to commit crimes. Of course, this doesn't explain what caused the weakening of ties in the first place and why ties were stronger in the 1950s than they were in the 1990s (Lafree 1998, 66–67).

Control theory also explains organizational crime. When applied to organizations, the theory goes like this: Organizations don't provide controls on deviance. Rules don't apply, especially at the top. The ends justify the means. According to control theory, the rules are seen as obstacles to a greater goal. So organizational criminals are freed from the bonds that would keep them in line (Stotland 1977, 179–196).

The Labeling Theory In his classic book *Outsiders,* Howard Becker (1973) developed the influential labeling theory. According to Becker, individuals don't commit crimes because they can't manage the stresses in society, associate with

▼ **TABLE 3.4 Four Ways to Curb the Natural Desire to Break Rules**

1. Attachment to others
2. Commitment to the conventional order
3. Involvement in legal activities
4. Belief in the conventional order

other criminals and learn crime from them, or break the social bonds that would keep in line their urges to break rules. Instead, outsiders—"moral entrepreneurs" like police, courts, and corrections officers trying to control crime—turn deviant episodes by individuals into criminal careers. In other words, the criminal justice system creates criminals. Whether "criminals" have actually broken the law doesn't matter. What does matter is once the "system" says they're criminals, they act like criminals. Society's actions shape their self-image.

Labeling theory shifts the emphasis from lawbreakers to lawmakers and law enforcers. This shift draws attention to the possible harmful effects of contacts with criminal justice agencies. The theory had a direct influence on public policy during the 1960s and 1970s in the creation of programs that diverted people out of the criminal justice system into alternative social programs (Cullen 1983, 125–128).

Developmental Theories

Before you learn about theories explaining the relationship between age and crime, you should be aware of three clear research findings (Laub and Sampson 2001, 16):

1. There's a link between juvenile delinquency and adult criminal behavior.
2. Most adult criminals have no juvenile delinquency record.
3. Most juvenile delinquents don't commit crimes as adults.
4. Almost all adult criminals sooner or later (mostly sooner) stop committing crimes.

Most of the theories you've learned about in this chapter assume that the variables in the theories have the same effect no matter what the offender's age. Developmental criminology focuses on changes in criminal behavior over time (Laub and Sampson 2003, 285). Specifically, it focuses on the criminal careers (the beginning, continuation, and end of criminal behavior). But theorists diverge into two groups when it comes to the *nature* of the change. Let's call them the early childhood theories and the life-course theories. We'll look at each as well as at desistance theories.

Early Childhood Theories Early childhood theories follow Shakespeare's insight that "the child is father to the man." Laub and Sampson (2003) sum up this perspective this way:

> The environment offers a "set of enabling conditions" that allow individual traits to express themselves. Although reciprocal interactions with the environment are allowed, life-course persistent offenders and adolescent-limited offenders follow a pre-programmed line of development—an unwinding, an unfolding, or an unrolling of what is fundamentally "already there." (285–286)

Biologist Richard Lewontin (2000) writes:

> If the development of an individual is an unfolding of a genetic program immanent in the fertilized egg, then variations in the outcome of development must be consequences of variations of that program. (17)

The heart of the early childhood perspective are early childhood (usually by the age of 8) traits that remain *stable* throughout life. According to Gottfredsen and Hirschi (1990, Chapter 10), criminal propensity (the proneness to commit crime because of low self-control) doesn't change over an individual's life. Of course, some individuals are more prone and some are less prone to commit crimes. And yes, propensity may show itself in a variety of behaviors, but this is because of chance or circumstance, not because of changes in propensity. So there's no need to get into the difficult (and very expensive and time-consuming) business of following individuals through their lives to map out their criminal

◄ Life-course theorists suggest that there are turning points that cause criminals to desist from a life of crime. Roddrick Marshall grew up in a neighborhood where crime was considered a respectable means of earning money. Incarcerated five times before the age of 18, he was allowed to attend a rehabilitative boot camp program instead of a three-year prison sentence. This militaristic lifestyle motivated him to improve his life once out of prison. He has since married and had a family (pictured here) and become a well-respected citizen of Savannah, GA, by volunteering in numerous organizations from his children's school boards to rape crisis centers to reentry aftercare programs.

careers. All we need to do is account for differences in propensity among (not within) individuals.

The Life-Course Theory Sociologists and prominent life-course theorists John H. Laub and Robert J. Sampson (2003) see the course of development very differently. Their **life-course theory** focuses on stability *and* changes in behavior throughout the life course.

> In our [life-course] theory of crime, development is better conceived as the constant interaction between individuals and their environment, coupled with the factor of chance or "random developmental noise." Recognizing developmental noise implies that the "organism is determined neither by its genes nor by its environment nor even between the interaction between them, but bears a significant mark of random processes." (286)

To test their theory, Laub and Sampson turned to a database of 500 delinquent and 500 nondelinquent boys born in lower-class Boston neighborhoods during the Great Depression in the 1930s. Sampson and Laub analyzed the data and followed the boys' lives up to 1997. (They were able to do this by reanalyzing the database and then following up on the 1,000 boys to 1997, when they were around 70 years old). Here's what they found:

> [W]e uncovered enormous heterogeneity in criminal offending over the life course. Some offenders start early and stop; others start early and continue for long periods of time.... Most important, long-term patterns of offending cannot be explained by individual differences (for example, low verbal IQ), childhood characteristics (for example, early childhood misbehavior), or adolescent characteristics (for example, chronic juvenile offending). In our conception of development ... the sum of the parts includes individual differences, environmental differences, social interactions, and random chance events. (286)

Desistance Theories and the Life Course Most of the theories you've learned about in this chapter try to explain why individuals *start* and *persist* in committing

life-course theory focuses on stability *and* changes in behavior throughout life

Source for quotations on pages 93 through 95: Reprinted by permission of the publisher from *Shared Beginnings, Divergent Lives: Delinquent Boys to Age 70* by John H. Laub and Robert J. Sampson, pp. 138, 139, 145, 285, 286, Cambridge, Mass.: Harvard University Press, Copyright © 2003 by the President and Fellows of Harvard College.

crimes. Developmental criminology does this too but it goes further and tries to explain desistance from crime. It asks the question, "Why do people *stop* committing crimes?" According to Gottfredsen and Hirschi (1990), the answer is biological; it's "due to the inexorable ageing of the organism" (141). Gove (1985) says physical strength, energy, psychological drive, and the need for stimulation closely track the rise and decline in criminal behavior. In other words, the answer is a combination of biology and psychology (136). Moffitt (1994) says the type of individual involved is the determining factor. Life-course persisters, who because of a variety of biological and psychological deficits, begin offending early in life and persist well into adult life. Adolescent-limited offenders engage in antisocial behavior only during adolescence.

Laub and Sampson (2003) offer an answer from the life-course perspective. When they asked the men in their study who were approaching 70 what were the "turning points" that led them to stop committing crimes, they came up with several, but the three most important were:

1. Marriage
2. Employment
3. Military service

Let's look at these three factors as well as at the influence of race and gender on desistance.

Marriage

> If I hadn't met my wife at the time I did, I'd probably be dead. It just changed my whole life...that's my turning point right there. (Laub and Sampson 2003, 134)

Why is marriage a turning point away from criminal behavior? Here are some of the explanations that came out of interviewing the men in Laub and Sampson's study.

First, marriage creates a deep attachment that promotes social bonds. These bonds are like an investment. As the investment grows, the incentive to avoid crime gets stronger because there's so much (social capital) at stake (Nagin and Paternoster 1994, 586–588). Second, marriage changes routine activities (see "Routine Activities Theory" earlier). Marriage lessens the time spent with friends, so individuals are cut off from delinquent friends. Marriage often means moving to a different neighborhood, or even a different town. Having children changes activities, too. Third, marriage can change the sense of who we are. For some, getting married means getting serious ("growing up").

Military Service

> The military cured me. It took a young hoodlum off the street. My neighborhood in East Boston was a jumping off place for jail (Laub and Sampson 2003, 49–50)

> I'd say the turning point was, number one, the Army. You get into an outfit, you had a sense of belonging, you made your friends. (132)

> I thought a turning point was joining the Navy. Oh, sure, everybody squawked about the food. I'm laughing...because I had nothing. Where the hell can you have roast beef on Monday for supper and then have roast pork. If we had roast beef [in Boston], we had it once a month....So, I appreciated it. I only had a couple of bad meals....(132)

So, according to Laub and Sampson's assessment of their data, military service (at least for juvenile delinquents from Boston's poor neighborhoods who served in World War II) was a turning point away from criminal behavior. They got the chance to learn technical and interpersonal skills in a new environment (134).

Work

> I had a paycheck coming in every week without fail. I always knew it was going to be there, even if I got sick. So that makes you stable and takes a lot of worry out of your life. (138)

> [My boss was] like a strict father. He went after me a few times. He also took me under his wing. We would have a few drinks together. (138–139)

> Being able to work, being able to get a paycheck. Being able to spend the money and not have to steal it. Being able to go to the store and buy something and not have to steal it. That's important in life...what changed my life is work. (139)

As the first quote shows, for these three former Boston delinquents, work was a means to an end—a way to pay bills and buy things they needed and wanted—but work also was a means of social control, as the second quote shows. Finally, for a few men, like the one in the third quote, work was how they defined themselves.

Laub and Sampson sum up what they learned from their study of the Boston men:

> Overall it appears that successful cessation from crime occurs when the proximate causes of crime are affected. A central element in the desistance process is the "knifing off" of individual offenders from their immediate environment and offering them a new script for the future. (145)

Race, Gender, and Desistance A very few studies examine race and gender differences in desistance. One of the few, Elliott (1994), found race differences over time. Whites desist earlier than Blacks. Elliott speculated the difference was because of where offenders lived and worked.

As for gender, Uggen and Kruttschnitt (1998) used arrest and self-report data to study the differences between desistance in men and women. They concluded that "women are more likely to make the transition out of crime and remain crime free for longer periods of time than similarly situated men" (361). They didn't have enough information to explain the gender difference, but they speculated that part of the reason is women "engag[e] in socially responsible activities (such as work and schooling)" (362).

▶ DECISION POINT ◀

Are criminals made or born?

Click on this Decision Point at http://cj.wadsworth.com/samaha_cj7e to explore the issue.

Criminal Law Theories

All the theories you've learned about up to now have focused on offenders and why and to what extent they choose to commit crimes; what biological, psychological, or social factors determine their criminal behavior; and how their criminal behavior changes over the course of their lives. Now, we'll shift our attention from the behavior of law *breakers* to the actions of law *makers* and law *enforcers*. You'll learn about the two major perspectives that lie behind all theories that explain how legislatures come to define behavior as criminal and how the criminal justice system responds to that behavior.

Throughout history, two contrasting views of the nature of society have prevailed in social theory. According to the consensus perspective, consensus is the normal state of society. The consensus of values and the need to uphold them are the glues that hold society together. That doesn't mean there's *total* agreement. One reason we have government is to mediate among groups with competing values. In the mediation, the state is the honest broker representing the values of the whole society, not those of any particular group(s).

According to the conflict perspective, conflict is the normal state of society. Conflict over interests (groups' wants and needs) and the efforts to satisfy them is how society operates. Conflict is rarely violent; revolution and civil war are hardly ever the means of choice to resolve conflict. Debate (sometimes very heated and emotional debate) and nonviolent pressure are the means most often used. The group(s) with the most power and resources win(s) the battles. Government is not an honest broker in the conflict over interests; it represents the interests of the most powerful group(s) (Bernard 1983; Chambliss 1975; Dahrendorf 1958; Hay 1980).

Criminal law theories include consensus theory, conflict theory, and radical theory. We'll look more closely at each.

The Consensus Theory

Consensus theory has an ancient heritage; it's at least as old as the teachings of Plato and Aristotle. But its modern version is most indebted to Émile Durkheim, the great nineteenth-century French sociologist whose ideas have greatly influenced the sociology of law and also contributed to criminal justice theory. Durkheim (1933) stated two propositions relevant to understanding the sociology of criminal law:

1. Crime is conduct "universally disapproved of by members of each society. Crimes shock sentiments which, for a given social system, are found in all healthy consciences."
2. "An act is criminal when it offends strong and defined states of the collective conscience."

Durkheim formulated two hypotheses of consensus theory based on the following two propositions:

1. *The **consensus hypothesis***. Criminal law is a synthesis of a society's essential morality, based on values that are shared by all "healthy consciences."
2. *The **boundary hypothesis**.* Society creates crime to establish moral boundaries that, if violated, threaten society's basic existence. In other words, defining *behavior* as "criminal" notifies ordinary people how far they can go without undoing social order. (Chambliss and Seidman 1982, 171–206)

consensus hypothesis criminal law is a synthesis of a society's essential morality, based on values that are shared by all "healthy consciences"

boundary hypothesis defining a behavior as "criminal" notifies ordinary people how far they can go without undoing the social order

▶ Empirical evidence supports the consensus hypothesis, indicating that people across ethnic, gender, and economic lines generally agree on what crimes are the most serious. While many people would consider drug control an important goal of law enforcement, the issues surrounding medical marijuana make it difficult to categorize. A jury had convicted San Franciscan Ed Rosenthal (center) of marijuana cultivation and other drug charges in federal court, but almost immediately questioned its verdict. Under tough federal drug laws, Rosenthal could have received up to 100 years in prison and been fined $4.5 million; instead the U.S. District judge sentenced Rosenthal to one day in prison and fined him $1,000.

AP/Wide World Photos

▼ **TABLE 3.5 Consensus on the Most Serious Crimes**

Severity Score	Offense—10 Most Serious
72.1	Planting a bomb in a public building (the bomb kills 20 people)
52.8	Forcibly raping a woman, who dies from the injuries
43.2	Robbing a victim at gunpoint, who dies after being shot while struggling with the robber
39.2	A husband stabbing a wife to death
35.7	Stabbing a victim to death
35.6	Intentionally injuring a victim, who dies as a result
33.8	Running a drug ring
27.9	A wife stabbing her husband to death
26.3	Skyjacking a plane
25.9	Forcibly raping a woman with no physical injury resulting

Source: Peter H. Rossi, Emily Waite, Christine E. Bose, and Richard E. Berk, "The Seriousness of Crimes: Normative Structure and Individual Differences," *American Sociological Review* 39(1974).

▼ **TABLE 3.6 Consensus on the Least Serious Crimes**

Severity Score	Offense—10 Least Serious
1.1	Disturbing the neighborhood with noisy behavior
1.1	Taking bets on the numbers
1.1	A group hanging around a street corner after police tell them to move on
0.9	Running away from home when under 16
0.8	Being drunk in public
0.7	Breaking the curfew law when under 16
0.6	Trespassing in the backyard of a private home
0.3	Being a vagrant
0.2	Playing hooky from school when under 16

Source: Peter H. Rossi, Emily Waite, Christine E. Bose, and Richard E. Berk, "The Seriousness of Crimes: Normative Structure and Individual Differences," *American Sociological Review* 39(1974).

The American sociologist Kai Erikson's (1966) classic study, *Wayward Puritans,* tested Durkheim's boundary hypothesis by examining witchcraft in seventeenth-century Puritan New England. He analyzed evidence about creating, prosecuting, and punishing witchcraft, concluding that the community created "crime waves" to solidify moral boundaries to keep itself from disintegrating. Puritans needed witchcraft to keep society from wandering outside settled behavioral boundaries.

Empirical evidence from modern times also supports Durkheim's consensus hypothesis. Blacks and Whites, ethnic groups, men and women, rich and poor, young and old, and well-educated and poorly educated people agree on what conduct amounts to serious crime. In 1983, researchers asked a selected sample to rank the seriousness of various crimes. The answers displayed a broad consensus on the following: Violent crimes were considered most serious, property crimes were less serious, and public-order crimes were the least serious (Rossi, Waite, Bose, Berk 1974). This compares favorably with rankings in most criminal codes. Tables 3.5 and 3.6 contain the results of this comprehensive survey of American opinion concerning the seriousness of offenses. Do your own rankings agree with these findings?

The Conflict Theory

conflict theory conflict is the normal state of society and social control requires active constraint, sometimes in the form of coercion

Consensus theory dominated mainstream criminology until the 1950s, when conflict theories reemerged. The conflict theorists challenged the notion that consensus is the "normal" state of society. Instead, **conflict theory** (which enjoys a history in social thought as old as consensus theory) assumes that conflict is the normal state of society. It assumes further that social control requires active constraint, sometimes in the form of coercion. Common values and interests can't maintain social control because they don't exist. Society is divided into competing classes and interest groups; the most powerful ones dominate legislatures and criminal justice agencies. They write criminal laws that further their interests and impose their values on the whole society. They use these laws to maintain their dominance and control conflict (Chambliss 1984, 16–31).

Conflict theory has many varieties, but they all shift the emphasis from law *breaking* to law *making* and law *enforcing*. Until modern conflict theory reemerged in the late 1950s, most criminologists began their study without questioning the culpability of criminal law. They considered *criminals*, not criminal *law*, to be the social problem. Conflict theory changed all that. The emphasis on lawmaking and law enforcing led to an examination of criminal law and its enforcement in a new and different light.

Conflict theory maintains that criminal law doesn't reflect absolute, agreed-on principles or universal moral values. Instead, criminal law defines, and criminal justice agencies preserve and protect, the interests and values of the dominant social groups. Criminal law and procedure are means of preserving the dominant group(s)' definition of social order (Greenberg 1981, 1–26, 90–94).

The Radical Theory

Dissatisfaction with consensus and conflict theory, and with mainstream criminology and criminal justice, contributed to the creation of a "new," or radical, criminology in the 1960s. It wasn't exactly new. It drew on the long tradition of social conflict theory. Radical criminology maintains that mainstream criminologists and criminal justice professionals are apologists, if not lackeys, for a capitalist ruling class that dominates the state. Radicals disagree over whether the dominant class consciously exploits the working class, or whether the structure of capitalist society inevitably determines their exploitative actions. Instrumentalists contend that the ruling class consciously decides to exploit. According to structuralist radical theory, capitalists don't *know* they're exploiters. Despite a lot of hot rhetoric (some called it hot air) in the 1960s and 1970s, radical criminologists (Quinney 1977) developed a coherent (even if widely rejected) radical criminal justice theory based on the following propositions:

1. The state's primary purpose is to protect the dominant class in society.
2. This purpose requires controlling the lower classes.
3. The ruling class exploits the working class by wringing profit from overworked laborers.
4. Criminal law controls workers so capitalists can get richer and secure protection for their accumulated riches.
5. Brute force isn't always necessary to protect these interests and control the workers.
6. Capitalists sometimes have to commit crimes to maintain the existing power arrangements. So police officers violate individuals' rights, government abuses its power, corporations fix prices, and so on. They try not to do this too often because it threatens the myth that law is neutral, evenhanded, and fair.
7. Workers commit crimes mainly out of necessity. They prey on other workers, and sometimes capitalists, to survive: They steal what they

cannot earn. Or, out of frustration with existing unjust arrangements, they erupt in violence against others. Occasionally, they commit "heroic crimes," like attacking the power structure. Their crimes are not bad or evil; they are utilitarian actions necessary to survive in a capitalist society.

These brief sections oversimplify the consensus, conflict, and radical social theories. Consensus theorists don't maintain that harmony and negotiation always prevail in politics and society; nor do they claim that their theories explain everything in criminal justice. Conflict theorists don't demand an interpretation of social interaction that totally excludes agreement and social cohesion. Radical criminologists don't contend that class determines *all* laws or that capitalists *always* win and workers *always* lose. But they *all* maintain that criminal law and criminal justice reflect *their* theory of social reality.

MAKE YOUR DECISION *Do Broken Windows Cause Serious Crime?*

In a now famous article, "Broken Windows," Professors James Q. Wilson and George L. Kelling (1982) set off a debate when they proposed their **"broken windows" theory** to explain serious crime. According to the theory, "small disorders" (like broken windows) don't just "bother" law-abiding people; they're actually linked to serious crime (robbery, felony assault, burglary, and felony theft). According to Professor Wilson:

> We used the image of broken windows to explain how neighborhoods might decay into disorder and even crime if no one attends faithfully to their maintenance. If a factory or office window is broken, a passerby observing it will conclude that no one cares or no one is in charge. In time, a few will begin throwing rocks to break more windows. Soon all the windows will be broken, and now passersby will think that, not only is no one in charge of the building, no one is in charge of the street on which it faces. Only the young, the criminal, or the foolhardy have any business on an unprotected avenue, and so more and more citizens will abandon the street to those they assume prowl it. *Small disorders lead to larger and larger ones, and perhaps even to crime.* [emphasis added] (Kelling and Coles 1996, xiv)

There's a long list of these "small disorders." Here's the part of the list that bothers most people, regardless of sex, race, class, or neighborhood (Skogan 1990a).

- Public drinking and drunkenness
- Begging and aggressive panhandling
- Threatening behavior and harassment
- Obstruction of streets and public places
- Vandalism and graffiti
- Street prostitution
- Public urination and defecation
- Unlicensed vending

DO BROKEN WINDOWS LEAD TO SERIOUS CRIME?

Read the three excerpts below; then, on the basis of your reading:

1. Summarize the evidence supporting the broken windows theory that minor disorders cause serious crime.
2. Summarize the evidence against the broken windows theory.

Source: Robert J. Sampson and Stephen Raudenbush, "Systematic Social Observation of Public Spaces: A New Look at Disorder in Urban Neighborhoods," *American Journal of Sociology* 105(3) (1999): 603–651. Reprinted with permission from the University of Chicago Press.

3. Assuming there's little or no evidence supporting the broken windows theory that minor disorder leads to serious crime, provide reasons why it's still a good idea to control disorder.
4. Assume you're a policy advisor to the mayor of your city. Stories about the success of broken windows policing has attracted her attention. She asks you to study and recommend the following:
   a. *Whether* your city should implement broken windows' policies.
   b. If so, *why;* if not, why not?

Disorder and Decline

When Wilson and Kelling wrote "Broken Windows," no one had empirically tested the broken windows theory. Professor Wesley G. Skogan (1990a) explored whether there's a statistical link between the level of crime and

▲ The "broken windows" theory suggests that *small* physical disorders, like empty bottles, graffiti, and broken windows lead to serious crimes like robbery and burglary. Would the state of the buildings on this street cause you to assume that the area was crime-ridden?

the level of disorder in neighborhoods by measuring the two using surveys. Residents were asked whether they thought disorder was a problem in their neighborhood. Then they were asked whether they'd been victims of rape, robbery, assault, or purse snatching. Skogan concluded that robbery and disorder were *strongly linked*, even when he controlled for the effects of poverty, stability, and race in the neighborhoods.

But is the link *causal*? Does disorder cause serious crime? Here's Skogan's (1990a) answer:

> The evidence suggests that poverty, instability, and the racial composition of neighborhoods are strongly linked to area crime, but a substantial portion of that linkage is through disorder: their link to area crime virtually disappears when disorder is brought into the picture. This too is consistent with Wilson and Kelling's proposition, and further evidence that direct action against disorder could have substantial payoffs.... Disorder needs to be taken seriously in research on neighborhood crime, and that both directly and through crime it plays an important part in neighborhood decline. "Broken windows" do need to be repaired quickly. (75)

Source: Wesley G. Skogan, *Disorder and Decline* (New York: Free Press, 1990a).

Illusion of Order

Professor Bernard E. Harcourt (2001) replicated Professor Skogan's data, and had some harsh things to say about his research and conclusions:

> Skogan's data are weak. Skogan patched together his data from five separate studies that were not entirely consistent, and as a result the study is missing a large amount of information. Robbery victimization is available in only thirty neighborhoods, and the disorder information is missing on average 30 to 40 percent of the time. The first point, then, is that the data are not reliable.
>
> But even more troubling is the fact that Skogan failed to disclose that there is no real connection between disorder and crime with regard to the other four crime variables in his study. Skogan focused on robbery victimization—where he found a connection with disorder—but failed to reveal that there is no similar connection between disorder and burglary, rape, physical assault, or purse-snatching victimization. In other words, in four out of five tests, there is no real connection between disorder and crime.
>
> Moreover, on close analysis, it turns out that the one place where there is a connection—the disorder-robbery nexus—is itself questionable. First, the survey question that was posed to neighborhood residents about robbery victimization was not neighborhood specific. In other

words, the question did not specify that the robbery victimization had to occur in the neighborhood in question, so as a result, it may have occurred in another neighborhood.

> Second, and more important, there is a set of five neighborhoods in Newark that exert excessive influence on Skogan's findings. When we take away those Newark neighborhoods, the tenuous connection to robbery disappears.
>
> As a result, Skogan's study does not support the broken windows hypothesis. In four out of five tests, there is no real connection between disorder and various crimes. In the only test where there is a connection, the nexus is itself highly questionable. It is fair to conclude that Skogan's study does not prove a connection between disorder and crime in general. (59–78)

Source: Bernard E. Harcourt, *Illusions of Order: The Broken Promise of Broken Windows Policing* (Chicago: University of Chicago Press, 2001).

"Systematic Social Observation of Public Spaces"

Professors Sampson and Raudenbush (1999) conducted what up to now is probably the most elaborate study of the "sources and consequences of public disorder" (603). Their study covered more than twelve thousand city blocks in 196 neighborhoods in Chicago. The sources for the study included census data, police records, *and* direct observation:

> In the spirit of the early Chicago school of urban sociology, we believe that direct observation is fundamental; to the advancement of knowledge.... One of the hallmarks of the Chicago school was its concern with observing public places—not just abstract variables, but the sights, sounds, and feel of the streets. (605–606)

They followed Albert J. Reiss's (1971) **systematic social observation (SSO) method** of observing police-citizen encounters. According to Reiss, SSOs have to follow "explicit rules that can be replicated, *and* the means of observation (whether persons or technology) have to be independent of what's being observed." Reiss pointed out that SSO can assess neighborhood physical conditions and social interactions that survey participants can't describe accurately. Besides, (and very important) almost all surveys linking signs of disorder with fear of crime and victimization are based on residents' subjective *perceptions*. ("How much of a problem do you feel disorder in your neighborhood is?") (606).

This is how Sampson and Raudenbush's (1999) SSO worked. For five months, observers trained at the National Opinion Research Center (NORC), drove an SUV at 5 miles an hour down every street in more than 12,500

Chicago city blocks. The blocks were selected for a maximum variety of race, ethnicity, and class among residents. Each SUV was equipped with a driver, a VCR operator and two VCRs facing each side of the street, and two observers. As the SUV drove slowly down each block, the cameras recorded social activities and physical features; the observers (one on each side) recorded their observations of each side of the block (616).

They coded the observations according to 10 items of physical disorder—"deterioration of urban landscapes, for example, graffiti on buildings, abandoned cars, broken windows, and garbage in the streets" (Figure 3.3)—and social disorder—"behavior usually involving strangers and considered threatening, such as verbal harassment on the street, open solicitation for prostitution, public intoxication, and rowdy groups of young males in public" (603–604) (Figure 3.4).

The results of a statistical analysis of the SSO revealed a positive correlation between physical and social disorder and concentrated poverty (.50). They also revealed a negative correlation between physical disorder and collective efficacy (–.49) and between physical disorder and social disorder (–.47). *Collective efficacy* means the ability of residents in a neighborhood to come together to achieve common goals (in this case to control disorder). According to Sampson and Raudenbush:

> One of the most central of common goals is the desire of community residents to live in safe environments free of predatory crime and disorder. There is no evidence of

which we are aware showing public approval of crime or disorder by any population group; if anything, the evidence suggests that residents of low-income, African-American, and high-crime neighborhoods are the *most* insistent on better police protection and demands for reducing violence.... Even active participants in criminal networks seek to achieve some semblance of order in their neighborhoods of residence.... Informal efforts to socially control local crime and disorder has long been reported in white working-class neighborhoods dominated by the mob. (611)

In contrast to externally or formally induced actions (e.g., a police crackdown [Chapter 5], housing code enforcement), our agency-oriented perspective on neighborhoods emphasizes the role of informal mechanisms by which residents initiate or achieve social control. Examples of...informal social control...include the willingness of residents to intervene to prevent acts such as truancy, drinking, vandalism, and street-corner disturbances (e.g., harassment, loitering, fighting). (611)

Importantly, however, actions of informal control need not involve direct confrontation or exclude the police or other formal channels of recourse. Recent ethnographic research has identified the creative ways in which socially organized communities react to disorder, including the establishment of "phone trees" among residents for calling the police upon observation of disorder; the organization of a group presence in court sentencing hearings for offenders caught defacing local public properties; voluntary "graffiti patrols" that log

▶ **FIGURE 3.3 Signs of Physical Disorder**

Source: Robert J. Sampson and Stephen Raudenbush, "Systematic Social Observation of Public Spaces: A New Look at Disorder in Urban Neighborhoods." *American Journal of Sociology* 105(3) (1999):617.

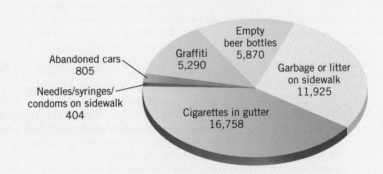

▶ **FIGURE 3.4 Signs of Social Disorder**

Source: Robert J. Sampson and Stephen Raudenbush, "Systematic Social Observation of Public Spaces: A New Look at Disorder in Urban Neighborhoods," *American Journal of Sociology* 105(3)(1999):618.

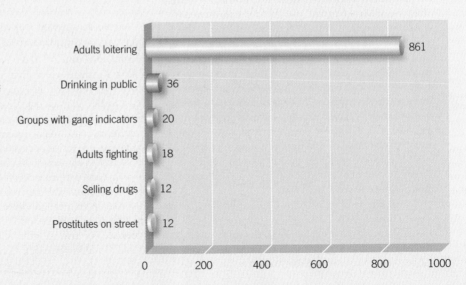

new incidents of disorder that are then presented to the police; and agitating for voting referendums to delicense bars where drug sales and disorder loom large (Carr 1998). The razing of a vacant "drug house" by housing authorities, if prompted by local complaints, would also fit this pattern. Ultimately, then, our perspective recognizes the articulation among the private (family), parochial (neighborhood), and formal (public) orders (Hunter 1985; Bursik and Grasmick 1993) but stresses the agency [initiative] of residents in establishing these connections. (612)

Completely separate from the SSO, Sampson and Raudenbush analyzed police records and census data and conducted a resident survey. Analyses of these data confirmed and strengthened the SSO conclusions. They found that concentrated disadvantage (including poverty, public assistance, unemployment, female-headed families, and mixed commercial and residential land use) "is the single most important predictor of disorder in Chicago neighborhoods" (625). And their data showed "a consistent negative relationship of collective efficacy with SSO disorder, both physical [–.26] and social [–.25] (626).

Summarizing their study as it relates to "broken windows" theory, Sampson and Raudenbush wrote that the:

observed disorder did not match the theoretical expectations set up by the main thesis of "broken windows" (Wilson and Kelling 1982; Kelling and Coles 1996). Disorder is a moderate correlate of predatory crime, and it varies consistently with antecedent neighborhood characteristics. Once these characteristics were taken into account, however, the connection between disorder and crime vanished in 4 out of 5 tests—including homicide, arguably our best measure of violence. The empirical results therefore support our contention that public disorder and most predatory crimes share similar theoretical features and are consequently explained by the same constructs at the neighborhood level, in particular the concentration of disadvantage and lowered collective efficacy. (637)

Although our results contradict the strong version of the broken windows thesis, they do not imply the theoretical irrelevance of disorder. After all, our theoretical framework rests on the notion that physical and social disorder comprise highly visible cues to which neighborhood observers respond. According to this view, disorder may turn out to be important for understanding migration patterns, investment by businesses, and overall neighborhood viability....

Put differently, the active ingredients in crime seem to be structural disadvantage and attenuated collective efficacy more so than disorder. Attacking public disorder through tough police tactics may thus be a politically popular but perhaps analytically weak strategy to reduce crime, mainly because such a strategy leaves the common origins of both, but especially the last, untouched. A more subtle approach...would look to how informal but collective efforts among residents to stem disorder may provide unanticipated benefits for increasing collective efficacy (Skogan and Hartnett 1998), in the long run lowering crime. (638)

Source: Robert J. Sampson and Stephen W. Raudenbush, "Systematic Social Observation of Public Spaces: A New Look at Disorder in Urban Neighborhoods," *American Journal of Sociology* 105(3)(1999):603–651.

REFERENCES

Bursik, Robert J., Jr., and Harold Grasmick. 1993. *Neighborhoods and Crime: The Dimensions of Effective Community Control.* New York: Lexington.

Carr, Patrick J. 1998. Keeping Up Appearances: Informal Social Control in a White Working-Class Neighborhood in Chicago. Ph.D. Dissertation. University of Chicago.

Hunter, Albert. 1985. "Private, Parochial, and Public School Orders: The Problem of Crime and Incivility in Urban Communities." In *The Challenge of Social Control: Citizenship and Institution Building in Modern Society,* edited by Gerald Suttles and Mayer Zald. Norwood, N.J.: Ablex Publishing.

Kelling, George L., and Catherine M. Coles. 1996. *Fixing Broken Windows.* New York: Free Press.

Reiss, Albert J., Jr. 1971. "Systematic Observations of Natural Social Phenomena." In *Sociological Methodology,* vol. 3, edited by Herbert Costner (pp. 3–33). San Francisco: Jossey-Bass.

Skogan, Wesley G., and Susan Hartnett. 1998. *Community Policing, Chicago Style.* New York: Oxford University Press.

Wilson, James Q., and George L. Kelling. 1982 (March). "Broken Windows." *Atlantic Monthly.*

KEY TERMS

"broken windows" theory minor physical and social disorder is linked to serious crime

systematic social observation (SSO) method observers have to follow explicit rules that can be replicated, *and* the means of observation (whether persons or technology) have to be independent of what's being observed

Chapter Summary

▶ The first explanations of crime were based on faith in supernatural forces; they equated sin with crime. Then came the natural explanations based on observations of things and events in this world. All modern scientific theories of crime descend from the natural theories, but spiritual explanations still exist. The spiritual theories don't appear in college textbooks, because they can't be proven by scientific observation; but this doesn't mean they're not true. The modern theories are called *scientific* because they focus on relationships between phenomena we can observe.

▶ The classical theory (now called rational choice) rests on two assumptions: individuals have free will (they choose to commit crimes) and reason (they choose decisions that benefit them). The rational choice theory doesn't say individuals have *total* freedom to choose or that they will make totally reasonable choices. The rational choice theory can lead to two contrasting public policies—increase the pain of committing crimes or increase the gains for lawful behavior (make washing cars more desirable than stealing them).

▶ Positivist theories of crime and their modern descendants grew out of disappointment that tailoring punishment to fit the crime didn't seem to reduce crime. The positivists looked for forces beyond the control of individual choice that caused or determined criminal behavior. These forces might be within the individual (biology and psychology) or external (social structure and process). Biological and psychological theories don't deny the importance of the social environment, so you'll often see the modern theories referred to as *biosocial* and *psychosocial theories*. Despite advances in our knowledge of the interaction among biology, psychology, and the social environment, we're a long way from having enough empirical support to build policies around them.

▶ Social structure theories link social class and structural conditions like poverty, unemployment, and poor education to criminal behavior. The original strain theory focused on how American culture defines goals of material success and the means to achieve them and how the social structure blocks many members of the lower classes from achieving them. This block creates strain that leads more people in the lower than in the upper classes to commit crimes. A lack of legitimate opportunities to succeed or the abundance of illegitimate opportunities to achieve material success can cause strain. Later, the strain theory expanded to include other goals; it also now applies the theory to upper-class strain and gender strain.

▶ Social process theory focuses on interactions among members of families, peer groups, schools, churches, neighborhoods, and other social institutions. Social process theorists agree that there's a link between social processes and criminal behavior but they don't agree on how.

▶ Social learning theories assume individuals are born like blank slates and can learn any values and behavior. Social control theory assumes everybody is born with the desire to break the rules. Labeling theory assumes the criminal justice system creates criminals.

▶ Developmental criminology focuses on changes in criminal behavior over time (the beginning, continuation, and end of criminal behavior). Early childhood theorists focus on the stability throughout life of traits set in childhood (usually by the age of 8). Life-course theorists focus on stability *and* changes in behavior throughout the life course.

▶ Criminal law and criminal justice theories shift the focus of explanations based on lawbreakers and lawbreaking to the law*makers* and law *enforcers*. Two contrasting views have dominated thinking about how behavior comes to be defined as criminal and how crime once defined is controlled. The consensus view takes consensus as the normal state of society; that consensus defines crimes as conduct that offends the "collective conscience." Society created crime to establish moral boundaries that when violated threaten the existence of society. The conflict view assumes that conflict is the normal state of society. Society is divided into competing groups. The most powerful groups get to define what's criminal and how to enforce criminal law. They define crime and enforce criminal laws to further their own interests.

Key Terms

correlation, p. 71
classical (utilitarian) theories, p. 71
positivist theories, p. 71
determinism, p. 71
criminal law theories, p. 71
rational choice theory, p. 72
routine activities theory, p. 78
foreground forces in crime, p. 79

background forces, p. 79
social structure theories, p. 88
anomie theory, p. 88
strain theory, p. 88
social process theories, p. 90
social learning theory, p. 90
social control theory, p. 90
labeling theory, p. 90

life-course theory, p. 93
consensus hypothesis, p. 96
boundary hypothesis, p. 96
conflict theory, p. 98
"broken windows" theory, p. 99
systematic social observation (SSO) method, p. 99

Web Resources

Go to http://cj.wadsworth.com/samaha_cj7e for a wealth of online resources related to your book. Take a "pre-test" and "post-test" for each chapter in order to help master the material. Check out the *Web Links* to access the websites mentioned in the text, as well as many others. Explore the *Decision Points* flagged in the margins of the text for additional insights. You can also access recent perspectives by clicking on *CJ in the News* and *Terrorism Update* under *Course Resources*.

Search Online with InfoTrac College Edition

For additional information, explore InfoTrac College Edition, your online library. Go to http://cj.wadsworth.com/samaha_cj7e to access InfoTrac College Edition from your book's website. Use the passcode that came with your book. You will find InfoTrac College Edition exercises and a list of key words for further research.

CHAPTER 4

Criminal Justice and the Law

FACT *or* FICTION?

- ► In our constitutional democracy any behavior can be made criminal as long as a majority votes for it.

- ► The criminal law is limited by the Constitution and by the elements of crime.

- ► The criminal act element limits criminal law to what people have done, not to what they agree to do.

- ► Criminal intent includes creating a risk of causing a criminal harm you didn't know you were creating.

- ► Defenses of justification focus on the wrongfulness of the defendant's actions.

- ► Defenses of excuse are based on the idea that defendants aren't responsible for what they did.

- ► Criminal procedure is aimed at telling police officers what they *can't* do.

- ► Due process commands that Blacks and Whites be treated alike before the law.

WAS HE JUSTIFIED IN KILLING HER BECAUSE OF HIS LAOTIAN VALUES?

A Laotian refugee living in this country for approximately two years was convicted of intentionally murdering his Laotian wife of one month. At trial, he tried to enter a defense of "extreme emotional disturbance" to mitigate the homicide on the theory that the stresses resulting from his status as a refugee caused a significant mental trauma. It affected his mind for a substantial period of time, simmering in the unknowing subconscious and then inexplicably coming to the fore. Although the immediate cause of the defendant's loss of control was his jealousy over his wife's apparent preference for an ex-boyfriend, the defense argued that under Laotian culture the conduct of the wife in displaying affection for another man and receiving phone calls from an unattached man brought shame on the defendant and his family sufficient to trigger the defendant's loss of control. The trial court refused to admit information regarding Laotian culture.

—*PEOPLE V. APHAYLATH*, 502 N.E.2D 998 (1986)

"No crime without law" and "No punishment without law" are two of the most ancient principles of our criminal law. Crime control in a constitutional democracy depends on these principles. If we lived in a pure democracy, the majority could do whatever it pleased, but we live in a *constitutional* democracy, which limits what the majority can do. The U.S. Constitution sets those limits. So none of the behavior discussed in Chapter 2 can be criminal without a specific law defining it as a crime and specifying a punishment for it. No action taken or decision made by any police officer, prosecutor, defense attorney, judge, jury, probation officer, corrections officer, or parole officer that you'll learn about throughout the rest of this book is allowed except by the authority of law. The sources of this authority are the national and state constitutions, federal and state statutes, and court decisions interpreting these constitutions and statutes.

Informally, the constitutional and legal framework and authority are broad and flexible enough to allow plenty of "play in the joints" of discretionary decision making. Legal terms, like all other words, are at best imperfect symbols of what they represent. No written rule defining criminal behavior can precisely describe all the behavior it's intended to prohibit. No provision defining the power of criminal justice agencies can fully account for all the actions that power allows. No rule can cover all contingencies that may arise after it's written. Finally, no rule, however clear and predictive, can—or should—eliminate the influences of ideology, economics, social structure and processes, and individual personality. In short, the tension between formal rules and informal, discretionary decision making—between formal and informal criminal justice—also applies to criminal law and criminal procedure.

This chapter examines the constitutional and legal framework in day-to-day criminal justice operations. Both criminal law and the law of criminal procedure affect these operations. **Criminal law** tells private individuals what behavior is a crime and lays down the punishment for it. **Criminal procedure** tells government officials the extent and limits of their power to enforce the criminal law, and it sets out the consequences for illegal official actions.

criminal law tells private individuals what behavior is a crime and lays down the punishment for it

criminal procedure tells government officials the extent and limits of their power to enforce the criminal law, and it sets out the consequences for illegal official actions

Criminal Law

Criminal law defines what behavior is criminal and spells out the punishment for committing crimes. In every society, there are people whose behavior we should condemn, but to condemn isn't necessarily to criminalize. To be blunt, we distinguish (and we *should*) between "creeps" and criminals. So everybody agrees that murder, rape, robbery, burglary, and theft should be crimes. But we also agree that creeps who cheat on their girlfriends or boyfriends and lie to their friends shouldn't go to jail. Why?

Criminal law has very high costs. It costs a lot of money, takes a lot of time, intrudes deeply into privacy and liberty, and more often than not fails to produce the result we want. Or if it does yield the desired result, we can achieve it at a lower cost with less expensive, less restrictive social control mechanisms like the disapproval of family, friends, and others we love and respect; informal discipline within social institutions like schools and workplaces; and private lawsuits. We call this limit on the use of criminal law by relying on the least expensive or invasive response to misbehavior the **principle of economy.**

The principle of economy isn't the only way we limit the power of government to define crime. Let's look at three others:

1. Constitutional limits
2. The elements of crime
3. The defenses to crime

Then, we'll look at the means for making sense of criminal law—classifying and grading crimes.

Constitutional Limits on Criminal Law

Four provisions in the U.S. Constitution limit the power of government to create criminal laws and set punishments:

1. "No...ex post facto law shall be passed." (Article I, Section 9)
2. "No person shall be...deprived of life, liberty, or property without due process of law...." (Amendment V)
3. "No state shall...deny any person life, liberty, or property without due process of law." (Amendment XIV)
4. "No state shall...deny any person within its jurisdiction the equal protection of the laws." (Amendment XIV)

The **ex post facto clause** bans retroactive criminal laws. Retroactive criminal laws make a crime out of behavior that wasn't criminal before the law was passed. For example, if a state passes a statute on January 2, 2005, raising the drinking age from 18 to 21, the state can't prosecute a 19-year-old who bought a beer on New Year's Eve in 2004. Why? People have to have fair warning their behavior is a crime; ex post facto laws obviously don't do that.

According to the **void-for-vagueness doctrine,** vague laws deny individuals life, liberty, and property without due process of law because vague laws don't give individuals fair warning. In *Lanzetta v. New Jersey* (1939), the U.S. Supreme Court explained that a law so vague that individuals "of common intelligence" have to "guess" what it means "violates the first essential of due process of law (453).

A Lincoln, Nebraska, city ordinance prohibited "any indecent, immodest, or filthy act in the presence of any person." The Nebraska supreme court, in *State v. Metzger* (1982), struck it down because it violated the Fourteenth Amendment due process clause. (The Fifth Amendment due process clause applies to the federal government; the Fourteenth Amendment due process clause applies to state governments.) A passerby saw Doug Metzger standing naked in front of his

FindLaw.com: Thousands of legal sites, cases, codes, forms, law reviews, law schools, and more. To reach this site go to "Web Links" on your Samaha CJ7 website: http://cj.wadsworth.com/samaha_cj7e.

principle of economy applying criminal law by relying on the least expensive or invasive response to misbehavior

ex post facto clause bans retroactive criminal laws

void-for-vagueness doctrine vague laws deny individuals life, liberty, and property without due process of law because they don't give individuals fair warning

window eating a bowl of cereal for breakfast; Metzger was arrested for indecency. According to the Nebraska supreme court, under the ordinance, there was "no way" for ordinary people to know what behavior the law prohibited. A few people might "believe persons of the opposite sex holding hands in public are immodest, and certainly more...might believe kissing in public is immodest."

The Fourteenth Amendment also bans states from denying individuals **equal protection of the laws.** Equal protection means criminal laws can only treat groups of people differently if the different treatment is *reasonable.* Distinctions based on race, ethnicity, religion, and national origin are *never* reasonable. Distinctions based on sex can be reasonable if there's a really good reason for the distinction; in other words, distinctions are *sometimes* reasonable. For example, a statute making it a crime for women (but not men) to smoke in public violated the equal protection clause. On the other hand, the U.S. Supreme Court ruled that California's statutory rape law, which applied only to men, didn't violate the equal protection clause. Why? Because California has a "compelling interest" in reducing "the tragic human costs of illegitimate teenage pregnancies" (*Michael M. v. Superior Court of Sonoma County* 1981).

Due process also protects the controversial right of privacy. But don't look for the word privacy in the U.S. Constitution—it's not there. The right is based on the idea that a free society maximizes human autonomy—the right of the people to be let alone by government, especially when it concerns their bodies, their homes, and their family relationships. So the U.S. Supreme Court, in *Griswold v. Connecticut* (1965), ruled that states can't make it a crime for married couples to use contraceptives. According to Justice William O. Douglas, the Constitution creates a "zone of privacy" around the "intimate relation of husband and wife," and the statute had a "destructive impact upon the relationship."

In 2003 (in a bitterly controversial decision), the U.S. Supreme Court extended the right to privacy to adult gay consensual sex in private. The case started when Houston police officers arrived at John G. Lawrence's home to investigate a neighbor's "weapons disturbance" report. When the officers got there, they found only two adult men, Lawrence and Tyrone Garner, having sex in the bedroom. (The neighbor was later convicted of filing a false police report.) Lawrence and Garner were arrested and later convicted and fined $200 each for violating the state's Homosexual Conduct law (Texas Penal Code 2004, §21.06).

▶ Tyrone Garner (left) and John Lawrence greet supporters at a victory rally in Houston after the U.S. Supreme Court struck down the Texas sodomy statute criminalizing adult consensual sex in private. The statute was struck down on the grounds that it violated the constitutional right to privacy (a word not found in the Constitution itself). Garner and Lawrence spent a night in jail and were fined $200 each for violating the law the Court struck down.

AP/Wide World Photos

According to the statute, "A person commits an offense if he engages in deviate sexual intercourse with another individual of the same sex." Lawrence and Garner appealed their case through the Texas and lower federal courts. It finally arrived in the U.S. Supreme Court (*Lawrence v. Texas* 2003). Five justices (it takes a majority of the nine justices to decide a case) voted to strike down the law because it violated Lawrence's and Garner's "fundamental right to privacy."

Several state constitutions do have specific provisions protecting privacy. The Alaska constitution provides "the right of the people to privacy is recognized and shall not be infringed." The Alaska supreme court ruled that a statute making it a crime for an adult to possess a small amount of marijuana at home for personal use violated the right to privacy. According to the court:

> The privacy amendment . . . was intended to give recognition and protection to the home. Such a reading is consonant with the character of life in Alaska. Our . . . state has traditionally been the home of people who prize their individuality and who have chosen to settle or to continue living here in order to achieve a measure of control over their own lifestyles which is now virtually unattainable in many of our sister states. (*Ravin v. State* 1975)

(The people of Alaska later overruled the decision by changing the law through a referendum.)

Constitutional limits on criminal law are commands; criminal justice officials have no choice but to obey them. However, as you'll learn, constitutional commands leave plenty of room for discretionary decision making when it comes to applying the commands to particular cases.

▶ DECISION POINT ◀

Can "sex" in private be protected from the law?

Click on this Decision Point at http://cj.wadsworth.com/samaha_cj7e to explore the issue.

The Elements of Crime

All serious crimes (criminal homicide, rape, robbery, burglary, theft, and the like) consist of three elements:

1. The criminal act (the physical element—*actus reus*)
2. The criminal intent (the mental element—*mens rea*)
3. The concurrence of the criminal act and the criminal intent (the relationship element)

A few crimes, like criminal homicide, require a fourth element:

4. Causing a particular result (for example, causing death in homicide)

The Constitution also commands that all crimes have to contain one of these elements—a criminal act—*and* that to convict defendants, the prosecution has to prove all the elements in the crime beyond a reasonable doubt (Chapter 10). A legislature doesn't have to include a criminal intent, but if it does, then the prosecution has to prove it beyond a reasonable doubt.

No matter what the Constitution allows, through long tradition (about 800 years), the criminal law has established limits of its own. These limits take the form of the elements in the preceding list, and you probably know by watching or reading crime dramas how very much alive these elements of crime still are. Because they're so entrenched, the principles are a form of command themselves. So *serious* crimes always contain at least the first three elements, and sometimes the fourth. Let's look at these elements of crime that are so old and still so much alive in our criminal justice system.

The Criminal Act The first element is the criminal act. Our criminal law can't punish people for what they *wish,* or *hope,* or *intend,* or for who they are (their inherited condition); it can only punish them for what they *do.* But this doesn't mean you have to complete a crime to satisfy the act requirement. So it was attempted murder when Ralph Damms chased his wife Marjorie with a gun he forgot to load, caught up with her, pointed the gun at her head, and pulled the trigger several times. "It won't shoot! It won't shoot!" he shouted (*State v. Damms*

1960). It's also a crime (conspiracy) to agree to commit a crime even if you never start to commit it. So a woman who agreed to buy "X" (the drug Ecstasy) was guilty of conspiracy even though the deal fell through. It's even a crime to encourage someone else to commit a crime (solicitation), even if they turn you down cold. So when Harold Furr offered Donald Owens $3000 to kill his wife Earlene, he was found guilty of solicitation even though Owens flatly refused the offer (*State v. Furr* 1977). It's also a crime to even have in your possession a long list of things, including certain types of weapons, drugs, and pornography, even if you don't use, sell, or for that matter do anything with them. Notice what all these crimes have in common—they all include some action: pulling the trigger, agreeing to buy Ecstasy, asking a friend to kill, and taking possession of, say, a gun.

Making crimes out of attempt, conspiracy, solicitation, and possession is justified as a way to prevent *future* harm. So we're punishing someone for what they *might* do, not for what they've done. There used to be strong objections to punishing future harm, but we're living in an age of prevention, as the "war on terror" after 9/11 and the "war on drugs" since the 1980s remind us. Throughout the rest of the book, you'll frequently meet up with this idea of crime prevention and how it influences decision making in all segments of the criminal justice system.

"Criminal act," as defined by the law, also includes the failure to act—but only if there's a legal duty to act. These are called criminal omissions. There are two kinds. Most common are failures to report when the law requires you to (not filing your income tax return, or an accident). Less common is the failure to intervene to help someone in danger, like a father who stands by while a mother abuses their baby. Legal duties can arise out of specific statutes (like income tax laws); contracts (an agreement to take care of a sick person); and special relationships (parents and minor children, doctors and patients).

One critical limit to the criminal law's generous definition of *act* is that the act has to be voluntary. So forcing Doug with a loaded gun to take Michelle's Ecstasy wasn't stealing. Nor, a court decided, was it murder in one bizarre case of sleepwalking when a mother killed her daughter Pat with an axe. (She was dreaming she was killing a man who was attacking Pat.)

The Criminal Intent In all serious crimes, like murder, rape, robbery, burglary, and theft, a criminal intent has to trigger the criminal act. The mental element is complicated because there are four levels of criminal intent (Table 4.1):

1. Purposeful
2. Knowing
3. Reckless
4. Negligent

purposeful intent (sometimes called specific intent) "you did it and/or caused a criminal result on purpose"

knowing intent you know you're committing an act or causing a harm but you're not acting for that purpose

Purposeful intent (sometimes called specific intent) means just what it sounds like—you did it on purpose and/or caused the result in crimes like murder that include the element of cause. **Knowing intent** means you know you're

▼ TABLE 4.1 Everyday Definitions of Model Code Levels of Culpability

Level of Culpability	Definition
Purposeful	"You did (or caused) it on purpose."
Knowing	"OK, so you didn't do it because you *wanted* to hurt me, but you *knew* you *were* hurting me."
Reckless	"OK, so you didn't *want* to hurt her, but you *knew* the odds were very high you *could* hurt her—and you did."
Negligent	"OK, so you didn't *mean* to hurt him, and you didn't even know how high the odds were you *would* hurt him, but you *should've* known the odds were very high—and he got hurt."

committing an act or causing a harm but you're not acting for that purpose. For example, a doctor who performed a hysterectomy on a pregnant woman to save her life knew he would kill the fetus, but he didn't remove the uterus for the very purpose of killing the fetus.

Reckless intent means consciously creating a risk of causing a criminal harm. Consider Brad who didn't tell his partner Monty he had AIDS because he was afraid Monty wouldn't have sex with him if he did. They had sex regularly. The last thing Brad intended was to give Monty AIDS, but he knew he created the risk of giving Monty AIDS every time they had sex—and he did it anyway.

reckless intent consciously creating a risk of causing a criminal harm

Negligent intent is like reckless in that it means taking actions that create a risk of causing harm. But *negligent* is unconsciously creating a risk, meaning you *should* know (or as it's often phrased, "a reasonable person *would* know") you're creating a risk. But in fact you don't know. Consider Tara who bought a car she found in a Minneapolis newspaper ad. She drove off in the car without having a safety check, which would've revealed the brakes were shot. On the way home, she hit and killed a pedestrian when the brakes failed. She was negligent; she didn't know about the brakes, but she should've known not to drive a car she knew nothing about.

negligent intent unconsciously creating an unreasonable risk of harm

Most *minor* crimes don't require intent; the act is enough. We call these crimes without intent **strict liability offenses.** Our criminal law didn't recognize strict liability until the Industrial Revolution when public transportation, factories, and large-scale consumer purchasing created high risks to health and safety. Shared managerial responsibility characterized these new enterprises and made the requirement of personal and individual culpability meaningless. The requirement of criminal intent prevented the punishment of these serious injuries, incurable diseases, and deaths. Legislatures responded by adopting strict liability offenses.

strict liability offenses crimes without criminal intent

The Concurrence of Act and Intent The element of concurrence means criminal intent has to trigger the criminal act. For example, Doug hates Nathan. He plans to kill him but changes his mind because he doesn't want to go to prison. As luck would have it, two months after he abandons his plan to kill Nathan, Michelle accidentally hits Nathan with her new VW and kills him. Doug's delighted when he hears Nathan's dead, but he's not guilty of murder. Why? Because his intent to kill Nathan didn't trigger Michelle's act of running over him (LaFave and Scott 1986, 267–277).

Causing a Criminal Harm In crimes that include an element of cause, the prosecution has to prove two kinds of cause: factual cause and legal cause. **Factual cause** means that the result wouldn't have happened if it weren't for (but for) the defendant's actions. More technically, the defendant's actions triggered a chain of events that eventually led to a criminal result. For example, Kibbe and his companion robbed Stafford and left him on a country road late at night. Blake, a college student driving back to school accidentally hit and killed Stafford. If Kibbe and his companion hadn't left Stafford on the road, Blake wouldn't have hit and killed him. So they're the factual cause of Stafford's death.

factual cause the result wouldn't have happened if it weren't for the defendant's actions

But factual cause isn't enough to prove causation; there has to be legal cause, too. **Legal cause** asks whether it's fair to blame defendants for the consequences of the chain of events their actions triggered. It's up to the jury to decide the "fair to blame" question. The jury (and probably you, too) decided it *was* fair to blame Kibbe and his companion for Stafford's death. But what about this example? In a jealous rage, Cameron shoves Rob who loses his balance and falls against the sharp edge of a glass table, suffering a nasty gash in his leg. Rob refuses to go to the doctor because he doesn't want to spend the money. Finally, after nearly a day, he's so weak from losing blood he goes to a hospital emergency room where he receives a transfusion. He develops an infection from a dirty needle used in the transfusion and dies three weeks later. Is Cameron guilty of criminal homicide? Probably not, because it's not fair to blame him for Rob's

legal cause asks whether it's fair to blame defendants for the consequences of the chain of events their actions triggered

negligent (possibly reckless) failure to get help *and* the hospital's negligent use of a dirty needle.

The Defenses to Crime

Even if the prosecution proves all the elements of a crime beyond a reasonable doubt, defendants can avoid conviction if they can prove one of three kinds of defenses:

1. Alibi
2. Justification
3. Excuse

defense of alibi defendants have to prove they couldn't have committed the crime because they were somewhere else when the crime was committed

defenses of justification defendants admit they're responsible for their actions, but, they argue, under the circumstances their actions were justified

defenses of excuse defendants admit what they did was wrong but, they argue, under the circumstances they weren't *responsible* for their actions

In the **defense of alibi,** defendants have to prove they couldn't have committed the crime because they were somewhere else when the crime was committed. In the defenses of justification and excuse, defendants admit they committed the crimes, but they argue they should be acquitted anyway. Why? In **defenses of justification,** defendants admit they're responsible for their actions but under the circumstances, they argue, their actions were justified. In other words, the *rightness* of their actions justifies what they did. The classic justification defense is self-defense: "I killed Cruz because he was just about to kill me." In **defenses of excuse,** defendants admit what they did was wrong but under the circumstances, they argue, they weren't *responsible* for their actions. In other words, the wrongfulness of their actions is *excused.* The classic excuse is insanity: "Killing Mai was wrong, but I was insane when I killed her." Let's take a closer look at the defenses of justification and excuse.

The Defenses of Justification The defenses of justification include self-defense, the defense of home and property, and consent. They're all *grudging* exceptions to the government's jealous monopoly on the use of force—that is, to the idea that you can't take the law into your own hands.

"Kill or be killed" is the idea behind the self-defense exception to the ban on taking the law into your own hands. But defendants can only avoid conviction if they can prove three conditions existed at the time they fought back.

1. They didn't provoke the attack.
2. They reasonably believed the attack was going to happen right then (it was imminent).
3. They used only enough force necessary to repel the attack.

The third condition points to two unacceptable reasons for taking the law into your own hands:

1. *Preemptive strikes.* To prevent future attacks, like killing someone who's going to kill you next week
2. *Retaliation.* To pay back someone who tried to kill you last week

Preemptive strikes and retaliation are always the government's business, never private individuals'.

"A man's home is his castle" is the ancient root of the modern defenses of home and property. Under the English common law (based on unwritten customs), killing nighttime intruders was justifiable homicide. Modern law still follows the common-law rule by granting occupants the right to use force to defend their homes. For example, Colorado's "make-my-day law" grants immunity from all legal action—including criminal prosecution—to occupants of homes who use force, including deadly force, against "one who has made an unlawful entry into the dwelling" (Colorado Statutes 1986).

In most states, you can also use force to protect your "stuff" (personal property). In Texas, you can even shoot to kill to protect your "stuff" if you can't protect it "by any other means" or if "the failure to use deadly force" would expose

Should Evidence of Rape Victims' Sexual Activities Be Off Limits in Rape Trials?

Both sides in basketball star Kobe Bryant's sexual assault trial agree he had sex with a 19-year-old hotel employee in his room at a Colorado resort. Bryant claims she consented; the woman and the state say it was rape. Prosecutors cite vaginal abrasions to prove that the sex was forced. The defense says DNA findings prove she could've been injured while having sex with someone else. The question for the judge was whether the evidence should be admitted. **Rape shield laws** were passed in the 1970s that banned testimony about victims' sex lives from the courtroom. With good reason. There was a time when the "type of panties a woman was wearing could be used to discount the claim of rape" (*Los Angeles Times* 2004, Editorial). The judge ruled to allow the evidence because the jury should have evidence of the woman's sexual activities during the hours before and after she had sex with Bryant.

The judge in the high-profile celebrity trial of professional basketball star Kobe Bryant's sexual assault trial made a controversial ruling that the defense could introduce evidence of the alleged victim's other sexual contacts. Rape victim advocates say the ruling will scare victims and embolden defense lawyers. Others say it's not a defeat for victims' rights; it's just recognizing how hard it is to get to the truth "in a bewildering era of shifting sexual mores." According to a *Los Angeles Times* editorial, it was "The Best Call, This Time":

> The ruling undermines the prosecution in this case, but its larger import is not so clear. It does not take us back to the day when the type of panties a woman was wearing could be used to discount the claim of rape. Other judges have made similar findings when the role of other sex partners seemed relevant. It is up to jurors to decide how much weight to give that evidence. Social science research suggests that they remain as likely to assess a defendant's guilt based on their view of the victim's virtue as on the physical evidence. But how do jurors assign virtue in an era when sexual freedom seems to have no boundaries, when group sex and "hooking up"—casual sex between virtual strangers—are not the norm but common enough to have lost shock value?

In Orange County, jurors—who had been asked on jury questionnaires whether they used sex toys, watched porno movies or were "sexually adventurous"—couldn't agree on whether a 16-year-old girl, videotaped lying motionless while three young men took turns having sex with her, poking and penetrating her with a juice bottle, a pool cue and a lighted cigarette, was a rape victim drugged unconscious or a willing participant playing porn star. After all, she had been known to use drugs and sleep around, defense lawyers said. The jury deadlocked a month ago, divided by conflicting views of her credibility.

In a recent case at UCLA, three high school football players on a campus tour talked their way into the dorm room of a freshman girl, then had sex with her, one after the other. She testified at their rape trial that she told them no repeatedly but didn't resist because she was scared. Their lawyers called the sex consensual, said she flirted and let them unbutton her pants. The jury found two of the boys not guilty and deadlocked on the other. A 23-year-old woman on the jury explained it this way: "It's not so far-fetched to me that today a female would go and have consensual sex with three men after 10 minutes of meeting them....I just didn't believe her."

The scenario in the Bryant case suggests a similar battle. Details of the woman's past—stories of suicide attempts and sexual escapades— have already been leaked to the media, and more is likely to emerge during trial. And the judge, struggling to be fair to both sides, has ruled that the woman cannot be referred to as "victim" because that might bias the jury against Bryant.

The judge's decisions seem prudent in the unemotional framework of the law. But in the real world, people bring their own prejudices and social values into the jury box. The urge to put the accuser on trial still lurks behind 30 years of rape law reform.

Source: http://www.latimes.com/news/opinion/editorials/la-ed-kobe01aug01,0,2906864.story?coll=la-news-comment-editorials

---

you or others to a "substantial risk of death or serious bodily injury" (Texas Criminal Code 1988, Section 9.42).

Are you justified in committing a crime against someone who consents to it? A few courts say consent is a justification for committing *minor* crimes. The reason is the high value placed on individual autonomy in a free society. If mentally competent adults want to be crime victims (so the argument goes), no paternal-minded government should interfere with their choice. Consent may make sense in the larger context of individual freedom and responsibility, but the criminal law is hostile to consent as a justification for committing crimes. (This isn't always evident in rape cases; see the In Focus box "Should Evidence of Rape Victims' Sexual Activities Be Off Limits in Rape Trials?") Individuals can take their

rape shield laws passed in the 1970s, they ban testimony about victims' sex lives from the courtroom

▶ Formally, the criminal law allows a long list of excuses as defenses to crime. But informally, almost every defendant who pleads an excuse is convicted. Here, Richard Keech, 77, a World War II veteran who pleaded the excuse of post-traumatic stress syndrome, speaks at his sentencing hearing after he was convicted and sentenced to 35 years in prison for killing his daughter's abusive ex-husband.

AP/Wide World Photos

own lives and inflict injuries on themselves, but they can't authorize others to kill them or beat them.

The few courts that allow this defense place three limits on its use: no serious injury results from the consensual crime; the injury happens during a sporting event; or the conduct benefits the consenting person, such as when a surgeon operates on a patient. Not only is consent limited to these three circumstances, but the consenting persons have to know they're consenting and consent of their own free will. Forgiveness after the crime has been committed doesn't count.

Now that you've learned some of the basics of some of the justifications, let's look at the excuses (the act was wrong, but the defendant wasn't responsible).

The Defenses of Excuse The defenses of excuse are based on the idea that the law should make allowances for the imperfections and frailties of human nature. In the real world, excuses aren't popular. I hear excuses from students almost every day. I often think (and sometimes say), "Excuses, excuses, excuses, I'm sick of excuses!!" The criminal law doesn't like them either, even though there's a long list of them, including age; duress; entrapment; intoxication; the best-known excuse, insanity or diminished capacity; and a number of so-called syndromes, like PMS (premenstrual syndrome), PTS (post-traumatic stress syndrome), and the culture of violence syndrome. The law's hostility to them is formally hidden, but you can detect it clearly in the failure of almost every defendant who pleads them to escape conviction.

The excuse of age (immaturity) reaches far back into the English common law brought by the colonists to America. The common law recognized three categories of maturity:

1. Individuals too young under all circumstances to be criminally responsible
2. Individuals mature to the extent that they might or might not be criminally responsible
3. Individuals mature enough to be criminally responsible in nearly all circumstances

The law still recognizes these categories (Chapter 15). In most states, the categories are synchronized with the jurisdiction (authority) of juvenile courts. So juvenile courts have exclusive jurisdiction up to age 15 or 16. Between 16 and 18, juveniles can either be tried as juveniles or certified (transferred) to the regular criminal courts for trial as adults. Certification is most common when juveniles are accused of murder, rape, aggravated assault, robbery, and drug-related offenses (Chapter 15).

Old age has occasionally provided an excuse to criminal liability. In one case, a husband asked his wife of 50 years to get him some bagels. She forgot. According to the prosecutor, "The guy goes berserk and he axes his wife; he kills the poor woman with a Boy Scout–type ax!" The prosecutor did not charge the man, saying: "What do we do now? Set high bail? Prosecute? Get a conviction and send the fellow to prison? You tell me! We did nothing. The media dropped it quickly and, I hope, that's it." Incidentally, this case provides another excellent example of discretion adapting law to social reality. The formal law provided no excuse of advanced age, but the prosecutor exercised his independent judgment as to what justice required in this individual case and how best to allocate scarce resources and balance the law and broad community values (Cohen 1985, 9).

If someone forces you to commit a crime, you might have the excuse of duress. In some states, duress is a defense to all crimes except murder; in others, it excuses only minor crimes. States also differ as to the definition of duress. Some say only threats to kill the defendant are enough to excuse the crime; others say threats to seriously injure will do. Threats to damage reputation or to destroy property aren't enough in any state. Most states say defendants have to face immediate harm if they refuse to commit the crime.

"Make it easy to do right and difficult to do wrong," Prime Minister William Gladstone told the English government. "Lead us not into temptation, but deliver us from evil" implores the Lord's Prayer. **Entrapment**—law enforcement officers' efforts to get people to commit crimes—defies both the great prime minister's advice and the Lord's Prayer, but the practice has an ancient pedigree. From the reign of Henry VIII, to Hitler and Stalin, to Slobodan Milosevic and Saddam Hussein, police states have relied on government agents (agents provocateurs) to trap opponents of the regime (Carlson 1987, 1011).

entrapment efforts by law enforcement officers to get people to commit crimes

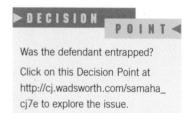

▶ DECISION POINT ◀

Was the defendant entrapped?

Click on this Decision Point at http://cj.wadsworth.com/samaha_cj7e to explore the issue.

Law enforcement encouragement occurs most often in crimes where there are no *complaining* witnesses (prostitution, gambling, pornography, official wrongdoing, and drug crimes) because officers have to use deception to detect these crimes. The argument in favor of entrapment (and against entrapment as an excuse for criminal behavior) was nicely summed up by one court more than a hundred years ago:

> We are asked to protect the defendant, not because he is innocent, but because a zealous public officer exceeded his powers and held out a bait. The courts do not look to see who held out the bait, but to see who took it. (*People v. Mills* 1904, 791)

Allowing the excuse of entrapment represents an intolerance of government pressures on law-abiding people to commit crimes they wouldn't have committed without the pressure (Marcus 1986, 5). Notice that *encouragement* isn't entrapment. So for the purpose of getting people to commit crimes, officers can ask people to commit crimes; form personal relationships with them; promise them benefits; and supply or help them get contraband. How do we separate encouragement from entrapment?

Most courts use the predisposition test to decide when officials have crossed the line between encouragement and entrapment. According to the test, if the defendant was ready and willing to commit the crime (predisposed) and the officer only provided her with the opportunity to commit it, that's encouragement, not entrapment. The crucial question is, Where did criminal intent originate? If it originated with the defendant, then the government didn't entrap but only encouraged the defendant (Tiffany, McIntyre, and Rotenberg 1967).

Sherman v. United States (1958) is a good example of entrapment. In this case, a government undercover agent, Kalchinian, met Sherman in a drug treatment center, made friends with him, and eventually asked Sherman to get him some heroin. Sherman, an addict in treatment, at first refused. After several weeks of Kalchinian's pleading, Sherman broke down and got the requested heroin. The U.S. Supreme Court ruled that Kalchinian entrapped Sherman, arguing that Sherman's reluctance and his being in treatment refuted the claim he was predisposed to commit the crime.

Johnny James was executed by lethal injection for kidnapping two women, forcing them to perform sex acts on each other, and then shooting them both in the head. One died, the other survived and identified James at trial. The criminal justice system turned a deaf ear to James's claim he was too drunk to know what he was doing when he committed the crime so he didn't deserve to die (Gibeaut 1997, 56).

According to Professor George Fletcher, the defense of intoxication is "buffeted between two conflicting principles":

1. *Accountability.* Those who get drunk should face the consequences of their actions.
2. *Culpability.* You can't punish someone who isn't responsible for his or her actions. (Fletcher 1978, 846)

The common law focused on the first principle:

As to artificial, voluntarily contracted madness, by drunkenness or intoxication, which, depriving men of their reason, puts them in a temporary frenzy; our law looks upon this as an aggravation of the offense, rather than as an excuse for any criminal misbehavior. (Blackstone 1803, IV, 25–26)

The Johnny James case proves the common-law principle is alive and well. John Gibeaut (1997) notes this contemporary emphasis on the principle of accountability in his article on the James case, "Sobering Thoughts: Legislatures and Courts Increasingly Are Just Saying No to Intoxication as a Defense or Mitigating Factor" (56–57).

We've been talking about voluntary intoxication, which isn't an excuse, but involuntary intoxication is. Involuntary intoxication refers to defendants who either don't know they're taking intoxicants or know but are forced to take them. So Augustus Penman was allowed the defense of intoxication when he killed a friend after taking breath mints he didn't know were laced with cocaine (*People v. Penman* 1915).

As for forced intoxication, only extreme force excuses. According to one authority, "[A] person would need to be bound hand and foot and the liquor literally poured down his throat, or . . . would have to be threatened with immediate serious injury." In *Burrows v. State* (1931), Richard Burrows was 18 and stranded on an Arizona highway with no money. (See the In Focus box "Was He Too Drunk to Be Guilty of Murder?") He hitched a ride to Phoenix with Jack Martin. Shortly after they got on the road, Martin began drinking beer and asked Burrows to have some. Burrows, who'd never had a drink, turned him down. Martin got belligerent and threatened to throw Burrows out in the desert if he didn't

Was He Too Drunk to Be Guilty of Murder?

FACTS

Allen Hall was hitchhiking in the West, and Gilford Meacham offered him a ride from Oregon to Chicago if Hall would drive. Hall was supposed to split off and hitchhike to his home in North Carolina, while Meacham was to drive on to Connecticut to get married. Hall drove all the way to Iowa without rest and was exhausted. When they got to Des Moines, Hall took a pill (later determined to be LSD) casual acquaintances in California had given him. (They told Hall it was a "little sunshine" and would make him feel "groovy.") It made him "feel funny, and the road turned different colors and pulsated."

Meacham was sleeping on the passenger side. Hall testified he heard strange noises from Meacham's throat, like growling. Meacham's face grew and his nose got long, and his head turned into a dog like the one defendant's stepfather had shot. Defendant testified he got scared, picked up Meacham's gun, and shot him three times. Hall said he didn't remember much that happened for awhile. The next time he clearly remembered anything he was in a cemetery at What Cheer, Iowa. He testified he had periods thinking Meacham was human and periods thinking Meacham was a dog. He drove Meacham's car to Davenport, abandoned it, took a bus to Chicago, hitchhiked through the Southwest, and turned himself in to officials in the State of Nevada. He voluntarily told officers about the incident.

The County Attorney of Jasper County, Iowa, charged defendant with murder, and a jury found him guilty of first-degree murder. Hall appealed, claiming involuntary intoxication was an excuse for the murder.

OPINION

Voluntary intoxication from alcohol does not constitute a complete defense. Defendant . . . argues that he did not take the pill voluntarily. But . . . according to his own testimony no one tricked him into taking it or forced him to do so. . . . Defendant did not take the pill by mistake—thinking, for example, it was candy. If his own testimony is believed, he knew it was a mind-affecting drug.

Defendant's next contention takes us another step into the legal effect of voluntary use of drugs. The trial court submitted to the jury forms of verdict for both first- and second-degree murder, for manslaughter, and for acquittal. In its instruction on defendant's claimed mental condition from taking a pill, the trial court instructed that "no amount of voluntary use of drugs can entirely excuse a Murder and thereby entitle a slayer to an acquittal."

Does voluntary drug intoxication permit a jury to reduce a homicide to manslaughter? Turning again to the analogy of intoxication resulting from alcohol,

> It is now generally held that intoxication may be considered where murder is divided into degrees, and in many states, may have the effect of reducing homicide from murder in the first degree to murder in the second degree. In fact, in most states the only consideration given to the fact of drunkenness or intoxication at the time of the commission of the homicide is to enable the court and jury to determine whether the prisoner may be guilty of murder in the second degree, rather than of murder in the first degree. The rule followed by most courts is that intoxication will not reduce a homicide from murder to manslaughter.

Affirmed.

DISSENT

. . . I cannot agree with the majority opinion. . . . It is only voluntary intoxication which may not be relied upon as a defense to the commission of a criminal act. The majority finds that the use of drugs here was voluntary. I believe that finding entirely overlooks the real import of the evidence. The testimony shows defendant took a pill which he knew to be a drug but which he did not know to be LSD and which he testified he thought to be harmless, although he had been told it would make him feel groovy. There is nothing to indicate he knew it could induce hallucinations or lead to the frightening debilitating effects of mind and body to which the doctors testified. The majority nevertheless holds the defendant's resulting drug intoxication was voluntary. I disagree.

Source: State v. Hall, 214 N.W.2d 205 (Iowa 1974).

---

drink some beer with him. Burrows took a drink because he was afraid of being stranded in the desert. Later, Martin started drinking whiskey and threatened to throw Burrows out again when Burrows said he didn't want to drink anymore. So Burrows took some. The situation quickly deteriorated after that; the man got more belligerent and Burrows now drunk, got more scared, and finally shot and killed Martin. At his trial for murder, Burrows contended "Any suggestion or influence which induces another to become intoxicated, when, if he had been left entirely to himself, he would have remained sober, excuses him from the consequences of a crime." The state argued that "the influence must go to the extent of actual coercion and abuse."

The jury convicted Burrows of murder. On appeal, the Arizona supreme court wrote:

> We are of the opinion that the true rule is that the influence exercised on the mind of a defendant must be such as to amount to duress or fraud. The law has always jealously guarded the effect of drunkenness as a defense in criminal cases, and, even with all the restrictions surrounding it, the doctrine is a dangerous one, and liable to be abused. In this case there is no suggestion of fraud, and it was for the jury to decide whether or not there was coercion and abuse to the extent of duress. (1035)

The insanity excuse attracts a lot of public, philosophical, religious, and scholarly attention, but it plays only a tiny part in the day-to-day operations of criminal justice. Defendants rarely plead insanity and rarely succeed if they do. Also, if they do succeed, they don't automatically "walk." In some jurisdictions, the verdict is "not guilty by reason of insanity"; in others, it's "guilty but insane." Guilty but insane means they will go to prison but with the chance for treatment while incarcerated. Not guilty by reason of insanity means they're not guilty but not free to go. Special proceedings to decide whether defendants are mentally ill and dangerous follow the verdict of not guilty by reason of insanity. If they are (and it's a rare court that finds they aren't), they're confined to maximum security hospitals (really just prisons). They're confined until they're no longer dangerous, which usually means a long time and often for life. John Hinckley, who attempted to assassinate President Reagan in the early 1980s, is typical. He's still detained in a maximum security hospital (although he's allowed occasional weekend furloughs).

Insanity is a legal, *not* a medical, term; it means a mental disease (for example, paranoia) or defect (retardation) that impairs reason and/or will. There are three main tests of insanity:

1. The right-wrong test
2. The right-wrong test supplemented by the irresistible impulse test
3. The substantial capacity or American Law Institute (ALI) test

right-wrong test an insanity defense focus on whether a mental disease or defect impaired the defendants' reason so that they couldn't tell the difference between right and wrong

The **right-wrong test** focuses on reason. The test, sometimes called the *M'Naughten rule,* comes from a famous English case. In 1843, Daniel M'Naughten had the paranoid delusion that the prime minister, Sir Robert Peel, had masterminded a conspiracy to kill him. M'Naughten shot at Peel in delusional self-defense but mistakenly killed Peel's personal secretary. The jury acquitted M'Naughten. On appeal, the House of Lords—England's highest court of appeal—formulated the right-wrong test. The test evaluates whether two necessary elements were present at the time the crime was committed:

1. A mental disease or defect caused such damage to the defendants' capacity to reason
2. That either they didn't know what they were doing, or if they knew what they were doing, they didn't know it was wrong (M'Naughten's Case 1843)

irresistible impulse test a test of insanity that focuses on whether mental disease affected the defendants' willpower (their capacity to control their actions at the time of the crime)

Several jurisdictions have supplemented the right-wrong test with the **irresistible impulse test.** The irresistible impulse test focuses on defendants' willpower, or their capacity to control their actions at the time of the crime. The test evaluates whether two necessary elements existed:

1. Defendants suffered from a mental disease or defect.
2. It caused them to lose the power to choose between right and wrong

In other words, defendants know what they're doing, they know it's wrong, but they can't stop themselves from doing it.

substantial capacity test a test of insanity that focuses on whether a mental disease substantially impaired the reason and/or will of the defendants

The **substantial capacity test** focuses on both reason and will. Formulated by the American Law Institute, it evaluates whether two necessary elements existed at the time of the crime:

1. Defendants had a mental disease or defect that caused them to lack substantial capacity
2. To either appreciate the wrongfulness (criminality) of their conduct or to conform their conduct to the requirements of the law

Notice the test focuses on *substantial* capacity; in other words, the mental disease or defect doesn't have to totally destroy defendants' reason or will.

Excuse defenses based on syndromes that supposedly affect mental capacity began to appear in the 1970s. The defense has led to some bizarre excuses, including such syndromes as policeman's, love, fear, chronic brain, and holocaust. Law professor and defense attorney Alan Dershowitz (1994, 3) wrote a book listing dozens of these syndrome excuses. The title, *The Abuse Excuse and Other Cop-Outs, Sob Stories, and Evasions of Responsibility,* underscores his low opinion of them. Dershowitz worries these excuses are "quickly becoming a license to kill and maim." His is probably a needless worry because defendants rarely plead these excuses, and except for a few infamous cases, they don't escape conviction by pleading "abuse excuses."

One famous syndrome excuse case took place in the late 1970s when Dan White, a San Francisco police officer and member of the city council, shot and killed gay activist and city councilman Harvey Milk and Mayor George Moscone. White's lawyer introduced the junk food syndrome, popularly called the "Twinkie defense." He argued junk food had diminished White's mental faculties. According to one psychiatrist's testimony:

> During these spells he'd become quite withdrawn, quite lethargic. He would retreat to his room. Wouldn't come to the door. Wouldn't answer the phone. And during these periods he found that he could not cope with people. Any confrontations would cause him to kind of become argumentative. Whenever he felt things were not going right he would abandon his usual program of exercise and good nutrition and start gorging himself on junk foods. Twinkies, Coca Cola.
>
> Mr. White had always been something of an athlete, priding himself on being physically fit. But when something would go wrong he'd hit the high sugar stuff. He'd hit the chocolate and the more he consumed the worse he'd feel, and he'd respond to his ever-growing depression by consuming even more junk food. The more junk food he consumed, the worse he'd feel. The worse he'd feel, the more he'd gorge himself. (Weiss 1984, 349–350)

The defense argued these depressions, which eating junk food aggravated, diminished White's capacity enough to reduce his responsibility. The jury returned a verdict of manslaughter, and White was sentenced to a relatively short prison term. After his release from prison, he committed suicide.

Women occasionally have claimed a premenstrual syndrome (PMS) (Chapter 3) as a defense to excuse their crimes. In a New York case, Shirley Santos called the police, telling them, "My little girl is sick" (*Newsweek* 1982, 111). The medical team in the hospital emergency room where she was taken found welts on the girl's legs and blood in her urine and diagnosed them as resulting from child abuse. The police arrested Santos, who explained, "I don't remember what happened. . . . I would never hurt my baby. . . . I just got my period."

At a preliminary hearing, Santos claimed PMS excused her assaulting and endangering the welfare of her child. She admitted beating her child but argued that PMS caused her to black out; hence, she could not have formed the intent to assault or endanger her child's welfare. After lengthy plea bargaining, the prosecutor dropped the felony charges and Santos pleaded guilty to the misdemeanor of harassment. Santos received no sentence, not even probation or a fine, even though her daughter spent two weeks in the hospital from the injuries. The plea bargaining prevented a legal test of the PMS defense in this case. Nevertheless, the judge's leniency suggests that PMS affected the outcome informally.

There are three legal obstacles to pleading the PMS defense:

1. Defendants have to prove that PMS is a disease; little medical research shows it is.

2. The defendant has to actually suffer from PMS; there are hardly ever any medical records to document it.
3. PMS has to cause the mental impairment; there's still too much skepticism about PMS to accept that it excuses criminal conduct. (Note 1983, 263–269)

Classifiying and Grading Crimes

The urge to make sense of criminal law is ancient. That urge has produced a lot of schemes to classify and grade the content of criminal law. We'll look at three classification schemes:

1. Felony, misdemeanor, and violation
2. *Mala in se* and *mala prohibita*
3. Crimes and torts

Felony, Misdemeanor, and Violation Crimes classified according to the type and duration of punishment are called felonies, misdemeanors, or violations. These are ancient classifications, demonstrating that the past still influences today's criminal law. The great legal historian Frederic William Maitland maintained that the reasons for old classifications may have died a long time ago, but their ghosts rule us from the grave. He meant that even when classifications have outlived their usefulness, they still shape how we think and what we do. Dividing crimes into felonies and misdemeanors is one example. Until 1600, felonies were all punishable by death. Today, we divide **felonies** into capital felonies, punishable by death or life imprisonment, and ordinary felonies, punishable by one year or more in prison. So felonies include serial killers at one extreme and individuals who steal $500 at the other. The breadth of its scope makes the classification largely meaningless in any sociological sense. It serves mainly as an

felonies capital felonies are crimes punishable by death or life imprisonment; ordinary felonies are crimes punishable by one year or more in prison

▶ The law punishes misdemeanors (minor crimes) with fines and/or jail time up to one year. Prostitution is only one of thousands of others called "crimes against public order" or "quality of life" crimes.

Are Some Crimes Inherently Evil?

The notion of inherently evil crimes suggests a consensus as to what serious crime is. Research does not confirm this conclusion. Not everyone agrees that activities such as drug use, gambling, and consensual adult sexual conduct are inherently evil, even if they are crimes. Consider these findings:

- More than one-third of all college men would rape if they thought they could get away with it.
- Most murders are committed by people who think they are righting some wrong done to them.

According to Donald Black (1983):

[M]ost intentional homicide in modern life is a response to conduct that the killer regards as deviant. Homicide is often a response to...matters relating to sex, love, or loyalty, to disputes about domestic matters (financial affairs, drinking, housekeeping) or affronts to honor, to conflicts regarding debts, property, and to child custody, and to other questions of right and wrong.

For example, one youth killed his brother during an argument about the brother's sexual advances toward their younger sisters.

- The vast majority of assaults occur between people who know each other.

In most cases, assailants believe they are redressing grievances. They take the law into their own hands to punish a wrongdoer. They do not believe that they were wrong in what they did, even though they may agree that it was against the law to do so. For example, some brothers attacked and beat their sister's boyfriend because he turned her into a drug addict. In another case, a gang member shot his gang leader for taking more than his proper share of the proceeds from a burglary. Years later, the same individual shot someone who had been terrorizing young women—including the avenger's girlfriend—in his neighborhood. Though he pleaded guilty to "assault with a deadly weapon" and was committed to a reformatory, not surprisingly he described himself as "completely right" and his victim as "completely wrong."

- Many property offenders know their victims.

They have taken or destroyed their victims' property because they believe their victims deserved it. For instance, a man broke into his ex-wife's apartment to take back property he believed was rightfully his. A former burglar noted, "We always tried to get the dude that the neighbors didn't like too much or the guy that was hard on the people who lived in the neighborhood. I like to think that all the places we robbed, that we broke into, was kind of like the bad guys."

- In many cases, vandalism turns out to be not wanton violence but an effort to punish what the vandals consider to be wrongdoing.

One young man found that someone had broken the radio antenna on his automobile. When he found out who did it, he slashed the culprit's tires in retaliation.

According to the criminal codes of virtually all jurisdictions, all of these examples are crimes. Yet, none of the perpetrators considered what they did to be evil. Quite the contrary; although they are "criminals" according to the law, they believed that they were exercising justified social control over "wrongdoers." The criminals considered themselves victims because they believed that they were forced to commit crimes to rectify wrongs against them.

Sources: Donald Black, "Crime as Social Control," *American Sociological Review* 48(1983): 34–46; Peter Rossi, Emily Waite, Christine E. Bose, and Richard E. Berk, "The Seriousness of Crime: The Normative Structure and Individual Differences," *American Sociological Review* 39(1974): 224–237.

---

administrative device to determine who gets the death penalty, life imprisonment, or incarceration in a state prison.

Misdemeanors are minor offenses punishable either by fines or up to one year in jail. Common misdemeanors include simple assaults and battery, prostitution, and disorderly conduct. Most jurisdictions divide misdemeanors into gross misdemeanors (30 days to one year in jail) and petty misdemeanors (a fine and/or up to 30 days in jail). **Violations** are punishable by a small fine, and they don't become part of your criminal history. (Remember criminal history is one of the major legitimate criteria for decision making in criminal justice.) The most common violations are traffic offenses.

misdemeanors minor offenses (simple assaults and battery, prostitution, and disorderly conduct) punishable either by fines or up to one year in jail

violations crimes punishable by a small fine; they don't become part of your criminal history

Mala in Se* and *Mala Prohibita This classification sorts crimes according to whether they are perceived as "evil." This old arrangement overlaps the felony, misdemeanor, and violation categories and defines some crimes as inherently bad (the Latin ***mala in se***). (See the In Focus box "Are Some Crimes Inherently Evil?") Crimes such as murder and rape fall into this category. Other behavior is

mala in se inherently evil behavior

mala prohibita behavior that is criminal only because the law defines it as a crime

a crime only because the law says so (the Latin ***mala prohibita***). Parking in a no-parking zone is *malum prohibitum.*

This ancient classification goes back to the roots of American criminal law in the religious and moral codes of England and colonial America. Although morality was frequently viewed as a preoccupation of the New England Puritans, the Anglicans of Virginia, Pennsylvania Quakers, and Maryland Catholics also infused criminal law with a moral component. The major felonies and the "morals" offenses—fornication, prostitution, sodomy, gambling, and public drunkenness—descend from this religious and moral heritage (Flaherty 1971, 203–253).

In practice, no clear line separates *mala in se* and *mala prohibita* offenses. Despite legal theories that cling to the distinction, and notwithstanding talk of an ethical core in the criminal law, empirical research has demonstrated that offenders consider many crimes that are formally classified as *mala in se* "justifiable." That is, they consider their "criminal" actions as informal means to put right a deeply felt wrong. They may concede that their conduct "technically" violates formal criminal law, but they believe that what they did definitely was not really evil. According to sociologist Donald Black (1983):

> There is a sense in which conduct regarded as criminal is often quite the opposite. Far from being an intentional violation of a prohibition, much crime is moralistic and involves the pursuit of justice. It is a mode of conflict management, possibly a form of punishment, even capital punishment. Viewed in relation to law it is self-help. To the degree that it defines or responds to the conduct of someone else—the victim—as deviant, crime is social control.

Crimes and Torts Some harms are the basis for lawsuits even though they're not crimes. These private or civil lawsuits differ from criminal actions in several respects. In criminal cases, the government and the defendant are the parties to the case. So the title of the criminal case is *State* (or *U.S., Commonwealth,* or *People*) *v. Munckton* (defendant). In private personal injury actions (called **torts**), plaintiffs sue wrongdoers (defendants) to get money for their injuries (called **damages**). Torts carry the names of the parties to the lawsuit; the plaintiff's name is first, as in *Chan* (plaintiff) *v. Gonzalez* (defendant). Criminal cases rest on the notion that crime harms society generally, leaving individual injuries to tort actions, but almost all crimes against persons and property are also torts. A burglary, for instance, consists of the tort of trespass; a criminal assault consists of the tort of criminal assault.

Criminal prosecutions and tort actions may arise out of the same event, but criminal and tort proceedings are not mutually exclusive. Victims can sue for, and the government can prosecute, injuries arising out of the same conduct. For example, a burglary victim can sue the burglar for trespass and, at least theoretically, collect damages. The government can prosecute the burglar and, if it obtains a conviction, impose punishment.

torts private personal injury actions

damages money for personal injuries awarded by courts

Legal Information Institute on Criminal Procedure: Overview of criminal law, including many links and resources. To reach this site go to "Web Links" on your Samaha CJ7 website: http://cj.wadsworth.com/samaha_cj7e.

The Law of Criminal Procedure

Criminal law tells private individuals what they can't do and lets them know the punishments for committing crimes. The law and rules of criminal procedure tell public officials what powers they have to enforce the criminal law, the limits of their powers, and the consequences for abusing them. (See the CJ & Technology box "Privacy and Terrorism: The Naked Crowd.") The law of criminal procedure is the formal side of decision making in criminal justice agencies (Chapter 1). It lays down rules for decisions made by officials at each step in the criminal process (Chapter 1). We'll examine the law of criminal procedure as it affects de-

U.S. Attorneys Manual: Go to the "Reading Room" on this site. To reach this site go to "Web Links" on your Samaha CJ7 website: http://cj.wadsworth.com/samaha_cj7e.

Privacy and Terrorism: The Naked Crowd

After the terrorist attacks of September 11, 2001, officials at Orlando International Airport began testing a remarkable new security device. Let's call it the Naked Machine, for that's more or less what it is. A kind of electronic strip search, the Naked Machine bounces microwaves and millimeter waves off the human body. In addition to exposing any guns or other weapons that are concealed by clothing, the Naked Machine produces a three-dimensional naked image of everyone it scrutinizes. Unlike the crude metal detectors used at airports today, the Naked Machine can detect ceramic and plastic as well as metal, allowing airport monitors to distinguish between lethal explosives and harmless nail clippers. The technologists who invented the Naked Machine hope that it will be deployed in the future not only at airports but also in schools, at public monuments, in federal buildings, and in prisons. Before we enter any vulnerable public space, the Naked Machine could strip us bare and confirm that we have nothing to hide.

The Naked Machine is a technology that promises a high degree of security, but it demands a correspondingly high sacrifice of liberty and privacy, requiring all travelers to expose themselves nakedly, even though they raise no particular suspicions and pose no particular threats. Many people feel that this is a small price to pay in an age of terror: What's a moment or two of embarrassment if terrorists are thwarted as a result? But the Naked Machine doesn't have to be designed in a way that protects security at the cost of invading privacy. With a simple programming shift, researchers at the Pacific Northwest National Laboratory in Washington State have built a prototype of a redesigned Naked Machine that extracts the images of concealed objects and projects them onto a sexless mannequin. The lurking image of the naked body is then scrambled into an unrecognizable and nondescript blob. (For most of us, this is an act of mercy.)

This more discreet version of the Naked Machine—let's call it the Blob Machine—guarantees exactly the same amount of security without depriving liberty or invading privacy. Unlike the Naked Machine, the Blob Machine is a silver bullet technology that promises dramatic benefits without obvious costs; if it were deployed at airports, or perhaps even on subways and buses, the most scrupulous defenders of liberty and privacy could greet it with gratitude and relief.

For those who care about preserving both liberty and security, the choice between the Blob Machine and the Naked Machine might seem to be easy. But in presenting a hypothetical choice between the Naked Machine and the Blob Machine to groups of students and adults since 9/11, I've been struck by a surprising pattern: There are always some people who say they would prefer, at the airport, to go through the Naked Machine rather than the Blob Machine, even if the lines for each were equally long. When asked why, the people who choose the Naked Machine over the Blob Machine give a range of responses. Some say they are already searched so thoroughly at airports that they have abandoned all hope of privacy and don't mind the additional intrusion of being seen naked. Others say they're not embarrassed to be naked in front of strangers, adding that those who have nothing to hide should have nothing to fear. (A few are unapologetic exhibitionists.) Still others are concerned that the Blob Machine would be less accurate in identifying weapons than the Naked Machine, and they would prefer not to take chances. And in each group, there are some people who say they are so afraid of terrorism on airplanes that they would do anything possible to make themselves feel better, even if they understand, on some level, that their reaction is based on emotions rather than evidence. They describe a willingness to be electronically stripped by the Naked Machine as a ritualistic demonstration of their own purity and trustworthiness in much the same way that the religiously devout describe rituals of faith. They don't care, in other words, whether or not the Naked Machine makes them safer than the Blob Machine because they are more concerned about feeling safe than being safe.

Source: Jeffrey Rosen, *The Naked Crowd* (New York: Random House, 2004), pp. 3–4.

---

cision making in law enforcement, courts, and corrections in later chapters where each specifically applies. Table 4.2 contains a list of the specific provisions in the Bill of Rights and the stages of the criminal process to which they relate. Here, we will focus on the principles that apply to all stages—due process and equal protection.

Due Process of Law

The bedrock of the formal law of criminal procedure is the principle of "due process of law." **Due process** in the law of criminal procedure means the right

CONCEPT | BUILDER

Visit http://cj.wadsworth.com/ samaha_cj7e for an interactive exploration of the issues surrounding **due process.**

due process the right to fair procedures

▼ TABLE 4.2 The Bill of Rights and Criminal Procedure

Agency	Amendment	Rights
Police	Fourth	Guarantee against unreasonable search and seizure
	Fifth	Right to a grand jury indictment Right against double jeopardy Right to due process (in federal proceedings) Right against self-incrimination
	Fourteenth	Right to due process (in state proceedings) Equal protection (in state proceedings)
Courts	Sixth	Right to a lawyer Right to a notice of charges Right to a speedy trial and public trial Right to a trial by jury Right to confront witnesses
	Eighth	Right against excessive bail Right against cruel and unusual punishment (in sentencing)
Corrections	Eighth	Prohibition against excessive fines Prohibition against cruel and unusual punishment

to fair procedures (Chapter 1). As we saw at the beginning of the chapter, both the Fifth and Fourteenth Amendments to the U.S. Constitution guarantee that neither the federal nor state governments can deny any person "life, liberty, or property without due process of law." (See also Chapter 1 on the tension between crime control and due process.)

But, as early as 1833, the chief justice of the U.S. Supreme Court, John Marshall, made clear that criminal procedure is a state and local matter. If Congress had meant to take the extraordinary step of applying the Bill of Rights (listed in Table 4.2) to the states, "they would have declared this purpose in plain…language." So Marshall concluded, whether the Bill of Rights applied to state and local procedure is a question "of great importance, but not of much difficulty": The federal Bill of Rights did not apply to the states. The states had their own bills of rights, which they could enforce as each state saw fit (*Barron v. Baltimore* 1833, 250).

Following the Civil War, a number of amendments were added to the U.S. Constitution to bring former slaves into full citizenship. As far as criminal justice is concerned, the Fourteenth Amendment due process clause is the most important of the "Civil War Amendments," because it specifically says, "No state shall deny any person of life, liberty, or property without due process of law." Despite this specific ban, states continued to make all decisions about criminal justice within their own borders, just as they'd done since the Revolution. However, this hands-off state criminal justice approach began to break down in the 1930s. It's probably not a coincidence that just as Hitler rose to power in Germany, the U.S. Supreme Court decided its first case applying the Fourteenth Amendment due process clause to the states. The German war machine of the First World War and the rise of fascism in its aftermath had already revived suspicions of arbitrary government held by Americans since the days of George III.

That first case began in northern Alabama one morning in March 1931, when seven scruffy White boys came into a railway station and told the stationmaster a "bunch of Negroes" had picked a fight with them and thrown them off a freight train (*Powell v. Alabama* 1932). The stationmaster phoned ahead to Scottsboro, where a deputy sheriff deputized every man who owned a gun. When the train got to Scottsboro, the posse rounded up nine Black boys and two White girls. The girls were dressed in men's caps and overalls. Five of the boys were from

The Scottsboro boys in jail during their trial for the rape (a capital offense) of two White women in Alabama in 1933. With them is their trial lawyer, Stephen Roddy, who came to the first day of their trial already drunk at 9 o'clock in the morning. The U.S. Supreme Court overturned their conviction on the grounds that they were denied a fair trial because they were put on trial for their lives without adequate representation.

Georgia and four from Tennessee. They ranged in age from 12 to 20. One was blind in one eye and had only 10 percent vision in the other; one walked with a cane; all were poor; and none could read or write. As the deputy sheriff was tying the boys together and loading them into his truck, Ruby Bates told him the boys had raped her and her friend, Victoria Price. By nightfall, a mob of several hundred people had surrounded the little Scottsboro jail, vowing to avenge the rape by lynching the boys.

When the trial began on Monday morning, April 6, 1931, 102 National Guardsmen struggled to keep several thousand people at least 100 feet away from the courthouse. Inside the courtroom, Judge Alfred E. Hawkins offered the job of defense attorney to anyone who would take it. Only Chattanooga lawyer Stephen Roddy accepted. Roddy, an alcoholic already drunk at 9:00 A.M., admitted he didn't know anything about Alabama law. Judge Hawkins then appointed "all members" of the local bar present in the courtroom as counsel. By Thursday, eight of the boys had been tried, convicted, and sentenced to death. The jury was divided on 12-year-old Roy Wright, with seven demanding death and five holding out for life imprisonment. Judge Hawkins declared a mistrial in Roy Wright's trial and sentenced the others to death by electrocution.

Liberals, radicals, and Communists around the country rallied to the defense of the "Scottsboro boys," as the case became popularly known. In March 1932, the Alabama Supreme Court upheld all of the convictions except for Eugene Williams, who was granted a new trial as a juvenile. In November, the U.S. Supreme Court ruled in *Powell v. Alabama* that Alabama had denied the boys due process of law. According to Justice Sutherland:

It has never been doubted by this court...that notice and hearing are preliminary steps essential to the passing of an enforceable judgment, and that they, together with a legally competent tribunal having jurisdiction of the case, constitute the basic elements of the constitutional requirement of due process of law. The words of [the great lawyer, Daniel] Webster...that by "the law of the land" is intended "a law which hears before it condemns" have been repeated...in a multitude of decisions....The necessity of due notice and an opportunity of being heard is...among the "immutable principles of justice which inhere the very idea of free government which no member of the Union may disregard."

There were passionate debates about just what the decision meant for state criminal justice, but by the end of the 1960s the meaning boiled down to this: The federal Bill of Rights sets a minimum standard that all states have to follow. They can raise this minimum by expanding rights, but they can't fall below it. For example, in one leading case, the U.S. Supreme Court ruled that DWI (driving while intoxicated) checkpoints at which all motorists are stopped and checked for signs of intoxication aren't "unreasonable seizures" under the Fourth Amendment to the U.S. Constitution (*Michigan v. Sitz* 1990). But the Michigan Supreme Court decided the Michigan constitution's seizure provision guaranteed more protection than the U.S. Constitution and that according to the state constitution DWI roadblocks are unreasonable seizures (*Sitz v. Department of State Police* 1993). According to the Michigan supreme court:

Our courts are not obligated to accept what we deem to be a major contraction of citizen protections under our constitution simply because the United States Supreme Court has chosen to do so....This court has never recognized the right of the state, without any level of suspicion whatsoever, to detain members of the population at large for criminal investigatory purposes....In these circumstances, the Michigan Constitution offers more protection than the United States Supreme Court's interpretation of the Fourth Amendment. (218)

The Equal Protection of the Law

It's an uncomfortable fact we have to live with, but our Constitution recognized Black slavery, excluded Native Americans from its protection, and provided no rights for women. But standing beside this caste system, written into the Constitution is the value of equality, which is deeply embedded in our ideology. In the years just before the Revolution, one commentator wrote, "The least considerable man among us has an interest equal to the proudest nobleman, in the laws and constitution of his country" (Inbau 1980, 209). In the 1960s, we described equality in criminal justice in harsher terms: "If the rich can beat the rap, then everyone should get to beat the rap."

Since 1868 (as you've already seen in the earlier section on constitutional limits on criminal law) equality has been more than a hope of the excluded or a slogan in criminal justice—it's a constitutional command. According to the Fourteenth Amendment to the U.S. Constitution, "No state shall...deny to any person within its jurisdiction the equal protection of the laws." In the law of criminal procedure, equal protection doesn't mean officials have to treat suspects, defendants, and offenders exactly alike in their efforts to control crime. It does mean they can't investigate, apprehend, convict, and punish people for unacceptable reasons. So courts look suspiciously at certain classifications, particularly those based on race and ethnicity, at least when they're the only reason for decision making.

But police officers can take ethnic background into account when they stop and frisk a Hispanic suspect, as long as being a Hispanic isn't the only reason for the stop and frisk. Prosecutors can take race into account when they decide to prosecute a Black crack dealer as long as it's not the only reason for the decision. (By the time you read this, you may be able to apply the "not the only reason" test to the investigations, detentions, charges, and prosecutions surrounding the September 11, 2001, attacks on the World Trade Center and the Pentagon.) As we move through the criminal justice decision-making process in the chapters on police, courts, and corrections, we'll run into other examples of the law treating people differently without violating the equal protection clause.

There's a lot of talk about how much better things are for battered women now than they used to be, but every day, husbands and boyfriends still beat their wives and girlfriends. Many of these women die from the beatings— but not all. A very small number strike back and kill their abusers. Judy Ann Norman was one of them. Here's her story.

Judy Ann Norman

Facts

Deputy Sheriff R. H. Epley found the victim, John Norman, lying on a bed in a rear bedroom with his face toward the wall and his back toward the middle of the room. He was dead, but blood was still coming from wounds to the back of his head. A later autopsy revealed three gunshot wounds to the head. The autopsy also revealed a .12 percent blood alcohol level in the victim's body.

Later that night Judy Ann Norman told Epley this story. Her husband had been beating her all day and had made her lie down on the floor while he slept on the bed. After he fell asleep, she took her grandchild to her mother's house; took a pistol from her mother's purse; walked back home; and pointed the pistol at the back of her sleeping husband's head. The gun jammed; she fixed it. Then, she shot him in the back of the head as he lay sleeping. After one shot, she felt her husband's chest; he was still breathing. She then shot him twice more in the back of the head. She told Epley, "she took all she was going to take from him, so she shot him."

At her trial for murder, Norman presented evidence of a long history of physical and mental abuse by her husband, caused by his alcoholism. At the time of the killing, the 39-year-old Norman and her husband had been married almost twenty-five years and had several children. Norman testified that her husband had started drinking and abusing her about five years after they were married. His physical abuse of her consisted of frequent assaults that included slapping, punching, and kicking her; striking her with various objects; and throwing glasses, beer bottles, and other objects at her. The defendant described other specific incidents of abuse, such as her husband putting her cigarettes out on her, throwing hot coffee on her, breaking glass against her face, and crushing food on her face. She presented no evidence she'd ever had medical treatment, but she did display several scars on her face.

Norman also presented evidence of other indignities inflicted upon her by her husband. Her husband didn't

Source: State v. Norman (1989)

work and forced her into prostitution to make money and then made jokes about it to family and friends. If she resisted going out to prostitute, he beat her; if he wasn't satisfied with the amount she made, he called her a "dog," "bitch" and "whore." Sometimes, he forced her to eat pet food out of the pets' bowls and to bark like a dog. He often made her sleep on the floor. Sometimes, he deprived her of food and refused to let her get food for the family. Throughout the long years of abuse, her husband threatened numerous times to kill her and to maim her in various ways.

Norman said her husband's abuse occurred only when he was drunk; they "got along very well when he was sober; he was a "good guy" when he wasn't drunk.

Early in the morning on the day before his death, her husband (drunk at the time) went to a rest area off a highway where Norman was engaging in prostitution. He assaulted her. A patrolman stopped him on the way home and jailed him on a DWI charge. Norman's mother got him out of jail at her request. He went home and started drinking and abusing Norman again.

Norman's evidence also tended to show that her husband seemed angrier than ever after he was released from jail and that his abuse of her was more frequent. That evening, sheriff's deputies were called to the Norman residence, and Norman complained that her hus-

▲ A very small number strike back at their abusers, sometimes savagely, like Judy Norman or Nancy Seaman, a respected fourth-grade teacher shown here testifying at her trial for murder in Pontiac, Michigan. Seaman hacked her husband to death with a hatchet some time after he'd savagely beaten her. A jury took only 5 hours to convict and sentence her to life in prison for first-degree murder.

band had been beating her all day and she couldn't take it anymore. They advised her to file a complaint, but she said she was afraid her husband would kill her if she had him arrested. The deputies told her they needed a warrant before they could arrest her husband, and they left the scene. The deputies were called back less than an hour later after Norman had taken a bottle of pills. As paramedics treated her, her husband cursed her and told them to let her die. One of the deputies finally chased him back into his house while the paramedics were putting Norman into an ambulance. After her stomach was pumped at the local hospital, Norman was sent home with her mother.

While Norman was in the hospital, she discussed with a therapist filing charges against her husband and having him committed for treatment. Before the therapist left, Norman agreed to follow up the next day. The therapist testified at trial that Norman seemed depressed in the hospital; that she expressed considerable anger toward her husband; and that she threatened several times that night to kill her husband and that she *should* kill him "because of the things he'd done to her."

The next day (the day she shot her husband), Norman went to the mental health center to talk about charges and possible commitment. She told her husband: "J.T., straighten up. Quit drinking. I'm going to have you committed to help you." She said her husband said he'd "see them coming" and cut her throat before they got to him. During the rest of the day, he continued his abuse, threatening to kill and to maim her, slapping her, kicking her, and throwing objects at her. At one point, he took her cigarette and put it out on her, causing a small burn on her upper torso. He would not let her eat or bring food into the house for their children.

That evening, Norman and her husband went into their bedroom to lie down, and he called her a "dog" and made her lie on the floor when he lay down on the bed. Their daughter brought in her baby to leave with Norman; Norman's husband agreed to let her baby-sit. After her husband fell asleep, the baby started crying and Norman took it to her mother's house so it wouldn't wake up her husband. She returned shortly with the pistol and killed her husband.

Norman testified she was too afraid of her husband to press charges against him or to leave him. She said she'd temporarily left their home several times, but he'd always found her, brought her home, and beaten her. Asked why she killed him, she answered:

> Because I was scared of him and I knowed when he woke up, it was going to be the same thing, and I was scared when he took me to the truck stop that night it was going to be worse than he had ever been. I just

couldn't take it no more. There ain't no way, even if it means going to prison.

Norman and other witnesses testified that for years her husband had frequently threatened to kill her and to maim her. When asked if she believed those threats, she replied, "Yes. I believed him; he would, he would kill me if he got a chance. If he thought he wouldn't a had to went to jail, he would a done it."

QUESTION

If you didn't know any law on the subject, what decision would you make?

a. Acquit Judy Ann Norman because she had a right to defend herself against her husband
b. Convict her of murder and recommend a less than maximum sentence
c. Convict her of voluntary manslaughter because her husband provoked her to kill him (Manslaughter is a serious felony but not as serious as murder.)
d. Convict her of murder without leniency

Now, read the court's opinion and the dissenting opinion.

Majority Opinion

The right to kill in self-defense is based on the necessity, real or reasonably apparent, of killing an unlawful aggressor to save oneself from *imminent* death or great bodily harm at his hands....The term "imminent,"... means "immediate danger, such as must be instantly met, such as cannot be guarded against by calling for the assistance of others or the protection of the law."...

No harm was "imminent" or about to happen to the defendant when she shot her husband. The uncontroverted evidence was that her husband had been asleep for some time...when she shot her husband three times in the back of the head.

...Stretching the law of self-defense to fit the facts of this case would...legalize the...killing of abusive husbands...solely on wives' testimony concerning their subjective speculation as to the probability of future felonious assaults by their husbands. Homicidal self-help would then become a lawful solution, and perhaps the easiest and most effective solution, to this problem.

Dissenting Opinion

Evidence...revealed no letup of tension or fear, no moment in which the defendant felt released from impending serious harm, even while her husband slept....Psychologists have observed and commentators have described battered woman's syndrome as a "constant state of fear" brought on by the cyclical nature of battering as well as the battered spouse's perception that her abuser is both "omnipotent and unstoppable." Constant fear means a perpetual anticipation of the next blow, a perpetual expectation that the next blow will kill. . . . Thus from the perspective of the battered wife, the danger is constantly immediate. For the battered wife, if there is no escape, if there is no window of relief or momentary sense of safety, then the next attack, which could be the fatal one, is imminent. . . .

QUESTIONS

1. Summarize the arguments of the majority opinion of the court.
2. Summarize the arguments of the dissenting judge.
3. Which opinion do you favor? Defend your answer.

PROS AND CONS OF A BATTERED WOMAN'S SELF-DEFENSE

"Few batterers ever see the inside of a jail cell, even when convicted of a serious offense"; probation is the most common punishment (160). Let's explore the arguments for and against allowing the justification of self-defense to women like Judy Ann Norman who kill their batterers at times when they're not being battered.

The Reasonableness Argument

Deny the Defense. Nonconfrontational killing is never reasonable. (Remember that taking the law into your own hands is only justified if it was reasonably necessary to kill or be killed *now*.) So the law would be giving women "special favors" if it agreed that it's reasonable to kill someone who's not threatening or trying to kill you right now.

Allow the Defense. Criminal law has always left it up to juries to decide what's reasonable in each case. Besides, the reasonableness requirement hides a gender bias; it assumes a "male model of behavior" that treats women claimants of the defense as if they're asking for "special favors" (167). They're not asking for special favors, so let the jury decide whether the killing was reasonable.

The "Battered Woman Syndrome" Argument

In 1979, psychologist Lenore Walker used the term "battered woman syndrome" to describe the effects of intimate-partner abuse. Women in abusive relationships suffer from low self-esteem, passivity, and traditional attitudes about male-female roles. There's a "cycle of violence": first tension-building, then a battering incident, and finally "loving contrition." Then the cycle starts over. Finally, according to her theory of "learned helplessness," once battered women learn they can't control or prevent the beatings, they feel they can't avoid the violence and that there is no way out of the abusive relationship. Battered women aren't masochists; they stay for lots of reasons, including learned helplessness; the support they get during the "loving contrition" stage; fear; lack of resources; concern for their children; love for their partner; shame; and lack of external support resulting from their batterer's efforts to isolate them from others (168).

Deny the Defense. The syndrome is out of date. There's no one-size-fits-all list of the effects of battering; women who fight back are hardly passive. Second, learned helplessness contradicts the use of self-defense; women taking the law into their own hands by killing their batterers have learned empowerment not helplessness. "It is hardly a sign of helplessness to acquire a gun and . . . kill one's psychological captor" (173).

Allow the Defense. Research *has* advanced, but that research supports the defense. For example, according to "active survivor theory," battered women start out looking for help in escaping but they can't find it. As violence escalates, they step up their self-help efforts, "attempting, in a very logical fashion, to assure themselves and their children protection and therefore survival" (176). The theory emphasizes the reasonableness of the battered woman's actions, not her psychological disability or weakness. This fits with traditional self-defense. Battered women aren't looking for special favors; they just want the same rules applied to them that apply to everybody else.

The Imminence Argument

Deny the Defense. It's probably true that battered women who kill under nonconfrontational circumstances reasonably fear abuse. But there's a catch; it's *future* danger. So they can't reasonably believe they're in imminent danger at the moment when they kill.

Allow the Defense.

1. Many battered women who kill pick up a signal that this time their batterer's really going to kill them; they recognize imminence before others without prior experience could.
2. Battered women may reasonably believe the only time to protect themselves is when their abuser is temporarily incapacitated (like when he's asleep). They've learned from past experience it's useless to try and fight back during a beating because fighting back makes the beating worse. Worse still, they may also have learned from experience that when they flee for help, the criminal justice system and social service agencies fail them; their husbands find and beat them even worse (181).
3. "Inevitable future harm" may not be the same as "imminent harm," but the battered woman who kills her sleeping husband satisfies the imminence requirement, just like the hostage who's being slowly poisoned over a period of time, or who's been told to expect to die later in the week, and suddenly seizes the opportunity to attack her kidnapper and save her life (182).

QUESTION

What's your final decision about the battered woman's self-defense justification?

1. List all the arguments in favor of a battered woman's self-defense justification.
2. List all the criticisms of the defense.
3. Now, put these answers together with the majority and dissenting opinions in *State v. Norman*.
4. Make your final decision, backing it up with your responses to questions 1–3:
   a. Acquit Judy Ann Norman because she had a right to defend herself against her husband
   b. Convict her of murder and recommend a less than maximum sentence
   c. Convict her of voluntary manslaughter because her husband provoked her to kill him

(Manslaughter is a serious felony but not as serious as murder.)
   d. Convict her of murder without leniency

Source: Based on Kit Kinports, "So Much Activity, So Little Change: A Reply to the Critics of Battered Women's Self-Defense," *St. Louis Public Law Review* 23(2004):155.

Was she justified in killing her batterer?

Click on this Decision Point at http://cj.wadsworth.com/samaha_cj7e to explore the issue.

Chapter Summary

▶ If we lived in a pure democracy, the majority could do whatever it pleased, but we live in a *constitutional* democracy, which limits what the majority can do. Constitutions, statutes, and court decisions interpreting them are the formal sources and framework for all decision making in criminal justice. Informally, the constitutional and legal framework and authority are broad and flexible enough to allow plenty of "play in the joints" of discretionary decision making.

▶ Criminal law defines what behavior is criminal and spells out the punishment for committing crimes. Criminal law is limited by the U.S. Constitution; the principle of economy; the elements of crime requirements; and the defenses to crime. The only element of crime required by the Constitution is a criminal act. Criminal intent consists of four states of mind: purposefulness, knowingness, recklessness, negligence. Defenses to crime consist of justifications focusing on the rightness of defendants' actions under the circumstances and excuses that focus on the responsibility of the defendants.

▶ Criminal procedure tells public officials what powers they have to enforce the criminal law, what the limits of those powers are, and the consequences of abusing their power. The Constitution guarantees due process (fair procedures) in both federal and state criminal justice systems. These procedures are those listed in the Bill of Rights. The Constitution also guarantees equal protection of the laws. Equal doesn't mean identical; it means that if groups are treated differently there has to be a good reason. Classifications based on race are probably never justified.

Key Terms

criminal law, p. 108
criminal procedure, p. 108
principle of economy, p. 109
ex post facto clause, p. 110
void-for-vagueness doctrine, p. 110
equal protection of the laws, p. 110
purposeful intent, p. 112
knowing intent, p. 112
reckless intent, p. 113
negligent intent, p. 113
strict liability offenses, p. 113

factual cause, p. 113
legal cause, p. 113
defense of alibi, p. 114
defenses of justification, p. 114
defenses of excuse, p. 114
rape shield laws, p. 115
entrapment, p. 117
right-wrong test, p. 120
irresistible impulse test, p. 120
substantial capacity test, p. 120
felonies, p. 122

misdemeanors, p. 123
violations, p. 123
mala in se, p. 123
mala prohibita, p. 124
torts, p. 124
damages, p. 124
due process, p. 125

Web Resources

Go to http://cj.wadsworth.com/samaha_cj7e for a wealth of online resources related to your book. Take a "pre-test" and "post-test" for each chapter in order to help master the material. Check out the *Web Links* to access the websites mentioned in the text, as well as many others. Explore the *Decision Points* flagged in the margins of the text for additional insights. You can also access recent perspectives by clicking on *CJ in the News* and *Terrorism Update* under *Course Resources*.

☝ Search Online with InfoTrac College Edition

For additional information, explore InfoTrac College Edition, your online library. Go to http://cj.wadsworth.com/samaha_cj7e to access InfoTrac College Edition from your book's website. Use the passcode that came with your book. You will find InfoTrac College Edition exercises and a list of key words for further research.

CHAPTER 5

Missions and Roles of the Police

FACT *or* FICTION?

▶ Criminal law enforcement was the only police mission until 1900.

▶ The top priority of the FBI in 2004 was to protect the U.S. against foreign intelligence operations.

▶ In day-to-day operations, police departments resemble hospitals and universities more than military organizations.

▶ People spend more time in their daily lives policed by nongovernment individuals and groups than by public police.

▶ Police use more discretionary decision making in maintaining order than in enforcing the criminal law.

▶ When it comes to college education, the bottom line is that officers have taken *some* college courses is a demonstrated benefit.

▶ The number of women police officers has almost doubled since 1995.

▶ There are now more Hispanic than Black police officers in the United States.

WHAT ARE THE POLICE?

- The police are a body of handsome young men and women...who bravely fight the forces of evil to make the world safe for decent people. [This definition was offered by a handsome and humorous young man who worked for the campus police.]

- The police are a bunch of hotshots who get their kicks from hassling Blacks, students, and most other people who are trying to have a good time. [This definition was the effort of a tall, thin, hairy fellow with a widely advertised appetite for controlled substances.]

- The police are an agency of government that enforces the law and keeps the peace. [This one came from a very serious young woman who always sat in the front row. She remembered it from another class.]

- The police are a weapon the state uses to oppress the working classes, the poor, and minorities. [The author of this definition was an intense young Marxist.]

- The police are the people who come into my father's restaurant to get free food. [This was from a second-generation Eastern European student.]

- The police are the people who drive police cars. [The effort of one of the brightest students I have ever taught. She went on to become a lawyer.]

Source: These are definitions of police offered by some of Professor Carl Klockars' (1986, 7–8) criminal justice students, together with his comments in brackets.

Every profession has a mission. The mission of armies is to win wars, of doctors to cure the sick, and of teachers to educate the young. Professionals play roles, become part of organizations, adapt to the group's subculture, and follow strategies to accomplish their missions. Yet, in reality, no profession sticks to a single mission or plays a single role. Armies sometimes "keep the peace." Doctors sometimes play the role of "ministers of mercy" by allowing or even helping terminally ill patients to die. Teachers help students through crises by assuming the role of counselor. Perhaps no profession has more missions than policing. And perhaps none has faced more controversy both from inside and outside about what its missions should be and what strategies it should follow to accomplish them.

To the public, to politicians, in most of the news media, on television, and in movie dramas, the police mission is simple and clear—to prevent crime and catch criminals—but the reality is a lot more complicated.

The History of Police and Policing

To get some perspective on the history of policing, notice how ancient the idea of policing really is. As far back as 1500 B.C., Egypt and Mesopotamia established police forces. We don't know much about them except they were efficient and effective, tortured suspects to obtain confessions, and mistreated prisoners. We also know that in 27 B.C. the Roman Emperor Augustus appointed an urban officer armed with the power to "maintain public order," and by A.D. 6, the Romans had established a "24/7" police force that patrolled the streets of Rome (Adamson 1991, 1–2). Let's look at the major, evolving forms of policing that followed.

The Constable/Night Watch System, 1066–1850

Fast forward to England after the Norman Conquest when in 1066 King William created the **constable/night watch system,** a police system based in the local community. It consisted of two elements—constables and night watch—in every local community. That system lasted until 1829 in England, came to the American colonies, and endured until the 1850s.

constable/night watch system a police system based in local communities during the first eras of policing, consisting of constables and night watch

Constables worked for the courts. They were paid fees for serving warrants and summonses and arresting suspects. They also made money by helping to prosecute criminals. Prosecution was private and widely used, especially by the poor, Black, and immigrant communities in 1800s' cities. Victims had to bring their own cases to court (they often did) and they paid constables to help them, even when it cost more to hire them than the value of the property stolen (Lane 1992, 7).

Night watchmen (they were all men) were supposed to patrol the neighborhood from dusk to dawn, calling out the hours ("8 o'clock and all is well!"); making sure the street lamps were lit; watching for fire; breaking up fights; and arresting "suspicious persons." Night watch was a public duty, but you could hire substitutes to do it for you.

Watchmen were the objects of ridicule, at least from the time of Shakespeare. The usual criticisms were they slept when they should've been watching; they shook their "rattles" only to scare off criminals instead of apprehending them; and they ran away from real danger. One newspaper said they were "idle, drunken, vigilant snorers," who never stopped a disturbance "in their lives; but would ... be as ready to join in a burglary as any thief in Christendom" (Monkkonen 1992, 549).

There's no way to tell how true these criticisms were, but it's hard to believe these amateurs or their substitutes were an effective law enforcement organization. Still, for all its faults, the constable/night watch system had two things going for it: it was cheap and it was weak. So it reduced the fear of two things mid-1800s Americans hated as much as crime: government taxes and government power.

But fear of disorder, especially mobs of urban rioters that grew in number and intensity between 1830 and 1860, led to less fear of government and more dread of disorder. There was plenty to spark outbursts from rioting mobs: "out" groups like the newest immigrants, unpopular politicians, merchants who sold food at high prices in hard times, and as the Civil War approached—slavery. The change to a market economy with its cycles of boom and bust; swarms of warring foreign immigrants and domestic "hayseeds" fresh from rural America pouring into cities; and growing hostility to free Blacks as the country approached civil war all contributed to make the period from 1830 to 1860 the most riotous in our history (Lane 1992, 7–8).

The Municipal Police Department Era, 1851–1920

After three major riots in four years, Boston had had enough. In 1838, the city established a **municipal police department system,** a formalized police force responsible to a central office and on duty "24/7." Most cities rapidly followed Boston's example. Riots triggered the creation of police departments, but city residents and city government quickly came to view them as a convenient tool for missions other than riot control. According to police historian Roger Lane (1992):

municipal police department system a formalized police force responsible to a central office and on duty "24/7"

The men on the beat gave directions, unsnarled traffic, returned lost children, aided victims of sudden accident, and escorted drunks either to the station house or home.... Homeless drifters...were given nightly lodging in the station houses....In hard times policemen sometimes ran soup kitchens for the hungry. (9)

The new police introduced four new features. First, they were formally organized like a military hierarchy with orders issued from the chief at the top and carried out by officers on the beats below. Informally, except for riot control, patrol officers spent most of their time alone walking beats acting on their own initiative with no orders (see "Criminal Law Enforcement" later); this was unlike soldiers who acted in groups under specific orders.

Second, the new departments were part of the executive branch of city government, not the courts as the constable/night watch system had been. This meant the end of fees collected for serving court documents. Instead, police officers were paid salaries (good salaries, good enough to lure many skilled laborers onto the force). But as part of the executive branch, police were divorced from preparing and prosecuting cases, which isolated them from courts and prosecutors and generated antagonism among the three major criminal justice agencies (Lane 1992, 13).

Third, officers wore uniforms. This made them the first (and for a long time the only) public official everybody identified as a public official. Officers hated and bitterly fought wearing uniforms. In New York, mass protests, resignations, and lawsuits greeted the introduction of uniforms in 1853 (Lane 1992, 12). Why such opposition? First, it was un-American. Uniforms were for lackeys of kings and queens, not for Americans who believed part of being an American was being able to dress as you pleased. One Philadelphia officer who refused to wear a uniform said it was "derogatory to my feelings as an American." Second, uniforms identified them not just to residents who needed them but to "street toughs looking for trouble" and probably, more important, to superior officers making sure officers were walking their beats and not hanging out in saloons and billiard rooms (Monkkonen 1992, 556–557).

Fourth, police practiced **proactive policing,** meaning they were supposed to prevent crime before it happened by going out looking for suspicious people and behavior. This was the opposite of **reactive policing** ("Don't call us; we'll call

proactive policing officers are supposed to prevent crime before it happens by going out looking for suspicious people and behavior

reactive policing officers respond when called ("Don't call us; we'll call you.")

▶ When turn of the twentieth-century police officers started wearing uniforms it made them the first (and for a long time the only) public officials everybody identified as public officials. In this 1907 photo, we see San Jose, California, officers sitting in their Model 21 Rambler in front of their precinct station.

Bettmann/Corbis

you"), used in the constable/night watch system, where constables and watchmen only acted when they were asked and paid to do it. Walking the beat (patrol) was supposed to scare off criminal wannabes, and salaries were supposed to make officers want to investigate crimes and victims to report crimes to the police (Monkkonen 1992, 556–557).

The major downside of municipal control was that police departments became the arms of the dominant political machines. So they participated in partisan politics, and that participation was often corrupt—like manipulating ballot boxes. Partisan politics wasn't the only corrupting influence. Money, too, often lured departments as well as individual officers into making deals with vice operations, like houses of prostitution, saloons, and gambling establishments. One New York City officer was delighted by his assignment to the vice district because it meant he'd be eating tenderloin instead of chuck steak. (I never knew until I heard this story why a friend who took me to a place in Chicago I'm not about to identify told me we were going to the "tenderloin.")

Nevertheless, on balance, police departments had several strengths. Communities supported them because officers policed the neighborhoods they lived in. They took charge of "whatever emergencies and crises crossed their paths." They provided needed services, such as ambulances, soup kitchens, garbage collection, and homeless shelters. Malcolm K. Sparrow and his colleagues (1995) summed up the contributions of municipal police this way in their excellent book on the police:

> In a time before widespread and well-supported social work and social programs, and before municipalities had assumed many of their routine obligations, the police often filled important vacuums. (34)

By the way, police reform got swept up in a new wave of reform in the early twentieth century, called the Progressive Era. A rash of investigations in cities throughout the United States from about 1895 to 1920 uncovered widespread incompetence and corruption in most city police departments.

At the same time, policing was changing from an all-purpose public service to the narrow mission of criminal law enforcement. This shift reflected a change in thinking by social welfare reformers and some police chiefs who were beginning to stop looking at unemployed people as members of the "dangerous classes," saving the description for criminals only. This wasn't just a change in viewpoint; it was a change in police officers' behavior. Until the late 1800s, the police didn't see any difference between housing the homeless, feeding the hungry, rounding up drunks, and arresting murderers, rapists, and robbers because they were all part of the mission to control the dangerous classes.

Historians Catrien C. J. H. Bijleveld and Eric H. Monkkonen (Monkkonen 1992) showed in their analysis of arrests in the largest cities in the country that as early as 1894 police departments were concentrating more on criminal law enforcement against murder and other felonies and less on broader social services like housing the homeless and minor public-order offenses. According to Bijleveld and Monkkonen, "By the end of World War I, police were in the business of crime control. Other city- or state-run agencies had taken over their former noncrime control activities" (Monkkonen 1992, 556–557).

Police missions may have changed, but police officers stayed the same. As the twentieth century opened, the typical urban police officer in the United States was a recent immigrant with little or no education, appointed by a local politician, and expected to enforce the law according to the ward's wishes. According to Richard A. Staufenberger (1980), officers

> knew who put them in office and whose support they needed to stay there. Their job was to manage their beat; often they became completely enmeshed in the crime they were expected to suppress. Corruption, brutality, and racial discrimination, although not universal, were characteristic of most big city departments. (8–9)

The Reform Model Era, 1921–1960

Recognizing this political dominance, corruption, and lack of training, three California police chiefs in the 1920s, August Vollmer, O. W. Wilson, and William Parker, encouraged what they called the **reform model of policing.** According to this model, the police are the "gatekeepers" to the criminal justice system; they decide who enters the system and who doesn't. So the police mission is clear and narrow: arrest people for committing the FBI's Index Crimes (Chapter 2) (Sparrow, Moore, and Kennedy 1995, 37–38).

By the 1950s, all of the following elements in the reform agenda were accepted and in place, at least in the larger departments:

1. *Centralization of police authority.* Police chiefs began to really run their departments.
2. *Shift from foot to motorized patrols.* Officers moved into squad cars.
3. *Technological advances.* Fewer officers could cover more territory because of squad cars, two-way radios, and telephone call boxes.
4. *Paramilitary organization.* Chiefs were in charge of a strictly disciplined hierarchy with formal authority descending from the top through the ranks to patrol officers.
5. *Specialized units.* These were mainly vice squads with the power to control police corruption throughout the department.
6. *UCR data.* FBI Uniform Crime Reports data (Chapter 2) became the measure of police performance.
7. *Reactive, incident-driven policing.* Responding to calls became the distinctive method of policing.
8. *Restrictions on police discretion.* Department rules, such as those regarding use of force and high-speed chases, lessened police discretion.
9. *Focus on criminal law enforcement.* As opposed to maintaining order and providing service, the focus became enforcing criminal law. (Sparrow, Moore, and Kennedy 1995, 38–40)

The results according to Malcolm K. Sparrow and his colleagues (1995):

> The reformers produced a conception of policing whose purpose has been largely focused on crime control and whose methods have been limited to law enforcement. Every discussion of the purpose of the police begins with crime control. For many the discussion ends there as well. Crime control is widely taken, both inside and outside the police, as the only important police function, with everything else they might do not only secondary but a dangerous and wasteful distraction. This is not in itself new; much thinking about the police has taken more or less this form for the last century. But the degree to which the reform model...has narrowed the debate is unprecedented. (41)

Public confidence in the reform model remains high and support from police professionals and politicians remains strong—but not without challenge. A small band of police chiefs around the country is fighting the reform model. These chiefs and their supporters in academic circles list the following reasons for their lack of confidence in the reform model.

1. Despite some reduction in the mid- to late 1990s, crime rates taken in the long run remain at historic highs. (Chapter 2)
2. Criminal justice is ineffective because even if the police arrest suspects, the likelihood is small they will serve time in prison. (Chapter 8)
3. Police tactics such as patrol, rapid response, follow-up investigation, and arrest don't work well to either control crime or reduce fear of crime.
4. Private security is outpacing public police as a means to control crime, fear, and disorder. (See "Private Police and Policing" later.) (Sparrow, Moore, and Kennedy 1995, 44–50)

reform model of policing police are the "gatekeepers" to the criminal justice system; they focus on the criminal law enforcement mission

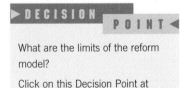

DECISION POINT

What are the limits of the reform model?

Click on this Decision Point at http://cj.wadsworth.com/samaha_cj7e to explore the issue.

The Turbulent 1960s

During the 1960s, a predominantly urban, pluralist, highly vocal, and mostly young group of protesters challenged the values of White Anglo-Saxon Protestant (we called them WASPs) men and their dominance. The challengers demanded their share of the promises of American life—material abundance, freedom, and justice. Their hopes were raised and quickly dashed. The belief that a "quick fix" could ensure everybody an opportunity to share the good life evaporated. Understanding the police in the 1960s requires appreciating the false hopes and the resulting frustration, anger, destruction, and, ultimately, adoption of more modest goals that were the legacy of those turbulent times of protests, riots, and soaring crime rates (Chapter 2) (Cronin, Cronin, and Milakovich 1981; Matusow 1984).

The police became easy scapegoats caught in the middle of disorder, riots, and crime-plagued cities. Of course, police couldn't remove or even significantly reduce deep racial, ethnic, class, and gender inequalities. Nor could they realistically be expected to calm the culture wars between social conservatives and social liberals that had ebbed and flowed long before the 1960s and are very much alive today. Police actions didn't create these divisions even if they sometimes helped to bring them into sharp and painful focus.

It's not surprising "law and order" was a major theme of the 1964 presidential election campaign. The significance of the Republican candidate Barry Goldwater's appeals for law and order weren't lost on Lyndon Johnson, despite his enormous landslide victory. Right after the election, President Johnson created the President's Commission on Law Enforcement and the Administration of Justice. The Crime Commission, as it was called, gave serious attention to six police problems:

1. The multiple and conflicting missions of policing
2. The fragmented nature of law enforcement
3. The poor training and minimal education of police officers
4. Police corruption, brutality, and prejudice
5. The separation of the police from the communities they serve
6. The lessening of the public support that effective policing depends on (President's Crime Commission 1967; Staufenberger 1980, 13–18)

By the late 1960s, police officers were frustrated, angry, and fed up with highly publicized and unrelenting criticism by the "reformers." But they had other complaints, too: poor pay, dictatorial chiefs, urban riots, unrealistic demands to solve the nation's social problems, and U.S. Supreme Court opinions that "handcuffed the police instead of the criminal" (Chapter 7). These complaints had one lasting effect—urban police unionization. Regardless of whether their complaints were justified and whether unions were the answer to their complaints, departments in almost all large cities, with the big exception of those in the South, became unionized.

Unionization had a major impact on police administration. Chiefs had to share their power by negotiating with unions. Furthermore, according to police historian Samuel Walker (1992b), the union movement "won dramatic improvement in salaries and benefits for officers along with grievance procedures that protected the rights of officers in disciplinary hearings." Not everyone favored unionization—and it still has its share of critics. Some reformers believed unions "resisted innovation and were particularly hostile to attempts to improve police community relations" (27–28). Nevertheless, the union movement represents a major concrete result of the troubled 1960s.

That's not all the 1960s left us. President Johnson's Crime Commission sparked great research activity. Thanks to evaluation research and police department cooperation with researchers, we've advanced enormously our knowledge of policing. More than courts and corrections, police departments have allowed and participated in evaluations of their work, even when research has criticized their practices. They've also worked with researchers to set up and conduct experiments that have led not just to better understanding but to improvements in policies and practices. So, clearly, the legacy of the 1960s includes more than riots, crime, and disorder. Of course, there's still a lot to criticize, and we'll examine some of those criticisms in this and the next two chapters (Feeley and Sarat 1980).

The Community Policing Era, 1970–

The social unrest of the late 1960s, coupled with the crime boom (Chapter 2), shook the confidence of practitioners, leading them to wonder if crime and disorder were beyond the control of law enforcement as it operated under the reform model. Scholars highlighted the failings of the most widely used reform model strategies (Chapter 6), further shaking the confidence of police professionals and prompting them to reassess their strategies (Zhao, Lovrich, and Thurman 1999, 74–75).

In this time of professional reassessment and scholarship evaluating the effectiveness of reform model policing, the community policing era was born. The 1970s and 1980s were marked by hot debate among cops and between the cops and the professors over what this new community policing should look like, whether it could work, and whether it was real or just talk. Scholars who supported it called community policing a "quiet revolution" (Kelling 1988); those who didn't said it could never work (Zhao et al., 75). Several successful community policing experiments (Chapter 6); strong support from President Clinton, who signed bills creating the federal programs into law; and billions of federal dollars approved by both major political parties have made community policing the *talk* if not the *walk* of policing in 2005. Here's how COPS (Community-Oriented Policing Services 2004), the U.S. government's official community policing agency, describes it:

> Community policing focuses on crime and social disorder through the delivery of police services that includes aspects of traditional law enforcement, as well as prevention, problem-solving, community engagement, and partnerships. The community policing model balances reactive responses to calls for service with proactive problem-solving centered on the causes of crime and disorder. Community policing requires both police and citizens to join together as partners in the course of both identifying and effectively addressing those issues.

As you can see from the definition, community-oriented policing (COP) boils down to three elements:

1. The community and the police working together to accomplish the missions of crime control, order maintenance, and other social services to the public
2. Identifying, analyzing, responding to, and evaluating community problems (including not just crime but disorder) by focusing on causes, not just specific incidents of crime and disorder
3. Bringing in other government agencies and private community resources from business and community service organizations to participate in working on problems

We'll save the discussion of the state of community policing for Chapter 6.

The History of Policewomen and Women Policing

You're going to learn about policewomen and women policing separately because it's difficult to weave it into the history we've already sketched. This is partly because until 1900 there were practically no policewomen, and until very

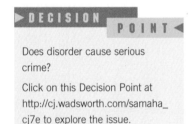

► DECISION POINT ◄

Does disorder cause serious crime?

Click on this Decision Point at http://cj.wadsworth.com/samaha_cj7e to explore the issue.

Community Oriented Policing Services (COPS): A national database for all things related to COPS. To reach this site go to "Web Links" on your Samaha CJ7 website: http://cj.wadsworth.com/samaha_cj7e.

recently, there were only a few, and these few were kept in minor roles. But in the 1990s, excellent histories of policewomen and women policing appeared. Thanks to these histories and the growing numbers of women police officers with responsibilities equal to those of policemen, it's now possible to outline the major developments in the history of policewomen and women policing.

In 1930, an unidentified woman wrote the following editorial in a Midwestern newspaper:

> There is to most of us something highly distasteful in the idea of a woman walking a beat, carrying a billy [club] and going into all sorts of low places.... Though we may feel ourselves equally capable as the men in many ways, it is better that we do our work well than to try to do men's poorly. Women have great power as law enforcers. But that power should be used in the home.... We can still do more good...as mothers and teachers than as policewomen. (Appier 1998, 2)

The idea that police work is "man's work" is central in the history of police in the United States, even though women have worked in law enforcement since 1820, when they commonly served as matrons in jails and prisons.

Police work throughout U.S. history has included a lot that's not "masculine": helping lost children, running soup kitchens, and providing lodging for the destitute and the homeless. Helping the helpless may have been the public image of women's work but it was also part of the reality in U.S. police departments (Appier 1998, 2). We'll look at how women have gradually changed the perception of police work as they became policewomen and saw their roles move from social worker to crime fighter.

Policewomen as Social Workers, 1900–1930 By 1900, a new attitude about women in law enforcement was developing. One of the pioneers in women policing was Alice Stebbing Wells. In 1910, Wells told her family and friends she wanted to become a police officer. Wells hardly fit the popular image of a police officer of her day (working-class, heavy-drinking, Irish Catholic men with lots of muscle). She was a middle-class, Protestant, college-educated, five-foot-tall member of the Women's Christian Temperance Union (Appier 1998, 2).

The women pioneers in police work argued that the compassionate nature of women uniquely qualified them for a crime prevention mission, particularly working with juvenile delinquents and female criminals. The best women for preventive police work, they contended, were women like them—middle-class social workers. They were good role models, and they were trained in improving people, particularly women and juveniles. Their argument ran something like this:

1. The highest form of police work is social work.
2. Prevention is the most important mission of police work.
3. Therefore, women's nature suits them to prevent crime best by means of social work. (Appier 1998, 3)

As a result of the pioneers' efforts, hundreds of middle-class women became police officers during the 1910s and 1920s. In her excellent history of women policing, *Policing Women*, the historian Janis Appier (1998) wrote:

> Despite women's presence in police departments, the anticipated gender- and class-based transformation of police work never took place. Instead, year after year, pioneer policewomen remained a tiny, beleaguered minority within police work, resented and even despised by most of their colleagues...the...entry of women into police work during the 1910s and 1920s fundamentally changed the nature and gendered representation of law enforcement in unintended ways. Whereas prior to the 1910s, the occupation of police work was presumed to be sex-specific (only men could be police officers), during the 1910s and 1920s it became an occupation with an array of gender-linked functions. According to pioneer policewomen and their advocates, men were best at performing certain police duties, while women were best at performing other police duties. (3)

International Association of Women Police: This site is the official publication of the IAWP and includes current issues and topics related to women in policing. To reach this site go to "Web Links" on your Samaha CJ7 website: http://cj.wadsworth.com/samaha_cj7e.

British Association for Women in Policing (BAWP): To reach this site go to "Web Links" on your Samaha CJ7 website: http://cj.wadsworth.com/samaha_cj7e.

► By 1968, the woman crime fighter was a reality. Betty Blankenship and Elizabeth Robinson were assigned to patrol in Indianapolis. They became the first female officers to wear uniforms, strap gun belts to their waists, drive a marked car, and answer general-purpose police calls on an equal basis with policemen.

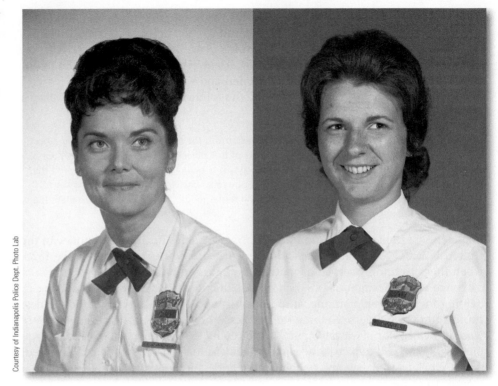

Courtesy of Indianapolis Police Dept. Photo Lab

From Social Workers to Crime Fighters, 1931–Present Policing underwent major changes during the Great Depression of the 1930s. FBI Director J. Edgar Hoover and the reform chiefs August Vollmer and O. W. Wilson led the way in deemphasizing the social service mission of policing, stressing criminal law enforcement as the only police mission. At the same time, working women were viewed less favorably than during the prosperous 1920s, and feminism no longer commanded the public support it once had. The Depression reinforced more traditional roles for women. According to historian Susan Ware (1982):

> Women were strongly encouraged to limit their aspirations to husband, family, and domesticity; work outside the home, especially for married women, was discouraged. Working women were considered selfish and greedy, who took money away from men—the real breadwinners. (13–14)

Women returned to police work during World War II, when there was a shortage of male officers. But they remained social service officers at a time when most departments minimized the social service mission because of the commitment to crime fighting. Women's reentry into policing doesn't compare to women's entry into the general workforce. "Rosie the Riveter" really did replace male riveters who were in the military, but there was no comparable "Connie the Crime Fighter" in police work. Women did not replace male crime fighters who served in World War II (Schulz 1995, 98).

The 1950s are commonly viewed as a time when the place of women was in the home, but for policewomen, it was a time of growth. Women's role was shifting from social worker to crime fighter. Women worked with men in undercover operations; they wore uniforms for the first time, and they were trained to use and were expected to carry firearms (98–99).

By 1968, the woman crime fighter was a reality. Betty Blankenship and Elizabeth Robinson were assigned to patrol in Indianapolis. They became the first female officers "to wear uniforms, strap gun belts to their waists, drive a marked car, and answer general purpose police calls on an equal basis with policemen" (Schulz 1995, 5).

In the mid-1990s, author Dorothy Moses Schulz (1995) declared:

Today's women police officers, like their male colleagues, are primarily working class high school graduates who enter policing for its salary, benefits, and career opportunities. Their demands no longer reflect the upper middle class, educated roots of the past, but reflect working-class concerns about pay, promotions, and pensions. Their law enforcement concept is also similar to that of their male peers; as crimefighters, they enforce the law, maintain order, and provide for the public safety, just as men do. Thus, not only is the role of women in the police service radically different from its historical roots, the women are also radically different from their foremothers. (5)

Schulz added these insights into job advancements for policewomen:

Although women are slowly moving up the ranks of police departments...women frequently do not avail themselves of promotion opportunities both for personal reasons but also because systemic discrimination against them still exists. The personal reasons women list involve not wanting to give up positions with daylight hours due to family and childrearing requirements. Systemic reasons involve lack of assignments to high-profile units, weighted seniority beyond the minimal eligibility requirements, negative supervisory evaluations, and general attitudes of male co-workers that psychologically discourage ambition. Sexual harassment and male resentment over affirmative action hiring goals and what many officers see as a dilution of physical standards are also of concern. These systemic reasons belie the legal equality women have achieved and highlight issues pertaining to the subtle discrimination women face as they compete with men on terms defined by and for men. (5–6)

What about women police chiefs? Is there a glass ceiling? Maybe, but in April 2004, Deputy U.S. Attorney General Deborah J. Daniels reported some promising numbers at the Women in Policing Conference (2004):

Today, as I'm sure every officer in this room is well aware, women head the police departments in five major U.S. cities—Boston, Detroit, San Francisco, Milwaukee, and Nashville. And a woman, Chief Mary Anne Viverette of Gaithersburg, Maryland, will soon take the reins as President of the International Association of Chiefs of Police. These are strong women, with tremendous leadership and management skills, who are leading their agencies to become models of modern policing. Equally noteworthy is the fact that each of these chiefs has the respect and admiration of the members of her force, and that of her fellow chiefs.

Many more women across the country today hold leadership positions in law enforcement: women like Chief Joanne Jaffe, the first woman at the NYPD to wear three stars; women like Chief Diana Pizzuti, commanding officer of your police academy; and women like Chief Joyce Stephen, NYPD's commanding officer for community affairs.

In closing this too brief sketch, you should know that

some feminist criminologists...are asking whether advocates of gender-neutral policing—including police managers—are doing themselves and other women a disservice and should, instead, be stressing their differences from, rather than their similarities to, the men who make up the overwhelming majority of the police. (Schulz 1995, 5–6)

Police Structure and Organization

Public police agencies in the United States are organized along the lines of our federalist system of government (Chapter 1). So we have a system of dividing crime control (not always harmoniously) among national, state, county, and municipal agencies. The enormous numbers of for-profit private law enforcement agencies further complicate this structure. Let's look at the broad outlines of this organizational structure of federal, state, county, municipal, and private law enforcement agencies in the United States.

Bureau of Justice Services: Statistics on Numbers of Officers in the U.S.: Click on "Law Enforcement" for these statistics. To reach this site go to "Web Links" on your Samaha CJ7 website: http://cj.wadsworth.com/samaha_cj7e.

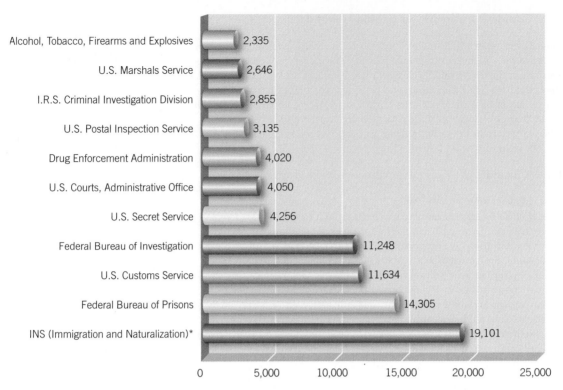

Agency	Number
Alcohol, Tobacco, Firearms and Explosives	2,335
U.S. Marshals Service	2,646
I.R.S. Criminal Investigation Division	2,855
U.S. Postal Inspection Service	3,135
Drug Enforcement Administration	4,020
U.S. Courts, Administrative Office	4,050
U.S. Secret Service	4,256
Federal Bureau of Investigation	11,248
U.S. Customs Service	11,634
Federal Bureau of Prisons	14,305
INS (Immigration and Naturalization)*	19,101

▲ **FIGURE 5.1 Number of Federal Law Enforcement Officers, June 2002**

*The INS no longer exists. There is now a Directorate of Customs and Border Security, which is under the direction of the new Department of Homeland Security.
Note: The totals exclude the numbers of officers serving outside the 50 states.
Source: Bureau of Justice Statistics, *Federal Law Enforcement Officers, 2002* (Washington, DC: Bureau of Justice Statistics, August 2003), Highlights, Table 1.

Federal Law Enforcement Agencies

In June 2002, there were 93,000 federal officers authorized to make arrests and carry firearms (Figure 5.1). (For security reasons, the total doesn't include Federal Air Marshals and CIA Security Protective officers; it also excludes officers assigned outside the 50 states.) The main work of federal law enforcement officers is criminal investigation, responding to calls and patrol (62 percent), followed by corrections (19 percent) (Bureau of Justice Statistics [BJS], August 2003, Figure 1). Let's look at a few of the largest agencies: the FBI, the DEA, other federal agencies, and the Department of Homeland Security (DHS).

Federal Bureau of Investigation (FBI) Here's the description of the FBI I wrote in most of the earlier editions of your book:

> The FBI investigates more than 200 categories of federal crime (mainly drug laws and corporate fraud, and other white-collar crime and racketeering). In addition, the FBI assists other federal, state, and local agencies through its extensive fingerprint files and other records. The FBI National Academy provides aid for some enforcement agencies throughout the country.

September 11, 2001, changed all that. The description and discussion that follow are based on a statement by FBI Executive Assistant Director of Counterterrorism/Counterintelligence John Pistole (2004) to the U.S. Senate Governmental Affairs Committee. Shortly after September 11, 2001, FBI Director Mueller put into effect a plan that

> transformed the FBI with one goal in mind: establishing the prevention of terrorism as the Bureau's number one priority. No longer are we content to concentrate on investigating terrorist crimes after they occur; the FBI is now dedicated to disrupting terrorists *before* they are able to strike. Director Mueller has overhauled our counterterrorism operations, expanded our intelligence capabilities, modernized our business practices and technology, and improved our coordination with our partners.

In line with the plan, the FBI mission statement now reads:

> The mission of the FBI is to protect the United States against terrorism and foreign intelligence threats, to uphold and enforce the criminal laws of the United States, and to provide leadership and criminal justice services to federal, state, municipal, [and] international agencies and partners.

And its top ten priorities are (FBI 2004, "FBI Priorities"):

1. Protect the United States from terrorist attack
2. Protect the United States against foreign intelligence operations and espionage
3. Protect the United States against cyber-based attacks and high-technology crimes
4. Combat public corruption at all levels
5. Protect civil rights
6. Combat transnational and national criminal organizations and enterprises
7. Combat major white-collar crime
8. Combat significant violent crime
9. Support federal, state, county, municipal, and international partners
10. Upgrade technology to successfully perform the FBI's mission

According to Assistant Director Pistole (2004), the priorities "strictly govern" how the FBI's money is spent. Field offices have to distribute their money to make sure that "all anti-terrorism-related leads are addressed before resources can be dedicated to other priorities." Here are some of the ways the resources were reallocated between September 11, 2001, and August 3, 2004:

- 111 percent increase in agents assigned to terrorism
- 86 percent increase in intelligence analysts
- 117 percent increase in linguists

(Pistole only reported the percentages, so we don't know the actual numbers of agents these reflect.)

The FBI also created the following new units:

- 24/7 Counterterrorism Watch (CT Watch) and National Joint Terrorism Task Force (NJTTF) to manage and share threat information
- Terrorism Financing Section (TFS) to centralize efforts to stop terrorism financing
- Document/media exploitation squads to exploit material found both domestically and overseas for its intelligence value
- "Fly teams" to lend counterterrorism expertise wherever its needed
- Terrorist Screening Center (TSC) and Foreign Terrorist Tracking Task Force (FTTTF), interagency units, to help identify terrorists and keep them out of the United States
- Terrorism Reports and Requirements Section to circulate FBI terrorism-related intelligence to the "intelligence community"
- Counterterrorism Analysis Section to "connect the dots" and assess the indicators of terrorist activity against the United States from a strategic perspective

According to Assistant Director Pistole (2004):

> We centralized management of our Counterterrorism Program at Headquarters to limit "stove-piping" of information [policymakers get information they want directly to top leadership without filtering it through those who might disagree with the information], to ensure consistency of counterterrorism priorities and strategy across the organization, to integrate counterterrorism operations domestically and overseas, to improve coordination with other agencies and governments, and to make senior managers accountable for the overall development and success of our counterterrorism efforts.

The DEA "Operation Web Tryp"

The DEA "Operation Web Tryp" investigated Internet sites selling "research chemicals" that were really hallucinogenic drugs like Ecstasy and Foxy Moxy. In one case, David Linder (Arizona) was charged in the U.S. District Court in Norfolk, Virginia, with conspiracy to distribute Foxy. Linder is expected to be extradited to Norfolk to face the charge. Linder could face more serious charges when the federal grand jury hears evidence about an 18-year-old man who died from a "research chemical" he got from Linder's web site. Linder's web site was called www.pondman.nu, which sold landscaping supplies. The site was linked to "Research Chemicals," according to a complaint filed against Linder in U.S. District Court. That page offered for sale a variety of chemicals, each developed to mimic the effects of Ecstasy and other hallucinogens, the complaint says. (The site was immediately shut down.) The site also offered the naturally occurring plant substance called Harmine, which itself is harmless but (according to the DEA) when mixed with another chemical becomes a powerful hallucinogenic called Ayahuasca used by South American indigenous people.

According to DEA Administrator Karen P. Tandy, "The Internet has become the street corner for many users and traffickers. Today's action (Linder's arrest in July 2004) will hopefully prevent future deaths and over-doses." Linder is accused of supplying chemicals to Richard L. Klecker, a former sailor who told Navy investigators that he purchased the drugs through Linder's web site, court records say. The records say that Klecker pressed the powder into Foxy pills and sold them to Navy personnel and others in the Norfolk area. Typically, according to the DEA, the drug was sold at rave parties. Klecker was arrested in 2002 along with another former sailor, Michael D. Wolfe, and Timothy C. Luken, who had worked for Sentara Norfolk General Hospital.

Luken pleaded guilty to a drug conspiracy charge and was sentenced last fall to 70 months in prison. His sentence later was cut in half for assistance that he provided to investigators in the case, court records show. Wolfe pleaded guilty to a similar charge and is serving a 48-month prison sentence.

Klecker also pleaded guilty but challenged the government's argument that Foxy was an illegal controlled substance. At the time of the case, Foxy was not listed as an illegal substance by the DEA. It is now.

Klecker took his case to the U.S. Supreme Court, but the court refused to hear it. He's serving an 84-month prison term. Officials said the Klecker case was instrumental in getting the DEA to list Foxy as an illegal drug.

Source: Tim McGlone, "Drug Web Site Tied to Sales in Norfolk, among Sailors." *The Virginian-Pilot,* July 22, 2004.

Drug Enforcement Administration (DEA): Federal agency that investigates drug offenses. To reach this site go to "Web Links" on your Samaha CJ7 website: http://cj.wadsworth.com/samaha_cj7e.

Drug Enforcement Administration (DEA) The Drug Enforcement Administration (DEA) (2004) mission is

to enforce the controlled substances laws and regulations of the United States and bring to the criminal and civil justice system of the United States, or any other competent jurisdiction, those organizations and principal members of organizations, involved in the growing, manufacture, or distribution of controlled substances appearing in or destined for illicit traffic in the United States; and to recommend and support non-enforcement programs aimed at reducing the availability of illicit controlled substances on the domestic and international markets.

To carry out its mission, the DEA lists the following responsibilities:

- Investigation and preparation for prosecution of major interstate and international controlled substance violators (See the CJ & Technology box "The DEA 'Operation Web Tryp.'")
- Investigation and preparation for prosecution of "criminals and drug gangs who perpetrate violence in our communities and terrorize citizens through fear and intimidation"
- Management of "a national drug intelligence program in cooperation with federal, state, local, and foreign officials to collect, analyze, and disseminate strategic and operational drug intelligence information"
- Seizure and forfeiture of assets derived from, traceable to, or intended to be used for illicit drug trafficking
- Coordination and cooperation with federal, state, and local law enforcement officials on mutual drug enforcement efforts and enhancement of such efforts through exploitation of potential interstate and international investigations beyond local or limited federal jurisdictions and resources

- Coordination and cooperation with federal, state, and local agencies, and with foreign governments, in programs designed to reduce the availability of illicit abuse-type drugs on the U.S. market through crop eradication, crop substitution, and training of foreign officials
- Responsibility, under the policy guidance of the Secretary of State and U.S. Ambassadors, for all programs associated with drug law enforcement counterparts in foreign countries
- Liaison with the United Nations, Interpol, and other organizations on matters relating to international drug control programs (Drug Enforcement Administration 2004)

Other Federal Law Enforcement Agencies Here are brief descriptions of some of the other federal law enforcement agencies (some are listed in Figure 5.1):

- *U.S. Marshals Service.* The Marshals Service is a separate agency within the Department of Justice. The marshals protect the federal courts, judges, and jurors; guard federal prisoners from arrest to conviction; investigate violations of federal fugitive laws; serve summonses; and control custody of money and property seized under federal law.
- *U.S. Customs Service.* Customs inspectors examine all cargo and baggage entering the country. Special agents investigate smuggling, currency violations, criminal fraud, and major cargo frauds. Special customs patrol officers concentrate on contraband, such as drugs and weapons, at official border crossings, seaports, and airports.
- *Bureau of Alcohol, Tobacco, Firearms, and Explosives (ATF)* (Explosives were added to the title following 9/11). The Bureau of Alcohol, Tobacco, Firearms, and Explosives (ATF) enforces federal laws related to firearms; the investigation of arson; explosives incidents and thefts of explosives; and alcohol and tobacco diversion. According to the ATF (Bureau of Alcohol, Tobacco, Firearms, and Explosives 2004), in 2003 the bureau initiated about 30,000 firearms investigations that resulted in about 6,000 convictions of firearms-related offenses, including more than 900 sentences for firearms trafficking offenses (1). The ATF is also responsible for investigating "outlaw motorcycle organizations" (OMO). In connection with this power, the ATF reported that "in July 2003 four ATF-lead investigations spanning nine states culminated in nine arrests, 118 search warrants and the seizure of 1001 firearms, $90,000 in currency, as well as narcotics and explosives" (1).

   After 9/11, the ATF's enforcement of explosives-related crimes was expanded. In connection with its expanded power, in 2003 the ATF "investigated nearly 400 bombings, more than 750 incidents involving recovered explosives or explosive devices, and more than 60 thefts of explosives. The effort resulted in 708 of these cases being forwarded for prosecution. The ATF's three laboratories worked on 630 bomb-related cases in 2003, an increase of 28 percent over the previous year" (2).

Department of Homeland Security (DHS) The events of 9/11 didn't just affect the FBI and the ATF. They also resulted in a huge new addition to the structure of federal law enforcement—the Department of Homeland Security (DHS)—in 2002. According to the DHS (2004), its "exceedingly complex mission" is to

prevent and deter terrorist attacks and protect against and respond to threats and hazards to the nation; ... [to] ensure safe and secure borders, welcome lawful immigrants and visitors, and promote the free-flow of commerce. (5)

According to the DHS, one reason for its creation "was to provide the unifying core for the vast national network of organizations and institutions involved in efforts to secure our nation." The DHS's *Strategic Plan* (DHS 2004) was developed

U.S. Marshals Service: These officers apprehend federal fugitives, protect federal judicial officials, and provide witness protection. To reach this site go to "Web Links" on your Samaha CJ7 website: http://cj.wadsworth.com/samaha_cj7e.

U.S. Customs and Border Protection: After 9/11, the Border Patrol and Customs merged into this department under the umbrella of the Department of Homeland Security. To reach this site go to "Web Links" on your Samaha CJ7 website: http://cj.wadsworth.com/samaha_cj7e.

Bureau of Alcohol, Tobacco, Firearms, and Explosives (ATF): ATF enforces the federal laws and regulations relating to alcohol and tobacco diversion, firearms, explosives, and arson. To reach this site go to "Web Links" on your Samaha CJ7 website: http://cj.wadsworth.com/samaha_cj7e.

Department of Homeland Security: The agency that oversees our homeland security and includes many federal law enforcement agencies. To reach this site go to "Web Links" on your Samaha CJ7 website: http://cj.wadsworth.com/samaha_cj7e.

► The effects of 9/11 included a huge new addition to the structure of federal law enforcement—the Department of Homeland Security (DHS). Homeland security is now a top priority of the federal, state, and local governments. In this photo, a 25-foot Homeland Security boat from the Coast Guard Station in Boston provides a security escort for the LNG Tanker MATTHEW in Boston Harbor. These escorts are a multi-agency priority, consisting of Coast Guard, local and state police, and the Massachusetts Environmental Patrol.

to accomplish its mission and to "provide guidance to the 180,000 DHS men and women who work every day on this important task."

The DHS's stated strategic goals include:

- *Awareness.* Identify and understand threats, assess vulnerabilities, determine potential impacts, and disseminate timely information to our homeland security partners and the American public.
- *Prevention.* Detect, deter, and mitigate threats to our homeland.
- *Protection.* Safeguard our people and their freedoms, critical infrastructure, property, and the economy of our nation from acts of terrorism, natural disasters, or other emergencies.
- *Response.* Lead, manage, and coordinate the national response to acts of terrorism, natural disasters, or other emergencies.
- *Recovery.* Lead national, state, local, and private sector efforts to restore services and rebuild communities after acts of terrorism, natural disasters, or other emergencies.
- *Service.* Serve the public effectively by facilitating lawful trade, travel, and immigration.
- *Organizational excellence.* Value our most important resource, our people. Create a culture that promotes a common identity, innovation, mutual respect, accountability, and teamwork to achieve efficiencies, effectiveness, and operational synergies. (9)

State Law Enforcement Agencies

All states have law enforcement agencies with statewide authority. They go by various names, but common ones are the State Police, State Highway Patrol, and State Bureau of Investigation. Whatever they're called, state police originated with the Texas Rangers, who in the early 1800s patrolled the Texas settlements. Following the Civil War, Massachusetts and Connecticut created state police agencies to combat vice. In the wake of labor-management strife resulting from rapid industrialization, Pennsylvania adopted a state police agency to quell industrial violence. These states overcame resistance generated by a fear that centralized state police agencies threatened both civil liberties and local autonomy.

After 1910, when the number of motor vehicles proliferated, the need for highway traffic control generated new calls for state police. States such as Texas,

Pennsylvania, Connecticut, and Massachusetts added a state trooper division to their existing organization. However, most states never overcame opposition to a centralized state police agency with comprehensive powers, but they did adopt special state highway patrol agencies with authority limited to traffic law enforcement. State highway patrol officers have only limited authority to perform general law enforcement duties, such as investigating crimes occurring in a state trooper's presence or on or near state highways.

Governors appoint the directors of state police or state highway patrols. Technological advances in traffic devices, alcohol testing, and communications systems all require officers to have greater ability and more training than their predecessors. Increasing numbers of states are setting statewide entry requirements and training standards for police officers, either through agency-established academies or in conjunction with institutions of higher learning. Following training, line officers advance in rank through either civil service or merit plans. In addition to enforcement agencies and training institutions, most states maintain "crime lab" or "criminalistics" services; some support investigative units.

County Law Enforcement Agencies

Sheriffs' departments enforce the criminal law in most rural and unincorporated portions of the more than three thousand counties in the United States. In most instances, sheriffs don't interfere in municipal law enforcement because most incorporated towns and cities have their own police forces.

Besides county law enforcement, sheriffs' departments have two other duties. They maintain the county jails, which hold pretrial detainees and most persons sentenced for misdemeanors (Chapter 13). They're also officers of the county court. In that capacity, the sheriff's office supplies bailiffs to provide security and management of detainees on trial; transports prisoners to and from court; and serves court papers (summonses, forfeiture and eviction notices, and court judgments).

Municipal Police Departments

More than 12,500 municipal police departments do the lion's share of policing and consume most of the law enforcement budget (Figure 5.2) in the United States, and they're the subject of most of what you'll learn about police and policing in this book. So we won't say any more about them here, except to note a few basic facts that you'll learn more about in this chapter and in Chapters 6 and 7:

- Municipal police departments range enormously in size. The largest, in New York City, has over 40,000 sworn officers; 5000 departments have fewer than 10 officers; 676 departments have only one. (Bureau of Justice Statistics [BJS] January 2003, 2)

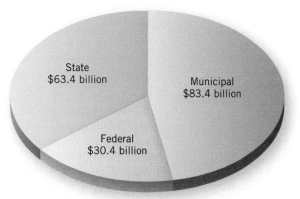

◀ FIGURE 5.2 Expenditures on Federal, State, and Local Agencies, 2001

Source: Bureau of Justice Statistics, *Justice Expenditure and Employment in the U.S., 2001* (Washington, DC: Bureau of Justice Statistics, May 2004), Table 1.

- The numbers of women, Black, and Hispanic sworn officers are increasing. (BJS May 2002)
- The percentage of departments requiring some college education is increasing. (BJS May 2002)
- The percentage of departments using computers is increasing. (BJS May 2002)
- The percentage of departments with special units devoted to full-time domestic violence and victims' assistance is increasing. (BJS May 2002)

Police departments have a formal structure but use an informal decision-making style; we'll examine these seemingly inconsistent characteristics.

Formal Police Structure Formally, law enforcement agencies resemble military organizations; we call this the **military model of policing.** Police departments use a hierarchical command structure, meaning authority flows from the chief who gives orders at the top down to officers on the beat who carry out the orders. Officers wear uniforms, and they're divided into ranks with military-sounding names like commander, captain, lieutenant, and sergeant. Also, disobeying orders is called insubordination, and it leads to punishment just like in the military. The police mission is defined as fighting "wars" against "enemies" who commit crimes, use drugs, and otherwise cause trouble. The following description of the New York City Police Academy is a little old but it still nicely captures this military model of police agency structure:

> "Attention," the drill sergeant yelled at 200 men and women. One man slouched. Another saluted with his left hand. "About face." A few turned the wrong way. A few more stumbled. The sergeant was not amused. "This is unbelievable!" the sergeant bellowed at a new crop of police recruits on their first day of gym class at the Police Academy. "Look straight ahead when you're at attention. Do things in unison. You're not civilians anymore," he told them. "You're in a military outfit." (Nix 1987)

The Informal Police Decision-Making Process The military model describes the formal, outward structure of police organization, but the informal reality of its decision-making process in its day-to-day operations is very different. Whereas soldiers wait for specific orders from officers before they act, and most orders are highly specific ("Go over that hill and attack that house"), police officers are left on their own to carry out vague commands like "keep the peace," "settle problems," and so on. Soldiers work together. They can't, don't, and shouldn't decide whether to move into an area, shoot at the enemy, and so on. In contrast, except for large public gatherings, demonstrations, disturbances, and riots, police officers work alone or with a single partner.

> Every day, out of their supervisors' sight, police officers at the lowest levels of their departments make…"low visibility decisions" that have great effects on…individuals.…At any moment…police officers throughout the United States are deciding whether to ticket or merely to warn this motorist; whether or not to destroy the marijuana cigarette that kid was found holding and send him on his way without marking his life history with a record of arrest; whether or not to arrest this abusive husband; whether to back off a bit or stand firm and shoot the oncoming emotionally disturbed person wielding the knife. (Skolnick and Fyfe 1993, 119)

In day-to-day operations, police departments resemble hospitals, universities, and law firms more than military organizations. Police chiefs, hospital administrators, college deans, and managing partners in law firms make sure there are enough personnel, money, and support so the officers, doctors, professors, and lawyers can do their jobs. But the "big" decisions are left to the doctors (medicate or operate), professors (pass or fail), trial lawyers (plead guilty or go to trial), and officers (arrest or let go) (Skolnick and Fyfe 1993, 118).

The military model does describe our image of the police as well as their image of themselves. But that image causes problems. The military image and

military model of policing organized in a hierarchical command structure where decisions (orders) are made by the chief at the top and are carried out by officers on the beat

the belief that "all's fair in war" leads some police officers to use excessive force or illegally invade the privacy and liberty of anyone they consider the "enemy" (Chapter 6). The enemy—people in the community in this case—may adopt the same maxim, putting the police in danger. According to Jerome Skolnick, a highly respected police expert, and James Fyfe (1993), a former police officer and now a criminal justice professor:

> However stirring this call [for a war on crime], it relies upon an inexact analogy and is far more likely to produce unnecessary violence and antagonism than to result in effective policing. The lines between friend and foe were clear in the Arabian desert, but police officers on American streets too often rely on ambiguous cues and stereotypes in trying to identify the enemies in their war. When officers act upon such signals and roust people who turn out to be guilty of no more than being in what officers view as the wrong place at the wrong time—young black men on inner-city streets at night, for example—the police may create enemies where none previously existed. (114)

Private (Nongovernment) Police and Policing

"Policing is being transformed... in the modern world," write police experts David H. Bayley and Clifford D. Shearing (2001, vii) in the most thorough and latest review of research on developments in worldwide policing. Here are two remarkable developments around the world Bayley and Shearing uncovered in their review:

1. Nongovernment police outnumber public police.
2. People spend more time in their daily lives in places policed by *nongovernment* individuals and groups than by public police agencies. (1)

Private police are nothing new. The first private security officer in the United States was Allan Pinkerton, who founded the legendary Pinkerton Agency in the mid-1800s mainly to protect business interests. He started out working for railroads because once trains left the station, they were open targets for train robbers. Soon, Pinkerton was also working for factory owners during the industrial strife of the 1880s. Although he was pro-labor, Pinkerton was against strikes. Business protection is also a major component of modern private policing, but it's not the only one (Bayley and Shearing, 6); Table 5.1 lists others.

Let's look at two of the major components in nongovernment policing: business and residential. We'll also discuss the private security business and its personnel.

Business Nongovernment Police Legal businesses act either individually or collectively to police their interests. Individually, they either set up their own internal security force or hire others to do it for them (Bayley and Shearing 2001, 6). Or they band with other businesses based on either geography or similar service offerings. Good examples of geographical bandings are BIDS (business

American Society for Industrial Security: This is the premier site for professional private security. Includes certification programs, training, and resources for security professionals. To reach this site go to "Web Links" on your Samaha CJ7 website: http://cj.wadsworth.com/samaha_cj7e.

▼ **TABLE 5.1 Components of Private Policing**

Components	Type of Nongovernment Policing
Business interests	Legal: Business Illegal: Criminal organizations, juvenile gangs
Residential communities	Gated communities Neighborhood Watch and the like
Cultural communities	Nation of Islam (Black Muslims)
Individuals	Self-defense Bodyguards

Source: David H. Bayley and Clifford D. Shearing, *The New Structure of Policing: Description, Conceptualization, and Research Agenda* (Washington, DC: National Institute of Justice, 2001).

improvement districts), which "tax" members to pay for police patrol. Good examples of bandings based on common services are banks, bars, and taxi companies. Common-service banding organizations don't usually hire and share police. Instead, they warn each other about potential threats, swap ideas about strengthening security, and support one another when they need it.

Illegal businesses also take charge of and provide security for places where they live and people they live with. In some places, they're the only police available. Governments may actually help these illegal businesses, with public police turning a "blind eye" to illegal activities to get information. For example, the Brazilian police tolerate the good Donos' (drug lords) illegal conduct because they maintain order in their communities. The bottom line: governments cut illegal businesses some slack provided they contribute to public safety in ways public police can't (Bayley and Shearing 2001, 7).

Residential Community Nongovernment Police Residential communities come in many varieties, and they provide for their own security in various ways. Gated communities take their cue from the ancient practice of "walling" (Chapter 6). The name tells you what they are: residences you have to go through gates to get to because walls surround them. Here's a description of wealthy gated communities in a New Orleans suburb:

> [W]ith names that whisper exclusivity: English Turn, Barkley Estates and Oakland Plantation. Six-foot brick walls and iron fences encircle these enclaves of luxury homes. Electronic gates and 24-hour security guards keep outsiders away. The streets are spotless, the landscaping lush. (El Nasser 2002)

Just in case you think gated communities are reserved for the rich, here's another example:

> A mile away, Gina Rojas, a waitress and single mom, also enjoys a gated lifestyle. But she lives in a one-bedroom apartment that rents for $492 a month. An iron fence surrounds her Harper's Ferry development. She needs a coded card to get past the electronic gates that guard all three entrances. (El Nasser 2002)

Gina Rojas isn't an isolated example. According to the U.S. Census Bureau's 2001 Survey of Housing (El Nasser 2002), wealthy homeowners aren't the only ones "retreating behind gates. The desire to lock out the outside world cuts across all income groups." According to Tom Sanchez, associate professor of urban affairs and planning at Virginia Tech, "We think of affluent people and mini-mansions in exclusive enclaves, but we don't think about the multifamily, higher density, lower-income residents also being in that type of development."

The 2001 Survey of Household showed that more than seven million households (6 percent of the U.S. population) are in gated communities. In some areas, it's higher. According to Ed Blakely, dean of the Milano Graduate School at New School University in New York and co-author of *Fortress America: Gated Communities in the United States*, about 40 percent of new homes in California are behind walls. And most of the subdivisions approved by Palm Beach County, Florida, between 1997 and 2002 are gated (El Nasser 2002).

Single-dwelling homes surrounded by gates are what we call horizontal-gated communities. Most of them are policed by realtor-managed security guards and hardware. The other kind of gated community, condominiums and "co-op" apartments, we call vertical-gated communities.

A third kind of private security takes place in nongated communities. Here, neighborhood cooperation is the basis for security; it's not hired out and managed by outsiders. Residents agree to watch one another's houses, call the police about suspicious strangers, patrol the streets at certain times of the day, improve dangerous physical conditions, and organize restorative justice conferences (Bayley and Shearing 2001, 7; Chapter 12).

© Bill Varie/Corbis

◀ Two remarkable developments are transforming police: There are more nongovernment than government police officers, and people spend more time in their daily lives in places policed by *non*government individuals and groups than by public police agencies. In many states, private security personnel like this guard checking monitors in a building that is serviced by a private security agency have the power to arrest, and they're not subject to the same restraints as public police officers.

The Private Security Business Except for the voluntary resident cooperative policing you just learned about, and the similar service business cooperation, most private security is a for-profit industry. It provides human resources (guards, investigators, couriers, bodyguards, employee monitoring, background checks, and polygraph and drug testing). It also supplies hardware (safes, locks, alarm systems, and closed-circuit television). Businesses or others can either hire private security directly or contract for specific services and equipment.

Private Security Personnel In many states, private security personnel have the power to arrest, and they're not subject to the same restraints as public police officers. For example, private police don't have to give arrestees the *Miranda* warnings (Chapter 7). Some states have special legislation authorizing private security to act as "special police" within a specific jurisdiction, such as a plant, store, or university campus (BJS 1988b, 66).

Sworn police officers can (and frequently do) "moonlight" for private security firms during their off-duty hours; most police departments permit moonlighting. Some departments even contract with private concerns to provide personnel and use the revenue for department needs. For example, Miami and St. Petersburg, Florida, allow off-duty police officers to work armed and in uniform; the departments even arrange jobs for their officers (BJS 1988b, 66).

In the business improvement districts (BIDS) in New York City, private security forces patrol various parts of the city and augment public police. For example, 29 uniformed but unarmed security guards patrol a 50-block section of Manhattan. A former police borough commander directs the force, and a self-imposed surtax by property owners pays for it. Security guards start at about $10 an hour, take a special 35-hour training course at John Jay College of Criminal Justice, and spend two more weeks training on the street. Squads patrol from 8 A.M. to midnight. Similar private security forces patrol other areas: A 285-member unit patrols Rockefeller Center; a 49-member unit patrols South Street Seaport; and Roosevelt Island has an unarmed 46-member force commanded by a former police official. New York City police officers are allowed to moonlight but not in NYPD uniforms (Blumenthal 1989).

🌐 **"Building Private Security/Public Policing Partnerships to Prevent and Respond to Terrorism and Public Disorder":** An article on the International Association of Police Chiefs' website. Select "Publications" twice to reach the article. To reach this site go to "Web Links" on your Samaha CJ7 website: http://cj.wadsworth.com/ samaha_cj7e.

DECISION POINT

Is private security worth the cost?

Click on this Decision Point at http://cj.wadsworth.com/samaha_cj7e to explore the issue.

In some precincts, there are more off-duty public police officers acting as private security officers than on-duty officers. Because they wear uniforms, off-duty employment increases both the availability and visibility of police officers. On the other hand, off-duty employment raises concerns about conflict of interest in serving private interests, fears of corruption, and possible lawsuits for alleged misconduct. To reduce the risk of these problems, department orders and regulations frequently limit the kinds of employment officers can accept (Reiss 1988).

Police Missions

"The police in modern society...have an 'impossible task,'" wrote police expert Peter K. Manning (1995, 103) in 1977. This is still true. So is his next comment:

> To much of the public the police are seen as...crime-fighters...that keep society from falling into chaos. The policeman himself considers the essence of his role to be the dangerous and heroic enterprise of crook-catching and the watchful prevention of crimes....They do engage in chases, in gunfights, in careful sleuthing. But these are rare events. (103)

As you've already learned from the history of policing, the police have three missions:

1. Criminal law enforcement
2. Order maintenance
3. Public service not related to either criminal law enforcement or maintaining order

Criminal law enforcement may be the most publicized mission, but it's in maintaining order and providing services not related to crime or disorder that discretionary decision making looms largest. It's also how officers spend most of their time and where most taxpayers' dollars go. Let's look more closely at each of the three police missions.

Criminal Law Enforcement

Criminal law enforcement is a "rare" police mission, but that doesn't mean it's unimportant. Guarding the gates of the criminal justice system and starting the criminal justice process in motion by deciding who will and who won't pass through those gates is by any measure very important. The police produce the first product of criminal justice decision making—the criminal suspect. Without that product, the criminal process never starts. The criminal law enforcement mission boils down to four duties:

1. Preventing crime from happening in the first place
2. Investigating crimes and identifying suspects after crimes have been committed
3. Finding and catching suspects after they're identified
4. Helping prosecutors build a case against defendants

full enforcement nondiscretionary enforcement of all criminal laws all the time

selective enforcement officers use their discretion to arrest *some* people, *sometimes,* for breaking *some* laws

Formally, police are supposed to enforce all the criminal laws all the time (it's called **full enforcement**). Informally, officers never make the impossible—and really stupid—effort to enforce every criminal statute all the time by setting the criminal process in motion every time there's probable cause (the legal standard) to arrest a suspect for any crime. In their day-to-day work, officers practice **selective enforcement;** they use their discretion to arrest *some* people, *sometimes,* for breaking *some* laws (Goldstein 1977, chaps. 3–4).

Selective enforcement doesn't mean police officers can do as they please in deciding when, how, and against whom they enforce the criminal laws. This is especially true of decision making about serious felonies. As gatekeepers of the criminal justice system, law enforcement officers *always* "open the gates" for se-

Which Laws Should the Police Enforce?

All of the following incidents took place in Chicago:

1. A 19-year-old fired three shots from the street at a woman standing in her doorway. Several neighbors saw the shooting. The woman asked the police not to arrest him.
2. A police officer witnessed an armed robbery. The victim asked him not to arrest the robber.
3. A police officer witnessed a shoplifting. The store owner asked the officer not to arrest the shoplifter.
4. An officer caught a juvenile throwing rocks through large windows. The youth agreed to pay for the damages.
5. A patrol officer saw a juvenile drinking.
6. An officer witnessed a man paying a prostitute for services.
7. A patrol officer saw a 21-year-old woman riding her bicycle on the sidewalk.
8. An officer saw customers smoking in the "no smoking" section of a restaurant.
9. A group of neighbors gathered in an apartment for a Saturday night poker game for money. A police officer, in the building on another call, saw the game in progress through an open door.
10. Two patrol officers saw a man spit on the sidewalk.
11. Two patrol officers came upon a young couple having sexual intercourse in their car while parked in a city park.
12. A patrol officer caught a 21-year-old man smoking marijuana. The only marijuana he had on him was the "joint" he was smoking when he was caught.
13. The police caught a cocaine user with cocaine in her possession. She was well known among big drug dealers and would make an excellent "snitch."
14. The police witnessed a physician and a lawyer engaging in homosexual sodomy in their car in a city park.

All of these incidents broke a state law and/or a city ordinance. And police board rules and general orders issued by the chief of police clearly stated officers have to enforce all the laws and city ordinances. The police didn't arrest anyone.

Source: Kenneth Culp Davis, *Police Discretion* (St. Paul: West, 1975), pp. 3–7.

---

rious felonies when there's probable cause to arrest. In other words, they always arrest suspected murderers, rapists, and armed robbers no matter what their race, ethnicity, gender, or social class (Chapter 1). In less serious felonies and minor offenses, their decision making is more discretionary. This is an example of how important the seriousness of the offense and the dangerousness of the offender are in decision making at every point in criminal justice. And, of course, the more discretion, the more room there is for unacceptable criteria to infect decision making (Chapters 1 and 4).

Order Maintenance

Maintaining order means police are supposed to "do something right now to settle problems." (See the In Focus box "Which Laws Should the Police Enforce?") Notice three major differences between maintaining order and criminal law enforcement:

> maintaining order police are supposed to "do something right now to settle problems"

1. "Do something" calls for discretionary decision making that includes a lot more choices than just arresting someone.
2. "Settle problems" also allows a wide range of discretionary decision making. Problems include more than crimes, and "settle" means more than putting the criminal justice process in motion.
3. "Right now" means to settle the problem in minutes. Criminal law enforcement takes days—sometimes weeks or even months—stretching from investigation before an arrest and the arrest itself by patrol officers to follow-up investigation by detectives. (Chapters 6 and 7)

In order maintenance, law enforcement officers have to use their judgment to "do the right thing," sometimes without clear guidelines and with lots of controversy over just what the right thing to do is (Wilson 1968, 4–5). But officers *do* know one thing for sure: they've got the power to back up their decisions with force. This monopoly of force is the defining feature of police work (Bittner 1970, 36–47). According to Skolnick and Fyfe (1993):

> The risk of physical injury is greater in many lines of industrial work than in policing, but cops are the ones to whom society accords the right to use, or to threaten to use, force. This assignment and the capacity to carry it out are said to be the central feature of the role of police in society. (94)

There are lots of definitions of order, but in this book, we mean behaving according to ordinary standards of decency when we're in public. This sounds like an awfully broad definition and open to all kinds of mischief in the hands of officers whose mission is to maintain these "ordinary standards of decency." And it *could* be. But we shouldn't be too alarmed. As you've already learned, people in all kinds of neighborhoods, of all ages, both sexes, across racial, ethnic, and economic groups believe order is central to the quality of life and that disorderly conduct threatens it. *And* just as (or more) important, these highly diverse groups agree on the meaning of behaving in public according to "ordinary standards" (Chapter 3).

As for doing something "right now," officers can't say, "Hold everything until I check the book on this one." Even if they've got time (which they usually don't), the answer won't be in the book. It can't be; no book can spell out how to respond to the countless kinds of problems officers face every day. So decision making to maintain order and public manners boils down to depending more on experience, community standards, and personal values than on the mechanical application of rules found in manuals, ordinances, statutes, constitutions, and court decisions.

Public Service

Police departments are the only government agency on call every day, all day, all year. It's useful to point out that in the 1800s the word *police* meant "local government." (To this day, the legal term *police power* refers to the state and local governments' power to make and enforce *all* laws, not just criminal laws [Black 1980, 29–32].) So it makes sense for people to call the police to solve all kinds of problems: to report fights, drunkenness, rowdy kids, prostitution, and panhandling on the streets; to stop a feud between neighbors outside; to settle a domestic disturbance and a noisy party inside; to find lost children and animals in distress anywhere; or to find the nearest hospital, football field, or dog show.

Calling the police for every imaginable reason is nothing new. In 1910, Brand Whitlock, the reform mayor of Toledo, Ohio, recognized this reality in his city. Whenever anything "bothered" people their instant reaction was, "It's time to call the police," the exasperated mayor complained (Whitlock 1914, 239). This community service mission is a central part of the history of policing (see "The History of Police and Policing" section). So it's clear, whether the police like or want to get involved in people's problems, the public wants (no, demands!) that they do get involved. In reality, police touch the lives of more people in more ways than any other public agency. It's not surprising police funding eats up the largest share of criminal justice expenditures (Chapter 1, Figure 1.1).

The Overlapping of Missions

In real life, police missions don't fit neatly into their own boxes of law enforcement, order maintenance, and public services. Instead, the three missions overlap and reinforce each other. According to police expert James Q. Wilson (1983):

> Though the law enforcement, order maintenance, and service provision aspects can be analytically distinguished, concretely they are thoroughly intermixed. Even in a routine law enforcement situation (for example, arresting a fleeing purse snatcher), how the officer

deals with the victim and the onlookers at the scene is often as important as how he handles the suspect. The victim and onlookers, after all, are potential witnesses who have to testify in court; assuring their cooperation is as necessary as catching the person against whom they will testify. The argument about whether "cops" should be turned into "social workers" is a false one, for it implies that society can exercise some meaningful choice over the role the officer should play. Except at the margin, it cannot. (111–112)

Others have suggested the crime-fighter image makes maintaining order and community service more effective. Police effectiveness boils down to the public having respect for officers' potential power to use force. For example, Elaine Cumming and her colleagues found wife beaters were less willing to obey unpleasant orders given by service-oriented police officers than by crime-fighter officers who make clear they're prepared to arrest and put them in jail. Cumming and her colleagues also found individuals "needing help" follow crime fighters' orders better than community service agents' commands (Cumming, Cumming, and Edell 1965, 285).

Respected police expert Herman Goldstein (1984), who for decades has studied what police really do out there in the field, concludes:

> We've learned that what the police do in their "order maintenance" function may have a very important bearing on their capacity to deal with crime; that citizen attitudes and cooperation are heavily influenced by the effectiveness of the police in providing the wide range of services that the public has come to expect from them. (11)

Possible Shifts in Mission Priorities

When I called St. Paul Assistant Police Chief Richard Gardell to ask him to talk to my "Introduction to Criminal Justice" class about the missions of the police, I began, "I'm sorry to interrupt you in your war on crime, which I know you spend all of your time fighting...." He interrupted me with a laugh and said, "Not anymore, at least not in this department where we have all kinds of other things to do." This exchange was just banter with my former student from the 1970s. But there's some evidence to suggest that the myth of the crime-fighting mission may have started to lose its grip even in the days when Assistant Chief Gardell was a young student here at the University of Minnesota.

Professor James Q. Wilson (1968, 236) noted in his study of police departments during the 1960s that at least some police administrators were aware of, and willing to talk openly about, maintaining order and providing services as higher priorities than law enforcement. Another study based on observing three California departments found patrol officers willing, even eager, to nurture their community service functions. They openly admitted they get a lot of satisfaction from pursuing the mission of community service. Some departments issue clear policy statements regarding the importance of maintaining order and providing service.

In 1981, police expert George Kelling offered the following excellent summary of the complexity of police functions—and it's still accurate:

> Although the crime-related functions of the police were historically important and continue to be so, it is insufficient to define the police either predominantly or exclusively on the basis of those functions. Their functions are far broader, and consist of peace-keeping and management functions essential to urban life. Taking this point of view the police are not just a part of the criminal justice system, but also are a key element of urban government. They are the primary contact citizens have with government.... [P]olice services constitute more than 30% of the cost of city government. The police are available 24 hours a day. They resolve conflicts between families, groups, interests and individuals. All police rhetoric about crime fighting aside, it is clear, from observing the needs of citizens and what the police actually do, that the order and service functions are the functional heart of policing. (Police Foundation 1981, 112)

Not everyone agrees police should perform such a wide variety of services. Many criminal justice professionals, the public, and politicians call for the police to narrow their focus to concentrating on serious crime. In 1967, Professors Norval Morris and Gordon Hawkins (1967) wrote what many believe is still true:

> The immense range of police obligations and duties must be drastically reduced. A variety of means are suggested here [transferring traffic control, most misdemeanors, and minor violations to other agencies] for both diminishing the range of their responsibilities and enabling the more effective use of their resources in the prevention and control of serious crime [murder, rape, robbery, and burglary in particular]. (9)

Police Officers

California Commission on Peace Officer Standards and Training: This site includes every facet of the selection process for police officers. To reach this site go to "Web Links" on your Samaha CJ7 website: http://cj.wadsworth.com/samaha_cj7e.

Before we get to the details, let's look at some basic facts about local police officers in 2000, the latest available data (BJS January 2003, iii):

- Local police departments had 441,000 sworn officers.
- Minorities made up 22.7 percent of local police department full-time sworn officers (up 17 percent from 1990).
- Almost all officers worked for departments that use criminal record checks, background investigations, driving record checks, personal interviews, and medical and psychological testing to screen applicants for police work.
- Fifteen percent of departments (employing one-third of all sworn officers) required new applicants to have completed *some* college.
- State-mandated field and academy training averaged about 750 hours. Additional training above the state requirements averaged about 300 hours.

Now, let's look more in depth at some of the details behind these and other aspects of local police officers: how they're selected, their "working personality," how that personality impacts their discretionary decision making, and the growing impact of women and minority officers.

Officer Selection, Training, and Promotion

It's easy to criticize a lot about the 1960s and 1970s, but during those troubled times (Chapter 1) two positive developments influenced the selection, training, and promotion of police officers:

1. *The report of President Lyndon Johnson's Crime Commission* (President's Commission on Law Enforcement and Administration of Justice 1967). The report documented widespread police corruption, discrimination, and failure to respond to the needs and demands of communities. It also challenged the assumptions that the "manly virtues" and the willingness to obey orders (premium qualities looked for in traditional police forces) were the qualities most needed to make a "good" police officer. It rejected the prevailing requirements of height, financial credit history, and the absence of *any* criminal record and the view that they accurately screened for competent officers. Instead, the commission argued, those requirements effectively (if not always consciously) excluded large segments of society from police work. As a result, the most visible form of law enforcement didn't represent women, Blacks, Native Americans, Asian Americans, and Hispanics. The commission recommended the adoption of screening devices that eliminate arbitrary and exclusionary effects.
2. *The passage of the Equal Employment Opportunity Act (EEO) P.L. 92-261* (U.S. Code 1972). The act banned discrimination in public employment. It also led to a number of federal court cases appraising hiring, promotion, and training practices of local police departments.

Disagreement about the definition of "good" police officers added to the challenges of the Crime Commission and the civil rights legislation. To some segments of society, good police officers maintain the status quo; to others, they change it. To some segments, good police officers aggressively fight crime; to oth-

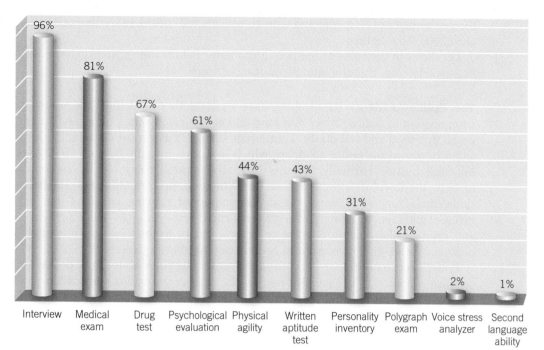

◀ FIGURE 5.3
**Screening Methods
Used by Local Police
Departments**
Source: Bureau of Justice
Statistics, *Local Police
Departments, 2000*
(Washington, DC: Bureau of
Justice Statistics, January
2003), Table 8.

Interview — 96%
Medical exam — 81%
Drug test — 67%
Psychological evaluation — 61%
Physical agility — 44%
Written aptitude test — 43%
Personality inventory — 31%
Polygraph exam — 21%
Voice stress analyzer — 2%
Second language ability — 1%

ers, they help people in trouble. To some, good officers follow the letter of the law; to others, they bend the rules to get results.

Despite such disagreements, no one denied that personality, selection of applicants, training, and promotion of officers matter when it comes to the effectiveness of police operations and police deviance (corruption and brutality, Chapter 7). Robert D. Meier and Richard E. Maxwell (1987) reported a growing consensus that psychological testing can determine the emotional and psychological fitness of recruits. More than half the nation's police departments now use some form of psychological testing.

Unfortunately, psychologists and psychiatrists disagree on what makes a good police officer and, so, don't agree on what they're looking for and how to find it in the tests. Also, a growing body of empirical research casts doubt on the accuracy of predictions of future officer performance based on psychological testing. Benjamin Wright and colleagues (1990) analyzed data from the Tallahassee Police Department to test the relationship between before-employment psychological test results and performance of recruits during their initial field training. The results showed no relationship between the results of the Minnesota Multiphasic Personality Inventory or the California Personality Inventory and field performance. The researchers concluded that the results suggest a need to reshape the police selection process. Despite these reservations, most departments use psychological testing, along with a number of other criteria to screen applicants to local police departments (Figure 5.3).

Most traditional departments also maintained stringent physical, mental, and character requirements that were subject to manipulation to favor White men. The minimum 5-foot 8-inch height and 150-pound weight requirements of those days made it difficult for women to enter police work. Traditional civil service examinations favored Whites. Physical agility tests—timed runs, carrying weights, and repeat trigger-pulling—favored men. Character investigations that eliminated potential recruits with even the most minor criminal records favored Whites. Oral interviews allowed gender and race to affect judgments. Traditional screening produced a homogeneous group of recruits: young, White men with blue-collar backgrounds and high school diplomas who entered police work because it promised job security. The height and weight requirements are no longer with us, but the others are (Figure 5.3). To what extent they infect selection decision making isn't clear, but the evidence *does* show that by 2000 the percentage of Black officers outnumbered their percentage of the general population; however, the percentages of Hispanic and women officers fell considerably short (BJS January 2003, Highlights).

Let's look at the roles of the police academy, field training, and higher education in selecting, training, and promoting officers.

The Police Academy Researchers have consistently found that "the transition from civilian to police officer is a long and complicated series of stages, inviting much upheaval and self doubt" (Lundman 1980, 73). For most officers, this transition begins in the police academy, which socializes recruits by both formal and informal means. Formally, recruits learn the written rules of the academy—namely, the laws of search, seizure, interrogation, and identification; technical skills, including crime scene preservation; pursuit driving; weapons use; self-defense; and report writing. Rules govern virtually everything in police academies, and military-like officers attempt to enforce them. Rules focus on punctuality, neatness, order, attentiveness, and obedience to authority (Harris 1978, 273–291).

Police recruits also learn the unwritten informal rules about how police officers are supposed to behave. But neither the rules of the traditional academy nor the formal laws of criminal procedure answer recruits' most pressing questions:

- "What's it really like out there on the streets?"
- "How do I arrest someone who doesn't want to be arrested?"
- "Exactly when do I use my baton, and how do I do it?"
- "What do the other patrol officers think of me?"

Recruits learn some of the answers from instructors or other experienced officers in the form of police war stories. Most of these stories, such as that told by Jonathan Rubenstein (1973) stress two themes: police defensiveness and police depersonalization:

> A jack is a beautiful weapon, but it is very dangerous, fellas. I remember once we were looking for a guy who had beaten up a policeman and escaped from a wagon. I found him hiding under a car. To this day I don't know if he was coming out to surrender or to attack me, but he was just coming out before I told him to move. He was a real big guy and I didn't wait. I had my jack ready, and as he came up I hit him as hard as I could. I thought I killed him. He was O.K., but since then I haven't carried a jack unless I was going on some dangerous job. I don't want to beat someone to death, and with a jack you can never be sure. You should get yourself a convoy and use it in your fist. If you punch for a guy's heart, the whipping action of the spring will snap it forward and break his collarbone. Then you've got him. (282)

This war story portrays both themes. Officers learn they have to defend themselves *and* develop defensiveness. They also learn not to trust "outsiders." According to Richard Harris (1978), a journalist who attended a police academy in New York City, instructors told recruits that "anyone who was not a law enforcement officer was not to be trusted" (53).

The story of using the blackjack also illustrates how the traditional academy encourages recruits to depersonalize individuals, as this instructor did by describing the use of force in such a cold, matter-of-fact manner. The themes of defensiveness and depersonalization stem in large part from the perceived danger of police work (see "The Police 'Working Personality'" section).

Field Training New police officers finish their academy training feeling insecure about whether what they've learned will help them on the street. Departments usually require field training, which places rookies in the hands of older officers who are supposed to help them transition from the academy and learn the craft of policing. But training involves more than learning skills and techniques. According to James Fyfe (1995):

> Everything that supervisors do or tolerate, every interpretation of broad departmental philosophy, every application of specific rules and policies is a training lesson that has at least

Does Field Training Make Better Cops?

IN FOCUS

Some departments provide broader educational experience than the traditional academy and field training. Some accept courses that are supposed to improve critical thinking because administrators believe that such courses improve the capacity of police officers to make sound discretionary judgments. Some departments accept liberal arts courses, and even degrees, as satisfying both entry and advancement criteria. Instructors in some law enforcement courses have adopted problem-solving approaches, the case method, and discussion to enhance prospective officers' ability to make judgments. Experienced officers sometimes act as guest lecturers, interacting with students who hope to become officers and with other students. The interaction can prove enriching to students, instructors, and officers.

Field experiences that broaden the perspectives of new officers are supposed to improve their understanding and effectiveness. Community service internships offer recruits the opportunity to gain a broader perspective on crime and criminal law enforcement. To improve understanding of the criminal justice system beyond the police department, some officers spend time in prosecutors' offices to appreciate the complexities of charging suspects; in public defenders' offices getting the defense point of view; and in judges' chambers learning about the difficulties of sentencing. Some departments give officers the opportunity to learn more about the cultural diversity in their district by assigning them to hospital emergency rooms, alcoholic detoxification clinics, psychiatric wards, welfare offices, and schools (Campbell 1986).

The San Diego Police Department (Boydstun 1975) introduced an innovative field experience aimed at sensitizing police officers to the authority they wield by subjecting them to it. Trainees and their supervisors traveled to San Jose, California, for the field training phase. In a stimulating and educational session, officers were placed in situations designed to attract the attention of the local police. The exercise attempted to give officers firsthand experience of police interrogation from a nonpolice perspective. Some officers felt they were harassed; others felt they were subjected to unnecessary physical handling or illegal arrest. But not all the contact experiences were negative; some very good interrogations were conducted. The San Diego officers in training had to think about what they had done to attract the attention of the local police. This led the trainees to examine their own motives for selecting particular individuals for field interrogations (11).

Training in improving discretionary decision making, whether by means of courses in critical thinking or field experiences, works best when departments recruit applicants adaptable to these innovations. Almost everyone agrees that police work requires officers intelligent enough to grasp difficult problems and to decide quickly on a response. Beyond that, controversy lies. Some want to improve the effectiveness of discretionary decision making generally, because it plays such a large role in all police missions—maintaining order, enforcing the criminal law, and providing other services. Others want to focus strictly on producing more effective crime fighters. John E. Boydstun, who studied field interrogation in San Diego, expresses the broad view of training:

> Recruits should be able to understand the cosmopolitan nature of an urban area and appreciate differences between cultures. They must learn to tolerate unconventional behavior and respect divergent life-styles. They must be able to appreciate the meaning of freedom and be sensitive to the awesome consequences stemming from the unbridled use of authority. They must take on the commitment to protect constitutional guarantees. They must subscribe to the value our society attaches to limiting the use of force, and they must learn to appreciate the controls exercised over the use of police powers and the role of the community in directing and reviewing police conduct. (263)

Source: John Boydstun, *San Diego Field Interrogation Final Report* (Washington, DC: Police Foundation, 1975).

as much impact on officers' performance as what they may have learned in their rookie days. (164)

Field training officers are fabled for telling rookies, "Forget what they told you in the police academy kid; you'll learn how to do it on the street." But when they do that, says Fyfe (1995),

> formal training is instantly and irreparably devalued. Worse, when officers actually see firsthand that the behavioral strictures in which they are schooled are routinely ignored in practice, formal training is neutralized and the definitions of appropriate behavior are instead made in the secrecy of officers' locker rooms. (164)

In teaching rookies the craft of policing, experienced officers emphasize that "real" policing involves "heavy" calls, such as "man with gun," "shots fired," and "officer needs assistance." The true test of a good officer, according to the traditional standards, is the ability and willingness to risk injury in these situations (Fyfe 1995, 164). (See the In Focus box "Does Field Training Make Better Cops?")

Some older officers are experienced in field training, and some departments establish structured field training and evaluation. In other departments, the officers have had little or no training in evaluating rookies. William G. Doerner and E. Britt Patterson (1992) describe field training in Tallahassee, Florida, before a court case prompted the department to improve it:

> Post-academy training consisted of a thirty-day observation period with a senior patrol officer. The veteran officer imparted words of wisdom as needed and answered any questions that the rookie had. At the end of the assignment, the senior officer would submit a recommendation....[T]here were no...standardized training modules. A sound performance rating system, particularly one anchored in actual job tasks, was absent. What this practice amounted to was an indefensible extension of the antiquated "good old boy" system. (25)

Higher Education The demands for police officers who possessed more than physical strength and the capacity to obey orders didn't begin with the recognition of the complexity of society and the police mission. August Vollmer, the famous reform police chief of Berkeley, California, recommended higher education for police officers as early as 1920. Little movement in that direction occurred until the 1960s, when training and education became the foremost measures to "upgrade" the police. In 1989, the Police Executive Research Forum (Carter, Sapp, and Stephens 1989) reviewed research, surveyed 502 departments, and visited 7 departments to determine the present state of police officer education in the United States. They reported that the national average educational level had risen from 12.4 years in 1967 to 13.6 years in 1989. Seventy-two percent of Blacks and 73 percent of Hispanics employed had attended college. By 2000, almost all departments required some education (Figure 5.4).

In 1990, a number of police chiefs commented on the importance of police education (Malcolm 1990, A1). Neil Behan, chief of police in Baltimore County, said, "When I was a rookie 43 years ago, we knew where we stood as officers. In those days, you spent an entire career in the same department with that department's same mind-set. It took a very special person to break away." But in 1990, Behan was telling his 1545-member department that he would promote no one to senior management without a college degree "or the imminent prospect of one." Charlie Johnson, chief of police in the Denver suburb of Lakewood, said, "I want disciplined, dedicated, tolerant people who understand how society works and want to solve problems, not just answer distress calls." Allen H. Andrews, Jr., chief of police in Peoria, Illinois, maintained that "society is more complicated now. Society and I expect officers not just to be law enforcers but to be the grease on the wheels of solving social conflicts." Andrews sends all recruits to special courses on courtesy and body language so they can read people's movements and focus on their own attitudes and intentions.

▶ **FIGURE 5.4 Minimum Education Requirements for New Police Officers, 2000**

Note: Total does not add to 100 percent because of rounding.
Source: Bureau of Justice Statistics, *Local Police Departments, 2000* (Washington, DC: BJS, January 2003), Table 10.

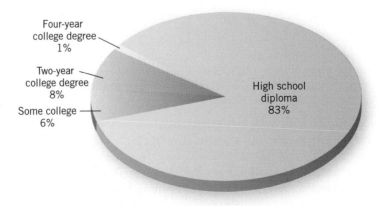

Four-year college degree 1%
Two-year college degree 8%
Some college 6%
High school diploma 83%

At about the same time, the Police Executive Research Forum (Carter and Sapp, 1991) listed the many *possible* ways higher education *can* benefit police officers; it:

- Develops a broader base of information for decision making
- Provides additional years and experience for increasing maturity
- Inculcates responsibility through course requirements and achievement
- Teaches the history of the country, the democratic process, individual rights, and the values of a free society
- Engenders the ability to handle difficult and ambiguous situations with creativity and innovation
- Teaches the "big picture" of the criminal justice system and provides a fuller understanding and appreciation of prosecution, courts, and corrections
- Develops a greater empathy for minorities and the impact of discrimination
- Encourages tolerance and understanding of differing lifestyles and ideologies
- Helps officers communicate with and respond to people and their problems in a competent, civil, and humane manner
- Develops officers who can deal innovatively and flexibly with problem-oriented and community policing
- Helps officers develop better communications and community relations skills
- Engenders a more "professional" demeanor and performance
- Enables officers to cope with stress
- Makes officers less authoritarian and cynical
- Prepares officers to accept and adapt to change
- Helps reduce the number of lawsuits against police departments, because college-educated officers know the law better

Of course, we who teach in these higher education institutions hope these possibilities turn into realities, but what does the research tell us? Robert Worden (1990) measured the attitudes and performance of officers who obtained bachelor's degrees before entering police work, officers who became police officers before obtaining a degree, and officers without college degrees. He surveyed both officers and private individuals in 24 police departments in three metropolitan areas: St. Louis, Rochester, and Tampa-St. Petersburg. He found only marginal differences in both attitudes and performance among the three groups:

> Although college-educated officers may be superior from the perspectives of supervisors, who find that such officers are more reliable employees and better report writers, they are not superior from the perspective of police clientele, who are concerned principally with effective and courteous contacts with police. Therefore this analysis suggests that patrol officers' performance and morale will be affected neither by policies that encourage in-service education nor by entry requirements that include college education. (565)

In another study, Worden (1995) relied on data collected from observations of more than five thousand police-citizen encounters. He looked at a number of officer characteristics and their relationship to the use of force. He found that officers who earned bachelor's degrees were more likely to use force *generally*. But Worden also found that officers with bachelor's degrees were less likely to use *excessive* force (45).

Victor Kappeler, Allen Sapp, and David Carter (1992), in an analysis of citizen complaints against officers in a medium-sized department, found that officers with college degrees produced fewer citizen complaints for rudeness than officers without college degrees, but they had more departmental complaints for rules violations.

Donald M. Truxillo and colleagues (1998) investigated the relationship between college education and work performance in a 10-year study of 84 police

Police Executive Research Forum: This site is a resource for law enforcement-related research, particularly for policy issues and model programs. To reach this site go to "Web Links" on your Samaha CJ7 website: http://cj.wadsworth.com/samaha_cj7e.

CONCEPT I BUILDER
Visit http://cj.wadsworth.com/ samaha_cj7e for an interactive exploration of **police professionalism.**

officers. They found that a bachelor's degree accounts for *some* promotions and supervisors' more favorable ratings of job knowledge. One reason "could be that the motivation for educational achievement may be the same as for promotions." Another explanation is that "those who have more education may have mastered some of the skills (e.g., study and test-taking) necessary to be promoted." Finally, it might be that "college education instills a degree of professionalism and maturity that is needed and valued at higher organizational levels." The study didn't show a relationship between higher education and lower disciplinary problems. The bottom line for criminal justice policy:

> Law enforcement jurisdictions may be justified in requiring educational qualifications or giving additional credit or compensation for them. However, they should not do so without the appropriate validity evidence, as these results may not generalize to all law enforcement jobs and organizations.... In addition, supporting college education among current officers may be useful to their development; because of their age at hire, many officers have not had the chance to obtain higher education. However, caution should be used in assuming a relationship between education and all aspects of police work. In this study, for example, education did not show a consistent relationship with disciplinary actions, a relevant performance dimension to police work. (Truxillo, Bennett, and Collins 1998, 278)

The Police "Working Personality"

> The day the new recruit walks through the door of the police academy he leaves society behind to enter a profession that does more than give him a job, it defines who he is. For all the years he remains he will always be a cop. (Skolnick and Fyfe 1993, 91)

This insight from New Haven, Connecticut, police chief James Ahern in 1972 described how policing becomes what Skolnick and Fyfe (1993, 91) call the "defining identity" of police.

The sociology of occupations teaches that our job affects the way we look at the world. Social scientists who've studied police all over the United States, in Europe, and in Asia have found three elements of police work always the same—danger, authority, and the power to use force. The combination of these three elements creates the **police working personality**—the way police look at the world; their standards of right and wrong; and their behavior while they carry out their missions, strategies (Chapter 6), and the law (Chapter 7) (Skolnick and Fyfe 1993, 92). We'll examine the way police look at the world and the stress of police work.

police working personality the way police look at the world; their standards of right and wrong; their behavior while they carry out their missions, strategies, and the law

How Police Look at the World The way the police working personality develops goes something like this: Danger makes them suspicious. Suspiciousness combines with their authority and the power to back it up with force to isolate them. This isolation makes police stick together, especially when they're in trouble. Let's fill in some details.

Explaining that the world cops work in is "unkempt, unpredictable, and sometimes violent," police experts David H. Bayley and Egon Bittner (1989) write:

> Police continually deal with situations in which physical constraint may have to be applied against people who are willing to fight, struggle, hit, stab, spit, bite, tear, hurl, hide, and run. People continually use their bodies against the police, forcing the police to deal with them in a physical way. While police seem to be preoccupied with deadly force, the more common reality in their lives is the possibility of a broken nose, lost teeth, black eyes, broken ribs, and twisted arms. Few officers are ever shot or even shot at, but all except the rawest rookie can show scars on their bodies from continual encounters with low-level violence. (93)

The potential for danger makes officers look for signs of danger, especially the chance of violence but other law-breaking and disorder, too. Police manuals teach officers where to look for the signs of danger: an adult hanging out where children play; several kids hanging out on street corners; known troublemakers in large groups of people; dirty cars with clean license plates; clean cars with dirty license plates; lights on in an office building at night. In other words, be suspicious of the unusual, the out of place (Baker 1985, 97).

When officers use their authority in unusual circumstances, it's usually applied to someone who at the very least doesn't like it and probably resents it (sometimes a lot!). Of course, officers would like to deal with "stable, well-dressed, normal, and unthreatening" people. Unfortunately, because they're our designated force-users, they're probably going to run into unstable, badly dressed, threatening, and all-around not very nice people. So, every exercise of authority is a volatile situation.

We have to add to this mixture of danger, suspiciousness, and authority, the power to back up authority with force. According to sociologist Egon Bittner (1970), who probably knows more about what police actually do than most observers:

> Whatever the substance of the task at hand, whether it involves protection against an un-desired imposition, caring for those who cannot care for themselves, attempting to solve a crime, helping to save a life, abating a nuisance, or settling an explosive dispute, police intervention means above all making use of the capacity and authority to overpower resistance. (40)

Police Stress Everyone feels stress; it's part of life. Some stress can be good. For example, the physical stress of "working out" improves your cardiovascular system, and feeling pressure that causes you to study harder for an exam can improve your score. But police stress refers to the negative pressures related to police work. Police officers are not superhumans. According to Gail Goolkasian (1985), research shows they're affected by their daily exposure to human indecency and pain; that dealing with a suspicious and sometimes hostile public takes its toll on them; and that the shift changes, the long periods of boredom, and the ever-present danger that are part of police work do cause serious job stress.

Dr. Hans Selye's classic *The Stress of Life* (1976) describes the effect of long-term environmental threats he calls "stressors." Dr. Selye maintains that the un-relieved effort to cope with stressors can lead to heart disease, high blood pressure, ulcers, digestive disorders, and headaches. Stress in police work falls into four categories:

1. Stresses inherent in police work
2. Stresses arising internally from police department practices and policies
3. External stresses stemming from the criminal justice system and the society at large
4. Internal stresses confronting individual officers

Police stress arises from several features of police work. Alterations in body rhythms from monthly shift rotation, for example, reduce productivity. The change from a day to a swing, or graveyard, shift not only requires biological adjustment but also complicates officers' personal lives. Role conflicts between the job—serving the public, enforcing the law, and upholding ethical standards—and personal responsibilities as a spouse, parent, and friend act as stressors. Other stressors in police work include:

- Threats to officers' health and safety (Figure 5.5)
- Boredom, alternating with the need for sudden alertness and mobilized energy
- Responsibility for protecting the lives of others
- Continual exposure to people in pain or distress
- The need to control emotions even when provoked
- The presence of a gun, even during off-duty hours
- The fragmented nature of police work, with only rare opportunities to follow cases to their conclusion or even to obtain feedback or follow-up information

▶ FIGURE 5.5 Reasons for
Assaults on Law Enforcement
Officers, 2002

Note: Total does not add to 100 percent
because of rounding.

Source: FBI, *Law Enforcement Officers
Killed and Assaulted, 2002* (Washington,
DC: FBI, 2003), p. 78.

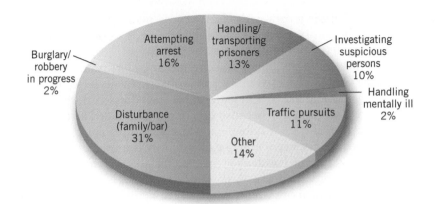

Administrative policies and procedures (which officers rarely participate in formulating) can add to stress. One-officer patrol cars create anxiety and a reduced sense of safety. Internal investigation practices create the feeling of being watched and not trusted, even during off-duty hours. Officers sometimes feel they've got fewer rights than the suspects they apprehend. Lack of rewards for good job performance, insufficient training, and excessive paperwork can also contribute to police stress (Russell and Biegel 1982, 280–298).

The criminal justice system adds to stress. Court appearances interfere with police officers' work assignments, personal time, and even sleeping schedules. Turf battles among agencies, court decisions limiting discretion, perceived leniency of the courts, and the release of offenders on bail, probation, or parole also lead to stress. Further stress arises from perceived lack of support and negative attitudes toward police from the larger society. (Most public opinion surveys, however, show strong support for and positive attitudes toward police.) Stress also stems from distorted and/or unfavorable news accounts of incidents involving police. The inaccessibility and perceived ineffectiveness of social service and rehabilitation agencies to whom officers refer individuals act as further stressors.

Women and minority officers face additional stress. They're more likely to face disapproval from fellow officers and from family and friends for entering police work. Supervisors, peers, and the public question women officers' ability to handle the emotional and physical rigors of the job, even though research indicates women can do so. The need to "prove themselves" to male officers and to the public constitutes a major stressor for women officers.

Stress contributes not just to the physical disorders previously mentioned but also to emotional problems. Some research suggests that police officers commit suicide at a higher rate than other groups. Most investigators report unusually high rates of divorce among police. And although some maintain that researchers have exaggerated the divorce rate among police, interview surveys demonstrate that police stress reduces the quality of family life. A majority of officers interviewed reported that police work inhibits nonpolice friendships, interferes with scheduling family social events, and generates a negative public image. Furthermore, they take job pressures home, and spouses worry about officers' safety. Systematic studies do not confirm the widely held belief that police suffer from unusually high rates of alcoholism, although indirect research has established a relationship between high job stress and excessive drinking. Finally, officers interviewed cited guilt, anxiety, fear, nightmares, and insomnia following involvement in shooting incidents.

In the past, departments either ignored officers with problems or dealt with them informally by assigning them to desk jobs. During the 1950s, some departments began to formalize their responses, usually by incorporating officer-initiated Alcoholics Anonymous groups made up exclusively of alcoholic officers. In the

1970s, departments instituted "employee assistance" programs to deal with problem officers, particularly those suffering from alcoholism. These programs have expanded into a broad range of responses to police stress. Some programs focus on physical fitness, diet, relaxation, and biofeedback to cope with stress. Others emphasize family counseling to involve spouses in reducing police stress, such as Kansas City's Marriage Partner Program or Minnesota's Couple Communications Program.

The Working Personality and Discretionary Decision Making

Steve Herbert (1998) rode along with Los Angeles police sergeants who supervise patrol officers and senior lead officers who monitor problem areas (like corners where drugs are sold and houses where gang members hang out). Herbert was interested not just in defining police subculture but in connecting it to police discretionary decision making. He found the following formal and informal subculture influences on police discretion:

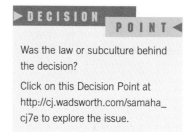

► D E C I S I O N
P O I N T ◄

Was the law or subculture behind the decision?

Click on this Decision Point at http://cj.wadsworth.com/samaha_cj7e to explore the issue.

1. Adventure/Machismo
2. Safety
3. Competence
4. Morality
5. Solidarity
6. Law and department rules

These influences interact and affect their standards of right and wrong and their behavior while they carry out their missions. Let's look at each of them.

Adventure/Machismo Los Angeles police officers see one another as either "hardchargers" or "station queens." Hardchargers are "willing to rush into dangerous situations" and look for "the adrenaline high" from a dangerous call. They "volunteer" to handle incidents that "threaten their well-being." They're "police warriors and exemplify such typically masculine characteristics as courage and strength." The LAPD has had a long reputation for being aggressive, especially in policing minority neighborhoods; hardchargers are sometimes called "ghetto gunfighters." Station queens are "wary of danger. They seek instead the refuge of inside to avoid the hazards of the streets. The term 'queen' clearly feminizes such officers—they do not possess sufficient strength to pass muster in accordance with the adventure/machismo normative order" (Herbert 1998, 355–356).

Safety Hardchargers may relish dangerous calls, but they don't want to die answering them. "It's better to be judged by twelve than carried by six," Herbert (1998, 357–358) heard officers say. Concern for their own safety shapes how they define situations and neighborhoods. Officers distinguish between "pro-police" and "anti-police" neighborhoods. When officers enter what they've decided is an anti-police neighborhood, they take their seat belts off for more mobility; they roll down their windows so they can hear better; they unlatch their shotguns; and they tell the dispatcher where they are in case they need backup. The Christopher Commission (1991) suggested an overconcern for safety made police overly suspicious of even remote threats by anyone. This in turn hurt their relations with neighborhoods, especially minority neighborhoods. So safety not only defines police subculture, it also explains tensions between police and some communities in Los Angeles.

Competence Competence means doing a good job. Doing a good job means getting the approval of other cops but, more important, it means pulling your own weight. Pulling your own weight means getting and keeping control of every situation officers run into without asking for help unless you really need it (Herbert 1998, 359–360).

Getting and keeping control isn't just a matter of solving problems, it means making sure the people they deal with respect police authority. Researchers have repeatedly found the high premium officers place on respect for their authority and the consequences for people who defy it. According to Paul Chevigny's (1969, 136) classic study of police in New York, "the one truly iron and inflexible rule" in all the cases of police abuse of power he reviewed was, "[A]ny person who defies the police risks the imposition of legal sanctions, commencing with a summons, on up to the use of firearms."

John Van Maanen (1978) describes how the importance of authority affects police decision making in his study of a large police force of over fifteen hundred officers. Officers divided the people they dealt with into three groups. Most people are *know-nothings*, ordinary people who aren't police and don't know anything about the world the police inhabit. Officers treat these "good citizens" with courtesy and efficiency. *Suspects* don't fit in their surroundings, like tall, Black, energetic, athletic, dreadlocked, disc jockey, promoter of rock music concerts Edward Lawson walking late at night in a White San Diego neighborhood, who the police usually treat in a brisk professional manner. They just want to confirm or remove their suspicion. Unless the suspicious person crosses the line into the third group, what Van Maanen says police call "assholes."

An *asshole* is anyone who questions police authority. Van Maanen gives this example: A cop stops a car for speeding and politely asks the driver for license and registration. "Why the hell are you picking on me and not somewhere else looking for real criminals?"

"'Cause you're an asshole, but I didn't know that until you opened your mouth."

Morality Seeking adventure, trying to stay alive, and maintaining their authority isn't all there is to the informal influence of the police working personality on decision making. There's also a powerful moral sense in the police working personality—the age-old struggle between good and evil. Steve Herbert (1998, 360) says "bad guy" comes up all the time in talk among LAPD officers. Of course, if there are bad guys there have to be good guys, too. And police officers see themselves as the good guys who fight the bad guys.

Sociologist Carl Klockars (1991a, 413) writes about a dilemma caused by this powerful moral component in the police working personality: Does the end justify the means? Klockars calls it the Dirty Harry problem. The name comes from the 1971 movie *Dirty Harry*, in which Clint Eastwood plays Dirty Harry Callahan, a cop who's on a psychopathic killer's trail. The psychopath is demanding ransom for a 14-year-old girl he kidnapped and buried alive with only enough air to live for a few hours. Dirty Harry brings the ransom to the kidnapper; the kidnapper takes back the offer, wounds Harry's partner, and escapes. Harry tracks him down, illegally searches his apartment, finds enough evidence to convict him, and captures the kidnapper on a football field. Harry shoots him in the leg and twists the injured leg until the kidnapper confesses where the girl is. Unfortunately, she's already dead, and almost as bad, the killer has to go free because Harry got the evidence and the confession illegally.

The movie presents a tough enough moral dilemma—breaking the law to save an innocent girl from an evil monster we know is guilty. Tougher still is when the evil isn't one clearly guilty person but a group (like a gang) and a mistake hurts innocent people. Skolnick and Fyfe (1993, 107–108) relate the tragedy of the LAPD Gang Task Force raid on four apartments they believed were crack houses controlled by gangs. Police also believed the gangs were terrorizing families who lived between the apartments and that the gang members were heavily armed.

A few days before the raid, the captain at roll call told officers to "hit hard"; he wanted the apartments to look "leveled" and "uninhabitable" after the raid. The police officers did just that. They raided the apartments with guns, axes, and sledgehammers. Nobody was killed, but they destroyed the apartments. They broke the toilets and tore them out of the floor, and water ran everywhere. They smashed the walls with their sledgehammers. They broke everything they could find—VCRs, TVs, and the bedroom and living room furniture. They cut the wires. They emptied wine and baby food on clothes and bedding. And they spray-painted "LAPD rules" on what was left of the walls.

Unfortunately, no gang members lived in the apartments, only a small amount of marijuana and cocaine was found, and there were no guns at all. An honest but tragic mistake. (Or very bad police work "outsiders" might say, behavior the officers should be held accountable for.)

Newsweek columnist Jonathan Alter (2001) poses the Dirty Harry dilemma as it relates to the investigation of the September 11 attacks and suspects who might have information about future attacks:

> In this autumn of anger, even a liberal can find his thoughts turning to . . . torture. OK, not cattle prods or rubber hoses, at least not here in the United States, but something to jump-start the stalled investigation of the greatest crime in American history. Right now, four key hijacking suspects aren't talking at all. Couldn't we at least subject them to psychological torture, like tapes of dying rabbits or high-decibel rap? (The military has done that in Panama and elsewhere.) How about truth serum, administered with a mandatory IV? Or deportation to Saudi Arabia, land of beheadings? (As the frustrated FBI has been threatening.) Some people still argue that we needn't rethink any of our old assumptions about law enforcement, but they're hopelessly "Sept. 10"—living in a country that no longer exists. (45)

Solidarity Danger, authority, and the power to use force—these three elements of the police subculture set the police apart, creating solidarity among them and isolating them from the people they police. The Christopher Commission (1991), which investigated the riots following the police use of force against Rodney King in Los Angeles in the early 1990s, picked up on what it called the siege mentality of the Los Angeles police—"us against them." Isolation and the us-against-them attitude is especially strong when police are being criticized and the police code of silence (don't ever tell on another cop) kicks in.

The National Institute of Ethics (2000) conducted the most extensive research ever on the police code of silence. Between February 1999 and June 2000, the institute asked 3714 officers and academy recruits from 42 states to participate. One part of the study determined academy recruits' views; the other part identified officers who'd taken part in the code, then asked why and how it occurred. Some of the key findings are listed in Tables 5.2 through 5.4.

We often hear police officers that break the code risk their lives. This has probably happened sometime in someplace besides cop shows and movies, but Skolnick and Fyfe say they know of only one case where police shot other officers to

▼ **TABLE 5.2 Recruits' Responses in Code of Silence Study, 1999–2000**

Facts about Academy Recruits
1. 79% said that a law enforcement Code of Silence exists and is fairly common throughout the nation.
2. 52% said that the fact a Code of Silence exists doesn't really bother them.
3. 24% said the Code of Silence is more justified when excessive force involves a citizen who's abusive.
4. 46% said they would not tell on another officer for having sex on duty.
5. 23% said they wouldn't tell on another cop for regularly smoking marijuana off duty.

Source: National Institute of Ethics, "Police Code of Ethics Facts Revealed" (International Association of Chiefs of Police [IACP], 2000 Conference, 2000). http://www.aele.org/loscode2000.html.

▼ **TABLE 5.3 Current Officers' Responses in Code of Silence Study, 1999–2000**

Facts about Current Officers

1. "Please describe the first time you witnessed misconduct by another employee but took no action." 46% (532) said they'd witnessed misconduct but concealed what they knew.

2. "At the time the incident occurred, what did you think would happen if you revealed what had taken place?" The most listed answers:
   a. I'd be ostracized. (177 times)
   b. The officer who committed the misconduct would be disciplined or fired. (88 times)
   c. I'd be fired from my job. (73 times)
   d. I'd be "blackballed." (59 times)
   e. The administration wouldn't do anything even if I reported it. (54 times)

3. 73% of the individuals pressuring officers to keep quiet about the misconduct were leaders.

4. 8% (40) of the 509 officers who admitted to intentionally withholding the information about officer misconduct were upper administrators. The upper administrators of the average American police department compose only 5% of the agency.

5. 449 of the 532 officers were male; 74 were female.

6. Excessive use of force was the most frequent situation where the Code of Silence occurs.

7. The five most frequently offered solutions for controlling the Code of Silence from the 532 officers who confessed to taking part in it were:
   a. Conduct good ethics training (46 times)
   b. Require more consistent accountability (20 times)
   c. Ensure open communication between officers and leaders (16 times)
   d. Provide an anonymous reporting system (14 times)
   e. Protect whistleblowers (10 times)

Source: National Institute of Ethics, "Police Code of Ethics Facts Revealed" (International Association of Chiefs of Police [IACP], 2000 Conference, 2000). http://www.aele.org/loscode2000.html.

punish them for "squealing." In the isolation of the us-against-them world of police, there's enormous pressure to remain loyal, so there's no need to shoot people to guarantee their loyalty. The most common ways to enforce the code are the threat of shunning and blowing the whistle on informants' own wrongdoing. Robert Leuci's testimony put his whole squad and about seventy other NYPD narcotics officers in jail. Here's a conversation Leuci had with his wife before he talked:

LEUCI: I'm not going to implicate anyone close to us.

GINA: Do you think they will allow you to do whatever you choose to do? Do you think they will say: Okay Bob, whoever you want to tell us about. You decide. I don't think they will allow you to do that [short pause]. I know you feel guilty. Other people are responsible, not you. They are guiltier than you are.

LEUCI [in a low voice]: I want to end this life I have been living.

GINA: Then quit the Police Department.

LEUCI: And do what? Sell insurance? Work in a bank?

GINA: I know you. It's going to kill you. They will force you to hurt friends, people who have done no harm to you, only good. When you were sick they all came. They called me every day. I know what kind of man you are. I know what you can live with and what you can't live with. This will kill you. You tell me the feelings you have for informants, and now you are going to be an informant. How are you going to live with that? (Skolnick and Fyfe 1993, 111–112)

Notice Leuci doesn't mention safety. Why? Because he didn't believe—and he turned out to be right—the people he "hurt" would *physically* shut him up. At the end of the day he had to face the reality that he could never be what he once was—the "Prince of the City," a hotshot member of the most envied and prestigious detectives in the biggest police department in the country (Skolnick and Fyfe 1993, 112).

Some Conclusions from the Researchers
1. Some form of a Code of Silence will develop among officers in virtually any agency.
2. Because the code is an essentially natural occurrence, attempts to stop it all together will be futile.
3. Whistleblowers are generally not supported by the administration of law enforcement agencies.
4. The Code of Silence among administrators, although better camouflaged and less well known, is more destructive than when nonranking personnel do the same thing.
5. The majority of officers who've been in law enforcement for several years have directly participated in the Code of Silence.
6. The Code of Silence is prompted by excessive use of force incidents more than for any other specific circumstance.
7. The "us versus them" mentality is usually present within the minds of those who participate in the Code of Silence.
8. The belief that rookie officers across the nation are routinely told that one of the most basic rules they must abide by is that they can never "rat out" another officer, especially by testifying against them, is false.
9. Although structured role modeling will probably become the most effective corrective tool for preventing the Code of Silence, it will be necessary to begin the process of making change through training.
10. A culture that acts as fertile ground for the destructive features of the Code of Silence to grow is one that promotes loyalty to people over integrity.
11. Many police officers feel a great sense of alienation. This often acts as a catalyst for officers to rationalize that taking part in the Code of Silence is not particularly wrong.
12. One of the most powerful "root causes" of officers throughout the nation participating in a Code of Silence is that they deeply believe they have been victimized by their own workplace.
13. Some police agencies have shown they are incapable of policing themselves.
14. To be successful at preventing the Code of Silence, we must be able to develop cultures in which the bad officers are the ones who are alienated.
15. Officers should be fired for not reporting officers who commit criminal acts.

Source: National Institute of Ethics, "Police Code of Ethics Facts Revealed" (International Association of Chiefs of Police [IACP], 2000 Conference, 2000). http://www.aele.org/loscode2000.html.

Codes of silence aren't unique to police work (Skolnick and Fyfe 1993, 110). Do you know of at least one student who's cheated on an exam or plagiarized a paper? Did you turn him or her in? I think I know your answer.

Law It should be clear by now how much discretion police officers have and how important the informal influence of the police working personality is on individual officers' discretionary decision making. But broad and important as police subculture is, the law (and department rules) is also key to decision making (Herbert 1998, 352–363).

First, the law creates and defines police power; it sets the boundaries of discretionary decision making. Second, the law defines order—the "disorderly conduct" ordinances. Third, the law is the way officers define a problem. And fourth, it tells them how to resolve a problem. Many have written how officers handle an incident and *then* find some law to back up how they handled it. But often it works just the other way around: Officers use the law to decide whether and how to respond. Of course, broad terms like "disorderly conduct" leave officers lots of room to roam according to their occupational values and sometimes thumb their noses at the law they're sworn to uphold (Chapter 6), but these excesses don't mean the law isn't important.

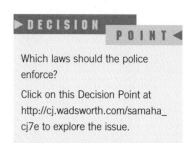

▶ DECISION POINT ◀

Which laws should the police enforce?

Click on this Decision Point at http://cj.wadsworth.com/samaha_cj7e to explore the issue.

Women and Minority Officers

You learned in "The History of Police and Policing" section that women police and policing have received little attention by researchers. You also learned in the preceding sections that adequate training and intelligent recruits do not by themselves produce "good" police officers and effective policing, but we do know that police departments perform best when they have strong public support. Hiring competent personnel who reflect the cultural diversity and gender division of the community is one way to get that public support. Calls for establishing closer connections between the police and the community, the law requiring equal employment opportunity, and the values of an open and diverse society have all encouraged hiring and advancing women and minorities in policing. Successfully recruiting minorities and women has challenged police administrators for decades. Empirical and impressionistic evidence suggest a weakening, but by no means a removal, of barriers in police departments based on race, ethnic origin, and gender (Bayley and Bittner 1989, 311).

Women Officers

When Ella Bully-Cummings became a Detroit police officer in 1977, police departments across the nation were stepping up their efforts to hire more women—often because the departments were under court orders to do so, or were being threatened with discrimination lawsuits. The resentment Bully-Cummings faced within the department's macho, paramilitary culture is still fresh in her mind. Some male officers feigned illness to avoid working with her. Some on patrol with her sometimes would call for backup even before arriving at crime scenes. But Bully-Cummings stuck it out, and rose through the ranks. And now, at 46, she is Detroit's new police chief, in charge of 4,600 officers in a city that is battling a surge in violent crime.

Three decades after U.S. police departments began hiring women in significant numbers, Bully-Cummings is part of an unprecedented wave of women who have ascended to police chief posts. Since November, women have been appointed to lead five of the largest local police departments in the nation: those in Detroit, San Francisco, Milwaukee, Boston and Fairfax County, Va., in suburban Washington. (Leinwand 2004)

▶ There are more women police officers than there used to be, but they're still greatly outnumbered by male officers in most departments. And there are only a tiny handful of female chiefs. One is Ella Bully-Cummings, Chief of the Detroit Police Department, here showing her new chief's badge at a news conference. Bully-Cummings is the first female ever to hold the office of chief in Detroit. She took over when former Chief Jerry Oliver resigned because of controversy over reports he failed to declare a loaded pistol in his luggage and was charged with the misdemeanor of possessing an unlicensed handgun.

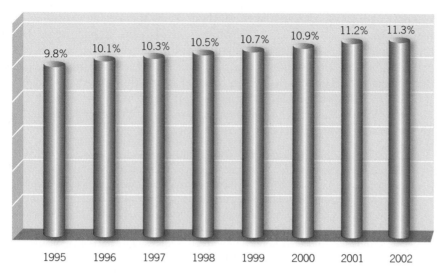

◀ **FIGURE 5.6 Percentage of Female Sworn Officers, 1995–2002**

Source: FBI, Crime in the U.S., 1995–2002 (Washington, DC: FBI, 2003), Section VI.

These chiefs are among hundreds of women who've made their way to the high ranks of police command, but "policing remains largely a man's domain"; only 1 percent of police chiefs are women (Leinwand 2004). In fact, what Susan E. Martin (1989) concluded after surveying the 1970s and 1980s is still true: the available evidence on women in policing presents a "mixed picture." The number of women sworn officers is creeping up. Between 1995 and 2002, the percentage of women cops rose from 9.8 to 11.3 percent, an increase of only 1.5 percent (Figure 5.6). You can see another part of the mixed picture in Figure 5.7 (later); the 11.3 percent is an *average,* which masks the fact that most departments fall below the average.

The skepticism among traditional police departments and officers, and among the public, about women police officers generated considerable questions about their effectiveness. The research shows the skepticism wasn't based on fact. Nine surveys representing a broad cross section of the country's police departments demonstrated that women patrol officers perform as well as men patrol officers. For example, performance ratings of women after their first year in the Washington, D.C., Police Department were similar to those of men in their first year of service. Women stood up to difficult circumstances as well as men, and they resigned or were terminated at about the same rate as men (Martin 1989, 316).

The empirical research regarding the performance of women police officers also led to questions and research about their attitudes. One theory explaining the attitudes of women police officers is the **gender model of police attitudes.** The gender model predicts differences in attitude between women and men police officers because of their different early socialization into gender roles. According to Carol Gilligan, women develop a "morality of care," which depicts "society as an interdependent and interconnected web of personal relationships." The theory predicts that the morality of care leads women to take a broad view of the police mission—that is, to provide service. Men, on the other hand, the theory predicts, develop a "morality of justice," which concentrates on law enforcement, hierarchy, rules, and discipline (Worden 1993, 205–206).

A second theory, the **job model of police attitude,** predicts that women and men don't differ in their attitudes toward police work because socialization to work overrides prior socialization into gender roles. In other words, women may come into police work with attitudes different from men's, but after attending the academy, going through field training, and especially after working as police officers for a period of time, the attitudes of men and women converge into a similar police officer attitude.

▶ DECISION POINT ◀

How would you recruit, retain, and promote women into policing?

Click on this Decision Point at http://cj.wadsworth.com/samaha_cj7e to explore the issue.

gender model of police attitudes predicts differences in attitude between women and men police officers exist because of their different early socialization into gender roles

job model of police attitudes predicts that women and men don't differ in their attitudes toward police work because socialization to work overrides prior socialization into gender roles

Alissa Pollitz Worden tested these theories by measuring attitudes in a large data set that surveyed 1435 police officers in 24 police departments. She found that women and men officers had similar attitudes on a range of subjects concerning policing. Both favored uniform over selective law enforcement; women did not define the police mission in broader terms than men; the longer women worked, the more their views of people converged with the views of men; the views of women and men also converged over time with respect to their willingness to accept legal restrictions on their work. According to Worden:

> The most striking finding in this study is the failure of gender to explain much or any variation in the array of attitudes examined, even when potentially confounding variables are controlled. Overall, female as well as male police officers were predictably ambivalent about restrictions on their autonomy and the definition of their role, only mildly positive about their public clientele, complimentary of their colleagues, and unenthusiastic about working conditions and supervisors. What should one conclude from this about theories of gender differences and their applicability to policing? ... [T]aken as a whole, these findings offer little support for the thesis that female officers define their role or see their clientele differently than do males, and one must therefore remain skeptical ... about claims that women bring to their beats a distinctive perspective on policing. (228–229)

Minority Officers Dr. Elysee Scott, executive director of the National Organization of Black Law Enforcement Executives (NOBLE), remembers that as she was growing up in a small Louisiana town in the 1950s, Black police officers rode around in police cars marked "Colored Only." Black officers could arrest only "colored" people; if a white person committed a crime in a Black neighborhood, Black officers had to call for a White officer to make the arrest. Beginning in the 1960s, following brutality by White officers against Blacks, civil rights legislation, lawsuits brought by Blacks, and demands for minority hiring, the position of Black and other minority officers began to change (Sullivan 1989, 331).

Since the 1960s, the number of minority police officers has grown (Figure 5.7). Samuel Walker (1989) surveyed police departments in the nation's 50 largest cities. He found that between 1983 and 1988, those departments "made uneven progress in the employment of African American and Hispanic officers." While nearly half the big-city departments made significant progress in employing Black officers, another 17 percent reported declines in the percentage of Black and Hispanic officers. Similarly, 42 percent of the departments hired more Hispanics, whereas 11 percent reported declines.

▶ **FIGURE 5.7 Black and Hispanic* Sworn Officers, 1960–2000**

*Numbers for Hispanic officers weren't recorded until 1990. Percentages are of all sworn officers.

Source: Samuel Walker, Cassia Spohn, and Miriam DeLone, *The Color of Justice* (Belmont, CA: Wadsworth, 2000), p. 112; Bureau of Justice Statistics, *Local Police Departments, 2000* (Washington, DC: Bureau of Justice Statistics, January 2003), Table 7.

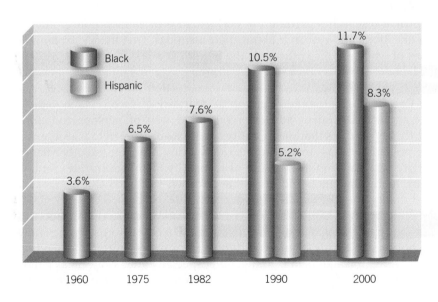

Affirmative action plans played a significant role in police employment trends, according to Walker. Nearly two-thirds of the departments reported operating under such plans. Twenty-three of the plans were court ordered; seven were voluntary. Despite the unevenness of the progress in hiring Black and Hispanic officers, a survey of all police departments in the country revealed that by 2000, the percentage of Black officers was approaching their percentage of the general population; the percentage of Hispanic officers wasn't.

Black police chiefs have increased significantly in numbers since the 1960s. In 1976, Hubert Williams, chief of the Newark, New Jersey, Police Department, was the only Black police chief in the country. By 1990, Blacks headed one-quarter of the 50 largest city police departments, including New York, Chicago, Philadelphia, Baltimore, Detroit, Washington, and Miami (Malcolm 1990, A12). By 2004, seven Blacks and one Hispanic headed the 20 largest police departments (Joy 2004).

Business Improvement Districts are growing fast, and they're very popular. Thousands have appeared since New York City's Grand Central Partnership, the one we focus on for your decision. BIDs started when business owners began to see their business districts becoming less pleasing and less safe (Barr 1997, 395). Let's look at two excerpts discussing the pros and cons of BIDs as public policy.

BUSINESS IMPROVEMENT DISTRICTS (BID), NEW YORK CITY

Daniel Biederman, 43, roams the streets of midtown Manhattan as if he ran the place—and, in some ways, he does. They call him "the mayor of Midtown." He holds no political office, but he levies taxes, effects vast changes on the urban landscape, and employs a raft of private workers to perform services the city government can no longer afford. His powers are widely tolerated, even in the face of a recent scandal, because nearly everyone agrees on a vital fact: If one person can claim credit for the cleanup and renewal of the center of New York City over the past couple years, Biederman is that man. He is president of the city's three largest Business Improvement Districts, or BIDs, a new, unorthodox amalgam of private money and public action that could become a model of urban planning in an era of budget cuts.

Anyone who strolled through midtown three or four years ago would hardly recognize the place today. Bryant Park, a square-block space behind the New York Public Library on 42nd Street and Fifth Avenue, has been transformed from an open drug bazaar into a flowery, tranquil, safe urban haven. Before the park closed in 1989 for reconstruction, it was the scene of 144 reported muggings. Last year, after the reopening, there was one.

Grand Central Station, once a dirty, dreary cavern, is undergoing a grand renovation. For several blocks around the station, sidewalks are clean and clear, scam artists have fled the taxi stands, new lamps shine brightly, and 300 trees line the streets. "Before," Biederman said, standing outside Grand Central at the start of a walking tour across his domain, "if foreigners came to the United States and wanted to see a beautiful city, they went to Boston. Boston has all these sensational developments—Faneuil Hall, Post Office Square, the seaport. Now, they can also come to New York."

As the walk began, he stepped over to greet by name two street sweepers wearing uniforms bearing the logo "Grand Central Partnership," the neighborhood BID. "We have 50 sweepers in the district," Biederman said. "Most of our curbs are swept every 30 or 45 minutes,

Source: Fred Kaplan, "Business Activist Gives a Lift To Midtown NYC," *The Boston Globe,* October 20, 1995, 1.

none less often than every hour. Our guys empty the trash bins up to five times a day and put in new plastic bags. They've got solvents in their belts to remove graffiti. There's no graffiti on the mail boxes anymore.... People feel safe not because they read about reduced crime statistics but because of the way a place looks. When people feel safe, they stay out later at night. Shops and restaurants stay open later. People feel like coming here. Businesses don't feel compelled to flee."

The specter of companies fleeing New York City has haunted and fueled the Business Improvement Districts (BIDs) from the beginning. The concept was devised 10 years ago by the corporate lawyer Peter Malkin. His in-

AP/Wide World Photos

▲ Business Improvement Districts are very popular because of their promise to improve the appearance and safety of a community. Thousands have appeared since New York City's Grand Central Partnership, the subject of this Make Your Decision. In this photo, security officers from the Wilshire Business Improvement District in California stand watch with police officers and private security guards as Jews enter the Wilshire Boulevard temple for Rosh Hashanah services one week after the terrorist attacks on the World Trade Center.

spiration was Mobil Oil, which moved out of New York because the area around its headquarters, just across from Grand Central, was so run-down. Malkin's solution was Grand Central Partnership, the first BID. The city government agreed to donate $50,000 if Malkin could raise $100,000 from the area's private property owners. Malkin raised $1 million. He used some of the money to hire Boston architect Jane Thompson, who had designed the renovation of Faneuil Hall and other sites, to design a master plan. The plan took 18 months to clear myriad city agencies. The organization was chartered in 1988.

By that time, Biederman, a former neighborhood commissioner, had been working for five years on a similar deal to rebuild Bryant Park. The city kicked in $250,000. By the time the park opened, private businesses were contributing nearly $2 million. Malkin brought Biederman onboard Grand Central Partnership to replicate what he had done for Bryant Park. Other businesses asked them to form a third BID around Penn Station. Others since have created BIDs in Times Square, the garment district along Seventh Avenue, downtown near Wall Street, all over town.

Once the city council approves a BID charter, every commercial property owner in the district must pay a surcharge, amounting to about 6 percent, on their real-estate taxes. The surcharge is collected by the city government, which turns it over to the BID, which spends the money on its own budget. "At first, we got a lot of resistance," Malkin said. "People said, 'Why should we pay more money? We're already paying taxes.' But once the improvements were clear, the support was overwhelming."

Malkin and Biederman's three BIDs have an annual budget of $22 million, 90 percent of which comes from the property-tax surcharge; only $2 million comes from the city government. The BIDs also have issued $55 million in bonds. They hired street sweepers, taxi-stand patrols, and 100 security guards. "There used to be 50 drug dealers on this corner at any one time," Biederman said, standing outside the public library. "People said that would never change. It did. There's no drug dealing here now. We did this with our private security force. It's our pride and joy." They also built new, pink granite, handicap-access curbs on the corners and new Victorian-style lamp posts with white streetlights. Biederman said: "Yellow light makes people look sickly and isn't good for security."

They also started a homeless shelter, which feeds 300 to 400 people a day and helps them find jobs and housing. This project created a scandal earlier this year, when BID employees were accused of beating up homeless people to force them to come to the shelter. Biederman and Malkin deny the charge or say their employees, some former homeless people themselves, were provoked. The incidents appear to be isolated....

Some critics...worry that Biederman is turning New York into a homogenized, over-renovated showcase for tourists and rich people, at the expense of the city's native, funkier culture. "I don't see how getting rid of filth and crime destroys a city's character," he said. "The randomness of New York is great. Nobody's arguing for office parks, but there are things we can learn from them—things like trees and flowers. They don't take anything away from the rakishness of New York."

STRENGTHS AND WEAKNESSES OF PRIVATIZATION

Strengths of Private Police

Private security has advantages over public police but it also has disadvantages. The advantages include:

[1 through 4 are omitted]
5. Private security agencies tend to be more receptive to innovation and risk than do municipal police departments.
6. Private agents have the authority to stop and challenge any person, without probable cause, for trespassing in a designated private area, and they can make arrests without having to give *Miranda* warnings to arrestees.
7. Municipal police departments may be able to reduce patrols in areas covered privately, thus freeing up resources for other public needs.
8. The delivery of police services and specific police functions (such as vehicle towing and laboratory analysis of forensic evidence)...are subject to economies of scale...that private organizations are more likely forces to achieve than public.

Weaknesses of Private Police

...Private security agents are not generally bound by the same set of constraints that are imposed on sworn police officers. They enjoy the powers to arrest, to search for and seize evidence, and to file criminal charges in court, but they are not held to due process requirements routinely followed by the police, such as those specified in *Mapp v. Ohio* [Chapter 7].

This latitude offers to private agents a degree of immunity from criminal or civil liability charges arising from false arrests that sworn officers must often face. Unlike sworn officers, who are bound to file criminal charges when probable cause exists, private security personnel have discretion to prosecute offenders under either civil (advantageous to stores in cases involving affluent shoplifters) or criminal statutes (generally used for poor offenders), thus raising questions about equal protection and due process.

Affluent voters have been willing to tax themselves for police services in their communities at prevailing margins and to augment those funds with private security expenditures targeted on specific needs, but many have been less than thrilled to see their tax dollars leave their immediate communities to go elsewhere within the jurisdiction. Obviously, a private citizen has substantially more control over funds spent on private protection services than over funds aimed at public police that must traverse convoluted governmental processes, and it should not be surprising that they would vote accordingly. A common self-interested attitude seems to go along the following line: "I'm tired of trying endlessly to bail out the inner cities with my tax dollars; let them take care of themselves for a change. I can keep pretty much to my neighborhood and be responsible for my own protection, public and private." As good jobs have left urban centers over the past twenty years, it has become all too easy for upper- and middle-class voters to separate themselves from the problem of inner-city crime. Federal and state expenditures on policing are more easily distributable to inner cities than are local expenditures, but political pressures often intervene to thwart even those redistributions.

Thus one of the acute problems of privatization has been to allow areas most in need of protective services to go without them, which only adds to the vulnerability of the residents of those neighborhoods to crime and disorder. The Metropolitan Police Department of Washington, D.C. has come under extreme financial stress in the late 1990s while neighborhoods in many of the District of Columbia's affluent northwest area can protect themselves privately and as the suburbs surrounding the nation's capital experience low crime rates and well-financed police departments. Police departments operating within the metropolitan areas of New Orleans, Detroit, Richmond, Virginia, and other places with extremes of inner-city crime in the general vicinity of wealthy suburbs have come to experience similar disparities in protection.

...Another [problem] is that a private corporation and its employees can be difficult to supervise, especially when the contracts are awarded to different companies periodically. This can become a noxious matter when the private agents have access to sensitive information. Though public officials occasionally violate privacy..., government employees...are accountable...in ways that private individuals are not.

Another potential problem with privatization derives from one of the most basic aspects of our criminal justice system: the adversarial system of legal procedure reduces the role of vengeance by interposing the state in the place of the victim as the offender's legal opponent.... This feature of our system surely contributes to the breach between the police and legal cultures. Several scholars have noted that this cultural divergence lies beneath episodes of police brutality delivered as "curbside justice," an act of using dirty means to achieve what some individuals view as worthy ends.

...The extralegal retributive behaviors that have become a too-familiar feature of our policing culture could conceivably become more widespread under further privatization.... The security agent working directly for a client victim...may be more inclined to do the client's bidding for brutal tough justice, especially when his job security may be strengthened by the activity. Bar bouncers and bodyguards are rarely known for their reputations as civil libertarians, and an expansion of these uncontrolled and often overly aggressive branches of the private security industry would not bode well for the goal of a more civil society.

Perhaps the most difficult problem of private security personnel is that the potential for incompetence and misbehavior is enormous. The screening for many private hirings is often lax and the training nil. Poor screening has been known to result in the hiring of private security personnel with criminal records. Security guards may receive guns without having received adequate instruction on their usage. They may receive uniforms and be assigned beats to patrol when they are unprepared for even routine situations. And poorly managed agencies and unscrupulous operators have been known to go bankrupt or otherwise fail to honor contractual assurances that their services and products—alarm systems, locking devices, and so on—are up to par.

The fundamental issue is that of legitimacy. Police officers take an oath of office in which they swear to serve the public at large; they are neither narrowly nor tentatively employed.... Few private security agents are bound by solemn vows to serve the public. Such a commitment not only may serve the public more effectively but may produce the side benefit of contributing to the building of character—a trait that has, regrettably, lost currency in contemporary matters—perhaps even inducing citizens to participate more in the democratic process.

Source: Brian Forst, "Policing with Legitimacy, Equity, and Efficiency," *The Privatization of Policing: Two Views,* edited by Brian Forst and Peter K. Manning (pp. 20–24) (Washington, DC: Georgetown University Press, 1999).

QUESTIONS

1. What's New York City's Grand Central Partnership BID according to Excerpt 1?
2. What are BIDs' strong points, according to the two excerpts?
3. What are BIDs' weak points, according to the two excerpts?
4. What's your decision? Are BIDs good policy? Back up your answer with facts and arguments from the two excerpts.

Chapter Summary

- Policing was private in the beginning; became mixed with public policing in the 1800s; and now is more nongovernment than government. Early 1900s reformers worked hard to professionalize public policing by training officers, restricting the police mission to criminal law enforcement, and promoting formal decision making. By the 1950s, the reform agenda was accepted (at least in larger departments). In the 1960s, order maintenance, working with communities, and building up neighborhood control became popular ideas.

- The structure and organization of public police organizations reflect our federalist system, so there are federal, state, county, and municipal crime control agencies. Federal law enforcement is growing rapidly, especially since 9/11 shifted counterterrorism and national security to top priorities. But state and local policing still do the lion's share of policing and consume 80 percent of tax dollars. The military model command structure defines the formal organization and decision making of police departments, but informally their structure and decision making is more like hospitals and universities.

- Nongovernment police outnumber public police, so people spend more time in places policed by nongovernment individuals and groups than by public police departments. Nongovernment policing includes protecting business interests, residential communities, cultural communities, and individuals.

- The missions of the police are to enforce the criminal law, maintain public order, and provide other public services. In day-to-day operations, police officers spend a lot more time maintaining order and providing help to people who ask for it than they do enforcing the criminal laws.

- Personality, selection, training, and promotion matter when it comes to the effectiveness and deviance of police officers. There's little empirical evidence that a college education improves the effectiveness of police officers' performance. The police "working personality" is determined by three elements: danger, authority, and the power to use force. These elements determine how police look at the world, their standards of right and wrong, and their behavior while they carry out their missions of criminal law enforcement, order maintenance, and public service. Six influences in police subculture shape police formal and informal decision making: machismo, safety, competence, morality, solidarity, and law and department rules.

- Empirical evidence demonstrates that female officers are as effective as male officers. The numbers of women and minority officers are growing. On average, minority officers are now or nearly representative of their numbers in the general population. Despite some high-profile women chiefs in large departments, their numbers are far below their numbers in the general population, *and* the growth in female officers has slowed significantly since 1995.

Key Terms

constable/night watch system, p. 139
municipal police department system, p. 140
proactive policing, p. 140
reactive policing, p. 140

reform model of policing, p. 142
military model of policing, p. 154
full enforcement, p. 158
selective enforcement, p. 158
maintaining order, p. 159

police working personality, p. 168
gender model of police attitudes, p. 177
job model of police attitudes, p. 177

Web Resources

Go to http://cj.wadsworth.com/samaha_cj7e for a wealth of online resources related to your book. Take a "pre-test" and "post-test" for each chapter in order to help master the material. Check out the *Web Links* to access the websites mentioned in the text, as well as many others. Explore the

Decision Points flagged in the margins of the text, as well as the *Concept Builders* for additional insights. You can also access recent perspectives by clicking on *CJ in the News* and *Terrorism Update* under *Course Resources*.

Search Online with InfoTrac College Edition

For additional information, explore InfoTrac College Edition, your online library. Go to http://cj.wadsworth.com/samaha_cj7e to access InfoTrac College Edition from your

book's website. Use the passcode that came with your book. You will find InfoTrac College Edition exercises and a list of key words for further research.

CHAPTER 6

Policing Strategies

FACT *or* FICTION?

▶ During the 1960s, a public fed up with the crime boom demanded that researchers tell them "now" why it was happening.

▶ Ninety percent of the time police officers go out looking for crimes on their own initiative.

▶ The Kansas City Preventive Patrol Experiment showed that crime rates stayed the same no matter how many patrol cars were on the street.

▶ Most men suspected of battering their wives don't re-assault their original victim whether they're arrested or not.

▶ Community policing is popular because research has shown that it reduces crime.

▶ Problem-oriented policing focuses on solving violent crime by finding out its causes.

▶ Collecting DNA samples from the general population would not help to solve most crimes.

CAN THE POLICE REDUCE CRIME?

Over half of all crime comes from less than 3% of the addresses in a city, and crime at those "hot spot" addresses is bunched by "hot" days of the week and times of day. Thus, most addresses, and most blocks, in a city will go for years without any crime—even in high crime neighborhoods. Spreading patrol visibility or even undercover police evenly across space and time means applying police officers *unevenly* to crime. While all citizens get their "fair share" of policing equally, this strategy may be as useful as giving everyone their fair share of penicillin—regardless of whether they are sick. And by reducing the "penicillin dosage" received by those who are "sick," its net effect may be to raise crime for everyone.... A more sensible question ... is whether police activity can make a difference if concentrated in high-crime places and times.

—LAWRENCE SHERMAN (2004, 159)

one-size-fits-all approach to crime control law enforcement reacts the same way to all crimes in all places at all times in the same way

crime-attack strategies police home in on specific types of suspicious people in specific places at specific times to prevent or interrupt crimes and arrest suspects for committing specific crimes

community policing strategy based on the idea that the police can best carry out their missions by helping communities help themselves by getting at the causes of and finding solutions to community problems

Now that you've learned about police missions and police officers, we'll take the next logical step and examine police strategies for carrying out their missions. Two reactive strategies—preventive patrol and criminal investigation—have dominated U.S. policing since the 1800s. Uniformed police officers patrol the streets to prevent crimes. Detectives investigate crimes to catch suspects for prosecution, conviction, and punishment. For most of their history, both strategies have followed a **one-size-fits-all approach to crime control— react the same way to all crimes in all places at all times.** However, since the 1970s, a convincing body of research has shown clearly the limits of the one-size-fits-all approach.

Research; public fear, frustration, and anger over violence, guns, and illegal drugs (Chapter 5); and the crime and social disorder boom (Chapter 3) combined to create a public mood of "enough is enough." That fed-up public sent a strong message to politicians and cops: "Do something *now!*" Police leaders got the message, and they responded. One response was to refine patrol and investigation. Another was to supplement preventive patrol and criminal investigation with proactive policing strategies—a bolder, more provocative, and more controversial response. **Crime-attack strategies** (the narrowest) home in on specific types of suspicious people in specific places at specific times to prevent or interrupt crimes and arrest suspects for committing specific crimes. Some call these narrowly tailored crime-attack strategies "smarter law enforcement." But how "smart" crime-attack strategies really are depends on the answers to empirical questions about their effectiveness; constitutional questions about whether they violate rights of privacy and liberty; and ethical questions about whether they intrude upon dignity and autonomy in a free society.

There's also a far more ambitious and sweeping proactive strategy afoot. The **community policing strategy** "promises to change radically the relationship between the police and the public" (Eck and Rosenbaum 1994, 3). The strategy (some call it a whole new philosophy) is based on the idea that the police can best carry out their missions by helping communities help themselves, not (or at least not *just*) to enforce the criminal law but to prevent crime, reduce the fear of crime, maintain order, *and* improve the quality of community life by getting at the causes of and finding solutions to community problems. In this chapter, we'll look at each of these strategies and at how technology is changing law enforcement.

Patrol: The "Backbone" of Policing

The medieval word *patrol* means "to walk or paddle in mud or dirty water." Today, patrol officers move through the streets, sometimes on foot, but mostly in vehicles. **Preventive patrol** consists of officers moving through their beats making themselves visible. It has two objectives: controlling crime and reassuring law-abiding people that they're safe. Patrol cars move either slowly (prowling) to prevent crime or speeding through the streets, with sirens screaming and red lights flashing, to pursue suspects. Crime control assumes that just seeing uniformed officers and knowing they might appear anytime will prevent criminal wannabes from committing crimes. It also improves the chance that officers might see and catch criminals in the act. The second objective, reassuring law-abiding citizens they're safe, also assumes the effectiveness of the visible presence of uniformed officers. Patrol dominates police strategy; it's what officers are supposed to be doing whenever they're not "compelled to operate differently" (Scott 2000, 86). Let's look at how patrol officers mobilize and the different types of patrol.

> **preventive patrol** officers move through their beats on foot or in vehicles, making themselves visible to control crime and reassure law-abiding people they're safe

Mobilizing Patrol

Ninety percent of the time mobilization is reactive; officers go into action only *after* victims report crimes. The other 10 percent of the time, mobilization is proactive; officers go out looking for crimes and go into action when they find them. There are four decision points in police mobilization:

1. Victims and witnesses decide to call the police. (Chapters 1 and 2)
2. Civilian police operators decide whether to forward calls to dispatchers. About half the callers don't get beyond the operators. Their decisions aren't reviewed, but we know their main criterion—the more serious the crime the more likely operators will forward the call to dispatchers.
3. Dispatchers decide whether to mobilize the police. They have wide discretion, too, but the seriousness of the crime determines whether they assign cars at all and, if they do, what priority to give the calls.
4. Patrol officers decide how to respond to the calls dispatchers give them. They can drop some calls, hurry to the scene in others, or proceed with no particular urgency, depending on their reading of the situation. (Scott 1980, 59–67)

Faster is better. At least, that's what police used to think about their response to calls. They assumed the faster they got to crime scenes the more criminals they could catch, the more injuries they could prevent, and the more satisfied the public would be. Departments relied on two tactics to speed up response time: (1) the emergency 911 telephone number and (2) a computer-assisted automobile vehicle monitoring (AVM) system (National Advisory Committee on Criminal Justice Standards and Goals 1973, 193).

Then several empirical studies shattered the belief that faster is better. Researchers discovered police response time has no effect on apprehension, charge, and conviction rates. They also found people's satisfaction doesn't depend on how fast police answer calls (Forst, Leahy, Shirhall, Tyson, and Bartolomeo 1982; Forst, Lucianovic, and Cox 1977; Kelling and Fogel 1978, 166–167; U.S. Department of Justice 1978).

Police departments dropped the one-size-fits-all approach to calls, adopting instead a **differential response approach.** This approach varied their response according to the type of crime. They used rapid response for serious crimes like rape and robbery and other responses, like 30-minute delays, telephone reporting,

> **differential response approach** varying police mobilization according to the type of crime

walk-in reporting, and scheduled appointments, for less serious offenses (Petersilia 1989, 234).

The respected Police Executive Research Forum (PERF) designed a model response system. In this model, civilian complaint-takers answer all calls and classify them as critical or noncritical. They transfer the critical calls to dispatchers for immediate response and ask callers to file reports of their noncritical calls later. Evaluation of the model found:

1. Fast police response accounted for less than 5 percent of arrests for serious crimes.
2. Most service calls don't require a fast response.
3. Different responses don't alienate people if they know in advance how the police will handle their calls.
4. The differential response approach saved the Garden Grove, California, Police Department 8000 labor-hours during its first year. (Petersilia 1989, 235)

Types of Preventive Patrol

There are two types of patrol: vehicle patrol and foot patrol. Foot patrol dominated the first century of public policing. Then came the car, which by the 1940s replaced foot patrol to become the dominant patrol until the 1970s when foot patrol and the hybrid bicycle came back into use. (The hybrid bicycle has a few of the advantages of vehicles and practically all the benefits of foot patrol.) Let's look at vehicle patrol and then foot patrol.

Vehicle Patrol How does vehicle patrol work in practice? It depends on the city or town, the beat, the time of day, and the individual officer. According to Gary Cordner and Robert Trojanowicz (1992):

> Patrolling can be stationary or mobile; slow-, medium-, or high-speed; and oriented toward residential, commercial, recreational, or other kinds of areas. Some patrol officers intervene frequently in people's lives by stopping cars and checking out suspicious circumstances; other officers seem more interested in...parked cars and the security of closed businesses; still other officers rarely interrupt their continuous patrolling. Some officers devote all of their uncommitted time to loafing or personal affairs. (5)

Vehicle patrol has serious drawbacks. It contributes to poor police-community relations, especially in poor neighborhoods, where many residents think of the police as a hostile occupational force. Isolated in their "rolling fortresses," with windows rolled up to protect them from the smells, the dangers, and even the temperatures, they seem out of touch and "unable to communicate with the people they presumably serve" (Police Foundation 1981, 11).

The eminent police sociologist Professor Albert J. Reiss, Jr. (1992) says this about the price of vehicle preventive patrol:

> Insulation of the police came at a high price. The patrol officer in his air-conditioned and heated car no longer got out of the police vehicle to do preventive patrol or to learn more about the community being policed. The insulation of the police from the public to control corruption and to respond rapidly to their calls had served primarily to insulate the police from the public they were to serve. No longer did the public have confidence that the police were handling, or could handle their problems, and many, particularly minority groups, felt alienated from the police. (53)

Beginning in the 1970s, a series of empirical evaluations uncovered several deficiencies in preventive patrol besides isolation and poor community relations. Prisoners told interviewers the presence of police didn't frighten them; obviously, it didn't deter them from committing crimes (Kelling, Pate, Dieckman, and Brown 1974, 9–10). Attempts to increase perceived police presence by letting officers use squad cars for their personal use had little, if any, deterrent effect. Patrol can't stop crimes committed inside buildings. Even when preventive patrol deters, its effect is limited to main streets and buildings, leaving side and back streets, alleys, and even the backs of buildings on main streets unaffected (Goldstein 1977, 49–54).

These evaluations also found crimes of passion are largely beyond the reach of preventive patrol. Enraged or demented individuals don't take patrol officers into account when their impulses explode into violence. Also, skilled criminals quickly discover where the police concentrate their efforts and avoid those places or at least wait until a squad car drives by before they make their moves. According to Andrew Halper and Richard Ku (1975), a police officer

> performs the functions of a scarecrow. . . . In this respect his presence can be as reassuring to criminals as to the law-abiding. The potential felon, knowing where a policeman is, can safely deduce where he is not, and guide himself accordingly." (1–2)

David Bayley (1998) adds:

> The relatively small effects of police patrolling on crime, arrests, or the fear of crime may be due to the relatively small numbers of patrol officers compared with population. . . . Most people are unaware just how thinly police are spread out in most places. . . . In American cities, the average is about 400 people per police officer. The ratio of visible patrol officers—cops on the street—to population at any given moment is, however, much less. In fact, it is less than one-tenth of total police strength. There are several reasons for this. In the first place, only about 60% of police officers are assigned to patrol. So visible strength is already four-tenths less than the total. But all patrol officers do not work all the time; they work in shifts. Usually, there are four shifts—three 8-hour shifts on duty, and one shift off duty. This means that only 15% of police strength is available during most 8-hour periods (60% divided by 4). (29)

The most famous (and probably the most influential) study of preventive patrol, the Kansas City Preventive Patrol Experiment, tested the effectiveness of this dominant police strategy. Researchers divided 15 beats into three groups matched for similar crime rates and demographic characteristics. For one year, the police applied three patrol strategies to each group. In the control group, they applied traditional preventive patrol; one car drove through the streets whenever it wasn't answering calls. In group 2, proactive patrol, they greatly increased patrol activity; cars drove through the beats two to three times more often than in the control group. In group 3, reactive patrol, they eliminated preventive patrol entirely; a patrol car stayed at the station until someone called for assistance.

Before and after the experiment, interviewers asked businesspeople and neighborhood residents if they'd been crime victims; their opinion about the quality of law enforcement; and about their fear of crime. To the surprise of many, no matter the strategy:

- Crime rates stayed the same.
- Rates of reporting crime to the police remained constant.
- People's fear of crime stayed the same.
- Opinions about the effectiveness of police services didn't change.
- Respect for the police increased in the control beats (traditional preventive patrol!). (Kelling et al. 1974) (See the In Focus box "Is Preventive Patrol a Waste of Police Time and Taxpayer's Money?")

Foot Patrol Police returned to the old practice of patrolling on foot in the 1970s and 1980s because it brought them closer to the community. Why does getting closer to the community matter? According to Stephen Mastrofski (1990):

> Imbued with a proprietary interest in the neighborhood's well-being and armed with a rich knowledge of its people and places, the officer is expected to enlist citizens' assistance and thus reinforce the informal social control mechanisms of the community. Ultimately these efforts are expected to contribute to more positive police-community relations, less fear of crime and disorder, and an actual reduction in crime and disorder. (37)

Police Foundation Research Brief on the Kansas City Preventative Patrol Experiment: This report was a benchmark of the effectiveness of patrol. To reach this site go to "Web Links" on your Samaha CJ7 website: http://cj.wadsworth.com/samaha_cj7e.

CONCEPT | BUILDER
Visit http://cj.wadsworth.com/samaha_cj7e for an interactive exploration of **police effectiveness: myths versus facts.**

Is Preventive Patrol a Waste of Police Time and Taxpayers' Money?

Some critics have rushed to the conclusion the Kansas City Preventive Patrol Experiment was a waste of police time and taxpayers' money. But Gary Cordner and Robert Trojanowicz (1992) caution that the Kansas City study merely "demonstrated that varying the level of motorized patrol between zero cars per beat and 2–3 cars per beat, for one year in one city, had no effect" (6–7). And James Q. Wilson (1983b, 65–66), author of the influential *Varieties of Police Behavior*, warns the experiment didn't prove police presence of all kinds is useless in controlling crime; it only showed patrol in marked cars did little good. Results might have been different if officers had responded to calls faster in unmarked cars or on foot. Reported crime did decline in Flint, Michigan, when the Flint Police Department adopted foot patrols (Sherman 1992, 153–154).

The Kansas City Preventive Patrol Experiment did have several definitely positive effects:

1. It showed the willingness of police departments to engage in research to evaluate the effectiveness of their programs. According to police expert Herman Goldstein (1977), the experiment also "demonstrated that the police can undertake complex experiments that require altering routine operations with results that are beneficial to the agency . . . and to the entire police field" (52).
2. The experiment also opened up the possibility of freeing expensive patrol resources for other police activities; administrators might be able to divert as much as 60 percent to investigation, surveillance, and community service without diminishing the effectiveness of patrol.

3. By challenging traditional practices, according to J. L. Ray LeGrande of the Miami Beach Police Department, "It was a breakthrough in research—as important as using the police radio for the first time" (Petersilia 1989, 232).
4. The experiment set off a wave of empirical studies pointing out the shortcomings of reactive policing, spurring the increase of variations on existing proactive strategies, and introducing several new ones.

Most of the discussion of evaluations of the reactive strategies of preventive patrol and criminal investigation and the analyses of proactive strategies in the rest of this chapter stem from the findings and questions raised by the Kansas City Preventive Patrol Experiment.

The findings of the Kansas City Preventive Patrol Experiment were and still are widely accepted. Nevertheless, according to policing expert David H. Bayley (1998):

> Motorized patrol is still the mainstay of policing, with police departments continuing to assign the bulk of their personnel to random motor patrolling. . . . In sum, the Kansas City preventive patrol research is famous; its findings are generally accepted as being true; its research strategy is considered to be seriously flawed; it has never been replicated; it has not lessened appreciably the reliance of the police on random patrolling, but it has encouraged a rethinking of police purposes and methods. The curiously mixed, indeed paradoxical impact of the Kansas City research represents a failure, in my view, of police professionals, as well as social scientists. One group or the other should have acted on it, and neither really has. (15)

Does foot patrol make police more "street smart," reduce crime and disorder, and reduce the fear of crime, too? Two major evaluations tried to answer these questions. In Flint, Michigan, foot patrol reduced the fear of crime and actual crime rates. It was so popular that in spite of Flint's severe financial problems, the city voted three times for special tax increases to expand the program. On the other hand, the Newark Foot Patrol Experiment produced mixed results. Fear of crime went down and public satisfaction with police went up, but crime rates stayed the same (Cordner and Trojanowicz 1992, 10).

Single-Officer Patrol Patrol is labor-intensive; it relies heavily on people, not labor- and cost-saving equipment. Salaries make up 80 percent of police budgets, making patrol the most expensive police operation. This is particularly true of two-officer patrols, which prevailed in American policing until the 1980s. Faced with declining budgets, the cost-effectiveness of one-officer patrols appealed to budget-conscious administrators, who saw the chance to cut the cost of patrol in half. But officers vigorously opposed the idea because of their strong belief that

© Jonathan Nourok/Photo Edit

◀ First there was foot patrol, then vehicle patrol, and now there's the hybrid bicycle patrol. Here, two officers on bike patrol watch over the Cinco de Mayo festival on Olivera Street in Los Angeles. Bike patrol has a few of the advantages of vehicles and practically all the benefits of foot patrol.

partners backing each other up increased their safety. However, when the respected Police Executive Research Foundation evaluated one-officer patrols in San Diego, it found this wasn't true. The study reported that compared to two-officer units, one-officer units:

- Saved money
- Resulted in fewer resisting-arrest situations
- Resulted in fewer assaults against officers
- Resulted in fewer injuries to officers
- Generated fewer citizen complaints
- Completed about the same number of traffic warnings, field interrogations, business checks, arrests, and crime report filings (Mastrofski 1990, 31)

▶ DECISION POINT ◀

Are one-officer patrol units as effective as the San Diego study found?

Click on this Decision Point at http://cj.wadsworth.com/samaha_cj7e to explore the issue.

Criminal Investigation

Crime stories, whether on TV or in novels, always start with detectives. From Sherlock Holmes in the 1800s to *CSI* and *Law and Order* in 2005, detectives sleuth clues in dirty, dangerous places; subject their clues to laboratory analysis and their own intuition; and, lo and behold, catch the bad guy. To most people, police work *is* criminal investigation. Detectives, who make up about 15 percent of officers, are also the prestige elements in police subculture. They don't have to wear uniforms, keep their own hours, get paid more, and are the envied group.

Sound research complicates (as it often does) the popular image of criminal investigation. Since the 1960s, research has found "detective work is often boring, usually requires only normal decision-making powers, and seldom leads to solutions." But is detective work really that boring and useless? Research from the

▶ Criminal investigation is a major police strategy and indispensable in gathering evidence of crimes. Here, Fremont, California Crime Scene Specialist Donna Gott investigates the scene of a double homicide. A woman and her daughter were bludgeoned to death with the branch of a tree as they walked 4 miles through the night.

AP/Wide World Photos

1980s and 1990s indicates criminal investigation isn't as exciting as the crime stories depict it, but it's more effective than the 1960s and 1970s research suggested (Brandl and Frank 1994, 149–168; Eck 1992, 19). Let's look more closely at what really happens during preliminary and follow-up investigations and the roles of patrol officers and detectives in each.

Preliminary Investigation

preliminary investigation patrol officers collect information at crime scenes and write incident reports describing what they learned

incident reports written reports describing what patrol officers found during preliminary investigations

Most departments divide a criminal investigation into a preliminary investigation by patrol officers and a follow-up investigation by detectives. In **preliminary investigations,** patrol officers collect information at crime scenes and write **incident reports** describing what they learned. Police departments and prosecutors rely heavily on incident reports in deciding whether to continue the criminal process. Incident reports that contain "good" information, such as (1) the names and addresses of several witnesses, (2) the names and addresses of suspects (or at least good descriptions of them) and (3) detailed descriptions of stolen property, raise the chances of successful prosecution and conviction. Police incident reports containing the names of two witnesses instead of one raise conviction rates by 60 percent! Furthermore, good preliminary investigation also reduces the chance of involving innocent people as suspects (Forst et al. 1977, 24–32; 1982, 23).

Patrol officers make most arrests. They either arrest suspects at the scene of the crime or later based on identifications from victims or witnesses. Detectives, on the other hand, make only a small number of arrests, and detective investigations almost never lead to the identification of unknown criminals. As a result of these findings, many police departments now train patrol officers to conduct more extensive investigations. Some departments even provide patrol officers with feedback from prosecutors' offices regarding the final outcome of cases the officers investigated (Brandl and Frank 1994; Eck 1983; Greenwood, Chaiken, and Petersilia 1977; Greenwood and Petersilia 1975) (Chapter 1).

Follow-Up Investigation

Follow-up investigation consists of investigation by detectives after the preliminary investigation by patrol officers. TV and movies tell stories where the detectives always solve the crime and catch the bad guys, but researchers who've studied detectives in real life tell a more complicated story. First, most cases aren't solved by detective work, according to researchers who examined arrests in Los Angeles, Miami, and Washington, D.C. Then, how are they solved?

1. Patrol officers have already arrested the suspect.
2. Detectives have identified suspects before they get the case.
3. Arrested suspects confess to other crimes they've committed. (Greenwood, Chaiken, and Petersilia 1977, 72)

In a study of the importance of detective work in solving crimes, John Eck (1983) collected data from four police departments: DeKalb, Illinois; County, Georgia; St. Petersburg, Florida; and Wichita, Kansas. Cases fell into three categories. In two of the categories—weak cases with little evidence and strong cases with a lot of evidence—police effort didn't matter. They didn't have to do anything in the strong cases and no matter how hard they worked on weak cases, they couldn't solve them. In the third group—cases with moderate evidence— the more time detectives spent, the greater their chances of making an arrest.

Police experts Jerome H. Skolnick and David H. Bayley (1986) sum up detective work this way:

> Crimes are not solved—in the sense of offenders arrested and prosecuted—through criminal investigations conducted by police departments. Generally, crimes are solved because offenders are immediately apprehended or someone identifies them specifically—a name, an address, a license plate number. If neither of these things happens, the studies show the chances that any crime will be solved fall to less than one in ten. Despite what television has led us to think, detectives do not work from clues to criminals; they work from known suspects to corroborating evidence. Detectives are important for the prosecution of identified perpetrators and not for finding unknown offenders. (5)

follow-up investigation an investigation by detectives after the preliminary investigation by patrol officers

► DECISION POINT ◄

When is undercover work ethical?

Click on this Decision Point at http://cj.wadsworth.com/samaha_cj7e to explore the issue.

Proactive Policing

Can police reduce crime? The public thinks so. So do politicians, but criminologists are skeptical. Their research has demonstrated clearly the limits of preventive patrol and criminal investigation. But it goes deeper than that. Some criminologists doubt the police can do *anything* about crime. According to these criminologists, police can answer emergency calls and maintain order, but they can't control crime. Why? Because they believe cops can't do anything about the "root causes" of crime (Chapter 3).

Not all criminologists are so pessimistic. They concede preventive patrol and criminal investigation have their limits, but those limits are mainly due to strategies based on a one-size-fits-all approach to crime control—respond to all crimes in all places at all times the same way. We've already seen how research led to refinements in patrol and investigation. The same research also led to adopting proactive crime-attack strategies (officers initiate actions to prevent crime and catch criminals) tailored to specific crimes and types of criminals, in particular places, at certain times. Let's look at some of these strategies, including "hot spots" patrol, police crackdowns, field interrogations, and crime-specific lines of attack.

"Hot Spots" Patrol

"Hot spots" patrol is based on a simple idea: Some addresses at certain times need special attention. Why? Because crime isn't distributed evenly in place and time. For example, in Minneapolis, more than half the 911 calls reporting serious crimes came from only 3 percent of its 115,000 addresses (hot spots). All rapes came from 1.2 percent of the addresses; all robberies from 2.2 percent; all car thefts from 2.7 percent; and all domestic disturbances from 9 percent. So deciding to give every resident an equal share of patrol wasn't smart. Lawrence Sherman (1995, 331) assisted the Minneapolis Police Department in designing a major experiment to test how "smart" hot spots patrol is.

Sherman and his colleagues at the Crime Control Institute (Sherman 1995) evaluated the experiment. They collected addresses based on calls for assistance and crimes reported to the police during one year for the Minneapolis Hot Spots Patrol Experiment. Then, the police applied "three hours a day of intermittent, unpredictable police presence" to a random selection of the "worst" hot spot intersections in the city (333). Robbery fell 20 percent, and crimes overall fell 13 percent in these intersections. The number of fights and disturbances was cut in half in the experimental areas. The Minneapolis police officers on hot spots patrol just drove around; they didn't get out of their cars to talk to people or to interrogate suspects. According to Sherman (1995), "More aggressive efforts may have reduced crime even further—or made it worse" (333–334).

Crackdowns

Lawrence Sherman and Dennis Rogan (1995) also found calls to the police came on "hot" days of the week at "hot" times of the day. According to Sherman, "Most addresses, and even most blocks, in any city go for years without any crime—even in high-crime neighborhoods" (331). **Police crackdowns** consist of sudden increases in police activity at places during these "hot" days and times.

How effective are crackdowns? The evidence is mixed. Some research shows crackdowns on drunk driving, robbery, drug dealing, and prostitution reduce crime—but (and it's a big but) only at the crackdown location and only for a short time. Why? Because crime moves to another location (a result called the **displacement effect**) and then comes back to its old location after the crackdown. However, Sherman's review of evaluations of crackdowns in 18 U.S. locations and 5 other countries shows 15 worked with little evidence of displacement. For example, in London, England, there was no evidence a crackdown on prostitution pushed prostitutes to other areas of London (Sherman 1995, 332).

Sherman (1995) contends crackdowns have the opposite effect of displacement:

> Rather than displacing crime to surrounding areas, crime prevention measures reduce crime in nearby areas where they had not been implemented. . . . The key to making crackdowns work is to keep them short and unpredictable. Long-term police crackdowns all show a "decay" in their deterrent effects over time. Short-term crackdowns, in contrast, show a free bonus of "residual deterrence" after the crackdown stops, while potential offenders slowly figure out that the cops are gone. Random rotation of high police visibility across different short-term targets can accumulate free crime prevention bonuses and get the most out of police visibility. Even if displacement to other spots occurs, the unpredictable increases in police presence at any hot spot may create generally higher deterrent effects from the same number of police officers. (332)

Crackdowns raise questions about the right balance between crime control and individual liberty and privacy in a constitutional democracy (Chapter 1). Crackdowns intrude deeply into people's daily lives. As a result, they interfere with everybody's right to come and go as they please and to be let alone by government. Some residents complain about crackdowns turning their neighborhoods into "police states." Young Black men complain officers "hassle" them simply because they're young, Black, and in the neighborhood. Inevitably, crackdowns affect innocent people who have no intention to commit crimes or cause trouble (Sherman 1990, 2–6).

Field Interrogation

Field interrogation means to stop, question, and sometimes search people who "don't look or act right" (Chapter 7). Does field interrogation reduce crime? The San Diego Field Interrogation Experiment tried to find out. The experiment compared three patrol areas. One area continued field interrogations as usual. In the second, only officers specially trained to reduce conflicts with the individuals they stopped did the questioning. The third area stopped all field interrogations for nine months and then started it up again. Total reported crime stayed the same in both areas where field interrogations continued. But total crime went up 20 percent during the nine months that interrogations stopped in the third area, and then went down when interrogations started up. Quality-of-life crimes (disorderly conduct, public drunkenness, petty theft, and prostitution) went up even more during the suspension of field interrogations (Boydstun 1975).

But did the benefits of field interrogation come at the expense of bad relations with the community? No. Surveys showed reducing interrogations had no effect on people's attitudes toward the police. But attitudes toward police were most favorable in the area where specially trained officers did the questioning. So it looks like aggressive field interrogation can reduce crime and maintain good relations with communities where it's practiced professionally (Boydstun 1975). (See the In Focus box "Were the Field Interrogations Appropriate?")

field interrogation police stop, question, and sometimes search people who "don't look or act right"

Specific Crime Attack

We've emphasized that proactive policing tries to provide "smarter law enforcement" by moving from one-size-fits-all strategies to crime-attack strategies that focus on times, places, and people. Now let's look at how police use smarter law enforcement to attack three types of crimes—gun violence, drugs, and domestic assault.

Gun Violence Most gun research focuses on *gun density* (how many guns there are within a defined area), but it takes *gun carrying* to translate the number of guns into gun violence. So cities with a high gun density can have lower gun-crime rates than cities with a low gun density. James Q. Wilson hypothesized that police can reduce gun violence by seizing guns in "gun hot spots." (Hot spots are high-crime locations, like intersections and street addresses, identified by crime patterns at certain times, like weekend nights.) But most police departments count on reactively finding guns during routine searches following arrests for other crimes. Departments don't use the number of guns seized as a measure of police performance and "few officers go out of their way to try and find guns on the street" (Sherman and Rogan 1995, 673, 675).

The Kansas City Gun Experiment tested the hypothesis that greater enforcement of gun-carrying laws in gun-crime hot spots could reduce gun crimes overall in two Kansas City, Missouri, Police Department beats (144 and 242) with identical drive-by shooting rates. The control beat, 242, did business as usual, while beat 144 directed extra patrols on gun-crime hot spots. Here are three examples of what the extra patrol officers actually did:

1. *Safety frisk during traffic stop.* When the officer asked the driver for his license, the driver leaned over to the glove compartment, revealing a bulge under the jacket on the left arm. The officer grabbed the bulge, felt a hard bulk in the shape of a gun, and reached into the jacket to pull the gun out.

Were the Field Interrogations Appropriate?

Two field interrogations conducted by New York City police officers as part of the NYPD "zero tolerance" for quality-of-life violations (Chapter 3) are reproduced here. Keep in mind, these are written from the perspective of two of the individuals who were interrogated, not the police who conducted them.

PERSONAL NARRATIVE

John Reyes

John Reyes is a 22-year-old Hispanic male who resides in East Harlem with his ill mother and teenage sister. Mr. Reyes graduated from a New York City public high school in 1996 and matriculated at a community college in Westchester that same year. After only one semester, he could no longer afford the school and was forced to leave. To pay for college, Mr. Reyes entered the federal Americorps scholarship program. In accordance with the program's requirements, he worked at a community-based program site for approximately 1200 hours to earn scholarship money. Mr. Reyes' "stop & frisk" experience occurred late one night in the summer of 1997.

After working a late shift, Mr. Reyes left the community center at approximately 12:30 A.M. He arrived at his building at approximately 1:00 A.M. Mr. Reyes entered his apartment building, walked to the elevator bank, and was waiting for the elevator when four or five men appeared. "I felt like they came from nowhere. Although they were not in uniform, a few of the men had their badges on, so I knew that they were police officers." The police officers questioned him about where he was coming from. They frisked him and searched his bag. In the midst of a search of his bag, the officers asked Mr. Reyes if he lived in the building. He told them that he did.

"Once the police officers seemed satisfied that I was not in possession of any contraband, and that they were going to let me go on my way, I felt comfortable to ask them what was going on.... They told me that they had received a report that shots had been fired, and that I fit the description of the perpetrator. They didn't give me any more details."

Mr. Reyes reported that this was his first encounter with the police. As he explained, "I was nervous about being stopped and searched. I thought that only happened to criminals." The officers searched his bag. He was embarrassed and somewhat afraid. "It felt strange when the police told me to place my hands against the wall, patted down my body, and then rifled through my things. I was somewhat embarrassed because I knew I had done nothing wrong....I was also glad that none of my neighbors witnessed this incident, because they might have gotten the wrong idea." Mr. Reyes added, "I did not tell my mother what had just happened because I didn't want to upset her."

Jean Davis

Jean Davis is a 54-year-old African American woman who resides in Brooklyn. Davis works as a home health aide for elderly persons. Her encounter with the NYPD

2. *Plain view.* As the officer approached a car he had stopped for speeding, he shined a flashlight onto the floor in front of the back seat and saw a shotgun. Ordering the driver and the passenger out of the car, he found the shotgun was loaded.

3. *Search incident to arrest on other charges.* After stopping a driver for running a red light, the officer asked for his driver's license. A computer check revealed that the driver was wanted for a failure to appear on domestic assault charges. The officer arrested the driver, searched him, and found a gun hidden under his shirt. (Sherman and Rogan 1995, 681)

What were the results? Hot spots patrol officers increased the total guns found in beat 144 by 65 percent in six months (29 guns). Most of the guns never went back into the streets; they were destroyed by the police. Gun crimes fell by 49 percent in the same six months, including reductions in drive-by shootings and homicide. Residents said they were less afraid and more satisfied with their neighborhoods. There was no sign of displacement either. Rather than gun crimes moving to the beats next to 144, gun crimes went down in two of them. The results of the control beat told a different story: Gun seizures fell slightly and gun crimes went up slightly; homicide and drive-by shootings stayed the same. Residents felt more fear and less satisfaction than residents in beat 144 (Sherman and Rogan 1995, 688–689).

Despite these favorable results, Sherman and Rogan (1995), who conducted the research, caution:

occurred in March 1999 at about 10:30 P.M. That evening, Ms. Davis had worked as an aide at a client's home five blocks away from her house. At the end of her shift, she left the client's home and walked on foot toward her house.

Two blocks from her home, she noticed a White man walking in the street. Ms. Davis thought it was strange to see a White person in her predominately Black neighborhood. Since there recently had been reports of crimes in the area, Ms. Davis quickened her pace. She was almost at her home when the man suddenly approached her from behind and grabbed her around her neck. "I screamed. I thought I was being attacked, so I screamed. I was only a few houses away from where I lived, and I thought I could scream loud enough that my son would hear me, and come to my rescue."

"The man told me to be quiet because he was a police officer, but I really didn't know whether to believe him because he did not show me any identification...the next thing I knew, the man was forcing me to walk down the street, back towards the direction he came from. He pulled me down the street towards a car. As we got closer to the car, I saw another man get out of it. The man who was holding me forced me to put my hands on the hood of the car, and patted down the sides of my body and legs."

By this time, Ms. Davis knew that the two men were police officers. Her original fear began to subside as her anger grew. Ms. Davis stated that the officer then conducted a full search of her person, removing the contents of her jacket pockets, shaking her pants legs, removing the baseball hat she was wearing, and shaking that out as well.

At this point, Ms. Davis asked the officers for an explanation. One officer explained that the officers had gotten a call informing them that someone had purchased drugs in the area, and that she fit the description of the alleged purchaser. The officer was not specific about the description. The officer then walked up and down the street looking for drugs. Ms. Davis, now suspicious of the officers and irritated by her continuing detention, feared that an officer might plant drugs on her to cover up his mistake. Ultimately, the officer told Ms. Davis that she was free to go.

"I was shocked and humiliated at being treated like a common criminal," Ms. Davis said. She went home immediately and called her co-worker, who in turn called their employer. The employer accompanied Ms. Davis to the police precinct, where she filed a complaint. She also filed a complaint with the Civilian Complaint Review Board. "I don't trust police officers. Following the incident, I couldn't sleep well for months...Eventually, I went to the doctor who prescribed sleeping pills." Ms. Davis added that, rather than walk the five blocks to her job site, now she takes a taxi.

Source: Eliot Spitzer, *The New York City Police Department's "Stop & Frisk" Policy Practices: A Report to the People of the State of New York from the Office of the Attorney General* (Albany, NY: State Attorney General's Office 1999).

We offer our findings with appropriate cautions. Intensified gun patrols in some neighborhoods conceivably could harm police-community relations, even though no complaints and no legal challenges to the experiment were ever filed in Kansas City....Gun hot spot patrols could pose great risks to officers' safety, although no officers were injured in the limited period of the experiment. Most worrisome is the possibility that field interrogations could provoke more crime by making young men subjected to traffic spots more defiant toward conventional society and thus commit more crimes. (692)

Drug Hot Spots Policing drug crimes has created the most innovative strategies in police work since the 1980s: police crackdowns; raids on crack houses; and new tactics like "jump-out" squads intercepting public drug deals, condemning buildings, and fining landlords for drug dealing. Which police strategies work in drug law enforcement? To find out (and let's be honest, to answer public pressure), the National Institute of Justice established the Drug Market Analysis Program (DMA).

David Weisburd and Lorraine Green (1995, 715–717) evaluated a DMA experimental strategy to enforce drug laws in Jersey City, New Jersey. Drug hot spots were responsible for a "substantial portion" of calls for service, drug-related crimes, and arrests. For example, the hot spots amounted to only 4.4 percent of streets and intersections but 46 percent of drug sales arrests and emergency calls for narcotics. Before the project, the Jersey City Police Department narcotics squad had relied on unsystematic tactics, including surveillance, arrests, search warrants, and "street pops" (field interrogations of suspected dealers on street corners). Although these activities increased, they didn't have any impact on the drug problem.

According to Jersey City Captain Frank Gajewski, the traditional drug enforcement strategy maintained the street-level drug problem as much as it combated it:

> One can look at these drug markets as vineyards. The arrests made within their borders can be symbolized as the fruit from the vine. Each vineyard is capable of producing a continual supply of "fruit" as long as the vine is left intact. Some vineyards are larger than others. The arrest strategy sees the pickers (the police) traveling from vineyard to vineyard harvesting the fruit. There are many vineyards so the pickers never stay too long at any particular site. As demand increases from irate citizens...the police respond by picking more fruit. Police administrators seeking to assuage the public, display the high harvest numbers as evidence of their commitment and the efficiency of their organization. But the vines are never uprooted, indeed police activity may contribute to their health. (Weisburd and Green 1995, 717)

The ineffectiveness of their traditional strategies frustrated the Jersey City Police Department. That's when they turned to DMA and the creation, implementation, and evaluation of the drug hot spots experiment. The experimental strategy aimed at getting business owners and residents involved; cracking down on drug hot spots; and creating a maintenance program to patrol the hot spots after the crackdowns. Comparing the seven months before and after the experiment, Weisburd and Green (1995) found:

1. Significant reductions in emergency calls to the police
2. Little displacement of crime to areas near the experimental hot spots
3. Reduced crime in areas around the experimental hot spots (diffusion of benefits) (714–717)

According to Weisburd and Green (1995, 721), the reduction in emergency calls is important because "recent studies suggest emergency calls are a more reliable measure of crime and crime-related activity than are other official indicators."

Domestic Violence "I hate those domestic disputes. There's not a thing you can do with them" (Black 1980, 146). What *can* police do about domestic violence disputes? A 1968 study found some New York City Police officers specially trained to handle domestic violence calls believed counseling batterers was more effective than arresting them. A report by the National Institute of Law Enforcement and Criminal Justice endorsed the NYPD approach. However, by the 1970s, many law enforcement officials had started rejecting the counseling approach, claiming it didn't work. At the same time, the growing women's movement rejected it as "soft" on batterers (Brown 1988, 289).

During the 1980s, states began to change ancient laws that only allowed officers to arrest suspects without warrants if they witnessed a misdemeanor firsthand. About the same time, police departments began to adopt policies allowing officers to arrest batterers even if they hadn't witnessed misdemeanor assaults or didn't have evidence a felony was committed. These new laws and policies made it easier for police to arrest batterers.

In 1980, the Minneapolis Domestic Violence Experiment tested the effectiveness of nonarrests in domestic assault cases. Officers agreed to give up their discretion and decide according to a random system whether to arrest, mediate, or temporarily separate couples. Using victim interviews and official police records of assaults, experiment evaluator Lawrence Sherman and his associates reported arrests cut assaults by 50 percent in the six months after the first assault (Sherman, Schmidt, and Rogan 1992).

Scholars claimed this was one of the "most influential results ever generated by social science" (Maxwell, Garner, and Fagan 1991, 3). But six replications of the Minneapolis Experiment in other places between 1981 and 1991 failed to du-

▶ D E C I S I O N   P O I N T ◀

Should kids report their parents to the police?

Click on this Decision Point at http://cj.wadsworth.com/samaha_cj7e to explore the issue.

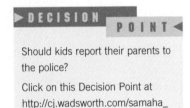

National Institute of Justice, "Batterer Intervention Programs": This report describes the issues of mitigating or preventing recidivism among those who batter their families. To reach this site go to "Web Links" on your Samaha CJ7 website: http://cj .wadsworth.com/samaha_cj7e.

plicate these results. In three studies, assaults by arrested batterers went up; in three others, assaults by arrested batterers went down—a little bit (1). However, when researchers reworked the data from the replication studies, they found the following:

- Arresting batterers was related to fewer aggressive acts against female intimate partners.
- Age and criminal history were more strongly related to future assaults than arrests.
- Arrests reduced future aggression about equally in all locations.
- Most suspects committed no new crimes against their original victim whether they were arrested or not.
- There was no association between arresting the offender and an increased risk of subsequent aggression against women generally. (2)

Department of Justice Office on Violence Against Women: A national site for research, statistics, and more on the issue of violence against women, particularly domestic violence. To reach this site go to "Web Links" on your Samaha CJ7 website: http://cj.wadsworth.com/samaha_cj7e.

Community-Oriented (COP) and Problem-Oriented (POP) Policing

Community-oriented policing (COP) and problem-oriented policing are two very popular, widely talked about, new, and well-funded strategies (sometimes called a "quiet revolution"). Touted by police management, criminal justice academics, and politicians, both reflect a partnership between police and the communities they police to identify and solve community problems. Both emphasize shifting decision-making power from top executives at headquarters down to local precincts. **Community-oriented policing (COP)** is first and foremost concerned with establishing a working relationship with the community. **Problem-oriented policing (POP)** has as its top priority identifying and solving community problems (Roberg 1994, 249). But they usually go hand in hand. Problem-oriented policing is almost always an essential strategy in community policing, and it's rarely seen outside of community policing. Table 6.1 contrasts COP with traditional patrols, and Table 6.2 contrasts POP with COP. Let's look at both strategies and then at evaluations of their effectiveness.

community-oriented policing (COP) police strategy primarily concerned with establishing a working relationship with the community

problem-oriented policing (POP) police strategy primarily concerned with identifying, analyzing, responding to, and assessing community problems related to crime and neighborhood quality of life

◀ The idea of community-oriented policing (COP) is that partnerships between police and the community can reduce crime and increase security. It emphasizes that residents are the main line of defense against crime, disorder, fear, and the deterioration of the quality of life in their neighborhoods. Here, Yesenia Valasquez watches as Providence, Rhode Island, Police Explorer Robinson Cardona fingerprints her younger sister Karlyn during Operation Safe Child at the Providence Mall. Hundreds of children gave DNA samples and fingerprints for child identification kits that can aid authorities if children are reported missing.

AP/Wide World Photos

▼ TABLE 6.1 Traditional Patrol and Community-Oriented Policing

Element	Traditional Patrol	Community Oriented
Decision making	Police	Police and the community
Organization	Centralized	Local
Authority	From the chief down to the officers	Officers at the beat level
Mission	Crime control	Crime control, fear reduction, order maintenance, and improved neighborhood living conditions
Strategy	Respond to specific incidents	Respond to underlying causes of community problems

Source: Michael S. Scott, *Problem-Oriented Policing: Reflections on the First 20 Years* (Washington, DC: U.S. Department of Justice, Office of Community-Oriented Policing Services [COPS], 2000), Table 10, p. 99.

▼ TABLE 6.2 Problem-Oriented and Community-Oriented Policing

Principle	Problem Oriented	Community Oriented
Primary emphasis	Substantive social problems within police missions (Chapter 5)	Engaging the community in the policing process
Police and community collaboration	Determined on a problem-by-problem basis	Always or nearly always
Emphasis on problem analysis	Highest priority given to thorough analysis	Encouraged but less important than collaboration with the community
Preference for responses	Strong preference for exploring alternatives to criminal law enforcement	Preference for collaborative responses from the community
Role for police in organizing and mobilizing the community	Advocated only if warranted in the specific problem being addressed	Emphasizes strong role for police
Importance of geographic decentralization of police and continuity of officer assignment to the community	Preferred but not essential	Essential
Degree to which police share decision-making authority with the community	Strongly encourages input from the community while preserving the ultimate decision-making authority for police	Emphasizes sharing decision-making authority with the community
Officers' skills	Emphasizes intellectual and analytical skills	Emphasizes interpersonal skills
View of the role or the mandate of the police	Encourages broad, but not unlimited, role for police; stresses limited capacities of police and guards against creating unrealistic expectations of police	Encourages expansive role for police to achieve ambitious social objectives

Source: Michael S. Scott, *Problem-Oriented Policing: Reflections on the First 20 Years* (Washington, DC: U.S. Department of Justice, Office of Community-Oriented Policing Services [COPS], 2000), Table 10, p. 99.

▶ **DECISION** **POINT** ◀

How can the police fix "broken windows"?

Click on this Decision Point at http://cj.wadsworth.com/samaha_cj7e to explore the issue.

Community Oriented Policing (COP): A national database for all things related to COP. To reach this site go to "Web Links" on your Samaha CJ7 website: http://cj.wadsworth.com/samaha_cj7e.

Community-Oriented Policing (COP)

The idea of community-oriented policing (COP) is that partnerships between police and the community can reduce crime and increase security. It emphasizes that residents are the main line of defense against crime, disorder, fear, and the deterioration of the quality of life in their neighborhoods. So, in community-oriented policing, residents identify and participate in the solutions to the problems in their neighborhood. When police talk to residents, they find residents don't always put serious crime at the top of their list of concerns; they often say fear is as important as victimization, and what to police seems like minor stuff (kids hanging out on corners, drunks in the street, and graffiti) usually triggers their fear more than serious crime (Moore 1992, 123; Chapter 3, Make Your Decision: "Broken Windows").

Crime control isn't the only mission in community-oriented policing; achieving community satisfaction and harmony is also critical. This doesn't mean police do whatever neighborhood residents want. Suppose angry neighbors want to drive a suspected child molester out of the neighborhood. The police can't allow it because they have to uphold the suspect's rights. Police can't just listen to the most outspoken individuals or groups in the neighborhood either. The "squeaky wheel" doesn't "get the grease" in community-oriented policing unless the police believe it should. And residents have to help in the solutions, too. They can't just nominate a problem and expect the police to solve it alone. So police listen to neighborhood demands, but they don't (and shouldn't) automatically give in to them (Moore 1992, 123).

Community policing is very popular and enjoys wide support from both major political parties—support that translates into billions of federal tax dollars (Zhao, Lovrich, and Robinson 2001, 365; Chapter 5). In 2000, 68 percent of larger police departments had a full-time community policing unit (similar to 1997); 94 percent of all police departments had full-time sworn community police officers (up from 80 percent in 1997); and 79 percent trained all new recruits in community policing (BJS April 2004, vi).

Many programs qualify as part of community policing. Tables 6.3 and 6.4, taken from a survey of over two hundred police departments in cities with populations over twenty-five thousand (Zhao, Lovrich, and Robinson 2001, 374–375) give you some idea of how broad (and flexible) community policing is.

▼ **TABLE 6.3 Externally Focused COP Programs**

Externally Focused Change—Reorientation of Police Operations and Crime Prevention
1. Department sponsorship of community newsletter
2. Additional officers on foot, bicycle, or horse patrol
3. Use of storefronts for crime prevention
4. Use of a task unit for solving special problems in a targeted area
5. Victim contact program
6. Crime prevention education of the general public
7. Fixed assignment of officers to neighborhoods or schools for extended periods
8. Permanent reassignment of some sworn personnel from traditional patrol to crime prevention
9. Use of citizen survey to keep informed about local problems
10. Neighborhood watch
11. Business watch
12. Increased hiring of civilians for non–law enforcement tasks
13. Community service officers (uniformed civilians who perform support and community liaisons)
14. Unpaid civilian volunteers who perform support and community liaison activities

Source: Jihong Zhao, Nicholas P. Lovrich, and T. H. Robinson, "Community Policing: Is It Changing the Basic Functions of Policing? Findings from a Longitudinal Study of 200+ Municipal Police Agencies." *Journal of Criminal Justice*, 29(5)(2001):365–377.

▼ **TABLE 6.4 Internally Focused COP Programs**

Internally or Managerially Focused Change
1. Reassessment of rank and assignments
2. Reassignment of some management positions from sworn to civilian personnel
3. Addition of the position "Master Police Officer" to increase rewards for line officers
4. Formation of quality circles (problem-solving among small groups of line personnel)

Source: Jihong Zhao, Nicholas P. Lovrich, and T. H. Robinson, "Community Policing: Is It Changing the Basic Functions of Policing? Findings from a Longitudinal Study of 200+ Municipal Police Agencies." *Journal of Criminal Justice*, 29(5)(2001):365–377.

> **DECISION**
> **POINT** ◀

Is community-oriented policing good policy?

Click on this Decision Point at http://cj.wadsworth.com/samaha_cj7e to explore the issue.

According to Professor Mark Moore (1994, 285–286), a community policing expert, it's not hard to understand the popularity of the programs (and others not included) in Tables 6.3 and 6.4. They're answers to the limits of the "reform model" of policing: heavy use of a reactive response to crime control; reliance on arrests to reduce crime and disorder; lack of working relationships with the community; and the restrictions of the military model of police organization. In Professor Moore's words:

> In contrast, the new ideas point to a new set of possibilities: the potential for crime prevention as well as crime control; creative problem solving as an alternative to arrest; the importance of customer service and community responsiveness as devices for building stronger relations with local communities; and "commissioning" street level officers to initiate community problem-solving efforts. To many, these ideas seem more likely to ameliorate the wide variety of crime and disorder that are now tearing the heart out of America's communities. (286)

A key to community policing is that police can't go it alone; but they can help communities help themselves. Success depends on commitment from *all* of what the late community policing expert Robert C. Trojanowicz (1994, 238–239) called the "Big Five" (police, community residents, social service agencies, political leaders, and the media). According to Professor Trojanowicz:

> Citizens need to do more for themselves and volunteer to help rejuvenate their neighborhoods; social agencies need to do their share; political leaders need to provide long-term commitment and support; the media needs to educate the public; and the police cannot conduct "business as usual." (259)

Problem-Oriented Policing (POP)

Center for Problem-Oriented Policing: Problem-oriented policing is designed to identify and remove the causes of recurring crime and disorder problems that harm communities. This is a sister site to the COP site; both are full of data, training, and resources for the serious criminal justice student and aspiring police officer. To reach this site go to "Web Links" on your Samaha CJ7 website: http://cj.wadsworth.com/samaha_cj7e.

Problem-oriented policing is another proactive strategy that stems from the research pointing out the limits of the traditional preventive patrol, rapid response, and follow-up criminal investigations. According to Herman Goldstein (2001), the "father of problem-oriented policing," the research findings provided the following insights, which led to problem-oriented policing:

- Police deal with a range of community problems, many of which are not strictly criminal in nature.
- Arrest and prosecution alone—the traditional functions of the criminal justice system—do not always effectively resolve problems.
- Giving the officers, who have great insight into community problems, the discretion to design solutions is extremely valuable to solving the problems.
- Police can use a variety of methods to redress recurrent problems.
- The community values police involvement in noncriminal problems and recognizes the contribution the police can make to solving these problems.

Table 6.5 lists the four elements (SARA) of problem-oriented policing.

Notice that "problems" include crimes *and* disorder, fear, and any other threat to the quality of neighborhood life. Also, single incidents like a loud party or the burglary of a particular house are *not* problems. A series of burglaries on a particular street or ongoing loud parties in an apartment building near a college are. Police officers and residents participate (in fact, residents may take the lead) in identifying and analyzing problems. The "Big Five" (police, businesses and landlords, social service agencies, politicians, and the media) may all participate in the solution to the problem, which may be arrest and criminal prosecution, but it can be (and often will be) some nonpolice or criminal justice response. (See the In Focus box "Problem-Oriented Policing in Chicago" on page 204.)

▼ TABLE 6.5 The Elements of Problem-Oriented Policing (SARA)

Scanning	Identifying recurring problems of concern to the public and the police
	Identifying the consequences of the problems for the community and the police
	Prioritizing those problems
	Developing broad goals
	Confirming that the problems exist
	Determining how frequently a problem occurs and how long it has been taking place
	Selecting problems for closer examination
Analysis	Identifying and understanding the events and conditions that precede and accompany the problem
	Identifying relevant data to be collected
	Researching what is known about the problem type
	Taking inventory of how the problem is currently addressed and the strengths and limitations of the current response
	Narrowing the scope of the problem as specifically as possible
	Identifying a variety of resources that may be of assistance in developing a deeper understanding of the problem
	Developing a working hypothesis about why the problem is occurring
Response	Brainstorming for new interventions
	Searching for what other communities with similar problems have done
	Choosing among the alternative interventions
	Outlining a response plan and identifying responsible parties
	Stating the specific objectives for the response plan
	Carrying out the planned activities
Assessment	Determining whether the plan was implemented (a process evaluation)
	Collecting pre- and post-response qualitative and quantitative data
	Determining whether broad goals and specific objectives were attained
	Identifying any new strategies needed to augment the original plan
	Conducting ongoing assessment to ensure continued effectiveness

Source: Herman Goldstein, 2001, "What Is Problem-Oriented Policing?" http://www.popcenter.org/about-whatisPOP.htm.

Evaluating Community- and Problem-Oriented Policing

Do community-oriented and problem-oriented policing work? If by "work" we mean do they improve community life by reducing crime, disorder, and fear, there's no convincing empirical evidence that they do. But there's another important question that we'll try to answer here: Do the impressive numbers of departments with community policing units, officers, and training mean that they're *practicing* community policing?

According to the optimists, the answer for the numbers is pretty straightforward. First, police leaders faced up to the reality that traditional policing was getting more and more ineffective by the late 1960s. Second, by the 1970s the social environment had changed: Public trust in government had declined; there were efforts to "reinvent" government and drives to stimulate efforts of communities to solve their own problems (Zhao, Lovrich, and Robinson 2001, 366). Police had to respond to the new environment and the shortcomings of their old ways. Community- and problem-oriented policing was their response. The response was genuine and it was revolutionary (Goldstein 1977). That's what the numbers mean.

Skeptics (some call them pessimists) aren't so sure. Some see obstacles to implementing community- and problem-oriented policing in the structure of police departments. Roy R. Roberg (1994, 250), who's written extensively about police organizations, says that despite great variety in size and quality among U.S. municipal police departments, the bottom line is they're paramilitary organizations (Chapter 5). As a result, training and rewards concentrate on criminal law

Problem-Oriented Policing in Chicago

Here's an excellent example of problem-oriented policing:

One cold March evening, several Chicago beat-team police officers visited a four-story apartment building in a decaying section of their district. For months, neighbors had been complaining about the building at the area's community beat meetings (formal gatherings of police and citizens), so the officers decided to make a careful inspection of it as they followed up on a specific incident.

They were appalled at what they found. Inside, the building was in a state of collapse. The doors had been torn off most of the apartments, and the appliances and electrical fittings had been scavenged. Ceilings in the top-floor units were coming down. The halls were littered with hypodermic syringes. None of the exterior doors locked, but that would have made little difference because garbage was piled so high in the alley that anyone could clamber through a rear window. One resident later reported that cockroaches in the building "look like little Volkswagen cars." The officers soon found that the paying tenants had all fled and that they had been replaced by a rotating cast of squatters, gang members, drug dealers and users, and runaway youths.

One of the beat-team officers got the district's commander involved. He had already heard complaints about the building and its landlord at beat meetings he attended, and when he got the whole picture, he became furious. He later noted, "Guys like these are just as bad as the criminals that were arrested in this building. They...don't care for their building and just milk these people dry. I'm not going to stand for that!"

He brought a police photographer with him during a walk-through inspection of the building and later took the area's alderman on a guided tour. A search of police records found an enormous number of 911 calls about the building, and a long list of arrests associated with it. There was quick follow-up action by the city's building inspection department, and within two months, the prosecutor's office had delivered an ultimatum to the landlord—a list of what needed to be done to the building. Meanwhile, residents picketed the landlord's office, and the district commander sent a team to back them up.

When the landlord did not comply, he was charged and hauled into court. A group of approximately 15 residents, representing the district's court advocacy committee, attended each hearing and made its presence known to the judge and the prosecutor. The landlord was convicted of reckless conduct that violated the state's criminal housing management statute, and he was eventually fined and sentenced to perform 200 hours of community service.

Source: Wesley G. Skogan and Susan M. Hartnett, *Community Policing, Chicago Style* (New York: Oxford University Press, 1997), pp. 3–4.

---

enforcement and strict obedience to department rules and regulations that come from the top command and flow down to officers at the bottom. Furthermore, because of the high skill level and innovative methods required, in the near future only a very few "elite" departments will be able to put *real* community- and problem-oriented policing into effect (256).

Michael Buerger (1994), a former police officer with a doctor's degree in criminal justice sees huge (probably impossible) shortcomings in the "community" part of community policing. According to Buerger, our view of community is a myth:

The nostalgic sense of community embedded in the language of community policing is largely absent in the neighborhoods beset by crime. Despite all the problems related to doing so, reversing an area's economic decline may be a necessary precursor to restoring a sense of community; at the very least, some mechanism other than "crime prevention" is needed to galvanize the uncommitted.

The vast number of the silent members of the community are neither disposed nor respond to clarion calls. They may have seen past successes celebrated to no great effect; they may know firsthand the costs of taking on an activist role. Without a greater stake in the geographically defined community they will likely ignore all symbolic statements directed at them. (272)

Most fundamental in the skeptics' view is that community- and problem-oriented policing isn't "real" police work; in fact, it violates the very nature of police work. The late plainspoken police expert Professor Carl Klockars (1988) called community policing a sham:

The modern movement toward what is currently called "community policing" is best understood as the latest in a fairly long tradition of circumlocutions whose purpose is to conceal, mystify, and legitimate police distribution of coercive force. (41)

One Chicago police commander agreed; he dismissed his city's community policing program as a "'warm and fuzzy' public relations program designed to make civilians feel better about the police" (Skogan and colleagues 2000, 16). What Klockars' criticism boils down to is pretty strong stuff: community policing can't work because it renounces the very nature of police work—coercive force (Chapters 5, 7).

So much for the theories of optimists and skeptics. What about the evidence? One thing seems pretty clear. Departments with community- and problem-oriented programs haven't shifted their priorities or their resources away from crime control to solving problems of fear, disorder, and neighborhood quality of life apart from crime control. A survey (Zhao, Lovrich, and Robinson 2001) of 245 municipal police departments serving populations of more than twenty-five thousand people during the 1990s found:

1. Police departments rated crime control far above order maintenance and service, even though crime rates were *falling* (370–371). This finding held true no matter the size of the city or its geographical location. (373)
2. An increase in community policing programs translated into a *slight* shift in priorities away from crime control toward order maintenance. This shift took place during the 1990s, a time when "community policing became a broadly diffused innovation across the country. The primary findings of this research clearly indicate that the core functional priorities of American policing largely remain closely modeled after the professional model; these priorities were not significantly affected by changes such as the addition of officers, the provision of funds for COP training or the adoption of COP programs." (372)

Supporting the theory that force is the nature of policing is Kraska and Kappeler's (1997) study of special weapons and tactics (SWAT) units. Kraska and Kappeler asked a sample of 690 police departments (excluding federal agencies) in jurisdictions with more than fifty thousand people and 100 sworn officers about military tactics and ideology in law enforcement agencies. They also conducted follow-up unstructured interviews with 81 respondents (5). They found that 89.4 percent of the responding departments had a SWAT unit in 1995; over 20 percent of departments without a unit said they were "planning on establishing one in the next few years." Most departments created SWAT units in the 1970s; by 1982, 59 percent had adopted one; by 1990, 78 percent had (6).

In 2000, the number of SWAT units was still 89 percent in municipal police departments, but in county police departments, it was 97 percent (BJS April 2004, vi). (In the same year, about two-thirds of county and municipal departments had community policing units.)

SWAT units didn't just expand in numbers; they also were used in more kinds of cases (Kraska and Kappeler 1997, 6). When they were introduced in the 1960s and early 1970s, SWAT units were confined to rare events like "civil riots, terrorism, barricaded suspects, and hostage situations." By 1995, they could be used in any situation departments considered "high risk." Here's the percentage breakdown of types of cases SWAT units responded to in 1995: civil disturbances, 1.3; terrorist incidents, .09; hostage situations, 3.6; barricaded persons 13.4; "high risk warrant work," (mostly "drug raids"), 75.9 (7).

Kraska and Kappeler's story of policing in the era of community- and problem-oriented policing is captured in the metaphor of war; it helps us organize our thoughts and values regarding social problems. The war metaphor is widespread throughout U.S. history: We've had wars on alcohol since the 1700s, wars on crime beginning in the late 1800s and throughout the twentieth century, wars on poverty in the 1960s, wars on drugs since the 1970s, and now the war on terrorism.

If Kraska and Kappeler are right about the prevalence of the war metaphor in policing, what does this say about the place of community- and problem-oriented policing? During the 1980s and 1990s, they wrote:

> Most police academics have fixated on the professed turn toward community and problem-oriented policing. While transfixed on the "velvet glove" few have inquired into the possibility of a simultaneous strengthening of the "iron fist" as a type of "backstage" phenomenon. Despite the overtly militaristic nature of U.S. paramilitary units (PPUs), and their continued growth since the early 1970s, little academic research or discussion examines these units. (2–3)

What then can we make of these bold theories and few pieces of research as they relate to *practicing* community- and problem-oriented policing? Here's what Professor Wesley G. Skogan and his colleagues (2000) said about the practical difficulties of implementing community policing in Chicago:

> Translating the abstract concepts of community policing into day-to-day steps that police officers can follow is complicated, and motivating officers to follow those practical instructions is difficult. It is just as difficult to rebuild the collective efficacy [Chapter 3] of communities that have lost it and to involve residents of poor and previously disenfranchised neighborhoods in partnership with the police. (1)

Finally, listen to the careful conclusion of criminal justice policy and public management expert Mark H. Moore (1994). His words are a fitting way to close this section (See also "In Focus: Problem-Oriented Policing in Chicago"):

> Something is clearly afoot in the field of policing. Throughout the country (even the world), police executives are committing their organizations to something called "community" or "problem-solving" policing. Indeed, popular enthusiasm for these ideas is so great that in a few cases in which police executives have been slow to embrace them, communities have forced the ideas upon them.
>
> Predictably, rhetorical commitment[s] to these ideas have outpaced the concrete achievements. Still, as one looks across the country, one finds many examples of departments that have introduced important new operational programs and administrative systems that are consistent with the spirit of the wider reforms (and are often the first steps in changing operational philosophy of an entire department)....Community policing has become the new orthodoxy for cops; and community policing is the only form of policing available for anyone who seeks to improve police operations, management, or relations with the public. (285)

Law Enforcement Technology

"Cops Combine Old and New Techniques"
"Biometric Technology Creeping into Everyday Life"
"Police Test New ID Gadget"
"Sheriffs' Offices Can Get Tips Online"
"Public Safety Wireless Experts Talk the Talk"
"UnWired We Stand"

These headlines from just a few of the stories appearing in newspapers around the country during August 2004 will give you some idea of the rapid advance in technology that has affected not just law enforcement but all of our daily lives. The list of specific advances is very long (Figure 6.1 and Table 6.6). In this section, we'll concentrate on the enormous advance in computers and information systems. (We'll discuss advances in technology related to the use of force in Chapter 7.) (See the CJ & Technology box "3-D Mug Shot" on pages 210–211.)

Are computers and information systems "godsends" to law enforcement, as authors Paul Tracy and Vincent Morgan (2000, 636) describe them? According to a National Institute of Justice report (June 2004, 1), computers and other new

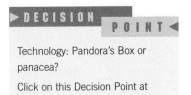

▶ DECISION POINT ◀

Technology: Pandora's Box or panacea?

Click on this Decision Point at http://cj.wadsworth.com/samaha_cj7e to explore the issue.

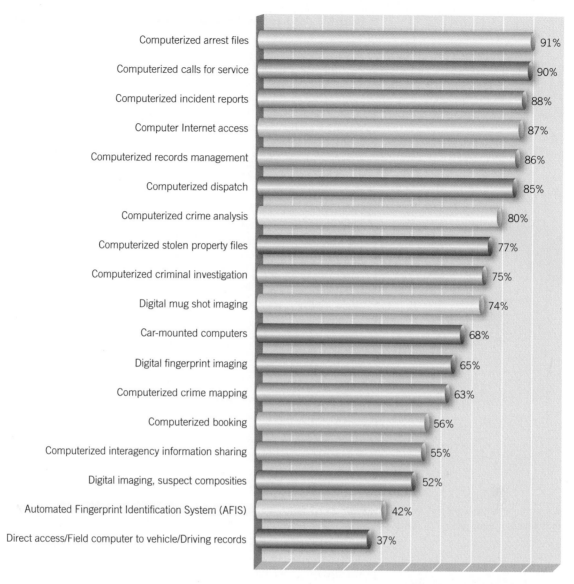

FIGURE 6.1 Computers and Information Systems in Large Police Departments, 2000

Source: Bureau of Justice Statistics, *Law Enforcement Management and Administrative Statistics, 2000* (Washington, DC: Bureau of Justice Statistics, April 2004), viii.

technologies can help reduce crime rates, catch criminals, and make officers, suspects, and the public safer. But, the authors point out, some call the same technologies "evil" because they're not perfect; they can be very expensive; and they can invade privacy (636). Let's look at two of these new technologies, DNA and crime mapping.

DNA

Every human being carries with him from his cradle to his grave certain physical marks which do not change their character, and by which he can always be identified—and that is without a shade of doubt or question. These marks are his signature, his physiological autograph, so to speak, and this autograph cannot be counterfeited, nor can he disguise it or hide it away, nor can it become illegible by the wear and the mutations of time. This signature is not his face—age can change that beyond recognition; it is not his hair, for that can fall out; it is not his height, for duplicates of that exist; it is not his form, for duplicates of that exist also, whereas this signature is every man's very own—there is no duplicate of it among the swarming populations of the globe! (Twain, 1980, 108)

If you thought you just read a description of DNA, you'd be wrong; it's Mark Twain describing fingerprints in 1894 (Figure 6.2). The definitions of fingerprints and DNA are a lot alike (in fact, DNA is sometimes called *DNA* fingerprints).

Integrated Automated Fingerprint Identification System (IAFIS): The IAFIS provides automated fingerprint search capabilities, latent searching capability, electronic image storage, and electronic exchange of fingerprints and responses, 24 hours a day, 365 days a year. To reach this site go to "Web Links" on your Samaha CJ7 website: http://cj.wadsworth.com/samaha_cj7e.

▼ TABLE 6.6 Computers and Information Systems in Small Police Departments, 2000

Technology	Often (%)	Sometimes (%)	Never (%)
Communications—mobile radios	98.7	0.0	1.3
Communications—portable radios	95.3	2.1	2.6
Communications—base station radios	82.5	7.7	9.8
Personal computer (PC/microcomputer)	66.4	11.1	22.6
Communications—cellular phones	59.5	30.8	9.7
Mainframe computer	43.6	9.4	47.0
Video camera (in patrol cars)	33.6	18.1	48.3
Digital imaging—mug shots	31.2	14.1	54.7
Minicomputer	25.8	10.0	64.2
Car-mounted mobile digital/data terminal	15.9	3.1	81.1
Car-mounted mobile digital/data computer	12.9	1.3	85.8
Laptop computer (in field)	11.3	15.2	73.5
Digital imaging—fingerprints	9.6	7.9	82.5
Video camera (fixed-site surveillance)	8.3	30.9	60.9
Video camera (mobile surveillance)	8.3	31.0	60.7
Digital imaging—suspect composites	6.9	30.2	62.9
Night vision/electro-optic (image intensifiers)	3.5	38.2	58.3
Night vision/electro-optic (infrared—thermal imagers)	1.8	23.7	74.6
Vehicle (stolen-vehicle tracking)	1.3	5.3	93.4
Global positioning systems—mobile surveillance	1.3	7.4	·91.3
Night vision/electro-optic (laser rangefinders)	1.3	8.4	90.3
Global positioning systems—vehicle location	0.9	1.8	97.4
Handheld digital terminal	0.9	1.8	97.4

Note: Figures may not sum to 100 due to rounding.

Source: National Institute of Justice, *Law Enforcement Technology* (Washington, DC: NIJ, June 2004), p. 3.

DNA the building block for each individual's unique genetic makeup

DNA is the building block for your entire genetic makeup, which is unique. Every cell in your body has the same DNA. This is a unique law enforcement identification tool because every person's DNA is unique (except for identical twins). So, just like fingerprints, DNA evidence collected at crime scenes can point the finger at or eliminate a suspect.

When labs link DNA from one crime scene with evidence at another crime scene using CODIS (Combined DNA Index System), they can link these crimes to a single suspect anywhere in the country. **CODIS** is a software program that operates databases of DNA profiles from convicted offenders, unsolved crime scene evidence, and missing persons. It can electronically link crime scenes.

According to a National Institute of Justice Special Report:

CODIS (Combined DNA Index System) a software program that operates databases of DNA profiles of convicted offenders, unsolved crime scene evidence, and missing persons

> Every law enforcement department throughout the country has unsolved cases that could be solved through recent advancements in DNA technology. Today, investigators who understand which evidence may yield a DNA profile can identify a suspect in ways previously seen only on television. Evidence invisible to the naked eye can be the key to solving a residential burglary, sexual assault, or murder. The saliva on the stamp of a stalker's threatening letter, the perspiration on a rapist's mask, or the skin cells shed on a ligature of a strangled child may hold the key to solving a crime. (NIJ July 2002, 1)

DNA has another advantage. With the newer technology, it is possible to analyze biological evidence that was collected and stored properly, even if the sample is decades old (NIJ July 2002, 6). Originally, to create a DNA profile, labs had to have fairly fresh samples that were at least as big as a quarter. Now, even highly degraded evidence will do because only tiny amounts (like a few skin cells) are enough. Also, older DNA technology could only use the nucleus of a cell; now, other parts can also be used. So old cells with decayed nuclei and cells

CODIS National Database for DNA: The FBI Laboratory's Combined DNA Index System (CODIS) enables federal, state, and local crime labs to exchange and compare DNA profiles electronically, thereby linking crimes to each other and to convicted offenders. To reach this site go to "Web Links" on your Samaha CJ7 website: http://cj.wadsworth.com/samaha_cj7e.

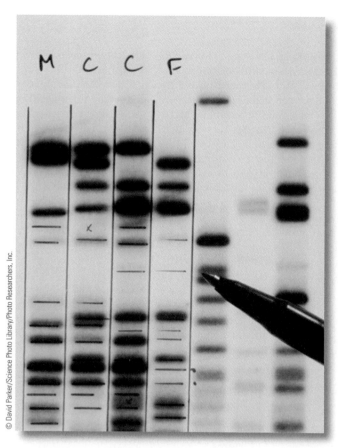

◄ DNA is a unique law enforcement identification tool because every person's DNA is unique (except for that of identical twins). So, just like fingerprints, DNA evidence collected at crime scenes can point the finger at or eliminate a suspect. Here, DNA fingerprints are marked "M" for mother, "C" for child, and "F" for father. Both children share *some* bands with each parent, proving they they're in fact related.

Fingerprints | DNA Strands

◄ **FIGURE 6.2 Fingerprints and DNA Strands**

Source: National Institute of Justice, *Using DNA to Solve Cold Cases* (Washington, DC: NIJ, July 2002), p. 6.

3-D Mug Shot

Sam Reese Sheppard, who has long maintained that his father, Dr. Sam Sheppard, had nothing to do with the killing of Mrs. Sheppard on a July night 45 years ago, might well have wished that a crime-fighting tool now under development at MIT's Lincoln Laboratory existed back in 1954. Because that tool is sophisticated enough that, if it had been employed at the Sheppard crime scene, it would very likely have ferreted out evidence missed by investigators of the day—evidence that might have altered the jury's decision.

The tool in question is a laser-imaging system that provides pictures in three dimensions of target objects using a technique known as Accordion Fringe Interferometry (AFI). Nathan Derr, a physicist and member of the team that invented AFI, says that in the future, detectives might bring a portable version of one of these 3-D cameras to crime scenes, where they could photograph everything from footprints to tooling marks—

scratches or nicks left by tools or other hard objects (Figure 6.3).

The system is quick—producing a picture takes seconds—and its images are sharp: each is accurate to 200 microns, or one-fifth of a millimeter. Further, the device does not damage or contaminate the evidence itself, allowing future detectives the ability to, as environmentalists like to say, "take only photographs."

One of the most promising applications for the new technology is the three-dimensional mug shot. Traditional 2-D mugs, long the standard in suspect identification, have obvious limitations. Authorities typically photograph a suspect from only two angles, under a single lighting condition. A witness to the crime, however, may have caught a fleeting glimpse of the suspect in the dark, or a security camera may have captured his or her blurry image from only one unnatural angle. What if police could access a database of 3-D mug shots that offered them the ability to rotate a suspect's head and adjust the source of light shining on his or her face to simulate different lighting conditions? Well, let's just

▶ **FIGURE 6.3 AFI Prototype**

Source: Rob Meyer, "Killer's Trail," *NOVA* (Boston: WGBH, October 19, 1999). http://www.pbs.org/wgbh/nova/sheppard/mugshot.html. Reprinted with permission of MIT Lincoln Laboratory, Lexington, Massachusetts.

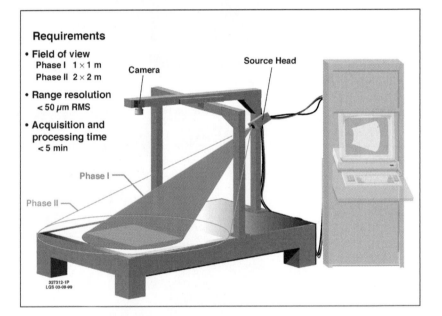

Requirements

- **Field of view**
  Phase I 1 × 1 m
  Phase II 2 × 2 m
- **Range resolution**
  < 50 μm RMS
- **Acquisition and processing time**
  < 5 min

Camera

Source Head

Phase I

Phase II

327312-1P
LGS 03-08-99

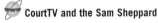

CourtTV and the Sam Sheppard Murder Case: This case was the basis for the TV show and film "The Fugitive." To reach this site go to "Web Links" on your Samaha CJ7 website: http://cj.wadsworth.com/samaha_cj7e.

that don't have nuclei, like hair shafts, bones, and teeth, can be used (6). The bottom line: DNA testing is a "godsend," at least when it comes to matching an evidence sample from a crime scene with a *known* suspect's for the purpose of eliminating (not including) the suspect in a specific case (Tracy and Morgan 2000, 637).

But what about collecting DNA samples for DNA data banks to help solve older cases where the police couldn't identify a suspect (called cold cases)? Samples come from two sources, "donors" (all individuals in particular groups, like all prisoners convicted of certain felonies) and crime scene evidence. DNA

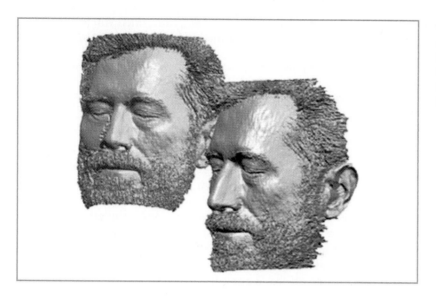

◄ **FIGURE 6.4 3-D Mug Shot**
Source: Rob Meyer, "Killer's Trail," *NOVA* (Boston: WGBH, October 19, 1999). http://www.pbs.org/wgbh/nova/sheppard/mugshot.html. Courtesy of Dimensional Photonics.

say the FBI, for one, is very interested in what Lincoln Laboratory is up to.

Acquiring and processing all the data necessary to render an image precisely in 3-D used to take weeks; using the Lincoln Laboratory technique, a computer can record all of the necessary information in seconds. The subject sits in a dentist's chair facing a camera, all but oblivious to a zebra pattern of near-infrared light illuminating his face. The system takes a rapid series of still images and sends the information to a computer, which runs some novel processing algorithms developed by Dr. Lyle Shirley, head of the group that invented AFI. Within seconds, a 3-D rendering of the subject's head appears on the screen (Figure 6.4). (Presently, the engineers are unable to capture the very back of the head, but they're exploring the possibility of taking two such pictures simultaneously in order to get a full 360° view.)

Measuring the dimensions of a human face with such precision presents unique problems. Minute movements of individual hairs make exact measurement impossible, and because complex shapes such as a person's nose block illumination from the laser source, the source must be rigged so as to ensure optimal coverage of the face. Moreover, any system for real-world usage needs to be lightning fast. (As team member Matt Kavalauskas

notes, "You're not going to get a suspect to hold perfectly still for five seconds.") The Lincoln Laboratory engineers feel confident that with faster cameras now on the market, they will be able to get their device to work in under a second.

Soon, too, they hope to produce such 3-D mug shots in color. Because their system records the x, y, and z coordinates of every point on the face, they feel confident that, with the proper equipment, they should be able to record the color values for every point as well, offering photo-realistic renderings in full, living color. Authorities could install such a useful instrument in police stations, where suspects would supply fingerprints, then sit in a special chair for a 3-D mug.

Source: Rob Meyer, "Killer's Trail," *NOVA* (Boston: WGBH, October 19, 1999). http://www.pbs.org/wgbh/nova/sheppard/mugshot.html.

labs analyze the samples and put them into the data bank. Now, labs can compare every sample in the bank with all the others. Despite huge backlogs of samples waiting to be analyzed (Tracy and Morgan 2000, 643), there have been some stunning successes. In one case, a young guy was raped, shot in the head, and left for dead. A year and a half later, the cops still had no solid leads. Forensic specialists got a sample of the perp's semen, made up a profile, and compared it with the Illinois database. The DNA from the semen matched the DNA of a recently released sex offender (644). Case solved! Supporters say, great, let's do it.

Chief Ronald S. Neubeuer, president of the reform-minded International Association of Chiefs of Police, made this optimistic assessment of DNA's potential:

> I think it's one of the most important developments in forensic science in law enforcement....And in the 21st century, I not only see DNA being a tool to solve crimes, but as a way to insure that innocent people are not being convicted of crimes they did not commit. (Tracy and Morgan 2000, 637)

The problem with this claim (sincere as I'm sure it is) is that it's backed up mostly by anecdotes (admittedly, really powerful anecdotes like the Illinois murderer-rapist). But what does the empirical research say? Is Chief Neubeuer's optimism warranted? When it comes to known suspects, we can be *very* optimistic (assuming the technicians doing the testing and storing do it right). The "cold cases" are another matter; there are questions about the effectiveness of sampling and storing in solving them. The cost of sampling and storing is very high, and there are questions concerning whether they're worth the cost. Let's look at what some of the research has to say.

Keep in mind that before evidence containing DNA can solve crimes, three conditions have to be met:

1. Criminals have to leave evidence containing DNA behind, either at the crime scene or on the victim or the victim's clothes.
2. A trained technician has to search for the evidence.
3. Investigators have to find evidence containing DNA. (Tracy and Morgan 2000, 649)

Solving Crimes The bottom line: DNA data banks aren't going to help much to solve the vast majority of crimes (Chapter 3). Why? First, law enforcement already solves most violent crimes without DNA. Second, in the vast majority of crimes, which are nonviolent, criminals don't leave evidence containing DNA behind (Tracy and Morgan 2000, 650). Third, assuming there is such evidence, police are probably not going to look for it because they don't have the time or the money to spend on the time-consuming expensive search for evidence containing DNA in nonviolent crimes.

Cost-Effectiveness If evidence containing DNA can't help solve the vast majority of nonviolent crimes and law enforcement is already solving most violent crimes without it, is it worth the cost? The answer is important because DNA testing is definitely here to stay and shows every sign of expanding to include more groups of donors, like all prisoners, everyone convicted of a felony, everyone convicted of any crime, or everyone arrested for a felony or any crime.

Eventually, we'll have to decide at what point DNA testing (and mining the data for "hits") isn't worth the cost, especially if successful hits run few and far between. Here's the way Tracy and Morgan (2000, 668) see how the future of data mining for unknown suspects might look:

> Convicted sex-offenders? No problem here. They're all a bunch of sick recidivists anyway. All convicted felons? Sure, why not? Maybe they'll think twice next time. All people arrested? Well, it's a little tougher here, but sure, the cops are good guys and they can't arrest you without probable cause anyway. Everyone at birth or when we get our driver's license renewed? Well, maybe this is what is needed to end crime altogether. After all, if everybody knows that their DNA is on file and, consequently, that they will be caught every time for every crime, then no one would commit crimes.

But what about two other parts of the cost-effectiveness debate—loss of privacy and misuse of DNA data banks? Former Attorney General Janet Reno asked a national commission to study whether it was legal to collect DNA samples from everyone arrested, instead of just the convicted sex offenders and violent felons, which federal law and some state laws allowed (Tracy and Morgan 2000, 669). Some say we should collect a sample of everyone's DNA. It seems like state legislatures have thought about privacy and abuses in their statutes. Here are some database issues and state statutes regarding them:

1. *Who has access to these databases?* In most states, access is limited to law enforcement agencies, court proceedings, and to a defendant in connection with the defense of the charge(s) that gave rise to the DNA sample.
2. *What security measures are commonly utilized?* Most states have penalties designed to combat unauthorized use and tampering.
3. *Is reasonable force allowed to obtain a sample?* Missouri is one of only eight states that allow the use of reasonable or necessary force to obtain a sample from uncooperative subjects.
4. *Who pays the fees for analyzing DNA?* More than a dozen states allow for making offenders pay for tests.
5. *Does the statute allow for expunction of DNA records?* Over three dozen states have included expunction provisions expressly related to the DNA database. (Tracy and Morgan 2000, 683–684)

Tracy and Morgan (2000, 685–686) conclude their analysis of DNA this way:

> We have no quarrel whatsoever with the earliest and most basic of DNA applications in the criminal law: known suspect testing and post-conviction relief. We agree that there is unparalleled value to the use of DNA testing to match a particular suspect's DNA with that extracted from trace evidence left behind at a crime scene. Similarly, can there be a more justice-oriented application for DNA than to use its exculpatory capabilities to exonerate persons who were wrongfully accused and convicted? . . . Each of these DNA applications should be used as extensively as possible, not only as effective crime control measures, but more importantly, as definitive tests of whether an accused, or even a previously convicted person, is actually innocent.
>
> Beyond these two applications of DNA testing . . . , our inquiry concerning the spreading craze over DNA databases as a crime control measure does not offer similar support. In fact, the analysis . . . of the best available government crime data raises serious concerns that DNA databases are proliferating and becoming ever more inclusive, and the costs associated with collecting, testing, and storing the information are rising into the hundreds of millions of dollars. These developments are occurring all across the country despite the absence of convincing evidence that the DNA mining process will strike gold as proponents have claimed.

COMPSTAT (Computerized Statistics)

"I can cut crime in half in any city in this country," Police Chief Jack Manion announced as his first words in the 2001 series opener of CBS's cop series, *The District*. In the series, the aggressive Chief Manion emphasized using innovative tactics to reduce crime. At the end of the first show, Manion unveiled COMPSTAT, a crime-mapping tool that enabled the fictional Washington, D.C. police department to view crime patterns.

The District was fiction, but **COMPSTAT** is a real-life crime-mapping program created by the New York Police Department in 1994. COMPSTAT may seem like it's only a technology, but in reality it consists of five components: computerized crime-mapping technology, a management style, response tactics, follow-up, and accountability. It has spread to other (mostly large) departments. Almost 60 percent of departments with 500 or more sworn officers have implemented COMPSTAT; less than 10 percent of departments with fewer than 100 sworn officers have done so (Weisburd, Mastrofski, Greenspan, and Willis 2004, 1). Using maps to display crime information isn't new, but it's growing fast, thanks to desktop (as opposed to mainframe) computers, user-friendly, cheap software, and the Violent

COMPSTAT consists of five components: computerized crime-mapping technology, a management style, response tactics, follow-up, and accountability

Crime Control and Law Enforcement Act (1994, Sections 30202–30208). Computerized searching has dramatically increased the speed and efficiency of crime mapping.

Let's look at COMPSTAT's use in New York City because most departments follow this version closely, hiring former NYPD experts either to help them set it up or permanently as chiefs or other administrators (Dewan 2004, 1A). The description that follows is based mostly on the NYPD's COMPSTAT website page, "COMPSTAT Process" (NYPD n.d.).

Under COMPSTAT, power over discretionary decision making shifted down to precinct commanders because they're in a position to understand better than headquarters the needs of their community. They're also in a better position than beat cops to understand the policies and the dynamics of their precincts. With expanded power goes increased accountability.

Now, let's look at how computerized statistics fit in with this downward shift in power and accountability for crime and quality-of-life control. Every week, all precincts compile a statistical summary of the week's crime complaints, arrest and summons activity, and a write-up of "significant cases," crime patterns, and police activities. The data also include the specific time and location of crimes and enforcement activities. The data are forwarded to the chief of the COMPSTAT unit where they're collated, loaded into a citywide data bank, and analyzed by COMPSTAT software. The analysis generates a weekly COMPSTAT Report that includes week-to-date, prior 30-day, and year-to-date activities, with comparisons to previous years' activities. The report ranks each precinct in each complaint and arrest category. With this information in hand, precinct commanders and top executives can see emerging and established crime patterns, as well as deviations and anomalies. They can also compare commands.

The department conducts a weekly "COMPSTAT Meeting," which provides a forum for commanders to tell top executives about the problems in their precincts and to share crime reduction tactics with other commanders. The meeting also allows top executives to monitor what's happening in the precincts; to evaluate the skills and effectiveness of commanders; and to distribute resources to "reduce crime and improve police performance." The Weekly Report and the COMPSTAT Meeting don't just focus on the FBI Crime Index offenses (Chapter 3). They also include the number of shooting incidents and gun arrests and arrests and summonses for quality-of-life offenses (public drinking, public urination, panhandling, loud radios, prostitution, and disorderly conduct).

The meeting is held in the department's hi-tech Command and Control Center, which features its impressive computerized "pin mapping." This displays crime, arrest, and quality-of-life data in several visual formats (comparative charts, graphs, and tables). Through MAPINFO software and other computer technology, executives can access the COMPSTAT database, and project a precinct map, depicting an array of combinations of crime and/or arrest locations or crime "hot spots" onto the center's large projection screens. They can also project comparative visuals simultaneously. These visuals allow commanders and top executives to "instantly identify and explore trends...."

At the meetings, commanders can expect to be called on at random to make a presentation about once a month. During the presentation, top executive staff members grill commanders about crimes and arrests, as well as initiatives they've taken to reduce crime and enforce quality-of-life offenses. Commanders "are expected to demonstrate a detailed knowledge of the crime and quality of life problems...within their own commands and to develop innovative and flexible tactics to address them."

The NYPD "COMPSTAT Process" concludes on this very positive note:

> The process described here truly represents a revolution in the way police agencies are managed and has been adapted for use in many other law enforcement agencies throughout the nation and overseas. Although the process has been revolutionary, it is not static.

The New York City Police Department will continue to adjust, refine and enhance the process to respond swiftly and effectively to the changing demands we encounter in the "Greatest City in the World." (NYPD n.d.)

You can understand the pride expressed here (and also claims not included about how COMPSTAT has reduced crime and improved the quality of life in New York City). After all, New York City's crime rates have fallen dramatically since COMPSTAT; and, by all accounts, New York is now a beautiful, clean, and orderly city to visit and live in. But there's no systematic, independent empirical research verifying COMPSTAT's impact in all this. The whole nation experienced a "crime bust" beginning in the mid-1990s (Chapter 3), and that continues to this day. Most places didn't then (and still don't) have COMPSTAT. Although nearly all the press and police opinion is positive, there are opposing opinions over COMPSTAT. This chapter's Make Your Decision presents opposing views of COMPSTAT.

COP Report: Crime Analysis in America—Findings and Recommendations: In 2000, the University of South Alabama's Center for Public Policy conducted an extensive study of crime analysis operations in American law enforcement agencies. To reach this site go to "Web Links" on your Samaha CJ7 website: http://cj.wadsworth.com/samaha_cj7e.

MAKE YOUR DECISION *Are the Streets "Less Mean" Because of COMPSTAT?*

YES

Ten years ago, a lieutenant would have been scoffed at or reprimanded for going door to door on Mott Street in search of unlicensed produce vendors...and kebab carts parked too close to the curb: "Don't you have something better to do? Shouldn't you be out catching bad guys?" But this is the job in one Manhattan precinct, 10 years after crime in the city began its precipitous drop. All but gone are the chalk outlines, the cooling bodies draped in plastic. The command to "move along, folks, nothing to see here" has taken on a new meaning: there truly is nothing to see. Instead, police officers pursue a variety of tasks that just a decade ago, when 2,000 New Yorkers were killed each year, would have seemed unimaginably minor. The drop in crime has reshaped the face of policing in ways small and large, obvious and surprising.

At the heart of the changes is COMPSTAT, a means of statistically analyzing where and when crimes are occurring, a new philosophy that transformed crime-fighting in 1994 and is, today, as deeply embedded in the identity of the Police Department as its badges. COMPSTAT is the boss who never goes home, never takes a day off. COMPSTAT decides when officers sleep. A little spike in a precinct's numbers sends squads of officers to the night shift. "COMPSTAT's like religion," Lieutenant Fanale says. "It's a really, really good idea, like religion....To spend months with the men and women of the Fifth Precinct is to see how COMPSTAT and the changes it has wrought have altered the lives of those who protect the city....

Violent crime in the precinct has dropped 70 percent since 1993, the first year recorded by the COMPSTAT system. It is Captain William Matusiak's job to keep that number down, and make it even lower. He is the precinct's 23rd commanding officer since 1969, when its official liaison to the Asian community, Shuck Seid, 78, began keeping track. Across from Captain Matusiak's desk is the wipe-off board of the week's crimes, a more important view of the precinct than a picture window twice its size: assault, robbery, grand larceny, auto theft, burglary, rape and murder. The last two are less frequent than parades. This year's only killing so far was on Jan. 17. Xiang Ving Jiang was shot to death on East Broadway. At this time in 1994, there were nine.

...[Matusiak] puffs a cigar and looks at a little spike of seven grand larcenies, defined as thefts of goods worth more than $1,000. "No good," he says. "No good."...He thinks about what it must have been like to be the commanding officer of the precinct when he became a beat officer 20 years ago: "It would have been a much nicer job. They worried about crime, but they didn't worry about crime like I worry about crime. They worried about summonses, corruption. They weren't so focused on reducing crime. That's something COMPSTAT did. I

mean, don't get me wrong. It's a good thing, but it's an odd thing. I was on vacation last week. I was on the phone for hours, worrying about every complaint report," he says. "I guess I'm still going through that insecurity. Am I worthy? Am I doing enough?"...

Captain Matusiak marked his first anniversary as commanding officer last week. The tug-of-war with COMPSTAT continues: This week, he will try to keep the number of crimes below 24, the figure for the same week last year....

Source: Michael Wilson, "The Precinct Life in the Fifth: Policing a City Where Streets Are Less Mean," *New York Times,* August 8, 2004. Copyright © 2004 by The New York Times Co. Reprinted by permission.

WE NEED MORE INFORMATION

A Bronx baseball bat attack in which the victim suffered a fracture was wrongly classified as a misdemeanor, which could have allowed the suspect to walk free, *Newsday* has learned. The error, which prompted sharp questioning during a recent Police Department COMPSTAT meeting, comes at a time when the department has been accused by critics, including its unions, of downgrading felonies to misdemeanors to make the crime rate appear lower. According to sources familiar with COMPSTAT, the computerized system used to track crime trends, it also highlights

▲ Using maps to display crime information isn't new, but it's growing fast thanks to desktop (as opposed to mainframe) computers, user-friendly, cheap software, and the Violent Crime Control and Law Enforcement Act of 1994. Almost 60 percent of departments with 500 or more sworn officers have implemented COMPSTAT. Here, an officer examines a report of crime mapping statistics.

the difference in attention paid to felonies and misdemeanors and how public safety is potentially affected.

The incident took place in the 40th Precinct, where crime is up 9.94 percent for the year. The precinct covers Mott Haven and is commanded by Deputy Insp. Kevin Walsh. At an April 1 COMPSTAT meeting—a gathering where precinct brass are grilled about crime in their commands—Walsh was questioned about why the bat attack, in which the victim suffered a fracture, was classified as a misdemeanor. Assaults are classified as felonies if they result in a serious physical injury or if a weapon is used.

At some point after the assault, the details of which were not immediately clear, the suspect was taken into custody, but the detective on the case did not know that because a "want card" was never filed on the suspect. Such a card, typically filed in felony cases, lets police know that the person named on the card is suspected of committing a crime and should be held. "The squad noted that if the [report] was properly classified as a felony, a want card would have been dropped and the perp would have been found right away," according to an internal police memo obtained by *Newsday*.

The details of the suspect's arrest were not clear, but officers eventually determined he was wanted in the assault case and kept him in custody. Walsh referred *Newsday* to the department's press office, whose chief spokesman, Deputy Commissioner Paul Browne, stressed that the error was immediately rectified and the suspect never left police custody. Browne also called Walsh "an outstanding commander with an outstanding record of honest, accurate crime reporting."

The incident comes amid accusations by the unions representing police officers and sergeants that the department has pressured commanders to "cook the books" to make the crime rate appear lower. *Newsday* has reported that more than 1,000 crime reports filed in the 112th Precinct in Forest Hills last year are being reviewed under suspicion that felonies such as grand larceny were filed as misdemeanors. *Newsday* has also reported that some officers from the 50th Precinct in Riverdale contend their former commander harassed some crime victims and regularly sought to downgrade felonies. Since *Newsday*'s story, 50th Precinct supervisors have ordered the room where copies of all criminal complaints are stored to be locked, according to one police source familiar with precinct operations.

Source: Leonard Levitt and Rocco Parascandola, "NYPD Crime Stats; Charge Bungle in Bronx," *Newsday* (April 30, 2004), p. A16. Reprinted with permission.

QUESTIONS

1. List all the arguments in favor of COMPSTAT in the first excerpt.
2. List the evidence backing up the arguments.
3. List all the criticisms made of COMPSTAT in the second excerpt.
4. List all the evidence backing up the criticism.
5. Write your own evaluation of COMPSTAT. Rely on the main text section and the two excerpts to explain your evaluation. Include what more you'd need to know before you would feel confident in your evaluation.

How Law Enforcement Agencies Can Make Geographic Information Technologies Work for Them: A geographic information system (GIS) is a powerful technological tool for municipal police departments and other law enforcement agencies. Typical GIS users in law enforcement include crime analysts, computerized crime records management personnel, police executives, shift supervisors, patrol sergeants, and even patrol officers. To reach this site go to "Web Links" on your Samaha CJ7 website: http://cj.wadsworth.com/samaha_cj7e.

Chapter Summary

▶ Two reactive strategies have dominated policing for 150 years. The first, preventive patrol, still consumes about 90 percent of police time. During most of the remaining time, patrol officers conduct preliminary investigations and detectives conduct follow-up investigations.

▶ A combination of dissatisfaction with the ineffectiveness of traditional patrol and investigation during the 1960s crime boom and research showing the limits to the one-size-fits-all approach of traditional patrols and investigations led to the adoption of proactive crime-attack strategies. Empirical research provides some tentative support for the effectiveness of some crime-attack strategies tailored to specific crimes like cracking down on gun violence, shutting down illegal drug "hot spots," and arresting domestic partners for assault.

▶ Community-oriented policing (COP) based on police-community partnerships and shifting power down from top police executives to commanders in local police precincts is very popular. Problem-oriented policing (POP), almost always practiced in community policing departments and also popular, is based on the idea that you can't solve problems of crime and neighborhood quality of life by responding to single incidents of crime and disorder. So police and the community work together to identify, analyze, respond to, and assess the effectiveness of solving problems of crime and disorder.

▶ It's not clear to what extent departments who've subscribed to community- and problem-oriented policing actually *practice* them. Optimists say they're part of a quiet revolu-tion in policing; pessimists say you can't change the very nature of policing, which is the monopoly on and use of coercive force (captured in the metaphor of war to describe the nature of policing).

▶ A couple of things are clear: Most departments that have adopted COP and POP haven't shifted their priorities away from crime control to order maintenance and community service. And departments seem to rely more on SWAT units than on COP and POP. But revolutions take time, and it's still very early in the revolution; so it's really too early to pass judgment on whether the nature of policing is changing.

▶ The list of technological advances affecting law enforcement is very long. To mention only a few, it started with fingerprints, the telephone, the car, and the two-way radio, and it now includes DNA testing, computerized statistical crime analysis, and 3-D "mug shots." The claims and the anecdotes "proving" their effectiveness have always been high, but there isn't enough reliable empirical evidence to back up the claims that they control crime and reduce cost effectively. Also, it's still not clear how much they invade privacy and liberty.

Key Terms

one-size-fits-all approach to crime control, p. 186
crime-attack strategies, p. 186
community policing strategy, p. 186
preventive patrol, p. 187
differential response approach, p. 187
preliminary investigation, p. 192
incident reports, p. 192

follow-up investigation, p. 193
"hot spots" patrol, p. 194
police crackdowns, p. 194
displacement effect, p. 194
field interrogation, p. 195
community-oriented policing (COP), p. 199
problem-oriented policing (POP), p. 199

DNA, p. 208
CODIS (Combined DNA Index System), p. 208
COMPSTAT, p. 213

Web Resources

Go to http://cj.wadsworth.com/samaha_cj7e for a wealth of online resources related to your book. Take a "pre-test" and "post-test" for each chapter in order to help master the material. Check out the *Web Links* to access the websites mentioned in the text, as well as many others. Explore the *Decision Points* flagged in the margins of the text, as well as the *Concept Builders* for additional insights. You can also access recent perspectives by clicking on *CJ in the News* and *Terrorism Update* under *Course Resources*.

Search Online with InfoTrac College Edition

For additional information, explore InfoTrac College Edition, your online library. Go to http://cj.wadsworth.com/samaha_cj7e to access InfoTrac College Edition from your book's website.

Use the passcode that came with your book. You will find InfoTrac College Edition exercises and a list of key words for further research.

© Spencer Grant/Photo Edit

CHAPTER 7

Police and the Law

FACT *or* FICTION?

▶ The authors of our Bill of Rights weren't very clever when they set up a system that favored criminals' rights over victims' rights.

▶ Not all searches backed up by probable cause are reasonable.

▶ Stops and frisks are reasonable as long as they turn up evidence of crime.

▶ In most cases, proving a crime was committed is easier than identifying the perpetrator.

▶ The use of force out of malice or prejudice turns an otherwise reasonable seizure into an unreasonable seizure.

▶ Unfortunately, most police departments "don't know how" to analyze properly the information they've collected.

▶ Most police misconduct is also a crime.

▶ The exclusionary rule throws out "good" evidence because of "bad" police behavior.

No Court "Control" Over Police?

What the courts offer to police is the opportunity, if they wish to take advantage of it, to seek the state's capacity to punish. In effect, the courts say to the police that if they wish to make use of that capacity, they must demonstrate to the courts that they have followed certain procedures in order to do so.... Only on those occasions that the police wish to employ the state's capacity to punish do courts and police have any relationship of any kind. Despite the enormous growth in police law in the past quarter century, the courts have no more "control" over the police than local supermarkets have over the diets of those who shop there....

Empirically, however, we know two major things about the terms of this relationship between the police, the law, and the courts. The first is that the felony arrest rate for patrol officers is very, very, low even in areas in which felony offense rates are very high. For example...40 percent of the 156 officers assigned to a very high crime area in New York City did not make a single arrest during the entire year under study.... The second empirical fact...has to do with the frequency with which police choose not arrest when they have every legal right and all the necessary evidence to do so, or, alternatively, choose to make arrests when they have no legal grounds to do so whatsoever.... Collectively, they constitute the major empirical discovery of police research...: the discovery of selective enforcement and the enormous influence on police discretion of such things as suspect demeanor, complainant preferences, and a host of other factors that have nothing to do with "the law."

—CARL B. KLOCKARS, police expert (1991b, 532)

Police officers usually don't take advantage of the opportunity to bring cases to prosecutors, as discussed by Professor Klockars in the opening quotation. One year, half the officers assigned to a high-crime neighborhood in New York City didn't make a single felony arrest; 68 percent made only three. Sociologist Donald Black (1980) found officers usually don't arrest suspected violent felons even when they've got plenty of evidence. So police, the gatekeepers to the criminal justice system, usually don't open the gates to criminal prosecution. Instead, they exercise their discretionary decision making against starting the formal criminal justice process. This shouldn't surprise you, and don't think it means police aren't doing their job. Remember, maintaining order and providing 24/7 services take up most of their time (Chapter 5).

It may not seem like it from what you hear, read in the news, and see on television, but contacts of any kind with the police are unusual, and contacts involving criminal suspects are extremely rare (Figure 7.1). This is one of the findings in *The Police-Public Contact Survey II* (PPCSII) (BJS February 2001). In the PPC-SII, the U.S. Department of Justice, Bureau of Justice Statistics (BJS), surveyed

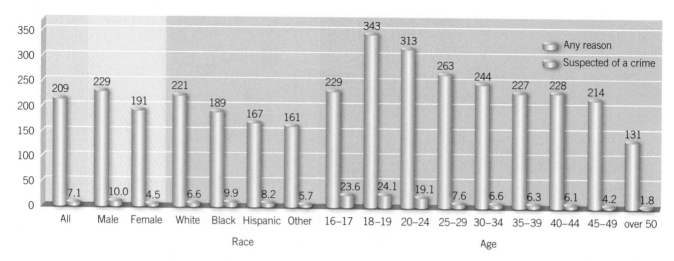

a sample of individuals over 16 in the National Crime Victim Survey (NCVS), 1999 (Chapter 2). The sample represents fairly the gender, race, ethnicity, and age distribution among the 209,350,600 individuals over 16 in the United States.

▲ FIGURE 7.1 Contacts between the Police and the Public (Per 1,000 People Ages 16 and Over)
Source: Bureau of Justice Statistics, *Contacts between Police and the Public, Findings from the 1999 Survey* (Washington, DC: Bureau of Justice Statistics, February 2001), p. 5, Figure 1.

Law Enforcement and the Constitution

Several years ago, a Japanese police reporter took my criminal procedure class. He told me how amazed he was at one difference between policing in Japan and in the United States: "In Japan, if I'm sitting on a park bench minding my own business, and a police officer comes up to me, and asks me to come with her, *I* have to justify to her why I shouldn't do it. In your class, I've learned that in the same situation, *she* has to justify why to me." What he was referring to is that under our constitutional system, police can't on a whim or a hunch (the law calls it "mere suspicion") interfere with our rights to come and go as we please and to be free from physical invasions of our bodies, our houses, and our "stuff" (Table 7.1). They have to back up their interferences with facts. We call this requirement the **objective basis** for official searches, seizures, interrogation, and identification procedures. Of course, checking out suspicious people and circumstances; gathering evidence of crime; and apprehending suspects is very important business.

objective basis government officials have to back up with facts their encroachments on liberty and privacy

▼ TABLE 7.1 The Bill of Rights and Police Powers

Amendment	Rights Protected
Fourth Amendment	The right of the people to be secure in their persons, houses, papers, and effects against unreasonable searches and seizures shall not be violated, and no warrants shall issue but upon probable cause, supported by oath or affirmation, and particularly describing the place to be searched and the persons or things to be seized.
Fifth Amendment	No person . . . shall be compelled in any criminal case to be a witness against himself, nor be deprived of life, liberty, or property, without due process of law. . . .
Sixth Amendment	In all criminal prosecutions, the accused shall enjoy the right . . . to be confronted with the witnesses against him . . . and to have the assistance of counsel for his defense.
Fourteenth Amendment	No state shall make or enforce any law which shall abridge the privileges or immunities of citizens of the United States; nor shall any state deprive any person of life, liberty, or property, without due process of law; nor deny to any person within its jurisdiction the equal protection of the laws.

FindLaw.com: Each amendment is reviewed in detail along with relevant case law. To reach this site go to "Web Links" on your Samaha CJ7 website: http://cj.wadsworth.com/samaha_cj7e.

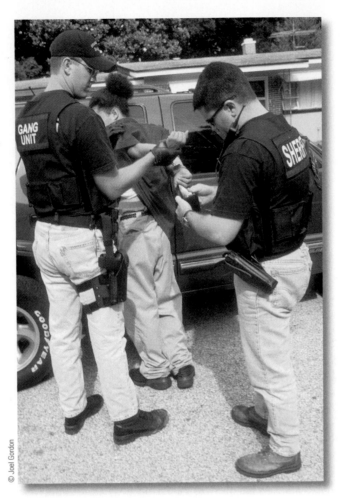

© Joel Gordon

► The framers of the Bill of Rights didn't ban *all* seizures, only *unreasonable* ones. A reasonable arrest under the Fourth Amendment allows officers to use the amount of force necessary to get and keep control of a suspect who they have probable cause to arrest. If these two Gang Unit officers have probable cause to arrest this suspect, then it looks like they're using reasonable force to make the arrest.

The framers of our Bill of Rights, while protecting criminal suspects' rights, also left plenty of play in the joints for informal decision making by individual officers to enforce the criminal law. The framers were very clever: they didn't ban *all* government searches and seizures, only *unreasonable* ones; they didn't ban *all* confessions, only *compelled* ones. The significance of the many police cases that come to local courts, and the few that wind up in the U.S. Supreme Court, boils down to maintaining the balance between the need for enough government power to control crime against the liberty and privacy rights of individuals.

The main (but as you'll soon learn, not the only) objective of searches and seizures, police interrogation, and other activities like identification procedures is to find and collect evidence. It's no exaggeration to say that information drives and controls the formal criminal justice process. It's only natural that the police would like to control the discovery and the use of this information. Suspects and defendants, of course, would like to manage if, when, what, and how the police get the information. And innocent people, understandably, don't want to be arrested, searched, put in jail, interrogated, or stand in lineups unless the police can objectively justify their right to interfere with their liberty, privacy, and property.

Let's look at police actions that call for balancing government power to control crime and individuals' right to be let alone by the government. These include making arrests and other seizures of individuals; conducting searches of persons, houses, and "stuff"; interrogating suspects; and managing procedures regarding eyewitnesses' identification of strangers. Later in the chapter, we'll examine the police use of force, racial profiling, and police misconduct.

Arrest

When police officers arrest you, it's a Fourth Amendment seizure, so it has to be reasonable (Table 7.1). What's a reasonable arrest? The answer boils down to three elements:

1. *Probable cause.* Officers must have an objective basis for the arrest.
2. *Reasonable force.* Officers can't use excessive force to make an arrest. (See the "Police Use of Force" section.)
3. *Warrant.* Officers have to get a warrant before they enter a house to arrest someone.

The Definition of Arrest

Police actions can affect our right to come and go as we please in several ways that don't amount to arrest. **Arrest** means to take you into custody without your consent. So an officer who comes up to you and asks, "Who are you and what are you doing here?" hasn't arrested you. But the officer who comes up to you and says, "You're under arrest," takes you to the station, books you, takes your "mug shot," and locks you up overnight *has* arrested you. In the first example, you're free to decline to answer—and even to walk away. (You may feel the pressure of a moral and civic duty to stay and answer, but you're not *legally* bound to.) In the second example, the Fourth Amendment ban on unreasonable seizures protects you, meaning the officer has to back up her actions with probable cause *and* use only reasonable force in taking you into custody.

> **arrest** taking an individual into custody without her consent

Whether an arrest is reasonable comes down to two elements: the objective basis (probable cause) and the manner of the arrest (the use of arrest warrants and/or reasonable force). Let's look at the elements of probable cause and the warrant requirement (we'll discuss the use of force later on in the chapter).

DECISION POINT

When did the police arrest Royer?

Click on this Decision Point at http://cj.wadsworth.com/samaha_cj7e to explore the case *Florida v. Royer*.

Probable Cause The Fourth Amendment says arrests are unreasonable unless officers back them up with probable cause. **Probable cause to arrest** means there are enough facts for a reasonable officer in light of her expertise to believe the person she is arresting has committed, is committing, or is about to commit a crime. What kind of facts are needed to make the cause for the arrest "probable"? It definitely means officers need more than a hunch, and it definitely doesn't mean they need proof beyond a reasonable doubt (Chapter 10). Practically speaking, it means officers have to have enough facts that would justify detaining a suspect long enough to give prosecutors time to decide if there's enough evidence to charge. (The leading U.S. Supreme Court case is old but still cited frequently. See an excerpt in the In Focus box "Was There Probable Cause to Arrest?")

> **probable cause to arrest** facts and circumstances that would lead a police officer in the light of her training and experience to believe that a crime has been, is being, or is about to be committed and that the person suspected has committed it

Arrest Warrants The vast majority of arrests are reasonable without warrants. There's one big exception: entering homes to arrest suspects. Why? According to the U.S. Supreme Court, entering homes is the "chief evil" the Fourth Amendment protects against, and "a principal protection against unnecessary intrusions into private dwellings is the warrant requirement imposed by the Fourth Amendment on agents of the government who seek to enter the home for purposes of search or arrest (*Welsh v. Wisconsin* 1980, 748).

In one of the leading cases, *Riddick v. N.Y.* (1980), officers had probable cause to believe Obie Riddick had committed two armed robberies. They went to the Queens house where he was living and knocked on the door. When his young son opened the door, they saw Riddick sitting on a bed, went in, and arrested him. It was an unreasonable arrest ruled the U.S. Supreme Court. Why? Because the officers didn't have an arrest warrant. According to the majority of the Court:

CONCEPT BUILDER

Visit http://cj.wadsworth.com/samaha_cj7e for an interactive exploration of **probable cause.**

Was There Probable Cause to Arrest?

FACTS

Marsh, a federal narcotics agent with 29 years' experience, was stationed at Denver. Hereford, an informant for about six months, was paid for giving information to Marsh about illegal drug trafficking. The information was always accurate and reliable. Hereford told Marsh that James Draper "was peddling narcotics to several addicts." Four days later, on September 7, Hereford told Marsh "that Draper had gone to Chicago the day before (September 6) by train; that he was going to bring back 3 ounces of heroin; and that he'd return to Denver by train either on the morning of the 8th or 9th of September. Hereford described Draper to Marsh this way: He's a Black man with a light brown complexion, 27 years old, and 5 feet 8 inches tall; he weighs about 160 pounds; he'll be wearing a light colored raincoat, brown slacks, and black shoes; he'll be carrying "a tan zipper bag"; and he habitually "walks real fast."

On the morning of September 8, Marsh and a Denver police officer went to the Denver Union Station and saw a person who matched the exact description Hereford had given Marsh. Marsh and the police officer, overtook, stopped, and arrested him.

OPINION

The crucial question for us is whether the facts and circumstances gave Marsh "probable cause" within the meaning of the Fourth Amendment to believe Draper had committed or was committing a violation of the narcotics laws....

"In dealing with probable cause...as the very name implies, we deal with probabilities. These are not technical; they are the factual and practical considerations of everyday life on which reasonable and prudent men, not legal technicians, act."...We believe that, under the facts and circumstances here, Marsh had probable cause to believe that Draper was committing a violation of the laws of the United States relating to narcotic drugs at the time he arrested him.

DISSENT

...The officers had no evidence—apart from the mere word of an informer—that Draper was committing a crime. The fact that Draper walked fast and carried a tan zipper bag was not evidence of any crime. The officers knew nothing except what they had been told by the informer. If they went to a magistrate to get a warrant of arrest and relied solely on the report of the informer, it is not conceivable to me that one would be granted. For they could not present to the magistrate any of the facts which the informer may have had. They could swear only to the fact that the informer had made the accusation. They could swear to no evidence that lay in their own knowledge. They could present, on information and belief, no facts which the informer disclosed. No magistrate could issue a warrant on the mere word of an officer, without more....

Source: Draper v. U.S., 358 U.S. 307 (1959).

The Fourth Amendment protects the individual's privacy in a variety of settings. In none is the zone of privacy more clearly defined than when bounded by the unambiguous physical dimensions of an individual's home—a zone that finds its roots in clear and specific constitutional terms: "The right of the people to be secure in their...houses...shall not be violated." That language unequivocally establishes the proposition that "at the very core of the Fourth Amendment stands the right of a man to retreat into his own home and there be free from unreasonable governmental intrusion."...The Fourth Amendment has drawn a firm line at the entrance to the house. Absent [an emergency], that threshold may not reasonably be crossed without a warrant. (589–590)

Searches

The right against unreasonable searches is ancient. In 57 B.C., Cicero spoke of citizens' homes as "sacred." Under Byzantine Emperor Justinian's Code of A.D. 533, a "freeman could not be summoned from his house" because it's "everyone's safest place, his refuge, and his shelter." In 1505, John Fineux, chief justice of the English Court of King's, held "the house of a man is for him his castle and his defense" (Cuddihy 1990, xc–xcvi).

But the *practice* of government searches is as much a part of history as the lofty rhetoric claiming the *right* against unreasonable searches. Most of the early controversy over searches in England was about religion and politics. When Catholics were in power, they ransacked the houses of Protestants to find proof of their blasphemy; when Protestants were in power, they did the same to Catholics' houses. When subjects criticized the kings and queens, their ministers ransacked the subjects' houses looking for "seditious libels." (Seditious libels are written criticisms of the government.) No one cared much about the rights of ordinary criminals—the subject of our book; the power to search them and their "houses, papers, and effects" (to use the words of the Fourth Amendment) was pretty much unlimited.

In the 1700s, the numbers of seditious libels increased because of the low respect the English had for their imported German kings (the four Georges). The kings granted general warrants (blank checks good for the life of the king issued to officials) authorizing their officers to break into shops and homes to look for seditious libels. General warrants also became a weapon in the war against smuggling a growing list of taxable goods—most of them very popular, like salt, beer, and cider—into the American colonies. The use of general warrants provoked William Pitt in 1777 to speak the most famous words ever uttered against the power of government to search the houses of its people:

> The poorest man may in his cottage bid defiance to all the forces of the Crown. It may be frail; its roof may shake; the wind may blow through it; the storm may enter; but the king of England may not enter; all his force dare not cross the threshold of the ruined tenement without a lawfull warrant. (Hall 1993, 4)

In the British American colonies, the great colonial trial lawyer James Otis argued a famous general warrant case in Boston in 1760. He claimed the general warrants were illegal; only searches with specific dates, naming the places or persons to be searched and seized, and based on probable cause were lawful where free people lived. The future president John Adams was at the trial. Many years later Adams recalled how moved he was by Otis's words: "There was the Child Independence born" (Smith 1962, 56). Hostility to general warrants led to the adoption of the Fourth Amendment. But remember the opposition to these warrants was about their use in religion, politics, and taxation—not to what we call ordinary crime.

The Fourth Amendment "unreasonable searches" clause limits the power of law enforcement to get information to control crime, but it still leaves the government with plenty of power. According to former prosecutor John Wesley Hall, Jr. (1993):

> The raw power held by a police officer conducting a search is enormous. An officer wielding a search warrant has the authority of the law to forcibly enter one's home and search for evidence. The officer can enter at night and wake you from your sleep, roust you from bed, rummage in your drawers and papers and upend your entire home.... The power of an officer conducting a stop or warrantless search is also quite intense. Nothing can be more intimidating or frightening to a citizen than being stopped by the police and being asked or told to submit to a search. (ix)

The Definition of Search

Wherever people have a reasonable expectation of privacy, government intrusions are searches. Remember, the Fourth Amendment only bans *unreasonable* searches. What makes up a reasonable expectation of privacy is left to the courts to decide on a case-by-case basis. In *Katz v. U.S.* (1967), FBI agents bugged a public telephone booth to listen to bookie Charles Katz giving odds on college football games in his gambling operation. According to the U.S. Supreme Court, "One who occupies a public telephone booth, shuts the door, and pays the toll that permits him to place a call is entitled to assume that his conversation is not being intercepted."

This probably sounds to you like a boost for privacy (we sure thought so way back then), but the U.S. Supreme Court quickly let us know that reasonable expectation of privacy is very narrow. According to the Court, none of the following

► **DECISION**
POINT ◄

Were they plain-view searches?

Click on this Decision Point at http://cj.wadsworth.com/samaha_cj7e to explore the issue.

actions is a search, so the decision to undertake them is left to the discretion of individual law enforcement officers:

- Looking for evidence in plain view
- Obtaining bank records, including savings and checking accounts and loans (*U.S. v. Miller* 1976)
- Getting a list of all numbers dialed from or to a specific telephone (*Smith v. Maryland* 1979)
- Going through trash looking for criminal evidence (*California v. Greenwood* 1988)
- Wiring a paid informant for sound so law enforcement officers can listen to conversations (*U.S. v. White* 1971)

According to the plain-view doctrine, it's not a search if officers' discovery of evidence meets three conditions:

1. Officers discover the evidence by means of their ordinary senses—sight, smell, hearing, and touch.
2. Officers have a right to be where they are and are doing what they have a right to do.
3. Officers discover the evidence inadvertently.

Applying these conditions, the U.S. Supreme Court decided that it was a plain-view search when officers stopped a car for running a red light and saw a plastic bag of marijuana on the front seat. But it wasn't a plain-view search when officers used a high-powered telescope to see into the apartment of a suspect hundreds of feet away or turned a TV set upside down to get its serial number and check to see if it was stolen. Why? According to the Court, the first was a plain-view search because officers discovered the marijuana by their ordinary sense of sight while they were doing what they had a right to do in a place they had a right to be. In the second case, officers relied on a technological enhancement of their sense of sight to look into the apartment. In the third case, the discovery wasn't accidental: they had to upend the TV to get the serial number.

In *Kyllo v. U.S.* (2001), the Court decided it was a search when officers parked outside Danny Kyllo's house and employed a thermal imaging device to detect heat lamps he used to grow marijuana in his house. By a bare majority of 5–4, the Court decided the home is a special place where the reasonable expectation of privacy is so high officers need a warrant to sit outside and point the device at someone's home (Chapter 1).

The Meaning of Unreasonable Search

Like the question of what's an unreasonable arrest, the question of what's an *unreasonable* search is complicated, and the answer fills even more pages of the U.S. Supreme Court's written decisions. But for us, the answer boils down to this. In the everyday work of police officers, searches are reasonable if they:

1. Back them up with probable cause
2. Get a warrant backed up with probable cause before they search houses
3. Conduct the search at the time of arrest
4. Get consent to search if they don't have probable cause

The vast majority of searches are searches at the time of arrest and consent searches, meaning that most searches are without warrants.

Probable cause to search is similar to probable cause to arrest, except the facts and circumstances have to support a reasonable belief officers will find evidence of crime, weapons, or contraband on the person or places they search. Of course, a reasonable belief doesn't mean officers will find any of these items (Figure 7.2). The Constitution doesn't require that officers' beliefs turn out to *right;* it only requires that their beliefs be *reasonable* (*Illinois v. Rodriguez* 1990).

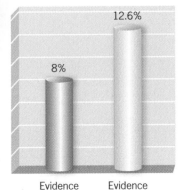

▲ **FIGURE 7.2 Percentage of Physical and Vehicle Searches That Bear Fruit**

Source: Bureau of Justice Statistics, *Contacts between Police and the Public* (Washington, DC: Bureau of Justice Statistics, February 2001), p. 20, Table 13.

◀ Homes are special places, and the U.S. Supreme Court recognizes the high value we place on being safe and secure in our homes. So, warrants are required before officers can search them—but not always. These officers are searching a public housing project apartment without warrants. On March 29, 2004, the U.S. Court of Appeals for the 5th Circuit approved searches of public housing units like this one without warrants in Texas, Lousiana, and Mississippi.

Searches of Homes Searches of houses are reasonable only if officers get warrants and, in most cases, only if they knock, announce their presence, and give occupants a chance to get to the door before they go in. They don't have to wait long because suspects might run out the back door, grab a weapon, and/or destroy evidence or contraband. So, according to the **knock-and-announce rule,** a search is reasonable if officers get a warrant; knock on the door saying, "Open up, police"; wait 10 seconds; knock down the door; enter; and arrest the suspect (*Wilson v. Arkansas* 1995).

knock-and-announce rule a search of a home is reasonable if officers get a warrant; knock on the door saying, "Open up, police"; wait 10 seconds; knock down the door; enter; and arrest the suspect

Officers don't always have to follow the knock-and-announce rule. According to the U.S. Supreme Court: "The Fourth Amendment's flexible requirement of reasonableness should not be read to mandate a rigid rule of announcement that ignores countervailing law enforcement interests." There are three exceptions to the rule:

1. When there's a threat of violence
2. When officers are in hot pursuit of a fleeing suspected felon
3. When there's a threat that occupants will destroy evidence (*Wilson v. Arkansas* 1995)

Searches at the Time of Arrest Once an officer lawfully arrests a suspect, the officer at the time of (technically called "incident to") the arrest can thoroughly search the suspect and the area under her control without either a search warrant or probable cause (*Chimel v. California* 1969). The **search incident to arrest rule** raises three questions: First, what's the purpose for setting aside the warrant and probable cause requirements? Three purposes: to protect officers from suspects reaching for a weapon; to preserve evidence or contraband that suspects might destroy; and to prevent suspects from trying to escape. Second, what time period does "incident to" cover? It includes the time leading up to the arrest and enough time after the search to give officers time to get control of the situation. Third, what area does "under the suspect's control" include? It includes the suspect's body and the "grabbable area" around her; in other words, it is as far as she can reach for a weapon, evidence, or some means of escape.

search incident to arrest rule an officer who *lawfully* arrests a suspect can search the suspect and the area under her control without either a search warrant or probable cause

Much more extensive searches of vehicles at the time drivers and passengers are arrested are reasonable. In the very important case *New York v. Belton* (1981), Trooper Douglas Nicot stopped Roger Belton and three other college students for speeding on the New York Thruway. When he approached the car, he smelled marijuana. He arrested all four, ordered them out of the car, and split them up so they couldn't get near each. Then, he searched the entire passenger compartment and a black leather jacket in the back seat. To search the jacket he had to unzip the pockets; he found cocaine in one of the pockets.

Belton argued the search went beyond the "grabbable area." The U.S. Supreme Court disagreed:

> We hold that when a policeman has made a lawful custodial arrest of the occupant of an automobile, he may, as a contemporaneous incident of that arrest, search the passenger compartment of that automobile. It follows from that conclusion that the police may also examine the contents of any containers found within the passenger compartment.

Consent Searches Officers don't need either probable cause or warrants if the person they search consents to the search. According to the **consent search rule,** you can give up your right against unreasonable searches—but only if you do it voluntarily. In the leading U.S. Supreme Court consent search case, *Schneckloth v. Bustamonte* (1973), police officers didn't have either a warrant or probable cause to search a car, so they asked if it was "okay to look in the trunk of the car." "Sure, go ahead," the driver said.

The Court ruled the consent was voluntary, so the Fourth Amendment warrant and probable cause requirements didn't kick in. The dissent argued consent searches should only be legal if officers warn people they have a right to say no to the search (like the *Miranda* warnings discussed later on). Why? Because ordinary people see requests by police officers as polite commands backed up by the power to use force.

Stops and Frisks

Stopping suspicious persons and demanding to know whom they are and why they're out and about is an old practice. Ancient statutes and court decisions empowered English constables to detain "suspicious nightwalkers" and hold them until morning to investigate their suspicious behavior. You've already learned about this old practice in its modern form—the proactive police strategy of field interrogation (Chapter 6). Fourth Amendment stops are briefer detentions than arrests, and they take place in public (Table 7.2). (See the In Focus box "Do You *Have* to Identify Yourself to Police Officers?")

Fourth Amendment frisks consist of outer clothing pat downs for weapons and are less invasive than full-body searches (Table 7.3).

consent search rule individuals can give up their right against unreasonable searches, if they do so *voluntarily*

DECISION POINT

Should the right against "unreasonable seizures" be reduced during emergencies?

Click on this Decision Point at http://cj.wadsworth.com/samaha_cj7e to explore the issue.

▼ TABLE 7.2 Comparison between Stops and Arrests

	Stops	Arrests
Length	Minutes	Hours, maybe days
Location	On the spot; they take place in public places	The suspect is moved to the intimidating atmosphere of the police station
Invasiveness	A few on-the-spot questions	Mug shot, full interrogation, lineup

▼ TABLE 7.3 Comparison between Frisks and Full Searches

Frisks	Full Searches
Once over pat down of outer clothing	Thoroughly feeling all parts of the body
The sole purpose is to check for weapons that might harm the officer	The purposes are to protect officers, preserve evidence, and prevent the suspect's escape

Do You *Have* to Identify Yourself to Police Officers?

FACTS

The sheriff's department in Humboldt County, Nevada, received an afternoon telephone call reporting an assault. The caller reported seeing a man assault a woman in a red and silver GMC truck on Grass Valley Road. Deputy Sheriff Lee Dove was dispatched to investigate. When the officer arrived at the scene, he found the truck parked on the side of the road. A man was standing by the truck, and a young woman was sitting inside it. The officer observed skid marks in the gravel behind the vehicle, leading him to believe it had come to a sudden stop.

The officer approached the man and explained that he was investigating a report of a fight. The man appeared to be intoxicated. The officer asked him if he had "any identification on [him]," which we understand as a request to produce a driver's license or some other form of written identification. The man refused and asked why the officer wanted to see identification. The officer responded that he was conducting an investigation and needed to see some identification. The unidentified man became agitated and insisted he had done nothing wrong. The officer explained that he wanted to find out who the man was and what he was doing there. After continued refusals to comply with the officer's request for identification, the man began to taunt the officer by placing his hands behind his back and telling the officer to arrest him and take him to jail. This routine kept up for several minutes: the officer asked for identification 11 times and was refused each time. After warning the man that he would be arrested if he continued to refuse to comply, the officer placed him under arrest.

The man turned out to be Larry Dudley Hibel. He was charged with, convicted [of], and fined $250 for "willfully resisting, delaying, or obstructing a public officer in discharging or attempting to discharge any legal duty of his office." The "legal duty" in question is Nevada's "stop and identify" statute (NRS § 199.280 (2003)) which defines the right and duties of police officers when they make investigative stops. (Twenty states have similar statutes.) The statute provides:

1. Any peace officer may detain any person whom the officer encounters under circumstances which reasonably indicate that the person has committed, is committing or is about to commit a crime.
   . . . .
3. The officer may detain the person pursuant to this section only to ascertain his identity and the suspicious circumstances surrounding his presence abroad. Any person so detained shall identify himself, but may not be compelled to answer any other inquiry of any peace officer."

OPINION

Terry v. Ohio . . . permits a State to require a suspect to disclose his name in the course of a *Terry* stop. . . . The [Nevada "stop and identify" statute] requires only that a suspect disclose his name. It apparently does not require him to produce a driver's license or any other document. If he chooses either to state his name or communicate it to the officer by other means, the statute is satisfied and no violation occurs. . . . The stop, the request, and the State's requirement of a response did not contravene the guarantees of the Fourth Amendment.

DISSENT

". . . An officer may ask [a person stopped on reasonable suspicion] . . . a moderate number of questions to determine his identity and to try to obtain information confirming or dispelling the officer's suspicions. But the detainee is not obliged to respond." A name itself—even if it is not "Killer Bill" or "Rough 'em up Harry"—will sometimes provide the police with "a link in the chain of evidence needed to convict the individual of a separate offense."

Source: Hibel v. Sixth Judicial District Court of Nevada, 124 S.Ct. 2451 (2004).

Constitutionally, stops are Fourth Amendment seizures and frisks are Fourth Amendment searches (*Terry v. Ohio* 1968). Stops and frisks that begin and end on the street are a lot more frequent than arrests and full searches, which usually end up with suspects at the police station (Figure 7.3). For example, the New York City Police Department recorded 175,000 stops between January 1998 and March 1999; only 19,000 of these stops led to arrests (Spitzer 1999, 112).

The objective basis for backing up stops and frisks is less than probable cause; it's called reasonable suspicion. **Reasonable suspicion** to stop consists of facts and circumstances that would lead a reasonable officer in the light of her training and experience to *suspect* that a crime *might* be afoot. Compare this definition with the one for "probable cause to arrest," which requires enough facts and circumstances to *believe* that a crime *is* afoot (Table 7.4). "Suspect" isn't as strong a conclusion as "belief"; and "might" isn't as certain as "is."

reasonable suspicion facts and circumstances that would lead an officer (in light of her training and experience) to suspect that a crime might be afoot

► FIGURE 7.3 The Fourth
Amendment and Police-Individual
Contacts

► FIGURE 7.3 The Fourth
Amendment and Police-Individual
Contacts

Source: Criminal Procedure, 6th ed., by
Samaha. © 2005. Reprinted with permission
of Wadsworth, a division of Thomson
Learning, Inc.

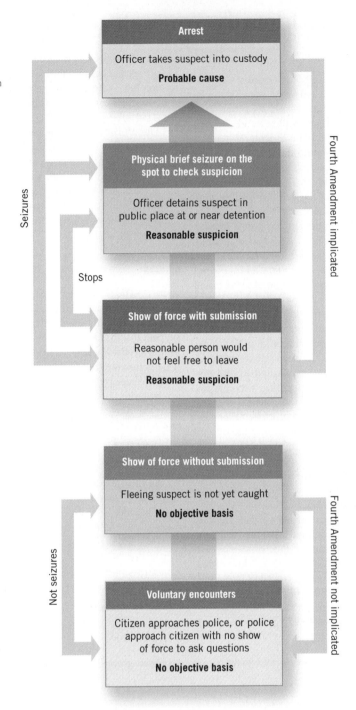

Reasonable suspicion to frisk consists of facts and circumstances that would
lead an officer to suspect that a person lawfully stopped might be armed (*Terry v.
Ohio* 1968).

The U.S. Supreme Court hears more Fourth Amendment search and seizure
cases than the other police practice cases you'll learn about in the next two sections, interrogation and identification procedures. The Court's term ending in
July 2004 included several important other search and seizure cases summarized
in the paragraphs that follow.

1. "Knock and Announce" Rule: *U.S. v. Banks,* **124 S.Ct. 521 (2003)** When
federal and local law enforcement officers went to Lashawn Lowell Banks's

▼ TABLE 7.4 Elements of Reasonable Suspicion to Stop and Probable Cause to Arrest

Reasonable Suspicion	Probable Cause
Facts and circumstances	Facts and circumstances
Reasonable officer in light of her training and experience	Reasonable officer in light of her training and experience
Suspects	Believes
Crime *might* be afoot	Crime *is* afoot

apartment to execute a warrant to search for cocaine, they called out "police search warrant" and rapped on the front door hard enough to be heard by officers at the back door, waited for 15 to 20 seconds with no response, and then broke open the door. Banks was in the shower and testified that he heard nothing until the crash of the door. The District Court denied his motion to suppress the drugs and weapons found during the search, rejecting his argument that the officers waited an unreasonably short time before forcing entry, in violation of the Fourth Amendment. Banks pleaded guilty but reserved his right to challenge the search on appeal. In reversing and ordering the evidence suppressed, the Ninth Circuit found, using a four-part scheme for vetting knock-and-announce entries, that the instant entry had no exigent circumstances, making forced entry by destruction of property permissible only if there was an explicit refusal of admittance or a time lapse greater than the one here.

The U.S. Supreme Court (9–0) reversed. The Court held that the officers' 15-to-20-second wait before forcible entry satisfied the Fourth Amendment. According to the Court, the standards bearing on whether officers can legitimately enter after knocking are the same as those for requiring or dispensing with knock and announce altogether. This Court has fleshed out the notion of reasonable execution on a case-by-case basis but has pointed out factual considerations of unusual, although not dispositive, significance. The obligation to knock and announce before entering gives way when officers have reasonable grounds to expect futility or to suspect that an exigency, such as evidence destruction, will arise instantly upon knocking. Since most people keep their doors locked, a no-knock entry will normally do some damage, a fact too common to require a heightened justification when a reasonable suspicion of exigency already justifies an unwarned entry.

This case turns on the exigency revealed by the circumstances known to the officers after they knocked and announced, which the government contends was the risk of losing easily disposable evidence. After 15 to 20 seconds without a response, officers could fairly have suspected that Banks would flush away the cocaine if they remained reticent. Each of Banks's counterarguments—he was in the shower and didn't hear the officers, and that it might have taken him longer than 20 seconds to reach the door—rests on a mistake about the relevant enquiry. As to the first argument, the facts known to the police are what count in judging a reasonable waiting time, and there's no indication that they knew Banks was in the shower and thus unaware of an impending search. As to the second, the crucial fact isn't the time it would take Banks to reach the door but the time it would take him to destroy the cocaine. It's not unreasonable to think that someone could get in a position to destroy the drugs within 15 to 20 seconds. Once the exigency had matured, the officers weren't bound to learn anything more or wait any longer before entering, even though the entry entailed some harm to the building.

2. Car Search: *Thornton v. U.S.*, 124 S.Ct. 2127 (2004) Before Officer Nichols could pull over Marcus Thornton, he parked and got out of his car. Nichols then parked, accosted Thornton, and arrested him after finding drugs in his pocket.

Incident to the arrest, Nichols searched Thornton's car and found a handgun under the driver's seat. Thornton was charged with federal drug and firearms violations. In denying his motion to suppress the firearm as the fruit of an unconstitutional search, the District Court found, that the automobile search was valid under *New York v. Belton*, in which this Court held that, when a police officer makes a lawful custodial arrest of an automobile's occupant, the Fourth Amendment allows the officer to search the vehicle's passenger compartment as a contemporaneous incident of arrest. Thornton appealed his conviction, arguing that *Belton* was limited to situations where the officer initiated contact with an arrestee while he was still in the car. The Fourth Circuit affirmed.

The U.S. Supreme Court (7–2) affirmed. The Court held that *Belton* governs even when an officer doesn't make contact until the person arrested has left the vehicle. In *Belton*, the Court placed no reliance on the fact that the officer ordered the occupants out of the vehicle, or initiated contact with them while they remained within it. And here, there's simply no basis to conclude that the span of the area generally within the arrestee's immediate control is determined by whether the arrestee exited the vehicle at the officer's direction, or whether the officer initiated contact with him while he was in the car. In all relevant aspects, the arrest of a suspect who is next to a vehicle presents identical concerns regarding officer safety and evidence destruction as one who is inside. Under petitioner's proposed "contact initiation" rule, officers who decide that it may be safer and more effective to conceal their presence until a suspect has left his car would be unable to search the passenger compartment in the event of a custodial arrest, potentially compromising their safety and placing incriminating evidence at risk of concealment or destruction. The Fourth Amendment doesn't require such a gamble. *Belton* allows police to search a car's passenger compartment incident to a lawful arrest of both "occupants" and "recent occupants." While an arrestee's status as a "recent occupant" may turn on his temporal or spatial relationship to the car at the time of the arrest and search, it certainly doesn't turn on whether he was inside or outside the car when the officer first initiated contact with him. Although not all contraband in the passenger compartment is likely to be accessible to a "recent occupant," the need for a clear rule, readily understood by police and not depending on differing estimates of what items were or were not within an arrestee's reach at any particular moment, justifies the sort of generalization which *Belton* enunciated. Under Thornton's rule, an officer would have to determine whether he actually confronted or signaled confrontation with the suspect while he was in his car, or whether the suspect exited the car unaware of, and for reasons unrelated to, the officer's presence. Such a rule would be inherently subjective and highly fact specific, and would require precisely the sort of ad hoc determinations on the part of officers in the field and reviewing courts that *Belton* sought to avoid.

U.S. Customs and Border Protection Agency: This group is now part of the Department of Homeland Security. To reach this site go to "Web Links" on your Samaha CJ7 website: http://cj.wadsworth.com/samaha_cj7e.

3. Border Searches: *U.S. v. Flores-Montano*, **124 S.Ct. 1582 (2004)** At the international border in southern California, customs officials seized 37 kilograms of marijuana from Manuel Flores-Montano's gas tank by removing and disassembling the tank. After respondent was indicted on federal drug charges, he moved to suppress the drugs recovered from the gas tank, relying on a Ninth Circuit panel decision holding that a gas tank's removal requires reasonable suspicion under the Fourth Amendment. The District Court granted the motion, and the Ninth Circuit summarily affirmed.

The U.S. Supreme Court (9–0) reversed. The Court held that the search didn't require reasonable suspicion. In the decision relied on below, the Ninth Circuit panel seized on language from *U.S. v. Montoya de Hernandez*, that used "routine" as a descriptive term in discussing border searches. The panel took "routine," fashioned a new balancing test, and extended it to vehicle searches. But the reasons that might support a suspicion requirement in the case of highly intrusive searches of persons simply don't carry over to vehicles. Complex balancing tests to determine what's a "routine" vehicle search, as opposed to a more "intrusive" search of a person, have no place in border searches of vehicles. The government's interest in preventing the entry of unwanted persons and effects is at its zenith at the international border. Congress has always granted the Executive plenary authority to conduct routine searches and seizures at the border, without probable cause or a warrant, in order to regulate the collection of duties and to prevent the introduction of contraband into this country. Flores-Montano's assertion that he has a privacy interest in his fuel tank, and that the suspicionless disassembly of his tank is an invasion of his privacy, is rejected, as the privacy expectation is less at the border than it is in the interior, and this Court has long recognized that automobiles seeking entry into this country may be searched. And while the Fourth Amendment "protects property as well as privacy," the interference with a motorist's possessory interest in his gas tank is justified by the government's paramount interest in protecting the border. Thus, the government's authority to conduct suspicionless inspections at the border includes the authority to remove, disassemble, and reassemble a vehicle's fuel tank.

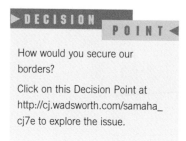

▶ DECISION POINT ◀

How would you secure our borders?

Click on this Decision Point at http://cj.wadsworth.com/samaha_cj7e to explore the issue.

4. Roadblock: *Illinois v. Lidster,* **124 S.Ct. 885 (2004)** Police set up a highway checkpoint to obtain information from motorists about a hit-and-run accident occurring about one week earlier at the same location and time of night. Officers stopped each vehicle for 10 to 15 seconds, asked the occupants whether they had seen anything happen there the previous weekend, and handed each driver a flyer describing and requesting information about the accident. As Robert Lidster approached, his minivan swerved, nearly hitting an officer. The officer smelled alcohol on Lidster's breath. Another officer administered a sobriety test and then arrested Lidster. He was convicted in Illinois state court of driving under the influence of alcohol. He challenged his arrest and conviction on the ground that the government obtained evidence through use of a checkpoint stop that violated the Fourth Amendment. The trial court rejected that challenge, but the state appellate court reversed. The State Supreme Court agreed, holding that, in light of *Indianapolis v. Edmond,* the stop was unconstitutional.

The U.S. Supreme Court reversed. The Court held that the checkpoint stop didn't violate the Fourth Amendment. In *Edmond,* this Court held that, absent special circumstances, the Fourth Amendment forbids police to make stops without individualized suspicion at a checkpoint set up primarily for general "crime control" purposes. Specifically, the checkpoint in *Edmond* was designed to ferret out drug crimes committed by the motorists themselves. Here, the stop's primary law enforcement purpose was *not* to determine whether a vehicle's occupants were committing a crime, but to ask the occupants, as members of the public, for help in providing information about a crime in all likelihood committed by others. *Edmond's* language, as well as its context, makes clear that an information-seeking stop's constitutionality was not then before this Court.

The checkpoint stop was constitutional. In judging its reasonableness, this Court looks to "the gravity of the public concerns served by the seizure, the degree to which the seizure advances the public interest, and the severity of the interference with individual liberty." The relevant public concern was grave, as the police were investigating a crime that had resulted in a human death, and the stop advanced this concern to a significant degree given its timing and location. Most importantly, the stops interfered only minimally with liberty of the sort the Fourth Amendment seeks to protect. Viewed objectively, each stop required only a brief wait in line and contact with police for only a few seconds. Viewed subjectively, the systematic contact provided little reason for anxiety or alarm, and there is no allegation that the police acted in a discriminatory or otherwise unlawful manner.

Interrogation

According to the Fifth Amendment, "No person shall be compelled in any criminal case to be a witness against himself." There's a lot of controversy over police interrogation. Supporters believe a safe society depends on questioning suspects. Critics argue a free society doesn't convict people with evidence out of their own mouths. Supporters of interrogation reply that it doesn't just convict the guilty, it frees the innocent, too. Critics argue police use unethical tactics like lying, deceit, and tricks to get confessions; officers reply that interrogating criminal suspects isn't (and shouldn't be treated like) a conversation between friends and pressure isn't the same as force.

Empirical data will probably never fully resolve this debate, partly because we don't know what really goes on in interrogation rooms. According to U.S. Supreme Court Chief Justice Earl Warren, an experienced former prosecutor, "Interrogation takes place in privacy. Privacy results in secrecy and this in turn results in a gap in our knowledge as to what in fact goes on in the interrogation room." Fortunately, sociologist Richard Leo's (1996) research has begun to close the gap. After spending more than five hundred hours inside the interrogation rooms of a major urban police department and analyzing videotaped custodial interrogations from two other departments, Leo made the following important findings:

1. Very few interrogations are coercive.
2. One in five suspects invokes one or more *Miranda* rights to avoid cooperating with the police.
3. Interrogators use tactics advocated in police training manuals (fabricated evidence, "good guy–bad guy") to undermine the confidence of suspects and overbear their rational decision making.
4. Interrogators have become increasingly skilled in eliciting incriminating evidence during custodial interrogation.
5. The overwhelming majority of custodial interrogations last less than one hour.
6. Suspects who provide incriminating information are likely to be treated differently at every stage of the criminal process from suspects who don't. (266, 302)

Let's look at the impact of the landmark case *Miranda v. Arizona* and the ban on forced self-incrimination.

Miranda v. Arizona

In one of the most famous cases in U.S. Supreme Court history, *Miranda v. Arizona* (1996), the Court decided police have to give suspects in custody four warnings before they interrogate them:

1. You have a right to remain silent.
2. Anything you say will be used against you.
3. You have a right to a lawyer.
4. If you can't afford a lawyer, one will be provided for you.

"*Miranda* has become embedded in routine police practice to the point where the warnings have become part of our national culture," said Chief Justice of the U.S. Supreme Court William Rehnquist on June 26, 2000. What was the occasion for the Chief Justice's comment? He was reading the Court's decision in *Dickerson v. U.S.* (2000), a case that decided whether Congress had overstepped its power when it overruled *Miranda v. Arizona* in 1968. In that year, in a burst of "get tough on criminals" legislation, Congress overruled the requirement that police officers had to give the now famous warnings.

The law was ignored until 1997 when a Virginia federal court relied on the statute to admit Charles Dickerson's confession, obtained by FBI agents after giving him defective warnings. The 1968 law, the 1997 case relying on it, and the Supreme Court's decision declaring the law unconstitutional are part of a long and impassioned debate over the right against self-incrimination (Levy 1968). The U.S. Supreme Court continues determining just how to apply *Miranda v. Arizona* to police practices, as the interrogation cases in the Court's term ending in July 2004 that follow clearly demonstrate.

1. Delay in Giving Warnings: *Missouri v. Seibert*, 124 S.Ct. 2601 (2004) Seibert feared charges of neglect when her son, afflicted with cerebral palsy, died in his sleep. She was present when two of her sons and their friends discussed burning her family's mobile home to conceal the circumstances of her son's death. Donald, an unrelated mentally ill 18-year-old living with the family, was left to die in the fire to avoid the appearance that Seibert's son had been unattended. Five days later, the police arrested Seibert but did not advise her of her rights under *Miranda v. Arizona*. At the police station, Officer Hanrahan questioned her for 30 to 40 minutes, obtaining a confession that the plan was for Donald to die in the fire. He then gave her a 20-minute break, returned to advise her of her *Miranda* warnings, and obtained a signed waiver. He resumed questioning, confronting Seibert with her prewarning statements and getting her to repeat the information.

Seibert moved to suppress both her prewarning and postwarning statements. Hanrahan testified that he made a conscious decision to withhold *Miranda* warnings, question first, then give the warnings, and then repeat the question until he got the answer previously given. The District Court suppressed the prewarning statement but admitted the postwarning one, and Seibert was convicted of second-degree murder. The Missouri Court of Appeals affirmed, finding the case indistinguishable from *Oregon v. Elstad*, in which this Court held that a suspect's unwarned inculpatory statement made during a brief exchange at his house did not make a later, fully warned inculpatory statement inadmissible. In reversing, the state Supreme Court held that, because the interrogation was nearly continuous, the second statement, which was clearly the product of the invalid first statement, should be suppressed; it distinguished *Elstad* on the ground that the warnings had not intentionally been withheld there.

The U.S. Supreme Court (5–4) affirmed. Justice SOUTER, joined by Justice STEVENS, Justice GINSBURG, and Justice BREYER, concluded that, because the midstream recitation of warnings after interrogation and unwarned confession in this case could not comply with *Miranda*'s constitutional warning requirement, Seibert's postwarning statements are inadmissible. Justice KENNEDY concluded that when a two-step interrogation technique is used, postwarning statements related to prewarning statements must be excluded unless curative measures are taken before the postwarning statement is made. Not every violation of *Miranda v. Arizona* requires suppression of the evidence obtained. Admission may be proper when it would further important objectives without compromising *Miranda*'s central concerns.

2. Warnings to a 17-Year-Old: *Yarborough v. Alvarado*, 124 S.Ct. 2140 (2004)
Michael Alvarado helped Paul Soto try to steal a truck, leading to the death of the truck's owner. Alvarado was called in for an interview with Los Angeles detective Comstock. Alvarado was 17 at the time, and his parents brought him to the station and waited in the lobby during the interview. Comstock took Alvarado to a small room where only the two of them were present. The interview lasted about two hours, and Alvarado was not given a warning under *Miranda v. Arizona*. Although he at first denied being present at the shooting, Alvarado slowly began to change his story, finally admitting that he had helped Soto try to steal the victim's truck and to hide the gun after the murder. Comstock twice

asked Alvarado if he needed a break and, when the interview was over, returned him to his parents, who drove him home.

After California charged Alvarado with murder and attempted robbery, the trial court denied his motion to suppress his interview statements on *Miranda* grounds. In affirming Alvarado's conviction, the District Court of Appeal (state court) ruled that a *Miranda* warning wasn't required because Alvarado hadn't been in custody during the interview under the test which requires a court to consider the circumstances surrounding the interrogation and then determine whether a reasonable person would have felt at liberty to leave. The Federal District Court agreed, but the Ninth Circuit reversed, holding that the state court erred in failing to account for Alvarado's youth and inexperience when evaluating whether a reasonable person in his position would have felt free to leave the interview. The U.S. Supreme Court held that the state court considered the proper factors and reached a reasonable conclusion that Alvarado was not in custody for *Miranda* purposes during his police interview.

3. Suspect Interrupts Warnings, Says He Knows His Rights: ***U.S. v. Patane*, 124 S.Ct. 2620 (2004)** After Officer Fox began to investigate Samuel Francis Patane's apparent violation of a temporary restraining order, a federal agent told Fox's colleague, Detective Benner, that Patane, a convicted felon, illegally possessed a pistol. Officer Fox and Detective Benner went to Patane's home, where Fox arrested him for violating the restraining order. Benner attempted to advise Patane of his rights under *Miranda v. Arizona*, but Patane interrupted, asserting he knew his rights. Benner then asked about the pistol and retrieved and seized it. Patane was indicted for possession of a firearm by a convicted felon. The U.S. District Court granted his motion to suppress the pistol, reasoning that the officers lacked probable cause to arrest him and declining to rule on his alternative argument that the gun should be suppressed as the fruit of an unwarned statement. The Tenth Circuit reversed the probable cause ruling, but affirmed the suppression order on Patane's alternative theory.

The U.S. Supreme Court (5–4) concluded that a failure to give a suspect *Miranda* warnings does not require suppression of the physical fruits of the suspect's unwarned but voluntary statements. According to the Court, the *Miranda* rule is a prophylactic employed to protect against violations of the Self-Incrimination Clause, U. S Const., Amdt. 5. That Clause's core protection is a prohibition on compelling a criminal defendant to testify against himself at trial. It cannot be violated by the introduction of nontestimonial evidence obtained as a result of voluntary statements.

4. Incriminating Statements at Home before Warnings at Jail: ***Fellers v. U.S.*, 124 S.Ct. 1019 (2004)** Police officers went to John F. Fellers's home and advised him they'd come to discuss his involvement in drug distribution. They told him they had a federal warrant for his arrest and that a grand jury had indicted him for conspiracy to distribute methamphetamine. During the course of a brief discussion, Fellers made several incriminating statements. Once at the county jail, Fellers was advised of his rights under *Miranda v. Arizona*, signed a waiver of those rights, and reiterated his earlier statements. Before trial, he moved to suppress the incriminating statements he made at his home and at the jail. A Magistrate Judge recommended that the home statements be suppressed because the officers had not informed Fellers of his rights, and that portions of his jailhouse statements be suppressed as fruits of the prior failure to provide *Miranda* warnings. The District Court suppressed the unwarned home statements but admitted the jailhouse statements, concluding that Fellers had knowingly and voluntarily waived his *Miranda* rights before making the statements. The Eighth Circuit affirmed the conviction, holding that Fellers's jailhouse statements were properly admitted.

The U.S. Supreme Court (9–0) held that the Eighth Circuit erred in holding that the absence of an "interrogation" prevented Fellers from claiming that his jailhouse statements should've been suppressed as fruits of the statements taken from him at his home. An accused is denied the protections of the Sixth Amendment "when there [are] used against him at his trial...his own incriminating words, which federal agents...deliberately elicited from him after he had been indicted and in the absence of his counsel."

The Chief Justice was right that *Miranda* is part of our culture; he didn't mention that it's also part of our culture wars. Perhaps no procedure has generated more hostility among the public. On *NYPD Blue*, the good cops, Andy Sipowitz and whoever his current partner was (he had several) waged an unrelenting "war on *Miranda*." In almost every episode, a "scumbag" murderer—or his lawyer—made a "mockery of the system" by taunting the cops with his rights. Then Sipowitz and his partner threatened, shoved, and often beat a confession out of the "worthless animal" called a suspect. We all knew he was guilty (it was always a man), and we were invited to hate not just the murderer but also the system that gave rights to such lowlifes.

This pop culture picture of saintly cops handcuffed by *Miranda* in their war against satanic criminals hides the complexity of the real picture of interrogation in at least four ways:

1. ***Custodial interrogation.*** Police don't have to warn suspects if they only take them into custody (almost always the police station) *and* interrogate them.
2. ***Public safety exception.*** Officers don't have to give the warnings when giving them could endanger officers and/or citizens.
3. *Waiver.* Most suspects give up their rights to remain silent and to have a lawyer and agree to be interrogated.
4. *Causal link.* Police coercion by itself doesn't mean courts throw out confessions; police coercion has to cause suspects to make incriminating statements (see the next section).

custodial interrogation *Miranda* warnings required if suspects are in custody *and* officers interrogate them

public safety exception *Miranda* warnings not required if giving them could endanger officers or others nearby

The Ban on "Compelled" Self-Incrimination

Remember, the Fifth Amendment bans compelling suspects to confess. A confession is compelled only if the facts of the case prove (1) coercion by law enforcement officers and (2) a causal link—that is, coercion by law enforcement officers has to cause the incriminating statements. (See the In Focus box "Do Officers Have to *Mirandize* Suspects When It Would Endanger an Officer or Someone Nearby?")

In *Colorado v. Connelly* (1986), Francis Connelly came up to Officer Patrick Anderson in downtown Denver and said he'd murdered someone and wanted to talk about it. Anderson immediately "mirandized" Connelly. Connelly said he understood his rights but he still wanted to talk about the murder. Shortly after that, homicide detective Stephen Antuna arrived and "mirandized" Connelly again. After the warnings, Connelly told Antuna he'd come all the way from Boston to confess to murdering Mary Ann Junta. Connelly readily agreed to take the officers to the scene of the murder. Later, Connelly said he wanted to confess because God had told him to either confess or commit suicide.

Connelly was charged with murder, and the case eventually arrived at the U.S. Supreme Court, where the issue was whether the confession was voluntary. The Court said it was. God may have compelled Connelly to confess, but the Fifth Amendment only applies to *police* coercion:

> Cases considered by this Court over...50 years...have focused on the crucial element of police overreaching. While each confession case has turned on its own set of factors

Do Officers Have to *Mirandize* Suspects When It Would Endanger an Officer or Someone Nearby?

Do officers have to give the warnings anyway? No, said the U.S. Supreme Court in *Quarles v. New York* (1984), a case that created a public safety exception to *Miranda*. In *Quarles*, a woman came up to two NYPD officers and told them she'd been raped by a man carrying a gun who'd just gone into a supermarket across the street. Officer Kraft ran to the market and saw Benjamin Quarles, who fit the woman's description. Kraft briefly lost sight of Quarles, then saw him again, pulled his own gun, and ordered Quarles to stop and put his hands over his head. He frisked him, discovered an empty shoulder holster, and handcuffed Quarles. Without mirandizing Quarles, Kraft asked him where the gun was. Nodding to some cartons, Quarles said, "The gun's over there." Kraft found a loaded .38 caliber revolver.

By a 5–4 vote, the Court decided Officer Kraft didn't have to warn Quarles. According to the Court, the cost of *Miranda* is that some guilty people will go free, a cost worth paying in most cases because of the premium we put on the right against coerced self-incrimination. But the cost is too high if giving the warning endangers public safety. According to the majority:

> The need for answers to questions in a situation posing a threat to the public safety outweighs the need for the...rule protecting the...privilege against self-incrimination. We decline to place officers such as Officer Kraft in the untenable position of having to consider, often in a matter of seconds, whether it best serves society for them to ask the necessary questions without the *Miranda* warnings and render whatever probative evidence they uncover inadmissible, or for them to give the warnings in order to preserve the admissibility of evidence they might uncover but possibly damage or destroy their ability to obtain that evidence and neutralize the volatile situation confronting them. (657–658)

So the Court created the public safety exception to the *Miranda* rule:

> In recognizing a *narrow exception* [my emphasis] to the *Miranda* rule in this case, we acknowledge that to some degree we lessen the desirable clarity of that rule....The exception will not be difficult for police officers to apply because in each case it will be circumscribed by the exigency which justifies it. We think police officers can and will distinguish almost instinctively between questions necessary to secure their own safety or the safety of the public and questions designed solely to elicit testimonial evidence from a suspect. (658)

Justice O'Connor, who agreed the exception made sense, dissented because of the confusion making exceptions to *Miranda*'s "bright line" rule (a specific rule that enables determination of reasonableness) would cause:

> Since the time *Miranda* was decided, the Court has repeatedly refused to bend the literal terms of that decision....Wherever an accused has been taken into "custody" and subjected to "interrogation" without warnings, the Court has consistently prohibited the use of his responses for prosecutorial purposes at trial. As a consequence, the "meaning of *Miranda* has become reasonably clear and law enforcement practices have adjusted to its strictures."...
>
> In my view, a "public safety" exception unnecessarily blurs the edges of the clear line heretofore established and makes *Miranda's* requirements more difficult to understand...The end result will be a fine spun new doctrine on public safety exigencies incident to custodial interrogation, complete with the hair-splitting distinctions that currently plague our Fourth Amendment jurisprudence. (662–664)

Source: Quarles v. New York, 467 U.S. 649 (1984).

justifying the conclusion that police conduct was oppressive, all have contained a substantial element of coercive police conduct. Absent police conduct causally related to the confession, there is simply no basis for concluding that any state actor has deprived a criminal defendant of due process of law....As interrogators have turned to more subtle forms of psychological persuasion, courts have found the mental condition of the defendant a more significant factor in the "voluntariness" calculus. But this fact does not justify a conclusion that a defendant's mental condition, by itself apart from its relation to official coercion, should ever dispose of the inquiry into constitutional "voluntariness."

Eyewitness Identification of Strangers

In most cases, proving a crime was committed is easier than identifying the perpetrator. But not always. Some suspects are caught red-handed; victims and witnesses personally know other suspects; and others confess. Crimes perpe-

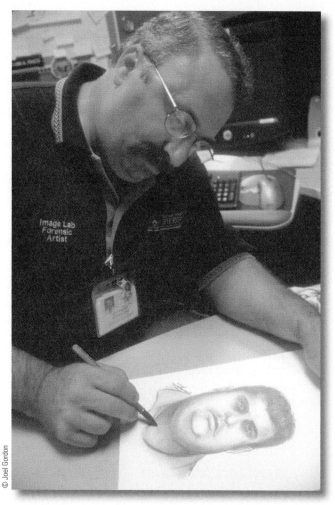

◄ Faulty identification of strangers is the "greatest single threat to our ideal that no innocent man shall be punished." Best guesses are that faulty identification by witnesses account for half of all wrongful convictions. In this photo, forensic artist Stephen A. Fusco makes a composite sketch that will be scanned and distributed to local agencies and the news media in and around Orlando, Florida. Hopefully, it'll help identify the right person.

trated by strangers present the greatest challenge to law enforcement and victims. Eyewitnesses' identifications of strangers are sometimes unreliable. According to one expert, faulty identifications of *strangers* is the "greatest single threat to the achievement of our ideal that no innocent man shall be punished." Best guesses are eyewitness error accounts for half of all wrongful convictions. Let's look at the dangers of eyewitness misidentifications and at how lineups impact identifications.

The Dangers of Mistaken Identifications

In one classic case (*National Law Journal* 1979, 1), seven eyewitnesses swore Bernard Pagano, a Roman Catholic priest, robbed them with a small, chrome-plated pistol. In the middle of Pagano's trial, Ronald Clouser admitted that he, not Father Pagano, had committed the robberies. Improper suggestion by law enforcement officers probably accounts for some errors. But, according to widely accepted findings of psychologists (Note 1977, 970), the biggest problem is we're just not very good observers, and our memories too often add to our inaccurate observations. This is particularly true when we're under stress, which most crime victims are.

Psychologists have known for more than a century that the eye isn't like a video camera that records exact images on the brain. Cameras have no expectations; people do. And their expectations influence what they think they see. Add to these problems the troubling finding by psychologists that we're even worse at identifying strangers of a different race. Blacks can identify Whites better than

Whites can identify members of other races, because Whites are more prone to the "they all look alike" phenomenon. In one famous experiment, researchers showed observers a photo of a White man brandishing a razor blade in an altercation with a Black man on a subway. When asked immediately afterward to describe what they saw, over half the observers reported that the Black man was carrying the weapon (Note 1977, 982).

Memory fades over time, and it fades most in the first few hours after seeing a stranger and then remains stable for several months. What happens after seeing the stranger can dramatically alter what witnesses remember seeing; they can be highly susceptible to the power of suggestion. The mind stores all information about an event—whether it was learned at the time of the event or later—in the same "bin." According to the highly respected eyewitness research expert Elizabeth Loftus, in a study she conducted, witnesses embellished their stories depending on how she described an incident. Later, they drew this information out of the bin during the identification process (Yant 1991, 91).

Steven Penrod, an identification researcher at the University of Wisconsin, says this embellishment is natural. "A witness tells his story to the police, to the family, then to friends, then to the prosecutor." As the story gets retold, it becomes less reality and more legend. "Witnesses feel very confident about what they now think happened and that confidence is communicated to the jury" (Yant 1991, 100).

Unfortunately, witnesses' confidence about the image grows, while their memory is fading. That false confidence is especially dangerous because witness confidence has such a strong effect on judges and juries. For once TV has it right: When the prosecutor asks, "Do you see who did this to you?" and the witness, pointing directly at the defendant, strongly proclaims, "There he is," it's usually all over.

Lineups and Mistaken Identifications

Now, add the pressure created by police lineups and photographic displays. Witnesses think the suspect has to be in the lineup or in the mug shots or the police wouldn't have bothered to call them in. So they treat the procedure like multiple-choice tests without a "none of the above" choice. They're afraid they might look foolish if they "don't know the answer." Despite knowing of these problems, courts hardly ever reject eyewitness identification testimony.

Lineups depend for their reliability on their makeup *and* the way the police conduct the identification process. Let's look at each of these elements of reliability and at how issues of due process affect lineup misidentifications.

The Makeup of Lineups It's important that there are enough people in the makeup of the lineup and that the participants resemble each other. The International Association of Chiefs of Police (IACP) recommends that lineups be made up as follows:

1. 5–6 participants
2. Same race, ethnicity, and skin color
3. Similar age, height, weight, hair color, and body build
4. Similar clothing

However, real lineups often fall short of these recommendations. (Don't jump to the conclusion that police purposely set up defective lineups; the reason is almost always because the only people available to put in lineups are police officers and jail inmates.) Partly because of the difficulty in complying with the recommendations, most courts don't throw out lineup identifications. For example, in *McFadden v. Cabana* (1988), the lineup consisted of four Black men, including Alan McFadden. McFadden was only 5'6" and weighed 130 pounds. Two of the other men in the lineup were 6'6" and 6'5" and weighed almost 200 pounds

The Innocence Project: A non-government agency that works to exonerate the wrongfully convicted through post-conviction DNA testing and develop and implement reforms to prevent wrongful convictions, including cases of eyewitness testimony. To reach this site go to "Web Links" on your Samaha CJ7 website: http://cj.wadsworth.com/samaha_cj7e.

each. The fourth was 5'10". According to the court, "while the height and weight disparities were serious and unnecessary, they are...insufficient to overcome the indicia of reliability." Perhaps even more important, courts rely on prosecutors and defense lawyers' skills in pointing out the strengths and weaknesses in the lineups, and they trust jurors' common sense and daily experience to weed out bad lineups.

Unfortunately, a significant, consistent, and convincing body of empirical research demonstrates courts have misplaced their trust in lineups. Jennifer Davenport and Steven Penrod (1997) surveyed the state of our knowledge on the point and concluded:

> Jurors tend to rely on factors that are not diagnostic of eyewitness accuracy, such as an eyewitness's memory for peripheral details and eyewitness confidence, tend to overestimate eyewitness accuracy, and have difficulty applying their commonsense knowledge of lineup suggestiveness to their verdict decisions. (353)

And, according to one study in their survey, "the numbers for inaccurate eyewitnesses are quite disturbing, because they suggest jurors may believe "three out of four mistaken identifications" (348).

Administering Lineup Identification The way police administer lineups is also critical to reducing the risk of picking the wrong person. Most of the difficulties in administering the lineup come from the power of suggestion. Let's be clear, just like in making up the lineup, most suggestion during the administration of lineups isn't intentional; in fact, it's not even conscious. Officers hardly ever conduct a lineup like the officer in charge of the notorious Lindburgh kidnapping murder case who told the witness, "We've got the right man. There isn't a man in this room who isn't convinced he's the man. Don't say anything until I ask you if he's the man" (Dressler 1997, 484). But unconscious suggestion is no less powerful; maybe it's more powerful. To weaken the power of suggestion, researchers (Wells and Selau 1995, 765) recommend police departments follow these rules for conducting lineups (and photo arrays, too):

1. Tell the witness the offender may or may *not* be in the lineup.
2. Someone who doesn't know who the suspect is should conduct the lineup.
3. If a witness identifies the suspect, immediately ask the witness how sure she is of the identification *before* other information contaminates her decision.

Due Process and Lineup Misidentifications Despite research findings and recommendations (largely the work of psychologists), the U.S. Supreme Court has set a high standard for throwing out eyewitness identifications. To throw out an identification, it has to deny a defendant "due process of law." What does due process have to do with identification procedures? The basic idea behind the application of the due process clause is that unreliable identification procedures can convict innocent people, and convicting innocent people deprives them of life (if they're executed), liberty (if they're imprisoned), and property (if they're fined) without due process of law.

The Court created a two-step test to implement the due process violation standard. The defendant has to prove by a preponderance of the evidence (more evidence than not) that:

1. The lineup, show-up, or photographic array was unnecessarily and impermissibly suggestive.
2. The totality of circumstances proves the unnecessarily and impermissibly suggestive procedures created a very substantial likelihood of misidentification. (Twenty-Sixth Annual Review of Criminal Procedure 1997, 944–945)

Five circumstances (factors) enter into the "totality":

1. *Witnesses' opportunity to view* defendants at the time of the crime
2. *Witnesses' degree of attention* at the time of the crime
3. *Witnesses' accuracy of description* of defendants prior to the identification
4. *Witnesses' level of certainty* when identifying defendants at the time of the identification procedure
5. *Length of time between the crime and the identification procedure* (Twenty-Sixth Annual Review of Criminal Procedure 1997, 945–946)

If the totality of circumstances shows the identification was reliable, it's admissible, even if it was unnecessarily or impermissibly suggestive (*Rodriguez v. Young* 1990).

Police Use of Force

The defining characteristic of police is the legitimate use of force (Chapter 5). Police use legitimate force to gain control of resisting or fleeing suspects and to protect themselves or others from injury and death (Williams 1993, 5–6). *Excessive force* means officers use more than the amount of force necessary to get control of suspects and protect themselves and others.

Before we examine excessive force (the focus of this section), you need some facts to help you keep the discussion in balance. First, police rarely use any force at all in making Fourth Amendment seizures. Why? They don't have to because suspects submit to police authority without resistance. (Of course, this isn't to say they submit without complaining about it, Figure 7.4.) And when they do, they don't often cause serious injury. According to a well-conducted national sample of individuals ages 16 and over who police used force against, 12 out of 100 said they suffered broken bones or teeth knocked out; 13 percent said they received cuts and bruises; and over 63 percent they either received no care or treated themselves (BJS February 2001, 26).

The use (or perception) of excessive force has sparked some of the worst riots in American history—Harlem in 1935, Watts in 1965, Miami in 1980, and Los

▶ The defining characteristic of police is the legitimate use of force. Officers can use the amount of force necessary to the circumstances to get control of resisting or fleeing suspects, and to protect themselves and others in danger. Here is a single frame from an incident in which White Oklahoma City police officers used their batons, pepper spray, and "physical beating" to subdue this Black suspect lying on the ground. It's very difficult to tell from this single frame whether the use of force was reasonable, but the officers faced disciplinary action based on the video taken by Brian Bates. Bates, who calls himself a "video vigilante," usually films men soliciting prostitutes and then calls police to have them arrested.

© Reuters/Corbis

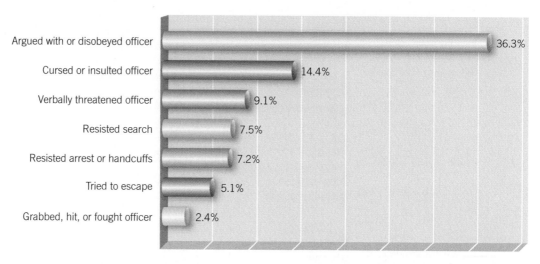

▲ **FIGURE 7.4 Actions Taken by Individuals 16 and Over during Officers' Use of Force**

Source: Bureau of Justice Statistics, *Contacts between Police and the Public* (Washington, DC: Bureau of Justice Statistics, February 2001), p. 28, Table 28.

Angeles in 1992. The police use of force against Rodney King and the riots following the acquittal in 1992 of the officers who used that force brought out the public's mixed feelings about police use of force (legitimate or not). We actually saw the police use force instead of just hearing descriptions of it (by chance, a young guy trying out his new camcorder recorded a group of LAPD officers using clubs, boots, and other means to keep King down). Seeing the tape night after night on TV etched the picture in our minds. And it provoked a huge public debate over police use of force.

The beating, then the acquittal, and the death and destruction caused by the riots highlighted three points about police use of force:

1. The legitimate use of coercive force—the defining characteristic of police work—is critical to effective police work. (Chapter 5)
2. The need for *legitimate* force is also the source of the *excessive* use of force.
3. The *perception* that police use excessive force routinely is held by many members of racial minority groups. (Kerstetter 1985, 149–182)

Bringing these points out into the open generated research showing us what we *know* (and *don't* know) about the kinds and amounts of force police use in their day-to-day operations; about department use-of-force policies; and about the effectiveness of these policies and practices. But the debate over police use of force didn't begin with Rodney King. New York journalist Lincoln Steffens opened the twentieth century with a series of articles reporting the brutality of NYPD officer "Clubber Williams." In 1930, President Hoover's Wickersham Commission reported shocking abuses of police use of force. In 1967, President Johnson's Commission on Law Enforcement found some police were still abusing their power to use force. The debate started by Lincoln Steffens in 1900 continues today, and I'm sure will continue for as long as there are police.

In this section, we'll look at the types of force police use, how the Constitution applies in issues of police use of force, and race and the use of deadly force.

The Types of Force

The respected Police Foundation conducted the most thorough study yet of the kinds and amounts of police use of force (Pate and Fridell 1993, 21–25, 73–78). Figure 7.5 shows the results of this survey. Let's look at three kinds of force: nondeadly knockdown force, deadly force, and high-speed chases.

Knockdown Force Knockdown force is enough force to "cause the suspect to fall to the ground." Greg Meyer (1991), a Los Angeles Police Department officer,

knockdown force enough force to cause a suspect to fall to the ground

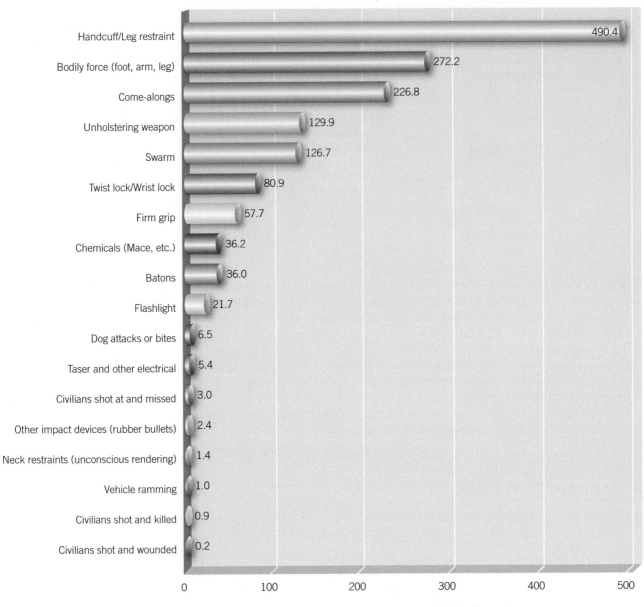

▲ **FIGURE 7.5 Types of Force Used
by City Police**

Source: Anthony M. Pate and Lorie A.
Fridell, *Police Use of Force: Official
Reports, Citizen Complaints, and Legal
Consequences* (Washington, DC: Police
Foundation, 1993), based on Table 6.1.

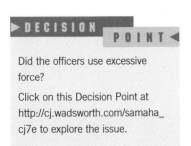

Did the officers use excessive
force?

Click on this Decision Point at
http://cj.wadsworth.com/samaha_
cj7e to explore the issue.

examined the types of force used by LAPD officers, the success of each in getting control of suspects, and the injuries caused to officers and suspects by each. He found Tasers and chemical sprays, two types of knockdown force, are as (or more) effective as other kinds and also a lot safer. Meyer's data showed Tasers and tear gas didn't injure a single suspect or officer (29). According to the Police Foundation, using more Tasers, stun guns, and tear gas would result in "fewer citizen injuries and deaths, fewer officer injuries and deaths, improved police-community relations, reduced exposure to departmental liability for wrongful police actions, and improved police morale" (29). The CJ and Technology box "Are Tasers Safe?" discusses the issue of Taser safety.

Deadly Force Police kill on average about 600 people every year, shoot and wound another 1200, and fire at, but miss, another 1800. However, the numbers vary from city to city and from neighborhood to neighborhood in the same city. For example, New Orleans police are 10 times more likely to kill people than Newark police. Chicago's near west side, for example, is 27 times more likely than the near north side to experience a police shooting in an average year. Deadly force not only kills suspects, officers die as well; 52 were killed in 2003

Are Tasers Safe?

The advent of pulsed energy weapons (most commonly known as Tasers) has had an enormous impact on reducing police use of deadly force by giving officers another less-than-lethal option in dealing with suspects. However, the popularity of the device has raised new issues for police executives. Both the Miami and Seattle police departments reported that there were no police-involved shootings in their respective agencies in 2003. As PERF staff explores less-than-lethal use of force options, it has become clear that the Taser will continue to garner more attention.

Advancements in technology have always changed the way in which people live. As human knowledge expanded, tools were developed to make people more efficient both at home and in the workplace. Police weapons technology, such as the Taser, has mirrored these advancements. Police defensive weaponry has come full circle; it began with a reliance on less-than-lethal weapons during the mid-1800s when clubs were issued to officers in New York and Boston. In the late 1800s, police forces began issuing firearms in response to criminal and riot-related threats. More recently, police departments in the United States (and the United Kingdom) have returned to more less-than-lethal options, including the collapsible baton, oleoresin capsicum (OC) spray, and pulsed energy weapons like the Taser.

Taser International, Inc., reports that more than four thousand police departments have armed themselves with Taser devices (with more than five hundred agencies equipping all of their patrol officers). According to new Police Commissioner Kathy O'Toole, the Boston Police Department is one of many agencies considering equipping patrol supervisors and tactical teams with nonlethal options such as Tasers.

However, criticism of the Taser-type devices has emerged. The ACLU of Colorado has complained that pulsed energy weapons often are being used in a manner that "constitutes unnecessary and unreasonable force that may constitute cruel, inhuman, or degrading treatment" (www.aclu-co.org/docket/200319/ACLU_letter_Taskforce_taser_abuses.pdf). But Taser International claims that "in over 30,000 actual field uses…there has never been a documented death…directly attributed to the TASER device" (www.taser.com)….

As the citizenry continues to hold law enforcement agencies accountable for their officers' use of force, there will be a need for continued development and standardized guidelines for less-than-lethal technologies like pulsed energy weapons. As with any service weapon, police executives will have to manage how such devices are used. Of course, any police service weapon has to be used prudently and responsibly and cannot be used punitively or in an abusive manner. Within the law enforcement profession, guidelines such as how often, and in what circumstances, Taser deployment is appropriate need to be standardized. Department policies vary on the use of a Taser on actively resisting suspects versus passively resisting suspects. Additionally, questions such as where on the body the Taser should be used, as well as prohibitions of its use (such as on pregnant women or juveniles for example) have to be explored.

These less-than-lethal devices are playing an important role in reducing police use of deadly force. As we move forward, and to maintain credibility with the public, law enforcement will likely need independent means to establish less-than-lethal weapons guidelines. Many agencies have begun this process.

Source: Josh Edermheimer and Jason Cheney, Police Executive Research Forum Newsletter, *Subject to Debate*, July 2004, p. 5.

(FBI 2004, 5). Contrary to what you might think, it's not always suspects who kill officers; they often die in friendly fire—officers accidentally shoot other officers (Geller and Scott 1992, 59–60; O'Donnell 1983, 14).

Departments that adopt strict deadly force rules and enforce them show steep drops in citizen and officer deaths. After the Kansas City, Missouri, department adopted a rule banning police from shooting juveniles except in self-defense, the number of youths under 18 shot by the police dropped dramatically. Former NYPD officer and now criminal justice professor James Fyfe showed that not only police shootings dropped sharply after the New York City Police Department adopted a rule, but the numbers of police officers shot at also dropped (*Criminal Justice Newsletter* 1996 [Nov. 15], 5; Geller 1985; Milton 1977, 10).

Formulating, implementing, and enforcing deadly force rules is difficult. Patrol officers suspect changes, and police unions fight them. Administrators don't want to put firearms policies in writing because they're worried about lawsuits. In fact, some courts have given them reason to worry. The California Supreme Court (*Grudt v. Los Angeles* 1970) allowed the LAPD written firearms policy to be used as evidence by a plaintiff who was suing an officer for wrongful death. (The officer had broken the deadly force rule.)

However, compared with the total number of contacts police have with individuals, shootings are rare. A study of New York City patrol officers found officers used force of all kinds in less than one-tenth of 1 percent of all encounters with private individuals. Civilians were shot at 5 of the 1762 times observers saw officers use any physical force (Geller and Scott 1992, 60). We have to be careful not to give the impression that rare means not serious because, of course, every death, every wound, even every miss is serious.

High-Speed Chases

> During our years in police cars, we have been at the cop's end of more than thirty high-speed chases. Younger cops, hotshot cops, aggressive cops, relish the exhilaration of these pursuits. People who haven't ridden in patrol cars for a full shift cannot appreciate how tedious policing can be even in the world's most crime-ridden cities. Patrol policing, like military combat and the lives of cowboys, consists mostly of periods of boredom, broken up by interludes of excitement and even of terror. For police, a chase is among the most exciting of all work experiences: the sudden start of a chase is a jolt not unlike that experienced by the dozing fisherman who finds suddenly that he has a big and dangerous fish on the other end of his line. (Skolnick and Fyfe 1993, 11)

Why is the topic of high-speed chases in this section on police use of force? Because vehicles are deadly weapons that can hurt and kill people. According to police specialist Gordon E. Misner (1990), "If the circumstances don't reasonably permit the use of deadly force, they also do not warrant engaging in a high-speed chase!" (15) (Figure 7.6).

Is the risk of injury and death worth the chase? Geoffrey P. Alpert and Roger G. Dunham (1990, 38; Alpert 1987, 298–306) found 54 percent of high-speed chases in Florida's Metro-Dade County Police Department were for traffic violations; 32 percent were for suspected felonies; 12 percent were because of calls "to be on the lookout for" a named suspect; and 2 percent were for driving while

▶ **FIGURE 7.6 IACP Model Pursuit Policy**

Pursuit
Submitted by: Highway Safety Committee
AHSO18.a96

WHEREAS, police pursuits have become an increased focus of attention for public safety officials, the news media and the public at large; and

WHEREAS, an acceptable balance must be obtained between the capture of fleeing suspects and the responsibility of law enforcement to protect the general public from unnecessary risks; and

WHEREAS, there is no uniform reporting criteria or system in place to accurately account for all pursuits; and

WHEREAS, many agencies have excellent comprehensive policies in place while others have minimal or no policies at all dealing with pursuits; and

WHEREAS, some states have enacted serious penalties for consciously attempting to elude the police while others have not; and

WHEREAS, there is a need to adopt a generic "sample" policy that can serve as a minimum guideline for all agencies involved with pursuits; now, therefore, be it

RESOLVED, that the International Association of Chiefs of Police (IACP), duly assembled at its 103rd annual conference in Phoenix, Arizona, encourages all agencies to adopt written policies governing pursuits, and that these policies contain at a minimum all the elements put forth in the IACP "sample" policy and that all members of the agency receive familiarization training in the policy; and be it

FURTHER RESOLVED, that the IACP and the National Highway Traffic Safety Administration (NHTSA) develop a uniform pursuit reporting criteria and form to accurately document pursuit involvements and results nationwide; and be it

FURTHER RESOLVED, that the IACP and NHTSA encourage the state legislatures to make it a criminal offense with severe punishments to evade arrest by intentionally failing to comply with the lawful order of a police officer to stop a motor vehicle; and be it

FURTHER RESOLVED, that the IACP, NHTSA and the National Association of Motor Vehicle Manufacturers work together to apply technology that will disable fleeing vehicles and minimize the need for pursuits; and be it

FURTHER RESOLVED, that the IACP adopt the attached pursuit policy as its sample and that it be made a part of the Manual of Model Police Traffic Services Policies and Procedures maintained by the Highway Safety Committee, and that this policy replace and rescind all prior IACP policies on this subject.

CALEA Standard Ref: 41.2.2, 61.3.4

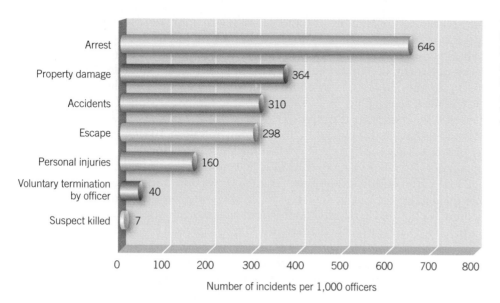

◄ **FIGURE 7.7 Results of High-Speed Chases, Dade County Police Department, 1985–1987**
Source: Geoffrey P. Alpert and Roger G. Dunham, *Police Pursuit Driving: Controlling Responses to Emergency Situations* (New York: Greenwood Press, 1990), based on Table 1, p. 37.

intoxicated (DWI). Accidents occurred in more than half the pursuits. But Alpert also found many traffic violation chases produced arrests for unrelated serious felonies (Figure 7.7).

Still, Lee P. Brown, when he was chief of the Houston Police Department, in a cover message to a new pursuit policy, wrote:

> Remember the criminals will continue to be out there in the future and they can be found and arrested by other means. So if you decide not to chase based on the risks involved, you will not be subject to criticism. However, if you decide that you should chase, we will support you and offer acceptable standard operating procedures to assist you. The safety and well-being of our officers and the public we serve is the first and foremost priority in our minds, and we will continue to work toward that end with you. (Misner 1990)

The Use of Force and the Constitution

Constitutionally, police use of force is a Fourth Amendment seizure (*Tennessee v. Garner* 1985). You learned in the section on arrests that the Fourth Amendment bans *only* "unreasonable" seizures. According to the U.S. Supreme Court, only the use of *excessive* force is an unreasonable seizure. What this means in practice is that officers can use the amount of force reasonably necessary to get and keep control of fleeing and resisting suspects and to defend themselves and others against force used by suspects. According to the Court:

> Our Fourth Amendment jurisprudence has long recognized that the right to make an arrest or investigatory stop necessarily carries with it the right to use some degree of physical coercion or threat thereof to effect it. . . . With respect to a claim of excessive force, the . . . standard of reasonableness at the moment applies: "Not every push or shove, even if it may later seem unnecessary in the peace of a judge's chambers," violates the Fourth Amendment. The calculus of reasonableness must embody allowance for the fact that police officers are often forced to make split-second judgments—in circumstances that are tense, uncertain, and rapidly evolving—about the amount of force that is necessary in a particular situation. (*Saucier v. Katz* 2001, 210)

Throughout most of our history, states followed the ancient common-law rule that allowed officers to use deadly force when it's necessary to apprehend fleeing felons. By the 1960s, many police departments had adopted rules that restricted the common-law rule. The gist of these rules is that officers can use deadly force only when (1) it's necessary to apprehend "dangerous" suspects, and (2) it doesn't put innocent people in danger. In *Tennessee v. Garner* (1985), the U.S. Supreme Court "constitutionalized" these rules into an **objective standard of reasonable force** to decide the case. According to the standard, the Fourth Amendment permits

Civil Rights Violations by Police: Law and procedures followed when investigating civil rights violations allegedly committed by the police. To reach this site go to "Web Links" on your Samaha CJ7 website: http://cj.wadsworth.com/samaha_cj7e.

objective standard of reasonable force Fourth Amendment permits officers to use the amount of force necessary to apprehend and bring suspects under control

officers to use the amount of force necessary to apprehend and bring suspects under control. The standard is objective because it doesn't depend on officer's intent or motives. So if an officer uses a reasonable amount of force, using that force out of malice or prejudice doesn't make it unreasonable. By the same token, no amount of good intentions and noble motive will make the use of excessive force reasonable.

▶ D E C I S I O N
P O I N T ◀

Can the police shoot to kill a fleeing burglar?

Click on this Decision Point at http://cj.wadsworth.com/samaha_cj7e to explore the case *Tennessee v. Garner*.

Here's what happened in the *Garner* case. At about 10:45 P.M. on October 3, 1974, Memphis Police Officers Elton Hymon and Leslie Wright were dispatched to answer a "prowler inside call." When they got there, they saw a woman standing on her porch gesturing toward the adjacent house. She told them she'd heard glass breaking and that "they" or "someone" was breaking in next door. While Wright radioed the dispatcher to say that they were on the scene, Hymon went behind the house. He heard a door slam and saw someone run across the backyard. The fleeing suspect, Edward Garner, stopped at a 6-feet-high chain link fence at the edge of the yard. With the aid of a flashlight, Hymon was able to see Garner's face and hands. He saw no sign of a weapon, and though not certain, was "reasonably sure" and "figured" that Garner was unarmed. He thought Garner was 17 or 18 years old and about 5 feet 5, or 5 feet 7 inches tall. While Garner was crouched at the base of the fence, Hymon called out "police, halt" and took a few steps toward him. Garner began to climb over the fence. Convinced that if Garner made it over the fence he'd escape, Hymon shot him. The bullet hit Garner in the back of the head. Garner was taken by ambulance to a hospital, where he died on the operating table. Ten dollars and a purse taken from the house were found on his body.

Applying its objective standard of reasonable force, the Court decided the shooting was a Fourth Amendment "unreasonable seizure." According to the Court:

> Whenever an officer restrains the freedom of a person to walk away, he has seized that person.... There can be no question that apprehension by the use of deadly force is a seizure subject to the reasonableness requirement of the Fourth Amendment.... The use of deadly force to prevent the escape of *all* felony suspects, whatever the circumstances, is constitutionally unreasonable. It is not better that all felony suspects die than that they escape. Where the suspect poses no immediate threat to the officer and no threat to others, the harm resulting from failing to apprehend him does not justify the use of deadly force to do so.
>
> It is no doubt unfortunate when a suspect who is in sight escapes, but the fact the police arrive a little late or are a little slower afoot does not always justify killing the suspect. A police officer may not seize an unarmed, nondangerous suspect by shooting him dead....
>
> Officer Hymon could not reasonably have believed that Garner—young, slight, and unarmed—posed any threat. Indeed, Hymon never attempted to justify his actions on any basis other than the need to prevent escape.... The fact that Garner was a suspected burglar could not, without regard to the other circumstances, automatically justify the use of deadly force. Hymon did not have probable cause to believe that Garner, whom he correctly believed to be unarmed, posed any physical danger to himself or to others.

Three justices dissented. They agreed that shooting Garner was a seizure but argued it was reasonable under the Fourth Amendment. According to the dissenters:

> Whether that seizure was reasonable and therefore permitted by the Fourth Amendment requires a careful balancing of the important public interest in crime prevention and detection and the nature and quality of the intrusion upon legitimate interests of the individual....
>
> The public interest involved in the use of deadly force as a last resort to apprehend a fleeing burglary suspect relates primarily to the serious nature of the crime. Household burglaries represent not only the illegal entry into a person's home, but also "pose a real risk of serious harm to others."...
>
> Against the strong public interests justifying the conduct at issue here must be weighed the individual interests implicated in the use of deadly force by police officers.... The police officer, in the course of...investigating a nighttime burglary, had reasonable cause to arrest the suspect and ordered him to halt. The officer's use of force resulted because the suspected burglar refused to heed this command and the officer reasonably believed that there was no means short of firing his weapon to apprehend the suspect.... "The policeman's hands should not be tied merely because of the possibility that the suspect will fail to cooperate with legitimate actions by law enforcement personnel."

The same objective standard of reasonable force applies to cases of nondeadly force. The In Focus box "Interrogating Terrorist Suspects: Does the Constitution Allow It?" examines the issue of how much force police should be allowed to use when interrogating terrorist suspects.

Race and Deadly Force

Does race play a role in the use of deadly force? The most common type of incident in which police and civilians shoot one another in urban America involves an on-duty, uniformed, White, male officer and an armed, Black, male civilian between the ages of 17 and 30, at night, in a public location in a high-crime precinct, in connection with a suspected armed robbery or a "man with a gun" call (Geller and Scott 1992, 143). Nearly all related studies report that the police shoot at more Blacks than Whites:

- Chicago police officers shot at Blacks 3.8 times more than at Whites during the 1970s.
- New York City police officers shot at Blacks 6 times more than at Whites during the 1970s.
- Dallas police officers shot at Blacks 4.5 times more than at Whites during the 1970s and 1980s.
- St. Louis police officers shot at Blacks 7.7 times more than at Whites from 1987 to 1991.
- Memphis police officers fatally shot at Blacks 5.1 more times than at Whites from 1969 to 1974; 2.6 times more from 1980 to 1984; and 1.6 times more from 1985 to 1989. They were 9.4 times more likely to shoot at Blacks than at Whites in relation to suspected property crimes from 1969 to 1974 and 13 times more from 1980 to 1984; and Blacks were the only property crime suspects shot at from 1985 to 1989. (Geller and Scott 1992, 147–148)

Is the decision to shoot suspects infected with racism? The numbers definitely show there's a disparity between decisions to shoot Blacks and Whites. But you've already learned that disparity doesn't have to mean discrimination. The empirical research is mixed. In their widely cited *Split-Second Decisions,* when William A. Geller and Kevin J. Karales (1981, 119) controlled for violent felonies (murder, rape, armed robbery, and aggravated assault and battery) in decisions to shoot, racial disparities disappeared.

But James Fyfe (1982, 707–722) found shooting data in Memphis showed race did infect decisions to shoot in some kinds of cases. The data strongly supported

> the assertion that police did differentiate racially with their trigger fingers, by shooting blacks in circumstances less threatening than those in which they shot whites....[The] black death rate from police shootings while unarmed and non-assaultive (5.4 per 100,000)...18 times higher than the comparable white rate (0.3). (715)

After Memphis police officer Elton Hymon shot and killed 13-year-old Edward Garner (*Tennessee v. Garner* 1985), Memphis adopted a strict shooting policy—police could only shoot to apprehend suspected "violent felons" who "posed a threat of serious physical harm to the officer or to others unless he is immediately apprehended." Jerry R. Sparger and David J. Giacopassi (1992) reviewed records of police shootings before and after the restriction. They found after the strict policy was adopted:

1. Overall police shootings dropped sharply.
2. Racial disparity in shootings almost disappeared.
3. Black deaths from police shootings declined.

But they also found the rate of Black deaths from police shootings was still 56.5 percent higher than the rate for Whites (211–225). Also, few will disagree with the Black officer who voiced this opinion after the Rodney King case:

Interrogating Terrorist Suspects: Does the Constitution Allow It?

FBI and Justice Department investigators are increasingly frustrated by the silence of jailed suspected associates of Osama bin Laden's al-Qaeda network, and some are beginning to say that traditional civil liberties may have to be cast aside if they are to extract information about the September 11 attacks and terrorist plans. More than 150 people rounded up by law enforcement officials in the aftermath of the attacks remain in custody, but attention has focused on four suspects held in New York who the FBI believes are withholding valuable information.

FBI agents have offered the suspects the prospect of lighter sentences, money, jobs, and a new identity and life in the United States for them and their family members, but they have not succeeded in getting information from them, according to law enforcement sources. "We're into this thing for 35 days and nobody is talking," a senior FBI official said, adding that "frustration has begun to appear." Said one experienced FBI agent involved in the investigation: "We are known for humanitarian treatment, so basically we are stuck. . . . Usually there is some incentive, some angle to play, what you can do for them. But it could get to that spot where we could go to pressure . . . where we won't have a choice, and we are probably getting there."

Among the alternative strategies under discussion are using drugs or pressure tactics, such as those employed occasionally by Israeli interrogators, to extract information. Another idea is extraditing the suspects to allied countries where security services sometimes employ threats to family members or resort to torture. Under U.S. law, interrogators in criminal cases can lie to suspects, but information obtained by physical pressure, inhumane treatment, or torture cannot be used in a trial. In addition, the government interrogators who used such tactics could be sued by the victim or charged with battery by the government.

The four key suspects, held in New York's Metropolitan Correctional Center, are Zacarias Moussaoui, a French Moroccan detained in August initially in Minnesota after he sought lessons on how to fly commercial jetliners but not how to take off or land them; Mohammed Jaweed Azmath and Ayub Ali Khan, Indians traveling with false passports who were detained the day after the World Trade Center and Pentagon attacks with box cutters, hair dye, and $5,000 in cash; and Nabil Almarabh, a former Boston cabdriver with alleged links to al-Qaeda.

Unanswered questions asked of "the two with the box cutters and others have left us wondering what's the next phase," the FBI official said. One former senior FBI official with a background in counterterrorism said recently, "You can't torture, you can't give drugs now, and there is logic, reason, and humanity to back that." But, he added, "you could reach a point where they allow us to apply drugs to a guy. . . . But I don't think this country would ever permit torture, or beatings." He said there was a difference in employing a "truth serum," such as sodium pentothal, "to try to get critical information when facing disaster, and beating a guy till he is senseless. If there is another major attack on U.S. soil, the American public

---

There are many fine white officers who are doing their job and do not harbor racist sentiments. However, there is still a significant group of individuals whose old line, deep-seated biases continually manifest themselves on the job. (Christopher Commission 1991, 80)

Racial Profiling

- Out of desperation, a young Black woman trades her new sports car in for an older model; cops repeatedly stopped her because they suspected she stole it.
- An elderly Black couple on their way home from a social event in formal dress are stopped and questioned at length because their car resembles one identified in a robbery.
- A prominent Black lawyer driving a luxury car is stopped repeatedly on various pretexts.
- A Hispanic deputy police chief is stopped numerous times "on suspicion" when he's outside his jurisdiction.
- A young Hispanic man working the evening shift drives the same way home every night; police stop him almost every night.
- Officers stop a Black judge away from her jurisdiction, handcuff her, and lay her face down on the pavement while they search her car. They find nothing and let her go without a citation.

could let it happen," he said. "Drugs might taint a prosecution, but it might be worth it."

Even some people who are firm supporters of civil liberties understand the pressures that are developing. David Cole, a professor at Georgetown University Law Center who obtained the release of Middle Eastern clients after they had been detained for years based on secret information, said that in the current crisis, "the use of force to extract information could happen" in cases where investigators believe suspects have information on an upcoming attack. "If there is a ticking bomb, it is not an easy issue, it's tough," he said.

Kenneth W. Starr, the independent counsel during the Clinton administration, wrote recently that the Supreme Court distinguished terrorism cases from cases where lesser threats are involved. He noted that five justices in a recent deportation case recognized that the "genuine danger" represented by terrorism requires "heightened deference to the judgments of the political branches with respect to matters of national security."

Former attorney general Richard L. Thornburgh said, "We put emphasis on due process and sometimes it strangles us." In the aftermath of September 11, he said, "legally admissible evidence in court may not be the be-all and end-all." The country may compare the current search for information to brutal tactics in wartime used to gather intelligence overseas and even by U.S. troops from prisoners during military actions.

Extradition of Moussaoui to France or Morocco is a possibility, one law enforcement official said. The French security services were quick to leak to journalists in Paris that they had warned the CIA and FBI in early September, before the attacks, that Moussaoui was associated with al-Qaeda and had pilot training. The leak has irritated U.S. investigators in part because "it was so limited," one FBI official said. "Maybe we should give him [Moussaoui] to them," he said, noting that French security has a reputation for rough interrogations.

The threat of extradition to a country with harsh practices does not always work. In 1997, Hani Abdel Rahim al-Sayegh, a Saudi citizen arrested in Canada and transferred to the United States under the promise that he would tell about the bombing of the Khobar Towers military barracks in Saudi Arabia, refused to cooperate in the investigation when he got here. The FBI threatened to have al-Sayegh sent back to Saudi Arabia, where he could have faced beheading, thinking it would get him to talk. "He called their bluff and went back, was not executed and is in jail," a government official said.

Robert M. Blitzer, former chief of the FBI counterterrorism section, said offers of reduced sentences worked to get testimony in the cases of Ahmed Ressam, caught bringing explosives into the country for millennium attacks that never took place, and Ali Mohammed, the former U.S. Army Green Beret who pleaded guilty in the 1998 embassy bombings and provided valuable information about al-Qaeda. The two former al-Qaeda members who testified publicly in the 1998 bombing trials were resettled with their families in the United States under the witness protection program and given either money or loans to restart their lives. Torture "goes against every grain in my body," Blitzer said. "Chances are you are going to get the wrong person and risk damage or killing them." In the end, he said, there has to be another way.

Source: Walter Pincus, "Silence of 4 Terror Suspects Poses Dilemma," *Washington Post*, October 21, 2001. © 2001, The Washington Post. Reprinted with permission.

Stories like these are told, reported in the news, and cited in the enormous commentary on (and hot controversy over) **racial profiling** (law enforcement decisions based on race or ethnicity) that has been cascading down on us for more than a decade now (Fridell 2004, 2; Fridell, Lunney, Diamond, and Kubu, 2001, 2–3; Harris 2002; Wilson, Dunham, and Alpert 2004, 896). The practice is part of the larger problem of decision making infected by race and ethnicity throughout the criminal justice system. Race- and ethnicity-infected decision making isn't new; it's part of the "long history of sometimes tense and even volatile police-minority relations" (Fridell 2004, 2). But the current debate and the strongest feelings are directed at the decisions to stop, interrogate, and search drivers and vehicles (Harris 2002 and too many others to cite here). Let's look more closely at the controversy surrounding "driving while Black or Brown" (DWB) and how constitutional issues impact profiling.

> racial profiling law enforcement decisions based on race or ethnicity

"Driving While Black or Brown"

The question is how widespread are the stories at the beginning of this section. That's an extremely difficult and complex question to answer. But because of the desire to know the answer (and, let's admit, responding to public pressure and state laws) many police departments require officers to collect information on all vehicle stops. The information includes race or ethnicity of drivers; reason(s) for the stop (traffic violations, suspicion of crime); disposition (citation, warning, arrest); whether drivers, passengers, and/or vehicles were searched; and whether any contraband or evidence of crime was found during the search. By 2003,

> **Human Rights Watch: "Shielded from Justice":** National report on police abuse and misconduct. To reach this site go to "Web Links" on your Samaha CJ7 website: http://cj.wadsworth.com/samaha_cj7e.

about half the states had passed racial profiling laws with data collection requirements; similar laws were pending in other states (Fridell 2004, 3).

Unfortunately, most departments "don't know how to" analyze properly the information they've collected. According to Lorie Fridell, Director of Research at the Police Executive Research Forum (PERF):

> They are either ill-equipped or misinformed about what should be done. An overwhelming majority of the data analyses reviewed by PERF...were based on substandard methods. Most agencies are using models for their analyses that fall far short of minimal social science standards. (Fridell 2004, 3)

One of the basic problems is one you've learned about already: disparity is taken for discrimination. For example, police stop, interrogate, arrest, and search more Blacks and Hispanics more often than Whites, or in greater proportions than their representation in the general population. Too often, analysts jump to the conclusion that race or ethnicity infects these decisions. But in fact the analysts' job has only just begun. Race or ethnicity is just one of several hypotheses that might explain the disparity. The analysts have to rule out the "alternative hypotheses." To illustrate, let's look at gender disparity. We know that police stop men more often than women. Suppose that 65 percent of the drivers they stop are men and 35 percent are women. We'd be foolish to jump to the conclusion that gender infected these decisions. Here are some alternative hypotheses we'd have to rule out before we could blame the decision to stop on drivers' sex:

1. *Quantity hypothesis.* Men drive more than women.
2. *Quality hypothesis.* Men violate traffic laws more than women.
3. *Location hypothesis.* More men than women drive in places where police are likely to make traffic stops.

Controlling for driving quantity, quality, and location are the strongest benchmarks to take into account in analyzing the problem of "driving while Black or Brown" (Fridell 2004, 6).

Important as research is so we can know how much disparity there is, and the reasons for it, knowing those answers aren't the only path to grounding police decisions to stop, question, arrest, and search drivers and vehicles on legitimate criteria which should be familiar to you by now. (Try and name the criteria before you read the next sentence.) Those criteria, as they apply here include the seriousness of the drivers' suspected offense; the dangerousness of the drivers; and the strength of the objective basis. The other paths to legitimate decision making include the standards for recruiting and hiring officers; the quality and amount of police training; police procedures; police performance measures; and officer accountability (see Chapter 5 and "Remedies" later in this chapter).

Racial and ethnic disparity in decisions to stop, interrogate, arrest, and search drivers and their vehicles (whether it's intentionally discriminatory or not) leads many Black and Brown Americans to *perceive* that they're routinely stopped and searched because of their skin color, not because of their behavior (Wilson, Dunham, and Alpert 2004, 896). PERF Director of Research Lorie Fridell and her colleagues (2001) underscore the importance of this perception:

> Racial and ethnic minorities constitute a substantial and growing segment of the U.S. population. Strength is in diversity, and we look to minority communities to participate fully in all aspects of society. Police are now looking to the public for partnerships and collaborative problem-solving solutions to community ills [Chapter 6]. If substantial segments of the community are the victims of police bias, or even perceive that they are, the likelihood of success is dim. We all know that racial profiling is unacceptable and is at variance with the standards and values inherent in ensuring a fair and dignified response to all. (1)

Looking at the big picture, Fridell and her colleagues put profiling in the context of policing in a constitutional democracy:

> If prejudice, arbitrary decisions, treatment disparity, and disrespect are to be replaced by universal respect and equitable use of police powers, then we must begin a process of

bringing all policing into accord with democratic principles. We must insist that protection of human rights is a fundamental responsibility of police. We must ensure at all costs the primacy of the rule of law, and scrupulously monitor the use of police authority for compliance. We must carefully examine our beliefs regarding the role of police, and eradicate from the police culture the mentality that leads to the use of bias in dealing with citizens. We must do this everywhere, and all of the time. (10)

Profiling and the Constitution

The Fourteenth Amendment commands that "no state shall deny any citizen the equal protection of the laws." You've already learned (Chapter 4) that equal protection doesn't mean identical protection. But if decisions to interfere with someone's right to come and go as they please (like traffic and street stops) are based on group characteristics (**profiles**), instead of individual actions, the question immediately comes up: Did race, or ethnicity, or sexual orientation, infect the decision? Or to put the question in constitutional terms, "Did the decision deny a citizen equal protection of the laws?"

profiles decisions based on group characteristics instead of individual behavior

In practice, it's very difficult to prove claims that officials denied equal protection (*U.S. v. Armstrong* 1996). Challengers have to prove two difficult facts: First, the official action had a discriminatory *effect*. Specifically, this means proving race or some other illegal group characteristic (not some legitimate criterion like seriousness of the offense or criminal record) was behind the official decision.

Second, and much more difficult, is proving discriminatory *intent;* namely, individual officials intended to discriminate against the challenger because of the challenger's race or other illegal criteria. What makes it so difficult is the **presumption of regularity.** The presumption is that government actions are lawful and free of discrimination. Challengers have to prove the actions were illegal by "clear evidence" (*U.S. v. Armstrong* 1996, 464). For example, proving an official said (and meant) "I hate Hispanics" isn't good enough to win an equal protection case brought by a Hispanic who claims the cop stopped him because he was Hispanic. The challenger would have to prove the cop said (and meant) something like "I stopped him because he was Hispanic." But how likely is it in a time of political correctness that any cop would say that, and, if he did, how likely is it that the challenger could prove it?

presumption of regularity government actions are presumed to be lawful and free of discrimination

Police Misconduct

Police misconduct can include everything from something as minor as accepting a free cup of coffee in a local restaurant to things as serious as arresting someone just because she's Hispanic and selling drugs. There are many explanations of police misconduct. First, there's the rotten apple theory, which says there are a few bad officers that recruitment and training can't identify. Another is that some officers start out as idealists but become "bad" because of the socialization processes of training and field experiences (Chapter 5). In this section, we'll look at police corruption, remedies for police misconduct, the exclusionary rule, and other responses to police misconduct.

Police Corruption

Police corruption is a form of occupational crime: misusing police authority for private gain (Chapter 2). Corruption can be limited to one or two officers or spread throughout a whole department. And it can include everything from a top official extorting thousands of dollars a month from vice operations to a patrol officer accepting a free cup of coffee from a neighborhood restaurant (Sherman 1978, 30–31). In former New York Police Commissioner Patrick Murphy's broad definition, "Except for your paycheck, there is no such thing as a clean buck" (Goldstein 1977, 201).

The most common corrupt practices include:

- *Mooching.* Free meals, alcohol, groceries, or other items
- *Chiseling.* Demands for free admission to entertainment
- *Favoritism.* Getting immunity from traffic violations
- *Prejudice.* Giving non-Whites less than impartial treatment
- *Shopping.* Stealing small items from stores left unlocked after business hours
- *Extortion.* Demanding money in exchange for not filing traffic tickets
- *Bribery.* Receiving payments of cash or "gifts" for past or future assistance in avoiding arrest or in falsifying or withholding evidence
- *Shakedown.* Taking expensive items for personal use and attributing their loss to criminal activity during the investigation of a break-in or burglary
- *Perjury.* Lying to provide an alibi for fellow officers apprehended in illegal activity
- *Premeditated theft.* Executing a planned burglary to gain forced entry to acquire unlawful goods (Stoddard 1983, 340–341)

Police corruption has serious consequences. It damages public confidence and lessens residents' willingness to help the police. It also hurts policing from inside. Officers "on the take" have less time for police work and even resent how it interferes with their moneymaking. Corrupt supervisors also weaken administrative control over patrol officers. Weak supervisors encourage officers to "respond more slowly to calls for assistance, avoid assigned duties, sleep on the job, and perform poorly in situations requiring discipline" (Goldstein 1977, 190–192).

We can't write off the cause of corruption as simple greed (Goldstein 1977, 197–199). Police officers deal with not very nice people in a day's work. So it may not be surprising that some officers believe everybody's "on the take." Officers sometimes also look at criminal justice as hopeless. They watch offenders pass through the lower courts. They see prosecutors, defense attorneys, and judges take their share of "dirty money," and they swallow the bitter pill of seeing them immune from scandalous exposure (Knapp Commission 1972, 5–6; Rubenstein 1973, 282).

But does seeing corruption by other public officials justify or excuse their own corruption? Of course not. This is especially true when we take into account what this chapter teaches us: Police officers are different from the rest of us—only they have the legal power and the technology to take away what we dearly prize—our right to come and go as we please and even our lives—before there's proof beyond a reasonable doubt that we're guilty of crimes. As every Spider-Man® comic book reader knows because it appears in every issue: "With great power comes great responsibility."

Exposing and correcting corruption are difficult. For one thing, discretionary decision making not to enforce laws (necessary as this may be) is usually hidden from public view. Further, "a code of silence brands anyone who exposes corruption a traitor. . . . It is easier for . . . a rookie to become corrupt than to remain honest" (Chapter 5; Knapp Commission 1972).

Remedies for Police Misconduct

One day, when I was a member of a Minneapolis mayor's committee to examine police misconduct, we held a neighborhood meeting. One resident made this comment, "We all know what happens when we break the law—we get arrested and prosecuted." Then, he asked, "What I want to know is what happens when the *police* break the law? What recourse do we have?" The answer is there are four possible remedies for police misconduct:

1. *Criminal law.* Prosecute the officer.
2. *Civil law.* Sue the officer, the police department, or the government.
3. *Administrative.* Discipline the officer as a result of internal or external review.
4. *Procedural.* Throw illegally obtained evidence out of court.

Formally, all four remedies are available in the same case. For example, the state can prosecute a police officer for breaking and entering when he illegally searches a house. The homeowner can sue the officer for damages. The police department can fire or suspend the officer. Finally, if the "victim" of the illegal entry is prosecuted, the court can throw out any evidence the officer found during the illegal search. However, in practice, it's rare to see all of these remedies pursued in the same case. Let's look at each of the remedies.

Criminal Punishment Most police misconduct is also a crime. A police officer who illegally shoots and kills a person has committed criminal homicide. Illegal arrests might be false imprisonment. Illegal searches can be breaking and entering or trespassing. Corruption might be theft, extortion, or even robbery. But how likely is it police officers will be charged with crimes, convicted, and punished when they break the law? Not very. Why? First, witnesses are hard to come by and when they are they usually don't get much jury sympathy. Many people who are the objects of police illegality are probably criminals themselves. Rarely will a prosecutor or a jury (or, for that matter, the public) side with a "real" criminal over police officers who, after all, are "only trying to do their job." Even totally innocent people run up against the thick wall of resistance to criticizing police officers. There's a strong presumption they're acting properly, and it's tough to show they're not.

Civil Lawsuits Most police criminal misconduct is also a private injury (tort). Plaintiffs can go into a state court to sue individual officers and sometimes their departments and municipalities to recover money (damages) to compensate them for their injuries. But just as it's hard to convict police officers of crimes, it's also hard to win lawsuits in state courts. According to the **doctrine of official immunity,** police officers aren't liable unless their misconduct was intentional and malicious. Why? Because, as the Minnesota supreme court (*Susla v. State* 1976, 912; *Pletan v. Gaines et al.* 1992, 40) put it, "To encourage responsible law enforcement . . . police are afforded a wide degree of discretion precisely because a more stringent standard could inhibit action." So, the court decided, a police officer wasn't liable for the death of a small boy killed during a high-speed chase where the officer was trying to catch a fleeing shoplifter. Official immunity protected the officer; otherwise, the court maintained, officers in the future might hold back in their vigorous enforcement of the law.

Plaintiffs can also sue in federal courts if officers violate their constitutional rights. The Civil Rights Act gives individuals the right to sue state and local governments, their agencies, and their agents for violations of rights guaranteed by the U.S. Constitution. The act provides:

> Every person who, under color of any statute, ordinance, regulation, custom, or usage, of any State or Territory, subjects, or causes to be subjected, any citizen of the United States or other person within the jurisdiction thereof to the deprivation of any rights, privileges, or immunities secured by the Constitution and laws, shall be liable to the party injured in an action at law, suit in equity, or other proper proceeding for redress. (U.S. Code 1994)

It's even harder for plaintiffs to recover damages under the Civil Rights Act than it is in state courts. The U.S. Supreme Court has created a **defense of qualified immunity** for officers whose actions are "objectively reasonable." According to the Court, qualified immunity has to strike a balance between protecting individuals' constitutional rights and law enforcement's power to do its job. In the leading qualified immunity case, *Anderson v. Creighton* (1987), FBI agents searched the Creightons' home without a warrant and without probable cause, looking for one of their relatives. The Court agreed FBI Agent Anderson violated the Creightons' rights when he illegally came in and searched their house. But unreasonable searches don't automatically translate into civil liability under section 1983. If Anderson could have believed his unreasonable search was reasonable, he wasn't liable. So the Creightons lost their case.

doctrine of official immunity officers aren't liable for their misconduct unless it's intentional

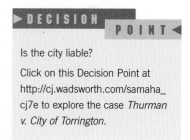

Is the city liable?

Click on this Decision Point at http://cj.wadsworth.com/samaha_cj7e to explore the case *Thurman v. City of Torrington.*

defense of qualified immunity officers aren't liable for their "objectively reasonable" actions

Internal Review The most common accountability procedure for police misconduct is internal review. In most large and mid-sized departments, special internal affairs units (IAU) review police misconduct. According to Professor Douglas W. Perez (1994, 88–89), a former deputy sheriff, "Most cops do not like internal affairs." They don't trust IAU, and some even think IAU investigators are traitors. Still, most officers believe IAU operations are a necessary evil. For one thing, they're a good defense against external review (see next section). The famed Chicago chief of police O. W. Wilson said, "It is clearly apparent that if the police do not take a vigorous stand on the matter of internal investigation, outside groups—such as review boards consisting of laymen and other persons outside the police service—will step into the void" (Griswold 1994, 215–221).

There are four stages of internal review:

1. Intake
2. Investigation
3. Deliberation
4. Disposition

The Internal Affairs Section of the Oakland, California, Police Department is considered an excellent unit, so we'll use it as an example of how internal review proceeds through these four stages. Although the unit is housed in the department building, the department's intake policy is "anyone anywhere should accept a complaint if a citizen wishes it taken." All complaints alleging excessive force, police corruption, and racial discrimination are followed up (Perez 1994, 92–93).

Someone besides the intake officer investigates complaints. The investigator gathers evidence, usually interviewing the officer involved last. If officers refuse to cooperate, they're subject to discipline, like dismissal for refusing to obey an order of the chief.

Completed investigations go to the IAU supervisor. If the supervisor approves, complaints go to the decision-making or deliberation stage. There are four possible decisions (Figure 7.8):

1. *Unfounded.* The investigation proved that the act did not take place.
2. *Exonerated.* The acts took place, but the investigation proved that they were justified, lawful, and proper.
3. *Not sustained.* The investigation failed to gather enough evidence to clearly prove the allegations in the complaint.
4. *Sustained.* The investigation disclosed enough evidence to clearly prove the allegations in the complaint. (Perez 1994, 96)

If the decision is "unfounded," "exonerated," or "not sustained," the case is closed. If the decision is "sustained," the supervisor recommends disciplinary action. Recommended disciplinary actions ranked from least to most severe include (1) reprimand, (2) written reprimand, (3) transfer, (4) retraining, (5) counseling, (6) suspension, (7) demotion, (8) fine, and (9) dismissal (Figure 7.9).

After the initial disposition, the case goes up the chain of command until it finally reaches the chief. In about half the cases, there's a discrepancy between the chief's recommendations and those of the immediate supervisor. These discrepancies are important because the immediate supervisor, usually a sergeant of patrol, works on the street with other patrol officers. The supervisors of sergeants usually go along with the recommendations of sergeants. Chiefs of police, on the other hand, are removed from the day-to-day street operations of patrol officers and their immediate supervisors. They have departmentwide perspectives and are responsible to "local political elites" for their department's performance. So chiefs may find the disciplinary penalty too light and make it heavier.

According to Perez, "Oakland chiefs are often seen from below as abusive of police officers, always increasing punishments, never going along with the lighter recommendations." Oakland, however, may not be typical in this respect

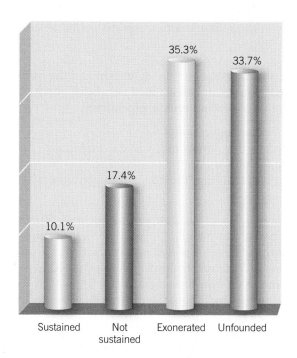

▲ FIGURE 7.8 Disposition of Excessive Force Complaints

Source: Anthony M. Pate and Lorie A. Fridell, *Police Use of Force: Official Reports, Citizen Complaints, and Legal Consequences* (Washington, DC: Police Foundation, 1993), p. 116.

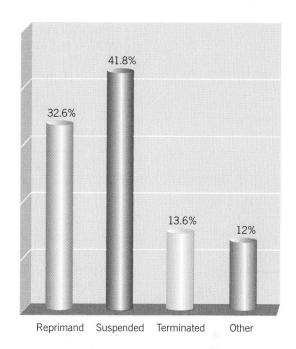

▲ FIGURE 7.9 Distribution of Disciplinary Actions

Source: Anthony M. Pate and Lorie A. Fridell, *Police Use of Force: Official Reports, Citizen Complaints, and Legal Consequences* (Washington, DC: Police Foundation, 1993), p. 116.

(Perez 1994, 96–97). Figure 7.9 shows the distribution of disciplinary measures taken in a national sample of city police departments.

External Review The fundamental objection to internal review is that police shouldn't police themselves. To the question, "Who will watch the watchmen?" the answer is, "Not the watchmen!" In response, we've seen the external review grow. In external review, individuals who aren't sworn police officers participate in the review of complaints against the police. Usually called civilian review, it has sparked controversy for nearly half a century. Police oppose external review because it invades their independence; they have no confidence outsiders know enough about police work to review it; and they know outside scrutiny would pierce the "blue curtain" that hides their "real" work from public view (Chapter 5).

Strong police unions, chiefs who opposed external review, and the creation of internal review procedures (discussed in the last section) successfully prevented external review during the 1960s, when it became a popular proposal of some reformers and citizen groups. However, by 1994, 72 percent of the 50 largest cities had created civilian review procedures of some sort (Walker and Bumpus 1992, 1, 3–4). Let's look at the various types of civilian review boards and how well they work.

Types of External Review The differences among civilian review procedures all turn on the point in the decision-making process when nonofficers may participate, including

1. The initial investigation to collect the facts
2. The review of the investigation reports
3. The recommendation for disposition to the chief
4. The review of decisions made by the chief

Still, no matter at what point nonofficers participate, civilian review boards can only recommend disciplinary action to police chiefs, because under civil service

National Association for Civilian Oversight of Law Enforcement: NACOLE is a nonprofit organization of civilian oversight practitioners and supporters working to promote fair, firm, and consistent law enforcement in the United States through the practice of civilian oversight. To reach this site go to "Web Links" on your Samaha CJ7 website: http://cj.wadsworth.com/samaha_cj7e.

laws, only police chiefs can decide on disciplinary action against police officers (Walker and Bumpus 1992, 3–4).

Does Civilian Review Work? The answer depends on the definition and the measures of effectiveness. "Effectiveness" can mean at least four things, all of which are important in determining the value of civilian review procedures:

1. Maintaining effective control of police misconduct
2. Providing resolutions to complaints that satisfy individual complainants
3. Preserving public confidence in the police
4. Influencing police management by providing "feedback from consumers" (Walker and Bumpus 1992, 8)

It's difficult to measure the effectiveness of civilian review because official data are ambiguous. Take the number of complaints, for example. A large number of complaints might mean a large volume of police misconduct. But it can also indicate confidence in the review procedures. Following the Rodney King incident in Los Angeles, observers noted that San Francisco, a city known for its strong review procedures, received more complaints than the much larger city of Los Angeles. In contrast, the Independent Commission heard a number of citizen complaints that the LAPD created "significant hurdles" to filing complaints, that they were afraid of the process, and that the complaint process was "unnecessarily difficult or impossible." The ACLU collected evidence suggesting that the LAPD "actively discouraged the filing of complaints." The beating of Rodney King, in fact, would never have come to public attention without the video, according to the Independent Commission, because the efforts of his brother Paul to file a complaint following the beating were "frustrated" by the LAPD (Pate and Fridell 1993, 39).

The numbers and rates of complaints are also difficult to assess because we don't know the numbers of incidents where people don't file complaints. In one national survey, of all the people who said the police mistreated them, only 30 percent said they filed complaints. One thing, however, is clear. Misconduct isn't distributed evenly among individuals and neighborhoods. In one survey, only 40 percent of the addresses in one city had any contact with the police in a year. Most contacts between private individuals and the police occur in poor neighborhoods. In New York City, the rate of complaints ranges from one to five for every 10,000 people, depending on the neighborhood.

Official data have consistently indicated racial minority males are disproportionately represented among complainants. So the perception of a pattern of police harassment is a major factor in conflict between the police and racial minority communities (Walker and Bumpus 1992, 10).

Whatever the ambiguity of numbers and rates in the official statistics, observers have noted civilian review procedures rarely sustain complaints. Furthermore, the rates of complaints sustained in civilian review are about the same as the rates in internal affairs units (Walker and Bumpus 1992, 16–17).

The Exclusionary Rule

The exclusionary rule throws out "good" evidence because of "bad" police behavior. It bans the government from using confessions obtained in violation of the right against self-incrimination; evidence gathered by unreasonable searches and seizures; evidence gotten in violation of the right to counsel; and eyewitness identifications gotten by unreliable procedures.

Most countries don't have an exclusionary rule (except for England, Canada, and Germany; Slobogin 1998, 552–553), so why do we? There have been several justifications for the exclusionary rule over the years, but the U.S. Supreme Court says only one is acceptable—to deter unconstitutional police behavior. The Court weighs the social cost of letting criminals go free by throwing out

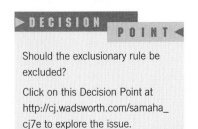

► DECISION POINT ◄

Should the exclusionary rule be excluded?

Click on this Decision Point at http://cj.wadsworth.com/samaha_cj7e to explore the issue.

good evidence of guilt against the possible deterrent effect throwing out evidence has on law enforcement officers. If the social costs outweigh the deterrent effect (which in virtually every case the Court says it does), then the evidence can come in (Schroeder 1981, 1378–1386).

Empirical research doesn't support the Court's view that throwing out evidence has hardly any effect on deterring police misconduct. In an extensive study of the exclusionary rule among Chicago narcotics officers, Myron W. Orfield, Jr. (1987) reported several important findings:

- Chicago narcotics officers are always in court when judges suppress the evidence.
- They always understand why the court excluded the evidence.
- This experience has led them to seek search warrants more often and to be more careful when they search for and seize evidence without warrants.

Before *Mapp v. Ohio* (1961), which applied the exclusionary rule to state and local law enforcement, police officers rarely obtained warrants. By 1987, the narcotics division of the Chicago Police Department ordered that "virtually all pre-planned searches that are not 'buy busts' or airport-related searches occur with warrants." Orfield's (1987) study also demonstrated the exclusionary rule "punishes" officers. Getting evidence thrown out can negatively affect both assignments and promotions (1017–1018, 1029).

Orfield found that some officers lie in court so their illegally seized evidence won't be thrown out. Admittedly, this limits the effectiveness of the exclusionary rule, but strong responses to police perjury by both the police department and the courts have reduced the instances of perjury. Finally, every officer in Orfield's (1987) study believed the courts should keep the rule. They said the rule has just about the right amount of a deterrent element. They believed a tort remedy (suing the police) would "overdeter" the police in their search for evidence (1027–1028).

The social costs of excluding evidence aren't nearly as high as the Supreme Court (and most people) thinks. Researchers have shown the rule affects only a tiny number of cases in just a few crimes. Less than one-tenth of 1 percent of all criminal cases will be dismissed because the police illegally got the evidence. And most of these are drug offenses, not murder, rape, and other violent crimes. Property crimes, too, are unaffected (National Institute of Justice 1982, 12).

Other Responses to Misconduct

Every remedy we've discussed up to now centers on punitive measures. One positive approach to dealing with police misconduct relies on training and other socialization measures to change police behavior. For example, advocates for the positive approach argue the effectiveness of convincing officers to use unflappable responses to unpleasant behavior. Taking an insult without reaction wins more respect and obedience than responding emotionally to insults. James Q. Wilson (1983b), a supporter of the positive approach, recommends that recruitment, training, and the police subculture should aim at producing police officers

who can handle calmly challenges to their self-respect and manhood, are able to tolerate ambiguous situations, have the physical capacity to subdue persons, are able to accept responsibility for the consequences of their own actions, can understand and apply legal concepts in concrete situations, and are honest. (112)

Facts

At 2:40 A.M. on 11 August 2001, Trooper C. J. Carroll stopped defendant Juan Villeda, a Hispanic male, for a seatbelt violation on Highway 70 near the Highway 15–501 intersection in Durham, North Carolina. Villeda was arrested for driving while impaired (DWI), charged and found guilty in district court and appealed to the superior court on 11 January 2002. On 18 April 2002, he filed a motion to suppress the evidence obtained during the traffic stop. The motion alleged violations of his rights under the "4th, 5th, and 14th Amendments" to the United States Constitution and Article I, Section 19 of the North Carolina Constitution, stating defendant's detention had been motivated "in part by [his] race or national origin." Based on these grounds, Villeda also filed a motion to dismiss the DWI charge on 17 September 2002.

At the hearing on defendant's motions, defendant presented the testimony of three attorneys who had come into contact with Trooper Carroll in the past while defending clients arrested for various driving violations. Attorney Kenneth Duke (Duke) testified that in 1998 he had represented a client charged with DWI. At the first court appearance in that case, Duke ran into Trooper Carroll in the hallway of the courthouse. Duke asked Trooper Carroll the reason for stopping his client, to which the officer replied: "[I]f they're Hispanic and they're driving, they're probably drunk." At the hearing in traffic court, Duke requested and was allowed to question Trooper Carroll about his statement in the hallway. Trooper Carroll denied having made such a statement; but when questioned by the trial court, Trooper Carroll admitted that after having seen Duke's client, a Hispanic, walk into a gas station, he parked his vehicle, turned off his lights, and just watched the gas station. Upon seeing Duke's client walk out of the gas station with beer in his arms, get into his vehicle, and start to drive away, Trooper Carroll stopped him as he was leaving the parking lot. The trial court reacted in outrage to this account of the events and dismissed the DWI charge against Duke's client.

Attorney Frances Miranda Watkins testified at the suppression hearing that she had been present at the hearing for Duke's client and confirmed Trooper Carroll's account of the stop and the trial court's reaction to it.

Attorney Leonor Childers (Childers) testified she had represented a client, Elvin Javier Ayala, in 2001 charged with DWI and driving with a revoked license. Prior to trial, Childers contacted Trooper Carroll by telephone to question him about his stop of her client. Trooper Carroll explained he had been driving on Miami Boulevard when he observed her client exit the Circle K® store with a carton of beer in his hands. Trooper Carroll followed Childers' client, observed a broken tail-light, and ran the vehicle's tags through the computer. The computer search indicated the vehicle was uninsured. Trooper Carroll then stopped Childers' client, issued a ticket for the insurance violation and subsequently arrested him for driving while impaired. When asked by Childers if he had been staking out the Circle K, Trooper Carroll replied that on that particular occasion he had not done so, "but on other occasions he does stake out that Circle K on Miami Boulevard as well as another location on U.S. 70" near LaMaraca, a Hispanic nightclub. Trooper Carroll told Childers he patrols those two areas of Durham "for the purpose of looking for Hispanic males." Childers further inquired, if all her client had done was exit the store with a carton of beer, why did Trooper Carroll stop him. Trooper Carroll responded: "Everyone knows that a Hispanic male buying liquor on a Friday or a Saturday night is probably already drunk"; "Mexicans drink a lot because they grew up where the water isn't good"; and that he did not care what happened in court "as long as I get them [(i.e. Hispanic males)] off the road and in jail for one night." Finally, when asked if he targets Hispanics, Trooper Carroll stated: "I'm not targeting Hispanics. Most of my tickets go to blacks." At the hearing on the charges against Childers' client, although Trooper Carroll denied having made the above statements, the trial court dismissed the charges.

▲ According to empirical research, most officers' decisions to arrest suspects are not infected by discrimination. Even if officers are prejudiced, they don't usually act on their prejudices when they make decisions regarding suspects. However, it's very difficult to prove whether officers' decisions are infected with a discriminatory purpose. What do you think?

Source: Facts: Adapted from the Court's opinion in *State of North Carolina v. Juan Villeda*, North Carolina Court of Appeals, No. COA03-772.

Childers further testified that, following her discussion with Trooper Carroll, she began looking into his citation history. She pulled up all of Trooper Carroll's citations from 1 January 2001 to 24 March 2002, a total of 716 citations, and found that 71% of DWI citations issued by Trooper Carroll involved Hispanic individuals. Only 16% of DWI stops were of Caucasians, 9% of African-Americans, and 2% of other racial backgrounds. After Trooper Carroll came under investigation by Internal Affairs in the spring of 2002 for racial profiling, no Hispanics were cited by him for DWI violations.

In plotting the DWI stops on a map, Childers noted "two fairly concentrated areas": Area 1—the U.S. 70–Hillsborough Road–Main Street area in Durham (within a two-to-three-mile radius of LaMaraca), and Area 2—encompassing Miami Boulevard, East Durham, Geer Street, and Holloway Street (including Circle K). According to the 2000 census data Childers reviewed, the Hispanic population in Durham County amounts to approximately 7% of the general population. However, the census data for LaSalle Street in the city of Durham, which is located in Area 1 and a quarter mile from LaMaraca, reveals a population of 32% Hispanics and 36% African-Americans....

Lieutenant Edward Vuncannon with the Highway Patrol's Internal Affairs Section testified regarding his investigation of Trooper Carroll following allegations of racial discrimination. His interviews of Trooper Carroll were recorded on tape and later transcribed. Lieutenant Vuncannon testified Trooper Carroll told him that in his personal opinion "Hispanics are more prone than other races to get in a car after they have been drinking" and that "[i]t's the lifestyle they live. They work Monday through Friday and...." During the interview with Lieutenant Vuncannon, Trooper Carroll denied having made any of the statements testified to by Childers....

The trial court concluded that there was no credible evidence of "reasonable suspicion to justify the traffic stop" and "the investigatory detention...violated the Fourth and Fourteenth Amendments to the United States Constitution." The trial court further concluded that defendant offered sufficient evidence to support a *prima facie* showing [a showing that if not rebutted by the state proves] that Trooper Carroll engaged in racial profiling and that defendant "was stopped pursuant to intentional racially discriminatory law enforcement conduct." Accordingly, the trial court suppressed all evidence seized as a result of the stop, and dismissed the DWI charge against defendant....

[The North Carolina Court of Appeals affirmed the trial court's decision as to there being no reasonable suspicion. It didn't decide whether Trooper Carroll's stop was infected with Villeda's Hispanic ethnicity. The briefs for both the state of North Carolina and the defendant Villeda did get into the race profiling issue. Read the excerpts from the briefs of the state and Villeda. As you read the excerpts, summarize the arguments for and against whether ethnic profiling infected Trooper Carroll's decision to stop Juan Villeda.]

North Carolina's Brief

The Equal Protection Clause prohibits selective enforcement of the law based on considerations such as race. In order to prevail on a selective prosecution claim, a defendant must show that enforcement against him "had a discriminatory effect and...was motivated by a discriminatory purpose." The defendant must establish both (1) that he has been "singled out" while others similarly situated have not; and (2) that the decision was "invidious or in bad faith, i.e., based upon such impermissible considerations as race, religion, or the desire to exercise his constitutional rights." A claimant can demonstrate discriminatory effect by naming a similarly situated individual who was not investigated or through the use of statistical or other evidence which addresses the crucial question of whether one class is being treated differently from another class that is otherwise similarly situated. Discriminatory purpose can be shown by demonstrating that the decision maker selected or reaffirmed a particular course of action at least in part because of, not merely in spite of, its adverse effects upon an identifiable group.

Although the "similarly situated" requirement places a heavy evidentiary burden on a claimant, the similarly situated requirement does not make a selective-prosecution claim impossible to prove. Difficulty of proof does not justify a slackening of the claimant's burden of proof.

Discriminatory effect can be proved in one of two ways. First, when the claim is selective enforcement of the traffic laws or a racially-motivated arrest, the plaintiff must normally prove that similarly situated individuals were not stopped or arrested in order to show the requisite discriminatory effect and purpose. Ms. Childers' study made no attempt to identify individuals who were similarly situated to defendant, thus eliminating any need for further discussion of that method of proof.

Secondly, discriminatory effect may also be shown through statistical evidence. Of course, parties may not prove discrimination merely by providing the court with statistical analyses. The statistics must address the crucial question of whether one class is being treated differently from another class that is otherwise similarly situated. Further, statistics are not irrefutable; they come in infinite variety and, like any other kind of evidence, they may be rebutted. Defendant's statistical evidence completely fails to meet the foregoing criteria.

First, defendant's data does not identify the racial composition of the motoring public who were committing minor traffic infractions but were not stopped. Such proof is necessary in order to meet the "similarly situated" requirement. Statistics may be used to make out a case of targeting minorities for prosecution of traffic offenses provided the comparison is between the racial composition of the motorist population violating the traffic laws and the racial composition of those arrested for traffic infractions on the relevant roadway patrolled by the police agency.

Secondly, there was no rationale for lumping together the numbers of African-Americans, Hispanics and Others to determine that 83% of Trooper Carroll's DWI arrests were of a "person of color." The case before Judge Hudson was a DWI and seat belt case in which Juan Villeda, an Hispanic, was the defendant. Even so, defendant's census data discloses that 79.5% of the residents of the LaSalle Street Tract are non-Caucasian and 84.6% of the residents of the Holloway Street Tracts are non-Caucasian. The fact that 83% of Trooper Carroll's stops were of non-Caucasians is not statistically significant compared to the population data.

Third, the fact that 93% of Trooper Carroll's DWI arrests were on the weekend is meaningless. Common sense dictates that more DWI arrests are made on weekends than weekdays. Even so, Sergeant Rose testified that "SHP [State Highway Patrol] officers work mainly on weekends...And we try to concentrate most of our Troopers on the weekends."

Finally, Ms. Childers calculated the number of Trooper Carroll's DWI arrests from the time he returned from his leave of absence during the IA investigation to the date of the hearing on the motions to suppress and dismiss, demonstrating that Trooper Carroll's arrests of Caucasians had increased from 16.7% to 50% and that his DWI arrests of Blacks had increased from 9.5% to 50%. Since these percentages of Caucasian and Black arrests are based on precisely two (one White and one Black) arrests during the period surveyed, the statistics are patently invalid on their face and do not account for the geography Trooper Carroll was assigned to patrol during that period.

In addition to showing discriminatory effect, a defendant must also prove the conduct was motivated by a discriminatory purpose. Defendant must demonstrate that the government's discriminatory selection of him for prosecution has been invidious or in bad faith." To establish discriminatory purpose plaintiffs must show that the policymaker selected or reaffirmed a particular course of action at least in part because of, not merely in spite of, its adverse effects upon an identifiable group."

Defendant's only evidence as to discriminatory purpose consisted of the hearsay statements offered by the three attorneys and the statements extracted from the investigation transcript.

Neither the SHP management nor individual troopers are required to avoid patrolling areas which have a high concentration of minority populations. It cannot be assumed that, because a trooper patrols such areas, he is improperly "stalking" minorities and engaging in racial profiling. Following a vehicle after a law enforcement officer has seen a person exit a convenience store late at night carrying a carton of beer is not improper conduct. The legitimacy of any subsequent stop is based upon a reasonable articulable suspicion that a crime is or has occurred which is based on the totality of the circumstances.

Defendant has failed to prove either the discriminatory effect or the discriminatory purpose prong of the selective enforcement claim.

Source: North Carolina's Brief: Adapted from the brief of the State of North Carolina, *State of North Carolina v. Juan Villeda,* North Carolina Court of Appeals, No. COA03-772.

Villeda's Brief

(R)ace alone cannot create a reasonable suspicion for a *Terry* stop....Citizens are entitled to the equal protection of the laws at all times. The rationale for universal application of the Equal Protection Clause appears patent when one considers the type of nation to which we aspire and in which we expect to live. This is a free society, criminal suspects are a minute part of the traveling public, and the rights of innocent persons who might also be stopped must be considered.

To prevail under the Equal Protection Clause, a defendant must prove that the decision makers in his case acted with a discriminatory purpose. Because often it is difficult to prove directly the invidious use of race, discrimination can be proved through direct evidence, which seldom exists, or inferences can be drawn from valid relevant statistical evidence of disparate impact or other circumstantial evidence. Statistical evidence alone rarely proves racial discrimination....

Once the defendants expose a prima facie case [enough evidence (if not rebutted) to prove the defendant's case] of selective enforcement, the State generally cannot rebut it by merely calling attention to possible flaws or unmeasured variables in the defendants' statistics. Rather the State must introduce specific evidence showing that either there actually are defects which bias the results or that the missing factors, when properly organized and accounted for, eliminate or explain the disparity. Nor will mere denials or reliance on the good faith of the officers suffice....

As discussed above, one may prove equal protection violations through the use of circumstantial or direct evidence. Mr. Villeda does not contend that he has proved his case through the use of statistics alone. Mr. Villeda does not even need to use statistics. Unlike most claimants, Mr. Villeda has substantial direct evidence of discrimination.

Direct evidence alleviates the need for statistics altogether.... Two attorneys testified that Trooper Carroll admitted to targeting Hispanics for DWI stops. Trooper Carroll demonstrated his bias with statements such as "everyone knows that a Hispanic Male buying liquor on a Friday or Saturday night is probably already drunk" and "Mexicans drink a lot because where they grew up, the water isn't good." Attorney Ken Duke testified that when he asked Trooper Carroll why he stopped his client, he said "well he's a Mexican wasn't he." Appalled by the racist actions to which Trooper Carroll testified, a Durham District Court Judge dismissed another DWI charge against an Hispanic male....

Given the persuasive direct evidence of discriminatory intent, one need not even address the statistics. Nonetheless, the State's arguments reflect a misunderstanding of the use of statistics to show discriminatory intent.

The State argues that Villeda's statistics contain flaws because they do not include the numbers of legally intoxicated non-Hispanic drivers that Trooper Carroll did not stop. Of course, the statistics are silent on such data. It is impossible to determine the number of intoxicated drivers that escape detection by law enforcement. One could never establish a violation of the Equal Protection Clause should courts require such proof.

Significantly, Trooper Carroll never testified. The State offered no explanation whatsoever as to why Trooper Carroll investigated Mr. Villeda for driving under the influence. Thus, the State failed to rebut the substantial direct and circumstantial evidence that Trooper Carroll investigated Mr. Villeda for DWI because of his race.

Source: Villeda's Brief: Adapted from "Brief of Appellee, Juan Villeda," *State of North Carolina v. Juan Villeda,* North Carolina Court of Appeals, No. COA03-772.

QUESTIONS

1. Summarize the state's arguments in favor of reversing the trial court's decision that Villeda made a prima facie case that his Hispanic ethnicity infected Trooper Carroll's decision to stop him.
2. Summarize Villeda's arguments in favor of affirming the trial court's decision that he made a prima facie case that his Hispanic ethnicity infected Trooper Carroll's decision to stop him.
3. Assume you're the judge in the case. Write an opinion in the case supporting your view of the arguments.

Chapter Summary

▶ Under our constitutional system, police can't interfere with individual liberty and privacy on hunches; they have to back up interferences with facts. The Bill of Rights, while protecting criminal suspects' rights, also leaves plenty of room for individual officers' discretionary decision making.

▶ Arrests are reasonable if they're backed up by probable cause; only reasonable force is used to get and keep control of arrested persons; and arrests warrants are obtained before entering homes to make arrests.

▶ Searches are reasonable only if they're backed up by warrants and probable cause, *unless* they fall into one of the exceptions to the warrant and/or probable cause rule. (The vast number of searches fall within the exceptions.) Neither probable cause nor warrants are required for the most common searches (searches incident to arrest and consent searches). Stops are Fourth Amendment seizures, and frisks are Fourth Amendment searches, but they're less invasive than arrests and full searches, so they need only reasonable suspicion to back them up.

▶ There's disagreement over how important police interrogation is to crime control, and empirical data will probably never fully resolve it. The Fifth Amendment bans only *compelled* (coerced) statements; pressure isn't coercion. *Miranda v. Arizona* ruled that custody is inherently coercive without the famous warnings. The public safety exception allows officers to interrogate suspects in custody without the warnings if giving them would endanger officers or those nearby. Even coerced confessions are admissible unless police coercion caused suspects to incriminate themselves. Most suspects waive their right to remain silent and agree to be interrogated.

▶ In most cases, it's easier to prove a crime was committed than to identify the perpetrator. The danger of mistaken identification of strangers is high (maybe as high as 50 percent of wrongful convictions) because of deficiencies in perception, memory, and recall. These deficiencies are made worse by the power of suggestion (almost never intentional) by officers administering lineups, show-ups, and photo identifications. According to the U.S. Supreme Court, identification procedures violate due process only if they're unnecessarily suggestive *and* if the suggestive procedure creates "a very substantial likelihood" of misidentification.

▶ Police use of force is a Fourth Amendment seizure. Officers can use the amount of force necessary to get and maintain control of suspects. Only *excessive* force is an unreasonable seizure. The intent of the officer is irrelevant. No amount of malice or prejudice can turn a reasonable use of force into an unreasonable seizure. And no amount of good intention will make excessive force a reasonable seizure.

▶ The evidence shows a clear disparity between the use of force against Whites and Blacks; the evidence is mixed as to whether the cause of the disparity is that the decision to use force is infected by race and ethnicity.

▶ Racial, ethnicity, and gender disparities in individuals stopped, interrogated, and searched during traffic stops are widely documented. Proving the disparity in decision making is infected by discrimination (race profiling) is difficult and hasn't yet been demonstrated.

▶ Most police misconduct is also a crime and a private personal injury. Some police officers commit ordinary crimes (mostly occupation related, like theft and corruption). Other misconduct is violating the constitutional rights of those they're in charge of protecting (like excessive force).

▶ There are four remedies for police misconduct, all possible but not practical: criminal prosecution; private lawsuits against individual officers, and/or departments, and the government; administrative discipline; and procedural (the exclusionary rule). Most actions against the police are unsuccessful because of public support for the police, the presumption of regularity, the doctrine of immunity, and the limits to the exclusionary rule.

Key Terms

objective basis, p. 223
arrest, p. 225
probable cause to arrest, p. 225
knock-and-announce rule, p. 229
search incident to arrest rule, p. 229
consent search rule, p. 230

reasonable suspicion, p. 231
custodial interrogation, p. 239
public safety exception, p. 239
knockdown force, p. 245
objective standard of reasonable force, p. 249

racial profiling, p. 253
profiles, p. 255
presumption of regularity, p. 255
doctrine of official immunity, p. 257
defense of qualified immunity, p. 257

Web Resources

Go to http://cj.wadsworth.com/samaha_cj7e for a wealth of online resources related to your book. Take a "pre-test" and "post-test" for each chapter in order to help master the material. Check out the *Web Links* to access the websites mentioned in the text, as well as many others. Explore the *Decision Points* flagged in the margins of the text for additional insights. You can also access recent perspectives by clicking on *CJ in the News* and *Terrorism Update* under *Course Resources.*

🕊 Search Online with InfoTrac College Edition

For additional information, explore InfoTrac College Edition, your online library. Go to http://cj.wadsworth.com/ samaha_cj7e to access InfoTrac College Edition from your book's website. Use the passcode that came with your book. You will find InfoTrac College Edition exercises and a list of key words for further research.

CHAPTER 8

Courts and Courtroom Work Groups

FACT *or* FICTION?

- ▶ Speed is bad when it comes to providing justice in court.
- ▶ There's no constitutional right to appeal a criminal conviction.
- ▶ Courts are one place in the criminal justice system where law trumps discretion.
- ▶ The U.S. Supreme Court never reviews whether convicted defendants are guilty or innocent.
- ▶ Judges, prosecutors, *and* defense lawyers agree defendants are guilty; all they have to do is agree on a punishment.
- ▶ Prosecutors are the most powerful members of the courtroom work group.
- ▶ It's a defense lawyer's duty to block the search for the truth.

JUSTICE BY CONSENT?

Americans expect the...courthouse...to live up to the promise of its marble exterior. It is to be a palace of justice, with no secret closets or hidden corridors. Anyone should be able to walk in and see the rules of law being uniformly applied. Prosecutors and defense attorneys are to be vigorous advocates, but must place above all else their commitment to truth and law. Judges and juries are to wisely and justly apply the law to the particular facts of each case.

But most Americans also know that the courthouse must deal with the brutish and bloody aspects of life. Among the criminals it confronts are cheats, robbers and murderers. This reality leads to a very different set of expectations and demands. Now the public gives allegiance to a crime control system that has force and punishment at its base....When seen this way the courthouse is not a majestic palace. It is a harsh and seamy place, sometimes more cruel than just, where guilt is assumed, and men are prodded from station to station like cattle in a slaughterhouse.

—ROSETT AND CRESSEY (1976, 1–2)

After arrests, decision making moves from police departments to courts. The formal and informal stories of courts and how they operate are very different. In the *formal* story, courts are legal institutions—"palaces of justice." In the courtrooms, aggressive prosecutors fight for the "people," vigorous defense lawyers fight for their clients, and neutral judges act as umpires to make sure their work group accomplishes its mission to find the truth by due process of law. Judges let both sides fight *hard* but make sure they fight *fair*. Juries convict the guilty and free the innocent. In the *informal* version of the story, the courtrooms are almost always dark and empty; they're lit up and occupied only for the rare trial and to ratify decisions already made in judges' chambers, halls, and even in closets and restrooms (Nardulli, Eisenstein, and Flemming 1988, 373–374).

In this chapter, we'll look at the criminal court structure, criminal court missions, and courtroom work group roles.

CONCEPT | BUILDER

Visit http://cj.wadsworth.com/ samaha_cj7e for an interactive exploration of the **dual court system.**

The Criminal Court Structure

In our federal system, there are national and state courts separated into three tiers (Figure 8.1):

1. *Lower courts (trial courts of limited jurisdiction).* They have the power to decide the facts and apply the law in misdemeanor cases and conduct pretrial proceedings in felony cases.
2. *Felony courts (trial courts of general jurisdiction).* They have the power to decide the facts and apply the law in felony cases.
3. *Appellate courts (appeals courts).* They have the power to review trial courts' application of the law to the facts.

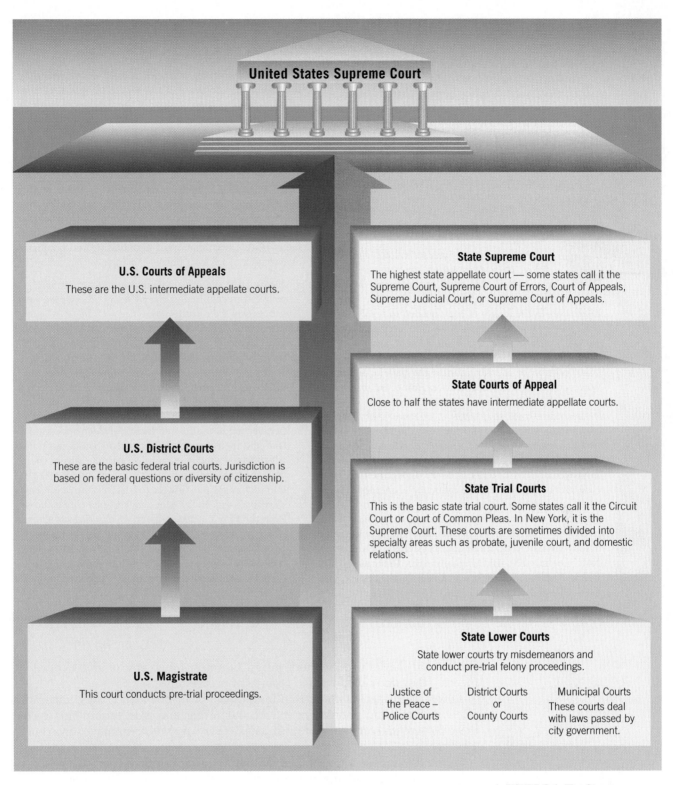

United States Supreme Court

U.S. Courts of Appeals
These are the U.S. intermediate appellate courts.

State Supreme Court
The highest state appellate court — some states call it the Supreme Court, Supreme Court of Errors, Court of Appeals, Supreme Judicial Court, or Supreme Court of Appeals.

U.S. District Courts
These are the basic federal trial courts. Jurisdiction is based on federal questions or diversity of citizenship.

State Courts of Appeal
Close to half the states have intermediate appellate courts.

State Trial Courts
This is the basic state trial court. Some states call it the Circuit Court or Court of Common Pleas. In New York, it is the Supreme Court. These courts are sometimes divided into specialty areas such as probate, juvenile court, and domestic relations.

U.S. Magistrate
This court conducts pre-trial proceedings.

State Lower Courts
State lower courts try misdemeanors and conduct pre-trial felony proceedings.

| Justice of the Peace – Police Courts | District Courts or County Courts | Municipal Courts These courts deal with laws passed by city government. |

▲ **FIGURE 8.1 The Structure of the U.S. Judicial System**

Source: Adapted with permission from William T. Schanz, *The American Legal Environment* (St. Paul, MN: West Publishing, 1976).

Lower Courts

Lower courts (called by many different names, such as misdemeanor, superior, municipal, county, justice of the peace, and magistrate's courts) only have the power (jurisdiction) to decide misdemeanors and conduct preliminary proceedings in felony cases. That's why they're called courts of **limited jurisdiction.** Formally, defendants in lower criminal courts have the same rights as defendants in felony courts. In practice, most cases are tried less formally than in felony

limited jurisdiction power (jurisdiction) to decide misdemeanors and conduct preliminary proceedings in felony cases

IN FOCUS

Does Speed Trump Justice?

The Sixth Amendment to the U.S. Constitution guarantees the fundamental right to "a speedy and public trial," yet balancing the pace of the legal process with quality case processing remains a formidable challenge. Other equally vital and fundamental values, such as due process, equality, and protections against double jeopardy, excessive bail, and self-incrimination, demand time and attention. Indeed, conventional thinking holds that these two values—the timeliness and the quality of justice—are in conflict, with a gain in one coming only at a loss in the other.

In response to widespread concern about delays in case resolution, an extensive body of research in this field has emerged in recent decades. Most of these efforts sought to explain disparities in the length of time needed to resolve criminal cases by comparing caseload characteristics and aspects of court organization, management, and resources. When these factors failed to account for more than a small portion of the variation in the pace of litigation, however, researchers began to examine the qualitative social and political dynamics of court systems.

Despite efforts to identify the sources of delay in felony case processing and find ways to alleviate it, the problem persists. Indeed, much of its apparent intractability can be traced to the long-standing belief that improvements in timeliness compromise the quality of case processing. To test the influence of factors thought to affect case processing time, the National Institute of Justice supported a study that measured the relative impact of each factor, alone and in combination, within and across nine state criminal court systems (Albuquerque, NM; Austin, TX; Birmingham, AL; Cincinnati, OH; Grand Rapids, MI; Hackensack, NJ; Oakland, CA; Portland, OR; and Sacramento, CA). Researchers also interviewed and surveyed judges, attorneys, and other court officials to ascertain attitudes toward court resources, management, and the skill and tactics of opposing counsel. Researchers then compared these opinions with the overall processing speed of their respective jurisdictions.

KEY FINDINGS

The study challenges conventional thinking that the timeliness and quality of justice are mutually exclusive, arguing instead that courts can exercise considerable control over how quickly cases move from indictment to resolution without sacrificing advocacy or due process. Other highlights of this examination of quantitative and qualitative characteristics of case processing include the following:

- Meaningful and effective advocacy was more likely to occur in criminal justice systems, where case resolution was the most timely.
- The relative pace of litigation depended largely on the local legal culture—that is, the expectations and attitudes of judges, prosecutors, and defense attorneys. In the more expeditious courts, personnel had more efficient work orientations, including clear case processing time goals. Attorneys in these courts had more positive views about resources, management policies, and the skill and tactics of their opposition than did their counterparts in less expeditious courts.
- All courts treated cases proportionately, giving each case the time and attention that it deserved. More complex cases took longer to resolve than less complex cases did. In the more expeditious courts, however, the time needed to reach resolution was shorter.
- The combined influence of four factors—a violent felony charge, the issuance of a bench warrant, pretrial release on bond, and resolution by trial—produced a significant increase in case processing time in all nine courts.

courts, and they're tried without juries. Lower criminal courts aren't courts of record—they don't keep written records of proceedings.

Lower courts decide minor (but in numbers by far the most) cases, like traffic offenses, drunk and disorderly conduct, shoplifting, and prostitution. This makes them the first and only contact most people ever have with criminal courts (Forer 1984, 3).

In the 1800s, observers complained that in lower criminal courts in big cities judges rushed defendants through cramped, noisy, undignified courtrooms. Things were pretty much the same in the 1950s when Professor Caleb Foote (1956, 605) watched one Philadelphia magistrate decide 55 cases in 15 minutes. Four defendants were tried, convicted, and sentenced in 17 seconds! As the magistrate read off each of the four defendants' names, he took one look and said, "Three months." In the 1970s, a sociologist who observed lower courts in another city for three months found judges decided 72 percent of the cases in less than a minute each (Mileski 1971, 479).

Observers in the 1990s told much the same stories. Describing a New York criminal court in 1991—where most cases were decided in less than 4 minutes—Professor Harry I. Subin (1991) wrote that the court was

- All courts can become more efficient by maximizing attorney skills, management techniques, and available technology. Increases in efficiency will simultaneously improve the timeliness and quality of felony case processing.

POLICY IMPLICATIONS

This research suggests that the court community can achieve efficiency, timeliness, and quality by adopting a three-step process of self-diagnosis, communication, and education.

- *Self-diagnosis*. The first step requires that court officials examine case processing practices and reach a consensus on the court's goals. To be efficient, a court needs meaningful time standards and continuous monitoring of both disposition timeframes and the size of pending caseloads. Proportionality, a fundamental underpinning of criminal justice, is another important subject for discussion. Both efficiency and due process require proportionality in the amount of time attorneys and judges devote to the preparation and resolution of criminal cases (16). Such an examination would likely sharpen a court's knowledge of how different case and defendant characteristics affect case processing times.
- *Communication*. This study's survey of prosecutors and defense attorneys revealed a significant difference between faster and slower courts in the clarity of goals for case processing time. This finding suggests that effectively communicating a court system's goals is essential to attorney receptivity to and shared understanding of those goals. Courts could conduct a similar survey to help determine the clarity of their own message among judges, prosecutors, and criminal defense counsel. The more a court understands about the attitudes of its attorneys, the better the court can tailor management strategies to improve efficiency.

- *Education*. National, state, and local judicial and attorney training programs should emphasize how judges and attorneys can become more efficient and how gains in efficiency can be used to secure timeliness and quality in felony case processing. Such programs should not focus simply on delay reduction. Indeed, one reason that delay is such a formidable problem for courts, despite the development of delay reduction techniques, is that successful delay reduction continues to be viewed as a threat to quality. Promoting both delay reduction and enhanced quality as natural consequences of efficiency will help courts overcome this resistance to change and, ultimately, achieve higher levels of timeliness and quality in felony case processing.

HOW FAST IS FAST ENOUGH?

An important role of courts is to balance the competing interests of speed and due process. But what is the optimal combination of expedition and quality justice?

The American Bar Association (ABA), the Conference of Chief Justices (CCJ), and the Conference of State Court Administrators (COSCA) addressed this question...The ABA standards suggest that, from the date of arrest to the date of disposition (e.g., entry of guilty plea, verdict, or dismissal), courts should dispose of 90 percent of their felony cases in 120 days; 98 percent in 180 days; and 100 percent within 1 year. This study modified the ABA standard calling for 98 percent of all felonies to be resolved within 180 days of the initial arrest to a standard calling for the disposition of 98 percent of all cases within 180 days of indictment or bindover. No court in this study met the unmodified ABA standards.

Source: Brian J. Ostrom and Roger A. Hanson, *Efficiency, Timeliness, and Quality: A New Perspective from Nine State Criminal Trial Courts* (Washington, DC: National Institute of Justice, June 2000).

overwhelmed by a flood of cases...[and, therefore, it] accomplishes very little. It does not dispense justice. It simply disposes of each day's business in any way it can, so it can be ready to dispose of the next day's business. And because substantive action would slow things down, the court very rarely conducts legal proceedings or imposes punishment on the guilty.

Is speed bad? A lot of judges also complain about it. According to one experienced trial judge, "For many years I have been dismayed by the fact that cases were allocated only fifteen to twenty minutes." The emphasis on speed, according to critics, has produced "assembly-line justice" rather than the deliberation that justice requires. Still, some pretty convincing research says that slowing down the rate at which criminal cases are disposed of isn't as important to the mission of justice and efficiency as these critics of speed say it is. (See the In Focus box "Does Speed Trump Justice?")

Besides deciding minor criminal cases (as fast or as slow as due process requires), lower criminal courts conduct four important pretrial proceedings in both misdemeanor and felony cases:

1. They decide whether to release defendants on bail.
2. They assign lawyers to indigent (poor) defendants.

3. They preside over preliminary hearings to test the government's case against defendants.
4. They decide whether confessions, searches, and seizures can be admitted as evidence.

Felony Courts

Felony courts (usually called district or circuit courts) are where felony cases are tried (Chapter 10). They're courts of **general jurisdiction,** meaning they can decide all felony cases from capital murder to theft and also review the decisions of lower courts. Felony courts are courts of record, and they follow the rules of the adversary process more than proceedings in lower courts.

Appellate Courts

The main distinction between the trial (lower criminal and felony) courts and appeals courts is that **appellate courts** don't decide questions of guilt or innocence. They review the proceedings in the trial court to make sure the trial courts followed the rules of procedure and didn't violate defendants' constitutional rights. Defendants don't have to (and most don't) appear when appellate courts hear their cases. Proceedings in the appellate court are the most formal of all three levels of courts.

Most states and the federal judiciary have two levels of appellate court—intermediate (usually called courts of appeals) and last resort (usually called supreme courts). The intermediate appellate courts review the objections of defense and prosecution, the rulings trial courts have made on the objections, and whether the government has proved its case beyond a reasonable doubt. Supreme courts review the most serious cases—like death penalty cases—the most complicated legal questions, and all constitutional questions.

There's no constitutional right to appeal a trial or intermediate appellate court's decisions, but all states have created a statutory right to review. Many states allow the automatic appeal of death sentences. Overturning the decisions of the lower courts doesn't automatically close the case. The government can retry defendants. State appellate courts decide about 80 percent of all appeals.

The U.S. Supreme Court

> The judicial Power of the United States, shall be vested in one supreme Court, and in such inferior Courts as the Congress may from time to time ordain and establish. The Judges, both of the supreme and inferior Courts, shall hold their Offices during good Behavior, and shall, at stated Times, receive for their Services a Compensation which shall not be diminished during their Continuance in Office. (U.S. Constitution, Article III, Section 1)

This is all the Constitution has to say about the federal courts, except for a few words guaranteeing a jury in all criminal trials (Article III, Section 2) and the definition of treason (Article III, Section 3; Chapter 3). The Judiciary Act of 1789 created the U.S. Supreme Court, but the Court assumed to itself the source of its greatest power—the power of judicial review (the Court's power to decide whether federal and state laws and court decisions violate the U.S. Constitution).

The U.S. Constitution is the "supreme law of the land"; unfortunately, it doesn't come with an instruction manual telling us what its provisions mean. Many provisions don't need an instruction manual because they're perfectly clear, like the minimum age requirement for the president (35), members of the Senate (30), and members of the House of Representatives (25). But others aren't so clear, like some you've already run into—"due process of law," "equal protection of the laws," and "unreasonable searches and seizures"—and others you'll learn about in the remaining chapters.

AP/Wide World Photos

◀ Justices of the U.S. Supreme Court. Front row, left to right: Associate Justices Antonin Scalia and John Paul Stevens, Chief Justice William Rehnquist, Associate Justices Sandra Day O'Connor and Anthony Kennedy. Back row, from left to right: Associate Justices Ruth Bader Ginsburg, David Souter, Clarence Thomas, and Stephen Breyer.

The U.S. Supreme Court's decisions are our instruction manual. You need to be clear about several points regarding cases that reach the Court for decision:

1. You have no constitutional right to a review of your case.
2. The Court doesn't decide whether you're guilty or not.
3. Almost everything the Court does is secret, except for the lawyers' arguments before the Court, the briefs they file, and the Court's published opinions.
4. Criminal cases come to the Court by way of two petitions. (They're called petitions because there's no right to the Court's review.) The **petition for a writ of habeas corpus** asks the Court to order some official (usually a prison warden or jail supervisor) to come to a trial court and justify a prisoner's imprisonment. The **petition for a writ of certiorari** asks the Court to order a lower court to send up the record of its proceedings for the Supreme Court to review. The Court issues the writ if four justices vote to issue it.

petition for a writ of habeas corpus asks the U.S. Supreme Court to order some official (usually a prison warden or jail supervisor) to come to a trial court and justify a prisoner's imprisonment

petition for a writ of certiorari asks the U.S. Supreme Court to order a lower court to send up the record of its proceedings for review

The Court usually agrees to review cases for two reasons:

1. A conflict exists among the U.S. Circuit Courts (the intermediate federal appellate courts) on the law's position on the issues.
2. An important constitutional question has not been resolved.

The U.S. Supreme Court gets many thousands of petitions every term; it decided only 80 cases during its 2003 term (October 2003 to July 1, 2004). So, you see, the Court denies the vast number of petitions it receives.

The National Center for State Courts (NCSC): The NCSC provides research, consulting services, publications, and national educational programs to state courts. These services provide solutions that enhance court operations with the latest technology. The group also collects and interprets the latest data on court operations. To reach this site go to "Web Links" on your Samaha CJ7 website: http://cj.wadsworth.com/samaha_cj7e.

Criminal Court Missions

We all know courts are supposed to administer justice according to the rule of law. That's their formal mission (we'll call it their due process mission; Chapter 1), but courts also have informal missions. One is crime control—the public expects courts to make sure guilty people are convicted and punished. Another is social justice—the public expects courts to do what's "best" for victims and offenders. A third informal mission stems from the reality that courts are not just legal institutions, they're social organizations made up of a professional **courtroom work group**—prosecutors, judges, and defense lawyers. The courtroom work group mission is to keep the organization running smoothly, efficiently, and, above all, harmoniously. This informal mission (we'll call it the court's organizational mission) dominates the everyday operations of our criminal courts (Chapter 10, "Conviction by Trial and Guilty Plea"). A final mission (we'll call it the career advancement mission) focuses on providing the work group an avenue to advance their own careers either within the group or in private law practice or political office. (You'll learn about this career advancement mission later on, pp. 286, 289.) First, let's examine the other four missions.

The Due Process Mission

The criminal courts' **due process mission** consists of making sure the process of turning suspects into defendants, then turning defendants into offenders, and finally sentencing offenders to punishments is fair (Chapter 1). In the words of the U.S. Constitution, *fair* means the criminal process won't "deny any person life, liberty, or property without due process of law." According to the due process mission, the best way to obey that constitutional command is to stick to **adjudication**—decision making in open court according to the adversary process. Fairness is more important than convicting guilty people, because in our constitutional system the ends don't justify the means—at least not formally (Chapter 1).

The adversary process used to be called the "sporting theory of justice," because it's a lot like a sporting event. There are two teams—the people's and the defendant's. Prosecutors represent the people's team (also called the government's, the state's, and the commonwealth's team). The defense counsel represents the defendant's team. Both fight hard to win. It's OK for them to fight hard, but they have to fight fair. Fighting fair means fighting according to the rules (the Constitution, statutes, and rules of court). Under the rules, it's fair for the lawyers on both sides to tell only their side of the story and to spin it as best they can to their advantage, but they have to back up their spinning with evidence (Chapter 9).

The judge is the umpire. She interprets and enforces the rules impartially as the law commands (and we hope in practice, too). Juries decide the facts—what the story really was—and whether they add up to guilt beyond a reasonable doubt (Chapter 10). This image reflects the highest ideals of U.S. justice—an open, fair, impartial, dignified conflict that sorts out the guilty from the innocent, punishes the guilty, and sets the innocent free (Pound 1912, 302–328).

According to the adversary system, if all goes according to plan, competition over the facts guarantees (or at least greatly improves the odds) the true story will win. But in practice, the adversary system doesn't always operate according to plan, mainly because the sides aren't always evenly matched and because judges (especially trial judges who have to face periodic elections) aren't always neutral. Individual lawyers vary in their talents, skills, training, and experience. More money can hire better lawyers. Guilt or innocence can depend on who has the best lawyer more than on the facts of the case. And, as you'll learn in the "Organizational Mission" section, the missions of the courtroom work group might conflict with the inefficient, time-consuming, adversary process (Rosett and Cressey 1976, 53–55).

The Crime Control Mission

The law controls the due process mission under the rules of the adversary process. The crime control mission responds to public opinion, and it's shaped by the "nasty, brutish" side of life seen in criminal courts. According to one judge, "There's no use kidding yourself. We have a particular type of clientele in

Gun Courts: Breaking the Cycle?

Swift adjudication and consistent sentencing are the hallmarks of the few gun courts operating in the country. The first two gun courts, which were very different in design, were created in 1994. After a decade-long lull, three more have been launched recently. [They're]...controversial because of their limited flexibility....

Adult courts in three of the five boroughs of New York City and in Rhode Island deal out swift justice..., and the consequences are...severe. Brooklyn's gun court, which began about a year ago, was New York's first. It has handled only gun possession cases. It is the brainchild of John Feinblatt, the city's criminal justice coordinator. Five percent of the precincts in Brooklyn accounted for 50% of the gun arrests in Brooklyn and 25% of the gun arrests in the entire city, Feinblatt said. "There's no greater threat to public safety than people who carry guns," he asserted. "And there's no better way to send a clear and unequivocal message to those who carry guns that we are going to focus our best police, prosecutorial and judicial resources on them."

Brooklyn has assigned three prosecutors to the court. Amy Feinstein, the chief assistant district attorney in Brooklyn, laid out the office's straightforward approach: A one-year sentence if there's no prior felony; a determinate sentence of five to seven years if there's a prior violent felony; and three to seven years if the prior felony is nonviolent. "Very few people will get probation over our objection," said Feinstein. And it's "unusual for us to bargain in these cases."

As an example of the court's accomplishments, Feinblatt said that before the dedicated court, there was a 78% incarceration rate for offenders with no prior felony. Now it's up to 97%. The median jail time was 90 days, and is now one year. But a University of Chicago Law School professor questions the court's process. "Hardly exercising discretion—or 'one size fits all'—takes the concept of 'justice' out of our justice system." In 1994, Rhode Island created the first gun court in the nation. Its goal was to shorten the time it takes to adjudicate any crime involving the use or possession of a firearm and to ensure a certain prospect of prison for those convicted. Since then, the time to dispose of these kinds of cases has fallen to 155 days from 518 days.

Source: Leonard Post, "Gun Courts Aim to Break Cycle," *The National Law Journal,* May 31, 2004. Page printed from: http://www.nlj.com.

---

this court: The criminal court is a cesspool of poverty." The public expects criminal justice to punish these "bad" people. Prosecutors are supposed to be ruthless; defense lawyers shouldn't "get their clients off on technicalities"; and judges shouldn't be "soft on criminals" or "handcuff the police" in their fight against crime (Levin 1977, 60). (See the In Focus box "Gun Courts: Breaking the Cycle?")

The Social Justice Mission

Here's how one trial judge describes the social justice mission: "You have to consider what type of person the defendant is. I try to glean from the background, [from] the kind of woman he is married to, from the nature of his offense, from his relationship to his children, and from his associations" (Levin 1977, 129–130). With social justice in mind, one judge granted probation to an armed robber because the victim provoked the defendant, and the defendant's wife was a "neatly dressed woman in her twenties who appeared mature and seemed to have a settling effect on the defendant." Due process can get in the way of social justice when individual cases don't fit neatly into the rigid rules of the adversary process. These cases need the room provided by discretion so courts can take into account mitigating and aggravating circumstances (Levin 1977, 129–130; Padgett 1985, 753–800).

Social justice and crime control are combined in Miami Florida's Drug Courts, created to deal with the huge number of drug cases in Dade County. The idea behind creating the court was that "an effective and flexible program of court-supervised drug treatment could reduce demand for illicit drugs and hence involvement in crime and reinvolvement in the court system" (Goldkamp and Weiland 1993). The Miami Drug Court accepts only first-time offenders charged with third-degree felony drug possession. John S. Goldkamp and Doris Weiland studied a sample cohort of defendants for 18 months. They found Drug

Drug Courts (NCJRS): Drug courts vary somewhat from one jurisdiction to another in terms of structure, scope, and target populations, but they all share three primary goals: (1) to reduce recidivism, (2) to reduce substance abuse among participants, and (3) to rehabilitate participants. To reach this site go to "Web Links" on your Samaha CJ7 website: http://cj.wadsworth.com/samaha_cj7e.

Court defendants were re-arrested less than other felony drug defendants and, when they were re-arrested, the length of time to their first re-arrest was two to three times longer than for other defendants. Drug Court defendants did fail to appear more often than other defendants, but this was because courts ordered them to appear far more often than other defendants.

The Organizational Mission

Courts aren't just legal organizations following the rules; they're complex social organizations that place a high premium on accomplishing their mission of smooth, efficient, and harmonious decision making. Chief Judge Lawrence H. Cooke of the New York State Court of Appeals shows obvious pride in the part he played in carrying out the organizational mission of the court in this summary of his achievements:

> New York has become one of the few states where the courts are disposing of more cases than they are taking on. We've made the courts more manageable. The courts are working much better than they did, they're producing much more, and they're more nearly up to date than they were six years ago. (Margolick 1984, 10)

This mission is difficult to accomplish in adversary proceedings, especially when courts face heavy criminal caseloads, which most of them do. So discretion and negotiation, not adversary proceedings and written rules, are the means to accomplish the organizational mission. (See the In Focus box "Drug Courts: A Good Idea for the Federal Justice System?") But it's not just necessity and convenience that encourage the use of discretion and negotiation; they're more pleasant, too, as you're about to find out in the operations of the courtroom work group.

The Courtroom Work Group

The courtroom work group—judges, prosecutors, and defense attorneys—carries out the organizational mission of deciding (disposing of) cases. This is a difficult mission to accomplish in adversary proceedings, especially because there are so many criminal cases in most courts. The courtroom work group has a lot more in common than the due process mission suggests. Decision making takes place within a close working and personal environment. Judges, prosecutors, and defense attorneys see one another regularly and have similar backgrounds and career ambitions. According to Peter F. Nardulli (1978), who extensively studied the courtroom work group in Chicago:

> In many courtrooms daily sessions were frequently preceded (as well as followed) by "coffee klatches" held in the judge's chambers. The coffee klatches were usually attended by the judge, public defender, the two assistant attorneys and a handful of private defense attorneys, who may or may not have had a case in that courtroom on the day in question. Conversations ranged from the fate of the Blackhawks or Bulls the night before, the potential impact of some changes in criminal law or procedure, the cases scheduled for that day, to what happened in the annual football game between the state's attorney's office and the public defender's office. "War stories" concerning unusual criminal cases in which the various participants had been involved were also related frequently, and occasionally some political gossip was exchanged. Oftentimes these klatches evolved into plea bargaining sessions involving concerned participants, with opinions and comments by bystanders freely registered. In short, these sessions were not unlike those that might take place in any office or shop. (179)

Paul B. Wice (1985), after interviewing more than five hundred judges, prosecutors, and defense attorneys in major cities throughout the country, concluded:

> Despite their locations in a hectic urban setting, the criminal courts which I visited seemed like traditional villages. The high level of intimacy and frequency of interaction between

Drug Courts: A Good Idea for the Federal Justice System?

In 2003, there were more than 1,500 [state] drug courts either in operation or in the planning stages. Drug court graduates have substantially lower rates of criminal recidivism than offenders who are imprisoned. In New York, for example, the re-arrest rate among 18,000 drug court graduates was 13 percent, compared with 47 percent for the same type of drug offenders who served prison time without treatment. Drug courts also cost less than incarceration and have high retention and completion rates. Even Congress recognizes their worth; since 1994, it has authorized the attorney general to make grants to states, state and local courts, and local and tribal governments to establish drug courts.

Years ago, Chief Judge James L. Oakes of the United States Court of Appeals for the Second Circuit and I, as chief judge of the Eighth Circuit, sponsored a sentencing institute. At that institute, I asked the chairman of the United States Sentencing Commission why an 18-year-old who had received some drugs by mail for a friend should face a mandatory minimum sentence of 10 years, under the commission's federal sentencing guidelines set by the commission. The chairman responded that because this teenager would be in prison during his 20's, the age when the likelihood of recidivism is greatest, the sentence would cut down on re-arrests. The head of the Bureau of Prisons whispered to me, "Doesn't he realize when that young man gets out of prison, he will be nothing more than a hardened criminal?"

Mandatory minimum sentences, enacted by Congress, have contributed to the rising costs of imprisonment and crowding in federal prisons. In federal drug cases, defendants could face a minimum of 5 to 10 years in prison, while a similar offense in some state courts would allow a court, depending on the circumstances, to place the defendant on probation. Justice Anthony Kennedy and several other scholars, judges, professors and law reviews have openly criticized the use of mandatory minimum sentences in federal criminal cases. To make matters worse, a bill has been proposed in the Senate that would set a mandatory sentence of 10 years for a first drug conviction and mandatory life imprisonment for a second.

According to the Federal Bureau of Prisons' Web site (as of September 4, 2004), the total federal inmate population is 180,318. About 54 percent of that population are drug felons. The total cost for each prisoner was $61 per day; for the entire population, almost $11 million a day or $4 billion a year. It is predicted that by 2010 there will be more than 216,000 individuals serving time in federal prisons.

Unlike the states, the federal criminal justice system offers no alternatives for nonviolent offenders charged with drug-related crimes. In the federal system, it is almost a certainty that a convicted drug offender will be incarcerated rather than going through a community-based treatment program. It is little wonder then that the federal prison system will continue to be overburdened. Given the success of drug courts in the states, the federal government should study how to modify its sentencing to incorporate elements of the drug court model and to assess the effectiveness of community-based alternatives to imprisonment for nonviolent federal drug felons.

Source: Donald P. Lay, senior judge for the United States Court of Appeals for the Eighth Circuit, "Rehab Justice," *New York Times*, November 18, 2004. Copyright © 2004 by The New York Times Co. Reprinted with permission.

---

nearly all of the courtroom work group made many defendants and outsiders unfamiliar with the court's inner workings incredulous as to the possible existence of adversary proceeding. Although the "kibitzing" is curtailed during the time when court is in session, it is never completely absent. In the hallways, around the snackbars, in the courtrooms during recesses, and before and after the day's business, the friendly joshing never seems to end. Whether this exaggerated conviviality serves as a type of necessary social lubricant to disguise actual tensions, or is an accurate measure of their camaraderie, is difficult to discern. Whichever purpose it serves, it is an omnipresent style of interaction that typified almost every city visited. (48)

To the courtroom work group, defendants are outsiders (even to their own lawyers). Once defendants are charged, judges, prosecutors, and defense lawyers usually agree that defendants are guilty of *something*. So all that's left for the group to do is agree on a punishment. This is usually not hard to do because:

- There's a large volume of cases, and they all have deadlines.
- Most cases are routine.
- The group definitely prefers friendly negotiation to disputation.
- The pull of other business makes negotiation attractive.

Against the strong pull of these realities, due process, crime control, and social justice definitely have to compete with the time and effort the group commits to informal decision making. The mission to dispose of cases and the desire to maintain good work group relationships soften formal role conflicts among prosecutors, defense counsel, and judges (Nardulli 1979; Wice 1985, 110–113, 152). According to James Eisenstein and Herbert Jacob (1977):

> Pervasive conflict is not only unpleasant; it also makes work more difficult. Cohesion produces a sense of belonging and identification that satisfies human needs. It is maintained in several ways. Courtroom work groups shun outsiders because of their potential threat to group cohesion. The work group possesses a variety of adaptive techniques to minimize the effect of abrasive participants. For instance, the occasional defense attorney who violates routine cooperative norms may be punished by having to wait until the end of the day to argue his motion; he may be given less time than he wishes for a lunch break in the middle of a trial; he may be kept beyond usual court hours for bench conferences. Likewise, unusually adversarial defense or prosecuting attorneys are likely to smooth over their formal conflicts with informal cordiality. Tigers at the bench, they become tame kittens in chambers and in the hallways, exchanging pleasantries and exuding sociability. (24–25)

The "justice" negotiated behind the scenes in the courthouse corridors, judges' chambers, or even the restrooms is far more typical than the criminal trial that looms so large on TV and movie screens. "Justice by consent" dominates the reality of criminal courts, not the criminal trial. This reality that due process, crime control, and social justice have to fit in with the work group's organizational and personal agenda confuses those who aren't part of it, often to the point of exasperation. Deals prosecutors and defense attorneys make and judges approve are inconsistent (or so they appear to be) with both due process and crime control (Levin 1977, 3; Rosett and Cressey 1976, 2).

As parts of an organization, judges, prosecutors, and defense attorneys don't oppose one another in competition for the truth. They're a team, negotiating the best settlement possible with minimal dispute and maximum harmony within the courtroom work group. They have the thankless job of doing what they can to balance an array of competing, often irreconcilable, demands and values. Such balancing rarely satisfies anyone, because no one gets everything he or she wants—that's what settlement (as opposed to victory) means. In the adversary system, the goal is victory, and there's always a winner—or at least it seems that way from the outside. In negotiation, the goal is settlement, and the result is always at best "only half a loaf." Don't think negotiation and settlement have to mean injustice. They usually represent the best outcome possible in the real world (Nardulli, Eisenstein, and Flemming 1988, 373–374).

In any event, although the evils of speed and bargaining are often trumpeted by defense lawyers, the history of criminal justice records persistent complaints about the evil of legal foot-dragging. When Shakespeare's Hamlet tries to decide whether to commit suicide ("To be or not to be?"), he lists putting up with "law's delays" as an argument against killing himself. Why? Because

> the dread of something after death,
> The undiscover'd country from whose bourn
> No traveller returns, puzzles the will
> And makes us rather bear those ills we have
> Than fly to others that we know not of? (Act 3, Scene 1, Lines 23–27)

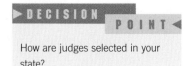

▶ DECISION POINT ◀

How are judges selected in your state?

Click on this Decision Point at http://cj.wadsworth.com/samaha_cj7e to explore the issue.

Judges

"The decision as to who will make the decisions affects what decisions will be made," Jack Peltason (1955), scholar of federal courts, wrote in 1955. This statement is still true. Even though we pride ourselves on being a "government of laws" and not individuals, judges play a major policy-making role in American criminal justice. The personal characteristics of judges affect decision making, so we need to know something about these characteristics (Slotnick 1995, 200).

◄ The number of female *trial* judges in the U.S. is growing. Still, there are fewer women than men in the top judicial positions, fewer with life tenure, and fewer minority women. Does gender matter in decision making? The small amount of research available suggests it doesn't.

States select judges by four methods: popular election (21 states), appointment (6 states), the merit (Missouri Bar) plan (16 states), and a mixture of methods (9 states) (American Judicature Society January 2004, 2). Missouri created the merit plan idea in 1940 to overcome the widespread use of political patronage in judicial selection. Under the **merit system,** a commission made up of lawyers, citizens, and an incumbent judge draws up the list of nominees. From this list, governors appoint judges to fill a short initial term. After it expires, the judges have to be elected. The merit system doesn't *eliminate* political influence, but it does *minimize* it by eliminating the need for fund-raising, advertising, and making campaign promises (American Judicature Society, September 2004).

Supporters of the merit system argue that impartial decision making depends on knowing the law and the ability to judge according to the law (Figure 8.2). Elections and their dependence on party loyalty stand in the way of impartial decision making. Supporters of the elective system promote its democracy, arguing elected judges are responsive and responsible to the community they serve. Voters will (and should) throw out judges who don't respond to community values (American Judicature Society, September 2004).

Whether elected or appointed, interest groups—political parties, bar associations, businesses, police unions, civil rights organizations—try their best to influence the selection of judges, because they want policy to benefit their particular interests. Members of women's and minority groups, like other interest groups, seek the appointment of women and minority judges who will represent their interests. Minority groups especially feel the need for representation on state courts, because they're most likely to come in contact with state criminal justice and they make up such a small proportion of judges (less than 3 percent of each group) compared with their percentage in the general population (about 12 percent) (ABA Task Force 1997).

In 2000, 18 percent of U.S. District Court judges were women—double the percentage in 1990. We don't have complete numbers for state judges, but limited data show similar progress. For example, the majority of the Massachusetts

merit system (Missouri Bar plan) a commission initially nominates and governors select judges from the list; then, judges have to be elected after a term of service

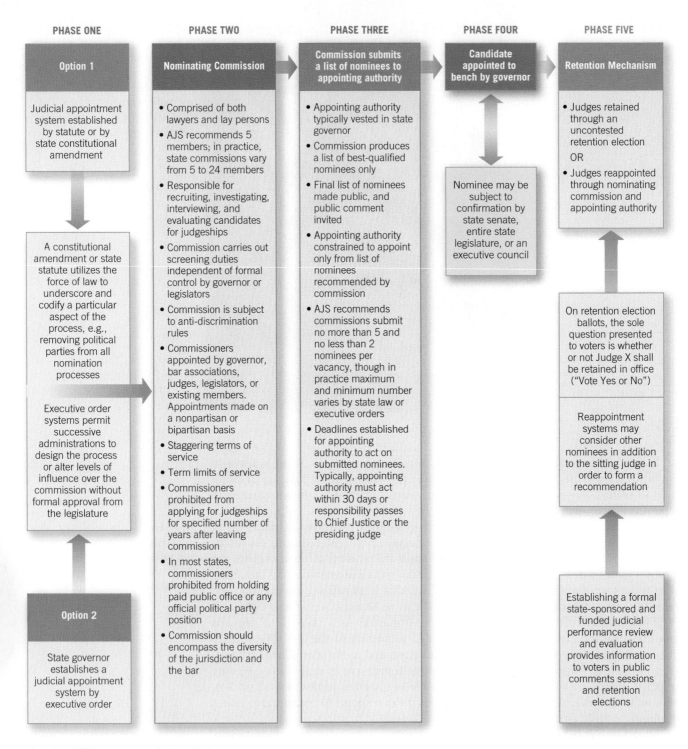

PHASE ONE	PHASE TWO	PHASE THREE	PHASE FOUR	PHASE FIVE
Option 1	**Nominating Commission**	**Commission submits a list of nominees to appointing authority**	**Candidate appointed to bench by governor**	**Retention Mechanism**

Option 1

Judicial appointment system established by statute or by state constitutional amendment

A constitutional amendment or state statute utilizes the force of law to underscore and codify a particular aspect of the process, e.g., removing political parties from all nomination processes

Executive order systems permit successive administrations to design the process or alter levels of influence over the commission without formal approval from the legislature

Option 2

State governor establishes a judicial appointment system by executive order

Nominating Commission

- Comprised of both lawyers and lay persons
- AJS recommends 5 members; in practice, state commissions vary from 5 to 24 members
- Responsible for recruiting, investigating, interviewing, and evaluating candidates for judgeships
- Commission carries out screening duties independent of formal control by governor or legislators
- Commission is subject to anti-discrimination rules
- Commissioners appointed by governor, bar associations, judges, legislators, or existing members. Appointments made on a nonpartisan or bipartisan basis
- Staggering terms of service
- Term limits of service
- Commissioners prohibited from applying for judgeships for specified number of years after leaving commission
- In most states, commissioners prohibited from holding paid public office or any official political party position
- Commission should encompass the diversity of the jurisdiction and the bar

Commission submits a list of nominees to appointing authority

- Appointing authority typically vested in state governor
- Commission produces a list of best-qualified nominees only
- Final list of nominees made public, and public comment invited
- Appointing authority constrained to appoint only from list of nominees recommended by commission
- AJS recommends commissions submit no more than 5 and no less than 2 nominees per vacancy, though in practice maximum and minimum number varies by state law or executive orders
- Deadlines established for appointing authority to act on submitted nominees. Typically, appointing authority must act within 30 days or responsibility passes to Chief Justice or the presiding judge

Candidate appointed to bench by governor

Nominee may be subject to confirmation by state senate, entire state legislature, or an executive council

Retention Mechanism

- Judges retained through an uncontested retention election
  OR
- Judges reappointed through nominating commission and appointing authority

On retention election ballots, the sole question presented to voters is whether or not Judge X shall be retained in office ("Vote Yes or No")

Reappointment systems may consider other nominees in addition to the sitting judge in order to form a recommendation

Establishing a formal state-sponsored and funded judicial performance review and evaluation provides information to voters in public comments sessions and retention elections

Copyright 2000 American Judicature Society

▲ **FIGURE 8.2 Model Merit System Plan for Selecting State Judges**

Source: American Judicature Society, *Model Merit Selection Plan in Theory and Practice* (Des Moines, IA: American Judicature Society, 2003). Reprinted with permission.

supreme court are women, and one-third of all judges are women. Still, there are fewer women judges at the top, fewer with life tenure, and fewer minority women. Does gender matter in decision making? The little available research suggests it doesn't (ABA Commission on Women and the Legal Profession 2001).

Prosecutors

Judges are the most visible and certainly look like they're the most important members of the courtroom work group, but looks are probably deceiving. According to Professor of Criminal Justice Candace McCoy (1998), prosecutors are the most powerful members:

> The prosecutor is the government's representative and advocate in all phases of criminal adjudication. Except for the daily operations of public police, prosecution is the most powerful component of the criminal justice process because of the number of offenders and victims it affects and because it dominates decision making about the legal course of every case. In the United States, the prosecutor reviews the cases of all defendants arrested by the police, exercises independent investigatory powers, determines the factual and legal sufficiency of each case and whether to dismiss or pursue it, officially files the charges, negotiates the conditions of guilty pleas, and serves as the trial attorney whose client is the state. (457)

Prosecutors are a vital link between police and courts and between courts and corrections. Police bring arrests to prosecutors, not to judges. Prosecutors, not judges, decide whether these cases ever get to court (Chapter 9). Enormous power results from this connection. By deciding not to charge, prosecutors can stop a police investigation in its tracks, rendering courts and corrections powerless. Even when they charge, prosecutors direct the course of events inside the work group by what crimes they decide to charge defendants with, what plea arrangements they make with defense attorneys, and what sentences they recommend to judges (Buchanan 1989, 2–8; Greenwood, Wildhorn, Poggio, Strumwassder, and DeLeon 1973; Jacoby 1980).

The following facts will give you some idea about prosecution in the United States. In 2001 (the latest available figures), 2341 local prosecutors' offices employed over 79,000 attorneys, investigators, victims' advocates, and support staff. Forty-two percent of prosecutors reported they prosecuted computer-related crimes; two-thirds reported using DNA evidence during plea bargaining or trial (compared to half in 1996); about one-quarter said they'd assigned prosecutors to community prosecution (DeFrances 2002, 1).

Prosecution in the United States is local; in most cases, counties elect prosecutors. Prosecution is local because American colonists hated the appointment of prosecutors by English kings thousands of miles away. The colonists also opposed private prosecutors because they denied equal access to justice. As soon as the Revolution was over, the new United States put into effect locally elected prosecutors paid for with public funds (McCoy 1998, 458).

The federal system is different. The president appoints federal prosecutors (U.S. attorneys) for all 94 federal districts. Despite this uniform centralized

◀ Prince William County, Virginia, prosecutor Paul Ebert holds a map as witness Ingrid M. Shaw points to her apartment during her testimony in the trial of D.C. sniper suspect John Allen Muhammad. A high-profile case such as this naturally leads to trial, but for the majority of cases prosecutors make the decision as to whether the cases will ever get to court. Even when they do charge the suspects, the prosecutors direct the course of events inside the work group by what crimes they decide to charge defendants with, what plea arrangements they make with defense attorneys, and what sentences they recommend to judges.

Getty Images

Chapter 8 Courts and Courtroom Work Groups 283

formal system, informal practice varies dramatically among the districts, especially, "considering that the U.S. attorneys in each district are drawn from the ranks of the party faithful with close ties to local political constituencies" (McCoy 1998, 458). Let's look next at the formal and informal missions of prosecutors, the structure and management of prosecutors' offices, and community prosecution.

District Attorney of New York County: This office investigates and prosecutes more than 130,000 criminal cases annually and employs more than 550 assistant district attorneys and approximately 700 support staff, making it one of the largest law firms—public or private—in the nation. To reach this site go to "Web Links" on your Samaha CJ7 website: http://cj.wadsworth.com/samaha_cj7e.

Formal and Informal Missions Prosecutors pursue multiple and conflicting missions. Formally, they're the chief law enforcement officer in the criminal courts. Sixty-five years ago, U.S. Supreme Court Justice George Sutherland described their function in this classic statement:

> The mission of the prosecutor is not that he shall win a case, but that justice shall be done. As such, he is in a peculiar and very definite sense the servant of the law, the twofold aim of which is that guilt shall not escape or innocence suffer. He may prosecute with earnestness and vigor—indeed, he should do so. But while he may strike hard blows, he is not at liberty to strike foul ones. (*Berger v. U.S.* 1935)

Along with administering justice, prosecutors are also office administrators, formulating policy and managing cases and their office staff. They're also careerists. They have their eye on gaining higher public office, entering high-paying prestigious private practice, or maybe just keeping their comfortable work group relations until they retire.

Most of us think of prosecutors as law enforcers. This isn't surprising because it's how we most often see and hear about them in the news and TV drama. In the real world, prosecutors' power to choose what crimes and suspects to prosecute is an essential part of law enforcement. Prosecutors use various standards to measure how successfully they're accomplishing their law enforcement mission. For example, they may decide welfare and corporate fraud deserve high priority and measure their success in dealing with them by either the number of convictions, the ratio of convictions to acquittals, or the types and lengths of sentences offenders get.

If prosecutors see themselves as the people's representative, public opinion influences their decisions. So if welfare recipients "ripping off the taxpayers" arouse the public, prosecutors prosecute welfare-related offenses. If the community believes drunk drivers are "getting off too easy," the representative-of-the-people-type prosecutors seek a high conviction rate and harsh sentences for drunk drivers (Carter 1974; Mellon, Jacoby, and Brewer 1981, 52; Neubauer 1974, 45; Skoggin 2004).

Other prosecutors see themselves as public interest lawyers, experts elected by the public to control crime as their professional judgment dictates. So they and not the public decide what crimes to prosecute, what sentences to ask for, and how to measure success. They work to serve the community's interest, not to satisfy the public's desires. When asked how he views the public, one prosecutor who considers himself a trustee of the public's best interest replied, "With a jaundiced eye" (Mellon, Jacoby, and Brewer 1981).

Prosecutors may be law enforcement officers, but they don't always get along with local police departments. (See the In Focus box "Is Police-Prosecutor Cooperation Worth the Effort?") This is nothing new. More than seventy years ago, President Hoover's National Commission on Law Observance and Enforcement found "frequent lack of cooperation between investigating and prosecuting agencies in the same locality." Why? Prosecutors work in different surroundings from the police. The police work on the streets; prosecutors work in and around the criminal courts with other lawyers. Prosecutors focus on legal guilt—enough admissible evidence to win cases; police officers act on factual guilt—when they "know" individuals are guilty. Legal rules and the professional legal subculture that prosecutors work in can seem not just like a rebuke to police work but a system that sacrifices the interests of victims, cops, and the public by making

Is Police-Prosecutor Cooperation Worth the Effort?

Police-prosecutor teams have overcome some of the problems arising out of their different interests. The teams—police investigators and prosecutors—work closely from the early stages of investigation all the way to conviction. Maine created an entirely new agency, the Bureau of Intergovernmental Drug Enforcement, to require police-prosecutor cooperation. The agency was responsible for "the integration and coordination of investigative and prosecutorial functions in the State with respect to drug law enforcement." For the first time, state law "mandated that prosecutors and investigators team up to create a more efficient and effective drug law enforcement strategy. It's not an investigation and then a trial; it's a unitary process, a case throughout," according to Assistant U.S. Attorney for Maine John Gleason (Buchanan 1989, 2–3).

The agency has reduced basic misunderstandings arising from the different worlds of police and prosecutors. According to bureau supervisor Dan Ross (Buchanan 1989):

> We have had to change some of our ideas because the attorney's perspective is that of the courtroom. Officers may not be concerned with how things appear in court because they tend to concentrate on just the facts. But the attorney has to care because appearances are so important in getting a conviction. (2–3)

For example, to get evidence in drug cases, police officers in Maine depended heavily on informants. Prosecutors didn't want to call informants as witnesses because jurors react negatively to them. Once they worked together, police began to realize this and get evidence to back up what informants told them. Prosecutors also benefit from the teamwork. One prosecutor said, "The insights I have gained into case investigation translate into better courtroom performance." For example, prosecutors working closely with drug cops learned officers often have to decide on the spot to search when they've got limited information. Knowing this, prosecutors can make more effective arguments for the good faith exception to the search warrant requirement, an area, according to one prosecutor in Maine, "where prosecutors are sometimes weak" (Buchanan 1989, 4).

Laconia, New Hampshire, adopted a police-prosecutor cooperation approach to test its effectiveness in battling quality-of-life crimes, which don't get publicity but use up the lion's share of police budgets (Chapter 3). In Laconia, a prosecutor with an office in the police department prosecutes all misdemeanor arrests. Officers consult with the prosecutor about filing criteria and investigative practices, and the prosecutor lets police know how cases are decided in court. Knowledge about case dispositions has helped cops' decision making enough to close legal loopholes in cases of driving while intoxicated (DWI), disorderly conduct, theft, and assault. According to the chief of police in Laconia, the close contact between police and prosecutors has also reduced the number of lawsuits against the police. The chief says, "A higher degree of legal awareness has developed, and it is reflected in the officers' actions on the street" (Buchanan 1989, 7).

A New York police-prosecutor program to prepare felony cases was supposed to reduce the number of felony cases dropped or thrown out. Did it? To find out, James Garofolo (1991, 439–449) examined felony arrests and interviewed prosecutors and liaison officers in a sample of six county prosecutor's offices and the New York State Police. Four of the counties instituted the liaison program; two didn't. The program had little effect on felony case attrition and liaison officers had little effect on whether cases produced convictions. But liaison officers did cut down case "slippage"—conviction for an offense less than the charge, such as from a Class E felony to a Class A misdemeanor. And it improved communication between prosecutors and arresting officers.

"deals" with criminals and their lawyers (see Chapter 10, "Plea-Bargaining Criteria"). For prosecutors, who see the world through the eyes of the work group, a plea of guilty to a lesser crime than the offender really committed might be enough. To police, who see the world through the eyes of the police working personality (Chapter 5), the government should prosecute, convict, and punish criminals for the crimes they actually committed, not make deals for something less (Feeley and Lazerson 1983, 229–232; Feeney 1981, 4–6; Forst 1981, 1–3).

Prosecutors aren't just law enforcement officers, as officers of the court they're also supposed to do justice. Doing justice includes protecting defendants' constitutional rights (remember prosecutors can fight hard but they have to fight fair, which is shorthand for fighting according to the Constitution). Doing justice also includes tailoring the law to suit individual defendants' needs. Sometimes, this means deciding not to prosecute—like diverting drunk drivers into alcohol treatment. Or it might mean asking for a sentence of probation for a first-time drug offender.

Prosecution offices are organizations, which means that high on their list of priorities are efficiency, economy, and smooth-working relations among staff and between staff and other public agencies and the community. As heads of this organization, prosecutors put a premium on cases and crimes that produce the greatest impact for the quickest and most economical processing. Prosecutors as administrators also favor rules that foster routine, regular, and predictable results. So they emphasize the uniformity of cases, rather than the uniqueness of individuals (Nardulli 1979, 108–111).

Prosecutors want to get ahead in the legal profession. If they want to be career prosecutors, they build friendly relationships with their superiors and members of related agencies, mainly the police, public defenders, and judges. If they want to move up the political ladder, making the right political connections influences their decision making. If it's private practice they're after, they seek the goodwill of members of private law firms (Carter 1974, 71–74).

Structure and Management Prosecution management varies according to jurisdiction size, geography, resources, and technology. Every jurisdiction has a chief prosecutor, usually elected to a four-year term. In small jurisdictions, prosecutors work alone or with a few assistants who know one another personally and who work together closely. These prosecutors usually have their own private practices, too. In large jurisdictions, prosecutors' offices are large agencies with lots of assistant district attorneys (ADAs) whom chief prosecutors rarely see and probably don't even know. Chief prosecutors (DAs or county attorneys) in states, and U.S. attorneys in federal jurisdictions, hardly ever appear in court. They set general office policy, deal with the public, and manage relations with other criminal justice agencies. Some chief prosecutors are career prosecutors, but most eventually wind up in private practice, become judges, or run for higher political office (Bureau of Justice Statistics 1992a, 1).

Most assistant prosecutors are fresh out of law school. They're usually appointed because of the law school they graduated from, where they ranked in their class, and their political connections. Democrats usually appoint Democratic assistant prosecutors; Republicans appoint Republicans.

Most assistant prosecutors don't make prosecution a life career. They stay fewer than five years and then go into private practice. "You're not supposed to stay too long. Sixty percent leave after three years. The longer you stay the less career value is the ADA [assistant district attorney] experience," said one (Wice 1985, 63). When they leave, most don't go to prestigious corporate law firms; rather they usually stay in criminal law practice, often becoming defense attorneys. A few become judges, but they hardly ever run for political office.

Prosecution offices assign assistant prosecutors according to two operating systems. In **prosecutor horizontal case assignment** offices, assistants are assigned to manage one stage of the prosecution—drafting criminal charges, working on pretrial motions, negotiating pleas, trying cases, or handling appeals. Under **prosecutor vertical case assignment,** assistant prosecutors are assigned to manage all stages of specific defendants' cases from charge at least through trial and often through appeal. Horizontal system assistants get to be experts in criminal procedure (arraignment, preliminary hearing, pretrial motions, and trial); vertical system assistants become experts in criminal law (homicide, rape, burglary) (Jacoby 1980, 3).

prosecutor horizontal case assignment assistant prosecutors are assigned to manage one stage of the prosecution

prosecutor vertical case assignment assistant prosecutors are assigned to manage all stages of specific defendants' cases

Community Prosecution You've learned in the earlier chapters about major changes in crime (increase in violence and drug crimes), changes in public opinion about crime (tougher attitudes toward punishment), and changes in criminal justice policy regarding crime (proactive crime attack, community- and problem-oriented policing strategies). Prosecutors have moved with the times, too; almost half of prosecutors' offices have adopted a proactive approach to prosecution (at

▼ TABLE 8.1 The Evolving Missions and Responsibilities of Prosecutors

Traditional Missions	Current Missions	Future Missions
Representing the state in criminal cases	Increasing use of noncriminal responses	Serving as a community leader
Holding offenders accountable	Doing justice	Implementing review and management of prosecutors
Imposing appropriate penalties	Introducing special community prosecution units	Becoming a policymaker
Reducing crime		
Promoting public safety	Adopting innovative approaches to prosecution	Embracing innovative ideas
Preventing crime	Increasing investigative powers	Continuing to embrace technology to solve crimes
Rehabilitating offenders	Expanding discretionary powers	Continuing to expand prosecutors' knowledge of current problems and issues
	Implementing technological and scientific advances	

Source: M. Elaine Nugent, *The Changing Nature of Prosecution: Community Prosecution v. Traditional Prosecution Approaches* (Alexandra, VA: American Prosecutors Research Institute, 2004), p. 16. Reprinted with permission.

least when it comes to minor crimes and disorder), and like the police, they've shifted from prosecuting cases to solving community problems (Nugent 2004, 1) (Table 8.1).

Community prosecution means taking a "grass-roots approach to justice," which involves the community, law enforcement, and other government agencies in solving neighborhood crime, public safety, and quality-of-life problems (Nugent 2004, 3). Community prosecution consists of five elements:

- Proactive approach to crime
- Specific community or neighborhood focus
- Emphasis on problem-solving, neighborhood public safety, and neighborhood quality of life
- Partnerships between the prosecutor and the police, the community, and other government agencies
- Use of a variety of enforcement methods (not just prosecution)

community prosecution a "grass-roots approach to justice," in which the community, law enforcement, and other government agencies work together to solve neighborhood crime, public safety, and quality-of-life problems

Defense Counsel

Defense lawyers, like the other members of the courtroom work group (and all other criminal justice professionals for that matter), pursue formal and informal missions. We're all familiar with their formal mission to defend their clients. Their informal mission is to bargain with prosecutors to get the best deal for their clients. Another important informal organizational mission is to get along with the courtroom work group. And, like prosecutors, defense attorneys have to focus on the career advancement mission.

"In all criminal prosecutions, the accused shall enjoy the right to...have the Assistance of Counsel for his defense," so the Bill of Rights to the U.S. Constitution commands. To this, the U.S. Supreme Court has added: Defendants have the right to *effective* counsel (Chapter 9). And the lawyers' code of ethics says defense lawyers have to "zealously" defend their clients. So formally, defense lawyers have the constitutional duty and professional responsibility to make sure the government plays by the rules. Specifically, that means seeing to it that the government proves every element of its case beyond a reasonable doubt based on evidence that was legally obtained.

An effective and zealous defense can go so far as to "actually frustrate the search for truth. Indeed, defense counsel may be ethically required to do so," says Rodney J. Uphoff (1995, 16). This may be especially true when lawyers know their clients are guilty. One defense lawyer in Arthur Lewis Wood's (1967) classic study of the defense bar summed up the formal mission this way:

 American Bar Association:
Professional association of attorneys. Resources, law school information, internships, and more. To reach this site go to "Web Links" on your Samaha CJ7 website: http://cj .wadsworth.com/samaha_cj7e.

► Defense counsel are ethically and legally bound to defend their clients vigorously. They're also bound to get along with the other members of the courtroom work group. Can they do both? Defense attorney Roger Diamond shows a bottle of herbal ecstasy to expert prosecution witness Dr. Jo Ellen Dyer (a pharmacist and toxicologist who specializes in sexual assault) during cross examination in the trial of Max Factor heir Andrew Luster. Luster was convicted of raping three women, and before the end of the trial jumped bail and fled to Mexico, where he was captured six months later. How could the nature of Luster's crimes and his jumping bail make this case difficult for the defense attorney to handle?

It's a criminal lawyer's function to get a criminal off or help him get a lighter sentence. He's helping him preserve his freedom. Whether it's good for society to have a criminal loose is another question. It may not be good for society, but that is the lawyer's job. It's his duty to the client; everybody knows it. His job is to preserve his client's freedom. (67)

In the 1960s, Abraham Blumberg (1967, 22) called the practice of criminal defense law "a confidence game." According to Blumberg, organizational pressures generated by the courtroom work group lead criminal defense lawyers to abandon their role of zealous advocate for the accused. Relationships with judges and prosecutors, he believed, outweigh the needs of clients. To maintain good relations, judges, prosecutors, and defense lawyers join together in an "organized system of complicity" (20).

It's true defense lawyers, especially public defenders, aren't just lawyers, they're members of the courtroom work group. According to one observer, they're "surrogates of the prosecutor, a member of their 'little syndicate.'" The government pays public defenders, so it's no surprise some people view them as agents of the government—a suspicion shared by indigent defendants. The "friendly adversary" relationship between defense counsel and their supposed opponents—prosecutors—feeds this suspicion. Opponents, after all, aren't supposed to be friends (Caspar 1972, 107, 110–111).

David W. Neubauer (1974), who has studied day-to-day decision making in criminal justice systems in "middle America," puts it this way:

If they are friendly adversaries, then we begin to suspect something is amiss. For example, if you visit most courtrooms, you will see the prosecution and defense exchange pleasantries before, after, and during the court appearances. You may even see two lawyers strenuously arguing their case in court, and then having lunch together. Some commentators interpret such actions to mean that the defense has closer ties to the prosecution than to the client, and the client suffers. (78)

►DECISION
POINT◄

Should lawyers defend "guilty" defendants?

Click on this Decision Point at http://cj.wadsworth.com/samaha_cj7e to explore the issue.

Can lawyers vigorously defend clients they've never seen before and probably will never see again, especially when it might antagonize professional peers they have ongoing relationships with? Some empirical evidence suggests defense lawyers can wage a hard fight in the adversary system, drive a hard bargain in plea-negotiating sessions, and still maintain close professional, peer, and personal relationships with prosecutors and judges. Defense lawyers shouldn't (and most don't) take personally either the fights over defending clients in court or the arguments for clients out of court. In fact, it's quite the opposite, because it's the heart of the adversary system (McIntyre 1987, 148).

I saw this firsthand when I was a first-year law student. On the advice of my brilliant criminal law professor, Claude Sowle, I went to watch a criminal trial. An inexperienced young prosecutor prosecuted and an experienced defense lawyer defended a teacher accused of murdering his wife. They went at each other so hard the judge finally said, "Boys, boys control yourselves or I'm gonna hold you both in contempt." Then came a lunch break and I saw an astonishing thing: the defense lawyer put his arm around the kid prosecutor, told him what a good job he was doing, and they went off to lunch together. After lunch, they came back and slugged it out for the rest of the afternoon.

How can this be? The answer lies in something else Professor Sowle taught us by his brutal attacks on our arguments and reasoning—don't take it personally, and if you can't learn not to, don't be a lawyer. Confrontation, argument, and conflict are part of being a lawyer. One judge said, "Yesterday two lawyers started arguing about their case in the corridor after the hearing. That just shouldn't happen. Lawyers have to know how to channel disagreement" (McIntyre 1987).

Many criminal defense lawyers face daunting concerns beyond defending their clients' rights or maintaining good working relationships with prosecutors and judges: They're trying to make a living. According to one study, most criminal defense lawyers practice criminal law because it's the only way they can make a living in the law. They didn't graduate at the top of their law school classes, so they couldn't get jobs in large law firms or in corporations. They went into general practice and let minor criminal work help pay their bills. This is especially true of the majority of private criminal defense attorneys. These lawyers form an outer ring, beyond the elite corporate lawyers, with the less elite but still middle-status lawyers such as personal injury and labor lawyers who oppose corporations (Ladinsky 1963, 128).

Some don't like their work, and they don't believe it accomplishes anything noble for anybody: "It's not a very acceptable way of earning a living—at least according to many other lawyers. You are always dealing with shady characters. I take criminal cases but I would just as soon get away from it" (Ladinsky 1963, 64).

Other defense lawyers look at defense work (especially the trial experience they can get as public defenders) as a good credential to land positions in prestigious corporate law firms. In a sense, these lawyers treat criminal defense work as an apprenticeship for private law practice. Except in high-paying public defender's offices like the one in Los Angeles, where some attorneys in the mid-1990s were earning close to $100,000 a year, most public defenders leave public defense work after a few years and go into private practice. A lot of prosecutors go to the same private law firms defenders enter (Barker 1993, 83; Platt and Pollock 1974).

The National Association of Criminal Defense Lawyers (NACDL): This organization advances the mission of the nation's criminal defense lawyers: to ensure justice and due process for persons accused of crime or other misconduct. To reach this site go to "Web Links" on your Samaha CJ7 website: http://cj .wadsworth.com/samaha_cj7e.

"If the courts were organized to promote justice," Clarence Darrow told the inmates of the Cook County Jail in 1902, "the people would elect somebody to defend all these criminals, somebody as smart as the prosecutor—and give him as many detectives and as many assistants to help, and pay as much money to defend you as to prosecute you."

Darrow's vision will probably never be fully realized, as justice is never as popular as order. Still, Darrow would have been impressed by the system in Washington, D.C., where the courts operate in a reasonably just fashion: most of the guilty are convicted, and nearly all of the innocent go free.

By no means should one conclude that justice prevails in Washington. Ninety-nine percent of the injustice associated with crime occurs before the principals come into contact with the criminal justice system: the victim has already been victimized; the defendant, more often than not, has been subjected to every kind of abuse, from inadequate prenatal care to exclusion from the work force. The police, courts, and prisons are just mop-up operations.

"Now, no intelligent physician would consider treating an ailment without trying to discover its cause." Darrow wrote, yet that is how we treat crime, concentrating on the symptomatic relief we think the criminal justice system should bring—fast, fast, fast....The only limit on the number of people in prison is the space available. When we get more space, we lock up more people. New prisons generally reach capacity by the second year they are open.

The courts cannot reduce crime or establish justice. They are just a sorting mechanism between the front end of the system—the police—and the back end—the prisons. To the extent that the public supports adequate judicial resources and effective representation for the accused, the sorting can be done in a just and equitable manner.

I am proud of the role I played in that process.

Source: James S. Kunen, "Afterword," in *"How Can You Defend Those People?"* (New York: Random House, 1983).

CONFESSIONS OF A CRIMINAL LAWYER

My mind drifted to my preoccupations of the last months—I wondered how many times I had been asked what I got out of being a criminal lawyer. "You spend most of your time with monsters," "You're in and out of depressing places like prisons all day long," "The pay isn't extraordinary," "You're looked down upon by judges, other lawyers, and the public." It wasn't hard to explain why very few lawyers did criminal work and even fewer went on doing it for any length of time. I struggled to understand why I had remained in this work for more than fifteen years.

Most criminal lawyers I had met over the years were extraordinarily perceptive about the personalities of oth-

ers. They could impressively predict how a person would respond to certain kinds of pressures or questions. But in their personal lives these same lawyers, with their enormous egos, fed by the "power" available to them in the courtroom, and reinforced by their "victories," often had little understanding of their own behavior. And as a psychological defense mechanism, they concealed even from themselves their failure to understand their own motivation by claiming to have little interest in it.

The courtroom was a forum in which the lawyer could act out a whole range of intense emotions....Over the past years I had often expressed rage, or indignation, or joy, or sadness in a courtroom. At one level these displays had been fake or, at least, suspect: they were controlled and purposeful. I'm sure I wasn't the only trial lawyer who knew exactly when he was going to "lose his temper," what he would say or do while his temper was "lost," and how long it would be before he recovered.

▲ Defense lawyers frequently have to defend some "not very nice" people. Gary Leon Ridgway, the "Green River" serial killer, is one of them. Ridgway was suspected of murdering up to 48 prostitutes and runaways between 1982 and 1984. After a 19-year investigation, Ridgway was arrested and charged with four murders. He first pleaded not guilty in 2001. Then, following plea bargaining, he pleaded guilty, and was sentenced to life imprisonment without chance of parole in 2003.

The Supreme Court of Tennessee once said in a written opinion that the use of tears is "one of the natural rights of counsel which no court or constitution can take away," and that "indeed, if counsel has them at his command, it may be seriously questioned whether it is not his professional duty to shed them whenever proper occasion arises...."

At another level, I realized, this display of contrived emotions had been as real as anything else in my life. I had felt genuine rage during an outburst when I had trapped a cop lying; I'd had real tears in my eyes when describing a horrible wound.

For years I had been troubled by my difficulty in expressing the same range and depth of feeling outside the courtroom. A personal relationship seemed infinitely more threatening than a packed courtroom. Frequently, the problem wasn't just in the expression of feeling but in a failure to experience those feelings, or to experience them with sufficient intensity to recognize them.

What was there about the courtroom that made the expression of emotions possible? The lawyers knew the rules and the acceptable limits of any emotional outburst. We were given license to be demonstrative, in fact, we were encouraged to be, because that was the way the system operated; that was the way lawyers had always acted; it was only a performance anyway, and everybody knew it; and it was all done on behalf of someone else—the client. But getting angry in a personal confrontation could mean actually losing control and becoming vulnerable, and that could be terrifying. We never lost control in the courtroom. Quite the opposite, we showed virtuoso skill at appearing transported by emotion, while every moment keeping it all on a tether.

All the emotions and skills on that tether were supposed to be deployed for one purpose—winning. During the cross-examination, all available energy was spent on beating the witness. With a tough witness, the duel could be dramatic. Only rarely, and with great reluctance, would a lawyer admit that more than the pleasure of good craftsmanship had been involved in his subduing of a witness, but I had seen lawyers work a witness over, control him, dominate and humiliate him, then torment him. Deriving enjoyment from inflicting that unnecessary measure of pain might be rare, but not that rare. If the witness was a woman, there might even be sexual overtones to the encounter. With some lawyers, perhaps sometimes with me, similar patterns could be played out in personal relationships.

...For years..., I'd had no difficulty separating myself from my clients, and even from aspects of my own behavior that I found distasteful. But although I had been unaware of the extent of my detachment, and, at times, had even taken pride in my ability to keep so many things from touching me, I had been paying a heavy price. Yes, I'd had to adjust to the world I had been part of for so much of the last fifteen years. I had adjusted to the violence and the inhumanity. I had adjusted to the lies, the incompetence, and the brutality.

It would be false to attribute all these new grievances about myself to some kind of delayed reaction to my work. Obviously much of my personality had been formed before I stepped into law school, and it had been no accident that I had chosen such a career. But what problems I had brought into adult life with me had been exacerbated over the years by the fact that I was a criminal lawyer.

The constant exposure to so many lies had made me suspicious of people. I had formed the habit of automatically sizing up character and trustworthiness, searching out motives. I had developed a reflex of recalling all inconsistent statements, no matter how trivial. These were good habits for a criminal lawyer—if only they hadn't bled into my personal life.

Destroying witnesses had led to an arrogance, to an inflated sense of control over people, that I found difficult, at times, to leave behind in the courtroom. The temptation to dominate a social situation or individual encounter was sometimes irresistible. This arrogance would betray itself in an impatience with people who were not speaking "relevantly" or "responsibly."

Even more dismaying, the need to function dispassionately had widened the distance between my emotional and my intellectual reactions. In this latest murder case, for which I was about to deliver a summation, I had been making a constant effort not to call the two-year-old daughter "it" in front of the jury—but "it" was what I was usually thinking. With a cold detachment concealed inside me, I had screamed at my client about his feelings for his daughter, and the same cold detachment had been behind my outrage at that "prostitute," Mrs. Lewis, for "slandering" my client's good name by claiming rape. My detachment had been of an even colder sort because I had been conjuring up false emotions in an effort to influence the jury. I was suddenly, overwhelmingly aware of just how much these contrived emotions had been deceitful performances—calculated lies. Too many of the performances had been successful, and, as a result, I had become suspicious of my own emotions in other contexts. And certainly I had been suspicious of the emotions expressed by others for years.

About a month earlier, an acquaintance had come to see me, filled with enthusiasm about a rehabilitation project he wanted to launch. As he excitedly explained his plan to set up a center to help drug addicts, I found myself pulling away physically, leaning back in my chair. Here was someone I had known for several years, someone who should have been an intimate friend, speaking with concern and insight about a subject I knew well and should have cared more about.

Coldly I marshaled statistics and logic and, with lawyerly skills developed over the years, demolished his plan—never considering with generosity whether the plan had any merit. After my acquaintance left my office deflated, as perhaps others had done before him, I realized I envied his optimism, admired his eagerness to do something about an outrageous problem.

My own capacity for outrage, genuine outrage, had long ago been traded for cynicism. What had once been a shield of self-protection separating me from a psychologically threatening criminal world had assumed the pretension of a personal philosophy. The chances for intimacy with new friends or new ideas had diminished slowly over the years without my noticing it. With lower expectations of people and ideas, I could no longer be disappointed easily. Aside from the self-defeating limits this attitude imposed on my relationships, it was a depressing world view to be alone with. . . .

I knew it would be a while before I would try another case. My career had taken an important turn. Of course I still believed everyone was entitled to the best defense, and entitled as well to a competent lawyer. But not necessarily to me. I would have to screen my cases from now on. I had never turned down a case because the crime or the criminal were despicable—but now that would change. I could no longer cope with the ugliness and brutality that had for so long, too long, been a part of my life.

I also knew that I couldn't deal with the same volume of cases. I couldn't constantly be in court, on my feet, arguing, fighting, struggling to win. I needed to find a way to step back from the aggression of the courtroom battles and the violence that was usually the subject over which those battles were fought. I had to examine in a disciplined way the sources of my anger, the anger that was peculiar to me rather than to criminal lawyers generally.

Source: Seymour Wishman, *Confessions of a Criminal Lawyer* (New York: Times Books, 1981), pp. 231–233, 238–241. Reprinted with permission from the Wendy Lipkind Agency, agent for Seymour Wishman.

THE BEST DEFENSE

The zealous defense attorney is the last bastion of liberty—the final barrier between an overreaching government and its citizens. The job of the defense attorney is to challenge the government: to make those in power justify their conduct and defend the right of those who lack the ability or resources to defend themselves. (Even the rich are relatively powerless—less so, of course, than the poor—when confronting the resources of a government prosecutor.)

One of the truest tests of a free country is how it treats those whose job it is to defend the guilty and the despised. In most repressive countries there is no independent defense bar. Indeed, a sure sign that repression is on the way is when the government goes after the defense attorneys. Shakespeare said, "The first thing we do, let's kill all the lawyers." Hitler, Stalin, the Greek colonels, and the Chinese Cultural Revolutionaries may not have killed all the lawyers first, but they surely placed defense attorneys—especially vigorous and independent ones—high on their hit lists.

One of the surest ways of undercutting the independence of defense attorneys is to question the propriety of their representing the guilty. Those who argue that defense attorneys should limit their representation to the innocent, or indeed to any specific group or category, open the door to a system where the government decides who is, and who is not, entitled to a defense. Granting the power to the government, to the bar, or to any establishment, marks the beginning of the end of an independent defense bar—and the beginning of the end of liberty. . . .

Justice . . . is a process, not only an end; and that for the process to operate fairly, all persons charged with crime must have the right to a defense. Since not all defendants are created equal in their ability to speak effectively, think logically, and argue forcefully, the role of a defense attorney—trained in these and other skills—is to perform those functions for the defendant. The process of determining whether a defendant should be deemed guilty and punished requires that the government be put to its proof and that the accused have a fair opportunity to defend. . . .

To me the most persuasive argument for defending the guilty and the despised is to consider the alternative. Those governments that forbid or discourage such representation have little to teach us about justice. Their systems are far more corrupt, less fair, and generally even less efficient than ours. What Winston Churchill once said about democracy can probably also be said about the adversary system of criminal justice: It may well be the worst system of justice, "except [for] all the other [systems] that have been tried from time to time."

Attorneys who defend the guilty and the despised will never have a secure or comfortable place in any society. Their motives will be misunderstood; they will be suspected of placing loyalty to clients above loyalty to society; and they will be associated in the public mind with the misdeeds of their clients. They will be seen as troublemakers and gadflies. The best of them will always be on the firing line, with their licenses exposed to attack.

There will never be a Nobel Prize for defense attorneys who succeed in freeing the guilty. Indeed there are few prizes or honors ever bestowed on defense lawyers for their zealousness. The ranks of defense attorneys are filled with a mixed assortment of human beings from the most noble and dedicated to the most sleazy and corrupt. It is a profession that seems to attract extremes. The public sometimes has difficulty distinguishing between the noble and the sleazy; the very fact that a defense lawyer represents a guilty client leads some to conclude that the lawyer must be sleazy. Being so regarded is an occupational hazard of all zealous defense attorneys. The late Supreme Court Justice Felix Frankfurter once commented that he knew of no title "more honorable than that of Professor of Law at the Harvard Law School." I know of none more honorable than defense attorney."

Source: From *The Best Defense* by Alan Dershowitz. Copyright © 1982 by Alan M. Dershowitz. Reprinted by permission of Random House.

QUESTIONS

1. List the authors' reasons both for and against being a defense lawyer.
2. Based on your list in question 1, how would you answer the question, "How can you defend these people?"?

Chapter Summary

- The judiciary in a federal system is divided into U.S. and state courts in three tiers: lower courts, felony courts, and appeals courts. Lower courts have limited jurisdiction to try and conduct pretrial felony proceedings. Felony courts have general jurisdiction to try all criminal cases. Appeals courts review trial courts' application of law to facts. The U.S. Supreme Court has the last word in interpreting the U.S. Constitution. The Court hears only a tiny fraction of all petitions to review cases. The Court doesn't accept cases to review whether defendants are guilty.

- The criminal courts' formal mission is to provide due process of law. They also have informal missions, including crime control, tailoring justice to suit individual defendants, and an organizational mission.

- The main mission of the courtroom work group (judges, prosecutors, and defense lawyers) is to dispose of cases efficiently and harmoniously. Speed in disposing of cases isn't necessarily bad. Nor is the adversary system necessarily the best way to achieve justice. Justice by informal negotiation within the courtroom work group is far more common than justice by means of formal trials.

- Judges play a major policy as well as judicial role in our criminal justice system. Most judges are responsible to the electorate either initially or at periodic points in their careers.

- Prosecutors pursue multiple missions, including law enforcement, ensuring justice for defendants, getting along with the other work group members, and pursuing their careers. Community prosecution is a proactive varied response to dealing with minor crime.

- Defense counsel's formal mission is to defend their clients vigorously; their informal missions mirror those of the prosecution: get along with the work group and pursue their careers.

Key Terms

limited jurisdiction, p. 271
general jurisdiction, p. 274
appellate courts, p. 274
petition for a writ of habeas corpus, p. 275
petition for a writ of certiorari, p. 275

courtroom work group, p. 276
due process mission, p. 276
adjudication, p. 276
merit system (Missouri Bar) plan, p. 281
prosecutor horizontal case assignment, p. 286

prosecutor vertical case assignment, p. 286
community prosecution, p. 287

Web Resources

Go to http://cj.wadsworth.com/samaha_cj7e for a wealth of online resources related to your book. Take a "pre-test" and "post-test" for each chapter in order to help master the material. Check out the *Web Links* to access the websites mentioned in the text, as well as many others. Explore the *Decision Points* flagged in the margins of the text for additional insights. You can also access recent perspectives by clicking on *CJ in the News* and *Terrorism Update* under *Course Resources*.

Search Online with InfoTrac College Edition

For additional information, explore InfoTrac College Edition, your online library. Go to http://cj.wadsworth.com/samaha_cj7e to access InfoTrac College Edition from your book's website. Use the passcode that came with your book. You will find InfoTrac College Edition exercises and a list of key words for further research.

CHAPTER 9

Proceedings before Trial

FACT *or* FICTION?

► The prosecutor has *nearly* total discretion to charge suspects with crimes.

► The main formal criterion in the decision to charge is the strength of the case against suspects.

► The evidence clearly demonstrates that race and gender influence the decision to charge.

► The main function of the first appearance is to take defendants' pleas of guilty or not guilty in felony cases.

► There's a constitutional right to counsel but not to *effective* counsel.

► The only legitimate reason for denying bail is to make sure defendants show up for trial.

► Grand juries are being used increasingly to help fight the war on terror.

EXAMINING A WITNESS THE WRONG WAY

> Q. [DEFENSE COUNSEL]: How do you remember that the man said that? How do you remember that? You still remember?
>
> A. [THE VICTIM]: I don't know.
>
> Q. [DEFENSE COUNSEL]: I give you—I['m] gonna give you one candy, one Valentines lollipop if you can tell us if you do remember or not, no? . . .

Thereafter, counsel sought permission to sit in the witness chair and continue his cross-examination while the victim sat in his lap. The transcript between the court and Smith's counsel reads:

> THE COURT: What do you propose to do?
>
> [DEFENSE COUNSEL]: I'm going to be sitting on the chair and she can sit on my lap so she can see the jurors, so the jurors can see her.
>
> THE COURT: What is this reference to candy or something?
>
> [DEFENSE COUNSEL]: I have candy, you know, just to open things up a little bit more. It's up there. . . .

—*STATE V. SMITH*, 712 P.2D 496 (1986)

O nly one out of ten people arrested for committing a felony goes to prison. Table 9.1 shows the decisions and decision makers who determine whether arrested suspects go free or become defendants and possibly convicted offenders. Figure 9.1 shows the funnel effect of decision making after arrest. In this chapter, you'll learn about the decision making behind this funnel effect, including the decision to charge, the appointment of defense counsel, the decision to detain or release defendants before trial, testing the government's case against defendants, and arraignment and pretrial motions.

The Decision to Charge

More than fifty years ago, the former prosecutor and Supreme Court Justice Robert Jackson (1940) said the power to charge people with crimes gives prosecutors "more control over life, liberty, and reputation than any other person in America" (32–33). Why? Because prosecutors have *nearly* total discretion to make three decisions:

1. To charge and—just as important—not to charge suspects with crimes
2. The specific crime to charge suspects with, like first- or second-degree murder
3. Whether to transfer the case from the criminal justice system to social services, like drug treatment—known as diversion

The decision to charge starts formal court proceedings (adjudication). Once adjudication starts, prosecutors represent the government in all the following proceedings:

1. Deciding whether to bail or detain defendants
2. Presiding over grand jury reviews and presenting the government's case in preliminary hearings
3. Presenting the government's case in trials
4. Negotiating guilty pleas with defense lawyers
5. Negotiating sentences with judges and defense lawyers

Prosecutors' discretion to charge is wide but not total. One reason is that prosecutors share the decision to charge (or just as important, the decision *not* to charge) with other decision makers, including:

- Members of the public who complain to the police (Chapter 2)
- Patrol officers who respond to the complaints (Chapter 6)
- Detectives who investigate complaints to gather evidence and witnesses (Chapter 6)
- Victims and other witnesses who provide testimony and other information (discussed later in this section)
- Judges who conduct the first appearance and other preliminary proceedings (later in this chapter)
- Grand jurors who hand up indictments (later in this chapter)
- Defendants who agree to plead guilty, or refuse to plead guilty, to a specific crime (Littrell 1979, 32–33; Chapter 10)

Let's look further at what influences the decision to charge; how race and gender affect the decision to charge; and the consequences of being charged with a crime.

▼ TABLE 9.1 Decisions and Decision Makers from Arrest to Sentencing

Decision Makers	Decisions
Prosecutor	Charge with a crime
	Divert to social service agency
	Dismiss case
	Test case by grand jury or judge
	Plea-bargain (Chapter 10)
	Try case (Chapter 10)
	Recommend sentence (Chapter 11)
Judge	Set bail
	Assign counsel
	Bind over for trial
	Rule on motions and objections before, during, and after trial
	Sentence defendants (Chapter 11)
Bail bondsman	Put up money bail
	Pursue defendants who fail to appear
Grand jury	Indict
	"No bill" (decline to indict)
Defense counsel	Advise defendant on how to plead (Chapter 10)
	Plea-bargain with prosecutor (Chapter 10)
	Develop strategy to defend client's interest (Chapter 10)
Defendant	Plead guilty or not guilty (Chapter 10)
	Accept plea bargain (Chapter 10)
Court personnel	Conduct bail investigation
	Conduct presentence investigation and report (Chapter 11)
Trial jury	Convict (Chapter 10)
	Acquit (Chapter 10)

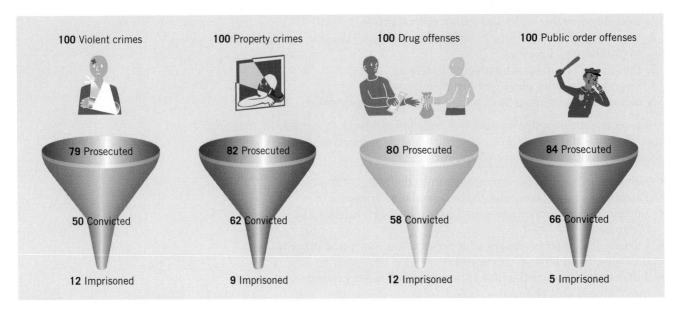

100 Violent crimes	100 Property crimes	100 Drug offenses	100 Public order offenses
79 Prosecuted	82 Prosecuted	80 Prosecuted	84 Prosecuted
50 Convicted	62 Convicted	58 Convicted	66 Convicted
12 Imprisoned	9 Imprisoned	12 Imprisoned	5 Imprisoned

▲ **FIGURE 9.1 The Funnel Effect after Arrest**

Source: Bureau of Justice Statistics, *Sourcebook of Criminal Justice Statistics, 1991* (Washington, DC: Bureau of Justice Statistics, 1992), Table 5.53.

The Influences on the Decision to Charge

"Let the punishment fit the crime," the famous eighteenth-century Italian criminal law reformer Cesare Beccaria urged. In other words, focus on behavior the law defines as criminal and fit the punishment to the behavior. Ironically, modern prosecutors have stood Beccaria's idea on its head: They fit the crime to the punishment. They decide how much punishment the "badness" of the act and the "sinisterness" of the suspect deserve, and then they look for a crime to fit the deserved punishment. The bottom line: The decision to charge is the most discretionary decision (meaning it's the least subject to review) in all of criminal justice (Albonetti 1986, 624).

Most experts believe prosecutors need this broad discretion because not all arrests should result in criminal charges. Some victims don't want prosecution. In other cases, there might not be enough evidence to prove defendants are guilty beyond a reasonable doubt. Maybe counseling or other noncriminal responses are better. Maybe resources can be spent better on prosecuting other cases (Gottfredson and Gottfredson 1988, 113–114).

What criteria do prosecutors use in deciding whether to charge and what to charge suspects with? Empirical research (Gottfredson and Gottfredson, 1988, 119–128; Miller, Dawson, Dix, and Parnas 2000, 661–663) points to four criteria we're familiar with by now. One is formal—the strength of the case against the suspect. Three are informal—the seriousness of the offense, the criminal history of the suspect, and the relationship between the suspect and the victim.

The Strength of the Case Let's look at the formal (legal) criterion—the **strength of the case.** The "strength of the case" means the amount of evidence against the suspect. All the research puts this criterion at the top of the list of influences on prosecutors' decision to charge. So answers to the questions, Are there witnesses? Are they believable? Will they show up in court? Is there physical evidence? and Is it admissible? are all important. If the evidence adds up to what prosecutors believe is proof beyond a reasonable doubt they'll charge suspects; if it doesn't, they won't.

Of course, the evidence has to be obtained legally or it'll be thrown out (Chapter 7, "Exclusionary Rule"). Keep in mind that research repeatedly shows that law enforcement officers' violation of suspects' constitutional rights (got evidence by illegal searches and seizures, by coerced confessions, or illegal lineups)

strength of the case the amount of evidence against the suspect

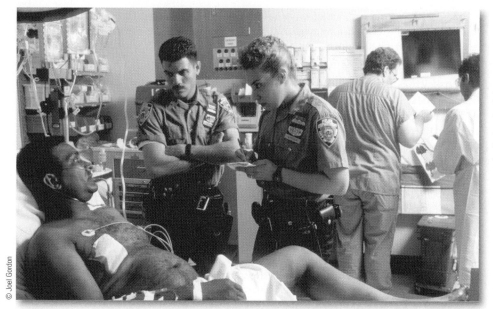

◀ Practically speaking, the quality and amount of evidence is a bigger problem than its admissibility. In this emergency-trauma room at Lincoln Hospital, South Bronx, two officers gather evidence from a gun shot victim. What they learn will be instrumental in the prosecutor's decision to charge, what to charge the defendant with, and whether the case goes to trial or is plea bargained.

© Joel Gordon

practically never (less than one-tenth of 1 percent of all cases) influences prosecutors' decision to charge.

Prosecutors *do* have a concern about evidence, but it's about the amount, not the admissibility, of it. The concern boils down to whether the police got enough physical evidence (like stolen property) or witnesses to prove guilt beyond a reasonable doubt (Chapter 10). For every 1 case prosecutors drop because police violated suspects' constitutional rights, they drop 20 because the police didn't get enough evidence to prove the suspects are guilty (Forst 1995, 367).

Brian Forst (1995), who studied the decision to charge for 20 years, sums up the real problems with evidence this way:

> In short, whether an arrest ends in conviction depends in the first place on factors over which the prosecutor has no control: the strength of the evidence as presented to the police officer, the effectiveness of the officer in bringing the best available evidence (both tangible and testimonial) to the prosecutor, and the seriousness of the offense. Nonetheless, prosecution resources and practices—and the exercise of discretion—do play a significant role in determining whether arrests lead to conviction. (367–368)

Let's now turn to the informal (extralegal) influences on the prosecutor's discretionary decision to charge.

Informal Influences According to sociologist of law Donald Black (1989), "The strength of the case is a sociological as well as a legal question" (24). The sociological question consists of three extralegal influences on the prosecutor's decision to charge:

1. Seriousness of the offense
2. Sinisterness of the defendant
3. Organizational pressure to "win" cases

Black calls these three influences the **social structure of the case.** In their charging decision, prosecutors have to answer these sociological questions about the structure of the case:

social structure of the case extralegal influences on the prosecutor's decision to charge

> Who allegedly killed whom? That is, what were the characteristics of the alleged victim and the accused? Was this an upward or a downward murder (was the social status of the accused below or above the social status of the victim)? Or was it a lateral murder (between equals)? If lateral, at what status level were the principals: low, intermediate, or high? And what was the relational structure of the crime? Were the victim and the accused acquainted? If so, how well? Who are the witnesses for each side?... Anyone who ventures

into the legal world without knowing how to assess the sociological strengths and weaknesses of a case has a disadvantage. Any law school that does not offer a course on this subject is denying its students valuable knowledge about how the law actually works. (Black 1989, 24)

Prosecutors are wary of charging in cases where there's some kind of relationship between suspects and victims. For example, New York City prosecutors decided not to charge in more than half the assault cases in which suspects and victims had some kind of prior relationship (Vera Institute of Justice 1977). Why? One assistant district attorney' relates an example:

> This woman was charged on the complaint of her common-law husband. She then filed a complaint against him for assault. I don't know which of them called the police first. The charge against her was reduced in the Complaint Room to assault in the third degree [a misdemeanor]. Because they were both complainants in court, I was able to speak to them both. They told me they did not wish to continue prosecution. They told me that they were both drinking and apparently they both started to insult each other. It wasn't clear who struck first, but the common-law husband struck his wife with a shovel, hitting her in the eye, and she struck him in the arm with an exacto knife, causing injury. Neither said they were injured seriously, though the arresting police officer had written up her assault against her husband as assault in the second degree, while his assault against her was a third-degree assault. She was also charged with possession of a weapon as a misdemeanor, which was also dropped because the husband refused to testify as to how the knife was used. The knife was not classified as a dangerous instrument per se.
>
> When I had satisfied myself that neither had been injured seriously, I looked at their past records. He had one previous arrest ten years ago, I don't recall for what, and she had no prior arrests. I felt that since there had not been problems with the law, and neither one had any sort of record, there was no reason to keep this case in court. (31–32)

This case shows a mix of the formal and informal criteria we've been examining. Of course, the relationship is important, but so is the seriousness of the offense—there weren't any serious injuries. The strength of the case also played a part in the decision—the victim didn't want her husband convicted and she wouldn't make a good witness because she wasn't entirely innocent herself. Whether the suspect had a criminal history was also considered—he had only one prior arrest and that was ten years ago; she had none.

The real world of criminal justice justifies the wide discretion of prosecutors to charge. Most statutes can't account for variations in individual cases. Legislatures pass many criminal laws, making crimes out of virtually everything that "bothers" particular groups without regard to whether they can be enforced. Some prosecutors believe that criminal codes are "society's trash bin." The charging process gives prosecutors a way to scour it. Also, prosecutors have to "individualize justice." Possessing 1 ounce of marijuana for personal use isn't the same as possessing 150 ounces for sale. Prosecutors do, and probably should, respect the wishes of victims who want to forgive those who have harmed their persons and property. Burglars who break into stores to steal compact disc players haven't caused the same harm as those who break into homes in the dead of night, terrorizing occupants in their beds.

Not prosecuting suspects can sometimes serve justice better than prosecuting them. A minor property offender willing to return a stolen television set and pay for the inconvenience to the victim probably fares better if not prosecuted. Scarce resources demand that prosecutors set priorities because they can't prosecute all cases. Accordingly, they prosecute the most serious crimes and, among the most serious crimes, pick the most "dangerous" offenders.

Lisa Frohmann (1991, 213–226) observed the screening process in more than 300 sexual assault cases in two branch offices of a West Coast district attorney's office. One office served a white middle- to upper-class community, the other an African American and Hispanic lower-class community. Frohmann found that the organizational pressure to win cases influenced the screening process. The promotion policy in the prosecutor's office encourages prosecutors to accept

"If You Can't Measure It, You Can't Manage It"

Harry Connick was elected as the District Attorney for Orleans Parish in 1974. He has remained in that office for the past twenty-eight years. Connick first ran for office in 1969 against incumbent Jim Garrison, the flamboyant District Attorney made famous in the film *JFK*. . . . As in other American cities, the criminal courts in New Orleans deal with enormous volume. In the face of this large urban caseload, Connick . . . started speaking publicly about a . . . screening procedure that "would weed out those cases really not worthy of being on the criminal docket, so more courtroom emphasis can be devoted to the violent offender." . . .

Connick's screening techniques he chose to pursue [his goal of weeding out cases] would by themselves make NODA (New Orleans District Attorney) practices an important case study. But Connick added another critical tool to his administrative kit. From the earliest times, he relied on computerized information systems. Connick often invoked the slogan, "If you can't measure it, you can't manage it." During his first term in office, he combined this interest in data with his commitment to screening cases and suppressing negotiated guilty pleas.

This data system operates primarily as an internal office management tool. The office does not issue standard public reports based on the data. The system collects details about each step of the process, from intake through final disposition. It identifies both the decision maker (such as the screening attorney) and the reasons for each processing decision along the way. A standardized set of codes capture the reasons attorneys invoke most frequently to explain their choices.

Data systems are not cheap. In addition to the costs of hardware, software, and expertise to run the system, Connick employs as many as five people to enter data. Why would a prosecutor in an environment with sharply limited resources invest in data systems?

Information systems respond to limited resources and rapid turnover of lawyers since they make it easier to supervise the constant stream of new attorneys. In part because the NODA data system operates for internal administration purposes, it provides reliable information to test the claims of the office. The attorneys fill out the required forms and staff members enter the data routinely, at the same time that their cases unfold. Line attorneys know that their supervisors will summarize and review the data, and monitor the quality of the data they enter. Although Connick refers occasionally to summary statistics, no detailed reports go to the public regarding particular cases or particular units of the office. The system exists more for management than for public relations purposes. Thus, there is little temptation to obscure important decisions in the data.

Source: Ronald Wright and Marc Miller, "The Screening/Bargaining Tradeoff," *Stanford Law Review* 55:65–67 (October 2002).

---

only "strong" or "winnable" cases. Promotions are based on conviction rates, and the office gives more credit to convictions than to guilty pleas. The stronger the case, the better the chance for a guilty verdict, the better the "stats" for promotion. The office discourages taking risks on weaker cases. It treats high ratios of not guilty verdicts as an indicator of incompetence. On the other hand, it gives credit to prosecutors for the number of cases they reject, because the rejections reduce the caseload of an overworked court. (See the CJ & Technology box "If You Can't Measure It, You Can't Manage It.")

Race, Gender, and the Decision to Charge

Do improper criteria like race and gender infect the decision to charge? Rarely, some researchers say. Celesta A. Albonetti (1986, 639) found race had no effect, and gender had only a little (women had a 7 percent better chance than men of having charges against them dropped) in the Washington, D.C. trial courts. Barbara Boland and her colleagues (1989) reported the strength of the case against the defendants (number of witnesses, amount of physical evidence, use of a weapon), not defendants' race or gender, affected the decision to charge in a nationwide sample of jurisdictions. W. Boyd Littrell (1979, 32–33) also found little evidence of race or gender influencing the decision to charge in the New Jersey jurisdictions he examined.

Other researchers say race, gender, and ethnicity *do* infect the decision to charge. Cassia Spohn, John Gruhl, and Susan Welch (1987, 175–181) examined the decision to charge Black, White, and Hispanic female and male defendants in over 33,000 Los Angeles cases. Controlling for age, seriousness of the offense,

▶ **FIGURE 9.2 Percentage of Sexual Assault Cases Charged by Race, Ethnicity, and Gender of Suspect**

Source: Cassia Spohn, Dawn Beichner, Erika Davis Frenzel, and David Holleran, "Prosecutors' Charging Decision in Sexual Assault Cases: A Multi-State Study, Final Report" (Washington, DC: National Criminal Justice Research Service, 2002).

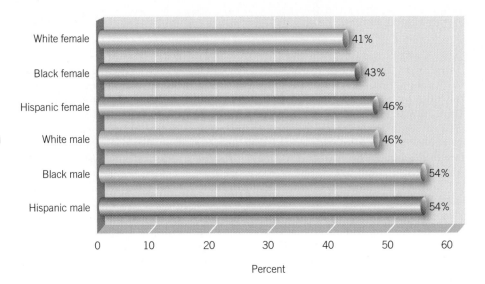

criminal history of the defendant, and whether defendants were armed, they found discrimination in favor of women and against Hispanics and Blacks (Figure 9.2). But they infect decisions only in borderline cases. So where the evidence is strong enough definitely to charge or too weak to charge at all, race and gender have no effect.

What are we to make of these conflicting findings among respectable researchers? According to Spohn and her colleagues (1987), we shouldn't get too comfortable with reassuring findings that race, ethnicity, and gender don't infect decision making, especially in highly discretionary, low-visibility decisions like charging suspects with crimes. "While [our] findings are certainly not definitive, even for [Los Angeles], they do call for the kind of scrutiny in the pretrial stages that has been so rightly given to the convicting and sentencing stages" (187). In a later study of charging in sexual assault cases in Kansas City, Philadelphia, and Miami, Spohn and her colleagues (2002), found there was definitely a race (and gender) disparity in the decision to charge (Figure 9.2).

The Consequences of the Decision to Charge

The decision to turn suspects into defendants by charging them with crimes has far-reaching consequences, even if the charges don't end up in convictions. The consequences for the defendants can include losing time at work or maybe even getting fired; getting locked up during court proceedings; and suffering damages to their reputation even if they're acquitted. After he was acquitted, one former U.S. Secretary of Agriculture asked bitterly, "How do I get my reputation back?"

Becoming a criminal defendant is a form of "degradation ceremony," to borrow Erving Goffman's phrase. According to Abraham S. Blumberg (1970):

> The accused is confronted by definitions of himself which reflect the various worlds of the agent-mediators yet are consistent for the most part in their negative evaluation of him. The agent-mediators have seized upon a wholly unflattering aspect of his biography to reinterpret his entire personality and justify their present attitude and conduct toward him. Even an individual with considerable personal and economic resources has great difficulty resisting pressures to redefine himself under these circumstances. For the ordinary accused of modest personal, economic and social resources, the group pressures and definitions of himself are simply too much to bear. He willingly complies with the demands of agent-mediators, who in turn will help "cool him out." (69)

The power to decide what specific crimes to charge enjoys wide latitude, and the choice has serious consequences, too. For example, prosecutors can decide to charge first-degree murder, second-degree murder, voluntary manslaughter, or

Courts on the National Criminal Justice Reference Service (NCJRS): Virtual library of information, resources, and statistics on courts in the U.S. To reach this site go to "Web Links" on your Samaha CJ7 website: http://cj.wadsworth.com/samaha_cj7e.

involuntary manslaughter. They can charge aggravated assault, attempted murder, or simple assault and battery. They can charge armed robbery, simple robbery, larceny from the person, or simply larceny. Because the penalties vary for each of the specific crimes, prosecutors in effect set the upper limits of criminal punishment. (Prosecutors rarely decide to reduce a crime involving violence to one that doesn't, like simple theft instead of armed robbery [Israel, Kamisar, and LaFave 2002, 523].)

The First Appearance

After prosecutors file charges, defendants make their first appearance in court. (Don't confuse the first appearance with the arraignment discussed later; the first appearance comes *before* arraignment.) Misdemeanor defendants frequently enter pleas at the first appearance; felony defendants hardly ever do. The first appearance judge does three things:

1. Reads the charges against defendants and informs them of their rights
2. Appoints lawyers for indigent (poor) defendants
3. Decides whether to bail or detain defendants prior to trial and sets the initial terms for bail or detention

The Appointment of Defense Counsel

Lawyers are everywhere in the criminal justice system today. But that wasn't always true. In fact, during colonial times and for some time afterward, victims had to find and hire their own private prosecutors, and defendants in felony cases didn't even have the right to a lawyer to defend them during their trials. Until the 1960s due process revolution (Chapter 1), a lawyer's job was to represent people once they got to court, not before they were charged or after they were convicted. Since the due process revolution, which extended constitutional protections, even police departments and corrections agencies have to hire lawyers, because the Constitution protects people on the street, in police stations, and when they're locked up before trial. The right to a lawyer reaches even into prison cells—and to the death penalty.

Here, we'll concentrate on counsel for suspects and defendants. The Sixth Amendment to the U.S. Constitution provides: "In all criminal prosecutions, the accused shall enjoy the right . . . to have the assistance of counsel for his defense." U.S. courts have always recognized criminal defendants' Sixth Amendment right to **retained counsel** (a lawyer paid for by the client), but they didn't recognize the right to **appointed counsel** (lawyers assigned to people who can't afford to hire their own) until well into the 1930s. The story begins in northern Alabama one morning in March 1931, when seven scruffy White boys came into a railway station in northern Alabama and told the stationmaster that a "bunch of Negroes" had picked a fight with them and thrown them off a freight train. The stationmaster phoned ahead to Scottsboro, where a deputy sheriff deputized every man who owned a gun. When the train got to Scottsboro, the posse rounded up nine Black boys and two White girls. The girls were dressed in men's caps and overalls. Five of the boys were from Georgia and four from Tennessee. They ranged in age from 12 to 20. One was blind in one eye and had only 10 percent vision in the other; one walked with a cane; all were poor and illiterate. After the deputy sheriff had tied the boys together and was loading them into his truck, Ruby Bates told the sheriff that the boys had raped her and her friend, Victoria Price. By nightfall, a mob of several hundred people surrounded the little Scottsboro jail, vowing to avenge the rape by lynching the boys.

When the trial began on Monday morning April 6, 1931, 102 National Guardsmen struggled to keep several thousand people at least 100 feet away from the

retained counsel a lawyer paid for by the client

appointed counsel lawyers assigned to people who can't afford to hire their own

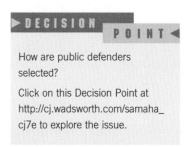

How are public defenders selected?

Click on this Decision Point at http://cj.wadsworth.com/samaha_cj7e to explore the issue.

courthouse. Inside the courtroom, Judge Alfred E. Hawkins offered the job of defense attorney to anyone who would take it. Only Chattanooga lawyer Stephen Roddy—an alcoholic already drunk at 9:00 A.M., who admitted he didn't know anything about Alabama law—accepted. Judge Hawkins then appointed "all members" of the local bar present in the courtroom as counsel. By Thursday, eight of the boys had been tried, convicted, and sentenced to death. Only 12-year-old Roy Wright remained because the jury hung, with seven demanding death and five holding out for life imprisonment. Judge Hawkins declared a mistrial in Roy Wright's trial and sentenced the others to death by electrocution.

Liberals, radicals, and Communists around the country rallied to the defense of the "Scottsboro boys," as the case became popularly known. In March 1932, the Alabama Supreme Court upheld all of the convictions except for Eugene Williams, who was granted a new trial as a juvenile. In November, the U.S. Supreme Court ruled in *Powell v. Alabama* (1932) that Alabama had denied the boys due process of law. According to Justice Sutherland, the right to counsel is part of due process that states are required to provide:

> In the light of the...ignorance and illiteracy of the defendants, their youth, the circumstances of public hostility, the imprisonment and the close surveillance of the defendants by the military forces, the fact that their friends and families were all in other states and communication with them necessarily difficult, and above all that they stood in deadly peril of their lives—we think the failure of the trial court to give them reasonable time and opportunity to secure counsel was a clear denial of due process. But passing that, and assuming their inability, even if opportunity had been given, to employ counsel, as the trial court evidently did assume, we are of opinion that, under the circumstances just stated, the necessity of counsel was so vital and imperative that the failure of the trial court to make an effective appointment of counsel was likewise a denial of due process within the meaning of the Fourteenth Amendment.

In *Johnson v. Zerbst* (1938), the Supreme Court elaborated the reasons for the right to counsel announced in *Powell v. Alabama:*

> [The right to counsel is] necessary to insure fundamental human rights of life and liberty. Omitted from the Constitution as originally adopted, provisions of this and other Amendments were submitted by the first Congress...as essential barriers against arbitrary or unjust deprivation of human rights. The Sixth Amendment stands as a constant admonition that if the constitutional safeguards it provides be lost, justice will not "still be done." It embodies a realistic recognition of the obvious truth that the average defendant doesn't have the necessary professional legal skills to protect himself when brought before a tribunal with power to take his life or liberty, wherein the prosecution is represented by experienced and learned counsel. That which is simple, orderly, and necessary to the lawyer—to the untrained layman—may appear intricate, complex, and mysterious. (462)

Despite the glowing words, *Zerbst* recognized only a very narrow right to counsel. According to the Court, the Sixth Amendment guarantees poor defendants a right to a lawyer at their *trial* in *federal* courts. It said nothing about a right to counsel either *before* trial in federal courts or to any proceedings at all in *state* courts.

The U.S. Supreme Court confronted the right to counsel in *state* courts in *Betts v. Brady* (1942). Betts was convicted of robbery and sentenced to prison. At his trial, he asked for a lawyer, claiming that he was too poor to afford one. The judge denied his request because Carroll County, Maryland, the site of the trial, provided counsel only in murder and rape cases. Hearings on Betts's petition for habeas corpus eventually reached the Supreme Court. The Court decided that the denial of counsel deprives a defendant of a fair trial only in "special circumstances."

So most indigent defendants (defendants too poor to hire their own lawyers) had to rely on counsel *pro bono* (lawyers willing to represent clients at no charge). That was supposed to change after the U.S. Supreme Court overruled *Betts v. Brady*, which the Court did in *Gideon v. Wainwright* (1963), when it ac-

▼ **TABLE 9.2 "Critical Stages" and the Right to Counsel**

Stage of Process	Right to Counsel?
Investigative stop	No
Frisk for weapons	No
Arrest	No
Search	No
Custodial interrogation	Yes
Lineups before charge	No
First appearance	No
Lineup after charge	Yes
Grand jury review	No
Preliminary hearing	Yes
Arraignment	Yes
Pretrial hearings	Yes
Trial	Yes
Appeals	Yes

cepted Clarence Gideon's (a Florida drifter) handwritten petition for certiorari. Here's part of what Clarence Gideon wrote:

> Respondent [Florida attorney general] claims that I have no right to file petitions for a Writ of Habeas Corpus. Take away this right to a citizen and there is nothing left. It makes no difference how old I am or what color I am or what church I belong too if any. The question is I did not get a fair trial. The question is very simple. I requested the court to appoint me attorney and the court refused. All countrys try to give there Citizens a fair trial and see to it that they have counsel.
>
> Petitioner asks of this court to disregard the response of the respondent because it was out of Time and because the Attorney General did not have one of his many assistant attorney generals to help me a citizen of the State of Florida to write my petition or this brief. But instead force me to write these petitions under duress. On this basis it is respectfully urged that the petition for Writ of Certiorari shall be issue.

Let's look more closely at when the right to counsel kicks in, the meaning of the Sixth Amendment's words "all criminal prosecutions," the right to "effective" counsel, the standard of indigence for obtaining counsel, and how the defense of the poor works in practice.

When the Right to Counsel "Kicks In" The Sixth Amendment guarantees the right to counsel in all criminal "prosecutions." What proceedings are prosecutions? Definitely trials and appeals, when defendants most need special legal expertise. But what about before trial? According to the Supreme Court, the right attaches to all "critical stages" of criminal proceedings. Table 9.2 shows the stages in the criminal process and indicates the ones the U.S. Supreme Court has declared critical stages. It's clear from the table that defendants have the right to counsel to represent them at all procedures after the first appearance.

But what about what happens in the police station *before* the first appearance? Specifically, do you have a right to a lawyer during police interrogation and identification procedures (lineups, show-ups, and photo identification, Chapter 7)? The U.S. Supreme Court first applied the right to a lawyer in police stations in *Escobedo v. Illinois* (1964). The Court held that the right to counsel attached at the accusatory stage of a criminal case—namely, when general investigation focused on a specific suspect. According to the Court, that point was reached in *Escobedo* when the police made up their minds that Danny Escobedo had committed the murder they were investigating. After they made up their minds he was the murderer, Chicago police officers tried to get him to confess by interrogating him. During the interrogation, Escobedo asked to see his lawyer, who was in the police station. The officers refused. Eventually, he confessed and was tried and convicted with the help of the confession. The U.S. Supreme Court said the confession was not admissible because it was obtained during the accusatory stage without the help of Escobedo's lawyer.

Just two years later, in *Miranda v. Arizona* (1966), the Court decided that police officers have to tell suspects that they have a right to a lawyer during custodial interrogation (Chapter 7). As for identification procedures, those conducted after indictment are a critical stage; those conducted before indictment are not (Chapter 7).

The Meaning of "All Criminal Prosecutions" We've looked at what kinds of proceedings are prosecutions. Now, let's look at what kinds of cases are included (Table 9.3). As we saw in *Powell v. Alabama,* due process commands that appointed counsel represent poor defendants in capital cases. In *Gideon v. Wainwright* (1963), the Court extended the right to counsel to poor defendants prosecuted for felonies against property. In 1972, the Court went further, ruling that all poor defendants prosecuted for misdemeanors punishable by jail terms have a right to an appointed lawyer. In *Argersinger v. Hamlin* (1972), Jon Richard Argersinger, a Florida indigent, was convicted of carrying a concealed weapon, a misdemeanor punishable by up to six months' imprisonment, a $1,000 fine, or both. A Florida rule limited assigned counsel to "non-petty offenses punishable by more than six months imprisonment." The Court struck down the rule, holding that states have to provide a lawyer for defendants charged with any offense punishable by incarceration no matter what the state's criminal code calls it (misdemeanor, petty misdemeanor, or felony).

Notice what the Court did *not* say in *Argersinger:* Poor people have a right to a lawyer paid for by the government in *all* criminal cases. Why? Because the Court was well aware of a practical problem: there isn't enough money to pay for everyone to have a lawyer. Of course, strictly speaking, constitutional rights can't depend on money but, as a practical matter, money definitely affects how many people get their rights in real life. We know many poor people who have a right to a lawyer don't get one because counties and other local governments simply don't have the money to pay for them. Why? Because taxpayers don't want their tax dollars spent on lawyers for "criminals." This mix of practical reality and constitutional rights surfaced in *Scott v. Illinois* (1979). The Court specifically ad-

▼ **TABLE 9.3 The Leading Right to Counsel Cases**

Case	Year	Definition
Powell v. Alabama	1932	Appointed counsel for poor, illiterate, "ignorant," isolated defendants in state capital cases
Johnson v. Zerbst	1938	Appointed counsel in *federal* cases at trial (not before or after)
Betts v. Brady	1942	Appointed counsel in state cases under "special circumstances"
Chandler v. Fretag	1954	*Retained* (paid for) counsel in all criminal cases
Gideon v. Wainwright	1963	Appointed counsel in state felony cases (overruled *Betts v. Brady*)
Argersinger v. Hamlin	1972	Appointed counsel in misdemeanors punishable by over six months incarceration
Scott v. Illinois	1979	No right to counsel for sentences that don't result in actual jail time

dressed the question, "Does the right to assigned counsel extend to offenses that don't actually result in prison sentences?" The Court answered no.

The Right to "Effective" Counsel In 1932, the U.S. Supreme Court said due process requires not just counsel but effective counsel. But the Court didn't tell us what "effective" means, so lower federal courts and state courts stepped in and adopted what was called a "mockery of justice standard." Under this standard, only lawyers whose behavior is so "shocking" that it turns the trial into a "joke" are constitutionally ineffective. One lawyer called it the "mirror test." (Put a mirror under the lawyer's nose; if it steams up he passes.)

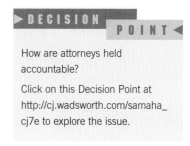

DECISION POINT

How are attorneys held accountable?

Click on this Decision Point at http://cj.wadsworth.com/samaha_cj7e to explore the issue.

What prompted this professional "dissing"? In actual cases, appellate courts ruled that lawyers who slept through trials; came to court drunk; couldn't name a single precedent related to the case they were arguing; or were released from jail to represent their clients hadn't turned the proceedings into a joke. Thus, they hadn't met the mockery of justice standard. When one defendant claimed he got ineffective representation because his lawyer slept through the trial, the judge said, "You have a right to a lawyer; that doesn't mean you have a right to one who's awake." That decision was affirmed by the reviewing court.

Courts and commentators have criticized the mockery of justice standard for being too subjective, vague, and narrow. The standard's focus on the trial excludes many serious errors lawyers make preparing for trial. Besides, in the overwhelming majority of cases disposed of by guilty pleas, the standard is totally irrelevant. Judge Bazelon, an experienced and respected federal judge, said the test requires "such a minimal level of performance from counsel that it is itself a mockery of the Sixth Amendment." He continued, "I have often been told that if my court were to reverse in every case in which there was inadequate counsel, we would have to send back half the convictions in my jurisdiction."

Courts don't like to get involved in the touchy question of judging the performance of defense attorneys. Why? For one thing, too much interference can damage not only professional relationships but also the professional independence of defense lawyers and even the adversary system itself. Furthermore, judges who criticize defense lawyers are criticizing fellow professionals, lawyers who appear in their courts regularly.

Most jurisdictions have abandoned the mockery of justice standard, replacing it with the "reasonably competent attorney standard." According to this standard, judges measure lawyers' performance against the "customary skills and diligence that a reasonably competent attorney would perform under similar circumstances." Attorneys have to be more diligent under the reasonably competent attorney standard than under the mockery of justice standard. Nevertheless, both the mockery of justice and the reasonably competent attorney standards are "vague to some appreciable degree and . . . susceptible to greatly varying subjective impressions."

The U.S. Supreme Court tried to increase the clarity of the reasonably competent attorney test by creating a two-pronged (reasonableness and prejudice) effective counsel test to evaluate the effectiveness of counsel. The test was announced in *Strickland v. Washington* (1984). In 1976, David Leroy Washington went on a 10-day crime spree that ended in three murders. After his lawyer, William Tunkey, was appointed, Washington confessed; he also pleaded guilty at his trial. Washington waived his right to an advisory jury to decide whether he should get the death penalty. During the sentencing phase of the proceedings, Tunkey didn't present any character evidence, didn't present any medical or psychiatric evidence, and only cross-examined some of the state's witnesses. The judge sentenced Washington to death. Washington went through the state and then the federal courts claiming ineffectiveness of counsel.

When the case finally reached the Supreme Court, the Court applied its new two-pronged test and rejected Washington's claim that his counsel was ineffective. Under the first prong (reasonableness), defendants have to prove their lawyer's performance wasn't reasonably competent, meaning the lawyer was so deficient she "was not functioning as the 'counsel' guaranteed the defendant by the Sixth Amendment." Under the reasonableness prong, reviewing courts have to look at the totality of the facts and circumstances to decide whether the defense lawyer's performance was reasonably competent. Reviewing courts have to start with a presumption in favor of the defense lawyer's competence, meaning they have lots of leeway to make tactical and strategic decisions that fall within the wide range of available professional judgment. As long as defense counsel's choices fall within that wide range, representation is presumed reasonable.

If the defendant proves his lawyer's performance was unreasonable, she still has to prove the second prong of the test (prejudice). Under the prejudice prong, defendants have to prove their lawyer's incompetence was *probably* responsible for their conviction. (See the In Focus box "Did His Lawyer Represent Him 'Effectively'?")

The Standard of Indigence There are three kinds of indigent defense:

public defenders full-time defense lawyers paid for by local taxpayers

assigned counsel lawyers in private practice selected from a list on a rotating basis either for a fee or pro bono (donated time)

contract attorneys private attorneys under contracts with local jurisdictions to represent indigent defendants for an agreed-upon fee

1. **Public defenders.** Full-time defense lawyers paid for by local taxpayers
2. **Assigned counsel.** Lawyers in private practice selected from a list on a rotating basis either for a fee or pro bono (donated time)
3. **Contract attorneys.** Private attorneys under contracts with local jurisdictions to represent indigent defendants for an agreed-upon fee

The U.S. Supreme Court has never defined "indigence." (What does poor mean?) However, U.S. Courts of Appeals have established some general guidelines on how to determine whether defendants are poor enough to qualify for a lawyer paid for by the government:

1. Poor defendants don't have to be completely destitute.
2. Earnings and assets count; help from friends and relatives doesn't.
3. Actual, not potential, earnings are the measure.
4. The state can tap defendants' future earnings to get reimbursement for the costs of counsel, transcripts, and fees for expert witnesses and investigators.

The Reality of the Criminal Defense of the Poor How does the defense of the poor work in practice? Only 5 percent of all indigent defendants see a lawyer before their first appearance. This means poor defendants usually don't get any legal advice before they're interrogated, have to stand in lineups, or are charged with crimes. Furthermore, the most inexperienced and least-trained lawyers usually defend the poorest defendants (Court 1993). In a symposium on the fortieth anniversary of *Gideon v. Wainwright*, Professor Ellen Podgor (2004) summarized the state of criminal defense this way:

> The Symposium was important for several reasons. It started by recognizing the status of *Gideon* as one of the landmark decisions in the history of the Court. Had the Court not issued the *Gideon* decision, accused individuals who could not afford an attorney might not receive any legal representation at trial. Second, the Symposium provided insight into the problems currently facing attorneys practicing in the indigent criminal defense system. Even today, the discussion demonstrated, caseloads in some indigent offices make it impossible to provide an adequate legal defense. Finally, the Symposium hammered home the existing crisis in indigent defense. It pointed out that people continue to remain in jail without counsel for long periods of time. And those who are finally afforded counsel may be merely provided a person who does little to assist in their defense. (133)

Despite these discouraging facts, some empirical evidence suggests that for poor defendants lucky enough to have lawyers, public defenders do as well for their clients as private defense counsel do for theirs. Roger A. Hanson and his

Did His Lawyer Represent Him "Effectively"?

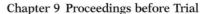

Smith lured a five-year-old girl who had been playing at a playground in South Hilo to the "laundromat room" of a nearby hotel with intent to have the child perform an act of fellatio, but this design was foiled by the sudden appearance of the owner of the liquor establishment located above the basement room. The bar owner testified that when he opened the door to the room he saw the girl kneeling in a corner with her back to the wall. Smith, the witness said, was in a crouched position over the kneeling child; her face, according to the witness, was several inches away from the defendant's groin area. When the bar owner approached the pair he saw the defendant's exposed and erect penis and the victim's frightened countenance. Smith hurriedly attempted to cover the exposed organ and fled despite the witness' attempt to question him. However, he was apprehended shortly thereafter by the police and identified by the witness as the culprit.

Michael Smith testified he had no intention of engaging in deviate sexual activity with the victim, he did not ask her to perform an act of fellatio, and he was only exposing himself when the witness entered the "laundromat room."

The testimony followed an opening statement delivered by Smith's lawyer. The statement included these remarks,

> My client is a loner. He is in a sense a hermit, a fantasizer. My client will be telling you folks that he has had a very tragic and distorted background. He's never really had a family. His mother is an alcoholic. And he's always had a hang-up about sex. He's always fantasized being with either little boys or little girls. Sixty percent boys, forty percent girls. That's the kind of fantasies he's had.
>
> He served time in prison before. But not for anything close to what we're charged with today, Attempted Sodomy in the Second Degree. He served time in prison at Oahu Prison. Served five years there. Just got out last year. Served time for burglaries. Also committed thefts in the past. He's done a whole bunch of stuff that you folks are going to be terribly offended by. But we picked you today because we feel that you folks will stick to what the evidence shows and not what my client's past background is.
>
> I just want to let you folks know now through my opening statement of this so that you folks don't get shocked by the testimony that will come out from my client. Please understand that we say this to you only on the premise that we're giving you everything we got. We're putting everything out on the table.
>
> My client is not a nice guy. He's a pervert if you want to put it that way. But he's never, he's never committed anything like attempted sodomy before. He's flashed himself up on the U.H. Hilo campus before, he's been an exhibitionist, if you want to call it, but he's never done anything like go and attempt to sexually molest or commit a deviate act such as having a little girl, you know, with her mouth over his penis. Nothing like that.

During direct examination of Smith, the following were among the questions asked and statements made by Smith's lawyer,

> Michael, you've been in trouble with the law before, correct? Well let's not "BS" with the jury, okay. What have you been in trouble for? Tell us about the past five years of your life.... Just tell it from your heart cause we don't hide nothing from the jury. [Defense counsel also]...adduced evidence of six prior burglary convictions and incarceration in the penitentiary as a consequence, as well as testimony about a "quirk" defendant had of exposing himself.

During the cross-examination of the young victim, the following exchange took place:

> Q. [DEFENSE COUNSEL]: How do you remember that the man said that? How do you remember that? You still remember?
> A. [THE VICTIM]: I don't know.
> Q. [DEFENSE COUNSEL]: I give you—I gonna give you one candy, one Valentines lollipop if you can tell us if you do remember or not, no?...

Thereafter, counsel sought permission to sit in the witness chair and continue his cross-examination while the victim sat in his lap. The transcript between the court and Smith's counsel reads:

> THE COURT: What do you propose to do?
> [DEFENSE COUNSEL]: I'm going to be sitting on the chair and she can sit on my lap so she can see the jurors, so the jurors can see her.
> THE COURT: What is this reference to candy or something?
> [DEFENSE COUNSEL]: I have candy, you know, just to open things up a little bit more. It's up there....

HAWAII SUPREME COURT'S OPINION

We are convinced from a review of the record that the assistance rendered by trial counsel was not within the range of competence demanded of attorneys in criminal cases and there were errors or omissions reflecting a lack of skill or judgment that substantially impaired a potentially meritorious defense.

Source: State v. Smith, 712 P.2d 496 (1986).

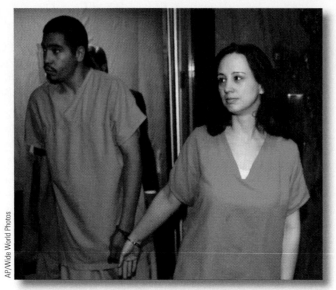

► Brenda Andrew, accused of plotting the murder of her advertising executive husband, arrives in court shackled to another prisoner. She's asking the court to declare her indigent (too poor to hire a lawyer) and appoint her a public defender. Although she may not appear to be too poor to hire a lawyer, the U.S. Supreme Court has ruled that poor defendants don't have to be completely destitute.

colleagues (1992) analyzed a random sample of 4000 felony cases from nine courts and interviewed 125 defense attorneys. They found public defenders:

- Disposed of their cases as fast as private lawyers
- Were as successful as private lawyers at obtaining favorable outcomes for their clients
- Were compensated and trained as well as prosecutors
- Received about the same level of support as prosecutors in the same jurisdictions

Former public defender David Lynch (1994) disagrees. Lynch studied defense lawyers in two counties and found the courtroom workgroup corrupts the relationship between public defenders and their clients:

> I have witnessed countless criminal defendants who claimed they were being "sold out" by their lawyers. Many asked the court, almost always unsuccessfully, to appoint new counsel. Some later filed collateral attacks, alleging coercion, to the entry of their guilty pleas. These allegations were almost always found to be unsubstantiated. Like mental institution inmates yelling "conspiracy," prison inmates yelling "conspiracy" were never taken credibly, even though the similarities of their tales of woe should have made people wonder. (124)

Vera Institute of Justice: The Vera Institute has conducted research, demonstration, and technical assistance projects in the areas of crime and victimization. Vera became nationally known through its very first effort, the Manhattan Bail Project, which ultimately led to President Johnson's signing of the Bail Reform Act. To reach this site go to "Web Links" on your Samaha CJ7 website: http://cj.wadsworth.com/samaha_cj7e.

The Vera Institute of Justice (Anderson 1997), a New York City criminal justice research institute, designed and implemented an experiment in public defender service, the Neighborhood Defender Service of Harlem (NDS), in 1990. NDS put its offices in a Harlem neighborhood "far from the courthouse, and made community involvement the core of its approach to defense." It used a "team-approach that united lawyers, community investigators, and caseworkers as equal partners in the process." Vera's evaluation of the NDS experiment showed NDS clients got "substantially shorter" jail and prison sentences than poor clients represented by traditional lawyers for the poor.

Bail and Detention

Almost all misdemeanor defendants and nearly two-thirds of all felony defendants remain free after they're charged, largely through the system of bail.

bail the release of defendants until their cases are decided

Bail, the release of defendants until their cases are decided, is ancient. More than two thousand years ago, the Greek philosopher Plato (1926) wrote that a "defendant shall provide three substantial securities [individuals] who guarantee to produce him at the trial, and if a man be unable or unwilling to provide these securities, the court must take, bind and keep him, and produce him at the trial of the case" (2:261). In 1682, the Pennsylvania constitution included a provision copied by the rest of the states. It commanded that all prisoners are "bailable" except in capital cases "where proof is evident" (Miller et al. 2000, 616).

By 1900, money had replaced individuals to guarantee defendants would show up in court. At first, defendants had to put up the full amount of bail. If defendants showed up for their court date, they got their money back. Soon, the money bail system replaced the demand for the full amount or direct financial surety. The Eighth Amendment to the U.S. Constitution bans "excessive bail," but the U.S. Supreme Court hasn't done much in the way of telling us what "excessive" means. So the kinds and amounts of bail are left mainly up to the states.

Let's look further at the money bail system, potential bias in bail decisions, preventive detention, and defendant misconduct while on bail.

The Money Bail System Under the money bail system, defendants pay bondsmen (most of them are men) 10 percent of the total amount of bail; bondsmen are legally liable for the full amount if defendants don't appear. Even if defendants show up, they don't get their 10 percent back—it's the bondsmen's fee. Technically, when defendants fail to appear on private bail bonds, courts can collect the full amount from the bondsmen, who then can recoup the amount paid from defaulting defendants. In practice, this rarely happens. Intricate and entrenched informal rules ensure that bondsmen won't forfeit the amount of bail bonds (Schlesinger 1986, 182).

Bondsmen in Connecticut, for example, avoid forfeiture in several ways. They can compromise by an agreement with the court to reduce the forfeited amount. They can also get delays from the court to look for defendants. Finally, they can find and bring their customers to court. From his observations of a Connecticut lower court, Malcolm M. Feeley (1979, 96–111) calculated bondsmen lost only about 3 percent of the face amount of bond forfeitures.

Formally, the amount of bail money is supposed to be just enough to make sure defendants show up in court. Extensive empirical research during the 1960s challenged the fairness of the money bail system in practice (Miller et al. 2000, 617). First, poor defendants were kept in jail; affluent defendants were freed on bail (Foote 1965; Freed and Wald 1964; Goldfarb 1965). Some spent more time in jail waiting for trial than the length of the sentence for the crimes they were charged with (Miller et al. 2000, 618). Second, it's expensive to run jails, and local communities had to pay for feeding, housing, supervising, and caring for sick, detained defendants. Third, detention affected the outcome of poor defendants' cases, because they couldn't help their lawyers as well as defendants out on bail. Many were sentenced to jail and prison instead of probation. Fourth, they tended to be sentenced to longer terms than bailed defendants because they couldn't show they were working, maintaining community ties, and obeying the law while they waited for trial (Rankin 1964, 641).

This research and the political temper of the 1960s led to a powerful bail reform movement. The heart of the movement was to shift bail decision making away from money and toward the characteristics of individual defendants. In 1961, the Manhattan Bail Project set off a wave of changes throughout the country. The Project staff personally interviewed arrested defendants to find out if they had ties to the community that would ensure they showed up in court. If they did, they were released solely on their promise to appear in court. Release in exchange for a promise to appear is called "release on recognizance" (ROR). Evaluation of the program was promising. According to Chris Eskridge's (1983) survey of research:

From the data now available, it appears likely that [pretrial release] programs in general are able to ensure the appearance of an accused individual for the appointed court hearings at least as well as the traditional money bail system, and probably a bit better due to the screening ability of programs. (99–100)

Many states and the federal government passed laws shifting decision making away from money to ROR and other nonmoney conditions of release on bail.

Race and Gender Bias in Bail Decisions Empirical research about bail decisions backs up what we've found about decision making by police and prosecutors: Most of the time, judges decide bail according to three appropriate criteria:

1. The seriousness of the charges against defendants
2. The strength of the prosecution's case against defendants
3. The criminal history of defendants (Goldkamp 1985, 8–9; LaFave and Israel 1984, 2:114; Wice 1974)

Some research challenges these findings. E. Britt Patterson and Michael J. Lynch (1991) examined how judges decided bail according to a bail schedule in a large western city. Bail schedules are lists setting the amount of bail a defendant has to pay according to the charged offense. Judges can raise or lower the amount on the schedule. What did they find? Whites, particularly White women, were more likely to receive bail below the schedule than non-Whites. When they controlled for seriousness of the offense and criminal history of the defendant, they found non-Whites and men had about the same chance as Whites and women to receive bail above the amount on the schedule. However, Whites and women were significantly more likely than non-White men to receive bail below the schedule (Figure 9.3).

Patterson and Lynch (1991) concluded, "Although minorities were not treated more harshly than whites, they were discriminated against because they were not given the same benefit of the doubt as were whites" (129).

Preventive Detention Whether getting individuals to vouch for defendants, demanding money from them, or getting promises from them, the purpose of bail was clear—making sure defendants came to court. Beginning in the 1980s, there was a growing demand to add a second purpose to bail—protecting public safety

Preventive detention: Is it a viable solution to public safety?

Click on this Decision Point at http://cj.wadsworth.com/samaha_ cj7e to explore the issue.

▶ **FIGURE 9.3 Race and Gender Differences in Bail Schedules**
Source: E. Britt Patterson and Michael J. Lynch, "Biases in Formalized Bail Procedures," in *Race and Criminal Justice*, edited by Michael J. Lynch and E. Britt Patterson (New York: Harrow and Heston, 1991).

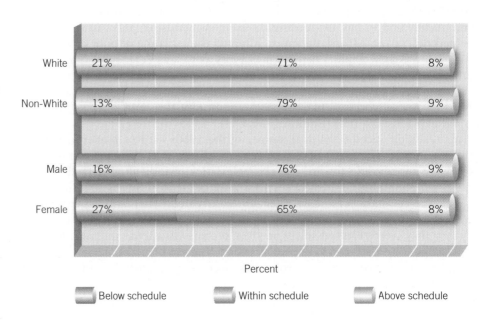

by preventing defendants on bail from committing crimes. In line with public safety, the federal government and many states amended their bail laws to provide for **preventive detention** (detaining defendants to protect public safety). South Dakota is typical. Its bail statute used to make appearance in court the purpose of bail. However, in the 1980s, South Dakota amended its bail statute to include conditions based on the "risk that defendants will pose a danger to any person in the community" (Miller et al. 2000, 631–632).

Setting conditions to ensure public safety may include banning defendants from certain neighborhoods or places or carrying weapons and requiring them to report to court periodically. But if judges decide these conditions (or others) won't protect the community, they can lock up defendants before and during trial. For example, the U.S. Bail Reform Act of 1984 directs judges to order defendants jailed if after a hearing they decide "no conditions or combination of conditions will reasonably assure...the safety of any other person and the community" (U.S. Code 1999, Title 18, §3142(f)).

Preventive detention provided the government with a useful tool in investigating the September 11, 2001, attacks on the World Trade Center and the Pentagon. For example, on November 9, 2001, a federal court ordered Mujahid Menepta preventively detained without bail. Menepta was an Oklahoma friend of Zacarias Moussaoui, who federal agents suspected was supposed to be the twentieth hijacker in the September 11 attack on the World Trade Center. The preventive detention order was issued after Jeffrey Whitney, a Bureau of Alcohol, Tobacco, and Firearms agent, testified Menepta "is dangerous and poses a flight risk." Whitney told the court Menepta had been born with the name Melvin Lattimore but had changed his name to Mujahid Menepta after he converted to Islam in 1989. Menepta defended Moussaoui (whom he met in a mosque), telling a newspaper reporter, on October 9, 2001, "I think he's a scapegoat" (Thomas 2001).

In *U.S. v. Salerno* (1987), the U.S. Supreme Court examined whether the preventive detention provision of the U.S. Bail Reform Act of 1984 violates the U.S. Constitution. The government charged "Fat Tony" Salerno and "Tony Ducks" Corallo, two of New York's most famous Mafia family bosses, with 29 counts of racketeering and conspiracy to commit murder (Toobin 2001, 58). At the arraignment, the government asked the judge to detain Fat Tony and Tony Ducks because no release condition could guarantee the safety of the community. Fat Tony argued the preventive detention provision violated his constitutional rights because detaining him was punishment before conviction. A majority of the U.S. Supreme Court disagreed, writing that preventive detention is a "regulatory device," not punishment. The Constitution allows for balancing individual liberty and community safety. In this case, according to the Court, the need for public safety outweighed Salerno's interest in pretrial release.

Justice Thurgood Marshall strongly dissented:

It is a fair summary of history to say that the safeguards of liberty have frequently been forged in controversies involving not very nice people. Honoring the presumption of innocence is often difficult; sometimes we must pay substantial social costs as a result of our commitment to the values we espouse. But at the end of the day the presumption of innocence protects the innocent; the shortcuts we take with those whom we believe to be guilty injure only those wrongfully accused and, ultimately, ourselves.

Throughout the world today there are men, women, and children interned indefinitely, awaiting trials which may never come or which may be a mockery of the word, because their governments believe them to be "dangerous." Our Constitution, whose construction began two centuries ago, can shelter us forever from the evils of such unchecked power. Over 200 years it has slowly, through our efforts, grown more durable, more expansive, and more just. But it cannot protect us if we lack the courage and the self-restraint to protect ourselves. Today, a majority of the Court applies itself to an ominous exercise in demolition.

► Millionaire Robert Durst (center) was acquitted in a trial for the murder of his neighbor. But he's still in jail. Why? Because he'd jumped bail before the acquittal, and was charged with bail jumping. Here he's in court with his lawyers, listening to Texas State Court Judge Susan Criss deny his appeal to lower his $2 million bond on the bail-jumping charge.

AP/Wide World Photos

Defendant Misconduct during Pretrial Release How big is the problem of defendants failing to show up for their court dates and committing crimes while they're on bail (Goldkamp 1979, 53–59; Thomas 1976; Toborg 1981)? Seventy-eight percent of all bailed defendants show up for all their court appointments (Hart and Reaves 1999, 26–27). Seventeen percent of those who miss their appointments, or fail to appear (FTA), show up later. So 95 percent of all bailed defendants eventually show up in court. Defendants charged with violent crimes do even better—98 percent eventually show up. Drug case defendants don't do as well—92 percent eventually show up. Still, most FTA defendants aren't fugitives. They forgot a date, got confused about where they should go, or missed the scheduled time. Sometimes, they were given the wrong time, date, or courtroom.

What about freed defendants committing crimes while they're on bail? Britt, Gottfredson, and Goldkamp (1992, 62–78) studied the value of monitoring the use of drugs by defendants on bail as a means to reduce not only their drug use but also their pretrial misconduct. They selected a control group and an experimental group of similar defendants on bail from a computerized case-tracking system in Pima and Maricopa counties in Arizona. The computerized system included information about prior record, court appearance history, offense, living arrangements, bail decision, failure to appear, and criminal behavior while on bail. The control group received normal supervision; the experimental group received drug monitoring during pretrial release.

No significant differences in failure to appear or re-arrest rates between the two groups occurred in Pima County, except members of the monitored group were slightly less likely to get re-arrested for the possession of drugs. In Maricopa County, arrests and failure-to-appear rates were higher in the monitored group than in the control group. On the basis of their findings, the authors concluded that systematic drug testing and monitoring in the pretrial setting... is not likely to achieve significant or major reductions in pretrial misconduct. At the same time that these programs fail to achieve their stated goal of reducing rates of pretrial misconduct, they carry a heavy price tag. In both Pima County and Maricopa County the cost of drug testing programs averaged from $400,000 to $500,000 per year. Given the high financial costs of these programs, including the testing and staffing required to accomplish them, it seems reasonable to question the effectiveness and cost-effectiveness of drug testing the released pretrial population. (Britt, Gottfredson, and Goldkamp 1992, 77)

Testing the Government's Case

After the first appearance, assigning counsel, and deciding bail, the prosecutor has to test the government's case before it can go to trial. **Test the government's case** means an independent review of the prosecutor's decision to charge is conducted to make sure there's enough evidence to put the community and the defendant to the time and expense (and for defendants, the additional burden of stigma and stress) of criminal prosecution. The two testing devices are the preliminary hearing and the grand jury review (Miller et al. 2000, 681) (Table 9.4).

test the government's case an independent review of the prosecutor's decision to charge to make sure there's enough evidence to put the community and the defendant to the time and expense (and for defendants, the additional burden of stigma and stress) of criminal prosecution

The Preliminary Hearing

Preliminary hearings follow the initial appearance. The length of time between the first appearance and the preliminary hearing varies from a few days in some jurisdictions to a few weeks in others. The formal function of the preliminary hearing is to test the government's case against defendants. It offers the first opportunity for judicial screening of cases—cases that up to this point only police and prosecutors have reviewed.

At **preliminary hearings,** judges review prosecutors' charging decisions to determine whether there's probable cause to continue the case against the defendant. If judges decide that cases deserve further action, they *bind over* defendants (order them to answer the charges against them). If they determine that the prosecution's case lacks probable cause, they dismiss charges. Although prosecutors can recharge in the future, as a practical matter, they rarely reopen cases dismissed at preliminary hearings.

preliminary hearings judges review prosecutors' charging decisions to determine whether there's probable cause to continue the case against the defendant

According to the *Federal Rules of Criminal Procedure* (2004):

Rule 5.1 Preliminary Hearing

...

(c) *Scheduling.* The magistrate judge must hold the preliminary hearing within a reasonable time, but no later than 10 days after the initial appearance if the defendant is in custody and no later than 20 days if not in custody.

...

(e) *Hearing and Finding.*... If the magistrate judge finds probable cause to believe an offense has been committed and the defendant committed it, the magistrate judge must promptly require the defendant to appear for further proceedings.

▼ **TABLE 9.4 Contrasts between Preliminary Hearing and Grand Jury Review**

Preliminary Hearing	Grand Jury Review
Public	Secret
Adversarial	Presents only the government's case
Judge presides	Prosecutor presides
Judge decides facts	Grand jurors decide facts

Federal Grand Jury: Handbook for Grand Jurors in the federal system. Includes history of grand juries and the differences between them and preliminary hearings in court. To reach this site go to "Web Links" on your Samaha CJ7 website: http://cj.wadsworth.com/samaha_cj7e.

(f) *Discharging the Defendant.* If the magistrate judge finds no probable cause to believe an offense has been committed or the defendant committed it, the magistrate judge must dismiss the complaint and discharge the defendant. A discharge does not preclude the government from later prosecuting the defendant for the same offense.

The Indictment

The government can also initiate criminal proceedings and test probable cause by **indictment,** a formal written accusation by the grand jury; this is an ancient practice originating in medieval England. Grand jury proceedings can he held in place of preliminary hearings, or they can follow preliminary hearings as a second screening device.

Dismissals at preliminary hearings don't prevent grand juries from reconsidering probable cause to send a case to trial. In other words, if magistrates dismiss cases, prosecutors can bring them to grand juries for another try, in the hope they will win a more favorable outcome. On the other hand, if judges bind over cases, grand juries can decide not to indict. Grand juries are composed of private citizens chosen to serve from one to several months. Traditionally, 23 sat on a grand jury; 12 to 16 most commonly sit today. Compared to the unanimous verdict usually required to convict, it takes a simple majority of grand jurors to indict.

Indicting by grand jury screening and binding over in preliminary hearings rest on the same objective basis: probable cause. However, major differences separate preliminary hearings from grand jury proceedings. Grand jury hearings are not adversarial proceedings: only the government presents evidence. Defendants can neither offer evidence nor appear before grand juries. Furthermore, grand jury proceedings are secret and closed; preliminary hearings are open and public. The disclosure of any information presented to grand juries warrants severe penalties for grand jurors or others who "leak" such information. Finally, magistrates preside in preliminary hearings; prosecutors oversee grand jury proceedings.

The Information

Prosecutors can bypass the grand jury and initiate proceedings following their own review of probable cause in an instrument called an **information.** Most states using the information procedure require that a preliminary hearing follow the filing of an information. The preliminary hearing prevents a criminal prosecution from proceeding solely on the prosecutor's probable cause determination. In other words, the preliminary hearing in information jurisdictions screens what a grand jury review screens in indictment jurisdictions.

The adoption of the information process followed long-standing criticisms of grand jury review. In the eighteenth century, the famous English law reformer Jeremy Bentham attacked the process, and objections to it have continued since. Some reformers demand its outright abolition; others call for severe restrictions on its power. Abolitionists consider grand jury review "essentially worthless," agreeing with the former prosecutor who said he could "indict anybody, at any time, for almost anything before a grand jury."

This criticism depicts grand juries as rubber stamps for prosecutors, and statistics indicate that grand juries rarely disagree with prosecutors. Between January 1 and June 30, 1974, 235 cases were presented to the San Francisco grand jury, and indictments were returned in all 235 (*Hawkins v. Superior Court* 1978). The ratio hasn't changed significantly since then. Also, according to critics, the grand jury "is costly in terms of space, manpower and money," and it delays case processing because grand juries are not as accessible as magistrates (LaFave and Israel 1984, 2:282).

Despite criticism, supporters—who count prosecutors among their numbers—claim several advantages of grand jury review. They maintain that grand

Grand Jury: Sword against Terror and Corporate Crime or Shield against Government Power?

The constitutional lore, nurtured by the Supreme Court, is that the federal grand jury is a "protective bulwark," whose central mission is to protect civil liberties and shield citizens from unfounded or abusive criminal charges. As a civil rights institution, however, the grand jury is an odd one. It is championed by the Department of Justice, which generally opposes any changes to grand jury procedures, even though it is federal prosecutors who are ostensibly being "checked" by the grand jury process. At the same time, the grand jury's operations frequently come under attack by the criminal defense bar, whose clients' rights are ostensibly being protected.

Most recently, the Department of Justice found new and expanded uses for the federal grand jury in the wake of September 11 and the Enron case. Following the September 11 terrorist attacks on American targets, federal prosecutors have arrested and detained numerous people without criminal charges as "material witnesses" in grand jury investigations. Congress has created a federal grand jury role in foreign intelligence matters.

Meanwhile, federal prosecutors responded to national outrage over allegations of accounting fraud at major companies, such as Enron Corporation and the Arthur Andersen accounting firm, by noticeably increasing grand jury investigations and indictments of white-collar defendants.

The grand jury has never been more important to the modern federal criminal justice system. Yet despite its importance, the grand jury remains mysterious, shrouded in secrecy, and clouded in ambiguity—some would argue, deliberately so. The strict rules of secrecy that apply to the federal grand jury's proceedings tend to shield from the public eye both the specifics of ongoing investigations and the nature of the grand jury process. When allegations of grand jury abuse come to light, the public is often surprised to learn of the one-sided rules, principles, and procedures that govern the modern federal grand jury rules, which are highly favorable to the government.

... The disconnect between the rhetoric and reality of the grand jury is not a coincidence, or an historical vestige, but a central and important feature of the modern federal criminal justice system. Most knowledgeable observers would describe the federal grand jury more as a handmaiden of the prosecutor than a bulwark of constitutional liberty. To quote the classic vignette, the grand jury is little more than a rubber stamp that would "indict a ham sandwich" if the prosecutor asked.

But the Supreme Court continues to affirm the supposed vitality of the defendant's right to be indicted by grand jury, ostensibly because the "grand jury right serves a vital function ... as a check on prosecutorial power." This disconnect raises the obvious question of why the Court persists in its romanticized and highly fictionalized vision of the institution.

... Legal fictions theory reveals that a fictional ideal of grand jury independence plays a useful, but ultimately dangerous, role in the federal system, allowing the grand jury not only to speed the criminal charging process but also to mask the expansion of governmental investigative powers and to minimize judicial pretrial procedures. ...

A federal prosecutor can harness the grand jury's broad powers to issue document subpoenas with virtually no relevance limitations, compel witnesses to testify in secret without their lawyers and with almost no objections permitted, "lock" defense witnesses into trial testimony, time indictment decisions in order to build the government's case for trial while delaying the disclosure obligations that will apply once the case is before the court, and avoid judicial pretrial hearings.

Ultimately, the grand jury gives the prosecutor the awesome power to indict (and the corresponding power to bargain for a guilty plea). For important constitutional reasons, however, these powers can be exercised by the prosecutor using the grand jury only if we pretend it is the grand jury that is actually exercising them.

Source: Niki Kuckes, Associate Professor, Roger Williams College of Law, "The Useful, Dangerous Fiction of Grand Jury Independence," *American Criminal Law Review* 41(1)1–3 (1994).

jurors do have minds of their own and that they effectively screen criminal cases. The low rate of refusals to indict has little or nothing to do with prosecutors dominating the grand jury room; instead, the many indictments result from careful preliminary screening. Prosecutors bring only strong cases that persuade the grand jury to indict. In fact, prosecutors say they present cases in which they have not only probable cause but also proof beyond a reasonable doubt. The high ratio of indictments to convictions—more than 98 percent result in conviction—supports this conclusion (LaFave and Israel 1984, 284). (See the In Focus box "Grand Jury: Sword against Terror and Corporate Crime or Shield against Government Power?")

A Summary of the Tests

The preliminary hearing, the indictment, and the information represent different ways to test the government's case against defendants before trial. The preliminary hearing places the decision in the magistrate's or judge's hands; the information, in the prosecutor's; and the indictment, in the community's representatives, the grand jurors. Each has a check on its authority to initiate the criminal process. The grand jury can review and reverse a preliminary hearing bind over or an information, and magistrates can review grand jury indictments. Despite its tenacious and occasionally truculent critics, the grand jury remains an alternative to an information and the preliminary hearing in serious and sensitive cases. In these cases, prosecutors can receive support and share the responsibility with the grand jury, a body that represents the community.

Arraignment and Pretrial Motions

If the government passes the tests posed by preliminary hearing bind overs, grand jury indictments, or prosecutorial informations, the criminal court has the authority to try defendants. It exercises the authority by arraigning defendants. **Arraignment** consists of bringing defendants to open court, reading the charges against them, and demanding that they plead not guilty, guilty, or *nolo contendere* (no contest) to the charges. The arraignment and plea to charges formally set the stage for the criminal trial. Informally, they provide the opportunity either to start, continue, or ratify a plea agreement already reached.

During the period between arraignment and the trial, the prosecution and the defense can file pretrial motions that lead to pretrial hearings. Most states require the defense to make objections to the indictment or information, request the prosecution's evidence (known as *discovery*), and object to the government's evidence (*fruits* of illegal searches and seizures) before trial. The government can also request discovery in the form of a pretrial motion.

arraignment bringing defendants to open court, reading the charges against them, and demanding that they plead not guilty, guilty, or *nolo contendere*

► Here's an excellent example of how technology is affecting the ancient pretrial procedure of arraignment (bringing the defendant to court to hear and answer charges against her). Melissa Ann Rowland and her public defender Mark Helm "virtually" appear in court before Judge Sandra Peuler by means of a closed-circuit television in the Salt Lake City jail. Her plea? Not guilty to murdering one of her children.

AP/Wide World Photos

Pretrial motions and hearings occur in only 10 percent of all felony cases and in less than 1 percent of misdemeanor prosecutions. Courts dismiss practically no misdemeanor cases and only about 5 percent of felony cases in pretrial hearings arising out of objections in pretrial motions. Pretrial motions, in the rare instances when they take place, occur mainly in cases involving noncomplaining victims, such as drug-related felonies. Critics greatly exaggerate the numbers of violent criminals set free by pretrial motions to exclude evidence illegally obtained under the search and seizure clause (LaFave and Israel 1984, 1:27).

Are Decisions to Charge in Sexual Assault Cases Infected by Race and Stereotypes of Women?

Widely accepted research concludes that when prosecutors are deciding whether to charge (or reject) sexual assault cases for prosecution, they're more likely to charge when

1. The offense is serious.
2. The suspect has a criminal record.
3. It's clear the victim has suffered "real harm."
4. There's strong evidence against the suspect.
5. The victim's willing to cooperate.
6. The odds in favor of conviction are high. (Spohn and colleagues 2002, 3–4)

The last criterion reflects prosecutors' concern with "winning" cases. This concern forces them to predict how the victim, the suspect, and the crime will come across to judges and juries. Prediction is a risky business, which leads prosecutors to develop a "perceptual shorthand" based on their beliefs as to what are typical sexual assault situations—namely *"real crimes"* and *"genuine victims."* So prosecutors consider not just the legal indicators of the seriousness of the offense and the criminal record of the *suspect* but the *victim's* background, character, behavior, and willingness to cooperate and the *relationship* between the victim and the suspect (Spohn and colleagues 2002, 5).

THE DECISION TO CHARGE, DADE COUNTY (MIAMI), FLORIDA

The following scenarios (actual cases) from Dade County, Florida, are divided by criteria prosecutors used in their decision to charge, reject, or dismiss sexual assault cases. Table 9.5 breaks down the number of sexual assault cases rejected (65 out of 140) or later dismissed by prosecutors. After the scenario, you'll find the prose-

cutor's written justifications for the decision. When you're finished reading each scenario, write *your* decision, identify each justification, and then explain why you believe the decision was based on appropriate criteria or was infected by unacceptable criteria.

Discrepant Accounts

One discrepant account case involved a white female victim and a white male suspect, who were ex-boyfriend and ex-girlfriend. The victim reported that the suspect came to her residence in an attempt to reconcile the relationship. Although the victim asked the suspect to leave the residence, he pushed his way into her apartment and refused to leave, despite numerous requests by the victim. The suspect subsequently held the victim against her will and would not allow her to leave the premises. He then bound her arms behind her back with duct tape and sexually assaulted her. Following the assault, the suspect unbound the victim and apologized for his actions. He then began to bang his head against the wall and later attempted to jump from an exterior stairwell. The victim stopped him from jumping, but during the struggle, the suspect fell down a flight of stairs.

At this point, the victim telephoned police. The suspect was arrested and taken into police custody outside of the victim's residence. Following review of the case, the ASA decided not to charge, using the following justifications:

There is insufficient evidence to convince a jury beyond a reasonable doubt that a sexual battery and burglary with assault were committed by the defendant. The victim made inconsistent statements as to whether or not the defendant penetrated her. She told fire rescue that

▼ TABLE 9.5 Prosecutors' Justifications for Rejecting Sexual Assault Cases in Dade County, Florida

Types of Justification	Explanation	Number of Cases
Discrepant accounts	1. Inconsistencies in the victim's accounts or between the victim's and the suspect's accounts	13
	2. Typification of rape behavior	
	a. Typical rape scenarios	4
	b. Inferences about victims based on typical rape scenarios	5
	c. Typical rape-reporting practices	2
Ulterior motives		7
Other justifications	1. Victim failed to appear or couldn't be found	15
	2. Victim wouldn't cooperate or asked the prosecutor to drop the case	10
	3. Victim recanted	5
Couldn't classify		4

Source: Cassia Spohn et al., "Prosecutors' Charging Decision in Sexual Assault Cases: A Multi-State Study, Final Report" (Washington, DC: National Criminal Justice Research Service, 2002, Table 4.2).

▲ Basketball star Kobe Bryant holds his wife Vanessa's hand at a news conference after he was charged with sexually assaulting a 19-year-old woman. Bryant denied the charge, claiming he was guilty of adultery but not sexual assault.

he didn't penetrate her and she told the uniformed officer that he did penetrate her. Additionally, the allegation is that the defendant bound the victim prior to the rape. The victim indicated during her profile conference that she has permitted the defendant to bind her and have sexual intercourse with her in the past. She indicated that the defendant has a video of this. The defendant told the officers that this was consensual sex. The duct tape used to bind the victim was kept in her home (in her bedroom closet). Additionally, after the act, the victim calls 911 and doesn't report the rape. She reports that the defendant might have injured himself because she saw him lying in the stairwell. Also the victim declined to go to the rape treatment center on the day of rape so there is no DNA evidence. The victim also said that a couple of days before the assault, she and the defendant had consensual sex although they had broken up. For the foregoing reason it is the undersigned belief along with the chief of the domestic crimes unit that there is insufficient evidence to file the case.

Typifications of Rape-Relevant Behavior

The next two cases illustrate prosecutorial case rejection based on incongruities between the victim's version of events and the prosecutor's existing knowledge of typical behavior in rape case scenarios.

The victim in one case is a white, 17-year-old female who made allegations of "date rape" against a black male teacher's aide at her high school. According to the victim's report to police, she accompanied the suspect to his residence to watch a movie. She stated that she and the suspect watched the movie while lying on his bed, during which time they engaged in consensual foreplay. Subsequently, the suspect attempted to convince the victim to engage in sexual intercourse. After the victim refused the suspect's requests, he attempted to force intercourse on her. The victim then demanded that the suspect take her home and he complied. The victim reported the incident nearly two weeks later by submitting an anonymous letter to the school principal. The prosecutorial rejection read:

> This case was no actioned because it is in this ASA's opinion that the charge of sexual battery by physical force cannot be proven beyond a reasonable doubt because there were several facts that would prevent the state from showing the defendant was on notice that his actions were against the victim's consent. See note in file regarding these actions by the victim. At no time during the alleged incident did the defendant threaten physical harm or prevent the victim from leaving the apartment.

The note alluded to in this justification provides 15 additional actions by the victim that are inconsistent with this ASA's construction of a genuine rape scenario:

1. In her letter, the victim admits to flirting with the defendant and finding him attractive.
2. In the telephone call leading up to the incident, the defendant had told the victim "that he was going to come over, pick [the victim] up and kidnap [her] and [he] made some sort of sexual remark after that," according to the victim's sworn statement to police. The victim responded in the following manner, "I laughed sarcastically and said this sounded good up to that part referring to, as it sounded good to go out with him somewhere."
3. The victim allowed the defendant to remain in the room wearing nothing other than boxer shorts.
4. The victim laid on the defendant's bed.
5. Prior to the start of the movie, the victim asked the defendant for a hug and received a hug.
6. The victim allowed the defendant to touch her throughout the beginning of the movie. While she kept her hand on top of his to guide his hand, at no time did she remove his hand so that it wouldn't be touching her.
7. The defendant was allowed to kiss the victim.
8. Even when the victim realized that the kisses were becoming more involved, the victim left to go to the bathroom but then came back, sat on top of the defendant and continued to kiss him.
9. In response to the defendant's questions about the color of her underwear, the victim showed him the top of her underwear.
10. In response to his requests to remove her pants, the victim indicates in her written letter that she "put up a little struggle but it was very little."

11. Due to his repeated requests, the victim allowed the defendant to kiss her breast.
12. After the defendant first kissed the victim's vagina, the victim remained in the room, on the bed, partially undressed.
13. Even after the defendant's first attempt at penetration, the victim remained in the room partially undressed and complied with his request to stand by the chair and his request to walk back again to the bed.
14. The victim allowed the defendant to drive her home.
15. Despite the requests of her ex-boyfriend, the victim did not immediately call the police and instead waited for a full disclosure until she was upset that the defendant had not been fired from the school.

Typifications of Rape Scenarios and Inferences about the Victim. In this case, the victim, a 31-year-old white female, advised that she, her boyfriend, the suspect (her half-brother), and several other people went out drinking together. When the victim arrived home, she was extremely intoxicated and went directly to bed. Soon after she went to bed, the suspect entered her bedroom, removed her clothing, and began engaging in sexual intercourse with her. The victim woke up and demanded that the suspect stop. The suspect then attempted to force the victim to engage in fellatio; when she resisted, he resumed having sexual intercourse with her. Due to her intoxication, the victim passed out during the incident. When she awoke, she reported the incident to the police. The prosecutor provided the following written justification:

> This case is being no actioned for the following reasons: (1) the victim was very intoxicated on the night of the incident. She had consumed 2 beers, 2 long island iced teas, 2 glasses of wine, a large glass of vodka and coke and medication for AIDS. (2) She told me under oath that she has no recollection of the events that took place in her bedroom that evening. There is no way to prove an essential element of the crime, which is the victim's lack of consent. She told me she's not sure whether she consented or not. It is the undersigned's belief that this case can not be proved beyond a reasonable doubt.

Typifications of Rape Reporting. Delay in reporting was a key factor in the rejection of a spousal sexual battery case. In this case, the victim, a white 38-year-old female, stated that her husband forced her to engage in vaginal intercourse against her will. The victim stated that after the assault, she remained in their bed and fell asleep. The victim stated that she did not attempt to make any noise or summon help because she did not want her guests to know what was happening. The victim did not contact the police immediately following the incident; in fact, she left the country and did not report the incident until she returned. The victim also stated that she had sex with the suspect after the rape. The prosecutor provided the following justification for case rejection:

> The victim reported the crime approximately six weeks after it occurred. The victim did not respond to the rape treatment center or call the police the night of the crime. The victim left the country and called the police upon her return. There is no physical or corroborating evidence. Given the lack of evidence and the time between the date of the incident and the date of the report the state has no choice but to no action this case.

Case Rejection Based on Ulterior Motives

Frohmann (1991, 221) notes, "Ulterior motives rest on the assumption that a woman consented to sexual activity and for some reason needed to deny it afterwards." One of the ulterior motive cases included in our study involved a 13-year-old black female who reported that her stepfather fondled her, digitally assaulted her as often as five times per week, and attempted to rape her. Although the felony review unit initially filed charges in this case, facts that came to light as the case moved toward trial caused the state's attorney to whom it was assigned to file a motion to dismiss the charges. The ASA filed the following justification for dismissing the charges prior to trial:

> The victim is the stepdaughter of the defendant. The victim disclosed to her school counselor that the defendant had sexually molested her starting in Kansas when she was eleven and continuing up until approximately one week before she disclosed to him. The victim when initially interviewed by this ASA was very credible as there was physical evidence of penetration. The defendant responded to the accusations by cleaning out the joint checking account, not showing up at his job, and was missing for a week. While preparing for trial, motives for the victim to fabricate became apparent. However, the most important issue was that the victim repeatedly told this ASA and the defense attorney (in deposition) that she had never been involved with anyone else and had never had a boyfriend. Sunday night before the trial was to begin, this ASA was contacted by defense counsel that he was adding two witnesses to the defense list. The first was [a sixteen year old male], who would testify that while visiting the defendant during the summer of 1997, he and the victim had consensual sex. The second was the victim's cousin by marriage, who would testify that she had overheard the victim threaten the defendant "that she would do to him what she had done to her grandfather." On Monday morning, the victim was confronted by this ASA with these allegations. The victim admitted that she and the stepbrother had made out, petted, and that she had "hunched" with him but had not had sex. The victim then became hysterical in the ASA's office and stated that she did not wish to go forward with the trial. The victim's mother was informed of what was going on and agreed that she did not want her daughter to go through with the trial. The ASA then announced a Nolle Posse in Court.

Case Rejection Based on Lack of Victim Cooperation

Prosecutors' options were limited in those cases in which the victim would not cooperate, asked that the case be dropped, or recanted. Although prosecutors are not legally precluded from pursuing a case with a reluctant victim, their goal of "avoiding uncertainty" (Albonetti 1986) makes this unlikely. The closeout memos filed in several of these cases suggested that the prosecutor assigned to the case believed that the victim had been sexually assaulted. One case, for example, involved a woman who claimed that she had been sexually assaulted by her ex-boyfriend, who broke into her house in the middle of the night. The prosecutor, apparently convinced that the victim was telling the truth, made numerous attempts to secure her cooperation and even had the victim arrested and held in jail for four days for failure to cooperate. Eventually, however, the victim recanted her testimony. The prosecutor explained that the case was rejected

> because the victim refused to assist in the prosecution of this case. She failed to appear in my office after personal service on August 5, 1997 and August 12, 1997.... Thereafter, I had the court issue a writ of bodily attachment against her. She was arrested on 9/19/97 and held for 4 days. On 9/23/97 I took a sworn statement from her where she recanted entirely. Therefore, it is impossible to prosecute this case without her cooperation. There is no physical evidence to prove this case without her cooperation.

Other cases in the "victim would not cooperate/asked that charges be dropped" category involved teenage girls who admitted under questioning that the sexual contact was consensual. In some of these cases, the complaint was filed, not by the alleged victim, but by the victim's parents. The written justifications filed in one of these cases included the following:

Victim is fourteen years old; defendant is nineteen years old. Both parties engage in consensual sex. Victim does not want to prosecute. Initially, victim's mother wants to prosecute but acknowledges later on that she just wanted to teach her daughter a lesson.

QUESTIONS

1. List and summarize each of the prosecutor's justifications for her decision to prosecute.
2. In your opinion, which justifications are based on appropriate criteria? Explain why.
3. In your opinion, which justifications are infected by inappropriate criteria? Explain why.
4. Make your decision whether to prosecute. Back up your decision with appropriate criteria.

► DECISION POINT ◄

Should the prosecutors charge the suspect with rape?

Click on this Decision Point at http://cj.wadsworth.com/samaha_cj7e to explore the issue.

Chapter Summary

▶ Prosecutors have *nearly* complete discretion to charge suspects with crimes. The criteria prosecutors use to make the charging decision include the strength of the evidence, the seriousness of the offense, and the criminal history of the suspect. The evidence is mixed as to whether race and gender influence charging decisions.

▶ Shortly after charging, defendants are brought to court for their first appearance. The three main events at the first appearance are to read the charges to defendants; to appoint lawyers for poor defendants; and to bail or detain defendants until trial.

▶ The Sixth Amendment guarantees the right to a lawyer in all criminal prosecutions. In most cases, the right kicks in as soon as suspects are charged with crimes. The right to counsel includes the right to *effective* counsel, but the standard for what's effective is low. The U.S. Supreme Court has never defined how poor defendants have to be before they're entitled to assigned counsel. In practice, many poor defendants (however defined) don't have lawyers.

▶ The Eighth Amendment bans "excessive" bail. The two purposes for denying bail are to make sure defendants appear in court and to prevent defendants from committing crimes while they're waiting for trial. Most bail decisions are free from the infection of race and gender bias, but some research challenges this conclusion. Most bailed defendants show up (eventually) in court, and few commit new crimes while on bail.

▶ The government's case against defendants has to be tested before it goes to trial. A preliminary hearing review tests the government's case in public, adversarial proceedings presided over by judges. The judge decides whether there's enough evidence to go to trial. A grand jury review tests the government's case in a secret proceeding, run by prosecutors, where only the government's case is presented. Grand jurors decide whether there's enough evidence to send the defendant to trial.

Key Terms

strength of the case, p. 298
social structure of the case, p. 299
retained counsel, p. 303
appointed counsel, p. 303
public defenders, p. 308

assigned counsel, p. 308
contract attorneys, p. 308
bail, p. 310
preventive detention, p. 313
test the government's case, p. 315

preliminary hearings, p. 315
indictment, p. 316
information, p. 316
arraignment, p. 318

Web Resources

Go to http://cj.wadsworth.com/samaha_cj7e for a wealth of online resources related to your book. Take a "pre-test" and "post-test" for each chapter in order to help master the material. Check out the *Web Links* to access the websites mentioned in the text, as well as many others. Explore the

Decision Points flagged in the margins of the text for additional insights. You can also access recent perspectives by clicking on *CJ in the News* and *Terrorism Update* under *Course Resources.*

☞ Search Online with InfoTrac College Edition

For additional information, explore InfoTrac College Edition, your online library. Go to http://cj.wadsworth.com/samaha_cj7e to access InfoTrac from your book's website. Use the passcode that came with your book. You will find InfoTrac exercises, and a list of key words for further research.

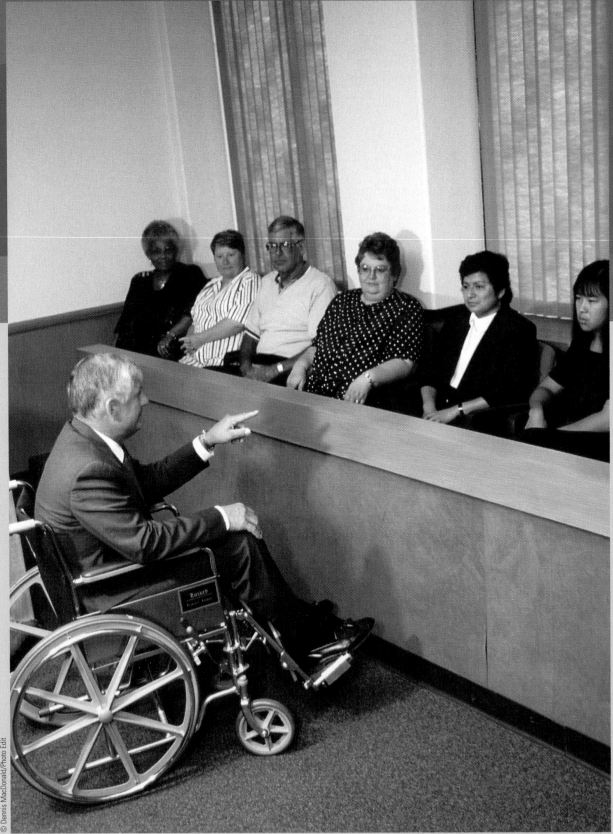

CHAPTER 10

Conviction by Trial and Guilty Plea

FACT *or* FICTION?

▶ Half of all cases are decided by trial.

▶ Jury verdicts have to be unanimous.

▶ The most important criterion governing plea bargaining is not the seriousness of the offense but the strength of the evidence against the defendant.

▶ The criminal justice system would break down if plea bargaining were banned.

▶ Most defendants *want* their lawyers to do full battle in court.

▶ Defendants convicted at trial receive longer sentences than those who plead guilty.

▶ Most defendants charged with crimes are guilty.

BARGAINING OVER THE PENALTY, NOT GUILT

Prosecutors come to distinguish between serious and nonserious cases, and between cases in which they are looking for [prison] time and cases in which they are not looking for time. These standards or distinctions evolve after the prosecutor has processed a substantial number of factually and legally guilty defendants. They provide a means of sorting the raw material—the guilty defendants. Indeed, one can argue that [in plea bargaining] the adversary component of the prosecutor's job is shifted from establishing guilt or innocence to determining the seriousness of the defendant's guilt and whether he should receive time. The guilt of the defendant is assumed, but the problem of disposition remains to be informally argued.

—HEUMANN 1978, 103

Criminal trials are the high point of formal criminal justice. They're public morality plays pitting good against evil, containing moments of high drama and displaying the gory details of the horrors people are capable of inflicting on each other. But only a few (5 out of 100) cases decide whether defendants are guilty (BJS June 2003, 1) (Figure 10.1). In the other 95, *guilt* isn't the issue (the courtroom workgroup already knows defendants are guilty); *punishment* is. In informal, low-visibility, private negotiations, they work out what the punishment will be. In these 95 cases, court proceedings just ratify formally and publicly what the courtroom workgroup (Chapter 8) has already decided informally in private. Let's look first at conviction (disposition) by formal trial, where guilt is the issue, and then at disposition by informal negotiation, where punishment is the issue.

Disposition by Trial

Criminal trials are powerful symbols. The "right" outcome stands for justice triumphant: Crime doesn't pay; the criminal justice system frees the innocent, punishes the guilty, and satisfies the victims; good conquers evil. Of course, the "wrong" outcome is a powerful symbol, too—a symbol of injustice in which the wicked win, the innocent lose, the victims are frustrated, and wealth and power can buy "fancy lawyers" or shape outcomes to their liking. For good or ill, then, the trial teaches a public, visible, and potent lesson about the integrity, fairness, and effectiveness of the criminal justice process.

Criminal trials are also searches for the truth. According to the adversary process, the government has to prove defendants are guilty beyond a reasonable doubt. Third, trials send messages to officials throughout the criminal justice system about the vast majority of cases that never get to trial. Expectations about what happens in trials shape police decisions to arrest, prosecutors' decisions to charge, defense lawyers' willingness to negotiate, and defendants' decisions to plead guilty. They all know "juries do not merely determine the outcome of the cases they hear; their decisions profoundly influence the 90 to 95 percent of cases that are settled through informal means" (Kalven and Zeisel 1966, 31–32; Silberman 1978, 283).

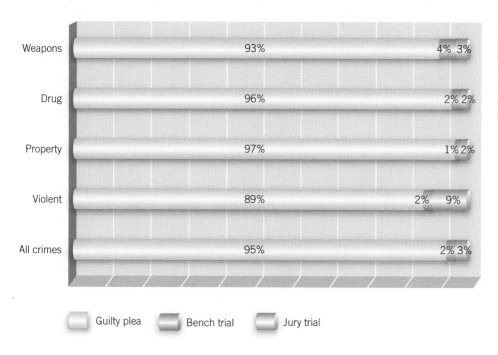

◀ **FIGURE 10.1 The Types of Felony Dispositions in State Courts, 2000**

Source: Bureau of Justice Statistics, *Felony Sentences in State Courts, 2000* (Washington, DC: Bureau of Justice Statistics, June 2003), Table 10.

Crime	Guilty plea	Bench trial	Jury trial
Weapons	93%	4%	3%
Drug	96%	2%	2%
Property	97%	1%	2%
Violent	89%	2%	9%
All crimes	95%	2%	3%

Guilty plea   Bench trial   Jury trial

Juries are the people's representatives in the "halls of justice," guarding against undue, improper, and vindictive government action. Leading jury experts have called this the "halo effect." Let's look more closely at trial by jury and the makings of a fair trial.

Juries

Trial by jury has ancient roots. In the Magna Carta of 1215, King John promised that "no free man shall be taken or imprisoned or in any way destroyed except by the lawful judgment of his peers." The Sixth Amendment to the U.S. Constitution guarantees the right to a trial "in all criminal prosecutions by an impartial jury of the State and district" where the crime was committed. In jury trials, juries decide the facts—whether the government's evidence proves defendants are guilty beyond a reasonable doubt. Their verdict (from the Latin to tell the truth) is their decision on that important question. Judges decide the law, meaning they apply the rules of the adversary system. Defendants who don't want juries to decide the facts can have bench trials, in which judges decide both the facts and the law. Let's look at juries as a reflection of community values, the power they exercise through jury nullification, how juries are selected, and unanimous verdicts.

The Jury as a Political Institution Juries are the democratic element of the court system; they represent the community and its values. The famous nineteenth-century French observer of America, Alexis de Tocqueville, put it this way: "The jury is, above all, a political institution, and it must be regarded in this light in order to be understood." De Tocqueville's observation is still true; but it must be qualified. In clear-cut cases, formal law, not informal politics, governs. But in cases that can go either way, extralegal influences enter the jury room and affect jurors' deliberations and decisions (Levine 1992, 14).

"I just stuck to the facts," most jurors say about their vote. And empirical studies show they're not lying. But *unconsciously* their value judgments affect their interpretation of the facts—but only in close cases. We call this unconscious influence of value judgment the **liberation hypothesis.** According to Harry Kalven and Hans Zeisel (1966, 163–167) in their classic study of the jury, determining the truth and making value judgments are intertwined. The facts in close cases are not clear-cut. The chance of reading the facts in two sharply contrasting ways

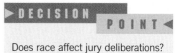

Does race affect jury deliberations?

Click on this Decision Point at http://cj.wadsworth.com/samaha_cj7e to explore the issue.

liberation hypothesis the unconscious influence of value judgments on jurors is heightened because of the adversary process—the prosecution spins the facts only toward "guilty," and the defense spins them only toward "not guilty."

According to the liberation hypothesis, the combination of the lack of clear-cut evidence and the fact-spinning of the adversary process "liberate" jurors to resolve doubts in favor of their personal values. This can lead to verdicts based on personal prejudice, but it's more likely their verdicts reflect the values of their community—as they should. Community values range across a broad spectrum, including views about the crime problem; the value of punishment; moral standards; police power (Levine 1992, 16); and surely after "9/11," terrorism.

The verdicts in cases involving the use of force by the police reflect the influence of community values. In communities with strong sentiments about law and order, jurors rarely convict the police on charges of police brutality. The Southern California community of Simi Valley, where police officers were tried for using force against Rodney King, is one of these. The jury, despite what looked like a clear case of excessive force to some who watched the videotape of the incident, acquitted the officers. They accepted the argument that the police are a "thin blue line" between respectable citizens and violence and disorder. Unpleasant as the use of force was, the police were using it to protect law-abiding citizens from criminals.

In other communities, the use of force by police looks different. In the Bronx, where juries are more than 80 percent Black and Hispanic, juries acquit Black defendants 47.6 percent of the time, nearly three times the national rate of acquittal. This is true even though most crime victims are also Black and Hispanic (Holden, Cohen, and de Lisser 1995). In one case, Larry Davis, an alleged major drug dealer and multiple murderer, was acquitted twice during a time when he was the most wanted fugitive in New York City. Davis's case and others like it led a Bronx prosecutor to comment, "It's bizarre. Everything here is truly stood on its head. The jurors are overwhelmingly suspicious of cops. If you have a case involving cops, you are almost certain to lose." The case produced an article entitled, "Bronx Juries: A Defense Dream, a Prosecutor's Nightmare" (Kifner 1988).

The acquittal of O. J. Simpson raised a spate of commentary about race influencing the decisions of juries. Commentators argue that the evidence, far more than race, determines verdicts. Jury watchers say otherwise. According to Benjamin A. Holden and his colleagues (1995), "race plays a far more significant role in jury verdicts than many people involved in the justice system prefer to acknowledge." Race-based verdicts, of course, aren't by any means limited to Black juries deciding in favor of Black defendants. All-White juries in the South for centuries convicted Blacks accused of committing crimes against Whites no matter what the evidence, while Whites who raped and killed Blacks were acquitted. In death penalty cases, Whites acquit White defendants accused of killing Blacks more often than they acquit Blacks accused of killing Whites (Chapter 11).

Social scientists see signs of another effect on jury decision making—September 11 (Dolan 2001). Jury consultant Arthur H. Patterson says their research shows juries are *usually* "calm and dispassionate, capable of logically sifting through evidence and evaluating it evenhandedly." "But at the moment [October 2001], America's jury pool is *not* calm or dispassionate. At this time, most jurors are angry and fearful and very sensitized to terrorism, injury, and death" (B2). Patterson sees signs that in ambiguous cases, juries will trust government witnesses, like police officers, more than defense witnesses, and they'll give the prosecution—not the defense—the benefit of the doubt.

Jury Nullification Jury nullification—juries' power to ignore the law and decide cases according to informal extralegal considerations—"fits neatly into a tradition of political activism by U.S. juries" (Case n.d.). It's also part of our history. William Penn benefited from nullification in 1670 when an English jury acquitted him for following his conscience in practicing his Quaker beliefs, a crime

jury nullification juries' power to ignore the law and decide cases according to informal extralegal considerations

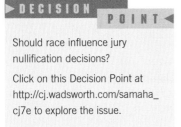

Should race influence jury nullification decisions?

Click on this Decision Point at http://cj.wadsworth.com/samaha_cj7e to explore the issue.

under English law. During colonial times, John Peter Zenger also violated the law by publishing material that criticized the British government. Zenger's lawyer told the jury they had the right "beyond all dispute to determine the law and the facts." The jury followed his suggestion and acquitted Zenger (Holden et al. 1995, 4).

In the first video of an actual jury deliberation ever made, we see jurors agonizing over whether to nullify the law in the case of a man who clearly was guilty of carrying a handgun—his lawyer even told the jury his client was guilty. But he also told them, "You should acquit him anyway." Why? He didn't break the law intentionally because he didn't know it was illegal for him to have it. He told the police he had the gun and even went home and brought it back to the police when they asked him to. He was mildly retarded and obviously didn't know much of what was going on in court. And finally, the prosecutor never should have prosecuted him in the first place. The jury's verdict: "Not guilty" (Levin and Hertzberg 1986).

Jury Selection The Sixth Amendment guarantees the right to an impartial jury. According to the U.S. Supreme Court, this means jurors have to be selected at random, from a "fair cross section of the community." To satisfy the random selection requirement, jurisdictions make a jury list; the names are taken from one of a variety of sources—voter registration lists, actual voter lists, tax rolls, telephone directories, or even lists of driver's license registrations. The jury list excludes minors, people who can't speak or write English, convicted felons, and recent residents. According to the Supreme Court, fair cross section doesn't mean jurors have to "mirror the community and reflect the various distinct groups in the population." For example, a jury doesn't have to include an 8 percent Hispanic makeup just because the community population is 8 percent Hispanic. It only bans the exclusion of recognized races, ethnic groups, or sexes from the chance to participate; it doesn't say they have to actually sit on juries (*Holland v. Illinois,* 1990; *Taylor v. Louisiana* 1975).

Many states "excuse" some potential jurors from jury *duty*—and jury service is a duty not a choice. Excuses include poor health, old age, economic hardship, and distance. Members of some occupations, like doctors, government workers, and members of the military, are also excused in many states (LaFave and Israel 1984, 2:708).

Analysis of the Jury Nullification Process: Prepared by the Constitutional Rights Foundation Chicago. To reach this site go to "Web Links" on your Samaha CJ7 website: http://cj.wadsworth.com/samaha_cj7e.

© Jack Kurtz/Reuters/Corbis

◀ Jury foreperson Lois Dopler stands in front of the jury as she reads their statement about the conviction of former Roman Catholic Bishop Thomas O'Brien in a Phoenix, Arizona court. The jury convicted O'Brien, head of the Phoenix Roman Catholic Church for 21 years, of leaving the scene of a fatal accident. The 68-year-old bishop faced up to three years and nine months in prison for being connected with the hit-and-run accident. Bishop O'Brien hit and killed Jim Reed, 43, who was jaywalking at the time.

Martin A. Levin (1988, 89–124), a political scientist who has studied juries, argues juries can't represent the community for two reasons: They're drawn from unrepresentative lists, and attorneys can remove prospective jurors by "peremptory challenge" (removing a prospective juror without a reason). According to Levin, multiple-source lists, including voters, public utility customers, driver's licenses, telephone directories, and tax rolls, would produce more representative jurors.

From the jury list, the jury panel (people from the jury list actually called for jury duty) is selected. The next step is the voir dire, the process of questioning the prospective jurors to pare the panel to actual juries. The voir dire gives prosecutors and defense counsel the chance to get the jurors they want and to exclude the ones they don't. They can remove jurors either by challenge for cause or peremptory challenge. In the challenge for cause, both prosecution and defense can object to as many prospective jurors as they like, as long as they can show prejudice to the judge's satisfaction, such as women in rape cases, bar owners in drunk-driving cases, and white men in gang-rape cases with Black defendants. The prosecution and the defense also have a specific number of peremptory challenges they can use to remove prospective jurors without having to give a reason why.

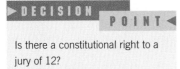

▶ DECISION POINT ◀

Is there a constitutional right to a jury of 12?

Click on this Decision Point at http://cj.wadsworth.com/samaha_ cj7e to explore the case *Williams v. Florida*.

12-Member Juries and Unanimous Verdicts Most of us think of juries as having 12 members and their verdicts as being unanimous. That was true for centuries but not anymore. In *Williams v. Florida* (1970), the Supreme Court held that 6-member juries didn't violate the Sixth Amendment. According to the Court, the Sixth Amendment aims to ensure accurate, independent fact-finding by preventing government oppression. Six-member juries, the Court concluded, don't affect juries' effectiveness. Not everyone agrees. Empirical research shows that 6-member juries are less reliable, don't save time, and are a lot less likely to represent a cross section of the community (LaFave and Israel 1984, 2:695–696). On the point of representing a cross section, the distinguished jury expert Professor Hans Zeisel had this to say:

> Suppose that in a given community, 90 percent of the people share one viewpoint, and the remaining 10 percent have a different viewpoint. Suppose further that we draw 100 twelve-member and 100 six-member juries. Using standard statistical methods, it can be predicted that approximately 72 of the twelve-member juries will contain a representative of the 10 percent minority, as compared to only 47 juries composed of six persons. This difference is by no means negligible. (LaFave and Israel 1984, 2:696)

Juries consisting of less than 12 members are most common in misdemeanor cases, but seven states also allow them in noncapital felonies.

What about 5-member juries? The Court drew the line at 6 in the unanimous decision *Ballew v. Georgia* (1978). Justice Blackman concluded that statistical data demonstrated:

1. Progressively smaller juries are less likely to foster group deliberation.
2. Smaller and smaller panels raise doubts about the accuracy of jury verdicts.
3. Verdicts will vary as juries become smaller.
4. The variance will hurt the defense.
5. The opportunity for minority representation decreases with the size of juries.

The Supreme Court has also decided that the right to jury trial doesn't include the right to a unanimous verdict. According to the Court, in *Apodaca v. Oregon* (1972), neither 11-to-1 nor 10-to-2 votes to convict in felony cases violates the Sixth Amendment. Why? The commonsense judgment of peers doesn't depend on whether *all* jurors agree to convict:

[There's] no difference between juries required to act unanimously and those permitted to convict by votes of 10-to-2 or 11-to-1. [In] either case, the interest of the defendant in having the judgment of his peers interposed between himself and the officers of the state who prosecute and judge him is equally well served.

In a companion case, *Johnson v. Louisiana* (1972), the Court rejected the argument that proof beyond a reasonable doubt required a unanimous verdict; it decided that a 9-to-3 guilty verdict in a robbery case complied with the right to an impartial jury:

Nine jurors—a substantial majority of the jury—were convinced by the evidence. Disagreement of the three jurors does not alone establish reasonable doubt, particularly when such a heavy majority of the jury, after having considered the dissenters' views, remains convinced of guilt.

Critics of the *Apodaca* and *Johnson* decisions argue that unanimity instills confidence in the system, ensures participants' careful deliberation, and guarantees the hearing of minority viewpoints. Furthermore, unanimity prevents government oppression and supports the established legal preference for freeing 100 guilty persons rather than convicting one innocent individual. Finally, unanimity comports better with the requirement that criminal conviction rest on proof beyond a reasonable doubt. Most states seem to agree. Despite the Court's green light on the constitutionality of less than unanimous verdicts, only two states also allow less than unanimous verdicts (11–1 and 10–2) in noncapital felony cases (LaFave and Israel 1984, 2:698).

A Fair Trial

Fair trials require an atmosphere that doesn't prejudice the jury against defendants. In a notorious case, the State of Ohio tried Dr. Sam Sheppard for brutally murdering his socialite wife. The newspapers were filled with "evidence" (actually rumors) about Sheppard's "guilt"; nearly all editorials were against him, and reporters even disrupted the trial proceedings to scoop "sensational" stories. The jury convicted him, but the U.S. Supreme Court overruled the verdict, finding Sheppard couldn't get a fair trial in such a "carnival atmosphere" (*Sheppard v. Maxwell* 1966).

To guarantee an atmosphere that minimizes prejudice, trial judges can transfer the trial to a calmer location (change of venue). They can also sequester the jury (put them in hotel rooms under guard where they can't read newspapers, watch TV, or talk on the telephone) (Phillips 1977, 218). Trial judges can also put gag orders on the press and lawyers and even keep reporters out of the courtroom. Further, they can remove "unruly" spectators and "troublesome" members of the press. However, judges have less freedom to control disruptive defendants, because the Sixth Amendment guarantees defendants the right to be present at their own trials. But they can remove defendants if it's impossible to proceed with them in the courtroom. More often judges keep disruptive defendants in the courtroom gagged and bound to keep "order in the court" (*Illinois v. Allen* 1970).

Although it's probably not obvious to most outsiders, the elaborate rules for every procedure in the criminal trial—choosing jurors; presenting lawyers' opening statements examining and cross-examining witnesses; introducing and presenting evidence; presenting lawyers closing arguments; charging the jury, and jury deliberations—are all aimed at deciding whether defendants are guilty. Whether they're guilty depends on proving guilt beyond a reasonable doubt. We have looked at the impact of juries; next we'll examine these other procedures.

Proving Guilt "Beyond a Reasonable Doubt" Proof beyond a reasonable doubt is the burden prosecutors have to carry to turn defendants into offenders. Defendants don't have to prove their innocence, and they don't have to help the

► Fair trials have to take place in an atmosphere that doesn't poison the jury against defendants. Michael Jackson's trial for child sex abuse is a case in point. Jackson has passionate supporters who believe he's innocent and equally passionate people who believe he's guilty. Here Michael Jackson gestures to some of his fans from the top of his SUV after his arraignment at the courthouse in Santa Maria, California.

state prove its case. They can even throw roadblocks in the way of the government's efforts to prove its case. In other words, defendants are innocent until proven guilty; they enjoy a presumption of innocence (Chapter 1). To win acquittal, all defendants have to do—and only if they choose to—is cast a reasonable doubt on the government's case (Black 1983, 635; *In re Winship* 1970).

According to the U.S. Supreme Court in the landmark case *In re Winship*, defendants have a constitutional right to proof beyond a reasonable doubt because it reduces the risk of convicting innocent people. Criminal defendants have so much to lose—property, liberty, and sometimes life itself—as well as suffering the stigma of being labeled "criminals," that without the right to proof beyond a reasonable doubt, conviction would deny them due process of law (Chapter 4). Less than proof beyond a reasonable doubt also weakens the criminal law's moral force and casts doubt on the courts' capacity to condemn guilty and vindicate innocent people (*In re Winship* 1970).

How much proof is proof beyond a reasonable doubt? Courts, including the U.S. Supreme Court, have struggled to define it. Here's one judge's struggle to instruct the jury on what proof beyond a reasonable doubt means:

> The phrase "beyond a reasonable doubt" has no technical or unusual meaning. You can arrive at the real meaning of it by emphasizing the word "reasonable." A reasonable doubt is a doubt for which a valid reason can be assigned. It's a doubt which is something more than a guess or a surmise. It's not a conjecture or a fanciful doubt. It's a reasonable doubt. It's not a doubt which is raised by somebody simply for the sake of raising doubts, nor is it a doubt suggested by the ingenuity of counsel or any of the jurors which is not justified by the evidence or lack of the evidence. A reasonable doubt is a doubt based on reason and not on the mere possibility of innocence. It is a doubt for which you can in your own mind conscientiously give a reason.
>
> A reasonable doubt, in other words, is a real doubt, an honest doubt, a doubt which has its foundation in the evidence or the lack of evidence. It's the kind of doubt which in the serious affairs which concern you in everyday life you would pay heed and attention to.

Now, of course, absolute certainty in the affairs of life is almost never attainable and the law does not require absolute certainty on the part of the jury before you return a verdict of guilty. The state does not have to prove guilt beyond all doubt or to a mathematical or absolute certainty. What the law does require, however, is that after hearing all the evidence, if there's something in that evidence or lack of evidence which leaves in the minds of the jury as reasonable men and women a reasonable doubt about the fault of the accused, then the accused must be given the benefit of that doubt and acquitted. Any conclusion reasonably to be drawn from the evidence which is consistent with the innocence of the accused must prevail. If there's no reasonable doubt, then the accused must be found guilty. The test is one of reasonable doubt, a doubt based on reason and common sense. (*State v. Vicente* 2001, 630)

After he was convicted, Ruperto Vicente appealed complaining about the judge's "drumbeat repetition" in the instructions about reasonable doubt. Although the court agreed the instruction was long, it didn't prejudice the jury.

Opening Statements In their opening statements, prosecutors and defense lawyers give an overview of their side of the case. Prosecutors use the opening statements to give the jury a road map of what they're going to prove. This helps juries follow the case because prosecutors can't always present their evidence in a logical order. If they can follow the case, jurors are less likely to get confused, bored, and irritated by evidence that doesn't make sense without the opening statement. Defense lawyers can use their opening statement to take advantage of weaknesses in the prosecution's view of the case. Defense lawyer Seymour Wishman (1981) reports this incident from his own experience:

> The D.A., overly confident, had made a mistake in his opening statement. Instead of giving a general statement broadly outlining the kind of evidence he would present to the jury, he had been specific, naming witnesses and the details of what each would say. He had a strong case, but he was taking an unnecessary risk: I might be able to poke holes in some of his facts, and if I could, my performance would have more impact than it would have had otherwise. (169–170)

Calling and Examining Witnesses Both the defense and the prosecution have broad powers to subpoena (command by a court order) witnesses to testify. Ordinary witnesses usually get travel money and a small daily fee (rarely enough to pay them for lost wages). Expert witnesses (fingerprint specialists, psychiatrists, psychologists, and so on) are well paid for their testimony. (See the CJ & Technology box "The Remote Defendant.")

The rules for direct examination—examination of witnesses on the side of the case the lawyers represent—differ from *cross-examination*—examination of witnesses on the opposing side. Answers to questions on direct examination call for narratives, like the answer to "Where were you on October 8 at about 8:00 P.M.?" In direct examination, lawyers can't ask leading questions—questions steering witnesses to the answers the lawyers want. Leading questions, which call for simple "yes" or "no" answers, during cross-examination are common.

Criminal law professor George P. Fletcher (1988), a respected writer on criminal law, describes the differences between direct and cross-examination this way:

> Lawyers at trial are directors as well as performers in presenting their client's version of the truth. They make theatrical decisions about the order in which to present their witnesses, they coach them like directors in rehearsal, and they lead their witnesses gently through their parts. Their presentation of the truth reflects art and rhetoric as well as rational argument. (116)
>
> Their role [in direct examination] stops short of prompting their witnesses when they do not perform as expected. Prompting falls under the ban against asking "leading questions." A lawyer disappointed in his witness may not try to put words in his mouth. He cannot ask (assuming that the witness would be prepared to answer "yes"), "Isn't it true that you saw the gunman smiling as he was shooting?" He must try to elicit this testimony

Criminal Trial Process: Prepared by the Cook County Courts (Illinois). To reach this site go to "Web Links" on your Samaha CJ7 website: http://cj.wadsworth.com/samaha_cj7e.

The Remote Defendant

The defendant's case is called for arraignment, but the defendant is not in court. The defendant is in a room in the jail where the defendant is incarcerated awaiting trial. During the proceeding, the court will inform the defendant of the charges, set or review bail, and possibly take the defendant's guilty plea. The defendant appears by videoconferencing technology on a screen visible to the judge and others in the courtroom. In the remote location, the defendant views a video monitor to learn what is happening in court and to hear the judge. Any colloquy between the judge and the defendant takes place by videoconference. The defendant's only eye into the court proceedings is the television monitor.

Few resources have been devoted to assessing the impact of videoconferencing. Researchers in other disciplines have attempted to determine the strengths and weaknesses of various forms of communication, including videoconferencing. They have generated interesting results. For some tasks, simple telephone communication is as effective as a link with a visual channel. For others, even videoconferencing is inferior to face-to-face communication. The data from other disciplines raise concerns that the assessment of the defendant as well as the defendant's experience of the justice system may be skewed by the reliance on videoconferencing.

The impact of videoconferencing on the justice process, however, is hard to assess. The impact of technology is often subtle. Videoconferencing is unlikely to produce measurable changes in the outcomes of proceedings. Nevertheless, we cannot and should not assume that videoconferencing technology is entirely benign. For example, the mere fact that video bail hearings sometimes result in bail amounts that the defendants can meet does not signify that the technology has no impact; the amounts may be higher or the conditions of release more restrictive than they would have been had the defendants appeared in person. The decisions in criminal cases involve many variables. In the criminal justice system, a negative impact will harm the quality of justice.

While videoconferencing transmits a wider range of verbal and nonverbal cues than teleconferencing, it still falls short of in-person interactions. The question is whether its social presence is sufficient to preserve the quality of justice. The research on the use of videoconferencing has not addressed this question.

Armed with information about the subtle effects of videoconferencing, the system should attempt to diminish or contain those effects. All personnel, judges in particular, who deal with defendants appearing through videoconferencing, must be carefully trained to reduce negative impacts. Not only should they be instructed in how to conduct a videoconferencing hearing but they should also be educated in the effect generated by including the defendant only through video.

If the criminal justice system invests in videoconferencing technology to expedite court proceedings, it should offer that technology to defense counsel, particularly public defenders, faced with the challenge of providing appropriate representation to incarcerated clients. The system should not merely allow the brief consultation by video in preparation for a specific court appearance that is currently the norm. Instead, defense counsel should have access to clients through videoconferencing during noncourt hours to work on all aspects of the case.

The criminal justice system should not continue to rely on, and to expand its reliance on, videoconferencing without recognizing that the technology may introduce negative effects. The system should address this possibility in two ways. First, the government should commission careful studies of the subtle impact of this technology on the quality of justice. Second, the government must take steps to ameliorate the negative impact of videoconferencing through design of videoconferencing systems and training of those who participate in videoconference proceedings.

In addition, the government should employ its videoconferencing capacity for the defendants' benefit. The courts should make videoconferencing available to defendants and their attorneys to enhance the interaction between incarcerated defendants and their counsel, which is often characterized by neglect and disengagement. Making technological connections to the jail available for attorney-client consultation may improve the attorney-client relationship and the quality of representation.

In the end, we should ask what we gain and what we lose through videoconferencing. Without videoconferencing, court proceedings can involve the defendant appropriately. The courtroom setting puts the defendant in appropriate physical relation to other actors, providing opportunities for consultation with defense counsel, direct interaction with the judge, and general observation of the proceeding. When courts replace in-court appearances with videoconferencing, they sacrifice that courtroom dynamic in exchange for possible cost savings and gains in efficiency and security, and, doing so, they diminish the quality of justice.

Source: Anne Bowen Poulin, "Criminal Justice and Videoconferencing Technology: The Remote Defendant," *Tulane Law Review* 78:1090–1091, 1157–1158, 1164, 1166 (March 2004).

◄ Expert witnesses are often an essential element in criminal trials. Shannon Novak, a research assistant in anthropology at the University of Utah, testifies during Cody Nielson's murder trial in First District Court in Logan, Utah. As expert witness for the state, she explained cut marks on human bones found in Melville, Utah.

without giving away the script. But when they turn into critics on cross-examination, lawyers can ask all the leading questions they want and insist, often contemptuously, that the witness answer "yes" or "no." (231)

Fletcher (1988) describes defense attorney Barry Slotnick's skill in leading witnesses in cross-examination in the trial of Bernhard Goetz, the "subway vigilante" case in New York City in 1986. Slotnick wanted to establish that Goetz fired shots against four youths in rapid succession, not pausing between shots:

> The tactic became clear on the cross-examination of ... Victor Flores, who claimed actually to have seen Goetz fire at two of the youths as they were running toward him and away from Goetz. He heard four shots "one after another." On cross-examination, Slotnick took advantage of his legal option to restate Flores's testimony in his own language and ask Flores to answer "yes" or "no" whether that was his view of what happened. Thus he reformulated Flores's first statement about the pattern and rapidity of the shots by asking, "And the three shots or the four shots ... that you hear in rapid succession after the first shot, were all going in your area, is that correct?" Having gained Flores's assent to the phrase "rapid succession," Slotnick began using the label over and over again in cross-examination. The jury heard Flores say "yes" to this description so often—five more times—that the words came to seem like his own. (121–122)

Slotnick made his intention clear by asking the following question purely for the jury's benefit:

> So it is fair to say that as far as your witnessing what occurred, the fact that he might have walked over to a rear seat and shot somebody and said something to them, like "you don't look bad, here's another," something like that, that really never happened? (Fletcher 1988, 121–122)

Admissible Evidence The law of evidence recognizes two types of evidence: physical evidence (weapons, stolen property, and fingerprints) and testimonial

relevant evidence evidence that helps prove the elements of the crime

prejudicial evidence evidence whose power to damage the defendant is greater than its power to prove the government's case

hearsay evidence evidence not known directly by the witness

jury instructions instructions from the judge that explain the role of the jury, the law, and what proof beyond a reasonable doubt means

evidence (witnesses' spoken, written, or symbolic words). Lawyers can't use just any evidence they want to present. Evidence has to help prove the elements of the crime; that is, it must be **relevant evidence.** But even relevant evidence isn't admissible in three instances:

1. If its power to damage the defendant is greater than its power to prove the government's case, called **prejudicial evidence**
2. If the government got it illegally, as in an unreasonable search (Chapter 7)
3. If it's **hearsay evidence**—evidence not known directly by the witness, like a police officer who testifies to the facts of a robbery told to him by the bank teller who actually witnessed it

Closing Arguments After both sides have presented all their evidence, they make their closing arguments. The experienced prosecutor Steven Phillips (1977) explains the importance of the closing argument:

> It is one of the few arts left in which time is of no consequence. Standing before 12 people, a lawyer can be brief or lengthy—the choice is his own; there are no interruptions, and a captive audience. All that matters are those 12 people; they must be persuaded, or everything that has gone before is in vain. Summation is the one place where lawyers do make a difference; if an attorney can be said to "win" or "lose" a case, the chances are that he did so in his closing argument to the jury. (196–197)

Charging the Jury After the closing arguments, the judge "charges" the jury. The charge is given in the form of jury instructions. **Jury instructions** explain the role of the jury—to decide whether facts prove the elements of the crime; explain the law—define the elements of the crime they have to apply the facts to; and explain what proof beyond a reasonable doubt means. This sounds simple enough, but, in reality, the often long, complex, and technical legalese found in instructions demands a lot—maybe too much—from jurors. According to prosecutor Steven Phillips (1977):

> A judge's charge to the jury is an amazing exercise in optimism. For two or three hours he reads to twelve laymen enough law to keep a law student busy for a semester. Twelve individuals, selected more or less at random, sit there, unable to take notes or ask questions. Somehow, just by listening, it is presumed everything spoken by the judge will take root in their collective intelligence. (213)

Jury Deliberations After the charge, the jury retires to a room to decide whether the prosecution proved its case beyond a reasonable doubt. When they've decided, they go back to the courtroom to reenact the centuries old scene of giving the court their verdict. Formally, judges have the last word—if the verdict is "Guilty," they turn defendants into offenders by entering a judgment of guilty; if the verdict is "Not guilty," they turn defendants into ordinary individuals by entering a judgment of acquittal.

Disposition by Negotiation

The criminal trial you've just learned about is the way cases are decided on TV in almost every crime drama. But in real life, it describes only 5 out of 100 cases, where the question is, "Is she guilty?" You're about to learn about the other 95 out of 100 cases, where defendants are guilty, and the question is, "What's the punishment?"

The domination of decision by guilty plea is nothing new. In my analysis of criminal justice in Essex County, England, more than 90 percent of defendants were pleading guilty. That was 450 years ago (Samaha 1974)! A survey of 1920s Cleveland, Ohio, showed that guilty pleas disposed of half the felony cases scheduled for criminal court (Pound and Frankfurter 1922, 93). Malcolm Feeley (1979) showed that in 1974, there "were no trials in my sample of 1,640 lower court cases" (310) in New Haven, Connecticut. Milton Heumann found that in the same New Haven between the years 1880 and 1954, less than 10 out of 100 cases went to trial (Heumann 1975, 519). We assume that negotiation lies behind these guilty pleas, but we don't know for sure, especially in those that took place 450 years ago.

Professors Robert Scott and William Stuntz (1992) at the University of Virginia Law School describe plea bargaining (which they assume is behind the guilty pleas) as "scandalously casual":

> A quick conversation in a prosecutor's office or courthouse hallway between attorneys familiar with the basics of the case, with no witnesses present, leading to a proposed resolution that is then "sold" to both the defendant and the judge. To a large extent, this kind of horse trading determines who goes to jail and for how long. That is what plea bargaining is. It is not some adjunct to the criminal justice system; it is the criminal justice system. (1911–1912)

Until the 1970s and 1980s, scholars ignored this overwhelming dominance of informal disposition of cases by guilty plea instead of formal disposition by trial (Alschuler 1979, 211; Rosett and Cressey 1976; Sanborn 1986, 111). What most "outsiders" (the general public, most guilty-plea scholars, and incidentally, most of my students) see in this "street bazaar" justice, they don't like (to put it mildly). One critic compared the choice for defendants in plea bargaining to a threat at gunpoint (Kipnis 1976, 97–99); the historian and expert on the law of torture John Langbein (1978) called plea bargaining "medieval torture." However, the *insiders* in the courtroom workgroup like informal justice by plea bargaining just fine.

We'll examine the reasons outsiders and insiders see plea bargaining so differently, in the "The Plea-Bargaining Debate" section. But first, let's look at the types of guilty pleas; plea-bargaining criteria; the courtroom workgroup (prosecutors, defense lawyers, judges) and plea bargaining; defendants and guilty pleas; and the Constitution and guilty pleas.

The Types of Guilty Pleas

All guilty pleas aren't alike. In **straight pleas** ("mercy of the court" pleas), defendants plead guilty, hoping for a more lenient sentence *after* pleading guilty. In **negotiated pleas,** defendants arrange some kind of deal for a reduced charge or sentence *before* pleading guilty (Boland and Forst 1985, 10–15; Heumann 1979a, 651; Rubenstein, Clarke, and Wright 1980, 81; Wright and Miller 2002). Let's look at each type.

straight pleas defendants plead guilty, hoping for a more lenient sentence *after* pleading guilty

negotiated pleas defendants arrange some kind of deal for a reduced charge or sentence *before* pleading guilty

Straight Pleas Most pleas are straight (mercy of the court) pleas. Why do defendants plead guilty without a promise of getting something in return? Michael Rubenstein and his colleagues (1980) tried to answer this question by analyzing data from police, jail, and court records in Alaska. They also interviewed every judge, prosecutor, and criminal defense attorney in Anchorage, Fairbanks, and Juneau, asking why defendants give up their right to jury trial without getting anything from the state. The strength of the case of clear guilt against them (called dead-bang cases) was the most common reason. One experienced defense lawyer described a dead-bang case:

> Well, where you've got a nineteen-year-old kid who's ripped off somebody else's stereo and he confessed to it, what do you gain from going to trial? You can go to jury trial and your client gets on the stand and says, "I didn't do it," and you say, "Well, you confessed to it, and we found the stereo in your house." You know what's going to happen then? I mean, your client is either going to have to perjure himself, or he's not going to take the stand. And, if he doesn't take the stand, and if it takes you four days to try the case, you have nothing to argue at the end. The judge is going to say, "What happened here? Why did you

waste thousands of dollars putting us all through this?" You know, they're going to pay a price for this—it's only natural. (Rubenstein et al. 1980, 81)

Another reason for a straight plea is the "boy scout" reason—hoping that cooperating without bargaining will speak well for the defendant at sentencing:

> Now if the guy is a "boy scout" [said one defense lawyer] I might advise him to enter a guilty plea. Keep the image consistent that way. Take this guy charged with a first-offense burglary in a dwelling. He confessed when he was arrested and he helped the cops retrieve the property. He had no real defenses. If he had exercised all his constitutional rights it would have hurt him. He'd have gone to jail. I could advise him that if he continued in the cooperative mode in which he had already begun when I started representing him he'd have the best chances of probation. He got straight probation and a suspended imposition of sentence. He could never have gotten that disposition if he had exercised his constitutional rights. (Rubenstein et al. 1980, 85)

Straight pleas don't always stem from such noble reasons. Defense attorneys admit that guilty pleas benefit them as much as they do their clients. Guilty pleas help lawyers "avoid the three or four grueling courtroom days usually required for a felony trial, not to mention more time spent in pretrial preparation." According to one assistant public defender:

> You really have to watch yourself if you have three or four trials scheduled over the next month, and you are picking up new cases. If a case looks bad you may automatically say, "Well, that person is going to plead guilty." There is only so much you can take. As a defense attorney you have a wide range of rationalizations for not going to trial. The defense attorney does not misrepresent, so much as he comes up with rationalizations why clients shouldn't go to trial. And it isn't difficult to do this in any given case. (Rubenstein et al. 1980, 86)

Sometimes a lawyer will advise a client to plead guilty because of the only too human reluctance to appear foolish in public. One defense lawyer admitted candidly, "fear of embarrassment was one of the big things that I have had to get over as a trial attorney. Some cases are just embarrassing" (Rubenstein et al. 1980, 87).

Another lawyer said:

> You know, that's got to be the toughest thing, when you just don't have very much to argue at all, and you're sitting through a trial just searching for something to say at the end of the case. There are a lot of attorneys that wouldn't subject themselves to that, who would rationalize that their clients would gain something by entering their pleas. (Rubenstein et al. 1980, 88)

Defense attorneys also believe (and some empirical findings back them up) that insisting on a trial results in harsher penalties (Figure 10.2). In the words of one assistant public defender:

> In violent crimes the judge sees the victim and hears the whole ugly story. Naturally he's going to give a tougher sentence. In fraud cases the judge has a chance to sit and think, "Boy, this guy really premeditated this fraud; he's too slick to trust." (Rubenstein et al. 1980, 91)

One plainspoken judge put it this way:

> The defendant played the odds; they went against him. He played and he declined to plead. He put the state to the burden of proof, and the state won. There is nothing wrong with [giving him a harsher sentence for losing the gamble]. (Rubenstein et al. 1980, 92)

Finally, going to trial is expensive. Those who can afford a lawyer can measure that cost in dollars. According to one defense attorney, private lawyers "simply have to inform their client how much it will cost them to pursue their claim of innocence at trial. This causes a lot of defendants to sober up." Not even indigent defendants want to draw out their cases for months. They want to get the case over with as soon as possible for the perfectly understandable rea-

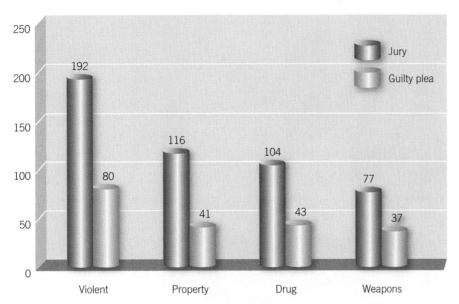

◄ **FIGURE 10.2 Average Months of Prison Sentence by Jury and by Guilty Plea, 2000**

Source: Bureau of Justice Statistics, State Court Sentencing of Convicted Felons, 2000 Statistical Tables (Washington, DC: Bureau of Justice Statistics, June 2003). Table 4.5.

son that it makes life easier (Feeley 1979, 186; also see below "Defendants and Plea Bargaining").

Negotiated Pleas In negotiated pleas, defendants make a deal with the government; they plead guilty in exchange for less punishment. The exact deal is accomplished by bargaining over the charges, the number of charges (called "counts"), or the sentence:

1. *Charge bargaining.* Prosecutors file charges less serious than the facts justify in exchange for defendants' guilty pleas. For example, a defendant who has committed a first-degree murder carrying a mandatory life term might plead guilty to second-degree murder with a term of 20 years to life. The plea to second-degree murder gives the judge discretion to sentence the defendant to less than life imprisonment.
2. *Count bargaining.* Prosecutors drop some of the charges (counts) against the defendant in exchange for a guilty plea. For example, a defendant is charged with five robberies; the prosecutor drops two of them in exchange for the defendant's guilty plea.
3. *Sentence bargaining (pleading guilty "on the nose").* Defendants plead guilty to charges actually justified by the facts in the case but with the understanding the judge will grant (or at least the prosecutor will request) a lenient sentence, such as probation instead of jail time for writing a bad check.

Plea bargaining can be either express or implicit. In express bargaining, prosecutors, defense lawyers, and sometimes trial judges meet face to face to work out the deal. Implicit bargaining involves no direct meetings. Instead, the "going rate for guilty pleas" informally accepted within the courthouse workgroup (local legal culture) dictates the terms of the deal. According to Milton Heumann (1979b), the going rates are

> products of the individual courthouse and community, and are not primarily shaped by state or national considerations. In one jurisdiction an armed robber may receive eight years after a trial and five years if he pleads; in another, the comparable figures may be seven and four, or ten and eight, and so on. (208–210)

In implicit bargaining, defense attorneys can fairly assume that if their clients plead guilty to "normal" crimes, they'll receive concessions in line with the going rate. According to one Detroit judge familiar with the practice, "The system

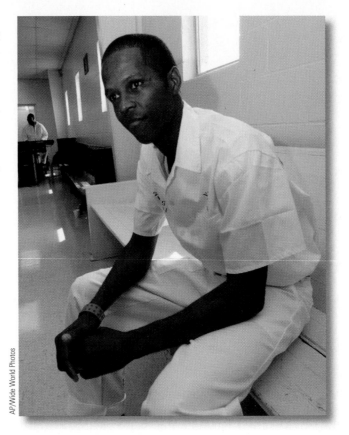

AP/Wide World Photos

► You've learned that pleading guilty to crimes one didn't commit can meet the constitutional requirement that guilty pleas be voluntary. Medell Banks is an example of an innocent person pleading guilty. Banks, who's retarded, pled guilty to killing his new-born baby—a baby that may never have existed. By a vote of 3 to 2 the Alabama Court of Criminal Appeals threw out the conviction. According to the Court, "a manifest injustice has occurred in this case." Banks, his es-tranged wife Victoria, and her sister pled guilty to killing Victoria's baby in rural Choctaw County.

operates in terms of defense attorney and defendants' expectations—what is widely known as a rate. It's an expectation model" (Heumann 1978, 9).

Critics of plea bargaining compare implicit bargaining to a flea market where haggling over prices (type and length of sentence) varies with each transaction. But the reality of "going rates" isn't much like bargaining at all; it's more like going to Wal-Mart®, where the prices are set and we have to take them or leave them (Feeley 1979, 187). The negotiation centers on how the facts of the case fit the criteria for decision making now familiar to you (and which you'll read about in the next section).

Public opinion affects local legal culture, too. Cases the public doesn't care about are probably going to be decided by plea; sensational cases will probably go to trial. The distinguished former U.S. Attorney General Edward Levi gave this advice to U.S. attorneys:

[Consider] what the public attitude is toward prosecution under the circumstances of the case. There may be situations where the public interest might be better served by having the case tried rather than by being disposed of by means of a guilty plea—including situations in which it is particularly important to permit a clear public understanding that "justice is done" or in which a plea agreement might be misconstrued to the detriment of public confidence in the criminal justice system. For this reason, the prosecutor should be careful not to place undue emphasis on factors which favor disposition of a case pursuant to a plea agreement. (Heumann 1979a, 213–214)

According to James Eisenstein and Herbert Jacob (1977), the courtroom work-group also contributes to the local legal culture's influence on plea bargaining. They found defense attorneys, prosecutors, and judges have created norms for the "way things are done." Members of the workgroup rarely try to do things differently. They'd feel a lot discomfort if they insisted on going to trial when negotiating is the "way things are done" (286; Nardulli, Eisenstein, and Flemming 1988).

However accomplished, the exchange boils down to this: Defendants give up their chance of getting no punishment at all by taking the risk of pleading "Not

Guilty," and getting a "Not Guilty" verdict at trial. In return, they plead guilty and get a guarantee of *less* punishment than they'd get if they went to trial and got convicted. Here's one example:

> San Francisco defense attorney Benjamin Davis . . . represented a man charged with kidnapping and forcible rape. The defendant was innocent, Davis says, and after investigating the case Davis was confident of an acquittal. The prosecutor, who seems to have shared the defense attorney's opinion on this point, offered to permit a guilty plea to simple battery. Conviction on this charge would not have led to a greater sentence than thirty days' imprisonment, and there was every likelihood that the defendant would be granted probation. When Davis informed his client of this offer, he emphasized that conviction at trial seemd highly improbable. The defendant's reply was simple: "I can't take that chance." (Church 1979, 515)

Plea-Bargaining Criteria

The courtroom workgroup (prosecutors, defense lawyers, and judges) have different emphases when they bargain, but they've all got the same criteria in mind when they negotiate (Forst 1995, 366–368). Three criteria shouldn't surprise you: the strength of the case against the defendants, the seriousness of the offense, and the dangerousness of the defendant. Two other criteria, caseload pressure and defendant pressure (see "Defendants and Plea Bargaining"), also impact negotiations. Let's look at the three main criteria and how they're applied by prosecutors, defense counsel, and judges in negotiated pleas. We'll also examine the role of heavy caseloads in negotiations.

The Strength of the Case We begin with the strength of the case because prosecutors, defense lawyers, and judges repeatedly tell researchers (and when they talk to my class, my students) that this is the most important of all the criteria (Figure 10.3). According to Herbert Miller and his associates (1978) in their study of plea bargaining, "Virtually all prosecutors regard weak cases as prime targets for plea negotiations." This isn't surprising given that we're talking about lawyers here. Of all the criminal justice professionals, lawyers are most in touch with the use of evidence to prove a case (62; also McDonald 1985, 65).

What makes a strong case? Maybe the defendant really *did* commit the crime, but lawyers know there's a huge gap between committing a crime and proving it—especially proving it beyond a reasonable doubt, the highest standard of

Steps in a Trial/The Plea Bargain: Part of "How Courts Work" by the American Bar Association. To reach this site go to "Web Links" on your Samaha CJ7 website: http://cj .wadsworth.com/samaha_cj7e.

National Institute of Justice (NIJ): NIJ is the research, development, and evaluation agency of the U.S. Department of Justice. To reach this site go to "Web Links" on your Samaha CJ7 website: http://cj.wadsworth.com/ samaha_cj7e.

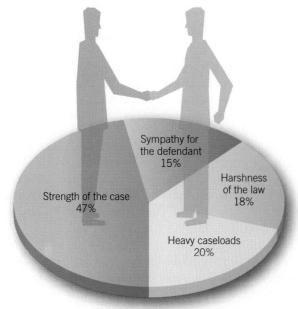

◀ **FIGURE 10.3 Reasons Prosecutors Negotiate**

Source: Based on data in Herbert S. Miller, James Cramer, and William McDonald, *Plea Bargaining in the United States* (Washington, DC: National Institute of Justice, 1978).

Sympathy for the defendant
15%

Harshness of the law
18%

Strength of the case
47%

Heavy caseloads
20%

proof known to our law. **Factual guilt**—what we know to be true outside court—isn't good enough; only **legal guilt**—what we can prove in court—counts. A St. Louis prosecutor (to his regret) ignored this distinction when he charged a defendant with murder on no more proof of legal guilt than a photograph a pawnbroker had taken of the defendant pawning the dead woman's TV set the day after her apartment was burglarized and she was murdered. When asked if he was worried that the defendant might be innocent, he replied he knew the defendant was guilty because:

> I sent two of my best investigators who are Black and competent men out on the street to check out the case. They went down to the section of town where this guy hangs out and they talked to the people down there about his involvement in this crime. They found out that the street talk says he's guilty. The guys down there on wise-guy alley say he did it, so I know he is guilty.

Not surprisingly, the defendant was acquitted (Miller et al. 1978, 93).

The Seriousness of the Offense How do prosecutors, defense lawyers, and judges decide how serious an offense is? The answer begins with the going rates for crimes—the local "market value" measured in jail time or the fine for particular crimes. Market values aren't the same as the punishments spelled out in the state's criminal code. According to one Detroit judge familiar with the practice, "The system operates in terms of defense attorney and defendants' expectations—what is widely known as a rate. It's an expectation model" (Heumann 1978, 9). Judge Ronald Lisk clearly was referring to the going rate in Santa Clara County, California, when he said to the prosecutor and defense lawyer, "It's a kilo case, guys. Everybody goes to the joint for two years for a kilo case. Sorry, there's not much I can do" (Schmitt 1991a).

How is the going rate determined? According to Milton Heumann (1979b), there's an informal understanding among prosecutors, defense lawyers, and judges about what punishment cases deserve. Each community has its own going rates, which are

> products of the individual courthouse and community, and are not primarily shaped by state or national considerations. In one jurisdiction an armed robber may receive eight years after a trial and five years if he pleads; in another, the comparable figures may be seven and four, or ten and eight, and so on. (208, 210)

The going rate may not be in writing, but the price of not pleading guilty is clear. According to Heumann (1978), "Defendants are told clearly by someone—usually their lawyers, but sometimes by judges, prosecutors, police officers, or others—that they had better plead guilty or they will be punished more severely if they go to trial" (7). Defendants can count on sentences in line with the going rate if they plead guilty.

Senior staff don't always help new lawyers learn how to incorporate informal local going rates into their decision making. In Delaware, Pennsylvania, the senior prosecutor instructed new prosecutors only to "Protect yourself. You're a lawyer first and a prosecutor second. Check with somebody. Don't be Mr. Nice-Guy. Don't make a fool of yourself or gain a reputation for poor judgment. Don't bring stuff into a judge and have it rejected" (Miller et al. 1978, 82). But they learn fast not to go above or below the going rates. One new prosecutor learned this the hard way. In his first case, he asked for the maximum sentence. Laughter broke out, a senior prosecutor stepped up, took the file from the novice's hand, and made clear to the judge the state wanted considerably less (in other words, the going rate) than the maximum (83).

The Dangerousness of the Defendant Until now, we've referred to defendants' criminal history (their past criminal behavior) as the sole criterion that affects decision making. Now, we extend the criterion to include not just "bad records" but also "bad defendants." We'll call this combination of bad records and bad people the dangerousness of the defendant (Institute for Law and Social Research 1977). Herbert Miller and his colleagues (1978) quote an experienced prosecutor on the point:

> I've got the police department record. I can see where the kid lives, what kind of neighborhood it is. I find out the place where the guy is hanging around and whether there are other scum in the area. I've got his prior arrests and their dispositions. (119)

A senior prosecutor in Delaware County, Pennsylvania, said prosecutors ask the arresting officer who brings them the case jacket "whether this guy is trouble." Sometimes the officer will "tell you that although he looks like trouble, he really is not a bad guy or vice versa. Sometimes the police can tell you that he is a known troublemaker" (Miller et al. 1978, 67–68). But prosecutors don't always accept what officers tell them. A senior prosecutor from Dade County, Florida, said:

> If the policeman says I don't like this guy and want to bust his ass and doesn't explain himself any further, I am not satisfied that he really tried to make the case. But on the other hand if the policeman reports that this guy is only the wheel man and won't give us the names of the two robbers who pulled the job, then I am willing to go along with a request for a tougher deal. Or if they say, the defendant told one story to the policeman at the crime scene and is now telling a different story, then I'll take this information into account as a legitimate concern of the police. (Miller et al. 1978, 67–68)

Lawyers don't look at the case strength, offense, and offender seriousness in isolation. In weak cases involving serious offenses and "bad news" offenders, some kind of guilty plea is likely, even if it's only half a loaf. In Miller and his associates' national survey of plea bargaining, one prosecutor reflected this attitude when he admitted he wouldn't dismiss murder, drug, and robbery cases (no matter how weak) because of their seriousness.

Heavy Caseloads We've now been reminded several times that the workgroup wants to dispose of cases efficiently, quickly, and harmoniously. But the workgroup subculture isn't all that pushes members. Heavy caseloads drive them to dispose of cases and to do it quickly and smoothly. As administrators, prosecutors manage caseloads, which most of them believe are too heavy. "We are running a machine here. We know we have to grind them out fast," said one Los Angeles prosecutor. A Manhattan prosecutor echoed his Los Angeles counterpart, "Our office keeps eight courtrooms extremely busy trying 5 percent of the cases. If even 10 percent of the cases ended in a trial, the system would break down. We can't afford to think very much about anything else" (Zimring and Frase 1980, 506–507).

Although the courthouse workgroup believes heavy caseloads force them to plea-bargain, empirical research casts doubt on this belief. No simple relationship exists between caseload pressure and guilty pleas. Comparing trial rates in districts with an extremely high volume and those with minimal caseload pressures revealed no significant differences between the percentage of cases disposed of by trial and those disposed of by guilty plea. In Connecticut, where court caseloads were cut in half with no corresponding reduction in personnel, the numbers of guilty pleas didn't drop at all (Heumann 1978, 29–31).

Now, let's look at the roles of each of the workgroup members and the defendant in plea bargaining.

The Prosecutor and Plea Bargaining

Plea bargaining varies according to the roles its key participants (prosecutors, defense counsel, and judges) play. Prosecutors' discretion in charging and sentencing decisions conditions their role in plea bargaining. Discretion not only affects decisions in individual cases but also orders general charging policies in prosecutors' offices. In small or rural jurisdictions, individual case discretion, not general charging policies, constitutes the norm. In large, urban jurisdictions, however, general charging policy includes plea bargaining.

Urban and rural policy differences have historical roots. As jurisdictions grow and become more complex, a transformation occurs; plea bargaining changes with it. Delaware County, Pennsylvania, for example, grew from a small, rural jurisdiction to a large, suburban one in about twenty years. Plea bargaining changed, too, from implicit bargaining with heavy judicial participation in the 1950s to explicit bargaining between prosecutors and defense counsel with little or no judicial participation by the 1970s (Miller et al. 1978, 56; Nardulli, Eisenstein, and Flemming 1988).

Defense Counsel and Plea Bargaining

Formally, defense counsel have to look at the effect their bargaining decisions have on their clients because plea bargaining is essential to their constitutional and professional duties to vigorously and effectively defend their clients (Chapter 8). As one expert put it:

> Experienced criminal lawyers know that one of defense counsel's most important functions, perhaps the most important, is working out with the prosecutor the best possible disposition of a client's case in situations in which there is no realistic prospect of acquittal. The lawyer not only may properly do this, but s/he violates the obligation to represent the client adequately if s/he does not. (Amsterdam 1984, 1:229)

But these formal professional duties run up against their informal connections to the workgroup (Chapter 8). In his description of what he calls "workgroup pathologies," David Lynch (1994), who worked both as a prosecutor and a public defender, reveals how much closer to the workgroup public defenders feel than they do to most of their clients:

> Part of "doing time" was having to put up with the constant stress and abuse heaped on us by ill-tempered and antisocial clients.... This was the sort of individual who made us love plea bargaining. Plea bargaining...makes cases "go away," taking with them some of the stress, work, combat, and (very important) the client—whose "companionship" one often wishes to minimize and whose guilt one often believes (correctly or incorrectly) to be so obvious.... (121–122)
>
> Defense attorneys knew all too well that if they brought too many cases to trial, they would be seen as either unreasonable and worthy of professional ostracism or as a fool who was too weak to achieve "client control." Many attorneys I knew became masters of the fine art of "chair therapy," in which a client who insists on a trial is made to sit in the hall of the courthouse (or in the courthouse lockup) for days on end during the courthouse trial terms, waiting for his day in court, until he accepts a deal. Some (usually unintentionally) resorted to "good cop/bad cop" routines, in which a resistant defendant is subjected to the screams of his or her attorney, followed by the lawyer's associate, who tries to calmly help the accused see the light. Usually, however, defense attorneys, aware that incredible trial penalties were attached to the "right" to a jury trial, only needed to tell a defendant of the unconscionable sentences that had been meted out to others who dared to create work for a judge. (123)

But don't overemphasize the desire for workgroup harmony and speed as an influence on plea bargaining. According to plea-bargaining expert Donald Newman:

> Negotiation can be quite adversary. The defense counsel may indicate to the prosecutor that he thinks the state has no evidence against his client except possibly a charge of disorderly conduct. The prosecutor in turn may state that he is not only going to push an armed robbery charge but plans to level a special count of being a habitual offender unless the defendant cooperates. Defense counsel then offers to have his client plead guilty to petty larceny with the prosecutor offering to reduce the charge to second-degree robbery. (Miller et al. 2000, 952)

Judges and Plea Bargaining

Judges enter into plea bargaining in one of two ways: They either participate during the negotiations or supervise after lawyers have struck bargains. Sometimes they do both (LaFave and Israel 1992, 928). Judicial participation in plea bargaining varies according to individual judges' styles and from jurisdiction to jurisdiction. Miller and his associates (1978) found four types of participation by judges:

1. They don't participate at all.
2. They gently lean on lawyers to move the bargaining along.
3. They put heavy pressure on lawyers to "force" guilty pleas.
4. They bargain with the lawyers over sentence recommendations.

Judges who refuse to participate at all just look over what the lawyers have already decided. These judges believe they can't supervise impartially a process they're an active part of. But are they always impartial? Most of these judges in Miller and his associates' study (1978, 244–245) found they agreed with prosecutors on sentencing in almost 100 percent of the cases. One judge admitted he'd never changed a prosecutor's recommendation. He occasionally told prosecutors the sentence wasn't in line with "going rates" to give them something to think about in future cases, but he never changed a recommendation in the current case.

The "gentle leaners" want to keep the flow of cases moving as smoothly and swiftly as possible. They have to "keep the pleas coming in" as one Oregon judge put it or "keep things from getting bogged down" as another said. "Gently leaning" usually means talking to the lawyers about the case, sometimes asking why the case was going to trial and expressing displeasure with the idea (Miller et al. 1978, 246–248).

Only a few "heavy leaners" try to "force" lawyers into bargains. The ones who do say heavy caseloads are the single most important reason they strong-arm defense lawyers and prosecutors into bargains. These judges make sure "no stone was left unturned to arrive at a plea of guilty," including "arm twisting, forcing, jerking the defense attorney around, and coming down on the defendant" (Miller et al. 1978, 249). A burglary case in New York City's criminal courts is an excellent example of arm-twisting by the judge. When the judge called the case, one of the two defendants didn't have a lawyer, so the judge just picked out a lawyer who happened to be in the courtroom. The district attorney offered a 2-to-4-year sentence in return for a guilty plea right then. The judge jumped in with, "After today, it's 3 to 6, after that it's 4 to 8. If they're ever going to plead, today is the time to do it." When the defense lawyer turned down the bargain (remember the judge had appointed him only moments before), the judge said, "We'll make it very easy. It's 4 to 8 after today. Let's play hardball" (Schulhofer 1985, 585).

Another hardball judge in Hartford, Connecticut, admitted he turned himself into a prosecutor

> when 835 cases were backlogged. He reduced the backlog to 299 cases by ordering the prosecuting attorney to select his two best assistants and setting up conferences at five-minute intervals day and night for six days. He enforced attendance of the prosecutor and defense attorney under threat of an arrest warrant. Under these conditions defense attorneys went to prosecutors and disposed of easy cases. The judge then ordered them into his chambers to discuss "sticky cases" and make a plea recommendation. They then marched back into court to recite the recommended disposition onto the record. He observed, somewhat ironically, that this practice "stinks" because a judge becomes a prosecutor. He did, however, indicate pleasure with the results. (Miller et al. 1978, 252)

Judges can participate in sentence bargaining either indirectly or directly. They bargain indirectly when they systematically impose heavier sentences on convicted defendants who demand a trial. Why the differential? Several reasons. Defendants who admit their guilt show remorse; remorse is the first step toward rehabilitation;

and so they deserve a lesser penalty. Other judges abide by the slogan, "If you want to win big, you'd better be prepared to lose big," so defendants who "burden" the state with a trial have to pay a price if the state wins. One Chicago judge says defendants who "waste" taxpayers' money and the court's time "deserve more time in jail for the problems they create" (Miller et al. 1978, 263–264).

Judges who bargain directly can offer general recommendations like "I'll give prison time as opposed to probation" or "I'll sentence in the upper instead of the lower range of prison time" (Miller et al. 1978, 260). Or they can offer specific sentences like five years of prison time or a $200 fine. Those who keep their offers general are balancing two values—they want predictability, believing defendants have a right to know what's going to happen to them, but they also want to maintain their independence as judges by not being just another party in the bargaining process (Miller et al. 1978, 250).

There's considerable opposition to judges participating in plea bargaining. The American Bar Association Standards say the "trial judge should not participate in plea discussions" (LaFave and Israel 1992, 928–929). Some statutes and court rules go so far as to ban judges from plea bargaining. For example, the *Federal Rules of Criminal Procedure* (2004) say judges "shall not participate in any such discussions." In *U.S. v. Werker* (1976), the court interpreted this rule to ban sentencing judges from taking any part "in any discussion or communication regarding the sentence to be imposed prior to the entry of a plea of guilty, conviction, or submission to him of a plea agreement."

Defendants and Plea Bargaining

It's a myth that the typical defendant wants her lawyer to do full battle in court for her. According to Malcolm Feeley's (1979) study of Connecticut's lower criminal courts, "The cost of invoking one's rights is frequently greater than the loss of the rights themselves, which is why so many defendants accept a guilty plea without a battle" (277). One defense lawyer explains it this way:

> Unfortunately, if you want to assert your rights, it's going to take time....It's very quick and easy if you want to plead guilty, but if you want to maintain your innocence, unfortunately people have to come another time. It's awful. Everything is done to make it easy and comfortable—quick—for the person who wants to plead guilty. To the person who wants to fight his case, you file a motion to fight it; in two or three weeks he comes back. The police officer doesn't show up, and they've got to come back again. Back and back and back. (Heumann 1978, 71)

Asserting the constitutional right to go to trial is more than time-consuming. For defendants not familiar with the criminal justice system, it's scary, embarrassing, and risky. According to Professor Rodney Uphoff (1995), an experienced public defender and associate director of a clinical legal program for law students planning to become defense lawyers:

> The prospect of actually going through a trial and having to take the witness stand is very intimidating. Fear, embarrassment, or the risk of adverse publicity drives defendants to negotiate and avoid trial. Unquestionably, the risk of a jail sentence or the prospect of a harsher sentence also deters defendants from viewing a trial as a desirable alternative to pleading guilty. For some, a pessimistic attitude or fatalistic mind-set dampens any enthusiasm for going to trial. (82)

Many defendants have been through the system before. Their prior experiences affect their attitude toward plea bargaining. For some (especially minorities and "outsiders"), these experiences have led them to believe that going to trial is a poor option because the system is "heavily stacked against them." For others, trials aren't worth their time because they think their cases aren't "that big a deal" or are "nothing to worry about." They just want to "get it over with" as soon as possible, and the way to do that is to plead guilty (Uphoff 1995, 82–83).

Defendants who've had experience with the system aren't naïve. They're familiar with the **penalties/rewards system** lesson: Defendants who go to trial pay a penalty for their adversary stance, and they get rewarded for pleading guilty (Heumann 1978, 66). Court personnel give some of the following explanations for the penalty/reward system:

penalties/rewards system defendants who go to trial pay a penalty for their adversary stance but get rewarded for pleading guilty

- Defendants who plead guilty save the state time and money.
- Defendants who plead guilty take the first step in their rehabilitation by owning up to their crimes. Don't overlook defendants who plead guilty because they're truly remorseful and want to take responsibility for what they did. They believe they did the crime so they should do the time.
- Defendants who plead guilty give up their chance of acquittal and make decision making more predictable.
- Defendants who plead guilty reduce the risk that judges will be embarrassed by having their rulings reversed on appeal.

The U.S. Supreme Court and Guilty Pleas

It may surprise you to learn that the U.S. Supreme Court never got around to approving plea bargaining until 1971 when Chief Justice Burger wrote:

> The disposition of criminal charges by agreement between the prosecutor and the accused, sometimes loosely called "plea bargaining," is an essential component of the administration of justice. Properly administered, it is to be encouraged. If every criminal charge were subjected to a full-scale trial, the States and the Federal Government would need to multiply by many times the number of judges and court facilities. (*Santobello v. N.Y.* 1971, 261)

The Court also made it clear that when prosecutors make promises during plea bargaining, they have to keep them (*Santobello v. N.Y.* 1971). According to Chief Justice Burger, "when a plea rests in any significant degree on a promise or agreement of the prosecutor, so that it can be said to part of the inducement . . . , such promise must be fulfilled" (262). (See the In Focus box "'Guilty but Not Guilty Because I'm Innocent': A Voluntary Plea?")

Constitutionally, defendants give up several fundamental rights when they plead guilty, including:

1. The right against self-incrimination (Amendment V)
2. The right to trial by jury (Amendment VI)
3. The right to confront the witnesses against them (Amendment VI)

The Court also recognized the huge constitutional significance of pleading guilty. According to Justice William O. Douglas:

> However important plea bargaining may be in the administration of criminal justice, . . . a guilty plea is a serious and sobering occasion inasmuch as it constitutes a waiver of the fundamental rights to a jury trial, to confront one's accusers, to present witnesses in one's defense, to remain silent, and to be convicted by proof beyond all reasonable doubt. . . . (*Santobello v. N.Y.* 1971, 264)

Because of their great constitutional significance, we can give up (waive) these rights only if we make the waiver:

1. *Knowingly.* We know what our rights are and know we're giving them up.
2. *Voluntarily.* We give up the rights of our own free will.

To make sure these conditions are met, judges have to "address the defendant personally in open court" (colloquy) to make sure they've knowingly and voluntarily waived their rights (*Boykin v. Alabama* 1969; *Federal Rules of Criminal Procedure* 2002, Rule 11). To satisfy the knowingly requirement federal judges (and most state judges) have to make sure defendants understand:

"Guilty but Not Guilty Because I'm Innocent": A Voluntary Plea?

Henry Alford was indicted for first-degree murder, a capital offense under North Carolina law. The court appointed an attorney to represent him, and this attorney questioned all but one of Alford's witnesses who said they'd back up his claim of innocence. Instead, they gave statements that strongly indicated his guilt. Faced with strong evidence of guilt and no substantial evidentiary support for the claim of innocence, Alford's attorney recommended that he plead guilty but left the ultimate decision to Alford. The prosecutor agreed to accept a plea of guilty to a charge of second-degree murder; Alford pleaded guilty to the reduced charge.

The North Carolina murder statute of the time operated under this penalty scheme:

1. *Death.* Conviction by jury for first-degree murder.
2. *Life in prison.* Pleading guilty to first-degree murder.
3. *Two to 30 years in prison.* Conviction for second-degree murder.

Before the plea was accepted finally by the trial court, the court heard the sworn testimony of a police officer who summarized the State's case. Two other witnesses besides Alford were also heard. Although there was no eyewitness to the crime, the testimony indicated that shortly before the killing Alford took his gun from his house, stated his intention to kill the victim, and returned home with the declaration that he had carried out the killing.

After the summary presentation of the State's case, Alford took the stand and testified he hadn't committed the murder but was pleading guilty because he faced the threat of the death penalty if he didn't. In response to his lawyer's questions, he acknowledged his lawyer had explained the difference between second- and first-degree murder and of his rights in case he chose to go to trial.

The trial court then asked Alford if, in light of his denial of guilt, he still wanted to plead guilty to second-degree murder and Alford answered, "Yes, sir. I plead guilty on [because of]...the circumstances that he [Alford's attorney] told me." After getting information about Alford's prior criminal record (a long one), the trial court sentenced him to thirty years' imprisonment, the maximum penalty for second-degree murder.

Alford claimed his plea of guilty was the "product of fear and coercion." A divided panel of the U.S. Fourth Circuit Court of Appeals agreed. It reversed his conviction because the North Carolina statute encouraged defendants to waive constitutional rights by the promise of no more than life imprisonment if a guilty plea was offered and accepted. The Court of Appeals then ruled that

1. The charge and the punishment for the crime they're pleading guilty to
2. They have a right to a lawyer
3. They have a right to plead not guilty, the right to a jury trial, the right to a lawyer at the trial, the right to confront and cross-examine witnesses, and the right against self-incrimination
4. Once the court accepts the guilty plea, there will be no trial because the defendant has given up that right

To meet the voluntariness requirement, judges have to satisfy themselves by "addressing the defendant personally in open court" that the plea isn't the result of threats, force, or promises (except of course for those in the plea bargain). Before finally accepting the guilty plea, judges also have to make sure there's a "factual basis" (some evidence in addition to the plea itself) that defendants are really guilty.

The Plea-Bargaining Debate

For more than a generation, plea bargaining has generated fierce debate. Supporters make three main arguments. First, many supporters accept the caseload pressure explanation, even though most of the empirical research casts doubt on it (see "Heavy Caseloads"). Second, plea bargaining is constitutional (see the last section) as long as both parties voluntarily agree to it (which they most often do because it's to the benefit of everyone involved). Third, it's inevitable; it exists (and has existed) pretty much in its present form since the 1850s, and in all kinds of courts with all levels of caseloads and all kinds of local legal cultures.

Plea Bargaining: Information on the effectiveness of plea bargaining from the Public Broadcasting Service. To reach this site go to "Web Links" on your Samaha CJ7 website: http://cj.wadsworth.com/samaha_cj7e.

Alford's guilty plea was involuntary because its principal motivation was fear of the death penalty.

U.S. SUPREME COURT

After Alford's plea of guilty was offered and the State's case was placed before the judge, Alford denied that he had committed the murder but reaffirmed his desire to plead guilty to avoid a possible death sentence and to limit the penalty to the thirty-year maximum provided for second-degree murder. Ordinarily, a judgment of conviction resting on a plea of guilty is justified by the defendant's admission that he committed the crime charged against him and his consent that judgment be entered without a trial of any kind. The plea usually includes both elements even though there is no separate, express admission by the defendant that he committed the particular acts claimed to constitute the crime charged in the indictment. Here Alford entered his plea but accompanied it with the statement that he had not shot the victim.

State and lower federal courts are divided on whether a guilty plea can be accepted when it is accompanied by protestations of innocence and hence contains only a waiver of trial but no admission of guilt. Some courts, giving expression to the principle that "our law only authorizes a conviction where guilt is shown," require that trial judges reject such pleas. But others have concluded that they should not "force any defense on a defendant in a criminal case," particularly when advancement of the defense might "end in disaster...." They have argued that, since "guilt, or the degree of guilt, is at times uncertain and elusive," "an accused, though believing in or entertaining doubts respecting his innocence, might reasonably conclude a jury would be convinced of his guilt and that he would fare better in the sentence by pleading guilty...." As one state court observed nearly a century ago, "reasons other than the fact that he is guilty may induce a defendant to so plead and he must be permitted to judge for himself in this respect."

Alford now argues in effect that the State should not have allowed him this choice but should have insisted on proving him guilty of murder in the first degree. The States in their wisdom may take this course by statute or otherwise and may prohibit the practice of accepting pleas to lesser included offenses under any circumstances. But this is not the mandate of the Fourteenth Amendment and the Bill of Rights. The prohibitions against involuntary or unintelligent pleas should not be relaxed, but neither should an exercise in arid logic render those constitutional guarantees counterproductive and put in jeopardy the very human values they were meant to preserve.

While most pleas of guilty consist of both a waiver of trial and an express admission of guilt, the latter element is not a constitutional requisite to the imposition of criminal penalty. An individual accused of a crime may voluntarily, knowingly, and understandingly consent to the imposition of a prison sentence even if he is unwilling or unable to admit his participation in the acts constituting the crime.

Source: North Carolina v. Alford, 400 U.S. 25 (1970).

Why then, do critics disapprove of plea bargaining? The list of objections is long; here are a few (Hessick and Saujani 2002, 189):

1. Guilty defendants get lighter sentences than they deserve.
2. Innocent defendants get punished for crimes they didn't commit.
3. Defendants are coerced into giving up their constitutional rights against self-incrimination and unreasonable searches and seizures, effective assistance of a lawyer, the presumption of innocence, and a jury trial.
4. Judges don't protect defendants from unfair, pressured guilty pleas, and they join in the pressure by threatening defendants with harsher punishment if they go to trial.

Most (but not all) of the critics work *outside* the criminal justice system. Most supporters are *insiders* (the courtroom workgroup) (Feeley 1979, Chapter 8; Hessick and Saujani 2002). According to Scott and Stuntz (1992, 1909–1910):

> There is something puzzling about the polarity of contemporary reactions to this practice. Most legal scholars oppose plea bargaining, finding it both inefficient and unjust. Nevertheless, most participants in the plea bargaining process, including (perhaps especially) the courts, seem remarkably untroubled by it.

The reasons for the insiders' support for plea bargaining are probably the strong incentives to negotiate rather than fight. Prosecutors can handle more cases; conviction rates go up; criminals are removed from the street faster; and public confidence increases (Hessick and Saujani 2002, 191–192). Defense lawyers benefit, too. One major incentive is that getting along with prosecutors and judges in the courtroom workgroup is crucial to getting the best deal for their clients; it also makes their own lives easier by relieving some of the pressure from prosecutors and judges to keep the case processing moving (Hessick and Saujani 2002, 210). Judges benefit by keeping their dockets from backing up with cases in time-consuming trials.

Admittedly, these incentives apply mainly to lesser offenses, but these cases make up most of the courts' business, not the tiny minority of violent crimes, where of course the stakes for all members of the workgroup and the defendants are higher, and where more cases go to trial. Criminal law professor George P. Fletcher (1995) sums up the attitude in his interesting book *With Justice for Some:*

> Though roughly 90% of all cases are disposed of consensually without trial, there is something unseemly about the prosecution's trading a lower charge in return for the defendant's cooperating and waiving his right to trial. The very idea that the authorities cut special deals with particular defendants offends the rule of law. Many legal systems on the Continent, Germany most strongly, have long rejected this kind of discretionary justice.... Germans refer to American-style discretionary justice as the ... principle of expediency as opposed to the ... principle of legality, which demands prosecution according to the extent of the perceived legal violation. Even-handed justice under the law should mean that everyone receives the same treatment: no leniency for those who promise something in return. (191)

The public agrees with Professor Fletcher. (So do most of my students. Every year when we discuss the pros and cons of plea bargaining, they agree with Professor Fletcher.) Do you? See if your position changes after you read the next sections and again after you read this chapter's Make Your Decision.

The heart of the debate over plea bargaining boils down to two questions:

1. Do *innocent* defendants get punishments they don't deserve?
2. Do *guilty* defendants escape the punishment they deserve?

All criminal defendants (guilty or not) have to decide whether to plead guilty or go to trial. The overwhelming motive behind the choice (for most defendants) is getting the least punishment. So the choice is about weighing the risks. Defendants have to balance the sentence they expect will follow conviction in a trial (discounted by the chance of acquittal) against the sentence they expect to get in exchange for a guilty plea. The less the expected sentence in exchange for the guilty plea is, the more attractive pleading guilty becomes.

We'll look at this issue of whether plea bargaining punishes the innocent and is too lenient with the guilty. We'll also examine pretrial settlement conferences, in which parties traditionally excluded from negotiations have an opportunity to observe; administrative rule making; and whether plea bargaining should be banned.

Punishing Innocent Defendants Practically speaking, when innocent defendants plead guilty, they're trading their chance of being acquitted at trial and getting no punishment in exchange for getting less punishment than they'll get if they're convicted (Church 1979, 513–514). (Kind of like a bird in the hand is worth two in the bush.) And we're not just talking about the punishment of the sentence itself. Trials are expensive and psychologically stressful, especially for innocent defendants with no experience in the criminal justice system. To borrow Malcolm Feeley's (1979) phrase, "the process is the punishment."

The higher the risk of conviction, the greater is the stress. So the incentive for defendants and the prosecution is to settle for a more comfortable resolution whereby the

> benefits of success at trial are discounted by the possibility of failure.... If the sole benefit a defendant expects from trial is the chance for acquittal, it is difficult to argue that the state somehow burdens the right to trial merely by posing an alternative that may be more attractive. (Church 1979, 514)

The right to trial isn't the only right that innocent defendants who plead guilty give up. Some—for example, the right against self-incrimination and to cross-examine witnesses and the presumption of innocence—are intended especially to protect innocent defendants. According to the prestigious U.S. National Advisory Commission (1973):

> The plea negotiation system creates a significant danger to the innocent. Many of the rights it discourages are rights designed to prevent the conviction of innocent defendants. To the extent these rights are rendered nonoperative by the plea negotiation system, innocent defendants are endangered. (48)

But these rights are taken into account during plea negotiation. Almost every study of plea bargaining proves that the strength of the case against defendants is high on the list of decision-making criteria (Church 1979, 515). So if a confession or other evidence is likely to be thrown out at trial, the bargain reflects that likelihood.

The biggest problem with the argument that plea bargaining punishes the innocent defendant is the assumption that innocent defendants are *always* acquitted at trial. That's not true. Witness the recurring stories about prisoners released because DNA evidence proved their innocence. If innocent defendants didn't risk conviction, they wouldn't negotiate in the first place (Church 1979, 516).

Punishing Guilty Defendants Less Than They Deserve The critics of plea bargaining argue that guilty defendants who plead guilty get less punishment than they deserve because prosecutors have to give them something in exchange for their guilty plea. On the surface, this is a convincing argument. You've already learned that defendants found guilty at trial get longer sentences than defendants who plead guilty (Figure 10.2).

You also know that by the time cases get to the plea-bargaining stage, they've survived three screenings (by the police after arrest, by the prosecutor before the charge, and by the grand jury or court after the charge). By that time, most defendants left in the system are guilty of *something* (even though it's not exactly the crime they're charged with).

Nevertheless, going to trial always risks that some guilty defendants will be acquitted. Judges might rule against the admissibility of evidence; witnesses might not show up or if they do, they might not be persuasive; defense lawyers might be talented advocates, and juries are sometimes unpredictable. Prosecutors with this risk of guilty defendants "walking" in mind might reasonably conclude that the best way to protect the public is choosing the *certainty* of *some* punishment over the *chance* of *none*. (It's the bird in the hand again, or half a loaf is better than none.)

Viewed in this light, the prosecutor isn't giving the defendant a concession; defendants are exchanging their chance of "walking" for a punishment less severe than they might get by going to trial. They're "exchanging the possibility of total victory for the certainty of avoiding total defeat" (Church 1979, 518).

Because of our commitment to the position of the great eighteenth-century English scholar of the law, William Blackstone, that "it is better that ten guilty men go free than that one innocent man be convicted," it's reasonable to assume (although never empirically proven) that more guilty defendants "walk" than innocent defendants get convicted. That probability led the supporter of plea bargaining Thomas W. Church to conclude:

> If we assume that the trial system will acquit a predictable number of factually guilty defendants..., the public policy question is not whether defendants who plead guilty receive sentences lighter than the optimum.... Rather, we must ask whether it is necessarily irrational... to allow procedures in which (1) proportionately more criminal defendants are convicted than would be if all cases went to trial, but (2) the sentences imposed are less severe. (518–519)

Of course no one believes plea bargaining is perfect. Thomas Church (1979, 519) recognizes that judges and prosecutors can (and *do*) "punish" defendants who refuse to plead guilty; that lawyers aren't always competent to assess risks and advise their clients; and that lack of resources in courts relying heavily on plea bargaining are "serious problems." Church recommends four solutions to these problems:

1. Cases should go to trial based on legitimate criteria, *not* to punish defendants for not pleading guilty.
2. Every defendant should be represented by effective lawyers throughout plea negotiations.
3. All information and evidence relevant to the trial outcome should be made available to both prosecution and defense lawyers.
4. Both the prosecution and the defense should have enough resources to take cases to trial. (520–521)

Pretrial Settlement Conferences Plea bargaining shuts out people with a vital interest in the case—victims, defendants, police officers, and sometimes judges—from the decision making. Pretrial settlement conferences try to make up for this important shortcoming. Dade County, Florida, set up an experiment with pretrial settlement conferences to restructure plea bargaining (Kerstetter and Heinz 1979). The Dade County pretrial settlement conferences took place in judges' chambers. Judges wore business suits instead of the forbidding black robes. Participants sat around the room or gathered about a table in an atmosphere more like a conference than a court proceeding.

Conference sessions were brief—from 10 to 25 minutes long. Topics included the seriousness of the case, the criminal history of the defendants, recommendations for punishment, and, less frequently, the personal backgrounds and circumstances of victims and defendants. Because most conferences generally lasted about 10 minutes, they only covered the topics superficially. Judges did most of the talking. In 40 percent of the cases, prosecutors didn't say anything about the facts of the case, and in over half the cases, prosecutors didn't say anything about defendants' prior records. Defense lawyers did discuss defendants' criminal history—usually to clear up misunderstandings—and defendants' personal characteristics in more than one-third of the cases. Police officers contributed facts relating to the crime in about 70 percent of the cases and added information about defendants' backgrounds in more than half the cases.

Most victims didn't come to the conference—two-thirds stayed away. Most who came were passive. Occasionally, they commented on the facts but practically never expressed views about disposition, except occasionally to approve what judges and lawyers recommended. Fear that victims would demand maximum sentences didn't materialize.

Two-thirds of the defendants came but, like victims, said little. If they said anything, it was usually about either the facts of the case or their background. They hardly ever mentioned recommended sentences.

The conferences didn't affect decision making. Before and after the experiment, the rate of cases going to trial, the sentences offenders got, and the time and expense of processing cases all stayed the same. However, the conferences did improve the attitudes of victims and police officers toward plea bargaining and the criminal justice system. Over half said they understood and approved of plea bargaining after they attended the conferences. Still, presettlement conferences clearly aren't a cure for everything that ails plea bargaining.

Administrative Rule Making Some experts have recommended reforming plea bargaining by subjecting it to written guidelines established by those who participate in it. Although not a widespread practice, increasingly, formal administrative rules are used as a device to control discretion in the bargaining process. The American Bar Association's *Standards Relating to Pleas of Guilty* (1968) includes rules for prosecutors, defense attorneys, and judges. The standards permit prosecutors to bargain over charges and sentence recommendations. They require defendants' approval to all plea bargains, and demand that defense counsel clearly outline to defendants all the alternatives available in the case. Although they prohibit judges from participating in plea bargaining, they allow prosecutors and defense counsel to submit written agreements to judges prior to guilty pleas. If judges initially accept agreements but later reject them, defendants can change their pleas.

Ban on Plea Bargaining Despite widespread commitment to plea bargaining inside the criminal justice system, strong public, and some professional insider, opposition has led to a few attempts to abolish it. In 1973, a distinguished panel appointed by President Richard Nixon called for a total ban on plea bargaining by 1978 (National Advisory Commission on Criminal Justice Standards and Goals 1973, 3.1). Alaska Attorney General Avrum Gross answered the call in 1975. A 1980 follow-up study to determine the effect found the ban had mixed results (Rubenstein, Clarke, and Wright 1980, 219–243; Rubenstein and Wright, 1979). Courts in Alaska didn't collapse under a crush of criminal trials. In fact, decision making actually speeded up after the ban. Why? Defendants continued to plead guilty at about the same rate, giving lawyers more time to prepare for cases that were going to trial.

It's no surprise that the ban wasn't a cure-all. The evils once blamed on plea bargaining were still there. Defendants' incomes still affected decision making. Defendants who went to trial still got stiffer punishments than those who pleaded guilty. Race, income, and employment status still infected sentencing decisions. The ban also took away some needed flexibility in charging and sentencing. For example, the ban stopped the practice of sentencing "clean kids" (first-time, nonviolent property offenses) to probation instead of prison. Professors Franklin Zimring and Richard Frase (1980) give a few more examples: "a shaky prosecution witness, a faulty police investigation, or an attractive defendant may provide irresistible inducements to bargain, and make negotiated settlements seem by far the most sensible recourse" (684).

A second follow-up in 1991 by Teresa Carns (1991) also found mixed results. The Alaska courts still haven't broken down under the ban. The ban had definitely improved prosecutors' charging decisions. Tighter screening standards had led to a "dramatic increase in the number of cases not accepted for prosecution." On the other hand, despite the absolute formal ban on bargaining and an initial compliance with the ban, charge bargaining was routinely practiced.

The finding that banning plea bargaining didn't break down the court blew a hole in the courtroom workgroup's cherished caseload hypothesis. According to the caseload hypothesis, the pressure to dispose of large numbers of criminal cases requires plea bargaining to keep the courts from breaking down. But hold on a minute; the controversy's not over. An evaluation of an experimental ban on plea bargaining in El Paso, Texas, supports (modestly) the caseload hypothesis. Malcolm D. Holmes, Howard C. Daudistel, and William A. Taggart (1992)—relying on annual numbers of felony cases pending at the beginning of each year, the number of cases added each year, jury trial dispositions each year, and convictions each year—found that although a majority of defendants still pleaded guilty, the number of jury trials increased, the rate of dispositions decreased, and the number of convictions stayed the same. The bottom line: Even a small increase in the number of trials slows down decision making. This chapter's Make Your Decision presents the arguments of one former defense lawyer and prosecutor (now a professor of criminal justice) for banning plea bargaining.

CONCEPT | BUILDER

Visit http://cj.wadsworth.com/ samaha_cj7e for an interactive exploration of the issues surrounding **plea bargains.**

▶ DECISION POINT ◀

Abolish plea bargaining?

Click on this Decision Point at http://cj.wadsworth.com/samaha_ cj7e to explore the issue.

THE IMPROPRIETY OF PLEA AGREEMENTS: A TALE OF TWO COUNTIES

Although there is a substantial literature on plea bargaining, little of it originates from the vantage point of someone who knows the system from the inside. Plea bargaining, by its very nature, is a closed-door affair that is not readily amenable to observation by outsiders. I bring to this discussion a perspective based on experience with the system: I worked...as a "professional plea bargainer."...I served as a full-time assistant public defender in..."Washington County" from April 1986 to July 1989 [117]....Washington County is a suburban county of a very large city....[It] has a population of nearly 350,000 people....

In this essay, I describe the role of plea bargains in the practice of criminal justice....My theme is that excessive use of plea bargains is both undesirable and unnecessary....Virtually all defendants are coerced into accepting negotiated sentences in exchange for guilty pleas.

As with all case studies, my findings may be difficult to generalize, and some may be unique to the counties involved. Nevertheless, I believe they can provide some insights about practice elsewhere.

CASELOADS, WORK AVOIDANCE, AND COERCION

...We courthouse regulars deluded ourselves and others into believing the popular wisdom that the system would disintegrate were plea bargaining to be eliminated [118]. The simple fact was that the evidence against most defendants was overwhelming, and many defendants, realizing this, probably would have pled guilty eventually with or without a bargain. To go to trial when the evidence is overwhelming would invite public humiliation. But more important, it would indicate an obvious lack of remorse to the judge, who presides not only at the trial but at the sentencing as well. Defendants who had little hope of winning at trial generally recognized that trials were not in their best interests and correctly guessed that judges would usually reward a plea of guilty (even one entered without a bargain) with a greatly reduced sentence.

When I was a public defender, most of my clients who were offered awful bargains by the prosecutor eventually entered open pleas of guilty before a judge (that is, pleading guilty without any bargain) rather than bring their "dead-bang loser" cases to trial. This strategy was not as risky as it might appear, since judges almost never punished defendants for entering open pleas of guilty by rendering sentences stiffer than those the prosecutor had been willing to live with. Indeed, defendants often got some further reduction for having shown a reasonable attitude by avoiding trial with a hopeless case.

...Even those few clients in Washington County who never would have pled guilty without a guaranteed concession of some sort would not have caused the system to break down had they been refused a plea bargain and been brought to trial. True, the public defender caseloads were sufficiently large that even these few cases (perhaps 15% or 20%) would seem "on paper" to be difficult to dispose of by trials. I believe, however, that handling the additional trials would not have been as difficult as it might appear to an outside observer.

We public defenders had a gift for seeming much busier than we really were. Defense attorneys (and prosecutors also) constantly requested and received continuances for cases because of minor problems—witness on vacation, more time needed to work out a deal, an open bed needed at some rehabilitation facility, and so on—delaying the case for weeks. But the case would remain on one's list of open cases, even though it required little or no further work. The more pending cases one had, the fewer new cases one would be assigned. Public defenders thus had an incentive to inflate their caseloads, giving the appearance of a burden much more onerous than it really was and that they were much too bogged down juggling the heavy load to do any significant number of trials.

To avoid work, attorneys often exaggerated their official caseloads in other ways. I recall a crisis during which

▲ Singer Courtney Love escaped jail time by pleading guilty to possession of a forged prescription and the drug oxycodone found in her home. She was sentenced to 18 months probation and ordered to continue with a drug rehabilitation program. According to her lawyer, Love had "turned her life around" and was now "clean and sober."

© Nick Ut/Pool/Getty Images

I had to go into another attorney's office to seek a file needed immediately in court. While flipping through his files, I noted that fully a third of his "open cases" had in fact already undergone final dispositions—some as long as six months earlier—and should have been "closed out" (taken off his list of open cases). During that same search, I also had to go into another attorney's office, and while flipping through his files, I observed an identical pattern. My secretary told me that nearly everyone carried open cases after they had been closed, and that I was just creating more work both for myself and for her by promptly closing out cases instead of "hanging onto them for awhile."

At times, the attorneys in my office worked hard—but only during trial terms, which were scheduled for roughly two weeks out of every six. Between trial terms we had plenty of time that could have been used to prepare cases for trial if we had wanted to. Instead, most of us chose instead to take things "slow and easy." In fact, we did about 80% of our work during the third of the time that was reserved on the judicial calendar for criminal trials. Attorneys often spent the periods between trial terms on private law work, golfing, long lunches, or just relaxing.

Much of the work done between trial terms was "brain-dead" work that any paralegal could have helped us do (drafting routine discovery motions or bills of particulars, assisting attorneys in the screening of files, etc.). With a very small investment, paralegals could have been hired to help us do this work, thus freeing up additional time for trial preparation....

The fact that judges were often lazy and wished to avoid trials initially greatly surprised me, especially when I saw courtroom after courtroom sitting idle during criminal trial terms. If asked why plea bargaining was necessary, most judges and attorneys would tell you that the system would break down if defendants started insisting on trials. Yet, during criminal trial weeks, judges spent most of their time in chambers while their courtrooms sat empty.

In some courtrooms, attorneys who tried occasionally to bring a case to trial would be punished for doing so.... After going for more than a year without a single criminal trial,...[one] judge encountered a defendant who refused to be intimidated and steadfastly insisted on a trial. The defendant lost his case, and when the smoke had cleared, he received a 30-year sentence, one so harsh (though perfectly legal) for the crimes committed that attorneys reacted with stunned disbelief on hearing about it. It was the talk of the courthouse for days. Even officials from other counties heard about it. That was the last time that any defense attorney dared to have a trial before that judge for a long, long time.

...My first major felony trial was assigned to another judge's courtroom. This judge wanted me to "request" a defense continuance so that the trial would be postponed so he would not miss any of his music lessons. I refused, since to continue the case (in which I believed there was reasonable doubt about my client's guilt) would result in my client waiting for nearly two additional months in jail for his day in court. The judge angrily "allowed" my client to have his jury trial, but was so openly hostile to the defendant and to me throughout the trial that the court stenographer began to cry because of his outbursts [121]....

Lawyers and judges weren't the only ones who sought to avoid work by plea bargaining more cases than they needed to. Police officers expressed displeasure at having to come to court to testify at trials. Officers seemed to take little interest in their cases once they sent them to the district attorney's office. When I first became a criminal lawyer, I thought prosecutors with whom I would deal would be getting pressure from police officers not to work out deals. I was surprised to learn...that the opposite was generally true. Officers usually had no interest in the cases that were "closed by arrest," and didn't like coming to court (often during times other than their official shifts) to testify.

No discussion of public defenders' motivations would be complete without an analysis of alienation. Rather than seeing their jobs as a calling, most public defenders in my office, like many other American workers, simply viewed their job as work and sought to accomplish their assigned tasks with as little pain and as much dignity as possible. Nearly all members of my office saw their positions as "doing time" before moving on to bigger and better things.

Part of "doing time" was having to put up with the constant stress and abuse heaped on us by ill-tempered and antisocial clients, whose sole audience for their angry outbursts against "the system" was their public defenders, whom they often considered to be incompetent, hired cronies of the state.

One such client was Joseph Miller, a violent, career criminal who had been arrested repeatedly for severely assaulting people for no apparent reason. Miller hated human beings in general, and public defenders in particular, because they apparently could not keep him from being locked up time and time again.... Soon after his arrest, Miller wrote my office a letter stating that he didn't want any of us "motherfucking pieces of shit" to represent him.... He also threatened physical harm to various members of my office. These threats caused us some concern, since we knew Miller was so violent that he once had tried to choke to death a state highway patrol officer....

Plea bargaining unfortunately plays right into the hands of alienated public defenders because it legitimizes their work avoidance. It makes cases "go away," taking with them some of the stress, work, combat, and (very important) the client—whose "companionship" one often wishes to minimize and whose guilt one often believes (correctly or incorrectly) to be so obvious. (Ironically, as stressful as the prolonged company of some defendants can be, trials are often not as stressful as "selling" plea bargains to reluctant clients.)...

In sum, it has been my experience that judges, lawyers, and even police officers often love plea bargaining. They love it not because it prevents the breakdown of the criminal justice system but because it helps them avoid work and stress.

WORKGROUP PATHOLOGIES

Individual laziness and coercive tendencies on the part of certain courthouse officials are cause for grave concern, but what is truly worrisome is that these individual traits can so easily turn into workgroup norms.... Prosecutors and defense counsel got to know each other quite well, saw each other frequently, and developed bonds of mutual loyalty. Attorneys and judges who worked together also developed close relationships [123]. Under these circumstances, it is naïve to think that a public defender or a private attorney would be an aggressive adversary on behalf of a nonpaying or poorly paying client. The price of such a strategy—a professional life of conflict and unpopularity—was simply too high to make it worthwhile. Defense attorneys universally collected their fees up front, public defenders were paid a set salary, and salaried prosecutors and judges all got paid no differently whether a case was settled in a 60-second negotiation or disposed of by a trial.... Defense attorneys all knew that if they brought too many cases to trial, they would be seen as either unreasonable and worthy of professional ostracism or as a fool who was too weak to achieve "client control."

Many attorneys I knew became masters of the fine art of controlling their clients. Some liked to engage in "chair therapy," in which a client who insists on a trial is made to sit in the hall of the courthouse (or in the courthouse lockup) for days on end during courthouse trial terms, waiting for his day in court, until he accepts a deal. Some (usually unintentionally) resorted to "good cop/bad cop" routines, in which a resistant defendant is subjected to the screams of his or her attorney, followed by the lawyer's associate, who tries to calmly help the accused to see the light. Usually, however, defense attorneys, aware that incredible trial penalties were attached to the "right" to a jury trial, only needed to tell a defendant of the unconscionable sentences that had been meted out to others who dared to create work for a judge."...

The constitutional interests of an accused are best served when the system works as it was designed: the formal presentation of evidence before a panel of 12 individuals who have absolutely nothing to do with courthouse machinations. In such a contest, attorneys feel that they have no choice but to go all out, and a real clash of competing interests can be presented to unjaded, lay fact-finders. But in much of present-day America, this apparently is not meant to be....

OTHER NEGATIVE ASPECTS OF PLEA BARGAINING

Although quality of defense counsel, in my opinion, never seemed to make much difference during trials (the witnesses, after all, do most of the talking), defense counsel quality seemed to make an enormous difference in plea bargaining. Some attorneys were skillful at power-coercive brinkmanship. Others were completely incompetent at negotiations. One defense attorney in particular was so bad that he would instantly agree to anything that we prosecutors would offer him. We felt so sorry for his clients that some of us adopted a policy of giving him the same sort of offers up front that we eventually would have given a competent negotiator after some discussion. But not all prosecutors were quite so liberal.

This defense attorney, like some others I dealt with as a prosecutor, was a poor negotiator. Although civility and intelligence are usually assets in most professions, plea bargaining tends to exalt the negative traits of human character. Some of the most effective negotiators were arrogant, aggressive, unreasonable, and even ill informed as to the law. These attorney traits formed part of the calculus that prosecutors used in deciding what to offer [131].

Fortunately (for the workgroup) most attorneys chose to be reasonably pleasant, but the more crude, hot tempered, and unreasonable an attorney was, the more many felt obliged to appease him or her with a better deal. Plea bargaining thus made the practice of criminal law one in which legal knowledge and civility took a back seat. One must question a system that exalts such negative characteristics and that places so much importance on defendants' skill or luck in choosing attorneys with the right mix of personality quirks rather than those with knowledge of rights and of the law....

CONVICTING THE INNOCENT

In the final analysis, perhaps the biggest problem I have with plea bargaining is the fear that some innocent people might be pleading guilty.... Even more frightening is what the future might hold for basic rights as plea bargaining continues to become more entrenched as an institution.

If I were innocent of a crime but appeared to be guilty, I would hate to have to decide whether to accept probation for something that I did not do, or else expose myself to the risk of a draconian jail sentence if I went to trial and somehow lost. I would be especially nervous at such a decision if I were black, poor, and had a public defender who, anticipating a quick resolution of the case by a plea bargain, introduced him or herself to me minutes before my time in court and who obviously was ill prepared to go to trial [132]. (One public defender I knew in Washington County was famous for preparing his trials in the elevator on the way to court.)

Criminally accused but innocent people are more likely to plead guilty as sentencing offers made to them become less and less painful relative to what they are threatened with should some jury convict them. Our system is designed to give some protection against the conviction of innocent people by requiring proof beyond a reasonable doubt. But arresting a person only requires "probable cause" (a much lower standard), and accepting a guilty plea generally only requires the low evidentiary standard of "factual basis." Because of plea bargaining, "factual basis" has almost universally replaced "beyond a reasonable doubt" as the standard for obtaining criminal convictions in the United States....

CONCLUSION

In sum, plea bargaining fosters all the wrong values among courthouse actors and almost certainly damages the integrity of our criminal courts. Unless my experiences are atypical, plea bargaining invites work avoidance, coercion, workgroup cooptation, and lack of proper sentencing standards. It exalts hyperaggressiveness and diminishes the importance of legal knowledge. Worst of all, it betrays the truly innocent on the altar of supposed practicality.

QUESTIONS

1. List and summarize Lynch's arguments against plea bargaining.
2. Compare his list with the arguments in favor of plea bargaining in "The Plea-Bargaining Debate" section of this chapter.
3. Consider Robert Weisberg's (1994) reaction to Lynch's article:

   Any essay that rests on admittedly personal and anecdotal evidence will face criticism for those who say their experience is opposite. Some lawyers reading Lynch surely will respond that their caseload pressure is real, not feigned—not all of them in inner cities of the sort Lynch does not describe. Others, I think, will challenge the "work group" idea, arguing that... there is a huge cultural divide between prosecutors and defense attorneys. (146)

4. On the basis of your text, Lynch's arguments, and Weisberg's reaction, should plea bargaining be banned, reformed, or do you need more information to make your decision?

Source: David Lynch, "The Impropriety of Plea Bargaining," *Law and Social Inquiry* 19 (1994).

Chapter Summary

▶ Only 5 out of 100 cases are decided by trial. These are cases where the issue is *guilt*. Criminal trials are powerful symbols for good (crime doesn't pay) or evil (crime *does* pay). Trials also influence the vast majority of cases that don't go to trial.

▶ Juries decide the facts of the case. Jurors try very hard to stick to the facts, but juries are political institutions (and they should be). They represent the community's values; they're the democratic part of court system. The Constitution doesn't require 12-member juries or unanimous verdicts.

▶ Ninety-five out of every 100 cases are decided by straight or negotiated guilty pleas. In these cases the issue isn't *guilt* (the courtroom workgroup already knows the defendants are guilty), it's *punishment*. Defendants plead guilty for several reasons, including wanting to take responsibility for their actions, hoping to get a more lenient sentence, wanting to "get it over with," being encouraged by their lawyers, and experiencing fear and anxiety.

▶ Bargaining criteria include the strength of the case, the seriousness of the offense, the dangerousness of the defendant, and heavy caseloads. According to the U.S. Supreme Court, defendants can give up their constitutional rights to trial by jury and self-incrimination if there's evidence defendants are guilty and defendants give up their rights voluntarily and knowingly.

▶ Plea bargaining generates fierce controversy. Critics (mostly academics and the public) claim guilty defendants get off easy and innocent ones get punished for crimes they didn't commit; the courtroom workgroup pressure defendants to give up their right to trial. Supporters (mostly the courtroom workgroup) claim negotiating is better than fighting; it saves time and money; it provides defendants the appropriate punishment.

▶ Efforts to ban plea bargaining have produced mixed results; less drastic reforms like pretrial settlement conferences and administrative rule making haven't fared well in practice.

Key Terms

liberation hypothesis, p. 329
jury nullification, p. 330
relevant evidence, p. 338
prejudicial evidence, p. 338

hearsay evidence, p. 338
jury instructions, p. 338
straight pleas, p. 339
negotiated pleas, p. 339

factual guilt, p. 344
legal guilt, p. 344
penalties/rewards system, p. 349

Web Resources

Go to http://cj.wadsworth.com/samaha_cj7e for a wealth of online resources related to your book. Take a "pre-test" and "post-test" for each chapter in order to help master the material. Check out the *Web Links* to access the websites mentioned in the text, as well as many others. Explore the *Decision Points* flagged in the margins of the text for additional insights. You can also access recent perspectives by clicking on *CJ in the News* and *Terrorism Update* under *Course Resources.*

ᐯ Search Online with InfoTrac College Edition

For additional information, explore InfoTrac College Edition, your online library. Go to http://cj.wadsworth.com/samaha_cj7e to access InfoTrac College Edition from your book's website. Use the passcode that came with your book. You will find InfoTrac College Edition exercises and a list of key words for further research.

CHAPTER 11

Sentencing

FACT *or* FICTION?

▶ Restorative justice starts with the proposition that crime is a harm to individuals, not to the society.

▶ "Three strikes and you're out" laws don't reduce crime.

▶ Sentencing guidelines focus on both the seriousness of the offenses and the criminal history of the offenders.

▶ There's disparity but not discrimination in sentencing Blacks, Hispanics, and women.

▶ The U.S. Supreme Court has declared that executing juveniles is cruel and unusual punishment.

▶ Public opinion favors life without any chance of parole over capital punishment for murderers.

▶ There's evidence that the death penalty prevents murders.

ATTRACTED, BUT OPPOSED, TO THE DEATH PENALTY

I admit that I am still attracted to a death penalty that would be applied to horrendous crimes, or that would provide absolute certainty that the likes of Henry Brisbon would never again satisfy their cruel appetites.... Like many others who have wrestled with capital punishment, I have changed my mind often, driven back and forth by the errors each position seems to invite. Yet after two years of deliberation, I seem to have finally come to rest. When ... asked whether Illinois should have a death penalty, I voted no.

—SCOTT TUROW (2003)

Every spring and fall, the scarlet-robed royal judges rode to all the county towns of eighteenth-century England to read proclamations, address the local bigwigs, and try all the felons held in the local jails. In the presence of the local bigwigs and surrounded by large crowds, they made their "jail delivery" a great spectacle. Nowhere was royal power more evident than when the judges put on their "black caps of death" to exercise their life and death power by pronouncing sentence on convicted felons (all felonies from murder to stealing were capital offenses). The judges rarely let felons hang. Most of the time, they took full advantage of the spectacle first to strike terror in the convicts and spectators by pronouncing the death sentence and then, at the last minute, to temper justice with mercy by saving repentant convicts from the hangman's noose in a dramatic stay of execution.

> Methinks I see him [recalled one observer in 1785] with a countenance of solemn sorrow, adjusting the cap of judgment on his head.... He addresses ... the consciences of the trembling criminals ... shows them how just and necessary it is, that there should be laws to remove out of society, those, who instead of contributing their honest industry to the public good and welfare of society, have exerted every art that the blackest villainy can suggest, to destroy both....
>
> He then vindicates both the mercy, as well as the severity of the law, in making such examples, as shall not only protect the innocent from outrage and violence, but also deter others from bringing themselves to the same ignominious end. He acquaints them with the certainty of speedy death and consequently with the necessity of speedy repentance. And on this theme he may so deliver himself, as not only to melt the wretches at the bar into contrition, but the whole auditory into the deepest concern. Tears express their feelings.... Many of the most thoughtless among them may ... be preserved from thinking lightly of the first steps into vice.... The dreadful sentence is now pronounced. Every heart shakes with terror. (Hay 1975, 17–19)

Sentencing no longer ends with the fanfare of public ceremonies conducted in the center of town with crowds gathered to watch and hear. Nevertheless, the judgment of punishment still fascinates us. Modern judges don't have the power of the eighteenth-century English judges because public demands to "get tough" on crime, reformers' dissatisfaction with judicial discretion, and scholars' research on the ineffectiveness of sentencing practices have produced reform laws limiting judges' sentencing power. Also, the structure of our criminal justice system distributes the power to sentence among legislatures, prosecutors, and judges. Finally, the Eighth Amendment to the U.S. Constitution bans "cruel and unusual punishments"; the denial of life, liberty, or property without due process of law; and the denial of the equal protection of the laws.

Sentencing also affects public policymakers, particularly during times of heightened concern about crime. Since the 1970s, politicians, criminologists, reformers, and the public have subjected sentencing to careful scrutiny. The public has demanded that we "get tough" on violence, illegal drugs, and juvenile crime. And although crime rates have fallen since the late 1990s, they haven't returned to the levels they were before the great crime boom of the 1960s to 1990s (Chapter 2). As a result of these influences, almost all legislatures have enacted some kind of sentencing reform laws. Certain justice *and* flexible mercy are still parts of the practical reality of sentencing in the twenty-first century.

In this chapter, we'll look at the purposes of sentencing, its history, the types of determinate sentencing, the presentence investigation, disparity and discrimination in sentencing, and the death sentence.

The Purposes of Sentencing

Billions of words have been written trying to answer the question: "What's the purpose of criminal punishment?" Or to put it another way, "What's criminal punishment good for?" There's a simple answer. Criminal punishment boils down to four purposes: retribution, prevention, restitution, and restoration. **Retribution** (sometimes called "just deserts") looks *backward* to punish criminals for their completed criminal *conduct* because they deserve it. **Prevention** looks *forward* to change criminals, punishing them to prevent future crimes. There are four kinds of prevention: general deterrence, special deterrence, incapacitation, and rehabilitation. **Restitution** looks backward to make offenders pay back victims for property losses. **Restoration** looks backward and forward to heal victims (not just pay them back in money what they lost) and restore relationships. Let's look at these four purposes of criminal punishment and their components.

retribution punishes criminals for past crimes because they deserve it

prevention punishes criminals to deter future crimes

restitution offenders pay back victims in money for losses they caused

restoration aims to heal victims and restore relationships

Retribution

Striking out to hurt what hurts us (retribution) is a natural impulse. It's why we kick the rock we stubbed our toe on. The Old Testament sums up the idea this way: "life for life, fracture for fracture, eye for eye, tooth for tooth" (Holy Bible 2000, Leviticus 24). The words of the famed Victorian judge and historian of the criminal law, Sir James F. Stephen, written in 1883, don't sound at all strange today:

> The criminal law...proceeds upon the principle that it is morally right to hate criminals... I think it highly desirable that criminals should be hated, that the punishments inflicted upon them should be so contrived as to give expression to that hatred, and to justify it so far as the public provision of means for expressing and gratifying a healthy natural sentiment can justify and encourage it (81–82).

From the Old Testament's philosophy of taking an eye for an eye, to the nineteenth-century Englishman's claim that it's right to hate and hurt criminals, to the modern idea of "three strikes and you're out" and "lock 'em up and throw away the key," the desire for retribution has run strong and deep in religion, in criminal justice, and in society. Retributionists see this long tradition as proof of its worth; tenacity validates it.

The long and strong life of retribution lies mainly in its dependence on two appealing ideas: culpability and free will. **Culpability** means offenders are responsible for their actions and have to suffer the consequences if they act irresponsibly. Simply put, we can't punish those we can't blame; and, we can't blame those who aren't responsible. But justice demands that we *do* punish the blameworthy. Retribution assumes we all have free will. Applied to the idea of culpability, offenders are free to choose between committing and not committing crimes. Because offenders have this choice, society can blame them for making

culpability assumes offenders are responsible for their actions and have to suffer the consequences if they act irresponsibly

the wrong choice. Retribution is two-edged: It benefits society by retaliation and it benefits criminals by "paying their debt to society." In the words of Andrew von Hirsch, in his influential book *Doing Justice* (1976):

> We should punish criminals simply for the crime committed. We should not do it either to reform them, or to deter them, or to deter others. In other words, punishment should fit the crime already committed, not the criminal—nor the crimes either the criminal or others might commit in the future.

There are three problems with retribution. First, it's difficult to translate abstract justice into specific penalties. What are a rapist's just deserts? Is castration justice? How many years in prison is a robbery worth? How much offender suffering will repay the pain of a disfigured assault victim? Critics of retribution answer, "We can't! And we shouldn't even try." Why? The answer lies in a second problem: Retributionists can't prove human nature craves revenge (Weihofen 1960, 116–120). Third, and probably the strongest argument against retribution, is that most criminal laws aren't based on moral blameworthiness because they don't require criminal intent (Diamond 1996, 111–131; Chapter 4, "The Elements of Crime").

Prevention

Like retribution, prevention inflicts pain, too, but for a totally different reason. Prevention looks *forward* and inflicts pain to stop criminals and criminal wannabes from committing crimes in the future. There are four types of prevention: special deterrence, general deterrence, incapacitation, and rehabilitation. The idea of prevention by deterrence was born in the eighteenth-century Enlightenment and is based on the English philosopher Jeremy Bentham's philosophy of utility. Utility starts with two assumptions about human nature: (1) people seek pleasure and avoid pain, and (2) they have the free will to choose their own actions (Chapter 3).

In deterrence, the aim of punishment is to inflict just enough pain (or the threat of pain) to make criminals (or wannabes) avoid the pain of committing crimes. **Special deterrence** hopes to teach convicted criminals the lesson that "crime doesn't pay" by inflicting actual pain on them—pain that "costs" more than the pleasure they got from committing the crime—so when they get out of prison, they won't commit more crimes. **General deterrence** "sends a message" to people thinking about committing crimes that "crime doesn't pay." Whether that message gets through depends on three things—the swiftness, the certainty, and the severity of the punishment. According to deterrence theorists and researchers, swiftness and certainty are more important than severity. For example, knowing that you're really going to prison next week for one year—no ifs, ands, or buts—is more effective than *maybe* you'll go to prison for five years starting in the year 2030.

Incapacitation is based on the straightforward idea that criminals can't commit crimes while they're locked up. It's *present* oriented because it's aimed at preventing locked-up criminals from committing crimes they'd be committing if they weren't locked up. It isn't concerned with what they might do in the future when they get out. The ultimate incapacitation is, of course, death. The basic idea of **rehabilitation** is to change criminals into people who "work hard and play by the rules." Rehabilitation inflicts pain but not on purpose—only as a necessary side effect of changing criminals.

In practice, none of these aims is either completely distinct from or in harmony with the others. So punishment in specific cases is usually based on several conflicting aims. For example, a rapist goes to prison to suffer the pain of confinement for its own sake, to send him a message that rape doesn't pay, to incapacitate him so he won't be raping while he's in prison, to send a message

special deterrence teaches convicted criminals that "crime doesn't pay"

general deterrence "sends a message" to people thinking about committing crime that "crime doesn't pay"

incapacitation confines criminals so they can't commit crimes while they're locked up

rehabilitation aims to change criminals into people who "work hard and play by the rules"

to rapist wannabes that if they rape they'll go to prison, and to subject him to sex-offender treatment to rehabilitate him. In Kathleen Daly's (1994) study of sentencing in New Haven, Connecticut's courts, she writes:

> I read the sentencing transcripts many times before I could identify the category (or categories) in which a sentencing justification fell. . . . What I found was that judges combine various punishment theories. For example, the general deterrence aim of punishment—to send a signal to others that crime will not go unpunished—may shade in a desert- or retribution-based rationale. (Daly 1994, 182)

Daly (1994) gives this example of Dorothy who set two fires to her apartment after a fight with her boyfriend. At her sentencing, the judge said:

> This could have been a disastrous . . . incident for the people that lived in the house—undoubtedly something you didn't give a moment's thought to at the time you did this. But how many times do we pick up the paper and read about fires that are started by people motivated like you to retaliate against somebody else for some grievance that result in serious injuries or deaths to people [retribution]. . . . This is the kind of conduct that we have an obligation to try to stop [special and general deterrence]. The only way that we know how to do it is to incarcerate the people that commit offenses like this [incapacitation], and this is the reason you are being incarcerated today: to demonstrate to you [special deterrence] and hopefully to other people who might be inclined to do the same thing [general deterrence] that kind of conduct is not going to be tolerated [retribution]. (184–185)

Like punishments based on retribution, punishments for the purpose of prevention raise difficult questions. Like how much and what kind of pain is a rape worth? Or how much pain exceeds the pleasure of satisfying the urge to rape? Does locking up a rapist really incapacitate him or just shift the pool of his victims? What sex-offender treatments work? And if they work, who do they work for and under what circumstances? These questions, like so many others we've encountered, and will encounter throughout the rest of the book, are difficult and still unresolved.

"National Assessment of Structured Sentencing": An analysis of the effects of structured sentencing from the National Criminal Justice Reference Service. To reach this site go to "Web Links" on your Samaha CJ7 website: http://cj.wadsworth.com/samaha_cj7e.

Restitution and Restorative Justice

Restitution means offenders (almost always property offenders) pay back their victims in money for losses they caused. Restorative justice is more ambitious than simply paying back victims' losses. It starts with the proposition that the basic nature of crime is a harm to individuals (victims, offenders, and their friends and families) and their relationships, a harm that has to be repaired and healed (McCold 2004). (Contrast this view of crime with retribution and prevention, where crime is a violation of the criminal law and all of society is the victim.) Furthermore, according to restorative justice:

> The conflicts arising out of crime are the "property" of those involved. Lawyers in courtrooms steal people's conflicts, taking from the opportunity to resolve those conflicts themselves. (14)

The goal of restorative justice is to heal and repair the damage to individuals and relationships directly involved. It replaces punishment of offenders with efforts to heal the injuries to crime victims, offenders, their families, and others who care about them. Retribution and prevention in the current criminal justice "respond to harm with more harm but restorative justice responds to harm with healing. Only acts of restoration, not further harm, will effectively counterbalance the effects of crime" (McCold 2004, 15).

To accomplish restoration, victims, offenders, their families, and others who care about them have to participate in resolving the conflict. Since the victim and offender "own the conflict," restoration is impossible without their participation. They have to work together (but of course not alone) to satisfy victims' needs and for offenders to realize the consequences of their behavior. According

▶ Restorative justice is based on the humane idea that crime injures not just victims but offenders, families, and friends. This injury has to be healed for everyone concerned. These two dogs visiting an inmate in Clark County Juvenile Justice Center in Vancouver, WA, are part of the center's emphasis on restorative justice, which recognizes the power of injecting more humanity into the criminal justice system.

to Paul McCold (2004), a research criminologist and Research Director at the International Institute for Restorative Practices:

> For restorative justice to be "restorative" it must involve those most directly affected. Every effort must be made to maximize the involvement and exchange of information between the affected parties. Neither the state nor any individual or group appointed by the state can restore people by replacing the primary stakeholders, doing things to them or for them. Restorative justice requires that justice be done with offenders, engaging them in an active and responsive way, and, whenever possible, with victims and others affected by the specific incident. (15)

The History of Sentencing

determinate sentencing legislatures attach specific punishments to crimes

indeterminate sentencing legislatures set only the outer limits of possible penalties, and judges and corrections professionals decide actual sentence lengths

Whether to fit sentences to the crime or tailor them to individual criminals has pestered officials, academics, and (in modern times) the public for more than a thousand years. In **determinate sentencing** (sometimes called fixed sentencing), legislatures focus on the crime and attach specific punishments to it, like a sentence of 25 years to the crime of armed robbery. In **indeterminate sentencing,** legislatures set only the outer limits of possible penalties, like 0 to 25 years for robbery. Corrections officials then tailor the actual time served using specialized programs to suit the individual offenders and release them when they're "corrected."

Both fixed and indeterminate sentencing are essential elements of criminal justice. Fixed sentences point to the desirability of the certainty, predictability, and evenhandedness of formal rules in administering criminal justice. Indeterminate sentencing responds to the need for flexibility, the "play in the joints" of informal discretionary decision making that's essential to fair criminal justice. We can see the tension between fixed and indeterminate sentencing as early as A.D. 700 in the Roman Catholic Church's penitential books, which sometimes laid down penance strictly according to the sin and at other times tailored penance to suit individual sinners (Samaha 1978).

Let's look at the history of sentencing during the periods before 1870, between 1870 and 1970, and after 1970 to the present.

Determinate and Indeterminate Sentencing, Before 1870

In U.S. history, the controversy over fixed and indeterminate sentencing began during the 1630s in the Massachusetts Bay Colony. The governor of the colony, the great Puritan founder John Winthrop, maintained that both fairness and justice demanded wide judicial discretion. Each sentence, he said, should depend on a combination of the facts of the case, the background and character of the defendant, and the general needs of the community. So, Winthrop argued, poor people should pay lower fines than rich people, religious leaders should suffer harsher penalties than laypersons for committing morals offenses, and powerful colonists should receive more severe penalties for breaking the law than weak individuals. How could abuse of this wide discretionary power be avoided? Appoint wise judges whose personal prejudices don't infect their sentencing, Winthrop answered. The Massachusetts Bay Colony legislature wasn't convinced. It passed a fixed sentencing law banning judicial discretion in sentencing (Samaha 1989).

Fixed sentencing was common until the Revolution, when fixed but moderate penalties became the norm. States abolished the death penalty for many offenses. Corporal punishment (whipping), mutilation (cutting off ears and slitting tongues), and shaming (the ducking stool) remained on the books but were never used. By 1850, state laws established fixed prison terms for most felonies. However, early release for "good time" and other devices allowed the use of informal discretionary judgment to alter formally fixed sentences (Rothman 1971). Fixed sentencing remained the norm until the 1870s, when organized voices proclaimed the need for change.

Indeterminate Sentencing, 1870–1970

The modern history of sentencing grew out of dissatisfaction with legislatively fixed harsh prison sentences. A growing band of prison administrators complained that prisons were nothing more than warehouses for the poor, immigrants, and other "undesirables." They also claimed that imprisonment didn't work. Released prisoners soon returned to prison, and crime continued at unacceptably high rates no matter how many offenders were locked up. A high point in the debate about the ineffectiveness of fixed prison sentences was the National Prison Congress, where a large group of prison officials eager for reform gathered in 1870 in Cincinnati. Its "Declaration of Principles" was based on the idea that sentencing shouldn't just punish criminals; it should reform them. How? Get rid of fixed sentences and put indeterminate sentences in their place. A "mere lapse of time" to "pay" for past crimes shouldn't determine sentence length, the Congress proclaimed; "satisfactory proof of reformation" should determine how long to keep criminals in prison (*Transactions of the National Congress* 1971).

According to one conference leader, Zebulon Brockway (1912):

> [A]ll persons in a state, who are convicted of crimes or offenses before a competent court, shall be deemed wards of the state and shall be committed to the custody of the board of guardians, until, in their judgment, they may be returned to society with ordinary safety and in accord with their own highest welfare. (401)

Even before the conference, Brockway, who was superintendent of the Detroit House of Correction, played an instrumental role in the enactment of the nation's first indeterminate sentencing law. A prototype statute appeared in Michigan in 1869. The statute authorized judges to sentence prostitutes to three years in houses of correction but permitted inspectors to terminate such sentences if, in their discretion, a prostitute "reformed" (Twentieth Century Fund 1976, 95).

New York enacted the first indeterminate sentencing law in 1878. It provided that:

> Every sentence to the reformatory of a person convicted of a felony or other crime shall be a general sentence to imprisonment in the New York State reformatory at Elmira and the courts...shall not fix or limit the duration thereof. The term of...imprisonment...shall be terminated by the managers of the reformatory...but...imprisonment shall not exceed the maximum term provided by law for the crime for which the prisoner was convicted and sentenced. (Twentieth Century Fund 1976, 95)

By 1922, all but four states had adopted an indeterminate sentencing law. Indeterminate sentencing laws were based on the confidence that professionals could transform criminals into hardworking individuals who played by the rules. A dedicated core of middle-class reformers accepted the findings (in fact, they were more beliefs than scientific findings) of contemporary social and physical scientists that both basic human "drives" and social "forces" controlled human behavior. According to these "findings," individuals didn't choose their actions; their heredity, physical characteristics, psyche, and environment thrust their behavior on them (Appier 1998, 16–17).

Indeterminate sentences weren't supposed to be "soft on crime"—far from it. According to the rehabilitation experts of the time, criminals were either corrigible or incorrigible. Reform measures could change the corrigibles—namely, first-time offenders under 30. The incorrigibles—over 30, repeat offenders—were hardened criminals beyond hope. What reform measures could change these criminals into hardworking citizens who obeyed the law? Professionals enforced strict rules and daily schedules of hard work, study, exercise, and healthy living habits. Prisoners who didn't comply got harsh punishment, like solitary confinement on a diet of bread and water, and/or whipping, hosing, and other corporal punishments.

Prison officials, parole officers, and reformers believed prisoners and parolees could easily fake reformation. So they made prisoners prove they'd reformed by following prison rules. When prisoners were released from prison it was only conditionally (Chapter 12). Parolees had to clinch the proof their reformation was genuine by keeping a job, living a clean life, and staying out of even minor trouble with the law. Incorrigibles couldn't reform. But that didn't mean incorrigible prisoners could "get away" without working. They had to pay their own way, usually by forced hard labor inside prison because they refused to willingly earn their keep. If force didn't work, well then they should be killed (Samaha n.d.).

According to these tough reformers, judges trained in law weren't qualified to decide who was corrigible and incorrigible or when corrigibles could safely return to society. Only the new professionals—criminologists, physicians, psychiatrists, social workers, corrections officials—had the expertise and judgment to classify, treat, and proclaim which criminals had really turned into hardworking citizens who followed the rules and paid their own way (Lindsey 1925, 16, 96).

In indeterminate sentencing states, prison officials and parole boards had more discretionary power to decide actual sentences than legislatures and judges. But judges could still make discretionary judgments. They could grant probation instead of imprisonment; suspend sentences in favor of community service; or pick confinement times within minimums and maximums prescribed by statutes, like 5 years under a statute that prescribed 0 to 10 years in prison. But parole boards and corrections officers determined the exact date of release and the conditions and length of parole (Chapter 12).

The Return to Determinate Sentencing, 1971–Present

Indeterminate sentencing remained dominant until the 1970s, when several forces combined to bring about a return to fixed sentencing. The country was in the midst of the biggest crime boom in its history (Chapter 2). Prison riots in the late 1960s made rehabilitation look like nothing more than talk and exposed prisons as seething cauldrons of discontent erupting into extreme violence (Chapter 14). Prisoners' rights advocates challenged the broad informal discretionary powers of criminal justice officials. And a band of activist judges demanded that criminal justice officials justify their decisions in writing and empowered defendants to dispute their sentencing.

At the same time, disillusionment with rehabilitation was spreading quickly among professionals and academics. Several statistical and experimental studies strongly suggested poor people and Blacks got harsher sentences than Whites and more affluent Americans. Disillusionment and the troubling statistical studies led to the creation of a distinguished panel of the National Research Council to review sentencing practices. The panel concluded that by the early 1970s, a "remarkable consensus emerged among left and right, law enforcement officials and prisoners groups, reformers and bureaucrats that the indeterminate sentencing era was at its end" (Blumstein, Cohn, Martin, and Tonry 1983, 48–52).

What led to this remarkable consensus? A powerful alliance between civil libertarians and conservatives who agreed that the aim of sentencing is swift and certain punishment. But there the agreement ended. They disagreed over two fundamentals: the length and the kind of sentences. To civil libertarians, determinate sentencing meant short, fixed sentences, with programs to prepare prisoners for playing by the rules and paying their way in life. To conservatives, punishment meant long, fixed uncomfortable sentences (prisons aren't "country clubs"). The public was firmly on the side of the conservatives. Political scientist James Q. Wilson (1983b), in his best-selling book *Thinking about Crime*, pointed to a public that was frustrated and fed up with judges who were "letting too many criminals off with a slap on the wrist."

The conservatives (Wilson 1983b) and the public view of fixed sentencing won. According to the National Council on Crime and Delinquency (1992):

> By 1990, the shift in goals of sentencing was complete. Virtually all new sentencing law was designed to increase the certainty and length of prison sentences to incapacitate the active criminal and deter the rest. (6)

By 1996 the United States was sentencing more people to prison for longer terms than almost any other country in the world.

The Types of Determinate Sentencing

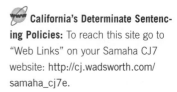 **California's Determinate Sentencing Policies:** To reach this site go to "Web Links" on your Samaha CJ7 website: http://cj.wadsworth.com/ samaha_cj7e.

There are two types of fixed sentences: (1) mandatory minimum sentences, in which convicted offenders have to spend at least some time in prison, and (2) sentencing guidelines, which base sentences on a combination of the severity of the crime and the criminal history of the offender. Let's look more closely at both types.

Mandatory Minimum Sentencing Laws

Under **mandatory minimum sentence laws** offenders have to spend at least some time (the mandatory minimum laid out in the law) in prison. At least as far as the mandatory minimum is required, the laws take away both judges' and corrections officials' discretionary power in sentencing. Judges can't suspend the minimum, and they can't substitute probation for it. Prison and parole authorities can't release offenders until they've served the minimum.

Mandatory penalties have a long history. The Old Testament "an eye for an eye" is a mandatory penalty. The Anglo-Saxon king Alfred prescribed a detailed mandatory penalty code, including such provisions as "If one knocks out another's eye, he shall pay 66 shillings, 6 1/3 pence. If the eye is still in the head, but the injured man can see nothing with it, one-third of the payment shall be withheld."

mandatory minimum sentence laws offenders have to spend at least some time (the mandatory minimum laid out in the law) in prison

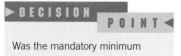
California's Rules of Court:
Rules of the court in cases heard in California's Superior Courts. To reach this site go to "Web Links" on your Samaha CJ7 website: http://cj.wadsworth.com/samaha_cj7e.

Mandatory minimums have had an on-and-off history in the United States (U.S. Sentencing Commission 1991, 14–16). They were used frequently during the 1800s but then fell into disuse from 1900 to 1950. Then fear of crime and illegal drugs became part of the Cold War in the 1950s. (Some members of Congress were convinced there was a Communist plot to get Americans "hooked" on an especially potent "pure Communist heroin" from China, [U.S. Congress 1954, 7].)

In 1956, Congress enacted a mandatory minimum drug law to make sure that offenders who did the drug crime would "do the time"—in this case, 5 years in prison for a first-time heroin sale. According to the House Committee considering the bill:

> [The Committee] therefore recommends an increase in maximum sentences for first as well as subsequent offenses. With respect to the mandatory minimum features of such penalties, and prohibition of suspended sentences or probation, the committee recognizes objections in principle. It feels, however, that, in order to define the gravity of this class of crime and the assured penalty to follow, these features of the law must be regarded as essential elements of the desired deterrents, although some differences of opinion still exist regarding their application to first offenses of certain types. (U.S. Sentencing Commission August 1991, 6)

The statute imposed stiff mandatory minimum sentences for narcotics offenses, requiring judges to pick within a range of penalties. Judges couldn't suspend sentences or put convicted offenders on probation; they had to sentence them to at least 5 years in prison. Offenders weren't eligible for parole if they were convicted under the act. For second offenders, the mandatory minimum was raised to 10 years. The penalty for the sale of narcotics to persons under 18 years of age ranged from a mandatory minimum of 10 years to a maximum of life imprisonment or death (U.S. Sentencing Commission August 1991, 6).

Congress repealed the 1956 law in 1970 (U.S. House of Representatives 1970, 11), because it concluded that increased sentence lengths "had not shown the expected overall reduction in drug law violations." Further, they alienated youths from the general society; hampered the rehabilitation of drug law offenders; infringed on judicial discretion; and reduced the deterrent effect of drug laws. Prosecutors stopped charging offenders because even they believed the laws were too severe (U.S. Sentencing Commission 1991, 6).

The 1970 retreat from mandatory minimum sentences didn't last long. By 1991, 46 states and the federal government had enacted mandatory minimum sentencing laws, mainly aimed at drug and weapons offenses. According to Senator Orrin Hatch:

> The reason why we went to mandatory minimums is because of these soft-on-crime judges...who just will not get tough on crime, get tough especially on pushers of drugs that are killing our youth. And so that's why the mandatory minimums...within which judges have to rule, rather than allowing them to just put people out on probation who otherwise are killing our kids. (*Frontline* 1999)

► **DECISION** **POINT** ◄

Was the mandatory minimum sentence appropriate?

Click on this Decision Point at http://cj.wadsworth.com/samaha_cj7e to explore the issue.

Criminal justice officials told the U.S. Sentencing Commission (1991) that mandatory minimum sentences further five fundamental principles of criminal punishment:

1. *Equality.* Similar offenses receive similar sentences.
2. *Certainty.* Offenders and the public know that offenders will really do the minimum prison time the statute prescribes.
3. *Just deserts.* Violent and drug offenders, habitual criminals, and criminals who use guns to commit crimes deserve mandatory long prison terms.
4. *Deterrence.* Mandatory prison sentences deter crime by sending the strong message that those who "do the crime" really will "do the time."
5. *Incapacitation.* Mandatory prison terms protect public safety by locking up drug dealers and violent armed criminals.

But do mandatory minimum sentences really work? Let's look more closely at this issue. Then we'll examine two types of mandatory minimum sentencing laws: "truth in sentencing" and "three strikes and you're out" laws.

Do Mandatory Minimum Sentence Laws Work? Mandatory minimum sentences are supposed to satisfy three aims of criminal punishment: retribution, incapacitation, and deterrence. They promise that serious crimes will receive severe punishment so violent criminals, criminals who use weapons, and drug offenders can't harm the public if they are in prison. Also, the knowledge that committing mandatory minimum crimes will bring certain, severe punishment will deter criminal wannabes.

Evaluations suggest that mandatory minimum penalties in practice don't live up to these promises. The National Institute of Justice (1982) assessed two mandatory minimum sentence laws, one in New York and one in Massachusetts. In 1973, the New York legislature enacted "the nation's toughest drug law." For example, the possession of two ounces of heroin or the sale of a single ounce carried a minimum 15 to 25 years in prison. A second conviction for the unlawful possession of any "stimulant, hallucinogen, hallucinogenic substance, or LSD," with intent to sell carried a minimum term of 1 to 813 years. Conviction for the possession of one ounce of marijuana carried a 1- to 5-year minimum prison sentence.

The results of the New York drug law were disappointing. Drug offense conviction rates dropped 30 percent. Heroin use following enactment was as widespread as before. Serious property crime—the kind generally believed to be linked to drug use—increased sharply, despite the tough legislation. The law probably did not deter convicted felons from committing further crimes. A rigorous Department of Justice evaluation concluded that "the threat embodied in the words of the law proved to have teeth for relatively few offenders" because "mandatory sentencing laws directly affect only an end product of a long criminal justice process—the convicted offender." The statute also had some serious

Reuters/Corbis

◀ In 1973, New York passed "the nation's toughest drug laws." The Rockefeller Drug Laws require judges to give drug offenders mandatory minimum sentences regardless of their background, character, role in the offense, or threat to society. Furthermore, these laws restrict the ability of judges to divert appropriate offenders into treatment. In April 2004 the New York State Assembly and Senate formed a conference committee to discuss Rockefeller Drug Law reform. Real Reform 2004 is a coalition of advocates, activists, and Rockefeller Drug Law survivors and their families like Veronica Flournoy, shown here with her two kids, hip hop musician Russell Simmons, and former Cabinet Secretary Andrew Cuomo. The group welcomes the conference committee but is committed to making sure serious, meaningful reform is enacted.

side effects. It slowed down the criminal process and worked a real hardship in some cases. One 38-year-old woman with no prior criminal record, for instance, was sentenced to life imprisonment for possessing one ounce of heroin (Walker 1989, 89).

In 1974, Massachusetts enacted the Gun Control Act. The law imposed a mandatory minimum one-year sentence on anyone who failed to comply with the state's long-time requirement that handgun owners license their weapons. The law allowed no chance of reducing the minimum by probation, parole, or judicial manipulation. The National Institute of Justice evaluation showed more positive results from the Massachusetts gun control law than from the New York drug law. Despite widespread predictions that the law wouldn't work, officials didn't evade the law and more persons were imprisoned for violating it. Finally, fewer people carried firearms as a result of the stiff new penalties (Wilson 1983b, Chapters 7–10).

Why these mixed results in Massachusetts and New York? First, the number of gun control cases was very small—the Massachusetts law increased the overall caseload by only about seventy cases a year, whereas the New York drug act covered thousands of cases. Second, the Massachusetts law enjoyed much more support than the New York law. Mandatory minimum sentences, it seems from these results, depend for their effectiveness on the conditions in which they are implemented.

Research on Michigan's Felony Firearm Statute further complicates matters. Michigan's gun law mandated an additional two-year minimum sentence for carrying a gun during the commission of a felony. A popular law because it distinguished between lawful and unlawful use of guns (which the Massachusetts law did not), the Michigan statute enjoyed wide support. The statute didn't prohibit plea bargaining; nevertheless, the Wayne County prosecutor initiated a policy forbidding negotiations regarding the law. In a combined qualitative and quantitative analysis relying on interviews with judges, prosecutors, and defense attorneys, and on case dispositions in Detroit (Wayne County), Milton Heumann and Colin Loftin (1979) found that the law had little impact on the severity of sentences.

Federal Sentencing Guidelines: The guidelines are established by the United States Sentencing Commission, a group whose principal purposes are: (1) to establish sentencing policies and practices for the federal courts; (2) to advise and assist Congress and the executive branch in the development of effective and efficient crime policy; and (3) to collect, analyze, research, and distribute a broad array of information on federal crime and sentencing issues. To reach this site go to "Web Links" on your Samaha CJ7 website: http://cj.wadsworth.com/samaha_cj7e.

In 1990, Congress ordered the U.S. Sentencing Commission (1991) to evaluate federal mandatory minimum sentencing statutes. After studying presentence reports, sentencing hearings, plea agreements, sentencing guideline worksheets, and a random sample of drug and firearms cases, the commission reported:

- Only 41 percent of defendants who qualify for mandatory minimum sentences actually receive them.
- Mandatory minimum sentences increase disparity in sentencing.
- Whites are less likely than Blacks and Hispanics to be indicted or convicted at the mandatory minimum.
- Whites are also more likely than Blacks and Hispanics to receive reductions for "substantial assistance" in aiding in the prosecution of other offenders. (76)

Defendants who provide prosecutors with "substantial assistance" in investigating other offenders are eligible for an exception to the mandatory minimum sentences. The substantial assistance exception creates more than racial disparities. It also favors the very people the law was intended to punish ("drug kingpins") because underlings don't have anything substantial to offer the government. Stanley Marshall, who sold less than one gram of LSD, got a 20-year mandatory prison sentence. Jose Cabrera, on the other hand, who the government estimated made more than $40 million from importing cocaine and who qualified for life plus 200 years, got 8 years because he provided "substantial assistance" in the case of Panamanian dictator–drug dealer Manuel Noriega.

According to Judge Terry J. Hatter, Jr., "The people at the very bottom who can't provide substantial assistance end up getting [punished] more severely than those at the top" (Wallace 1993, 11). Joey Settembrino, in prison serving a 10-year mandatory minimum for a cocaine deal, reflected on the irony:

> They say that they want to get the big guy, they want to get the big fish, and that's why they go about getting all these little fish, because they eventually get the big fish. But what they don't realize is that when the big fish finally gets caught, he tells on the little fish, and he's free. (*Frontline* 1999)

Mandatory minimum sentences don't eliminate discretion either; they just shift it from judges to prosecutors. Prosecutors can use their discretion in a number of ways, including not charging defendants at all with mandatory sentence crimes (Chapter 10). Or they can charge them with less serious mandatory minimum crimes. They can also manipulate the substantial assistance exception to suit their purposes. Although the Sentencing Commission recommended further study before drawing any final conclusions about the effectiveness of mandatory penalties, their findings suggest that mandatory minimum penalties aren't the easy answer to the crime problem that politicians promise and the public hopes (Campaign for an Effective Crime Policy 1993; Schulhofer 1993, 199).

"Truth in Sentencing" and "Three Strikes and You're Out" Laws Despite the shortcomings of mandatory minimum sentences, they remain popular with the public and some professionals. Twenty-eight states have passed truth-in-sentencing laws (Turner, Greenwood, Chen, and Fain 1999, 76); 26 states have passed "three strikes and you're out" laws (Shepherd January 2002, 159). Truth-in-sentencing laws are intended to make sure serious offenders spend some time locked up. Three-strikes laws are supposed to make sure offenders who get convicted of a third felony get locked up for a very long time (sometimes for life). Supporters claim both types of laws will "help restore the credibility of the criminal justice system and will deter crime." Opponents believe the harsh penalties won't have much effect on crime and they'll cost states more than they can afford to pay (Turner et al. 1999, 75). Let's look at both types of laws and the research evaluating their costs and benefits.

Forty-three states have truth-in-sentencing laws mandating that *violent* offenders serve at least some of their sentence in prison (Sobel, Rosich, Kane, Kirk, and Dubin 2002, 8). Most of these state laws were passed after Congress passed the federal Violent Crime Control and Law Enforcement Act of 1994

State of Connecticut General Assembly Report on Sentencing History and Guidelines: An overview of the development of sentencing, including determinate versus indeterminate sentencing. To reach this site go to "Web Links" on your Samaha CJ7 website: http://cj.wadsworth.com/samaha_cj7e.

◀ California's three-strikes law is the toughest law of its kind in the country. Families to Amend California's Three-Strikes Law demonstrate outside the California Institute for Women (California's maximum security prison for women). Their mothers and daughters are locked up for 25-year minimum sentences for committing third non-violent and petty offenses.

(1994, Sections 20101–20109). The act awards grants to states to expand prison space to punish violent offenders, *if* they can prove that offenders convicted of violent crimes (murder, manslaughter, forcible rape, robbery, and aggravated assault) serve at least 85 percent of their sentences.

What's the effect of truth-in-sentencing laws? Joanna M. Shepherd (October 2002) applied sophisticated econometric statistical analyses to data from all 3054 U.S. counties between 1984 and 1996. She had *mostly* good news for supporters of truth-in-sentencing laws specifically and strict enforcement of mandatory sentences in general. "Truth-in-Sentencing laws decrease murders by 16 percent, [and] aggravated assaults by 12 percent" (509). The bad news is "offenders substitute into property crimes: burglaries increase by 20 percent and auto thefts by 15 percent" (509).

"Three strikes and you're out" may be a catchy phrase but the idea behind it is almost five hundred years old. In sixteenth-century England and in the American colonies, statutes imposed harsh penalties on habitual offenders. In 1797, New York expanded habitual offenders to include all repeat offenders, not just offenders who repeated the same crime. The New York law ordered a sentence of mandatory life imprisonment "at hard labor or in solitude, or both" for all offenders convicted of their second felony—no matter what that second felony was. Habitual offender laws flourished even in the era of the indeterminate sentence. By 1968, every state had some form of habitual felon statute (Turner, Sundt, Applegate, and Cullen 1995, 16).

Twenty-four states have three-strikes laws, but only California (the first to pass one) seriously enforces it (Shepherd, January 2002). California's law passed in 1994, after the kidnapping, brutal sexual assault, and murder of 12-year-old Polly Klaas in 1993 (Ainsworth 2004, 1). A bearded stranger broke into Polly Klaas's home in Petaluma California, and kidnapped her. He left behind two other girls bound and gagged. Polly's mother was asleep in the next room. Nine weeks later, after a fruitless search by hundreds of police officers and volunteers, a repeat offender, Richard Allen Davis, was arrested, and, in 1996, convicted and sentenced to death.

The California law is the toughest three-strikes law in the country (Ainsworth 2004, 1). Unlike the laws in other states, California's law includes both two- and three-strike provisions. Here's how the law works. Strike 1 is a conviction for one of the strikeable felonies listed in Table 11.1. Strike 2 is a later conviction for *any* felony. If you're "out" on two strikes the punishment is a mandatory sentence of double the length of the second strike offense. In strike 3 cases, strikes 1 and 2 must be convictions from the list of strikeable felonies in Table 11.1. Strike 3 is *any* felony. If you're "out" on a third strike, the penalty is a mandatory 25 years to life (Shepherd, January 2002, 161).

Liberals and conservatives, Democrats and Republicans, and the public all jumped on the three-strikes bandwagon, taking for granted they were a good idea. Why were they popular? Here are three reasons:

- They addressed the public's dissatisfaction with the criminal justice system.
- They promised a simple solution to a complex problem—the "panacea phenomenon."
- The use of the catchy phrase "Three strikes and you're out" was appealing; it put old habitual offender statute ideas into the language of modern baseball. (Benekos and Merlo 1995, 3; Turner et al. 1995)

What effects have three-strikes laws had? Everybody agrees that they incapacitate second- and third-strikers while they're locked up. But incapacitate them from doing what? Some critics argue that most strikers are already past the age of high offending (Chapter 3, "Age Theories"). Most of the debate centers on deterrence: Do the laws prevent criminals from committing further crimes? The conclusions are decidedly mixed: Three-strikes laws deter crime; three-strikes laws have no effect on crime; three-strikes laws *increase* crime.

Minnesota Three-Strikes Laws: Although Minnesota doesn't have an official three-strikes law, it does have a law mandating a life sentence for certain sexual offenders who commit a third sexual offense. Minnesota requires a mandatory sentence of "at least the length of the presumptive sentence under the sentencing guidelines" for persons convicted of two or more prior felony convictions for violent crimes. To reach this site go to "Web Links" on your Samaha CJ7 website: http://cj.wadsworth.com/samaha_cj7e.

"Three Strikes and You're Out: The Implementation and Impact of Strike Laws": A Department of Justice report on the effects of three-strikes laws. To reach this site go to "Web Links" on your Samaha CJ7 website: http://cj.wadsworth.com/samaha_cj7e.

▼ TABLE 11.1 California "Strikeable Offenses"

• Murder	• Any felony resulting in bodily harm
• Rape	• Arson causing bodily injury
• Lewd act on a child	• Carjacking
• Continual sexual abuse of a child	• Exploding a device with intent to injure
• Penetration by foreign object sexual	• Exploding a device with intent to murder
• Penetration by force	• Kidnapping
• Sodomy by force	• Mayhem
• Oral copulation by force	• Arson
• Robbery	• Burglary of an occupied dwelling
• Attempted murder	• Grand theft with a firearm
• Assault with a deadly weapon on a peace officer	• Drug sales to minors
• Assault with a deadly weapon by an inmate	• Any felony with a deadly weapon
• Assault with intent to rape or rob	• Any felony where a firearm is used

Source: John Clark, James Austin, and D. Alan Henry, *"Three Strikes and You're Out": A Review of State Legislation* (Washington, DC: National Institute of Justice: Research Brief, September 1997), Exhibit 1.

Joanna Shepherd concluded that three-strikes laws deter crime. She tested the application of rational choice theory (Chapter 3) to California's two- and three-strikes laws. Specifically, she says her results show that "*all* potential offenders," even before they commit their first-strike offense (Table 11.1), "consider the threat of the law in their decisions.... Criminals vigorously seek to avoid a first or second strike" (161–162). Applying sophisticated statistical econometric models to California's counties, Shepherd confidently concluded:

> Theory-based empirical results indicate that strike sentences deter crimes covered by the laws. During the first 2 years of the legislation [1994–1996], approximately eight murders, 3952 aggravated assaults, 10,672 robberies, and 384,488 burglaries were deterred in California. (159)

There's more good news according to Shepherd. Strict sentencing in one county decreases crime in neighboring counties. "Why would criminals in one county care about sentencing in another county?" Shepherd speculates the reasons may be (199–200):

- News reports of stricter sentencing practices might not identify a specific county.
- Criminals aren't sure of where county lines are.
- Criminals don't know exactly what county they'll be tried in.

Whatever the reason, Shepherd concludes, the empirical results allow us to conclude that "strike sentences not only deter criminals within a county but also deter criminals in surrounding counties" (200).

One other piece of good news. Shepherd estimated that the deterrent effect of the laws saved California taxpayers a minimum of $889 million in the first two years of its operation (201).

Shepherd reports only one piece of bad news among her findings: Thefts went up by 17,770. Why? "Criminals substituted out of strikeable offenses and into nonstrikeable offenses" (200–201).

John L. Worrall (2004) didn't reach the same encouraging conclusions that Shepherd did. Using county data from 1989 to 2000, Worrall explored the effect of California's strikes law on serious crime. Serious crime was defined as the list of FBI Index crimes (homicide, aggravated assault, robbery, rape, burglary, and theft; Chapter 2). After controlling for economic variables (income, welfare, and unemployment) and demographic variables (age groups, race, population density, resident mobility, and high school dropout rate), Worrall concluded: Three strikes legislation appears to have virtually no effect on serious crime (293).

Tomislav V. Kovandzic and his colleagues (2002) concluded that three-strikes laws *increase* homicide rates. Their results (based on data from 188 large U.S. cities) were similar to those of another study (Marvell and Moody 2001) based on *statewide* sentencing and homicide rate data. Using sophisticated regression analysis, they concluded that cities in states with three-strikes laws experienced short-term increases of between 13 and 14 percent in homicide rates and between 16 and 24 percent in the long term (399). How can this be? The answer is based on the same theory as Shepherd's work—rational choice. But Kovandzic and colleagues found choice theory working quite differently from Shepherd's application of the theory:

> Criminals facing lengthy prison terms upon conviction for a third strike may take steps to try and reduce the chances of being caught, prosecuted, and convicted by changing their *modus operandi*. That is, during the commission of an ordinarily nonlethal offense, an offender may decide to kill victims, witnesses, or police officers to reduce the chances of apprehension. (400)

These unintended negative consequences of three-strikes laws led Kovandzic and his colleagues to draw the following conclusion on the implications for criminal justice policy:

> Despite their public support and political popularity, policy makers should seriously consider repealing three-strikes laws. They are simply not the panacea for the nation's violent crime problem, and according to a growing body of scientific research, they may actually exacerbate the most serious crime—homicide. (418)

As you can see from these conflicting results of careful research, the effect of three-strikes laws on crime rates hasn't been answered definitively yet. Californians placed an initiative on the 2004 election ballot that proposed softening its law. Instead of 25 years to life for *any* third felony under the present law, the ballot measure would've imposed 25 years to life only if the third felony was a *serious* or *violent* crime. It also would've allowed courts to retroactively reduce sentences of those locked up. Polls showed a large majority favored the changes, but the measure was soundly defeated (Ainsworth 2004, A1). (See the In Focus box "Three-Strikes Law: Time for Change?")

Besides the effect on crime rates, there's the question of whether sentencing decisions in three-strikes laws are infected by race and ethnicity. The Justice Policy Institute (Ehlers, Schiraldi, and Ziedenberg 2004), "a non-profit research and public policy organization dedicated to ending society's reliance on incarceration and promoting effective and just solutions to social problems," analyzed data from the Uniform Crime Reports (Chapter 2), the U.S. Census Bureau, the California Department of Corrections, and the California attorney general's office. The results are depicted in Figure 11.1.

▶ **FIGURE 11.1 The Race and Ethnicity of California "Striker" Prisoners per 100,000 State Residents, 2004**

Source: Scott Ehlers, Vincent Schiraldi, and Jason Ziedenberg, *Still Striking Out* (San Francisco: Justice Policy Institute 2004), Figure 5, p. 12.

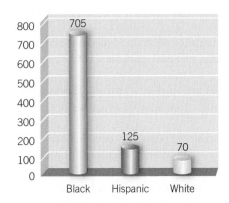

Three-Strikes Law: Time for Change?

Half a dozen tombstone-shaped placards stood on easels at the front of a South Los Angeles meeting hall this month, each bearing the photo of a convict incarcerated under the state's 1994 three-strikes law. Filling the row of folding chairs and standing in the aisles were community activists, relatives of convicted felons and a few repeat offenders who had served their time. They were all here to make their case for Proposition 66, which would greatly reduce the number of felons eligible for sentencing under three strikes. "Buried Alive" read the posters, with the prisoners' time served written like life spans on grave markers. The caption on a grainy photo of one young man read: "Brian Smith received 25 years to life for 'aiding' a shoplifting."

In Santa Barbara last week, those opposing changes to California's mandatory sentencing requirements marshaled their own resources, displaying mug shots of third-strikers who would be eligible for reduced sentences. One was of Steve Matthews, a convicted murderer who also raped his mother. He was sentenced as a third-striker when he was caught with two deadly weapons, including a 2-foot-long machete etched with an antigay slur. "Under Proposition 66, Mr. Matthews' sentence would be reduced to a maximum of three years," opponents said in a news release distributed at the event. "Because of time served and 'good time' credits, he would be eligible for release in early 2005."...

The "Three Strikes and You're Out" law was considered unlikely to gain much support when it was proposed more than a decade ago. But in 1994, in the aftermath of the kidnapping and murder of 12-year-old Polly Klaas in Petaluma, scores of politicians backed the measure, which then-Gov. Pete Wilson signed into law, and voters ratified it by a ratio of 3 to 1....

Now, many Californians appear inclined to reconsider. A Field Poll taken last month [August 2004] found nearly seven in 10 likely California voters said they would vote to change the law, with the numbers for both Republicans and Democrats well above the threshold for passage....

On both sides are passions and deeply held beliefs. Proponents of the measure, who include prominent civil rights and religious organizations, call some of the punishments meted out under three-strikes sentencing requirements "cruel and unusual." They argue that minorities have been disproportionally affected. And they say the state is spending tens of millions of dollars to incarcerate petty thieves and drug addicts who are no real threat to society.

Opponents of the measure, who point out that two of the strikes must have been violent or serious to trigger a term of 25 years to life, say the cost of crime to victims and their families is immeasurable. They say that if voters change the law, some of those released will kill again. Gov. Arnold Schwarzenegger and state Atty. Gen. Bill Lockyer are among the prominent politicians urging voters to defeat the measure.... "Those felons are going to be moved into your neighborhood," said Kelly Moran, whose group, California Organization of Police and Sheriffs, formed one of two committees opposing Proposition 66.

"Proponents want to make you believe they're pot smokers and bread stealers, but the fact is they are convicted felons," Moran said. "The question is whose mother is going to be raped or who's going to get killed over a drug deal because there are going to be people who don't belong back out on the street?" Each side accuses the other of lying and misleading voters. Those backing the initiative repeatedly accuse their opponents of trying to scare voters into keeping the law intact. Asked about Matthews and other felons used as examples by anti-Proposition 66 forces, Steve Hopcraft, campaign consultant for the side favoring the measure, referred to the early-release list as a "boogeyman," saying, "Looks like Halloween came early this year."

Beyond rhetoric and sad stories, the two sides disagree on...the law's effectiveness. Santa Barbara County Dist. Atty. Tom Sneddon said he and other district attorneys throughout the state have no doubt that the law has helped reduce crime, and noted that courts have given prosecutors discretion in using strikes against defendants. Proponents of the initiative cited a study released last week by the Washington-based Justice Policy Institute that found California's law to be the only one in the country that allows the third strike to be a minor offense. In California, 42,000 people are serving time under three strikes, nearly as many as in all other states combined. The study, conducted by an advocacy group that says it is committed to "ending society's reliance on incarceration," found that 57% of third-strikers had their 25-years-to-life sentences triggered by a nonviolent offense.

Brian Gurwitz, an assistant district attorney in Orange County who has taken a leave to fight the initiative, said voters are being asked to put their sympathy in the wrong place. "How hard is it not to commit another felony?" he asked. "I don't think it's that hard."

But Dorothy Erskine, whose nephew Brian Smith is serving 25 years to life on a third strike for shoplifting, said she sees a different reality. She said her nephew's criminal history was connected to drugs, an addiction that began after his mother died of cancer when he was 17. Erskine said Smith had prior convictions for stealing a car, using force on the driver and burglarizing an unoccupied house. In 1994, he was with two women at a mall in Cerritos when they were all stopped for stealing hundreds of dollars worth of sheets. The women served a few years and have long since been released, she said. Her nephew—who is no longer on drugs and has been trained to repair air conditioners—is still in prison. "I do feel Brian should have served time for each and every crime he committed," the retired schoolteacher said. "But I believe the time should fit the crime."

Source: Megan Garvey, "Initiative Fight Puts Focus on Felons," *Los Angeles Times,* September 27, 2004, p. B1. Reprinted with permission.

Figure 11.1 definitely shows wide *disparity*, but it doesn't prove discrimination because we don't know the effects of legitimate criteria (the seriousness of offense, the details of the criminal history of the offenders, and the strength of the case).

There are several evaluations of California's 1994 three-strikes law (King and Mauer 2001), which mandates life in prison for any third felony (like auto theft, or even as in one case—stealing a pizza). By June 1, 2001, more than 50,000 offenders were in prison under the law (6271 for "three strikes" and 43,800 for "two strikes"). The Sentencing Project, a research and advocacy group, analyzed official data on California's two- and three-strike sentencing and found the law:

1. Has not significantly contributed to reducing crime
2. Has increased the number and severity of sentences for nonviolent crime
3. Is rapidly expanding an aging and costly prison population, a population that doesn't contribute to violent crime
4. Has no relation to California's 1990s crime bust (King and Mauer 2001)

Prior to its passage, a RAND Corporation study (Greenwood, Rydell, Abrahamse, and Caulins 1994) found the California three-strikes legislation would reduce murder, rape, and aggravated assault by about 11 percent and other serious crimes like robbery and residential burglary. The study predicted that the cost of the law would be high, between $4.5 and $6.5 billion a year in 1994 dollars to pay for added prison space.

Sentencing Guidelines

Sentencing guidelines are fixed (but flexible) sentences based on balancing the seriousness of the offense and the criminal history of the offender. Guidelines establish the narrow ranges that judges can sentence offenders to. Guidelines have four purposes:

- *Uniformity.* Improving the chances that similar offenders who have committed similar offenses will receive similar penalties
- *Neutrality.* Reducing the chances that race, gender, ethnicity, age, and class affect sentencing by restricting the criteria for sentencing to the seriousness of the offense and the criminal history of the offender
- *Truth.* Ensuring that the type and length of sentences that offenders actually serve nearly equal the sentences judges impose—that is, "You do the crime, you do the time"
- *Control.* Preventing rapidly growing prison populations from overtaking prison space and state resources

Let's look at the types of sentencing guidelines and then specifically at the Minnesota sentencing guidelines.

The Types of Guidelines In presumptive sentencing guidelines, either legislatures or special commissions set the types and ranges of sentences. Judges have to contain their sentences within the prescribed ranges, unless they can justify in writing their departures from the guidelines according to criteria usually prescribed in a guidelines manual. Voluntary sentencing guidelines merely suggest possible sentences. Judges can (and often do) follow the suggested sentences, but they don't have to. The specific types and exact ranges of sentences are either descriptive or prescriptive. In descriptive sentencing guidelines, the guidelines are based on existing sentencing practices within the state; they merely state in writing what judges have actually been doing. Prescriptive sentencing guidelines develop new sentencing norms based on what decision makers decide the type and range of penalties should be. (See the In Focus box "Sentencing Guidelines: Denial of the Right to a Jury Trial?" on page 382.)

Lockyer, Attorney General of California v. Andrade: The Supreme Court case on the constitutionality of three-strikes laws. To reach this site go to "Web Links" on your Samaha CJ7 website: http://cj.wadsworth.com/samaha_cj7e.

sentencing guidelines fixed (but flexible) sentences based on balancing the seriousness of the offense and the criminal history of the offender

380   **Part 3 The Courts**

SEVERITY LEVEL OF CONVICTION OFFENSE		0	1	2	3	4	5	6 or more
Murder, 2nd Degree (intentional murder; drive-by-shootings)	XI	306 *299–313*	326 *319–333*	346 *339–353*	366 *359–373*	386 *379–393*	406 *399–413*	426 *419–433*
Murder, 3rd Degree Murder, 2nd Degree (unintentional murder)	X	150 *144–156*	165 *159–171*	180 *174–186*	195 *189–201*	210 *204–216*	225 *219–231*	240 *234–246*
Criminal Sexual Conduct, 1st Degree† Assault, 1st Degree	IX	86 *81–91*	98 *93–103*	110 *105–115*	122 *117–127*	134 *129–139*	146 *141–151*	158 *153–163*
Aggravated Robbery 1st Degree Criminal Sexual Conduct 2nd Degree (c), (d), (e), (f), (h)†	VIII	48 *44–52*	58 *54–62*	68 *64–72*	78 *74–82*	88 *84–92*	98 *94–102*	108 *104–112*
Felony DWI	VII	36	42	48	54 *51–57*	60 *57–63*	66 *63–69*	72 *69–757*
Criminal Sexual Conduct, 2nd Degree (a) & (b)	VI	21	27	33	39 *37–41*	45 *43–47*	51 *49–53*	57 *55–59*
Residential Burglary Simple Robbery	V	18	23	28	33 *31–35*	38 *36–40*	43 *41–45*	48 *46–50*
Nonresidential Burglary	IV	12*	15	18	21	24 *23–25*	27 *26–28*	30 *29–31*
Theft Crimes (Over $2,500)	III	12*	13	15	17	19 *18–20*	21 *20–22*	23 *22–24*
Theft Crimes ($2,500 or less) Check Forgery ($200–$2,500)	II	12*	12*	13	15	17	19	21 *20–22*
Sale of Simulated Controlled Substance	I	12*	12*	12*	13	15	17	19 *18–20*

Presumptive commitment to state imprisonment. First Degree Murder is excluded from the guidelines by law and continues to have a mandatory life sentence. See section II.E. Mandatory Sentences for policy regarding those sentences controlled by law, including minimum periods of supervision for sex offenders released from prison.

Presumptive stayed sentence; at the discretion of the judge, up to a year in jail and/or other non-jail sanctions can be imposed as conditions of probation. However, certain offenses in this section of the grid always carry a presumptive commitment to state prison. These offenses include Third Degree Controlled Substance Crimes when the offender has a prior felony drug conviction, Burglary of an Occupied Dwelling when the offender has a prior felony burglary conviciton, second and subsequent Criminal Sexual Conduct offenses and offenses carrying a mandatory minimum prison term due to the use of a dangerous weapon (e.g., Second Degree Assault). See sections II.C. Presumptive Sentence and II.E. Mandatory Sentences.

* One year and one day
† Pursuant to M.S. §609.342. subd. 2 and 609.343, subd. 2, the presumptive sentence for Criminal Sexual Conduct in the First Degree is a minimum of 144 months and the presumptive sentence for Criminal Sexual Conduct in the Second Degree—clauses c, d, e, f, and h—is a minimum of 90 months (see II.C. Presumptive Sentence and II.G. Convicitions for Attempts, Conspiracies, and Other Sentence Modifiers).

The Minnesota Sentencing Guidelines Minnesota, a pioneer guidelines state, adopted its guidelines to reduce judicial discretion and sentencing disparity without increasing prison populations. The Minnesota guidelines incorporate a modified deserts sentencing model; they base sentences on a combination of the severity of the convicted offense and the criminal history of the offender. The guidelines regulate both the kind of disposition (incarceration or probation) and the length of jail and prison terms. Figure 11.2 reproduces the Minnesota grid (also called a matrix) for determining sentences under the modified deserts model.

▲ **FIGURE 11.2 Minnesota Sentencing Guidelines**

Source: Adapted from Minnesota Sentencing Guidelines Commission, *Minnesota Sentencing Guidelines and Commentary,* revised August 1, 2004, p. 49.

Sentencing Guidelines: Denial of the Right to a Jury Trial?

FACTS

Ralph Howard Blakely, Jr. married his wife Yolanda in 1973. He was evidently a difficult man to live with, having been diagnosed at various times with psychological and personality disorders including paranoid schizophrenia. His wife ultimately filed for divorce. In 1998, he abducted her from their orchard home in Grant County, Washington, binding her with duct tape and forcing her at knifepoint into a wooden box in the bed of his pickup truck. In the process, he implored her to dismiss the divorce suit and related trust proceedings.

When the couple's 13-year-old son Ralphy returned home from school, Blakely ordered him to follow in another car, threatening to harm Yolanda with a shotgun if he did not do so. Ralphy escaped and sought help when they stopped at a gas station, but Blakely continued on with Yolanda to a friend's house in Montana. He was finally arrested after the friend called the police.

The State charged Blakely with first-degree kidnapping. Upon reaching a plea agreement, however, it reduced the charge to second-degree kidnapping involving domestic violence and use of a firearm. Blakely entered a guilty plea, admitting the elements of second-degree kidnapping and the domestic-violence and firearm allegations, but no other relevant facts. The case then proceeded to sentencing.... Washington's Sentencing Reform Act specifies, for Blakely's offense of second-degree kidnapping with a firearm, a "standard range" of 49 to 53 months. A judge may impose a sentence above the standard range if he finds "substantial and compelling reasons justifying an exceptional sentence."... When a judge imposes an exceptional sentence, he must set forth findings of fact and conclusions of law supporting it. A reviewing court will reverse the sentence if it finds ... there is insufficient evidence in the record to support the reasons for imposing an exceptional sentence.

Pursuant to the plea agreement, the State recommended a sentence within the standard range of 49 to 53 months. After hearing Yolanda's description of the kidnapping, however, the judge rejected the State's recommendation and imposed an exceptional sentence of 90 months—37 months beyond the standard maximum. He justified the sentence on the ground that petitioner had acted with "deliberate cruelty," a statutorily enumerated ground for departure in domestic-violence cases. Blakely appealed, arguing that this sentencing procedure deprived him of his federal constitutional right to have a jury determine beyond a reasonable doubt all facts legally essential to his sentence. The State Court of Appeals affirmed. The Washington Supreme Court denied discretionary review. Blakely appealed to the U.S. Supreme Court.

U.S. SUPREME COURT

Justice Antonin Scalia for the majority (5 justices)

Blakely was sentenced to more than three years above the 53-month statutory maximum of the standard range because he had acted with "deliberate cruelty." The facts

The rows on the grid contain offenses and the columns represent a score for criminal history. The bold line, called the disposition line, represents the boundary separating presumptive stayed sentences—that is, those cases in which judges suspend prison sentences for the number of months specified in the grid. The numbers above the bold line are the presumptive executed sentences (prison sentences). The numbers in the cells present the range of months judges can sentence offenders to. For example, a first-time aggravated robbery conviction carries a recommended sentence of 48 months, but the judge can choose any time between 44 and 52 months without formally departing from the guidelines.

Allowing judges to choose within a range without departing from the guidelines builds flexibility into the system, allowing for differences in individual cases. Characteristics like the amount of money stolen, the extent of personal injury inflicted, and the criminal history of the offender can affect the sentence judges impose without undermining the basic goals of uniformity and equity.

What if judges want to sentence a first-time robber to more than 52 months or less than 44 months? (Going outside the recommended range is called a departure). Judges can depart from the range when the "individual case involves substantial and compelling circumstances." What are "substantial and compelling circumstances"? Circumstances justifying downward departures include the victim was the aggressor in the crime (Kunume starts a fight with Jessica and Jessica stabs Kunume); the offender played only a minor role in the crime (Christian

supporting that finding were neither admitted by Blakely nor found by a jury. . . . When a judge inflicts punishment that the jury's verdict alone does not allow, the jury has not found all the facts "which the law makes essential to the punishment." Because the State's sentencing procedure did not comply with the Sixth Amendment [the right to trial by jury, Chapter 10], Blakely's sentence is invalid.

[The right to trial by jury] is no mere procedural formality, but a fundamental reservation of power in our constitutional structure. Just as suffrage ensures the people's ultimate control in the legislative and executive branches, jury trial is meant to ensure their control in the judiciary. ("Were I called upon to decide whether the people had best be omitted in the Legislative or Judiciary department, I would say it is better to leave them out of the Legislative," Letter from Thomas Jefferson to the Abbe Arnoux, July 19, 1789, reprinted in 15 Papers of Thomas Jefferson 282, 283, J. Boyd ed. 1958). . . . The judge's authority to sentence derives wholly from the jury's verdict. Without that restriction, the jury would not exercise the control that the Framers intended. . . . The Framers would not have thought it too much to demand that, before depriving a man of three more years of his liberty, the State should suffer the modest inconvenience of submitting its accusation to the unanimous suffrage of twelve of his equals and neighbours.

The judgment of the Washington Court of Appeals is reversed, and the case is remanded for further proceedings not inconsistent with this opinion.

Justice Breyer, Dissenting Opinion (4 justices)

. . . The Court says to Congress and state legislatures: If you want to constrain the sentencing discretion of judges and bring some uniformity to sentencing, it will cost you—dearly. Congress and States . . . will either trim or eliminate altogether their sentencing guidelines schemes and, with them, 20 years of sentencing reform. The "effect" of today's decision will be greater judicial discretion and less uniformity in sentencing. . . .

The consequences of today's decision will be as far reaching as they are disturbing. Washington's sentencing system is by no means unique. Numerous other States [Alaska, Arkansas, Florida, Kansas, Michigan, Minnesota, North Carolina, Pennsylvania] have enacted guidelines systems, as has the Federal Government. Today's decision casts constitutional doubt over them all and, in so doing, threatens an untold number of criminal judgments. Every sentence imposed under such guidelines in cases currently pending on direct appeal is in jeopardy. The numbers available from the federal system alone are staggering. . . . Between June 27, 2000 . . . and March 31, 2004, there have been 272,191 defendants sentenced in federal court. Given that nearly all federal sentences are governed by the Federal Sentencing Guidelines, the vast majority of these cases are Guidelines cases.

The practical consequences for trial courts, starting today, will be equally unsettling: How are courts to mete out guidelines sentences? Do courts apply the guidelines as to mitigating factors, but not as to aggravating factors? Do they jettison the guidelines altogether? The Court ignores the havoc it is about to wreak on trial courts across the country.

What I have feared most has now come to pass: Over 20 years of sentencing reform are all but lost, and tens of thousands of criminal judgments are in jeopardy. I respectfully dissent.

Source: Blakely v. Washington, 124 S.Ct. 2531 (2004).

drives Charles to a convenience store so Charles can rob it); or the offender lacked the capacity of judgment due to physical or mental impairment (Ben is a borderline schizophrenic but not insane when he steals Amirthini's cell phone).

Circumstances justifying upward departure include the victim was vulnerable (Keeley beat up an elderly man who has to use a walker); cruelty was inflicted on the victim (Eddie shot in the feet and the hands a victim he had just mugged); the crime was a major drug offense; or the crime was committed for hire (Brandon hired Jocelyn to shoot his wife). Judges who depart have to give written reasons for their departures. Defendants can appeal upward departures; prosecutors can appeal downward departures (Minnesota Sentencing Guidelines Commission 2001).

Terance D. Miethe and Charles A. Moore (1985, 357–361) evaluated the impact of the Minnesota sentencing guidelines. They found one major positive outcome—a shift in prison populations from property offenders to violent criminals (an outcome in line with the Minnesota legislature's intent to move property offenders into community corrections). But they also found that guidelines don't eliminate race, gender, marital status, income, and other biases from infecting sentencing decisions. Judges can hide their biases in their discretionary departure decisions. This is true even though their discretion is open to public view because they have to put their reasons for departing in writing. And prosecutors can even more easily hide their bias in their invisible reasons for charging and plea bargaining with defendants.

🌐 **California's Rules of Court on the Role of the Probation Officer and the Presentencing Report:** To reach this site go to "Web Links" on your Samaha CJ7 website: http://cj.wadsworth.com/samaha_cj7e.

The Presentence Investigation

Judges rely on information about offenders' backgrounds when they make their sentencing decisions. This is certainly true in indeterminate sentencing where judges have broad discretion, but it also applies to fixed sentencing because although mandatory minimum sentencing and guidelines sentencing *reduce* judicial discretion, they don't *eliminate* it. Also (and frequently overlooked), fixed sentences are aimed almost completely at reducing discretion in felony sentencing; that leaves judges with lots of leeway in misdemeanor sentencing. (Remember, misdemeanor cases vastly outnumber felony cases; Chapter 2). So even in felony cases but much more so in misdemeanor cases, judges don't just automatically apply sentences in statutes and guidelines; they use their discretion.

This leeway in sentencing allows judges to take into account the individual offender. That's where the presentence report comes in to guide judges' discretion in sentencing. The presentence report (PSR) based on a presentence investigation (PSI) contains information about offenders' prior criminal record (criminal history); their social history; and, mental health history and psychiatric evaluation. The first part of the PSR enumerates the facts of the case based on both the police report and the defendant's version of what happened. As you might expect, police and defendants' versions often conflict. Judges tend to accept the police version. (Critics say this isn't fair to defendants.)

The second part of the PSR includes the offender's prior criminal record, including prior convictions, dropped charges, and arrests. (Critics say histories shouldn't include arrests because they only require probable cause whereas convictions require proof beyond a reasonable doubt.) Social histories include family history, employment record, and education. Judges say social histories help them predict the offender's potential for rehabilitation and future behavior. Psychiatric evaluations include the defendant's history of mental illness, hospitalizations, treatment, and recommendations (Rosecrance 1985, 539–554).

The quality of information in PSRs can be a problem. Probation officers, who are in charge of presentence investigations and who write the PSRs, have to do these jobs while they're supervising heavy caseloads of probationers (Chapter 12). Always pressed for time, they often can't get all the information they need or, equally important, make sure the information they do get is correct.

Another problem is that probation officers have less influence on sentencing than the presentence investigation and report suggest. Based on his 15 years of experience as a probation officer and on interviews with probation officers, Professor John Rosecrance (1985, 539–554; 1988, 236–256) concluded that they write presentence reports for three audiences: the court, the prosecutor, and the probation supervisor. They use the report to maintain their credibility, looking for cues from these audiences and providing them with recommendations their audiences want to hear. So probation officers make recommendations not so much to influence their audiences' perceptions of defendants but to legitimate the officers' own claim to being "reasonable."

Disparity and Discrimination in Sentencing

We've already learned from empirical research surveyed earlier in the book that decisions in criminal justice (arrest, charge, and disposition) depend on three appropriate criteria: the seriousness of the offense, the criminal history of the offender, and the strength of the case. We've also learned that these are the *main* but not the *only* ingredients in decision making. Let's examine to what extent sentencing decisions are infected with inappropriate ingredients. Remember the distinction we've referred to earlier between discrimination and disparity. Sentencing *discrimination* means the use of unacceptable criteria, usually race, ethnicity, or gender, to determine sentences. Sentencing *disparity* includes inequality of three different types:

1. *Different sentences for similar offenders.* Two burglars the same age, with similar records, break into stores after hours and each takes $100 from the cash register. One burglar goes to prison, the other gets probation.
2. *Similar sentences for different offenders.* Both a five-time burglar and a first-time burglar receive five years in prison.
3. *Similar offenders receiving different sentences for minor differences.* An armed robber who takes $1000 receives a 10-year sentence; another armed robber who takes $750 gets a 5-year sentence. (Schulhofer 1992, 835–836)

Let's look at disparity as it applies to Blacks, Hispanics, and women.

Blacks and Disparity

Adult Black males account for less than 5 percent of the general population of the United States, according to the 2000 census. But they made up 18 percent of violent offenders, 25 percent of property offenders, and 42 percent of drug offenders sentenced in state courts in 2000, the latest figures available (Durose and Langan 2003, Table 5).

How do we explain this racial gap? Early research on the connection between race and sentencing suffered from two shortcomings. First, most sentencing research depended on aggregate sentencing data (lumping together data from all places studied). Aggregate data obscure local variations. For instance, conclusions based on all sentences in a state might hide racially determined sentences in particular counties; one county can obscure the racism of individual judges (Alabama Law Review Summer Project 1975, 676–746; Daly 1989, 136–168; Kruttschnitt 1984, 213–232; Nagel and Weitzman 1971, 171–198; Petersilia 1985, 15–35).

Martha A. Myers and Susette M. Talarico's (1987, 80–81) study of sentencing in Georgia clearly demonstrates the strengths of disaggregating data. They compared a random sample of 16,798 Georgia felons throughout the whole state with a comparable random sample of 1685 Georgia felons from Fulton and DeKalb counties. They found few systemwide differences in sentences of Black defendants:

> We expected that sanctions would be more severe in counties characterized by pronounced inequality, a sizeable percentage of black unemployed residents, and relatively high crime rates. In actuality, we found little evidence to support these expectations.... We found no consistent relationship with punitiveness in sentencing. Nor did the presence of large economically subordinate populations, whether black or unemployed, foster more severe sanctions. (Myers and Talarico 1987, 80–81)

But after Myers and Talarico looked more closely at different communities, they found racial discrimination in specific communities, where the seriousness of the crime combined with the racial composition to create disparities. But the disparity might mean more leniency as well as more severity:

> There were many instances in which blacks received disproportionately lenient punishment. Although this pattern may suggest a paternalism that is just as discriminating as disproportionate punitiveness, it nevertheless indicates that courts in Georgia do not have a heavy hand with black defendants in the general systemic sense or in every context where differential treatment is observed. (170–171)

Hispanics and Disparity

Gary D. Lafree (1985) analyzed 755 defendants in Tucson, Arizona, and El Paso, Texas, to find out whether there was discrimination in the sentencing of Hispanic defendants. He found major differences between the two cities in robbery

"**Prison Population and Harsh Sentencing**": An American Civil Liberties Union report on sentencing disparity. To reach this site go to "Web Links" on your Samaha CJ7 website: http://cj.wadsworth.com/samaha_cj7e.

"**Sentencing Rules Haven't Solved Disparities**": An MSNBC report on sentencing disparity. To reach this site go to "Web Links" on your Samaha CJ7 website: http://cj.wadsworth.com/samaha_cj7e.

and burglary sentences. In Tucson, there were no significant differences between sentences of Hispanics and non-Hispanics. In El Paso, on the other hand, Hispanics received longer sentences. Interviews with criminal justice officials suggested that the established Hispanic population in Tucson, versus the less-established Mexican American and Mexican national populations in El Paso, accounts for the difference. According to one El Paso prosecutor:

> We're sitting here on a border. Across the river from us, which is nothing more than an oversized mud puddle, is the city of Juarez, with over a million and a quarter residents.... Our police force is geared to the size of this city and what it can afford. El Paso does not have the economic base to support the city itself. In other words, we perceive El Paso as the city north of the Rio Grande, but bullshit, we're talking about another million and a quarter people that go back and forth like a tide. (228)

Women and Disparity

Until the 1990s, most research on sentencing women showed a clear gender gap that favored women—they got more lenient sentences than men. Much of that research was based on data sets from the 1960s and 1970s before the move toward more fixed sentencing and more sophisticated research methods were developed to sort out the effects of gender from the effects of the seriousness of offenses and the criminal history of offenders.

Darrell Steffensmeier, John Kramer, and Cathy Streifel (1993, 411–446) analyzed later data from Pennsylvania during 1985 to 1987. Pennsylvania adopted sentencing guidelines in 1982 based on the combination of the seriousness of offense and the criminal history of the offender. They applied regression analysis to sort out the effects of gender from offense and criminal history. They asked two important questions: Did gender affect the decision whether to sentence to incarceration? And did gender affect the decision of how long to incarcerate?

They found no gender gap in sentencing. The seriousness of the offense and the criminal history of the offender overwhelmed gender in both the decisions to sentence defendants to incarceration and how long the incarceration should be. So here we have it again—the right reasons for decisions trump the wrong ones in criminal justice decision making. But gender wasn't completely irrelevant; men were 12 percent more likely to get prison sentences than women (Steffensmeier et al. 1993, 426–428).

What about downward departure decisions? Do judges give women breaks they don't give men? At first, it might look like they do. Steffensmeier and his colleagues (1993) found that 29 percent of women got a break in their departures contrasted with 15 percent of the men. But when examined more closely, offense and history, not gender, were the reasons. In the words of one of the judges:

> Maybe some judges *do* give women a break because they feel sorry for the woman or because she has children. But the main thing for me is that sometimes you're comparing "apples and oranges." A woman coming before you in court may have the same prior record score or the same offense score as a man but her score involves all property offenses—no violent priors at all. And many times the woman's part in the offense is small, more the follower than the leader. I don't know where they find these guys but some of these women get hooked up with such losers you can hardly imagine it. Another thing that doesn't show up [in the official record] is that the women I see in court fairly often have health problems or mental problems. What are we going to do? The jails can't handle that. (434)

How do Steffensmeier and his colleagues explain the absence of a gender gap while so much of earlier research identified one? The authors offer several possibilities. Maybe sentencing decisions have gotten more gender-neutral because of greater concern about equal application of the law. Or maybe Pennsylvania's sentencing guidelines led to greater equality by reducing judges' discretion. Part of the explanation is probably the more sophisticated statistical analysis that controlled for the seriousness of offenses and criminal history. Past studies with the fewest controls show the biggest gender gap (Steffensmeier et al. 1993, 435–437).

The Death Sentence

 Death Penalty Information Center: A compendium of material and links related to the death penalty. To reach this site go to "Web Links" on your Samaha CJ7 website: http://cj .wadsworth.com/samaha_cj7e.

"Thou shalt not kill!" commands the Old Testament. But "Vengeance is mine," said the Old Testament God, and "not the Lord Chief Justice's," added the British playwright George Bernard Shaw. "Forgive thine enemies," Jesus implored in the New Testament. In North Carolina, visitors can hear or download audio clips of members of the media and the public who have witnessed an execution. In Florida, photographs of the electric chair and execution gurney can be downloaded. And in Oregon, an extensive narrative details how the condemned spend their last hours—and minutes. There's even a photo of a stopwatch to accompany the narrative.

The Georgia Department of Corrections recently updated its death row site, which provides not only its always popular "virtual jail cell" tour but now also offers photos and a roster of condemned inmates. Until recently, you could go to the Texas website and see the menu of death row prisoners' last meal.

"I don't know if we'll ever go back to the death penalty as we knew it, as long as I'm governor," said Illinois governor George Ryan, who stopped all executions after 13 men were sent to death row before being exonerated by new evidence. (See Make Your Decision.) "Serious questions are being raised about the death penalty." U.S. Supreme Court Justice Sandra Day O'Connor (2001) told a group of Minnesota lawyers. Minnesota "must breathe a big sigh of relief every day," she told the audience (Minnesota has no death penalty).

The previous three paragraphs will give you some idea of the passion swirling around capital punishment, passion on all sides of the issue. In the face of all this passion, let's look at some facts and then try to examine soberly several issues surrounding the sentence of death. We'll look at the death penalty and the Constitution, public opinion and the death penalty, and tough questions we should ask when evaluating whether we should keep, modify, or ban the death penalty.

Facts about the Death Sentence

 California's Department of Corrections: This site contains a balanced history of executions in California and includes the current protocols for the lethal injection process. To reach this site go to "Web Links" on your Samaha CJ7 website: http://cj .wadsworth.com/samaha_cj7e.

The American public stands firmly behind the death penalty (see "Public Opinion and the Death Penalty"). Also, an increasingly exasperated majority of the U.S. Supreme Court has repeatedly reminded stubborn defense lawyers that the U.S. Constitution doesn't forbid the death penalty. Yet, in the face of this strong public support, and the clear rulings of the U.S. Supreme Court, the reluctance to actually kill criminals convicted of capital offenses is strong. Figure 11.3 shows the growth in the numbers of prisoners on death row between 1976 and 2003. On December 31, 2002, there were 3562 prisoners on death row (Bonczar and Snell 2004, Table 4). Sixty-five of them were executed between January 1 and December 31, 2003, and they'd been waiting on death row an average of 10 years and 10 months (Bonczar and Snell 2004, Table 11)!

The Death Penalty and the Constitution

The Eighth Amendment to the U.S. Constitution prohibits "cruel and unusual punishments." The death penalty was well established before the Eighth Amendment was adopted and was widely practiced afterward. The U.S. Supreme Court didn't decide a single case challenging the constitutionality of the death penalty until 1890 in the case of William Kemmler. In 1889, shortly after New York introduced the electric chair to replace hanging, the state convicted Kemmler and sentenced him to death for murdering his wife. In 1885, the governor had asked the state legislature "whether the science of the present day cannot provide a means for taking life in a less barbarous manner" than hanging, which "has come down to us from the dark ages." A commission appointed by the legislature found one—the newly invented electric chair. The commission reported that electrocution is "the most humane and practical method of execution known to modern science" (*In re Kemmler* 1890, 444).

Numbers of Prisoners on Death Row

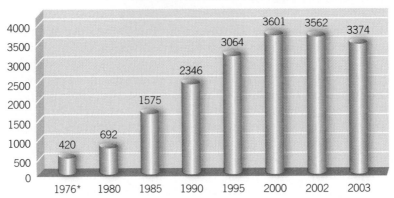

▶ FIGURE 11.3 Numbers of Prisoners on Death Row

*The U.S. Supreme Court allowed reinstatement of the death penalty.
Source: Bureau of Justice Statistics, *Capital Punishment, 2003* (Washington, DC: Bureau of Justice Statistics, November 2004), Table 4; Death Penalty Information Center, *Facts about the Death Penalty* (Washington, DC: October 8, 2004), p. 1.

The case of *In re Kemmler* (1890) came to the U.S. Supreme Court because Kemmler claimed electrocution was a cruel and unusual punishment—notice that he didn't argue that capital punishment itself was cruel and unusual, only the method. The Court agreed that electrocution was unusual but to violate the Eighth Amendment, it had to be unusual and cruel. But was it cruel? Absolutely not, said the Court. Punishments aren't cruel as long as they don't go further than "the mere extinguishments of life." The Court spelled out what this phrase means. First, death has to be instantaneous and painless. Second, it can't involve unnecessary mutilation of the body. According to the Court, beheading is cruel because it mutilates the body. Crucifixion is doubly cruel because it causes lingering death and mutilates the body.

In 1910, in *Weems v. U.S.*, the Court added the principle of proportionality—namely, that punishments should fit the crime—to the meaning of cruel. Paul Weems was convicted of falsifying a public document. The trial court sentenced him to 15 years of hard labor in chains and took away his civil rights for life. The U.S. Supreme Court overturned the sentence because the punishment was too harsh for the crime and therefore cruel. So far, the Court has taken the position that only the crime of murder fits the punishment of death. But the Louisiana Supreme Court has decided that the death penalty for raping a child under 12 isn't cruel or unusual because it fits the crime (*State v. Wilson* 1996). A jury convicted and sentenced Patrick Kennedy to death for repeatedly raping his 8-year-old stepdaughter; he's on Louisiana's death row. His lawyers expect to appeal (Axtman 2003, 2).

The U.S. Supreme Court has also decided that the sentence of death doesn't violate two other provisions in the U.S. Constitution: (1) It doesn't deny individuals life without due process of law (Fifth and Fourteenth Amendments) if both mitigating and aggravating circumstances are considered before the sentence is imposed. And (2) it doesn't deny equal protection of the law (Fourteenth Amendment) as long as the sentence isn't discriminatory; that is, race and other unacceptable criteria didn't play a part in the decision to impose the death sentence.

To meet these requirements, most death penalty states have passed **guided discretion death penalty statutes.** These statutes list the aggravating and mitigating circumstances that juries have to consider before they decide whether defendants should receive the sentence of death or life imprisonment. The usual aggravating circumstances include killing someone while committing some other felony; prior convictions for homicide; killing strangers; killing multiple victims; especially cruel killings; and killing law enforcement officers. Typical mitigating circumstances include no prior criminal history; mental or emotional stress; victim participation in the crime; and playing only a minor part in the murder.

Defendants charged with capital crimes under guided discretion statutes are tried in two stages (bifurcated trials). The first stage decides whether defendants are guilty; the second decides the sentence. It's during this second stage that ju-

guided discretion death penalty statutes These statutes list the aggravating and mitigating circumstances that juries have to consider before they decide whether defendants should receive the sentence of death or life imprisonment

ries consider the aggravating and mitigating circumstances before they decide whether defendants should receive the death penalty or life imprisonment.

Is it constitutional to execute mentally retarded offenders and juveniles? We'll turn to these issues next.

Executing Mentally Retarded Offenders Thirty-five mentally retarded persons were executed between 1976 when the death penalty was reinstated and 2001 (Human Rights Watch 2001). The American Association on Mental Retardation (AAMR) includes three elements in its definition of mental retardation:

1. Substantial intellectual impairment
2. The impact of that impairment on the everyday life of the mentally retarded individual
3. Retardation is present at birth or during childhood (*Atkins v. Virginia* 2002, 308).

In 2002, in *Atkins v. Virginia*, the U.S. Supreme Court ruled that executing anyone who proved the three elements in the AAMR definition applied to them violated the ban on cruel and unusual punishment. The decision grew out of a grisly case. On August 16, 1996, Daryl Atkins and William Jones were drinking alcohol and smoking "pot." At about midnight, they drove to a convenience store to rob a customer. They picked Eric Nesbitt, an airman from Langley Air Force Base, abducted him, took him in their pickup truck to an ATM machine, and forced him to withdraw $200. Then they drove him to a deserted area. Ignoring his pleas not to hurt him, they ordered Nesbitt to get out of the car. Nesbitt took only a few steps when (according to Jones, who made a deal with prosecutors to testify against Atkins in exchange for a life instead of a death sentence), Atkins fired eight shots into Nesbitt's thorax, chest, abdomen, arms, and legs (338).

Atkins v. Virginia: The Supreme Court decided against executing the mentally retarded in this recent case. To reach this site go to "Web Links" on your Samaha CJ7 website: http://cj.wadsworth.com/samaha_cj7e.

The jury convicted Atkins of capital murder. At the penalty phase of Atkins' trial, the jury heard evidence about his 16 prior felony convictions, including robbery, attempted robbery, abduction, use of a firearm, and maiming. He hit one victim over the head with a beer bottle; "slapped a gun across another victim's face, clubbed her in the head with it, knocked her to the ground, and then helped her up, only to shoot her in the stomach (339).

The jury also heard evidence about Atkins's mental retardation. After interviewing people who knew Atkins, reviewing school and court records, and administering a standard intelligence test which revealed Atkins had an IQ of 59, Dr. Evan Nelson, a forensic psychologist concluded that Atkins was "mildly mentally retarded." According to Nelson, mental retardation is rare (about 1 percent of the population); it would automatically qualify Atkins for Social Security disability income; and that "of the over 40 capital defendants that he had evaluated, Atkins was only the second" who "met the criteria for mental retardation." Nelson also testified that, "in his opinion, Atkins' limited intellect had been a consistent feature throughout his life, and that his IQ score of 59 is not an 'aberration, malingered result, or invalid test score'" (309).

In reversing the death sentence, the U.S. Supreme Court based its decision on a change in public opinion since its 1989 decision that it's not cruel and unusual punishment to execute retarded offenders (*Penry v. Lynaugh*). How did the Court measure this change in public opinion? First, since 1989, 19 states and the federal government passed statutes banning the execution of mentally retarded offenders (*Atkins v. Virginia* 2002, 314). Second, it's not just the number of bans that's significant, it's "the consistency of the direction of the change:

> Given the well-known fact that anticrime legislation is far more popular than legislation providing protections for persons guilty of violent crime, the large number of States prohibiting the execution of mentally retarded persons (and the complete absence of States passing legislation reinstating the power to conduct such executions) provides powerful evidence that today our society views mentally retarded offenders as categorically less culpable than the average criminal.

The evidence carries even greater force when it is noted that the legislatures that have addressed the issue have voted overwhelmingly in favor of the prohibition.

Moreover, even in those States that allow the execution of mentally retarded offenders, the practice is uncommon. Some States, for example New Hampshire and New Jersey, continue to authorize executions, but none have been carried out in decades. Thus there is little need to pursue legislation barring the execution of the mentally retarded in those States.

And it appears that even among those States that regularly execute offenders and that have no prohibition with regard to the mentally retarded, only five have executed offenders possessing a known IQ less than 70 since we decided *Penry*. The practice, therefore, has become truly unusual, and it is fair to say that a national consensus has developed against it. (315–316)

Third, executing retarded offenders doesn't serve the main purposes for having death sentences: retribution and deterrence. Mentally retarded offenders aren't as blameworthy or as subject to deterrence as people with normal intelligence because of their "diminished capacity to understand and process information, to learn from experience, to engage in logical reasoning, or to control their impulses" (319–320).

Executing Juvenile Offenders The execution of juveniles began in 1642, when Plymouth Colony hanged 16-year-old Thomas Graunger for bestiality with a cow and a horse (Rimer and Bonner 2000). It continued at a rate of about one a year until Oklahoma executed Scott Hain on April 3, 2003, after the U.S. Supreme Court refused to hear his appeal. Hain and a 21-year-old acquaintance killed two people in the course of a carjacking and robbery. He was a "deeply troubled" 17-year-old kid who dropped out of seventh grade after repeating the sixth grade three times. As a teenager, Scott's father got him a job in a warehouse so he could steal stuff and give it to his father, who sold it. At the time of the carjacking murders, Scott was living on the street in Tulsa, drinking, and using other drugs daily, but he'd never committed a violent crime (Greenhouse 2003, A18).

Just a few months before the U.S. Supreme Court refused to hear Scott Hain's case, four Supreme Court justices (John Paul Stevens, David Souter, Ruth Bader Ginsburg, and Stephen Breyer) had called the death penalty for juveniles a "shameful practice. The practice of executing such offenders is a relic of the past and is inconsistent with the evolving standards of decency in a civilized society" (Greenhouse 2003, A18).

The Court adopted the "evolving standards" to test whether sentences run afoul of the Eighth Amendment ban on "cruel and unusual punishments" in *Trop v. Dulles* (1958). In 1944, U.S. Army private Albert Trop escaped from a military stockade at Casablanca, Morocco, following his confinement for a disciplinary violation. The next day, Trop willingly surrendered. A general court martial convicted Trop of desertion and sentenced him to three years at hard labor, loss of all pay and allowances, and a dishonorable discharge. In 1952, Trop applied for a passport. His application was rejected on the ground that he lost his citizenship due to his conviction and dishonorable discharge for wartime desertion. The Court decided the punishment was "cruel and unusual." Why? Because, "the words of the Amendment are not precise, and their scope is not static. The Amendment must draw its meaning from the evolving standards of decency that mark the progress of a maturing society" (100–101).

The Court applied the "evolving standards of decency" approach in 1988, in *Thompson v. Oklahoma*, to ban the execution of juveniles under 16. But the next year, in *Stanford v. Kentucky* (1989), the Court ruled that executing juveniles between 16 and 18 didn't offend "evolving standards of decency." (After serving 14 years on death row, Stanford was granted clemency in 2003 and is now serving a life sentence.)

In 2005, the Court decided that the standards of decency had evolved enough since 1989 to be offended by executing Christopher Simmons for a carjacking murder he committed when he was 17 (*Roper v. Simmons* 2005). The justices most certainly considered the following (Streib 2004, 3–5):

1. Twenty out of the 39 death penalty jurisdictions set the minimum age at 18, 5 at age 17, and 14 at age 16.
2. Most nations in the world have signed international agreements banning the execution of juveniles. (Figure 11.4).
3. Death sentencing for juveniles has been declining rapidly; it's at its lowest point since 1989.
4. Only 21% of the public favors death over life in prison for juveniles who murder.
5. Since 1989, Texas has executed 13 juveniles, only 9 have been executed throughout the rest of the country. (Figure 11.4 does not reflect two U.S. executions that took place during 1989.)

The Court's decision probably won't affect the arguments for and against juvenile executions, which seem to have remained constant since the 1980s. (See the In Focus box "U.S. Supreme Court Ban on Capital Punishment for Juveniles: Who's Next?) These arguments are listed in Table 11.2.

Roper v. Simmons: In this March 2005 decision, the Supreme Court stated that those who were minors (under 18) at the time they committed a homicide cannot be executed when they are older. To reach this site go to "Web Links" on your Samaha CJ7 website: http://cj.wadsworth.com/samaha_cj7e.

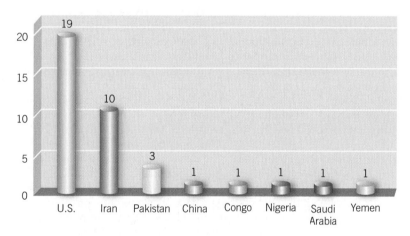

◀ **FIGURE 11.4 Recorded Executions of Juveniles from 1990–2004**

Source: Amnesty International, "Executions of Child Offenders Since 1990," 2004. http://web.amnesty.org/pages/deathpenalty-children-stats-eng).

▼ **TABLE 11.2 Arguments For and Against Capital Punishment for Juveniles**

FOR	AGAINST
1. Violent juvenile crime, especially homicide, is much worse in the U.S. than it is in the rest of the world.	1. Almost all teenage offenders had terrible childhoods, which they haven't grown out of yet.
2. Juvenile homicide rates increased dramatically in mid- and late-1990s. (They've dropped dramatically since 2000, but fear is still high.)	2. Medical research since 1990 shows that the adolescent brain doesn't mature organically until the late teens and early twenties, with impulse control being the last to develop fully. (See the CJ & Technology box "Crime, Culpability, and the Adolescent Brain" on page 394.)
3. Juvenile murderers are especially brutal and don't respond to calls for them to stop killings.	3. The threat of death doesn't deter teenagers who don't grasp the finality of death; they see themselves as immortal.
4. Almost every political leader calls for harsher punishments for juvenile crime.	4. The desire for retribution by extremely harsh punishment is blunted when a "child" is the offender.
5. Correcting the social conditions that breed violent juvenile crime is a huge task seemingly impossible to achieve.	5. Harsh punishments for violent juvenile crimes are only temporary band-aid solutions; the only true solution is cleaning up the neighborhoods, schools, and other societal conditions that breed violent juvenile crime.

Source: Adapted with permission from Victor L. Streib, "The Juvenile Death Penalty Today," pp. 13–14, October 5, 2004. © 2003 Victor L. Streib. http://www.law.onu.edu/faculty/streib.

U.S. Supreme Court Ban on Capital Punishment for Juveniles: Who's Next?

After a decade of relative quiet, the Supreme Court has in the last several years fundamentally re-shaped the nation's capital justice system. It has narrowed the class of people eligible for execution, excluding juvenile offenders yesterday as it had previously the mentally retarded. It has rebuked lower courts for sending people to their deaths without adequate safeguards. And it has paid increasing attention to the international opposition to capital punishment. "Early in the 1990's, we reached the high point in deregulating death," said Franklin E. Zimring, a law professor at the University of California, Berkeley, alluding to decisions in which the court refused to hear defendants' claims of innocence because they were raised too late. "Then there was very little from the Supreme Court through the 1990's. Now, in a whole series of substantive and procedural decisions, you have a re-regulation taking place."

Opinions vary about where the process will end.

"The trend seems to be pushing toward the abolition of capital punishment," said Rory K. Little, a former Justice Department official who is now a professor at Hastings College of Law in San Francisco. "But it would be a mistake to predict that these decisions are leading inexorably to abolition. It could be that they cut out all the edges and leave the core that everyone is comfortable with."...

All 72 men on death row for murders they committed when they were 16 or 17 will be spared their lives under the latest decision and will instead receive the harshest punishment available, typically life without the possibility of parole. "These people will all spend the rest of their lives in prison," said Victor L. Streib, a law professor at Ohio Northern University whose studies of the juvenile death penalty were cited in yesterday's decision. "Nobody's getting out."

Similarly, people who had faced capital prosecutions for crimes they committed as juveniles can now be sentenced, at worst, only to life terms. That group includes Lee Malvo, the teenage sniper serving a life term in Virginia. Prosecutors in Alabama and Louisiana had wanted to try Mr. Malvo on capital charges for killings there.

Supporters of the death penalty said they were braced for further, incremental attacks on the use of capital punishment—whether it should be applied to the mentally ill, older teenagers and defendants claiming racial discrimination.

"The next battle is the mentally ill," said Prof. Robert Blecker of the New York Law School. Given the decisions on the mentally retarded and on juveniles, Professor Blecker said, "it has a certain appeal."

Professor Blecker said he also expected opponents of the death penalty to try to move up the age separating juveniles from adults. In 1988, the Supreme Court set the line at age 16. Yesterday, it rose to 18.

"The interim attack may be to go after the so-called teenage death penalty, so they'll go after 19-year-olds," he said. "Then they will redefine juveniles to say it should extend to those under 21."

Richard C. Dieter, the executive director of the Death Penalty Information Center, a research group opposed to the death penalty, said he expected the role of race in capital punishment to re-emerge.

"Among the issues the Supreme Court decided around the same time as the juvenile death penalty was race and the death penalty," Mr. Dieter said, alluding to a 1987 decision holding that the disparities between whites and nonwhites at the time did not offend the Constitution. "They may be ready to take another look."

Professor Zimring said he also expected more attention on procedural safeguards.

"The areas to watch for large developments in are the adequacy of representation of counsel and harmless error," he said. Opponents of the death penalty are often critical of the quality of appointed counsel for capital defendants and the willingness of courts to overlook some prosecutorial misconduct by calling it harmless....

Source: Adam Liptak, "The Supreme Court: The Context; Another Step in Reshaping Capital Punishment," *New York Times*, March, 2, 2005, p. A13. Copyright © 2005 by The New York Times Co. Reprinted with permission.

Public Opinion and the Death Penalty

Attitudes toward the death penalty shift with the mood of the country. During the conservative 1950s, about two-thirds of the people favored it. Then, during the brief interlude of the mid-1960s liberalism, support slipped to 42 percent, the lowest in 50 years. The quick return to conservatism in the wake of the 1960s crime boom (Chapter 2) brought support back to 51 percent in 1969. Support continued to grow from the 1970s to the mid-1990s as the country's tough stand on punishment hardened. By 1994, support for the death penalty reached an all-time high—80 percent (Kohut 2001, 33).

 Support for the death penalty began to falter because of technological advances like DNA analysis, which proved many death row inmates innocent and highlighted the fallibility of the sentence's application. According to Jane Bohman, executive director of the Illinois Coalition Against the Death Penalty, "The whole system has been so called into question that it would only be appropriate for prosecutors to act with caution."

AP/Wide World Photos

After 1994, support began to falter for a number of reasons. First, DNA testing drove home the obvious fact that human beings make mistakes, including sentencing innocent people to death (see "Fallibility" on page 397). There's also a growing belief that the penalty isn't administered fairly; rich people can escape it and poor people can't. This is especially troubling because so many death penalty defendants are racial and ethnic minorities (see "Fairness" on page 399). At the same time, there is growing doubt among the public that the death penalty prevents murder. For the first time since 1986, an ABC/Washington Post poll, taken in 2001, showed that a majority believes the death penalty doesn't prevent murder. Finally, religious beliefs are increasingly cited as the main reason for opposition among social conservatives, Catholics, and white evangelical Protestants (Kohut 2001, 33).

You should keep in mind that support for the death penalty depends on the questions interviewers ask the people polled. The Gallup Poll, which has polled the public about the death penalty since the 1930s, had always asked just one question: "Are you in favor of the death penalty for a person convicted of murder?" In the last few years, they've also asked: "If you could choose between the following two approaches, which do you think is the better penalty for murder: the death penalty (or) life imprisonment with absolutely no possibility of parole?" In Gallup's May 2004 poll, 70 percent favored the death penalty when asked only if they favored it for murder (Figure 11.5). But support dropped to 50 percent when they got to choose between death and life without any chance of parole (Polling Report.com 2004) (Figure 11.6).

So despite public uneasiness about the penalty, support remains at 50 percent even when those polled are given the choice between death and life with no chance of parole. One other thing, the support goes up when some horrible crime is at issue. For example, 81 percent supported the death penalty for Timothy McVeigh, including 58 percent of the people who said they were death penalty opponents! Obviously, a huge majority of the public had no problem with the death penalty in his case. Why? Three reasons: The public was convinced we weren't killing an innocent person (remember he confessed in public

Crime, Culpability, and the Adolescent Brain

In 2004, the U.S. Supreme Court considered whether the death penalty for teenagers under 18 violates the Eighth Amendment ban on "cruel and unusual punishment." The argument is based partly on brain studies.

The case is based on a brutal murder. When he was 17 years old, Christopher Simmons persuaded a younger friend to help him rob a woman, tie her up with electrical cable and duct tape, and throw her over a bridge. He was convicted of murder and sentenced to death by a Missouri court in 1994. In a whipsaw of legal proceedings, the Missouri Supreme Court set the sentence aside last year. Now 27, Simmons could again face execution: The state of Missouri has appealed to have the death penalty reinstated. The U.S. Supreme Court will hear the case in October, and its decision could well rest on neurobiology.

At issue is whether 16- and 17-year-olds who commit capital offenses can be executed or whether this would be cruel and unusual punishment, banned by the Constitution's Eighth Amendment. In a joint brief filed on 19 July, eight medical and mental health organizations including the American Medical Association cite a sheaf of developmental biology and behavioral literature to support their argument that adolescent brains have not reached their full adult potential. "Capacities relevant to criminal responsibility are still developing when you're 16 or 17 years old," says psychologist Laurence Steinberg of the American Psychological Association, which joined the brief supporting Simmons. Adds physician David Fassler, spokesperson for the American Psychiatric Association (APA) and the American Academy of Child and Adolescent Psychiatry, the argument "does not excuse violent criminal behavior, but it's an important factor for courts to consider" when wielding a punishment "as extreme and irreversible as death."

...In arguing for leniency, Simmons's supporters cite some of the latest research that points to the immaturity of youthful brains, such as a May study of children and teens, led by NIMH's Nitin Gogtay. The team followed 13 individuals between the ages of 4 and 21, performing magnetic resonance imaging (MRI) every 2 years to track changes in the physical structure of brain tissue. As previous research had suggested, the frontal lobes matured last. Starting from the back of the head, "we see a wave of brain change moving forward into the front of the brain like a forest fire," says UCLA's Thompson, a co-author. The brain changes continued up to age 21, the oldest person they examined. "It's quite possible that the brain maturation peaks after age 21," he adds....

Adults behave differently not just because they have different brain structures, according to [neuroscientist Ruben Gur of the University of Pennsylvania in Philadelphia, Ruben] Gur, but because they use the structures in a different way. A fully developed frontal lobe curbs impulses coming from other parts of the brain...: "If you've been insulted, your emotional brain says, 'Kill,' but your frontal lobe says you're in the middle of a cocktail party, 'so let's respond with a cutting remark.'"

As it matures, the adolescent brain slowly reorganizes how it integrates information coming from the nether regions. Using functional MRI—which lights up sites in the brain that are active—combined with simple tests, neuroscientist Beatriz Luna of the University of Pittsburgh has found that the brain switches from relying heavily on local regions in childhood to more distributive and collaborative interactions among distant regions in adulthood....

Although many researchers agree that the brain, especially the frontal lobe, continues to develop well into teenhood and beyond, many scientists hesitate to weigh in on the legal debate. Some...say the data "just aren't there" for them to confidently testify to the moral or legal culpability of adolescents in court. Neuroscientist Elizabeth Sowell of UCLA says that too little data exist to connect behavior to brain structure, and imaging is far from being diagnostic. "We couldn't do a scan on a kid and decide if they should be tried as an adult," she says....

Source: Reprinted with permission from Mary Beckman, "Crime, Culpability, and the Adolescent Brain," *Science Magazine,* July 30, 2004. Copyright 2004 AAAS.

---

interviews); McVeigh himself said he wanted to die; and the crime was horrific (killing 168 innocent people, including many children). These findings led Frank Newport (2001) of the Gallup Poll to write:

> We thus end up with a sociological hypothesis: Americans' support for the death penalty will increase to the degree that it is made clear that no mistake has occurred and that the death penalty is being applied to a truly guilty person. One corollary to this hypothesis: support may actually end up increasing in the years to come, rather than decreasing, as new DNA testing techniques become widely used. Why? Because, while this evidence may prove that some on death row are in reality innocent, it also may reduce any chance of a mistake in future cases.

For years we assumed the death penalty saved money. Not anymore. We've learned it's expensive to charge and try death sentence cases. In federal cases, the

CJ & TECHNOLOGY

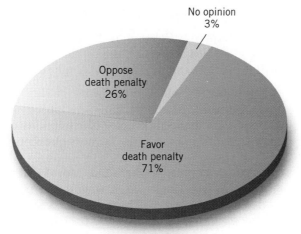

No opinion
3%

Oppose
death penalty
26%

Favor
death penalty
71%

◄ **FIGURE 11.5 Public Opinion and the Death Penalty, 2004**

"Are you in favor of the death penalty for a person convicted of murder?"

Source: PollingReport.com, "Crime: Death Penalty," May 2004; found at http://www.pollingreport.com/crime.htm (visited October 15, 2004).

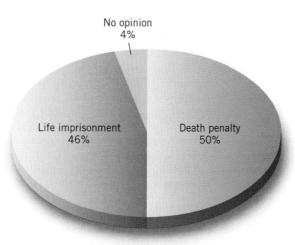

No opinion
4%

Life imprisonment
46%

Death penalty
50%

◄ **FIGURE 11.6 Public Opinion on the Death Penalty vs. Life without Parole**

"If you could choose between the following two approaches, which do you think is the better penalty for murder: the death penalty or life imprisonment with absolutely no possibility of parole?"

Source: PollingReport.com, "Crime: Death Penalty," May 2004; found at http://www.pollingreport.com/crime.htm (visited October 15, 2004).

average cost of defending a negotiated death sentence is $192,333; the amount rises to $269,000 if the case goes to trial. Prosecuting a federal death penalty case costs an average of $365,000. These amounts don't include the cost of investigation, expert assistance, or law enforcement assistance (Judicial Conference of the United States 1998).

Keeping prisoners on death row until they're executed is also high. According to an article in the *Columbus Dispatch:*

> The State of Ohio spent $1.5 million to kill one mentally ill man who wanted to be executed. Among the costs were: $18,147 overtime for prison employees and $2,250 overtime for State Highway Patrol officers at the time of the execution. This does not include overtime for 25 prison public information officers who worked the night of the execution. The state spent $5,320 on a satellite truck so that the official announcement of Wilford Berry's execution could be beamed to outside media, and $88.42 for the lethal drugs. Attorney General Betty Montgomery had 5 to 15 prosecutors working on the case. Between 5 and 10% of the annual budget for the state's capital-crimes section was devoted to the Berry case for 5 years. Keeping Berry in prison for his entire life would have cost approximately half as much. (Johnson 1999, A1)

In 1995, the estimated cost of one execution was $2 million. Asked why, the noted criminologist Frank Zimring replied, "Lawyers cost more than prison guards" (Baldus 1995, 1035).

Four Tough Questions about Capital Punishment

The U.S. Supreme Court may have settled the constitutional questions surrounding the death penalty; the public may support it; and the cost might be worth it. But let's examine four other questions about the sentence of death:

1. Is it right? (the moral question)
2. Does it work? (the utilitarian question)
3. Does it kill innocent people? (the fallibility question)
4. Does it discriminate? (the fairness question)

Is the Death Penalty Right? (The Moral Question) Death penalty supporters point to two Old Testament passages: one from Genesis, "Whoever sheds the blood of man, by man shall his blood be shed" (Gen. 9:6); the other from Exodus, "Eye for eye, tooth for tooth, hand for hand, foot for foot, burn for burn, wound for wound, stripe for stripe" (Ex. 21:24–25). Opponents invoke the New Testament passage where Jesus admonishes the crowd before stoning an adulteress: "He that is without sin among you, let him first cast a stone at her" (John 8:7). They also point to the Old Testament, in which God warns, "Vengeance is mine" (meaning it's not ours to inflict) (Deut. 32:35). Sister Helen Prejean (the nun who was the inspiration for the role played by Susan Sarandon in the movie *Dead Man Walking*) put the moral question this way: "When you hear of the terrible things people have done, you can say they deserve to die, but the key moral question is 'Do we deserve to kill?'" (*Frontline* 1996).

Supporters of capital punishment also rely on moral arguments to bolster their positions. According to Professor Ernest van den Haag:

> The life of each man should be sacred to each other man....It is not enough to proclaim the sacredness and inviolability of human life. It must be secured as well, by threatening with the loss of their own life those who violate what has been proclaimed as inviolable—the right of innocents to live. (Bedau 1982, 331)

At the end of the day, the moral debate over capital punishment can't be a matter of science or logic; it boils down to values. Some people believe deeply it's wrong for the state to kill anyone for any reason; others believe just as deeply that it's wrong not to execute the worst criminals.

Does It Work? (The Utilitarian Question) Way back in the 1600s, the tough-as-nails judge Sir Edward Coke said it made him "weep" that hanging 500 English felons in one year didn't reduce crime but instead encouraged it to grow by example. In the 1700s, both the great Italian criminologist Cesare Beccaria and the American reformer Benjamin Rush agreed with Lord Coke and opposed the death penalty at least in part because it didn't work to reduce crime. A hard core of abolitionists has crusaded against the death penalty ever since. The abolitionist crusade continued but the death penalty endured because of the strong public support for it, much of that support based on confidence that executions prevented murder.

The crusaders couldn't prove that killing criminals didn't reduce crime and the public couldn't prove it did. Then, in the 1950s, the distinguished and highly respected sociologist Thorsten Sellin (1959, 24; 1967) decided to study the deterrent effect of the death penalty. He compared homicide rates in states that had abolished the death penalty with carefully matched similar states next to and/or similar to states that retained the death penalty. He found that "Homicide rates are conditioned by other factors than the death penalty."

Other sociologists (Bowers 1974; Reckless 1969, 54) got similar results by comparing homicide rates before and after in (1) states that abolished the death penalty; (2) states that imposed a moratorium on the death penalty; (3) states with highly publicized executions; and, (4) states with mandatory death penalties against states with discretionary death penalties. They, too, found no deterrent effect. As if this weren't impressive enough social science evidence, Sellin even found there's no statistical support for the proposition that law enforcement officials are safer in death penalty states than those in states without it. With this impressive array of studies, the sociologists seemed to have answered the deterrence question.

Then the accomplished University of Chicago economist Isaac Ehrlich (1975, 397) got into the debate in 1975 when he published the findings from his econometric study that "an additional execution per year...may have resulted, on average, in 7 or 8 fewer murders." Careful and responsible researcher that he is, he added this warning, "[T]he weakness inherent in these predicted magnitudes is that they may be subject to relatively large prediction errors." Of course, the headline was more exciting than the warning. Death penalty supporters turned it into the bumper sticker, "One execution saves eight innocent lives!" (Albert 1999, 354–355). Opponents pounced on it. A cottage industry in death penalty research was born, and an ideological battle broke out. The economists backing up Ehrlich's findings grew bolder. Steven K. Layson (1985, 68), in another elaborate econometric analysis based on homicide data from 1936 to 1977, concluded that every execution prevents 18 murders!

Ehrlich's study set off a firestorm of debate. The sociologists savaged the econometric analyses by pointing out all kinds of flaws. Even the U.S. Supreme Court joined the fray. Justice Thurgood Marshall (1976) wrote in one dissenting opinion:

> The study is defective because it compares execution and homicide rates on a nationwide, rather than a state-by-state, basis. The aggregation of data from all States including those that have abolished the death penalty obscures the relationship between murder and execution rates. Under Ehrlich's methodology, a decrease in the execution risk in one State combined with an increase in the murder rate in another State would, all other things being equal, suggest a deterrent effect that quite obviously would not exist. Indeed, a deterrent effect would be suggested if, once again all other things being equal, one State abolished the death penalty and experienced no change in the murder rate, while another State experienced an increase in the murder rate. (235)

The debate continues as you read this. Professor Craig J. Albert (1999, 354–355) applied regression analysis to state-by-state homicide data from 1982 to 1994. His regression variables included economic conditions, demography (youth and race), population, and alcohol consumption. His conclusion: "The data do not support any conclusion that execution deters homicides." But Professor Albert has enough reservations (we won't list them here) to assure us that his research isn't the last word on whether the death penalty reduces murders.

Does the Death Penalty Kill Innocent People? (The Fallibility Question) In 8,048 rape and rape-and-murder cases referred to the FBI crime lab from 1988 to mid-1995, a staggering 2,012 of the primary suspects were exonerated by DNA evidence alone. Had DNA analysis not been available (as it wasn't a decade earlier), several hundred of the 2,012 would probably have been tried, convicted, and sentenced for crimes they didn't commit (National Institute of Justice 1996a).

Does this startling finding of the U.S. Department of Justice mean that innocent people are actually killed? If so, how many wrong executions are acceptable? Abolitionists quickly answer zero because, they argue, you can't say, "Whoops, wrong person, let's take this one back." It's too late for that. Supporters say, first, there's nothing to worry about because the last innocent person was executed in the 1930s. And second, that single mistake proves the death penalty is almost perfect, which is all we can expect from any human institution. Besides, they say, the demand for perfection is only a smoke screen for death penalty opponents to hide their real motive, to get around the U.S. Supreme Court's firm majority position that sentences of death and capital punishment are constitutional. (See the In Focus box "To Kill or Not to Kill?")

We really don't *know* how many innocent people are executed. We hear and read about innocent people released at various stages in the criminal process—arrest, charge, trial, and conviction. We hear especially about close calls on

To Kill or Not to Kill?

When Joseph Hartzler...was appointed the lead prosecutor in the trial of Timothy McVeigh, the Oklahoma City bomber, he remarked that Mc-Veigh was headed for Hell, no matter what. His job, Hartzler said, was simply to speed up the delivery. That was also the attitude evinced by the prosecutors vying to be first to try the two Beltway sniper suspects. Given the fear and fury the multiple shootings inspired, it wasn't surprising that polls showed that Americans favored imposing what Attorney General Ashcroft referred to as the "ultimate sanction." Yet despite the retributive wrath that the public seems quick to visit on particular crimes, or criminals, there has also been, in recent years, growing skepticism about the death-penalty system in general. A significant number of Americans question both the system's over-all fairness and, given the many cases in which DNA evidence has proved that the wrong person was convicted of a crime, its ability to distinguish the innocent from the guilty.

Ambivalence about the death penalty is an American tradition. When the Republic was founded, all the states, following English law, imposed capital punishment. But the humanistic impulses that favored democracy led to questions about whether the state should have the right to kill the citizens upon whose consent government was erected....One need only glance at a TV screen to realize that murder remains an American preoccupation, and the concomitant questions of how to deal with it challenge contending strains in our moral thought, pitting Old Testament against New, retribution against forgiveness....

* * *

Supporters of capital punishment in Illinois, particularly those in law enforcement, often use Henry Brisbon as their trump card. Get rid of the death penalty, they say, and what do you do about the likes of Henry?

On the night of June 3, 1973, Brisbon and three "rap partners" (his term) forced several cars off I-57, an interstate highway south of Chicago. Brisbon made a woman in one of the cars disrobe, and then he discharged a shotgun in her vagina. He compelled a young couple to lie down in a field together, instructed them to "make this your last kiss," and shot both of them in the back. His role in these crimes was uncovered only years later, when he confessed to an inmate working as a law librarian in the penitentiary where he was serving a stretch for rape and armed robbery. Because the I-57 killings occurred shortly after the Supreme Court declared capital punishment unconstitutional, Brisbon was not eligible for the death penalty. He was given a sentence of one thousand to three thousand years in prison, probably the longest term ever imposed in Illinois.

In October, 1978, eleven months after the sentencing, Brisbon murdered again. He placed a homemade knife to the throat of a guard to subdue him, then went with several inmates to the cell of another prisoner and stabbed him repeatedly. By the time Brisbon was tried again, in early 1982, Illinois had restored capital punishment, and he was sentenced to death. The evidence in his sentencing hearings included proof of yet another murder Brisbon had allegedly committed prior to his imprisonment, when he placed a shotgun against the face of a store clerk and blew him away. He had accumulated more than two hundred disciplinary violations while he was incarcerated, and had played a major role in the violent takeover of Stateville prison, in September, 1979. Predictably, the death sentence did not markedly improve Brisbon's conduct. In the years since he was first condemned, he has been accused of a number of serious assaults on guards, including a stabbing, and he severely injured another inmate when he threw a thirty-pound weight against his skull....

* * *

The members of the [Illinois Governor's Commission on Capital Punishment] knew that capital punishment would not be abolished in Illinois anytime soon. Accordingly, our formal recommendations, many of which were made unanimously, ran to matters of reform. Principal among them was lowering the risks of convicting the innocent. [See Make Your Decision on page 400 for a list of these reforms.]

* * *

Yet our proposals sidestepped the ultimate question. One fall day, Paul Simon, the former U.S. senator who was one of the commission's chairs and is a longtime foe of the death penalty, forced us to vote on whether Illinois should have a death penalty at all. The vote was an expression of sentiment, not a formal recommendation. What was our best advice to our fellow-citizens, political realities aside? By a narrow majority, we agreed that capital punishment should not be an option.

I admit that I am still attracted to a death penalty that would be applied to horrendous crimes, or that would provide absolute certainty that the likes of Henry Brisbon would never again satisfy their cruel appetites. But if death is available as a punishment, the furious heat of grief and rage that these crimes inspire will inevitably short-circuit any capital system. Now and then, we will execute someone who is innocent, while the fundamental equality of each survivor's loss creates an inevitable emotional momentum to expand the categories for death-penalty eligibility. Like many others who have wrestled with capital punishment, I have changed my mind often, driven back and forth by the errors each position seems to invite. Yet after two years of deliberation, I seem to have finally come to rest. When Paul Simon asked whether Illinois should have a death penalty, I voted no.

Source: Excerpts from "Annals of Law: To Kill or Not to Kill," by Scott Turow, first appeared in *The New Yorker*, January 6, 2003, and was later revised and published in the book, *Ultimate Punishment*, by Scott Turow. Copyright © 2003 by Scott Turow. Reprinted by permission of Farrar, Straus and Giroux, LLC.

death row—convicts who escape execution by days or sometimes even hours (Bedau, Radelet, and Putnam 2004, 589–594). As of February 2001, DNA tests had led to the release of 82 prisoners, 10 of them on death row (LoLordo 2001, 3A). These releases have generated lots of news coverage and heated up the debate on the death penalty to furious proportions.

Death penalty opponents argue these close calls are too close. Take the case of Florida half-brothers William Jent and Ernest Miller who came within 16 hours of execution. Supporters say they prove the system works (Radelet and Bedau 1998, 232). Calls for reform are growing louder as people from all parts of the religious, cultural, and political spectrum grow uneasy about the fallibility of the system. In *Criminal Justice 6* (Samaha 2003, 171), I wrote, "By the time you read these words, there may be a federal law providing for mandatory DNA testing in all capital cases." We're still waiting (March 26, 2005)!

Does the Death Penalty Discriminate? (The Fairness Question) You don't see wealthy people, or even middle-class people, on death row. Since John Webster, a famous professor of medicine at the Harvard Law School, was sentenced to death and hanged in 1850, businesspeople, professors, lawyers, and doctors have escaped death row almost completely. Mostly unskilled workers (almost all men), including many Blacks and Hispanics, are found on death row. But are they there unfairly—that is, because they're poor, men, and Black, Hispanic, or some other racial minority? There's not a single case in the twentieth century and so far in the twenty-first where a court decided a death sentence was based on class, sex, racial, or ethnic discrimination. Still, there's plenty of empirical evidence to cast doubt on whether there's no discrimination in death sentences (Black 1981, 94; Lewis 1979, 203–204).

The U.S. General Accounting Office (GAO) (1990) reviewed 28 empirical studies of the death penalty to find out whether either the race of the defendant or the race of the victim mattered in the decision to impose a death sentence. What did the studies show?

1. The race of the victim mattered. Those who murder Whites are more likely to get sentenced to death than those who murder nonwhites. This finding was "remarkably consistent across data sets, states, data collection methods, and analytic techniques."
2. The race of the defendant sometimes mattered and sometimes didn't. The influence of the defendant's race varied across studies, like one study that showed Black defendants were more likely to get death sentences in rural areas but White defendants were more likely to get death sentences in urban areas.

The GAO published its results in 1990. All of the studies at that time were of southern states. Since then, law professor David Baldus and statistician George Woodworth (1998, 385, 399–400) have examined both the period before and after the GAO study. Their study included all death penalty states that had imposed a death sentence (Kansas, New York, and New Hampshire hadn't done so at the time) and had an available study (28 states). They found that in 25 of the 28 states, there's evidence of race-of-the-victim disparities. There was some evidence of race-of-the-defendant disparity in 10 states. Disparities aren't limited to the South: They were found also in Philadelphia and in New Jersey in the 1990s.

"The most in-depth and detailed study of race and the death penalty in North Carolina's history" found that between 1993 and 1997 "defendants whose victims are white are 3.5 times more likely to be sentenced to death than defendants whose victims are non-white." ... "Despite a generation of legal and cultural efforts to eliminate discrimination, these results show that racial bias still dramatically affects the most final of judgments—who gets the death penalty," according to law professor and principal investigator of the study, Jack Boger (Common Sense Foundation 2001).

A bit more than a year after George Ryan, then the governor of Illinois, declared the state's capital punishment system broken and emptied death row, the struggle over the death penalty is returning here.

On one side of the new debate are legislators and prosecutors who say landmark reforms state lawmakers have adopted in recent months mean it is time to begin executions again. On the other side are critics of capital punishment who praise the reforms but say many more must be made before Illinois can be certain it is not executing an innocent person—if that can ever be assured.

Caught somewhere in the middle is Rod R. Blagojevich, a Democrat, who was sworn in as governor two days after Mr. Ryan, a Republican, condemned the state's system and cleared death row last January. For now, Mr. Blagojevich, a former prosecutor who supported the death penalty in the past, says that he is in no rush to move forward and that a statewide moratorium on executions—put in place four years ago by Mr. Ryan—stands. But he has begun facing pressure from both sides.

The possibility of killing an innocent man set off Illinois's struggle in 2000 and drew the attention of other states' leaders. By then, 13 condemned prisoners, including one man who came within 50 hours of execution, had been freed from death row because of exonerations and appeals—more than the number the state had actually executed since the death penalty was reinstated in 1977. If the truth, as Mr. Ryan then said, was that the system was broken, answers seem murkier now: Is it fixed? Can it ever be? And who gets to decide when that time has come? "We did the death penalty reform bill," said State Senator Peter J. Roskam, a Republican from Wheaton, who said he was urging Governor Blagojevich to at least consider execution dates of new death row inmates once their cases reach the end of appeals. Since death row was cleared 14 months ago, only three people have been sentenced to death in the state, and it will be years before their cases make their way through the appeals process, but legislators like Mr. Roskam say it is time to begin setting that process in motion. "We went through months of negotiations," Mr. Roskam said. "If the governor has substantive concerns about the bill that he has signed, we didn't hear about them. Now I think the time has come to lift the moratorium and enact the law."

That attitude deeply troubles others, like Edwin Colfax, executive director of the Illinois Death Penalty Education Project. "Our big concern is that people see the substantial progress we've had to date and are under the

impression that the death penalty has been fixed," Mr. Colfax said. "That would be a tragedy. The reality is that there is such a long way to go. We are not on the cusp of a death penalty system that deserves our confidence."

In January, Governor Blagojevich signed the last piece in a package of legislative changes to the system. The police will be required to audiotape or videotape their interrogations of murder suspects. Judges may now rule out execution in cases that depend on only a single jailhouse informant; moreover, such testimony must now be subject to screening before it is admitted in court. Defendants are granted more access to DNA databases and have more time to petition the court with new evidence. "I couldn't have gotten one of these passed five years ago," said Senator John J. Cullerton, Democrat of Chicago, who helped guide the package through the Legislature. "This was really a big deal."

Still, the legislation by no means included all of the more than 80 recommendations made by a panel Governor Ryan appointed to review the system. Among those not adopted were these: a requirement that the public defender be assigned during police interrogations of death-eligible cases if a suspect requests it; the separation of

AP/Wide World Photos

▲ Aaron Patterson (left), was pardoned in 2003 by then Illinois Governor George Ryan "by reason of innocence" after 17 years in prison. He stands here with Nathson Fields (right) as Fields' sister happily looks on. Patterson and Fields had met on death row and became fast friends. Shortly before this photo was taken, Patterson had walked into the Cook County Jail with a cashier's check for $100,000, the 10 percent of Nathson Fields' required $1 million bond. Fields, a former El Rukn gang member, was convicted of the murder of rival gang members. The Illinois Supreme Court overturned the conviction after the judge in the case, Thomas Maloney, was himself convicted of bribery. Fields was sent back to Cook County Jail where he was waiting for more than 5 years when Patterson posted bail for him.

the evidence laboratory from the state police; a significant reduction of the number of crimes that carry the death penalty; and the creation of a statewide review panel to consider each capital case brought by local prosecutors.

Supporters of the death penalty insist there is another agenda underlying the continuing moratorium and all the talk of more revisions. Kevin W. Lyons, the Peoria County prosecutor, said that opponents of the death penalty wanted to end capital punishment in Illinois altogether, not reform it. "This debate was birthed as a question of certainty—we wanted to be certain that we were executing the right people," Mr. Lyons said. "But it has been raised as a political issue. The death penalty abolitionists hopped the train, derailed it, and it became a hope to abolish the death penalty."

If Mr. Lyons and others are pressing Mr. Blagojevich to reconsider the moratorium, another group is pressing for more revisions. Aaron Patterson, who left death row 14 months ago, is one of that number. While Mr. Ryan commuted more than 160 of the condemned to sentences of life in prison, he pardoned Mr. Patterson and a handful of others outright and sent them home. Mr. Patterson, Mr. Ryan said, had been wrongly convicted in the 1986 stabbing deaths of an elderly couple.

Since he emerged from death row, Mr. Patterson, 39, has not gone away quietly. He has disrupted news con-

ferences held by Mayor Richard M. Daley of Chicago and Patrick J. Fitzgerald, the United States attorney here. He set up a tea service on the lawn of Richard Devine, the Cook County state's attorney, in an effort to get Mr. Devine's attention. "These people are unapologetic about what they did," he said, "and somebody has to hold their feet to the fire."

After 17 years behind bars, Mr. Patterson is running for the State Legislature in Tuesday's primary. It bothers him, he said, to watch what he considers the slowness of reforms to the death penalty and to the state's justice system in general. "They've been touching the surface," Mr. Patterson said of legislation in Springfield, the state capital. "I just don't see the tide turning fast enough. I feel like I should go down there to the source of the problem and change it."

QUESTIONS

1. List and summarize the arguments in favor of continuing the death penalty moratorium.
2. List and summarize the arguments against lifting the moratorium.
3. If you were governor, what would be your decision: lift or continue the moratorium? Back up your answer.

Chapter Summary

▶ Criminal punishment has three purposes. Retribution looks *backward* to punish criminals for their completed criminal *conduct* because they deserve it. There are three problems with retribution: Translating justice into specific penalties; proving human nature craves revenge; and most criminal laws aren't based on moral blameworthiness. Prevention looks *forward* to change criminals, punishing them to prevent future crimes. Restitution requires offenders to pay back monetary losses they caused to victims. Restorative justice starts with the proposition that the basic nature of crime is a harm to individuals (victims, offenders, and their friends and families) and their relationships, a harm that has to be repaired and healed.

▶ Both fixed and indeterminate sentencing are essential elements of criminal justice. Fixed sentences point to the desirability of the certainty, predictability, and evenhandedness of formal rules in administering criminal justice. Indeterminate sentencing responds to the need for flexibility, the "play in the joints" of informal discretionary decision making that's essential to fair criminal justice.

▶ Mandatory minimum sentences are supposed to satisfy three aims of criminal punishment: retribution, incapacitation, and deterrence. Evaluations suggest that mandatory minimum penalties in practice don't live up to these promises. Some evaluations of truth-in-sentencing laws and three-strikes-and-you're-out laws have found they reduce crime; some have found they have no effect; and some have found they increase homicides.

▶ Sentencing guidelines are fixed (but flexible) sentences based on balancing the seriousness of the offense and the criminal history of the offender. Their purposes include uniformity, neutrality, truth, and control. One evaluation of the Minnesota sentencing guidelines found they resulted in a shift in prison populations from property offenders to violent criminals. But it also found that guidelines don't eliminate race, gender, marital status, income, and other biases from infecting sentencing decisions.

▶ Presentence reports provide judges with information about offenders' criminal, social, and mental history. Use of reports *reduces* but doesn't *eliminate* judicial discretion. The quality of information varies, depending on the workload of the probation officers responsible for investigating and writing the report and on the amount of influence they have on judicial decision making.

▶ Disparity in sentencing refers to different sentences for similar offenders; similar sentences for different offenders; and similar offenders receiving different sentences for minor differences. There's disparity in sentencing Blacks, Hispanics, and women, but the evidence is mixed as to whether this disparity is infected with discrimination—that is, the use of unacceptable criteria, usually race, ethnicity, or gender, to determine sentences.

▶ The U.S. Supreme Court has ruled that the death penalty doesn't violate the Eighth Amendment ban on "cruel and unusual punishment," as long as it's fairly imposed and doesn't include mentally ill or mentally retarded prisoners or those who were juveniles under 15 when they committed the crimes they're imprisoned for. The public strongly supports the death penalty, although support drops when there's an option for life in prison with absolutely no chance of parole. It's expensive to charge and try death penalty defendants, and to confine prisoners on death row.

▶ Four tough questions surround the death penalty: Is it right? Does it work? Does it kill innocent people? Does it discriminate?

Key Terms

retribution, p. 365
prevention, p. 365
restitution, p. 365
restoration, p. 365
culpability, p. 365
special deterrence, p. 366

general deterrence, p. 366
incapacitation, p. 366
rehabilitation, p. 366
determinate sentencing, p. 368
indeterminate sentencing, p. 368

mandatory minimum sentence laws, p. 371
sentencing guidelines, p. 380
guided discretion death penalty statutes, p. 388

Web Resources

Go to http://cj.wadsworth.com/samaha_cj7e for a wealth of online resources related to your book. Take a "pre-test" and "post-test" for each chapter in order to help master the material. Check out the *Web Links* to access the websites mentioned in the text, as well as many others. Explore the *Decision Points* flagged in the margins of the text for additional insights. You can also access recent perspectives by clicking on *CJ in the News* and *Terrorism Update* under *Course Resources*.

Search Online with InfoTrac College Edition

For additional information, explore InfoTrac College Edition, your online library. Go to http://cj.wadsworth.com/samaha_cj7e to access InfoTrac College Edition from your book's website. Use the passcode that came with your book. You will find InfoTrac College Edition exercises and a list of key words for further research.

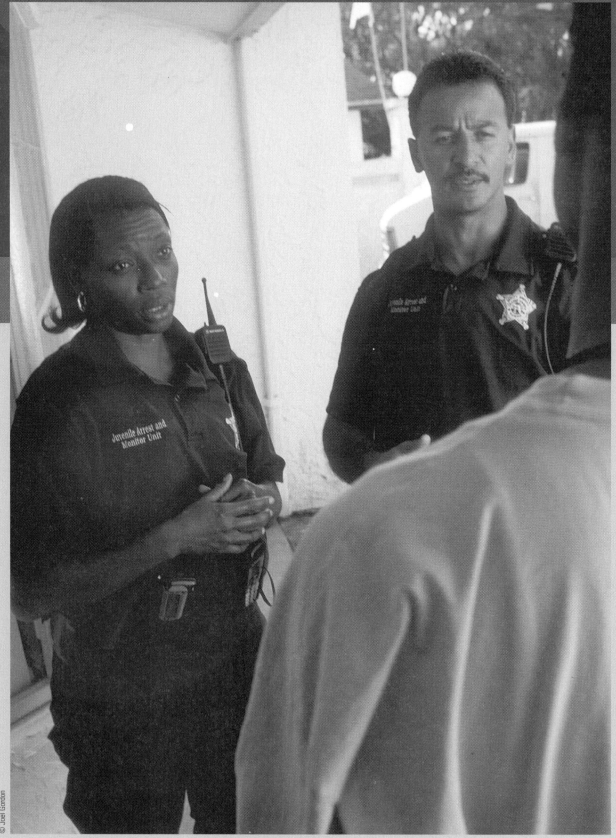

CHAPTER 12

Community Corrections

FACT *or* FICTION?

▶ The core mission of probation is leniency for first-time offenders.

▶ Felons on probation are a significant risk to public safety.

▶ Most probation and parole violators remain in the community.

▶ Probationers and parolees are entitled to *Miranda* warnings before they're interrogated.

▶ Empirical research proves that poor supervision accounts for most crimes committed by offenders released on probation and parole.

▶ Researchers haven't proven to what extent parole reduces parolees' future employment and income.

▶ The basic idea of intermediate punishments is to answer the popular demand for harsher punishments.

▶ Intermediate punishments are popular but not widely used.

▶ Correctional boot camps significantly reduce recidivism.

PROBATION AND PAROLE: COMMUNITY PROTECTION OR OFFENDER SECOND CHANCE?

Only a small percentage of men *have* to go back to prison. I think that many convicted fellows deserve another chance. However, we not only have to play fair with the fellows who's [*sic*] gotten bad breaks, but we must also consider the rights of the taxpayers and our duties to them. We don't want anyone in jail who can make good.

—LOU GEHRIG, MEMBER NEW YORK CITY PAROLE COMMISSION 1940–41, BASEBALL HALL OF FAME (QUOTED IN CULLEN, ECK, AND LOWENKAMP 2002, 28)

corrections the final stage of the criminal process—incarceration, probation and parole, or intermediate punishments

Once they're convicted, offenders are sentenced and moved to the final stage of the criminal process—**corrections.** Corrections can take place in prisons and jails (incarceration); in the community (probation and parole); or in a combination of confinement and community supervision (intermediate punishments). Incarceration—especially confinement in prisons—gets the lion's share of public attention, tax dollars, research efforts, and most textbook space (including this one). But most convicted offenders aren't in prison or jail; they're serving their sentences in the community. Four million adults were on probation at the beginning of 2004 and 775,000 were on parole; 1.4 million were in prison and 691,000 were in jail (Glaze and Palla 2004, 1) (Figure 12.1). About 100,000 offenders are sentenced to intermediate punishments; they remain in the community but under stricter supervision than ordinary probationers.

All community corrections—probation, parole, and intermediate punishments—have multiple and demanding missions:

- Punish offenders
- Rehabilitate offenders
- Protect the community
- Reduce crime
- Save money
- Relieve jail and prison crowding

In this chapter, we'll examine probation and parole and intermediate punishments.

Probation and Parole

Many people confuse probation with parole, so let's clear up the confusion before we discuss them:

probation a *substitute* for confinement in prison or jail

parole *follows* confinement in prison

1. **Probation** is a *substitute* for confinement in prison or jail; **parole** *follows* confinement in prison.
2. Probation is a *sentencing* option for *judges*, who set the conditions of release; parole is a *release* option for *administrators* (parole board), who set the conditions of release.
3. Probation is a local *or* state decision made in over two thousand probation departments; parole is *always* a state decision administered by one state agency (parole board). Local judges decide whether and under

◀ **FIGURE 12.1 Number of Persons under Correctional Supervision, 2004**

Source: Lauren E. Glaze and Seri Palla, *Probation and Parole in the United States, 2003* (Washington, DC: Bureau of Justice Statistics, July 2004), p. 1.

what conditions to put offenders on probation; state parole boards decide whether and under what conditions to release prisoners. (Petersilia 2004, 483)

Despite these differences, probation and parole have a lot in common:

1. Both gather and present information to decision makers.
2. Decision makers have the power to release offenders into the community, to set the conditions of their release, and to revoke the release of probationers and parolees and order them to confinement.
3. Both include the core missions of holding offenders accountable for their crimes, protecting public safety, and reintegrating offenders into the community—turning them into responsible people who support themselves and obey the law. (Petersilia 2004, 484)

In the next several sections, you'll learn about the history of probation and parole; their missions; the granting, conditions, and revocation of probation and parole; the Constitution and probation and parole; how effective each is; and the role of race, ethnicity, and gender in probation and parole.

The History of Probation and Parole

Supervision in the community instead of confinement in prisons and jails is an ancient practice. Justices of the peace in sixteenth-century England commonly released minor offenders from custody if they promised to "be of good behavior" and some responsible person agreed to make sure they kept their promise. If they broke it, they were locked up. Settlers brought the "good behavior bond" to the American colonies, and it continued in use after the Revolution in the new United States (Samaha 1981, 189–204).

The History of Probation In the 1840s, John Augustus, a Boston shoemaker, earned the title of "first probation officer" by expanding on the good behavior bond. Augustus visited the Boston police court, where he saw "a ragged and wretched looking man" charged with being a "common drunkard." The man begged Augustus to save him from the House of Correction; "I'll never take another drink if you save me." Deeply moved, Augustus asked the judge to release the man into his custody for 30 days. During that time, Augustus fed the man and found him a job. After that, the man stopped drinking and supported himself (Champion 1988, 1–3).

Encouraged by his success, Augustus gave up shoemaking and devoted the rest of his life to "saving" Boston criminals. Magistrates released 2000 people into his custody—mostly drunks, prostitutes, juveniles, and gamblers. Augustus treated them all the same; he took them into his home, found them jobs, and inspired

The Bostonian Society

▲ In the 1840s, former shoemaker John Augustus became the United States' first probation officer. Augustus was compelled to take on this job when he visited the Boston police court. There he saw "a ragged and wretched man" charged with being a "common drunkard" who begged Augustus to save him from the House of Correction: "I'll never take another drink if you save me." Deeply moved, Augustus asked the judge to release the man into his custody for 30 days. During that time, Augustus fed the man and found him a job; after that, the man stopped drinking and supported himself.

them to "purify" their lives. He had great success, probably because of the powerful combination of his devotion to reform and his skill in selecting the right offenders. He threw himself totally into his "calling," and he accepted only "good risks"—first-time, minor offenders who showed promise of success (National Probation Association 1983).

A half century later, probation became a favorite of reformers during the great Progressive reform wave of the early 1900s. By 1930, the federal government and 36 states had enacted probation legislation. By 1940, all but the most rural areas in the country had embraced probation (Rothman 1980, 82–83).

The History of Parole Alexander Maconochie, a Scottish geographer and captain in the British Royal Navy, introduced the modern idea of parole when, in 1840, he was appointed superintendent of the infamous English penal colonies in Norfolk Island, Australia. Believing prisoners were capable of reform, he developed a plan to prepare them for their eventual return to society. He divided his system into three grades, with each offering more life outside prison. Prisoners could earn promotions through labor, study, and good behavior.

The third grade in Maconochie's system was what we call parole—conditional liberty with a "a ticket of leave." With ticket in hand, prisoners could live outside prison as long as they obeyed the conditions of release attached to the ticket. Violating the rules of release meant returning to prison and starting all over again through the ranks. So conditional liberty, like the grades inside prison, was tied to successfully living according to the rules outside prison walls. Vast improvements in the conditions of confinement were reported, but the British government didn't appreciate Maconochie's reforms and replaced him in 1844, after which it's said, prison conditions sank to the low they were in before he took over (Wilcox 1927, 5–6).

The penologist Zebulon Brockway introduced parole to the United States when he became superintendent of the famous Elmira Reformatory in New York (Chapter 11). Brockway was determined to manage prison populations and reform prisoners. To accomplish these missions, he adopted a two-prong strategy: indeterminate sentences and parole releases (Chapter 11). Within a short time, parole came to include three elements, all based on the indeterminate sentence:

1. Conditional release from confinement before sentences expire
2. Supervision until sentences expire
3. Revocation for violations of the conditions of the release

Parole has always provoked controversy (usually heated). Clair Wilcox (1927), in his masterful survey of parole in Pennsylvania in the 1920s, examined newspapers and magazine articles about parole. He found headlines like "Turning the Criminals Loose" and "Uplifters and Politicians Free Convicts" (1). Even former Chief Justice and U.S. President William Howard Taft piled on, telling the widely popular *Collier's Weekly* magazine:

> Paroles have been abused and should be granted with greater care. It is discouraging to read of the arrest and prosecution of one charged with a new felony who had committed some prior offense, had secured parole after a short confinement and then had used his release to begin again his criminal life. (Wilcox 1927, 2)

These criticisms were made during the 1920s, but they could just as easily have come from today. Most of us remember the outrage following the kidnapping and murder in 1993 of 12-year-old Polly Klaas (Chapter 11), who was snatched from a slumber party by a parolee who had a criminal record for attacking children. Of course, the reality of parole is more complex than the critics admit. A closer look at the missions of probation and parole will give us insight into that reality.

The Missions of Probation and Parole

The core missions of probation and parole are sentencing (Chapter 11) and those you'll learn about in discussions on prisons (Chapters 13–14) and juvenile justice (Chapter 15). You've already learned the core missions of all community corrections (discussed further in Chapters 13–14):

1. *Punish.* Hold offenders accountable for their crimes by punishing them.
2. *Protect public safety.* Make sure offenders don't commit new crimes against law-abiding people.
3. *Rehabilitate offenders (reintegration).* Help offenders by connecting them with resources that turn them into responsible people who support themselves and obey the law.

Let's look at how probation and parole carry out these common missions.

American Probation and Parole Association: The international APPA is actively involved with probation, parole, and community-based corrections in both adult and juvenile sectors in local, state/provincial, and federal agencies. To reach this site go to "Web Links" on your Samaha CJ7 website: http://cj.wadsworth.com/samaha_cj7e.

The Missions of Probation Until the end of World War II, the mission of probation was to show leniency to first-time, minor offenders. After the war, doubts that prison was "correcting" offenders led to the adoption of another mission—rehabilitation. Judges started putting repeat and even violent offenders on probation to reform them. But by the 1970s, there was a backlash against probation. The public, fed up with crime and judges who were "soft on criminals," demanded probation accomplish a third mission—punish and protect the public from "felons on the streets." But there was a problem standing in the way of accomplishing the punish-and-protect mission—paying the high price of exploding prison populations (Clear and Braga 1995, 422; Petersilia 2004, 487–488; Chapter 13).

Despite worries about its "softness," probation is still the clear punishment of choice (Figure 12.1), probably because the public's not willing to pay the high costs of confinement. According to Joan Petersilia (1995):

> When the prison population began to overwhelm existing facilities, probation and "split sentences" (a jail sentence followed by a term on probation) became the de facto disposition of all misdemeanors. As prison overcrowding becomes a national crisis, the courts are being forced to use probation even more frequently. Many felons without criminal records are now sentenced to probation. (481)

Federal probation officer Edward J. Cosgrove (1994) describes the complexity the conflicting missions of rehabilitation and leniency and punishment and controlling prison populations creates:

> When Gannon and Friday were the role models for police officers, probation officers were an extension of the law. We kept "order" by seeing that people just did the right things. In the '70s, rehabilitation was the goal of supervision. The medical model taught us to diagnose a problem and then provide treatment. Help meant counseling; understanding the hardships of poverty, illiteracy, and broken homes; rendering the necessary support to address these symptoms; and coping with the bad feelings and making changes.
>
> As client needs seemed ever expanding, the '80s brought us the philosophy of reintegration. Probation officers could not expect to service all needs; so, the answer became brokering services: identify the problem and make the appropriate referral. By the end of the '80s, the pendulum had swung from primary care to clients to listening to the needs of the community. Mercy was not to be forgotten, but disparity must be eliminated. Guidelines achieved this with a focus on retributive justice, with scant attention focused to rehabilitation of the individual. The offender will be held accountable. Society will be protected. The Probation Service responded with the development of Enhanced Supervision. The goals were ranked: enforce court orders, provide risk control, address the correctional treatment needs of the offender.
>
> What does a probation officer do? To this day, I suffer a violent visceral pain whenever I hear some visiting academic discuss the "two hats" of the probation officer: cop or counselor. At last count, we wear at least 33 hats and the number is growing. (29)

The Missions of Parole From the brief history of parole sketched earlier, you can see a conflict between the original and ancient mission of rehabilitation and the more modern ones of punishment and public safety. Warren F. Spalding put it this way in an address to the American Prison Association in 1916:

> A parole does not release the parolee from custody; it does not discharge him from the penal consequences of his act; it does not mitigate his punishment; it does not wash away the stain or remit the penalty.... Unlike a pardon, it is not an act of grace or mercy, of clemency or leniency. The granting of parole is merely permission to a prisoner to serve part of his sentence outside the walls of the prison. He continues to be in the custody of the authorities, both legally and actually, and is still under restraint. The sentence is in full force and at any time when he does not comply with the conditions upon which he was released, or does not conduct himself properly, he may be returned, for his own good and in the public interest. (Wilcox 1927, 21)

Spalding doesn't mention one mission: controlling prison populations. But in the 1800s, when prisons became "warehouses for the poor," parole became a way to relieve prison crowding by making room for new prisoners. (It still is, even though you won't often see it on official lists.)

The missions of parole sometimes are at odds with one another. Releasing more prisoners reduces prison populations but also may increase the risk to public safety. Close supervision outside prison might enhance public safety but increase costs from rehabilitating and reintegrating offenders into the community.

Granting Probation and Parole

Over 2.5 million offenders entered probation in 2003 (Glaze and Palla 2004, Table 3); almost 500,000 entered parole (Glaze and Palla 2004, Table 5). Who decides whether offenders will spend their time behind bars or in the community? Who decides if and when offenders already behind bars will return to the community before the end of their sentences? These are the questions probation and parole authorities have to answer. Who are these authorities, and what criteria do they base their decisions on? Let's look at these questions and the answers to them.

Granting Probation Formally, probation is a criminal sentence imposed by judges. Probationers are in the custody of the state; they're legally accountable to the state and subject to conditions that limit their freedom and privacy. The judge can change the conditions of and revoke probation if probationers violate the conditions of their release. Informally, probation consists of discretionary decision making to accomplish the missions we discussed in the previous section. Probation isn't a suspended sentence (release of convicted offenders without conditions or supervision). The possibility of being locked up is still "hanging over their heads," because at any time judges can revoke the suspension and send them to jail or prison (Allen, Eskridge, Latessa, and Vito 1985, 81).

Formally, judges sentence offenders, but behind the sentencing decision is the influence of probation offices. Most judges' formal sentence only approves what probation officers have recommended in their presentence investigation report (Chapter 11). What criteria do probation officers use to decide? Two won't surprise you—the more serious the offense and the longer the criminal history of the offender the less the chances of getting probation (Gottfredson and Gottfredson 1988, 194). The other criteria are indirectly related to these. The Iowa Department of Corrections Scoring Guide (Iowa Department of Corrections n.d.) lists the following:

- *Employment.* Employment is a primary risk factor in that low levels of vocational achievement highly correlate with recidivism (committing another crime).

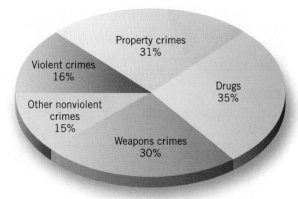

◀ **FIGURE 12.2 Felons on Probation, 2000**

Note: The percentages don't add up to 100 because the figure represents the percentage of each type of offender (violent, property, etc.) sentenced to probation. For example, of the 100% of offenders convicted of violent offenses in 2000, 16% were sentenced to probation; 84% were sentenced to prison. *Source:* Matthew R. Durose and Patrick A. Langan, *State Court Sentencing of Convicted Felons, 2000 Statistical Tables* (Washington, DC: Bureau of Justice Statistics), Table 3.6.

- *Education.* Overall academic achievement is germane to the stability of a crime-free lifestyle.
- *Financial condition.* Financial problems...may be indicative of...inappropriate ways to get money.
- *Marital or equivalent situation.* A satisfying family or marital situation... [is] negatively correlated with criminal risk.

Felons on Probation Do you think probation is for minor offenders? If you thought yes, you're *half* right. In 2003 (the latest available numbers), half of all adults on probation were minor offenders; half were felons, some violent (Glaze and Palla 2004, Table 4). Figure 12.2 shows what percentage of each type of offender was on probation in 2000.

Joan Petersilia (1998), a leading expert on community corrections, worries about the risk felons on probation create for both the public and probation officer safety:

> How far from John Augustus's vision we have moved. In his autobiography Augustus wrote that "probation officers just need a good heart." Today it appears they believe they need much more. Two-thirds of parole and probation agencies now permit officers to carry weapons. (578)

Are felons on probation a danger to public safety? Demands to get tough on crime and toughen up judges who are soft on criminals have produced a heated policy debate about whether felons should be on probation. On one side are the numbers that show that within three years of sentencing, 43 percent of felons on probation are arrested for a new crime; half of those arrests are for violent or drug offenses (cited in Petersilia 2004, 490). On the other hand, researchers Geerken and Hayes (1993) analyzed data on arrests, incarceration, and probation supervision for burglary and armed robbery in New Orleans. They found that probationers accounted for 8 percent of burglary and armed robbery arrests. According to Geerken and Hayes:

> These percentages are contrary to expectations and surprisingly low. They suggest that even the complete elimination of probation...would have a very negligible effect on the burglary and armed robbery rates since more than 90 percent of all burglaries and armed robberies were committed by persons not on probation...at the time of the arrest....We argue...that since a low percentage of all burglary and armed robbery arrests are of persons on probation...at the time, policy changes tightening or eliminating...probation can affect only a small percentage of these crimes. (557)

Granting Parole The United States sentences more people to prison and keeps them there longer than any "major" country in the world (Chapter 13). But most prisoners spend less than two years in prison before they're released. They're released in three ways:

▶ On March 3, 2005, Alex Kelly appeared before the Connecticut parole board, which denied his request for parole. Kelly, a former high-school wrestling star, skied the slopes of Europe for eight years as a fugitive before he was caught and convicted in 1997 for two rapes he committed in 1987. Kelly asked to be paroled halfway through his 16-year prison term. His victims Adrienne Bak (background left) and Hillary Buchanan (background right) watched as the board announced its decision.

AP/Wide World Photos

discretionary release parole boards decide the date of prisoners' release and set the conditions of their community supervision until their sentence expires

mandatory release legislatures and judges set the date of prisoners' release and the conditions of their community supervision until their sentence expires

expiration release prisoners are released unconditionally when their sentence expires

1. **Discretionary release.** Parole boards decide the date of release and set the conditions of their community supervision until their sentence expires.
2. **Mandatory release.** Legislatures and judges set the date of release and the conditions of their community supervision until their sentence expires.
3. **Expiration release.** Prisoners are released unconditionally when their sentence—less good time—expires.

You'll learn about mandatory and expiration release in Chapter 14, so we'll concentrate on discretionary decision making here.

Judges make the final probation decision; parole boards decide whether to release prisoners. State governors appoint about ten men and women to sit on the board, which has broad discretionary decision-making power. They review files (usually consisting of work done by probation officers); interview prisoners; and decide the date, conditions, and when necessary, the revocation of parole. They can also issue warrants and subpoenas; order the payment of restitution to victims and fees to the state to help pay the costs of their supervision; rescind release dates; restore (or continue to deny) prisoners' civil rights; and grant (or deny) final discharges from state custody (Petersilia 1998, 574).

What criteria drive the discretionary decision making of parole boards? An American Paroling Authorities' survey found the major criteria (listed here in order of importance to decision makers) to be:

1. Seriousness of the prisoner's offense
2. History of violence
3. Previous felony convictions
4. Possession of a firearm
5. Previous incarceration
6. Prior parole adjustment
7. Prison disciplinary record
8. Psychological reports
9. Victim input (Runda, Rhine, and Wetter 1994)

No surprises here. The ranking follows what you've learned throughout the criminal justice process: the seriousness of the offense and criminal history top the list, followed by criteria indirectly related to the top two.

Parole boards use two methods of decision making in granting parole. In the **case study method,** "the board member, case worker, or parole agency collects as much information as possible, combines it in a unique way, mulls over the results, and reaches a decision" (Petersilia 1998, 575). Case studies were the standard method of decision making until attempts to restrict parole boards' discretion led to the adoption of the **risk assessment method.** This method is a statistically based prediction. Information is collected about the seriousness of the crime offenders are imprisoned for and their criminal history.

The idea behind risk assessment is that the more serious the offense and the longer the criminal history the less the chances parolees will succeed in becoming law-abiding people who can support themselves. By 1994, half of the state parole boards had adopted a risk assessment method.

Supporters say decision making by risk assessment has several advantages. Predictions are based on objective legitimate criteria—the seriousness of the offense and criminal history. Because they're objective, they're also fair; they prevent the infection of decision making based on gender, race, and class. They're also cheaper; imprisonment costs more than parole. And they're best for the public; they confine the most dangerous offenders who've committed the worst crimes and release offenders who threaten public safety the least (Atkinson 1986, 54–55; Lombardi and Lombardi 1986, 86–87).

Objectively, which method is better? The empirical evidence shows the risk assessment method is better at predicting what drives all release decision making—the answer to the question, "Will parolees commit crimes when they're released?" But how *much* better? When Stephen Klein and Michael Caggiano (1986) applied six widely used risk assessment models to recidivism data from Texas, California, and Michigan, they found "They did not predict more than 10 percent of the variance on any of the measures of recidivism" (31). Kevin N. Wright, Todd R. Clear, and Paul Dickson (1984, 122–123) studied a risk assessment instrument developed for Wisconsin that the National Institute of Corrections called a "model system"; a number of other states had also adopted the instrument. They concluded that no matter what instrument was used all predictions are "fairly weak."

The Conditions of Probation and Parole

Probationers and parolees are not free to do as they please. There are strings attached to their release, because they're offenders both still under criminal sentences and in state custody. (See the In Focus box "Required Church Attendance: An Unconstitutional Condition of Probation?") They face three types of conditions (Figure 12.3):

- *Standard conditions.* Obey the law; don't carry a weapon; don't associate with criminals; report to your probation or parole officer; notify the office if you change your address; work or go to school; support your family; and don't leave the jurisdiction without permission.
- *Punitive conditions* (Usually reserved for felony probationers). Pay your fines; report daily to your probation office; do community service; pay victims back (restitution); don't leave the house (house arrest); and get drug tests.
- *Treatment conditions.* Go through a substance abuse program; get family counseling; and go through job training.

The conditions in Figure 12.3 are common, but they're not realistic because the money and personnel aren't there to enforce them. "We design systems so

case study method a professional collects information, combines it in a unique way, mulls over the results, and reaches a decision

risk assessment method a statistical prediction based on the seriousness of the crime offenders are imprisoned for and their criminal history

Required Church Attendance:
An Unconstitutional Condition of Probation?

From some time in 1993 until November 1994, Judge Thomas Quirk sentenced 540 defendants, who appeared in his court for various traffic offenses and misdemeanors, to attend a church of their choosing once a week as a condition of probation. Not one of these defendants objected at the time of sentencing. After a complaint challenging this practice was filed against Judge Quirk with the Judiciary Commission in November 1994, he began offering church attendance, as a condition of probation, only to those who specifically requested it. Approximately 969 defendants were sentenced in this fashion.

After the complaint was filed, Judge Quirk sent a letter, dated December 5, 1994, to the 540 defendants previously sentenced to attend church, advising them that if they objected to the sentence of church attendance, he would provide to them the opportunity to be resentenced. Ten defendants elected to be resentenced.

Judge Quirk testified he employed church attendance as a condition of probation only in cases where he perceived the defendants to be unable to afford a fine or court costs, and the church sentence was given in lieu of jail time, a fine, court costs, or some other typical condition of probation. Judge Quirk also testified the total number of people given church attendance as a condition of probation constituted about 3 percent of his docket.

The defendants sentenced to attend church were required to pay a $25.00 administrative fee to the Safety Council of Southwest Louisiana, which monitors attendance on behalf of the court of defendants at various programs made conditions of probation, such as defensive driving classes, alcoholics studies classes, and the community service program. With respect to the church attendance monitoring program, the defendant is given a card to be returned to the Safety Council, which must be signed by a "church official" verifying the defendant has attended church for that week.

There is no evidence to dispute Judge Quirk's testimony that the defendants could attend a church or religious institution of their choosing; they could attend any church function, such as a "men's meeting," and not just religious services; and they were not required to profess any belief in any religion. During the hearing before the Judiciary Commission, Judge Quirk explained he adopted this sentencing practice because the normal sentence for certain offenders of jail and/or payment of fines and court costs was not an option. He had been informed there was no room in the jail for these types of offenders; also some offenders could not afford the fines or court costs. He preferred attendance at church as a condition of probation because it was a free service; it was usually "open" and "readily available," even during travel out of town; and the Safety Council monitoring fee was only $25.00 as compared to the $75.00 fee required for participation in the community service program.

The Judiciary Commission, after a hearing, issued Findings of Fact and Conclusions of Law in which it found that Judge Quirk's "church sentences" are "clearly" unconstitutional under the First Amendment of the United States Constitution and Article I, Sec. 8 of the Louisiana Constitution of 1974 ("No law shall be enacted respecting an establishment of religion or prohibiting the free exercise thereof.") and that Judge Quirk's imposition of these illegal sentences violates Canons 2 A, 3 A(1) and 3 A(4) of the Code of Judicial Conduct because it constituted a pattern of committing egregious legal error in violation of defendants' constitutional rights made in bad faith in order to further a bias toward religion.

Source: In re Judge Thomas P. Quirk, 705 So.2d 172 (La. 1997).

---

that almost all parolees are likely to fail at some point.... Unfortunately parole [and probation] conditions serve as much to comfort agencies and parole boards, and help the release decision withstand public scrutiny, [as] to establish realistic expectations for the parolee" (Holt 1998, 10). You can substitute "probationer" for "parolee" because the criticism applies to both.

Revoking Probation and Parole

What happens if probationers and parolees violate the conditions of their release? They can be sent to prison to serve the rest of their sentences. Probation and parole are revoked for one of two reasons: **recidivism**—arrest or conviction for a new crime—or **technical violations**—violations of conditions that aren't crimes, like not notifying probation and parole officers of a change of address. Judges and parole boards can revoke probation and parole; but they usually

recidivism arrest, charge, or conviction for a new crime

technical violations violations of conditions that aren't crimes

PROB 7A (Revised 4/2004)

Conditions of Probation
UNITED STATES DISTRICT COURT
FOR THE
DISTRICT OF MINNESOTA

Docket No.

Name: _____
Address: _____

Sentence Date: _____

Under the terms of this sentence, the defendant has been placed on * by the Honorable * for the District of Minnesota. The defendant's term of supervision is for a period of * (*) **years,** commencing * immediately upon sentencing.

While on probation, the defendant shall not commit any federal, state, or local crime. The defendant shall not illegally possess a controlled substance.

If the judgment imposed a fine or a restitution obligation, it shall be a condition of probation that the defendant pay any such fine or restitution that remains unpaid at the commencement of the term of supervision in accordance with any schedule of payments set forth in the Criminal Monetary Penalties sheet of the judgment. In any case, the defendant should cooperate with the probation officer in meeting any financial obligations.

The defendant shall report in person to the probation office in the district to which the defendant is released within seventy-two (72) hours of release from the custody of the Bureau of Prisons.

* The defendant shall not possess a firearm as defined in 18 U.S.C. § 921.

For offenses committed on or after September 13, 1994:

The defendant shall refrain from any unlawful use of a controlled substance. The defendant shall submit to one drug test within fifteen (15) days of release from imprisonment or placement on probation and at least two periodic drug tests thereafter.

* The above drug testing condition is suspended based on the Court's determination that the defendant poses a low risk of future substance abuse.

It is the order of the Court that the defendant shall comply with the following standard conditions:

1. The defendant shall not leave the judicial district without the permission of the Court or probation officer;
2. The defendant shall report to the probation officer and shall submit a truthful and complete written report within the first five (5) days of each month;
3. The defendant shall answer truthfully all inquiries by the probation officer and follow the instructions of the probation officer;
4. The defendant shall support his or her dependents and meet other family responsibilities;
5. The defendant shall work regularly at a lawful occupation unless excused by the probation officer for schooling, training, or other acceptable reasons;
6. The defendant shall notify the probation officer ten days prior to any change in residence or employment;
7. The defendant shall refrain from excessive use of alcohol and shall not purchase, possess, use, distribute, or administer any controlled substance or any paraphernalia related to any controlled substance, except as prescribed by a physician;
8. The defendant shall not frequent places where controlled substances are illegally sold, used, distributed, or administered;
9. The defendant shall not associate with any persons engaged in criminal activity and shall not associate with any person convicted of a felony unless granted permission to do so by the probation officer;
10. The defendant shall permit a probation officer to visit him or her at any time at home or elsewhere and shall permit confiscation of any contraband observed in plain view by the probation officer;
11. The defendant shall notify the probation officer within seventy-two (72) hours of being arrested or questioned by a law enforcement officer;
12. The defendant shall not enter into any agreement to act as an informer or a special agent of a law enforcement agency without the permission of the Court;
13. As directed by the probation officer, the defendant shall notify third parties of risks that may be occasioned by the defendant's criminal record or personal history or characteristics and shall permit the probation officer to make such notifications and to confirm the defendant's compliance with such notification requirement.

The special conditions ordered by the Court are as follows:

1. The defendant shall refrain from possessing a firearm, destructive device, or other dangerous weapon.*
2. *[Other special conditions, if any are added here.]

Upon a finding of a violation of probation, I understand that the Court may (1) revoke supervision or (2) extend the term of supervision and/or modify the conditions of supervision.

These conditions have been read to me. I fully understand the conditions and have been provided a copy of them.

Signed

_____   _____
Defendant   U.S. Probation Officer/Designated Witness

don't. Half of all probationers commit technical violations, but only 20 percent of these have their probation revoked.

Critics say the gap between technical violations and revocations is just one more example of criminals getting away with breaking the rules and threatening the safety of innocent people. But criminologists like Todd R. Clear and Anthony A. Braga (1995, 442) see it differently. They say technical violations prove only probationers' lack discipline, not that they're a threat to public safety—just because a probationer doesn't tell her probation officer she moved doesn't mean she's going to commit a crime.

Probation, Parole, and the Law

►DECISION POINT◄

Are probationers' homes their "castles"?

Click on this Decision Point at http://cj.wadsworth.com/samaha_cj7e to explore the case *Griffin v. Wisconsin.*

Prison and Parole Information from the Department of Justice: To reach this site go to "Web Links" on your Samaha CJ7 website: http://cj.wadsworth.com/samaha_cj7e.

Probationers and parolees are convicted offenders still in state custody. So—according to the U.S. Supreme Court—they have fewer rights than law-abiding people. In the words of the Court, probationers and parolees are subject to "special restrictions" on their rights (*Griffin v. Wisconsin* 1987, 874–875). For example, probation and parole officers don't have to give them *Miranda* warnings (*Minnesota v. Murphy* 1984). Also, probationers and parolees have diminished rights against unreasonable searches and seizures guaranteed by the Fourth Amendment to the U.S. Constitution.

Don't mistake *fewer* rights for *no* rights. One right they still possess is that parole and probation can't be revoked without due process of law (*Morrissey v. Brewer* 1973, 485–486). Due process guarantees probationers and parolees the right to a hearing to decide, first, whether they violated the conditions of their release and, second, if they did, whether the violation justifies revocation. Due process also guarantees suspected violators:

1. Written notice of the alleged violations *before* the revocation hearing
2. The right to see and hear the evidence against them
3. The opportunity to be heard in person and to present witnesses and documentary evidence in their favor
4. The right to confront and cross-examine the witnesses against them
5. A hearing panel made up of neutral members
6. A written statement by the hearing panel, including the evidence relied on and the reasons for revoking probation (*Morrissey v. Brewer* 1973, 487–489)

The Effectiveness of Probation and Parole

Probation and Parole in the United States, 2003: This Bureau of Justice Statistics site reports the number of persons on probation and parole by state at year-end 2003 and compares the totals with year-end 1995 and 2002. To reach this site go to "Web Links" on your Samaha CJ7 website: http://cj.wadsworth.com/samaha_cj7e.

Fifty-nine percent of probationers successfully complete their sentence in the community (Glaze and Palla 2004, Table 4); 47 percent of parolees successfully complete their conditional release (Glaze and Palla 2004, Table 7) (Figure 12.4). Not surprisingly, young, new offenders do best, and success goes down as time from release goes up (Bureau of Justice Statistics 1997, Table 3.6). What accounts for these numbers? Is it probation and parole supervision? Or something else? Let's look at the research on the effectiveness of probation and parole and the side effects of parole.

The Effectiveness of Probation Many people think probation's a joke. Criminals, they believe, are walking around without supervision, free to commit more crimes and violate their probation. The truth is many probationers are low-risk offenders with no criminal history (Clear and Braga 1995, 430). In fact, some scholars argue these low-risk offenders would succeed without any supervision.

But we also know there's a subgroup of probationers who commit crimes at a high rate. James Byrne and Linda Kelly (1989) estimated this group at 10 per-

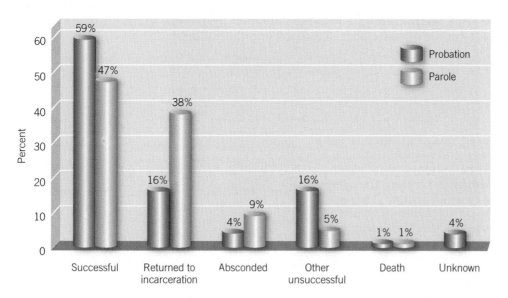

◀ **FIGURE 12.4 Adults Leaving Probation and Parole, 2003**
Source: Lauren E. Glaze and Seri Palla, *Probation and Parole in the United States, 2003* (Washington, DC: Bureau of Justice Statistics), Tables 4, 7.

cent and that 60 percent of this group will be charged with new crimes within a year of their release.

Joan Petersilia, Susan Turner, and James P. Kahan (1985) generated a storm of criticism of probation when they found that 65 percent of *felons* on probation were re-arrested for serious crimes like robbery and burglary. But they only examined two counties in California and the state of Massachusetts. When Gennaro Vito (1986, 17–25) applied Petersilia and her colleagues' methodology to Kentucky, he found felony re-arrest rates were 22 percent. Although this is still higher than the public would like, it's not nearly as alarming as 65 percent. In their summary of recidivism studies, Geerken and Hayes (1993, 549–564) found recidivism ranged from Petersilia and her colleagues' high of 65 percent to as low as 12 percent, for an average of about 40 percent.

Is it supervision that accounts for probation success or failure? We don't know the answer to this important question, because most researchers ignore the effects of supervision on ordinary probation (Taxman 2002). They're more interested in the effects of intermediate punishments (which you'll learn about later in the chapter). (See the In Focus box "Is Probation Dreaded More than Prison?")

The Effectiveness of Parole Less than half of all prisoners successfully completed parole in 2003 (Glaze and Palla 2004, 6). Are recidivism rates affected by the amount of supervision? Empirical findings don't clearly answer this important question (Taxman 2002). A Connecticut court decision gave Howard R. Sacks and Charles H. Logan (1979) a unique opportunity to measure the effect of supervision on recidivism. In the case of *Szarwak v. Warden* (1974), the Connecticut superior court ordered suspended sentences for all prisoners confined more than one year for unarmed robbery, burglary, or illegal possession of drugs.

The released prisoners became an experimental group in a natural experiment because eventually they would've been paroled. The control group consisted of prisoners released on parole at the ordinary time. What effect did parole have? Not much. Parolees avoided conviction for all offenses at a slightly higher rate (about 7 percent), but parole had no significant effect on the seriousness of the offenses committed. And the modest effects of parole supervision didn't last:

> Parole had no preventive effects after two (or three) years following release. Parole seems to affect recidivism while the parolee is on parole (and for a short period thereafter) but these effects soon begin to dissipate and tend to disappear by the time parolees have finished two years in the community. (Sacks and Logan 1979, 14–15)

Is Probation Dreaded More than Prison?

For many offenders, it may seem preferable to get that short stay in prison over rather than spend five times as long in an ISP.... Taking Marion County, Oregon, as an example, consider the alternatives facing convicted offenders:

- *ISP (intensive supervised probation)*. The offender will serve two years under this sanction. During that time, the offender will be visited by a probation officer two or three times per week, who will phone on the other days. The offender will be subject to unannounced searches of his home for drugs and have his urine tested regularly for alcohol and drugs. He must strictly abide by other conditions set by the court—not carrying a weapon, not socializing with certain persons—and he will have to perform community service and be employed or participate in training or education. In addition, he will be strongly encouraged to attend counseling and/or other treatment, particularly if he is a drug offender.
- *Prison*. A sentence of two to four years will require that the offender serve about three to six months. During his term, he is not required to work nor will he be required to participate in any training or treatment, but may do so if he wishes. Once released, he will be placed on two years routine parole supervision, where he sees his parole officer about once a month.

For these offenders, as for any of us, freedom is probably preferable to imprisonment. However, the ISP does not represent freedom. In fact, it may stress and isolate repeat offenders more than imprisonment does. It seems reasonable that when offenders return to their communities, they expect to return to their old lives. The ISP transforms those lives radically.

Their homes can be searched and they must submit regularly to urine testing. Offenders may well consider such invasions of their homes and lives more intrusive and unbearable than the lack of privacy in prisons—where it is an expected condition of life. The same is true of discipline and social isolation. By definition, imprisonment limits freedom of movement and activity, but once a person is in his own community, curfew and other restrictions may seem harder to take. Ironically, he may be less socially isolated from his peers in prison than in ISP.

Why do offenders' perceptions matter? Having established the counter-intuitive fact that some serious offenders prefer imprisonment to ISPs, what are we to make of it? Whatever else, it does argue for reconsidering the range of sanctions this country has and the assumptions they reflect. The point is not to insist that on any absolute scale ISP is "worse" than prison. Rather, it is to suggest that the scale we currently use needs reexamining. For the people who are likely to come under either sanction, how society at large views those sanctions is largely irrelevant. How offenders view punishment ought at least to be considered (23–27).

Source: Joan Petersilia, "When Probation Becomes More Dreaded Than Prison," *Federal Probation* 54 (1990): 23–27. Reprinted with permission.

Sacks and Logan concluded, "Parole does not prevent a return to crime, but it does delay it" (20).

They looked at parole supervision in general, but what about the kind of supervision? Does it matter? Yes, says Mark J. Lerner (1977); no, says Deborah Star (1979, 2–3, 52, 132; 1981). Lerner evaluated parole in New York State, where the public safety mission definitely comes first. At the time of his study, parole officers were "armed with .38 caliber revolvers [and] have even more extensive investigative and surveillance powers than those of policemen." Lerner divided 195 misdemeanor offenders into two groups, one in a control group released at the end of their sentences and the other released on parole. Based on arrests for two years after their release, Lerner found "parole supervision reduces criminal behavior of persons released from local correctional institutions."

Lerner (1977) concedes his study didn't try to explain why parole supervision reduced recidivism; he speculated the "effect is probably due to the deterrent or law-enforcement effect of parole supervision and not to the popular notions of rehabilitation" (220).

Star disagrees; her conclusion that the type of supervision doesn't matter is based on two experimental studies of parole by the California Department of Corrections. In the first, felons (excluding prisoners convicted of murder, rape, and some other serious offenses) were randomly assigned to either an experimental group of parolees or a control group. The first group received less supervision than the control group, who received normal supervision. The experimental group had significantly fewer face-to-face contacts initiated by parole officers to check up on their parolees. After six months, and again after one year, the researchers found no significant difference between either the frequency or the severity of criminal activity committed by the control group on regular parole and the experimental group on reduced supervision.

The second experiment (Star 1981, i–ii, 168, 251, 257)—the High Control Project—evaluated the effects of increased surveillance and investigation of parolees to control their criminal activities. The High Control Project differed from regular parole in four ways:

1. It emphasized control, not service.
2. It emphasized investigating parolees' possible criminal activities before arrest. (Ordinary supervision stresses investigation after arrest.)
3. It targeted "high risk" cases.
4. It used parole officers specially trained in law enforcement.

The High Control Project relied on two tactics to test the effectiveness of high levels of control. In the first tactic, criminal investigation, high-control parole officers investigated parolees suspected of crimes, apprehended them, and helped to prosecute them. In the second tactic, intensive supervision, officers with reduced caseloads closely monitored parolees with serious prior criminal records to prevent them from committing new crimes.

Using a quasi-experimental design, researchers compared high-control parolees with regular parolees. The result? Neither aggressive criminal investigation nor intensified supervision made a difference. The researchers did find that criminal investigation in the High Control Project was better than ordinary parole in verifying criminal behavior after it took place, even if it didn't reduce the frequency and seriousness of criminal behavior.

The Side Effects of Parole Almost all the research on parole focuses on its effect on criminal behavior, but parole failure can have more negative social consequences than creating threats to public safety. Here's a list of some of the *possible* consequences; it can:

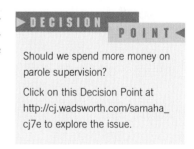

DECISION POINT

Should we spend more money on parole supervision?

Click on this Decision Point at http://cj.wadsworth.com/samaha_cj7e to explore the issue.

- Reduce parolees' future employment and income
- Deny parolees the right to vote or hold office
- Affect family stability and childhood development
- Contribute to community instability in neighborhoods where there's a high recycling of parolees in and out
- Increase community health-care costs because of the poor health of parolees (hepatitis, HIV, and tuberculosis) (Petersilia 2004)

Keep in mind that the extent of these consequences is not known because the empirical research on each of them is at this point fragmentary (Petersilia 2004, 494–495) (Chapter 14).

Race, Ethnicity, Gender, and Community Corrections

The same racial, ethnic, and gender differences we've seen in criminal behavior and in other parts of criminal justice are also true of probation (Figure 12.5) and parole (Figure 12.6). But are these differences the result of discrimination injected into decisions to grant probation or parole, impose conditions, and revoke sentences? Unfortunately, there's not enough research to answer this question.

FIGURE 12.5 The Gender, Race, and Ethnicity of Probationers

Source: Lauren E. Glaze and Seri Palla, *Probation and Parole in the United States, 2003* (Washington, DC: Bureau of Justice Statistics, July 2004), Table 4.

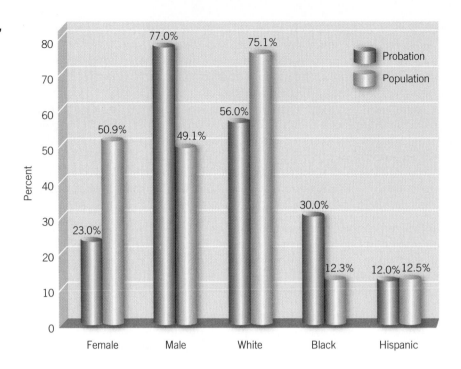

FIGURE 12.6 The Gender, Race, and Ethnicity of Parolees

Source: Lauren E. Glaze and Seri Palla, *Probation and Parole in the United States, 2003* (Washington, DC: Bureau of Justice Statistics, July 2004), Table 5.

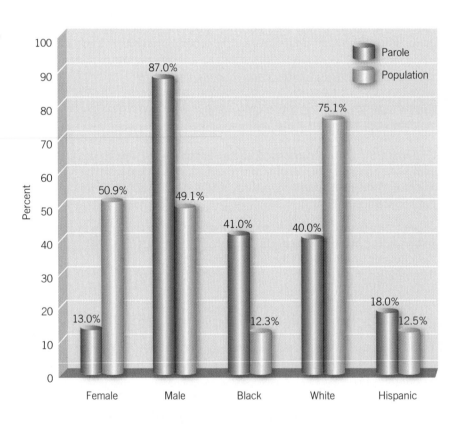

Intermediate Punishments

either/or corrections (also called **in-or-out corrections**) convicted offenders are either locked up or put on probation

For most of the twentieth century, convicted offenders were either locked up or put on probation. This **either/or corrections** (also called **in-or-out corrections**) policy ignored the reality that imprisonment is too harsh for a lot of criminal behavior, and, for some offenders, probation is too lenient. In other words, proba-

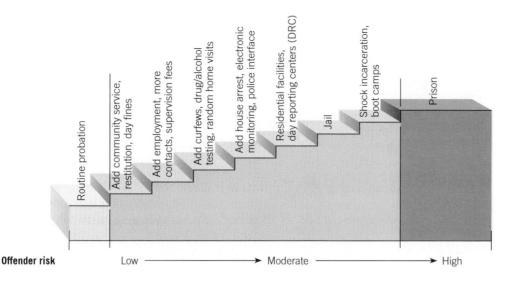

◀ **FIGURE 12.7 A Model of a Graduated Punishment System**

Source: Joan Petersilia, "Probation and Parole," in *Handbook of Crime and Punishment,* edited by Michael Tonry (New York: Oxford University Press, 1998), p. 583, Table 21.4.

Offender risk   Low ────────▶ Moderate ────────────▶ High

| Annual cost/ offender | $200–900 | $1,000–3,000 | $3,000–5,000 | $5,000–10,000 | $9,000–14,000 | $16,000–22,000 |

tion and confinement weren't accomplishing the mission of doing justice—fitting the punishment to the crime and tailoring the penalty to suit the offender. **Intermediate punishments,** which are harsher than probation but milder than imprisonment, allow us to accomplish the mission of justice.

Justice isn't the only mission that intermediate sanctions are supposed to accomplish. Proponents have "sold" them to legislators and the public on the claims that the sanctions can reduce prison crowding, protect the public, and punish and rehabilitate offenders—all while saving tax dollars. But intermediate sanctions can't completely accomplish all these far-reaching missions; they're not a panacea (Byrne, Lurigio, and Petersilia 1992, ix, xiii–xiv).

An ideal graduated punishment system would work like Figure 12.7, which depicts three important elements. First, there is a range of punishments, graduating in severity from the most lenient (probation) to the harshest (prison). Judges would choose the punishment that best fit the crime and the offender. Second, offenders wouldn't go straight to prison if they failed at a lower severity; they'd move up one level on the severity stairs. Third, the costs of punishment increase with the harshness of the punishment, from as low as $200 a year for each offender on routine probation to as high as $22,000 a year for every inmate in prison (Petersilia 1998, 582).

There's a fairly long list of intermediate punishments available (Table 12.1), but despite the compelling justification for a graduated punishment system depicted in Figure 12.7, intermediate punishments are only used rarely. The latest numbers available when this book went to press were 124,815 offenders serving sentences for intermediate punishments (intensive supervision—103,618, electronic monitoring—19,377, and correctional boot camps—1520) (BJS Statisticians 2002, Table 3.10). That's about 10 percent of the adult probation and parole population (Petersilia 2004, 496).

The Types of Intermediate Punishments

Now, let's look at several intermediate punishments that local, state, and federal governments adopted during the 1980s and 1990s:

- Intensive supervised probation (ISP)
- Home confinement (often called house arrest or home detention)
- Shock incarceration (correctional boot camps)

intermediate punishments harsher than probation but milder than imprisonment, they allow us to accomplish the mission of justice

Arizona's Community Corrections Program: The Community Supervision Bureau uses parole officers to supervise inmates released on any type of community supervision and conducts pre-placement investigations, including job placement and referral to contracted transitional services. The Bureau also administers the Home Arrest Program. To reach this site go to "Web Links" on your Samaha CJ7 website: http://cj.wadsworth .com/samaha_cj7e.

The American Community Corrections Institute (ACCI): This group publishes and distributes cognitive life skills workbooks for youths and adults. Their main purpose is to help people overcome distorted thinking and self-defeating behaviors. To reach this site go to "Web Links" on your Samaha CJ7 website: http://cj.wadsworth .com/samaha_cj7e.

Type	Characteristics	Goals	Empirical Evaluation
Intensive Supervision	Frequent contacts (e.g., daily)	Protect public safety	More technical violations
	Less privacy and freedom (e.g., unannounced officer visits; drug testing)	Punish	Little or no effect on arrest rates
		Reduce prison crowding	Little or no effect on the kinds of crimes arrested for
	Have to work, go to school, and/or get treatment	Save money	Punished appropriately, fulfilling the justice mission (Petersilia, Turner, and Deschennes 1992, 19)
		Rehabilitation	
Home Confinement/ Electronic Monitoring	24/7 surveillance	Confine without imprisonment	Reduce costs
	Ankle monitor		Participants found or kept employment
		Maintain family ties and employment	Participants supported their families
		Save money	Younger participants failed more frequently than older participants
		Public safety	No reduction in jail populations
			Technical problems with equipment
Correctional Boot Camps	Strict discipline	Deterrence	Deterrence? Mixed empirical results
	Physical training	Punishment	Succeed in punishing offenders
	Drill and ceremony		
	Military atmosphere		
	Physical labor		
	Punishment for minor violations		
Fines	Money punishment	Pay debt to victim (restitution)	Mixed empirical results
		Punishment	
		Deterrence	
Community Service	Order to work on public property (e.g., clean parks, sweep streets, clean jails)	Punishment	Not enough evaluations to comment
		Help community	
		Restitution	
		Rehabilitation	

- Fines
- Community service
- Day reporting centers

►DECISION POINT◄

Should felons serve time in the community?

Click on this Decision Point at http://cj.wadsworth.com/samaha_cj7e to explore the issue.

Intensive Supervised Probation (ISP) Crowded prisons, budget crunches, and the perceived threat to public safety led to the adoption of intensive supervised probation (ISP). Intensive supervised probation is a tougher version of traditional probation in several respects. Most programs include the following ingredients:

- Daily contact with probation officers
- Frequent alcohol and other drug testing
- Unannounced visits by probation officers
- Intolerance of even minor violations of the conditions of probation

Intensive supervised probation has several ambitious visible missions:

- Reducing prison crowding
- Increasing community protection
- Rehabilitating offenders
- Proving that probation can work and that probation is punishment
- Saving money

It also has some hidden missions:

- *Institutional.* Probation has an image problem; it's often regarded as a "slap on the wrist." ISP claims to be "tough" on criminals and promises to protect the community.
- *Professional.* ISP is supposed to generate more money for probation departments so probation officers can make a difference in probationers' lives.
- *Political.* ISP allows probation departments to get in tune with the public "get tough on crime and criminals" attitude. This harmony with the public makes probation—and probation budgets—more saleable to the public.

Does ISP work? In a solid empirical evaluation of one of several early programs, federal probation authorities divided offenders into four levels of supervision:

1. "Intensive," which assigned only 20 offenders to each probation officer
2. "Ideal," which assigned 50 offenders to each officer
3. "Normal," which assigned 70 to 130 offenders to each officer
4. "Minimum," which assigned several hundred offenders to each officer

The results weren't promising (Lurigio and Petersilia 1992):

> After two years, it was shown that smaller caseloads did little except generate more technical violations. Crime rates were about the same for all categories of supervision.... As similar evidence accumulated, federal funding for criminal justice projects began to evaporate.... Under these circumstances, most of the earlier ISP projects were dismantled; they remained dormant until the early 1980s. (7–8)

This didn't discourage ISP supporters. Intensive supervised probation is now the most popular and the most widely used intermediate punishment (Petersilia 2004, 496).

Evaluations of the many programs started up in the 1980s are mixed. In one of the most respected evaluations (Petersilia and Turner 1993), a randomized field experiment evaluated a national ISP demonstration project set up in 14 jurisdictions in nine states. Researchers found that:

- The frequency and seriousness of arrest offenses remained the same.
- Technical violations increased.
- Incarceration rates increased because technical violations rose.
- Program costs increased compared with ordinary probation. (281)

Home Confinement: Electronic Monitoring *Home confinement*—sentencing offenders to remain in their homes—is an old practice. Henry VIII confined his wife, Queen Catherine of Aragon, to home, and modern dictators do the same to their political enemies. During the 1980s, home confinement became popular with advocates of intermediate punishments. Most people sentenced to home confinement have committed misdemeanors, like DWI.

The benefits of home confinement include:

- Reducing the stigma of incarceration while still punishing offenders
- Maintaining family ties and occupational roles that improve chances for rehabilitation
- Saving money from reduced jail and prison maintenance and construction costs and from payments by offenders
- Protecting the public by keeping offenders "off the street"
- Satisfying the demand for punishment (Schmidt and Curtis 1987, 141–142)

Some critics of home confinement claim that it violates the right to privacy and the rights against self-incrimination, search and seizure, and cruel and unusual punishment. But since 1929, the U.S. Supreme Court has ruled that there's no constitutional ban on electronic surveillance. This is especially true under the

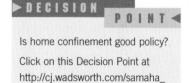

DECISION POINT

Is home confinement good policy?

Click on this Decision Point at http://cj.wadsworth.com/samaha_cj7e to explore the issue.

District of New Jersey Pretrial Services: Home Confinement with Electronic Monitoring Procedures: To reach this site go to "Web Links" on your Samaha CJ7 website: http://cj.wadsworth.com/samaha_cj7e.

© John B. Boykin/Corbis

► Correctional boot camps (one form of shock incarceration) provide an alternative to prison for young, first-time, nonviolent offenders, particularly drug offenders. The camps are based on the assumption that they deter and rehabilitate offenders more effectively than prisons. They're modeled on basic training in the military. These Texas boot camp inmates face inspection as they stand at attention.

"Home Confinement": A brief overview of electronic monitoring by the U.S. Probation and Pretrial Services group. To reach this site go to "Web Links" on your Samaha CJ7 website: http://cj.wadsworth.com/samaha_cj7e.

Georgia Department of Corrections: Boot Camp: A look at what a boot camp is and what the young inmates face. The camps are highly structured with a military regimen. Offenders work during the day in the facility or in the local community doing public service work. Risk-reduction programming, particularly in the area of substance abuse, is provided in the evening hours. To reach this site go to "Web Links" on your Samaha CJ7 website: http://cj.wadsworth.com/samaha_cj7e.

doctrine that convicted offenders enjoy only diminished constitutional rights (Chapter 14).

Correctional Boot Camps Correctional boot camps (one form of shock incarceration) provide an alternative to prison for young, first-time, nonviolent offenders, particularly drug offenders. They're based on the assumption that they deter and rehabilitate offenders more effectively than prisons. Boot camps are modeled on basic training in the military. Like other intermediate punishments, correctional boot camps are a response to the combined influences of prison crowding, the demand for more severe punishment, and budgetary restraints (MacKenzie and Parent 1992, 103–119).

Correctional boot camps stress a number of features in common with military boot camps:

- Strict discipline
- Physical training
- Drill and ceremony
- Military bearing and courage
- Physical labor
- Summary punishment for minor misconduct (103–104)

According to a camp sergeant in a Georgia correctional boot camp, "Here being scared is the point. You have to hit a mule between the eyes with a two-by-four to get his attention…and that's exactly what we're doing with this program" (104).

The use of militarism, hard labor, and fear in prisons has a long history. In 1821, John Cray, the deputy keeper of Auburn prison, turned away from using solitary confinement because it led to high rates of suicide and mental breakdowns. He replaced it with the requirement that prisoners maintain downcast eyes, march in lockstep, be silent, and work long hours of hard work under close supervision. At Elmira Reformatory, Zebulon Brockway adopted Auburn's basic idea, with some "modern" twists, in the 1890s (105). (See the In Focus box "Boot Camps: Do They 'Work'?" on p. 426.)

Fines Fines are monetary punishment that date back to the Old Testament notion of "an eye for an eye." Fines prevailed in England for much of the early part of the Middle Ages, when a price was put on all kinds of offenses, including maiming and murder. Fines have a lot to recommend them as appropriate criminal punishment. They're clearly aimed at both retribution and deterrence. They emphasize accountability by requiring offenders to pay their "debt to society" literally, in the form of money. All these aims are consistent with current sentencing policies (Ruback 2004, 21).

Fines also fulfill the aims of fairness and proportionality in punishment by allowing the size of the debt to society to be adjusted to the seriousness of the offenses in our criminal law. The flexibility of monetary penalties also allows for the adjustment of the fine to the ability of the offenders to pay. Moreover, fines are already a current sentencing option in all American courts, whether large or small, urban or rural. Finally, and far from least important, fines generate revenue (Ruback 2004, 21).

Fines are also consistent with basic American values. According to Michael Tonry and Kate Hamilton (1995):

> It seems odd, in a country where economic incentives and rational calculation are so widely celebrated, that monetary penalties play so small a part in punishment of offenders. Although in practice fines are generally set in amounts too small to be commensurate to the seriousness of nontrivial crimes, in principle they can vary from small change to economic capital punishment. Although in practice fines are often collected haphazardly or not at all, in principle they can be collected with the same vigor and solicitude that characterize our friendly neighborhood finance companies. Although in practice increased use of fines seems to be unfair to the poor and unduly lenient to the rich, in principle amounts can be tailored to individuals' assets and incomes so as to constitute roughly comparable financial burdens. (15)

Why haven't fines figured prominently in the repertoire of intermediate punishments? Some of the reasons are they have no effect on wealthy offenders; they're unfair to poor offenders; and poor offenders can't (or don't) pay them (Ruback 2004, 21). Also, according to Sally T. Hillsman and Judith A. Greene (1992):

> Among American criminal justice practitioners, there lingers a deep skepticism about the usefulness of fine sentences that focuses on the absolute size of the fine: Don't fines need to be large in order to be punitive and to deter? This emphasis on large fines leads to further issues about the fairness of fine sentences: If fines are large enough to punish and deter, how can they be collected from the majority of offenders who come before American courts? And if only those who can pay sizable amounts are fined, are not these more affluent offenders buying their way out of the more punitive sentences to imprisonment? (125–126)

According to some experts, the answer to problems with fines is a system that most European countries have put into effect—the day fine. **Day fines** base fines on the daily income of offenders. The imposition of day fines is a two-step process. In the first step, judges assign fine units. The more serious the offense, the more units are assessed. In the second stage, they attach monetary amounts to the units. The amount of money each unit costs depends on offenders' daily income (Hillsman and Greene 1992, 127–128).

day fines base fines on the daily income of offenders

Lower criminal courts have always been the primary users of fines. To determine the usefulness of day fines in the United States, a planning group established an experiment in New York's Staten Island Criminal Court. The group comprised judges, prosecutors, public and private defense attorneys, court administrators, and planners from the Vera Institute of Justice. They assigned fine units according to the seriousness of the offenses for which the court imposed sentences. They then created a method for attributing a monetary value to the fine units, basing it on a "fair share" of the daily, after-tax income of offenders. A fair share takes into account the offender's number of dependents and whether the offender's income is below the poverty line. According to Sally T. Hillsman (1995):

Boot Camps: Do They "Work"?

Correctional boot camps are extremely popular with the public and, therefore, with state and national politicians. Even presidents have repeatedly advocated correctional boot camps as part of their crime control programs. One political candidate produced an effective commercial promising that young offenders who didn't want to obey the law would "wind up breaking up rocks" in a correctional boot camp instead.

Empirical evidence, however, doesn't back up the conclusion that correctional boot camps deter offenders through their use of fear, or that you can "scare offenders straight." After surveying a considerable amount of the available research, Mary Morash and Lila Rucker (1990) concluded that

> the boot camp model is unlikely to provide a panacea for...the pressures arising from the problems of both prison overcrowding and public demands for severe punishment. Whether the point is to provide rehabilitation, to deter, or to divert people from prison, alternatives other than boot camp should be given careful consideration. (218)

The General Accounting Office, the National Institute of Justice, and several states have independently evaluated boot camps. After interviewing officials and reviewing NIJ data regarding boot camps in Florida and Georgia, the General Accounting Office (1988) concluded, somewhat more cautiously than Morash and Rucker, that

> available data are not sufficient to determine if boot camps reduce prison overcrowding, costs, or recidivism....Boot camps may reduce prison overcrowding and prison costs if they involve offenders who would have otherwise been sent to prison, the offenders are incarcerated for a shorter time, and they are not readmitted to prison after their release at a greater rate than prisoners sentenced to regular prisons. However, the possibility that some offenders sent to boot camps would have been put on probation if they had not been sent to boot camps would affect any potential savings. (3)

Dale K. Sechrest (1989) reviewed shock incarceration reports based on National Institute of Justice research and gave boot camps the most negative assessment:

> Regardless of the media hype, there is no evidence that shock incarceration "works" for the offenders that need to be reached any more than scared straight or shock probation worked to any great degree. None. Yet these types of "quick-fix" solutions linger on. Shock programs like scared straight and boot camps appear to be "right" methods based on our middle-class understanding of how punishment works. The American Correctional Association [however] notes that "This deeply-rooted social problem cannot be eradicated by exposing [young criminals] to threats of force, intimidation, verbal abuse, or other practices that are meant to shock youths out of [undesired] behavior." (19)

Doris Layton MacKenzie, Robert Brame, David McDowall, and Claire Souryal (1995) found mixed results at best when they compared boot camp graduates with comparison samples of prison parolees, probationers, and boot camp dropouts in eight states (Florida, Georgia, Illinois, Louisiana, New York, Oklahoma, South Carolina, and Texas). All the programs were chosen because they contained the core components of boot camps—military drill and ceremony, hard labor, physical training, strict rules, and discipline. The programs, however, differed in other respects that can affect recidivism, including length of stay and the amount of time devoted each day to treatment. MacKenzie and her colleagues measured recidivism in a number of ways, including arrest, revocation for technical violations, and revocation for committing new crimes.

Using regression analysis and other measures of the performance of boot camp graduates and comparison groups, MacKenzie and her colleagues concluded:

> Using this method, the day-fine amounts in the Staten Island court could range from as low as $25 for a welfare recipient with three children who was convicted of the least serious offense in the court's jurisdiction, to $4,000 for a single offender with no dependents and a gross income of $35,000 who was sentenced for the most serious offense. (23)

The results of an interim evaluation of the experiment were promising. The court implemented day fines smoothly, replacing virtually all fixed fines with day fines during the pilot year of the experiment. Revenue from fines rose 14 percent during the experiment because of the larger day fines imposed on affluent offenders. Despite the higher fines, collection rates remained as good under the experiment with day fines as they were under the old fixed-fine system. The court enforced the sentences of 84 percent of day-fine offenders. Most offenders paid their fines, or a substantial part of them. Thirteen percent originally sentenced to day fines were returned to court for resentencing because they did not pay. These offenders were usually sentenced to community service or to jail (Hillsman and Greene 1992, 133–134).

If [the core] components [of boot camp] effectively reduce the recidivism of offenders, we would likely have observed a consistent pattern across states. That pattern would be one of lower recidivism rates for boot camp graduates in contrast to those of comparison groups. *This did not occur* [emphasis added]. As a result, we conclude that these components in and of themselves do not reduce the recidivism of participating offenders. (351)

MacKenzie and her colleagues suggest why boot camp graduates of some programs do better than others. One possibility is the selection process. Boot camp identifies and selects

> offenders who were at lower risk of recidivism in the first place. That is, boot camp completers may be at lower risk than the dropouts for some unanswered reason at the start of the program, and the boot camp program merely separates those who are low risks (the completers) from those who are higher risks (the dropouts). (353)

It may be that the key to boot camp success is not the military drill, strict discipline and rules, hard labor, and heavy physical exercise. Georgia, where boot camp graduates did worse than the comparison groups, had little treatment in the daily schedule. Louisiana boot camp graduates had the lowest arrest rate of all the programs in the study, fewer revocations than either parolees or dropouts, fewer crimes than parolees, and fewer technical violations than dropouts. One possible explanation is that the Louisiana program devoted three or more hours every day to treatment. The researchers call for more research on this aspect of boot camps and ask the critical question: Would programs that incorporate treatment without the military atmosphere do as well as those with the military atmosphere (352–353)?

In a related study of some of the boot camps just discussed, MacKenzie and Brame (1995) tried to answer that question. They compared a sample of those who completed boot camp and those who dropped out of boot camp with groups who were eligible for boot camp but didn't attend. The researchers subjected the data collected from the samples to several statistical evaluations. They found "little conclusive evidence that" boot camps "had a positive effect on offender behavior." However, they did find that "supervision intensity plays an important role in shaping offenders' activities during community supervision." They conclude:

> The relatively weak association between shock incarceration [boot camp] and positive adjustment [meaning avoiding illegal activities, obtaining work and education, and meeting financial and family responsibility] should give policymakers reason for pause. While efforts to identify circumstances where shock incarceration is effective might be useful, it seems that the evidence weighs against concluding that shock incarceration programs are broadly effective at enhancing the ability of offenders to adjust more successfully in the community. (138)

Sheldon X. Zhang (1998) reviewed a wide range of evaluations of the effectiveness of shock incarceration by means of boot camps. He concluded:

> Although some have found positive changes in participants' attitudes, few program evaluations have found "hard" evidence of the effectiveness of these camps in terms of rehabilitation or reducing recidivism. According to the most comprehensive study to date [MacKenzie and her colleagues discussed above], based on a comparative analysis of programs in eight states, no clear-cut statements can be made about the effectiveness of boot camps. In general, boot camp graduates do not fare better or worse after release than their counterparts in the conventional correctional system.... Empirical efforts have also failed to produce consistent findings on other program effectiveness indicators such as increased prosocial behavior, reduction in technical violations, or reduced drug involvement of camp graduates. At present, the only summarizing statement one can make about boot camps is the lack of any consistent effect either positive or negative. (315)

Community Service Sentences of **community service** order offenders "to work without pay at projects that...benefit the public or...public charities" (McDonald 1992, 183–184). These sentences hark back to two ancient practices: restitution and hard labor.

community service intermediate punishment that orders offenders "to work without pay at projects that benefit the public

Restitution is paying back victims for the injuries and other losses caused by offenders. The laws of the ancient Babylonians, Greeks, Romans, and Jews and of medieval Europe all provided for specific compensation that offenders had to pay their victims. When victims lost their central place in criminal justice (Chapter 2), the use of restitution fell into disuse. Society as a whole took the place of individuals as the victim of crime. Community service orders took the place of restitution.

In ancient times, "offenders could avoid worse punishment if they performed hard manual labor on public projects (such as road building) or manned oars on galleys" (183–184).

Community service has several underlying purposes that have varied over time. During the 1970s, community service was acclaimed as a mechanism to

► Community service is viewed mainly as a way to punish criminals who deserve intermediate punishment; that is, they deserve to suffer more than ordinary probationers but not as much as offenders in jails and prisons. These three nonviolent offenders are doing their time sorting food at a local food bank.

© Jeff Greenberg/Photo Edit

DECISION POINT

Are community service sentences appropriate?

Click on this Decision Point at http://cj.wadsworth.com/samaha_ cj7e to explore the issue.

day reporting centers intermediate punishment that combines high levels of surveillance and extensive services, treatments, or activities

serve a variety of utilitarian purposes. It was touted as a form of restitution; instead of paying back individual victims, however, community service paid back the entire community. Furthermore, community service was supposed to rehabilitate offenders. Reformers hoped that by working beside law-abiding people, offenders would develop a sense of responsibility. Judge Dennis Challeen, a booster of community service sentences, argued that

> they require offenders to make efforts toward self-improvement, thus removing them from their roles as losers and helping them to address their personal problems and character defects that alienate them from the mainstream of society. (McDonald 1992, 187).

These justifications began to sound outdated in the atmosphere of the tougher attitudes toward crime and criminals that began in the 1970s. The philosophy of "just deserts" replaced utilitarian aims such as rehabilitation. Community service came to be seen mainly as a way to punish criminals who deserve intermediate punishment; that is, they deserve to suffer more than ordinary probationers but not as much as offenders in jails and prisons (McDonald 1992, 186).

Day Reporting Centers A handful of states have introduced day reporting centers as an intermediate punishment (Parent 1995). **Day reporting centers** can reduce jail and prison crowding by requiring offenders to report every day instead of confining them. Day reporting centers "combine high levels of surveillance and extensive services, treatments, or activities." Their clients include:

1. Defendants denied bail before conviction
2. Prisoners released conditionally from prison
3. Offenders sentenced to day reporting instead of confinement in jails

Dale G. Parent (1995) gives one example of (3): The Connecticut Prison Association reviewed "Frank's" case and recommended that the judge release him to Alternative Incarceration Center (AIC) in Hartford. The judge agreed:

> [H]e ordered Frank to report to the AIC every morning and to file an itinerary showing where he would be, and how he could be contacted, for each hour of each day. The judge ordered Frank to look for a job (Frank used the association's employment project to find a job as a custodian in a local factory) and to attend drug-use counseling sessions at AIC. Finally, the judge ordered Frank to submit to random drug-use tests. (125)

Jack McDevitt and his colleagues (*Criminal Justice Abstracts* 1998, 105–106) evaluated the Metropolitan Day Reporting Center (MDRC) in Boston. The center deals with inmates released early from jails. The researchers used the records of inmates and interviews with both inmates and staff members. The MDRC found that

- "MDRC inmates were twice as likely to remain crime-free as those released directly from a jail."
- Only 1 percent committed a crime while they were in the program.
- Nearly 80 percent were either working or looking for a job.
- Most inmates were suffering from serious alcohol or other drug abuse.
- About 60 percent of the MDRC clients who had been incarcerated three or more times in the past didn't commit new crimes.

Evaluating Intermediate Punishments

Intermediate punishments, especially ones that seem like they're really punishing offenders instead of coddling them—like correctional boot camps—are enormously popular with the public. But do they punish offenders? Do they deter crime? Do they rehabilitate offenders? Do they protect the public? There's a substantial amount of research (and mixed results) on the effectiveness of intermediate punishment programs, but we can boil it down into four findings researchers agree on:

1. *Intermediate punishments add tougher conditions to probation; they don't just divert offenders from prison.* This is good if the tougher conditions are added to offenders on probation who deserve harsher penalties and don't let serious prisoners out of prison. But it's not good if it's what we call *net widening,* meaning harsher penalties are added to offenders who need only ordinary supervision while intermediate punishments are denied to prisoners whose crimes and history merit them. Unfortunately, net widening is a problem in most intermediate punishment programs. So intermediate punishments haven't reduced prison populations. (Petersilia 2004; Tonry and Lynch 1996)
2. *Intermediate punishments do justice by implementing a graduated punishment system.* Policy makers, judges, corrections personnel, and the public strongly support intermediate punishment for nonviolent offenders, especially first-time offenders. Offenders see intermediate punishments as tougher than being locked up, especially if they have to work and get regular drug tests. (Petersilia 2004; Petersilia 1998, 583)
3. *Intermediate punishments can be cost-effective.* Intermediate punishments are cost-effective if they're managed well; are directed at nonviolent offenders; and aren't net widening. (Tonry and Lynch 1996, 107, 137)
4. *Most intermediate punishment programs fail.* According to Michael Tonry and Mary Lynch (1996), "There is no free lunch. The failure of most intermediate sanctions to achieve promised reductions in recidivism, cost, and prison use were never realistic. . . . Intermediate sanctions can reduce costs and divert offenders from imprisonment, but those results are not easy to obtain." (137–138)

> **▶ DECISION POINT ◀**
>
> Do intermediate sanctions punish offenders enough?
>
> Click on this Decision Point at http://cj.wadsworth.com/samaha_cj7e to explore the issue.

A major fear of criminal justice officials is that probationers, parolees, and other community-supervision detainees will commit new crimes while under their watch. The traditional probation and parole systems have had many problems, especially the fact that many of those under supervision commit new crimes.... Solutions have ranged from limiting the use of community sanctions while sending more to prison, to finding better ways to supervise those in the community. The former has resulted in massive expansions of our state and federal prison systems over the past 20 years. However, at the same time, the total population under community control has increased dramatically as well....

[One method used to improve the effectiveness of supervision is house arrest.] House arrest programs required probationers and parolees to remain in their homes unless authorized to make trips to work, school, shopping, etc. In recent years, house arrest has been combined with monitoring systems. Passive systems require offenders to report in themselves, usually by telephone. Active systems can send messages directly to the probation or parole department, alerting them that the client has absconded....

GLOBAL POSITIONING SYSTEMS (GPS)

In the late 1990s Florida and several other locations began experimenting with the use of satellite technologies to track the exact geographical location of offenders using global positioning systems. The Global Positioning System (GPS) consists of 24 military satellites that orbit 11,000 miles above the Earth. It takes three to five satellites to pinpoint the exact location of a GPS receiver anywhere in the world. In 1997, Florida described its initial program this way: The implementation of the offender tracking by use of GPS has expanded the surveillance capabilities of the department in tracking offenders on "house arrest."

Electronic monitoring using radio frequency monitors the offender's presence or absence from the home telephone but lacks the ability to know the offender's whereabouts while away from the residence. The enhanced technology utilizing the Global Positioning Satellites (GPS) to track the location of offenders in standard time and provide mapping for retrieval upon

Source: Cecil E. Greek, "Tracking Probationers in Space and Time: The Convergence of GIS and GPS Systems," *Federal Probation*, June 2002, Vol. 66, Issue 1, p. 51. Reprinted with permission.

demand adds a new dimension to supervision. The ability to track and know an offender's whereabouts in standard time also allows for early warning to victims if offenders enter restricted areas. The department is conducting two pilot programs in Hillsborough and Pinellas Counties and has probation officers on 24 hour on call pay to investigate and apprehend, along with local law enforcement, any program violators.

By 1999, police departments in at least 16 states were using a system known as SMART (Satellite Monitoring and Remote Tracking), including departments in Lackawanna County, Pa.; Genesee County, N.Y.; and Oakland County, Mich.; in addition to the Florida and Michigan corrections departments. In this system, the offender must wear an ankle or wrist bracelet that lets the GPS receiver know the inmate is close to it. The typical range

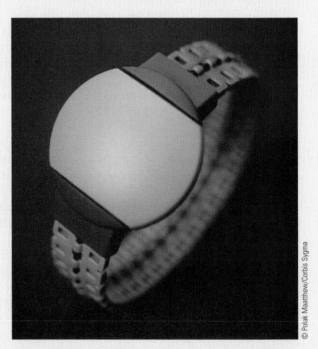

© Polak Maatthew/Corbis Sygma

▲ This Personal Identity Device (PID) manufactured by Geografix is a battery-powered, radio frequency transmitter that secures to a person's ankle or wrist. The PID emits a regular encoded radio signal that has a practical range of over 300 feet; is detected by a receiver located in the home or other place of detention; and confirms a person is within the boundaries of the detention location during curfew hours. If the signal from the PID isn't detected during hours of curfew, the person's absence is immediately reported to the Control Center.

is about 100 feet. If an offender strays too far from the GPS receiver, a notification will be sent.

For GPS to function, an offender must carry a GPS receiver, complete with a microprocessor and antennae, to record locations. The offender typically carries the device in a waist pack. The recorded data is fed to a data center or a monitoring station via cell phone or via a phone line when the device is charging at the offender's home. The microprocessor in the unit can be programmed to create inclusion zones (places the offender must be at certain times) and exclusion zones (places where the offender is not allowed). If either zone is violated, the receiver sends an alarm via pager to the monitoring station and the victim.

Costs

The biggest problem in implementing such a system is the equipment and set up costs. Typically, offenders are expected to pay at least a portion of the daily costs of the system. "In Fresno County, for example, probationers who once paid $7 to $10 a day for the electronic ankle bracelet system now pay up to $16 a day for GPS monitoring. If the convicts were to remain in jail, the state and county could pay as much as $75 a day for adults and $100 a day for juveniles." Prices drop as more offenders are added to the system. As of January 2002, only about 1,200 offenders nationwide are on GPS systems, out of 150,000 offenders in the United States who are subject to more established forms of electronic supervision, such as home monitoring systems and mandatory telephone checks.

The other way to cut costs is to avoid real-time location reporting. Having a phone line or cell phone repeatedly calling the reporting station or continuously connected is expensive, as anyone using cell phone minutes can verify. A newer device developed by Veridian Information Solutions and using a software system called VeriTracks, simply records the GPS data of its wearer at periodic intervals (typically every 10 or 15 minutes). At night the GPS receiver is placed into its base unit and the log of daily location information is phoned into the system and stored in a database application.

This is important because this data will be cross-tabulated the next morning with crime incident data being reported by participating law enforcement agencies. Finally, crime-mapping software can be used to pinpoint whether monitored offenders were in the vicinity of a reported crime close to the time it was committed.

GIS CRIME MAPPING

The key to finding out whether monitored offenders are indeed committing new crimes is the use of crime mapping software, the primary visual analysis tool that geographical information systems (GIS) software provides. (An excellent set of linked resources on crime mapping is available from Michigan State University at http://www .lib.msu.edu/harris23/crimjust/crimemap.htm.) Widespread use of crime mapping software did not occur until the mid-1990s because refinements in both the software and in personal computers had to take place.

Obstacles to Crime Mapping

Two obstacles remained to the type of multi-jurisdictional crime mapping that would be useful to agencies attempting to monitor community correctional clients. As offenders can easily move across the boundaries of several jurisdictions on their way to work, etc., complete access to multi-agency data is needed.

The first obstacle is a prepared crime map that includes all the participating communities. This is typically created through coordinated effort of the agencies or an outside consultant group.

The second is an even bigger hurdle. All agencies need to provide crime incident report data daily in a format that can be imported into the database application that is linked to the crime mapping output software. Because most agencies have their own proprietary records-keeping systems, trying to get agreement by all to change their procedures would be very difficult.

Two solutions are possible. One involves the use of XML to mark up databases so that they can be shared. The JNET (http://www.pajnet.state.pa.us/jnet/site/default .asp) in Pennsylvania is an example. According to the JNET project overview: The goal of the Pennsylvania Justice Network (JNET) is to enhance public safety by providing a common on-line environment whereby authorized state, county, and local officials can access offender records and other criminal justice information from participating agencies. The JNET System is also expected to promote cost-effectiveness and reduce redundancy and errors by making it possible, where appropriate, to enter new offender information only once as subjects proceed through the criminal justice process.

Using open Internet/World Wide Web technologies and standards, the JNET System links information from diverse hardware/software platforms under a common, web-browser interface. Each participating agency controls what information it shares and who is authorized to see it. Network firewalls, secure communication protocols, data encryption, and authentication based on digital signatures and certificates protect information on the JNET System from unauthorized access.

JNET is a state-based system that integrates state agencies that were mandated by the government to participate. Getting multiple local police agencies to cooperate is much more difficult. For example, in Pinellas County, Florida, one of the pilot sites for GPS/GIS integration, there are 13 city agencies, the county sheriff, and multiple state agencies with law enforcement arrest powers. The solution in this case was to have each agency create a nightly data dump of their input crime statistics and send it to a county-run third-party service provider.

As described by Veridian (http://www.veridian.com/veritracks/product.html): With VeriTracks, crime incident data is collected from Computer Aided Dispatch (CAD) and Records Management Systems (RMS) through an automated process that extracts, transforms, and loads the crime incident data from local law enforcement agencies to a database (data warehouse) on a centralized server. The local jurisdiction provides the crime data (which is automatically geo-coded) and other characteristics of the incident as determined by the agencies.

Basically, this involved writing a script that would export data from local agency databases into a format that could be imported into the centralized database. Once the GPS data from the previous day and the crime incident data are in the database, queries can be run that will provide the following information:

- Notification of the presence of a tracked offender at or near a crime incident through a "hit" report.
- Maps that display the time/location of crime incidents in combination with the time/location of tracked offenders.
- Time tracking of the inclusion and exclusion zones to make sure that the offender went to work, required treatment, etc., and avoided forbidden places or persons.

IS IT EFFECTIVE?

Preliminary reports show that monitored offenders are less likely to recidivate during the probation supervision period. In Hillsborough County, Florida, 70 percent of all offenders violate parole or probation. But only 40 percent of those under satellite surveillance are violators.

While initial studies have shown that satellite monitoring can be a good behavior-modification tool during the period in which the offender is tracked, it is still too new to tell whether offenders lapse back into criminal behavior patterns after they are no longer required to use it. To date, no long-term evaluation study of the Florida system has been instituted.

CIVIL LIBERTIES CONCERNS

To civil libertarians, the discussion of such systems conjures up images of Orwell's 1984 and "Big Brother." However, the law permits restrictions on the behavior of those free in the community who would otherwise be in prison or jail. In *Jones v. Cunningham*, 371 U.S. 236 (1963), the Supreme Court explained that a parolee is "in custody" because, "[w]hile petitioner's parole releases him from immediate physical imprisonment, it imposes conditions which significantly confine and restrain his freedom." The Court added: "It is not relevant that conditions and restrictions such as these may be desirable and important parts of the rehabilitative process; what matters is that they significantly restrain petitioner's liberty to do those things which in this country free men are entitled to do." Also, a convict released on his own recognizance pending execution of his sentence is "in custody" because he is obligated to appear at times and places ordered by the court (*Hensley v. Municipal Court*, 411 U.S. 345, 351 (1973)). "He cannot come and go as he pleases."

Few would want such systems used for all offenders in the community. Certainly it is not necessary for most and the added costs paid by offenders can be avoided. But monitoring allows more serious offenders to be supervised without the expense of prison. Those with a history of violence or sex-related crimes can be tracked, and brought in if they are going places they shouldn't or failing to meet court-ordered tasks. With these electronic tools, probation officers can assist in preventing new crimes before they happen or catching the criminal after the first offense of what otherwise might become a crime spree.

THE FUTURE

Systems such as these are likely to be widely adopted in the United States. Particularly as budgets for correctional institutions continue to grow, the public may demand a shift towards effective and safe community alternatives. As the technology becomes more sophisticated and less expensive, and a greater number of criminal justice agency databases are made available via secure networks, the implementation of systems approaching real-time integration may be possible. Rather than waiting for overnight data, law enforcement responders will be tracking monitored offenders in real time and getting access to crime report data as soon as it is filed. As many agencies now have computers in cars for data entry, wireless connections to agency databases could be updated immediately upon filing the report on an Internet available report form that sends data directly to the database.

QUESTIONS

1. Summarize the arguments in favor of monitoring by GPS (Global Positioning Systems).

2. Does it work?
3. Is it constitutional?
4. Assume you're a probation officer. Would you want your department to use it? Defend your answer.

British System of Home Electronic Tracking Using Satellite Technology: An overview of the British use of innovative technology to track those under home confinement or limited movement. To reach this site go to "Web Links" on your Samaha CJ7 website: http://cj.wadsworth.com/samaha_cj7e.

Chapter Summary

- All community corrections—probation, parole, and intermediate punishments—have multiple and demanding missions: punishment and rehabilitation of offenders; public safety; crime reduction; controlling costs; and relieving prison and jail crowding.

- Both probation and parole involve supervision in the community, *not* in jails and prisons. Probation is a *substitute* for incarceration; parole *follows* incarceration. They share the core missions of holding offenders accountable, protecting public safety, and reintegrating offenders into the community.

- Supervision in the community instead of confinement in prisons and jails is an ancient practice. Probation began in the United States in Boston in the 1840s; by 1940, all but the most rural areas had adopted it. Parole started in the 1870s; its elements included conditional release from confinement before sentences expire. Both probation and parole's elements included supervision until sentences expire and revocation for violations of release conditions.

- Until 1950, the dominant aim of probation was leniency for first-time offenders; from 1950 to 1970, it was rehabilitation; since then it's been retribution and public safety.

- Formally, probation is a criminal sentence imposed by judges; informally, granting probation is a discretionary decision by probation officers. The decision-making criteria include the familiar seriousness of the offense and the criminal history of the offender, as well as the employment, education, financial condition, and marital (or equivalent) relationship of offenders.

- Half of all probationers are felons. Some experts worry about the public safety risks of felons on probation. The empirical research is mixed.

- Most prisoners spend less than two years in prison; then they're released on parole or some other kind of supervised release. They're released early based on the seriousness of the offense and criminal history. Risk assessment is a more objective method for granting parole than case study, but both are weak predictors of which parolees will succeed on parole.

- The standard conditions of probation and parole include obey the law; don't carry a weapon; don't associate with criminals; notify your supervising officer of changes of address, work, or school; support your family; and don't leave the jurisdiction without permission. The conditions are reasonable, but they're not realistic because there aren't enough resources to supervise offenders in the community.

- Probationers and parolees who violate the conditions of their release are subject to incarceration for the remainder of their sentences. Most violators (especially technical violators) aren't incarcerated. Some say these are examples of offenders getting away with breaking the rules. Others say technical violations demonstrate a lack of self-discipline but they don't threaten public safety.

- Probationers and parolees have reduced constitutional rights (against self-incrimination and unreasonable searches and seizures) because although they're out of jail or prison, they're still convicted offenders in state custody. They *are* protected by the right to due process at revocation hearings, which includes the rights to receive written notice before the hearing; to see and hear evidence against them; to be heard to present evidence in their favor; to confront and cross-examine witnesses against them; to have an impartial hearing panel; and to have a written statement of the hearing proceedings.

- About 60 percent of probationers successfully complete probation; less than half of parolees do. The reasons for these percentages aren't clear according to existing evidence. Parole has several *possible* side effects, including effects on employment and income; the right to vote and hold office; family stability and child development; community stability; and health-care costs.

- There are gender, race, and ethnicity disparities in probation and parole, but there's not enough empirical evidence to answer whether these disparities are the result of legitimate decision making or decision making infected by discrimination.

- Intermediate punishments (between probation and incarceration) are intended for offenders for whom standard probation is too lenient but incarceration is too harsh. The missions of intermediate punishments include doing justice; reducing crime; reducing prison and jail populations; protecting the public; and saving money.

- Although there's a fairly long list of intermediate punishments available, they're not used very much. The empirical results of their effectiveness is mixed. They add tougher conditions to probation; they do justice by implementing a graduated punishment system; and they *can* be cost-effective. But most fail in their missions to reduce recidivism, cut costs, and better use prison space.

Key Terms

⊘ Web Resources

Go to http://cj.wadsworth.com/samaha_cj7e for a wealth of online resources related to your book. Take a "pre-test" and "post-test" for each chapter in order to help master the material. Check out the *Web Links* to access the websites mentioned in the text, as well as many others. Explore the *Decision Points* flagged in the margins of the text, as well as the *Concept Builders* for additional insights. You can also access recent perspectives by clicking on *CJ in the News* and *Terrorism Update* under *Course Resources*.

⊘ Search Online with InfoTrac College Edition

For additional information, explore InfoTrac College Edition, your online library. Go to http://cj.wadsworth.com/samaha_cj7e to access InfoTrac College Edition from your book's website. Use the passcode that came with your book. You will find InfoTrac College Edition exercises and a list of key words for further research.

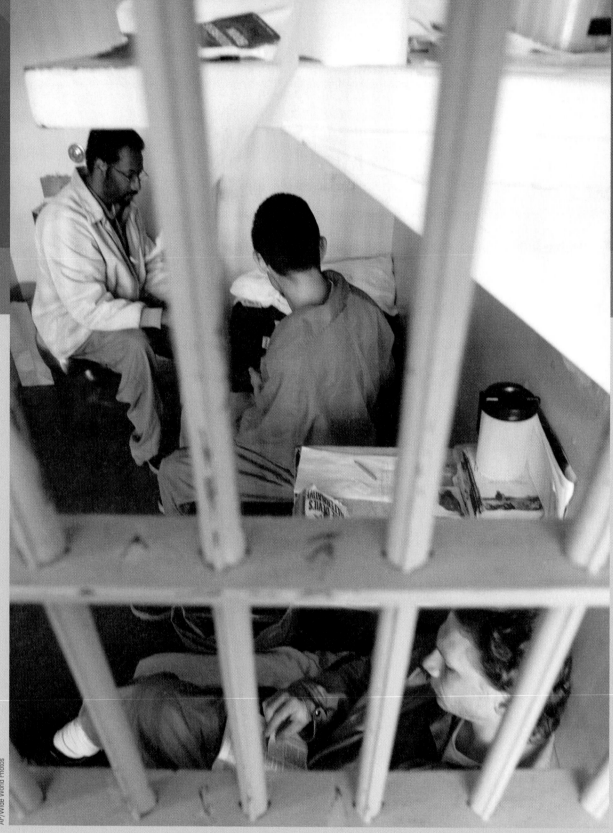

CHAPTER 13

Prisons, Jails, and Prisoners

FACT *or* FICTION?

▶ Women make up about 25 percent of all prisoners.

▶ Most prisoners committed nonviolent offenses.

▶ The history of U.S. prisons is one of trying to rehabilitate (not punish) criminals.

▶ The reason for the prison population boom is the increase in crime.

▶ Prisoners who are fathers rarely saw their children before they came to prison.

▶ New-generation prisons focus on both architecture *and* management.

▶ Female corrections officers are as effective as male officers in guarding *male* prisoners.

▶ The reason for jail programs is to reform jail inmates.

▶ Violent offenders return to prison for committing new crimes more frequently than property offenders.

▶ More prisoners are going to prison and staying there longer than they did in 1990.

IS "LOCK 'EM UP" GOOD PUBLIC POLICY?

Turning the other cheek has lacked popular acceptance, so that at all times and all places, when human beings have violated the core interests of others, those others have felt it necessary or prudent and proper to respond in punitive ways.... Serious wrongs have usually elicited reactions, and the reactions have generally hurt. The Biblical injunction "an eye for an eye, a tooth for a tooth" was intended to limit...punishment, not to encourage severity (only an eye for an eye, not a crucifixion for stealing).

—MICHAEL TONRY AND NORVAL MORRIS (TONRY 2000, VII)

Over the past twenty years, the fifty American states have engaged in one of the great policy experiments of modern times. In an attempt to reduce intolerably high levels of reported crime, the states doubled their prison capacity, and then doubled it again, increasing their costs by more than $20 billion per year. The states and the federal government have given up a lot to get to this point: that $20 billion could provide day care for every family that cannot afford it, or a college education to every high school graduate, or a living wage job to every unemployed youth.

—WILLIAM SPELMAN (2000)

On January 1, 2004, there were 2.2 million prisoners in U.S. prisons and jails. The prison incarceration rate was 482 prisoners for every 100,000 U.S. residents. Put another way, 1 out of every 140 U.S. residents was locked up (Harrison and Beck 2004, 2) (Figure 13.1). In some states the rate was higher. The top five were Louisiana with 801; Mississippi, 768; Texas, 702; Oklahoma, 636; and Alabama, 635. The bottom five were Maine with 149; Minnesota, 155; North Dakota, 181; Rhode Island, 184; and New Hampshire, 188 (Harrison and Beck 2004, Highlights). Here are some other highlights about imprisonment in the United States in 2004:

- Most prisoners were convicted of nonviolent crimes. (Harrison and Karberg 2004; Table 13.1)
- A total of 3000 state prisoners were under 18. (Harrison and Karberg 2004)
- A total of 90,700 prisoners were noncitizens. (Harrison and Karberg 2004)
- Women made up 6.9 percent of U.S. prisoners. (Harrison and Beck 2004)
- Almost 10 percent of all Black men between ages 25 and 29 were locked up. (Butterfield 2004)
- State prisons were operating above their capacity, as admissions continued to exceed releases. (Harrison and Beck 2004, Highlights)
- Private prisons held 95,522 prisoners. (Harrison and Beck 2004, Highlights)

Overview of Corrections in the U.S.: By the Bureau of Justice Statistics. To reach this site go to "Web Links" on your Samaha CJ7 website: http://cj.wadsworth.com/samaha_cj7e.

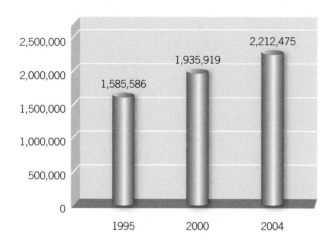

◀ **FIGURE 13.1 Prisoners in U.S. Prisons and Jails, 1995–2004**
Source: Paige M. Harrison and Allen J. Beck, *Prisoners in 2003* (Washington, DC: Bureau of Justice Statistics, November 2004), p. 1.

- About 1 in 3 Black men, 1 in 6 Hispanic men, and 1 in 17 White men will probably go to prison at some time during their lifetime. (Bonczar 2003)

Finally, the number of individuals in the general population who at some time in their lives have spent time in prison almost tripled between 1974 (1.8 million) and 2001 (5.6 million); author Thomas Bonczar refers to this as the **prevalence of imprisonment** (2003, 2).

Now that you've gotten a brief look at some highlights, let's examine prisons, jails, and prisoners more in depth. We'll begin by briefly telling the history of prisons, followed by analyzing the boom in the prison population and the side effects of imprisonment. Then, we'll look individually at prisons, corrections officers, jails, and prisoners. Last, we'll examine issues related to the length of imprisonment.

prevalence of imprisonment the number of individuals in the general population who at some time in their lives have spent time in prison

The History of U.S. Prisons

Punishment is as ancient as recorded history. One of the earliest known writings, the Code of Hammurabi, contains a list of penalties chipped in stone. These penalties strongly resemble the mandatory sentences of our own day (Chapter 11), with one huge exception: they don't include imprisonment. Prisons are ancient, too, but until 1700, they weren't used for punishment; they confined suspects and defendants to make sure they showed up in court. Prisons weren't used for punishment throughout most of North American colonial history either. Capital punishment was an option but wasn't used frequently. Occasionally, early American judges sentenced offenders to whipping or mutilation, including cropping their ears or slitting their nostrils. Judges also used public shaming—stocks, ducking stools, pillories, dunce caps, or signs such as "I'm a fornicator" and the like. Less dramatic, but still the punishments of choice, were fines and restitution (Bowker 1982).

Let's look at the origins of the penitentiary, the correctional institution, and finally, modern-day prisons.

The Penitentiary, 1785–1890

Massachusetts, Pennsylvania, and New York each contributed to the development of what was known as the *penitentiary,* during the period from 1785 to 1890.

The Massachusetts System Massachusetts was the first state to use prisons to punish convicted offenders. In 1785, the state passed a law allowing judges to

▼ TABLE 13.1 The Crimes for Which Prisoners Were Convicted, 2002

	All	Male	Female	White	Black	Hispanic
Total	1,208,700	1,132,500	76,200	424,200	548,800	205,300
Violent Offenses	596,100	571,700	24,400	208,100	267,700	102,600
Murder	159,200	150,700	8,500	51,500	77,100	27,800
Manslaughter	16,900	15,000	1,900	6,300	6,300	3,500
Rape	30,900	30,600	300	15,100	11,700	2,700
Other sexual assault	87,600	86,600	1,000	50,700	21,300	12,600
Robbery	155,200	150,100	5,200	34,100	91,100	26,200
Assault	118,800	113,200	5,600	38,700	50,300	25,300
Other violent	27,400	25,500	1,900	11,700	10,000	4,700
Property Offenses	233,000	213,100	20,000	101,800	92,300	32,500
Burglary	104,700	101,300	3,400	45,700	41,200	14,700
Larceny	45,500	39,600	5,800	17,400	20,300	6,100
Motor vehicle theft	18,000	17,300	700	6,900	6,700	4,200
Fraud	33,700	25,400	8,400	17,100	13,000	3,100
Other property	31,100	29,500	1,600	14,700	11,100	4,500
Drug Offenses	246,100	222,900	23,200	57,300	139,500	47,000
Public-Order Offenses	130,000	121,700	8,300	55,900	47,200	22,300
Other/Unspecified	3,600	3,200	400	900	1,700	800

Source: Paige M. Harrison and Allen J. Beck, *Prisoners in 2002* (Washington, DC: Bureau of Justice Statistics, 2003), Table 15.

sentence offenders to long-term confinement instead of the older punishments. The law named the Castle Island fortress built to guard Boston Harbor as the nation's first prison. According to the law, prisoners had to work at "hard labor," because "Whereas idleness is often the parent of fraud and cheating...confinement to hard labor may be a means of reclaiming such offenders." Convicts were ruled by a competent staff, including a doctor and a chaplain, and subjected to military discipline and strict dietary and sanitary conditions. The basic idea was to remove offenders from a corrupting environment and make them work. Isolation from society and hard work were supposed to redeem their souls, reform their bodies, and instill in them the habits of law-abiding citizens. Armed with these, they'd be ready, willing, and able to pay their way and stay out of trouble (Hirsch 1992, 11).

The Pennsylvania System The Pennsylvania Quakers soon stole the limelight from Massachusetts as prison innovators. The Quakers believed that inflicting pain for the sake of retribution was barbaric and cruel. To reclaim "fallen" citizens, the Quakers designed the Walnut Street Jail in Philadelphia. The jail was completed in 1790, followed by the Western Penitentiary in 1826 and the Eastern Penitentiary in 1830.

The Walnut Street Jail was the first penitentiary in the world. The basic idea of the **penitentiary** was to isolate offenders in their cells. In solitary confinement, they could think about what they did wrong and how they'd make it right by living useful lives when they went back into the world. To encourage prisoners to think, they weren't allowed to talk. They got adequate food, shelter, clothing, bedding, and medical care for free. This was a major reform because before this prisoners had to pay for their keep in money. And they worked—alone in their cells, making nails and cutting stones. Working all day in silent, solitary confinement and meditating in silent, solitary confinement the rest of the time was called the *Pennsylvania system*.

penitentiary places of confinement to remove offenders from a corrupting environment and make them work, isolating them in cells

◀ The Walnut Street Jail (Goal) in Philadelphia, Pennsylvania, considered the birthplace of the modern prison system and of the Pennsylvania system of solitary confinement, was built from 1773 to 1776 and demolished about 1835. In 1790, a penitentiary house with 16 cells was built in the yard of the jail. During the 1790s the jail and the Pennsylvania system of solitary confinement were greatly admired throughout the world. By 1800, however, mounting disciplinary problems caused by overcrowded facilities brought an end to the jail's finest years.

The Auburn System In 1817, New York built its own version of the penitentiary based entirely on solitary confinement in small cells and a strict rule of silence. But since so many prisoners committed suicide or had mental breakdowns because of being locked up in tiny cells with nowhere to go and nothing to do, authorities modified the system. Under the Auburn system (named after the town where the penitentiary was built) or congregate system, prisoners worked in silent groups during the day and meditated and slept in solitary confinement at night. Anyone who broke the rules was whipped on the spot.

Except for working together versus working alone, the Pennsylvania and Auburn penitentiary systems were alike. Prisons were separate worlds of huge, walled fortresses ruled by wardens with absolute power where breaking the rules of silence and work spelled instant, hard punishment. Both were considered humane—and they were, compared with capital punishment, mutilation, and whipping. Their missions were noble. They wanted to reform prisoners by means of silent meditation, hard work, healthy food, and proper religion. Once reformed, the penitentiary would send them back into the free world as people who worked for a living and obeyed the law instead of preying on others to survive.

The penitentiary system was part of a fundamental change taking place in the 1800s—the institutionalization of life outside the home. Historically, people worked, played, were educated, and were punished at home. After about 1820, these activities began to move from homes to bigger and impersonal buildings—factories, gymnasiums, hospitals, schools, "reformatories," and penitentiaries (Grob 1973; Rothman 1971).

However, most observers quickly noticed penitentiaries weren't accomplishing their mission of reforming prisoners. They also discovered reforming prisoners wasn't their only—maybe not even their primary—mission. If prisons weren't penitentiaries, then what were they? They were custodial warehouses for criminals where, despite the honest reform efforts and humanitarian rhetoric, the keepers were sometimes awfully cruel. One prisoner from the Elmira

Reformatory, a penitentiary for young offenders lavishly praised around the world for its reform ideals, reported what happened when he didn't finish a job:

> I knew I was in for a beating and I had a terror of what was coming. I refused to leave my cell. They stuck into the cell an iron rod with a two-foot hook on the end, heated red hot, and poked me with it. I tried to defend myself, but my clothing took fire, and the iron burned my breast. I finally succumbed, was handcuffed and taken to the bathroom. I asked Brockway [the famous born-again Christian superintendent] if I had not been punished enough. He laughed at me. I got half a dozen blows with the paddle right across the kidneys. The pain was so agonizing that I fainted. They revived me, and when I begged for mercy, Brockway struck me on the head with a strap, knocked me insensible. The next thing I knew I was lying on a cot in the dungeon, shackled to an iron bar. The next day I was again hoisted and beaten, returned to the dungeon, and after one day's rest, beaten again. Then I was put in the cell in Murderer's Row, where I remained for twenty-one days on bread and water. (Pisciotta 1983, 621)

The "Correctional" Institution, 1891–1970

The Progressive reformers attacked penitentiaries as cruel and barbaric, just as the creators of the penitentiary had attacked capital, corporal, and mutilation punishments as cruel and barbaric. The Progressives' mission was to reform (now called rehabilitate) offenders into law-abiding people who worked to support themselves. Their strategy was to combine the tactics of humane treatment, counseling, vocational training, and discipline into a coherent, scientifically sound program in **correctional institutions.**

correctional institution places of confinement to reform offenders into law-abiding people who worked to support themselves through a coherent, scientifically sound program

The Progressives led a successful campaign to establish the indeterminate sentence (Chapter 11) and the pillars of community corrections, probation, and parole (Chapter 12). According to the Progressives, if they were going to accomplish their mission, they had to first rid criminal justice of rigid formal decision making by legislators, lawyers, and judges. Next, they had to arm experts in the new social and medical sciences with discretionary decision-making power to "diagnose," "treat," and "cure" offenders, who were "sick" with the "disease" of criminal behavior. The Progressive reforms became known as the **medical model of corrections.** According to the model, decisions about whether to send offenders to prison in the first place; what kind of prison to send them to; and when to release them conditionally and then finally from state custody should depend on their rehabilitation, not on their past crimes (Rothman 1980).

medical model of corrections decisions about offenders' custody should depend on their rehabilitation, not on their past crimes

By the 1940s, the correctional institution, which was based on the mission of rehabilitation, had replaced the penitentiary. In principle, correctional institutions were more humane and accommodating than "big houses," the name for old penitentiaries. They provided softer discipline; more yard and recreational privileges; more liberal visitation and mail policies; more amenities, such as movies; and more programs, like education, vocational training, and therapy (Irwin 1980, Ch. 2).

Not everyone agrees with this benign description of the correctional institution. According to prison scholar Robert Johnson (1996):

> The benefits of correctional institutions are easily exaggerated. To my mind, the differences between the Big Houses and correctional institutions are of degree rather than kind. Correctional institutions did not correct. Nor did they abolish the pains of imprisonment. They were, at bottom, simply more tolerable warehouses than the Big Houses they supplanted, less a departure than a toned-down imitation. Often, correctional institutions occupied the same physical plant as the Big Houses. Indeed, one might classify them as Big Houses gone soft. (74–75)

During the 1960s, politicians dragged the issue of correctional institutions (as they did crime, police, plea bargaining, and sentencing) into politics. Both conservatives and liberals attacked them—sometimes ferociously (American Friends Society 1971; Gaylin, Marcus, Rothman, and Glasser 1978; Johnson 1996; Morris 1974; Sherman and Hawkins 1981). Liberals attacked correctional institutions because they put prisoners' needs over their rights. According to liberals, prison treatment programs were unjustified invasions of prisoners' privacy and autonomy. They also attacked the broad discretionary decision making of probation, parole, and prison officials as badly infected with individual, ethnic, racial, gender, and class discrimination. Conservatives attacked correctional institutions as "soft on crime," describing them as "country clubs" where prisoners were free-loading on hardworking, honest people's money. With prisons like these, conservatives asked, how can we expect them to deter criminals and send a message to criminal wannabes that crime doesn't pay? It's surprising people aren't breaking in instead of breaking out of prison.

Academics joined the chorus of criticism by claiming indeterminate sentences for the purpose of rehabilitation didn't work and it was time to do something about it. Liberals and conservatives could agree with that. So could a frightened, frustrated, and angry public. And so could politicians who saw criminal justice problems as red-meat political issues (Chapter 1). And they had a point. The 1960s witnessed a wave of prison riots (Chapter 14), a huge crime boom (Chapters 1–2), and high rates of recidivism.

There, the agreement ended. What to do became a heated controversy. Liberals wanted fewer people locked up, and they wanted those who were to stay behind bars for a short, fixed time. Further, liberals wanted prisoners' lives in confinement to be rich with programs to improve their chances of returning to productive and law-abiding lives outside prison. They called this process reintegration. Conservatives wanted long, fixed sentences under conditions that would punish offenders for their crimes (retribution), keep them from committing crimes (incapacitation or specific deterrence), and be unpleasant enough to make prisoners never want to come back (general deterrence) (Chapter 11).

Prisons, 1971–Present

The debate over prisons was hot and loud and political, but the future was with the conservatives. By the end of the 1970s, the dominant missions of prisons had become retribution, incapacitation, and general deterrence. Rehabilitation was still around but more as an incidental than a central mission.

The conservative victory accompanied (some say caused) four major changes in U.S. prisons:

1. Massive growth in prison populations (see Figure 13.2 and next section)
2. Heavy reliance on prison time for drug offenses (see "Prisoners" later)
3. Increasing proportions of Black and Hispanic prisoners (see "Prisoners" later)
4. Rising power and influence of prison gangs (Chapter 14)

The Prison Population Boom

Commentators on American culture were surprised at the immediate and strong national unity that followed the attacks on the World Trade Center and the Pentagon on September 11, 2001. Maybe not as much noticed or dramatic, but still important to those of us who work in and study criminal justice, is the strength and unity of support for the prison population boom that began in 1975, following 50 years of stable prison populations (Blumstein 2004).

The conscious decision by all 50 states and the federal government to break with the past and grow prison populations sharply and quickly is remarkable enough, but it's nothing short of amazing to witness a quarter century of strong and unshakeable support among the public for spending more tax dollars on prisons during a time when its support for other government programs (except

► **FIGURE 13.2 Imprisonment Rates per 100,000 People, 1925–2003**

For those imprisoned one year or more.

Source: Sourcebook of Criminal Justice Statistics Online (Washington, DC: Bureau of Justice Statistics), Table 6.22; http://www.albany.edu/sourcebook/ last visited Nov. 5, 2004.

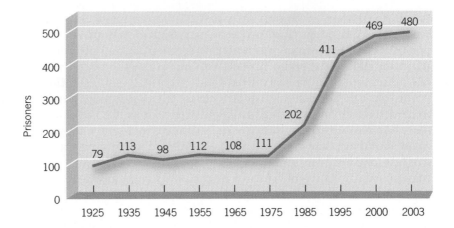

Social Security and Medicare), and the officials who administered them, was falling.

It's easy to track the pattern of stability in prison populations from 1925 to 1975, which was broken by the boom in prison populations from 1975 to 2000 (Figure 13.2). It's quite another matter to explain this pattern. In the explanations that follow, keep in mind one thing the experts agree on: policy makers *decided* to increase prison populations; it didn't just happen. So the question we want to answer is, "Why decide to increase the prison population?" To find some answers, let's look at the public's response to the crime boom, the role of political opportunism in the change, the impact of the drug war, the effects of a more efficient law enforcement system, and how racial and ethnic groups were affected by this change.

Public Response to the Crime Boom

The most common explanation for the imprisonment boom that began in the 1970s is the crime boom that began in the 1960s (Chapter 2). The public's reaction to the crime boom—"get tough on crime" by locking up criminals—was the combination of society's natural moral outrage and a rational desire to control crime (DiIulio 1996). Legislatures' and criminal justice agencies' decisions to "get tough" by locking up criminals followed. But the "do the crime, do the time" response to crime wasn't invented in the 1970s. It's part of a long and distinguished sociological approach to crime control, explained by the great nineteenth-century sociologist Emile Durkheim's theory that punishment is a collective moral response to the violation of social norms (Chapter 3).

Still, rising crime rates are only *part* of the explanation for the prison population boom (Caplow and Simon 1999, 64). We've had other crime booms in the twentieth century—Prohibition in the 1920s and 1930s and drug offenses during the 1950s—and the public demanded a "lock 'em up" response then, too. But none of these times produced explosions in prison populations. Significantly, the prison population boom and public support for it lasted right through the high-crime plateau of the 1980s and the crime bust of the 1990s (Chapter 3).

Political Opportunism

To conflict theorists, another group of social scientists and penal experts with a distinguished history (Chapter 3), morality may have driven the community's demand for punishment, but the decision by legislatures and criminal justice agencies to increase prison populations was motivated by political opportunism. Politicians preyed on public outrage and fear to get votes. They exploited the crime boom as a symbol to channel anxieties about the social order spurred by the dismantling of racial and gender hierarchies, economic restructuring, and large scale immigration. From this perspective the mobilization of laws and resources for imprisonment is political opportunism rather than rational public policy. (Caplow and Simon 1999, 65)

But there's more to the story of the decision making behind the prison population boom than political opportunism and community demands to control crime.

The "War" on Drugs

Another element in the story is the decision to fight still another war on drugs (Blumstein 2004, 453–454). Getting tough on crime can only raise prison populations if there are available offenders to lock up. Most murderers, rapists, robbers, burglars, and thieves aren't available to keep the population boom growing. Why? The worst criminals are already caught and locked up (or in rare cases, executed), leaving only a few roaming around uncaught, on probation, parole, or furlough. (Of course, when these few are discovered, they, their disgusting crimes, and criminal justice's failure to lock them up are blasted all over TV.) So that left drug offenders to keep the prison populations growing—and they did (Blumstein 2004, 453–454). Also, legislatures lengthened sentences for violent offenses, and keeping violent offenders locked up longer further contributed to the prison population growth (Zimring and Hawkins 1991).

We won't tell here the story of devastation caused by the spread of "crack" cocaine in the 1980s and the violence associated with the trafficking of it. We'll concentrate on the response to it, which was to pass mandatory sentencing laws that created new drug crimes with stiff prison sentences and lengthened the sentences of drug laws already on the books.

The result of tougher drug laws was that in any large city there was a pool of potential prisoners so large law enforcement officers could arrest as many as they had time and resources to go after. The same was definitely not true of violent and property crimes. According to Caplow and Simon (1999):

> Thus while more prison time for violent crime accounts for much of the growth in incarceration, a significant portion (how much is difficult to estimate) is associated with a . . . supply with few apparent constraints. This allows growth to continue, even if at a slower pace, during cycles when for whatever reason violent crime declines. (72)

Improved Criminal Justice System Efficiency

In 1960, state criminal justice agencies were inefficient offices run in highly personal ways by highly independent officials. By the 1980s, these same agencies had become modernized bureaucracies that could respond faster to public demand and political pressures. At the same time, the mission of criminal justice agencies was shifting from changing offenders into law-abiding citizens to controlling what was believed increasingly to be a permanent criminal class (Chapter 1). So the efficient, modern agencies could respond quickly to the public demand to control crime by locking up criminals (Caplow and Simon 1999, 97–110).

All criminal justice agencies—police, prosecution, defense lawyers, courts, and corrections—formed a rapid response team to satisfy public demand and political pressure for more incarceration. Police could make more arrests and make them stick because they were more efficient and knew the law better than they did in 1960 (Blumstein 2004, 460–466). The courtroom workgroup could process greater numbers of defendants into offenders because they were more efficient (Chapter 8). Judges could no longer use their discretionary sentencing power to put the brakes on the new efficiency in locking up more people. Just the opposite was true: Mandatory sentencing laws and sentencing guidelines put the brakes on judges by restricting their discretion to sentence (Chapter 11).

▶ **FIGURE 13.3 The Gender, Race, and Ethnicity of Prisoners, 2003**

Note: These percentages don't add up to 100% because some groups are counted in more than one category (e.g., Black women), and the total number of prisoners includes American Indians, Alaska Natives, Asians, Native Hawaiians, and other Pacific Islanders not included here.

Source: Paige M. Harrison and Allen J. Beck, *Prisoners in 2003* (Washington, DC: Bureau of Justice Statistics, November 2004), calculated from numbers in Table 5.

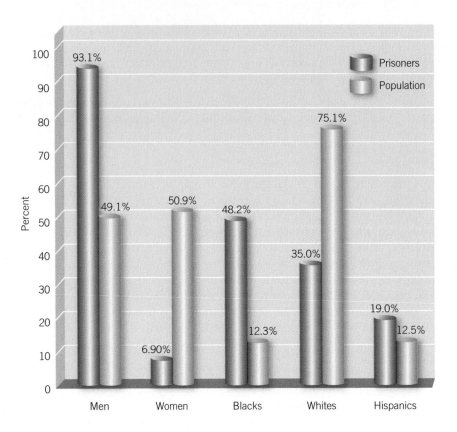

▶ DECISION POINT ◀

Is there a "better way" than imprisoning young Blacks?

Click on this Decision Point at http://cj.wadsworth.com/samaha_cj7e to explore the issue.

Race and Ethnicity

What part—if any—did the infection of discriminatory decision making play in the prison population explosion? It's easy to document the disproportionate numbers of Black and Hispanic prisoners and even how the disproportion increased (Figure 13.3). But why did this occur? One theory is the prison population reflects the reality that Blacks and Hispanics commit more crimes than Whites and other races and ethnic groups (Chapter 2). There's also research showing that street gangs are spreading from major to smaller cities, that they commit crimes routinely, and that their members are mainly Black (Decker and Van Winkle 1996; Klein 1995).

Other theories emphasize how tough it is to root out the infection of race and ethnicity from decision making that promotes locking up Blacks and Hispanics. Take minor offenses, where decision making is mainly discretionary. It's inevitable that race and ethnicity infect some police officers' decisions to arrest Blacks and Hispanics. Even if these arrests don't lead to jail time, arrest records can "tip sentencing decisions from probation to prison" after conviction for other offenses, and they can count as a strike in three-strikes laws (Caplow and Simon 1999, 90–91). According to Theodore Caplow and Jonathan Simon (1999):

> In the aggregate and over time, a systematic effect of subjecting African Americans to greater scrutiny for minor offenses will produce effects in the imprisonment rates (although how much of the racial disproportion they account for would be difficult to estimate). (91)

The Side Effects of Imprisonment

Most discussion and research about the decision to put our hopes and money in a crime policy based on locking up more offenders focuses on two direct effects of imprisonment—crime reduction and costs. As we'll shortly see, crime reduction is measured by how many prisoners return to crime when they leave prison.

The costs of imprisonment are measured by how much it costs to build prisons and maintain prisoners.

Here we'll discuss some of the side effects of the *growth* in imprisonment, or the "imprisonment binge" as some critics call it. We'll look at the effects of diverting resources from other services, diverting resources to other communities, the loss of income to offenders' communities, and offenders' imprisonment on their children. Let me warn you in advance that, important as this subject is, the research is scanty on these side effects. So much of what follows isn't backed up by solid empirical proof.

Diverting Resources from Other Public Services

The billions of new dollars spent on prisons probably didn't come from more tax dollars but from cuts in other spending. For example, California built about a prison a year for 20 years and one university; it spent $34,000 on every prison inmate in 1997 but only $6,000 on every college student. Florida increased corrections spending over higher education by three to one. The bottom line, say Hagan and Dinovitzer (1999), is "when we invest in prisons we often in effect make choices to disinvest in other social institutions as well as individuals who would otherwise receive assistance from them" (131).

Diverting Resources to Other Communities

Towns all over the country are competing for new prisons, just as they once competed for new car plants. Prisons are a booming business that brings money and jobs; they're a community resource. But one community's resource is another community's loss. Most prisoners come from poor city neighborhoods. And most probationers and parolees are supervised in these neighborhoods, making it more likely that kids know a criminal than a doctor, lawyer, or teacher. According to Hagan and Dinovitzer (1999):

> As large numbers of inmates return to their communities, so too does the prison subculture, which...may be "intensely hostile to established authority."...It is a cruel irony that when young minority males are taken from their communities and imprisoned, they become a novel resource in the investment/disinvestment equation that shifts resources from one location to another, disadvantaging the minority community to the relative advantage of another community, usually in a majority group setting. (133)

The Loss of Income

It surprises many students to learn that offenders get their money illegally *and* legally. More than half of state prisoners had a job when they were arrested. Maybe it wasn't a "good" job or a "full-time job," but it was legal. And—like it or not—crime generates wealth, too, sometimes bringing it in from the outside in the drug trade. So when offenders go to prison, their families and community lose an income producer. The reality is "many offenders drift back and forth over time between legal and illegal work" (Fagan and Freeman 1999).

Of course, illegal income is a mixed benefit—it brings bad behavior with it. But keep in mind there's a high demand for illegal work. For example, the demand for illegal drugs doesn't go to prison with the dealer. Plenty of substitutes are waiting in line to satisfy the demand. Sadly, the demand for legal jobs isn't as strong. So often when an offender leaves a legal job to go to prison, employers don't fill the job—it disappears (Wilson 1996). John Hagan and Ronit Dinovitzer (1999) summarize the problem this way:

> Imprisonment is part of a process through which minority males in particular become embedded in social networks of crime that lead away from opportunities for legal work. At the same time that imprisonment weakens links into legal employment for these youth, the

effect of the prison inmate culture is to strengthen their connection into gangs and the criminal underworld more generally.

The problem is that legal and illegal forms of work each create their own chainlike possibilities for future engagement and activity. . . . It is often the first job that establishes a mobility ladder within the same adjoining occupational networks. The chances of moving onward and upward in the labor market increase as a function of learning and being exposed to the new opportunities that employment in a work sector brings. Unfortunately, this is no less true of illegal work than it is of legal employment, and as individuals become involved in one or the other kind of setting, it is opportunities within that sector that are enhanced. Imprisonment can be a particularly consequential event in this kind of employment history. A number of studies now confirm that as time spent in prison increases . . . the subsequent likelihood of disengagement from the legal economy increases. This is not surprising given that even those who do not have criminal records have difficulty finding employment. (136)

The Effects on Offenders' Children

Two-thirds of women prisoners and more than half of men prisoners have children under 18. More than 1.5 million children have parents locked up in jails and prisons. The families left behind suffer financial, emotional, and psychological difficulties. "By getting tough on crime, the United States has also gotten tough on children," is the way Susan Phillips and Barbara Bloom (1998, 539) put it. Let's look, in turn, at how the incarceration of fathers and mothers affects the families they leave behind.

The Effects of Incarcerated Fathers You've already learned that many fathers involved in crime are also earning money legally. Even when they don't live in their children's homes, they buy them toys and diapers and "baby-sit" them. In their interviews with gang members, Decker and Van Winkle (1996) found all but one gang member with children saw their children every, or nearly every, day. Lanier (1993) found that 74 percent of 188 maximum security prisoners

▶ Half of male prisoners have children under 18. According to researchers Susan Phillips and Barbara Bloom, "By getting tough on crime the U.S. has also gotten tough on children." Families left behind don't suffer from just financial hardship; they also develop emotional and psychological problems. What price will this daughter pay for her father's imprisonment?

lived with their kids before they came to prison, and 75 percent said they spent a lot of time with them. That's the good news. The bad news is we don't have enough research to know if these fathers are a good influence on their children.

The Effects of Incarcerated Mothers Women represent a small part of the prison population, but their share is growing. More women are going to prison instead of receiving probation, and they're staying longer. This tougher attitude toward women offenders is captured in a comment by U.S. District Court Chief Judge Julian Cook, Jr. (1995) as he refused to consider parental duties while sentencing a pregnant mother of two small children convicted on a drug conspiracy charge:

> To grant her request would have the practical effect of establishing a precedent whereby the recent birth of a baby, coupled with the fear of being unable to identify an "adequate" family member to care for the minor children, would form the basis for vacating a term of incarceration in favor of probation. (145–147)

What are the consequences of sending more convicted mothers to prison? All we can say for sure in the sad absence of hard data is that locking up women will separate them from their children because most children live with their mothers. There's speculation that children of women in prison have problems of low self-esteem, lack of motivation, low achievement, and poor relationships with their peers. They feel guilt, shame, anxiety, sadness, grief, and isolation. When they reach adolescence, they start "acting out," like getting involved with drugs and gangs. All this may be true, but there's practically no empirical research to back it up (Hagan and Dinovitzer 1999, 146–148).

Prisons

It's expensive to lock up offenders; in 1999, the last year for which we have data, the average cost was over $21,000 per offender a year. The costs can be a lot higher (Alaska, $41,400!) or lower (Alabama, $8,500) (Camp and Camp, 2000, 87). Costs also vary a lot by the type of prison; the higher the security classification of the prison, the higher the cost (Table 13.2). To better understand the issues surrounding prisons, we'll look at the various types of prison security levels, women's prisons, private prisons, and prison management. (See the CJ & Technology box "Corrections Data Mining.")

Prison Security Levels

There are many types of prisons in the United States. We'll concentrate on four—minimum security, medium security, maximum security (Figure 13.4), and supermaximum security. Notice the word *security* in all of them; it tells us

CONCEPT | BUILDER

Visit http://cj.wadsworth.com/ samaha_cj7e for an interactive exploration of **"collateral damage" in relation to prison and the family.**

Federal Bureau of Prisons: An overview of the federal prison system. To reach this site go to "Web Links" on your Samaha CJ7 website: http://cj.wadsworth.com/samaha_cj7e.

▼ **TABLE 13.2 Daily Costs to House Minnesota Prisoners, 2004**

Security Level	Daily Cost per Prisoner
Oak Park Heights (men, level 6 maximum security)	$133.63
Shakopee (women, all security levels)	$89.09
St. Cloud (intake facility, also house general population inmates 19 and under with short criminal histories)	$88.42
Stillwater (men, level 5, close security)	$75.39
Average cost (includes all Minnesota Correctional Facilities, not just those listed here)	$76.80

Source: Lisa Cornelius, Agency Chief Financial Officer, Minnesota Department of Corrections, November 15, 2004.

Corrections Data Mining

Scattered among the thousands of inmates in a State's correctional system are a few who receive monthly visits from the same woman. Shortly after she makes her visits, these inmates deposit large sums of money. Because the inmates are in different facilities, no one notices that the woman is one inmate's "aunt," another inmate's "wife," and yet another inmate's "sister." Soon, however, a National Institute of Justice (NIJ) initiative, the Corrections/Law Enforcement Intelligence Gathering and Sharing Project, will help correctional administrators identify and evaluate data analysis/data mining software to sort through massive amounts of information from different sources to find patterns and in turn share information and partner with law enforcement to stop, and even prevent, crime.

Today's age of information technology could also be called an age of information overload. With so much information at everyone's fingertips, finding and sharing the right information has become critical. Data analysis/data mining tools make it easier to analyze the vast amounts of information contained in large databases by finding patterns and deviations much more quickly than any team of analysts. Many corrections departments want to move toward adding these tools to their intelligence operations, but they feel uncertain about which steps to take next and criteria to use. The goal of NIJ's Intelligence Gathering and Sharing Project is to make the selection and implementation process easier.

As part of that project, a team of information technology experts from NIJ's Border Research and Technology Center (BRTC), part of the National Law Enforcement and Corrections Technology Center system, and its technical partner, the Space and Naval Warfare Systems Center-San Diego (SSC-SD), go through the same data analysis/data mining tool selection process faced by corrections departments. The project will eventually not only help correctional administrators across the country select the data analysis tools that meet their needs but also improve their intelligence gathering and sharing capabilities. Once the project is completed, the team will issue a report and offer a workshop on lessons learned. Other major players in the project are State correctional personnel from Nebraska and Iowa..., who say their departments already had information sharing projects but that NIJ's involvement smoothed the process and sped up their timetables. (Both States have project advisory teams that include local units of the FBI and U.S. Immigration and Customs Enforcement, as well as local law enforcement.)

"The project helped us increase our networking efforts even before the testing began, and that's what we want to see happen," says Laura Scheffert James, Iowa's Assistant Deputy Director for Eastern Operations. "If there is information we can provide that will be of benefit to other agencies, there will also be benefits for us. We

security is the first mission of all prisons. Security against what? Three things: escape, harm to staff and other prisoners, and smuggling contraband into the prison. Security is the dominant criterion for building prisons and managing prisoners. The amount of security distinguishes the four types of prisons. We'll look at maximum, new-generation maximum, medium, and minimum security prisons.

maximum security prisons the highest priority security (preventing prisoners from escaping, hurting staff or each other, and keeping out contraband)

Maximum Security Prisons Maximum security prisons focus almost exclusively on security—preventing prisoners from escaping, hurting staff or one another, and keeping out contraband. Maximum security prisons can be traditional facilities, supermaxes, or new-generation facilities.

▶ **FIGURE 13.4 Breakdown of Prison Types by Security Levels, 2000**

Source: Criminal Justice Institute, *Corrections Yearbook 2000: Adult Corrections* (Middletown, CT: Criminal Justice Institute, Inc., 2001), p. 68.

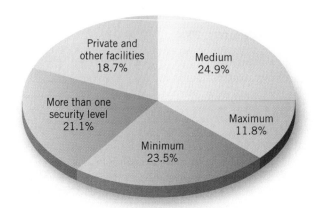

Private and other facilities 18.7%

Medium 24.9%

More than one security level 21.1%

Maximum 11.8%

Minimum 23.5%

see this as a two-way information flow. This particular project applies the [analysis] tool to our database, and it will impact what information we can make available. However, the biggest benefit to us comes from the whole process of learning what our partners need—of learning what information is most pertinent to them."

"NIJ is giving us good feedback and good ideas and keeping us focused," says B. J. Spring, administrative assistant at the Intelligence Division of the Nebraska Department of Correctional Services. "The sharing will happen in a better fashion than if we had just muddled through it ourselves." BRTC's Dr. Wadad Brooke Dubbleday says the project has shown her that much of what happens within jails and corrections facilities influences what happens on the outside. "Corrections may be able to share information with law enforcement, and it will turn out that each had a piece of the puzzle, and the picture is now complete," she says.

The completed picture includes pieces provided by the mining and analysis software, which finds previously undiscovered relationships and patterns, enabling both corrections and law enforcement to use their resources more effectively and intelligence analysts to perform their jobs at a higher level. In Nebraska, reaching that higher level became a long-term goal several years ago when the State created B. J. Spring's position (Spring is administrative assistant in the Intelligence Division at the Nebraska Department of Correctional Services) compiling statistics potentially related to drug use and looking for patterns.

Although Spring and his analysts had recorded some success, he says the NIJ project came along just when Nebraska wanted to move on. Before involvement with the NIJ project, Nebraska had compiled databases on

- Incidents suspected of having a drug-related link.
- Exchanges of large amounts of cash.
- Suspicious phone calls (culled from reports on all phone calls by a manual review).
- Visitors to inmates who had previously been flagged as exhibiting suspicious behavior.
- Account information.
- Vital statistics such as all inmates' height, weight, and date of birth.

When Nebraska became an evaluation site, these categories expanded and changed. The State now collects information on every visitor and every phone call, additional inmate incidents, and additional inmate identifiers such as scars, tattoos, and other marks. "With the addition of the analytical software, we hope we can take this copious amount of information, run it through the process, and have it tell us something that we didn't already know—that it will draw some relationships we wouldn't have seen otherwise," Spring says. "Will it be something as precise as 'There will be a buy Thursday at 2?' We don't know, we are really anxious to see what it will do." ...

Source: National Law Enforcement and Corrections Technology Center, "Corrections Data Mining," *TechBeat*, Fall 2004.

Traditional Facilities Traditional maximum security prisons are like fortresses, surrounded by thick, high walls or fences topped by electrified barbed or razor wire. Armed guards in fortified towers watch the walls at all times, using searchlights and even electronic devices to prevent prisoner escapes. Inside maximum security prisons, supervision, surveillance, and control are extensive. Prisoners are moved only in groups under close guard by officers.

In older maximum security prisons, large cell blocks arranged in tiers permit a single guard to observe hundreds of cells at one time. Bars replace doors and windows. Television surveillance makes it easier to watch prisoners, not only in their cells but also in the shower, at meals, and even in the toilet. Officers may strip-search prisoners before and after visits, and even visitors are subject to pat downs. Officers also take "head counts" throughout the day; anyone not accounted for prompts major efforts to locate the "missing" prisoner. Metal furniture built into the walls and floors improves security by preventing chairs and tables from being used as obstacles and weapons. Scraping, clashing, and echoing metal causes high noise levels. It's an understatement to say that prisons aren't quiet places.

Prisons have always had "jails within prisons" (Riveland 1999, 1). Just because people are locked up doesn't stop some of them from trying to escape, assaulting others, and causing disturbances. As long as they threaten prison safety and order, administrators have to remove them from the general prison population. In the old days, they were put into special units called "the hole." Today, we call segregation in units away from the general prison population "special housing units" if the units are inside prisons.

supermaximum security prisons ("supermaxes") prisons for "the worst of the worst"

⟨icon⟩ **Range of Security Levels of Federal Prisons:** To reach this site go to "Web Links" on your Samaha CJ7 website: http://cj.wadsworth.com/samaha_cj7e.

⟨icon⟩ **History of Alcatraz:** Origins, history, and famous escapes from Alcatraz. To reach this site go to "Web Links" on your Samaha CJ7 website: http://cj.wadsworth.com/samaha_cj7e.

Supermaximum Facilities Sometimes, we build whole prisons for "the worst of the worst." These special prisons are called **supermaximum security prisons,** or just **supermaxes.** The National Institute of Corrections defines supermax prisons this way:

> A freestanding facility, or a distinct unit within a freestanding facility, that provides for the management and security and control of inmates who have been officially designated as exhibiting violent or seriously disruptive behavior while incarcerated. Such inmates have been determined to be a threat to safety and security in traditional high security facilities and their behavior can be controlled only by separation, restricted movement, and limited access to staff and other inmates. (Riveland 1999, 3)

The legendary federal Alcatraz prison built in 1934 on an island off the coast of San Francisco was the first supermax prison, although it wasn't called that. Until 1963 when it closed, Alcatraz housed the nation's most notorious criminals, "most sophisticated prison escape artists," prison riot leaders, and most violent prisoners. The prison was based on the philosophy of "lock 'em up and throw away the key."

Alcatraz introduced the concentration model of managing prisoners who most threatened prison security and safety. The model assumes it's easier to manage troublemakers if they're completely removed from the general prison population (Riveland 1999, 5). When Alcatraz was closed in 1963, rehabilitation was still the dominant penal policy. Authorities then spread Alcatraz prisoners around the country in many different prisons, according to what sociologist and former Director of the Federal Bureau of Prisons David Ward (1994) calls the *dispersion model* of handling troublesome prisoners. Several assumptions lie behind the dispersion model. Spreading problem prisoners around prevents them from joining to cause trouble. This relieves prison staff from having to spend all their time controlling the same troublemakers. It also allows the prison administration to break up cliques and gangs, and prisoners can participate in rehabilitation programs (Riveland 1999, 1).

By 1978, a combination of rising assaults on staff, prison unrest, and "get tough on criminals" attitudes (discussed earlier) led to a return to the concentration model. In that year, the U.S. Bureau of Prisons opened a "special high security control unit" in the federal prison at Marion, Indiana. The unit housed the nation's most dangerous prisoners. Assaults on staff and prisoners increased sharply around the country and at Marion in the early 1980s. At Marion, there were 54 serious inmate-on-inmate assaults, 8 prisoner killings, and 28 serious assaults on staff—not counting group disturbances.

On July 8, 1983, two prisoners armed with knives stabbed an officer they'd taken hostage. The next week, prisoners stabbed a general population prisoner five times because he had more privileges than they did. Several days later, while prisoners were returning to their cells from the dining hall, two prisoners attacked two officer escorts, stabbing one officer 12 times. After this stabbing, the prison was put on lockdown status—the temporary suspension of all activities, including recreation. Prisoners received sack lunches in their cells for breakfast, lunch, and dinner. As soon as these restrictions were lifted, one prisoner was stabbed and staff were threatened. The lockdown was reinstated. This pattern continued, more or less—lockdowns, some letup followed by prisoner violence, and then a reinstated lockdown (Ward 1990).

Marion remained the nation's only supermax until 1994, when the U.S. Bureau of Prisons opened the Administrative Maximum Penitentiary at Florence, Colorado. Florence (ADX) became the nation's (and probably the world's) state-of-the-art supermax. According to the Office of Public Affairs of the Federal Bureau of Prisons:

> Florence (ADX) has been designed to operate in a humane, safe manner that is in accord with all applicable legal standards and sound correctional practices.... Unusually high security prisons are necessary at institutions like Marion and Florence because they confine

the most serious escape and assault risks in the Bureau, as well as some equally dangerous inmates from a number of states. Most Marion inmates have demonstrated by highly assaultive, predatory, or serious escape-related behavior that they are in a stage of their institutional career where they cannot function in traditional, open population institutions of lower security. They are simply the most violent and dangerous inmates in the entire system, and most of them have proven it repeatedly. (Federal Bureau of Prisons 1993, 1)

So, according to the Federal Bureau of Prisons (1993):

An unfortunate but real aspect of modern correctional administration in America is that many prison populations include growing numbers of extremely violent, predatory individuals. This, in part, is due to the emergence of prison gangs that seek to control internal drug trafficking and other illicit activity, and rely on threats, intimidation, assault, and murder to accomplish their objectives. Another threat to prison security comes from major offenders, who have immense outside assets, or lead sophisticated criminal organizations with resources that make violent, outside-assisted escapes a very real possibility. Furthermore, the lack of an enforceable Federal death penalty for murderous activity in prison means that, especially for inmates already serving life without parole, there is little effective deterrent to murder while incarcerated. (1)

Prisoners don't necessarily see what Bureau of Prisons officials see when they look at supermaxes. One prisoner described life in a supermax at Marion this way:

Some men at Marion have grown up here in the harshest hole ever constructed. Deprived for so long of a normal existence, our measure of self-worth is gauged by our capacity to endure whatever physical or psychological torture is thrust upon us. Men along the tiers boast of surviving brutal riots, of running gauntlets of club-wielding guards, of being starved and beaten in places like San Quentin, Attica and Huntsville. It is both an indictment of society and a human tragedy that the state of imprisonment in America has been allowed to degenerate to this level. (Bingham n.d., 25)

Supermaxes fascinate and horrify (depending on your point of view) the press, the public, and politicians. According to Professor David A. Ward, author of the forthcoming definitive work on Alcatraz and nationally known prison expert, despite the small number of prisoners they have confined (Alcatraz, 250 prisoners and Marion, 350 prisoners), supermaxes

have been responsible for more newspaper and magazine articles, more movies and television spots, more hearings before congressional committees, and more debates among criminologists and penologists than have been produced by all other federal prisons combined. (Ward 1994, 91–92)

Alcatraz confined some of the most notorious crime figures in our history, including Al Capone, John Dillinger, Pretty Boy Floyd, and Baby Face Nelson.

According to Professor Ward, "Marion contained a small, special unit to hold the country's high-visibility spies, an 'avowed racist' serial killer, and the country's most famous prison writer, Jack Abbott, author of *In the Belly of the Beast*" (Ward 1994). Marion is the "end of the line" for the "worst of the worst" prisoners. In supermaxes, prisoners are locked in their cells for 23 hours a day. Whenever convicts leave their cells, they are handcuffed, their legs are chained, and three guards armed with nightsticks surround them. There are no programs and most prisoners are there indefinitely, many of them for the rest of their lives (Earley 1992, 30; Ward 1994, 81, 90).

Supermaxes cost a lot of money, about twice as much as maximum security prisons (Kurki and Morris 2001, 394). Chase Riveland (1999), who headed the Washington State correctional system for over a decade and surveyed supermaxes for the National Institute of Corrections, explained why supermaxes are so expensive:

These facilities are significantly more expensive to build than traditional general population prisons, due in part to the enhanced and extensive security features on locks, doors, and perimeters; reinforced walls, ceilings, and floors; and, frequently, the incorporation of advanced electronic systems and technology. Their operating costs have proven to be much greater also. Providing meals and other services at individual cell fronts, multiple-officer escorts and maintenance of the elaborate electronic systems are examples of things that add up quickly. The number of correctional officers required to assure both internal and external security, movement of inmates, security searches of cells, and the delivery of food and other supplies and services to individual cells generally drives staffing ratios—and therefore operating costs—much higher than those of general population prisons. (2)

Are supermaxes worth the price? Relying on anecdotes, supporters of supermaxes say they've reduced assaults and other serious incidents against prisoners and staff throughout the prison system, not just in the supermaxes. But Commissioner Riveland says there's no hard data "comparing" these anecdotal claims of success with the costs of obtaining them. Further, in a long but important commentary on what we know about the impact of supermaxes, Commissioner Riveland (1999) writes:

> The cost, cost benefit, operating, legal, and ethical/moral issues of such facilities also raise a great deal of debate. Little is known about the impact of locking an inmate in an isolated cell for an average of 23 hours per day with limited human interaction, little constructive activity, and an environment that assures maximum control over the individual. Are potential negative effects greater after an individual has been in such a facility for three months, one year, three years, five years or more? Do extended isolation, absence of normal stimuli, and a controlling environment result in damage to an inmate's psyche? Research in this area is sparse. That which does exist tends to focus on the eventual recidivist criminal behavior—either in or out of prison—rather than on the potential psychological damage to the inmate....
>
> The impact of supermax facilities on staff working there has also been the subject of much discussion over the last several years ranging from the need to pick very experienced staff to the heightened levels of stress they experience. Having to deal on a daily basis with inmates proven to be the most troublesome—in an environment that prioritizes human control and isolation—presents line staff supervisors and facility and administrators with extraordinary challenges. Correctional administrators with experience in operating supermax facilities talk about the potential for creating a "we/they syndrome" between staff and inmates. The nature and reputation of the inmate and frequently the behavior combined with ultra-control and rigidity magnify the tension between inmates and staff. When there is little interaction except in control situations, the adversarial nature of the relationships tends to be one of dominance and, in return, resistance on both sides. (2)

New-Generation Maximum Security Prisons Not all maximum security prisons fit the description of either the traditional or the supermax prisons. In the 1970s, a new idea for both building and managing maximum security prisons arose. **New-generation maximum security prisons** are based on the idea that offenders are sent to prison *as* punishment, not *for* punishment (Chapter 14). These prisons are built to allow architecture and management to contribute to a safe, humane confinement where the confinement itself is supposed to be the punishment. (See "Prison Management" on page 458.)

New-generation prisons usually contain six to eight physically separated units within a secure perimeter. Each unit contains 40 to 50 prisoners, with a cell for each inmate. Each also has dining rooms, a laundry, counseling offices, game rooms, and an enclosed outdoor recreation yard and work area. Because these units are only two levels high, there is continual surveillance from secure "bubbles," monitoring all prisoners' interactions with one another and staff. These self-contained units can keep many prisoners secure in groups small enough to participate in group activities. The design also permits specialization. One unit focuses on drug dependency. Another houses prisoners attending school. A third concentrates on work projects. Another is reserved for those with disciplinary problems (Ward and Schoen 1981, 9–11).

New-generation prisons are still maximum security prisons. For example, prisoners at Oak Park Heights (Minnesota's state-of-the-art new-generation prison) are under constant surveillance and can't move anywhere without offi-

"Supermax Prisons: Overview and General Considerations": A report by the National Institute of Corrections. To reach this site go to "Web Links" on your Samaha CJ7 website: http://cj.wadsworth.com/samaha_cj7e.

new-generation maximum security prisons a combination of architecture and management to provide a safe, secure, humane environment based on the idea that offenders are sent to prison *as* punishment, not *for* punishment

▼ TABLE 13.3 Daily Schedule, Oak Park Heights New-Generation Maximum Security Prison

Time	Activity
6:30	Wake up
6:45–6:55	Live count—must show movement
7:00–7:20	Breakfast
7:35	Report to work
7:35–11:25	Work or program—receiving and orientation
11:25–11:40	Return to unit—stand-up count
11:40–12:15	Lunch
12:15	Return to work
12:15–3:25	Work or program—receiving and orientation
1:50–2:00	Education only—down to gym
2:00–3:30	Education only—mandatory gym
2:50–3:00	Verification count
3:25–3:35	Return to unit—verification count
3:35–4:50	Free time
4:50–5:00	Stand-up count
5:00–5:30	Dinner
5:30–8:30	Evening program
8:30–9:55	Evening program—free time
10:00	Stand-up count—inmates are locked up
10:55–11:55	Shift change—live count
1:00	Live count
3:00	Live count
5:00	Live count

Source: Lisa Cornelius, Agency Chief Financial Officer, Minnesota Department of Corrections, November 15, 2004.

cers. Prisoners do have some choices—they can work, go to school, or get treatment. But there are lots of things they can't do, like sit in their cells doing nothing (Table 13.3).

Medium and Minimum Security Prisons Most prisoners are not in maximum security prisons (Figure 13.4); they're confined in medium security prisons surrounded by barbed wire fences. **Medium security prisons** are less focused on security than maximum security prisons. Newer medium security facilities are commonly dormitories or other shared living quarters. Prisoners work without constant supervision. But medium security prisons do have several security practices that resemble maximum security prisons—like head counts and surveillance (Singer 1983, 1204).

medium security prisons less focused on security than maximum security prisons and more programs

Minimum security prisons tend to be newer than maximum and medium security prisons; most were built after 1950. Vocational training and treatment, not security, are their main focus. Minimum security prisoners are mainly first-time, nonviolent, white-collar and younger offenders who are not considered dangerous or likely to escape.

minimum security prisons for young, first-time and other offenders not considered dangerous or likely to escape, where vocational training and treatment, not security, are emphasized

Minimum security prisons look a lot like college campuses, with low buildings surrounded by a recreational area. Critics call them country clubs or, in the case of federal minimum security prisons, "Club Fed" because of incarcerated Wall Street inside traders caught spending their afternoons there sunbathing and playing tennis.

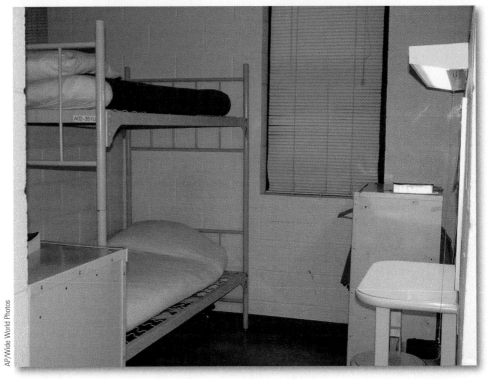

► This is a cell in the minimum security Alderson Federal Prison Camp in Alderson, West Virginia, the prison where Martha Stewart served her time. Minimum security prisons are usually newer than maximum and medium security prisons. Vocational training and treatment, not security, are their primary focus. Minimum security prisoners are usually first-time, nonviolent, white-collar offenders who aren't considered dangerous or escape risks.

AP/Wide World Photos

Minimum security prisons emphasize trust and a normal lifestyle. Prisoners eat in small groups, often at tables for four, instead of at long rows of tables that all face in one direction, a common feature of maximum and medium security prisons. Minimum security prisoners also have some privacy, including private rooms with doors prisoners can lock.

Most minimum security prisons also offer some programs, including vocational training, academic education, and counseling. A fair number of prisoners are released for the day on work-study programs that allow them to hold jobs and attend neighboring schools and colleges. Some provide family visiting facilities for conjugal visits where prisoners can stay with their families for up to three days at a time (Singer 1983, 1203–1204).

 **Women in Prison:** A report by the Bureau of Justice Statistics. To reach this site go to "Web Links" on your Samaha CJ7 website: http://cj.wadsworth.com/samaha_cj7e.

Women's Prisons

Most women's prisons combine maximum, medium, and minimum security levels in the same prison. Most of the time, a single cottage, dormitory, or wing is all that's needed to house maximum security women prisoners. At the other end of the security level, "honor cottages" confine minimum security prisoners. There are separate sections based on age groups, programs, and sentence lengths. Most women's prisons are less gloomy than men's because they tend to be located in rural settings, there's hardly any security equipment, and many have a cottage architecture and private rooms.

►DECISION POINT◄

Should we privatize jails and prisons?

Click on this Decision Point at http://cj.wadsworth.com/samaha_cj7e to explore the issue.

Private Prisons

Private prisons are built and managed by private companies under contract with the government. In 1989, Texas became the first state to open a private prison in the United States—four of them, in fact—two operated by Corrections Corporation of America and the other two by Wackenhut Corrections Corporation. At the end of 2002 (latest available numbers), privately operated prisons housed 93,771 prisoners, or 12.4 percent of federal and 5.8 percent of state prisoners (Harrison and Beck 2003, Highlights).

Private participation in the administration of criminal justice is nothing new in our history. From colonial times until the 1850s, police patrols and detective work were private (Chapter 5). So was prosecution; until the 1850s, victims had to hire lawyers to prosecute their cases (Chapter 8). Private defense attorneys still play a major role (Chapter 8). Probation began as a private and often charitable operation in the middle of the nineteenth century (Chapter 12).

Private prison management isn't new either. In 1825, a merchant, Joel Scott, offered to pay the state of Kentucky $1000 to lease him all the prisoners in the inefficiently run and costly Frankfort prison. In return for the right to work the prisoners, Scott agreed to house, clothe, and feed them; and he promised further to pay the state half the profits made from the convict labor. This arrangement, which lasted until the 1880s, reported profits and no mistreatment of prisoners. Throughout the South and West, states followed Kentucky's example, contracting prisoners out to work in coal mines and factories and to build roads and railroads. Under pressure from organized labor and manufacturers who didn't hire contract prison labor, most states abandoned the contract labor system by 1900; these groups opposed the system because it competed unfavorably with free labor (McDonald 1992, 380).

Private companies have contracted with government to provide health care, prison industry, counseling, education, and food service for decades without controversy (Harding 2001, 267). We should keep this long history of private participation in criminal justice in mind as we discuss private prisons (and jails), which became a highly controversial issue in the 1980s when corporations got into the country's biggest growth industry—imprisonment of adults for profit.

When Corrections Corporation of America made a gutsy proposal to take over the whole state of Tennessee's corrections system in 1985, it set off a full-blown debate among corrections professionals and policy makers (McDonald 1992, 362). They raised several key issues:

1. Are private prisons constitutional?
2. Do they save money?
3. Do they work?

The constitutional question boils down to whether the state can give up its responsibility to punish criminals. No, say some, like Professor John DiIulio (Harding 2001):

> To remain legitimate and morally significant, the authority to govern behind bars, to deprive citizens of their liberty, to coerce (and even kill) them must remain in the hands of government authorities. Regardless of which penological theory is in vogue, the message that those who abuse liberty shall live without it is the brick and mortar of every correctional facility—a message that ought to be conveyed by the offended community of law abiding citizens through its public agents to the incarcerated individual. (274)

Yes, the state can delegate its power to punish, says Charles Logan (quoted in McDonald 1992), one of the pioneer researchers of private prisons:

> The state does not own the right to punish; it merely administers it in trust on behalf of the people and under the rule of law. Because the authority does not originate with the state it does not attach inherently or uniquely to it, and can be passed along to private agencies. (408)

Who's right? We don't know because the U.S. Supreme Court hasn't spoken on the matter.

We do know that more important than legalities to most legislatures and the public is whether private corporations can save tax dollars. On one side, we have those who believe private businesses can do everything better than government and, on the other side, those who believe businesses are only interested in growing and making money and so they can't possibly do what's best for the people. Unfortunately, we don't have hard evidence to back up either side (Harding 2001, 283–285).

Corrections Corporation of America (CCA): Largest private corrections company in the U.S. To reach this site go to "Web Links" on your Samaha CJ7 website: http://cj.wadsworth.com/samaha_cj7e.

"Corrections Corporation of America: A Critical Look at Its First Twenty Years": An analysis by the Open Society Institute. To reach this site go to "Web Links" on your Samaha CJ7 website: http://cj.wadsworth.com/samaha_cj7e.

"**Prison Privatization and the Use of Incarceration**": A comparison of private prisons by The Sentencing Project. To reach this site go to "Web Links" on your Samaha CJ7 website: http://cj.wadsworth.com/samaha_cj7e.

Emerging Issues on Privatized Prisons: This NCJRS study offers a review of the history of privatization, presents a review of relevant research on the issues involved, and analyzes some of the major findings from the *National Survey of State Prison Privatization, 1997.* To reach this site go to "Web Links" on your Samaha CJ7 website: http://cj.wadsworth.com/samaha_cj7e.

control model of prison management emphasizes prisoner obedience, work, and education

The final and maybe the most important question is, "Do private prisons *work*?" Before we answer the question, we have to define what we mean by "work." A prison that "works" is one where prisoners don't leave in worse shape than when they arrived. According to Richard Harding (2001):

> The prison experience is notorious for causing further deterioration in offenders' ability to cope upon release into the outside world. Public antagonism or indifference to humanitarian issues and philosophical disillusionment with rehabilitation should not distract from this fundamental point. A penal objective . . . to suit the temper of our times would be to try to insure that prisoners do not undergo further social or character deformation while incarcerated. (325)

Do prisoners leave prison in worse shape than when they arrived? Once again, the answer (as I write this) is, we don't know. McDonald and his colleagues (1998) summed up the state of our knowledge this way:

> Perhaps the most striking aspect of this research literature is that it is so sparse and that so few government agencies have chosen to evaluate the performance of their contractors formally. Even though there exist overall over a hundred privately operated secure confinement facilities [in the United States], there have been very few systematic attempts to compare their performance to that of public facilities. Most government agencies have been satisfied with monitoring compliance with the terms of the contracts. (65)

Prison Management

Administrators use a variety of management styles to run prisons. Dr. George Beto, former director of the Texas Department of Corrections, adopted a **control model of prison management,** a style started during the 1800s at the famous Elmira Reformatory. The control model emphasizes prisoner obedience, work, and education. Beto ran every prison in Texas as a maximum security prison. He believed prisoners needed order, and that only through order could they develop work and educational skills that would make their lives in prison more productive and also help them return successfully to life outside prison. Beto ran a tight prison. The warden made the rules, and they were enforced through a strict line of authority that ran from Beto through the assistant wardens all the way down to the most junior correctional officers. Prisoners and staff had to live and work according to rules spelled out in writing. Prisoners walked between painted lines in the corridors; loud talking was a punishable offense. Life in Beto's prisons was a busy routine of numbering, counting, checking, locking, and monitoring prisoner movement to and from work, training, education, and treatment.

Professor John DiIulio (1987), who studied prison management styles in Texas, Michigan, and California, found that under Beto's control model of management:

> Officers had a sense of mission, an esprit de corps, and an amazing knowledge of the prison's history. Treatment and work opportunities were offered on a regular basis and well administered. . . . In short, life inside the Walls [the oldest prison in Texas] was in general safe, humane, productive, calm, stable, and predictable. (105)

Prisoners who broke the rules got the stick of quick and specific punishment—solitary confinement and heavier work. Prisoners who followed orders, worked, and "did their own time" got the carrot of the most liberal good time (time taken off prison time for good behavior) rules in American prisons—two days off for every productive, problem-free day served (DiIulio 1987, 107).

Despite Beto's masterful use of it, the control model has its shortcomings. In Texas, it suffered from the building-tender system, which relied on prisoners to help officers manage cell blocks. According to Dr. Beto:

> In any contemporary prison, there is bound to be some level of inmate organization, some manner of inmate society. . . . The question is this: who selects the leaders? Are the inmates to select them? Or is the administration to choose them or at least influence the choice? If the former, the extent of control over organized and semi-organized inmate life is lessened; if the latter, the measure of control is strengthened. (DiIulio 1987, 112)

In practice, the building-tender system was a not very pretty prisoner-boss system: race and ethnic prison gangs ran major parts of the Texas prison system; violence, exploitation, fear, and disruption followed (Martin and Ekland-Olson 1987).

At the other extreme, the Michigan prison system adopted a **responsibility prison management model,** which stresses prisoners' responsibility for their own actions. All prisoners—even in maximum security prisons—should get a significant degree of freedom and then be held accountable for their actions. According to one Michigan administrator:

> We go by the idea that prison should be as unrestrictive as possible. Don't misunderstand. Order comes first. You have to keep control. Security is number one through one thousand. But we don't have to smother people to keep things under control. We try to show inmates respect and expect it in return. We are more willing than Texas to give them air and then hold them accountable.... We attempt to operate safely in the least restrictive environment possible.... If Texas opts for the most restrictive, we opt for the least restrictive. (DiIulio 1987, 119–120)

The responsibility model isn't free of problems. For one thing, it requires enormous paperwork. Also, it has caused animosity among officers toward the "brass" at corrections department headquarters in Lansing. According to one 30-year veteran officer:

> I'd love to have a prison that could run the way the model says. But we've got a little problem: impulsive convicts and human nature.... This system deprives inmates of the right to safety in the name of giving them other rights.... A cellblock should be like a residential street. Would you want to live on a street where your neighbors were always shouting? Where most of what they shouted was vulgar and violent? Would you permit your neighbors to assault you and each other? (DiIulio 1987, 127)

Of course, it's not perfect, but Michigan prisons have provided more humane, safe, and secure confinement than many other state prisons.

The **confinement model of imprisonment** is based on the idea that offenders are sent to prison *as* punishment, not *for* punishment. That means that the loss of freedom is enough punishment; there's no need to pile on more suffering. The Minnesota supermax at Oak Park Heights is a prison based on the confinement model. The architecture is one part of the confinement model (see "Supermaximum Security Prisons"), but there's more to it; the management style at Oak Park Heights also contributes to its low level of serious violence, suicide, and drug use (Crist 2004). Warden Frank Wood (and his successors) exemplified this new management philosophy, which requires personal interaction among the warden, inmates, and staff. Wood spent more than 25 percent of his time, in his words, "eyeball to eyeball" with inmates and staff. According to Warden David Crist (2004) who worked under him, Wood personally conducted the final prisoner orientation meeting that makes them "understand their responsibilities and the prison's responsibilities to them."

Now retired, Wood still has great charisma. (When he entered the room at a retirement dinner for one of my colleagues all heads turned toward him, even those who didn't know who he was.) He inspired many of his staff, several of whom are now wardens. They're firmly committed to the management style Wood started in the 1970s (Crist 2004). The following principles and practices guide this management style:

- "Staff should treat the inmates as we would want our sons, brothers, or fathers—and in women's prisons our daughters, sisters, and mothers—to be treated."
- If inmates don't work or go to school, they can't watch TV and "roam around their units"; they're locked in their cells.
- The response to troublemaking is individual—not group—punishment.
- Lock up units on a random, regular basis for three to four days to "purge contraband."
- Test every lock every day.

responsibility prison management model stresses the responsibility of prisoners for their own actions instead of administrative control of prisoners' behavior

confinement model of imprisonment safe, secure, humane incarceration where architecture and management are based on the idea that prisoners are locked up *as* punishment not *for* punishment

- Keep inmates very busy.
- Listen to every inmate request, however unimportant the requests may appear.
- Periodically rotate inmates into the prison's mental health unit for observation and a change of environment and for relief from nearby inmates and staff. (Ward 1987)

Corrections Officers

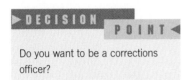
DECISION POINT

Do you want to be a corrections officer?

Click on this Decision Point at http://cj.wadsworth.com/samaha_cj7e to explore the issue.

Occupational Analysis of Correctional Officers: An overview by the U.S. Department of Labor—what you should know if you're interested in working as a correctional officer. To reach this site go to "Web Links" on your Samaha CJ7 website: http://cj.wadsworth.com/samaha_cj7e.

DECISION POINT

What are the advantages of working as a corrections officer?

Click on this Decision Point at http://cj.wadsworth.com/samaha_cj7e to explore the issue.

Corrections officers used to be called "guards" because of the belief that their primary missions were protecting the public by preventing escape and controlling prisoners by keeping order. Newer thinking takes into account the reality that officers have to do a lot more than "merely opening and closing doors." Stan Stojkovic and Rick Lovell (1992) say corrections officers have to play the roles of "father, mother, babysitter, counselor, priest, and police officer to prisoners." Still, their primary missions remain to watch and guard prisoners. They watch them while they work, go to school, eat, exercise, relax, and sleep. They escort them to the doctor when they're sick or injured, to court when they have hearings, and to visits with their families on visiting day. They sit in towers to watch the prison walls and in cubicles to guard the areas inside prison and the gates between the outside world and prison (Jacobs 1983, 115–132).

The most important duty officers have is accounting for every prisoner at all times (called "the count"). Even one prisoner unaccounted for shuts down all operations and movement. Officers face disciplinary action for miscounting.

Guarding and watching prisoners is dangerous. Prisoners outnumber officers by as much as 50 to 1, so officers have to depend more on their communication skills than on their physical power to protect themselves, control prisoners, and prevent escape. On "ordinary" days, prisoners could assault and injure them. During riots, prisoners might take them hostage, beat, rape, and kill them (Ross 1981, part I).

For officers on tower duty, it's also lonely and isolated. These officers have no contact with anyone except by telephone or walkie-talkie. They can't read, listen to the radio, or watch television. Tower guards remind prisoners as no one or nothing else can of the difference between themselves and those keeping them locked up (Toch 1978, 19–37).

To better understand the world of corrections officers, let's look more closely at the supervision hierarchy, women and minority corrections officers, officer training, and the growing power of their unions.

The Supervision Hierarchy Sergeants, lieutenants, and captains supervise the line officers. Sergeants supervise cell blocks, work units, kitchens, and hospitals. They check correctional officers' work, assign them to specific tasks, and even fill in for absentees. In traditional prisons, social distance separates line officers from lieutenants and captains. True to the operations of any paramilitary organization, corrections officers receive orders from their superior officers and are expected to carry them out efficiently and effectively.

Lieutenants act as prison police officers who keep the peace by stopping fights and other prison disturbances. They have to maintain order by "walking" prisoners to isolation or forcibly removing them from cells when necessary. When they're not settling disturbances, they go on preventive patrol, checking and "shaking down" prisoners for weapons and other contraband. Lieutenants police not only the prisoners but also the line officers. They search lower-ranking officers for contraband and weapons, just as they do prisoners. Lieutenants check on both prisoners and officers to make sure they're doing their jobs. Lieutenants also write disciplinary reports, called "tickets," on officers, just as officers write them on prisoners. The few captains manage the loads of paperwork required by bureaucracy—personnel evaluations, budget preparations, and disciplinary committee reports.

Women and Minority Corrections Officers Traditionally, the process for selecting officers gave high priority to physical standards—height, weight, and general strength. So male officers always guarded male prisoners until the 1970s when affirmative action lawsuits and federal and state legislation started to change that. By 1986, 6 percent of corrections officers were women (Zimmer 1986, 1). By 2000, women made up one-third of the ranks (Stephan and Karberg 2003, 14).

At first, prison administrators resisted having women officers in men's prisons because they believed women's physical weakness would allow male prisoners to overpower and assault them. There has been little evidence to support this belief. Research showed that none of the 39 women officers and 28 women trainees serving in medium and maximum security men's prisons in Illinois were attacked by men prisoners (Hunter 1986, 12–13). And other research revealed that corrections officials in New York regard gender integration as a success, despite one knife attack on a woman officer in Attica (Jacobs 1983, 178–201).

A female correctional officer in San Quentin suggests that despite men's reluctance to have women colleagues, the presence of women officers has made male correctional officers less brutal:

> [Having women in the pen] brings about a calmer setting. It also forces male officers not to act as "big, bad and tough" because here they have this little 5′2″, 115 lb. woman standing beside them, putting a guy that is 6′4″, 230 lbs. in cuffs saying, "Come on now, act right," and not having any problem doing it. Whereas he might have to go in there with two or three other guys and tackle him down to cuff him. It also forces them to recognize that they can't go home and talk about how bad and mean they are and what a tough day they have had because some little chickie can do the same thing he is doing. (Owen 1985, 158)

About 25 percent of corrections officers are Black and about 6 percent are Hispanic, considerably less than their representation among prisoner populations but growing rapidly (Bureau of Justice Statistics 2001e, 3). Some say adding non-White officers will improve guard work, but it's not clear whether this is true. Psychologists Craig Haney, Curtis Banks, and Philip Zimbardo (1973) found:

> Although the black corrections officers are younger, more urban, better educated, and more liberal than their white colleagues, there were no consistent differences in their attitudes toward prisoners, staff, correctional goals, or their occupation. (163)

The famous Stanford Prison Experiment suggests the role officers play is far more important than their sex or race in determining how they do their work. In

Stanford Prison Experiment: Features an extensive slide show and information about this classic psychology experiment, including parallels with the recent abuse of Iraqi prisoners. To reach this site go to "Web Links" on your Samaha CJ7 website: http://cj.wadsworth.com/samaha_cj7e.

►DECISION POINT◄

How would you recreate the Stanford Prison Experiment?

Click on this Decision Point at http://cj.wadsworth.com/samaha_cj7e to explore the issue.

that experiment, some students acted as officers and others as prisoners. Regardless of their gender or race, some officers just enjoyed their dominant position and harassed prisoners:

> In less than a week the experience of imprisonment undid (temporarily) a lifetime of learning: human values were suspended, self-concepts were challenged and the ugliest, most base, pathological side of human nature surfaced. We were horrified because we saw some boys (guards) treat others as if they were despicable animals, taking pleasure in cruelty. (Owen 1985)

Officer Training The U.S. Bureau of Prisons conducts a prison officer training program that covers typical subjects like custodial care, disciplinary procedures, report writing, and other people-processing duties. But it does more; it offers a 40-hour introduction to interpersonal communications, with a 12-hour segment devoted to improving staff relations. According to some experts, training also ought to include "a liberal component" to help officers "to be more tolerant, more capable of accepting difference, and generally more sympathetic (in the best sense) to the prisoner's position" (Hawkins 1976, 105).

But training isn't a cure-all according to the Joint Commission on Correctional Manpower and Training. The commission maintains that "too often [officers] receive little useful direction from management or professionally trained staff, and they find themselves in something of a sink-or-swim situation" (Hawkins 1976, 81). Gordon Hawkins says this problem is hard to solve because

> unfortunately, there is little scientific knowledge about handling offender populations, few principles for consistent practice, and almost no provision for assessing the value of particular measures in various situations. Custodial staff generally operate on the basis of lore which has made for continued improvements in practice in other fields and occupations. Very little has been written on group management practices with confined offenders. What there is has come mainly from social scientists and has little relevance for the line practitioner. (101)

American Correctional Association: A professional organization of correctional officers. To reach this site go to "Web Links" on your Samaha CJ7 website: http://cj.wadsworth.com/samaha_cj7e.

Corrections Officers' Unions One of the side effects of the prison population boom is the dramatic reversal of fortune of corrections officers' unions. In 1980, the unions were weak, disorganized, and ineffective. Now they're a powerful force. For example, the California Correctional Peace Officers Association grew from a membership of 4000 to 23,000 officers. Their officers now make a lot more money than California schoolteachers and associate professors at the University of California. With its newfound power, the Illinois union was able to kill legislation to make Illinois prisons private (King 1998, 618–619).

Jails

jail a county or municipal facility for *either* keeping adults while they wait for trial *or* for punishing them for less than a year after they're convicted

prisons state institutions where prisoners are locked up after they're convicted if their sentence is for more than a year

Don't confuse jails with prisons. A **jail** is a county or municipal facility for *either* keeping adults while they wait for trial *or* for punishing them for less than a year after they're convicted. In contrast, **prisons** are state institutions where prisoners are locked up after they're convicted if their sentence is for more than a year. That's the formal definition. However, in practice, according to Professor Richard Frase (1998):

> Jails lie at the center of the criminal justice system. They are intimately related to every stage of pretrial and post trial procedure and are the detention facility that affects the community most directly and most frequently. (474)

In addition to detention before and incarceration after conviction, jails hold all of the following people:

- Juveniles waiting to be transferred to juvenile facilities
- Adults waiting to be transferred to facilities in other counties, states, the federal government, or the military

- Adults waiting for mental facility commitment hearings
- Adults held as material witnesses
- Adults in protective custody
- Adults in contempt of court
- Probationers waiting for revocation hearings (Chapter 12)
- Parolees waiting for revocation hearings (Chapter 12)
- Felons waiting for transfer to prison after conviction
- Prison inmates waiting for trial on new charges, to testify as witnesses, or as plaintiffs in lawsuits against the government (Chapter 12) (Stephan 2001, 2)

American Jail Association: Professional organization of those who work in local jails. To reach this site go to "Web Links" on your Samaha CJ7 website: http://cj.wadsworth.com/samaha_cj7e.

Looking at this long list of what jails do, it's easy to see why Professor Frase (1998) says jails are "at the center of the criminal justice system" and the "detention facility that affects the community most directly and most frequently." It's also easy to understand why he calls jails "the custodial dumping ground of last resort" (474).

To better understand the role of jails in the punishment of offenders, let's look at women incarcerated in jails, jail programs, jail conditions, and new-generation jails.

Women in Jail

Almost all of what we said about prison populations is true of jails, and what we're going to say about prisoners is true of the people detained in jail, so we won't repeat that here. But one difference does need emphasizing: According to the last jail census (Stephan 2001, Table 5), most jails hold both men and women (90 percent men, 10 percent women), and the proportion of women in jails is growing (from 6 percent in 1983 to 11.2 percent in 1999). Despite their growing numbers, women in jail are at a disadvantage:

> Women are frequently denied access to the cafeteria and recreational facilities and confined to a specific floor, wing, or cell for the duration of their confinement. By far the most common medical problems of incarcerated women are gynecological or obstetric.... Yet medical services of jails, when provided, are usually [by] physicians accustomed to and primarily concerned with men. (Advisory Commission 1984, 14)

This quotation comes from a 1984 report, but it was still true in 1995, even in separate jails for women (Gray, Mays, and Stohr 1995, 187).

Jail Programs

According to the latest jail census (Stephan 2001, Table 15), jails offer a variety of programs for their detainees (Table 13.4).

What the numbers and percentages in Table 13.4 *don't* tell us is anything about the *quality* of these services. Notice, too, there's nothing in the census about exercise and recreation. The American Correctional Association Standards say jail inmates should receive at least one hour of exercise and exercise outside their cells (weather-permitting, outdoors) every day. The reason for the standard isn't to entertain prisoners; it's to maintain order. Idleness, especially without radios and TV sets to relieve it, raises tension and violence and weakens mental and physical health (Advisory Commission 1984, 21).

Jail Conditions

Some jails are modern, safe, clean, and efficiently and humanely administered. In 1975, Ronald Goldfarb, a leading jail expert, described one that wasn't:

> I was shocked to discover conditions [in the Atlanta jail] so horrible I could not believe them. The jail was far worse than the state prisons I had just seen. Inside a relatively modern exterior in a modest, busy part of town was a cramped, dark, dank interior. Large four-sided cages each held sixteen men, with disheveled beds and an open toilet. Inmates are

TABLE 13.4 Jail Programs, 1999

	Program	Number	Percent
Education	Secondary	1,545	55%
	Basic adult	696	25
	Special	303	11
	Study release	260	9
	Vocational	182	6
	College	94	3
Counseling	Religious/Spiritual	1,960	70%
	Alcohol	1,724	61
	Drug	1,528	54
	Psychological	1,306	47
	Life skills	601	21
	Domestic violence	488	17
	Pretrial services	468	17
	Job seeking	411	15
Health-Care Delivery System	Fee-for-service	1,101	39%
	On-site staff	882	31
	Managed care	500	18
	Local government		
	Physicians	338	12
	Mental health services		
	Screening at intake	2,152	78%
	Psychotropic medication	1,832	66
	24-hour care	1,309	47
	Routine therapy/Counseling	1,283	46
	Psychiatric evaluation	1,044	38

Source: James J. Stephan, *Census of Jails, 1999* (Washington, DC: Bureau of Justice Statistics, 2001), Table 15.

California Board of Corrections:
The BOC controls local city and county jails in California. To reach this site go to "Web Links" on your Samaha CJ7 website: http://cj.wadsworth.com/samaha_cj7e.

kept inside these cages twenty-four hours a day throughout their often prolonged stays at the Atlanta jail. There is no privacy... and artificial air and light. A dismal atmosphere, a constant din, and a wretched stench pervaded the place. (27)

In 1998, a grand jury found the Atlanta jail still a lot like Goldfarb described it in 1975. "Hundreds of inmates sleep shoulder-to-shoulder on bedrolls crammed into every open space on the concrete floors.... The walls leak when it rains. Toilets don't work. Medical care is wanting. 'It's falling apart,' said one lawyer in a lawsuit against the jail." After hearing this kind of testimony, U.S. District Judge Marvin Shoob ordered the jail to make sweeping changes. By October 2000, when Sheriff Jackie Barrett took Judge Shoob on a tour of the jail, Judge Shoob liked what he saw:

During the tour, Barrett was able to show Shoob the ongoing renovation of the jail, now more than half finished. Shoob saw some cellblocks with drab walls and stained ceilings and some hallways with concrete floors. He was then taken to the renovated units with fresh coats of paint and newly tiled floors. Walls and ceilings are highlighted with paintings of flowers and butterflies. "The judge's involvement has been helpful to us," Barrett said. "We hope this will set a trend, set a model for other counties. It's been a good thing."

[Former medical director of the jail Robert] Greifinger showed Shoob the medical records room, which he said was once so disorganized he could find only one out of five files he was seeking. The files, now color-coded and well-organized and categorized, are easy to locate, the doctor said. Greifinger then showed Shoob a small room used to clean dental equipment. When he was appointed in January, Greifinger said, equipment was dumped in a sink and hardly cleaned before being used on the next patient. "It was as if they were taking soiled instruments and reusing them in the next person's mouth," he said, noting that this could easily spread HIV, hepatitis and many other transmittable diseases. The room is now sparkling clean with proper sterilization equipment. Greifinger also noted that, previously, there were no sinks in the medical examination rooms, so doctors and nurses couldn't wash their hands between patients. "It seemed like the medical staff at the Fulton County Jail had not learned those basic hygienic lessons of the 19th century," he said. That has since been addressed. (Rankin 2000, 3b) (See the In Focus box "Atlanta Jail: Time for the Sheriff to Go?")

New-Generation Jails

The scene resembles a college dormitory with a student union lounge attached. At one end of a large, colorful room, a handful of young men are watching television; in another area, a second group watches a different set. Two inmates are playing ping-pong. A group of inmates goes up to the uniformed deputy, who is chatting amiably with someone, and asks him for the volleyball. He gives it to them, and they rush out the door to the recreation yard. Another man pads from the shower room to his private room, where he closes the door for privacy.

The area is bright, sunny, and clean. The furniture—sofas and chairs—is comfortable and clean. The carpet on the floor is unstained. No one has scratched his initials in the paint or on the butcher-block tables and desks. Windows allow a view of the outside. Despite all the activity, the room is relatively quiet. The television volume is low, and no one is shouting. (Gettinger 1984, 1)

This quotation describes a new-generation jail, a concept supported by prestigious bodies like the Advisory Board of the National Institute of Corrections, the American Jail Association, the American Institute of Architects' Committee on Architecture for Criminal Justice, and the American Correctional Association. **New-generation jails** combine a new approach to architecture, management philosophy, operation, and training. This combination has changed a few jails. When the Federal Bureau of Prisons, traditionally an innovative force in American corrections, developed the new-generation jail concept based on the confinement model of imprisonment (lock people up *as* punishment, not *for* punishment), its basic directive was, "If you can't rehabilitate, at least do no harm." Three federal Metropolitan Correctional Centers (MCCs) were built in Chicago, New York, and San Diego to provide humane, secure detention (Weiner, Frazier, and Farbstein 1987, 40).

Architecturally, new-generation jails have a podular design, which allows constant surveillance (Figure 13.5) compared to traditional jails, which have a linear design (a corridor lined with cells) officers can see into only when they walk down the hallways (Figure 13.6). So in traditional jails, officers can only control the area they see; prisoners control the rest. In new-generation jails, officers control most of the jail most of the time.

The podular design includes the following characteristics:

- Security concentration along the outside perimeter with impregnable walls and windows
- Restricted movement inside the jail—unit officers do not have keys; an officer in a control booth can allow movement in and out of the unit by closed-circuit TV and intercom
- Free movement and as few barriers as possible inside living units
- Living units with fewer than fifty prisoners to give officers an unobstructed view of the entire area
- Private rooms for prisoners
- Standard building materials for both cost and appearance

At first, new-generation jails were viewed as soft on criminals; critics accused them of providing inmates with a luxury motel at public expense. But the new

new-generation jails combine architecture, management philosophy, operation, and training based on the goal of incarceration *as,* not *for,* punishment

Atlanta Jail: Time for the Sheriff to Go?

In July 2004, a federal judge demanded to know why he should not replace the sheriff as head of the Fulton County Jail (Atlanta), which is severely understaffed, crowded with nearly three times the inmates it was intended to hold, unsanitary, hot and, as one court-appointed monitor said, in need of "immediate intervention."

Last Tuesday, just before a scheduled hearing on the issue, the sheriff, Jacquelyn H. Barrett, gave her response: Go right ahead. In a letter delivered to the judge, Marvin H. Shoob of Federal District Court, Sheriff Barrett said appointing a receiver to oversee the jail, which holds about 3,000 inmates, would be a "positive step." Ted Lackland, one of her lawyers, said, "The sheriff saw no reason to oppose bringing in a third party if a third party can bring people together to address the issues." He said the sheriff wanted to dispel accusations that she had exaggerated the difficulties of running the jail.

The sheriff is also accused of losing $2 million in public money to bad investments and is under federal investigation because of reports that the investments were illegal and possibly made in exchange for campaign contributions. Through her lawyer, she has said she was the innocent victim of fraud.... The embarrassing headlines have blighted a barrier-breaking career. Sheriff Barrett was first elected in 1992, becoming, as was widely reported, the country's first black female elected sheriff. She enjoyed great popularity and faced no significant opposition in her two re-election campaigns....

Problems at the jail began long before Sheriff Barrett took office, even before the jail opened in the mid-1980s. While it was under construction, it was determined to be too small, and the number of bunks were [sic] doubled, even though the number of showers, toilets and other utilities remained the same, said Stephen Bright, director of the Southern Center for Human Rights, which sued on behalf of inmates. Since then, a third bunk has been added to many cells, and some inmates sleep on mattresses in the common area.

In descriptions from court papers, the conditions sound more out of the 19th century than the 21st: windowless, steamy rooms, where the air-conditioning is broken; 59 inmates in one cellblock sharing two showers; backed-up sewage; inmates without clean underwear and uniforms due to broken laundry service; faulty record-keeping that leaves inmates locked up although they have served their time; attacks; beatings; escapes. Blocks designed to have 14 guards have only 2, Mr. Bright said.

Sheriff Barrett has long maintained that conditions at the jail are beyond her control, blaming, among other things, a county-imposed hiring freeze and the refusal of the Georgia Department of Corrections to take custody of about 200 inmates who belong in state prison. By allowing someone else to take over, she hopes to prove her point.... In May, a court-appointed monitor who is part of a settlement from an earlier lawsuit reported, "Jail staff appears to be doing everything they can with limited resources."

But the county commission says the sheriff has mismanaged resources and failed to take full advantage of money the county has provided for hiring, allowing the Sheriff's Department to become top-heavy. The commission chairwoman, Karen Handel, has called for Sheriff Barrett's resignation. "No amount of money or staffing is going to take care of gross mismanagement," she said.

The county and the sheriff each say the other is responsible for the dismal physical condition of the jail. Mr. Bright said that there was "a lot of blame to go around" for the problems at the jail, but that his concern was improving conditions for the prisoners. "I don't care how it got that way," he said.

Source: Shaila K. Dewan, "Sheriff Accepts Takeover of a Troubled Jail," *New York Times*, July 12, 2004, p. 12. Copyright © 2004 the New York Times Co. Reprinted with permission.

---

jails report as much as 90 percent fewer violent incidents. Private rooms allow prisoners to go to their own rooms to cool off, thereby preventing violent responses to incidents. Homosexual rape has almost disappeared. Vandalism and graffiti have nearly vanished. For example, the jail at Pima, Arizona, reported:

- Damaged mattresses dropped from 150 a year to none.
- Repairs to TV sets dropped from two repairs a week to two repairs in two years.
- Destroyed prisoner clothes dropped from an average of 99 sets of clothes every week to 15 in two years. (Weiner et al. 1987, 42)

These reductions have occurred without increases in construction and maintenance costs.

Architecture isn't the only reason for the success of new-generation jails; direct supervision has replaced old-style management. "You can't run a new-generation jail with old-generation management," said one new commander whose revamped podular design "had turned into a nightmare for staff and in-

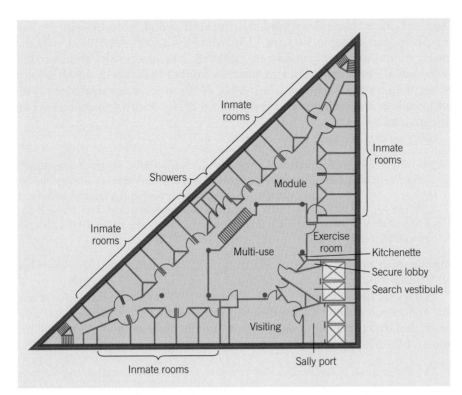

◀ **FIGURE 13.5 New-Generation Jails: Podular Design**

Source: Figure supplied by Federal Bureau of Prisons, Metropolitan Corrections Center, Chicago.

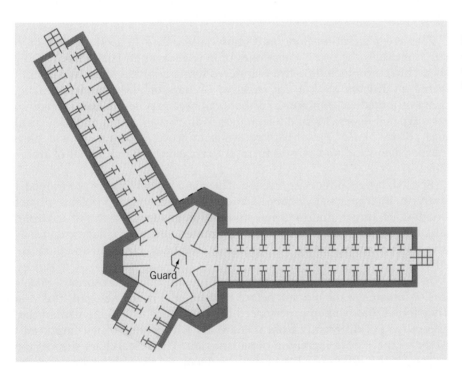

◀ **FIGURE 13.6 Traditional Jails: Linear Design**

Source: Figure supplied by Federal Bureau of Prisons, Metropolitan Corrections Center, Chicago.

mates." Direct supervision places officers in constant contact with prisoners, which allows them to get to know prisoners and thereby recognize and respond to trouble before it escalates into violence. Negotiation and verbal communication replace physical force. Women officers, who make up 40 percent of direct supervision officers in jails, are as effective in this role as male officers (Gettinger 1984, 20–21).

New-generation jails have had positive effects not only on prisoners and budgets but also on staff. Better surroundings benefit staff as much as, perhaps more than, prisoners, because in the long run, staff spend more time in the jail than prisoners. According to Richard Weiner and his associates (1987), jails that are clean, vandalism- and graffiti-free, carpeted, less noisy, safe, and peaceful also help staff morale: "Officers and inmates [agree] that direct supervision works better than traditional approaches. Most of the officers acknowledged that what was good for the inmates helped them as well, by improving conditions and reducing tension" (42).

Stephen H. Gettinger (1984) reports:

> The relatively pleasant atmosphere of the new-generation jail is designed with the officer in mind even more than the inmate. Without fear of assault, officers can relax and pay attention to their jobs. They are encouraged to mix actively with the inmates and are given authority to solve problems on their own. Officers learn leadership skills that will serve them well on the streets and equip them for management roles in the future. This job is more satisfying. (5)

Another side benefit to officer satisfaction is operating costs go down because staff absenteeism drops, in some places by as much as 40 percent.

Patrick G. Jackson and Cindy A. Stearns (1995) evaluated the new-generation jail in Sonoma County, California. Sonoma County built their jail after a federal court declared the conditions in the old jail unconstitutional. According to Jackson and Stearns:

> The cramped and poorly ventilated old jail was dirty, was loud, smelled, and, for most of the 225-or-so inmates and a much smaller staff, had all the negative trappings that go along with intermittent surveillance in linear facilities: a climate of fear, an absence of privacy, a lack of positive leadership, and so on. (205–206)

The new-generation Sonoma County jail opened in 1991. A state-of-the-art jail, it includes the two cornerstones of new-generation jails. First, it has podular architecture, including five two-tiered living quarters shaped in a semicircle facing an officers' station not enclosed by bars or glass barriers. Each "pod" contains a medical unit and a recreational area exposed to natural light, showers, carpeted floors, TV, and telephones. Wall-to-wall carpet and acoustical ceilings reduce noise, pastel-painted walls improve appearance, and plenty of inexpensive wood and plastic furniture replace the harsh metal of traditional jails.

Second, it uses direct supervision. The correctional officers are trained extensively in interpersonal communications. They manage problems proactively. Continuous, direct, and personal supervision is supposed to put control of the jail in the hands of the officers, not the inmates. Officers manage inmates by positive reinforcement, not by "brute force or steel bars" (Jackson and Stearns 1995, 207).

Jackson and Stearns (1995) measured the attitudes, perceptions, and behaviors of inmates in the old jail, before transfer, and in the new jail, after transfer. They found that women experienced the conditions of confinement in the new-generation jail differently from men. Men's perceptions of jail improved while women experienced increased dissatisfaction. The researchers suspect that the reason for this difference lies in the new-generation jail philosophy that seeks to lessen the development, breadth, intensity, and/or continuity of interpersonal networks or peer groups that might be perceived as supportive of inmate control of an institution. It is precisely these kinds of relationships between inmates that past research suggests has been of differential importance to female and male inmates (215).

New-generation jails are a lot more expensive than traditional jails. Besides, they're harder to "sell" to the public because they're viewed as not harsh enough and therefore susceptible to the charge that they "coddle criminals." Also, administrators and managers remain skeptical of direct supervision, despite support among hard-line corrections officers and criminal justice professors (Logan and Gaes 1993, 256–257).

 **National Institute of Corrections:** Resources, research, and information on correctional issues. To reach this site go to "Web Links" on your Samaha CJ7 website: http://cj.wadsworth.com/ samaha_cj7e.

Prisoners

Recent information tells us that prisoners numbers have vastly increased and that a growing proportion are being locked up for drug offenses. We also know that most prisoners are male, young, and Black or Hispanic, although women and Hispanic prisoners are making up a larger proportion of the prison population (Harrison and Beck 2003).

Our other demographics come from 1991, the latest official numbers, when the U.S. Bureau of Justice Statistics conducted a survey of state prisoners (Beck et al. 1993). According to the numbers in that survey, which probably haven't changed a lot, we can say:

- Most didn't live with both parents when they were growing up.
- Over a quarter had parents who were substance abusers.
- A third had a brother who served time in jail or prison.
- Less than half have been married.
- Almost three-quarters haven't graduated from high school.
- Most are not gang members.
- A third weren't employed when they were arrested.
- A third were using drugs and a third were drinking alcohol when they committed the crime they're serving time for.
- Less than half were making more than $10,000 a year at the time they committed the crime they're serving time for.
- Ninety-four percent have committed crimes (not counting minor offenses) before the crime they're serving time for.
- The number of older prisoners is increasing.

To learn more about prisoners, let's look more closely at women prisoners, repeat offenders, and special management prisoners.

Women Prisoners

From 1925 until 1980, the rate of women in prison never exceeded 10 for every 100,000 people. However, since 1980, the rate of women prisoners has sharply increased, from 11 to 62 in 2003 (Harrison and Beck 2003, 5; Kruttschnitt and Gartner 2003, 4). Just to keep this steep rise in perspective, at the beginning of 2004, men were 15 times more likely to be imprisoned than women; and only 6.9 percent of prisoners in 2003 were women (Harrison and Beck 2003, 4).

What are the reasons for the increase in women prisoners? Many are the same ones driving up the general prison population boom. But according to Barbara Owen and Barbara Bloom (1995), who profiled women prisoners in California, it's also because of the growing numbers of women prosecuted and convicted of drug offenses, the increasingly harsh sentences for drug offenses, and the lack of both treatment and community sanctions for women drug offenders. In fact, Owen and Bloom argue that the "war on drugs" is really a war on women (166).

The increase in women prisoners isn't distributed evenly according to race and ethnicity. The rate for White women increased the least (19 to 27); the rates for Black women (117 to 212) and Native American women (35 to 80) almost doubled. The rate for Hispanic women was in between (50 to 87). There's some indication that the growth in imprisonment for drug offenses was disproportionately high for Black women (Kruttschnitt and Gartner 2003, 8–9).

Repeat Offenders

Which offenses count in calculating **recidivism** (repeat offending) depends on the researcher. The three main measures are re-arrest for another crime, reconviction, and recommitment to prison. The re-arrest, reconviction, or recommitment doesn't have to be for the same crime; any other felony or "serious misdemeanor" counts (Langan and Levin 2002).

recidivism repeat offending

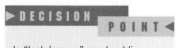

Is "lock 'em up" good public policy?

Click on this Decision Point at http://cj.wadsworth.com/samaha_cj7e to explore the issue.

The longer former prisoners remain out of prison, the less likely they are to return. Also, recidivism varies according to offense. Property offenders return to prison more frequently (33.5 percent) than violent offenders (22.5 percent). Burglars return most frequently, followed by robbers. Drug offenders, forgers, embezzlers, and sex offenders follow robbers; homicide is last with the lowest recidivist rates (Langan and Levin 2002, 2). The more times prisoners are confined, the greater the likelihood they'll return to prison. About one-quarter of all prisoners with no prior record will return to prison; 37 percent of all prisoners with one or two prior prison terms will return; and 42.7 percent of those with three or more prior terms will be back in prison (Immarigeon and Chesney-Lind 1992).

Recidivism also varies according to age, gender, and race. The younger prisoners are when they leave prison, the greater the chance they'll be back. In Massachusetts, for example, 31 percent of prisoners under age 25 will return to prison; between the ages of 25 and 29, 28 percent recidivate. At 30 and older, only 17 percent return to prison (Wallerstedt 1984, 5).

Gender also affects recidivism (Figure 13.7). Men recidivate at substantially higher rates than women. In New York State, for example, 36 percent of released men return to prison; 12.1 percent of women return. Women are less likely to recidivate when support services are available in the community. Most imprisoned women have "serious economic, medical, mental health, and social difficulties which are often overlooked and frequently intensified" in prison (Immarigeon and Chesney-Lind 1992). Community programs more effectively enable women to lead law-abiding lives than do imprisonment. In Pennsylvania, for example, the Program for Women Offenders found that its services reduced recidivism. In a random sample of more than one thousand clients, 3.2 percent recidivated. Intermediate sanctions such as home confinement and intensive supervision may also provide alternatives to imprisonment, if they include direct services (Immarigeon and Chesney-Lind 1992.)

▼ **FIGURE 13.7 Recidivism Rates Three Years After Release, 1994**

Source: Patrick A. Langan and David J. Levin, *Recidivism of Prisoners Released in 1994* (Washington, DC: Bureau of Justice Statistics, June 2002), compiled from Table 8.

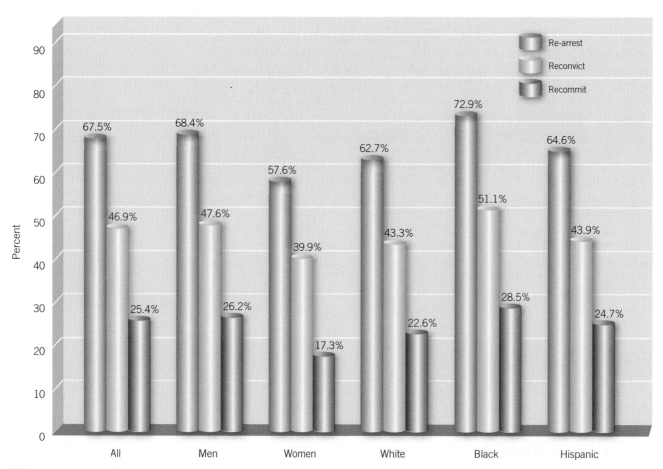

Special-Management Prisoners

Special-needs prisoners fall into three groups:

1. *Vulnerable.* A rapidly growing group of inmates who need protection from other prisoners to survive in prison
2. *Troublemaker.* Prisoners who need added restraints to protect other inmates, staff, or the security of the institution
3. *Mentally abnormal.* Prisoners with mental problems or retardation who can't function in the general population without assistance or who need professional treatment and medication

Special-needs prisoners create problems for the prison administration. According to a report of the National Institute of Justice (1985), "Prisons must handle large numbers of people in standardized ways if they are to stay within their budgets and if equity issues are not to be raised" (2).

"You have three choices," said one prison administrator. "You can pitch your program to the majority of inmates, in which case the needs of special groups will not be met. You can tailor your efforts to the minority of special inmates, which means that the majority will suffer. Or you can run two separate programs" (National Institute of Justice 1985, 2).

The Length of Imprisonment

Earlier in the chapter, we stressed that we're sending many more people to prison. Here we look at another aspect of prisoners—how long we keep them there. Between 1985 and 1990, the average time prisoners stayed locked up increased only slightly—from 20 to 22 months. Between 1990 and 1999, the average increased to 28 months. Also, since 1990, the number of prisoners serving less than six months has dropped and the number serving at least ten years has risen. And the projected length of actual time prisoners admitted in 1998 will serve has grown to 43 months (Bureau of Justice Statistics 1999a, 12; 1999c).

Several factors affect the length of time prisoners serve. We've already discussed mandatory minimum sentences set by legislatures (Chapter 11). Judges and parole boards in indeterminate sentencing states still have discretion in deciding how long prisoners will stay locked up (Chapter 11). Forty states have good-time laws that allow prisoners to reduce their sentences.

There are three types of good-time release. Statutory good time is awarded at the time of sentencing; credits are deducted for misbehavior. In earned credit, prisoners start with no good time and earn it by positive behavior and participation in prison programs like education or vocational training. Special credits are awarded for exceptional acts like donating blood, for serving as subjects in medical experiments, or for exemplary behavior during emergencies. In most states, prisoners can get one day off their sentence for every good-time credit, but in some states they can get up to half their prison time off; in others, they get no days.

The most common reasons given for granting good time are that it's necessary to control prison populations and it helps rehabilitate prisoners. No empirical research supports either the control or rehabilitation of prisoners' hypotheses; empirical research does support the control prison population hypothesis. But research also has demonstrated that prisoners released early because of good time are no more likely to commit crimes than prisoners released after serving their full sentences (Criminal and Juvenile Justice Coordinating Council 1996).

The prison population explosion has made early release a controversial practice. More people are sentenced to prison for longer times, but prison administrators are coping with crowded prisons by releasing them early.

Does Sending More People to Prison Reduce Crime Rates?

One of the great policy experiments in modern history was the 50 states' and the federal government's use of imprisonment to lower crime rates and make the public safer. Did the experiment work? "Yes," say some. "No," say others. Read the following excerpt from William Spelman's excellent survey of research on imprisonment and crime, and then make *your* decision.

WHAT RECENT STUDIES DO (AND DON'T) TELL US ABOUT IMPRISONMENT AND CRIME

Over the past twenty years, the fifty American states have engaged in one of the great policy experiments of modern times. In an attempt to reduce intolerably high levels of reported crime, the states doubled their prison capacity, then doubled it again, increasing their costs by more than $20 billion per year [420]. The states and the federal government have given up a lot to get to this point: that $20 billion could provide day care for every family that cannot afford it, or a college education to every high school graduate, or a living wage job to every unemployed youth. But crime levels have (at last) responded, dropping to their lowest level in years. Thus recent history provides [somewhat of] a . . . case for the effectiveness of prisons.

Not everyone has found this evidence persuasive. Some argue, quite convincingly, that recent crime reductions had nothing to do with the prison buildup. Crime has dropped because the number of poverty-stricken youths has dropped, or because police are more effective, or because of any number of other reasons. This correlation does not necessarily guarantee causation.

Perhaps more important, *whether* more prisons reduce crime matters less than *how much*. Crime is not the only problem the American public is grappling with. Policy makers may decide to spend taxpayer dollars on child care, college educations, jobs programs, or (for that matter) childhood immunization, infrastructure for decaying cities, subsidies to tobacco farmers, or B2 stealth bombers. (Occasionally, they even decide that the best use of the money is to give it back to taxpayers.) It is not enough to have a small effect on the crime problem if that means forgoing a big effect on an equally thorny social problem.

And prisons are no longer the only way to fight crime. Policy makers may decide to spend money on other agencies in the criminal justice system (e.g., more judges, better-managed police, or better-trained probation officers); on changes in the physical environment

that make it more difficult to commit a crime; on community organizing and education efforts that improve the public's capacity to intervene; on education and jobs programs that reduce would-be offenders' motivations to commit crimes; and on a host of other equally plausible alternatives.

With few exceptions, we have been unable to determine the benefit-cost ratios associated with these policies and programs. Nevertheless, we can be fairly sure that most do more good than harm; a few (childhood immunization is a classic case) may yield benefit-cost ratios as high as 5.0. Thus it is no longer sufficient, if it ever was, to demonstrate that prisons are better than nothing. Instead, they must be better than the next-best use of the money.

"Better than nothing" may be a minimal requirement, but it has taken decades to establish whether even this is true. . . . The mold for most future studies was cast in 1973 . . . when Ehrlich applied [the death penalty] state-of-the-art econometric methods and a plausible economic model to a cross section of American states. A raft of similar studies followed, each using similar methods, models, and data sets. In 1978, the National Research

▲ These prisoners in Tutwiler Women's Prison in Montgomery, Alabama, are part of one of the great policy experiments of modern times—locking up more offenders to reduce intolerably high crime rates. Since the 1970s, states have doubled their prison capacity, then doubled it again, increasing their costs by more than $20 billion a year. Did it work? Read on, and then make your own decision.

Source: William Spelman, "Prisons and Crime," in *Crime and Justice: A Review of Research,* edited by Michael Tonry (Chicago: University of Chicago Press, 2000), 419–494.

Council (NRC) published an analysis of this burgeoning literature....Researchers...showed that they provided inaccurate or biased results....

The rate of econometric studies dropped after the NRC report was published....Recently, however, the sheer expense of maintaining a million-plus prison population has stimulated...new studies [that] rely on new theoretical underpinnings; they employ new statistical methods, including the burgeoning array of time-series techniques; they recognize that statistical estimates can be fragile, because crime has many causes and because the prison population may be both a cause and an effect of crime. Collectively, these studies have succeeded in overcoming many of the objections of previous efforts. [422]

Whether closer to the truth or not, they are certainly more defensible than the studies of the 1960s and 1970s....As it happens, it is not difficult to put reasonable upper and lower bounds on the most important figures....We can be fairly sure that...doubling state prison...would probably reduce the Index Crime rate by somewhere between 20 and 40 percent.

This is still a wide range, and it falls in an awkward spot. If we could be sure that doubling the prison capacity would reduce crime by less than 20 percent, it is not hard to show that the costs of further prison construction exceed the benefits. If doubling capacity would reduce crime by more than 30 percent, we could be fairly sure that the benefits exceeded the costs, at least in the average state. Within this range, however, the policy implications hinge on controversial dollar estimates, statistical assumptions, and similarly unsatisfying issues.

Nevertheless, the results are sufficiently precise to suggest that most states should take a hard look before committing the money to building more prisons. Some have claimed that prison construction is an easy decision to make. Their claims are almost certainly false. The decision is difficult and will become more difficult unless and until alternative means of dealing with crime become politically realistic and demonstrably cost-effective.

The process of improving our estimates of prison effectiveness will continue indefinitely. The best study of twenty years ago would look hopelessly out of date in an academic journal today. Old problems, now largely solved, have been replaced with new and thornier problems. Nevertheless, estimates could be improved considerably if the best data and methods currently available were used consistently....[Spellman reviewed the major problems in explaining the relationship between imprisonment and crime. Only some are included here.]

The Specification Problem

The association of two variables is one of the most basic forms of analysis, and it has been used for years in efforts to explain changes and differences in crime rates....Consider, for example, the wide variety of ad hoc explanations offered for the recent reduction in New York City's crime rate. New York Mayor Rudy Giuliani, for instance, claimed the reduction was due to the New York Police Department's strict enforcement or "quality of life" strategy. By cracking down on smoking on buses and drinking in public, the police presumably stifled burglary and robbery as well. John Jay College professor Andrew Karmen credited the "little brother syndrome." "I'm more and more convinced that there's a shift in values among 20-somethings," said Karmen. "Having seen what the crack wars and violence caused to their friends and older brothers, they're more and more willing to give the world of legitimate work a try." University of Missouri at St. Louis professor Scott Decker believed crack addicts shifted from burglary to robbery. Burglary took too much planning and yielded goods that must be fenced; robbery was faster and yielded cash....

Finally, the usual suspects reared their ugly heads: the economy was good and unemployment was down; fewer young people were smoking crack cocaine; there were fewer young people, crackheads, or otherwise. All of these explanations derive ultimately from a (perhaps casually observed) association of the variable in question with the prevalence of crime. All appear plausible. None is definitive.

As a glance at any introductory criminology text will confirm, crime is a complex phenomenon, with many varied causes. The increases (and recent decreases) in crime that we are trying to explain are part of a long-term trend, not just short-term fluctuations. Our first task, then, must be to identify and account for as many alternative explanations as possible.

One reason for looking for alternative explanations is to find the right one. But there is an even more important reason: failure to control for some explanations—leaving out critical variables—biases our estimates of the effects of the remaining, included variables. What makes this problem especially ugly is that it is impossible to fix completely and that the bias is often of unknown size and direction. Nevertheless, careful modeling can mitigate the problem....

The Simultaneity Problem

Simply put, the simultaneity problem is this: If prison affects crime, and at the same time crime affects prison, how can we separate the two effects? If we cannot separate them, our results are uninterpretable. Of all the statistical issues, this has proved by far the thorniest. Unlike most issues, there is as yet no clear consensus as to the best solution.

One reason this is a hard problem is that the relationships probably work in opposite directions. Theories of incapacitation and deterrence suggest that more prisons reduce crime (i.e., that the relationship between the two variables is negative); at the same time, judges and state legislatures can be expected to respond to increases in crime with increased prison populations (a positive relationship). Unless the two effects can be separated, any attempt to estimate either relationship alone is bound to bring in the effects of the other—thus averaging the two. The net effect may be positive, negative, or zero, depending on which is larger. Whatever the result, it will not generally be useful, or even meaningful. . . .

Differences among States

Without exception, studies of the effectiveness of prison, even those relying on state panel data, have produced estimates that approximate a national average. This simplifies the analysis considerably; as detailed above, the basic estimation issues are sufficiently detailed that simplicity is an important virtue. Nevertheless, prison construction and use decisions are not made at the national level but at the state level. If states differ in their use of imprisonment, our policy implications are incomplete.

. . . Some states focus scarce prison resources on the most violent offenders; others incarcerate many offenders convicted only of drug and property crimes. Some states have implemented policies to focus special attention on repeat offenders ("three strikes, you're out" laws) or on especially frequent offenders (selective incapacitation). Some states give long sentences to a few (focusing presumably on desert and incapacitation at the expense of deterrence), while others give shorter sentences to many offenders (maximizing deterrence at the expense of incapacitation). It is very likely that some of these options yield better results than others. . . . If these differences can be sorted out, empirical research could be far more helpful than simply justifying a build/not build decision.

States differ considerably in the strategies they pursue. . . . Some states, such as Hawaii, New York, Massachusetts, and Wisconsin, incarcerate a small proportion of their offenders but hold them for long terms—a de facto incapacitation strategy. Other states, such as Alabama, Georgia, Mississippi, and North Carolina, incarcerate more offenders for shorter terms—a deterrence strategy. If one of these strategies is more effective than the other, this should be reflected in each state's elasticity and marginal offense rate. Thus we may exploit differences among states to draw conclusions about the relative effectiveness of each strategy.

. . . Each state's strategy is always evolving. For example, the biggest determinant of prison population growth in the 1970s and early 1980s was an increase in imprisonment rates. Increases in reported crime and arrest rates, in drug arrest and imprisonment rates, and in the at-risk population were relatively unimportant; the median sentence actually decreased slightly over the period. Thus most states were moving toward a deterrence strategy. More recent evidence suggests a shift to incapacitation. By the 1990s, reported crime rates, arrest rates, and incarceration rates for most violent and property crimes were stable or in decline; yet the number of violent and property offenders in prison continued to increase due to large increases in time served. . . .

Finally, sentence practices may be inherently more flexible in some states than in others. Indeterminate sentencing statutes and parole and early release guidelines give judges and prison officials broad discretion to fit their sentencing practices to current capacity. States with strict sentencing guidelines may have little choice but to respond, one for one, to any change in the crime rate. The details of the punishment equation are primarily of academic, rather than practical, interest.

Nevertheless, there is an important practical reason for considering these differences in the punishment equation. Failure to do so will bias our estimates of the crime equation. For example, suppose an increase in crime leads to an especially large and rapid increase in punishment in the politically conservative southeastern states. If we look for differences among states in the crime equation, but not in the punishment equation, this effect will appear, erroneously, in the crime equation. We may thus mistakenly conclude that an increase in punishment leads to an especially large and rapid increase in crime in the Southeast. We may even tentatively go on to speculate on the counterproductive effects of punitive scale and deterrence strategies, when in fact criminals respond exactly the same way in Mississippi and Alabama as they do everywhere else. . . .

Conclusions

. . . Policy makers looking for a single, best estimate are in error. We will never know enough about the relationship between prisons and crime to reduce our knowledge to a single point. Still, the recent studies suggest that our best guess as to the nationwide elasticity should be in the neighborhood of −0.30. Any figure between −0.20 and −0.40 can be defended, and we should not be too surprised to find that the result is anywhere between −0.10 and −0.50. Because theory is too weak to allow us to distinguish among different crime types, and because the empirical estimates are not statistically significantly different from one another, the most prudent course would be to assume the elasticity for each crime type is about the same, on average.

What, then, can we say about the cost-effectiveness of further prison construction? As a back-of-the-envelope analysis suggests, not much. . . . In a nutshell . . . , what the studies of the past ten years tell us is that crime responds to prison capacity and that continued expansion of prisons nationwide will reduce the crime rate. What the studies do not tell us is whether the reduction is large enough to warrant continued expansion. . . . Until better instruments surface, critics will be justified in viewing all estimates with suspicion. . . .

Finally, it is critical that we stop considering prison expansion decisions in a vacuum. Even if we could be certain that prison construction was cost-effective, it may still be true that some other program or policy was more cost-effective. Certainly many primary prevention programs at least appear to be worth their salt: family intervention, Head Start, self-paced education, and job apprenticeship programs are all examples. Many secondary prevention programs, including environmental design initiatives, community organizing, victim training, and even some offender rehabilitation programs, have shown tremendous promise when applied to the offenders, victims, and environments they fit best. It is easily conceivable that initiatives such as these will yield benefit-cost ratios much greater than the 1.50 to 2.00 that is the best we can expect from continued prison expansion.

Of a dullard, Samuel Johnson once proclaimed, "That fellow seems to me to possess but one idea, and that is a wrong one." The criminal justice community possesses many ideas. If we are to serve the public well, we must stop pretending otherwise.

QUESTIONS

1. How much do you think doubling the prison population should have to reduce crime rates before you would support doubling the prison population? 10 percent? 20 percent? 30 percent? 40 percent? 50 percent? Defend your answer.

2. Would it be good enough for you to support doubling the population if you knew the percentages were anywhere from 10 to 50 percent? Defend your answer.

3. How would you rank the priorities in spending public money on increasing prison populations or other things like education, national defense, or lower taxes?

4. Does this survey of research influence your answer to question 3? Why? Why not?

"Diverting Children from a Life of Crime: Measuring Costs and Benefits": A report by the Rand Corporation on the effectiveness of incarceration. To reach this site go to "Web Links" on your Samaha CJ7 website: http://cj.wadsworth.com/samaha_cj7e.

Chapter Summary

- The prevalence of imprisonment in the United States has almost tripled since 1974. Most prisoners are locked up for property, not violent crimes.

- In colonial America, prisons weren't used for punishment; they were used to hold defendants until trial. Massachusetts was the first state to use prisons to punish convicted offenders.

- The penitentiary system was based on the idea of reforming criminals by removing them from corrupting environments outside prison so they could work either alone or in groups, pray, and think about their past crimes and prepare for returning to society.

- In the correctional system, the idea was also to reform prisoners by a medical model of diagnosing, treating, and curing individual criminals and training them for a return to society as law-abiding, hardworking members of the community.

- After heated debate in the early 1970s between those who think prisons are for punishing, incapacitating, and preventing future crime and those who favor rehabilitation, the dominant (but not the only) mission is retribution, incapacitation, and prevention.

- After 50 years (1925–1975) of stable prison populations, the United States experienced an enormous prison population boom that started in 1975 and continues (at a slightly slower pace) in 2005. The boom was not forced on policy makers. It resulted from a conscious decision to adopt a policy of responding to crime by spending "as much as it takes" to lock up more offenders and keep them there longer. This decision reflected a strong consensus among federal and state governments and the public based on the public's "get tough" on crime attitude; political opportunism; the "war" on drugs; improved criminal justice efficiency; and possibly some racial and ethnic discrimination.

- Imprisonment has side effects beyond booming populations. They include diverting resources from other public services and from one community to another and loss of income to offenders and their families. These side effects are not yet well-documented empirically.

- It's expensive to lock up prisoners. And the greater the security level, the higher the cost. Supermaximum security prisons are the most expensive, and there are increasing numbers of them. Women's prisons house all security levels in one prison.

- Private prisons are not new; they're an integral part of our history. Private prisons raise three important questions: Are they constitutional? Do they save money? Do they work? There's a lot of emotional heat but little empirical light in the debate over the answers to these questions.

- Some prisons are managed according to an administrative control model; others are managed according to a prisoner responsibility model. Both models can "work," depending a lot on the individuals who operate them. But management style isn't the only key to well-run, safe, humane, secure prisons. Architecture matters, too. The success of prisons boils down to management *and* architecture.

- Corrections officers' main missions are to watch and guard prisoners, and their most important duty is conducting the "count." Officers are organized according to a hierarchy of supervisors (captains, lieutenants, and sergeants) and line officers (corrections officers) who do the actual work of guarding prisoners.

- Traditionally, officers were White men selected because of their physical size and strength. Now, about one-third of officers guarding male prisoners are women, one-quarter are Black, and 6 percent are Hispanic. The research is mixed, but it suggests the role officers play is more important than sex or race in determining how they do their work.

- Jails are facilities for *either* detaining before trial or some other kind of disposition *or* for punishing convicted minor offenders for less than a year. Most jails hold far more men than women, but women are at a disadvantage when it comes to jail services.

- Jails offer a long list of educational, counseling, and health-care programs, but there's little information about their *quality*. Jail conditions vary greatly; some are modern, safe, clean, and efficiently and humanely administered; others are the opposite.

- New-generation jails combine a new approach to architecture, management philosophy, operation, and training that follows a confinement model (lock up people *as* punishment, not *for* punishment). Research demonstrates that new-generation jails have positive effects not just on prisoners but on jail staff.

- Prisoners have greatly increased in numbers; a growing proportion are locked up for drug offenses; most are male, young, and Black or Hispanic. Most had deficient families, education, training, and employment. The number of older and women prisoners is growing, but they're still a small minority of prisoners.

- A significant number of prisoners return to prison. The number varies according to offense, age, gender, race, and ethnicity.

- The length of imprisonment has grown from 22 months for prisoners admitted in 1990 to 43 months for prisoners admitted in 1998. Several factors determine the length of imprisonment: mandatory minimum sentences; judicial discretion in indeterminate sentencing states; early release for good time; and prison crowding.

Key Terms

prevalence of imprisonment, p. 439
penitentiary, p. 440
correctional institution, p. 442
medical model of corrections, p. 442
maximum security prisons, p. 450
supermaximum security prisons
    ("supermaxes"), p. 452
new-generation maximum security
    prisons, p. 454

medium security prisons, p. 455
minimum security prisons, p. 455
control model of prison management,
    p. 458
responsibility prison management
    model, p. 459
confinement model of imprisonment,
    p. 459
jail, p. 462

prisons, p. 462
new-generation jails, p. 465
recidivism, p. 469

Web Resources

Go to http://cj.wadsworth.com/samaha_cj7e for a wealth of online resources related to your book. Take a "pre-test" and "post-test" for each chapter in order to help master the material. Check out the *Web Links* to access the websites mentioned in the text, as well as many others. Explore the *Decision Points* flagged in the margins of the text, as well as the *Concept Builders* for additional insights. You can also access recent perspectives by clicking on *CJ in the News* and *Terrorism Update* under *Course Resources*.

Search Online with InfoTrac College Edition

For additional information, explore InfoTrac College Edition, your online library. Go to http://cj.wadsworth.com/samaha_cj7e to access InfoTrac College Edition from your book's website. Use the passcode that came with your book. You will find InfoTrac College Edition exercises and a list of key words for further research.

CHAPTER 14

Prison Life

FACT *or* FICTION?

▶ Most criminal justice professionals believe prisons aren't tough enough on criminals.

▶ Judging by the "pains of imprisonment," it looks like men's prisons are "working."

▶ There's a ban on *consensual* sex in prison.

▶ Prison gangs are linked to gangs outside prison.

▶ The majority of male prisoners cope with prison by avoiding most other prisoners.

▶ The *quality* of jobs isn't related to recidivism of male prisoners.

▶ One reason life for women prisoners differs from that of men is that women are more "reformable" than men.

▶ The daily lives of women prisoners are radically different today from in the 1960s.

▶ Prisoners have fewer rights today than they did in the 1970s but more than they did in the 1950s.

▶ Prisoner reentry problems have decreased in the 2000s because of tough punishment in prison and because crime rates have fallen.

PRISON LIFE: *FOR* OR *AS* PUNISHMENT?

The standards of a nation's civilization can be judged by opening the doors of its prisons.

—FYODOR DOSTOYEVSKY (1860)

The first duty of a prison... is to perform the function assigned to it by law..., to insure that a sentence of imprisonment is a form of punishment. It must, however, be clear that it is the imprisonment, and not the treatment in prison, that constitutes the punishment. Men come to prison *as* a punishment, not *for* punishment.

—SIR ALEXANDER PATERSON (1951, 23)

punishment model of imprisonment offenders are sent to prison *for* punishment

What should life in prison be like? Ask my students (and those at other colleges I've visited), and you'll get some tough answers: "Torture chambers!" "Miserable!" "Horrible!" "Hellholes!" Listen to most people on the street and politicians who are only too happy to follow the public's lead, and you'll get similar answers. This is what we call the **punishment model of imprisonment,** or the punishment "plus" model of imprisonment. In other words, locking criminals up isn't enough punishment; you have to add something more. We refer to the punishment-plus model as sending offenders to prison *for* punishment, not *as* punishment.

But ask corrections professionals (who know a lot more about prisons than the rest of us) the same question, and you'll get a very different answer. They'll remind you that most people locked up aren't staying for life. Almost all of them are going to get out, even though they're spending more time behind bars than they used to. In 1995, prisoners were locked up an average 23 months; by 2002, the number had risen to 30 months (Harrison and Beck 2004, 8). Will torture, misery, and deprivation make released prisoners less dangerous when they're sitting beside us on the bus, going to the same movie, drinking at the same bar, or going to the same football game? Will it transform them from lawbreakers who prey on the rest of us into people who work hard, play by the rules, and pay their own way?

Corrections professionals will probably also ask you to consider the welfare of corrections officers—the "other prisoners"—who spend most of their time in prison, too (Chapter 13). What do you think *their* lives should be like? Does it matter that corrections professionals also have to spend their time in those "hellholes" you want for prisoners? Does it concern you that if the prisoners are miserable this makes the work of the professionals harder, too?

Unfortunately, the state of our knowledge doesn't help us answer the question, "Does punishment-plus make prisoners more criminal or punish them into becoming law-abiding, responsible people?" Nor does the available empirical evidence give us a clear answer to the question, "Do prison programs work?" But we *do* know one thing: Safe, secure, humane imprisonment makes the lives of corrections officers better, and in safe, secure, humane prisons, the level of disorder, violence, and gang activity is lower than in brutal, unsafe prisons.

confinement model of imprisonment offenders are sent to prison *as* punishment

This is one reason a number of corrections professionals recommend Sir Alexander Paterson's (1951, 23) **confinement model of imprisonment,** as quoted in the chapter opener: Send offenders to prison *as* punishment, not *for* punishment. Disciplined, safe, secure, orderly confinement that provides the basic necessities of life *is* punishment, even if it's also humane. We don't have to add brutal, filthy, unsafe, disorderly conditions to confinement.

What kind of lives do prisoners really lead behind bars? In this chapter, we'll look at the realities of male and female prison societies, the role of law in prison society, and the problems of recidivism and prisoners' reentry into society.

Male Prison Society

Male prison society (you'll learn about female prison society in "Life in Women's Prisons," on page 500) was the primary focus of early prison research (Gartner and Kruttschnitt 2004, 22–23). According to these researchers, there were two worlds where two completely separate societies existed—free society and the prison society. They thought of prisons as **total institutions** (whole societies, separate and isolated from free society). Inside prison walls, prison administrators had enough power to make prisoners give up their personalities and live completely controlled lives.

total institutions prisons are societies, separate and isolated from free society

To better understand the world of male prison society, let's look more closely at some theories of how these prisons were created; the deprivations of imprisonment; how prisoners cope with stresses inside prison; violence behind bars, committed both individually and collectively; and programs for prisoners.

Indigenous and Importation Theories

The theory that prison society was created inside prison walls independent of the outside world we call the **indigenous theory imprisonment.** The early indigenous theory researchers concentrated on how prisoners adapted to life in prison. Donald Clemmer's 1940 classic *The Prison Community* introduced what he called the concept of prisonization, the process by which prisoners adapt to the prison world. Clemmer based his prisonization theory on detailed observations he made when he worked at Menard Penitentiary in Illinois. The standard explanation for how prisoners adapted to life in prison was the inmate code, the unwritten law based on the values of "noncooperation and hostility toward staff." In author Kenneth Adams's (1992) words:

indigenous theory imprisonment prison society is created inside prison walls independent of the outside world

> The oppositional code, which governs inmate-staff interactions, was seen as a functional response to "reject their rejecters" and to salvage a sense of self-worth in the face of intense pressures. (278)

Don't confuse this unwritten informal inmate code with either formal prison rules or the informal adaptations of the written rules of the prison to the lives of prisoners. In a second classic, *Society of Captives,* Gresham Syke's (1958) study of life in a New Jersey prison during the 1950s, Sykes identified the unwritten rules of inmate code, including "Never rat on a con," "Be cool," "Do your own time," and "Don't exploit inmates." Although Sykes (1995, 82) saw the code as an ideal, not a description of how prisoners actually behaved, it became the basis of most indigenous theory research (Gartner and Kruttschnitt 2004, 24).

Prisons have changed a lot since the indigenous theory was introduced by Clemmer and Sykes in their powerful classics and developed by their followers. Prisons got bigger and so did the proportion of the public locked up. The numbers of Black and Hispanic prisoners outpaced that of Whites, increasing an already disproportionate number of minorities in prison (Chapter 13). Prison gangs got a lot bigger, too; their influence got stronger; and their connections with the outside world got firmer. More staff joined unions, and unions got a lot more powerful. The chance increased that courts would interfere with prison management and life in prison. And prisons and imprisonment became hot political issues.

CONCEPT | BUILDER
Visit http://cj.wadsworth.com/ samaha_cj7e for an interactive exploration of **prison life.**

All these changes led to a new theory to explain prison society, the **importation theory of imprisonment.** The theory assumes that the roots of prison society lie outside prison. All prisoners bring with them a long history of life in
public institutions—almost all have gone to school, many have spent time in juvenile and adult facilities, and some have been confined in psychiatric hospitals
and other treatment facilities. They also bring to prison other individual attributes—their race, ethnicity, and criminal history. Once in prison, prisoners still
watch TV, read magazines, listen to music, talk to visitors, bring lawsuits, and
maintain contacts with gangs outside prison. All these parts of their background
and life in prison break down the clear lines (if there ever were any) between life
inside and outside prison.

The "Pains" of Men's Imprisonment

In *Society of Captives*, Sykes (1958) identified five deprivations at the core of life
in a male maximum security prison:

- Goods and services
- Liberty
- Straight sexual relationships
- Autonomy
- Security

According to Sykes, recognizing these deprivations (he called them the **pains
of imprisonment**) is essential to understanding the way prisoners deal with confinement. Researchers have confirmed Sykes's findings. They've also identified
how painful these deprivations are and how prisoners *handle* them. Edward
Zamble and Frank Porporino (1988) interviewed and surveyed 133 prisoners to
identify the problems they faced in prison. Figure 14.1 shows the problems and
the percentage of prisoners who identified each as the most significant problem
they faced.

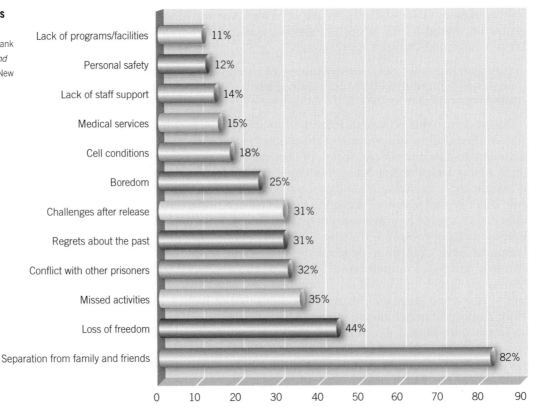

▶ **FIGURE 14.1 Problems
Prisoners Worry About**
Source: Edward Zamble and Frank
Porporino, *Coping, Behavior, and
Adaptation in Prison Inmates* (New
York: Springer-Verlag, 1988).

Let's look at some details behind Figure 14.1. First, based on inmates' own answers, it looks like prison is "working." Prisoners are *supposed to* feel pain for the crimes they've committed. Second, the problems prisoners identify when they arrive in prison stay with them throughout their imprisonment, with one exception—inmates serving long sentences worry more about permanently losing the close relationships they had before they came to prison; about making new friends inside prison; and about dealing with prison staff and bureaucracy. Hispanics worry more about separation from family than other ethnic and racial groups, maybe because of the importance of family relationships in Hispanic culture (Adams 1992, 285).

Prisoners *do* develop coping skills to handle these deprivations. Let's look at how they cope with two: deprivations of goods and services, by substituting their own prison economy, and the absence of straight sexual relationships, by substituting them with consensual sex behind bars.

Enforced Poverty Prisoners aren't supposed to be comfortable in confinement. It's part of their punishment to lose their freedom, their privacy, and also the "extras" connected to the good things in life. Prisons are supposed to be islands of poverty in a sea of plenty. This means prisoners live lives of enforced poverty, where the state provides only the bare essentials—plain food, clothing, medical care, and shelter (Williams and Fish 1974, 40). (See the CJ & Technology box "Is There a Doctor in the House?")

Of course, in movies, in the news, and on TV, prisons aren't exactly "islands of poverty." We see TV sets in prison cells and prisoners working out in well-equipped exercise rooms. We hear of "Club Feds" where "prisoners" play golf and lounge around swimming pools. We read of prisoners who are drunk on alcohol or high on other drugs. How can such comforts exist in these islands of poverty?

Prisoners obtain some amenities legally. For example, they're allowed to receive gifts from friends and relatives. They can also buy some of the comforts of life from the prison commissary. Prisoners don't buy these comforts (cash is banned) but get them with scrip or credit drawn on accounts supplied with money from the outside or that they've earned in prison (discussed on page 493 in "Men's Prison Programs").

Still, the approved list of gifts and the stock of items in the commissary are hardly enough to satisfy the wants of most prisoners. Prisoners are well aware of

▶ DECISION POINT ◀

Should prisoners be allowed contraband goods and services?

Click on this Decision Point at http://cj.wadsworth.com/samaha_cj7e to explore the issue.

© Shepard Sherbell/Corbis Saba

◀ Prisoners live lives of enforced poverty, where the state provides only the bare essentials—plain food, clothing, medical care, and shelter—no goodies. Does this 65-year-old prisoner who's serving two life sentences in the maximum security prison in Buckingham County, Virginia, look like he's getting only the basics, or is he getting goodies too?

Is There a Doctor in the House?

...Reggie Wilkinson, president of the 20,000-member American Correctional Association and director of the Ohio Department of Rehabilitation (ODRC),...has dedicated much of his energy to bringing technology behind prison walls.... "Our goal is to provide tools that will allow our staff to be more efficient and effective...." One of ODRC's—and Wilkinson's—greatest accomplishments is the department's move into telemedicine....

According to Wilkinson, telemedicine allows ODRC to provide remote medical services to prisoners. From the prison's clinic, a health care professional presents the patient and operates the scopes and cameras that transmit the video images in real-time to a doctor at another location. The advantages of telemedicine, Wilkinson says, are many. Prisoners receive care without incurring the cost of escorted hospital visits.

Telemedicine gives the prison access to a wider range of outside medical sources and specialized doctors. And, telemedicine provides a visual record of the visit, ensures the safety of the doctors, and reduces the potential for escape. This is important, he notes, since it was recently reported that more than 50 escape attempts occurred in this country from offsite medical facilities in one 12-month period. "We can do consultations, post-operative medical reviews, and routine doctor's visits. We can read x-rays, or zero in and magnify certain areas of the body so the doctor can get a very clear picture. We can actually hear the heartbeat of a person through the system," Wilkinson says.

... "In just 3 years we've done 4,000 medical consultations." Those consultations, Wilkinson notes, include a successful foray into telepsychiatry, something to which the inmates have responded well. He says, "It totally debunks the myth that you have to be in a room and on a couch to address your problems. The prisoners have been extremely responsive. They've answered questions and are not intimidated by the equipment at all."

In telemedicine, the equipment is so sophisticated it is as if the doctor were right there. Examples of telemedicine technologies include a "derm" camera that sees through the outer layer of skin and a highly sensitive electronic stethoscope that allows the doctor to listen to a patient's heart. Telemedicine also employs faxing capabilities as well as accessing a patient's chart onscreen. "These things don't come cheaply," Wilkinson says. But from his point of view, anything that makes ODRC more efficient is worth it....

But the additional magic of telecommunications is that it can offer more than just telemedicine services.

ODRC uses the same equipment to conduct wardens' meetings, parole hearings at maximum-security units, and videoconferences with potential inmate employers. The department is also considering televisiting for family members and attorneys of prisoners on death row or in administrative segregation.

The Missouri Department of Corrections is already experimenting with televisiting. By teaming up with Sprint Communications and Kinko's, Inc., family, friends, and attorneys can go to their local Kinko's for a "virtual" visit with inmates housed in the State's Farmington, Jefferson City, and Western Missouri correctional centers. Missouri officials expect the cost savings to be tremendous.... While videoconferences are not expected to replace face-to-face visits, they do allow out-of-State relatives, as well as those who have been banned from entering a correctional facility, to visit inmates....

ODRC recently purchased a drug detector for use during sweeps in the units and already does its own drug testing inhouse. Its Intranet and Internet system is one of the largest in the country, with about 1,700 pages. ODRC's policies and procedures are all online—printing of hard copies is minimized. Eventually department forms will be online, allowing them to be filled out and filed electronically.

Another database tracks gang members. It enables corrections personnel to instantly tell which prisoners are gang members, information readily shared with law enforcement. The Intranet system is accessible only to prison personnel. The ODRC's Internet site is equally sophisticated, allowing the public to keep up with parole information or track the movements of a specific prisoner.

Wilkinson is a member of the Corrections Operations Subcommittee of LECTAC and serves as president of the American Correctional Association. He also works closely with his State legislature to secure funding for projects that will make the prison run more smoothly and efficiently. "Our super maximum security prison will be one of the most technologically advanced ever. We'll use palm readers for access control. Our surveillance devices will be very sophisticated, and our control systems will be state-of-the-art," Wilkinson says. "We haven't had a problem getting funding for these projects, primarily because the citizens of Ohio see them as a service, something that actually is a cost savings instead of just another expense."

Source: "Is There a Doctor In the House?" *TechBeat* (Washington, DC: National Law Enforcement and Corrections Technology Center, Spring 1998), pp. 1–2.

all the comforts of life that they're not allowed to have. It's hard to satisfy their desires with available resources and within the enforced poverty of confinement. According to Susan Sheehan (1978), most of the men she studied in a New York prison were there "precisely because they were not willing to go without on the street. They are no more willing to go without in prison, so they hustle to obtain what they cannot afford to buy" (91).

Hustling contraband goods and services—mainly food, clothing, weapons, drugs, and prostitution—breaks prison rules and frustrates the goal of punishment by enforced poverty. Deprived of luxuries, prisoners do their best to get them. Getting what may seem like small luxuries eases the pain of imprisonment and promotes prison stability. Because contraband goods and services contribute to stability, and therefore make prisons and prisoners easier to manage, they're tolerated to some extent by the authorities.

Prisoners put great stake in these amenities, and trouble looms when they don't get them. Trouble also brews when prisoner leaders lose the profits from controlling contraband goods and services. In some prisons, these leaders form symbiotic relationships with correctional officers. Both have an interest in maintaining stability, so they make trade-offs: Officers allow some illegal trafficking, usually in "nonserious" contraband such as food; prisoner leaders, in return, maintain peaceful cell blocks (Kalinich 1986).

Ban on Sex There's a ban on sex in all prisons. Why? Because it's another legitimate pain of imprisonment. There may be a formal ban, but anecdotes about prison life for generations have told of routine consensual sex behind prison walls. The early records of Stillwater prison and the St. Cloud reformatory in Minnesota are full of celibacy code violations (Samaha, n.d.). But the spread of AIDS has created a sense of urgency, spurring a demand for more knowledge about consensual sex in prison. Empirical research varies in its assessment of how much consensual sex there is in prison—from rampant to rare.

▶ DECISION POINT ◀

Can we really know how widespread sex in prison is?

Click on this Decision Point at http://cj.wadsworth.com/samaha_cj7e to explore the issue.

Here are some comments from a study of Delaware male prisoners (you'll learn about consensual sex among female prisoners in "Pains of Women's Imprisonment") in 1994 (Saum, Spratt, Inciardi, and Bennett, 1997, 413):

- "There's an unspoken ridicule of inmates who engage in sex today."
- "Sex still goes on in here. People I know don't use protection because it's not available. People are knowledgeable [about HIV] but still have sex."
- "Most people that do it are lifers..., they don't care."
- "Just like on the streets, you can get sex anytime if you have money."

In another study, Christopher Hensley (2000, 1–4) conducted face-to-face interviews with 174 male prisoners in Oklahoma prisons to "explore the amount of consensual homosexual activity in male prisons" (Figure 14.2). (See the In Focus box "Ban Sex in Prison?")

But can we really know how much consensual sex there really is in prison? Methodological problems make it difficult. According to Christine Saum and her colleagues (1997), the major difficulty is inaccurate reporting because:

- Most incidents aren't recorded.
- Definitions of sex vary.

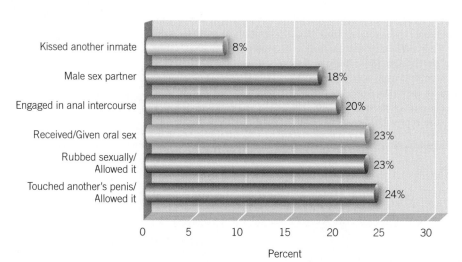

◀ **FIGURE 14.2 Consensual Homosexual Sex in Male Prisons**
Source: Christopher Hensley, "Consensual Homosexual Activity in Male Prisons," *Corrections Compendium* 26(2000): 1–4.

Ban Sex in Prison?

Thirteen million Americans have been convicted of felonies and spent time in prison. The prison system now releases an astonishing 650,000 people each year—more than the population of Boston or Washington. In city after city, newly released felons return to a handful of neighborhoods where many households have some prison connection. The so-called prison ZIP codes have more in common than large populations of felons or children who grow up visiting their mothers and fathers in jail. These neighborhoods are also public health disaster areas and epicenters of blood-borne diseases like hepatitis C and AIDS. Infection rates in these areas are many times higher than in neighborhoods short distances away.

No one can say how many infections begin in prison. But the proportion could be high given the enormous concentrations of disease behind bars and the risky behaviors that inmates commonly practice. They carve tattoos in themselves using contaminated tools borrowed from other inmates. They inject themselves with drugs using dirty syringes. The most common source of infection could easily be risky, unprotected sex, which, despite denials by prison officials, is clearly a regular occurrence behind bars. A recent study of male inmates in several prisons, for example, found that more than 40 percent had participated in sexual encounters with another man. Most of these inmates, by the way, viewed themselves as heterosexual and planned to resume sex with women once they got out of prison.

...Public health officials who favor needle exchanges in the United States are fully aware that this country has just emerged from a presidential election that witnessed heightened activism by conservative Christians. Indeed, even nonreligious Americans would prefer to see prisons shut off the flow of illegal drugs and provide addicts with treatment instead of syringes.

The condom issue, however, seems somehow less explosive. But as of now, condoms are banned or unavailable in 48 of 50 state prison systems, on the theory that distributing them would condone illicit sex. When confronted with public health data from abroad, American prison officials have blithely suggested that all the fuss is overblown—because there is little sex to speak of in jail. Congress seemed comfortable with this fiction until 2001, when the Human Rights Watch organization issued a grisly report titled "No Escape: Male Rape in U.S. Prisons." The study suggested that rape accompanied by horrific violence was a regular aspect of American prison life. Based partly on the accounts of more than 200 prisoners in nearly 40 states, the report told of prison officials who stood by while sexual predators raped fellow inmates and sometimes sold them—as sex slaves—to gangs and other inmates.

The study led directly to the Prison Rape Elimination Act of 2003, which sailed through Congress and was signed into law by President Bush. The law, which requires the Justice Department to collect data on prison rape and develop a national strategy for combating it, provided a much-needed mechanism for weeding out sexual predators behind bars. But this law is, at its heart, a public health law. It provides for grants that could be used to underwrite public health initiatives—including sorely needed studies of disease transmission in the criminal justice system. The law has already resulted in fruitful discussions about expanding disease testing and prevention behind bars.

Lawmakers find it easy to discuss prison sex in the context of rape because everyone agrees that sexual assault is horrible and needs to be rooted out. The conversation about consensual sex among inmates will be trickier to handle. Even so, the law will inevitably force prison officials to confront all the varieties of sexual contact that public health researchers have known about for a long time. The commission created by Congress to oversee the new law is just getting started. But it has already brought some honesty to the historically dishonest conversation about sexual behavior in prison. Commission members who have spent time in the public health world, for example, are well aware that people who participate in sex behind bars do so for a variety of reasons. Some barter their bodies—and risk disease—in exchange for protection from marauding gangs. Others perform sex acts in exchange for necessities like soap, food and access to telephone calls.

Not all sex in prison, however, can be attributed to rape or bartering. Recent research suggests that some of it is consensual among lonely inmates who experience same-sex encounters for the first time—and for many of them, the only time—while in prison. The new law is pushing some states to create new strategies for dealing with sexual assault in prison. But common sense tells us that sex among inmates will not disappear even if rape and coercion are taken out of the equation. That said, prison officials need to revisit rules that outlaw condoms behind bars. These rules aid the spread of diseases that flourish in prison—and then make the leap to the world outside.

Source: Brent Staples, "The Federal Government Gets Real About Sex Behind Bars," originally published in *The New York Times*, November 27, 2004. Reprinted with permission.

- Prisoners underestimate the amount of sex because they're afraid they'll get into trouble.
- Prisoners are embarrassed to admit they have sex with other men.
- Prisoners are afraid of being labeled weak or gay. (418)

Coping with Stress from the Pains of Imprisonment

In *The Felon* (1987), based on ex-convict turned sociologist John Irwin's interviews in Soledad men's prison in California (you'll learn about stress in female prison life in "Life in Women's Prisons" later), the author writes that all new inmates ask themselves, "How shall I do my time?" Or "What shall I do in prison?" A few can't cope at all; they either commit suicide or sink into psychosis. Irwin found those who can cope fit into two groups:

1. Those who identify with the world outside prison.
2. Those who identify primarily with the prison world. (426)

Those "who do not retain or . . . never acquired any commitment to outside social worlds" and "tend to make a world out of prison" are known as "jailers." One jailer told Mark Fleisher (1989), who studied life in the maximum security federal penitentiary at Lompoc, California:

> Beating the system is the best game in town. Middle-class Americans will never understand it. You know, I feel "extracultural." I live on the same planet you do. We speak the same language, but that's where our similarity ends. That's right, I live outside this culture. This is your culture. This is your prison. You have to live with all the f—— rules in this society. I don't. You have to obey the rules, Mark. That's how you live. But, I don't have to obey anybody's f—— rules. The worst that can happen to me is that they put me back in prison. And who gives a f—! When they do that, you got to pay for me. I win. If this is all this society can do to me, then I'm gonna do whatever I want to do. How you going to stop me? I'm invincible. (8, 29)

Another jailer, this one in the federal prison at Leavenworth, Kansas, put it this way:

> As the years go by and you get older, you realize that your life is considered a failure by society's standards. . . . You're a jailbird. You don't have any money, no house, no job, no status. In society's eyes you're a worthless piece of s—, or you can say, "F— society, I'll live by my own rules." That's what I did. I decided to live by my own standards and rules. They aren't society's but they are mine and that's what I've done. In your society, I may not be anybody, but in here, I am. (Johnson 1996, 164)

Prisoners who identify with the outside world adapt in two ways:

1. *Doing time.* Those who for the most part want to maintain their former life patterns and identities
2. *Gleaning.* Those who desire to make significant changes in their life patterns and identities and see prison as a chance to do this

"Time-doers" try to get through their prison terms with "the least amount of suffering and the greatest amount of comfort." They avoid trouble, find activities to occupy their time, secure a few luxuries, and make a few friends. The "gleaners" follow a plan of self-improvement.

According to one gleaner:

> I got tired of losing. I had been losing all of my life. I decided that I wanted to win for a while. So I got on a different kick. I knew that I had to learn something so I went to school, got my high school diploma. I cut myself off from my old . . . buddies and started hanging around with some intelligent guys who minded their own business. We read a lot, a couple of us paint. We play a little bridge and talk, a lot of the time about what we are going to do when we get out. (Irwin 1996, 430–431)

Deciding whether to be a time-doer, a gleaner, or a jailer can be difficult. Consider Piri Thomas, who was forced to decide whether to participate in a riot:

> I stood there watching and weighing, trying to decide whether or not I was a con first and an outsider second. I had been doing time inside yet living every mental minute I could outside; now I had to choose one or the other. I stood there in the middle of the yard. Cons passed me by, some going west to join the boppers, others going east to neutral ground.... I had to make a decision. I am a con. These damn cons are my people. Your people are outside the cells, home, in the streets. No! That ain't so....Look at them go toward the west wall. Why in hell am I taking so long in making up my mind? (Irwin 1996, 426)

In his review of the literature on coping, Kenneth Adams refers to research that asked inmates how they handle problems. Most male inmates choose "real-man strategies," relying heavily on personal strength and self-reliance. (We'll discuss "real-woman strategies" later.) Some long-term prisoners choose another coping strategy—sticking to minimum expectations based on focusing on today and not hoping for too much tomorrow. Hispanics sometimes join gangs as family surrogates to ease the pain of separation from their real families (Adams 1992, 286–287).

Individual Male Violence

Racial and ethnic conflict, gangs and violent prisoners, bans on consensual sex, and enforced poverty can lead to violence against other prisoners. Assaults and homicides in maximum security men's prisons have grown to the point that "the possibility of being attacked or killed has loomed as the major concern of offenders incarcerated in these prisons or anticipating going to one." According to one prisoner in California during the 1990s:

> I've been on the yard watching people get shot, watching people die. You know how hard it is coming out with tears in your eyes knowing that you're going to get hit, knowing that someone is going to physically hurt you, or try to kill you....Eighty-two, 83, 84, people were dropping like flies, people getting stuck. After two or three years of that, it's hard. People on the outside say, ah, that doesn't happen. You weren't there, man. (Irwin and Austin 1997, 72)

Economic victimization occurs when violence or threats of it accompany gambling, fraud, loan sharking, theft, robbery, protection rackets, con games, delivery of misrepresented contraband, or failure to deliver promised goods. When promised commodities aren't delivered—or are not as promised—victims may retaliate. Drug trafficking is a good example. To get drugs into prisons requires sophisticated smuggling operations. Violence results if drugs are stolen, misrepresented, overpriced, or not delivered. Prisoners use violence to prevent these distribution irregularities from happening in the first place or to retaliate for them if they do take place (Bowker 1983, 1230–1231).

Crowding is a common characteristic of prison life that probably accounts for some of the increased violence. On January 1, 2004, the federal prison system was operating at 139 percent capacity; state systems were operating between 100 and 116 percent capacity (Harrison and Beck 2004, 7). The prison population boom (and the reasons for the boom) are behind crowded prisons (Chapter 13), but there's more to the explanation; it's the public's unwillingness to pay for more prisons.

Escalating prison violence is seen in prisoner-officer violence, sexual assaults, the growing strength of gangs, and racial and ethnic divisions. We'll look at each of these, in turn, and then we'll look at how prisoners cope with violence.

Prisoner-Officer Violence Prisoners don't just attack each other; they attack officers, too. Officers take risks attempting to break up fights, managing intoxicated prisoners, and escorting them to segregation. These situations are known to provoke assaults. But not all violence is predictable, especially random violent acts like throwing dangerous objects at officers or dropping items from catwalks above as officers patrol cell blocks below (Bowker 1983, 1231).

Officers also attack prisoners. According to Todd R. Clear and George F. Cole (1994):

> Unauthorized physical violence against inmates by officers to enforce rules, uphold the officer-prisoner relationship, and maintain order is a fact of life in many institutions. Stories abound of guards giving individual prisoners "the treatment" outside the notice of their superiors. Many guards view physical force as an everyday operating procedure and legitimize its use. (275–276)

Sexual Assault Some prisoners are victims of sexual assault. More than 80 percent of the victims are young White men; 16 percent are Black; 2 percent are Hispanic. Most of the attackers are Black (80 percent); some are Hispanic (14 percent); and a few are White (6 percent). What explains these numbers? In Daniel Lockwood's (1980) study of sexual violence in prisons, one Black prisoner told Lockwood it's because Whites are weak:

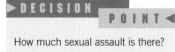

How much sexual assault is there?

Click on this Decision Point at http://cj.wadsworth.com/samaha_cj7e to explore the issue.

> If you come in here alone then they [Black prisoners] will try to crack on you for something. But if they know that you know people that have been here for awhile, then they know better. They try to pick on some of the weak ones. They like to pick on them. (29)

Another reason, according to Lockwood, is White prisoners are less organized, less likely to know other Whites in prison, and less willing to band together for protection. Also, class divisions among White prisoners are stronger than they are among Blacks. Middle-class Whites look down on other White prisoners they believe are their social inferiors. Some Whites don't even consider themselves criminals at all. All this isolates them and makes them more vulnerable to attacks (Lockwood 1980, 30).

Prisoners who don't respond to unwanted sexual approaches are going to become victims:

> You see a young pretty dude who doesn't come in here on a violent record. Now, he is probably in the worst situation than the guy that comes in here on a violent record. Because if you know that a guy has murdered someone on the street, and has taken a life, and is in here for life, you are going to think three or—not just once but three or four times—before you go up against him. Somebody that shows he's timid, who is real quiet. That is basically it. Someone who is real quiet and withdrawn and looks scared. He looks frightened you know. He is most apt to be approached. (Lockwood 1980, 33–34)

In view of these Black perceptions of White physical weakness, weak group solidarity, and Black prisoners' pent-up rage against what they perceive as White oppression, Lockwood (1980, 33–34) was surprised to learn that

> sexual aggression in prisons is not more widespread. Even in men's prisons where sexual violence is most concentrated, estimates of the incidence of sexual assault run as low as less than 1 percent. In some prisons, of course, the numbers are higher. In New York State, 28 percent of the prisoners reported some form of aggression—threats, propositions, and some physical contact. Even here, however, only one prisoner reported actually being raped. (33–34)

These low numbers are probably one reason why personal safety was ranked 11th out of the 12 problems prisoners said were the most important they face in prison (Figure 14.1).

Prison Gangs and Violence Prison gangs are a part of men's prison life, despite strong prohibitions against them. Gang members rob, assault, and otherwise prey on members of other gangs and members of the general prison population. Prisons have always had violent prisoners, usually youths recently "graduated" from juvenile prison as well as unskilled, lower- and working-class criminals.

► Two members of the Texas branch of the White prison gang Aryan Brotherhood relax in the prison yard separating them from rival gangs. As confirmed members of the gang, they're locked in their cells 23 hours a day. Although many other White gangs compete with it, the Aryan Brotherhood still remains one of the toughest prison gangs.

© Andrew Lichtenstein/Corbis

Before the 1960s, a strong majority of prisoners opposed to violence kept them in check. Since then, however, the number of tough young prison graduates and unskilled prisoners has increased (Knox 1991, 283).

Gang members are already hostile to authority when they come to prison. Unlike with older prisoners, little rewards, like sneaking extra cups of coffee, don't satisfy gang members. Gang members care about status and gang rivalry, so they challenge authority. According to James Jacobs (1977) in his study of Stateville Prison outside Chicago:

> When a lieutenant was called to "walk" an inmate, he was often confronted with ten or twelve of the inmate's fellow gang members surrounding him, challenging his authority. One Stateville guard explained: "The inmate will say, 'I'm not going.' Then a group of his gang will gather around him. I'll have to call a lieutenant. Sometimes one of the leaders will just come over and tell the member to go ahead." (161)

Prison is the ultimate test of manhood in the eyes of many young prisoners. A man in prison is able to secure what he wants and protect what he has: "In here, a man gets what he can" and "nobody can force a man to do something he don't want to" are key elements of their belief system. Any prisoner who doesn't meet these standards isn't a man, "has no respect for himself," and so doesn't deserve respect (Irwin 1980, 193–194).

Race, Ethnicity, and Violence in Men's Prisons During the 1960s and early 1970s, increased racial and ethnic consciousness, assertiveness, confrontation, solidarity, and violence marked U.S. society (Brakel 1982, 113). These developments were imported into male prison society, leaving men's prisons "fragmented, tense, and often extremely violent" (Irwin 1980, 181). (We'll see how different women's prison society is later in the chapter.)

Prison populations were also changing. By the late 1970s, Blacks, Hispanics, Native Americans, and other minorities in the general population were heading toward becoming the majority in American prisons. For example, by the early 1980s, 80 percent of Stateville's (Illinois' maximum security prison just outside Chicago) prisoner population was Black (Irwin 1980, 182).

With increased racial consciousness outside prison and among the minority prisoners in prisons came increased racial and ethnic hatred. Prisoners stick to their own race and ethnicity in choosing friends, cliques, and gangs. Of course, committing similar crimes, coming from the same neighborhood, doing time in another state prison or institution, living in the same cell block or working in the same prison workshop are also elements in individual and group relations in prison. But race and ethnicity are the overriding elements in forming social groups in prisoner society (Irwin 1980, 1982).

Racial hatred between White and Black prisoners, their cliques, and gangs is the most volatile dynamic in prisons. Since the 1960s, Black prisoners have become more assertive. According to one Black prisoner at Stateville Prison in Illinois:

> In the prison, the black dudes have a little masculinity game they play. It has no name, really, but I call it whup a white boy—especially the white gangsters or syndicate men, the bad juice boys, the hit men, etc. The black dudes go out of their way to make faggots out of them. And to lose a fight to a white dude is one of the worst things that can happen to a black dude. And I know that, by and far, the white cats are faggots. They will drop their pants and bend over and touch their toes and get had before they will fight. (Robinson 1971, 29)

Another said: "Every can I been in that's the way it is. It's gettin' even I guess. You guys been cuttin' our b—s off ever since we been in this country. Now we're just gettin' even" (Jacobs, 1980, 16).

White prisoners become bigoted or more bigoted if they were already racially prejudiced before coming to prison. According to a White California prisoner:

> After 10:30, the voice dropped a decibel or two, and from the morass of sound Ron began to recognize certain voices by timbre and catch snatches of conversation. Above him, perhaps on the second tier, he picked up a gumboed black voice saying he'd like to kill all white babies, while his listener agreed it was the best way to handle the beasts—before they grew up. A year earlier, Ron would have felt compassion for anyone so consumed by hate and whenever whites casually used "nigger" he was irked. Now he felt tentacles of hate spreading through himself—and half an hour later, he smiled when a batch of voices began chanting: "Sieg Heil! Sieg Heil!" (Bunker 1977, 92)

In the emphasis on Black and White prisoner conflicts we shouldn't overlook a third element—Hispanic prisoners. James B. Jacobs (1980) refers to this mix at Stateville, Illinois, maximum security prison:

> Afro-American, Caucasian-American and Mexican-American inmates lived side by side but maintained three distinct ethnic cultures. Inmates did not eat at the same table, share food, cigarettes or bathroom facilities with individuals of other ethnic groups. They would not sit in the same row while viewing television or even talk for more than brief interchanges with members of a different ethnic group. (13–14)

Coping with Violence Some older prisoners have established reputations for being tough; they can circulate throughout violent prisons without fear. Some young first-timers join gangs (gangbanging) for protection. But the majority of prisoners cope by avoiding most prisoners and most settings where large groups of prisoners congregate. According to John Irwin and James Austin (1997), they:

> shy away from most prisoners and settings where masses of prisoners congregate and withdraw into small groups or virtual isolation. Although they may occasionally buy from the racketeers, place bets, or trade commodities on a small scale with other unaffiliated prisoners, they stay out of the large-scale economic activities and dissociate themselves

from the violent cliques and gangs. They stick to a few friends whom they have met in the cell blocks, at work, on the outside (homeboys), in other prisons, or through shared interests. Either alone or with their few trusted friends, they go to work and/or attend meetings of various clubs and formal organizations that the prison administration allows to exist in prison. Otherwise, they stay in their cells. (78)

Collective Male Violence (Riots)

Riots are part of U.S. history; they're part of U.S. prison history, too. Two modern examples are Attica State Prison in New York in 1970 and the bloody riot at New Mexico Penitentiary in 1980. Although riots like Attica and New Mexico rightly deserve their notorious reputation, riots are a rare part of prison life. Some riots are spontaneous; others are planned in advance. A highly organized inmate force held together by racial solidarity and political consciousness planned and executed the famous Attica riot in 1971. To a considerable extent, that riot was a product of the 1960s—a political protest against "White oppression."

Other riots, like the bloody New Mexico riot in 1980, were spontaneous, disorganized outbursts. According to its historian, Mark Colvin (1982, 449), the New Mexico prison riot was the most brutal, destructive, and disorganized prison riot in U.S. history. In 36 hours, prisoners killed 33 fellow prisoners and beat and raped up to two hundred more. After drinking too much homemade whiskey, drunk prisoners overpowered four guards. Seven guards were taken hostage, beaten, stabbed, or sodomized before being released by their captors.

There was no plan. Prisoners stumbled on an open dormitory door, an open security grill, and blowtorches accidentally left behind by renovation crews. Storming through the prison, rioters tortured 12 inmates with blowtorches, set them on fire, and mutilated them. They beheaded one with a shovel. Their victims were suspected "snitches" (prisoners who inform on other prisoners' misbehavior), child rapists, and "mentally disturbed" prisoners whose screaming kept their killers awake at night (Colvin 1992).

Prisoners riot for complicated reasons. Some argue that riots break out when prison administrators take actions that disrupt existing prison society. This is particularly true when administrators try to alter power-sharing arrangements between staff and prisoners, arrangements that increase prisoners' status and comforts.

According to Colvin (1982), three situations create administrative disruptions:

1. Discovering and exposing corruption, such as narcotics traffic inside prisons
2. Policy conflicts, such as those between reformist, rehabilitation-oriented administrators and old-line, security-oriented staff
3. Policy changes brought about by new prison administrations, such as wardens who decide they're going to "crack down" on minority prisoner assertiveness (450)

If all three conditions occur simultaneously, trouble is almost certain to follow. Cohesion arising out of power, status, and wealth erodes badly. Conflict between prisoners' social structure and administrators' control structure erupts in various forms. Prisoner protests and strikes are organized to get back their privileges. If they do, order returns.

Sometimes, administrators don't give back lost privileges. Instead, for political or ideological reasons, they respond to protests with more restrictions. Prisoners' resentment grows, and administrators find it increasingly difficult to restore lost privileges. Hostility between guards and prisoners escalates; administrations change and guard turnover increases. Administrative actions don't restore order. On the contrary, they only raise tensions. As administrative staff divide into warring bureaucratic camps, prisoners' social structure disintegrates into self-protective, hostile cliques. Eventually, rioting breaks out.

Burt Useem and Peter Kimball (1989), in their stimulating study of prison riots, list the following eight popular theories of the causes of prison riots:

1. Violent, depraved prisoners
2. Prison conditions
3. Liberal judges giving prisoners too many rights
4. Radical prisoner organizations stirring up trouble
5. Prisoners crowded as if in cages
6. Racism
7. Gang plots
8. Prisoners' "cry for help" (3–4)

Men's Prison Programs

If there's one thing prisoners have, it's "time on their hands." Several years ago, I visited a prison with a colleague who for 17 years had also been Director of the Federal Bureau of Prisons. After we'd been there a while I said, "There's sure a lot of sitting around and sleeping going on here." He told me the average prisoner sleeps 17 hours a day. And this isn't new. In 1982, Chief Justice of the U.S. Supreme Court Warren Burger warned:

> We can continue to have largely human "warehouses," with little or no education and training, or we can have prisons that are factories with fences around them...to accomplish the dual objective of training inmates in gainful occupations and lightening the enormous load of maintaining the prison system of this country. (Flanagan 1989, 135)

As you read about prison programs, keep in mind that in too many prisons there are disappointingly few programs, or maybe it's more accurate to say there are too many programs with far too little money and staff (Lipton 1995, 4). It may surprise you to learn this, especially in view of two important missions prison programs are supposed help accomplish:

1. Rehabilitate prisoners
2. Manage prisons by keeping prisoners busy and out of trouble (As my mother used to warn me—"Get busy, Joel. Idle hands tempt the devil. Besides, it's good for what ails you.")

Why are there too many prisons either without programs or programs without enough support? The easy answer is the enthusiastic public (and often not informed) response to a 1974 article written by Robert Martinson, "What Works? Questions and Answers about Prison Reform." It concluded: "With few and isolated exceptions, the rehabilitative efforts that have been reported so far have no appreciable effect on recidivism" (25). Martinson was one of three respected sociologists who'd conducted the most extensive review of prison programs (231 programs) in the history of evaluation research. The professionals and the public saw the facts and concluded, "'Nothing works,' so why do anything?"

But wait a minute; that conclusion sounds too simple. And it is. First, Martinson unforgivably spinned the findings of the study. The study actually said, "[T]he field of corrections has *not as yet* found satisfactory ways to reduce recidivism by *significant* amounts." (I added the italics so you can see better the spin.) Second, the article shored up the popular view that prison programs are "soft on crime" and so they undermine the prison mission to punish criminals. According to Douglas Lipton (1995), the principal author of the study Martinson worked on:

> The phrase "nothing works" became a watchword and entered the corrections vocabulary. It was treated as fact. The belief that "nothing works" still has widespread acceptance and is one of the main reasons treatment programs are given low priority. (4)

Heated scholarly debate followed the knee-jerk reaction to the "nothing works" pronouncement. The outcome of this debate led to a more balanced assessment of the effectiveness of rehabilitation programs. Here's what two scholars deeply involved in rehabilitation research said:

> Martinson's finding, which was picked up by the mass media (for example, "Big change in prisons" [*U.S. News and World Report*], was used by critics of prison programs to argue against rehabilitation as a primary justification for incarceration. Soon, however, Martinson's critics pointed out that he was premature in dismissing all forms of intervention. Although few programs can succeed in rehabilitating all inmates, more moderate successes may be possible. (Gerber and Fritsch 1995, 120)

And

> Rather than ask, "What works for offenders as a whole?" we must increasingly ask, "Which methods work best for which types of offenders and under what conditions or in what types of setting?" (Palmer 1975)

The public and the politicians paid no attention to this debate; they were too heavily swayed by the view that "nothing *but* punishment works." Let's not fall for the shallow spin of "nothing works" but instead listen to researchers like those just quoted in assessing prison programs.

Most people and some professionals in corrections probably agree with the distinguished National Academy of Science's definition of rehabilitation as "the result of any planned intervention that reduces an offender's further criminal activity" (Gaes, Flanagan, Motuik, and Stewart 1998, 4). But prison programs have broader missions than reducing recidivism, like reducing misbehavior in prison; contributing to peaceful, humane punishment; and improving prisoners' chances of getting a job when they get out of prison. Practically, rehabilitation programs are aimed at "correcting" deficiencies that have the strongest links to criminal behavior. We'll focus here on five types of programs—education, work, recreation, religious programs, and substance abuse. We'll also take a closer look at the cognitive model of rehabilitation and the debate over prison programs.

Education in Men's Prisons Let's divide education into three categories: academic, vocational, and social (see "Cognitive Model of Rehabilitation" later). Teaching prisoners to read and write is the oldest rehabilitation program; it's been a prison mission and a part of prison life since the birth of the reformato-

► Academic education can reduce recidivism by improving the chances that parolees can get jobs, by contributing to their maturity and desire to achieve, and by enhancing their decision-making skills. These inmates are taking a computer-assisted GED class in Corrections Corporation of America's private prison in Tennessee.

© A. Ramey/Photo Edit

ries in the 1870s (Chapter 11). By the 1930s, primary and secondary education had become primary rehabilitation programs. By the 1960s, college education had been added (Gaes et al. 1998, 57).

Academic education can reduce recidivism in three ways. First, education improves the chances of getting a job, and getting a job reduces the chances of recidivism. Second, the process of learning itself makes inmates more mature, conscientious, and committed to achievement. These qualities can lead to better decision making, and better decision making reduces the chances of returning to prison. Third, the classroom is a chance for inmates to "interact with civilian employees in...a nonauthoritarian, goal-directed relationship" (Gaes et al. 1998, 56–57).

But does academic education reduce recidivism? Some research says yes, other research says no. Jorg Gerber and Eric Fritsch (1995) reviewed 13 studies of primary and secondary education programs they determined were conducted rigidly enough to deserve consideration; 9 of the studies found a modest relationship between the program and recidivism. As for college education, the answer was also mixed—there was a modest positive relationship in some studies and no relationship in others (123–130).

What about vocational education? Here the results are less mixed and more positive. According to Gerber and Fritsch (1995):

> Most of the research conducted in recent years shows a correlation between vocational training and a variety of outcomes generally considered positive for either society or correctional institutions: lower recidivism rates, lower parole revocation rates, better post release employment patterns, and better institutional disciplinary records. (131)

Besides the modest positive relationship between academic and vocational programs and recidivism, Gerber and Fritsch (1995) also found:

> a fair amount of support for the hypotheses that adult academic and vocational correctional education programs lead to fewer disciplinary violations during incarceration...increases in employment opportunities, and to increases in participation in education after release. (136–137)

But these positive effects aren't automatic; they depend on:

- *"The more extensive the educational program the more likely it is to achieve its stated objectives.* For instance, research in New York State showed that inmates who earned their G.E.D. were less likely to recidivate than those who attended G.E.D. classes but did not earn the diploma."
- *"Programs that are separate from the rest of the prison are more likely to succeed.* Successful programs had a designated area for providing vocational education and only vocational education."
- *"Programs that provide follow up after release are more likely to succeed.* Successful programs had systematic procedures for providing rate placement services."
- *"Programs that are successful in attracting an appropriate audience are more likely to achieve their intended objectives.* For instance, the 'Reading to Reduce Recidivism' program in Texas was hampered because it was designed for inmates who would serve short sentences and would be released quickly into the community, whereas the median sentence served by program participants was fifteen years."
- *"With respect to vocational education, programs that provide skills relevant to the contemporary job market are more likely to achieve their stated objectives.* Administrators claim that their programs offer inmates saleable skills, which will enhance their probability of obtaining and maintaining employment in the free world. But critics often maintain that vocational training programs fail because what they teach bears so little relationship to an offender's subsequent life outside of prison." (Gerber and Fritsch 1995, 135–136)

The bottom line: There's reason for some optimism that academic and vocational education have a modest effect on reducing recidivism and misbehavior in prison and increasing job opportunities and further education after prison if they're designed, carried out, and followed up right.

Work in Prison Education is the oldest rehabilitation program, but work is the oldest prison activity. And just as prisoners come to prison with major educational deficiencies, they also bring major deficiencies in their work history—poor to no work records, few if any marketable skills, and a poor to no work ethic (Gaes et al. 1998, 62). So work programs have multiple missions. Some of these missions are directed at inmates, such as developing positive attitudes toward work, self-discipline, and marketable skills. Two other missions are aimed at prison management:

1. Maintain order and safety by keeping prisoners busy and out of trouble.
2. Reduce the cost of imprisonment by using prison labor.

Prisons have to provide all the services most communities in the outside world have to provide—and more. They have utilities (sewer and water, electricity, telephones), restaurants, bakeries, laundries, hospitals, mail delivery, fire protection, record keeping, and janitorial services. Prisoners do most of the work that provides these services. Obviously, the resources of prisoner labor and time are in great supply in prisons. Prison jobs tell a lot about the prestige of the prisoners who hold them. The most prestigious are jobs closest to decision makers. Record keeping is the most prestigious because it puts inmates in charge of a valuable commodity—information (who's eligible for release or reclassification to lower or higher security prisons). Desk jobs provide regular access to administrators; food and other commodities service jobs give prisoners better food and other amenities *and* stuff they can sell to other prisoners. The lowest prestige job is also the most available—janitorial work. This work is menial, like mopping floors, and there's no access to information, goods, and services (Clear and Cole 1994, 334).

Prison work also includes working in prison industries that produce for the outside world. Prison industries were a major part of prison life from 1900 to 1925. They were considered a major element in the rehabilitation of prisoners. Work was not only useful, it was also therapeutic, according to the Progressive prison reformers. But prison industries faced stiff opposition from labor and small business, because they took jobs away from union labor and profits away from small businesses. They ran into the firmly entrenched principle of less eligibility (prisoners can't make as much money as free workers).

Prison industries returned to prison life in the 1980s (Hawkins 1983, 98–103). By 2000, prisons were engaged in a long list of enterprises, including car repair, lumbering, ranching, meat processing, making flags, printing, data entry, telephone answering services, Braille translation, microfilming, and CD-ROM copying (*Corrections Compendium Journal* 2000, 8).

The major justification for returning prison industries to prison life is the idea that prisoners should pay for their imprisonment. But this rarely happens; only a few prisoners work in prison industries. Further, many of the prison industry programs cost taxpayers more money than they save. People in charge of prison industries say that potential profits are eaten away by security and other concerns, such as rehabilitating inmates and protecting private businesses from unfair competition. "The goal is really to create work, reduce idleness, and help manage the prison," said Pamela Jo Davis, president of Florida's PRIDE (Prison Rehabilitative Industries and Diversified Enterprises) and chair of Correctional Industries Association, a national umbrella group for prison industries (Hoskinson 1998).

In 1997, 76,519 prisoners were working in prison industries, more than twice the number in 1980. Sales of products from prison industries more than tripled—

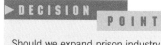

► D E C I S I O N
 P O I N T ◄

Should we expand prison industry programs?

Click on this Decision Point at http://cj.wadsworth.com/samaha_cj7e to explore the issue.

from $392 million in 1980 to $1.62 billion in 1997. Nevertheless, according to a National State Auditors Association's evaluation of prison industries in 13 states, many prison industries aren't self-sufficient (Hoskinson 1998).

Prison Work Programs Prison work provides all the essential services to keep prison society, and it occupies prisoners' time and keeps them out of trouble. But what about work *programs* aimed at reducing crime when prisoners leave prison? Some of these programs have focused on vocational training (already discussed); others emphasize job placement, subsidized employment, or temporary financial assistance (Uggen and Staff 2001, 3).

Most evaluations of well-designed programs (randomly selected, strongly matched experimental groups and control groups, and some nonexperimental) from the 1970s until recently have shown little difference in future criminal behavior between experimental groups that received job training or financial assistance and control groups that didn't (Uggen and Staff 2001, 5). But not *all* programs. Arrests for domestic abuse had a greater deterrent effect on *employed* men (Chapter 6). Also, an observational study found sex-offender treatment programs were more effective for probationers who had a steady employment history than those who didn't (Kruttschnitt, Uggen, and Shelton 2000). In another study, researchers found that federal offender participants in a nonexperimental vocational apprenticeship had higher employment rates when they left prison than a comparison group. And compared to a control group, participants in prison industries and participants who completed either vocational or apprenticeship training were 24 percent and 33 percent less likely to recidivate, respectively (reported in Uggen and Staff 2001, 5).

These mixed and weak results have led some criminologists to argue that "high quality" or "satisfying employment" can reduce recidivism (Uggen and Staff 2001, 8). Does it? The answer depends on whether individuals who get the jobs are also the least likely to commit crimes. In other words, it's not the job quality but the individuals who get the jobs that's related to crime.

Experimental programs can best separate the effect of job quality from the effect of individuals who get the jobs. But some nonexperimental evidence is promising. Chris Uggen (1999) made statistical corrections for the influence of individual selection in supported work data. He found that a shift from food service work (job quality score of .57) to skilled crafts work (job quality score of 1.08) decreases the probability of recidivism by 11 percent. Shifting from food service to the less satisfying job of machine operator increased the probability of recidivism by 14 percent. Other nonexperimental research suggests that securing high-quality work can be a turning point in criminal offenders' criminal careers (Uggen and Staff 2001, 9).

Uggen and Staff (2001) warn us that there's a lot we don't know about the employment-crime connections, particularly the answers to four questions:

1. What are the long-term job prospects 10, 20, or 30 years after release?
2. Are ex-offenders better off working among other ex-offenders or with nonoffenders?
3. Do ties to work and family alter the effectiveness of correctional interventions?
4. What features of employment and training programs are most attractive to offenders? (14)

Still, they conclude with a hopeful bottom line:

Despite these unanswered questions, we can reach the following provisional conclusion: Postrelease employment and training programs, especially those providing jobs of moderate high quality, are particularly promising for reducing recidivism among older and drug-involved offenders. We hesitate to conclude, however, that work programs cannot be beneficial for younger offenders, only that existing initiatives have been less successful for this group. (14–15)

Recreation Most prisons have athletic teams; many prisoners work out in prison exercise rooms; virtually all watch movies; and some participate in drama, music, art, and journalism. Recreation is an important—and, of course, desired by most prisoners—part of prison life. Recreation programs are good for prisoners: They help to accomplish the mission of rehabilitation to the extent they teach inmates social skills like fair competition, working together, and building self-esteem. They're also part of the reward and punishment system that helps to enforce prison discipline. Few inmates want to lose the privilege of recreation. Finally, recreation definitely fits in with the philosophy of humane punishment. Perhaps nothing more humanizes prisons than allowing prisoners to participate in social activities they really enjoy. Of course, recreation programs also create safety risks. Fights can—and do—erupt during competitive sports, for example. And there's considerable controversy over whether recreation is consistent with punishment. (See Make Your Decision.)

Religious Programs The scholarly literature doesn't pay much attention to prison religious programs, but they exist in every prison. The First Amendment guarantees the "free exercise" of religion, so prisons have to provide religion programs. Like most other prison programs, religious programs help prisoners fill time, are supposed to aid in rehabilitation, and contribute to a humane punishment.

Todd Clear and his colleagues (1992) conducted one of the few national studies of religion in prison. Interviews with inmates indicated that religion helps prisoners by providing a psychological and physical "safe haven." Religion also enables inmates to maintain ties with family and religious volunteers. The study also found that participation in religious programs contributed both to helping prisoners adjust to prison and reducing disciplinary infractions.

Drug Treatment There's compelling evidence that drug use increases criminal activity among significant numbers of offenders (Gaes et al. 1998, 386). Almost two-thirds of state prisoners say they use drugs regularly; nearly half of federal prisoners say the same (Pelissier et al. 2001). This has created enormous pressure on corrections departments to create drug treatment programs for prisoners. Most of these programs are therapeutic communities (TCs), which isolate drug-dependent prisoners from the general prison population. This isolation is supposed to increase group pressure on prisoners to commit themselves to the program and decrease peer pressure from outside the group to use drugs.

Let's look at the federal prison system because only a few state programs have been evaluated, and those evaluations have flaws (Pelissier et al. 2001). In the federal therapeutic communities programs, each community contains about one hundred prisoners. Treatment lasts for half the day; during the rest of the day participants mingle with the general population, participating in normal prison activities—work, school, meals, recreation. The programs follow the cognitive model (discussed in the next section). They try to "identify, confront, and alter attitudes, values, and thinking patterns that led to criminal behaviors and drug or alcohol abuse" (Pelissier et al. 2001, 319).

Do the programs work? Bernadette Pelissier and her colleagues (2001) compared participants with nonparticipants to find out how many were arrested or used drugs or alcohol within six months after they were released from prison. They found treated inmates were 73 percent less likely to be arrested and 44 percent less likely to use illegal drugs or alcohol than untreated inmates.

But treatment wasn't the only variable related to arrest and use. Older inmates, inmates with short criminal histories, inmates with full-time jobs, and those who lived with their spouses did better than their opposites. Researchers didn't (or maybe couldn't) sort out which of these elements contributed most to reduced arrests and drug and alcohol use. Also, the researchers didn't figure out how much each of the elements in the programs—cognitive skills, therapeutic community, or the intensity and quality of the treatment experience—contributed to the positive outcomes (Pelissier et al. 2001).

The Cognitive Model of Rehabilitation "Target thinking, not behavior" is the core value of the **cognitive model of rehabilitation.** The mission of cognitive skills programs is "rehabilitation through clearer thinking." The cognitive model of rehabilitation is backed up by extensive research showing that "faulty thinking patterns" are related to recidivism. (Of course, we all have faulty thinking patterns, but for most of us, they don't lead us to prison.) The assumption behind the model is if you can correct prisoners' faulty thinking patterns you can reduce their recidivism. Prisoners' faulty thinking patterns include acting on impulse instead of thinking problems through; thinking about now instead of planning for the future; looking at the world through their eyes instead of seeing others' perspectives; acting before they think about the consequences of their actions; and thinking their bad actions are someone or something else's fault (Fabiano, Porporino, and Robinson 1990).

> **cognitive model of rehabilitation** rehabilitation by means of developing clear thinking skills

The Cognitive Thinking Skills program developed by Robert Ross and Elizabeth Fabiano is the most widely used program following the cognitive model. Coaches meet with groups of 4 to 10 inmates for two hours, two to four times a week for 35 weeks. To keep participants motivated, coaches use a number of techniques, including role playing, videotaped feedback, modeling, group discussion, and games, that help avoid making the sessions like therapy or school.

Participants are tested to assess their cognitive skills and attitudes toward criminal behavior at the beginning and the end of the 35 sessions. Results indicate statistically significant improvement in several areas: Participants

- Appreciate other people's perspectives better
- Accept criticism better
- Consider more options in resolving conflicts with others
- Have less negative attitudes toward law, courts, and police

Participants were satisfied with the program. Seventy-four percent said the program "was much better than any other program" they'd participated in. Three weeks after the program, 97 percent said they were using the skills they'd learned. Maybe most important, participants believed the program was "highly relevant to their lives" (Figure 14.3).

Did the program reduce recidivism? A follow-up showed that 19.7 percent of released inmates who completed the program were convicted of a new crime and returned to prison within a year compared with 24.8 percent of a control group of similar offenders who wanted to get in the program but couldn't. For offenders who completed the program in the community instead of prison, the results were

▼ **FIGURE 14.3 Areas Where Offenders Felt They Functioned Better after Completing the Cognitive Thinking Skills Program**
Source: Elizabeth Fabiano, Frank Porporino, and David Robinson, "Rehabilitation Through Clearer Thinking: A Cognitive Model of Correctional Intervention," Correctional Service of Canada (1990). http://www.csc-scc.gc.ca/text/rsrch/briefs/b4/b04e.shtml.

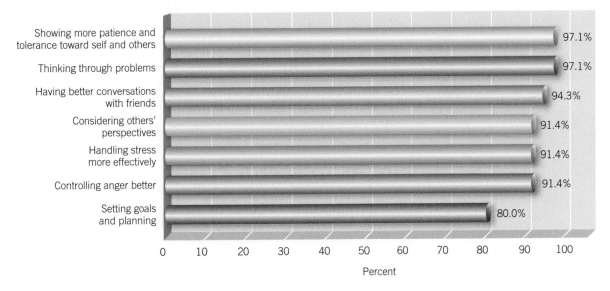

better: 8.4 percent of participants who completed the program in the community compared with the 24.8 percent who completed the program in prison were convicted. The bottom line: There was "some modest evidence of the effectiveness of the program" (Gaes et al. 1998, 29).

Program Debate Education, vocational training, prison work, and religious programs are broadly supported, so they don't stir up much controversy. Recreation programs are a different story (see Make Your Decision). They symbolize the deep division of opinion over the confinement model (prison as punishment) and the punishment model (prison for punishment) discussed earlier in the chapter. Those who believe prisoners are supposed to suffer confinement plus more pain resent recreation programs that allow prisoners to "work out," compete in sports, and watch movies.

Rehabilitation programs also arouse controversy, both from an ideological perspective—Should we rehabilitate prisoners?—and from a practical standpoint—Can we rehabilitate prisoners? We've already discussed how Robert Martinson's article started a war between rehabilitationists and retributionists. The truth is somewhere between nothing works and all treatments work. Ted Palmer (1992) reviewed a wide range of rehabilitation programs. He found that between one-quarter and one-third of the programs "work" (reduce recidivism). In view of the discussion of prison programs included in this section, I think Palmer got it just about right: Rehabilitation programs work, "but they don't work spectacularly" (1–11). Like the 1960s optimism that treatment was a panacea, the pessimism that "nothing works" is unwarranted.

Charles H. Logan, of the University of Connecticut, and Gerald G. Gaes, of the Federal Bureau of Prisons (1993, 247), dismiss Palmer's study and other meta-analyses (studies of studies) of rehabilitation programs. Because of a host of definitional, methodological problems and the pro-rehabilitation bias of most meta-analysis scholars, Logan and Gaes say the studies of studies of rehabilitation can't be trusted.

If we're just looking at whether prison programs turn prisoners into people who work hard and play by the rules in and after they leave prison, then the results of the research are mixed at best. But prison programs have missions besides rehabilitating prisoners. They also keep prisoners busy, and keeping them busy keeps them out of trouble—even if it doesn't turn them into law-abiding people. And "constructive" activity is consistent with an orderly, safe, humane confinement. According to Logan and Gaes (1993):

> "Constructive" activity is not defined here as "contributing to the betterment of inmates" but as activity that is, on its face, consistent with the orderly, safe, secure, and humane operation of a prison. Idleness and boredom can be considered wrong from a work ethic standpoint, or as unnatural because human beings are not meant to be idle, or as so fundamentally related to mischief as to be undesirable for that reason. In any case, prison programs can be defended as forms of constructive and meaningful activity and as antidotes to idleness, without invoking claims of rehabilitative effectiveness. This is not to say that it does not matter whether the programs have any rehabilitative effects; it would be fine if they did so. But when we say that the primary purpose of the prison is to punish through confinement, we become more interested in the operation of these programs inside the prison gates and less concerned about their effects beyond. (261)

Life in Women's Prisons

Life in prison is very different for women than for men. Why? Several reasons, including the fact that there are fewer women criminals than men; women commit lesser offenses; the belief that women are more "reformable" (some say "tractable") than men; assumptions about women's psyche; and conceptions about the role of women (Kruttschnitt and Gartner 2003, 1).

Most women prisoners are poor, undereducated, and unskilled Blacks or Hispanics with little or no work experience, locked up in Texas, California, and the federal prisons. They're also mostly young, single mothers with at least two children under 18. And they have many medical, psychological, and financial problems and needs. According to Barbara Owen and Barbara Bloom (1995), "Substance abuse, compounded by poverty, unemployment, physical and mental illness, physical and sexual abuse, and homelessness, often propel women through the revolving door of the criminal justice system" (167).

More than two-thirds of women prisoners are serving time for nonviolent crimes, mainly drug offenses and minor property crimes (Durose and Langan 2004, 6). More than half of the increase in women prisoners is due to the imprisonment of drug offenders. According to Owen and Bloom (1995), "the legal response to drug-related behavior has become increasingly punitive, resulting in a flood of less serious offenders into the state and federal prison systems" (167). Since 1991, the number of women serving time for violent offenses actually has dropped. One-third of the women serving time for either murder or manslaughter had killed relatives (168). Let's look at the pains of imprisonment in women's prisons; how women adapt to and cope with prison life; how women "do time," and women's prison programs.

The "Pains" of Women's Imprisonment

Women cope with prison life differently from men. David A. Ward and Gene G. Kassebaum's (1965) path-breaking study of the California Institution for Women (at the time the largest women's prison in the world) found that women responded to the pains of imprisonment by forming intimate (sometimes sexual) relationships that mimicked family relationships outside prison. But unlike in men's prisons, female prisoners didn't coerce their partners into homosexual relationships, and their relationships weren't necessarily sexual in nature.

Rose Giallombardo's (1966) study of the Federal Reformatory for Women supported Ward and Kassebaum's findings. Giallombardo showed that women reproduced outside family relationships in prison—father, mother, daughter, sister. Unlike the subculture of men's prisons, women's prison subculture fostered mutuality and harmony, not competition and dissension. In Giallombardo's words, women "resist the destructive effects of imprisonment by creating a substitute universe within which the inmates may preserve an identity relevant to life outside the prison" (129).

Esther Heffernen (1972) found a heterogeneous population in the District of Columbia's Reformatory. For women who grew up in foster homes, prison became the center of their lives. They continuously struggled with staff and other inmates for control of their lives and to obtain illegal food, drugs, clothing, and letters. Women imprisoned for situational offenses, such as murder of an abusive husband, rejected any criminal self-identification, attempting to recreate conventional life inside prison and maintain contacts outside. These prisoners accepted rules and regulations and identified with the staff. Professional criminals tried to keep busy to pass time quickly and avoided trouble to get released as soon as possible to their former lives of crime.

Heffernen's research demonstrates that women's response to imprisonment doesn't depend entirely on traditional gender roles; their lives outside prison were also important as their role identities. The variety of the roles adopted to cope with imprisonment demonstrates another important point. These women weren't just passive recipients of what prison administrations handed out; they were active agents with at least some control over their lives. According to Candace Kruttschnitt and Rosemary Gartner in their survey of women's imprisonment (2004), Heffernen's research shows that "women exercised some autonomy in choosing particular adaptations and styles of doing time, and shaped these in an active...manner" (26).

Barbara Owen documents a degree of active agency (sometimes for their good and sometimes not) in *Surviving the Mix: Struggle and Survival in a Women's Prison* (1998), a combined ethnographic and survey study of the largest women's prison in the United States (and probably the world). The Central California Women's Facility holds more than four thousand women. It has all levels of security, from the murderers on death row to the minor drug and property offenders. Two themes run throughout her research. First, when women enter prison, they realize the importance of developing some kind of program to help them cope with doing their time.

According to Owen (1998):

> Successful programming...involves settling down and developing a routine that provides satisfying...personal relationships and routine activities that offer constructive stimulation and protection from the dangers of the prison environment. (97)

Programming is to inmates what following a daily routine is to most people outside prison. According to one inmate:

> Programming means to me that I get up every morning, shower, brush my teeth, and get ready for work. I come to work, do my work. I go home for lunch, I come back. I get off, go home, shower and kick back. Either I read a book, or I kick back with some of my friends and bullshit. I stay in my room sometimes, but I go to the day room. It depends on the kind of mood I am in. I got in a fight once and lost my privileges for thirty days. This changed my whole attitude...as far as getting in trouble, going off on people. I have been able to come to myself, to sit in my room and think about my goals and stuff in life. (Owen 1998, 97)

According to Owen (1998):

> Most women want to do their time, leave the prison, and return to the free world. They want to avoid the mix of risky and self-defeating behaviors such as drug use and fighting or damaging relationships that interfere with one's program or limit freedom through placement in restrictive housing or the addition of time to one's sentence. (8)

But not all women; some refuse to program, spending their time getting around expectations. Trying to get around the program leads to loss of jobs, time spent in detention, and loss of "good time" (reduction in sentence length).

Some dip into "the mix"—risky and self-defeating behaviors such as drug use and fighting or damaging relationships—in the beginning of their prison terms, leaving the mix when they establish a more productive program. Others invest permanently in the destructive spiral of the mix and its attendant activities. For a small minority of women, the lure of the mix, with its emphasis on the fast life and the excitement of drug use, fighting, and volatile intimate relationships, proves too hard to resist (8). For some, the mix is too tempting to overcome.

The second theme of Owen's research is the importance of personal relationships. The play family is one of these relationships. It contains interpersonal satisfactions, a combination of social and material responsibilities, and a sense of belonging. According to Owen (1998), the play family "creates the sense of community and protection that the...cliques and gang structure provide for male prisoners" (8).

Female Prisoners' Control over Their Lives

In her study of Latina prisoners in New York, Juanita Diaz-Cotto (1996) criticizes most scholarship for highlighting prison family and kinship relationships because it portrays women as passive, when in fact they're quite the opposite. In the two prisons she studied, prison authorities tried lots of ways to block Latina prisoners' prison reform efforts, like using male guards to physically subdue "activist" prisoners. Latina prisoners didn't just stand by and take it, they rebelled against traditionally imposed gender roles and oppressive prison policies in a number of ways. In addition to forming prison family groups and kinship networks, they created other informal and formal prisoner groups, participated in rebellions, work strikes and hunger strikes, filed petitions and class action suits, wrote for prisoners' rights newsletters, published their autobiographies, physically resisted the attacks of their keepers, and escaped. (5)

Continuity and Change in Women Prisoners' "Doing Time"

Rosemary Gartner and Candace Kruttschnitt (2004, 267–304) also broke away from the family and kinship dominance in the literature when they revisited Ward and Kassenbaum's (1965) analysis of how women do time (discussed earlier). They suspended the focus on intimate play families and homosexual relationships. They developed a major prison research theme that applies to both men's and women's prisons. In the words of Gartner and Kruttschnitt (2004):

> The ways prisoners think about and relate to other prisoners, to their keepers, and to the prison regime—is affected by prisons' external and internal environments. With shifts in the political, cultural, and economic climate of the larger society, the relationship of prisons to society as well as the actors within the prison change. Similarly, official regimes, structures, and practices inside prisons shape the responses and adaptations of prisoners. (268–269)

Most of women's imprisonment research focuses on how changes outside and inside prison, over time and among women's prisons with different management, change women prisoners' daily lives (Diaz-Cotto 1996; Greer 2000; Rierden 1997). The changes include the shift from the ideology of rehabilitation to one of punishment (Chapters 1, 11); prison management styles (Chapter 13); and the prison population explosion (Chapter 13).

But despite the talk of change and its effects, there's good reason to believe there are also forces of continuity at work. For one thing, frontline workers and prisoners have a way of shaping (some say mangling) in practice the ideological goals and official policies made in places by people far removed from prisoners' daily lives (Lynch 1998, 839–870; 2000, 40–65). In David Garland's (2003) words:

> The rapid changes manifest at the level of government representations and rhetoric must not be mistaken for alterations in working practices and professional ideologies, nor should it be assumed that the discrediting of a particular vocabulary (such as "rehabilitation") means that the practices that it once described have altogether disappeared. (46)

Also, prisoners don't manage their lives according to abstract phrases and prison policies. They look more to how they can do their time in the face of elements of imprisonment that don't change: loss of freedom; isolation from the world outside prison; loss of control over body and time; and deprivations of material amenities and legal rights (Gartner and Kruttschnitt 2004, 272). (Gartner and Kruttschnitt call the list "a core of dreary consistency" [272].)

Another force for continuity at work: the belief that women prisoners are different is entrenched. And research backs up the belief. Women's prison research since the 1960s has shown that violence, gangs, and racial tensions are unusual; intimate and consensual sexual relationships and prison families are common; and cooperation with staff is typical. Women prisoners don't riot; they resist individually and secretly. According to Gartner and Kruttschnitt (2004):

> These studies suggest that some aspects of the ways women choose to do their time may be anchored in basic needs for a measure of comfort and control in a highly restrictive and depriving environment, and that these may vary little with changes in penal ideologies or a prison's regime. (273)

Gartner and Kruttschnitt (2004) tested how changes between the 1960s and the 1990s affected how women prisoners did (and probably still do) their time in the California Institution for Women (CIW). In the 1960s, CIW housed about 800 prisoners; by 1995, the number had doubled to over 1600. In the 1960s, there was no fence around the prison, the women lived in cottages with their own rooms, could wear street clothes, and were called "residents." By the 1990s, the prison was surrounded by a fence reinforced with razor wire and four towers staffed with armed guards; the women lived two to a cell, had to wear state-issued clothing (denim jeans and T-shirts or muumuus), and were called "inmates." In the 1960s, the prisoners were supervised only by women; by the 1990s, half the supervisors were men.

The dominant philosophy (if not always the practice) in the 1960s was rehabilitation, and there were several rehabilitation programs; by the 1990s, the philosophy (not always the practice) was retribution, and programs were aimed at personal responsibility. In the warden's words, "We're not rehabilitating anyone. We're creating an atmosphere in which women can change themselves.... We have a culture of responsibility here" (Gartner and Kruttschnitt 2004, 282). In the 1960s under indeterminate sentences, women's release dates depended on when parole boards decided they were rehabilitated; in the 1990s, under fixed and mandatory sentencing, women knew their release date from their first day in prison.

How, if at all, did these changes affect how prisoners did their time? Gartner and Kruttschnitt tried to answer this question. They had Ward and Kassebaum's (1965) research data from CIW in the 1960s (p. 501). They compared those data with their own collected in interviews and surveys of the women in the 1990s. Despite the seemingly dramatic differences in architecture, population, philosophy, and management, they found mostly continuity in women's perceptions of doing time, of other prisoners, and of staff. Table 14.1 compares the results of their survey data from the 1990s with that of Ward and Kassebaum's (1965) in the 1960s.

▼ TABLE 14.1 Prisoner Perceptions of Doing Time, of Other Prisoners, and of Staff (1960s and 1990s)

Survey Statements[†]	CIW 1963[‡] (n = 293)	CIW 1998[§] (n = 887)
The best way to do time is mind your own business and have as little to do with other inmates as possible.	72%	88%**
When inmates stick together, it's easier to do time.	77%	80%
Most inmates aren't loyal when it really matters.	72%	83%**
In some situations, it's OK to inform on another inmate.	43%	35%*
A good rule to follow is to share extra goods with friends.	56%	38%**
If you reveal too much about yourself to staff, the information will be used against you.	53%	72%**
Correctional officers have to keep their distance in dealing with inmates.	32%	51%**
An inmate should stick up for what she feels is right and not let staff set her standards.	92%	92%
The best way to do time is grin and bear it and not let staff know when you're down.	61%	61%
Staff have made it clear how they expect you to behave if you're to stay out of trouble.	68%	78%**

[†]Columns 2 and 3 show the percentages in the survey agreeing with the statement.

[‡]Ward and Kassebaum's 1963 data.

[§]Gartner and Kruttschnitt's 1998 survey.

*$p < .05$.

**$p < .001$.

Source: Rosemary Gartner and Candace Kruttschnitt, "A Brief History of Doing Time," *Law and Society Review* 38 (2004), Table 2, p. 290.

According to the interviews, in both periods, the most common response to how to do time and relate to other prisoners added up to "Mind your own business. Stay to yourself. Have a few friends, but don't trust anyone" (290). According to a 23-year-old Black woman doing two years for burglary, "You make one friend, you know what I'm saying, out of all these people here and that friend turns out to be just as scandalous as the rest of them" (291). According to a 50-something White woman with eight prior commitments, prisoners are "treacherous, dangerous, and out for themselves," especially the younger ones "who have no morals, no code, or anything to live by" (291).

Distrust of staff in both the 1960s and the 1990s also showed through in the interviews (as it did in the surveys, Table 14.1). According to one pregnant woman serving time for selling methamphetamines, "I'll do whatever it takes when it comes to one of my rights, because we have very little rights. But what little rights we need to stick by them, you know?" (294).

Let's end this section on the change and continuity theories with the words of a prisoner who'd served time in CIW during both periods:

> The faces have changed, the words have changed, the clothes have changed. But the way women do time has not changed that much. The way the institution offers what should be done with time and society's expectation of what happens when the person comes out has changed completely, and that's sad. (298)

Women's Prison Programs

Practitioners and scholars agree that most of the programs you learned about in "Men's Prison Programs" don't meet women prisoners' needs. But it's not at all clear what "works" for women prisoners, because there are so few evaluations of women's prison programs (Kruttschnitt and Gartner 2004, 44). Let's look at the needs, the programs, and the "what works" question.

Needs of and Programs for Women Prisoners To fill the gap in information about the needs of women offenders, and the programs designed to meet those needs, Merry Morash and her colleagues (1998) conducted the most comprehensive survey of women's prison programs in the United States. Morash and her colleagues report that women offenders have special program needs that men offenders don't. Why? Several reasons. First, 43 percent of women (12 percent of men) reported they'd been sexually or physically abused *before* they were admitted to prison. Second, women serving sentences for violent crimes were twice as likely as men to have committed the crime against someone close to them. Third, 75 percent of women (10 percent of men) in prison had children younger than 18 living with them before they came to prison. Finally, women used illegal drugs, and used them more frequently (54 percent) than men (50 percent).

Morash and her colleagues report significant differences between the kinds of, and participation in, women's and men's education, work, medical and mental health, and legal assistance programs. More women than men participated in all education programs (adult basic, secondary, and college). They also had more work assignments. *But* compared with men, women were assigned to janitorial and kitchen work; men were paid more often than women; and vocational training was more available to men than women (Krutschnitt and Gartner 2004, 45). Women were better off than men when it came to having access to and receiving medical services. One reason (but definitely not a justification) for not meeting the special needs of women offenders is that they make up such a small fraction of the prison population (Chapter 13) that it's easy for state corrections agencies to overlook them (Morash, Bynum, and Koons 1998, 2).

Angela West's (2001) assessment of the needs of Hispanic women prisoners points to an area of increasing (and important) attention: ethnic and cultural differences and the need for sensitivity in responding to the special needs created by the differences. To explore HIV needs and concerns, West conducted focus

► In Colorado's Women's Correctional Facility in Canon City, one prisoner changes the diaper on her 1-1/2-year-old; the other visits with her newborn baby. The two mothers get to visit their children three hours every week through the New Horizon Ministries, a Mennonite group that cares for children during the mothers' imprisonment. Seventy-five percent of female inmates had children younger than 18 living with them before they went to prison.

group interviews with groups of women prisoners in a medium security women's prison that holds 90 percent of a northeastern state's women prisoners. Content analysis pointed out general concerns common to all groups but highlighted cultural differences. Hispanic women are most at risk of entering prison with HIV infection. And the rates keep going up. Discussions of machismo (dominant male stereotype), marianismo (submissive female stereotype), and the role of the Roman Catholic Church emphasize the difficulties in creating and implementing effective prevention programs for Hispanic women prisoners (20).

What "Works" in Women's Prison Programs? "Almost nothing is known about its effectiveness," Candace Kruttschnitt and Rosemary Gartner (2004, 47) write about programming *inside* women's prisons. For the few evaluations available, they urge caution in interpreting them because some are based on very small samples (20 or fewer women offenders); also, randomized assessments and adequate follow-up periods (16 weeks maximum) are rare (48). Merry Morash and her colleagues (1998) summarized the "what works" component of the innovative programs intended to meet women's needs in their survey:

> Although corrections administrators could identify programs they considered innovative and program administrators could list program characteristics conducive to success, few outcome evaluations have been conducted so far. The review of both published and unpublished literature that preceded this study revealed written reports on the outcomes of just 68 [out of 212 cited] programs, actual measurement for 12, and measurement of recidivism for just 6 of these. (11)

The overall picture regarding evaluations of effectiveness is pretty dismal, but there are exceptions. Like Tessa Hale's (2001) evaluation of the Women in Community Services (WICS) Life Skills Program. WICS provides women a 9-to-12 week curriculum before their release. According to Hale, re-arrest rates for WICS graduates are significantly lower (35 percent) than for women in other programs (48 percent). But this evaluation has problems, too; Kruttschnitt and Gartner warn us that Hale doesn't "provide information about the length of the follow-up period and whether the assignment to treatment and control groups was randomized" (48).

Law in Prison Society

Conviction for a crime results in a fundamental transformation in constitutional and legal status for the criminal. It turns a defendant who at least formally is armed with all the rights of a free person into an offender stripped of constitutional rights (Chapter 9). But are defendants stripped bare, or are they left with some rights? The Thirteenth Amendment to the U.S. Constitution has something to say about this: It abolishes slavery, "except as a punishment for crime whereof the party shall have been duly convicted." Shortly after the amendment was adopted after the Civil War, a Virginia court in *Ruffin v. Commonwealth* (1871) explained what the Thirteenth Amendment means to prisoners:

> The bill of rights is a declaration of general principles to govern a society of freemen, and not of convicted felons and men civilly dead. Such men have some rights it is true, such as the law in its benignity accords to them, but not the rights of freemen. They are the slaves of the State undergoing punishment for heinous crimes committed against the laws of the land. While in this state of penal servitude, they must be subject to the regulations of the institution of which they are inmates, and the laws of the State to whom their service is due in expiation of their crimes.

The U.S. Supreme Court has gone so far as to say that "prison brutality...is part of the total punishment to which the individual is being subjected for his crime." These strong words don't mean prisoners have no rights; it does mean they have minimal rights.

According to the principle of **civil death,** a practice going back to ancient Rome, the law treats felons as if they were dead when it comes to political and legal rights. The practice survives today in taking away felons' right to vote. But the details of this lost right are a mosaic of state laws, summed up by The Sentencing Project (2005):

civil death denial of political and legal rights to felons

State Disenfranchisement Laws

- Forty-eight states and the District of Columbia prohibit inmates from voting while incarcerated for a felony offense.
- Only two states—Maine and Vermont—permit inmates to vote.
- Thirty-five states prohibit felons from voting while they are on parole, and 31 of these states exclude felony probationers as well.
- Six states deny the right to vote to all ex-offenders who have completed their sentences. Eight others disenfranchise certain categories of ex-offenders and/or permit application for restoration of rights for specified offenses after a waiting period (e.g., five years in Delaware and Wyoming, and three years in Maryland).
- Each state has developed its own process of restoring voting rights to ex-offenders, but most of these restoration processes are so cumbersome that few ex-offenders are able to take advantage of them. (1)

The Sentencing Project lists the following results of disenfranchisement:

- An estimated 4.7 million Americans, or 1 in 43 adults, have currently or permanently lost their voting rights as a result of a felony conviction.
- Approximately 1.4 million Black men, or 13 percent, are disenfranchised— a rate seven times the national average.
- An estimated 676,730 women are currently ineligible to vote as a result of a felony conviction. (1)
- More than 2 million white Americans (Hispanic and non-Hispanic) are disenfranchised.
- In six states that deny the vote to ex-offenders, 1 in 4 Black men is permanently disenfranchised.
- Given current rates of incarceration, 3 in 10 of the next generation of Black men can expect to be disenfranchised at some point in their lifetime.

- In states that disenfranchise ex-offenders, as many as 40 percent of Black men may permanently lose their right to vote.
- Approximately 1.7 million disenfranchised persons are ex-offenders who have completed their sentences. The state of Florida had an estimated 600,000 ex-felons who were unable to vote in the 2000 presidential election.

We'll further explore the consequences of disenfranchisement *after* ex-offenders leave prison, in "The Right to Vote and Reentry" section on page 522.

So what rights do prisoners have while they're still *in* prison? We'll look at the policy of hands-off prisons taken by the courts at various periods, an overview of which rights prisoners do maintain, their rights in practice, and how prison grievance procedures work when prisoners argue their rights have been violated.

The Hands-Off Doctrine

Until the 1960s, courts practically never interfered with prison life. Courts adopted a **hands-off doctrine;** prison administrators determined how prisons were run and the way prisoners were treated. According to the hands-off doctrine, the law didn't follow convicted offenders into prison; it left them at the prison gate. Prison conditions and prison society were none of the courts' business.

The main justification for this policy was that judges weren't qualified to run prisons. They weren't trained in prison administration, and they were far removed from prison life. So it didn't make sense for judges to substitute their judgments for those of the experts—wardens and officers. Another reason for the doctrine was the mission of punishment. Prisons are supposed to be unpleasant. Finally, the doctrine was necessary for prison security. Prisoners' rights backed up by judicial intervention would have been a recipe for prison unrest and even riots (Baker et al. 1973, 454).

However, in the 1960s, a combination of forces led to limiting the hands-off doctrine. Prisoners' rights were added to the agenda of the civil rights movement. Black and Hispanic prisoners sued wardens and states over prison conditions and the treatment of minority prisoners. Disillusionment with rehabilitation shifted the emphasis from the needs of prisoners to their rights.

The prisoners' rights movement got help from a few activist federal judges who gave prisoners a forum by letting them bring their grievances to their courts. Having as respected a grievance forum as the federal courts generated great solidarity among prisoners, and this prisoner solidarity made the prisoners' rights movement even stronger. However, without the support of a new breed of prison lawyers—specialists who knew how to voice complaints and frame grievances in legal and constitutional terms—the prisoners' rights movement would have died "aborning." According to James B. Jacobs (1983), a leading scholar of prisons and the rights of prisoners:

> A platoon, eventually a phalanx, of prisoners' rights lawyers, supported by federal and foundation funding, soon appeared and pressed claims. They initiated, and won, prisoners' rights cases that implicated every aspect of prison governance. In many cases the prisoners' attorneys were more dedicated and effective than the overburdened and inexperienced government attorneys who represented the prison officials. (39)

Overview of Prisoners' Rights

Ever since the 1960s, courts have made it clear that prisoners don't leave their constitutional rights at the prison gates—but their rights are severely restricted. Too many people believe prisoners are always suing over every little thing they don't like and are winning their lawsuits. (We'll see later how far from reality this is.) In defining the limits of these rights, courts use a balancing test of prisoners' rights: they look at all the facts of each case and weigh the shrunken rights of prisoners against the prison's powerful missions of punishment, security, order, and discipline. It shouldn't surprise you to learn that the powerful prison missions almost always trump the shrunken rights of prisoners.

With all that said, here is the list of rights prisoners keep in shrunken form:

1. Access to the courts
2. Due process of law
3. Equal protection of the laws
4. First Amendment rights of free speech, association, and religion
5. The Eighth Amendment right against "cruel and unusual punishment"
6. Fourth Amendment rights against unreasonable searches and seizures

The Right to Go to Court Prisoners keep the right to go to court. The right to go to court includes the right to challenge the legality, the length, and the conditions of their confinement; the right to a lawyer, including a jailhouse lawyer (prisoners who help other prisoners on points of law); and access to law libraries, transcripts of their cases, and other materials they need to present their claims.

Due Process of Law The Fifth and the Fourteenth Amendments guarantee that neither the federal government nor state governments can "deprive any person of life, liberty, or property without due process of law" (Chapter 3). Compared with free people, prisoners are "due" a lot less "life, liberty, and property" and a lot less process to protect them from deprivation of what little life, liberty, and property they have a right to. So in determining whether state officials have deprived prison inmates of these rights, courts look at how great the deprivation of life, liberty, or property is and decide how shrunken the procedures to deprive inmates of life, liberty, or property can be.

According to the U.S. Supreme Court, "certain changes in conditions may be so severe or so different from ordinary conditions of confinement . . . the state authorities" can't make the changes "without complying with the minimum requirements of due process of law" (*Sandin v. Conner* 1995, 493). So involuntarily committing an inmate to a mental hospital, forcing a prisoner to take antipsychotic drugs in prison, and taking away "good time" are severe enough to be protected by the due process clause. But most deprivations don't qualify. (See the In Focus box "Do Death Row Prisoners Have a 'Right' to Watch TV?") According to U.S. Supreme Court Justice David Breyer:

> Prison by design restricts the inmate's freedom. And one cannot properly view unimportant matters that happen to be the subject of prison regulations as substantially aggravating loss that has already occurred. Indeed, a regulation about a minor matter, for example, a regulation that seems to cabin the discretionary power of a prison administrator to deprive an inmate of, say, a certain kind of lunch may amount simply to an instruction to the administrator about how to do his job, rather than a guarantee to the inmate of a "right" to the status quo. Thus, this court has never held that comparatively unimportant prisoner "deprivations" fall within the scope of the Due Process Clause. . . . I recognize that, as a consequence, courts must separate the unimportant from the potentially significant. . . . It seems to me possible to separate less significant matters such as television privileges, "sack" versus "tray" lunches, playing the state lottery, attending an ex-stepfather's funeral, or the limits of travel when on prison furlough, from more significant matters. (*Sandin v. Conner* 1995, 499–500)

The Court also has decided some matters that might seem serious aren't serious enough to qualify for due process protection, like solitary confinement for 30 days or transferring prisoners from medium to maximum security prisons and even to supermaxes.

Assuming prison authorities have deprived prisoners of rights protected by due process, how much process are prisoners due? The Supreme Court has ruled that prisoners are definitely not entitled to the "full panoply of rights due" an ordinary person in a criminal trial. The state can satisfy the requirements of due process by providing prisoners:

Do Death Row Prisoners Have a "Right" to Watch TV?

A proposal to give death row inmates access to television is getting poor reception from the head of the state prison system's board of directors.

Of the 38 states that have capital punishment, Texas is the only one that does not allow condemned prisoners at least limited access to TV, say attorneys with the Texas American Civil Liberties Union. They also are the only Texas inmates who aren't allowed some amount of viewing time, a privilege that some experts believe helps ease behavior problems.

The ban doesn't appear likely to change in the near future, say ACLU officials, who can't get the chairwoman of the Texas Board of Criminal Justice to even discuss the subject.

In May, ACLU prison project litigation director Yolanda Torres attempted to broach the idea in a letter to Chairwoman Christina Melton Crain.

"We believe it is significant that every other death row in the country has successfully developed and implemented policies and practices that allow death row prisoners access to television, while at the same time maintaining the safety and security of their employees and institutions," Torres wrote.

Crain responded two months later that the issue was not open for debate.

"I appreciate the passion and energy that you bring to matters for which you advocate," Crain wrote. "But as the Board and the current Administration do not wish to entertain this issue further, dialogue between you and me on this subject is now closed."

Crain did not respond to requests from the *Houston Chronicle* for an interview. However, through a spokesman, she e-mailed a brief statement.

"The Texas Department of Criminal Justice does not provide television privileges to offenders (on)...death row," she stated, "and the board of criminal justice has no plans to amend this policy."

STARK DIFFERENCE

Life on death row has been drastically different since 1999, when the condemned inmates were moved from the Ellis Unit in Huntsville, where they were allowed to watch television, to what is now the Polunsky Unit in Livingston.

Privileges for death row inmates were reduced to the level of administrative segregation, or solitary confinement.

Now condemned prisoners are confined for 23 hours each day in their cells, which measure 6 1/2 feet by 10 feet. They receive one hour of daily recreation, either in an inside recreation yard or outdoor recreation area. They also receive their meals in their cells, are escorted to showers once daily and are escorted to the infirmary if they need medical care.

Death row inmates no longer participate in work programs.

They can be interviewed by the news media on Wednesdays and are allowed to meet with their attorneys Monday through Friday and occasionally on weekends through special arrangement.

Condemned inmates also may have visits from approved spiritual advisers and one general visit per week for a two-hour period. That period can be extended if a visitor has traveled more than 300 miles.

Death row prisoners also can receive newspapers and magazines through subscriptions and are allowed to spend $75 every 14 days in the unit's commissary on hygiene supplies and snacks.

SOME DON'T SEE A PROBLEM

The lack of TV viewing time is just fine with victims' rights activists.

"Convicted felons lose certain rights and privileges, and even more so for death row inmates," said Andy Kahan, victims' rights advocate for the city of Houston.

---

1. An unbiased review board or committee
2. Notice of the proposed action and the grounds for it
3. An opportunity to "present reasons why the proposed action should not be taken" (*Sandin v. Conner* 1995, 490)

Due process *doesn't* include the right to a lawyer or to confront the witnesses against them.

Equal Protection of the Laws The Fourteenth Amendment guarantees all individuals, including prisoners, equal protection of the laws. However, as you learned in Chapter 3, the equal protection clause doesn't guarantee all groups will be treated exactly alike. Groups can be treated differently if there's a good reason for doing so. The most common equal protection claim prisoners make is racial and ethnic discrimination. In ordinary circumstances, race is never a good enough reason to treat people differently. But prison is different. Accord-

"The pain, misery and grief that death row inmates have caused, committing some of the worst crimes known to mankind, should not be rewarded."

Kahan suggests that the inmates take out Book of the Month Club memberships and be required to write monthly book reports.

Dianne Clements of the group Justice For All adds that death row's configuration would require putting TV sets in individual cells.

That, she says, would provide another hiding place for contraband and a source for makeshift weapons. On Aug. 18, condemned murderer Jorge Salinas stabbed a prison guard 13 times with a metal rod from a typewriter. The guard was not seriously injured.

But the ACLU's Torres contends that, if 37 other prison systems found ways to provide TV access for death row, Texas officials should be able to do so.

Another supporter of TV on death row is Chase Riveland, the former director of the state prison systems in Washington and Colorado. He says some degree of access to television can be an important tool for keeping prisoners in line.

"In most jurisdictions, in order to have a television, an inmate has to have a good disciplinary record," said Riveland, now a consultant who has 36 years of correctional experience.

"If the inmates know they're going to lose their television if they misbehave, they're going to be very cautious about it, especially if they're in a lockdown situation (as in Texas), because that's their only real connection with the real world."

Riveland added that, in most other states, inmates' families pay for the TV sets.

"I can't even fathom why one wouldn't want to use such an inexpensive tool," he said.

He also suggests that the use of televisions on death row might actually ensure that inmates are mentally fit to be executed.

If kept in isolation, he said, "the odds of inmates becoming mentally ill are greatly enhanced."

"That, of course, then leads to all types of challenges against whether you can execute them," Riveland said.

"And so, by not having televisions or other means of keeping them mentally alert, it may add to the taxpayer drain through additional litigation."

RECONSIDERATION REQUEST

Texas ACLU Executive Director Will Harrell recently asked Crain to reconsider her "summary dismissal" of the organization's attempt to discuss the TV issue with prison officials.

Meredith Martin Rountree, the Texas ACLU's prison project director, believes Crain's decision is based on misguided popular opinion.

"TDCJ's job is not to pander to public misunderstandings and misconceptions about criminal justice," Rountree said.

"Its job is to run a safe and constitutional prison system and to make decisions based on sound, penological justifications.

"Every death row in the country has not only investigated this issue but has found that televisions are good management tools," Rountree said. "Why is TDCJ different?"

WHAT'S ALLOWED

Texas death row inmates can keep these items in their cells:

- *Miscellaneous:* radios, fans, hot pots, typewriters, religious and legal materials, mail, art supplies, and books
- *Games:* chess and checkers boards; inmates can play by numbering the positions on the boards and shouting their moves to each other

Source: Steve McVicker, "Proposal for TVs on death row tuned out; Backers say state is ignoring a tool to control the condemned," *The Houston Chronicle,* September 5, 2004, p. A1. Copyright 2004 Houston Chronicle Publishing Company. Reprinted with permission. All rights reserved.

ing to the Supreme Court, prison administrators have "the right, acting in good faith and in particularized circumstances, to take into account racial tensions in maintaining security, discipline, and good order" (*Lee v. Washington,* 1968, 334).

Free Speech, Association, and Religion Prisoners keep their First Amendment rights to expression, association, and religion only so far as they don't conflict with the prison's missions. In other words, courts balance prisoners' shrunken First Amendment rights against the broad need to accomplish the missions of prisons to punish prisoners and maintain security, safety, and discipline. So prison administrators can censor the correspondence of prisoners. In *Procunier v. Martinez* (1974), the U.S. Supreme Court ruled that California's prison censorship rules were constitutional because they were designed to maintain security, order, and rehabilitation and because First Amendment freedoms were restricted only enough to ensure security, order, and rehabilitation.

Do Prisoners Have a Right against Unreasonable Searches and Seizures?

FACTS

Russell Palmer Jr. is an inmate at the Bland Correctional Center in Bland, Virginia, serving sentences for forgery, uttering, grand larceny, and bank robbery convictions. On September 16, 1981, Ted Hudson, an officer at the Correctional Center, with a fellow officer, conducted a "shakedown" search of Palmer's prison locker and cell for contraband. During the "shakedown," the officers discovered a ripped pillowcase in a trash can near the respondent's cell bunk. Charges against Palmer were instituted under the prison disciplinary procedures for destroying state property. After a hearing, Palmer was found guilty on the charge and was ordered to reimburse the State for the cost of the material destroyed; in addition, a reprimand was entered on his prison record.

U.S. SUPREME COURT OPINION

We have repeatedly held that prisons are not beyond the reach of the Constitution. No "iron curtain" separates one from the other. Indeed, we have insisted that prisoners be accorded those rights not fundamentally inconsistent with imprisonment itself or incompatible with the objectives of incarceration. For example, we have held that invidious racial discrimination is as intolerable within a prison as outside, except as may be essential to "prison security and discipline."

However, while persons imprisoned for crime enjoy many protections of the Constitution, it is also clear that imprisonment carries with it the loss of many significant rights. These constraints on inmates, and in some cases the complete withdrawal of certain rights, are "justified by the considerations underlying our penal system." The curtailment of certain rights is necessary, as a practical matter, to accommodate a myriad of "institutional needs and objectives" of prison facilities, chief among which is internal security. Of course, these restrictions or retractions also serve, incidentally, as reminders that, under our system of justice, deterrence and retribution are factors in addition to correction.

We have not before been called upon to decide the specific question whether the Fourth Amendment applies within a prison cell.... We hold that society is not prepared to recognize as legitimate any subjective expectation of privacy that a prisoner might have in his prison cell and that, accordingly, the Fourth Amendment proscription against unreasonable searches does not apply within the confines of the prison cell. The recognition of privacy rights for prisoners in their individual cells simply cannot be reconciled with the concept of incarceration and the needs and objectives of penal institutions.

Prisons, by definition, are places of involuntary confinement of persons who have a demonstrated proclivity for anti-social criminal, and often violent, conduct. Inmates have necessarily shown a lapse in the ability to control and conform their behavior to the legitimate standards of society by the normal impulses of self-restraint; they have shown an inability to regulate their conduct in a way that reflects either a respect for law or an appreciation of the rights of others.

Right against Cruel and Unusual Punishment The Eighth Amendment prohibits "cruel and unusual punishments." This prohibition is aimed specifically at the protection of prisoners. Nevertheless, the Eighth Amendment doesn't ban "every government action affecting the interests or well-being of a prisoner." According to the Court:

> Only the unnecessary and wanton infliction of pain constitutes cruel and unusual punishment forbidden by the Eighth Amendment.... It is obduracy and wantonness, not inadvertence or error in good faith, that characterize the conduct prohibited by the Eighth Amendment clause, whether that conduct occurs in connection with establishing conditions of confinement, supplying medical needs, or restoring official control over a tumultuous cellblock. The infliction of pain in the course of a prison security, therefore, does not amount to cruel and unusual punishment simply because it may appear in retrospect that the degree of force authorized or applied for security purposes was unreasonable. (*Whitley v. Albers* 1986, 319)

In *Whitley v. Albers*, prisoners took a correctional officer hostage during a riot at the Oregon State Penitentiary and held him in the upper tier of a two-tier cell block. Prison officials developed a plan to free the hostage. According to the plan, the prison security manager entered the cell block unarmed. Armed prison officials followed him. The security manager ordered one of the officers to fire a "warning shot and to shoot low at any inmates climbing the stairs to the upper

The administration of a prison, we have said, is "at best an extraordinarily difficult undertaking." But it would be literally impossible to accomplish the prison objectives identified above if inmates retained a right of privacy in their cells. Virtually the only place inmates can conceal weapons, drugs, and other contraband is in their cells. Unfettered access to these cells by prison officials, thus, is imperative if drugs and contraband are to be ferreted out and sanitary surroundings are to be maintained.

Determining whether an expectation of privacy is "legitimate" or "reasonable" necessarily entails a balancing of interests. The two interests here are the interest of society in the security of its penal institutions and the interest of the prisoner in privacy within his cell. The latter interest, of course, is already limited by the exigencies of the circumstances: A prison "shares none of the attributes of privacy of a home, an automobile, an office, or a hotel room."

We strike the balance in favor of institutional security, which we have noted is "central to all other corrections goals." A right of privacy in traditional Fourth Amendment terms is fundamentally incompatible with the close and continual surveillance of inmates and their cells required to ensure institutional security and internal order. We are satisfied that society would insist that the prisoner's expectation of privacy always yield to what must be considered the paramount interest in institutional security. We believe that it is accepted by our society that "loss of freedom of choice and privacy are inherent incidents of confinement."

DISSENTING OPINION

Prison guard Hudson maliciously took and destroyed a quantity of Palmer's property, including legal materials and letters, for no reason other than harassment. Measured by the conditions that prevail in a free society, neither the possessions nor the slight residuum of privacy that a prison inmate can retain in his cell can have more than the most minimal value. From the standpoint of the prisoner, however, that trivial residuum may mark the difference between slavery and humanity.

Personal letters, snapshots of family members, a souvenir, a deck of cards, a hobby kit, perhaps a diary or a training manual for an apprentice in a new trade, or even a Bible—a variety of inexpensive items may enable a prisoner to maintain contact with some part of his past and an eye to the possibility of a better future. Are all of these items subject to unrestrained perusal, confiscation or mutilation at the hands of a possibly hostile guard? Is the Court correct in its perception that "society" is not prepared to recognize any privacy or possessory interest of the prison inmate—no matter how remote the threat to prison security may be?

It is well-settled that the discretion accorded prison officials is not absolute. A prisoner retains those constitutional rights not inconsistent with legitimate penological objectives. There can be no penological justification for the seizure alleged here. There is no contention that Palmer's property posed any threat to institutional security. Hudson had already examined the material before he took and destroyed it. The allegation is that Hudson did this for no reason save spite; there is no contention that under prison regulations the material was contraband. The need for "close and continual surveillance of inmates and their cells," in no way justifies taking and destroying non-contraband property; if material is examined and found not to be contraband, there can be no justification for its seizure.

Source: Hudson v. Palmer, 468 U.S. 517 (1984).

---

tier" since he would be climbing the stairs to free the hostage. Assistant Warden Harold Whitley, after firing the warning shot, shot inmate Gerald Albers in the knee when he tried to climb the stairs. Albers contended that shooting him was cruel and unusual punishment. The Court agreed that, in hindsight, the use of deadly force was probably excessive, but it wasn't "cruel and unusual punishment" if the officers acted in "good faith." Why? Because shooting him wasn't an "intentional and wanton infliction of pain" (313).

Right against Unreasonable Searches and Seizures The Fourth Amendment protects the people against unreasonable searches and seizures by any agent of the government (see Chapter 7). But the right of prisoners against unreasonable searches and seizures is extremely limited. (Some critics say it's nonexistent.) Surveillance, cell and strip searches, monitored visits, censored mail, and other restrictions on privacy are basic parts of prison life, justified on the grounds that prisoners are in prison as punishment; besides the invasions help to ensure secure, safe, and orderly prisons.

In the leading case on the Fourth Amendment rights of prisoners, *Hudson v. Palmer,* the U.S. Supreme Court ruled that prisoners have *no* right to privacy in their cells, even if the motive for the search was malice against the prisoner whose cell was searched. (See the In Focus box "Do Prisoners Have a Right against Unreasonable Searches and Seizures?")

Prisoners' Rights in Operation

Beginning in the late 1970s and continuing into the 2000s, the U.S. Supreme Court further limited prisoners' rights, returning to prison administrators most of the discretion they enjoyed during the hands-off era. Typical of this move is the important case of *Bell v. Wolfish* (1979), in which the Court ruled that prisoners had no right to a single cell. Justice Rehnquist wrote:

> The deplorable conditions and draconian restrictions of our Nation's prisons are too well known to retell here, and the Federal courts rightly have condemned these sordid aspects of our prison systems. But many of these same courts have, in the name of the Constitution, become increasingly enmeshed in the minutiae of prison operations. Judges, after all, are human. They (like the rest of us) have a natural tendency to believe their individual solutions to tough problems are better and more workable than the officials who have to run the particular institution under examination.
>
> The first question isn't whose plan is best, but which branch of government the Constitution charges with designing the plan. This doesn't mean constitutional rights are not to be scrupulously observed. What it *does* mean is that the inquiry of federal courts into prison management can't go further than inquiring whether a particular system violates any ban in the Constitution (or in Federal prisons, a Federal statute). The wide range of "judgment calls" that meet constitutional and statutory requirements are left to administrative officials outside the courts.

Not only has the Supreme Court restricted the rights of prisoners and returned discretionary judgment to prison officials, but most prisoners fail in their lawsuits even when the Court has accepted that they have rights against discretionary decision making by prison administrators. Most prisoners' cases never get beyond the earliest stages of the proceedings. In California, for example, the court terminated 80.4 percent of prisoners' cases shortly after they filed their suits and before prison administrators even responded. Nationwide, 68 percent of all prisoners' cases were dropped at this early stage. Due to early dismissal, only 4.2 percent of all cases filed ever get to trial (Thomas 1989, 27–54).

Even when prisoners succeed in getting their cases into court, they practically never "win." In one sample of 664 cases, only three court orders were issued regarding confinement conditions; only two prisoners were awarded minimal money damages. In a few more cases, seven temporary restraining orders and five preliminary injunctions were issued. Most cases that get to trial are cases of prisoners who have lawyers; lawyers are probably a necessity. In the two cited cases awarded damages, the prisoner with a lawyer received $200; the one without a lawyer got only $6! (Thomas 1989, 27–54).

On the other hand, Jack E. Call found that prisoners meet with greater success in prison crowding cases. Courts issued favorable rulings in 73.8 percent of all cases, 80 percent in federal district courts, and 66 percent in courts of appeals. According to Call (1988), many courts have made it clear that prison administrative discretion in managing prisons will not shield prisons from litigation involving "gruesome living conditions" (34–41).

In fairness, although prisoners win few victories in lower federal courts, court cases still affect life in prisons. Even a lost case can lead to prison reform. Prison administrators don't want courts to intrude into their domain, so they sometimes make changes to avoid the intrusions. Jim Thomas (1989), in his analysis of prisoner litigation, quotes one prison administrator on the effects of prisoner lawsuits:

> Where only a few years ago prisons operated without written rules and with only the most rudimentary record keeping systems, today prison authorities are engulfed in bureaucratic paper. There are regulations, guidelines, policy statements, and general orders; there are forms, files, and reports for virtually everything. (27)

Litigation has also increased centralization and oversight by correctional administrations.

Although, in the short term, court orders may reduce staff morale and even cause prison violence, court restrictions on crowding have increased prison and jail construction, according to Malcolm Feeley and Roger Hanson (1987). Court orders have also mitigated the most extreme abusive conditions in prisons. A detailed study of four major prison condition cases found that compliance, although grudging, slow, and incomplete, led all four states to spend substantial amounts of money responding to court orders. In some cases, new prisons were built following litigation. It is unlikely this would've occurred if prisoners hadn't sued their keepers (Harris and Spiller 1977).

Internal Grievance Mechanisms

Lawsuits aren't the only redress for prisoners who have grievances against prison administration. Every prison has some kind of internal grievance mechanism operated by prison officers and sometimes outside participants, including former prisoners. Although not totally supported by either prisoners or prison critics, internal grievance proceedings play a significant part in prison governance and life (Brakel 1983, 394).

Most state prison systems have broad powers to hear complaints. Illinois, for example, opens its Institutional Inquiry Board (IIB) to any prisoner who wants "resolution to complaints, problems, and grievances which [he or she has] not been able to resolve through other avenues available at the institution or facility" (Brakel 1982, 117). Let's look at some common grievances and grievance procedures.

Common Grievances and Disciplinary Violations Grievances, such as these raised in Illinois, are common:

- Claims for early release
- Charges that guards issued disciplinary "tickets" improperly
- Complaints that work or program assignments were not right
- Claims that prisoners were classified wrong
- Charges that property was lost, stolen, or confiscated

Common disciplinary actions against prisoners include "tickets" for:

- Creating dangerous disturbances
- Disobeying a direct order
- Undertaking unauthorized movement
- Assaulting another prisoner or an officer
- Destroying or damaging property
- Possessing dangerous contraband
- Engaging in sexual misconduct (Brakel 1982, 117)

The Minnesota Department of Corrections (n.d.) gives all prisoners a written statement of 10 procedures they're guaranteed in all grievance proceedings:

1. A published list of the charges and penalties
2. A prompt and full statement of the nature of the alleged violation no later than five days after the prisoner is charged with a prison rule violation
3. The right to adequate notice prior to the hearing
4. The opportunity for a prisoner to appear in person before the disciplinary hearing board and be heard
5. The right to bring witnesses and present evidence to the hearing
6. The right to an impartial hearing board
7. The right to counsel or substitute counsel throughout the process
8. A written notice of the board's findings

9. The right to appeal to the warden or another designated person
10. The right to a record of the proceedings at the hearing for review and appeal

Most prisoners' complaints are registered against their classification and the amount of good time they're entitled to. For example, under the Illinois good-time rule, prisoners get their sentences reduced one day for every day of good time they served. Discipline violations can reduce this good time. Also in Illinois, prisoners are classified either as A, B, or C. Grade A entitles prisoners to maximum freedom and privileges; C is for maximum security and the least freedom. Disciplinary tickets might lead to downgrading a prisoner's security level. A challenge to a disciplinary ticket might be, therefore, grounds to grieve reduced good time and a security reclassification. For example, violating the Illinois prison rule against forced sexual contacts can reduce good time by 360 days and downgrade prisoners to grade C security for 360 days (Brakel 1983, 412).

Another ground for complaint is when administrators deny prisoners' requests to be put into protective custody. Protective custody means living in a segregation unit for protection from other prisoners. One grievance arose when prison officials denied a request for protective custody to a 6'4" White man weighing 210 pounds against Black gang members. Prison officials argued he was big enough to protect himself (Brakel 1983, 414–415).

Missing prisoners' property is another source of complaint. Most commonly, these complaints arise because the administration has confiscated unauthorized property or contraband. Other common cases involve lost or stolen prisoner property. According to the prisoner, the administration didn't protect the property or didn't pay for damage or loss. Even though property cases don't usually involve a lot of money, they're important. First, they make up a considerable number of grievances filed. Second, items such as photographs, jewelry, and jackets may have sentimental value to the prisoner. These items may be all that provides individuality in an otherwise very impersonal and regulated place.

Ending the Abusive Treatment of Prisoners: Overview of the treatment of prisoners worldwide by the Human Rights Watch. To reach this site go to "Web Links" on your Samaha CJ7 website: http://cj.wadsworth.com/samaha_cj7e.

Grievance Procedures and Their Effects Grievance decision making is two-tiered. Members of a local grievance committee, drawn entirely from within the prison, initially decide for or against the prisoner. Prisoners can appeal decisions against them to a board made up of private citizens and correctional administrators. Proceedings are formal, governed by written rules and regulations. Prisoners have basic due process rights, usually including the right to be present at the hearing, sometimes the right to have witnesses and to challenge adverse evidence, and the right to have a decision in writing within a specified time period. This written decision has to give the reasons for the board's ruling. Prisoners have to go through the whole internal grievance procedure before they can take their cases to court, a requirement called exhausting administrative remedies.

Prisoners hardly ever win their grievance cases. One prisoner overestimated the win ratio when he said, "You don't win more than 1 in 10." In fact, it's less. One review of grievances in several cell blocks showed that prisoners won only 1 case out of 12 in one block, 1 of 19 in a second, 1 of 25 in a third, and only 1 of 28 in a fourth. On appeal to a review board, the results were also low. In one maximum security prison, prisoners "won" 17 percent of the appeals and lost 75 percent. Another 8 percent had mixed results (Brakel 1982, 124–126).

Grievance procedures in prisons have several missions, to:

- Improve prison management and help identify problems
- Reduce inmate frustration and prison violence
- Aid prisoner rehabilitation
- Reduce the number of cases prisoners take to the courts
- Bring "justice" to prisons

Existing grievance mechanisms may or may not accomplish their missions. Research has raised several questions. To improve prison management by identifying problems, the first aim, prison administrators have to take the time periodically to review caseloads to determine what kinds of grievances prisoners have. Only by reviewing the grievances can something be done about them. This takes time and resources most prisons simply don't have. To achieve this aim might require prisoners to bring grievances more selectively; instead of using grievance procedures to express "rights consciousness" or harassment, they might have to "purify" their complaints. According to prison litigation expert Jan Brakel (1982):

> The message to inmates should be that abusing the procedures for frivolous, repetitive grievances harms the chances of other inmates, and ultimately their own, of having important things changed. (129)

Few prison officials go so far as to say grievance procedures *eliminate* violence from prisons. They may provide a "safety valve" for prisoner discontent and "keep the lid on" violent prison outbreaks, but there's no proof this is true. Correlations between violence levels and prison grievance mechanisms simply don't exist. Through grievance procedures, an inmate here and there might develop more respect for procedures and be willing to follow them. These inmates are probably "rehabilitated," in the sense that they're more ready to live inside (and outside) prison without breaking the rules. However, most prisoners don't see grievance mechanisms positively. In many cases, prisoners see them only as proof that institutions rig decisions to maintain the establishment against dissidents—in this case, prison officials against prisoners (Brakel 1982, 130).

Proving grievance mechanisms reduce the load of cases in courts is also difficult. Grievance mechanisms may reduce caseloads by resolving grievances inside prison but they're likely to increase litigation because prisoners who are more conscious of their rights are more apt to demand them. If they don't win in prison, they'll take their fights to the courts. The bottom line (as we've learned so many times in this book) is there's no empirical support for any of these speculations.

Finally, it's not clear that grievance mechanisms bring justice to prisons. For that to be the case, according to Jan Brakel (1982, 133), administrators and prisoners have to use them to their best advantage,

> instead of playing games with them, games of power, games of psychology, harassment games, legalistic games, passing time games, and so forth. At neither Vienna nor Stateville were the procedures used to full advantage—the staff failed to maximize both the problem-identification and the problem-disposition potential of the process, and far too many of the inmates abused the process with groundless or frivolous claims.

Several recommendations aim at bringing the reality of grievance mechanisms closer to their proclaimed missions. One suggests changing the composition of the grievance body. Prisoners and other critics commonly complain that prison officials dominate grievance mechanisms. They call for more outside participation, either by citizens or prisoners. However, although outsiders may be impartial, they're also naive and ignorant of prison society and can therefore be "conned" by both prisoners and administration. Prisoners aren't necessarily a good choice either. They can be partial and subject to intimidation and physical danger if they rule against another prisoner.

Other reformers call for formal decision making, including written rules of procedure, adherence to decisions in prior cases, more documentation of proceedings, and putting decisions in writing. Some believe, however, that there's already enough "paper"; the real problem is how to use the documentation to achieve fair and just results. Demands for more investigation, more listening to the prisoners' side of the story, and so on accomplish little if all they do is add to an already heavily burdened grievance body (Brakel 1982, 136–137).

Perhaps the severest criticism is that too many frivolous and trumped-up grievances, or ones brought only to harass, are filed. Grievances have to be screened more carefully, but no one's quite sure how to do this. How does anyone decide, before hearings begin, whether a complaint has merit or is a farce—something "cooked up to obstruct the system, harass the staff, pass dead time"? Once proceedings begin, however, frivolous claims often come to light. At that point, they could be penalized, and such penalties might take several forms. Privileges such as movies, TV, or visits to the commissary could be taken away. Refiling restrictions could be imposed if present grievances are decided to be frivolous or spurious. Extreme cases might even call for the levy of fines (Brakel 1982, 139).

Leaving Prison

Let's be clear on an important point: When it comes to offenders who go to prison, "they all come back" home (Travis 2000, 1). Well, *almost* all—5 percent are executed or die before they leave. In 2004 (and for several years before), over 600,000 prisoners and 10,000,000 jail inmates went home (Solomon, Waul, Van Ness, and Travis 2004, 12). Of course, prisoners have always gone home; and corrections officials have always struggled with the problem of **prisoner reentry** (the process of leaving prison and returning to society). But beginning in the 1990s, reentry changed a lot. The huge increase in the numbers of released prisoners (the highest in our history) has stretched resources to the point where officials worry that they can't carry out their two main missions: protect the public and assist in successfully reintegrating released prisoners.

Research confirms that today's reentering prisoners need more supervision and assistance than prisoners in the past (Table 14.2). Why? According to Amy Solomon and her colleagues at the Urban Institute (2004) in a survey of reentry programs:

> Not only are more prisoners returning home than ever before, but they are also returning less prepared for life outside the walls. Many will have difficulty managing the most basic ingredients for successful reintegration—reconnecting with jobs, housing, and their families, and accessing needed substance abuse and health care treatment. Most will be arrested in three years, and many will be returned to prison for new crimes or parole violations. The cycle of incarceration and reentry into society carries the potential for profound adverse consequences for prisoners, their families, and communities. (12)

prisoner reentry the process of prisoners' leaving prison and returning to society

Ready4Work Prisoner Reentry Initiative: An overview of this program by the Center for Faith-Based and Community Initiatives, U.S. Department of Labor. To reach this site go to "Web Links" on your Samaha CJ7 website: http://cj.wadsworth.com/samaha_cj7e.

▼ TABLE 14.2 Problems More Acute among Today's Reentering Prisoners Than for Past Reentering Prisoners

• More disconnected from the potential support of their families and friends	• Less employable
• More health problems linked to untreated substance abuse and physical and mental illnesses	• Barred from receiving public assistance, like food stamps, health care, and housing
• Less educated	

Source: Joan Petersilia, "What Works in Reentry? Reviewing and Questioning the Evidence," *Federal Probation* (September 2004), 4; Amy Solomon, Michelle Waul, Asheley Van Ness, and Jeremy Travis, *Outside the Walls: A National Snapshot of Community-Based Prisoner Reentry Programs* (Washington, DC: Urban Institute, 2004), 12.

Since the 1980s, reentering prisoners have served more time in prison, especially for drug crimes (Lynch and Sabol 2001, 8). But that hasn't deterred two-thirds of all prisoners from getting arrested and half from committing another crime within three years (Solomon et al. 2004, 128). Paradoxically, while the number of "churners" (offenders who are returned to prison for technical violations or for committing new crimes) is rising, so is the number of prisoners released for the first time (Lynch and Sabol 2001, 8).

The potential "ripple effects" of today's reentry on released prisoners, their families, and their communities has caught the attention of policymakers, practitioners, and researchers. It even caught the attention of the president of the United States. President George W. Bush addressed it in the 2004 State of the Union address:

> In the past we've worked together to bring mentors to children of prisoners and provide treatment for the addicted, and help for the homeless. Tonight I ask you to consider another group of Americans in need of help. This year, some 600,000 inmates will be released from prison back into society. We know from long experience that if they can't find work, or a home, or help, they are much more likely to commit crime and return to prison. So tonight, I propose a four-year, $300 million prisoner reentry initiative to expand job training and placement services, to provide transitional housing, and to help newly released prisoners get mentoring, including from faith-based groups. America is the land of the second chance, and when the gates of the prison open, the path ahead should lead to a better life.

Let's look more closely at where these reentering prisoners go when they leave prison, which reentry programs work, and the issues surrounding released prisoners' right to vote.

Where Do Released Prisoners Go?

The vast majority of prisoners go back to where they came from. That means they reenter high-crime, large-city neighborhoods with high unemployment rates, few affordable housing choices, and hardly any social services. Let's take Texas as a typical example of this concentration of released prisoners (Watson, Solomon, LaVigne, and Travis 2004). Almost 60 percent of Texas prisoners are released to five counties (Figure 14.4). More than 25 percent go to Houston, the largest city in the state, and Harris County (Watson et al. 2004, 65). Not only does Houston have the highest rate of supervised released prisoners per 100,000 residents (3.1), they're concentrated in neighborhoods in five zip codes (Figure 14.5).

What do we know about these neighborhoods? They're among Houston neighborhoods' most affected by poverty, unemployment, crime, and other characteristics linked to crime and other problems, including high school dropouts, low owner-occupied housing, and much higher than average female-headed households (Watson et al. 2004, 69–72). Here's how Watson and her colleagues describe the neighborhood included in zip code 77026:

> 38 percent of its residents live below the poverty level, which is 102 percent higher than the city average; the neighborhood has a 39 percent unemployment rate, which is 410 percent higher than the city average; and female-headed households account for 16 percent of its households. Eighteen percent of Third Ward housing is vacant, and 64 percent is renter-occupied. Fifty-six percent of its residents are high school graduates, which is 21 percent lower than the city average of 70 percent. The population in the Third Ward neighborhood is 79 percent non-Hispanic black, 10 percent Hispanic, 7 percent non-Hispanic white, and 4 percent other races and ethnicities. With regard to crime, the Third Ward experienced violent crime at a rate of 23.9 crimes per 1,000 residents, which is 96 percent higher than the city average of 12.2. The property crime rate occurred at a rate of 25.5, which is 59 percent lower than the city average of 61.6. The Third Ward's drug crime rate is 25.5, 390.4 percent higher than the city average of 5.2. (74)

Planned Reentry: Descriptions of the California Department of Corrections' reentry programs. To reach this site go to "Web Links" on your Samaha CJ7 website: http://cj.wadsworth.com/samaha_cj7e.

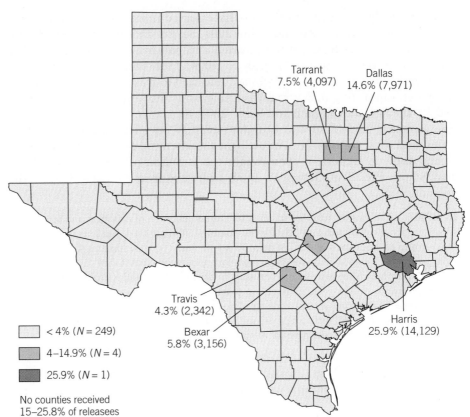

"A Portrait of Prisoner Reentry in Texas": This report is part of a larger Urban Institute initiative entitled "Returning Home: Understanding the Challenges of Prisoner Reentry." The purpose of the initiative is to develop a deeper understanding of the reentry experiences of returning prisoners, their families, and their neighborhoods. To reach this site go to "Web Links" on your Samaha CJ7 website: http://cj.wadsworth.com/samaha_cj7e.

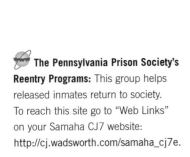

The Pennsylvania Prison Society's Reentry Programs: This group helps released inmates return to society. To reach this site go to "Web Links" on your Samaha CJ7 website: http://cj.wadsworth.com/samaha_cj7e.

Which Reentry Programs "Work"?

Opinions vary widely about the best program for prisoner reentry. Some say programs with more community involvement are the answer; others recommend that judges control reentry (see Make Your Decision at the end of the chapter). Others would put the responsibility on the reentering prisoners themselves. Some advise a mixed strategy of increasing supervision for high-risk offenders and reducing it for the rest; still, others would follow a "broken windows" theory of reentry, putting safety first and enforcing even small violations (Lynch and Sobal 2001, 4).

Joan Petersilia (Sept. 2004, 7) estimates in her review of "what works in prisoner reentry" research that, since 1975, states have tried more than 10,000 programs. Which ones work? It's hard to tell because hardly any program evaluations are based on scientific methodology (meaning evaluations based on large samples of participants who've been randomly assigned to program participants and control or comparison groups). The respected researcher Doris Layton MacKenzie (1998) and her colleagues identified 184 evaluations between 1978 and 1998 that were based on some kind of control or comparison group. According to those criteria, she found six programs that reduced recidivism and two that were promising. She also found that intensive supervision and electronic monitoring *by themselves* didn't reduce recidivism.

Even more dismal was Richard Seiter and Karen Kadela's (2003) review of published *and* unpublished "what works" evaluations between 1975 and 2001. Using the same criteria as Mackenzie, they found only 19 evaluations that contained any control or comparison group (10 of the 19 were drug treatment programs). In Petersilia's (Sept. 2004) words:

> This means that during a 25-year period, when hundreds of work release, halfway houses, job training, education programs, prerelease classes, and so forth, were implemented in the U.S., the literature contains only 9 credible evaluations! This is a disgrace. (6)

The news from Seiter and Kadela wasn't all bad. Among the nine credible evaluations, they *did* find a few programs that reduced recidivism: vocational training and work release; halfway houses; and drug treatment. They also found that education programs increased achievement scores even if they didn't reduce recidivism. And there's *some* evidence that prerelease programs reduce recidivism.

Petersilia sees a problem with answering the question, "What works in reentry?" on the basis of "so few rigorous evaluations" (7):

> Seiter and Kadela were able to identify just 19 reentry program evaluations that contained a comparison group. Only two of these evaluations were randomized experiments. Without this methodology, virtually every finding of program impact is open to criticism. If we assume that each state operated a minimum of 10 reentry programs . . . each year during this 26-year period, then there were close to 10,000 programs nationwide that were implemented during this time period. . . . Yet, just 19 evaluations (less than 1 percent of the total) were published from this experience and the majority of those use weak methodology and pertain to drug programs. Using this "body" of research to conclude anything about which reentry programs "work" or "don't work" seems misguided. (7)

Petersilia also sees as a problem the almost complete use of recidivism as the sole measure of effectiveness. Recidivism is an important (maybe even the *most* important) measure, but it's not the only one:

> After all, the ultimate goal of reentry programs is reintegration, which clearly includes more than remaining arrest-free for a specified time period. . . .
>
> If we wish to truly measure reintegration, we need to build into our evaluations measures of attachment to a variety of social institutions. Research shows that these factors are related to long-term criminal desistance. For example, evaluations should measure whether clients are working, whether that work is full or part time, and whether the income derived is supporting families. We should measure whether programs increase client sobriety and attendance at treatment programs. We should track whether programs help convicts become involved in community activities, in a church, or in ex-convict support groups or victim sensitivity sessions.
>
> There are many outcomes that reentry programs strive to improve upon, and these are virtually never measured in traditional recidivism-only outcome evaluations. Jeremy Travis (2003) makes this point powerfully when he writes of the far-reaching impacts of drug courts. He notes that one of the positive impacts of an offender's participation in a drug court is that the children born to drug court participants are much less likely to be born addicted to drugs. Drug courts reduce participants' drug use, and result in healthy children being born to sober mothers. When we use recidivism as the sole criterion for judging whether reentry programs "work" or "don't work," we often miss the more powerful impacts of program participation. (7)

Source for quotes: Petersilia, Joan. 2004. "What Works in Reentry? Reviewing and Questioning the Evidence." *Federal Probation*, September, p. 7. Reprinted with permission from *Federal Probation*.

The Right to Vote and Reentry

On November 7, 2004, the U.S. Supreme Court declined to review cases from New York and Washington State challenging the right of states to take away felons' right to vote. The plaintiffs in the case (state prisoners) claimed that the voting ban discriminates against the more than one-third of Black men denied the right to vote under state laws. The Federal Voting Rights Act bans states from applying voting qualifications in a racially discriminatory manner. The Court's action doesn't mean the matter is over. Plaintiffs in a Florida case are challenging the state's lifetime ban on felon voting. The plaintiffs presented evidence that Florida's law, passed in 1868, was passed with the intent to keep newly franchised Blacks from voting. Many lawyers following the case believe it has a chance of succeeding in the Supreme Court because the lawyers handling the case have built a convincing case of the state's history of discrimination (Greenhouse 2004).

Several social scientists have examined the origins and consequences of laws banning felons from voting (Uggen and Manza 2004). State laws vary widely, ranging from states with no restrictions to those with life-long bans, but researchers have identified a large (and growing) number of felons who can't vote because of their felony convictions. The ban affects minorities most heavily (2 million Blacks in 2002).

Most studies have focused on the *political* (not the criminogenic) effects of voting rights bans (Uggen and Manza 2004). For example, there's some evidence that the ban has affected the outcome of elections. Also, voting can affect felons' reintegration into life outside prison. The right to vote defines our membership in a democratic society. "Participation in democratic rituals such as elections affirms membership in the larger community..." (Uggen and Manza 2004, 2).

But more important for criminal justice, does participation in community life have some connection to avoiding criminal behavior after prisoners reenter society? You've already learned (Chapter 3) that there's solid evidence that ex-offenders who have steady jobs and family relationships and who participate in community life are less likely to commit crimes. The idea behind this reduced criminal behavior is informal social control (attachment to social institutions, work, and families increases their stake in conforming behavior, Chapter 3). Shad Maruna (2001) points out that the desire to "be productive and give something back to society" (88) is part of the motivation not to commit crimes.

Uggen and Manza (2004) ask whether voting might be another form of informal social control. They examined whether a cohort of former Minnesota public school students who voted in the 1996 presidential election had lower rates of arrest, incarceration, and self-reported criminal behavior after the election than those who didn't vote. First, they established a definite association between not voting and criminal behavior. Convicted felon Steven referred to losing his right to vote as a powerful symbol of his "outsider" status, "On top of the whole messy pile, there it was. Something that was hardly mentioned, and it meant a lot" (4). Pamela (a prisoner in her 40s) said losing her right to vote was "salt in the wound," "another loss to add to the pile" (4–5) of the problems she was running into because of her convictions.

Of course, this doesn't mean that voting is the *only* ingredient in not voting and crime. Larry (in his 20s) said, "People that are gonna get into crime are gonna do it whether they have the right to vote or not" (5). Alex (in the middle of a long sentence) said:

> I don't think that would have anything to do with it [committing future crimes], the right to vote.... I mean I had the right to vote before I came to prison, but I still let my crime happen. I don't go around beating up people as a hobby or anything. But I don't see voting as having an effect on criminal behavior. (5)

Still, after controlling for other possible explanations (like race, gender, employment, and marital status), Uggen and Manza conclude on this hopeful note:

Taken as a whole, this analysis suggests that a relationship between voting and subsequent crime and arrest is not only plausible, but also that it receives some degree of empirical support. We find consistent differences between voters and non-voters in rates of subsequent arrest, incarceration, and self-reported criminal behavior. While the single behavior act of voting is unlikely to be the single factor that turns felons' lives around, it is likely that the act of voting is tapping into something real, such as a desire to participate as a law-abiding stakeholder in larger society. At a minimum, our multivariate analysis suggests that the political participation effect is not entirely attributable to preexisting differences between voters and non-voters in criminal history, class, race, or gender. (17)

MAKE YOUR DECISION *A Provocative Proposal: Reentry Courts*

Let's imagine a world unconstrained by budgetary realities, legal conventions, or implementation considerations. In that world, let's consider a model of reentry that draws on and applies the lessons learned from the innovations described here. We make two assumptions: that people are still sent to prison, and that they are released back into the community with some portion of their sentence still to be served.

JUDGES AS REENTRY MANAGERS

If a new vision were written on a clean slate, the role of reentry management would best be assigned, in my view, to the sentencing judge, whose duties would be expanded to create a "reentry court." At the time of sentencing, the judge would say to the offender, "John Smith, you are being sentenced to X years, Y months of which will be served in the community under my supervision. Our goal is to admit you back into our community after you pay your debt for this offense and demonstrate your ability to live by our rules.

Starting today, we will develop, with your involvement, a plan to achieve that goal. The plan will require some hard work of you, beginning in prison and continuing—and getting harder—after you return to the community. It will also require that your family, friends, neighbors, and any other people interested in your welfare commit to the goal of your successful return. I will oversee your entire sentence to make sure the goal is achieved, including monitoring your participation in prison programs that prepare you for release.

Many other criminal justice agencies—police, corrections, parole, probation, drug treatment, and others—will be part of a team committed to achieving the goal. If you do not keep up your end of the bargain, I will further restrict your liberty, although only in amounts proportionate to your failure. If you commit a crime again after your release, all bets are off. If you do keep up your end of the bargain, it is within my power to accelerate the completion of your sentence, to return privileges that might be lost (such as your right to hold certain kinds of jobs or your right to vote), and to welcome you back to the community."

At the time of sentencing, the judge would also convene the stakeholders who would be responsible for the offender's reentry. They would be asked to focus on that day, perhaps years in the future, when John returns home. How can he be best prepared for that day and for a successful reentry? What does his support network

Source: Jeremy Travis, *But They All Come Back: Rethinking Prisoner Reentry* (Washington, DC: U.S. Department of Justice, May 2000).

commit to doing to ensure that success? A "community justice officer" (who could be a police officer, probation officer, or parole officer) would also be involved, since there might be special conditions, geared to the neighborhood, that the offender would have to meet.

The judge-centered model described here obviously borrows heavily from the drug court experience [Chapter 8]. Both feature an ongoing, central role for the judge, a "contract" drawn up between court and offender, discretion on the judge's part to impose graduated sanctions for various levels of failure to meet the conditions imposed, the promise of the end of supervision as an occasion for ceremonial recognition.

INCARCERATION AS A PRELUDE TO REENTRY

If John goes to prison, a significant purpose of his activities behind bars would be preparation for reentry. What does that mean? It depends on the type of offender and the offense, and could include sex offender treatment, job readiness, education and/or training, a residential drug treatment program, and anger management. These activities would also involve people, support systems, and social service and other programs based in John's neighborhood. Drug treatment in prison should be

▲ Should a significant purpose of a prisoner's time in prison be preparing for reentry into society? Here prisoners soon to be released from Mississippi State Penitentiary at Parchman work on basic life skills. An HIV/AIDS Task Force recommended that the prisons open vocational and education programs to help inmates with the AIDS virus learn job skills they can use when they reenter their communities after release.

linked to drug treatment in the community, job training should be linked to work outside, and so forth. In other words, mirror support systems should be established so that John can move from one to the other seamlessly upon release.

Even while in prison, John would continue to pay restitution to his victim or to the community he has harmed—tangible, measurable restitution. A lot of time would be spent with John's family, to keep family ties strong and to talk about what John will be like when he returns home. As the release date approached, the circle would widen, as the support system was brought into the prison to discuss how to keep the offender on the straight and narrow after release. Buddy systems would be established and training in the early warning signs of relapse provided. Again, the community justice officer could broker this process. All the while, the judge would be kept apprised of progress.

SETTING THE TERMS OF RELEASE

When released, John would be brought back to court, perhaps the same courtroom where he was sentenced. A public recognition ceremony would be held, before an audience of family and other members of the support team, and the judge would announce that John has completed a milestone in repaying his debt to society. Now, the judge would declare, the success of the next step depends on John, his support system, and the agencies of government represented by the community justice officer.

The terms of the next phase would be clearly articulated. If John's case were typical, he would have to remain drug free, make restitution to his victim and reparation to his community, work to make his community safer, participate in programs that began in prison (work, education, and the like), avoid situations that could trigger relapse, and refrain from committing crime. He would be required to appear in court every month to demonstrate how well the plan was working.

MAKING THE CONTRACT WORK

The judge presiding over a reentry court would be responsible for making sure that John held up his end of the bargain and that the government agencies and the support system were doing their parts. As in drug courts, the court appearances need not be long, drawn-out affairs; the purpose of invoking the authority of the court would be to impress on John that he has important work to do and to mobilize the support network.

The power of the court would be invoked sparingly when John failed to make progress. The court would view relapse in its broadest sense and would use the powers at its disposal (to impose prison sentences, greater restrictions on liberty, fines, and similar sanctions) to ensure that John toes the line. His family and other members of his support system would be encouraged to attend these court hearings.

The community justice officer would keep the court apprised of neighborhood developments involving the offender. To the extent John became involved in programs that made his community safer, there would be occasion for special commendation. The judge would be empowered by statute to accelerate the end of the period of supervision, to remove such legal restrictions as the ban on voting, and to oversee John's "graduation" from the program—his successful reentry into the community.

This approach would have several benefits. It cuts across organizational boundaries, making it more likely that offenders are both held accountable and supported in fulfilling their part of the reentry bargain. By involving family members, friends, and other interested parties in the reentry plan, it expands the reach of positive influences upon the offender. By creating a supervisory role for judges, the approach gives them far greater capacity to achieve the purposes of sentencing. Most important, by focusing on the inexorable fact that the prison sentence will one day be completed and the offender will come back to live in the community, the approach directs private and public energies and resources toward the goal of successful reintegration.

QUESTIONS

1. List the arguments in favor of using judges as reentry managers.
2. Explain why incarceration should be a prelude to reentry.
3. How are the terms of release set under the reentry courts determined?
4. How can a reentry contract be made to "work" under the reentry court model?
5. Based on your answers to questions 1–4, would you favor the establishment of reentry courts? Explain.

Chapter Summary

▶ There's a fundamental difference between male and female prison society and between the lives men and women prisoners live in prison.

▶ Male prison society depends on the conditions inside prison *and* the conditions of the larger society outside prison. A variety of deprivations account for the "pains" of imprisonment, which are a legitimate part of punishment; they include enforced poverty, a ban on consensual sex, no liberty, and reduced autonomy, privacy, and security. Male prisoners rely on a number of ways to cope with the stress caused by the pains of imprisonment, but most do so by avoiding other prisoners and places where large numbers of prisoners congregate.

▶ Racial and ethnic conflict, gangs and violent prisoners, bans on consensual sex, and enforced poverty can lead to violence against other prisoners. Prisoners don't just attack each other; they attack officers, too. Prison gangs are a part of men's prison life, despite strong prohibitions against them. Racial hatred between White and Black prisoners, their cliques, and gangs is the most volatile dynamic in prisons. Riots are part of U.S. history; they're part of U.S. prison history, too.

▶ There are disappointingly few prison programs, or at least too many programs with far too little money and staff. According to the best research, *some* programs reduce recidivism for *some* prisoners, under *some* conditions; they also occupy prisoners' time and keep them out of trouble while they're in prison. Recreation is controversial, but most experts agree it's good for prisoners and keeps prison society more peaceful.

▶ Life in women's prisons is very different from life in men's prisons, because there are fewer women prisoners, they commit less serious crimes, and they're considered more "tractable" than men. Women don't cope with the "pains" of imprisonment in the same way men do.

▶ According to earlier research, women responded to the pains of imprisonment by forming intimate (sometimes sexual) relationships that mimicked family relationships outside prison. But unlike in men's prisons, women prisoners didn't coerce their partners into homosexual relationships, and they weren't necessarily sexual in nature. Later research points to women prisoners as active agents (not just passive objects) in coping with prison life and its pains.

▶ Despite the shift from rehabilitation to punishment philosophies, the explosion in prison populations, and the development of tougher prison management styles, there are forces of continuity at work in the reality of women prisoners' daily lives. Women prisoners under the new and old regimes and social conditions believe the best way to do time is, "Mind your own business. Stay to yourself. Have a few friends, but don't trust anyone."

▶ Most male prison programs don't meet women prisoners' needs. But it's not at all clear "what works" for women prisoners, because there are so few evaluations of women's prison programs.

▶ Conviction for a crime turns a defendant formally armed with all the rights of a free person into an offender stripped of many constitutional rights. In defining the limits of these rights, courts use a balancing test: they look at all the facts of each case and weigh the shrunken rights of prisoners against the prison's powerful missions of punishment, security, order, and discipline. Prisoners' rights include the right to go to court and get due process and equal protection of the law. Prisoners keep their First Amendment rights to expression, association, and religion only so far as they don't conflict with the prison's missions. Prisoners' right against unreasonable searches and seizures is extremely limited.

▶ Practically, prisoners never succeed when they sue the government for violating their rights. They also lose most of their internal grievance complaints against staff and prison management.

▶ Almost all prisoners who go to prison sooner or later leave and reenter society. The number of prisoners reentering society has skyrocketed since the late 1990s. Research confirms that today's reentering prisoners need more supervision and assistance than prisoners in the past. The vast majority of prisoners go back to where they came from. That means they reenter high-crime, large-city neighborhoods with high unemployment rates, few affordable housing choices, and hardly any social services. It's very hard to estimate what reentry programs work, because so few are properly evaluated, but the few that have been are disappointing.

Key Terms

punishment model of imprisonment, p. 480

confinement model of imprisonment, p. 480

total institutions, p. 481

indigenous theory imprisonment, p. 481

importation theory of imprisonment, p. 482

pains of imprisonment, p. 482

cognitive model of rehabilitation, p. 499

civil death, p. 507

hands-off doctrine, p. 508

prisoner reentry, p. 518

Web Resources

Go to http://cj.wadsworth.com/samaha_cj7e for a wealth of online resources related to your book. Take a "pre-test" and "post-test" for each chapter in order to help master the material. Check out the *Web Links* to access the websites mentioned in the text, as well as many others. Explore the

Decision Points flagged in the margins of the text, as well as the *Concept Builders* for additional insights. You can also access recent perspectives by clicking on *CJ in the News* and *Terrorism Update* under *Course Resources*.

Search Online with InfoTrac College Edition

For additional information, explore InfoTrac® College Edition, your online library. Go to http://cj.wadsworth.com/samaha_cj7e to access InfoTrac College Edition from your

book's website. Use the passcode that came with your book. You will find InfoTrac College Edition exercises and a list of key words for further research.

CHAPTER 15

Juvenile Justice

FACT *or* FICTION?

▶ Solid evidence shows a rising tide of anger at teen-age killers.

▶ The U.S. Supreme Court has ruled that juvenile suspects are entitled to the same constitutional rights as adult criminal suspects.

▶ Juvenile delinquency is easy to measure, thanks to complete statistics.

▶ Despite media hype about spiraling juvenile crime, the juvenile crime rate is declining.

▶ In about half the cases, police counsel and release juvenile suspects.

▶ Transfers of cases from juvenile to adult criminal courts have increased since the 1990s.

▶ The number of status offenders in locked facilities has decreased since the 1990s.

▶ Juvenile suspects are detained in separate juvenile detention centers, not in jails for adult suspects.

JUVENILE CRIME STATISTICS: CAN WE TRUST THEM?

While many media stories may give the impression that both the number and seriousness of juvenile crimes are on the rise, we have only the most rudimentary of measures to tell whether or not this is the case. The most widely cited measure of crime, the FBI's Uniform Crime Reports (UCR), tells us nothing about the level of juvenile crime because it contains no information about the characteristics of offenders. The only indirect sources of information on juvenile crime rates are arrest rates and surveys of victims or high-risk youth.

—PETER GREENWOOD (2004), 75

A 12-year-old-boy attacks a woman walking down the street and grabs her purse. A 16-year-old boy does the same thing to another woman on another street. A 19-year-old young man attacks a third woman and takes her purse. The police arrest all three. Do their ages make a difference in what happens to them following arrest? Yes. In all U.S. jurisdictions, age determines which institutions will process these cases, what procedures will govern their process, and what policies will shape their disposition. Why? Because the United States has the structure and process we discussed in Chapters 1 through 12 for adults and the one we'll discuss here for juveniles.

In this chapter, we'll look back at the history of juvenile justice, examine juvenile justice and the Constitution, and discuss law enforcement, the courts, and corrections as they relate to the juvenile justice system.

The History of Juvenile Justice

For centuries, the law has treated children and adults differently. In early English history, the law put people into three categories:

1. Children under 7, who couldn't form criminal intent so they couldn't be tried for criminal behavior.
2. Children between 7 and 14, who were *presumed* incompetent to form criminal intent unless evidence showed otherwise; then they could be tried for crimes.
3. Adults over 14, who the law presumed were *competent* to form criminal intent unless they were insane or retarded.

doctrine of *parens patriae* allowed the government to intervene in family life to protect children's estates from dishonest guardians

The ancient **doctrine of *parens patriae*** allowed the government to intervene in family life to protect children's estates from dishonest guardians. This principle expanded over time to include the power to intervene to protect children against parental neglect, incompetence, and abuse. The doctrine of *parens patriae* and the legal presumptions against children's capacity to form criminal intent came to North America with the English colonists (Schlossman 1977).

The ferment of social reform during the 1800s produced a romantic "child saving" movement. At the same time, a great social, economic, and intellectual transformation was taking place. People were increasingly getting their education, livelihood, and entertainment not at home with their families but in

◀ New York's Elmira Reformatory was the first and most famous of the youth prisons based on the Progressive idea that young offenders could be "saved" by taking them out of their "bad" homes and away from their "unhealthy" associations, and through education, training, and discipline could be turned into law-abiding citizens who supported themselves. The woodworking shop shown in this 1898 photo was supposed to provide vocational training that would lead to a job after release.

schools, factories, and places of public amusement. The child-saving movement relied on two institutions, the house of refuge and the reform school, to "save" children. Both institutions were based on the nineteenth-century idea that children's environments made them bad. Houses of refuge and reform schools would take them out of their bad homes and away from their unhealthy associations and turn bad children into law-abiding people (Platt 1969).

Child saving was also on the agenda of the Progressive Era (about 1900 to 1914) reformers. According to the Progressives, children misbehaved because they lived in unhealthy homes with unhealthy families. "Healthy" meant homes where parents lived according to middle-class values. They worked hard, saved their money, went to church, didn't drink or smoke, and obeyed the laws of God and the state. The Progressives maintained that families who didn't have these values—particularly immigrants—should acquire these values. How would they learn the right values? From the good examples set by the Progressives and with a lot of help from Progressive government experts.

The Progressives had enormous (and naïve) confidence in both the state and in experts. This confidence led them to call on the state to supply experts to "save" children by "curing" their "unhealthy" home lives. The Progressives distrusted traditional institutions dominated (they claimed) by outdated, inefficient, and ineffective formal rules. So they turned away from the criminal courts, which emphasized criminal behavior, and created a new institution. The **juvenile court** concentrated not on behavior but on children and what they needed to make them responsible.

In juvenile court, judges didn't sit on benches above children but next to them. Proceedings were informal. Their aim was not to affix blame but to find out what caused children to "go wrong" so that it could be put right. The Progressives were great fact collectors. They gathered information about children's home life, past behavior, health, and anything else that might help them diagnose and cure youths' problems.

The Progressives were also great optimists. They had a strong faith that government could cure delinquency by making sure experts could make professional judgments not hampered by formal rules. Their optimistic faith in government led to the adoption of what came to be called a **medical model of crime.** The medical model is based on the idea that crime is a disease that

juvenile court concentrated not on behavior but on children and what they needed to make them responsible

medical model of crime the medical model is based on the idea that crime is a disease that experts can diagnose, treat, and cure

experts can diagnose, treat, and cure. Based on these optimistic ideas, Chicago established the first juvenile court in 1899. By 1925, almost every jurisdiction in the country had one (Platt 1969; Rothman 1980; Ryerson 1978).

During the 1960s, the professional interest in children shifted from needs to rights. This shift was due both to the general rights movement and a growing skepticism about the capacity of government to meet the needs of children. The increased fear of crime and disorder during that turbulent time led critics to attack juvenile justice generally and juvenile courts specifically. In 1967, President Lyndon Johnson's Commission on Law and Enforcement and the Administration of Justice concluded:

> The juvenile court has not succeeded significantly in rehabilitating delinquent youth, in reducing or even stemming the tide of juvenile criminality, or in bringing justice to the child offender. Uncritical and unrealistic estimates of what is known can make expectation so much greater than achievement and serve to justify extensive official action, and to mask the fact that much of it may do more harm than good. Official action may help to fix and perpetuate delinquency in the child—the individual begins to think of himself as a delinquent and proceeds to organize his behaviors accordingly. The undesirable consequences of official actions are heightened in programs that rely on institutionalization of the child. The most informed and benign institutional treatment, even in well designed and staffed reformatories and training schools, thus may contain within it the seeds of its own frustration, and itself may often feed the very disorder it is designed to cure. (7)

During the 1970s, the fear of crime and youth rebellion continued to rise. Also rising was disillusionment with the juvenile justice system's capacity both to meet the needs of juveniles and to secure their rights. Fear and disillusionment contributed to a harsher public attitude toward youth crime and to a renewed confidence that retribution was the right response to crime and delinquency. A growing consensus among both criminal justice professionals and the public demanded that juveniles be tried as adults.

Fueling this consensus was a belief that if juveniles are old enough to commit crimes, they're old enough to take the consequences. Today, impressionistic evidence suggests there's "a rising tide of anger at teen-age killers" (Glaberson 1998, 14). According to juvenile justice exert, Professor Martin Guggenheim, "We've lost our faith in the rehabilitative ideal, and that loss of faith has come from both the left and the right" (Glaberson 1998, 14). During the 1990s, 49 states made it easier to prosecute juveniles as adults (Sickmund 2003, 7). (See the In Focus box "Life Sentence for 12-Year-Old?")

Juvenile Justice and the U.S. Constitution

Several landmark U.S. Supreme Court decisions have restricted the informal, discretionary powers of the juvenile court and other agencies dealing with juveniles. These restrictions granted to juveniles a number of rights enjoyed by adult criminal defendants. For example, in *Kent v. United States* (1966, a case involving a 16-year-old charged with housebreaking, robbery, and rape), the Court ruled that juvenile court proceedings have to provide juveniles with the basic due process right to a fair hearing.

The Court extended juvenile rights further in *In re Gault* (1967). The case involved proceedings against a 15-year-old Arizona boy who had made lewd remarks to an elderly woman on the telephone. The juvenile court confined the juvenile to a training school. The U.S. Supreme Court ruled that committing a juvenile to a correctional facility required:

1. Written notice that a hearing was scheduled
2. Advice about the right to counsel
3. The right to confront and cross-examine witnesses

Life Sentence for 12-Year-Old?

Prosecutors offered a plea bargain...to the 16-year-old whose life sentence for kicking, slamming and stomping a 6-year-old to death was overturned this month. The agreement would require the teenager, Lionel Tate, who was 12 when he killed, to serve as few as four more weeks in prison. His lawyers said Lionel and his mother were considering the deal. "They are going to continue considering the offer," Lionel's lead lawyer, Richard Rosenbaum, said, adding that the deal had been in the works since shortly after Dec. 10, when an appeals court panel ordered a new trial.

The plea agreement is virtually identical to one that Lionel and his mother rejected before his trial in 2001 in the murder of the 6-year-old, Tiffany Eunick, who was visiting his house near Fort Lauderdale on July 28, 1999. Lionel was convicted of killing her by stomping on her 48-pound body so hard that her liver was lacerated and her skull cracked. His original lawyers said he had accidentally killed Tiffany while play wrestling. The appeals lawyers later said he had mistakenly leaped on her while bounding down a staircase.

Under the first offer, Lionel would have been in prison three years and would have been free by now. The state attorney in Broward County said that under both offers Lionel would plead guilty to second-degree murder and be sentenced to three years in a juvenile prison. The state attorney, Michael J. Satz, said in a statement that Lionel had served 33 months, suggesting he would be released in late March under the deal.

But Mr. Rosenbaum said Lionel, who is being held in the maximum-security Okeechobee juvenile jail, would probably receive credit for an additional two months he served in a county jail and be released late next month. The new deal would also require Lionel to spend a year under house arrest, be on probation for 10 years and obtain psychological help. "I am very pleased that the state has extended the same offer," Mr. Rosenbaum said.

Rejection of the initial offer was a factor in the appeals ruling on Dec. 10 that found that Lionel's mental competency should have been evaluated before the trial. He was 14 when tried on murder charges. Supporters say Lionel did not understand the risk of going to trial, though others say he was acting on the advice of his mother, Kathleen Grossett-Tate, a state police trooper who insisted that Lionel was not guilty. Reached by telephone, Ms. Grossett-Tate declined to comment on Friday.

In Florida, a first-degree murder conviction requires a life sentence with no parole regardless of the defendant's age. Florida prosecutes more children as adults than any other state. Lionel is thought to be the youngest American to receive such a sentence, a circumstance that drew international attention to his case and to the thorny issue of treating juvenile offenders as adults.

Ms. Grossett-Tate met Pope John Paul II this year to ask his help in changing juvenile sentencing laws and moving Lionel out of prison. Mr. Satz, the prosecutor, said in his statement he had consulted with Tiffany's mother, Deweese Eunick-Paul, before making his offer. "Mrs. Eunick-Paul has a big heart and was willing to offer Lionel Tate the same opportunity that she agreed to three years ago before the trial," Mr. Satz said. Mrs. Eunick-Paul has said that Lionel did not deserve a life sentence and that 10 to 20 years in prison might be enough. But the lawyer who prosecuted Lionel, Ken Padowitz, said this month that the trial had been fair and that Mrs. Eunick-Paul had been upset by the appeals court's reversal. Mr. Padowitz did not return a call.

A spokesman for Mr. Satz, Ron Ishoy, said Mr. Satz had decided to reoffer the accord because "it was the right thing to do before the trial, and it's the right thing to do now." He said he did not know whether Gov. Jeb Bush had been consulted. Lionel's lawyers had asked Mr. Bush for an expedited clemency hearing in case their appeal failed. But the governor delayed action during the appeal. He said this month that he would keep waiting while the court process continued. Mr. Bush, a Republican, would almost certainly face criticism whether or not he granted clemency.

Mr. Satz's statement said he was requesting a rehearing of the appeal, in case Lionel rejected his offer. That means if Lionel rejects the offer, the state can appeal the voiding of his conviction, delaying a new trial. Mr. Rosenbaum said that in case Lionel did go to trial again he was assembling "a team of lawyers who would make the O. J. Simpson legal team look modest."

Source: Abby Goodnough, "Boy Serving Life Sentence Is Reoffered Plea Bargain," *New York Times*, December 27, 2003. Copyright © 2003 by The New York Times Co. Reprinted with permission.

In *In re Winship* (1970), a 12-year-old boy was charged with purse snatching. The U.S. Supreme Court ruled that due process required proof beyond a reasonable doubt to classify juveniles as delinquent.

Juveniles don't have *all* the rights enjoyed by adult criminal defendants, so juvenile proceedings aren't exactly like adult criminal court proceedings. In *McKeiver v. Pennsylvania* (1970), the Court ruled, for example, that juveniles don't have the right to a jury trial. In the Court's words, "We do not mean to indicate that the hearing must be held to conform with all the requirements of a criminal trial but we do hold that the hearing must measure up to the essentials of due process and fair treatment" (533–534).

Juvenile Delinquency

States vary considerably in their definitions of **juveniles.** Most states exclude children under 8 from juvenile justice jurisdiction. States differ about the upper age limit, some using 16 and others 18 as the dividing line between juvenile and criminal justice jurisdiction. In most states, "older" juveniles, those within a year or two of the upper age limit, qualify either as juveniles or adults, depending on the circumstances (discussed later).

Juvenile justice processes several types of juveniles: the needy, the dependent, the neglected, and the delinquent. In this chapter, you'll learn only about delinquents and their delinquency. **Delinquency** includes conduct that would be criminal if an adult engaged in it (Chapter 2) *and* **status offenses,** conduct that's illegal only if juveniles engage in it. Common examples include truancy, underage drinking, curfew violations, running away, and incorrigibility. So **"juvenile delinquent"** can refer to a youth who's committed either crimes or status offenses, or both. In other words, a "juvenile delinquent is a person who has been adjudicated as such by a court of proper jurisdiction" (Males and Macallair 1998, 3–4). (See The In Focus box "Juvenile Delinquency: Arrest or Detention for Wearing a Low-Cut Midriff Top?")

The California Welfare and Institutions Code (1981) shows just how broad the scope of delinquency is in the nation's most populous state:

> Any person who is under the age of eighteen when he violates any law of this state or the United States or any ordinance of any city or county of this state defining crime other than an ordinance establishing a curfew based solely on age, is within the jurisdiction of the juvenile court. Any person under the age of eighteen years who persistently or habitually refuses to obey the reasonable and proper orders or directions of his parents, guardian, or custodian, or who is beyond the control of such person, or who is under the age of 18 years when he violates any ordinance of any city or county of this state establishing a curfew based solely on age is within the jurisdiction of the juvenile court. (§§ 601, 602)

Let's look at how delinquency is measured and at juvenile arrests.

Measuring Delinquency

It's not easy to measure delinquency because of incomplete statistics. Most criticisms regarding adult crime statistics (Chapter 2) apply to measures of juvenile delinquency. In fact, juvenile statistics come from the same sources: the Uniform Crime Reports, the National Crime Survey, court records, and self-reports. Despite difficulties in measuring delinquency, several facts stand out.

First, youths are substantially more "crime-prone" than adults. The juvenile arrest rate for serious property crimes exceeds the adult rate by about six to one and for violent crimes by about two to one. The majority of youth arrests are for property crimes, such as theft and burglary, and youth-only offenses, such as truancy, runaway, and curfew (Mathias, DeMuro, and Allison 1984, 8; National Institute for Juvenile Justice and Delinquency Prevention 1980, 59).

Second, juvenile offenders tend to commit crimes in groups. For example, in New York City, among crimes committed by juveniles, 90 percent of the robberies, 86 percent of the burglaries, 78 percent of the homicides, 60 percent of the assaults, and 50 percent of the rapes were committed by groups (Snyder 2004, 2).

Third, juvenile offenders are frequently armed. Sociologists James Wright, Joseph Sheley, and M. Dwayne Smith interviewed male juveniles serving sentences and male students attending inner-city schools. They found that it's easy for city youths to get handguns; almost one-third have owned a gun at one time (Zimring 1981, 867–875). How do they get them? From friends, family, and street sources. Most of the guns were stolen and purchased at prices well below their retail value. Most youths claimed that they carried guns for protection (Zimring 1978, 38).

Juvenile Delinquency: Arrest or Detention for Wearing a Low-Cut Midriff Top?

The 14-year-old girl arrived at school here on Oct. 17 wearing a low-cut midriff top under an unbuttoned sweater. It was a clear violation of the dress code, and school officials gave her a bowling shirt to put on. She refused. Her mother came to the school with an oversize T-shirt. She refused to wear that, too. "It was real ugly," said the girl, whose mother did not want her to be identified.

It was a standoff. So the city police officer assigned to the school handcuffed the girl, put her in a police car and took her to the detention center at the Lucas County juvenile courthouse. She was booked on a misdemeanor charge and placed in a holding cell for several hours, until her mother, a 34-year-old vending machine technician, got off work and picked her up. She was one of more than two dozen students in Toledo who were arrested in school in October for offenses like being loud and disruptive, cursing at school officials, shouting at classmates and violating the dress code. They had all violated the city's safe school ordinance....

Craig Cotner, chief academic officer for the Toledo public schools, said he believed part of the problem was that schools were being called upon to educate a far wider range of students than before. Thirty years ago, he said, students who were not performing well were counseled to drop out, and they easily found jobs at auto plants and other factories. "For students who did not fit the mold—whatever mold that may be—there were many more options," Mr. Cotner said. "In some cases, those students who found it impossible to sit for five hours in a classroom could function very well in a labor environment." Today, he said, those students, with far fewer options, remain in school, but the school district has fewer resources to handle difficult students.

With a $15 million budget deficit last year, the district laid off 10 percent of the teaching force, or 231 teachers. Class size increased. With a $16 million deficit this year, more cuts must be made, Mr. Cotner said. In addition, he said, a significant percentage of the district's resources must be used to fulfill federal mandates like the No Child Left Behind law, with its emphasis on accountability and testing.

Judge Ray of the county juvenile court says he sympathizes with school officials. "The schools have been called upon to fix everything that hasn't been working up to this point," he said. However, he said, juvenile court is not the appropriate place to solve adolescent problems. Judge Ray has Mr. Whitman, the court's intake officer, and other court officers handle minor nonviolent offenses, offering counseling and referrals to the proper programs.

Mr. Whitman, 50, said he believed that no young person should ever be written off. "If a kid's not doing well, I think we need to sit down and find out what we can do to help him or her out," he said.

Mr. Whitman talked at length with the 14-year-old girl who had worn the midriff top and with her mother. "She didn't come across as a major problem at all," he said. "She knew the shirt was inappropriate. She just wanted to show off a certain image at the school. Probably she just copped an attitude. I expect that from a lot of girls."

An official of the girl's school said he could not discuss her case. He referred a reporter to the principal, who did not return calls to his office. The girl's mother, who declined to be named, said she had not objected to the decision to arrest her daughter. "She wants to push authority to the hilt," she said.

The girl said of her encounter with school officials and the police: "I don't like to get yelled at for stupid stuff. So I talk back."

Source: Sara Rimer, "Unruly Students Facing Arrest, Not Detention," *New York Times*, January 4, 2004. Copyright © 2004 by The New York Times Co. Reprinted with permission.

Juvenile Arrests

The picture of juvenile crime isn't pretty. Here are some of the highlights from the latest survey of juvenile arrests (Snyder 2004):

- Of the nearly 1,600 juveniles murdered, 38 percent were under 5 and almost half were killed with a firearm.
- Female arrests for aggravated and simple assault are near record levels.
- Between 1993 and 2002, DWI arrests rose 46 percent for males; the increase for females was 96 percent!

Another part of this not pretty picture is that juveniles who begin offending at an early age are more likely to become violent offenders (Figure 15.1).

The picture of juvenile crime may not be very pretty, but let's end this section on a cautiously optimistic note. Take the likelihood of becoming a violent offender, depicted in Figure 15.1. The bad news is that 16 percent of offenders who

> **DECISION POINT**
>
> Should the boys be charged with attempted murder and burglary?
>
> Click on this Decision Point at http://cj.wadsworth.com/samaha_cj7e to explore the issue.

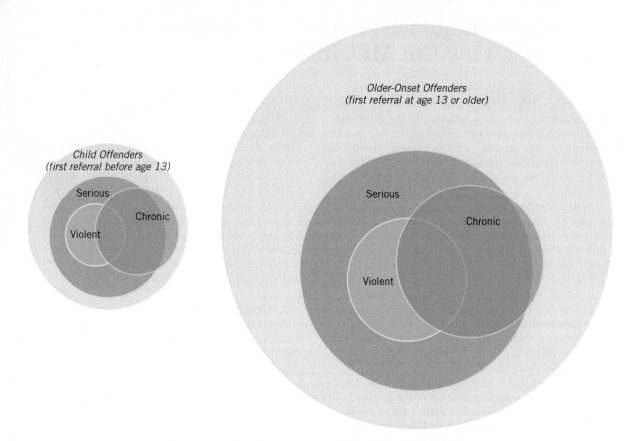

▲ FIGURE 15.1 Proportion of Serious, Violent, and Chronic Offenses among Children Younger Than 13 vs. Those 13 and Older

Child Offenders had a greater proportion of Serious, Violent, and Chronic careers than Older-Onset Offenders. Offenders outside the Serious, Violent, and Chronic circles (yellow areas) were referred to court 1 to 3 times but never for a serious offense. Overlapping circles represent offenders who committed multiple types of offenses. The circles and overlapping areas are drawn in proportion to the numbers of offenses of each type.

Violent offenders: Committed murder, kidnapping, violent sexual assault, robbery, or aggravated assault

Serious offenders: Committed violent offenses plus burglary, serious larceny, motor vehicle theft, arson, weapons offenses, or drug dealing

Chronic offenders: Were referred to court four or more times

Source: Melissa Sickmund, *Juveniles in Court* (Washington, DC: Office of Juvenile Justice and Delinquency Prevention, June 2003), p. 29.

entered the juvenile justice system when they're 9 years old will later become violent offenders. The good news is that 84 percent won't!

Also, despite a lot of media hype about the spiraling rate of juvenile crime (especially violent crime), the juvenile crime rate, like the rate for adults (Chapter 2) has fallen since the mid-1990s (Figure 15.2). Here are a few of the more positive highlights from the most recent survey of juvenile arrests, for the period 1995 through 2002 (Snyder 2004):

- The number of juvenile arrests for murder declined by almost two-thirds between 1993 and 2002.
- Juvenile violent crime was at its lowest level since 1980, and it was almost half the level it was in 1994.
- The gap between Black and White violent crime arrest rates closed substantially between 1980 and 2002.
- Juvenile property crime arrest rates reached their lowest rate since the 1960s.

OJJDP Statistical Briefing Book:
Statistical information on juvenile offending, victimization of juveniles, and involvement of youth in the juvenile justice system. To reach this site go to "Web Links" on your Samaha CJ7 website: http://cj.wadsworth.com/samaha_cj7e.

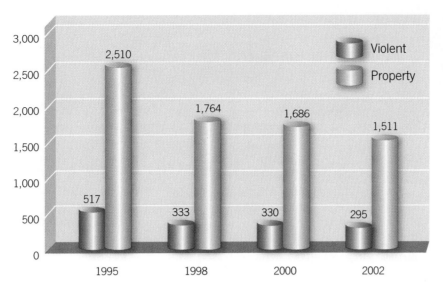

◀ **FIGURE 15.2 Juvenile Crime Rates, 1995–2002**

Source: Juvenile Justice Bulletin (Washington, DC: Office of Juvenile Justice and Delinquency Prevention, September 2000, 2002, 2004) for the years 1998, 2000, and 2002, respectively; James Q. Wilson and Joan Petersilia, eds., *Crime* (Oakland, CA: Institute for Contemporary Studies, 2004), Table 4.2, p. 78, for 1995.

The Juvenile Justice System: Law Enforcement, the Courts, and Corrections

The juvenile justice system is a state and a local affair. Like adult criminal justice, the juvenile system consists of law enforcement, courts, and corrections agencies (Figure 15.3). Legislatures define the scope of these agencies' legal authority, particularly what age span and what conduct falls within the jurisdiction of the juvenile justice system. Legislatures also determine when juveniles can be transferred to the criminal justice system to be tried and punished as adults. Finally, legislatures set the juvenile justice budget (Sickmund 2003, 5).

Let's take a closer look at juvenile law enforcement, courts, and corrections.

Law Enforcement and Juveniles

Most large-city police departments have special youth divisions. Juvenile units keep records on juveniles, investigate cases involving them, and initiate referrals to the juvenile court. Juvenile officers can detain juveniles in secure facilities for brief periods. Although these special youth divisions are responsible for juveniles, in practice, regular patrol officers encounter most juveniles and make the critical decisions whether to investigate and/or arrest them (Sickmund 2003).

How police handle juveniles depends on a combination of internal and external influences that differ from department to department and even among individuals within departments. Departments adopting a community-service approach emphasize helping juveniles, whereas departments stressing the crime-fighting role view rehabilitation differently. As one officer put it:

> I don't want to sound like a hardass, but we have some really bad young hoodlums on the streets in L.A. These aren't the nickel and dime kid shoplifters; they are hardcore. Some of them have dozens of arrests, but they're still out there ripping off people. These pukes are into juvenile hall and out twenty minutes later; seriously, some of these hoodlums are back on the street before I finish the paperwork. If you are going to correct kids they have to get their hands whacked the first time they put them in the cookie jar, not six months later. Juvenile justice is slow. Jesus, the rights these kids have got. They have more rights than I have. I'm not talking about the Mickey Mouse cases; I mean the serious hoodlums. (Carter 1976, 124)

Department policies and the outlook of individual officers also affect the way juveniles are processed. The general formalization of the criminal process has affected police discretion in processing juveniles less than it has in police dealing with

▶ **FIGURE 15.3 The Juvenile
Justice Process (Simplified)**

Source: South Carolina Department
of Juvenile Justice Web Page.
http://www.state.sc.us/djj/process
.html. Visited December 16, 2004.

**South Carolina Department
of Juvenile Justice:** Overview
of the state's juvenile justice
system and process. To reach
this site go to "Web Links"
on your Samaha CJ7 website:
http://cj.wadsworth.com/
samaha_cj7e.

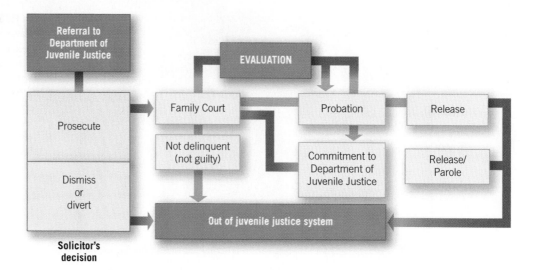

adults. The police have a range of options in deciding what to do with juvenile law-breakers. Their four major choices (Anderson, Garza, and Davis 2003) are to:

1. Ignore them
2. Counsel and release them
3. Refer them to other agencies
4. Process them further into the juvenile justice system (5)

If officers see juveniles together in a situation where the officers "sense something is wrong," for example, they may simply pass by or stop for a brief conversation. Or they may take further actions (Sickmund 2003, 2). From the least to the most invasive, the officers' actions might include:

1. Ask for their names, addresses, and what they're up to.
2. Search them.
3. Tell them to break up and move on.
4. Take them home and warn their parents to keep them off the street.
5. Take them to the station for further questioning without arresting them.
6. Take them to the station house and call in their parents. If the parents seem amenable, officers warn parents and kids of the consequences of further bad conduct and send them home.

None of these choices involves formal police action, because the police haven't arrested anybody (Carter 1984, 27).

In about half the cases, police decide to "counsel and release" (Greenwood 2004, 86). These actions may be *informal,* but informal handling can have greater consequences than you might expect. For example, police might treat this option like an informal probation system. So if juveniles who are counseled and released commit further offenses, they'll be arrested. Police also use the informal counsel-and-release option as a trade for information about other juveniles (Anderson et al. 2003).

Juveniles who aren't counseled and dismissed are either arrested and then released or referred to either a social service agency (diversion) or sent to juvenile court (referral). According to most estimates, about 50 percent of the juveniles who come into contact with police are referred to juvenile court. Police can also detain juveniles (detention) until they enter the juvenile court process (intake). Most juveniles are released while they wait for intake; about one-third are detained (Empey 1978, 432; Harris 1986, 107).

At least one criterion for deciding whether to release, divert, arrest, or refer to juvenile court should be familiar to you by now—the seriousness of the offense. The police are almost certain to arrest and refer to juvenile court juveniles suspected of serious crimes, such as murder, rape, or major theft. They're much more likely to dismiss or divert juveniles suspected of status offenses (Harris 1986, 107).

◄ How police handle juveniles depends partly on what part of the police mission an officer or department focuses on: providing service, maintaining order, or fighting crime. The fast food restaurant security guard taking this teenager into custody is probably most interested in fighting crime, but the police may have something else in mind. They might not arrest the juvenile but might rather counsel and/or and release him.

Citizen complaints also are important in police decisions to arrest juveniles. Police acquire most of their information concerning juveniles in the same way they do for adults—from private persons. If complainants are present and demand action short of arrest, police comply; if they ask for leniency, police grant it; if they demand formal arrest and processing, the officers usually accede. So the presence and wishes of those who complain influence whether juveniles are counseled and released, diverted to social service agencies, or arrested.

Department policy also affects police decision making. The numbers of arrested juveniles police refer to juvenile court vary widely. Some departments refer less than 10 percent, others as many as 80 percent. In a legalistic department (Chapter 5), to use James Q. Wilson's typology, impersonal legal standards are applied and more arrests will take place. In more service-oriented departments, or those that are less formalized, officers exercise wider discretion in releasing and diverting.

Inappropriate criteria can infect decision making. Take gender. Females commit the *same* kinds of offenses as males, even though they commit *fewer* delinquent acts—they use illegal substances, shoplift, skip school, destroy property, steal, and burglarize. But officers are less likely to arrest females than males for these offenses. On the other hand, they're more likely to detain female runaways and females who disobey their parents or are sexually active. In Honolulu, for example, only 6.1 percent of the females who committed serious criminal offenses were referred to juvenile court, whereas 33.7 percent of those arrested for status offenses were referred. Nationwide, 75 percent of the female delinquents referred to juvenile court were arrested for status, not criminal, offenses (Empey 1978, 426–427). (See the In Focus box "Arrest a 13-Year-Old for DWI?")

Also, racial minorities and the poor are overrepresented in the arrest statistics for juveniles, just as they are for adults. To what extent this overrepresentation is due to outright prejudice or inequalities in society and economy isn't clear. Naturally, inner-city dwellers and the police see matters very differently (Empey 1978, 427–428). Although now almost a half-century old, two contrasting assessments about race and juvenile justice still hold true. Black novelist and commentator on racism, James Baldwin (1962), wrote the following about police in the inner cities:

> Their very presence is an insult, and it would be, even if they spent their entire day feeding
> gum drops to children. They represent the force of the white world, and that world's criminal

Arrest a 13-Year-Old for DWI?

Even in a profession where few days can be considered routine, a state trooper's discovery of a drunken 13-year-old trying to drive away a crumpled vehicle was a rarity. The girl had an alcohol-concentration level of slightly more than 0.20 when she was arrested early Christmas morning, said State Patrol Capt. Jay Swanson. That is more than twice the legal limit for drivers 21 and over.

"We do arrest teens for drunken driving," Swanson said. "But usually they're 16 or 17. In 24½ years of doing this, I can't remember a case when a 13-year-old was arrested for DWI."

Authorities don't yet know where the girl got the alcohol or how she gained access to the car, Swanson said. No alcohol was found in the car. State trooper Beth Stanton saw a car stalled on northbound Interstate Hwy. 35W near 50th Street in Minneapolis about 3:30 a.m. Dec. 25. She first noticed a girl curled up on the ground near the center median crying. When Stanton went to the car, she found another girl in the driver's seat trying to put the car into gear, Swanson said. Stanton reached into the car, took the keys and pulled the girl from the car.

The teenage driver was taken to the Juvenile Detention Center, but she was so unruly that officials there asked that she be taken to Hennepin County Medical Center. The girl who was found crying in the median was distraught because her friend had been trying to leave without her, Swanson said....

After the girl's arrest, she continued to yell, swear and spit on Stanton, Swanson said.... "This is truly a sad situation," Swanson said. "My first question is what were these girls doing out at that time of night. The next is where did they get access to a car and alcohol."...

According to the Minnesota Department of Public Safety, in 2002 there were 32,948 drunken-driving arrests reported in the state. Of those arrests, 3,029 involved people under 21. Only six of those involved youths 14 and younger. While a 13-year-old drunken driver may be rare, addiction expert Carol Falkowski of the Hazelden Foundation said the widespread use of alcohol is such that "it was only a matter of time until a case like this showed up." A national survey done for the National Institute on Drug Abuse last year showed that 45.6 percent of eighth-graders said they had used alcohol at some point. It also showed that 20.3 percent of eighth-graders reported having been drunk. Those figures are down slightly, however, from 2002 when 47 percent of eighth-graders reported having used alcohol and 21.3 percent reported having been drunk.

Source: Howie Padilla, "Case of drunken driver, 13, surprises even troopers," *Star Tribune,* January 8, 2004, p. 1B. Republished with permission of *Star Tribune,* Minneapolis-St. Paul.

---

profit and ease, to keep the black man corralled up here, in his place. The badge, the gun in the holster, and the swinging club make vivid what will happen should his rebellion become overt. (66)

From the other side, criminologist James Q. Wilson (1978) wrote:

The patrolman believes with considerable justification that teenagers, Negroes, and lower income persons commit a disproportionate share of all reported crimes; being in those population categories at all makes one, statistically, more suspect than other persons; but to be in those categories and to behave unconventionally is to make oneself a prime suspect. Patrolmen believe they would be derelict in their duty if they did not treat such persons with suspicion, routinely question them on the street, and detain them for longer questioning if a crime has occurred in the area. To the objection of some middle-class observers that this is arbitrary or discriminatory, the police are likely to answer: "Have you ever been stopped or searched? Of course not. We can tell the difference; we have to tell the difference in order to do our job. What are you complaining about?" (40–41)

Juvenile Court

This court is a far more complex instrument than outsiders imagine. It is law, and it is social work; it is control, and it is help; it is the good parent and, also, the stern parent; it is both formal and informal. It is concerned not only with the delinquent, but also with the battered child, the runaway, and many others. The juvenile court has been all things to all people. (Rubin 1976, 66)

The juvenile court process starts with a referral. Law enforcement refers most (84%) of the cases to juvenile court; parents, schools, child welfare agencies, and probation officers refer the rest (Sickmund 2003, 2). From the time of referral, the juvenile court process consists of three-steps: (1) intake, (2) adjudication, and (3) disposition. Let's look at each.

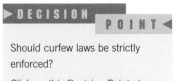

▶DECISION POINT◀

Should curfew laws be strictly enforced?

Click on this Decision Point at http://cj.wadsworth.com/samaha_cj7e to explore the issue.

Intake *Intake* consists of screening the cases referred to the court. Juvenile probation departments and/or prosecutors' offices are in charge of intake. Screening consists of making one of three choices (Sickmund 2003, 2):

1. Dismiss the case outright.
2. Handle the manner informally.
3. Request formal intervention by the juvenile court.

The decision-making process behind the choice begins with prosecutors and/or the probation department deciding whether there's enough evidence to prove the case against the juvenile. If there isn't, they dismiss the case outright.

If there's enough evidence, the next step is to decide whether formal court action (adjudication) is necessary. Intake officers dismiss about half of the cases with enough evidence; in the other half, juveniles voluntarily agree to and sign a written agreement (consent decree) to comply with specific conditions for a specific period of time (Sickmund 2003, 2). Typical conditions include victim restitution, school attendance, drug counseling, and/or curfew. Probation officers monitor compliance with the conditions. If the juvenile meets the conditions, the case is dismissed; if not, the case is referred for formal juvenile court hearing.

To start formal juvenile court proceedings, intake officers have to file one of two types of petition. **Delinquency petitions** request a trial (in juvenile court it's called an adjudicatory hearing) to find the youth a delinquent, and make him or her a ward of the court. **Transfer petitions** (discussed later) ask for a hearing to waive the juvenile court's jurisdiction and transfer the case to adult criminal courts. Let's look at the proceedings that follow a delinquency petition.

delinquency petitions requests for a trial (adjudicatory hearing) to find the youth a delinquent and make him or her a ward of the court

transfer petitions requests for a hearing to waive the juvenile court's jurisdiction and transfer the case to adult criminal courts

Adjudicatory Hearing During *adjudication*, judges (with a lot of help from probation officers) decide whether the allegations in the petition prove delinquency. If they do, juveniles are formally judged "delinquent." Since the U.S. Supreme Court opinions reviewed at the beginning of this chapter, the juvenile court's proceedings have become more formal than originally intended. Juveniles are notified of the pending delinquency charges, lawyers are more often present, evidence standards are stricter, and proceedings are more like criminal courts. Despite some increase in formality, juvenile justice expert Lamar Empey (1978) noted that:

> It is only in a minority of courts where attorneys and due process procedures are uniformly present. As more courts begin to adhere to this model, however, it seems likely that less attention will be paid to the moral condition of the child and more to the evidence in support of the charge. It is likely, moreover, that resistance will grow to the formal trials of status offenders, not only because they are not charged with crimes, but because status offenses are more difficult to prove. (457–458)

Disposition Once juveniles have been adjudicated delinquent, judges schedule **disposition hearings** to decide how best to resolve delinquency cases. In the meantime, probation officers conduct background investigations to assist judges in their disposition decisions. Juvenile court judges have wide discretion to choose from a broad range of alternative dispositions, ranging from unconditional dismissal to commitment to secure correctional facilities resembling adult prisons.

Judges may decide to order a **continuance in contemplation of dismissal.** If delinquents don't get into further trouble with the law within a specified period—often between six months and a year—judges will dismiss their cases. Continuance lets judges keep open their option for further action if juveniles don't obey the law. Judges might also continue cases until the fulfillment of specified conditions, including taking required diagnostic tests and treatment for disturbances stemming from emotional problems, substance abuse, and physical illness; observing curfew; paying restitution to victims; and providing community service. Delinquents usually are allowed one to six months to fulfill these conditions (Albanese 1985, 89).

Probation of delinquents strongly resembles adult probation (Chapter 12). For delinquents confined in juvenile correctional facilities for status offenses and minor

disposition hearing a hearing to decide how best to resolve delinquency cases

continuance in contemplation of dismissal dismissal of the case if the juvenile stays out of trouble for a specific time period

Florida Department of Juvenile Justice: Overview of Florida's juvenile justice process. To reach this site go to "Web Links" on your Samaha CJ7 website: http://cj.wadsworth.com/samaha_cj7e.

property crimes, confinement probably means training schools or camps. Or the confinement might consist of community-based programs, such as foster care, youth development centers, or independent living arrangements. For serious delinquency, juvenile corrections means secure facilities that resemble adult prisons.

Some observers believe juveniles aren't treated fairly; that is, they believe inappropriate factors infect disposition decisions. Some of these factors are based on attitudes that date back to the Progressives. Anthony Platt (1969) concluded that the Progressive "child savers" used dispositions to impose middle-class values on lower-class youths:

> The child saving movement had its most direct consequences on the children of the urban poor. The fact that "troublesome" adolescents were depicted as "sick" or "pathological," were "imprisoned for their own good," and were addressed in a paternalistic vocabulary, and exempted from criminal law processes did not alter the subjective experiences of control, restraint, and punishment. The "invention" of delinquency consolidated the inferior social status and dependency of lower-class youth. (176–178)

Sociologist Edwin Schur (1973) agreed:

> The philosophy of the juvenile court ensures that stereotypes will influence judicial dispositions. Sending the child who comes from a "broken home" in the slums to a training school, while giving probation to a youngster from a "good family" may not strike the judge as an exercise in stereotyping. However, such stereotypes tend to be self-confirming. Children from "broken homes" are likely to be committed to institutions because they are believed to be delinquency-prone; yet these very commitments, in turn, serve to reinforce that belief. (44)

Neither Platt nor Schur based his findings on empirical evidence. Lawrence E. Cohen made an effort to measure empirically the influences on juvenile court dispositions. He gathered information about nearly 13,000 juveniles who appeared before juvenile courts in three counties in Colorado, Tennessee, and Pennsylvania. Cohen measured the effects of juveniles' age, sex, ethnicity, socioeconomic status, and family situation; the seriousness of their offenses; the number of their prior referrals to juvenile court; their referral agent; whether the juveniles were in detention prior to hearings; and whether there were formal petitions or informal dispositions against them (Cohen 1975).

The jurisdictions varied considerably. In Colorado, the seriousness of the offense was most important. In Tennessee, offense seriousness was also most significant but was followed closely by whether the police referred the juveniles and whether they were in detention prior to adjudication. In Pennsylvania, the most important factors were whether juveniles were idle, from broken homes, and referred by agencies other than police (Cohen 1975).

Other investigators have found that minority youths are more likely to be incarcerated and less likely to be put on probation. Barry Krisberg and his colleagues (1986) took data collected nationally in a semiannual survey conducted by the U.S. Bureau of the Census, called Children in Custody (CIC), and compared the populations in juvenile correctional facilities with the arrest statistics in the Uniform Crime Reports. They found that in 1982, for example, Black youths were incarcerated at a rate of 8.6 per 100 compared with 5.1 per 100 for Whites, a ratio 69 percent higher. For Native Americans, the ratio was even higher—14.5. The researchers concluded that the reasons for this higher incarceration rate were not due to offense seriousness (23).

Offense seriousness (as we've repeatedly emphasized) is an appropriate reason for incarceration, but race and ethnicity clearly aren't. Equally inappropriate are idleness and broken homes, criteria that demonstrate that juveniles continue to be incarcerated according to attitudes prejudicial to those who are not from traditional, middle-class families (Albanese 1985, 91).

Transfer to Adult Criminal Court

dual system of justice one system of justice for adults and another for juveniles

Our **dual system of justice** for adults and juveniles is divided mainly according to age. What about juveniles who commit serious crimes? Are their murders, rapes, and robberies merely "delinquent acts"? Or should juveniles who commit these crimes be treated like adults—either partly or completely? The answers to these questions lie in the **transfer** of cases from the juvenile court (also called **waiver** of juvenile court jurisdiction or **certification** of juvenile cases for trial in adult criminal courts).

Here's how transfer works. The prosecutor or probation officer working in intake files a waiver petition when she believes an adult criminal court would handle the case "more appropriately" (Sickmund 2003, 3). After the intake officer files the petition, the juvenile court judge decides whether to waive jurisdiction of the juvenile court and transfer the case to adult criminal court. You shouldn't be surprised to learn that the criteria for the decision boil down to the strength of the case, the seriousness of the offense, and the juvenile's delinquency and criminal record. Juvenile courts waive about 1 percent of formal waiver petitions (Sickmund 2003, 3).

The practice of waiver of juvenile court jurisdiction and transfer to adult criminal courts is old, and all states allow it today. Some states' laws mandate transfer. Thirty-four states have "once an adult, always an adult" provisions, meaning that once a juvenile's been tried in adult criminal court, she has to be tried in adult court for subsequent offenses (Sickmund 2003, 7). Other mandatory transfer statutes target murder or crimes involving weapons.

Whatever the statutes say, transfers have increased since the 1990s (from 70% in the 1980s to 96% in 1994 in South Carolina), due in part to the shift from rehabilitation to punishment (Sickmund 2003, 8). Not surprisingly, the cases most likely to be waived are those where the offense is serious (the juvenile uses a weapon and injures someone) and the juvenile has a criminal history. This follows the practice approved by the U.S. Supreme Court in *Kent v. United States* (1966) discussed earlier: "An offense will be waived if it is heinous or of aggravated character, or even though less serious—if it represents a pattern of repeated offenses" (566).

transfer (also called **waiver** or **certification**) transfer of cases from juvenile court to adult criminal court

Youthful Offenders Program Information from Florida's Department of Corrections: Educational, counseling, and vocational programs offered to juveniles who have been convicted as adults and sentenced to prison. To reach this site go to "Web Links" on your Samaha CJ7 website: http://cj.wadsworth.com/samaha_cj7e.

▶ DECISION POINT ◀

How would you decide whether to charge a juvenile as an "adult"? Click on this Decision Point at http://cj.wadsworth.com/samaha_cj7e to explore the issue.

AP/Wide World Photos

◀ Jake Lee Eakin, 13 (foreground), of Moses Lake, Washington, looks at family members as he and his friend Evan Savoie, also 13, of Ephrata, Washington, attend a court hearing to decide whether they'll be tried as adults for first-degree murder. The victim was Craig Songer, a special education student, also 13, who was beaten and stabbed to death. The court eventually ordered the case transferred to adult criminal court, and in February 2005 the Washington state supreme court let stand the lower court's order. Estimates predict that a trial will cost more than $1 million. Transfers from juvenile to adult criminal court have been on the rise since the 1990s, especially in cases like this one where weapons and violence were involved.

Juvenile Corrections

The history of juvenile corrections has tracked pretty closely that of adult corrections (Chapters 12–14) and of criminal justice in general (Chapter 1). We won't go over that history again. Instead, we'll start our story of juvenile corrections in the 1950s, when a great interest arose in community-based alternatives to large, state-run institutions for delinquents, exemplified in the growth of local institutions, residential youth centers, group homes, and specialized probation services. From the late 1960s to the 1970s, in a second phase of this development, diversion and deinstitutionalization programs proliferated and were touted as the panacea to youth crime and delinquency. These community-based corrections rested on the conviction that state reformatories failed to prevent delinquency and, in fact, made it worse by stigmatizing youths exposed to it. Such youths became part of a "state youth subculture" heavily involved in patterns of both state dependence and criminality that were very difficult, if not impossible, to break (Cloward and Ohlin 1960).

The prison population "binge" and the shift from treatment to punishment in adult corrections (Chapters 12–14) have their parallels in juvenile corrections, like demands for more focus on punishment, deterrence, and community safety. Not that rehabilitation was ever the sole mission of juvenile justice—informally, punishment and community protection have always been missions, even if they're not admitted to up front. Still, there are differences between adult and juvenile corrections. Rehabilitation is still a major goal; probation is widespread; and there's more variety in juvenile correctional institutions (called "residential placements"), including training schools, treatment centers, boot camps, and group homes. Let's look at juvenile community (probation) and institutional placements.

Probation Most juvenile court delinquency cases result in probation (Puzzanchera 2003, 1). We won't discuss juvenile probation here because most of what you learned about probation in Chapter 12 applies here.

Institutional Corrections Let's start with some basic information about prisoners (in juvenile justice, they're called "residents") in juvenile institutions (usually called "juvenile custody facilities"). The latest survey (Sickmund 2004) highlights the following about juvenile custody facilities:

- Seventy percent of juvenile offenders are held in locked facilities. (16)
- Nearly 8 out of 10 residents are held for delinquency offenses. (3)
- Two out of three facilities are private, but they hold less than 1 out of 3 juvenile offenders. (3)
- The resident population has increased more than 50 percent since 1991. (4)
- The number of status offender residents has decreased since 1991, except for underage drinking, which has risen more then 68 percent. (5)
- Minority youths accounted for 7 in 10 residents held for a violent offense; rates for Blacks were highest. (9–11)
- Females make up a small part of juvenile residents. (14)

Juvenile correctional institutions cover a broad spectrum, from small, short-term, nonsecure facilities to long-term, highly secure facilities serving large areas. Foster homes—small, nonsecure substitutes for real families—are used at all stages in the juvenile justice process. Police might temporarily place arrested juveniles who can't be returned to their homes in foster homes instead of detention facilities. Courts might also assign juveniles to foster homes before, or after, adjudication. The National Advisory Commission (NAC) recommends foster care as the primary placement for minor delinquency. However, due to inadequate—and sometimes totally absent—accreditation and monitoring, some persons convicted of child abuse have received or retained foster home licenses (Finckenauer 1984, 151).

◄ Tim Muller laughs at a joke made by class valedictorian Matthew Graves during high school graduation in the gym of the Youthful Offenders Services prison for kids in Pueblo, Colorado. The prison holds minors convicted as adults of felonies like burglary and assault and offers job training and a high school education.

Shelters, nonsecure residential facilities, hold juveniles temporarily. These include juveniles who aren't sent home after arrest or who are waiting for placement after being adjudicated delinquent. Shelters are reserved mainly for status and property offenders.

Group homes, also nonsecure, relatively open community-based facilities, mainly hold juveniles who've been adjudicated delinquent. Group homes are larger and less familylike than foster homes. Small group homes serve from 4 to 8; large group homes serve from 8 to 12. Residents range in age from 10 to 17, but most are between 13 and 16. Group homes permit more independent living in a more permanent setting, and they are more treatment oriented than shelters. Group home residents usually attend school—in the home or in the community—or they work. They also participate in individual and group counseling and recreation. Group homes are intended to provide support and structure in nonrestrictive settings that facilitate reintegration into the community (National Institute of Corrections 1983, xvii).

Halfway houses are large, nonsecure residential centers. They provide both a place to live and a range of personal and social services. The typical halfway house serves from 12 to 20 residents, but some large programs serve as many as 40 residents. Residents' ages range from 14 to 18. "Halfway houses provide a range of services and emphasize normal group living, school attendance, securing employment, working with parents to resolve problems and general participation in the community" (National Institute of Corrections 1983, xvi).

Camps and ranches are nonsecure facilities located in rural and remote areas. Juveniles adjudicated delinquent are generally placed in camps as an alternative to the more secure training schools. The healthful setting, small numbers of residents, and close contact between staff and juveniles are supposed to develop good work and living habits that will facilitate rehabilitation. Ranches and camps emphasize outside activity, self-discipline, and the development of vocational and interpersonal skills. Juveniles assigned to them are not only supposed to develop good work habits, but they are also to perform "useful and necessary" work that benefits the community (National Advisory Committee 1980, 487–491).

Detention centers are temporary custodial facilities. But unlike shelters, detention centers are secure institutions—lockups—that hold juveniles both before and after adjudication. The three formal purposes of locking up juveniles in detention centers include:

1. To secure their presence at court proceedings
2. To hold those who cannot be sent home
3. To protect them from harming themselves or others or disrupting juvenile court processes

Juveniles who have committed more serious offenses are sent to detention centers; less serious offenders go to shelters (Finckenauer 1984, 151). (See the In Focus box "Juvenile Detention of Mentally Ill Juveniles: Substitute for Mental Health Care?")

Before adjudication, juveniles may stay in detention centers anywhere from a day to more than two weeks, raising the troubling question of the fairness of detention prior to proven delinquency. Detention is also sometimes used as informal punishment. Judges lock up juveniles to scare them, to show them what might happen to them, or to "teach them a lesson and give them a taste of jail." Some jurisdictions have formalized detention centers as jails for children. New Jersey, for example, permits sentencing juveniles who have been adjudicated delinquent for "repetitive disorderly persons offenses" to up to 60 days in detention centers (American Correctional Association 1983, xvii; New Jersey P.L. 1982, chap. 77, sec. 24).

Not all detained juveniles go to juvenile detention centers. Some are housed in adult jails—a situation criticized for more than a century. James O. Finckenauer (1984) visited one of these jails in Tyler, Texas, and reported the following:

> This author visited one such all purpose jail. On the upper floor of this jail (on a very humid day in late June, with the temperature soaring into triple figures) approximately a dozen juveniles were confined in a large bullpen cell. This cell was literally a "hot box," dark and without ventilation. Some of the juveniles were from out of the state, and the average stay for most was somewhere around forty-five days. Because these youth were confined in an adult facility, and because the sheriff was attempting to maintain physical separation of juveniles and adults, the youth had no place to go and nothing to do for just about the entire duration of their incarceration. The NAC referred to the jailing of juveniles as a "disconcerting phenomenon." This is certainly an understatement, to say the very least. Because they are intended to be temporary holding facilities, jails and detention centers offer little or nothing in the way of correctional treatment. (132)

Training schools are found in every state except Massachusetts, which abolished them in the 1970s. They vary greatly in size, staff, services, programs, ages, and types of residents. Most, however, house from one to several hundred juveniles committed by juvenile courts. Some training schools resemble adult prisons, with congregate-style living and emphasis on security and order, whereas others are relatively open facilities that focus on treatment and rehabilitation.

Training schools are the instrument of last resort in the juvenile correctional system. They contain the most serious delinquents: those who are security risks, have substantial prior records, or have exhausted other juvenile court dispositions. Almost all training schools are state-operated and controlled, unlike the other facilities discussed. Most legislation requires training schools to provide both safe custody and rehabilitative treatment (American Correctional Association 1983, xvii).

According to corrections expert Kenneth Wooden (1976):

> I found basically two types of training schools. The first is a miniature penitentiary with high walls surrounding the grounds. All the buildings and cell block wings therein are interlocked by long corridors. Not only are individual cell doors secured, but each wing is also locked at all times. There is almost always a self-sufficient industrial complex on the grounds—laundry, hospital, maintenance shop and any other facility needed to keep strangers out and the children in. Dubious educational and religious services are available to the children, along with the standbys of solitary confinement and of bloodhounds to locate any who run away.
>
> The second and more common type of training school is the cottage system. Its concept was introduced in 1856 to give children the closest thing to some form of home life. Those in charge are "house parents" rather than "guards." The outside area is usually quiet and

Juvenile Detention of Mentally Ill Juveniles: Substitute for Mental Health Care?

"Congressional investigators said Wednesday that 15,000 children with psychiatric disorders were improperly incarcerated last year because no mental health services were available.... The use of juvenile detention facilities to warehouse children with mental disorders is a serious national problem," said Senator Susan Collins, Republican of Maine, who sought the survey with Representative Henry A. Waxman, Democrat of California.

The study, presented at a hearing of the Senate Committee on Governmental Affairs, found that children as young as 7 were incarcerated because of a lack of access to mental health care. More than 340 detention centers, two-thirds of those that responded to the survey, said youths with mental disorders were being locked up because there was no place else for them to go while awaiting treatment. Seventy-one centers in 33 states said they were holding mentally ill youngsters with no charges. The 15,000 youths awaiting mental health services accounted for 8 percent of all the youngsters in the responding detention centers.

Dr. Ken Martinez of the New Mexico Department of Children, Youth and Families said the data showed "the criminalization of mental illness" as "juvenile detention centers have become de facto psychiatric hospitals for mentally ill youth." Mental health advocates, prison officials and juvenile court judges all testified and recommended three types of solutions: more community mental health services, financed in part by Medicaid; more cooperation between police officials and mental health agencies; and more extensive insurance coverage.

The witnesses included experts on psychiatry and juvenile justice. Judge Ernestine S. Gray of New Orleans Juvenile Court testified that 70 percent to 85 percent of the youngsters who appeared before the court had mental health or drug problems. "All too often," Judge Gray said, "children charged with delinquent behavior are identified early on as needing mental health services. But because the services are not available, the children are sent back home until there is another violation. After several brushes with the law, the children are incarcerated, so they might have a chance at getting mental health services."

Leonard B. Dixon, director of the Wayne County Juvenile Detention Facility in Detroit, said mentally ill children were "more difficult to manage, more explosive and more easily agitated." "Most juvenile detention centers," Mr. Dixon said, "do not have the luxury of separating youth with mental health problems from the general population."

Carol Carothers, executive director of the Maine chapter of the National Alliance for the Mentally Ill, told of a 13-year-old who was sent to a detention center even though he was suffering depression and had suicidal thoughts. He was held in isolation for 152 of his first 240 days there, Ms. Carothers said. He was sent to the youth center four more times, becoming more depressed and aggressive, and was punished for misbehavior, worsening the symptoms of his mental illness, she added.

Mr. Dixon, who is also president of the National Juvenile Detention Association, a professional organization, described a 16-year-old who was detained after having been accused of stabbing a classmate in the neck with a pencil. The youth was psychotic and severely depressed and had hallucinations, but was held in a detention center for months before going to a psychiatric hospital for treatment, Mr. Dixon said.

Dr. Steven S. Sharfstein, president-elect of the American Psychiatric Association, said: "We are in a much better position to diagnose and treat mental illness in children than we were just 15 years ago. Many kids who get in trouble should be in treatment. But because of the lack of money and the lack of services, they end up in the criminal justice system."

In an interview, Dr. Sharfstein, who is president of the Sheppard Pratt Health System in Baltimore, said: "It used to be thought that these were bad kids. But many of them are sick and could benefit from treatment such as medications, psychotherapy or therapeutic education—small classes and individualized attention that focuses on learning disabilities."

In California, 27 centers reported unnecessary incarcerations of youths awaiting mental health services; 19 reported that some of the children had attempted suicide.

Texas had 17 detention centers with children who could have been released if mental health services were available, according to the survey. New Jersey had 13, Florida and Illinois 7 each and New York 4.

Source: Robert Pear, "Many Youths Reported Held Awaiting Mental Help," *New York Times*, July 8, 2004. Copyright © 2004 by The New York Times Co. Reprinted with permission.

---

pleasant and bears little semblance to a penal facility. The cottages are usually small, aesthetically pleasing, dormlike structures. Unfortunately, those I have seen have no back or side doors, or if they do, the doors are always chained and locked. The windows are also secured with heavy wire. The cottage system always reserves one building for secure treatment, solitary confinement. Any child who acts up in solitary cottage is further isolated in a special single room for indefinite periods of time. (28–29)

MAKE YOUR DECISION *Juvenile Corrections: Rehabilitation or Punishment?*

There are no handcuffs, no razor-wire fences, no uniforms, no cells. Missouri does things differently in its prisons for young people, and it shows—in what you see and what you don't. Inmates, referred to as "kids," live in dorms that feature beanbag chairs, potted plants, stuffed animals and bunk beds with smiley-face comforters. Guards—who are called "youth specialists" and must have college degrees—go by their first names and don't hesitate to offer hugs.

At the maximum-security lockup in St. Joseph, two cats, Midnight and Tigger, curl up on laps as the state's toughest teenage offenders explore the roots of their anger, weep over the acts of abusive parents and swap strategies for breaking free of gangs. At another facility in Kansas City, boys who rack up months of good behavior earn the right to attend summer basketball camp.

"The old corrections model was a failure; most kids left us worse off than when they came in," said Mark Steward, the chief of Missouri's youth penal system. "So we threw away that culture, and now we focus on treatment, on making connections with these guys and showing them another way.... It works."

As California struggles to reshape a juvenile prison system so troubled and violent that some legislators want it closed down, Missouri—the Show Me State—is winning accolades as the national leader in handling kids who break the law. "Missouri is the best model we have out there," said Paul DeMuro, a New Jersey-based juvenile justice consultant and former chief of youth prisons in Pennsylvania.

"It works because they believe in the 'small is beautiful' theory," agreed Barry Krisberg, president of the National Council on Crime and Delinquency and the author of a recent report on California's juvenile system. "It's about high-quality treatment in an intimate setting." Comparing recidivism numbers is tricky, but Missouri is clearly a standout among states, Krisberg said. A 2003 study found that of the 1,400 teenagers released in 1999, only 8% wound up in adult prisons. California does not keep a comparable statistic. About half of those released from its juvenile prisons, however, will be back behind bars within two years, officials say. Missouri's system also delivers when it comes to another important measurement: cost. It spends about $43,000 a year per child. California's per capita tab is nearly twice that—$80,000—largely because its officers are paid almost twice as much, though the cost of living in the Golden State is near the top nationally, while Missouri's is among the lowest, statistics show.

Source: Jennifer Warren, "Spare the Rod, Save the Child: Missouri's Youth Prisons Focus on Small Groups, Therapy, Caring. Officials in California's Punishment-Oriented System Are Taking a Look," *Los Angeles Times*, July 1, 2004. Reprinted with permission.

Not one young inmate has committed suicide in the two decades since Missouri altered its approach to delinquent kids. In the California Youth Authority, meanwhile, 15 have killed themselves since 1996, including two boys found hanging by bedsheets last January in the isolation cell they shared.

Drawn by the success stories, delegations of corrections officials from around the nation are visiting Missouri for a closer look. Several states, including Louisiana, Georgia, Maryland, New Jersey and Illinois, have launched or are considering copycat programs.

Over the last 20 years, Missouri has replaced a traditional approach to young criminals—large, prison-like lockups with an emphasis on punishment and isolation—with small group settings that blend highly trained staff with constant therapy and positive peer pressure. Convinced that family connections are crucial, Missouri also takes pains to house children within 50 miles of their homes. If necessary, the government sends a van to enable parents to visit.

"The Missouri system is everything the California system isn't," DeMuro said. "It's a matter of philosophy and

▲ Director Mark Steward of the Missouri Division of Youth Services jokes with residents of the division's Rosa Parks Center as he passes out candy he brought to them. "We assess the risks and the needs of each person, while other states use the prison model, where they go into a cell and have three hots and a cot," said Steward. "We tried it that way in Missouri for more than 100 years, too. It didn't work." Missouri's model of placing youth offenders into nurturing settings for rehabilitation reports an 8 percent recidivism rate.

the will to do something right and appropriate, rather than warehousing kids and creating a hotbed for gangs and more violence."

Officials in California say the pervasive presence of gangs in the state, and the fact that the CYA (California Youth Authority) houses inmates as old as 25, makes the Missouri system unworkable in the Golden State. In Missouri, most inmates in juvenile prisons are younger than 18, though some are as old as 21.

"Everything I hear about Missouri tells me its programs work great for the population they have, but our demographics are very different," said Kevin Carruth, California's undersecretary of youth and adult corrections. Still, CYA Director Walt Allen plans to visit Missouri and several other states in the coming months, looking for ideas. Krisberg, who has been advising Allen on how to address the CYA's problems, agrees that California is "different from the rest of the world, so in some ways comparisons don't make much sense." He added, however, that the essence of Missouri's system—a commitment to small programs that emphasize treatment and rehabilitation—could be imported.

Last month two dozen youth advocates, former CYA inmates and parents with kids currently locked up in California toured the Missouri system. They were so impressed by the contrast that they met with Allen and lawmakers in Sacramento, pressing them to adopt a similar approach. "This place is like a dream," Katrina Allen, a Fresno minister whose 17-year-old son is in the CYA, said after visiting a medium-security facility in a woodsy park near Kansas City. "The whole focus is on treating kids so they can get a new start. In California, it's about trying not to get beat up and just doing time."

The Californians were particularly struck by the near absence of violence. Teenagers at one maximum-security center in Kansas City could recall only three scuffles in the last year, none serious. Asked if they worried about being jumped, they laughed. Staff assaults, too, are rare, said Steward, who could not remember any off the top of his head.

In California, meanwhile, a February report described the Youth Authority as a place permeated by fear among employees and inmates alike. At some prisons visited by a team of experts, youths attacked one another an average of 10 times a day. Officers at a CYA facility in Chino used Mace on youths four times a day during a four-month period in 2003, the report said.

California's present looks a lot like Missouri's past. For almost a century, the Midwestern state housed delinquent boys in a prison-like training school with a notorious solitary-confinement cell known as "the Hole." But in 1983, after a series of scandals and reports deploring conditions at the facility, the state decided to scatter its juveniles into groups of no more than 35 each. The move reflected research showing that in large-scale settings, youths tend to get lost and that relationships with counselors and other staff—a key to rehabilitation—are more difficult to forge.

After a fitful start, Missouri gradually settled on a formula, one heavy on therapy and anchored by a complex peer culture that helps teenagers resolve day-to-day problems, confront the roots of their criminality and seek a promising life path. The rehabilitative philosophy is reflected even in the aesthetics of the lockups. Dorm rooms overflow with homey touches—a piano and scented candle here, a fish tank and flowered shower curtain there.

The correctional officers look different too. Dressed in their own clothes, Missouri's staff members carry no Mace, no batons, no handcuffs—only walkie-talkies. "We don't need that stuff," said Courtney Collier, the system's regional director in Kansas City. If you do, she said, "you've got a problem."

To create such a safe environment, officials rely largely on a peer culture that engulfs youths the moment they enter a state facility. Assigned to 10-member teams with two counselors, the teenagers study, eat, sleep and exercise together. Several times a day, team members gather to "check in" with one another, a ritual that allows them to share concerns or complaints before they boil over into violence. More talk takes place after school in group treatment rooms. There, sitting together on floor pillows, youths revisit traumatic events in their lives and look for patterns that help explain what led them astray.

One exercise designed to unearth pain from the past is the creation of a "genogram," an elaborate family tree depicting violence, drug addiction and other ills suffered by relatives. Another requires teenagers to outline their bodies on a sheet of white paper and chart the emotional and physical wounds they've suffered. At the Northwest Regional Youth Center in Kansas City, for example, one boy's illustration featured marks on the head to reflect brain damage associated with methamphetamine use. Elsewhere, other scribbles symbolized scars and bruises, reflecting street fights and physical and sexual abuse by a parent.

Youths say the group therapy can be wrenching for newcomers. "Most of us come in with a fight mentality," said Eric White, 16, of Kansas City, a lanky youth who is doing time for burglary and was recently named student of the month at the Northwest Center. "But pretty soon you see there's no reason for that here." Occasionally, youths do fight—especially the newly arrived. When that happens, Missouri permits the juveniles, assisted by a staff member, to use a controversial tactic known as a "restraint"—wrestling the aggressor to the ground and holding fast until the youth calms down.

Some juvenile justice experts say offenders should not be permitted to lay hands on each other. Steward said it works here because of the intimate "team culture." There have been no injuries or lawsuits over the restraints, he said, adding that they rarely occur. Jerry Riley, 17, has never been restrained. But he arrived in the Missouri system with a defiant attitude and a long string of crimes under his belt. Initially, the youth said, he figured he could "fake the program, do my own thing." But as the months passed, his anger subsided and he spotted an opportunity. "Basically, this place allowed me the chance to be a child," said Riley, a garrulous teenager with broad shoulders and a wide grin. "My mom had five kids, she was living check to check, so I was always an adult, taking care of myself. I was always fighting, selling drugs, shooting at people, getting shot at—and I thought that was regular."

A year ago, he was arrested for selling crack cocaine and sent to the Northwest Center. "I'm glad I got caught," he said, "because I was on my way to doing bigger and bigger things." After months of exemplary behavior, Riley has earned top privileges, including daily phone calls, regular outings into the community and a week of basketball camp. He is so trusted by staff that he recently led the California visitors on a tour of the Northwest facility, dressed in a blue polo shirt and slacks. Like any good tour guide, he checked the clock frequently to make sure he stayed on schedule. Riley, who is weeks away from discharge and plans to attend college in the fall, will have a lot of help when he goes home, because intensive after-care is another uncommon hallmark of Missouri's approach.

From their first day in the state system to their last, youths are teamed with a single counselor, who develops a treatment plan tailored to their needs. Once out, a youth is assigned a second adult known as a "tracker," who acts somewhat like a big brother and meets with the parolee every few days to ensure he is staying straight.

Steward calls kids like Riley his goodwill ambassadors, and uses them to sell the story of Missouri's program in the Legislature and beyond. So far, political support has been steady and bipartisan. One big fan was the late Gov. Mel Carnahan, a Democrat, who was so taken with the program that he used to play host to a handful of boys in his statehouse office a few times a year. Another backer is conservative state Supreme Court Judge Stephen Limbaugh, cousin of radio commentator Rush Limbaugh.

Supporters say that beyond the recidivism numbers, they are captivated by the stories of lives turned around. One who embodies that transformation is Brian Laoruangroch, an ex-offender who was recently elected student body president at the University of Missouri. Earlier this year, he called his former counselor and volunteered to help promote the program. Steward wasted no time: "I said, 'See what he's doing next Tuesday,' and I brought him with us down to the House for our budget hearing."

Dressed sharply in suit and tie, the student leader recounted his lifelong struggle with drugs and other troubles, and explained the metamorphosis that took place inside Missouri's juvenile system. The legislators were smitten. Despite a budget deficit and cuts to agencies across state government, they left the youth corrections budget largely intact. Steward said he believes that his state's success can be replicated in California, despite the different mix of offenders. Older inmates, he said, have a maturity level that helps them "get" the program faster than younger kids. And Missouri's experience with youths from tough St. Louis gangs shows that such street ties are eroded by the strong peer bonds kids develop inside.

Krisberg, the president of the National Council on Delinquency, said the mission statement of the CYA would lead you to believe that it was "supposed to be doing the same thing they do in Missouri. But somewhere along the way, California went off track."

QUESTIONS

1. Describe the Missouri model of rehabilitation instead of punishment as it operates in the maximum security lockup in St. Joseph, Missouri.
2. According to Barry Krisberg, president of the National Council on Crime and Delinquency, why does the Missouri model work?
3. According to the California officials, why won't the Missouri model work in California?
4. List the arguments in favor of and against adopting the Missouri rehabilitation model in California.
5. Assume you're an advisor to the California governor. Present a plan for juvenile corrections in the state.

National Council on Crime and Delinquency (NCCD): NCCD conducts research, promotes reform initiatives, and seeks to work with individuals, public and private organizations, and the media to prevent and reduce crime and delinquency. To reach this site go to "Web Links" on your Samaha CJ7 website: http://cj.wadsworth.com/samaha_cj7e.

California Department of Youth Authority (CYA): One of the largest youth corrections agencies in the nation, with some 3,600 young men and women in institutions and camps, and approximately 4,100 more on parole. To reach this site go to "Web Links" on your Samaha CJ7 website: http://cj.wadsworth.com/samaha_cj7e.

Missouri Department of Youth Services: To reach this site go to "Web Links" on your Samaha CJ7 website: http://cj.wadsworth.com/samaha_cj7e.

Chapter Summary

- For centuries, the law has treated children and adults differently. The ferment of social reform during the 1800s produced a romantic "child saving" movement. Child saving was also on the agenda of the Progressive Era (about 1900 to 1914) reformers. The Progressives had enormous (and naïve) confidence in both the state and in experts. The Progressives had a strong faith that government could cure delinquency by making sure experts could make professional judgments unhampered by formal rules. Since the 1970s, a growing consensus among both criminal justice professionals and the public has demanded that juveniles be tried as adults. Fueling this consensus was a belief that if juveniles are old enough to commit crimes, they're old enough to take the consequences.

- The U.S. Constitution guarantees juveniles *some* rights that restrict the discretion exercised by juvenile justice officials, including due process rights to notice and a hearing, to counsel, to confront and cross-examine witnesses, and to proof beyond a reasonable doubt before classifying them as delinquent.

- Juvenile delinquency consists of both conduct that would be criminal if adults engaged in it and conduct that's illegal only if juveniles engage in it. Ages when juveniles can be judged delinquent vary among the states.

- It's difficult to measure delinquency because of inadequate statistics. But we know that youths are substantially more "crime-prone" than adults; juvenile offenders tend to commit crimes in groups; juvenile offenders tend to commit crimes in groups; and juvenile offenders are frequently armed. The picture of juvenile arrests isn't pretty, but it's not all ugly.

- The juvenile justice system consists of law enforcement, courts, and corrections agencies. Most large-city police departments have special youth divisions. How police handle juveniles depends on a combination of internal and external influences that differ from department to department and even among individuals within departments. The police have a range of options in deciding what to do with juvenile lawbreakers, including ignore them, counsel and release them, refer them to other agencies, and process them further into the juvenile justice system.

- Decision making in juvenile court proceedings consists of intake, adjudication, and disposition. Race and gender can infect decisions in criminal justice, but offense seriousness and a delinquency history are the main decision-making criteria.

- Our dual system of adult and juvenile criminal justice is divided *mainly* according to age. But depending on the seriousness of the offense and a history of delinquency, juveniles can be transferred to the adult criminal justice system. Transfers have increased since the 1990s.

- Juvenile correctional institutions cover a broad spectrum, from small, short-term, nonsecure facilities to long-term, highly secure facilities serving large areas, including shelters, group homes, halfway houses, camps and ranches, detention centers, and training schools.

Key Terms

doctrine of *parens patriae*, p. 530
juvenile court, p. 531
medical model of crime, p. 531
juveniles, p. 534
delinquency, p. 534

status offenses, p. 534
juvenile delinquent, p. 534
delinquency petitions, p. 541
transfer petitions, p. 541
disposition hearings, p. 541

continuance in contemplation of
  dismissal, p. 541
dual system of justice, p. 542
transfer (also called waiver or
  certification), p. 543

Web Resources

Go to http://cj.wadsworth.com/samaha_cj7e for a wealth of online resources related to your book. Take a "pre-test" and "post-test" for each chapter in order to help master the material. Check out the *Web Links* to access the websites mentioned in the text, as well as many others. Explore the

Decision Points flagged in the margins of the text, as well as the *Concept Builders* for additional insights. You can also access recent perspectives by clicking on *CJ in the News* and *Terrorism Update* under *Course Resources*.

Search Online with InfoTrac College Edition

For additional information, explore InfoTrac College Edition, your online library. Go to http://cj.wadsworth.com/samaha_cj7e to access InfoTrac College Edition from your

book's website. Use the passcode that came with your book. You will find InfoTrac College Edition exercises and a list of key words for further research.

Constitution of the United States

Preamble

We the People of the United States, in Order to form a more perfect Union, establish Justice, insure domestic Tranquility, provide for the common defence, promote the general Welfare, and secure the Blessings of Liberty to ourselves and our Posterity, do ordain and establish this Constitution for the United States of America.

Article I

Section 1. All legislative Powers herein granted shall be vested in a Congress of the United States, which shall consist of a Senate and House of Representatives.

Section 2. The House of Representatives shall be composed of Members chosen every second Year by the People of the several States, and the Electors in each State shall have the Qualifications requisite for Electors of the most numerous Branch of the State Legislature.

No Person shall be a Representative who shall not have attained to the Age of twenty five Years, and been seven Years a Citizen of the United States, and who shall not, when elected, be an Inhabitant of that State in which he shall be chosen.

Representatives and direct Taxes shall be apportioned among the several States which may be included within this Union, according to their respective Numbers, which shall be determined by adding to the whole Number of free Persons, including those bound to Service for a Term of Years, and excluding Indians not taxed, three fifths of all other Persons. The actual Enumeration shall be made within three Years after the first Meeting of the Congress of the United States, and within every subsequent Term of ten Years, in such Manner as they shall by Law direct. The Number of Representatives shall not exceed one for every thirty Thousand, but each State shall have at Least one Representative; and until such enumeration shall be made, the State of New Hampshire shall be entitled to choose three, Massachusetts eight, Rhode Island and Providence Plantations one, Connecticut five, New York six, New Jersey four, Pennsylvania eight, Delaware one, Maryland six, Virginia ten, North Carolina five, South Carolina five, and Georgia three.

When vacancies happen in the Representation from any State, the Executive Authority thereof shall issue Writs of Election to fill such Vacancies.

The House of Representatives shall choose their Speaker and other Officers; and shall have the sole Power of Impeachment.

Section 3. The Senate of the United States shall be composed of two Senators from each State, chosen by the Legislature thereof, for six Years; and each Senator shall have one Vote.

Immediately after they shall be assembled in Consequence of the first Election, they shall be divided as equally as may be into three Classes. The Seats of the Senators of the first Class shall be vacated at the Expiration of the second Year, of the second Class at the Expiration of the fourth Year, and of the third Class at the Expiration of the sixth Year, so that one third may be chosen every second Year; and if Vacancies happen by Resignation, or otherwise, during the Recess of the Legislature of any State, the Executive thereof may make temporary Appointments until the next Meeting of the Legislature, which shall then fill such Vacancies.

No Person shall be a Senator who shall not have attained to the Age of thirty Years, and been nine Years a Citizen of the United States, and who shall not, when elected, be an Inhabitant of that State for which he shall be chosen.

The Vice President of the United States shall be President of the Senate, but shall have no Vote, unless they be equally divided.

The Senate shall choose their other Officers, and also a President pro tempore, in the Absence of the Vice President, or when he shall exercise the Office of President of the United States.

The Senate shall have the sole Power to try all Impeachments. When sitting for that Purpose, they shall be on Oath or Affirmation. When the President of the United States is tried, the Chief Justice shall preside: And no Person shall be convicted without the Concurrence of two thirds of the Members present.

Judgment in Cases of Impeachment shall not extend further than to removal from Office, and disqualification to hold and enjoy any Office of honor, Trust, or Profit under the United States: but the Party convicted shall nevertheless be liable and subject to Indictment, Trial, Judgment, and Punishment, according to Law.

Section 4. The Times, Places and Manner of holding Elections for Senators and Representatives, shall be prescribed in each State by the Legislature thereof; but the Congress may at any time by Law make or alter such Regulations, except as to the Places of choosing Senators.

The Congress shall assemble at least once in every Year, and such Meeting shall be on the first Monday in December, unless they shall by Law appoint a different Day.

Section 5. Each House shall be the Judge of the Elections, Returns, and Qualifications of its own Members, and a Majority of each shall constitute a Quorum to do Business; but a smaller Number may adjourn from day to day, and may be authorized to compel the Attendance of absent Members, in such Manner, and under such Penalties as each House may provide.

Each House may determine the Rules of its Proceedings, punish its Members for disorderly Behavior, and, with the Concurrence of two thirds, expel a Member.

Each House shall keep a Journal of its Proceedings, and from time to time publish the same, excepting such Parts as may in their Judgment require Secrecy; and the Yeas and Nays of the Members of either House on any question shall, at the Desire of one fifth of those Present, be entered on the Journal.

Neither House, during the Session of Congress, shall, without the Consent of the other, adjourn for more than three days, nor to any other Place than that in which the two Houses shall be sitting.

Section 6. The Senators and Representatives shall receive a Compensation for their Services, to be ascertained by Law, and paid out of the Treasury of the United States. They shall in all Cases, except Treason, Felony and Breach of the Peace, be privileged from Arrest during their Attendance at the Session of their respective Houses, and in going to and returning from the same; and for any Speech or Debate in either House, they shall not be questioned in any other Place.

No Senator or Representative shall, during the Time for which he was elected, be appointed to any civil Office under the Authority of the United States, which shall have been created, or the Emoluments whereof shall have been increased during such time; and no Person holding any Office under the United States, shall be a Member of either House during his Continuance in Office.

Section 7. All Bills for raising Revenue shall originate in the House of Representatives; but the Senate may propose or concur with Amendments as on other Bills.

Every Bill which shall have passed the House of Representatives and the Senate, shall, before it become a Law, be presented to the President of the United States; If he approve he shall sign it, but if not he shall return it, with his Objections to the House in which it shall have originated, who shall enter the Objections at large on their Journal, and proceed to reconsider it. If after such Reconsideration two thirds of that House shall agree to pass the Bill, it shall be sent together with the Objections, to the other House, by which it shall likewise be reconsidered, and if approved by two thirds of that House, it shall become a Law. But in all such Cases the Votes of both Houses shall be determined by Yeas and Nays, and the Names of the Persons voting for and against the Bill shall be entered on the Journal of each House respectively. If any Bill shall not be returned by the President within ten Days (Sundays excepted) after it shall have been presented to him, the Same shall be a Law, in like Manner as if he had signed it, unless the Congress by their Adjournment prevent its Return in which Case it shall not be a Law.

Every Order, Resolution, or Vote, to which the Concurrence of the Senate and House of Representatives may be necessary (except on a question of Adjournment) shall be presented to the President of the United States; and before the Same shall take Effect, shall be approved by him, or being disapproved by him, shall be repassed by two thirds of the Senate and House of Representatives, according to the Rules and Limitations prescribed in the Case of a Bill.

Section 8. The Congress shall have Power To lay and collect Taxes, Duties, Imposts and Excises, to pay the Debts and provide for the common Defence and general Welfare of the United States; but all Duties, Imposts and Excises shall be uniform throughout the United States;

To borrow Money on the credit of the United States;

To regulate Commerce with foreign Nations, and among the several States, and with the Indian Tribes;

To establish an uniform Rule of Naturalization, and uniform Laws on the subject of Bankruptcies throughout the United States;

To coin Money, regulate the Value thereof, and of foreign Coin, and fix the Standard of Weights and Measures;

To provide for the Punishment of counterfeiting the Securities and current Coin of the United States;

To establish Post Offices and post Roads;

To promote the Progress of Science and useful Arts, by securing for limited Times to Authors and Inventors the exclusive Right to their respective Writings and Discoveries;

To constitute Tribunals inferior to the supreme Court;

To define and punish Piracies and Felonies committed on the high Seas, and Offenses against the Law of Nations;

To declare War, grant Letters of Marque and Reprisal, and make Rules concerning Captures on Land and Water;

To raise and support Armies, but no Appropriation of Money to that Use shall be for a longer Term than two Years;

To provide and maintain a Navy;

To make Rules for the Government and Regulation of the land and naval Forces;

To provide for calling forth the Militia to execute the Laws of the Union, suppress Insurrections and repel Invasions;

To provide for organizing, arming, and disciplining, the Militia, and for governing such Part of Them as may be employed in the Service of the United States, reserving to the States respectively, the Appointment of the Officers, and the Authority of training the Militia according to the discipline prescribed by Congress;

To exercise exclusive Legislation in all Cases whatsoever, over such District (not exceeding ten Miles square) as may, by Cession of particular States, and the Acceptance of Congress, become the Seat of the Government of the United States, and to exercise like Authority over all Places purchased by the Consent of the Legislature of the State in which the Same shall be, for the Erection of Forts, Magazines, Arsenals, dock-Yards, and other needful Buildings;—And

To make all Laws which shall be necessary and proper for carrying into Execution the foregoing Powers, and all other Powers vested by this Constitution in the Government of the United States, or in any Department or Officer thereof.

Section 9. The Migration or Importation of such Persons as any of the States now existing shall think proper to admit, shall not be prohibited by the Congress prior to the Year one thousand eight hundred and eight, but a Tax or duty may be imposed on such Importation, not exceeding ten dollars for each Person.

The privilege of the Writ of Habeas Corpus shall not be suspended, unless when in Cases of Rebellion or Invasion the public Safety may require it.

No Bill of Attainder or ex post facto Law shall be passed.

No Capitation, or other direct, Tax shall be laid, unless in Proportion to the Census or Enumeration herein before directed to be taken.

No Tax or Duty shall be laid on Articles exported from any State.

No Preference shall be given by any Regulation of Commerce or Revenue to the Ports of one State over those of another: nor shall Vessels bound to, or from, one State be obliged to enter, clear, or pay Duties in another.

No Money shall be drawn from the Treasury, but in Consequence of Appropriations made by Law; and a regular Statement and Account of the Receipts and Expenditures of all public Money shall be published from time to time.

No Title of Nobility shall be granted by the United States: And no Person holding any Office of Profit or Trust under them, shall, without the Consent of the Congress, accept of any present, Emolument, Office, or Title, of any kind whatever, from any King, Prince, or foreign State.

Section 10. No State shall enter into any Treaty, Alliance, or Confederation; grant Letters of Marque and Reprisal; coin Money; emit Bills of Credit; make any Thing but gold and silver Coin a Tender in Payment of Debts; pass any Bill of Attainder, ex post facto Law, or Law impairing the Obligation of Contracts, or grant any Title of Nobility.

No State shall, without the Consent of the Congress, lay any Imposts or Duties on Imports or Exports, except what may be absolutely necessary for executing it's inspection Laws: and the net Produce of all Duties and Imposts, laid by any State on Imports or Exports, shall be for the Use of the Treasury of the United States; and all such Laws shall be subject to the Revision and Control of the Congress.

No State shall, without the Consent of Congress, lay any Duty of Tonnage, keep Troops, or Ships of War in time of Peace, enter into any Agreement or Compact with another State, or with a foreign Power, or engage in War, unless actually invaded, or in such imminent Danger as will not admit of delay.

Article II
Section 1. The executive Power shall be vested in a President of the United States of America. He shall hold his Office during the Term of four Years, and, together with the Vice President, chosen for the same Term, be elected, as follows:

Each State shall appoint, in such Manner as the Legislature thereof may direct, a Number of Electors, equal to the whole Number of Senators and Representatives to which the State may be entitled in the Congress; but no Senator or Representative, or Person holding an Office of Trust or Profit under the United States, shall be appointed an Elector.

The Electors shall meet in their respective States, and vote by Ballot for two Persons, of whom one at least shall not be an Inhabitant of the same State with themselves. And they shall make a List of all the Persons voted for, and of the Number of Votes for each; which List they shall sign and certify, and transmit sealed to the Seat of the Government of the United States, directed to the President of the Senate. The President of the Senate shall, in the Presence of the Senate and House of Representatives, open all the Certificates, and the Votes shall then be counted. The Person having the greatest Number of Votes shall be the President, if such Number be a Majority of the whole Number of Electors appointed; and if there be more than one who have such Majority, and have an equal Number of Votes, then the House of Representatives shall immediately choose by Ballot one of them for President; and if no Person have a Majority, then from the five highest on the List the said House shall in like Manner choose the President. But in choosing the President, the Votes shall be taken by States, the Representation from each State having one Vote; A quorum for this Purpose shall consist of a Member or Members from two thirds of the States, and a Majority of all the States shall be necessary to a Choice. In every Case, after the Choice of the President, the Person having the greater Number of Votes of the Electors shall be the Vice President. But if there should remain two or more who have equal Votes, the Senate shall choose from them by Ballot the Vice President.

The Congress may determine the Time of choosing the Electors, and the Day on which they shall give their Votes; which Day shall be the same throughout the United States.

No person except a natural born Citizen, or a Citizen of the United States, at the time of the Adoption of this Constitution, shall be eligible to the Office of President; neither shall any Person be eligible to that Office who shall not have attained to the Age of thirty five Years, and been fourteen Years a Resident within the United States.

In Case of the Removal of the President from Office, or of his Death, Resignation or Inability to discharge the Powers and Duties of the said Office, the same shall devolve on the Vice President, and the Congress may by Law provide for the Case of Removal, Death, Resignation or Inability, both of the President and Vice President, declaring what Officer shall then act as President, and such Officer shall act accordingly, until the Disability be removed, or a President shall be elected.

The President shall, at stated Times, receive for his Services, a Compensation, which shall neither be increased nor diminished during the Period for which he shall have been elected, and he shall not receive within that Period any other Emolument from the United States, or any of them.

Before he enter on the Execution of his Office, he shall take the following Oath or Affirmation: "I do solemnly swear (or affirm) that I will faithfully execute the Office of President of the United States, and will to the best of my Ability, preserve, protect and defend the Constitution of the United States."

Section 2. The President shall be Commander in Chief of the Army and Navy of the United States, and of the Militia of the several States, when called into the actual Service of the United States: he may require the Opinion, in writing, of the principal Officer in each of the executive Departments, upon any Subject relating to the Duties of their respective Offices, and he shall have Power to grant Reprieves and Pardons for Offenses against the United States, except in Cases of Impeachment.

He shall have Power, by and with the Advice and Consent of the Senate to make Treaties, provided two thirds of the Senators present concur; and he shall nominate, and by and with the Advice and Consent of the Senate, shall appoint Ambassadors, other public Ministers and Consuls, Judges of the supreme Court, and all other Officers of the United States, whose Appointments are not herein otherwise provided for, and which shall be established by Law; but the Congress may by Law vest the Appointment of such inferior Officers, as they think proper, in the President alone, in the Courts of Law, or in the Heads of Departments.

The President shall have Power to fill up all Vacancies that may happen during the Recess of the Senate, by granting Commissions which shall expire at the End of their next Session.

Section 3. He shall from time to time give to the Congress Information of the State of the Union, and recommend to their Consideration such Measures as he shall judge necessary and expedient; he may, on extraordinary Occasions, convene both Houses, or either of them, and in Case of Disagreement between them, with Respect to the Time of Adjournment, he may adjourn them to such Time as he shall think proper; he shall receive Ambassadors and other public Ministers; he shall take Care that the Laws be faithfully executed, and shall Commission all the Officers of the United States.

Section 4. The President, Vice President and all civil Officers of the United States, shall be removed from Office on Impeachment for, and Conviction of, Treason, Bribery, or other high Crimes and Misdemeanors.

Article III
Section 1. The judicial Power of the United States, shall be vested in one supreme Court, and in such inferior Courts as the Congress may from time to time ordain and establish. The Judges, both of the supreme and inferior Courts, shall hold their Offices during good Behavior, and shall, at stated Times, receive for their Services a Compensation, which shall not be diminished during their Continuance in Office.

Section 2. The judicial Power shall extend to all Cases, in Law and Equity, arising under this Constitution, the Laws of the United States, and Treaties made, or which shall be made, under their Authority;—to all Cases affecting Ambassadors, other public Ministers and Consuls;—to all Cases of admiralty and maritime Jurisdiction;—to Controversies to which the United States shall be a Party;—to Controversies between two or more States;—between a State and Citizens of another State;—between Citizens of different States;—between Citizens of the same State claiming Lands under Grants of different States, and between a State, or the Citizens thereof, and foreign States, Citizens or Subjects.

In all Cases affecting Ambassadors, other public Ministers and Consuls, and those in which a State shall be a Party, the supreme Court shall have original Jurisdiction. In all the other Cases before mentioned, the supreme Court shall have appellate Jurisdiction, both as to Law and Fact, with such Exceptions, and under such Regulations as the Congress shall make.

The Trial of all Crimes, except in Cases of Impeachment, shall be by Jury; and such Trial shall be held in the State where the said Crimes shall have been committed; but when not committed within any State, the Trial shall be at such Place or Places as the Congress may by Law have directed.

Section 3. Treason against the United States, shall consist only in levying War against them, or, in adhering to their Enemies, giving them Aid and Comfort. No Person shall be convicted of Treason unless on the Testimony of two Witnesses to the same overt Act, or on Confession in open Court.

The Congress shall have Power to declare the Punishment of Treason, but no Attainder of Treason shall work Corruption of Blood, or Forfeiture except during the Life of the Person attainted.

Article IV
Section 1. Full Faith and Credit shall be given in each State to the public Acts, Records, and judicial Proceedings of every other State. And the Congress may by general Laws prescribe the Manner in which such Acts, Records and Proceedings shall be proved, and the Effect thereof.

Section 2. The Citizens of each State shall be entitled to all Privileges and Immunities of Citizens in the several States.

A Person charged in any State with Treason, Felony, or other Crime, who shall flee from Justice, and be found in another State, shall on Demand of the executive Authority of the State from which he fled, be delivered up, to be removed to the State having Jurisdiction of the Crime.

No Person held to Service or Labour in one State, under the Laws thereof, escaping into another, shall, in Consequence of any Law or Regulation therein, be discharged from such Service or Labor, but shall be delivered up on Claim of the Party to whom such Service or Labor may be due.

Section 3. New States may be admitted by the Congress into this Union; but no new State shall be formed or erected within the Jurisdiction of any other State; nor any State be formed by the Junction of two or more States, or Parts of States, without the Consent of the Legislatures of the States concerned as well as of the Congress.

The Congress shall have Power to dispose of and make all needful Rules and Regulations respecting the Territory or other Property belonging to the United States; and nothing in this Constitution shall be so construed as to Prejudice any Claims of the United States, or of any particular State.

Section 4. The United States shall guarantee to every State in this Union a Republican Form of Government, and shall protect each of them against Invasion; and on Application of the Legislature, or of the Executive (when the Legislature cannot be convened) against domestic Violence.

Article V
The Congress, whenever two thirds of both Houses shall deem it necessary, shall propose Amendments to this Constitution, or, on the Application of the Legislatures of two thirds of the several States, shall call a Convention for proposing Amendments, which, in either Case, shall be valid to all Intents and Purposes, as part of this Constitution, when ratified by the Legislatures of three fourths of the several States, or by Conventions in three fourths thereof, as the one or the other Mode of Ratification may be proposed by the Congress; Provided that no Amendment which may be made prior to the Year One thousand eight hundred and eight shall in any Manner affect the first and fourth Clauses in the Ninth Section of the first Article; and that no State, without its Consent, shall be deprived of its equal Suffrage in the Senate.

Article VI
All Debts contracted and Engagements entered into, before the Adoption of this Constitution shall be as valid against the United States under this Constitution, as under the Confederation.

This Constitution, and the Laws of the United States which shall be made in Pursuance thereof; and all Treaties made, or which shall be made, under the Authority of the United States, shall be the supreme Law of the Land; and the Judges in every State shall be bound thereby, any Thing in the Constitution or Laws of any State to the Contrary notwithstanding.

The Senators and Representatives before mentioned, and the Members of the several State Legislatures, and all executive and judicial Officers, both of the United States and of the several States, shall be bound by Oath or Affirmation, to support this Constitution; but no religious Test shall ever be required as a

Qualification to any Office or public Trust under the United States.

Article VII
The Ratification of the Conventions of nine States shall be sufficient for the Establishment of this Constitution between the States so ratifying the Same.

Amendment I [1791]
Congress shall make no law respecting an establishment of religion, or prohibiting the free exercise thereof; or abridging the freedom of speech, or of the press; or the right of the people peaceably to assemble, and to petition the Government for a redress of grievances.

Amendment II [1791]
A well regulated Militia, being necessary to the security of a free State, the right of the people to keep and bear Arms, shall not be infringed.

Amendment III [1791]
No Soldier shall, in time of peace be quartered in any house, without the consent of the Owner, nor in time of war, but in a manner to be prescribed by law.

Amendment IV [1791]
The right of the people to be secure in their persons, houses, papers, and effects, against unreasonable searches and seizures, shall not be violated, and no Warrants shall issue, but upon probable cause, supported by Oath or affirmation, and particularly describing the place to be searched, and the persons or things to be seized.

Amendment V [1791]
No person shall be held to answer for a capital, or otherwise infamous crime, unless on a presentment or indictment of a Grand Jury, except in cases arising in the land or naval forces, or in the Militia, when in actual service in time of War or public danger; nor shall any person be subject for the same offence to be twice put in jeopardy of life or limb; nor shall be compelled in any criminal case to be a witness against himself, nor be deprived of life, liberty, or property, without due process of law; nor shall private property be taken for public use, without just compensation.

Amendment VI [1791]
In all criminal prosecutions, the accused shall enjoy the right to a speedy and public trial, by an impartial jury of the State and district wherein the crime shall have been committed, which district shall have been previously ascertained by law, and to be informed of the nature and cause of the accusation; to be confronted with the witnesses against him; to have compulsory process for obtaining witnesses in his favor, and to have the Assistance of Counsel for his defence.

Amendment VII [1791]
In Suits at common law, where the value in controversy shall exceed twenty dollars, the right of trial by jury shall be preserved, and no fact tried by jury, shall be otherwise re-examined in any Court of the United States, than according to the rules of the common law.

Amendment VIII [1791]
Excessive bail shall not be required, nor excessive fines imposed, nor cruel and unusual punishments inflicted.

Amendment IX [1791]
The enumeration in the Constitution, of certain rights, shall not be construed to deny or disparage others retained by the people.

Amendment X [1791]
The powers not delegated to the United States by the Constitution, nor prohibited by it to the States, are reserved to the States respectively, or to the people.

Amendment XI [1798]
The Judicial power of the United States shall not be construed to extend to any suit in law or equity, commenced or prosecuted against one of the United States by Citizens of another State, or by Citizens or Subjects of any Foreign State.

Amendment XII [1804]
The Electors shall meet in their respective states, and vote by ballot for President and Vice-President, one of whom, at least, shall not be an inhabitant of the same state with themselves; they shall name in their ballots the person voted for as President, and in distinct ballots the person voted for as Vice-President, and they shall make distinct lists of all persons voted for as President, and of all persons voted for as Vice-President, and of the number of votes for each, which lists they shall sign and certify, and transmit sealed to the seat of the government of the United States, directed to the President of the Senate;—The President of the Senate shall, in the presence of the Senate and House of Representatives, open all the certificates and the votes shall then be counted;—The person having the greatest number of votes for President, shall be the President, if such number be a majority of the whole number of Electors appointed; and if no person have such majority, then from the persons having the highest numbers not exceeding three on the list of those voted for as President, the House of Representatives shall choose immediately, by ballot, the President. But in choosing the President, the votes shall be taken by states, the representation from each state having one vote; a quorum for this purpose shall consist of a member or members from two thirds of the states, and a majority of all states shall be necessary to a choice. And if the House of Representatives shall not choose a President whenever the right of choice shall devolve upon them, before the fourth day of March next following, then the Vice-President shall act as President, as in the case of the death or other constitutional disability of the President.—The person having the greatest number of votes as Vice-President, shall be the Vice-President, if such number be a majority of the whole number of Electors appointed, and if no person have a majority, then from the two highest numbers on the list, the Senate shall choose the Vice-President; a quorum for the purpose shall consist of two thirds of the whole number of Senators, and a majority of the whole number shall be necessary to a choice. But no person constitutionally ineligible to the office of President shall be eligible to that of Vice-President of the United States.

Amendment XIII [1865]
Section 1. Neither slavery nor involuntary servitude, except as a punishment for crime whereof the party shall have been duly

convicted, shall exist within the United States, or any place subject to their jurisdiction.

Section 2. Congress shall have power to enforce this article by appropriate legislation.

Amendment XIV [1868]
Section 1. All persons born or naturalized in the United States, and subject to the jurisdiction thereof, are citizens of the United States and of the State wherein they reside. No State shall make or enforce any law which shall abridge the privileges or immunities of citizens of the United States; nor shall any State deprive any person of life, liberty, or property, without due process of law; nor deny to any person within its jurisdiction the equal protection of the laws.

Section 2. Representatives shall be apportioned among the several States according to their respective numbers, counting the whole number of persons in each State, excluding Indians not taxed. But when the right to vote at any election for the choice of electors for President and Vice President of the United States, Representatives in Congress, the Executive and Judicial officers of a State, or the members of the Legislature thereof, is denied to any of the male inhabitants of such State, being twenty-one years of age, and citizens of the United States, or in any way abridged, except for participation in rebellion, or other crime, the basis of representation therein shall be reduced in the proportion which the number of such male citizens shall bear to the whole number of male citizens twenty-one years of age in such State.

Section 3. No person shall be a Senator or Representative in Congress, or elector of President and Vice-President, or hold any office, civil or military, under the United States, or under any State, who having previously taken an oath, as a member of Congress, or as an officer of the United States, or as a member of any State legislature, or as an executive or judicial officer of any State, to support the Constitution of the United States, shall have engaged in insurrection or rebellion against the same, or given aid or comfort to the enemies thereof. But Congress may by a vote of two thirds of each House, remove such disability.

Section 4. The validity of the public debt of the United States, authorized by law, including debts incurred for payment of pensions and bounties for services in suppressing insurrection or rebellion, shall not be questioned. But neither the United States nor any State shall assume or pay any debt or obligation incurred in aid of insurrection or rebellion against the United States, or any claim for the loss or emancipation of any slave; but all such debts, obligations and claims shall be held illegal and void.

Section 5. The Congress shall have power to enforce, by appropriate legislation, the provisions of this article.

Amendment XV [1870]
Section 1. The right of citizens of the United States to vote shall not be denied or abridged by the United States or by any State on account of race, color, or previous condition of servitude.

Section 2. The Congress shall have power to enforce this article by appropriate legislation.

Amendment XVI [1913]
The Congress shall have power to lay and collect taxes on incomes, from whatever source derived, without apportionment among the several States, and without regard to any census or enumeration.

Amendment XVII [1913]
Section 1. The Senate of the United States shall be composed of two Senators from each State, elected by the people thereof, for six years; and each Senator shall have one vote. The electors in each State shall have the qualifications requisite for electors of the most numerous branch of the State legislatures.

Section 2. When vacancies happen in the representation of any State in the Senate, the executive authority of such State shall issue writs of election to fill such vacancies: Provided, That the legislature of any State may empower the executive thereof to make temporary appointments until the people fill the vacancies by election as the legislature may direct.

Section 3. This amendment shall not be so construed as to affect the election or term of any Senator chosen before it becomes valid as part of the Constitution.

Amendment XVIII [1919]
Section 1. After one year from the ratification of this article the manufacture, sale, or transportation of intoxicating liquors within, the importation thereof into, or the exportation thereof from the United States and all territory subject to the jurisdiction thereof for beverage purposes is hereby prohibited.

Section 2. The Congress and the several States shall have concurrent power to enforce this article by appropriate legislation.

Section 3. This article shall be inoperative unless it shall have been ratified as an amendment to the Constitution by the legislatures of the several States, as provided in the Constitution, within seven years from the date of the submission hereof to the States by the Congress.

Amendment XIX [1920]
Section 1. The right of citizens of the United States to vote shall not be denied or abridged by the United States or by any State on account of sex.

Section 2. Congress shall have power to enforce this article by appropriate legislation.

Amendment XX [1933]
Section 1. The terms of the President and Vice President shall end at noon on the 20th day of January, and the terms of Senators and Representatives at noon on the 3d day of January, of the years in which such terms would have ended if this article had not been ratified; and the terms of their successors shall then begin.

Section 2. The Congress shall assemble at least once in every year, and such meeting shall begin at noon on the 3d day of January, unless they shall by law appoint a different day.

Section 3. If, at the time fixed for the beginning of the term of the President, the President elect shall have died, the Vice President elect shall become President. If the President shall not have been chosen before the time fixed for the beginning of his term, or if the President elect shall have failed to qualify, then the Vice President elect shall act as President until a President shall have qualified; and the Congress may by law provide for the case wherein neither a President elect nor a Vice President elect shall have qualified, declaring who shall then act as President, or the manner in which one who is to act shall be selected, and such person shall act accordingly until a President or Vice-President shall have qualified.

Section 4. The Congress may by law provide for the case of the death of any of the persons from whom the House of Representatives may choose a President whenever the right of choice shall have devolved upon them, and for the case of the death of any of the persons from whom the Senate may choose a Vice-President whenever the right of choice shall have devolved upon them.

Section 5. Sections 1 and 2 shall take effect on the 15th day of October following the ratification of this article.

Section 6. This article shall be inoperative unless it shall have been ratified as an amendment to the Constitution by the legislatures of three-fourths of the several States within seven years from the date of its submission.

Amendment XXI [1933]
Section 1. The eighteenth article of amendment to the Constitution of the United States is hereby repealed.

Section 2. The transportation or importation into any State, Territory, or possession of the United States for delivery or use therein of intoxicating liquors, in violation of the laws thereof, is hereby prohibited.

Section 3. This article shall be inoperative unless it shall have been ratified as an amendment to the Constitution by conventions in the several States, as provided in the Constitution, within seven years from the date of the submission hereof to the States by the Congress.

Amendment XXII [1951]
Section 1. No person shall be elected to the office of the President more than twice, and no person who has held the office of President, or acted as President, for more than two years of a term to which some other person was elected President shall be elected to the office of President more than once. But this Article shall not apply to any person holding the office of President when this Article was proposed by the Congress, and shall not prevent any person who may be holding the office of President, or acting as President, during the term within which this Article becomes operative from holding the office of President or acting as President during the remainder of such term.

Section 2. This article shall be inoperative unless it shall have been ratified as an amendment to the Constitution by the legislatures of three-fourths of the several States within seven years from the date of its submission to the States by the Congress.

Amendment XXIII [1961]
Section 1. The District constituting the seat of Government of the United States shall appoint in such manner as the Congress may direct:

A number of electors of President and Vice President equal to the whole number of Senators and Representatives in Congress to which the District would be entitled if it were a State, but in no event more than the least populous state; they shall be in addition to those appointed by the states, but they shall be considered, for the purposes of the election of President and Vice President, to be electors appointed by a state; and they shall meet in the District and perform such duties as provided by the twelfth article of amendment.

Section 2. The Congress shall have power to enforce this article by appropriate legislation.

Amendment XXIV [1964]
Section 1. The right of citizens of the United States to vote in any primary or other election for President or Vice President, for electors for President or Vice-President, or for Senator or Representative in Congress, shall not be denied or abridged by the United States, or any State by reason of failure to pay any poll tax or other tax.

Section 2. The Congress shall have power to enforce this article by appropriate legislation.

Amendment XXV [1967]
Section 1. In case of the removal of the President from office or of his death or resignation, the Vice President shall become President.

Section 2. Whenever there is a vacancy in the office of the Vice President, the President shall nominate a Vice President who shall take office upon confirmation by a majority vote of both Houses of Congress.

Section 3. Whenever the President transmits to the President pro tempore of the Senate and the Speaker of the House of Representatives his written declaration that he is unable to discharge the powers and duties of his office, and until he transmits to them a written declaration to the contrary, such powers and duties shall be discharged by the Vice President as Acting President.

Section 4. Whenever the Vice President and a majority of either the principal officers of the executive departments or of such other body as Congress may by law provide, transmit to the President pro tempore of the Senate and the Speaker of the House of Representatives their written declaration that the President is unable to discharge the powers and duties of his office, the Vice President shall immediately assume the powers and duties of the office as Acting President.

Thereafter, when the President transmits to the President pro tempore of the Senate and the Speaker of the House of Representatives his written declaration that no inability exists, he shall resume the powers and duties of his office unless the Vice President and a majority of either the principal officers of the executive department or of such other body as Congress may by law provide, transmit within four days to the President pro tempore of the Senate and the Speaker of the House of Representatives their written declaration and the President is unable to discharge the powers and duties of his office. Thereupon Congress shall decide the issue, assembling within forty-eight hours for that purpose if not in session. If the Congress, within twenty-one days after receipt of the latter written declaration, or, if Congress is not in session, within twenty-one days after Congress is required to assemble, determines by two thirds vote of both Houses that the President is unable to discharge the powers and duties of his office, the Vice President shall continue to discharge the same as Acting President; otherwise, the President shall resume the powers and duties of his office.

Amendment XXVI [1971]

Section 1. The right of citizens of the United States, who are eighteen years of age or older, to vote shall not be denied or abridged by the United States or by any State on account of age.

Section 2. The Congress shall have power to enforce this article by appropriate legislation.

Amendment XXVII
[Proposed 1789; Ratified 1992]

No law, varying the compensation for the services of Senators and Representatives, shall take effect until an election of Representatives have intervened.

Glossary

A

adjudication: decision making in open court according to the adversary process

adversary process: getting the truth by fighting in court according to the formal rules of criminal procedure

anomie theory: crime results from the breakdown of social norms

appellate courts: courts that review the proceedings in the trial court

appointed counsel: lawyers assigned to people who can't afford to hire their own

arraignment: bringing defendants to open court, reading the charges against them, and demanding that they plead not guilty, guilty, or *nolo contendere*

arrest: taking an individual into custody without her consent

assigned counsel: lawyers in private practice selected from a list on a rotating basis either for a fee or pro bono (donated time)

B

background forces: the underlying sociological causes

bail: the release of defendants until their cases are decided

bill of rights: a list of specific guarantees limiting the power of the government to enforce the criminal law

boundary hypothesis: defining a behavior as "criminal" notifies ordinary people how far they can go without undoing the social order

"broken windows" theory: minor physical and social disorder is linked to serious crime

C

career criminals: individuals who start committing crimes very early and continue to commit crimes throughout their lives

case attrition: at each stage, the numbers of people in the system shrink as they're sorted out of or into other parts of the formal system

case mortality: view that every case would end in conviction and punishment if it weren't for "technicalities," incompetence, softhearted judges, or even corruption

case study method: a professional collects information, combines it in a unique way, mulls over the results, and reaches a decision

civil death: denial of political and legal rights to felons

classical (utilitarian) theories: theories based on free will and reason

CODIS (Combined DNA Index System): a software program that operates databases of DNA profiles of convicted offenders, unsolved crime scene evidence, and missing persons

cognitive model of rehabilitation: rehabilitation by means of developing clear thinking skills

community policing strategy: based on the idea that the police can best carry out their missions by helping communities help themselves by getting at the causes of and finding solutions to community problems

community prosecution: a "grass-roots approach to justice," in which the community, law enforcement, and other government agencies work together to solve neighborhood crime, public safety, and quality-of-life problems

community service: intermediate punishment that orders offenders to work without pay at projects that benefit the public

community-oriented policing (COP): police strategy primarily concerned with establishing a working relationship with the community

COMPSTAT: consists of five components: computerized crime-mapping technology, a management style, response tactics, follow-up, and accountability

confinement model of imprisonment: offenders are sent to prison *as* punishment; safe, secure, humane incarceration where architecture and management are based on the idea that prisoners are locked up *as* punishment not *for* punishment

conflict theory: conflict is the normal state of society and social control requires active constraint, sometimes in the form of coercion

consensus hypothesis: criminal law is a synthesis of a society's essential morality, based on values that are shared by all "healthy consciences"

consent search rule: individuals can give up their right against unreasonable searches, if they do so *voluntarily*

constable/night watch system: a police system based in local communities during the first eras of policing, consisting of constables and night watch

constitutional democracy: balancing community security and individual liberty and privacy

continuance in contemplation of dismissal: dismissal of the case if the juvenile stays out of trouble for a specific time period

contract attorneys: private attorneys under contracts with local jurisdictions to represent indigent defendants for an agreed-upon fee

control model of prison management: emphasizes prisoner obedience, work, and education

corporate fraud: crimes committed by corporations or their officers, including falsification of corporate financial information, self-dealing by corporate insiders, and obstruction of justice

correctional institutions: places of confinement to reform offenders into law-abiding people who work to support themselves through a coherent, scientifically sound program

corrections: the final stage of the criminal process—incarceration, probation and parole, or intermediate punishments

correlation: observable phenomena that "*tend* to vary with each other systematically"

courtroom workgroup: social organizations made up of prosecutors, judges, and defense lawyers

crime-attack strategies: police home in on specific types of suspicious people in specific places at specific times to prevent or interrupt crimes and arrest suspects for committing specific crimes

crime control model: focuses on the need to protect people and their property for the good of the whole society

Crime Index: UCR statistics reporting numbers and rates of eight serious crimes reported to the police

crime rates: the number of crimes for every 100,000 individuals in the general population

criminal justice system: a series of decision points and decision making

criminal law: tells private individuals what behavior is a crime and lays down the punishment for it

criminal law theories: crime is whatever the law says it is

criminal procedure: tells government officials the extent and limits of their power to enforce the criminal law, and it sets out the consequences for illegal official actions

culpability: assumes offenders are responsible for their actions and have to suffer the consequences if they act irresponsibly

custodial interrogation: *Miranda* warnings required if suspects are in custody *and* officers interrogate them

D

damages: money for personal injuries awarded by courts

dark figure in crime: the number of crimes committed but not known

day fines: base fines on the daily income of offenders

day reporting centers: intermediate punishment that combines high levels of surveillance and extensive services, treatments, or activities

defense of alibi: defendants have to prove they couldn't have committed the crime because they were somewhere else when the crime was committed

defense of qualified immunity: officers aren't liable for their "objectively reasonable" actions

defenses of excuse: defendants admit what they did was wrong, but, they argue, under the circumstances they weren't *responsible* for their actions

defenses of justification: defendants admit they're responsible for their actions, but, they argue, under the circumstances their actions were justified

delinquency: includes conduct that would be criminal if an adult engaged in it

delinquency petitions: requests for a trial (adjudicatory hearing) to find the youth a delinquent and make him or her a ward of the court

determinate sentencing: legislatures attach specific punishments to crimes

determinism: forces beyond individual control

differential response approach: varying police mobilization according to the type of crime

discretionary release: parole boards decide the date of prisoners' release and set the conditions of their community supervision until their sentence expires

discriminatory decision-making criteria: characteristics that infect decision making to produce illegal, discriminatory, unfair decisions

displacement effect: crime moves to another location during crackdowns and comes back after the crackdown

disposition hearing: a hearing to decide how best to resolve delinquency cases

diversion: transferring individuals in the system to other agencies for alcohol and other treatment or family counseling programs

DNA: the building block for each individual's unique genetic makeup

doctrine of official immunity: officers aren't liable for their misconduct unless it's intentional

doctrine of *parens patriae*: allowed the government to intervene in family life to protect children's estates from dishonest guardians

dual system of justice: one system of justice for adults and another for juveniles

due process: the right to fair procedures

due process mission: to ensure the decision-making process is fair according to the law and Constitution

due process model: it's more important to guarantee the right of individuals to fair practices than to catch criminals

due process revolution: U.S. Supreme Court decisions during the 1960s to expand the rights of criminal defendants, apply the rights to federal and state criminal justice, and include protection for "outsiders"

E

either/or corrections (also called **in-or-out corrections**): convicted offenders are either locked up or put on probation

entrapment: efforts by law enforcement officers' to get people to commit crimes

equal protection of the laws: criminal laws can only treat groups of people differently if the different treatment is reasonable

espionage (spying): secret observation by special agents of a foreign country on people or their activities or enterprises (such as war production or scientific advancement in military fields)

expiration release: prisoners are released unconditionally when their sentence expires

ex post facto clause: bans retroactive criminal laws

F

factual cause: the result wouldn't have happened if it weren't for the defendant's actions

factual guilt: guilty in fact but not proven (or provable) in court

fair procedures: decision making according to formal rules growing out of the Bill of Rights and the due process clauses of the U.S. Constitution and state constitutions

false negatives: when attempts to predict accurately those who will become criminals based on their past behaviors fail

false positive problem: when prediction scales result in the substantial overprediction of future criminality

felonies: capital felonies are crimes punishable by death or life imprisonment; ordinary felonies are crimes punishable by one year or more in prison

field interrogation: police stop, question, and sometimes search people who "don't look or act right"

follow-up investigation: an investigation by detectives after the preliminary investigation by patrol officers

foreground forces in crime: the immediate causes

formal decision making: decision making open to public view, according to written rules

full enforcement: nondiscretionary enforcement of all criminal laws all the time

G

gender model of police attitudes: predicts differences in attitude between women and men police officers exist because of their different early socialization into gender roles

general deterrence: "sends a message" to people thinking about committing crime that "crime doesn't pay"

general jurisdiction: power to decide all felony cases from capital murder to theft and also review the decisions of lower courts

"good" criminal justice evaluation research: research that answers whether policies and practices are legal, fair, and smart

guided discretion death penalty statutes: statutes listing the aggravating and mitigating circumstances that juries have to consider before they decide whether defendants should receive the sentence of death or life imprisonment

H

hands-off doctrine: prison administrators (not courts) determine prison conditions, management, and how prisoners are treated

hate crimes: crimes motivated by prejudice against groups based on differences in race, ethnicity, religion, physical or mental capacity, or sexual orientation

hearsay evidence: evidence not known directly by the witness

"hot spots" patrol: based on the idea that some locations, like intersections and buildings, at certain times need special attention because they generate a substantial portion of calls for law enforcement services

hydraulic effect: compression of discretion at one point in the system causes discretion to pop up at another point

I

importation theory of imprisonment: the roots of prison society lie outside prison

incapacitation: confines criminals so they can't commit crimes while they're locked up

incidence of crime: the number of offenses

incident-based reporting: the collecting of detailed information about individual cases for each offense, including offense, victim, property, offender, and witnesses by local law enforcement agencies

incident reports: written reports describing what patrol officers found during preliminary investigations

indeterminate sentencing: legislatures set only the outer limits of possible penalties, and judges and corrections professionals decide actual sentence lengths

indictment: a formal written accusation by the grand jury

indigenous theory imprisonment: prison society is created inside prison walls independent of the outside world

informal decision making (discretionary decision making): professional decision making guided by education, training, and experience

information: a charging document initiated by the prosecutor alone

intermediate punishments: harsher than probation but milder than imprisonment, they allow us to accomplish the mission of justice

irresistible impulse test: a test of insanity that focuses on whether mental disease affected the defendants' willpower (their capacity to control their actions at the time of the crime)

J

jail: a county or municipal facility for *either* keeping adults while they wait for trial *or* for punishing them for less than a year after they're convicted

job model of police attitudes: predicts that women and men don't differ in their attitudes toward police work because socialization to work overrides prior socialization into gender roles

jury instructions: instructions from the judge that explain the role of the jury, the law, and what proof beyond a reasonable doubt means

jury nullification: juries' power to ignore the law and decide cases according to informal extralegal considerations

juvenile court: concentrated not on behavior but on children and what they needed to make them responsible

juvenile delinquent: can refer to a youth who's committed either crimes or status offenses, or both

juveniles: those under juvenile justice jurisdiction—children 8 to 16 (or 18 in some states)

K

knock-and-announce rule: a search of a home is reasonable if officers get a warrant; knock on the door saying, "Open up, police"; wait 10 seconds; knock down the door; enter; and arrest the suspect

knockdown force: enough force to cause a suspect to fall to the ground

knowing intent: you know you're committing an act or causing a harm but you're not acting for that purpose

L

labeling theory: criminal behavior is learned by being labeled a criminal by the criminal justice system

legal cause: asks whether it's fair to blame defendants for the consequences of the chain of events their actions triggered

legal guilt: guilt proven (or provable) in court

legitimate decision-making criteria: characteristics for decision making that produce legal, fair, and smart decisions

liberation hypothesis: the unconscious influence of value judgments on jurors

life-course theory: focuses on stability *and* changes in behavior throughout life

limited jurisdiction: power (jurisdiction) to decide misdemeanors and conduct preliminary proceedings in felony cases

M

maintaining order: police are supposed to "do something right now to settle problems"

mala in se: inherently evil behavior

mala prohibita: behavior that is criminal only because the law defines it as a crime

mandatory minimum sentence laws: offenders have to spend at least some time (the mandatory minimum laid out in the law) in prison

mandatory release: legislatures and judges set the date of prisoners' release and the conditions of their community supervision until their sentence expires

material support: the crime of providing aid to individual terrorists and terrorist organizations, including money, financial services, lodging, training, etc.

maximum security prisons: the highest priority security (preventing prisoners from escaping, hurting staff or each other, and keeping out contraband)

medical model of corrections: decisions about offenders' custody should depend on their rehabilitation, not on their past crimes

medical model of crime: the medical model is based on the idea that crime is a disease that experts can diagnose, treat, and cure

medium security prisons: less focused on security than maximum security prisons and more programs

merit system (Missouri Bar plan): a commission initially nominates and governors select judges from the list; then, judges have to be elected after a term of service

military model of policing: organized in a hierarchical command structure where decisions (orders) are made by the chief at the top and are carried out by officers on the beat

minimum security prisons: for young, first-time, and other offenders not considered dangerous or likely to escape, where vocational training and treatment, not security, are emphasized

misdemeanors: minor offenses (simple assaults and battery, prostitution, and disorderly conduct) punishable either by fines or up to one year in jail

municipal police department system: a formalized police force responsible to a central office and on duty "24/7"

N

National Crime Victimization Survey (NCVS): collects detailed information about violent and property crimes and publishes the survey results annually in *Criminal Victimization in the U.S.*

National Incident-Based Reporting System (NIBRS): the official report of crimes known to the police, which collects information about two groups of offenses, with details about each crime

negligent intent: unconsciously creating an unreasonable risk of harm

negotiated pleas: defendants arrange some kind of deal for a reduced charge or sentence *before* pleading guilty

new-generation jails: combine architecture, management philosophy, operation, and training based on the goal of incarceration *as,* not *for,* punishment

new-generation maximum security: a combination of architecture and management to provide a safe, secure, humane environment based on the idea that offenders are sent to prison *as* punishment, not *for* punishment

O

objective basis: government officials have to back up with facts their encroachments on liberty and privacy

objective standard of reasonable force: Fourth Amendment permits officers to use the amount of force necessary to apprehend and bring suspects under control

one-size-fits-all crime control approach: law enforcement reacts the same way to all crimes in all places at all times in the same way

P

pains of imprisonment: deprivations suffered by prisoners as part of life in prison society

parole: *follows* confinement in prison

penalties/rewards system: defendants who go to trial pay a penalty for their adversary stance but get rewarded for pleading guilty

penitentiary: places of confinement to remove offenders from a corrupting environment and make them work, isolating them in cells

petition for a writ of certiorari: asks the U.S. Supreme Court to order a lower court to send up the record of its proceedings for review

petition for a writ of habeas corpus: asks the U.S. Supreme Court to order some official (usually a prison warden or jail supervisor) to come to a trial court and justify a prisoner's imprisonment

police crackdowns: sudden increases in police activity at particular places during "hot" days and times

police working personality: the way police look at the world; their standards of right and wrong; their behavior while they carry out their missions, strategies, and the law

positivist theories: theories based on determinism or forces beyond individual control

prejudicial evidence: evidence whose power to damage the defendant is greater than its power to prove the government's case

preliminary hearings: judges review prosecutors' charging decisions to determine whether there's probable cause to continue the case against the defendant

preliminary investigation: patrol officers collect information at crime scenes and write incident reports describing what they learned

presumption of guilt: view that the people caught up in criminal justice are *probably* guilty

presumption of innocence: the government always has the burden to justify its use of power even against people who turn out to be guilty

presumption of regularity: government actions are presumed to be lawful and free of discrimination

prevalence of criminality: the number of offenders

prevalence of imprisonment: the number of individuals in the general population who at some time in their lives have spent time in prison

prevention: punishes criminals to deter future crimes

preventive detention: detaining defendants to protect public safety

preventive patrol: officers move through their beats on foot or in vehicles, making themselves visible to control crime and reassure law-abiding people they're safe

principle of economy: applying criminal law by relying on the least expensive or invasive response to criminal behavior

prisoner reentry: the process of prisoners' leaving prison and returning to society

prisons: state institutions where prisoners are locked up after they're convicted if their sentence is for more than a year

proactive policing: officers are supposed to prevent crime before it happens by going out looking for suspicious people and behavior

probable cause to arrest: facts and circumstances that would lead a police officer in the light of her training and experience to *believe* that a crime has been, *is* being, or is about to be committed and that the person suspected has committed it

probation: a *substitute* for confinement in prison or jail

problem-oriented policing (POP): police strategy primarily concerned with identifying, analyzing, responding to, and assessing community problems related to crime and neighborhood quality of life

profiles: decisions based on group characteristics instead of individual behavior

prosecutor horizontal case assignment: assistant prosecutors are assigned to manage one stage of the prosecution

prosecutor vertical case assignment: assistant prosecutors are assigned to manage all stages of specific defendants' cases

public defenders: full-time defense lawyers paid for by local taxpayers

public safety exception: *Miranda* warnings not required if giving them could endanger officers or others nearby

punishment model of imprisonment: offenders are sent to prison *for* punishment

purposeful intent (sometimes called **specific intent**): "you did it and/or caused a criminal result on purpose"

R

racial profiling: law enforcement decisions based on race or ethnicity

rape shield laws: passed in the 1970s, they ban testimony about victims' sex lives from the courtroom

rational choice theory: individuals make decisions according to what they *believe* is in their self-interest

reactive policing: officers respond when called ("Don't call us, we'll call you.")

reasonable suspicion: facts and circumstances that would lead an officer (in light of her training and experience) to *suspect* that a crime might be afoot

recidivism: arrest, charge, or conviction for a new crime; repeat offending

reckless intent: consciously creating a risk of causing a criminal harm

reform model of policing: police are the "gatekeepers" to the criminal justice system; they focus on the criminal law enforcement mission

rehabilitation: aims to change criminals into people who "work hard and play by the rules"

relevant evidence: evidence that helps prove the elements of the crime

responsibility prison management model: stresses the responsibility of prisoners for their own actions instead of administrative control of prisoners' behavior

restitution: offenders pay back victims in money for losses they caused

restoration: aims to heal victims and restore relationships

retained counsel: a lawyer paid for by the client

retribution: punishes criminals for past crimes because they deserve it

right-wrong test: an insanity defense focus on whether a mental disease or defect impaired the defendants' reason so that they couldn't tell the difference between right and wrong

risk assessment method: a statistical prediction based on the seriousness of the crime offenders are imprisoned for and their criminal history

routine activities theory: a focus on the influence of the location of targets and movements of offenders and victims in time and space on decision making by criminals

S

sabotage: the crime of destroying and damaging property for the purpose of interfering with and hindering preparations for and carrying on war and defense during national emergencies

search incident to arrest rule: an officer who *lawfully* arrests a suspect can search the suspect and the area under her control without either a search warrant or probable cause

sedition: to "stir up" others to overthrow the government by violence

selective enforcement: officers use their discretion to arrest *some* people, *sometimes,* for breaking *some* laws

self-reports: surveys of special groups in the general population

sentencing guidelines: fixed (but flexible) sentences based on balancing the seriousness of the offense and the criminal history of the offender

social control theory: individuals are rule breakers by nature

social learning theory: individuals learn behavior from others

social process theories: explanations of crime based on the interactions among members of families, peer groups, schools, churches, neighborhoods, and other social institutions

social structure of the case: extralegal influences on the prosecutor's decision to charge

social structure theories: explain the link between individual criminal behavior, social class, and structural conditions like poverty, unemployment, and poor education

special deterrence: teaches convicted criminals that "crime doesn't pay"

spousal and partner homicide exception: women commit fewer crimes than men, but women murder their spouses and intimate partners at about the same or higher rates

status offenses: conduct that's illegal only if juveniles engage in it

straight pleas: defendants plead guilty, hoping for a more lenient sentence *after* pleading guilty

strain theory: American culture defines goals, which the social structure blocks many members of the lower classes from achieving

street crime: violent and property crimes reported in the UCR

strength of the case: the amount of evidence against the suspect

strict liability offenses: crimes without criminal intent

substantial capacity test: a test of insanity that focuses on whether a mental disease substantially impaired the reason and/or will of the defendants

supermaximum security prisons ("supermaxes"): prisons for "the worst of the worst"

systematic social observation (SSO) method: observers have to follow explicit rules that can be replicated, *and* the means of observation (whether persons or technology) have to be independent of what's being observed

T

technical violations: violations of statutes or ordinances that aren't crimes

test the government's case: an independent review of the prosecutor's decision to charge to make sure there's enough evidence to put the community and the defendant to the time and expense (and for defendants, the additional burden of stigma and stress) of criminal prosecution

torts: private personal injury actions

total institutions: prisons are societies, separate and isolated from free society

transfer (also called **waiver** or **certification**): transfer of cases from juvenile court to adult criminal court

transfer petitions: requests for a hearing to waive the juvenile court's jurisdiction and transfer the case to adult criminal courts

treason: levying war against the United States, adhering to its enemies, or giving them aid and comfort

U

Uniform Crime Reports (UCR): official statistics of crimes known to the police, collected by the FBI, and published annually as *Crime in the U.S.*

V

value of crime control: criminal justice exists to reduce crime for the good of the whole society

value of due process: the mission of criminal justice is to guarantee fair procedures for every individual caught up in the system

violations: crimes punishable by a small fine; they don't become part of your criminal history

void-for-vagueness doctrine: vague laws deny individuals life, liberty, and property without due process of law because they don't give individuals fair warning

W

white-collar crime: crimes committed by respectable people, or at least respected business and professional people

Bibliography

ABA Commission on Women and the Legal Profession. 2001. *The Unfinished Agenda: Women and the Legal Profession*. Chicago: American Bar Association.

ABA Task Force on Minorities in the Judiciary. 1997. *Directory of Minority Judges in the United States*. Chicago: American Bar Association.

Adams, Kenneth. 1992. "Adjusting to Prison Life." In *Crime and Justice: An Annual Review of Research*. Edited by Michael Tonry. Chicago: University of Chicago Press.

Adamson, Patrick B. 1991. "Some Comments on the Origins of Police." *Police Studies* 14.

Advisory Commission. 1984. *Jails, Intergovernmental Dimensions of a Local Problem*. Washington, DC: Advisory Commission on Intergovernmental Relations.

Agnew, Robert. 1992. "Foundation for a General Strain Theory of Crime and Delinquency." *Criminology* 30(1): 47–87.

Agnew, Robert, and Lisa Broidy. 1997. "Gender and Crime: A General Strain Theory Perspective." *Journal of Research in Crime and Delinquence* 34(3): 275–306.

Ainsworth, Bill. 2004 (June 10). "Poll Finds Broad Support for Limits on 3-Strikes Law." *San Diego Union*.

Alabama Law Review Summer Project. 1975. "A Study of Differential Treatment Accorded Female Defendants in Alabama Criminal Courts." *Alabama Law Review* 27.

Albanese, Jay S. 1985. *Dealing with Delinquency: An Investigation of Juvenile Justice*. Lanham, MD: University Press of America.

Albert, Craig J. 1999. "Challenging Deterrence: New Insights on Capital Punishment Derived from Panel Data." *University of Pittsburgh Law Review* 60.

Albonetti, Celesta A. 1986. "Criminality, Prosecutorial Screening, and Uncertainty: Toward a Theory of Discretionary Decision Making in Felony Case Processings." *Criminology* 24.

Allen, Harry E., Chris W. Eskridge, Edward J. Latessa, and Gennaro Vito. 1985. *Probation and Parole in America*. New York: Free Press.

Alpert, Geoffrey P. 1987. "Questioning Police Pursuits in Urban Areas." *Journal of Police Science and Administration* 15.

Alpert, Geoffrey P., and Roger G. Dunham. 1990. *Police Pursuit Driving: Controlling Responses to Emergency Situations*. New York: Greenwood Press.

Alschuler, Albert W. 1979. "Plea Bargaining and Its History." *Law and Society Review* 13.

Alter, Jonathan. 2001 (November 5). "Time to Think about Torture." *Newsweek*.

American Academy of Political and Social Science. 1910. *The Administration of Justice in the United States*. Philadelphia: AAPS.

American Bar Association. 1968. *Standards Relating to Pleas of Guilty*. Chicago: University of Chicago Press.

American Correctional Association. 1983. *Standards for Juvenile Training Schools*. 2nd ed. Washington, DC: National Institute of Justice.

American Friends Society. 1971. *Struggle for Justice: A Report on Crime and Punishment in America*. New York: Hill and Wang.

American Judicature Society. 2003. *Model Merit Selection Plan in Theory and Practice*. Des Moines, IA: American Judicature Society.

American Judicature Society. 2004 (January). *Judicial Selection in the States Appellate and General Jurisdiction Courts*. Des Moines, IA: American Judicature Society.

American Judicature Society. 2004 (September). *Merit Selection: The Best Way to Choose the Best Judges*. Des Moines, IA: American Judicature Society.

Amnesty International. 2004. "Executions of Child Offenders Since 1990." http://web.amnesty.org/pages/deathpenalty-children-stats-eng.

Amsterdam, Anthony. 1984. *Trial Manual for the Defense of Criminal Cases*. Philadelphia: American Law Institute.

Anderson v. Creighton. 1987. 483 U.S. 635, 107 S.Ct. 3034, 97 L.Ed.2d 523.

Anderson, Curt. 2004 (July 13). "Corporate Fraud Task Force Gets Results." *Associated Press*.

Anderson, David C. 1997. *Public Defenders in the Neighborhood: A Harlem Law Office Stresses Teamwork, Early Investigation*. Washington, DC: National Institute of Justice.

Anderson, Louise, Sylvia Garza, and Tad Davis. 2003. *Juvenile Justice in California, 2003*. Sacramento: Criminal Justice Statistics Center (CJSC). http://caag.state.ca.us/cjsc/publications/misc/jj03/preface.pdf. Visited December 16, 2004.

Apodaca v. Oregon. 1972. 406 U.S. 404.

Appier, Janis. 1998. *Policing Women: The Sexual Politics of Law Enforcement and the LAPD*. Philadelphia: Temple University Press.

Argersinger v. Hamlin. 1972. 407 U.S. 25.

Atkins v. Virginia. 2002. 536 U.S. 304.

Atkinson, Donald. 1986 (February). "Parole Can Work!" *Corrections Today*.

Axtman, Kris. 2003 (September 8). "Judicial Rarity; Death Penalty in a Rape Case." *Christian Science Monitor*.

Baker, Donald P., et al. 1973. "Judicial Intervention in Corrections: The California Experience—An Empirical Study." *UCLA Law Review* 20:454.

Baker, Mark. 1985. *Cops: Their Lives in Their Own Words*. New York: Fawcett.

Baldus, David C. 1995. "Symposium: The Capital Jury Project, Keynote Address." *Indiana Law Journal* 70.

Baldus, David C., and George Woodworth. 1998. "Race Discrimination and the Death Penalty: An Empirical and Legal Overview." In *America's Experiment with Capital Punishment.* Edited by James R. Acker, Robert S. Bohm, and Charles S. Lanier. Durham, NC: Carolina Academic Press.

Baldwin, James. 1962. *Nobody Knows My Name.* New York: Dell.

Ballew v. Georgia. 1978. 435 U.S. 223.

Barker, Emily. 1993 (January/February). "Paying for Quality." *American Lawyer* 83.

Barr, Heather. 1997. "More Like Disneyland: State Action, 42 U.S.C. §1983, and Business Improvement Districts in New York." *Columbia Human Rights Law Review* 28:394.

Barron v. Baltimore. 1833. 32 U.S. 7 Pet. 243.

Bator, Paul. 1963. "Finality in Criminal Law and Federal Habeas Corpus for State Prisoners." *Harvard Law Review* 76.

Bayley, David H. 1998. *What Works in Policing.* New York: Oxford University Press.

Bayley, David H., and Egon Bittner. 1989. "Learning the Skills of Policing." In *Critical Issues in Policing.* Edited by Roger C. Dunham and Geoffrey P. Alpert. Prospect Heights, IL: Waveland Press.

Bayley, David H., and Clifford D. Shearing. 2001. *The New Structure of Policing: Description, Conceptualization, and Research Agenda.* Washington, DC: National Institute of Justice.

Beck, Allen J., Darrell Gilliard, Lawrence Greenfield, Caroline Harlow, Thomas Hester, Louis Jankowski, Tracy Snell, James Stephan, and Danielle Morton. 1993. *Survey of State Prison Inmates.* Washington, DC: Bureau of Justice Statistics.

Becker, Howard. 1973. *Outsiders.* New York: Free Press.

Beckman, Mary. 2004 (July 30). "Crime, Culpability, and the Adolescent Brain." *Science Magazine. www.sciencemag.org.*

Bedau, Hugo Adam. 1982. *Death Penalty in America.* New York: Oxford University Press.

Bell v. Wolfish. 1979. 441 U.S. 520.

Benekos, Peter J., and Alida V. Merlo. 1995 (March). "Three Strikes and You're Out!: The Political Sentencing Game." *Federal Probation.*

Bennett, William J., John J. DiIulio, Jr., and John P. Walters. 1996. *Body Count: Moral Poverty and How to Win America's War against Crime and Drugs.* New York: Simon & Shuster.

Berger v. United States. 1935. 195 U.S. 78.

Bernard, Thomas J. 1983. *The Consensus-Conflict Debate: Form and Content in Social Theories.* New York: Columbia University Press.

Betts v. Brady. 1942. 316 U.S. 455.

Bingham, T. D. n.d. "Maximum Transfer from Marion to Florence." *Prison Life* 25.

Bittner, Egon. 1970. *The Functions of the Police in Modern Society.* Cambridge, MA: Oelgeschlager, Gunn & Hain.

BJS Statisticians. 2002. *Correctional Populations in the United States, 1998.* Washington, DC: Bureau of Justice Statistics.

Black, Charles L., Jr. 1981. *Capital Punishment: The Inevitability of Caprice and Mistake.* 2nd ed. New York: W. W. Norton.

Black, Donald J. 1980. *The Manners and Customs of the Police.* New York: Academic Press.

———. 1983. "Crime as Social Control." *American Sociological Review* 48:34–45.

———. 1989. *Sociological Justice.* New York: Oxford University Press.

Black, Henry Campbell. 1983. *Black's Law Dictionary.* 5th ed. St. Paul: West.

Blackstone, Sir William. 1803. *Commentaries on the Laws of England.* London: T. Tegg. Pt. IV.

Blakely v. Washington. 2004. 124 S.Ct. 2531.

Blumberg, Abraham S. 1967. "The Practice of Law as Confidence Game: Organizational Co-Optation of a Profession." *Law and Society Review* 1.

———. 1970. *Criminal Justice.* Chicago: Quadrangle Books.

Blumenthal, Ralph. 1989 (August 22). "And Now a Private Midtown 'Police Force.'" *New York Times.*

Blumstein, Alfred. 1993. "Racial Disproportionality of U.S. Prison Populations Revisited." *University of Colorado Law Review* 64.

———. 2004. "Prisons: A Policy Change." In *Crime.* Edited by James Q. Wilson and Joan Petersilia, pp. 451–482. Oakland, CA: Institute for Contemporary Studies.

Blumstein, Alfred, Jacqueline Cohn, Susan Martin, and Michael Tonry. 1983. *Research on Sentencing: The Search for Reform.* Washington, DC: National Academy Press.

Blumstein, Alfred, David P. Farrington, and Soumyo Moitra. 1985. "Delinquency Careers." In *Crime and Justice: A Review of Research.* Edited by Michael H. Tonry and Norval Morris. Chicago: University of Chicago Press.

Boland, Barbara, Catherine H. Conly, Lynn Warner, Ronald Sones, and W. Martin. 1989 (June). *The Prosecution of Felony Arrests, 1986.* Washington, DC: Bureau of Justice Statistics.

Boland, Barbara, and Brian Forst. 1985. "Prosecutors Don't Always Aim to Pleas." *Federal Probation* 49.

Bonczar, Thomas P. 2003. *Prevalence of Imprisonment in the U.S. Population, 1974–2001.* Washington, DC: Bureau of Justice Statistics.

Bonczar, Thomas P., and Tracy L. Snell. 2004. *Capital Punishment, 2003.* Washington, DC: Bureau of Justice Statistics.

Bowers, William J. 1974. *Executions in America.* Lexington, MA: Lexington Books.

Bowker, Lee H. 1982. *Corrections: The Science and the Myth.* New Haven, CT: Yale University Press.

———. 1983. "Prisons: Problems and Prospects." In *Encyclopedia of Crime and Justice.* Edited by Sanford H. Kadish. New York: Free Press 3:1230–1231.

Boydstun, John. 1975. *San Diego Field Interrogation Final Report.* Washington, DC: Police Foundation.

Boykin v. Alabama. 1969. 305 U.S. 238.

Brain, Paul Frederic. 1994. "Hormonal Aspects of Aggression and Violence." In *Understanding and Preventing Violence.* Vol. 2, *Behavioral Influences.* Edited by Albert J. Reiss, Klaus A. Miczek, and Jeffrey A. Roth. Washington, DC: National Academy Press.

Braithwaite, John. 1979. *Inequality, Crime, and Public Policy.* London: Routledge and Kegan Paul.

Brakel, Samuel. 1982 (January). "Administrative Justice in the Penitentiary: Report on Inmate Grievance Procedures." *American Bar Foundation Research Journal.*

———. 1983 (January). "Ruling on Prisoners' Grievances." *American Bar Foundation Research Journal.*

Brandl, Steven G., and James Frank. 1994. "The Relationship between Evidence, Detective Effort, and the Disposition of Burglary and Robbery Investigations." *American Journal of Police* XIII.

Britt, Chester L., III, Michael R. Gottfredson, and John S. Goldkamp. 1992. "Drug Testing and Pretrial Misconduct: An Experiment on the Specific Deterrent Effects of Drug Monitoring

Defendants on Pretrial Release." *Journal of Research on Crime and Delinquency* 29.

Brockway, Zebulon. 1912. *Fifty Years of Prison Service.* New York: Charities Publication Committee.

Brown, Craig M., and Barbara D. Warner. 1992. "Immigrants, Urban Politics, and Policing in 1900." *American Sociological Review* 57.

Brown, Michael K. 1988. *Working the Street: Police Discretion and the Dilemmas of Reform.* New York: Russell Sage.

Brown, Stephen E. 1984. "Social Class, Child Maltreatment, and Delinquent Behavior." *Criminology* 22.

Brownstein, Henry H. 1996. *The Rise and Fall of a Violent Crime Wave.* Guilderland, NY: Harrow and Heston.

Buchanan, John. 1989 (May/June). "Police-Prosecutor Teams: Innovations in Several Jurisdictions." *National Institute of Justice Reports.*

Buerger, Michael E. 1994. "The Problems of Problem-Solving: Resistance, Interdependencies, and Conflicting Interests." *American Journal of Police* XIII.

Bunker, Edward. 1977. *Animal Factory.* New York: Viking Press.

Bureau of Alcohol, Firearms, Tobacco, and Explosives (ATF). 2004. *Snapshot.* Washington, DC: ATF. http://www.atf.gov/about/snap2004.htm.

Bureau of Justice Statistics. 1988b. *Report to the Nation on Crime and Justice.* 2nd ed. Washington, DC: BJS.

———. 1989a. *The Prosecution of Felony Arrests.* Washington, DC: BJS.

———. 1989b (January). *The Redesigned National Crime Survey: Selected New Data, Special Report.* Washington, DC: BJS.

———. 1992a. *Prosecutors in State Courts, 1990.* Washington, DC: BJS.

———. 1992b. *Sourcebook of Criminal Justice Statistics, 1991.* Washington, DC: BJS.

———. 1994. *Violence and Theft in the Workplace, 1987–1992.* Washington, DC: BJS.

———. 1997. *Correctional Populations in the United States.* Washington, DC: Bureau of Justice Statistics.

———. 1997 (July). *Implementing the National Incident-Based Reporting System: A Project Status Report.* Washington, DC: BJS.

———. 1998 (March). *Violence by Intimates.* Washington, DC: BJS.

———. 1999a (July). *Felony Sentences in the U.S., 1996.* Washington, DC: BJS.

———. 1999b. *Pretrial Release and Detention, 1996.* Washington, DC: BJS.

———. 1999c. *Prisoners in 1998.* Washington, DC: BJS.

———. 2000a (December). *Capital Punishment 1999.* Washington, DC: BJS.

———. 2000b. *Correctional Populations in the United States, 1997.* Washington, DC: BJS.

———. 2000c. *Criminal Victimization in the U.S., 1999.* Washington, DC: BJS.

———. 2001a. *Census of Jails, 1999.* Washington, DC: BJS.

———. 2001b. *Community Policing in Local Police Departments, 1997 and 1999.* Washington, DC: BJS.

———. 2001c. *Criminal Victimization 2000.* Washington, DC: BJS.

———. 2001d. *Prisoners in 1999.* Washington, DC: BJS.

———. 2001e. *Prisoners in 2000.* Washington, DC: BJS.

———. 2001 (February). *Contacts between Police and the Public: Findings from the 1999 Survey.* Washington, DC: BJS.

———. 2003 (January). *Local Police Departments, 2000.* Washington, DC: BJS.

———. 2003 (June). *Felony Sentences in State Courts, 2000.* Washington, DC: BJS.

———. 2003 (August). *Criminal Victimization, 2002.* Washington, DC: BJS, Table 1.

———. 2003 (August). *Federal Law Enforcement Officers, 2002: Highlights.* Washington, DC: BJS.

———. 2004 (April). *Law Enforcement Management and Administrative Statistics, 2000: Data for Individual State and Local Agencies with 100 or More Officers.* Washington, DC: BJS.

———. 2004 (May). *Justice Expenditure and Employment in the U.S., 2001.* Washington, DC: BJS.

Burrows v. State. 1931. 38 Ariz. 99, 297 P. 1029.

Bursik, Robert J., Jr., and Harold Grasmick. 1993. *Neighborhoods and Crime: The Dimensions of Effective Community Control.* New York: Lexington.

Butterfield, Fox. 1992 (November 13). "Study Cites Biology's Role in Violent Behavior." *New York Times.*

———. 2004 (November 8). "Despite Drop in Crime, an Increase in Inmates." *New York Times.*

Byrne, James M., and Linda Kelly. 1989. *Restructuring Probation as an Intermediate Sanction: An Evaluation of the Massachusetts Intensive Supervision Program.* Washington, DC: National Institute of Justice.

Byrne, James M., Arthur J. Lurigio, and Joan Petersilia. 1992. *Smart Sentencing: The Emergence of Intermediate Sanctions.* Newbury Park, CA: Sage.

California v. Greenwood. 1988. 486 U.S. 35.

California Welfare and Institutions Code. 1981. California Department of Youth Authority.

Call, Jack E. 1988. "Lower Court Treatment of Jail and Prison Overcrowding Cases: A Second Look." *Federal Probation* 52.

Camp, Camille Graham, and George M. Camp. 2000. *Corrections Yearbook 2000.* Middletown, CT: Criminal Justice Institute.

Campaign for an Effective Crime Policy. 1993 (October). "Evaluating Mandatory Minimum Sentences." Unpublished manuscript. Washington, DC: Campaign for an Effective Crime Policy.

Campbell, Michael S. 1986. *Field Training for Police Officers: State of the Art.* Washington, DC: National Institute of Justice.

Caplow, Theodore, and Jonathan Simon. 1999. "Understanding Prison Policy and Population Growth." In *Prisons.* Edited by Michael Tonry and Joan Petersilia. Chicago: University of Chicago Press.

Carlson, Jonathon C. 1987. "The Act Requirement and the Foundations of the Entrapment Defense." *Virginia Law Review.*

Carns, Teresa W. 1991. *Alaska's Plea Bargaining Ban Re-Evaluated.* Anchorage: Alaska Judicial Council. http://www.ajc.state.ak.us/Reports/pleafram.htm.

Carr, Patrick J. 1998. "Keeping Up Appearances: Informal Social Control in a White Working-Class Neighborhood in Chicago." PhD. Dissertation. University of Chicago.

Carter, David L., and Allen D. Sapp. 1991. *Police Education and Minority Recruitment: The Impact of a College Requirement.* Washington, DC: Police Executive Research Forum.

Carter, David L., Allen D. Sapp, and Darrell W. Stephens. 1989. *The State of Police Education: Policy Direction for the 21st Century.* Washington, DC: Police Executive Research Forum.

Carter, Lief H. 1976. *The Limits of Order.* Lexington, MA: Lexington Books.

Carter, Robert M. 1984. "The United States." In *Western Systems of Juvenile Justice*. Edited by Malcolm W. Klein. Beverly Hills: Sage.

Case, Travis. n.d. "O. J. Simpson." http://traviscase.org/Questions/Questions1–25/003-OJSimpson.html.

Casper, Jonathan D. 1972. *American Criminal Justice*. Englewood Cliffs, NJ: Prentice-Hall.

Chambliss, William J. 1975. *Criminal Law in Action*. Santa Barbara, CA: Hamilton.

———. 1984. *Criminal Law in Action*. 2nd ed. New York: Macmillan.

Chambliss, William J., and Robert Seidman. 1982. *Law, Order, and Power*. 2nd ed. Reading, MA: Addison-Wesley.

Chamlin, Mitchell B., and John K Cochran. 1998. "Causality, Economic Conditions, and Burglary." *Criminology* 36.

Champion, Dean J. 1988. *Felony Probation: Problems and Prospects*. New York: Praeger.

Chandler v. Fretag. 1954. 348 U.S. 3.

Chevigny, Paul. 1969. *Police Power: Police Abuses in New York City*. New York: Vintage.

Chimel v. California. 1969. 395 U.S. 752.

Christopher Commission. 1991. *Report of the Independent Commission on the Los Angeles Police Department*. Los Angeles: Independent Commission on the Los Angeles Police Department.

Church, Thomas W. 1979. "In Defense of 'Bargain Justice.'" *Law & Society Review* 13(2): 509–525.

Clark, John, James Austin, and D. Alan Henry. 1997 (September). *"Three Strikes and You're Out": A Review of State Legislation*. Washington, DC: National Institute of Justice, Research Brief. Exhibit 1.

Clarke, Ronald V., and Marcus Felson, eds. 1993. *Routine Activity and Rational Choice*. New Brunswick, NJ: Transaction Publishers.

Clear, Todd R., and Anthony A. Braga. 1995. "Community Corrections." In *Crime*. Edited by James Q. Wilson and Joan Petersilia. San Francisco: Institute for Contemporary Studies.

Clear, Todd R., and George F. Cole. 1994. *American Corrections*. 3rd ed. Belmont, CA: Wadsworth.

Clear, Todd R., Bruce Stout, Linda Kelly, Harry Dammer, and Patricia Hardyman. 1992. *Prisons, Prisoners, and Religion*. New Brunswick, NJ: Rutgers University Press.

Clemmer, Donald. 1940. *The Prison Community*. New York: Holt, Rinehart, & Winston.

Cloward, Richard, and Lloyd Ohlin. 1960. *Delinquency and Opportunity: A Theory of Delinquent Gangs*. New York: Free Press.

Cohen, Fred. 1985. *Criminal Law Bulletin* 21.

Cohen, Lawrence E. 1975. *Delinquency Dispositions: An Empirical Analysis of Processing Decisions in Three Juvenile Courts*. Washington, DC: Government Printing Office.

Cohen, Lawrence E., and Marcus Felson. 1979. "Social Change and Crime Rate Trends: A Routine Activity Approach." *American Sociological Review* 44.

Colorado v. Connelly. 1986. 479 U.S. 157.

Colorado Statutes. 1986. Section 18-1-704.5, 8b, C.R.S.

Colvin, Mark. 1982 (June). "The 1980 New Mexico Prison Riot." *Social Problems* 29.

———. 1992. *The Penitentiary in Crisis: From Accommodation to Riot in New Mexico*. Albany, NY: State University of New York Press.

Common Sense Foundation. 2001 (April 16). "Landmark North Carolina Death Penalty Study Finds Dramatic Bias." Raleigh, NC: Common Sense Foundation.

Community-Oriented Policing Service (COPS). 2004. "What Is Community Policing?" http://www.cops.usdoj.gov/Default.asp?Item=36.

Cook, Fay Lomax. 1979. "Crime among the Elderly: The Emergence of a Policy Issue." In *Reactions to Crime*. Edited by Dan E. Lewis. Beverly Hills: Wadsworth.

Cook, Julian Abele, Jr. 1995. "Family Responsibility." *Federal Sentencing Reporter* 8.

Cooke, Jacob E. 1961. *The Federalist*. Middleton, CT: Wesleyan University Press.

Cordner, Gary W., and Robert C. Trojanowicz. 1992. "Patrol." In *What Works in Policing?* Edited by Gary W. Cordner and Donna C. Hale. Cincinnati: Anderson.

Cornish, Derek B., and Ronald V. Clarke, eds. 1986. *The Reasoning Criminal: Rational Choice Perspectives on Offending*. New York: Springer-Verlag.

Corporate Fraud Task Force. 2004. *First Year Report to the President*. Washington, DC: Department of Justice. http://www.usdoj.gov/dag/cftf/first_year_report.pdf.

Corrections Compendium Journal. 2000 (September). Washington, DC: American Correctional Association.

Cosgrove, Edward J. 1994 (September). "ROBO-PO: The Life and Times of a Federal Probation Officer." *Federal Probation*.

Court, Andy. 1993 (January/February). "Is There a Crisis?" *American Lawyer*.

Criminal and Juvenile Justice Coordinating Council. 2000. "Working Paper No. 3, Executive Summary." http://www.cjjcc.org/download/wp03_es.pdf.

Criminal Justice Abstracts. 1998. New York: Monsey: Willow Tree Press.

Criminal Justice Institute. 2001. *Corrections Yearbook 2000: Adult Corrections*. Middletown, CT: Criminal Justice Institute, Inc.

Criminal Justice Newsletter. 1996 (February 15). New York: Pace Publications.

———. 1996 (November 15). New York: Pace Publications.

Crist, David. 2004 (August 2). "Managing Minnesota Prisons." University of Minnesota, Lecture.

Cronin, Thomas E., Tania Z. Cronin, and Michael E. Milakovich. 1981. *U.S. vs. Crime in the Streets*. Bloomington, IN: Indiana University Press.

Cuddihy, William J. 1990. "The Fourth Amendment: Origins and Original Meaning." Unpublished dissertation. Claremont, CA: Claremont Graduate School.

Cullen, Francis T. 1983. *Rethinking Crime and Deviance Theory*. Totowa, NJ: Rowman and Allenheld.

Cullen, Francis T., John E. Eck, and Christopher T. Lowenkamp. 2002. "Environmental Corrections—A New Paradigm for Effective Supervision." *Federal Probation* 66(2): 28–37.

Cumming, Elaine, Ian Cumming, and Laurel Edell. 1965. "Policeman as Philosopher, Guide, and Friend." *Social Problems* 12.

Currie, Elliot. 1998. *Crime and Punishment in America*. New York: Metropolitan Books.

Dahrendorf, Ralf. 1958. "Out of Utopia: Toward a Reorientation of Sociological Analysis." *American Journal of Sociology* 64.

Daly, Kathleen. 1989. "Neither Conflict nor Labeling nor Paternalism Will Suffice; Intersections of Race, Ethnicity, Gender, and Family in Criminal Court Decisions." *Crime and Delinquency* 35.

———. 1994. *Gender, Crime, and Punishment.* New Haven, CT: Yale University Press.

Davenport, Jennifer L., and Steven Penrod. 1997. "Eyewitness Identification Evidence: Evaluating Common-Sense Evaluations." *Psychology, Public Policy, and Law* 3:338–361.

Davey, Monica. 2004 (March 15). "Illinois Governor in the Middle of New Death Penalty Debate." *New York Times*, Sec. A, Col. 1, p. 14. http://www.nytimes.com.

Davis, Kenneth C. 1975. *Police Discretion.* St. Paul, MN: West.

Decker, Scott H., and Barrik Van Winkle. 1996. *Life in the Gang: Family, Friends, and Violence.* Cambridge: Cambridge University Press.

DeFrances, Carol J. 2002 (May). *Prosecutors in State Courts, 2001.* Washington, DC: Bureau of Justice Statistics.

Dershowitz, Alan. 1982. *The Best Defense.* New York: Random House.

———. 1994. *The Abuse Excuse and Other Cop-Outs, Sob Stories, and Evasions of Responsibility.* Boston: Little, Brown.

Dewan, Shaila K. 2004 (April 28). "New York's Gospel of Policing by Data Spreads across U.S." *New York Times.*

———. 2004 (July 12). "Sheriff Accepts Takeover of a Troubled Jail." *New York Times*, p. 12.

Diamond, John L. 1996. "The Myth of Morality and Fault in Criminal Law." *American Criminal Law Review* 34:111.

Diaz-Cotto, Juanita. 1996. *Gender, Ethnicity, and the State.* Albany, NY: State University of New York Press.

Dickerson v. U.S. 2000. 530 U.S. 428.

DiIulio, John. 1987. *Governing Prisons.* New York: Free Press.

———. 1996. "Help Wanted: Economists, Crime, and Public Policy." *Journal of Economic Perspectives* 10.

Doerner, William G., and E. Britt Patterson. 1992. "The Influence of Race and Gender upon Rookie Evaluations of Their Field Training Officers." *American Journal of Police* XI.

Dolan, Maura. 2001 (October 19). "Terrorism May Shift Jurors' Attitudes." *Los Angeles Times.*

Dostoyevsky, Fyodor. 1860. *House of the Dead.* London: Heinemann.

Draper v. U.S. 1959. 358 U.S. 307.

Dressler, Joshua. 1997. *Understanding Criminal Procedure.* New York: Matthew Bender.

Drug Enforcement Administration (DEA). 2004. "Mission Statement." Washington, DC: Drug Enforcement Administration. http://www.usdoj.gov/dea/agency/mission.htm.

Durkheim, Emile. 1933. *The Division of Labor in Society.* New York: Free Press.

———. 1951. *Suicide: A Study in Sociology.* New York: Free Press.

———. 1964. *The Division of Labor in Society.* New York: Free Press.

Durose, Matthew R., and Patrick A. Langan. 2003. *State Court Sentencing of Convicted Felons, 2000 Statistical Tables.* Washington, DC: Bureau of Justice Statistics.

———. 2004. *Felony Sentences in State Courts, 2002.* Washington, DC: Bureau of Justice Statistics.

Earley, Pete. 1992. *The Hot House.* New York: Bantam Books.

Easteal, Patricia. 1993. "Premenstrual Syndrome (PMS) in the Courtroom." Canberra: Australian Institute of Criminology. http://64.233.167.104/search?q=cache:o7XnLuSd_84J:www.aic.gov.au/publications/proceedings/16/Easteal2.pdf+&hl=en.

Eck, John E. 1983. *Solving Crimes: The Investigation of Burglary and Robbery.* Washington, DC: Police Executive Research Forum.

———. 1992. "Criminal Investigation." In *What Works in Policing?* Edited by Gary W. Cordner and Donna C. Hale. Cincinnati: Anderson.

Eck, John E., and Dennis P. Rosenbaum. 1994. "The New Police Order: Effectiveness, Equity, and Efficiency in Community Policing." In *The Challenge of Community Policing: Testing the Premises.* Edited by Dennis P. Rosenbaum. Thousand Oaks, CA: Sage.

Ehlers, Scott, Vincent Schiraldi, and Jason Ziedenberg. 2004. *Still Striking Out: Ten Years of California's Three Strikes.* San Francisco: Justice Policy Institute.

Ehrlich, Isaac. 1975. "The Deterrent Effect of Capital Punishment: A Question of Life and Death." *American Economic Review* 397.

Eisenstein, James, and Herbert Jacob. 1977. *Felony Justice.* Boston: Little, Brown.

Elliott, Delbert. 1994. "Serious Violent Offenders: Onset, Developmental Course, and Termination." *Criminology* 32:1–22.

El Nasser, Haya. 2002 (December 15). "Gated Communities More Popular, and Not Just for the Rich." *USA Today.*

Elton, Geoffrey R. 1974. *England under the Tudors.* 2nd ed. London: Methuen.

Empey, Lamar T. 1978. *American Delinquency: Its Meaning and Construction.* Homewood, IL: Dorsey Press.

Erikson, Kai T. 1966. *Wayward Puritans: A Study in the Sociology of Deviance.* New York: John Wiley & Sons.

Escobedo v. Illinois. 1964. 378 U.S. 478.

Eskridge, Chris. 1983. *Pretrial Release Programming: Issues and Trends.* New York: Boardman.

Eve, Raymond A., and Susan Brown Eve. 1984. "The Effects of Powerlessness, Fear of Social Change, and Social Integration on Fear of Crime among the Elderly." *Victimology* 9.

Fabiano, Elizabeth, Frank Porporino, and David Robinson. 1990. "Rehabilitation through Clearer Thinking: A Cognitive Model of Correctional Intervention." Correctional Service of Canada. http://www.csc-scc.gc.ca/text/rsrch/briefs/b4/b04e.shtml.

Fagan, Jeffrey, and Richard Freeman. 1999. "Crime and Work." In *Crime and Justice: A Review of Research.* Edited by Michael Tonry. Chicago: University of Chicago Press.

FBI. n.d. *CJIS Newsletter*, Vol. 4, No. 1. Washington, DC: U.S. Department of Justice.

———. 2003. *Crime in the U.S., 1995–2002.* Washington, DC: FBI. Section VI.

———. 2003. *Crime in the United States, 2002.* Washington, DC: FBI. Section IV, UCR Data, 2002.

———. 2003. *Hate Crime Statistics, 2002.* Washington, DC: Department of Justice.

———. 2003. *Law Enforcement Officers Killed and Assaulted, 2002.* Washington, DC: FBI.

———. 2004. "FBI Priorities." http://www.fbi.gov/priorities/priorities.htm.

———. 2004. *Law Enforcement Officers Killed and Assaulted, 2003.* Washington, DC: FBI.

Federal Bureau of Prisons. n.d. *Metropolitan Correctional Center.* Chicago.

———. 1993 (June 16). "Florence Background Paper." Washington, DC: Office of Public Affairs.

Federal Rules of Criminal Procedure. 2002. Washington, DC: U.S. Government Printing Office.

———. 2004. Washington, DC: U.S. Government Printing Office.

Feeley, Malcolm M. 1979. *The Process Is the Punishment.* New York: Russell Sage.

Feeley, Malcolm M., and Roger Hanson. 1987. "What We Know, Think We Know, and Would Like to Know about the Impact of Court Orders on Prison Conditions and Jail Crowding." In *Prison and Jail Crowding: Workshop Proceedings.* Edited by

Dale K. Sechrest, Jonathan D. Caspar, and Jeffrey A. Roth. Washington, DC: National Academy of Sciences.

Feeley, Malcolm M., and Mark H. Lazerson. 1983. "Police-Prosecutor Relationships: An Interorganizational Perspective." In *Empirical Theories about Courts*. Edited by Keith O. Boyum and Lynn Mather. New York: Longman.

Feeley, Malcolm M., and Austin D. Sarat. 1980. *The Policy Dilemma: Federal Crime Policy and Enforcement, 1968–1978*. Minneapolis: University of Minnesota Press.

Feeney, Floyd. 1981. *Case Processing and Police-Prosecutor Coordination*. Davis, CA: University of California, Davis, Center on Administration of Criminal Justice.

———. 1986. "Robbers as Decision-Makers." In *The Reasoning Criminals*. Edited by Derek B. Cornish and Ronald V. Clarke, pp. 53–71. New York: Springer-Verlag.

Fellers v. U.S. 2004. 124 S.Ct. 1019.

Felson, Marcus. 1986. "Linking Criminal Choices, Routine Activities, Informal Control, and Criminal Outcomes." In *The Reasoning Criminal*. Edited by Derek B. Cornish and Ronald V. Clarke, pp. 119–128. New York: Springer-Verlag.

———. 1998. *Crime in Everyday Life*. 2nd ed. Thousand Oaks, CA: Pine Forge Press.

Finckenauer, James O. 1984. *Juvenile Delinquency and Corrections: The Gap between Theory and Practice*. Orlando, FL: Academic Press.

Finkelhor, David, Richard J. Gelles, Gerald T. Hotaling, and Murray A. Straus. 1983. *The Dark Side of Families: Current Family Violence Research*. Beverly Hills: Sage.

Fishbein, Diana. 2001. *Biobehavioral Perspectives in Criminology*. Belmont, CA: Wadsworth.

Flaherty, David. 1971. "Law and Enforcement of Morals in Early America." In *Law in American History*. Edited by Donald Fleming and Bernard Bailyn. Boston: Little, Brown.

Flanagan, Timothy J. 1989. "Prison Labor and Industry." In *The American Prison: Issues in Research and Policy*. Edited by Lynne Goodstein and Doris Layton MacKenzie. New York: Plenum Press.

Flanagan, Timothy J., and Dennis R. Longmire, eds. 1996. *Americans View Crime and Justice*. Thousand Oaks, CA: Sage.

Fleisher, Mark. *Warehousing Violence*. 1989. Newbury Park, CA: Sage.

Fletcher, George P. 1978. *Rethinking Criminal Law*. Boston: Little, Brown.

———. 1988. *A Crime of Self-Defense: Bernhard Goetz and the Law on Trial*. New York: Free Press.

———. 1995. *With Justice for Some: Victims' Rights in Criminal Trials*. Reading, MA: Addison-Wesley.

Foote, Caleb. 1956. "Vagrancy-Type Law and Its Administration." *University of Pennsylvania Law Review* 104.

———. 1965. "The Coming Constitutional Crisis in Bail." *University of Pennsylvania Law Review* 113.

Forer, Lois. 1984. *Money and Justice*. New York: W. W. Norton.

Forst, Brian. 1981. *Improving Police-Prosecutor Coordination*. Washington, DC: Institute for Law and Social Research.

———. 1995. "Prosecution and Sentencing." In *Crime*. Edited by James Q. Wilson and Joan Petersilia. San Francisco: Institute for Contemporary Studies Press.

———, ed. 1993. *The Socio-Economics of Crime and Justice*. Armonk, NY: M. E. Sharpe, Inc.

Forst, Brian, F. J. Leahy, Jr., J. Shirhall, H. L. Tyson, and J. Bartolomeo. 1982. *Arrest Convictability as a Measure of Police Performance*. Washington, DC: National Institute of Justice.

Forst, Brian, Judith Lucianovic, and Sarah J. Cox. 1977. *What Happens after Arrest?* Washington, DC: National Institute of Law Enforcement and Criminal Justice.

Frase, Richard. 1998. "Jails." In *Handbook of Crime and Justice*. Edited by Michael Tonry. New York: Oxford University Press.

Freed, Daniel J., and Patricia M. Wald. 1964. *Bail in the United States: 1964: A Report to the National Conference on Bail and Criminal Justice*. Washington, DC: Vera Institute of Justice.

Fridel, Lorie A. 2004. *By the Numbers: A Guide for Analyzing Race Data from Vehicle Stops*. Washington, DC: Police Executive Research Forum.

Fridell, Lorie A., Robert Lunney, Drew Diamond, and Bruce Kubu. 2001. *Racially Biased Policing: A Principled Response*. Washington, DC: Police Executive Research Forum.

Frohmann, Lisa. 1991. "Discrediting Victims' Allegations of Sexual Assault: Prosecutorial Accounts of Case Rejections." *Social Problems* 38:213–226.

Frontline. 1996. "Angel on Death Row." Washington, DC: Public Broadcasting System.

———. 1999 (January 12). "Snitch." Washington, DC: Public Broadcasting System.

Fyfe, James J. 1982. "Blind Justice: Police Shootings in Memphis." *Journal of Criminal Law and Criminology* 73.

———. 1995. "Training to Reduce Police-Citizen Violence." In *And Justice for All: Understanding and Controlling Police Use of Force*. Edited by William A. Geller and Hans Toch. Washington, DC: Police Executive Research Forum.

Gaes, Gerald G., Timothy J. Flanagan, Laurence L. Motuik, and Lynne Stewart. 1998. *Adult Correctional Treatment*. Washington, DC: U.S. Bureau of Prisons.

Garland, David. 2003. "Penal Modernism and Postmodernism." In *Punishment and Social Control*. 2nd ed. Edited by Thomas G. Blomberg and Stanley Cohen, pp. 45–73. New York: Aldine De Gruyter.

Garofolo, James. 1991. "Police, Prosecutors, and Felony Case Attrition." *Journal of Criminal Justice* 19.

Gartner, Rosemary, and Candace Kruttschnitt. 2004. "A Brief History of Doing Time." *Law and Society Review* 38(2).

Garvey, Megan. 2004 (September 27). "Initiative Fight Puts Focus on Felons." *Los Angeles Times*, B1.

Gayarré, Charles. 1903. *History of Louisiana*. New Orleans: F. F. Hansell & Sons, Ltd.

Gaylin, Willard, Steven Marcus, David Rothman, and Ira Glasser. 1978. *Doing Good: The Limits of Benevolence*. New York: Pantheon.

Geerken, Michael R., and Hennessey D. Hayes. 1993. "Probation and Parole: Public Risk and the Future of Incarceration Alternatives." *Criminology* 31.

Geller, William A. 1985. *Crime File: Deadly Force*. Washington, DC: National Institute of Justice.

Geller, William A., and Kevin J. Karales. 1981. *Split-Second Decisions*. Chicago: Chicago Law Enforcement Study Group.

Geller, William A., and Michael S. Scott. 1992. *Deadly Force: What We Know and Don't Know*. Washington, DC: Police Executive Research Forum.

General Accounting Office. 1988 (September). *Prison Boot Camps: Too Early to Measure Effectiveness*. Washington, DC: U.S. General Accounting Office.

Gerber, Jorg, and Eric Fritsch. 1995. "Adult Academic and Vocational Correctional Education Programs: A Review of Current Research." *Journal of Correctional Rehabilitation* 22:1–2.

Gettinger, Stephen H. 1984. *New Generation Jails: An Innovative Approach to an Age-Old Problem.* Washington, DC: National Institute of Corrections.

Giallombardo, Rose. 1966. *Society of Women: A Study of a Women's Prison.* New York: Wiley.

Gibeaut, John. 1997 (May). "Sobering Thoughts: Legislatures and Courts Increasingly Are Just Saying No to Intoxication as a Defense or Mitigating Factor." *American Bar Association Journal.*

Gideon v. Wainwright. 1963. 372 U.S. 335.

Glaberson, William. 1998 (May 24). "Rising Tide of Anger at Teen-Aged Killers." *New York Times.*

Glaze, Lauren E., and Seri Palla. 2004. *Probation and Parole in the United States, 2003.* Washington, DC: Bureau of Justice Statistics.

Glueck, Sheldon, and Eleanor Glueck. 1930. *500 Criminal Careers.* New York: A. A. Knopf.

Goddard, H. H. 1914. *Feeblemindedness: Its Causes and Consequences.* New York: Macmillan.

Goldfarb, Ronald. 1965. *Ransom: A Critique of the American Bail System.* New York: Harper and Row.

———. 1975. *Jails: The Ultimate Ghetto.* New York: Archer Press.

Goldkamp, John S. 1979. *Two Classes of Accused.* Cambridge, MA: Ballinger.

———. 1985. "Danger and Detention: A Second Generation of Bail Reform." *Journal of Criminal Law and Criminology* 76.

Goldkamp, John S., and Doris Weiland. 1993. *Assessing the Impact of Dade County's Felony Drug Court: Final Report.* Philadelphia: Crime and Justice Research Institute.

Goldstein, Herman. 1977. *Policing a Free Society.* Cambridge, MA: Ballinger.

———. 1984. *The Future of Policing.* Seattle: William O. Douglas Institute.

———. 2001. "What Is Problem-Oriented Policing?" http://www.popcenter.org/about-whatisPOP.htm.

Goodnough, Abby. 2003 (December 27). "Boy Serving Life Sentence Is Reoffered Plea Bargain." *New York Times.*

Goolkasian, Gail. 1985. *Coping with Police Stress.* Washington, DC: National Institute of Justice.

Gottfredson, Michael R., and Don M. Gottfredson. 1988. *Decision Making in Criminal Justice.* 2nd ed. Sacramento, CA: Office of Attorney General of California.

Gottfredson, Michael R., and Travis Hirschi. 1990. *A General Theory of Crime.* Stanford, CA: Stanford University Press.

Gottfredson, Stephen D., and Don M. Gottfredson. 1992. *Incapacitation Strategies and the Criminal Career.* Sacramento, CA: Office of Attorney General of California.

Gove, Walter R. 1985. "The Effect of Age and Gender on Deviant Behavior." *Gender and the Life Course.* Edited by Alice S. Rossi. New York: Aldine.

Gove, Walter R., Michael Hughes, and Michael Geerken. 1985. "Are Uniform Crime Reports a Valid Indicator of the Index Crimes? An Affirmative Answer with Minor Qualifications." *Criminology* 23:451–501.

Gray, Tara, G. Larry Mays, and Mary K. Stohr. 1995. "Inmate Needs and Programming in Exclusively Women's Jails." *Prison Journal* 75:2.

Greek, Cecil E. 2002 (June). "Tracking Probationers in Space and Time: The Convergence of GIS and GPS Systems." *Federal Probation* 66(1): 51.

Greenberg, David, ed. 1981. *Crime and Capitalism: Readings in Marxist Criminology.* Palo Alto, CA: Mayfield.

Greenberg, Martin S., R. Barry Ruback, and David R. Westcott. 1983. "Seeking Help from the Police: The Victim's Perspective." In *New Directions in Helping.* Vol. 3. Edited by Arie Nadler, Jeffrey D. Fisher, and Bella M. DePaulo. New York: Academic Press.

Greenhouse, Linda. 2003 (January 27). "Justices Deny Appeal in Execution of Juveniles." *New York Times.*

———. 2004 (November 9). "Supreme Court Declines to Hear 2 Cases Weighing the Right of Felons to Vote." *New York Times.*

Greenwood, Peter W. 2004. "Juvenile Crime and Juvenile Justice." In *Crime: Public Policies for Crime Control.* Edited by James Q. Wilson and Joan Petersilia. Oakland, CA: Institute for Contemporary Studies.

Greenwood, Peter W., Jan Chaiken, and Joan Petersilia. 1977. *The Criminal Investigation Process.* Lexington, MA: D. C. Heath.

Greenwood, Peter W., and Joan Petersilia. 1975. *The Criminal Investigation Process.* Vols. I–III. Santa Monica, CA: Rand.

Greenwood, Peter W., C. Peter Rydell, Allan F. Abrahamse, and Nathan P. Caulins. 1994. *Three Strikes and You're Out: Estimated Benefits and Costs of California's New Mandatory-Sentencing Law.* Santa Monica, CA: Rand.

Greenwood, Peter W., Sorrel Wildhorn, Eugene C. Poggio, M. J. Strumwassder, and Peter DeLeon. 1973. *Prosecution of Adult Felony Defendants in Los Angeles County: A Policy Perspective.* Santa Monica, CA: Rand.

Greer, Kimberley. 2000. "The Changing Nature of Interpersonal Relationships in a Woman's Prison." *Prison Journal* 80: 442–468.

Griffin v. Wisconsin. 1987. 483 U.S. 868.

Griswold v. Connecticut. 1965. 381 U.S. 479.

Griswold, David B. 1994. "Complaints against the Police: Predicting Dispositions." *Journal of Criminal Justice* 22.

Grob, Gerald. 1973. *Mental Institutions in America.* New York: Free Press.

Grudt v. Los Angeles. 1970. 2 Cal.3d 575.

Hagan, John, and Ronit Dinovitzer. 1999. "Collateral Consequences of Imprisonment for Children, Communities, and Prisons." In *Prisons.* Edited by Michael Tonry and Joan Petersilia. Chicago: University of Chicago Press.

Halberstam, David. 1998. *The Children.* New York: Random House.

Hall, John W., Jr. 1993. *Search and Seizure.* 2nd ed. New York: Clark, Boardman, and Callaghan.

Halper, Andrew, and Richard Ku. 1975. *An Exemplary Project: New York City Police Department Street Crimes Unit.* Washington, DC: Government Printing Office.

Hamdi v. Rumsfeld. 2004. 124 S.Ct. 2623.

Haney, Craig, Curtis Banks, and Philip Zimbardo. 1973. "Interpersonal Dynamics in a Simulated Prison." *International Journal of Criminology and Penology* 1.

Hanson, Roger A., Brian J. Ostrom, William E. Hewitt, and Christopher Lomvardias. 1992. *Indigent Defenders Get the Job Done and Done Well.* Williamsburg, VA: National Center for State Courts.

Harcourt, Bernard E. 2001. *Illusions of Order: The Broken Promise of Broken Windows Policing.* Chicago. University of Chicago Press.

Harding, Richard. 2001. "Private Prisons." In *Crime and Justice: A Review of Research.* Edited by Michael Tonry. Chicago: University of Chicago Press.

Harris, David. 2002. *Profiles in Justice: Why Racial Profiling Cannot Work.* New York: New Press.

Harris, M. Kay, and Dudley P. Spiller, Jr. 1977. *After Decision: Implementation of Judicial Decrees in Correctional Settings.* Washington, DC: U.S. Department of Justice.

Harris, Patricia M. 1986. "Is the Juvenile Justice System Lenient?" *Criminal Justice Abstracts.*

Harris, Richard. 1978. "The Police Academy and Professional Self-Image." In *Policing: A View from the Street.* Edited by Peter K. Manning and John Van Maanen, Santa Monica, CA: Goodyear Press.

Harrison, Paige M., and Allen J. Beck. 2003. *Prisoners in 2002.* Washington, DC: Bureau of Justice Statistics.

———. 2004. *Prisoners in 2003.* Washington, DC: Bureau of Justice Statistics.

Harrison, Paige M., and Jennifer C. Karberg. 2004. *Prison and Jail Inmates at Midyear 2003.* Washington, DC: Bureau of Justice Statistics.

Hart, Timothy C., and Brian A. Reaves. 1999. *Felony Defendants in Large Urban Counties, 1996.* Washington, DC: Bureau of Justice Statistics.

Hawkins v. Superior Court. 1978. 586 P.2d 916.

Hawkins, Gordon. 1976. *The Prison: Policy and Practice.* Chicago: University of Chicago Press.

———. 1983. "Prison Labor and Prison Industries." In *Crime and Justice: An Annual Review of Research.* Edited by Michael Tonry and Norval Morris. Chicago: University of Chicago Press.

Hay, Douglas. 1975. "Property, Authority, and the Criminal Law." In *Albion's Fatal Tree.* Edited by Douglas Hay, Peter Linebaugh, John Rule, Edward P. Thompson, and Cal Winslow. London: Allen Lane.

———. 1980. "Crime and Justice in Eighteenth- and Nineteenth-Century England." In *Crime and Justice: An Annual Review of Research.* Edited by Norval Morris and Michael Tonry. London: Allen Lane.

Heffernen, Esther. 1972. *Making It in Prison: The Square, the Cool, and the Life.* New York: Wiley Interscience.

Henig, Robin Marantz. 1982 (March 7). "Dispelling Menstrual Myths." *New York Times Magazine.*

Hensley, Christopher. 2000. "Consensual Homosexual Activity in Male Prisons." *Corrections Compendium* 26:1.

Herbert, Steve. 1998. "Police Subculture Reconsidered." *Criminology* 36.

Herrnstein, Richard, and Charles Murray. 1994. *The Bell Curve.* New York: Free Press.

Hessick, Andrew F., III, and Reshma M. Saujani. 2002. "Plea Bargaining and Convicting the Innocent: The Role of the Prosecutor, the Defense Counsel, and the Judge." *Brigham Young University Journal of Public Law* 16:189.

Heumann, Milton. 1975. "A Note on Plea Bargaining and Case Pressure." *Law and Society Review* 9:515–528.

———. 1978. *Plea Bargaining: The Experience of Prosecutors, Judges, and Defense Attorneys.* Chicago: University of Chicago Press.

———. 1979a. "Author's Reply." *Law and Society Review* 13.

———. 1979b. "Thinking about Plea Bargaining. In *The Study of Criminal Courts.* Edited by Peter F. Nardulli. Cambridge, MA: Ballinger.

Heumann, Milton, and Colin Loftin. 1979. "Mandatory Sentencing and the Abolition of Plea Bargaining: The Michigan Firearm Statute." *Law and Society Review* 13:393.

Hibel v. Sixth Judicial District Court of Nevada. 2004. 124 S.Ct. 2451.

Hickman, Matthew J., and Brian A. Reeves. 2003 (January). *Local Police Departments, 2000.* Washington, DC: Bureau of Justice Statistics.

Hillsman, Sally T. 1995. "Day Fines in New York." In *Intermediate Sanctions in Overcrowded Times.* Edited by Michael Tonry and Kate Hamilton. Boston: Northeastern University Press.

Hillsman, Sally T., and Judith A. Greene. 1992. "The Use of Fines as an Intermediate Punishment." In *Smart Sentencing: The Emergence of Intermediate Sanctions.* Edited by James M. Byrne, Arthur J. Lurigio, and Joan Petersilia. Newbury Park, CA: Sage.

Hindelang, Michael. 1978. "Race and Involvement in Common Law Property Crimes." *American Sociological Review* 43.

Hindelang, Michael, Michael Gottfredson, and James Garofalo. 1978. *Victims of Personal Crime.* Cambridge, MA: Ballinger.

Hirsch, Adam Jay. 1992. *The Rise of the Penitentiary.* New Haven, CT: Yale University Press.

Hirschi, Travis. 1969. *Causes of Delinquency.* Berkeley: University of California Press.

Hirschi, Travis, and Michael Hindelang. 1977. "Intelligence and Delinquency." *American Sociological Review* 42:572–587.

Hoffmann, John, and Susan Su. 1997. "The Conditional Effects of Stress on Delinquency and Drug Use: A Strain Theory Assessment of Sex Differences." *Journal of Research in Crime and Delinquency* 34(1): 46–78.

Holden, Benjamin A., Laurie P. Cohen, and Eleena de Lisser. 1995 (October 4). "Color Blinded? Race Seems to Play an Increasing Role in Many Jury Verdicts." *Wall Street Journal.*

Holland v. Illinois. 1990. 493 U.S. 474.

Holmes, Malcolm D., Howard C. Daudistel, and William A. Taggart. 1992. "Plea Bargaining Policy and State District Court Loads: An Interrupted Time-Series Analysis." *Law and Society Review* 26.

Holt, Norm. 1998. "Parole in America." In *Community Corrections: Probation, Parole, and Intermediate Sanctions.* Edited by Joan Petersilia. New York: Oxford University Press.

Holy Bible: King James Version. 2000. http://www.bartleby.com/108/03/24.html.

Horney, Julie, and Ineke Haen Marshall. 1992. "Risk Perceptions among Serious Offenders: The Role of Crime and Punishment." *Criminology* 30.

Hoskinson, Charles. 1998 (December 1). "Prison Industries Often in the Red." *Associated Press.*

Hough, Mike. 1987. "Offenders' Choice of Target: Findings from Victim Surveys." *Journal of Quantitative Criminology* 3.

Howe, Frederic C. 1910 (July). "A Golden Rule Chief of Police." *Everybody's Magazine.*

Hudson v. Palmer. 1984. 468 U.S. 517.

Human Rights Watch. 2001. *Beyond Reason: The Death Penalty and Mental Retardation.* Vol. 13(1). Human Rights Watch. http://www.hrw.org/reports/2001/ustat.

Hunter, Albert. 1985. "Private, Parochial, and Public School Orders: The Problem of Crime and Incivility in Urban Communities." In *The Challenge of Social Control: Citizenship and Institution Building in Modern Society.* Edited by Gerald Suttles and Mayer Zald. Norwood, NJ: Ablex Publishing.

Hunter, Susan M. 1986. "On the Line: Working Hard with Dignity." *Corrections Today* 48:4.

IACP (International Association of Chiefs of Police). 2004. "Vehicular Pursuit, Model Policy." Alexandria, VA: IACP. http://www.theiacp.org/documents/pdfs/Publications/Vehicular%20Pursuit%20Policy.pdf.

IBR (Incident Based Reporting Center). 2004. "FBI's Status of NIBRS in the States." http://www.jrsa.org/ibrrc/status_nibrs/nibrs_states.html.

Illinois v. Allen. 1970. 397 U.S. 337.

Illinois v. Lidster. 2004. 124 S.Ct. 885.

Illinois v. Rodriguez. 1990. 497 U.S. 177.

Immarigeon, Russ, and Meda Chesney-Lind. 1992. *Women's Prisons: Overcrowded and Overused.* San Francisco: National Council on Crime and Delinquency.

Inbau, Fred E., James R. Thompson, and James B. Zagel. 1980. *Criminal Law and Its Administration.* 4th ed. Mineola, NY: Foundation Press.

In re Gault. 1967. 387 U.S. 1.

In re Judge Thomas P. Quirk. 1997. 705 So.2d 172 (La.).

In re Kemmler. 1890. 136 U.S. 436.

In re Winship. 1970. 397 U.S. 358.

Institute for Law and Social Research (INSLAW). 1977. *Curbing the Repeat Offender.* Washington, DC: INSLAW.

Iowa Department of Corrections. n.d. "Iowa Department of Corrections Scoring Guide." Mimeo produced by Iowa Department of Corrections.

Irwin, John. 1980. *Prisons in Turmoil.* Boston: Little, Brown.

———. 1987. *The Felon.* Berkeley: University of California Press.

———. 1996. "The Prison Experience: The Convict World." In *Criminal Justice.* Edited by George S. Bridges, Joseph G. Weis, and Robert D. Crutchfield. Thousand Oaks, CA: Pine Forge Press.

Irwin, John, and James Austin. 1997. *It's about Time: America's Imprisonment Binge.* 2nd ed. Belmont, CA: Wadsworth.

Israel, Jerold H., Yale Kamisar, and Wayne R. LaFave. 2002. *Criminal Procedure and the Constitution.* Eagan, MN: West.

Jackson, Patrick G., and Cindy A. Stearns. 1995. "Gender Issues in the New Generation Jail." *Prison Journal* 75.

Jackson, Robert. 1940. *Journal of the American Judicature Society* 34.

Jacobs, James B. 1977. *Stateville: The Penitentiary in Modern Society.* Chicago: University of Chicago Press.

———. 1980. "Race Relations and the Prisoner Subculture." In *Crime and Justice: An Annual Review of Research.* Edited by Norval Morris and Michael Tonry. Chicago: University of Chicago Press.

———, ed. 1983. *New Perspectives on Prisons and Imprisonment.* Ithaca, NY: Cornell University Press.

Jacoby, Joan. 1980. *The American Prosecutor: A Search for Identity.* Lexington, MA: D. C. Heath.

Jefferson, Thomas. 1853. *The Writings of Thomas Jefferson.* Edited by Albert Ellery Bergh. Washington, DC: U.S. Government.

Johnson v. Louisiana. 1972. 406 U.S. 356.

Johnson v. Zerbst. 1938. 304 U.S. 458.

Johnson, Alan. 1999 (February 28). "$88.42 in Drugs End Life of 'The Volunteer'; Wilford Berry's Case Cost Ohio $1.5 Million." *Columbus Dispatch.*

Johnson, Robert. 1996. *Hard Time: Understanding and Reforming the Prison.* 2nd ed. Monterey, CA: Brooks/Cole.

Joy, Kevin. 2004 (February 7). "A Minority Chief Would Be City's First." *Boston Globe.*

Judicial Conference of the United States. 1998 (September 15). *Federal Death Penalty Cases: Executive Summary.* Subcommittee on Federal Death Penalty Cases, Committee on Defender Services.

Juvenile Justice Bulletin. 2000 (September). Washington, DC: Office of Juvenile Justice and Delinquency Prevention.

———. 2002 (September). Washington, DC: Office of Juvenile Justice and Delinquency Prevention.

———. 2004 (September). Washington, DC: Office of Juvenile Justice and Delinquency Prevention.

Kalinich, David B. 1986. *Power, Stability, and Contraband.* Prospect Heights, IL: Waveland Press.

Kalven, Harry, Jr., and Hans Zeisel. 1966. *The American Jury.* Chicago: University of Chicago Press.

Kanarek, Robin. 1994. "Nutrition and Violent Behavior." In *Understanding and Preventing Violence: Behavioral Influences.* Vol. 2. Washington, DC: National Academy Press.

Kappeler, Victor E., Allen D. Sapp, and David L. Carter. 1992. "Police Officer Higher Education: Citizen Complaints and Rule Violations." *American Journal of Police* 11.

Karmen, Andrew. 1990. *Crime Victims.* 2nd ed. Pacific Grove, CA: Brooks/Cole.

Katz v. U.S. 1967. 389 U.S. 347.

Katz, Jack. 1988. *Seductions of Crime: Moral and Sensual Attractions in Doing Evil.* New York: Basic Books.

Kelling, George L. 1988. "Police and Community: The Quiet Revolution." *Perspectives in Policing*, No. 1. Washington, DC: National Institute of Justice and Harvard University.

Kelling, George L., and Catherine M. Coles. 1996. *Fixing Broken Windows.* New York: Free Press.

Kelling, George L., and David Fogel. 1978. "Police Patrol—Some Future Directions." In *The Future of Policing.* Edited by Alvin W. Cohn. Beverly Hills: Sage.

Kelling, George L., Tony Pate, Duane Dieckman, and Charles E. Brown. 1974. *The Kansas City Preventive Patrol Experiment: A Summary Report.* Washington, DC: Police Foundation.

Kent v. United States. 1966. 383 U.S. 541.

Kenyon, Jack P. 1986. *The Stuart Constitution.* 2nd ed. New York: Cambridge University Press.

Kerstetter, Wayne A. 1985. "Who Disciplines the Police? Who Should?" In *Police Leadership in America: Crisis and Opportunity.* Edited by William A. Geller. New York: Praeger.

Kerstetter, Wayne A., and Anne M. Heinz. 1979. *Pretrial Settlement Conference: An Evaluation.* Washington, DC: U.S. Department of Justice.

Kifner, John. 1988 (December 5). "Bronx Jurors: A Defense Dream, A Prosecutor's Nightmare." *New York Times.*

King, Roy D. 1998. "Prisons." In *Handbook of Crime and Punishment.* Edited by Michael Tonry. New York: Oxford University Press.

King, Ryan S., and Marc Mauer. 2001 (August). *Aging behind Bars: "Three Strikes" Seven Years Later.* Washington, DC: Sentencing Project.

Kinports, Kit. 2004. "So Much Activity, So Little Change: A Reply to the Critics of Battered Women's Self-Defense." *St. Louis Public Law Review* 23:155.

Kipnis, Kenneth. 1976. "Criminal Justice and the Negotiated Plea." *Ethics* 86:93.

Klein, Malcolm W. 1995. *The American Street Gang: Its Nature, Prevalence, and Control.* New York: Oxford University Press.

Klein, Stephen, and Michael Caggiano. 1986. *The Prevalence, Predictability, and Policy Implications of Recidivism.* Santa Monica, CA: Rand.

Klockars, Carl B. 1986. *The Idea of Police.* Beverly Hills: Sage.

———. 1991a. "The Dirty Harry Problem." In *Thinking about Police.* 2nd ed. Edited by Carl B. Klockars and Stephen D. Mastrofski. New York: McGraw-Hill.

———. 1991b. "The Rhetoric of Community Policing." In *Thinking about Police*. 2nd ed. Edited by Carl B. Klockars and Stephen D. Mastrofski. New York: McGraw-Hill.

Knapp Commission. 1972. *Report on Police Corruption*. New York: George Braziller.

Knox, George W. 1991. *An Introduction to Gangs*. Berrien Springs, MI: Van de Vere Publishing Ltd.

Kohut, Andrew. 2001 (May 10). "The Declining Support for Executions." *New York Times* 33.

Kovandzic, Tomislav V., John J. Sloan III, and Lynne M. Vieraitis. 2002. "Unintended Consequences of Politically Popular Sentencing Policy: The Homicide Promoting Effects of 'Three Strikes' in U.S. Cities, 1980–1999." *Criminology and Public Policy* 1(3): 399–424.

Kraska, Peter B., and Victor E. Kappeler. 1997. "Militarizing American Police: The Rise and Normalization of Paramilitary Units." *Social Problems* 44(1): 1–18.

Krisberg, Barry, Ira Schwartz, Gideon Fishman, Zvi Eisikovits, Edna Guttman, and Karen Joe. 1986. *The Incarceration of Minority Youth*. Minneapolis: University of Minnesota, Hubert H. Humphrey Institute of Public Affairs.

Kruttschnitt, Candace M. 1984. "Sex and Criminal Court Dispositions: The Unresolved Controversy." *Journal of Research in Crime and Delinquency* 30.

———. 2001. "Women's Involvement in Serious Interpersonal Violence." *Aggression and Violent Behavior* 7.

Kruttschnitt, Candace M., and Rosemary Gartner. 2003. "Women's Imprisonment." In *Crime and Justice: A Review of Research*. Edited by Michael Tonry, p. 30. Chicago: University of Chicago Press.

Kruttschnitt, Candace, Christopher Uggen, and K. Shelton. 2000. "Predictors or Desistance among Sex Offenders: The Interaction of Formal and Informal Social Controls." *Justice Quarterly* 17:61–87.

Kuckes, Niki. 1994. "The Useful, Dangerous Fiction of Grand Jury Independence." *American Criminal Law Review* 41(1): 1–3.

Kunen, James S. 1983. *"How Can You Defend Those People?"* New York: Random House.

Kurki, Leena, and Norval Morris. 2001. "The Purposes, Practices, and Problems of Supermax Prisons." In *Crime and Justice: A Review of Research*. Edited by Michael Tonry. Chicago: University of Chicago Press.

Kyllo v. U.S. 2001. October Term 2000, Slip Opinion. http://a257.g .akamaitech.net/7/257/2422/11june20011200/www.supreme courtus.gov/opinions/00pdf/99–8508.pdf.

Kyllo v. U.S. 2001. 533 U.S. 27.

Ladinsky, Jack. 1963. "The Impact of Social Backgrounds of Lawyers on Law Practice and the Law." *Journal of Legal Education* 16.

LaFave, Wayne R., and Jerold H. Israel. 1984. *Criminal Procedure*. St. Paul, MN: West.

———. 1992. *Criminal Procedure*. 2nd ed. St. Paul, MN: West.

LaFave, Wayne R., and Austin W. Scott, Jr. 1986. *Criminal Law*. 2nd ed. St. Paul, MN: West.

Lafree, Gary D. 1985. "Official Reactions to Hispanic Defendants in the Southwest." *Journal of Research in Crime and Delinquency* 22.

———. 1998. *Losing Legitimacy*. New York: Westview.

Lane, Roger. 1992. "Urban Police and Crime in Nineteenth Century America." *Crime and Justice* 15.

Langan, Patrick A. 1991. "America's Soaring Prison Population." *Science* 251.

Langan, Patrick A., and David J. Levin. 2002 (June). *Recidivism of Prisoners Released in 1994*. Washington, DC: Burea of Justice Statistics.

Langbein, John H. 1978. "Torture and Plea Bargaining." *University of Chicago Law Review* 46:3.

Lanier, C. S. 1993. "Affective States of Fathers in Prison." *Justice Quarterly 10*.

Lanzetta v. New Jersey. 1939. 306 U.S. 451.

Laub, John H., and Robert J. Sampson. 2001. "Understanding Desistance from Crime." In *Crime and Punishment*. Edited by Michael Tonry. New York: Oxford University Press.

———. 2003. *Shared Beginnings, Divergent Lives*. Cambridge, MA: Harvard University Press.

Lauritsen, Janet L., and Robert J. Sampson. 1998. "Minorities, Crime, and Criminal Justice." In *Crime and Punishment*. Edited by Michael Tonry. New York: Oxford University Press.

Lawrence v. Texas. 2003. 123 S.Ct. 2472.

Lay, Donald P. 2004 (November 18). "Rehab Justice." *New York Times*.

Layson, Stephen K. 1985. "Homicide and Deterrence: A Reexamination of the United States Time-Series Evidence." *Southern Economic Journal* 52.

Lee v. Washington. 1968. 390 U.S. 333.

Leinwand, Donna. 2004 (April 25). "Lawsuits of '70s Shape Current Police Leadership." *USA Today*.

Leo, Richard. 1996. "Inside the Interrogation Room." *Journal of Criminal Law and Criminology* 86.

Lerner, Mark Jay. 1977. "The Effectiveness of a Definite Sentence Parole Program." *Criminology* 15.

Levin, Alan M., and Stephen J. Hertzberg. 1986 (April 8). "Inside the Jury Room." *Frontline*. Public Broadcasting System.

Levin, Martin A. 1977. *Urban Politics and the Criminal Courts*. Chicago: University of Chicago Press.

———. 1988. "The American Judicial System: Should It, Does It, and Can It Provide an Impartial Jury to Criminal Defendants?" *Criminal Justice Journal* 11.

Levine, James P. 1992. *Juries and Politics*. Pacific Grove, CA: Brooks/Cole.

Levitt, Leonard, and Rocco Parascandola. 2004 (April 30). "NYPD Crime Stats; Charge Bungle in Bronx," *Newsday*, A16.

Levy, Leonard. 1968. *Origins of the Fifth Amendment*. New York: Oxford University Press.

Lewis, Peter W. 1979. "Killing the Killers: A Post-*Furman* Profile of Florida's Condemned." *Crime and Delinquency* 25.

Lewontin, Richard. 2000. *The Triple Helix: Gene, Organism, and Environment*. Cambridge, MA: Harvard University Press.

Lincoln, Alan J., and Murray A. Straus. 1985. *Crime and the Family*. Springfield, IL: Charles C. Thomas.

Lindsey, Edward. 1925. "Historical Sketch of the Indeterminate Sentence and Parole Systems." *Journal of Criminal Law and Criminology* 16.

Lipton, Douglas S. 1995. "CDate: Updating the Effectiveness of Correctional Treatment 25 Years Later." *Journal of Offender Rehabilitation* 22:1–2.

Littrell, W. Boyd. 1979. *Bureaucratic Justice: Police, Prosecutors, and Plea Bargaining*. Beverly Hills: Sage.

Lockwood, Daniel. 1980. *Prison Sexual Violence*. New York: Elsevier/ North Holland.

Logan, Charles H., and Gerald G. Gaes. 1993. "Meta-Analysis and the Rehabilitation of Punishment." *Justice Quarterly* 10.

LoLordo, Ann. 2001 (February 13). "DNA Testing Frees Va. Man Wrongly Imprisoned 18 Years; Release Comes Amid National Debate over Felons' Access to Tests." *Baltimore Sun.*

Lombardi, John H., and Donna M. Lombardi. 1986 (February). "Objective Parole Criteria: More Harm than Good?" *Corrections Today.*

Lombroso-Ferrero, Gina. 1972. *Criminal Man.* Montclair, NJ: Patterson Smith.

Los Angeles Times. 2004 (August 1). "Rape and Rights."

Lundman, Richard J. 1980. *Police and Policing.* New York: Holt, Rinehart & Winston.

Lurigio, Arthur J., and Joan Petersilia. 1992. "The Emergence of Intensive Supervision Programs in the United States." In *Smart Sentencing: The Emergence of Intermediate Sanctions.* Edited by James M. Byrne, Arthur J. Lurigio, and Joan Petersilia. Newbury Park, CA: Sage.

Lynch, David. 1994. "The Impropriety of Plea Bargaining." *Law and Social Inquiry* 19.

Lynch, James P., and William J. Sabol. 2001. *Prisoner Reentry in Perspective.* Washington, DC: Urban Institute.

Lynch, Mona. 1998. "Waste Managers: The New Penology, Crime Fighting, and the Parole Identity." *Law and Society Review* 32:839–870.

———. 2000. "Rehabilitation and Rhetoric: The Idea of Reformation in Contemporary Parole Discourse and Practices." *Punishment and Society* 2:40–65.

M'Naughten's Case. 1843. 8 Eng. Rep. 718.

MacKenzie, Doris Layton. 1998. "What Works in Corrections? An Examination of the Effectiveness of the Type of Rehabilitation Programs Offered by Washington State Department of Corrections." http://www.bsos.umd.edu/ccjs/corrections/What%20 Works%20In%20Corrections.htm. Visited December 5, 2004.

MacKenzie, Doris Layton, and Robert Brame. 1995. "Shock Incarceration and Positive Adjustment during Community Supervision." *Journal of Quantitative Criminology* 11:111.

MacKenzie, Doris Layton, Robert Brame, David McDowall, and Claire Souryal. 1995. "Boot Camp Prisons and Recidivism in Eight States." *Criminology* 33:351.

MacKenzie, Doris Layton, and Dale G. Parent. 1992. "Boot Camp Prisons for Young Offenders." In *Smart Sentencing: The Emergence of Intermediate Sanctions.* Edited by James M. Byrne, Arthur J. Lurigio, and Joan Petersilia. Newbury Park, CA: Sage.

Malcolm, Andrew H. 1990 (April 23). "New Police Chiefs Put New Ideas on the Force." *New York Times.*

Males, Mike, and Dan Macallair. 1998. "The Impact of Juvenile Curfew Laws in California." San Francisco: Justice Policy Institute.

Manning, Peter K. 1995. "The Police: Mandate, Strategies, and Appearances." In *The Police and Society: Touchstone Readings.* Edited by Victor E. Kappeler. Prospect Heights, IL: Waveland Press.

Mapp v. Ohio. 1961. 367 U.S. 643.

Marcus, Paul. 1986. "The Development of Entrapment Law." *Wayne Law Review* 33.

Margolick, David. 1984 (December 30). "Cooke, about to Retire, Looks Back in Satisfaction." *New York Times.*

Marshall, Justice Thurgood. 1976. *Gregg v. Georgia.* 428 U.S. 227.

Martin, Steve J., and Sheldon Ekland-Olson. 1987. *Texas Prisons: The Walls Came Tumbling Down.* Austin, TX: Texas Monthly Press.

Martin, Susan E. 1989. "Women on the Move? A Status Report on Women in Policing." In *Critical Issues in Policing.* Edited by Roger G. Dunham and Geoffrey P. Alpert. Prospect Heights, IL: Waveland Press.

Martinson, Robert. 1974 (Spring). "What Works? Questions and Answers about Prison Reform." *The Public Interest.*

Maruna, Shadd. 2001. *Making Good: How Ex-Convicts Reformed and Rebuilt Their Lives.* Washington, DC: American Psychological Association.

Mastrofski, Stephen D. 1990. "The Prospects for Change in Police Patrol: A Decade of Review." *American Journal of Police* 9.

Mather, Lynn. 1974. "Some Determinants of the Method of Case Disposition: Decision Making by Public Defenders in Los Angeles." *Law and Society Review* 8.

Mathias, Robert A., Paul DeMuro, and Richard S. Allison, eds. 1984. *Violent Juvenile Offenders: An Anthology.* San Francisco: National Council on Crime and Delinquency.

Matusow, Allen J. 1984. *The Unraveling of America: A History of Liberalism in the 1960s.* New York: Harper & Row.

Maxwell, Christopher, Joel H. Garner, and Jeffrey A. Fagan. 1991. *The Effects of Arrest on Intimate Partner Violence: New Evidence from the Spouse Assault Replication Program.* Washington, DC: National Institute of Justice.

McClam, Erin. 2004 (July 16). "Defiant Stewart Makes Her Case to the TV Cameras after Sentencing." *Associated Press.* http://www.usatoday.com/money/media/2004-07-16-stewart-optional-ap_x.htm.

McCold, Paul. 2004. "Paradigm Muddle: The Threat to Restorative Justice Posed by Its Merger with Community Justice." *Contemporary Justice Review* 7(1): 13–35.

McCoy, Candace. 1998. "Prosecution." In *The Handbook of Crime and Punishment.* Edited by Michael Tonry. New York: Oxford University Press.

McDonald, Douglas C. 1992. "Private Penal Institutions." In *Crime and Justice: A Review of Research.* Edited by Michael Tonry. Chicago: University of Chicago Press.

———. 1992. "Unpaid Community Service as a Criminal Sentence." In *Smart Sentencing: The Emergence of Intermediate Sanctions.* Edited by James M. Byrne, Arthur J. Lurigio, and Joan Petersilia. Newbury Park, CA: Sage.

McDonald, Douglas C., Elizabeth Fournier, Malcolm Russell-Einhorn, and Stephen Crawford. 1998. *Private Prisons in the United States: An Assessment of Current Practice.* Cambridge, MA: Abt Associates.

McDonald, William F. 1985. *Plea Bargaining: Critical Issues and Common Practices.* Washington, DC: National Institute of Justice.

McFadden v. Cabana. 1988. 851 F.2d 784 (Ca. 5).

McIntyre, Lisa J. 1987. *Public Defender.* Chicago: University of Chicago Press.

McKeiver v. Pennsylvania. 1970. 403 U.S. 528.

Meier, Robert D., and Richard Maxwell. 1987. "Psychological Screening of Police Candidates." *Journal of Police Science and Administration of Justice* 15:210–215.

Meier, Robert F., and Terance D. Miethe. 1993. "Understanding Theories of Criminal Victimization." In *Crime and Justice: A Review of Research.* Vol. 17. Edited by Michael Tonry. Chicago: University of Chicago Press.

Mellon, Leonard, Joan Jacoby, and Marion Brewer. 1981. "The Prosecutor Constrained by His Environment: A New Look at Discretionary Justice in the United States." *Journal of Criminal Law and Criminology* 72.

Merton, Robert K. 1968. "Social Structure and Anomie." *Social Theory and Social Structure*. Enl. ed. New York: Free Press.

Meyer, Greg. 1991. "Nonlethal Weapons versus Conventional Police Tactics: The Los Angeles Police Experience." Master's thesis. California State University, Los Angeles.

Meyer, Rob. 1999 (October 19). "Killer's Trail." *NOVA*. Boston: WGBH. http://www.pbs.org/wgbh/nova/sheppard/mugshot.html.

Michael M. v. Superior Court of Sonoma County. 1981. 450 U.S. 464.

Michigan v. Sitz. 1990. 496 U.S. 444.

Miczek, Klaus A., Allen F. Mirsky, Gregory Carey, Joseph DeBold, and Adrianne Raine. 1994. "An Overview of Biological Influences on Violent Behavior." In *Understanding and Preventing Violence 2*. Edited by Albert Reis, Klaus A. Miczek, and Jeffrey A. Roth. Washington, DC: National Academy Press.

Miethe, Terance D., and Robert F. Meier. 1994. *Crime and Its Social Context: Toward an Integrated Theory of Offenders, Victims, and Situations*. Albany, NY: State University of New York Press.

Miethe, Terance D., and Charles A. Moore. 1985. "Socioeconomic Disparities under Determinate Sentencing Systems: A Comparison of Preguideline and Postguideline Practices in Minnesota." *Criminology* 23.

Mileski, Maureen. 1971 (May). "Courtroom Encounters: An Observation Study of a Lower Criminal Court." *Law and Society Review*.

Miller, Frank W., Robert O. Dawson, George E. Dix, and Raymond I. Parnas. 2000. *Criminal Justice Administration*. New York: Foundation Press.

Miller, Herbert S., James Cramer, and William McDonald. 1978. *Plea Bargaining in the United States*. Washington, DC: National Institute of Justice.

Milton, Catherine H. 1977. *Police Use of Deadly Force*. Washington, DC: Police Foundation.

Minnesota v. Murphy. 1984. 465 U.S. 420.

Minnesota Department of Corrections. n.d. Grievance Hearings Procedures. Pamphlet supplied by Warden David Crist, Minnesota Department of Corrections.

Minnesota Sentencing Guidelines Commission. 2001. *Minnesota Sentencing Guidelines and Commentary*.

Miranda v. Arizona. 1966. 384 U.S. 436.

Misner, Gordon E. 1990 (December/January). "High-Speed Pursuits: Police Perspectives." *Criminal Justice, the Americas*.

Missouri v. Seibert. 2004. 124 S.Ct. 2601.

Moffitt, Terrie E. 1994. "Natural Histories of Deliquency." In *Cross National Longitudinal Research on Human Development and Criminal Behavior*. Edited by Elmar G. Weitekamp and Hans-Jurgen Kerner. Dordrecht: Kluwer Academic.

Monkkonen, Eric H. 1992. "History of Urban Police." In *Modern Policing*. Edited by Michael Tonry and Norval Morris. Chicago: University of Chicago Press.

Moody, Carl, and T. B. Marvell. 2001. "The Lethal Effects of Three-Strikes Laws." *Journal of Legal Studies* 30:89–106.

Moore, Mark Harrison. 1992. "Problem-Solving and Community Policing." In *Modern Policing*. Edited by Michael Tonry and Norval Morris. Chicago: University of Chicago Press.

———. 1994. "Research Synthesis and Policy Implications." In *Community Policing: Rhetoric or Reality?* Edited by J. Greene and Stephen Mastrofski, New York: Praeger.

Morash, Merry, Timothy S. Bynum, and Barbara A. Koons. 1998. "Women Offenders: Programming Needs and Promising Approaches." In *Research in Brief*. Washington, DC: National Institute of Justice.

Morash, Merry, and Lila Rucker. 1990. "A Critical Look at the Idea of Boot Camp as a Correctional Reform." *Crime and Delinquency* 36(2): 204.

Morris, Norval. 1974. *The Future of Imprisonment*. Chicago: University of Chicago Press.

Morris, Norval, and Gordon Hawkins. 1967. *The Honest Politician's Guide to Crime Control*. Chicago: University of Chicago Press.

Morrissey v. Brewer. 1973. 408 U.S. 471.

Myers, Martha A., and Susette M. Talarico. 1987. *The Social Contexts of Criminal Sentencing*. New York: Springer-Verlag.

Nagel, Stuart S., and Lenore J. Weitzman. 1971. "Women as Litigants." *Hastings Law Journal* 23.

Nagin, Daniel S., and Raymond Paternoster. 1994. "Personal Capital and Social Control: The Deterrence Implications of a Theory of Individual Differences in Criminal Offending." *Criminology* 32:581–606.

Nardulli, Peter F. 1978. *The Courtroom Elite*. Cambridge, MA: Ballinger.

———. 1979. "Organizational Analyses of Criminal Courts: An Overview and Some Speculation." In *The Study of Criminal Courts: Political Perspectives*. Edited by Peter F. Nardulli. Cambridge, MA: Ballinger.

Nardulli, Peter F., James Eisenstein, and Roy B. Flemming. 1988. *The Tenor of Justice: Criminal Courts and the Guilty Plea*. Urbana, IL: University of Illinois Press.

National Advisory Committee. 1980. *Standards for Administration of Juvenile Justice*. Washington, DC: Government Printing Office.

National Advisory Committee on Criminal Justice Standards and Goals. 1973. *Police*. Washington, DC: Government Printing Office.

National Council on Crime and Delinquency. 1992. *Criminal Justice Sentencing Policy Statement*. San Francisco: NCCD.

National Institute for Juvenile Justice and Delinquency Prevention. 1980. *Reports of the National Juvenile Justice Assessment Centers: A National Assessment of Serious Crime and the Juvenile Justice System*. Washington, DC: Law Enforcement Assistance Administration.

National Institute of Corrections. 1983. *Standards for Juvenile Community Residential Facilities*. Washington, DC: National Institute of Corrections.

National Institute of Ethics. 2000. "Police Code of Ethics Facts Revealed." International Association of Chiefs of Police (IACP), 2000 Conference. http://www.aele.org/loscode2000.html.

National Institute of Justice. 1982. *The Effects of the Exclusionary Rule: A Study of California*. Washington, DC: Government Printing Office.

———. 1985. *The Special Management Inmate*. Washington, DC: NIJ.

———. 1996a. *Convicted by Juries, Exonerated by Science: Case Studies in the Use of DNA Evidence to Establish Innocence after Trial*. Washington, DC: NIJ.

———. 1996b. *Measuring What Matters, Part I*. Washington, DC: NIJ.

———. 2002 (July). *Using DNA to Solve Cold Cases*. Washington, DC: NIJ.

———. 2004 (June). *Law Enforcement Technology*. Washington, DC: NIJ.

National Law Enforcement and Corrections Technology Center. 2004 (Fall). "Corrections Data Mining," *TechBeat*.

National Law Journal. 1979 (September 10). "Pagano Case Points Finger at Lineups."

———. 1990 (December 25, 1989–January 1, 1990).

National Probation Association. 1983. *John Augustus, First Probation Officer.* Reprint. New York: National Probation Association.

Neubauer, David W. 1974. *Criminal Justice in Middle America.* Morristown, NJ: General Learning Press.

New Jersey P.L. 1982. Chapter 77, Section 24.

Newport, Frank. 2001 (May 17). "What Can We Learn from Americans' Views about the Death Penalty?" Princeton, NJ: Gallup Poll.

Newsweek. 1982 (November 8). "Not Guilty Because of PMS?"

New York v. Belton. 1981. 453 U.S. 454.

New York Times. 1992 (November 8). "Victims' Rights Amendments Pass in 5 States."

Nix, Crystal. 1987 (February 6). "Police Academy Adapts to Changing New York." *New York Times.*

North Carolina v. Alford. 1970. 400 U.S. 25.

Note. 1977. "Notes: Did Your Eyes Deceive You? Expert Psychological Testimony on the Unreliability of Eyewitness Identification." *Stanford Law Review* 29.

Note. 1983. *Notre Dame Law Review* 59.

Nugent, M. Elaine. 2004. *The Changing Nature of Prosecution: Community Prosecution v. Traditional Prosecution Approaches.* Alexandra, VA: American Prosecutors Research Institute.

NYPD. n.d. "COMPSTAT Process." New York: NYPD. http://www .nyc.gov/html/nypd/html/chfdept/process.html.

O'Connor, Sandra D. 2001 (July 3). "Justice O'Connor Questions Death Penalty." *Washington Post.*

O'Donnell, Lawrence. 1983. *Deadly Force.* New York: William Morrow.

Ohlin, Lloyd E. 1993. "Surveying Discretion by Criminal Justice Decision Makers." In *Discretion in Criminal Justice: The Tension between Individualization and Uniformity.* Edited by Lloyd E. Ohlin and Frank J. Remington. Albany, NY: State University of New York Press.

Orfield, Myron W., Jr. 1987. "The Exclusionary Rule and Deterrence: An Empirical Study of Chicago Narcotics Officers." *University of Chicago Law Review* 54.

Ostrom, Brian J., and Roger A. Hanson. 2000. *Efficiency, Timeliness, and Quality: A New Perspective from Nine State Criminal Courts.* Washington, DC: National Institute of Justice.

Owen, Barbara. 1985. "Race and Gender Relations among Prison Workers." *Crime and Delinquency* 31.

———. 1998. *Surviving the Mix: Struggle and Survival in a Women's Prison.* Albany, NY: State University of New York Press.

Owen, Barbara, and Barbara Bloom. 1995. "Profiling Women Prisoners: Findings from National Surveys and a California Sample." *Prison Journal* 75.

Packer, Herbert L. 1964. "Two Models of the Criminal Process." *University of Pennsylvania Law Review.*

———. 1968. *The Limits of the Criminal Sanction.* Palo Alto, CA: Stanford University Press.

Padgett, John F. 1985. "The Emergent Organization of Plea Bargaining." *American Journal of Sociology* 90.

Palmer, Ted. 1975. "Martinson Revisited." *Journal of Research on Crime and Delinquency* 12.

Parent, Dale G. 1995. "Day Reporting Centers." In *Intermediate Sanctions in Overcrowded Times.* Edited by Michael Tonry and Kate Hamilton. Boston: Northeastern University Press.

Pate, Anthony M., and Lorie A. Fridell. 1993. *Police Use of Force: Official Reports, Citizen Complaints, and Legal Consequences.* Washington, DC: Police Foundation.

Paterson, Alexander, Sir. 1951. *Paterson on Prisons.* London: F. Mueller.

Patterson, E. Britt, and Michael J. Lynch. 1991. "Biases in Formalized Bail Procedures." In *Race and Criminal Justice.* Edited by Michael J. Lynch and E. Britt Patterson. New York: Harrow and Heston.

Pelissier, Bernadette, Susan Wallace, Joyce Ann O'Neill, Gerald Gaes, Scott Camp, William Rhodes, and William Saylor. 2001. "Federal Prison Residential Drug Treatment Reduces Substance Use and Arrests after Release." *American Journal of Drug, Alcohol Abuse* 27(2): 315–337.

Peltason, Jack. 1955. *Federal Courts in the Political Process.* New York: Random House.

Penry v. Lynaugh. 1989. 109 S.Ct. 2934.

People v. Aphaylath. 1986. 502 N.E.2d 998.

People v. Mills. 1904. 70 N.E. 786.

People v. Penman. 1915. 271 Ill. 82, 110 N.E. 894.

Perez, Douglas W. 1994. *Common Sense about Police Review.* Philadelphia: Temple University Press.

Petersilia, Joan. 1985. "Racial Disparities in the Criminal Justice System: A Summary." *Crime and Delinquency* 31.

———. 1989. "Influence of Research on Policing." In *Critical Issues in Policing.* Edited by Roger C. Dunham and Geoffrey P. Alpert. Prospect Heights, IL: Waveland Press.

———. 1990. "When Probation Becomes More Dreaded than Prison." *Federal Probation* 54.

———. 1995. "A Crime Control Rationale for Reinvesting in Community Corrections." *Prison Journal* 45.

———. 1998. "Probation and Parole." In *Handbook of Crime and Punishment.* Edited by Michael Tonry. New York: Oxford University Press.

———. 2004. "Community Corrections." In *Crime: Public Policies for Crime Control.* Edited by James Q. Wilson and Joan Petersilia, pp. 483–508. Oakland, CA: Institute for Contemporary Studies.

———. 2004 (September). "What Works in Reentry? Reviewing and Questioning the Evidence." *Federal Probation.*

Petersilia, Joan, and Susan Turner. 1993. "Intensive Probation and Parole." In *Crime and Justice Review: An Evaluation of Research.* Edited by Michael Tonry. Chicago: University of Chicago Press.

Petersilia, Joan, Susan Turner, and Piper Deschennes. 1992. "Intensive Supervision Programs for Drug Offenders." In *Smart Sentencing.* Edited by James M. Byrne, Arthur J. Lurigio, and Joan Petersilia. Newbury Park, CA: Sage.

Petersilia, Joan, Susan Turner, and James P. Kahan. 1985. *Granting Felons Probation.* Santa Monica, CA: Rand.

Phillips, Steven. 1977. *No Heroes, No Villains: The Story of a Murder Trial.* New York: Random House.

Phillips, Susan, and Barbara Bloom. 1998. "In Whose Best Interest? The Impact of Changing Public Policy on Relatives Caring for Children with Incarcerated Parents." *Child Welfare* 77.

Pincus, Walter. 2001 (October 21). "Silence of 4 Terror Suspects Poses Dilemma." *Washington Post.*

Pisciotta, Alexander W. 1983. "Scientific Reform: The 'New Penology' at Elmira, 1876–1900." *Crime and Delinquency* 29.

Pistole, John. 2004. "Statement to Senate Governmental Affairs Committee." http://www.fbi.gov/congress/congress04/pistole 080304.htm.

Plato. 1926. *Laws.* Cambridge, MA: Harvard University Press, 2:261.

Platt, Anthony. 1969. *The Child Savers: The Invention of Delinquency.* Chicago: University of Chicago Press.

Platt, Anthony, and Randi Pollock. 1974. "Channeling Lawyers: The Careers of Public Defenders." In *The Potential for Reform of Criminal Justice.* Edited by Herbert Jacob. Beverly Hills: Sage.

Pletan v. Gaines. 1992. 494 N.W.2d 38.

Plucknett, Theodore F. T. 1956. *A Concise History of the Common Law.* 5th ed. London: Butterworth & Company.

Podgor, Ellen S. 2004. "*Gideon* at 40: Facing the Crisis, Fulfilling the Promise." *American Criminal Law Review* 41:131.

Police Foundation. 1981. *Newark Foot Patrol Experiment.* Washington, DC: Police Foundation.

Polling Report.com. 2004. "Crime: Death Penalty." http://www.pollingreport.com/crime.htm. Visited October 15, 2004.

Post, Leonard. 2004 (May 31). "Gun Courts Aim to Break Cycle." *National Law Journal.* Page printed from http://www.nlj.com.

Poulin, Anne Bowen. 2004 (March). "Criminal Justice and Videoconferencing Technology: The Remote Defendant." *Tulane Law Review* 78:1090–1091, 1157–1158, 1164, 1166.

Pound, Roscoe. 1912. "The Administration of Justice in American Cities." *Harvard Law Review* 12.

———. 1921. "The Future of the Criminal Law." *Columbia Law Review* 21.

Pound, Roscoe, and Felix Frankfurter, eds. 1922. *Criminal Justice in Cleveland.* Cleveland: Cleveland Foundation.

Powell v. Alabama. 1932. 287 U.S. 45.

President's Commission on Law Enforcement and the Administration of Justice. 1967. *The Challenge of Crime in a Free Society.* Washington, DC: Government Printing Office.

President's Crime Commission. 1967. *The Police.* Washington, DC: Government Printing Office.

Procunier v. Martinez. 1974. 416 U.S. 396.

Puzzanchera, Charles M. 2003. *Juvenile Delinquency Probation Caseload, 1990–1999.* Washington, DC: Office of Juvenile Justice and Delinquency Prevention.

Quarles v. New York. 1984. 467 U.S. 649.

Quinney, Richard. 1977. *Class, State, and Crime: On the Theory and Practice of Criminal Justice.* New York: David McKay Co.

Radelet, Michael L., and Hugo Adam Bedau. 1998. "The Execution of the Innocent." In *America's Experiment with Capital Punishment.* Edited by James R. Acker, Robert S. Bohm, and Charles S. Lanier. Durham, NC: Carolina Academic Press.

Rankin, Bill. 2000. "Judge Tours Spruced-Up Jail." *Atlanta Journal and Constitution.*

Rankin, Charles. 1964. "The Effect of Pretrial Detention." *New York University Law Review* 39.

Rantala, Ramona R. 2000. *Effects of NIBRS on Crime Statistics.* Washington, DC: Bureau of Justice Statistics.

Ravin v. State. 1975. 537 P.2d 494 (Alaska).

Reckless, Walter. 1969. "The Use of the Death Penalty." *Crime and Delinquency* 15:43, 54.

Rehnquist, William H. 1974. "Is An Expanded Right of Privacy Consistent with Fair and Effective Law Enforcement? Or: Privacy, You've Come a Long Way Baby". *Kansas Law Review* 23.

Reiss, Albert J., Jr. 1971. "Systematic Observations of Natural Social Phenomena." In *Sociological Methodology.* Vol. 3. Edited by Herbert Costner, pp. 3–33. San Francisco: Jossey-Bass.

———. 1980. "Victim Proneness in Repeat Victimization by Time of Crime." In *Indicators of Crime and Criminal Justice: Quantitative Studies.* Edited by Steven E. Feinberg and Albert J. Reiss, Jr. Washington, DC: Bureau of Justice Statistics.

———. 1988. *Public Employment of Private Police.* Washington, DC: Bureau of Justice Statistics.

———. 1992. "Police Organization." In *Modern Policing.* Edited by Michael Tonry and Norval Morris. Chicago: University of Chicago Press.

Reiss, Albert J., Jr., and Jeffrey A. Roth. 1993. *Understanding and Preventing Violence.* Washington, DC: National Academy Press.

Remington, Frank, J. 1993. "The Decision to Charge, the Decision to Convict on a Plea of Guilty, and the Impact of Sentence Structure on Prosecution Practices." In *Discretion in Criminal Justice: The Tension between Individualization and Uniformity.* Edited by Lloyd E. Ohlin and Frank J. Remington. Albany, NY: State University of New York Press.

Remington, Frank J., Edward L. Kimball, Walter J. Dickey, Herman Goldstein, and Donald J. Newman. 1982. *Criminal Justice Administration.* Indianapolis: Bobbs-Merrill.

Rennison, Callie, and Michael R. Rand. 2003. *Criminal Victimization 2002.* Washington, DC: Bureau of Justice Statistics.

Reuter, Peter, Robert MacCoun, and Patrick Murphy. 1990. *Money from Crime.* Santa Monica, CA: Rand.

Riddick v. N.Y. 1980. 445 U.S. 573.

Rierden, Andi. 1997. *The Farm: Life Inside a Woman's Prison.* Amherst, MA: University of Massachusetts Press.

Rimer, Sara. 2004 (January 4). "Unruly Students Facing Arrest, Not Detention." *New York Times.*

Rimer, Sara, and Raymond Bonner. 2000 (August 22). "Whether to Kill Those Who Killed as Youths." *New York Times.*

Riveland, Chase. 1999. *Supermax Prisons.* Washington, DC: National Institute of Corrections.

Roberg, Roy R. 1994. "Can Today's Police Organizations Effectively Implement Community Policing?" In *The Challenge of Community Policing: Testing the Premises.* Edited by Dennis P. Rosenbaum. Thousand Oaks, CA: Sage.

Robinson, Billy "Hands." 1971 (September). "Love: A Hard Legged Triangle." *Black Scholar.*

Rodriguez v. Young. 1990. 906 F.2d 1153 (Ca. 7).

Roper v. Simmons. 2004. 124 S.Ct. 2198.

Rosecrance, John. 1985. "The Probation Officers' Search for Credibility: Ball Park Recommendations." *Crime and Delinquency* 31.

Rosen, Jeffrey. 2004. *The Naked Crowd.* New York: Random House.

Rosett, Arthur, and Donald Cressey. 1976. *Justice by Consent.* New York: J. B. Lippincott Co.

Ross, Edward A. 1907 (April). "The 'Criminaloid.'" *Atlantic Monthly.*

Ross, Robert R. 1981. *Prison Guard/Correctional Officer: The Use and Abuse of the Human Resources of the Prison.* Toronto: Butterworths.

Rossi, Peter H., Emily Waite, Christine E. Bose, and Richard E. Berk. 1974. "The Seriousness of Crimes: Normative Structure and Individual Differences." *American Sociological Review* 39.

Roth, Siobahn. 2003 (May 9). "Material Support Law: Weapon in the War on Terror." *Legal Times.*

Rothman, David. 1971. *The Discovery of the Asylum.* Boston: Little, Brown.

———. 1980. *Conscience and Convenience: The Asylum and Its Alternatives in Progressive America.* Boston: Little, Brown.

Ruback, R. Barry. 2004. "The Imposition of Economic Sanctions in Philadelphia: Costs, Fines, and Restitution." *Federal Probation* 68(1): 21–38.

Rubenstein, Jonathan. 1973. *City Police.* New York: Farrar, Straus, and Giroux.

Rubenstein, Michael L., Steven Clarke, and Theresa Wright. 1980. *Alaska Bans Plea Bargaining.* Washington, DC: U.S. Government Printing Office.

Rubenstein, Michael L., and Theresa Wright. 1979. "Alaska's Ban on Plea Bargaining." *Law and Society Review* 13.

Rubin, H. Ted. 1976. *The Courts: Fulcrum of the Justice System.* Pacific Palisades, CA: Goodyear Press.

Ruffin v. Commonwealth. 1871. 62 Va. 790.

Runda, John, Edward Rhine, and Robert Wetter. 1994. *The Practice of Parole Boards.* Lexington, KY: Association of Paroling Authorities.

Russell, Harold E., and Alan Biegel, 1982. *Understanding Human Behavior for Effective Police Work.* 2nd ed. New York: Basic Books.

Russell, Katheryn K. 1998. *The Color of Crime.* New York: New York University Press.

Ryerson, Ellen. 1978. *The Best Laid Plans: America's Juvenile Court Experiment.* New York: Hill and Wang.

Sacks, Howard R., and Charles H. Logan 1979. *Does Parole Make a Difference?* Storrs, CT: University of Connecticut Law School Press.

Samaha, Joel. n.d. Unpublished summary of reformatory records of Stillwater Prison and St. Cloud Reformatory, Minnesota, 1900–1920.

———. 1974. *Law and Order in Historical Perspective.* New York: Academic Press.

———. 1978. "Discretion and Law in the Early Penitential Books." In *Social Psychology and Discretionary Law.* Edited by Richard Abt. New York: W. W. Norton.

———. 1979. "Hanging for Felony: The Rule of Law in Elizabethan Colchester." *Historical Journal* 21.

———. 1981. "The Recognizance in Elizabethan Law Enforcement." *American Journal of Legal History* 25.

———. 1989. "John Winthrop and the Criminal Law." *William Mitchell Law Review* 15.

———. 2003. *Criminal Justice.* 6th ed. Belmont, CA: Wadsworth.

Sampson, Robert J. 1987. "Urban Black Violence: The Effect of Male Joblessness and Family Disruption." *American Journal of Sociology* 93.

———. 1995. "Toward a Theory of Race, Crime, and Urban Inequality." In *Crime and Inequality.* Edited by John Hagan and Ruth D. Peterson. Stanford, CA: Stanford University Press.

Sampson, Robert J., and Janet L. Lauritsen. 1997. "Racial and Ethnic Disparities in Crime and Criminal Justice in the United States." In *Ethnicity, Crime, and Immigration.* Edited by Michael Tonry. Chicago: University of Chicago Press.

Sampson, Robert J., and Stephen Raudenbush. 1999. "Systematic Social Observation of Public Spaces: A New Look at Disorder in Urban Neighborhoods." *American Journal of Sociology* 105(3): 603–651.

Sampson, Robert J., and William Julius Wilson. 1995. "Toward a Theory of Race, Crime, and Urban Equality. In *Crime and Inequality.* Edited by John Hagan and Ruth D. Peterson. Stanford, CA: Stanford University Press.

Sanborn, Joseph. 1986. "A Historical Sketch of Plea Bargaining." *Justice Quarterly* 3.

Sandin v. Conner. 1995. 515 U.S. 472.

Santobello v. N.Y. 1971. 414 U.S. 257.

Saucier v. Katz. 2001. 533 U.S. 194.

Saum, Christine A., Hilary Spratt, James A. Inciardi, and Rachael E. Bennett. 1997. "Sex in Prison: Exploring Myths and Realities." *Prison Journal* 75.

Savage, Charlie. 2004 (September 23). "Deal Frees Enemy Combatant." *Boston Globe.*

Savage, David, and Eric Lichtblau. 2001 (October 28). "Ashcroft Deals with Daunting Responsibilities."

Scannell, Kara. 2004 (July 17). "Stewart Is Sentenced to 5 Months in Prison." *Wall Street Journal.* http://online.wsj.com/article/0,,SB108931317411458779,00.html?mod=home_whats_news_us.

Schlesinger, Steven R. 1986. "Bail Reform: Protecting the Community and the Accused." *Harvard Journal of Law and Public Policy* 9.

Schlossman, Stephen. 1977. *Love and the American Delinquent: The Theory and Practice of "Progressive" Juvenile Justice, 1825–1920.* Chicago: University of Chicago Press.

Schmidt, Amnesty L., and Christine E. Curtis. 1987. "Electronic Monitors." In *Intermediate Punishments: Intensive Supervision, Home Confinement, and Electronic Monitoring.* Edited by Belinda R. McCarthy. New York: Willow Tree Press.

Schmitt, Christopher H. 1991a (December 8). "A Look Inside Where Deals Are Made: 2-Minute Discussion Decides the Future of Many Defendants." *San Jose Mercury.*

Schneckcloth v. Bustamonte. 1973. 412 U.S. 218.

Schneider, Victoria W., and Brian Wiersema 1991. "Limits and Use of the Uniform Crime Reports." In *Measuring Crime: Large Scale, Long Range Efforts.* Edited by Doris Layton MacKenzie, Phyllis Jo Baunach, and Roy R. Roberg. Albany, NY: State University of New York Press.

Schoenthaler, Stephen J. 1982. "The Effect of Sugar on the Treatment and Control of Anti-Social Behavior." *International Journal of Biosocial Research* 3:1–9.

———. 1983a. "Diet and Crime: An Empirical Examination of an incarcerated Juvenile Population." *International Journal of Biosocial Research* 4:25–39.

———. 1983b. "Diet and Delinquency: A Multi-State Replication." *International Journal of Biosocial Research* 5:70–78.

———. 1983c. "The Los Angeles Probation Department Diet-Behavior Program." *International Journal of Biosocial Research* 5:88–98.

———. 1985. "Nutritional Policies and Institutional Anti-Social Behavior." *International Journal of Biosocial Research. Nutrition Today* 20:16–25.

Schroeder, William A. 1981. "Deterring Fourth Amendment Violations." *Georgetown Law Journal* 69:1361, 1378–86.

Schulhofer, Stephen J. 1985. "No Job Too Small: Justice without Bargaining in the Lower Criminal Courts." *American Bar Foundation Research Journal* 3.

———. 1992. "Assessing the Federal Sentencing Process: The Problem Is Uniformity, Not Disparity," *American Criminal Law Review* 29.

———. 1993. "Rethinking Mandatory Minimums." *Wake Forest Law Review* 28.

Schulz, Dorothy Moses. 1995. *From Social Worker to Crimefighter.* Westport, CT: Praeger.

Schur, Edwin. 1973. *Radical Non-Intervention: Rethinking the Delinquency Problem.* Englewood Cliffs, NJ: Prentice-Hall.

Scott v. Illinois. 1979. 440 U.S. 367.

Scott, Eric J. 1980. *Calls for Service: Citizen Demand and Initial Police Response.* Washington, DC: U.S. Department of Justice.

Scott, Michael S. 2000. *Problem-Oriented Policing: Reflections on the First 20 Years.* Washington, DC: U.S. Department of Justice, Office of Community-Oriented Policing Services (COPS).

Scott, Robert E., and William J. Stuntz. 1992. "Plea Bargaining as Contract." *Yale Law Journal* 101:1909.

Sechrest, Dale. 1989 (September). "Prison Boot Camps 'Do Not Measure Up.'" *Federal Probation.*

Seiter, Richard P., and Karen L. Kadela. 2003. "Prisoner Reentry: What Works, What Does Not, and What Is Promising?" *Crime and Delinquency* 49(3): 360–388.

Sellin, Thorsten. 1959. "The Death Penalty." Appendix to American Law Institute, "Model Penal Code" (Tentative Draft No. 9).

———. 1967. "The Death Penalty and Police Safety." *Capital Punishment.* New York: Harper and Row.

Selye, Hans. 1976. *The Stress of Life.* New York: McGraw-Hill.

Sentencing Project. 2005. *Felony Disenfranchisement in the United States.* Washington DC: Sentencing Project. http://www.sentencingproject.org/pubs_05.cfm. Accessed February 10, 2005.

Shakespeare, William. *Hamlet.* http://www.shakespeare-literature.com/Hamlet.

Shaw, Clifford. 1966. *The Jack-Roller.* Chicago: University of Chicago Press.

Sheehan, Susan. 1978. *A Prison and a Prisoner.* Boston: Houghton Mifflin.

Shepherd, Joanna M. 2002 (January). "Fear of the First Strike: The Full Deterrent Effect of California's Two- and Three-Strikes Legislation." *Journal of Legal Studies* XXXI:159.

Sheppard v. Maxwell. 1966. 384 U.S. 333.

Sherman v. United States. 1958. 356 U.S. 369.

Sherman, Lawrence W. 1990 (March/April). "Police Crackdowns." *NIJ Reports.*

———. 1992. "Attacking Crime: Police and Crime Control." In *Modern Policing.* Edited by Michael Tonry and Norval Morris. Chicago: University of Chicago Press.

———. 1995. "The Police." In *Crime.* Edited by James Q. Wilson and Joan Petersilia. San Francisco: Institute for Contemporary Studies.

———. 2004. "Fair and Effective Policing." In *Crime: Public Policies for Crime Control.* Edited by James Q. Wilson and Joan Petersilia. Oakland, CA: Institute for Contemporary Studies.

Sherman, Lawrence W., Patrick R. Gartin, and Michael E. Buerger. 1989. "Hot Spots of Predatory Crime: Routine Activities and the Criminology of Place." *Criminology* 27.

Sherman, Lawrence W., and Dennis P. Rogan. 1995. "Effects of Gun Seizures on Gun Violence: 'Hot Spots' Patrol in Kansas City." *Justice Quarterly* 12.

Sherman, Lawrence W., Janell D. Schmidt, and Dennis P. Rogan. 1992. *Policing Domestic Violence.* New York: Free Press.

Sherman, Michael, and Gordon Hawkins. 1981. *Imprisonment in America: Choosing the Future.* Chicago: University of Chicago Press.

Shover, Neal. 1998. "White-Collar Crime." In *Crime and Punishment.* Edited by Michael Tonry. New York: Oxford University Press.

Shover, Neal, and David Honaker. 1992. "The Socially Bounded Decision Making of Persistent Property Offenders." *Howard Journal of Criminal Justice* 31.

Sickmund, Melissa. 2003. *Juveniles in Court.* Washington, DC: Office of Juvenile Justice and Delinquency Prevention.

———. 2004. *Juveniles in Corrections.* Washington, DC: Office of Juvenile Justice and Delinquency Prevention.

Silberman, Charles. 1978. *Criminal Violence, Criminal Justice.* New York: Random House.

Simon, William, and John H. Gagnon. 1976. "The Anomie of Affluence: A Post-Mertonian Conception." *American Journal of Sociology* 82.

Singer, Richard G. 1983. "Prisons: Typologies and Classifications." *Encyclopedia of Crime and Justice.* New York: Free Press.

Sitz v. Department of State Police. 1993. 506 N.W.2d 209 (Mich. App.).

Skogan, Wesley G. 1990a. *Disorder and Decline.* New York: Free Press.

———. 1990b. "Poll Review: National Crime Survey Redesign." *Public Opinion Quarterly* 54.

Skogan, Wesley G., and Susan M. Hartnett. 1997. *Community Policing, Chicago Style.* New York: Oxford University Press.

Skogan, Wesley G., and Susan M. Hartnett, Jill DuBois, Jennifer T. Comey, Marianne Kaiser, and Justine H. Lovig. 2000. *Problem Solving in Practice: Implementing Community Policing in Chicago.* Washington, DC: National Institute of Justice.

Skoggin, Paul. 2004. "Role of the Prosecutor." Lecture to Introduction to Crime and Justice Class, University of Minnesota.

Skolnick, Jerome H. 1994. *Justice without Trial.* 3rd ed. New York: Macmillan.

Skolnick, Jerome H., and David H. Bayley. 1986. *The New Blue Line.* New York: Free Press.

Skolnick, Jerome H., and James J. Fyfe. 1993. *Above the Law: Police and Excessive Use of Force.* New York: Free Press.

Slobogin, Christopher. 1998. *Criminal Procedure: Regulation of Police Investigation.* Charlottesville, VA: LEXIS Law Publishing.

Slotnick, Elliot E. 1995. "Review Essay on Judicial Recruitment and Selection." In *Courts and Justice.* Edited by G. Larry Mays and Peter R. Gregware. Prospect Heights, IL: Waveland Press.

Smith v. Maryland. 1979. 442 U.S. 745.

Smith, Page. 1962. *John Adams.* New York: Doubleday.

Snell, Tracy L., and Laura M. Maruschak. 2002. *Capital Punishment 2001.* Washington, DC: Bureau of Justice Statistics.

Snyder, Howard N. 2004. *Juvenile Arrests 2002.* Washington, DC: Office of Juvenile Justice and Delinquency Prevention.

Sobel, William J., and Katherine Rosich, Kamala Mallik Kane, David P. Kirk, and Glenn Dubin. 2002. *The Influence of Truth-in-Sentencing Reforms on Changes in States' Sentencing Practices and Prison Populations.* Washington, DC: Urban Institute Justice Policy Center.

Solomon, Amy, and Michelle Waul, Asheley Van Ness, and Jeremy Travis. 2004. *Outside the Walls: A National Snapshot of Community-Based Prisoner Reentry Programs.* Washington, DC: Urban Institute.

Sourcebook of Criminal Justice Statistics Online. 2004. Washington, DC: Bureau of Justice Statistics. http://www.albany.edu/sourcebook. Visited November 5, 2004.

South Carolina Department of Juvenile Justice Web Page. http://www.state.sc.us/djj/process.html. Visited December 16, 2004.

Sparger, Jerry R., and David J. Giacopassi. 1992. "Memphis Revisited: A Reexamination of Police Shootings after the *Garner* Decision." *Justice Quarterly* 9.

Sparks, Richard F. 1981. "Surveys of Victimization—An Optimistic Assessment." In *Crime and Justice: An Annual Review of Justice.* Edited by Michael Tonry and Norval Morris. Chicago: University of Chicago Press.

Sparrow, Malcolm K., Mark H. Moore, and David M. Kennedy. 1995. *Beyond 911: A New Era for Policing*. New York: Basic Books.

Spelman, William. 2000. "Prisons and Crime." In *Crime and Justice: A Review of Research*. Edited by Michael Tonry. Chicago: University of Chicago Press.

Spitzer, Eliot. 1999. *The New York City Police Department's "Stop and Frisk" Practices: A Report to the People of the State of New York from the Office of the Attorney General*. Albany, NY: New York State Attorney General's Office.

Spohn, Cassia, Dawn Beichner, Erika Davis Frenzel, and David Holleran. 2002. "Prosecutors' Charging Decision in Sexual Assault Cases: A Multi-State Study, Final Report." Washington, DC: National Criminal Justice Research Service.

Spohn, Cassia, and Jerry Cederblom. 1991. "Race and Disparities in Sentencing: A Test of the Liberation Hypothesis." *Justice Quarterly* 8.

Spohn, Cassia, John Gruhl, and Susan Welch. 1987. "The Impact of Ethnicity and Gender of Defendants on the Decision to Reject or Dismiss Felony Charges." *Criminology* 25.

Stanford v. Kentucky. 1989. 537 U.S. 938.

Staples, Brent. 2004 (November 27). "The Federal Government Gets Real about Sex Behind Bars." *New York Times*.

Star, Deborah. 1979. *Summary Parole*. California Department of Corrections.

———. 1981. *Investigation and Surveillance in Parole Supervision: An Evaluation of the High Control Project*. California Department of Corrections.

Star Tribune. 2004 (January 8). "13-Year-Old from Columbia Heights May Be Charged with DWI." *Minneapolis Star-Tribune*. http://www.startribune.com.

State v. Damms. 1960. 100 N.W.2d 592 (Wis.).

State v. Furr. 1977. 235 S.E.2d 193 (N.C.).

State v. Hall. 1974. 214 N.W.2d 205 (Iowa).

State v. Metzger. 1982. 319 N.W.2d 459 (Neb.).

State v. Norman. 1989. 378 S.E.2d 8.

State v. Smith. 1986. 712 P.2d 496.

State v. Vicente. 2001. 772 A.2d 680 (Conn.App.).

State v. Wilson. 1996. 685 So.2d 1063.

Staufenberger, Richard A. 1980. *Progress in Policing: Essays on Change*. Cambridge, MA: Ballinger.

Steffensmeier, Darrell, and Dana Haynie. 2000. "Gender, Structural Disadvantage, and Urban Crime: Do Macro-Social Variables Also Explain Female Offending Rates?" *Criminology* 38.

Steffensmeier, Darrell, John Kramer, and Cathy Streifel. 1993. "Gender and Imprisonment Decisions." *Criminology* 31.

Stephan, James J. 2001. *Census of Jails, 1999*. Washington, DC: Bureau of Justice Statistics.

Stephan, James J., and Jennifer C. Karberg. 2003. *Census of State and Federal Correctional Facilities, 2000*. Washington, DC: Bureau of Justice Statistics.

Stoddard, Ellwyn R. 1983. "Blue Coat Crime." In *Thinking about Police*. Edited by Carl B. Klockars and Stephen D. Mastrofski. New York: McGraw-Hill.

Stojkovic, Stan, and Rick Lovell. 1992. *Corrections: An Introduction*. Cincinnati: Anderson.

Stotland, Ezra. 1977. "White Collar Criminals." *Journal of Social Issues* 33.

Strachan-Davidson, James L. 1912. *Problems of the Roman Criminal Law*. Oxford: Clarendon Press.

Straus, Murray, Richard Gelles, and Suzanne Steinmetz. 1980. *Behind Closed Doors: Violence in the American Family*. New York: Doubleday.

Streib, Victor L. 2004 (January 1, 1973–September 30, 2004). "The Juvenile Death Penalty Today: Death Sentences and Executions for Juvenile Crimes." http://www.law.onu.edu/faculty/streib/juvdeath.pdf.

Strickland v. Washington. 1984. 184 S.Ct. 2052.

Stuntz, William J. 2002. "Local Policing after the Terror." *Yale Law Journal* 111.

Subin, Harry I. 1991 (December 19). "230,000 Cases, Zero Justice." *New York Times*.

Sullivan, Peggy S. 1989. "Minority Officers: Current Issues." In *Critical Issues in Policing*. Edited by Roger G. Dunham and Geoffrey P. Alpert. Prospect Heights IL: Waveland Press.

Sutherland, Edwin H. 1940. "White-Collar Criminality." *American Sociological Review* 5:1.

Sutherland, Edwin H., and Donald R. Cressey. 1978. *Criminology*. 10th ed. Philadelphia: J. Lippincott.

Sykes, Gresham. 1958. *Society of Captives*. Princeton, NJ: Princeton University Press.

Szarwak v. Warden. 1974. 330 A.2d 466.

Taxman, Faye S. 2002. "Supervision—Exploring Dimensions of Supervision." *Federal Probation* 66(2): 14–27.

Taylor v. Louisiana. 1975. 419 U.S. 522.

Tennessee v. Garner. 1985. 471 U.S. 1.

Terry v. Ohio. 1968. 392 U.S. 1.

Texas Criminal Code. 1988. Section 9.42.

Texas Penal Code. 2004. Section 21.06.

Thio, Alex. 1975. "A Critical Look at Merton's Anomie Theory." *Pacific Sociological Review* 18.

Thomas, Jim. 1989. "The 'Reality' of Prisoner Litigation: Repackaging the Data." *New England Journal on Criminal Law and Civil Confinement* 15.

Thomas, Jo. 2001 (November 10). "No Bail for Friend of Man Suspected of Preparing for Sept. 11 Hijackings." *New York Times*.

Thomas, Wayne H. 1976. *Bail Reform in America*. Berkeley: University of California Press.

Thompson v. Oklahoma. 1988. 487 U.S. 815.

Thornton v. U.S. 2004. 124 S.Ct. 2127.

Tiffany, Lawrence P., Donald M. McIntyre, Jr., and Daniel L. Rotenberg. 1967. *Detection of Crime*. Boston: Little, Brown.

Toborg, Mary A. 1981. *Pretrial Release: A National Evaluation of Practices and Outcomes*. Washington, DC: National Institute of Justice.

Toch, Hans B. 1978. "Is a 'Correctional Officer,' by Any Other Name, a 'Screw'?" *Criminal Justice Review* 3.

Tonry, Michael. 1995. *Malign Neglect: Race, Crime, and Punishment in America*. New York: Oxford University Press.

Tonry, Michael, ed. 2000. *Crime and Justice: A Review of Research*. Chicago: University of Chicago Press.

Tonry, Michael, and Kate Hamilton. 1995. *Intermediate Sanctions in Overcrowded Times*. Boston: Northeastern University Press.

Tonry, Michael, and Mary Lynch. 1996. "Intermediate Sanctions." In *Crime and Research: A Review of Research*. Vol. 20. Edited by Michael Tonry. Chicago: University of Chicago Press.

Toobin, Jeffrey. 2001 (November 5). "Crackdown." *New Yorker*.

Tracy, Paul E., and Vincent Morgan. 2000. "Big Brother and His Science Kit: DNA Databases for 21st Century Crime Control?" *Journal of Criminal Law and Criminology* 30:635.

Transactions of the National Congress of Prisons and Reformatory Discipline. 1971. Albany, NY: American Correctional Association.

Travis, Jeremy. 2000. *But They All Come Back: Rethinking Prisoner Reentry*. Washington, DC: U.S. Department of Justice.

Trojanowicz, Robert C. 1994. "The Future of Community Policing." In *The Challenge of Community Policing: Testing the Premises*. Edited by Dennis P. Rosenbaum. Thousand Oaks, CA: Sage.

Trop v. Dulles. 1958. 356 U.S. 86.

Truxillo, Donald M., Suzanne R. Bennett, and Michelle L. Collins. 1998. "College Education and Police Job Performance: A Ten-Year Study." *Public Personnel Management* 27(2): 269.

Tunnell, Kenneth D. 1990. "Choosing Crime: Close Your Eyes and Take Your Chances." *Justice Quarterly* 7.

Turner, Michael G., Jody L. Sundt, Brandon Applegate, and Francis T. Cullen. 1995 (September). "'Three Strikes and You're Out' Legislation: A National Assessment." *Federal Probation*.

Turner, Susan, Peter W. Greenwood, Elsa Chen, and Terry Fain. 1999. "The Impact of Truth-in-Sentencing and Three-Strikes Legislation: Prison Populations, State Budgets, and Crime Rates." *Stanford Law and Public Policy Review* 11:75.

Turow, Scott. 2003 (January 6). "To Kill or Not to Kill: Coming to Terms with Capital Punishment." *The New Yorker*. http://www.newyorker.com/fact/content/?030106fa_fact.

Twain, Mark. 1980. *Pudd'nhead Wilson and Those Extraordinary Twins*. New York: W.W. Norton.

Twentieth Century Fund. 1976. *Fair and Certain Punishment*. New York: McGraw-Hill.

Twenty-Sixth Annual Review of Criminal Procedure. 1997. *Georgetown Law Journal* 85.

Uggen, Christopher. 1999. "Ex-Offenders and the Conformist Alternative: A Job Quality Model of Work and Crime." *Social Problems* 46:127–151.

Uggen, Christopher, and Candace Kruttschnitt. 1998. "Crime in the Breaking: Gender Differences in Desistance." *Law and Society Review* 32(2): 339.

Uggen, Christopher, and Jeff Manza. 2004. "Voting and Subsequent Crime: Evidence from a Community Sample." http://www.soc.umn.edu/%7Euggen/Uggen_Manza_04_CHRLR2.pdf. Visited December 5, 2004.

Uggen, Christopher, and Jeremy Staff. 2001. "Work as a Turning Point for Criminal Offenders." *Corrections Management Quarterly* 5(4): 1–16.

Uphoff, Rodney J. 1995. "The Criminal Defense Lawyer: Zealous Advocate, Double Agent, or Beleaguered Dealer?" In *Courts and Justice*. Edited by G. Larry Mays and Peter R. Gregware. Prospect Heights, IL: Waveland Press.

U.S. v. Armstrong. 1996. 517 U.S. 546.

U.S. v. Banks. 2003. 124 S.Ct. 521.

U.S. v. Flores-Montano. 2004. 124 S.Ct. 1582.

U.S. v. Kenneth Lay. 2004. Indictment. U.S. District Court, Southern District of Texas, Houston Division. http://news.findlaw.com/hdocs/docs/enron/usvlay70704ind.pdf.

U.S. v. Martha Stewart and Peter Bacanovic. 2004. Indictment. United States District Court, Southern District of New York.

U.S. v. Miller. 1976. 425 U.S. 435.

U.S. v. Patane. 2004. 124 S.Ct. 2620.

U.S. v. Salerno. 1987. 481 U.S. 739.

U.S. v. Werker. 1976. 535 F.2d 198 (2d Cir. 1976), certiorari denied 429 U.S. 926.

U.S. v. White. 1971. 401 U.S. 745.

U.S.A. Patriot Act. 2001. http://frwebgate.access.gpo.gov/cgi-bin/getdoc.cgi?dbname=107_cong_bills&docid=f:h3162enr.txt.pdf.

U.S. Census. 2001. Profile of General Demographic Characteristics: 2000. http://www2.census.gov/census_2000/datasets/demographic_profile/0_National_Summary/2khus.pdf.

U.S. Code. 1972. Equal Employment Opportunity Act. P.L. 92-261. http://usinfo.state.gov/usa/infousa/society/landmark/eeoact.pdf.

———. 1994. 42 U.S.C.A. §1983, subs. 1.

———. 1999. Title 18, §3142(f).

———. 2003. Title 18, §§794, 2153, 2331–2339.

———. 2004. http://uscode.house.gov/usc.htm.

———. 2004. Title 28, § 234(b)(1). http://uscode.house.gov/uscode-cgi/fastweb.exe?search.

U.S. Congress. 1954. *Senate, Committee on the Judiciary, Hearing before the Subcommittee to Investigate Juvenile Delinquency*. Miami, Florida, 83d Cong., 2d sess.

U.S. Criminal Code. 2003. Title 18, Chapter 37, § 794.

U.S. Criminal Code. 2003. Title 18, Part I, Chapter 105, § 2153.

U.S. Department of Justice. 1978. *Response Time Analysis: Executive Summary*. Washington, DC: Government Printing Office.

U.S. General Accounting Office Report. 1990. *Death Penalty Sentencing*. Washington, DC: (GAO/GGD-90-57, 2/90).

U.S. House of Representatives. 1970. No. 1444, 91st Cong., 2d Sess. 11.

U.S. National Advisory Commission on Criminal Justice Standards and Goals. 1973. *Courts*. Washington, DC: Government Printing Office.

U.S. Sentencing Commission. 1991. *Mandatory Minimum Penalties in the Federal Criminal Justice System*. Washington, DC: U.S. Sentencing Commission.

Useem, Burt, and Peter Kimball. 1989. *States of Siege: U.S. Prison Riots, 1971–1986*. New York: Oxford University Press, pp. 3–4.

Van Maanen, John. 1978. "The Asshole." In *Policing: A View from the Street*. Edited by Peter K. Manning and John Van Maanen. New York: Random House.

Vera Institute of Justice. 1977. *Felony Arrests: Their Prosecution and Disposition in New York City's Courts*. New York: Vera Institute of Justice.

Violent Crime Control and Law Enforcement Act of 1994. 1994. http://search.netscape.com/ns/boomframe.jsp?query=violent+crime+control+and+law+enforcement+act+1994&page=1&offset=0&result_url=redir%3Fsrc%3Dwebsearch%26requestId%3D3e2957ea0f200ee7%26clickedItemRank%3D1%26userQuery%3Dviolent%2Bcrime%2Bcontrol%2Band%2Blaw%2Benforcement%2Bact%2B1994%26clickedItemURN%3Dhttp%253A%252F%252Fusinfo.state.gov%252Fusa%252Finfousa%252Flaws%252Fmajorlaw%252Fh3355_en.htm%26invocationType%3D-%26fromPage%3DNSSideBar%26ampTest%3D1&remove_url=http%3A%2F%2Fusinfo.state.gov%2Fusa%2Finfousa%2Flaws%2Fmajorlaw%2Fh3355_en.htm

Violent Crime Control and Law Enforcement Act of 1994. 1994. Public Laws. http://usinfo.state.gov/usa/infousa/laws/majorlaw/gun94.pdf.

Vito, Gennaro. 1986. "Felony Probation and Recidivism: Replication and Response." *Felony Probation* 50.

Vold, George B., Thomas J. Bernard, and Jeffrey B. Snipes. 2002. *Theoretical Criminology*. 5th ed. New York: Oxford University Press.

Von Hirsch, Andrew. 1976. *Doing Justice: The Choice of Punishments*. New York: Hill and Wang.

Walker, Samuel. 1980. *Popular Justice*. New York: Oxford University Press.

———. 1989. *Sense and Nonsense about Crime*. 2nd ed. Monterey, CA: Brooks-Cole.

———. 1992b. *The Police in America.* 2nd ed. New York: McGraw-Hill.

———. 1993. *Taming the System: The Control of Discretion in Criminal Justice, 1950–1990.* New York: Oxford University Press, 1993, pp. 8–20.

———. 1994. *Sense and Nonsense about Crime and Drugs.* 3rd ed. Belmont, CA: Wadsworth.

———. 1998. *Popular Justice.* 2nd ed. New York: Oxford University Press.

Walker, Samuel, and Vic W. Bumphus. 1992. "The Effectiveness of Civilian Review: Observations on Recent Trends and New Issues Regarding the Civilian Review of the Police." *American Journal of Police* XI.

Walker, Samuel, Cassia Spohn, and Miriam DeLone. 2000. *The Color of Justice.* Belmont, CA: Wadsworth.

Wallace, Henry Scott. 1993 (September). "Mandatory Minimums and the Betrayal of Sentencing Reform: A Legislative Dr. Jekyll and Mr. Hyde." *Federal Probation.*

Wallerstedt, John F. 1984. *Returning to Prison.* Washington, DC: Bureau of Justice Statistics.

Wall Street Journal. 1994 (March 22). "Death at Work."

Walters, Barbara. 2004 (July 16). *20/20.* ABC News.

Ward, David A. 1987. "Control Strategies for Problem Prisoners in American Penal Systems." In *Problems of Long-Term Imprisonment.* Edited by Anthony E. Bottoms and Roy Light. Brookfield, VT: Gower.

Ward, David A. 1990 (March 30). Personal conversation.

———. 1994. "Alcatraz and Marion: Confinement in Super Maximum Custody." In *Escaping Prison Myths: Selected Topics in the History of Federal Corrections.* Edited by John W. Roberts. Washington, DC: American University Press.

Ward, David A., and Gene G. Kassebaum. 1965. *Women's Prisons: Sex and Social Structure.* Chicago: Aldine.

Ward, David A., and Kenneth F. Schoen, eds. 1981. *Confinement in Maximum Custody.* Lexington, MA: Lexington Books.

Ware, Susan. 1982. *Holding Their Own: American Women in the 1930s.* Boston: Twayne.

Warren, Jenifer. 2004 (July 1). "Spare the Rod, Save the Child: Missouri's Youth Prisons Focus on Small Groups, Therapy, Caring. Officials in California's Punishment-Oriented System Are Taking a Look." *Los Angeles Times.*

Washington Post. n.d. "Revisiting Watergate."

Watson, Jamie, Amy L. Solomon, Nancy G. LaVigne, and Jeremy Travis. 2004. *A Portrait of Prisoner Reentry in Texas.* Washington, DC: The Urban Institute.

Weems v. U.S. 1910. 217 U.S. 349.

Weiner, Richard, William Frazier, and Jay Farbstein. 1987 (June). "Building Better Jails." *Psychology Today.*

Weihofen, Henry E. 1960. "Retribution Is Obsolete." In *Responsibility. Nomos.* No. 3. Edited by C. Friedrich. New York: Lieber-Atherton.

Weisberg, Robert. 1994. "The Impropriety of Plea Bargaining: An 'Anthropological' View." *Law and Social Inquiry* 19(1): 145–148.

Weisburd, David, and Lorraine Green. 1995. "Policing Drug Hot Spots: The Jersey City Drug Market Analysis Experiment." *Justice Quarterly* 12.

Weisburd, David, Stephen D. Mastrofski, Rosann Greenspan, and James J. Willis. 2004. *The Growth of COMPSTAT in American Policing.* Washington, DC: Police Foundation.

Weiss, Mike. 1984. *Double Play: The San Francisco City Hall Killings.* Reading, MA: Addison-Wesley.

Wells, Gary L., and Eric Selau. 1995. "Eyewitness Identification: Psychological Research and Legal Policy on Lineups." *Psychology, Public Policy, and Law.* 1:765.

West, Angela D. 2001. "HIV/AIDS Education for Latina Inmates: The Delimiting Impact of Culture on Prevention Efforts." *Prison Journal* 81(1): 20–41.

Welsh v. Wisconsin. 1980. 466 U.S. 470.

Whitley v. Albers. 1986. 475 U.S. 312, 319.

Whitlock, Brand. 1914. *Forty Years of It.* New York: D. Appleton.

Wice, Paul B. 1974. *Freedom for Sale.* Lexington, MA: Lexington Books.

———. 1985. *Chaos in the Courthouse: The Inner Workings of the Urban Criminal Courts.* New York: Praeger.

Wilcox, Clair. 1927. *Parole from State Penal Institutions.* Philadelphia: Pennsylvania State Parole Commission.

Williams v. Florida. 1970. 399 U.S. 78.

Williams, Hubert. 1993. "Foreword." In *Police Use of Force: Official Reports, Citizen Complaints, and Legal Consequences.* Vol. I. Edited by Anthony M. Pate and Lorie A. Fridell. Washington, DC: Police Executive Research Forum.

Williams, Virgil L., and Mary Fish. 1974. *Convicts, Codes, and Contraband.* Cambridge, MA: Ballinger.

Wilson v. Arkansas. 1995. 514 U.S. 927.

Wilson, George, Roger Dunham, and Geoffrey Alpert. 2004. "Prejudice in Police Profiling: Assessing and Overlooked Aspect in Prior Research. *American Behavioral Scientist* 47(7): 896–909.

Wilson, James Q. 1968. *Varieties of Police Behavior.* Cambridge, MA: Harvard University Press.

———. 1978. *Varieties of Police Behavior.* Cambridge, MA: Harvard University Press.

———. 1983a. *Crime File: Victims.* National Institute of Justice.

———. 1983b. *Thinking about Crime.* Rev. ed. New York: Basic Books.

Wilson, James Q., and George L. Kelling. 1982 (March). "Broken Windows." *Atlantic Monthly.*

Wilson, James Q., and Joan Petersilia, eds. 2004. *Crime.* Oakland, CA: Institute for Contemporary Studies.

Wilson, Margo I., and Martin Daly. 1992. "Who Kills Whom in Spouse Killings? On the Exceptional Sex Ratio of Spousal Killings in the United States." *Criminology* 30.

Wilson, Michael. 2004 (August 8). "Policing a City Where Streets Are Less Mean." *New York Times.*

Wilson, William Julius. 1996. *When Work Disappears: The World of the New Urban Poor.* New York: Knopf.

Wishman, Seymour. 1981. *Confessions of a Criminal Lawyer.* New York: Times Books.

Wolfgang, Marvin E., Terence P. Thornberry, and Robert M. Figlio. 1987. *From Boy to Man, from Delinquency to Crime.* Chicago: University of Chicago Press.

Women in Policing Conference. 2004. "Remarks of the Honorable Deborah J. Daniels, Assistant Attorney General, Office of Justice Programs." http://www.ojp.usdoj.gov/aag/speeches/womenpolice.htm.

Wood, Arthur Lewis. 1967. *Criminal Lawyer.* New Haven, CT: College and University Press.

Wooden, Kenneth. 1976. *Weeping in the Playtime of Others.* New York: McGraw-Hill.

Worden, Alissa Pollitz. 1993. "The Attitudes of Women and Men in Policing: Testing Conventional and Contemporary Wisdom." *Criminology* 31(2): 203–241.

Worden, Robert. 1990. "A Badge and a Baccalaureate: Policies, Hypotheses, and Further Evidence." *Justice Quarterly* 7:565.

Worden, Robert. 1995. "The 'Causes' of Police Brutality." In *And Justice for All: Understanding and Controlling Police Use of Force.* Edited by William A. Geller and Hans Toch. Washington, DC: Police Executive Research Forum.

Worrall, John L. 2004. "The Effect of Three-Strikes Legislation on Serious Crime in California." *Journal of Criminal Justice* 32:283–296.

Wright, Benjamin S., William G. Doerner, and John C. Spier. 1990. "Pre-employment Psychological Testing as a Predictor of Police Performance during an FTO Program." *American Journal of Police* 9:65–84.

Wright, James D. 1986. *The Armed Criminal in America.* Washington, DC: Bureau of Justice Statistics.

Wright, Kevin N., Todd R. Clear, and Paul Dickson. 1984. "Universal Applicability of Probation Risk-Assessment Instruments." *Criminology* 22.

Wright, Richard T., and Scott H. Decker. 1994. *Burglars on the Job: Streetlife and Residential Break-ins.* Boston: Northeastern University Press.

Wright, Ronald, and Marc Miller. 2002 (October). "The Screening/Bargaining Tradeoff." *Stanford Law Review* 55:65–67.

Yant, Martin. 1991. *Presumed Guilty: When Innocent People Are Wrongly Convicted.* Buffalo, NY: Prometheus Books.

Yarborough v. Alvarado, 124 S.Ct. 2140 (2004).

Zamble, Edward, and Frank Porporino. 1988. *Coping, Behavior, and Adaptation in Prison Inmates.* New York: Springer-Verlag.

Zhang, Sheldon X. 1998. "In Search of Hopeful Glimpses: A Critique of Research Strategies in Current Boot Camp Evaluations." *Crime and Delinquency* 44:315.

Zhao, Jihong, Nicholas P. Lovrich, and T. H. Robinson. 2001. "Community Policing: Is It Changing the Basic Functions of Policing? Findings from a Longitudinal Study of 200+ Municipal Police Agencies." *Journal of Criminal Justice* 29(5): 365–377.

Zhao, Jihong, Nicholas P. Lovrich, and Quint Thurman. 1999. "The Status of Community Policing in American Cities." *Policing: An International Journal of Police Strategies & Management* 72(1): 74–92.

Zimmer, Lynne E. 1986. *Women Guarding Men.* Chicago: University of Chicago Press.

Zimring, Franklin E. 1978. *Confronting Youth Crime—Report of the Twentieth Century Fund Task Force on Sentencing Policy toward Young Offenders: Background Paper.* New York: Holmes and Maier.

———. 1981. "Kids, Groups, and Crime: Some Implications of a Well-Known Secret." *Journal of Criminal Law and Criminology* 72.

Zimring, Franklin E., and Richard S. Frase. 1980. *The Criminal Justice System.* Boston: Little, Brown.

Zimring, Franklin E., and Gordon Hawkins. 1991. *The Scale of Punishment.* Chicago: University of Chicago Press.

Case Index

M

M'Naughten's case, 120
Mapp v. Ohio, 181, 261
Martha Stewart and Peter Bacanovic,
  United States v., 42
Martinez, Procunier v., 511
Maryland, Smith v., 228
Maxwell, Sheppard v., 333
McFadden v. Cabana, 242–243
McKeiver v. Pennslyvania, 533
Metzger, State v., 109–110
Michael M. v. Superior Court of Sonoma
  County, 110
Michigan v. Sitz, 128
Miller, United States v., 228
Minnesota v. Murphy, 416
Miranda v, Arizona, 13, 236–239, 306
Missouri v. Seibert, 237
Montoya de Hernandez, United States and,
  234
Morrisey v. Brewer, 416
Municipal Court, Hensley v., 432
Murphy, Minnesota v., 416

N

New Jersey, Lanzetta v., 109
New York v. Belton, 229–230, 234
New York, Quarles v., 240
New York, Riddick v., 225–226
New York, Santobello v., 349
Norman, State v., 130–132
North Carolina v. Alford, 350–351
North Carolina v. Juan Villeda, 262–265

O

Ohio, Mapp v., 181, 261
Ohio, Terry v., 231, 232
Oklahoma, Thompson v., 390
Oregon v. Elstad, 237
Oregon, Apodaca v., 332–333

P

Palmer, Hudson v., 512–513
Patina, United States v., 238
Penman, People v., 118
Pennsylvania, McKeiver v., 533
Penry v. Lynaugh, 389
People v. Aphaylath, 108
People v. Penman, 118
Pletan v. Gaines et al., 257
Powell v. Alabama, 126–128, 303–304, 306,
  306t
Procunier v. Martinez, 511

Q

Quarles v. New York, 240

R

Ravin v. State, 111
Riddick v. N.Y., 225–226
Rodriguez, Illinois v., 228
Roper v. Simmons, 390, WL
Royer, Florida v., 225, DP
Ruffin v. Commonwealth, 507
Rumsfeld, Hamdi v., 28–31

S

Salerno, United States v., 313
Sandin v. Conner, 509, 510
Santobello v. New York, 349
Schneckloth v. Bustamonte, 230
Scott v. Illinois, 306–307, 306t
Seibert, Missouri v., 237
Sheppard v. Maxwell, 333
Sherman v. United States, 118
Simmons, Roper v., 390, WL
Sitz v. Department of State Police, 128
Sitz, Michigan v., 128
Sixth Judicial District Court of Nevada,
  Hibel v., 124
Smith v. Maryland, 228
Smith, State v., 296, 309
Stanford v. Kentucky, 390
State v. Damms, 111–112
State v. Furr, 112
State v. Hall, 119
State v. Metzger, 109–110
State v. Norman, 130–132
State v. Smith, 296, 309
State v. Vicente, 334–335
State v. Wilson, 388
State, Burrows v., 118–120
State, Ravin v., 111
State, Sulsa v., 257
Strickland v. Washington, 307–308
Sulsa v. State, 257
Superior Court of Sonoma County,
  Michael M. v., 110
Supreme Court, Hawkins v., 316
Szarwak v. Warden, 417

T

Taylor v. Louisiana, 331
Tennessee v. Garner, 249–250, 251
Terry v. Ohio, 231, 232
Texas, Lawrence v., 110–111
Thompson v. Oklahoma, 390
Thorton v. United States, 233–234

Thurman v. City of Torrington, 257, DP
Trop v. Dulles, 390

U

United States v. Armstrong, 255
United States v. Banks, 232–233
United States v. Flores-Montano, 234–235
United States v. Kenneth Lay, 41–42
United States v. Martha Stewart and Peter
  Bacanovic, 42
United States v. Miller (1976), 228
United States v. Montoya de Hernandez, 234
United States v. Patane, 238
United States v. Salerno, 313
United States v. White, 228
United States, Cramer v., 38
United States, Dickerson v., 236–237
United States, Draper v., 226
United States, Fellers v., 238–239
United States, Katz v., 227
United States, Kent v., 532, 543
United States, Kyllo v., 7, 228
United States, Sherman v., 118
United States, Thorton v., 233–234
United States, Weems v., 388

V

Vicente, State v., 334–335
Virginia, Atkins v., 389, WL

W

Wainwright, Gideon v., 304–305, 306, 306t,
  308
Warden, Szarwak v., 417
Washington, Lee v., 511
Washington, Strickland v., 307–308
Weems v. United States, 388
Welsh v. Wisconsin, 225
White, United States v., 228
Whitley v. Albers, 512–513
Williams v. Florida, 332
Wilson v. Arkansas, 229
Wilson, State v., 338
Wisconsin, Griffin v., 416, DP
Wisconsin, Welsh v., 225
Wolfish, Bell v., 514

Y

Yarborough v. Alvarado, 237–238

Z

Zerbst, Johnson v., 304–306t

Name Index

Subject Index

crime control vs. rights, 6–8, 194
government power vs. liberty
wartime emergencies and, 29–30
Ban on plea bargaining, 355–359
Battered woman syndrome, 130–132
Battered woman's self-defense, 130–132, 133, DP
BAWP. *See* British Association for Women in Policing
Behavioral techniques, 85
Bell Curve, The, 87
Belly of the Beast, In the, 453
Bench trials, 329
Beyond a reasonable doubt, 328
proving guilt, 333–335
Beyond Self-Interest, 78
BIDS, 155–156, 157, 180–182
Bifurcated trials, 388–389
Big houses, 442
Bill of Rights, 25, 560, WL
criminal procedure and, 126
early republic and, 25
fair procedures and, 21
police power and, 223–224, 223t
wartime exception to, 28–31
Bind over, 315
Biological markers of violent behavior, 82–85
Biological theories, 80–86
BJS. *See* Bureau of Justice Statistics
Blacks. *See also* Race
disparity in sentencing and, 385
officers, 153
prison population and, 438
young, imprisonment of, 446, DP
Blame, 365
Blue curtain, 259
Bondsmen, 311
Boot camps
deterrence and, 426–427
effectiveness of, 426–427
Georgia Department of Corrections and, 424, WL
Border searches, 234–235
Boundary hypothesis, 96, 560
Boy scout reason, 339
Brain abnormalities, 83–84
Brain dysfunctions, 83–84
Bribery, 256
Bright line rule, 240
British Association for Women in Policing, 145, WL
British system of electronic tracking, 433, WL
Broken Windows, 100
Broken windows theory, 100–103, 560
police fixing and, 200, DP
Building-tender system, 458–459
Bureau of Alcohol, Tobacco, Firearms and Explosives (ATF), 151, WL
Bureau of Justice Statistics, 45, 48
crime and victims, 58, WL
officers in the U.S., 147, WL
probation and parole in the U.S., 416, WL
statistical data, 45, WL
Burglary

juveniles and, DP
motivation for, 74–75
shooting at suspects of, 250, DP
Business Improvement Districts (BIDs), 155–156, 157, 180–182
Business nongovernment police, 155–156
By the book decision making, 10, 12–13

C

California
determinate sentencing policies and, 371, WL
prison expenditures and, 447
probation officers, rules for courts and, 384, WL
three-strikes law, 380
California Board of Corrections, 464, WL
California Commission on Peace Officer Standards and Training, WL
California Department of Corrections, 387, WL
California Welfare and Institution Code, 534
California Youth Authority, 549, 550, WL
Calling witnesses, 335–337
Camps, 545
Capable guardian, 77, 79
Capital punishment, 387–401
Captains, 460
Car searches, 233–234
Career advancement, 276
Career criminals, 62–63, 560
crime patterns and, 65, DP
Case attrition, 18, 560
Case mortality, 18, 560
Case study method, 413, 560
Caseload pressure, 343, 345, 356–358
Castle Island fortress, 440
Causal link, 239
Causal relationship, 71
Causation, 71
Causes of Delinquency, 91
Causing a criminal harm, 111, 113–114
Celebrated cases, 16–18
Center for Problem-Oriented Policing, 202, WL
Centralization of police authority, 141
Certainty
deterrence and, 366
lineups and, 244
mandatory minimums and, 372
Certification, juveniles and, 543
Challenge for cause, 332
Change of venue, 333
Charge bargaining, 341
Charging as an adult, 543, DP
Charging the jury, 338
Child saving movement, 530–531
Children
criminal intent and, 530
criminal justice system and, 530
diverting from crime, 475, WL
Children in Custody (CIC), 542
Chiseling, 256
Christopher Commission, 171, 173
Chronic offenders, 62–63

Church attendance requirement, 414
CIC. *See* Children in Custody
Civil death, 507, 560
Civil law, 256
Civil lawsuits, 257
Civil Rights Act, 257
Civil rights movement, 508
Civil rights violations by police, 249, WL
Civil War Amendments, 126
Civilian review boards, 259–260
Class, decision making and, 14–15
Classical theories, 71, 72–80, 560
Classifying crimes, 122–124
Closing arguments, 338
Code of Hammurabi, 439
Code of silence, 173–175, 173t, 174t
CODIS, 52, 208, 560, WL
Coercion
interrogations and, 236
plea bargaining and, 356–358
Cognitive model of rehabilitation, 499–500, 560
Cognitive Thinking Skills Program, 499–500, 499f
Collateral damage, prison and, 448–449, CB
Collective male violence, 492–493
Collective moral response, 444
College education, police officers and, 153
Colloquy, 349–350
Colonial America, 25
Combined DNA Index System (CODIS), 52, 208, 560, WL
Commission on Law Enforcement
juvenile court and, 532
use of force and, 245
Common law
age and, 116–117
intoxication and, 118
use of force and, 249
Communities
felons serving time in, 422, DP
prevention and, 194, WL
Community corrections, 406, CB
ethnicity and, 419, 420f
felons serving time in, 422, DP
gender and, 419, 420f
race and, 419, 420f
Community oriented policing (COP), 144, 200, 560, WL
evaluating, 203–206
as policy, 202, DP
Community policing, 560
crime rates and, 52
era, 144
policing strategy, 186–187
Community prosecution, 286–287, 560
Community service, 421, 426–428, 560
sentences, 428, DP
Community Supervision Bureau, 421, WL
Compelled confessions, 239–240
Compensation, 60
Competence, 171–172
COMPSTAT, 213–217, 560
Computerized statistics, 213–217
Computers, 43
Concealing terrorists, 39

Concentration model of managing prisoners, 452
Concurrence, 111, 113
Conditions of parole, 413–414
Conditions of probation, 413–414, 415f
Condoms, prisons and, 486
Confessions, 236–240
Confinement
    as punishment, 439–440
    prisons and, 439
Confinement model of imprisonment, 459–460, 480–481, 500, 560
Conflict theory
    criminal law and, 95–96, 98, 560
    prison boom and, 444–445
Congregate system, 441–442
Connecticut, sentencing history and guidelines, 375, DL
Consensual sex in prisons, 485f
Consensus hypothesis, 96, 560
Consensus theory, 95–97
Consent
    defense of, 114, 115–116
    search rule, searches and, 230
    searches and, 228, 230
Consent search rule, 230, 560
Conspiracy, 112
Constable/night watch system, 139, 560
Constitution of the United States, 552–559. See also specific amendments
Constitutional democracy, 6, 560
    balance and, 6–8
    crime control in, 23
Constitutional limits on criminal law, 109–111
Continuance in contemplation of dismissal, 541, 560
Contraband, prisoners and, 483, DP
Contraceptives, privacy and, 110
Contract attorneys, 308, 560
Contract prison labor system, 457
Control, sentencing guidelines and, 380
Control model of prison management, 458, 560
Controlling crime, patrol and, 187
Convenience store robberies, 55, DP
Conventional order, crime and, 91
Convicting the innocent, plea bargaining and, 358–359
COPS Report: Crime Analysis in America, 215, WL
COPS. See Community-oriented policing
Corporate fraud, 41, 42, 561
Corporate Fraud Task Force, 42
Correctional boot camps, 421, 424
Correctional institution, 442–443, 561
Correctional supervision, number of persons under, 407f
Corrections, 406, 561
    data mining, 450,
    institutions and, 442–443, 561
    juveniles and, 544–547
    as producers, 9–10
    spending, 447
    in the United States, 438, WL
Corrections Corporation of America, 456, 457, WL

Corrections officers, 460–462
    advantages of, 460, DP
    as a career, 460, DP
    discretionary decision making and, 10
    occupational analysis, 460, WL
    prisoner violence against, 488–489
    training, 463
    unions, 463
Correlation, 71, 561
Corrigible criminals, 370
Corruption, 255–256
    police and, 141
    remedies for, 256–260
Cost-effectiveness, DNA and, 212–213
Counsel. See Defense counsel; Lawyers
Count, 460
Count bargaining, 341
County law enforcement agencies, 153
Court of Star Chamber, 25
Courtroom workgroup, 278–289, 561
    criminal courts and, 275–276
    defense counsel and, 287–289
    implicit bargaining and, 341–342
    judges and, 280–282
    plea bargaining and, 343–345
    prison population boom and, 445
    prosecutors and, 282–287
Courts, 276, WL
    appellate, 274
    due process mission, 276–277
    felony, 274
    juveniles and, 540–542
    missions of, 275–278
    National Criminal Justice Reference Service (NCJRS) and, 302, WL
    organizational mission and, 278
    proceedings, videoconferencing and, 336
    as producers, 9–10
    social justice mission and, 277–278
    structure of, 270–275, 271f
    trial process, 335, WL
    U.S. Supreme Court, 274–275
CourtTV, Sam Sheppard murder case, 210, WL
Crackdowns, 194–195, DP
Crime
    attachment, and, 91
    background factors and, 72f, 79
    characteristics of, 58, WL
    defenses to, 114–122
    determinism and, 80
    drugs and, 65, DP
    economic explanations of, 77, DP
    education and, 88
    elements of, 111–114
    free will and, 80
    genetics and, 81
    hedonism and, 80
    intelligence and, 86–87
    measuring, 45–51
    NCVS and, 48
    personality and, 87
    poverty and, 88
    against public order and morals, 36–37
    social class and, 88
    against the state, 38–40

    torts and, 124
    trends in, 51–53
    twins and, 81
    types of, 36–44
    victims, 58–61
    women and, 53, CB
Crime-attack strategies, 186, 561
Crime boom
    public response to, 444
    war on drugs and, 445
Crime causation theories, 71, WL
Crime control
    agencies, 8, 9, 9t
    balance with liberty and, 6–8,194
    in a constitutional democracy, 5–8, 108
    conveyor belt, 20f
    cost of, 4–5
    criminal courts and, 275
    expenditures for, 5f
    vs. individual rights, 6–8, 194
    levels of government and, 8
    mission, 276–277
    model, 19–21, 22–27, 561, CB
    return to, 26–27
    value of, 19
Crime Control Institute, 194
Crime control mission, 276–277
Crime control model, 19–21, 561, CB
    vs. due process model, 20t
    history of, 22–27
    return to, 26–27
Crime control/due process pendulum, 23f
Crime in the United States, 45
Crime Index, 45, 46t, 561
    offenses in 2003, 37f
    Part I offenses, 45
    Part II offenses, 45
Crime mapping, 213–217, 431–432
Crime patterns, 65, DP
Crime prevention, 60, DP
Crime rates, 561
    agency collaboration, and, 52
    community policing, and, 52
    Crime Index and, 45, 46t
    dark figure in, 45
    criminal justice agencies and, 52
    drop in, 51, DP
    gun violence and, 52
    imprisonment and, 52, 446
    juveniles and, 534, 537f
    objective or subjective, 45, DP
    people in prison and, 472–475
    prison boom and, 444
    sentencing reform and, 52
    simultaneity problem and, 473–474
    specification problem and, 473
    statistical data, 45, WL
    strain theory and, 90
    violent crime and, 51f
Crime reduction, imprisonment and, 446
Crime statistics
    juveniles and, 534
    objective or subjective, 45, DP
    sourcebook of, 296, WL
Crime theories, 71, WL
Crime-specific focus, 72
Criminal act, 111–112

Delinquency, 534, 561
Delinquency petitions, 541, 561
Delinquent personality, 87
Democracy
    constitutional, 6–8, 23
    pure, 6
Demographics
    of prisoners, 469
Department of Homeland Security, 9,
        151–152, 153, WL
Department of Justice
    parole information, 416, WL
    prison information, 416, WL
    violence against women, 199, WL
Departure, 382–383
Dependent variable, 85
Deprivations, prison and, 482
Description, lineups and, 244
Descriptive sentencing guidelines, 380
Desistance theories, 93–95
Detention 310–315, 462
Detention centers, 545–546
Determinate sentencing, 368, 561
    California and, 371, WL
    types of, 371–383
Determinism, 71, 80, 561
Deterrence
    boot camps and, 426–427
    certainty and, 366
    death penalty and, 396–397
    general, 366
    mandatory minimums and, 372, 373
    preventive patrol and, 188–189
    severity and, 366
    special, 366
    types of, 366
    three strikes law and, 376–377
Developmental theories, 92–95
DHS. See Department of Homeland
        Security
Diet, crime and, 84–85
Differences among states, imprisonment
        and, 473
Differential association theory, 91
Differential response approach, 187–188,
        561
Diminished rights, probationers and
        parolees and, 416
Direct examination, 335
Direct supervision, jails and, 467–468
Dirty Harry problem, 172, 173
Discharging defendant, 316
Disciplinary actions, police misconduct
        and, 258, 259f
Discovery, 318
Discrepant accounts, 320–321
Discretion, 10
    dispatchers and, 187
    judges, sentencing guidelines and, 384
    mandatory minimums and, 371–380
    officers and, 159–160
    prosecutors and, 296–297, 345–346
Discretionary decision making, 10, 13,
        14–15, 14t, 108, 561
    discrimination and, 14–15, DP
    funnel model and, 18–19
    police and, 171–175, 222
    prosecutors, 10

shifting of, 10
    wedding cake model and, 16–17
Discretionary release, 412, 561
Discrimination
    criminal justice system and, 14–15, DP
    death penalty and, 399
    decision making and, 14–15, DP
    in sentencing, 384–386
Disorder, 144, DP
Disorderly conduct arrests, 37t
Disparity in sentencing, 384–386
    Hispanics and, 385–386
    blacks and, 385
    in sentencing, 384–386
    sentencing rules and, 385, WL
    three-strikes law and, 378t, 380
    women and, 382
Dispatchers, 187
Dispersion model of managing prisoners,
        452
Displacement effect, 194, 561
Disposition
    internal review and, 258
    juvenile court and, 541–542
    by negotiation, 338–359
    by trial, 328–338
Disposition hearing, 541–542, 561
District Attorney of New York County, 284,
        WL
District of New Jersey Pretrial Services,
        423, WL
Diversion, 18, 296, 561
DNA, 207–213, 561
    cost-effectiveness and, 212–213
    death penalty and, 393, 397–399
    National Institute of Justice and, 208
    privacy and, 212–213
    solving crimes and, 212
    testing, The Innocence Project and,
        242, WL
Doctrine of official immunity, 257, 561
Doctrine of parens patriae, 530, 561
Doing Justice, 366
Doing time
    men and, 487
    women and, 503–504
Domestic violence, 198–199
Dopamine, 83
Double-blind procedures, 85
Dress code, arrest for, 535
Driving while black or brown, 253–254
Driving while intoxicated. See DWI
Drug courts, 277, WL
    federal justice system and, 279
    graduates of, recidivism and, 279
Drug dealing, 76, 150
Drug Enforcement Administration (DEA),
        150–151, WL
Drug hot spots, 197–198
Drug law, 372
Drug Market Analysis Program (DMA),
        197–198
Drug offenses
    internet and, 150
    mandatory minimums and, 372,
        373–374
    prisoners and, 469
    women and, 501

Drugs, 150–151
    crime and, 65, DP
    National Institute of Justice and, 197
    selling online, 150
    treatment for, 498–499
    use of, 48, DP
Drunkenness, arrests for in 2002, 37t
Dual court system, 270, CB
Dual system of justice, 542–543, 561
Due process, 19, 125–128, 561, DP
    death penalty and, 388
    juvenile courts and, 532, 533
    lineup misidentifications and, 243–244
    mission, 275, 276, 561
    model, 21–22, 561
    obstacle course, 23f
    prisoners and, 509–510
    privacy and, 110
    probationers and parolees and, 416
    proof beyond a reasonable doubt and,
        334
    revolution, 26, 303, 561
    wartime exception and, 28–31
Due process model, 21–22, 561
    vs. crime control model, 20t
    history of, 22–27
    obstacle course, 23f
Duration, interrogations and, 236
Duress, 117
Duties of criminal law enforcement, 158
DWI, 128
    arrests for in 2002, 37t
    juveniles and, 535
    thirteen year old and, 540

E

Early childhood theories, 92–93
Early release, 472
Earned credit, 471
Economic explanations of crime, 77, DP
Economic victimization, 488
Education
    correctional institutions and, 442
    crime and, 88
    granting probation and, 411
    men's prisons and, 494–496
    officers and, 153, 166–168, 166f
    youthful offenders and, 543, WL
Effective counsel, 309
    mirror test, 307
    mockery of justice standard, 307
    prejudice prong, 308
    reasonableness prong, 307–308
Eighteenth Amendment, 557
Eighth Amendment, 556
    cruel and unusual punishment and,
        364, 387
    excessive bail and, 311
    prisoners and, 512–513
Either/or corrections, 420, 561
Elective system, judges and, 281
Electrocution, 387
Electronic monitoring, 423–424
    home confinement and, 423, WL
Elements, routine activities theory and,
        77–79
Elements of crime, 111–114

Incident-driven policing, 141
Incident reports, 192, 562
Income, victimization and, 59
Incorrigible criminals, 370
Independent variable, 85
Indeterminate sentencing, 368, 562
Index Crimes, 45, 46t
Indictment, 316, 562
Indigence, standard of, 308
Indigenous theory of imprisonment, 481, 562
Individual strain, 88, 89
Industrialization, 26
Inferences about the victims, 322
Informal decision making, 10–13, 562
Informal decision-making process, 154–155
Informal influences, 299–300
Informal missions, 284–284
Informal rules, decision making and, 12t
Information, 316–317, 562
Information systems, decision to charge and, 301
Inmate code, 481
Inmates. See Prisoners
Innocent defendants, punishing, 352–353
Innocent people, death penalty and, 397–399
Innocent Project, The, 242, WL
In-or-out corrections, 420
Insanity, 120–121
Institutional corrections, juveniles and, 544
Insubordination, officers and, 153
Intake
    internal review and, 258
    juvenile court and, 541
Integrated Automated Fingerprint Identification System (IAFIS), 52, 207, WL
Intelligence Gathering and Sharing Project, 450–451
Intelligence, crime and, 86–87
Intelligent quotient, 86–87
Intensive supervised probation (ISP), 418, 421, 422–423
Intermediate appellate courts, 274
Intermediate punishment, 406, 420–433, 422t, 562
    evaluation of, 429
    punishment and, 429, DP
Intermediate sanctions. See Intermediate punishment
Internal affairs unit (IAU), 258
Internal review, 258–259
International Association of Police (IACP), lineup requirements and, 242
International Association of Women, 145, WL
Internet, crime and, 43, 150
Interrogation, 236–240
    coercion and, 236
    duration, 236
    Fifth Amendment and, 236
    Miranda warnings and, 236
    terrorist suspects, 252–253
Intimates, criminals and, 57–58
Intoxication
    common law and, 118

defense of, 118–120
involuntary, 118–120
Invasiveness, stops and, 230t
Investigation, internal review and, 258
IQ, 86–87
Iraqi prisoners, Stanford Prison experiment parallels, 461, WL
Irresistible impulse test, 120, 562
Isolation
    of offenders, 440
    police officers and, 168
ISP. See Intensive supervised probation

J

Jack-Roller, The, 90
Jailers, 487
Jails, 462–468, 562
    architecture and, 465–467, 467f
    conditions, 463–465
    podular design, 465–467
    vs. prison, 462
    programs, 463, 464t
    women and, 463
Job model of police attitude, 177, 562
Judges, 280–282
    appointment and, 281
    discretion and, 384
    discretion in sentencing and, 381, 445
    discretionary decision making and, 10
    elective system and, 281
    gender and, 281–282
    plea bargaining and, 347–348
    race and, 281
    selection of, 280, DP
    sentencing guidelines and, 384
Jump-out squads, 197
Junk fund abuse, as an excuse, 121
Juries, 329–333
    as political institutions, 329–330
    random selection and, 331
Jury deliberations, 329, 338, DP
Jury instructions, 338, 562
Jury list, 331–332
Jury nullification, 330–331, 562
    process, analysis of, 331, WL
    race and, 330, DP
Jury panel, 332
Jury selection, 331–332
Jury size, Sixth Amendment and, 332
Jury trial, 533
Jury verdicts
    jury nullification, 330–331, 562
    race and, 330
    September 11th attacks and 330
    terrorism and, 330
Just deserts, 365, 372
Justice by consent, 280
Justice for all or just us?, 14, DP
Justice process, videoconferencing and, 336
Justice, timeliness of trial and, 272–273
Justifications, defenses of, 114
    consent, 114, 115–116
    home and property, 114
    self-defense, 114–115
Juvenile corrections, 544–547
    rehabilitation or punishment, 548–550
Juvenile court, 540–542, 562

Commission on Law Enforcement and the Administration of Justice and, 532
    due process and, 532, 533
    history of, 531–532
    jury trial and, 533
    process, 541–542
Juvenile delinquents, 534–536, 562
Juvenile justice,
    history of, 530
    law enforcement and, 537–540
    process, 538f
Juvenile offenders
    execution of, 390–392, 391f, 391t
    groups and, 534
    Office of Juvenile Justice and Delinquency and, 534, WL
Juveniles, 534, 562
    arrests, 535–536
    attempted murder and, DP
    burglary and, DP
    certification, and 543
    charging as an adult, 543, DP
    crime statistics and, 534, 537f
    definition of, 534
    delinquency and, 534–536
    delinquency petitions and, 541
    dress code and, 535
    DWI and, 535
    handguns and, 534
    imprisonment binge and, 544
    jury trial and, 533
    life sentences for, 533
    mentally ill, 547
    probation and, 541–542, 544
    rehabilitation and, 544
    rights of, 532–533
    sentencing laws and, 533
    status offenses and, 534, 539
    transfer and, 543
    transfer petitions and, 541
    transfer to criminal courts an, 542–543
    victimization of, 536, WL
    waiver and, 543
    weapons and, 534
    youthful offenders, 534, CB

K

Kansas City Gun Experiment, 195–196
Kansas City Preventive Patrol Experiment, 189, 190, WL
Kids, reporting parents to police, 198, DP
Knock and announce rule, 229, 232–233, 562
Knockdown force, 245–246, 247, 562
Knowing intent, 112–113, 562
Knowingly, guilty pleas and, 349–350

L

Labeling theory, 90, 91–92, 562
Law enforcement
    juveniles and, 537–540
    officers, as producers, 9–10
    police and 159, 175, DP
    technology, 206–215
    U.S. Constitution and, 223–224

Sugar, violent behavior and, 84–85
Suggestion, lineup and, 242, 243
Suicide, police officers and, 170
Suitable target, 77, 78–79
Super predators, 62–63, 64–65
Supermaxes, 452–454, WL
Supermaximum security prisons, 449, 452–454, 565
Supervision hierarchy, 460
Supreme courts, 274
Survey of Household 2001, 156
Surviving the Mix: Struggle and Survival in a Women's Prison, 502
Suspects, as products, 9–10
Suspicion, arrests for in 2002, 37*t*
Sustained, internal review and, 258
SWAT, 205
Swiftness, 366
Syndromes, 121–122
Systematic social observation method, 101–103, 565

T

Taliban, American citizen and, 28–31
Tasers, 247
TCs, 498–499
Technical violations, 414, 416, 565
Technological advances, policing and, 141
Technology, criminal justice and
    3-D mug shots and, 210–211
    Britain and, 433, WL
    CODIS and, 52
    corrections data mining and, 450–451
    global positioning systems and, 430–433
    graphical information and, 217, WL
    IAFIS and, 52
    information systems and, 301
    MRI use, culpability and, 394
    National Institute of Justice and, 206–207
    operation Web Tryp and, 150
    Pandora's box or panacea, 206, DP
    satellite monitoring of prisoners and, 430–433
    SMART and, 430–433
    tasers and, 247
    telemedicine in prisons and, 484
    thermal imaging and, 7
    videoconferencing and, 336
    wireless access and, 43
Telemedicine, prisoners and, 484
Television, death row prisoners and, 510–511
Temptation, routine activities theory and, 77
Tenth Amendment, 556
Terrorism, 39–40. *See also* September 11th attacks
    building private security/public policing partnership to prevent, 157, WL
    jury verdicts and, 330
    material support and, 39–40, 40*t*
    Patriot Act and, 8–9, WL
    privacy and, 125
Terrorist crimes, Patriot Act and, 8–9, WL

Terrorist suspects
    concealing, 39
    September 11th attacks and, 252–253
    interrogation of, 252–253
Testimonial evidence, 337–338
Testing the government's case, 315–318, 565
Testosterone, violence and, 82
Texas, prisoner reentry and, 519, 520, 520*f*, WL
Texas Rangers, 153
The Sentencing Project, 458, WL
    civil death and, 507–508
Theoretical rationale, 71
Therapeutic communities, 498–499
Therapy, correctional institutions and, 442
Thermal imaging and privacy, 7
Thin blue line, 330
Thinking about Crime, 370
Third Amendment, 556
Third-tier crimes, 17, 17*f*
Thirteenth Amendment, 556–557
    prisoners and, 507
Three-strikes law, 375–380, CB, WL
    California and, 378, WL
    constitutionality of, 380, WL
    deterrence and, 376–377
    ethnicity and, 378*t*, 380
    race and, 378, 378*t*, 380
Time-doers, 487
Timeliness of trial, justice and, 272–273
Torts, 124, 257, 565
Total institutions, 481, 565
Totality of the circumstances, 243–244
Traditional facilities, 451
Training schools, 546
Transfer, 542–543, 565
Transfer petitions, juveniles and, 541, 542–543, 565
Treason, 38–39, 565
Treatment conditions, P&P and, 413
Treatment of prisoners, 516, WL
Trial
    adversary process and, 328
    presence at, 333
    steps in, 343, WL
Trial courts of general jurisdiction, 270, 274
Trial courts of limited jurisdiction, 270, 271–274
Troublemaker prisoners, 471
Truth in sentencing, 375–380
Tudor monarchs, criminal justice and, 24–25
Turf wars, 9
Twelfth Amendment, 556
Twelve member juries, 332–333
Twelve member jury, constitutional right to, 332, DP
Twentieth Amendments, 557–558
Twenty-fifth Amendment, 558–559
Twenty-first Amendment, 558
Twenty-fourth Amendment, 558
Twenty-second Amendment, 558
Twenty-seventh Amendment, 559
Twenty-sixth Amendment, 559
Twenty-third Amendment, 558
Twinkie defense, 84–85, 121

Twins, crime and, 81
Two-pronged effective counsel test, 307

U

U.S. Attorneys Manual, 124, WL
U.S. Bail Reform Act, 313
U.S. Bureau of Prisons, 452
U.S. Constitution, 552–559. *See also* specific amendments
    Amendments, 25, 223, WL
    church attendance requirement and, 414
    death penalty and, 387–392
    interrogating terrorist suspects and, 252–253
    juvenile justice and, 532–533
    privatization of prisons and jails and, 457
    profiling and, 255
    satellite monitoring of probationers, 430–433
    use of force and, 249–251
U.S. Courts, 276, WL
U.S. Customs and Border Patrol Protection Agency, 151, 234, WL
U.S. General Accounting Office, 399
U.S. judicial system, structure of, 271*f*
U.S. Marshals Service, 151, WL
U.S. prisons. *See also* Prison
    history of, 439–443
    prisoners incarcerated in, 439*f*
U.S. Sentencing Commission, 372, 374
U.S. Supreme Court decisions, 274–275, WL
    border searches and, 234–235
    car searches and, 233–234
    enemy combatants and, 28–31
    execution of mentally retarded, 389, WL
    execution of juveniles and, 390, WL
    gay consensual sex and, 110–111
    guilty pleas and, 349–350
    knock and announce rule and, 232–233
    Miranda warnings
        delay in, 237
        incriminating statements at home, 238–239
        interruption by suspect and, 238
        juveniles and, 237–238
        roadblocks and, 235
        thermal imaging and, 7
    wartime exception to the Bill of Rights and, 28–31
U.S. Victims of Crime Act, 60
UCR. *See* Uniform Crime Reports.
Ulterior motives, 322
Unanimous verdicts, 332–333
Undercover work, is it ethical, 193, DP
Understanding and Control of Violent Behavior Panel, 81, 82, 83–84, 86
Unemployment, 88
Unfounded, 258
Uniform Crime Reports (UCR), 45, 565, WL
    juveniles and, 534
    vs. NIBRS, 47*t*, 50*t*
    policing and, 141

Photo Credits

CJ & Technology image on pages 7, 43, 125, 150, 210, 247, 301, 336, 394, 450, and 484: Colin Anderson/Getty Images

In Focus image on pages 15, 78, 115, 119, 123, 159, 165, 190, 196, 204, 226, 231, 240, 252, 272, 277, 279, 285, 309, 317, 350, 379, 382, 392, 398, 414, 418, 426, 466, 486, 510, 512, 533, 535, 540, and 547: Colin Anderson/Getty Images

Make Your Decision image on pages 28, 62, 100, 130, 180, 216, 262, 290, 320, 356, 400, 430, 472, 524, and 548: "Lady Justice," © Benny De Grove/Getty Images Inc.

Chapter 1

2, © Comstock Images; 6, AP/Wide World Photos; 16, AP/Wide World Photos; 21, © San Francisco Chronicle/Michael Maloney; 22, © Frederic Larson/San Francisco/Corbis; 28, AP/Wide World Photos

Chapter 2

34, © Hutchings Stock Photography/Corbis; 39, AP/Wide World Photos; 42, AP/Wide World Photos; 48, © Michael Newman/Photo Edit; 52, AP/Wide World Photos; 62, © David Young-Wolff/Photo Edit

Chapter 3

68, © David Turnley/Corbis; 76, © Alamy Images; 80, AP/Wide World Photos; 92, Photo by Michael R. Strong Sr.; 96, AP/Wide World Photos; 100, © Cleve Bryant/Photo Edit

Chapter 4

106, © Robert Brenner/Photo Edit; 110, AP/Wide World Photos; 116, AP/Wide World Photos; 122, © Jim Varney/ Photo Researchers, Inc.; 127, The Granger Collection, New York; 130, AP/Wide World Photos

Chapter 5

136, © Henry Ray Abrams/Reuters/Corbis; 140, Bettmann/ Corbis; 146, Courtesy of Indianapolis Police Dept. Photo Lab.; 152, USCG photo by PA3 Kelly Newlin; 157, © Bill Varie/Corbis; 176, AP/Wide World Photos; 180, AP/Wide World Photos

Chapter 6

184, © Richard Lord/Photo Edit; 191, © Jonathan Nourok/ Photo Edit; 192, AP/Wide World Photos; 199, AP/Wide World Photos; 209 (above) © David Parker/Science Photo Library/ Photo Researchers, Inc., (below) National Institute of Justice; 210, Reprinted with permission of MIT Lincoln Laboratory, Lexington, Massachusetts; 211, Courtesy of Dimensional Photonics; 216, Todd Maisel/New York Daily News

Chapter 7

220, © Spencer Grant/Photo Edit; 224, © Joel Gordon; 229, © Getty Images; 241, © Joel Gordon; 244, © Reuters/Corbis; 262, © Bob Daemmrich/Photo Edit

Chapter 8

268, © Bob Daemmrich/The Image Works; 275, AP/Wide World Photos; 281, © Bob Daemmrich/The Image Works; 283, © Getty Images; 288, © C. Schneider/Ventura County Star/Corbis Sygma; 290, © Reuters/Corbis

Chapter 9

294, © Michael Newman/Photo Edit; 299, © Joel Gordon; 308, AP/Wide World Photos; 314, AP/Wide World Photos; 318, AP/Wide World Photos; 321, AP/Wide World Photos

Chapter 10

326, © Dennis MacDonald/Photo Edit; 331, © Jack Kurtz/ Reuters/Corbis; 334, AP/Wide World Photos; 337, AP/Wide World Photos; 342, AP/Wide World Photos; 356, © Nick Ut/Getty Images

Chapter 11

362, © Ted Sogul/Corbis; 368, AP/Wide World Photos; 373, © Reuters/Corbis; 375, © Ted Sogul/Corbis; 393, AP/Wide World Photos; 400, AP/Wide World Photos

Chapter 12

404, © Joel Gordon; 407, Courtesy of The Bostonian Society—Old State House Museum; 412, AP/Wide World Photos; 424, © John B. Boykin/Corbis; 428, © Jeff Greenberg/ Photo Edit; 430, © Polak Maatthew/Corbis Sygma

Chapter 13

436, AP/Wide World Photos; 441, © Getty Images; 448, © Joel Gordon; 456, AP/Wide World Photos; 461, AP/Wide World Photos; 472, © Robin Nelson/Photo Edit

Chapter 14

478, © Cary Wolinsky/Stock Boston; 483, © Shepard Sherbell/Corbis Saba; 490, © Andrew Lichtenstein/Corbis; 494, © A. Ramey/Photo Edit; 506, © Sean Cayton/The Image Works; 524, AP/Wide World Photos

Chapter 15

528, © Joel Gordon; 531, Eastern Kentucky University Library; 539, © Spencer Grant/Photo Edit; 543, AP/Wide World Photos; 545, © Sean Cayton/The Image Works; 548, AP/Wide World Photos